PIMLIC

7 ß

# DOWNING STREET DIARY

Lord Donoughue of Ashton was born in 1934 and educated at Northampton Grammar School, Oxford and Harvard. He worked on the editorial staff of *The Economist*, *Sunday Times*, *Sunday Telegraph* and *The Times*, and taught at the London School of Economics from 1963 to 1974, when he moved to 10 Downing Street as Senior Policy Adviser to Harold Wilson and then to James Callaghan. After working in the City, he served as Parliamentary Under-Secretary of State at the Ministry of Agriculture, Fisheries and Food between 1997 and 1999. His previous books include *British Politics and the American Revolution* (1964), *Herbert Morrison: Portrait of a Politician* (1973, with George Jones), *Prime Minister* (1987) and *The Heat of the Kitchen* (2003). He lives in London and Berkshire.

'Enjoyed it immensely – penetrating and honest.'
Lord (Denis) Healey, former Labour Chancellor of the Exchequer and Deputy Leader

'His diary becomes less a private journal and more a biography of his leader. And arguably one of the best ever written. Intimate, sincere and refreshingly candid, this is a memoir of supreme courage. If only all politicians were this truthful.'
*Good Book Guide*

'The machinations of the Labour party hierarchy and the sheer, bitchy hair-pulling jealousies puts one in mind of a Jilly Cooper novel.'
Mike Molloy, former editor of the *Daily Mail*

'Frank and revealing ... The most entertaining sections concern the vicious infighting within the kitchen cabinet, much of it provoked by Wilson's unstable private secretary, Marcia Williams.'
Andrew Lynch, *Sunday Business Post*

'A wonderful book.'
Lord (Jack) Ashley CH, former Labour MP

# DOWNING STREET DIARY

## With Harold Wilson in No. 10

---

# BERNARD DONOUGHUE

PIMLICO

Published by Pimlico 2006

2 4 6 8 10 9 7 5 3 1

Copyright © Bernard Donoughue 2005

Bernard Donoughue has asserted his right under the Copyright,
Designs and Patents Act 1988 to be identified as the author of this work

First published in Great Britain by Jonathan Cape in 2005

Pimlico edition 2006

Pimlico
Random House, 20 Vauxhall Bridge Road,
London SW1V 2SA

Random House Australia (Pty) Limited
20 Alfred Street, Milsons Point, Sydney,
New South Wales 2061, Australia

Random House New Zealand Limited
18 Poland Road, Glenfield,
Auckland 10, New Zealand

Random House South Africa (Pty) Limited
Isle of Houghton, Corner of Boundary Road & Carse O'Gowrie,
Houghton 2198, South Africa

Random House UK Limited Reg. No. 954009

A CIP catalogue record for this book is available from the British Library

ISBN 1844137457
ISBN 9781844137459 (From Jan 2007)

Papers used by Random House UK Ltd are natural, recyclable products
made from wood grown in sustainable forests. The manufacturing processes
conform to the environmental regulations of the country of origin

Printed and bound in Great Britain by William Clowes Ltd, Beccles, Suffolk

# Dedications

To my family, Carol, Rachel, Kate, Paul and Stephen, who gave me unstinting support and who may now understand why I was so often exhausted, irritable and absent – and after all these years may forgive.

And to dear Sarah, who, known earlier, would have helped me better to steer through these treacherous currents.

# Contents

Preface: The Diaries                                                      ix
Introduction: With Wilson in Downing Street                               1

1  Who Governs Britain? Harold Wilson Wins the
   Election of February 1974                                             20
2  The New Labour Government (March–April 1974)                          56
3  Preparing for the Next Election (April–May 1974)                     103
4  Lady Marcia; the Irish Problem (May–June 1974)                       119
5  Enter Left: Tony Benn and Industry Policy
   (June–August 1974)                                                   137
6  The Second 1974 Election (September–October 1974)                    174
7  Attack on the Policy Unit (October 1974)                             221
8  Back to Serious Government (October–November 1974)                   233
9  Edging Towards the European Nettle
   (November–December 1974)                                             242
10 New Year 1975: Scotland, the EEC and Escape
   to Washington (January–February 1975)                                270
11 To Dublin, and the EEC Renegotiation
   (February–March 1975)                                                306
12 The EEC Crunch in Cabinet (March–Easter 1975)                        333
13 The Budget – and Preparing for the Referendum
   (April 1975)                                                         347
14 Washington Again (May 1975)                                          368
15 The EEC Victory (May–June 1975)                                      377
16 A Botched Reshuffle (June 1975)                                      404
17 Crisis over Pay Policy (June–July 1975)                              418
18 Prime Minister to Retire? (July 1975)                                470
19 Party Conference at Blackpool (September–October 1975)               488
20 Autumn Miscellany (October–November 1975)                            516
21 Public Expenditure Crisis (November–December 1975)                   560

22   Irish Initiatives, Icelandic Retreats and Trying
     to Reform the Law (January–February 1976)            617
23   Drifting Towards Retirement (February–March 1976)     666
24   Resignation – With Such Honours (March–April 1976)    696

     List of Persons Mentioned in the Diary                725
     Index                                                 755

# Preface: The Diaries

Early in 1974, shortly after I began assisting the then Labour Party leader, Harold Wilson, I met a friend who had, when a civil servant, worked on some key negotiations with the Conservative Prime Minister, Edward Heath. Now a journalist, he told me that he deeply regretted not having kept a diary of those decisive events. He stressed how fallible is the human memory. Having myself been an academic historian who had used the diaries of prominent historical figures, I fully appreciated this argument. The point registered in the recesses of my brain and during the 1974 general election campaign I recalled it and began to jot down hurried notes late at night.

On that wet polling night of 28 February, touring a bleak Liverpool housing estate, when his election victory seemed for the first time seriously possible, Harold Wilson chatted with me about the style of his prospective government. He also pointed out to me how privileged I would be, as a then academic specialising in twentieth-century politics, to be able to observe the British political scene from the peak. (This was also his first, characteristically oblique, reference to his intention to employ me in his team in government.) He recalled the 1960–63 relationship between the US President, John F. Kennedy, and the Harvard Professor Arthur Schlesinger, who became historian to the Kennedy court. He urged me to retain 'a clear memory' of all that I witnessed. A little later in government in Number Ten he drew the same analogy and gave the same advice. I felt that the analogy flattered certainly me, and possibly even him, but I was further encouraged in my nightly writing.

Mr Wilson certainly did not actually suggest that I should keep a diary. That would have been quite out of character. He disliked the whole idea of personal revelations about himself – though like many people he was not averse to gossip about others – and he often made disapproving noises about ministerial colleagues who he knew were keeping diaries. Yet he knew that I was by profession a contemporary historian who had written on

Labour Party history, including a biography of a leading Labour politician with whom he had served in the Attlee Cabinet. It was my view that he was not averse to my preparing to write a record of his time as Prime Minister.

Harold Wilson always operated on several levels concurrently. I witnessed frequent examples of situations in Downing Street when he made it clear that he did not wish to know explicitly about certain proposed activities of his staff or colleagues and that he would have to disapprove of them publicly if they were brought openly to his attention. But he clearly hoped that they would happen without being brought to his attention. He was perhaps the most complex character I have met in my life.

I was content with that ambivalent understanding between us and at first saw the diary as most likely becoming the raw material for a detailed history of the 1974 Labour government, and possibly for a biography of Harold Wilson himself. In the event I chose a different career path and did not for many years have the time to undertake any such historical or biographical enterprise – by when the biographies written by others had made my own potential contribution seem less attractive. As the weeks, months and years slipped by in Number Ten, writing the diary became a habit and perhaps a therapy, regardless of any ultimate publishing objective.

On neither occasion when Mr Wilson and I discussed my role as an academic observer, did I mention that I had begun to keep a daily diary. It seemed best kept as a personal secret until I decided what, if anything, to do with it. I certainly did not want to alert the security services who were, according to the Prime Minister, prone to burgle those close to him. It was bad enough living at that time in Kentish Town, exposed to the local criminal profession, without also provoking the darker side and activities of MI5.

As time went on, I grew more systematic in my record-keeping, usually writing in my notebooks before falling asleep, however late, and also trying to write more fully with less recourse to abbreviated jottings. Sometimes I wrote in the mornings after returning from my dawn run across Hampstead Heath; temporarily forgotten incidents were added at weekends. My bedroom wardrobe and chest of drawers slowly filled. However, the legibility of my handwriting never improved.

For some time after ceasing in 1979 to keep a diary, I was uncertain what to do with the hoard of notebooks and supplementary sheets of scribbled paper. Finally, I consulted a publisher friend and we agreed to wait until sufficient time had passed for neither politics nor the careers of the individuals involved to be affected by the ever more distant events described.

I, of course, bore in mind the fifteen-year time-lapse recommended (though not prescribed) in the 1976 Radcliffe Report on ministerial and official memoirs – the uncertain and ambiguous introduction of which is described in this volume. I was equally aware that many ministers in the Cabinet which received that Report had overtly rejected it at the time (it was not formally approved by Cabinet) and had subsequently ignored its guidelines with respect to their own autobiographical writings. But in the event I decided, as a former special adviser in Whitehall, to abide by its recommended fifteen-year delay – that is fifteen years not only from the time of the events described (1974–76) but also from the date of my departure from public service (1979). As the years passed, there always seemed reason for further delay. Throughout the 1990s I was either a minister or a front bench spokesman and, to me, that ruled out publication.

By now in 2005 the main political participants in this diary have long left the electoral field of battle. The civil servants are all either retired or at the final peak of their official careers, well beyond any capacity I might conceivably have to affect their fates for good or ill. This has meant that the book has had to wait until long after Harold Wilson and many of his ministerial colleagues – and, indeed, the leading players in the subsequent Callaghan and Thatcher governments – have published their own memoirs and diaries. I am content with that, since this diary is simply a particular record and is not a reflective view of history, nor is it arguing part of a current debate, nor for or against any role in history. A further volume covering the prime ministership of James Callaghan 1976–79, which has also awaited the expiry of the various time constraints, will appear in due course.

Recently, professional historians and biographers have shown renewed interest in Wilson's remarkable political career and several biographies have been written. I trust that my personal record will have some additional interest and convey an authentic flavour of that special place, Number Ten Downing Street, during those particularly troubled times. Even if it does succeed in that, perhaps not all of what is written will give total pleasure to every one of the dramatis personae of Number Ten at that time – including the author, whose instant judgements do not always survive the test of historical hindsight. Such is the value and the weakness of diaries. They suffer from the pressures and the imbalances of a particular instant in time. They also reflect one locational viewpoint. Even in the power centre of Downing Street, one gets only part of the complex Whitehall picture. Another player in another department looking at the political prism from another angle will see a different picture which contains its own local truth.

This publication contains virtually the entirety of my handwritten note-books for this period, together with the inserted supplementary pages written at separate times (often in the office). A substantial number of editorial amendments have been made: particularly for stylistic reasons, where, for example, the insertion of prepositions and verbs omitted in the abbreviation of hurried writing makes the text more readable; and also in a number of cases on legal advice. Names and career positions have been elaborated more fully. Some inexplicably and unforgivably harsh observations on persons, some now dead, have been happily omitted – which might upset journalists seeking malicious copy but which I trust will find acceptance among the more civilised sections of the community and, especially, the families of those unfairly mentioned. In certain cases neither the typist nor I could read the handwriting and sentences have been omitted; occasionally elements of informed guesswork about the script have been accepted.

For better understanding and ease of reading, I have adopted two editorial practices. Brief biographies of people appearing in the diary (marked with an asterisk on first appearance in the text) are provided, listed at the back in alphabetical order. It is my observation that, apart from academic scholars, most readers do not enjoy a page cluttered with footnotes. I have also inserted background explanations of certain important events and developments which are referred to in passing in the text. It is chastening to my generation to realise how matters which seemed of great import and common knowledge at the time – the 'social contract', the 1975 pay policy and the EEC renegotiations are but a few major examples – are today beyond the recollection of all but a few readers with a special interest or experience. These insertions are distinct, clearly identified within square brackets, and where possible placed at the beginning or end of the relevant day's record.

Converting this almost illegible diary first on to a primitive early 1980s word processor and then a dozen years later on to a more sophisticated but apparently technically incompatible one, has proved a complex and tiresome task. For their assistance and discretion in completing that operation I express gratitude to Della Brotherstone and to Sandra Lee, as I do to my old friends Graham Greene and Joe Haines for their comments and unfailing friendship and support. My deepest retrospective appreciation goes to Carol and my children, who put up with a great deal during the exciting years described in this book.

Bernard Donoughue
November 2004

# Introduction:
## With Wilson in Downing Street

I had met Harold Wilson only rarely before joining his personal staff for the 1974 election campaign. The first time was when interviewing him in the early 1970s for a biography I was writing of the former Labour politician, Herbert Morrison. Then a year or so after that we chatted at a City lunch – specifically arranged by a mutual friend who felt that we might interest one another. These were our only communications until the autumn of 1973, when I was approached by a business acquaintance acting as intermediary and invited to join a small team advising the Labour leader on a series of opinion polls planned for the run-up to the next general election, due at the latest by the summer of 1975. As a teacher of political science at the London School of Economics I had some experience of polling, so I was interested and accepted.

I was also intrigued that Mr Wilson should look to me for help since, although a lifelong supporter of the Labour Party, I had never been identified with his brand of Labour politics. Indeed, I had worked closely with the supporters of Hugh Gaitskell in his battles against Wilson and the Left in the early 1960s. After Gaitskell's death in 1963, I continued to mix politically and socially with the Jenkins-Crosland wing of the party. I was then personally closest to Denis Howell and William Rodgers(*), both right-wing Gaitskellite MPs, and I frequently dissented from Wilson's 'soft' style of leadership. Since 1970, I had also acted as part-time adviser to Harold Lever(*), Labour's outstanding financial and economic spokesman and also identified with the party's moderate right wing. This personal approach to me from Harold Wilson was only the first of many examples I was to see of his remarkable tolerance of old opponents and commendable lack of interest in sectarian ideologies.

Characteristically, the Labour Party had at this time in 1973 set up two competing advisory groups on opinion polling. One group, containing a number of distinguished academics, together with stalwarts from the party organisation, was apparently advising the party on a formal and general basis. The second, set up primarily by Harold Wilson, met informally and more frequently. It was composed of Robert Worcester, the Canadian pollster employed periodically by the Labour Party, Percy Clarke, then Labour's press officer, Peter (later Lord) Lovell-Davis, who was an acquaintance of Harold Wilson and his personal and political secretary Marcia Williams, and myself. We were to report personally to the Labour leader and not directly to the party. In fact, the Labour Party's officers and activists had anyway grown increasingly disenchanted with opinion polls – mainly because the polls repeatedly showed that the electorate was itself increasingly disenchanted with the extreme policies preferred by the party's officers and activists.

Our group planned to conduct monthly surveys throughout 1974 into 1975 and then daily 'quickies' once the election was called. We drew up the detailed questions for the first poll in January 1974. When Robert Worcester's firm, MORI, had conducted and processed the questionnaire, we arranged to meet Mr Wilson for lunch to discuss the implications of its findings (which were not entirely encouraging to Labour).

The meeting was scheduled for lunchtime on Thursday, 7 February 1974. I recall that when I arrived at Westminster and walked up the steps and along the echoing corridor to the central lobby the atmosphere was buzzing with excitement. I was shown to the gloomy offices of the Leader of the Opposition, where Harold Wilson greeted me with the news that the Prime Minister, Edward Heath, had just dissolved Parliament. The election campaign would begin the following Monday, the 11th, and conclude on 28 February.

Mr Wilson apologised and said that he would not now be able to have lunch with Worcester and me since he had to go to discuss electoral arrangements. He asked us to eat with some of his colleagues in a Commons dining-room. There I sat with Wilson's amusing political aide from Bermondsey, Albert (later Lord) Murray, the former Labour MP for Gravesend, and wondered whether this was the beginning and end of my assignment.

However, immediately after lunch I was asked to go back to the leader's office. There I joined his personal team, who were sitting speculating on Labour's electoral chances. The atmosphere was informal, verging on chaotic, with people constantly wandering in and out and several telephones ringing at once. But the desultory discussion was strikingly dominated by two people to whom Harold Wilson readily deferred: Joseph Haines, Wilson's press secretary since previously in government in 1969, and Marcia Matilda Williams (later Baroness Falkender), his personal and political secretary since 1956, long before he became leader in 1963.

Joe Haines already had thirty years working in popular journalism behind him and was later to become the *Daily Mirror*'s outstanding political editor and columnist. He was in 1974 in his mid-forties, of medium height, wiry in build and hair, with quick, penetrating eyes behind rimless spectacles. He had the appearance of a coiled steel spring. I was aware of his reputation as a tough operator, hardened by a Rotherhithe childhood and a lifetime in the rough end of Fleet Street and at the grass roots of the Labour Party. He was not somebody lightly to be crossed. Later I learned that he could be a warm and loyal friend and very funny.

Although I had never met Marcia Williams, I remember as a young teenager frequently seeing her striding into Northampton's Derngate bus station, from where she travelled daily from the posh Northampton High School for Girls to her village some ten miles north of the town. (I had a similar daily routine from my school to another village to the south.) Then Marcia Field, daughter of a local builder, she struck me – admittedly younger and poorer than her and distinctly uncouth – as very tall, well dressed, very determined and perhaps having social aspirations a cut above most of my raucous Northamptonshire associates. She never mixed with our group of teenagers noisily gossiping and flirting in the dirty bus station. We did not actually meet, though we had mutual acquaintances and I eventually had a steady girlfriend who was her contemporary at her school, and so I was clearly aware of her.

She impressed me similarly in February 1974, as she dominated the proceedings and sliced through the election arguments like a knife. Around teatime, she rose from her chair and announced that we should all go home, since there was nothing more we could do today and we would be spending more than enough time with one another over the coming three weeks of the election campaign. Everybody, including Harold Wilson, obeyed. As we dispersed, he mentioned to me that we would all reassemble to discuss campaign strategy at his house nearby in Westminster on the following Sunday evening, 10 February.

That Sunday meeting was the first of my many visits to 5 Lord North Street, which immediately gave me the impression of not being really a home so much as a functional domestic base close to Parliament. Harold Wilson conducted the discussion in a very relaxed and democratic manner, asking everyone's views on the election issues that we should pursue and on various other tactical points. However, summing up, he decisively and eloquently outlined his strategy for the coming campaign. It would be, he said, similar to the English civil war battle of Marston Moor. We would spend the first week absorbing the Tory opening attacks on the trade unions, especially on the miners' strike, and dismissing Edward Heath's basic question of Who Governs Britain? Then we would counter-attack strongly on the issue of rising prices and the case for Labour's 'social contract' with the trade unions, assisted by skirmishes on the flanks over Britain's membership of the Common Market. He was witty and punchy and perceptive. For the first time it fleetingly crossed my mind that despite the adverse opinion polls Labour might win the election – though I sensed that Mr Wilson himself was perhaps less than convinced by his own arguments.

Nor did he seem enthusiastic for victory, for whoever won the election would face daunting problems in government. The British economic and industrial background was then bleaker than at any time since the immediate postwar period. Injudicious Tory Treasury management after 1970 threw away the benefits of Roy Jenkins's careful stewardship and saw the economy booming out of control in 1972, with output rising at an unsustainable 7%, and inflation rocketing into double figures in 1973. Relations between Edward Heath's Conservative government and the trade unions never recovered from the hostility engendered by his industrial relations legislation of 1970–72; and the number of days lost in strikes rose dramatically, inflated by the first national miners' strike since 1926, which led to a humiliating government capitulation in 1972. Readers of the following diary pages may justifiably feel that the next Wilson government was far from perfect in handling the succession of crises which befell Britain; but they should bear in mind its appalling inheritance from the previous Conservative government.

In this hostile economic and industrial environment – exacerbated by the Middle Eastern war of 1973 and a fourfold increase in OPEC oil prices – Mr Heath, contrary to his 1970 election pledge, announced a phased prices and incomes policy. A 7% pay norm was introduced in October 1973, precipitating another head-on confrontation with the miners, who refused to accept the norm.

The miners had begun their overtime ban on 12 November and the government responded in December with a state of emergency and a three-day working week to save electricity. On 17 December Chancellor Barber* introduced a mini-Budget of savage expenditure cuts and described the current situation as 'the gravest since the war'. Negotiations continued through January 1974, with the miners insisting on breaking the pay norm and the government, conscious of its humiliating 1972 climb-down, refusing to yield. On 4 February in the National Union of Mineworkers' ballot 81% voted for a strike.

Mr Heath called a sudden general election on 7 February 1974, posing the question of Who Governs Britain? This was curious in several ways. Mr Heath's government had a comfortable majority, had no difficulty in carrying through Parliament the programme on which it was elected in June 1970, and still had eighteen months to run. Its justification for a dissolution was the extremity of the multiple crises facing the nation: an energy crisis, an industrial relations crisis, an inflation crisis, an apparent social crisis and an alleged constitutional crisis. It was, and is still, not clear how holding a divisive election would have solved any or all of those problems. However, Mr Heath could feel that a clear victory would presumably give him a mandate for very tough action (though he never specified what that might be). Certainly the problems could only be solved, if at all, by exceptional wisdom, judgement and courage on the part of whichever politicians won power at the ballot box on 28 February.

On reflection and aided by hindsight, it strikes me now that few if any of us sitting there in 5 North Lord Street planning the February 1974 campaign fully appreciated the significance of the events which had precipitated this early election. Of course we understood that OPEC's dramatic increase in oil prices and cuts in production in 1973 had seriously damaging implications for the UK economy. But I doubt whether we had completely perceived the devastating combination of inflation and recession which the Arab oil producers had imposed on Britain. Of course, we grasped every detail of the miners' dispute, but probably did not realise that it had unwittingly launched a long power struggle between the unions and central government, which was not simply peculiar to Tory political obstinacy but would involve major abuses of unaccountable power by the trade union movement, and was progressively to break the postwar truce between capital and labour and would ultimately involve the unions losing many of their long-cherished privileges. I certainly knew from our polling evidence that the unions were unpopular, but did not see that our commitment to a 'social contract' with them meant that electorally Labour might ultimately be sunk with them – or in fact by them. I felt that the postwar social consensus was under pressure, but did not fully realise that violent confrontation was in fact becoming the new political style.

In the event, it was to prove a tactical mistake by the Conservative leader to try to make this a single-issue campaign on Who Governs Britain? Elections have their own personality and develop, as this one did, in ways which are difficult for politicians to control over three weeks of nationwide campaigning. But the Conservatives had with that slogan touched a deep concern and identified a profound industrial, social and political trend which would in coming years have to be either accepted or resisted by the democratically elected government. Either approach would involve tensions and unpopularities. That Labour in the immediate years ahead chose acceptance of union power and the Conservatives chose subsequently to confront and break it is not surprising, given their parties' distinct histories and philosophies. But it had major political and electoral consequences for the future fortunes of each party.

Sitting plotting our election strategy in February 1974, we certainly did appreciate the escalating inflationary danger faced by Britain, but probably not the extent to which it would come to obsess future government policy-making under whichever party; nor the way in which Labour's traditional Keynesian commitment to expanding the public sector and pursuing full employment was being rendered at best ineffective and at worst positively harmful by the new inflationary typhoon.

In Labour Party terms, we were a group of moderates, somewhat to the right of centre, with Mr Wilson well to the right. I personally was a 'revisionist' and considered myself on the radical right, with no attachments to the Marxist dogma then on the rise among party activists. Having City and transatlantic experience, I believed that Labour would have to come to terms with market forces and was convinced that the left wing's approach was sterile, too centralised, too authoritarian, too corporatist and too contemptuous of the individual citizen's wishes.

I had also for many years lectured at the London School of Economics on the steady decline in electoral support for both of Britain's main political parties. This alienation was to be an important part of the political atmosphere within which a future Labour government would operate and explains why we were so concerned with accommodating the growing Celtic nationalism within the kingdom. But, overall, I did not fully perceive the profound subterranean shifts which were in the 1970s altering the geography and geology of Britain's party system so that we would move into both a more multi-party system and, from 1979, one in which a single party would dominate government with a minority of the popular vote and the support of barely a third of the total electorate.

Perhaps Harold Wilson then possessed the vision to understand these underlying forces which were in 1974 affecting the British economic and political landscape. With his shrewd wisdom and six previous years of experience as Prime Minister he certainly understood more than the rest of us in his entourage. But in practice we were all then conditioned by our earlier assumptions, by traditional approaches to policy and by our tribal instincts and prejudices. So we invoked our familiar party political language – and Marston Moor.

There were reasons enough for us to be pessimistic about the outcome of the campaign ahead. Labour's 1970 general election defeat had been a great shock, and since then the party had not thrived in opposition. The ideological rift between the left and the right wings had grown wider and more bitter, with the Left gaining ground in the party organisation. The European Common Market provided a fresh divisive issue, splitting Labour in the 1972 Commons vote on entry, forcing its pro-European deputy leader, Roy Jenkins, to resign over the proposal to hold a referendum and leaving many other leading moderates in sullen disenchantment: some seeds of the future party split and the creation of the ill-fated Social Democratic Party were then sown.

Labour had not done well in recent by-elections and the opinion polls which Worcester, I and others analysed did not look promising. Among all the Labour politicians I talked with at the opening of the campaign, none expressed confidence that Harold Wilson would win. Perhaps some of the Gaitskellite Right were so hostile to Wilson and his compromising style of government that they did not mind if he lost – which would certainly have led to the change of leadership which they sought, though not inevitably in the direction which they wished. I came from that Gaitskellite tradition but did not share that view on the election, since I always preferred Labour to win. But I certainly did not begin as a fan of the Labour leader's political style.

At the close of our discussions that Sunday evening, 10 February 1974, Mr Wilson invited us all to gather again early the next morning for the first day of the campaign proper. I found this prospect exciting. Although I had for many years lectured academically on the conduct and outcome of post-1945 British general elections, this was to be my first direct political experience of an election at national level.

To begin with I found it confusing, but fortunately there was an established daily routine and regular timetable for the party leader with which I quickly became familiar. (The diary which follows below does not cover these opening days of the campaign, beginning only on 16 February.)

The day often began early at 5 Lord North Street with a discussion between Mr Wilson and his personal staff about overnight media coverage and the issues to be pursued and the speeches to be given that day. Then we all walked 200 yards along Lord North Street and across Smith Square to the party headquarters, then in Transport House, which were also the headquarters of the mighty Transport and General Workers' Union. There we attended the 9 a.m. daily meeting of the party's campaign committee, containing leading figures from the National Executive Committee, the trade unions and the party organisation. It discussed election tactics but was in fact too large, too unstructured and, in some cases, too ill-informed to be of much help. Afterwards Mr Wilson came to his campaign offices in Transport House for a further discussion with us prior to attending the daily press conference at which party spokesmen tried to get their views reported by the media – and to launch attacks on the Tories, who also held a morning press conference to the same journalists at their headquarters across the other side of the square.

The party leader then departed to distant cities, to tour marginal constituencies and to deliver the day's major speeches. He travelled with a secretary, a junior press officer, and a baggage carrier – his ever loyal and long-suffering assistant Albert Murray. While he was away for the rest of the day, the remaining three of his personal team – Joe Haines, Marcia Williams and myself – held the fort in Transport House, finally retiring to Lord North Street to await the travelling party's return, which was often around midnight.

One problem which immediately arose was how to get the leader's campaign speeches written in time for delivery. For the first couple of days Mr Wilson tried to dictate paragraphs in odd moments between meetings during the morning, sometimes while he was on the move, even in the bathroom while shaving or while being powdered and made up for television interviews. This inspired bouts of ill temper in the party leader and some very rough passages in the speeches. He was reluctant to give up this creative role because he had always boasted how he wrote his own speeches. But the pressure on him personally and the chaos surrounding the dictation and typing quickly forced him to surrender. In the middle of the first week he suddenly announced a radical change. We would collectively decide the main theme of each day's speeches well in advance and a first draft would be written – primarily by Joe Haines but with the assistance of Marcia Williams and myself – the day before it was to be delivered. This draft would be handed to Mr Wilson at our midnight gathering in Lord North Street for him to read overnight. When we met early the next morning he would propose changes, as might we in the light of overnight developments, which would be incorporated in the final draft while he was at the morning campaign committee and press conference.

This system worked beautifully, leaving Mr Wilson more time to think strategically and resulting in the speech usually being ready for distribution to the media well in advance of delivery from the platform. Joe Haines was a brilliant and speedy draughtsman, able to put arguments and jokes in perfect Wilsonian style. Soon journalists commented to me during the campaign that Harold was 'back on form with his speeches after a bad start' and how 'typical and inimitable' were his jokes and phrases attacking the Tories.

For myself, the speeches, the meetings, the discussions among the entourage at Transport House, the endless waiting for feedback from the party travelling with the leader, the late-night debriefings in Lord North Street – these became a total way of life, a daily treadmill beginning when I left home in the early morning and ending exhausted in the early hours of the following day. Fortunately I was then a university teacher, which meant that even in mid-term time a great deal of spare time was available to anybody reasonably energetic. I took taxis from Transport House to the LSE to meet my periodic teaching commitments. But actually none of my academic colleagues (some of whom for various reasons in those easier days themselves habitually followed a similar routine of only occasional professional attendance) was aware that I was working sixteen hours a day at the centre of the general election. In fact, I was never wholly confident myself that this activity would last beyond the current day – since Harold Wilson never specifically asked me to join his team for the campaign. It was simply a daily renewal: each night as I left Lord North Street he would say, 'I will see you in the morning as usual, then, Bernard,' and each day as he left for his travels he would wave to Joe, Marcia and me saying, 'I will see you all when I get back tonight.'

The daily repetition of this short-term invitation did after a while begin to feel like a slightly longer-term commitment. Certainly Joe and Marcia quickly treated me as a full member of the political family. It seemed I might hope to last the course till election day on 28 February. With this fascinating prospect ahead, I decided on 16 February to begin writing this diary. As a then professional historian I appreciated the unique opportunity offered by a vantage point at the centre of national affairs. Throughout my time working for Harold Wilson these two distinct professional roles, as temporary policy adviser and as a lifelong historian, ran exhaustingly in tandem. I also knew that, as so often in politics, it was not any unique personal merit but pure chance – the chance of availability and the fortune of being in the right place at the right time – which gave me that privileged opportunity to live the unique Downing Street life for the five tumultuous years that followed.

On rereading these diaries for the first time many years after the events, I was struck, as the reader will probably be struck, by what a peculiar world is there described and by the curious balance of priorities and concerns which is sometimes conveyed.

At times the internal office tensions between the then various sections of Number Ten – the private office, the political office, the press office and the Policy Unit – as well as between them and the Treasury and Cabinet Office elsewhere in Whitehall, seem to dominate the narrative. This will understandably seem petty in relation to the major issues of economic, social and foreign policy which were currently before the Prime Minister and his government (though the latter issues do, in fact, constitute the majority of the text). Yet such is the nature, the weakness and the strength of contemporary diaries. They record what especially absorbed or irritated the author at a particular time, and not always what posterity realises to have been the most important in public policy terms.

But there is a further factor, deriving from the special character and circumstances of the Wilson entourage in 1974–76, which needs elaboration in order to understand the context within which my diaries were written. The working reality of those two years was that on many days, while trying to cope with the major policy issues of the time, we were frequently diverted, delayed and even overwhelmed by the minor, extraneous but intensely irritating tensions generated within the Prime Minister's team. These absorbed a disproportionate amount of time and emotional energy and inevitably occupied an equally disproportionate amount of space in my writing relative to their ultimate global significance.

Any academic study written reflectively after the event and following the due sifting of measured priorities will bleach out such minor transactions and concentrate on only what is ultimately seen to be significant. Diaries are different and special. They reflect the realities, including the real trivialities, of daily life. They do suffer from the pressures, distortions and imbalances of a particular instant in time. To take an extreme example from the diary pages which follow, the casual reader might be excused for concluding that Mr Wilson's press secretary spent much of his time being angry with the political secretary, that I was permanently suffering from either a bronchial cold or a broken-down car. That was not the case, but when it occurred it tended to intrude on the daily narrative. Perhaps we should be reassured to find that even in Ten Downing Street not every hour is vibrant with great affairs of state, but often involves pointless endeavour relating to the ordinary routines of daily life.

Nor should the reader expect from diaries always a measured, fair and balanced view of every character participating in the action. References to, and descriptions of, individuals again reflect the particular pressures of that moment. All such references should be helpful in contributing to an overall portrait of each participant. But no reference on its own conveys the whole person, and some below are inevitably over-critical.

Wilson's Cabinet colleagues do not appear to suffer too badly in characterisation – perhaps because I was near enough to admire them but not sufficiently close to observe and perhaps exaggerate their warts. Certainly it was a remarkably impressive Cabinet. Harold Wilson, James Callaghan, Roy Jenkins, Denis Healey, Tony Crosland, Barbara Castle, Michael Foot and Tony Benn (to name but eight and to exclude others of great ability) composed a collective team of political experience, weight, skill and intellect which was remarkable then and today seems astonishing compared to some of their successors in more recent Cabinets. Each one either became or could easily have become a national party leader. Their place in history could not be harmed, and I hope will be modestly helped by their appearances in this diary.

But it is those who live and work in closest proximity to a diarist who experience the fiercest, though not always the fairest, light of scrutiny.

Harold Wilson, the central figure in this drama, is the most obvious and most important example. The diaries show him, often unguarded, during a brief period right at the end of his long and distinguished career (and when the author was often tired and frustrated).

These final years of 1974–76 were, anyway, an extremely difficult period in British history. It would have been nearly impossible for any Prime Minister and government to shine in the world economic crisis then prevailing, especially if, like Wilson, lacking an adequate parliamentary majority. It is not an accident nor a surprise that no democratic leader of a major nation who had to face the crisis following the four-fold increase in oil prices in 1973–74 survived in office until the end of the decade. Moreover, Harold Wilson was by 1974 old for his fifty-eight years, tired, often unwell, seeing nothing left to prove as a politician other than to achieve certain records of time in office – and knowing that after October 1974, he would not stand for office again.

He appears in these pages, warts and all. But the reader would be mistaken to count only the later warts. Wilson should be seen in the round and against the background of his whole remarkable career. Labour lost four successive general elections under the three leaders who followed Wilson. Compared to that dismal record, Wilson's electoral achievements during thirteen years of party leadership in winning four out of five general elections and leading four Labour administrations covering over eight years appears quite stunning.

As leader, he exhibited consummate skills in holding together a fissiparous party which was increasingly just a loose coalition of different and often conflicting interests and beliefs. He was similarly impressive as chairman of the Cabinet, giving every side an opportunity to voice a view, always seeking consensus, maintaining unity. These consensual skills are often seen on display in this diary. He himself would often dismiss them to colleagues by quoting, with a grin, his version of James Maxton's saying that 'if you cannot ride three horses at once you should not be in the circus'. But it was still a remarkable feat of party management. It was not just chance that within a few years of his retirement the Labour Party was openly split asunder.

His personal qualities were of great relevance to his successes as party leader. He could be accessible, warm, kind and humorous, which drew the affection and loyalty of those who worked for him. He had absolutely no side or any of the pretensions or assumptions of grandeur that sometimes accompany high office. Indeed, to the end he remained middle class, middlebrow, provincial in the best sense of the word, and a nonconformist, grammar school, 'Little Englander'.

He had no trace of snobbery or racism and was astonishingly tolerant of the sins, foibles and human weaknesses of others (though he did occasionally express mild distaste for what he saw as metropolitan glitz). His capacity for work remained spasmodically impressive and his mind, once of Rolls-Royce calibre, still showed flashes of quicksilver. But he was not an intellectual in the conventional sense, with little interest in theories, concepts or high-flown ideas. He had little interest in highbrow art and his cultural pleasures rarely extended beyond Gilbert and Sullivan or a popular novel. Like many of his social and educational background, he had ingrained habits of always doing his homework, almost 'swotting'.

Less attractive was his frequent boasting about his achievements (and, ironically in the light of his later medical experience, about his memory). In this, as in his delightful mischievousness, he was like a schoolboy, sometimes engagingly wicked, sometimes the boring Boy Scout. On the darker side were surly bouts of paranoid suspicion and a surrounding cloud of personal guilt with its attendant fears of exposure and scandal.

He was, for a politician, remarkably free of vindictiveness towards political opponents (though not towards journalists, for whom no revenge was too great). This enabled political wounds and bruises to heal quickly and meant that he did not, as some leaders do, build up over time a significant opposition of bitter enemies. Being so forgiving led others sometimes, though not in every case, to forgive him.

If he did not always exhibit overwhelming loyalty to those who had served him that is understandable within the jungle context of competitive politics, where too close an attachment can become an obstacle to advancement. Party politics is certainly tribal and it is often necessary to hunt in packs. But most politicians have limited lasting personal loyalties: instead they have shifting alliances of mutual interest. But within those constraints of the natural political habitat, Wilson was a team player, showing more continuity of alliance than most in his party. Several who had been his allies when he became leader in 1963 remained reasonably close to him and continued to have access to him two decades later (as is seen in the painful diary episodes describing his botched 1975 ministerial reshuffle). He also went out of his way to protect and promote parliamentary colleagues who had worked with him in the past. Later pages show how shortly before retiring he effected a minor reshuffle whose sole purpose was to provide better job security for some old supporters who might not expect to survive in office under a new Prime Minister.

The main reservations about Harold Wilson, expressed frequently by friends and critics alike, concern the actual use he made of his long tenure in prime ministerial office. It is felt that he had few lasting policy achievements and his governments made little real impact on British life. Some of this criticism is unfair, blaming him for the underlying national decline which had other, more fundamental, dynamics in those years. Even so, many who worked with him or observed him concluded that his lack of lasting achievement did derive from a lack of political principle; that he was almost wholly a political operator and manager; that because he apparently believed in so little he had few real policy commitments and objectives; that he was solely concerned with achieving and surviving in power and had no personal views on what actually to use that power to achieve. It has often been said that he was more a politician than a statesman.

Readers will find evidence for those criticisms in the pages that follow. He is seen to be most often concerned with Cabinet or party management. Only occasionally – as on the Northern Ireland issue in 1974–75 – is he described trying to initiate policy. But it should be remembered that he did at least create the Downing Street Policy Unit to provide him with policy ideas and, as with the Unit's proposals in 1975–76 to allow local authority tenants to buy their council houses, he immediately saw its significance and gave it encouragement and support against the opposition of ministers with less political foresight. It should also again never be forgotten that this period of 1974–76 was the tail-end of his career.

Those who have studied Wilson's administrations in the 1960s will note both the continuities and the differences of political style as described after 1974. Little of the earlier frenetic domestic activity or parading on the world stage remains. He occasionally reveals his interventionist instincts but rarely has the appetite to carry them through. His alleged earlier radicalism had by then faded, though he remained mildly anti-Establishment in a provincial kind of way. Most of his instincts were conservative and he was not simply joking when in the 1974 general election he said to me, with a hint of Stanley Baldwin, that his true personal manifesto was really to offer the British people a quiet life.

His skills as a Cabinet manager are shown as even more pronounced as he shrewdly balanced the main party factions within his government. He carefully built a close alliance with his most senior colleague, James Callaghan, burying old jealousies and disagreements, and so created a solid foundation for Cabinet stability at the heart of the government. Their joint conduct of the 1974–75 EEC renegotiations, narrated in some detail below, was little short of brilliant, keeping Britain in Europe while preserving unity in the Cabinet and the party when a majority of party and parliamentary members were certainly hostile.

Other less attractive features are seen to recur throughout his time as leader. In particular, his obsession with press criticism, his constant suspicion of 'leaks' of information to the media, his near paranoia about plots by various imaginary and genuine enemies – all these characteristics litter the diary pages in 1974–76 as they are reported to have clouded his earlier years. His dark suspicions were focused as much on those who worked for him as those who worked against, thus adding further stress to the immense pressures and workload which inevitably exist in Number Ten.

The single most important influence on Harold Wilson, common to all his previous eighteen years at the top of politics, was his personal and political secretary, Marcia Williams (elevated to Baroness Falkender in 1974). She features frequently and strongly in this record. Nobody can hope to understand Harold Wilson and to assess his career without attempting to comprehend her role in his life and work. From 1974–76 she probably spent less time in Number Ten than she had in 1964–70 (though I was not present during the earlier period to make precise comparisons). She almost certainly had less influence than previously on policy and on the Prime Minister's political decisions. Apart from her own avowed dislike of Downing Street, her sphere of activities was probably constrained both by the existence of the new Number Ten Policy Unit and also by the close alliance between the other two senior members of the Prime Minister's triumvirate of personal advisers, Joe Haines as press secretary and myself as senior policy adviser. But she remained the person closest to Harold Wilson and when she chose to intervene he usually gave her wishes priority over all others.

He listened to and accepted her views more readily than those from any other source. He often indulged her wildest whims almost like a daughter (for example treating honours like chocolates given to her to keep her quiet and happy) and equally feared her like a fierce mother (as when he is seen hiding from her menacing telephone calls). She, as I observed in the diary early in 1974, had the magical power both to switch on and switch off his lights. She was also very adept at mobilising his demons, stimulating his nightmares and evoking his alleged enemies.

Theirs was a relationship of great intensity and complexity which no one coming late to the scene as I did could presume fully to analyse and understand. But its existence mattered greatly to everyone who worked in Number Ten trying to serve Harold Wilson as Prime Minister. It inevitably pervades these diary pages, sometimes intruding merely as rumbles of distant thunder, sometimes striking centre stage like lightning. It was an influence which clearly met some deep need in Harold Wilson and may well have assisted him greatly in his rise to the top of British politics, providing the necessary aggression and jagged edge which was lacking in his own rather soft personality.

A number of people he respected attempted to wean him away from this relationship. He apparently told them, as reported below, that he neither desired nor dare face the consequences (whatever that might mean) of the liberation they advised. But viewing the influence overall, one cannot but note, despite its final flourish of exaggeration, the verdict expressed to the Downing Street press secretary at a dinner in 1975 by Lord Goodman, Wilson's longstanding and close personal adviser. 'Mr Haines,' the distinguished lawyer concluded, 'he [Wilson] will not go down in history as one of the great prime ministers, but if it had not been for that woman, he would have gone down as the greatest.'

The picture of Marcia Falkender which emerges from these pages is mixed, beginning with great admiration and evolving through sympathy to puzzlement and to eventual hostility. Overall it is not very flattering. As such it may underestimate her undoubted abilities – her sharp intelligence, her determination, her great manipulative skills, her shrewd political insight – although these were observed more often in earlier times before I knew Harold Wilson than in 1974–76. Again it must be stressed that these pages present a latter-day view, recorded in episodic exchanges, occasionally in vitriolic confrontation. They do not reflect her life's journey as Wilson's main adviser and confidante during much of his climb to the top of the slippery pole of British politics.

Nor should my passing diary comments lead to any underestimation of the dramatic power of her personality, exercised both creatively and destructively. This power was not only exercised through her bewitching domination of the Prime Minister himself. Once launched against any human obstacle or perceived personal enemy, her frenzied tirades were very impressive and virtually ungovernable. Victims of her bullying invective – whether grown men and women successful in their own spheres or defenceless female junior members of her staff – were at times reduced to silent, shivering and even blubbering wrecks. The sad experiences of the Prime Minister's assistant, Albert (later Lord) Murray, a former Member of Parliament and Minister of State and a kind and decent man, and of Bill Housden, Wilson's official driver, whom she often borrowed for her own personal use, were but two examples at different ends of the spectrum which feature in the pages below. The basis of her aggressive power lay in the realisation by her victims that she could normally mobilise the support of the Prime Minister for whatever she accused or demanded. Without that backing her style would have been less effective – indeed counterproductive and unacceptable in any normal working or social context. Those who refused to be controlled or manipulated by her, such as Arnold Goodman, Joe Haines, myself and, in earlier times, Derek Mitchell (Wilson's first principal private secretary), could find themselves subject to remorseless hostility and attack, at least behind their backs. As her sister is quoted, commenting to me at the team's last lunch in Downing Street in April 1976, it required some degree of steel to keep Marcia at bay.

The efforts of Joe Haines and myself, as well as the marginally less exposed secretaries in private office, to keep Marcia at bay may seem to the reader to occupy an excessive amount of the following text and to involve some trivial episodes. That was not from my choice, nor ever anticipated when I began to write this diary. I set out to write a historical record of Harold Wilson and his Labour government. I did not expect to set out so much personal detail nor so many particularities of office politics. In the event the multitude of minor daily matters had to be set down because they became such an important part of the Prime Minister's working life – and therefore of the working life of those who served him in Number Ten.

The everyday reality of our work was that anything we did or proposed for the Prime Minister – giving policy or political advice, suggesting meetings, writing speeches, fixing appointments, travelling to negotiations overseas with him, or indeed attending any engagements in relation to our jobs – was always subject to the political secretary's intervention. Because she had such influence on the Prime Minister, these were therefore always likely to be changed or rejected, often without apparent rational cause. Working for Wilson was like walking through an endless minefield, constantly wary, looking and listening for any signs of where the next hidden explosive might lie.

Exercising influence on the Prime Minister in Downing Street requires above all access to his ear and, to a lesser extent, the capacity to determine who else has access to him. The press of claimants to his ear is enormous. It has to be sifted and in many cases resisted. Those who have access have potential influence on the levers of power.

The then private office, containing a principal private secretary and several other secretaries specialising in foreign, economic, social and parliamentary affairs, together with a diary secretary, had automatic access to the Prime Minister. They also managed the access of others from the governmental side, including senior officials such as the Cabinet Secretary and ministerial colleagues. The press secretary has equally automatic entrée to his boss and arranges access from and to the media (which in 1974–76 was strictly limited because of Wilson's loathing of the press). Marcia controlled access from and to the whole political and personal side of the Prime Minister's life, including all organisational manifestations of the Labour Party, his constituency, most of his few leisure activities, much of his finances and his patronage. Any one of the team who inadvertently trespassed on her broad territory did so at considerable personal and professional peril – although she was not always as restrained in relation to their domains.

She tightly controlled the political and personal area of communication to and from Wilson, by telephone, on paper or in person. Anybody from outside (with the exception of a few special friends, his governmental colleagues and the press) wishing to see or talk to the Prime Minister was advised to make contact with and through her. Her personal approval secured access; her disapproval meant exclusion. Those who tried to gain access without first asking her permission would suffer a blackening of character and the slamming of the Prime Minister's door. Those previously privileged with access would be suddenly banished if incurring her displeasure. A similar experience faced those actually working in the entourage. This strategic position ensured her considerable power, since others had to please her in order to reach the Prime Minister. From her critically located offices, one opening on to the Cabinet Room lobby in Number Ten, the other adjacent to the Prime Minister's room in the Commons, she acted as an impressive and effective dragon at the gate.

To appreciate fully the stresses which these various personal and power factors could generate in the Downing Street team it is necessary to understand how Number Ten functions as an institution of central government. In fact I have described in some detail in an earlier book the then working of Number Ten and its component sections (see *Prime Minister*, Jonathan Cape 1987, esp. pp. 1–37). Here the main relevant point is that Number Ten is unlike any other department of British central government in that it is so small (around a hundred staff in total, with some dozen giving senior policy advice) and that its whole operation depends entirely on one person, the Prime Minister. There is no intervening departmental structure to cut off the Prime Minister from anything or anybody, no hierarchy to sift suggestions, cushion tensions or hide and disguise the workings of the house machine. The staff in Number Ten do not, as in other departments, work under layers of senior bureaucrats or in the shadow of the wider operations of Whitehall. We worked personally for and directly to the Prime Minister. Therefore the Prime Minister's mood, his personal views and reactions at any particular time wholly determined what we could or could not achieve or help him to achieve. Anything, however extraneous, however seemingly trivial (including press attacks), which affected the Prime Minister's mood or concentration, which diverted his attention or pre-empted his thinking, also affected our capacity to serve and advise him on the major policy issues of the day.

That is why those seemingly extraneous trivialities are so often recorded. They were important because they were all part of the pressures which operated on the Prime Minister. In affecting him they affected his team, and ultimately the central decision-making process. It was our view, as reflected in the diaries, fairly or unfairly, that the political secretary was at times a major source of distraction of the Prime Minister away from what we, rightly or wrongly, saw as his main government responsibilities and priorities. From her position, she undoubtedly saw it differently. But it was because she could exercise such supreme influence with, and even power over, the Prime Minister, however spasmodically practised during this later period, on whatever major or trivial issues, that her activities, wishes and whims mattered so much to the rest of the staff in Number Ten. Hence they at times preoccupied the diarist.

One final factor which should never be forgotten when reading the events which follow, especially when contemplating the examples of anger, irritation, unfairness and seeming misjudgements, in conduct and in writing, is the ceaseless treadmill of work which burdened the Downing Street team. Academics concerned with 'overload' in British central government will not lack evidence here. The long working days; the need to scan and quickly absorb a huge flow of papers usually equivalent to reading a heavy book a day; the endless conveyor belt of high-level committees; the pressure of having to take positions, make judgements and give hurried but accountable written or verbal advice on matters of considerable importance – all these accumulated over time to deplete one's innermost physical and nervous resources. This strain was made worse by the conflicts of internal office politics and especially when the external political climate was depressed by government failures and constant media hostility.

To some extent this burden can be deduced from the daily narratives. But the full weight and pressure can never be properly described or conveyed. Fortunately it was often eased or erased for a while by the countervailing sense of exhilaration derived from operating at the centre of political power and by the satisfaction of working together with people of very high calibre. Success, whether personally in the job or by the government as a whole, would also ease pain and help the adrenalin to flow. But always in the background there was a nagging sense of deep exhaustion, which only fully surfaced when stepping off the treadmill and taking a holiday, the first part of which was always in my case spent sleeping. It was even worse for the press secretary, who was bombarded with telephone calls night and day. Later he told me that after leaving Number Ten he noticed something very odd in his life and how he felt physically strange – that for the first time in several years he had been able to sleep a whole night uninterrupted by office worries or by the telephone.

Having experienced, suffered and above all enjoyed the pressures of Downing Street for over five years – pressures which were shared or far surpassed by other senior ministers and officials – I am finally impressed not by the number of errors made in British central government, but that there are not more. My observation of politicians also led me to conclude that to reach and survive at the top of politics requires more stamina (and luck) than genius. During my years in Number Ten I was blessed with relative youth and considerable physical and mental energy. My admiration for those, such as Harold Wilson and James Callaghan, who survived those pressures when much older and less obviously physically fit, was and is boundless.

After Harold Wilson's resignation as Prime Minister in April 1976, I was asked to remain in Number Ten to serve with growing admiration his successor, James Callaghan. I inevitably lost direct contact with Mr Wilson (although he did formally request that I act as secretary to a Royal Commission on the City of London which he was to chair; the request was declined by the new Prime Minister). However, my respect for him as an immensely professional politician remains undimmed, as is my affection for him as a warm and remarkably tolerant human being. Those feelings are reinforced by rereading these pages. Diaries, for all the reasons explained above, rarely do justice to those who appear in them. His reputation should grow.

# CHAPTER 1

# Who Governs Britain?
# Harold Wilson Wins the Election
# of February 1974

*Saturday 16 February 1974*

I arrived at the high gloomy room in Transport House at 10 a.m. Harold Wilson,* Marcia Williams* (Wilson's political secretary) and Joe Haines* (Wilson's press secretary) were already there. Wilson was dictating an extra section to add to the extract of tonight's Southampton/Portsmouth speech which would be released to the press. Too long and wordy – but the intention was to strengthen the paragraphs on what Labour would do about prices. Haines tried to cut and simplify: with his usual good sense of what ordinary people understand. Peter Davis* joined us and Tommy Balogh* crept in, hovered, lurked in corners.

Then on to discuss the statement for the daily press conference. Short and better. Accusing Ted Heath* of having no solutions to the economic crisis. I corrected this together with Marcia Williams, who has a mind like a hacksaw, fast and penetrating and very jagged. She had a cold this morning.

An Israeli woman arrived with a huge petition and a dozen cameramen asking for Harold Wilson's support for Russian Jewish women on hunger strike. Harold was photographed endlessly holding the petition and looking deeply concerned. He called a secretary to dictate his statement on this. At the same time Joe Haines was revising the speech press release and Marcia Williams and I were checking the press conference statement. Balogh hovered. Research assistants wandered in. Albert Murray* (Wilson's personal assistant) reported on whether the helicopter would be available. Ron Hayward* (general secretary of the Labour Party) came in about something organisational. Telephones rang. Like Euston station. Complete chaos.

When the Israeli deputation left it was almost time for the press conference (11.45 a.m.). HW asked me to boil down James Callaghan's* statement on incomes policy. The typing was slow. Nearly every photocopier in Transport House not working. Our office out of paper.

I went to the press conference, which had already started. I sent the

Callaghan summary to HW on the platform – in case of questions. Marcia refused to take it – says on principle she doesn't service him on public platforms.

Statement by Tony Crosland* (Labour's spokesman on Housing and the Environment) was good. Makes the responsibility for housing seem too small for him. Young Eric Deakins* then lectured the audience, mainly against the EEC.

It was a smaller audience today. Desultory air, people walking in and out. Tame questions, mainly to HW who began to attack the press, stung by an *Evening Standard* article saying he was old and tired. But he then retreated. The question on the EEC was very skilfully handled – renegotiate and put it to the people at the ballot box, no suggestion by HW of withdrawal.

Back to HW's room in Transport House. He was preparing to leave by helicopter at 2 p.m. Discussed conference speakers next week. Haines repeated my earlier suggestion of gathering Labour's whole economic team for the trade figures conference – Denis Healey,* Jim Callaghan, Roy Jenkins* and Wilson. HW agreed and Marcia Williams immediately set about arranging it. We also agreed the speakers for the rest of the conferences throughout the campaign – all solid men. Not an extreme left-winger mentioned. Marcia was very sound on all this.

HW ate a quick plate of ham with a can of beer. He pulled my leg about the French mustard, saying it proved he was 'not anti-foreigner'.

Rush and crisis as HW got ready to leave. The speech papers were muddled. He changed his shirt. He was furious that his wash-bag fell in the wash-basin and was full of water. Complaining his servicing not good enough. Nowhere to rest or work when he gets to meetings – he had to use the ladies' lavatory in Manchester. Marcia was trying to get a decision on tomorrow's strategy meeting – where, when, who? He doesn't want to go to the campaign committee. Says they had decided to meet *next* Sunday. It was leaked to the press who printed that it would be *this* Sunday. Now the committee feels his absence will help again to delay the repeated request for a 'Wedgy Benn* phone-in'.

Wilson looks tired and low. Marcia says he feels depressed and instructs him to cheer up. Finally he is brushed, combed and spruced in front of a battered old mirror which Bill Housden, his long-time chauffeur, produces. [Bill Housden, the Prime Minister's colourful driver for many years, also assisted Marcia in many capacities including chauffeuring her on shopping trips and ferrying her mail from Downing Street to her home. He was often unhappy and frequently held informative conversations with the author, Joe Haines and Albert Murray.]

He leaves 20 minutes late, so will have to go direct to meeting. Apparently

on leaving he thanks Marcia for handling Tommy Balogh's irritating interruptions so tactfully.

HW told Joe Haines and me to write his speech for Leicester tomorrow
and produced an old press release of an earlier speech a year ago and says
just reproduce it. Haines and I were relieved and went out to lunch at
Church House. I like him and get on well. He says it is a good sign that
HW is edgy. That HW thought he was losing in 1966 (when he won by a
landslide): Joe says that in the 1970 election the entourage was himself,
Marcia, Terry Lancaster, a political journalist representing the Mirror
newspapers, and Peter Shore.* Says HW keeps Shore out now because he
is 'barmy on the Common Market'. HW apparently gave Shore a terrible
rocket because he made such anti-Market speeches. Joe says HW needs
sleep – but his resilience and recovery are then remarkable. Joe doesn't
like handling the press, for whom he has little respect. He would like to
write the framework of all the speeches so that HW could get some time
to think about long-term strategy. But HW hates the idea of people writing
his speeches. That's why he dictated an extra piece this morning. 'He was
getting his own back on me for writing his speech.' Joe has total contempt
for the Transport House party headquarters (except for Reg Underhill,*
who is a lone beacon of sense and competence).

Back in the office Marcia was there saying she had just come from a
terrible row between Ron Hayward, the party secretary, and Percy Clarke,
the party press officer, and the latter had walked out. The phone then rang
and Hayward was on saying Clarke had just been to apologise, in tears. The
phone rang again and Clarke was on. Marcia offered him some of the tranquillisers she regularly takes to calm herself. Clarke came to collect them.

Marcia's sister, Peg, then arrived with coffee and bags of food.

Joe and I look at the old Leicester speech. No good – just a lot of statistics. We discuss a new speech on voluntary incomes policy. Joe sits down
to type. The speech was quickly taking shape. He is obviously at home
behind a typewriter. Then fast and fluent – in complete HW style. I decide
to go and make arrangements for tomorrow's programme. Marcia jokes
about dragging me away from my regular Sunday morning football. It is
quieter in the office as I go. Just Joe at his typewriter and Marcia at a desk
taking calls and giving instructions. I can see how HW depends so much
on them both. They each know what he wants and would say.

In the outer office, less intimidating, are the research assistant, two secretaries plus Peg, sitting, ready to do her younger sister's bidding. Joe is
short, slim, bristly black hair, with a direct piercing look in his eyes, very
quick in all his movements and thoughts. He is funny and obviously short
on temper and long on courage. Marcia is tall and rangy, with eyes like a
hawk and teeth like a hare. She frightens everybody (especially Harold

Wilson) except Joe. She is obviously neurotic, but there is also something else less obvious, but definitely there, about her. To do with power, which I detect but cannot yet identify. Not sure if it is healthy. But Joe and Marcia are an impressively intimidating pair if they work together. Otherwise mutually destructive.

Home for half an hour when Marcia and Joe phone me to discuss how to handle Heath's violent speech tonight accusing Labour of being reds and unconstitutional. I suggest we contact HW and get him to incorporate a statement in his speech saying that the Tory leader is rattled, being a bully and divisive again. I am most keen not to be diverted off the prices issues now we have them cornered there. The weakness of Harold Wilson and Marcia is that they cannot let a point pass, want to argue and deny every Heath accusation. This happened over the miners' strike throughout the week. In fact it gives Heath the initiative and leaves us always reacting. So he can influence the ground we fight on. Harold and Marcia want to issue a separate statement. I hope not. It will divert attention from HW's prices attack.

Really today is the quietest day so far. With much of the speech done in advance and HW leaving early. Yet still tremendous bustle and time flew.

All are encouraged by our private poll (4% behind the Tories as opposed to 12% previously) and by advance news of Sunday's poll showing us only 1–3% behind. It means we have contained the Tories' first attack. Yet I sense deep pessimism everywhere. Don't think anyone believes we will win. I do sometimes. But worried by the party's Scottish poll showing us doing badly, and worse than last time, with a strong trend to nationalist policies and a large majority wanting a Scottish Parliament. Scotland could be the wild card which kills us.

Twelve more days to polling day.


## *Sunday 17 February 1974*

Arrived at Transport House in Smith Square at 10 a.m. for the election 'Strategy' meeting. In fact Harold Wilson did not arrive till 10.30. Then we rapidly plunged into the correction of today's speeches (at Leicester and Nottingham). Present were Joe Haines, Marcia, Geoffrey Goodman (a journalist from the *Daily Mirror*), myself, Balogh and Ben Whitaker* (the former Labour MP for Hampstead). We decided to put stress on Labour's voluntary incomes policy, on the assumption that now prices are established at the centre of the campaign people would want to know what we would do about wages. Stress also on the social contract. Whitaker wanted dramatic headlines for the newspapers. Balogh was talking mainly about North Sea oil. Joe Haines, Marcia and myself were impatient to discuss broader strategy. HW was distracted by discussions about when the plane would take off for Leicester. Haines, who has a really very nice sense of humour, said it was like Euston station and twice shouted asking when the train was due to leave this platform. Finally he and I went out into the corridor to discuss the plan for himself, myself, Marcia, HW and Geoffrey Goodman to slip out to Wilson's home around the corner at 5 Lord North Street to hold a proper strategy meeting in private. We did this. I went with Marcia. She is constantly lively and bright and cynically realistic about HW, knowing all his faults, but seems always loyal and affectionate. Not at all what I expected – apparently a devoted supporter of Roy Jenkins and constantly working to get him and others like Callaghan and Shirley Williams* to appear at the press conferences. She gets on well with Jenkins's assistant, John Harris*. Clearly no respect for the Left. Always constructive, looking for decisions, handling people, with rather brutal honesty but always to get a solution. A much better politician than HW – or most other MPs. But sometimes very heavy on fools. Totally lacking in deference towards HW. Simply tells him the brutal truth as she sees it. E.g. today she told him he must use the Shadow Cabinet team and push his colleagues forward. He agreed.

In the private strategy meeting at Lord North Street I said that it was like last year's Arab-Israeli war: we had held the Syrians on the Golan Heights in the first week of the campaign – now we needed to counter-attack and to cross the Suez Canal. I suggested we must broaden the prices issue into wider and more positive issues – managing the economy, a fairer society, and something on the interrelationship between prices, wages and the unions. HW agreed. Haines was very constructive on precise day-to-day questions.

Wilson ate his cold salad lunch. He telephoned Sydney Jacobson*, the *Daily Mirror* boss. Then went upstairs to wash and change. Obviously in much better form than yesterday, when he left tetchy and, in his own words to Marcia, 'glum'. He had been encouraged by the crowds' enthusiasm in Portsmouth and Southampton. He had slept eight hours. He looked years younger, quicker and less slumped. In good shape to begin the central stage of the campaign – with the polls swinging our way. Though I still have this gut feeling that we shall lose.

HW left for the plane at 1.45 p.m. (possibly a helicopter). Goodman went back to the *Mirror*. Marcia, Joe and I went to lunch at St Ermin's Hotel. Spirits high, conversation amusing. I find them both very easy-going, though I know others don't. Marcia is totally direct and one can say anything to her.

I forgot to mention that this morning HW asked me to get Roy Jenkins to phone him. I did this and they discussed Jenkins's speech this evening and a press handout attacking Heath for his violent speech last night. Wilson seemed very nervous of contacting Jenkins and seemed to think I would be an acceptable go-between. Curiously I am more nervous of phoning Roy than Wilson. John Harris was helpful here. Odd how these personalities matter. Neither Wilson nor Jenkins will take the first move towards the other. Roy, I gather, is generally depressed, by death of mother-in-law, etc.

Also this morning Ron Hayward approached me to press on Wilson the importance of Scotland. Unless we can get our Scottish politicians to move towards devolution, we shall lose a lot of seats. Our special Scottish poll is very depressing – Labour is behind the Tories and everybody is demanding a Scottish Parliament. The problem apparently is Willie Ross*, the party spokesman on Scotland, who is adamantly against all Scottish Nationalist arguments. The relations between Hayward and Wilson are obviously not good. HW, Marcia and Joe have total contempt for the party organisation in Transport House. All the evidence is on their side – today Transport House ran out of paper and had messed up the TV coverage of the meeting at Nottingham.

I went back with Marcia and Joe to write Wilson's speech for tomorrow in the Kent marginals. On housing, etc., but also trying to get in something about the economic crisis and HW's better team. Joe wrote it despite frivolous interruptions from Marcia and myself. Then the Oxford speech for Tuesday, where I wrote the final section on 'the Fair Society'. Joe is very skilful at writing Wilsonian speeches. Wry humour. Gets on with the job under constant heckling from MW and myself.

Watch HW on TV from Leicester. Obviously in good form. Albert Murray phones in: reports a packed meeting, some interruptions, excellent reception.

We discuss the way to raise a question at the daily press conference on the two party leaders' wrangling – Wilson to regret and stress the quality of his team.

Also fix press conference speakers for next week. Marcia says Hayward is complaining that all are right-wingers 'while left-wingers do all the work'. I laugh. Marcia says we must do something. Decides to put Joan Lestor* on with David Owen* on Saturday, a quiet day – and Jim Callaghan and Harold Lever* on Friday, and Lever on Monday. Seems satisfactory.

I go home at 9 p.m. leaving Joe and Marcia there still working on Tuesday's speech.

*Our strategy for the second week is*:

(1) To counter-attack on strikes, by integrating it with inflation and arguing that more rising prices mean more strikes.

(2) To open a wider economic front, denouncing Barber's (the Tory Chancellor) catastrophic failures and demonstrating the strength of Labour's immensely superior economic team.

(3) To put it all in the context of an exposé of 'The Tory Unfair Society'.

## Monday 18 February 1974

Arrived at Transport House at 10 a.m. Harold Wilson, Marcia Williams, Joe Haines, Denis Lyons,* Tommy Balogh and Ben Whitaker were there.

Discuss North Sea oil. HW going to attack on this since we know the Tories will. To head them off.

Too many people. Joe furious. He was trying to get rid of T. Balogh and B. Whitaker. They won't go. Balogh drifts around. Spills his heart pills all over the floor. He keeps making complex and sophisticated suggestions. Impossible to include them in the speeches. Wilson has nearly lost his voice.

Go through Joe's draft for tonight's speech in Kent. Housing and the economy and the North Sea. Joe shouts at T. Balogh.

Shirley Williams comes in. Cheerful and blue-stocking as ever.

They go off to the press conference at Transport House. I stay and talk over the speeches with Denis Lyons. Decide we should offer to retire from the team if so many people continue to attend these meetings.

From 1–2 p.m. Wilson, Marcia, Joe and myself discuss his speech tonight and future general strategy. Get our private polls, which show us neck and neck 40–40 on Friday and 42–42 on the weekend panel. Encouraging. Must be prices. So we have held the first week's Tory attack. I am worried about the next few days. Not clear where is our next initiative now the prices issue has been exploited. May slip a little with unions to the front again.

After Wilson left I went to the LSE to teach for an hour, there and back in a taxi. Fortunately, university teachers of social science work very few hours. Nobody at the LSE realises that I am working full-time with Wilson.

Back at 7 p.m. and we discuss Joe's good draft on the Tory 'mean society' for tomorrow's speech at Oxford. Watch TV – not good. HW's voice is clearly still troubling him. Not good extracts. BBC coverage of the campaign still blatantly biased. Just does Tory party politicals.

Roy Jenkins's party political broadcast is impressive but too sombre. Silvia Rodgers (wife of Bill*) says Roy is depressed, and it shows.

Joe has a good idea for the Wednesday speech. Prices – but wider aspects. How inflation must be got right to get the rest of economic and social policy right. He thinks very quickly.

We sat around, Marcia, Joe and myself, joking and in good spirits.

Albert Murray phoned through to say they had a good meeting this evening, the best yet – as every night!

HW arrived back at Transport House at 10.40 p.m. Looked very tired and troubled by his voice, which apparently almost completely failed at the first meeting in Kent. He sat slumped with a whisky and a cigar. Discussing tomorrow's press conference and Wednesday's speech. Depressed with the Scanlon* and Lever clash about the social contract on television. I phoned Lever to say it was bad for Labour, but he was not home yet.

Marcia said it was time to go home and out we went. HW suddenly picked up and joked affectionately with Marcia. Outside she drove off and I walked with him to his house in Lord North Street. He said, 'It's a funny election. I don't know how it's going. But at least it's better organised with the speeches. And the spirit of the office is so good. I don't know if I will win or lose, but this is my happiest election.'

Joe Haines told me that the campaign was much better than 1970, particularly because Tommy Balogh had dropped his previous habit of crunching ice-cubes while HW was on the phone. Wilson would shout, 'Stop eating crisps, somebody. I can't hear.' Marcia would throw Balogh out and only allow him back when he had no more ice.

Marcia and Joe often discuss their time in government in 1964–70 – and how difficult the Civil Service then were. Say next time must have an inner office of Labour people. She thinks Derek Andrews* will be the principal private secretary again but is not sure. Says the Civil Service used to wear them down with obstruction. Also tried to slip a former employee from Tory Central Office into the No. 10 press corps. Joe threw him out.

She thinks Harold is too willing to be fair. She says he has thought a lot about how to do it better next time – 'But he won't reveal anything in case Balogh finds out'! [She made it clear to me later that this was a reference to his intention to set up a Policy Unit in 10 Downing Street.]

Marcia's sister Peg keeps us fed with beer, coffee, chocolate, sausages and apples.

## Tuesday 19 February 1974

Arrived at Transport House at 10 a.m. Usual problem of too many people in the room.

Discussed our press conference and the problem of how to lead on the social contract when Hugh Scanlon of the Engineers Union was denying that one existed between the unions and the Labour Party under which the unions would restrain wages in return for favourable legislation on social issues. HW was annoyed with Harold Lever for having gone on TV to debate it. Decide to reassert the validity of the social contract and try to get Len Murray,* the general secretary of the TUC, to go on TV to support it.

Then we went through HW's Oxford speech – on 'Mean Tories'. HW insisted on dictating 'a few lines on foreign policy'. He did it later – turned out to be 18 pages. Balogh was there, and Terry Pitt, the head of Transport House research, kept coming in with a few suggested snippets. HW was fairly relaxed but clearly irritated by Scanlon – who he said had not bothered to attend the relevant party committee which approved support for the social contract.

Press conference went quite well. I then went off for lunch with the Football Association and the Football League, whom I had known since I served on the Government Inquiry into Association Football in the 1960s.

I arrived back at Transport House at 6 p.m. Marcia and Joe were working on the Preston speech on prices. Poll news still good – 40–39 to them.

Lever had sent a lovely cake and wine from Harrods as a peace offering to make up for his TV mistake. Marcia asked me to refuse it, but Joe and I were not having any such nonsense. We cut up the cake with a pair of scissors (where was the notorious Transport House knife?) and drank the wine.

Joe did a second, better version of the Preston speech, now looking good. Watched TV. BBC still biased – Robin Day appeared a bit sycophantic to the Tory spokesman Hailsham* and rude to Ted Short,* who complained about 'double standards' of interviewing.

We tried to telephone to protest to the BBC but nobody answered. In fact we are getting very touchy and over-sensitive on media coverage.

HW phoned from Oxford. Great meeting. Two thousand locked out. Heckling but cheers. Obviously HW is always restored by public meetings. Necessary for his adrenalin. But his eye is getting bad – always does under strain. He phoned again as the night wore on until Marcia finally advised him to get in the car and come home 'or else I will come up there and bring you home'.

I was very tired. Walked to Victoria Street with Joe discussing how to cope with the Civil Service in government and the problem of even Labour supporters bending over backwards to be fair to the Establishment.

*Wednesday 20 February 1974*

Arrived late, 10.30 a.m. – press conference. Our spokesmen were trying to show the latest Tory party political broadcast as gutter politics. Quite good impact.

Lunch with John Harris. Intelligent. Good suggestions for showing HW in better light – speaking to camera. Also for a better projection of our policies on inflation.

Back to the office with just Wilson and Marcia. I asked HW how he would feel if we *didn't* have opinion polls. He said 'euphoric, because of the great reception at meetings'.

He thinks the Tory party political broadcast will damage them with the quality press corps, but might have influenced some ordinary voters.

Jeremy Isaacs,* whom I have known and respected since Oxford, passed through, to get HW to Thames TV, which has a strike.

HW is still keen to keep the campaign focused wholly on prices. Balogh and I want to broaden it out on to economic mismanagement. Really we are all searching for the issue to counter-attack with over the weekend. Not clear yet.

In the evening Joe wrote an article and a handout. I drafted something on prices and strikes. Watched TV. Depressed by latest polls – 5–6% Tory leads.

But Enoch Powell* has spoken attacking Heath – as promised to us by his intermediary, the journalist Andrew Alexander.*

## Thursday 21 February 1974

Arrived at Transport House at 10.10 a.m., the same time as Harold Wilson. He immediately asked Balogh and Ben Whitaker to leave the room so that he, Marcia, Joe and I could discuss campaign strategy in private.

He said he was not depressed by the polls. Some encouraging features. In contrast with canvassing and excited meetings. Also the polls showed that the public are most concerned with the policy issues which we are emphasising. The trade union issue is declining. Henceforward we would try to break through with (a) the government's economic mismanagement issue and (b) the Common Market.

Harold Wilson asked me to write the economic speech. I demurred. Joe does them better and it is important that one person maintains a unified theme. In the end we agreed HW would do an opening on general incompetence of government, Joe would do a '10 points of failure' part and I would do a warning about the coming economic crisis and a statement on the choice facing the electorate and concluding with a 'Labour uplift'.

Balogh came to the door and complained to HW that he did 'not want me any more'. HW lost his temper and shut the door.

Discussed the press conference statement. Mainly on the economy (unemployment figures today). HW also wanted a piece on how the

Trotskyites were voting Tory. I was against it. Also Marcia. She was passionately for 'all emphasis on the important issues. We must hit the central
issues, not be diverted into minor details.'

Tommy Balogh and Ben Whitaker were then invited to enter. We
discussed the words of the press statement. Denis Healey came in. Lots
of reports of good canvassing. HW was still dictating the press statement
while being powdered and made up for the television coverage of the press
conference.

Press conference went quite well. Packed. I talked with John Harris
about the news that Enoch Powell would speak in Birmingham recommending Tories to vote Labour because of its scepticism on the EEC. John
will attend the meeting and report to me.

Back in the office we began to write the speech for tonight's meetings
in Hampstead and Ilford: HW dictating his opening, Joe typing his part,
and I went in the outer room to write and get my part typed. By 3.15 we
had it finished.

HW and Joe went to 5 Lord North Street for lunch and invited me
along. Beef bourguignon at the ground-floor table. HW talked about being
Prime Minister: how he never saw draft minutes of the Cabinet. Discussed
handling of the South African arms crisis. All the leaking of news from
the Cabinet. HW said Churchill was a terrible chairman of Cabinet. Never
summed up. Once Edward Bridges, the then secretary to the Cabinet, asked
Wilson, who was then in the Cabinet secretariat, to write the Cabinet
minutes. HW said he couldn't remember what they had decided. Bridges
said, 'Write down what you think they ought to have decided – they'll
never know.'

I went off in a taxi to the LSE to lecture (HW stuffed a cigar in my
top pocket as I left).

Returned at 7.30 p.m. Joe was writing the Common Market speech for
Friday. Everybody was excited about tonight's news that the miners' wages
had been miscalculated by official figures and in fact had fallen further
behind the national average since the Wilberforce Report. We discussed
how to handle it – whether to send an open letter to Heath. Waited for
HW to phone and discuss. He was late – anyway he had left the second
half of the speech behind and it had to be rushed to him in Hampstead
while he read the first half extremely slowly.

TV excerpts were poor – as always only showed his gags, not the serious
parts. Albert Murray phoned: good meeting, heckling not too bad. HW
was against pressing the miners' issue till we had time to think it over and
make a considered response. Marcia was also nervy – 'We must make sure
these facts are right.'

Balogh went off to the Reform Club to meet vital contact, 'G.', from the Pay Board which issued the report, and to get the precise facts on the miners' wages.

Also a message from Enoch Powell's ambassador (Andrew Alexander) for Joe. Cryptic. His speech on Saturday would be 'cool, Monday hotter', and we 'would be pleased'. He was concerned that it wouldn't get on TV. Impression that the BBC would veto interviewing Powell, on the basis that any threats to Heath must not be publicised. We felt the veto could be news and we could publicise it. Powell advised us to wait and peak our campaign *after* his Monday speech.

Watched TV, quite good for us.

HW phoned in to Transport House after his meeting. Marcia told him to go straight to bed and not to come to the office. We finished the bottle of Harold Lever's Beaujolais and left. I walked to St Ermin's Hotel with Joe. Discussed HW's poor speech style and his lack of feel for words. Joe said Harold cannot remember words at all, only dates and statistics. This is why he has to read every word of every speech and is afraid of ad-libbing.

Told me how on the day after the last election defeat in June 1970 HW came to him and said he would write his memoirs: (a) to get the achievements on the record and (b) to earn money to run the office in Opposition. He sat down next day and began to write the first 12,000 words. He already had the chapter headings for the whole book.

Joe thinks HW is a good strategist but a bad tactician. Also thinks too fast for his own good.

One week to go to polling day.

## Friday 22 February 1974

Met early at Lord North Street to have quiet discussions. HW, Marcia, Joe and me. Discussed the polls. HW was consoled that the Liberals are now so strong it will hurt Tories more than us. Also discussed question of the Pay Board discovering that the government's calculations of miners' wages were wrong. HW wants to follow through on this. Apparently the party's campaign committee had not realised the significance. Wanted to ignore it and press only the Common Market issue.

Hayward, the party secretary, had told the constituency parties that HW would make a big speech on the EEC tonight. Now we decided not to. Would speak on prices, and the economic crisis and the government's error on miners' wages.

We walked along Lord North Street and westwards across Smith Square to Transport House. I went upstairs to Denis Lyons's room and drafted a bit of today's speech. Stayed there till after the press conference.

Back to HW's room. Terrible rush. Drafting the speech for tonight. Contacting Joe Gormley* of the miners' union and Len Murray on the miners' pay issue. Geoffrey Goodman of the *Mirror* was there, drafting a good peroration to the speech.

No lunch, as usual. Finished the speech by 3.15 when HW and Joe went to Lord North Street to eat and off to a TV studio for an interview. Then HW left for Bristol. Marcia went off, after meeting with Terry Pitt from Transport House when he complained of lack of consultation. Obviously the party organisation is bitter about us for not attacking the EEC, but also feels left out of discussions. Resentment at Wilson's 'Kitchen Cabinet'.

I was alone in the dreary office at Transport House taking phone calls on every conceivable subject. One from Harold Lever in Manchester saying they were worried up there. Joel Barnett* afraid he will lose. Lever did not realise his own seat in Central Manchester was on the list of possible Liberal gains – they hope to win 11 from Labour, mainly in north-west, and 25 from Tories.

The polls are depressing – we are now 8% behind. The Liberals are up to 22%.

Joe returned. We discussed the depressing outlook. Joe feels 'we may get a hiding'. What worries him is the effect of defeat on HW, the personal pain. Joe's main characteristic is loyalty. He sees that if we lose, all the hatred is trained on HW.

He thinks if we lose HW should resign on the Saturday after the election as quickly as possible.

But he is very angry at the thought that anybody might move in to precipitate a leadership crisis. Clearly has Roy Jenkins in mind. Thinks Jim Callaghan will only move if asked. And Benn not a serious candidate – HW wouldn't have it.

Joe and Marcia think HW would certainly have resigned after a couple of years if he had won in 1970. Marcia insists this is true. They had often discussed it and HW swore this was true. Marcia claims she definitely wants to lose – she doesn't want him to go through it all again in Downing Street.

We then agreed not to discuss our pessimistic prospects again. Joe tells me to go out to lunch (it is 6.15 p.m.).

When I return he has done a marvellous opening to tomorrow's speech. Marcia is there, very depressed. I am more optimistic, because the Liberals are worse for the Tories than for us. We sit and discuss the possibilities of a coalition and the way in which the two-party system is breaking up. Marcia says if we were not so involved, this would be the most exciting election she has known, because it is so different. She is the most shrewd, perceptive and intuitively intelligent female politician I have met.

Having finished the speech we watched TV. Good for us. Spirits rose. HW looked quite good. Heath looked bad over the miscalculations on the miners' pay.

HW phoned and we went across to join him at Lord North Street. Peg serving drinks and cheese. Mary Wilson* is there for a while, saying nothing, but then went to bed.

Discussed HW's Bristol meeting earlier tonight – marvellous reception. Then tactics for tomorrow's press conference. And possible newspaper strike. Marcia and I strongly advised him not to intervene.

Very relaxed. Drinks, chat and jokes. HW looking tired, smoking his cigar, voice hoarse, but not in bad spirits.

As we left Marcia said she could not assess his mood. Clearly puzzled. She drove me to her smart mews house in Wyndham Mews, Marylebone W1. Her mother was there and an Asiatic girl domestic servant and a Spanish maid and her sister Peg. Chatted to her mother about Northants – Blisworth where Marcia's brother Tony* lives and nearby Long Buckby and East Haddon, where the Field family come from – all familiar to me. A Northants evening. Very relaxed and happy. Smart modern house, full of women.

Then home by taxi with the Spanish maid, who lives nearby. Home 1 a.m. Quite a day. Looks bleak for the election. Yet nobody can assess the impact of the Liberals and Enoch Powell. Still everything to be won.

Bed at 1.40 a.m.

## Saturday 23 February 1974

Very interesting day. First to Harold Wilson's house. Just him there. We discussed the polls. He is still in good spirits. Still thinks the Liberals will help us.

Marcia, Joe and Peter Davis arrive and we discuss tactics – on union picketing (HW slipped up last night). Decided to do a campaign review at the press conference. Mentioning the enthusiasm, but people clearly puzzled, still to make up their mind.

Discussed his coming Birmingham speech. To swing the emphasis from criticism to the positive, from crisis to recovery (a theme suggested to Marcia by John Harris).

Backed by information that the Sunday opinion polls are close. Even a Labour lead in the *Observer*. But our own polls still show us 7% behind.

Morale very good. Feeling things are beginning to go our way. Tories on the defence. Much humour. HW said Joe and I were Morecambe and Wise. Peter Davis said like the Western Brothers. Joe said Rawicz and Landauer. [The first pair were contemporary comedians, the second pair comedians from the 1940s and the third were piano duettists popular in the Second World War.]

Then went to the office in Transport House where the rest are waiting. Difficulties typing the statement. Not finished till HW about to leave for the press conference. Small attendance. Quite friendly but slack.

On return to the office we sat around and talked and then HW set off for Scotland. Joe went off to lunch. I took Marcia's sister Peggy Field to lunch in a nearby pub. Joined other Transport House people. Afterwards I walked round Smith Square with Tom McNally,* an old friend, who is very happy with the campaign and annoyed by people inside Transport House who criticise it.

Joe joined us for a few more circuits then back to the office. Joe quickly wrote an article for the *Evening News*. Encouraged by Enoch Powell's speech getting big treatment over the tapes.

Marcia returned. The speech-writing went slowly. I did a piece on the Common Market. And the peroration. Joe did many drafts of the most difficult part with much help from Marcia. Also from Balogh.

Much hilarity and bawdy good humour.

Find myself naturally looking to Marcia for judgement on many things. Instinctively goes like a knife to the heart of matters. When she says she doesn't understand something it is because it is not clear.

Digress on the day of defeat last time (1970). Everybody weeping in No. 10. Packing the boxes. Except HW who went round cheering everybody up.

The devotion of Marcia and Joe is total.

Joe still concerned at the prospect of attacks on HW after defeat. Thinks he should resign straight away. Marcia not sure – perhaps HW should stay on till a successor emerges. Joe says *that* is HW's biggest concern, 'his ideology': keeping the party together.

Told me how a week after the 1970 defeat Barbara Castle* came to see Wilson and said she would stand against Jenkins as deputy leader. HW told her sharply not to and anyway she wouldn't get 10 votes. She was upset and said she would stand anyway. He said, if so, he would resign. She insisted, went away, but didn't stand.

Joe also said that the pro-marketeers have 'no idea of the shit which HW took in the past over the Common Market issue, always concerned to keep the party together'. That the Jenkins alternative of uncritical support for the EEC would have split the party. Only HW could have stopped the majority from going for withdrawal in the vote on whether to join the EEC in 1972.

Finished the speeches at midnight, surrounded by wineglasses, bits of Peg's pork pie and masses of paper from rejected drafts.

Joe went home early. Marcia and her sister Peggy took me home in the car. Called in on HW in Lord North Street on the way. He is pleased with the *Sunday Mirror* coming out for us. But he had bumped his head in Newcastle.

I am tired but fascinated. No sense of defeat. Excitement. Feeling that this election is different. And still can be won. Sense the press beginning to realise that HW's speeches are much better than Heath's. And the Tories have no new policies to offer.

## Sunday 24 February 1974

Another fascinating day. Met Harold Wilson at Transport House after the early morning campaign committee and walked with him to Lord North Street. He is still convinced the Liberals' advance will help us. Still enthused by canvass reports and good meetings.

Also obviously pleased with his speeches going down well.

At Lord North Street we met with Marcia, Peggy Field, Joe and Geoffrey Goodman. Joe and I both felt the trade union statement by David Basnett* and Clive Jenkins* was important. It restates support for the social contract between Labour and the unions. We decided to put this in the speech. Also to rewrite some of my peroration which looked a bit loose in the morning. Terrible rush to get it typed before Wilson left at 12.45 for Birmingham.

Joe, Marcia, Peggy and I went to St Ermin's Hotel for lunch. Very jolly and bawdy. But Marcia is really depressed. For the first time it has crossed her mind that we might lose and she is thinking of the wounds afterwards. I try to take her mind off it by arguing with her about Catholics and abortion. Also Joe and I recite Peggy Lee songs we like and Bob Newhart. Joe has all these records. He also calls her Lucretia Borgia, which I repeat – and later we regret it, saying she will come back at us later.

She took a purple heart earlier to keep awake, as she frequently does, and now has a headache. But her intelligence is undiminished. I can see why HW is fascinated by her. Like a father for a daughter – as Joe points out. Venetia Stanley and Asquith had nothing on this. [Venetia Stanley was the young friend and correspondent of the Prime Minister.] This is not – now at least – a sexual relationship. Harold is astounded by her endless nervous energy, her instinctive capacity to go to the heart of any issue. He loves it when she shouts at him, corrects him, opposes him. It is the nearly incestuous father-daughter relationship, with no mother and no guilt to intervene.

All this came out late at night, back in No. 5 Lord North Street, when we adjourned there to discuss tomorrow's television broadcast. Harold is tired. Obviously worried by the polls. But above all bewildered. Birmingham meetings went very well.

During the day we slogged away – I at tomorrow's speech, Joe at articles and the final party political broadcast on television. The author John Mortimer* had written the latter, but not quite good enough politically, though some excellent bits, so it was scrapped and Joe wrote it.

We were all a little neurotic about the Liberals being on TV to try to destroy the Labour Party.

Marcia and I constantly clashed, jokingly. Her nerves on edge. Very emotional.

We decided that a future Labour government must do something about the BBC being totally subservient to the Tories.

She also talked to me about how I got there with them. How I was repeatedly recommended. She had obviously been impressed. She said nobody could believe I did not have political ambitions to get into the House of Commons myself.

As usual no supper except one of Peg's sausages and some mediocre white wine which Tommy Balogh brought in.

Home 1 a.m.

## Monday 25 February 1974

The final week.

We gathered at Transport House. There had been a row at the earlier campaign committee over the Tony Benn piece on nationalisation in the previous Labour Party political broadcast.

HW slipped out and winked for me to follow. We went across Smith Square together and down Lord North Street to Wilson's home. There we discussed strategy together while waiting for Joe to bring the script for HW's final party political broadcast.

Marcia arrived and was tired but skittish.

The script very good and everybody was pleased. Marcia as usual picked on the only weak piece.

Back to Transport House. Went through the script again and discussed this evening's Birmingham speech, which was my draft, with HW's interpolations, all pulled together and put in more snappy language by Joe.

While HW was being made up for the press conference we got the latest poll – only 1% behind – 8% on Friday and 7% on Saturday. The Liberals' support is halved. Tories slipping since Thursday. I was very excited. Showed it to HW. He was impassive.

Good press conference with Peter Shore and John Silkin* excellent. HW was pressed on the prospects for a coalition. Said absolutely no. Joe says that if HW is in a minority his policy would be to govern until brought down.

Off to the LSE to lecture (where I write up today's diary so far).

On return just Joe and me.

There was a slight contretemps with Peter Jenkins, the political correspondent of the *Guardian*, who was waiting around in the outer office of Transport House. Albert despatched him. Later I telephoned Peter to apologise for any discourtesy and to smooth the ruffled feathers.

HW and Marcia returned from recording the party political broadcast. Very pleased.

Then a sudden crisis erupted about the *Express* and the *Mail* intending to print tomorrow a smear story about Marcia. HW was worried and dashed off to No. 5 Lord North Street. Marcia put on her coat, took some tranquillisers and announced melodramatically that she was 'leaving to catch a train' and would 'not return'.

Joe and I followed HW to No. 5. Telephone calls. Air of crisis. The last cheap trick of a desperate Tory press.

Joe and I went back to Transport House. Trying to soothe Marcia. Telling her it's nothing important. Coaxing her to take her coat off. Peg arrives with Guinness and snacks. Slowly settle. Joe writes HW's radio broadcast. We watch TV. The party political broadcast was excellent. The TV news full of the embarrassing trade deficit. (Early BBC news contained import and export figures but curiously omitted to mention the actual deficit.) Joe telephoned them and they later corrected it. Desperate efforts by the BBC interviewer to suggest it was all because of oil. But Healey deals with it well. And the extract from HW's speech is very good. ITV much better as usual.

Enoch Powell attacking the Tories again. Can't harm us.

HW summons us back to No. 5 at midnight. Stay nearly an hour. He was in a curious, slightly snarling mood. Not seen this before. Tired and slumped. Eyes brown and heavy. Walks very slowly as if completely exhausted. Still confident, but the confidence a beam of light shining from a tired hulk. Savage at Joe. Says his speeches are too sophisticated and so he dictates an awful piece about Trotskyite shop stewards.

Everybody knows it's no good. Just his resentment at having his speeches written for him. Cannot adjust to it. Always refers to it, always says how good the speeches are and clearly resents it.

Joe very angry and gets up to go home. Marcia sits by HW and ticks him off. He calls for Joe and tries to mollify him. Joe won't have it and is in a huff. Totally honest man. Does his job marvellously. Asks no credit. Completely loyal. But when he is annoyed he cannot be bought off. A man to go in the jungle with.

We order a taxi for the typist but it doesn't come. So Marcia and Peg drive me to Euston and wait till I get a taxi. Nervous about the newspapers. Pulling my leg.

To take away Marcia from him would be like removing the dynamo from an engine. She makes his lights go on (and off).

## Tuesday 26 February 1974

Remarkable day.

Meeting in the morning with HW, Marcia, Joe and Geoffrey Goodman. I walked across Smith Square with HW. He is pleased with the way things are going, especially in the office. He thinks the team of Joe, Marcia and me is working well.

Back at No. 5 we discussed polls and our strategy.

HW went off to do a broadcast.

We started tonight's speech at Huddersfield. Great rush. Must be finished by midday.

HW returned to dictate a large chunk – very good. He is in much better spirit today. Nothing in the papers about Marcia.

Roy Jenkins and Denis Healey came in before the press conference at Transport House. Roy read his statement on the balance of payments. Immensely impressive. On quite a different level from anything we can achieve.

Mounting excitement because of the feeling we can win. Canvass reports from everywhere reveal big swing to us.

Lunch with Joe, Marcia and Peggy at St Ermin's. Marcia still a bit jittery. But lively conversation and she and Joe score a number of points off me. I am now very, very tired. Had a row with a BBC producer this morning. He was going to put Lord Watkinson* on as an 'independent' businessman to discuss the damaging impact on business confidence of a Labour victory. Also wanted a 'Labour businessman'. I blew up and said we didn't have any Labour ex-Cabinet ministers sailing under the flag of businessmen. In fact he wanted to be helpful. I phoned after lunch to apologise – and again to press them to get a trade unionist. Mustn't get touchy. It is just that the BBC has been disgraceful, with a programme producer attending Heath's morning strategy meetings, and the news programme acting as an agent for the Tories each evening.

Went to sleep for an hour on Albert Murray's bed in St Ermin's.

Depressed because our latest poll showed a slip back to Tories. Don't believe it, but still depressing.

Joe and I went back to a bizarre situation at Transport House.

*Daily Mail* reporters and photographers were waiting at the entrance to photo Marcia arriving. They have photostats of a contract of her brother selling land at a profit. Obvious election smear. I wanted to take the chief reporter, a very creepy man, into a corner and work him over a little. I felt furious at their gutter behaviour and really would have belted him into the ground. Fortunately Joe restrained me and handled the reporter very carefully.

The press hounds left but waited in their car in Smith Square. Joe and I trailed them and waited in the cold and dark to intercept Marcia when she arrived. I was nearly knocked over stepping in front of a blue Triumph like hers. Driven by young man with long hair who nearly didn't see me.

Joe intercepted Marcia and sent her home, in tears. Reporters were around the rest of evening and telephoning for Marcia.

We were jittery and unable to write the Liverpool speech till very late. There were too many people. John (Scofield) Allen*, T. Balogh, various secretaries, T. Pitt, R. Hayward all drifting in and out. The television was on. Not the ideal situation for writing the final peroration of the election campaign.

Joe told me that when John Allen, a married man, worked for Wilson in the 1964–70 administration Marcia had an affair with Allen and wanted to marry him. HW strongly supported this and sent Allen to Africa for some months, nominally on an official visit, to consider it and to strengthen his resolve to accept. When Allen returned and declined he was, apparently as a punishment, effectively removed from the PM's staff. He is suspected, rightly or wrongly, of being close to *Private Eye*.

We finished after midnight and took the speech to No. 5 – HW was coming back on the overnight train and would read it in time for the morning meeting.

Then at Joe's suggestion, to help them forget the *Daily Mail*, I took a little of the champagne from Harold Lever to Marcia and Peggy at home – and we all drank it. She was gay and frivolous and seemed to forget the *Daily Mail* incident.

She tells me HW has discussed quite calmly what he will do on Friday–Saturday after the election. All travel plans, etc. for defeat or for victory.

Also that he will retire from the Labour leadership at 60 – because he has imposed that on others. [He did exactly that.]

Also *she* wants Roy Jenkins as Chancellor. But thinks it may be Lever. She claims she was decisive in Roy getting it rather than Crosland after Callaghan's resignation in 1967.

She argues passionately that the right wing don't understand the Labour Party and may well split it in a bid for leadership.

Ron Hayward, the general secretary, has discussed with her who would control Transport House if the party splits. She thinks he is no good.

Remarks that HW's overriding concern has always been to hold the party together – and that the Left hate him for it. And that Peter Shore's wife hates Harold and pushes Peter to the left. Perhaps Marcia doesn't like other women and friends' wives?

Home 2 a.m.

## Wednesday 27 February 1974

We quickly did the press conference statement and finished the speech for the Liverpool eve-of-poll rally.

HW left for Merseyside at 1 p.m. and I went off for lunch. Spent the afternoon at the LSE. And taught an MSc seminar in the early evening. Still nobody at the LSE knows that I am doing 16 hours a day in Westminster.

Back to Transport House at 8 p.m. Marcia and Joe were there and we sat and talked. Fresh rumours of a *Daily Mail* scandal story and Joe was in touch with Lord Goodman* (HW's lawyer).

Slack atmosphere. No more speeches to write. Sudden let-down. Everyone depressed. Momentarily I feared we might lose. The last opinion polls published showed us well behind – only, as we later that evening discovered, because the newspapers had doctored them. TV carried the polls and assumed Heath would win. First editions of next day's papers arrived after dinner with headlines about Heath's expected comfortable victory.

Sat around till well after midnight. Didn't feel like drinking – or eating, although had eaten no dinner and lost 10lb in the campaign.

Finally left an empty Transport House around 1 a.m. Marcia, Peggy, Joe and myself. After telephone calls from Liverpool that the final rally meetings went marvellously.

Tomorrow is the deciding day.

## Thursday 28 February 1974: Election Day

Taxi to Lord North Street. As I got out at 11 a.m. HW came out of the door with Mary and others to go around the corner to vote. He had flown back especially from his Huyton constituency in Liverpool – because his political office had characteristically forgotten to register his postal vote.

We walked together to the polling booth in Great Smith Street. Big crowd of journalists etc. A big lorry pulled out and the lorry driver leaned out and shouted, 'Good luck, Harold, my old son.' He was about 25.

Back to Lord North Street and then off to the airport. Beautiful spring day.

The jet plane was small. HW, Mary, Joe, Marcia. Terry Boston,* Albert and myself. Very cosy. Sandwiches and beer. Mary looked tired but the rest in good form. Albert especially full of wit and common sense. He and Joe are the very best kind of Londoners. Albert is physically round and rolls like a sailor as he walks. He has a beaming ruddy face beneath sandy hair, is jolly, extrovert, with a large cigar in his mouth, happily dealing with all the practical details. Joe more introverted, a completely impassive face, dark and sharp, behind his rimless spectacles, always somehow reminding me of Humphrey Bogart. Very slight in build, yet taut. Not somebody I would cross. Totally straight, incorruptible. Also very wryly funny.

Landed in grey Liverpool. Police escort to the Adelphi Hotel where we had a large suite of rooms. HW, Joe and Albert then went canvassing. I had a steak lunch and then went with Marcia and Terry Boston for a long walk along the Mersey waterfront. Getting mistier. Rain is forecast and I am afraid it will keep down our vote. I keep looking at my watch, hoping the rain will hold off. Every half-hour matters.

Back to the hotel at 5. Already beginning to snow. Poor Marcia has blisters. She is obviously very nervous about tonight. Terry Boston, who had joined the team to help handle the press and the baggage, is excellent calming company. Polite and balanced and always considerate. I tell her that Harold will be the next Prime Minister, though possibly of a minority government. She says she doesn't want that. Wants him out of it, so she can live an ordinary domestic life and so he can get out of it. She says she is only concerned that he should not be hurt like he was last time – which she constantly refers to as a most traumatic experience for her.

Mary had been sleeping and was now reading the new *Oxford Book of Poetry*.

I telephoned Roy Jenkins's headquarters in Birmingham and got a report. His agent was obviously impressed by the high turnout. Had no idea what was happening in the rest of Birmingham. Said it was like being isolated in a fortress with no idea of what was happening elsewhere. But encouraging – 50% turnout by 2 p.m. in one ward. The three-day week operating because of the miners' strike is helping by enabling our men to vote during the day.

We were in the main Adelphi Hotel suite, which has a large lounge and a bedroom. I wanted to watch the football results on TV and then realised it was Thursday not Saturday. Somehow it felt like Saturday, unreal.

HW and the others returned from visiting the polling booths. Encouraged by the high poll. They then began to discuss plans for returning to London afterwards. HW had most complicated schemes. After the count at Huyton he would tell the press he was going back to the Adelphi, but would in fact go to another hotel, the Golden Eagle in Kirkby. Stay there watching the results, have a brief sleep and then slip off quickly in the early morning to the plane – which would set off for London but be diverted in flight to a small airfield in Bedfordshire. HW would then race back to Grange Farm, his country house in Buckinghamshire, or even hide away at the cottage of a friend of Marcia's.

Albert laughingly suggested to HW that we should blindfold the pilot so he did not know where he was landing.

I suddenly realised what was behind all these bizarre plans – HW was preparing to lose! He was preparing his getaway plans. Unwilling to face the press, as anybody when beaten.

Marcia had hinted to me that he had discussed these arrangements the day before – and his intention to resign as leader on Saturday if beaten. Also that he would only stay in office for a couple of years if he won. Long enough to establish the government, see the party united and to leave the succession clear. Her firm preference was for Roy Jenkins. She did not say who HW wanted – but made it clear definitely not Benn or Callaghan. Hinted it was Roy.

I telephoned Transport House to get a run-down on how things were going. It looked good on turnout. Also phoned the London Labour Party. Already the regional differentials were showing. I like the high turnout. Have always believed that if the working class would only vote, we would win.

I was tired and went off to bed. Had just dropped off to sleep when phone rang – Alf Richman[*] to say it was dinnertime. I was not hungry, having only recently eaten a big steak and chips. But felt should go. To the suite. Most of them were already there round a large table. Joe and I sat at a small one – Rawicz and Landauer as HW insists on calling us. It was again steak and chips! I ate it.

They were again discussing escape plans. I could see Marcia was unhappy at this. She knows what is behind it. So does Joe. It gets too complicated to follow. Mention of trains and diversionary cars as well as the airplane. So many diversions, bluffs and cover that I cannot work out which hotel I am staying in or how I am going back to London if at all. Mention this to Marcia. She rebukes me and says that that is absolutely clear, I am going back with HW on the plane. I had not heard that. She simply knows what he wants and means in every situation. He doesn't give instructions. He drops hints. She is always ahead of them.

Harold asks me to phone Transport House again because he has been unable to get any common sense out of them. I do and get some encouraging answers.

HW sets off again to his Huyton constituency at 8.30 p.m. to tour the polling booths. He has had 20 minutes' sleep and looks and feels much better. Myself, Terry Boston and Alf Richman with him. The press follow in cars which constantly try to drive beside and behind him, separating him from the police.

For nearly two hours we tour the constituency, in rain and sleet, very dark, totally lost in miles of council house estates. At first there is almost nobody in the party offices and clubs. All still canvassing. Later there are more people and the reception gets better.

The press follow at a distance, but show little interest. The police are polite but do not treat HW especially well. He looks like the local candidate and I sensed that everybody saw him as a loser, finished, who would soon be just an old back-bench MP. At times we walked in the rain, just the two of us, HW and myself, rather lonely figures lost in anonymous wet streets. At one point I reminded him that he had earlier in the campaign said that he found the crowds enthusiastic, but didn't know whether it was 1945, when Labour won, or 1959, when we lost. I now said I thought it was like 1964 when we just scraped home. He agreed.

Finally back to the hotel. In the car he discussed the campaign, how it had gone the way we had planned, how happy it had been in the office. Also discussed with me his new government – perhaps first sign that he now sensed he might win. He said that he would run a low profile, no presidential stuff, no first 100 days. He said how lucky he was to have such a good and experienced team. He would leave the main ministers to get on with it. No more settling of strikes with beer and sandwiches at No. 10. How different this was from 1964, when none of his colleagues had previously been in the Cabinet in high office – only Jim Griffiths and Patrick Gordon Walker* briefly.

He talked about how fortunate I was to be an academic now watching practical politics from the inside. [He also said now – though I did not record the details in what was only part of a very long conversation, much of it concerned with his more immediately interesting views on current politics and how he would run his government – that I must retain 'a clear memory of everything and write it up later'. He mentioned the role of Arthur Schlesinger as President Kennedy's court historian. I felt that he flattered both of us, especially me. He repeated this analogy to me later in Downing Street while debriefing me on a particularly exciting Cabinet.]

Back at the hotel after the polling booths closed the press were gathering in the lobby, but still aloof and obviously not treating him seriously. Fortunately the BBC had sent Michael Charlton, who is nice and polite and serious and almost the only BBC man who is not out to knock the Labour Party and lick the Tories' arse. I said to him that we were pleased he had come and enquired if the rest of the BBC news team was perhaps down in Sidcup canvassing for Mr Heath. He smiled and clearly understood what was meant.

Back to the suite. Mary and Albert, Joe and Marcia are in their rooms sleeping. I knock on doors. We assemble, move the settee round, send for tea, serve whiskies and settle down for the television results. I sit on the settee between Marcia and Joe. She is trembling with nerves. Joe tense and silent. I sense their concern, almost terror, that this will be a repetition of last time. HW sits on a chair beside us, sipping a whisky, very calm now, beginning to get interested in percentages, doing sums quickly in his head, recalling precise majorities in various seats. In the car he told me that he could remember numbers but not words. That is why he has to read his speeches. Cannot remember any quotations or trust himself to say any sentences. Joe is the reverse. Can quote everything.

Suddenly the first result. Guildford. Comfortable Tory win. High Liberal vote. Labour bottom. Can read nothing into it. Obviously we won't do well in the south.

Then Salford. Stan Orme* – and a marvellous boost in Labour's majority. However you look at it, this is marvellous. The working classes are voting for us. I say to Joe, 'Don't worry. We can't lose now. It may be very close, but we won't lose.' Marcia is silent, not believing it. HW was clearly cheered. He immediately announces the string of Lancashire marginals which we will win – we do, every one.

After an hour it looks quite good, ahead and a possibility of an overall majority. Clear pattern – Labour takes north and Midlands, Tories south and south-west. The country is split in two in electoral geography.

We then all set off for the count in Harold's Huyton constituency. Outside the door are half a dozen men. HW pauses and I ask who they are – CID. There is another policeman holding the lift, more guarding the stairs. Downstairs the press is bubbling and crowd round him and wish him good luck. They know he might win and suddenly the police care and the press change sides. Massive motorcade, with police cyclist outriders.

At the Huyton count everybody is optimistic. I do not go to the count. Sit in a side-room with the radio taking results from elsewhere. Not so good now. East Midlands and south-west very disappointing.

Marcia and Mary, who seem to get on well, open a bottle of champagne.

Off to Huyton Labour Club, to tumultuous reception. Everybody singing and chanting. Packed. Woman next to me had tears streaming down her face and was shouting, 'I love him, I love him.' This is so far from London, the scepticism and coolness. Here HW comes alive, relaxes with them and they clearly think the world of him. Makes a nice speech. Marcia is clearly very moved and happy, quietly always in the background, willing it to go well. Resents being treated as one of the men, always feminine and wanting her femininity to be recognised and tended.

Finally away from the cheering crowds – off on the diversion to the Golden

Eagle in Kirkby – a small, miserable hotel, with poky modern rooms and no atmosphere whatsoever. I say to Marcia I don't like it, nor does she. Want to go. Hate the receptionist, clearly Tory. Upstairs to a drab lounge to watch the TV results. Starts going badly for us. Depression – and tiredness – set in. Have some sandwiches and drinks. But the uplift has gone. Cannot work out why. Then learn that the press have found out where we are and are downstairs. Ridiculous. What are we doing here? We are winning, not losing. The bizarre thing is that HW has not changed his getaway plans – to escape secretly – so we are still running from defeat although we have won!

We went to bed at 4.30 a.m. with it looking as if we will have a lead of nine over the Tories but no overall majority. HW showing signs of nervousness and interested in the constitutional position – what would the Queen do? Odd to get depressed. Really a marvellous result, considering all the final polls showed us losing. Marcia went up to HW and told him not to be silly, to cheer up, it was a great triumph.

I lay in bed, exhausted. Unhappy to be in this dismal hotel. No place to celebrate a marvellous victory. We should be at the Adelphi, with the Labour crowds celebrating, putting up two fingers to the press. This is wrong. So is the plan to slip away in the morning. Why should we? He should go back to the Adelphi.

Marcia phones. She cannot sleep and holds exactly the same views. We agree to call a meeting. I summon Albert, who comes in with the newspapers and some tea. Says the press are all camped in the hall downstairs so we could not slip off secretly anyway. We call Terry Boston, who is the only one actually asleep, while Marcia phones HW. Agreed not to go to the Adelphi now, as I wanted. That would be too bizarre, to run away from two hotels in one night. But to summon a press conference at the Adelphi in the morning and we would go there for coffee at 10. Terry Boston goes off to arrange it. Albert goes to mollify the press here. I do go to sleep – it is 4.50 a.m. I wake up 25 minutes later and get up.

Have breakfast and in the middle am paged. Marcia says Harold wants me. We discuss the draft to the press statement. Joe comes in and takes the shorthand, suggests improvements and goes off and types it. Then we all drive off to Adelphi, followed by cavalcade of press. Plenty of police.

To the Adelphi Hotel suite and finalise the press statement. I phone John Harris in Birmingham and Harold Lever in Manchester. A Shadow Cabinet has been called for this afternoon. Typically HW changed the words Shadow Cabinet to 'senior parliamentary colleagues'. 'There is no Shadow Cabinet now,' he said. Too many echoes of being in opposition.

At one point he told me he was pleased there had been an election (this before the result). Because he felt this Parliament had 'turned sour'. 'A nasty Parliament,' he said, 'nasty atmosphere.'

To the press conference. Good statement. Questions on coalition, but he would not be drawn. CID men everywhere.

Off to the airport. Crowds cheer. Raining and sleet. Nice flight back. Feeling of a job well done. Seems a lifetime since we arrived – less than 24 hours before. I sit with Mary and Marcia on the small aeroplane and we chat. Mary tells me she doesn't look forward to No. 10. Says she doesn't like this political life. Prefers the family.

Morale good. HW delighted at seeing the press running for cover. Reads out the *Daily Telegraph* City column with an article beginning 'The Tories have won, but not by as many as we would have wished.' Hilarity all round. Albert in marvellous form, singing songs. Terry Boston happy – has done excellent job handling the press. Joe more silent. Tells me he still fears we won't make it. Discuss Scotland, results still to come, which still worries me.

Several results and recounts are announced while we are up in the sky, cut off, making HW Prime Minister or not.

We get off the plane in London to face the TV and press. Cheers from airport workers. Better than sneaking off in defeat to some field in Bedfordshire! Met by large limousines. Drive 20 yards then stop and we leap into the VIP lounge to phone the Labour Party headquarters for the latest results. Transport House puts me through to wrong extension and nobody there seems to know results. So we telephoned the *Daily Mirror* and they tell us we have won three more seats and it looks good.

Two cars. I am in the second with Marcia and Albert. Joe is with HW and Mary. I say Heath won't give up easily. Will have to be forced out. Fear a deal with the Liberals over Common Market and moderation. Marcia tells me not to depress her. She is still bright as a new penny, sharp and funny. Never flat. Astonishing. Her intuition never sleeps. Always thinking, creating, what HW must do in every situation. She is afraid of what will happen when he gets back into government. Under pressure, him gossiping. That he will take decisions too hurriedly – 'as in 1964'. She keeps saying, 'He must have you friends around to protect him from himself. You know what he is like. You have got to restrain him and direct him. I don't want to do it. I have had enough of that. I only came back after 1970 to help him personally, but I want my private life, I want to be an ordinary person, I don't want to be sucked back into that madness.'

Crowds at Lord North Street. Cheering the next PM. Inside we watch TV. No more victories. Marginals we hope to win we don't. In fact we don't win any more seats. Now just a question of hoping we hold what we have and that the Tories lose some to Scots Nats and Liberals.

Caernarvon is recounting for fifth time.

Cold lunch at Lord North Street then off to Transport House for Shadow Cabinet. We all go into Ron Hayward's room for drinks. Shadow

Cabinet and others begin to drift in – Roy Jenkins, Reg Prentice,* Jack Jones* of the Transport Workers Union, Tony Benn. Also there are Harold's son and daughter-in-law, Tom Driberg* and others. An odd sort of party. Now Joe thinks we won't make it. Convinced – rightly – that Heath will try to hang on.

I leave the Shadow Cabinet and go to HW's room. Listen to the radio with Marcia, Albert and Joe. Discuss how to prise Heath out. What Liberals will do. What the Queen will do. Joined by Terry Lancaster of the *Mirror*, who produces a bottle of whisky, which we all drink. It is 3.30 p.m.

Make some phone calls. Hang around.

HW comes up and we draft the Shadow Cabinet statement. [The Labour Party statement said simply that since the Conservative Party had 'failed in their appeal for an increased majority they lacked the authority to give the lead the country was seeking. Therefore, the Labour Party is prepared to form a government and to submit its programme for the endorsement of Parliament.']

Transport House full of press and cameras.

*Sunday Telegraph* man arrives at our office. Joe takes him down the corridor. He says he has a story that Mrs Wilson doesn't want HW to take premiership. Joe tells him to f . . . off.

HW returns and does interview for the *Mirror*. People drifting in and out.

Now nobody is interested in the final results. We shall have a lead but no overall majority. Question is: what will Heath do?

My view is hang on. Beneath all the gloss, the Tories are interested in only one thing – power. They will try not to give it up. And the press and the BBC will cover for them, saying it is in the national interest.

We go back to Lord North Street. I go in the car with HW and Marcia.

There we sit down to discuss tactics. Whether to send a letter to Heath or to the Queen. Whether the party should make a statement saying Heath is cheating. Whether Harold should stay here or go to his farmhouse at Great Missenden. We are getting tired and slow. And tetchy. HW sends Mary and the children off to the farm. They had been all over the chairs and the floor. Impossible to hold a serious discussion.

Marcia is indignant with Heath. Because she claims that the working people are being cheated. Thinks HW should speak out and say this is disgraceful. I think we should play it more like a Prime Minister in waiting. Aloof. But perhaps send a letter tomorrow saying that the crisis requires that Britain has a government.

Press friends phone us with leaks from the Conservative Cabinet meeting.

Academic friends phone with interpretations of the constitution and citing precedents from 1923 and 1929.

One odd incident earlier at lunchtime. Heath's private secretary, Robert Armstrong,* phoned Marcia to say 'things are very confused here' and to ask for HW's movements that afternoon. Gave the impression they were about to resign.

Marcia phoned back at 7.30 to ask what was happening. Robert Armstrong was with Heath and clearly embarrassed. Appears that as the afternoon results were better for the Tories Heath changed his mind. Perhaps the first telephone message was without Heath's knowledge, the Civil Service preparing for the transition.

Now we are tired and incoherent. The election campaign had its own momentum, a timetable of speeches and meetings. This sitting and waiting was awful. Speculating on what would happen. When? This could go on for days.

Then a television announcement that Heath would see other party leaders tomorrow, Saturday. HW wonders if it includes him. We agree he must not go. Our position is clear. Heath has lost and must go. But we suspect the Liberals will play. A Liberal friend from Hampstead who knows Jeremy Thorpe* (John Pardoe*) tells me over the telephone from Cornwall that 'Jeremy's weakness has always been that he cannot resist getting his knees under any top table.' But surely the younger radical Liberals won't play. Much of their vote was anti-Heath.

HW gets ill-tempered.

Albert takes his shoes off and snores in the corner on the floor. I nearly drop off.

HW phones Jim Callaghan and asks him to issue a statement on behalf of members of Labour Party – that they are being cheated. Jim refuses bluntly.

Marcia intervenes and says we are all tired and should stop. I agree.

We leave together, walk down the Embankment to Parliament Square and take a taxi, with our suitcases. She is angry at how it is working out. She wants Labour to be in government. Wants Harold to win and be PM in order to wipe out the trauma of the defeat in 1970. But she doesn't actually want him to be in No. 10 and hates the prospect for herself. She wants to lead an ordinary life.

I drop her off at her house, decline to go in and go home.

Talk briefly with my wife Carol and collapse into bed.

[The final result of the 28 February 1974 general election was:

Labour: 301 seats (net gain 3) with 37.1% of vote;
Conservatives: 296 seats (net loss 16) with 37.8% of vote;
Liberals: 14 seats (net gain 1) with 19.3% of vote;

Others (including 11 Ulster Loyalists and 9 Celtic Nationalists) had a
net gain of 12.

It was the first election since 1929 which produced no overall majority and
the first time that even a combination of the winning party (Labour) and the
third party (Liberal) did not produce an overall majority.]

## Saturday 2 March 1974

I sleep till 9.30 in the morning when the phone starts ringing and rings
all day. Marcia (twice), HW (twice), John Harris, Harold Lever (twice).

I talk to Harold Evans,* who promises that the *Sunday Times* will say
Heath should go. Try the *Observer*, but David Astor* inaccessible.

Also decide to contact John Pardoe in Cornwall for more news of the
Liberals.

Marcia again worried about what will happen when Harold gets into
government again. Suggests I will be taken in and must be strong. Is really
complaining that we all lean on her, all phone her, all ask her to do things
or what to do. Keeps saying she wants to be left alone. HW is going round
to see her for tea at her nearby country house in Buckinghamshire.

## Sunday 3 March 1974

Marcia telephoned at 1 a.m. and said HW was very jumpy, wanted to know
what Liberals doing. Also he has big plans for me.

I spent ages telephoning John Pardoe in Cornwall. Spoke to his agent,
his secretary, a drunken constituent, but couldn't get hold of JP. Left a
message.

Next morning Pardoe phoned and said he would not support a Lib-
Con coalition and if he did, his constituents would repudiate him.

Also spoke to Harry Evans of the *Sunday Times*, who thought the Libs
would not support Heath. Also insisted Harold Lever must be in high
office overseeing finance in new Labour government.

Several phone calls to and from HW and Marcia. They are out at HW's
Grange Farm at Great Missenden in lovely sunshine. HW is now much
more relaxed and confident. I tell him I am sure Heath will fail and the
momentum of failure may mean he resigns on Tuesday.

HW said he might want me to go to see Roy Jenkins. Point is that he
cannot make Roy Chancellor of the Exchequer 'because he walked out of
the Shadow Cabinet over Britain's membership of the EEC. The party
won't have it.'

Apparently wants me to reassure Roy that the first Cabinet appointments are only for a year. Seems to intend to promote Roy then. He hints that he wants Roy to succeed him.

[Jenkins had resigned as Deputy Leader of the Labour Party in April 1972 in protest against the Shadow Cabinet's decision to support a referendum on British membership of the EEC. (Previously H. Wilson and the party had opposed a referendum, but the party leader now adopted it as a compromise vehicle to hold the party together while resisting pressure from the Left to commit itself to complete withdrawal from the EEC.) Jenkins rejoined the Shadow Cabinet in November 1973.]

I mention that I think Callaghan would then be best for the Department of Labour and dealing with the unions, and perhaps Healey to the Foreign Office. Then somebody else – Roy, Lever or Crosland – could go to Treasury. HW seems sympathetic but feels Callaghan won't allow it.

He is very concerned not to do anything which would upset party equilibrium. So his appointments will be orthodox, very much in line with Shadow Cabinet position.

In the afternoon I dealt with masses of correspondence accumulated during the campaign. Also a quick walk on Hampstead Heath, where I met Bill Rodgers.

Roy Jenkins had made a telephone call to Bill Rodgers. Obviously suspicious of my alleged 'betrayal' in going to work for Wilson. I let that pass. Must be better to have one of us at No. 10. After all, our Campaign for Democratic Socialism always believed that power was more important than dogma or prejudice. Foolish to behave like the Left.

[The Campaign for Democratic Socialism was a Labour Party pressure group operating in 1959–64 in support of Hugh Gaitskell and against the Labour Left and especially unilateral disarmament (and against Harold Wilson's bid for the party leadership in 1960 and less certainly in 1963). Its main officials included Bill Rodgers and Bernard Donoughue, with Roy Jenkins and Tony Crosland as prominent supporters. Donoughue, as secretary of CDS, issued its formal statement of dissolution in 1964 to encourage party unity behind Harold Wilson at the general election of that year.]

Went to HW at Lord North Street at 8 p.m. We discuss the next Cabinet (when I now suggested Michael Foot* for Labour Secretary of State) and my proposed job running the new Policy Unit in Downing Street.

Joe, Marcia and Albert arrived later. We sat down to discuss forming the new government:

1) How to take over No. 10. Apparently last time in 1964 was very humiliating, with the civil servants treating the political team contemptuously, refusing to allow them into any rooms in No. 10. They snatched away writing paper to prevent them writing letters. And locked the door between the Cabinet Office and No. 10 to prevent any communication.

HW said this time the four of us would go in together – through the front door – and he would interview the civil servants and tell them to take instructions from the four of us. We decide on rooms. He says that if the civil servants, like last time, ask Marcia to leave, we will say OK and will all leave with her.

Discuss plans to change various civil servants who have shown themselves over-enthusiastic for Heath.

2) Discuss my job, in charge of a new Policy Unit. Staff of around six plus two personal assistants.

To act as 'eyes and ears' for HW. To see *all* Cabinet papers and alert him of anything politically difficult. To make sure nobody slips from the manifesto. To liaise with all ministers' private offices. Liaise with Transport House and outside experts. To feed in new policy ideas. Pick up anything being missed by other ministries.

My rank to be deputy secretary.

3) Discuss Cabinet. Same problems as discussed earlier.

Main problem now is Education – possibly Merlyn Rees?*

Chairman of PLP – Arthur Bottomley?*

PPS for HW? Keep it open till Albert Murray gets a seat – presumably when Elwyn Jones* made Lord Chancellor.

Also discuss patronage and need to keep an eye on it.

Harold thinks Roy Hattersley* is 'an opportunist'. Says he prefers people who oppose him openly to his face.

Albert states his principle of government – 'In defeat malice, in victory revenge.'

Happy relaxed atmosphere. HW insistent that this team must go into No. 10 and stick together.

Lots of phone calls. John Silkin to say that Eric Lubbock* of the Liberals is in touch with him. Lord Wigg* to say that Jeremy Thorpe is in touch with him. Also reports from what went on in the Tory Cabinet this evening.

Drove home at half past midnight.

[During the long weekend while Harold Wilson waited patiently at Grange Farm the attempts by Prime Minister Edward Heath to persuade other political parties to support the continuance in office of his Conservative government moved towards their doomed conclusion.

On Friday 1 March he went to Buckingham Palace to report to the Queen on the proposal for a coalition. On Sunday 3 March Jeremy Thorpe, the Liberal leader, travelled from Devon to Downing Street at Mr Heath's invitation. After two hours of discussions Thorpe stated that he could say nothing in public until he had consulted his senior Liberal colleagues next day. At that Liberal gathering, aware of strong hostility among Liberal activists, the Liberal leaders unanimously rejected any coalition with the Tories. However, they said they were not opposed to the possibility of supporting a Conservative minority government on an agreed programme – presumably including the introduction of proportional representation. The Prime Minister rejected that suggestion.

The political reality was that the Liberals did not actually hold the decisive balance of power in the new Parliament. Even with their support, Heath would have been eight short of an overall majority (and the seven dissident Ulster Unionists had already responded discouragingly to his invitation to take the Conservative Whip).

After two meetings of his Cabinet on Monday 4 March Mr Heath accepted that it was not practical for him to proceed and he went to the Palace at 6.30 p.m. to tender his resignation.]

## Monday 4 March 1974

I went to LSE to lecture in the morning while we waited for the outcome of Heath's coalition discussions. HW is still at Grange Farm.

Lunch at St Ermin's. HW, Joe, Marcia, myself and Gerald Kaufman,* whom Marcia had invited to join us.

In the morning I had, on HW's request the previous day, phoned Roy Jenkins to ask his movements. Now HW was concerned I get him again and talk to him to say:

1) Roy to have the Home Office and Northern Ireland;
2) Must be 'detached' for a while;
3) Only for a time at the Home Office – then promotion;
4) Soon – say 18 months – HW will retire and hopes Roy will succeed him. But thinks Roy can only succeed after successful spell in office.

I promise to convey this. HW suggests by telephone. I think not and decide to see Roy personally after lunch.

Lunchtime cheerful chatter. I feel removed, thinking of my new Policy Unit and appointments to it. My *first real* job.

They discuss giving peerages to Terry Pitt from the research department at party headquarters and John Harris. HW had promised T. Pitt to come into Downing Street and meant to put him in my unit. I decline and Marcia suggests a peerage as a way out.

I leave lunch at 2 p.m. to go and find Roy Jenkins. After I have gone Kaufman apparently (Marcia told me) presses that Roy should go to the

Treasury instead of Denis Healey. HW apparently white with rage walks out. Says the party balance won't stand it.

I see Roy in the corridor of the House of Commons and tell him the message. Roy was obviously nervous. Says nothing except thanking me and walks away. I find it difficult to talk to him. It cannot be pleasant for him receiving this news from a young messenger.

Tony Crosland comes across and congratulates me on the campaign. He can make people feel relaxed and warm.

To the LSE to see my tutees. At 4.10 p.m. I hear that the Liberals' message about not joining a coalition is in with the Shadow Cabinet. I cancel a class and set off to HW's room in the Commons.

Talk to Jim Callaghan and Harold Lever. Then Wilson sends me to Roy Jenkins again. I meet him in the corridor and say that HW would like to see him.

Roy explodes in an extraordinary fashion, shouting, 'You tell Harold Wilson he must bloody well come to see me and if he doesn't watch out, I won't join his bloody government. He repeated this several times, on a public staircase. He was very angry. I was also angry and embarrassed. I said I would *politely* suggest that HW come to see Roy and I implied that I was not altogether happy about being a messenger between them. But I suspected HW felt that sending a 'Jenkinsite' was a sign of good will. I should have declined. Certainly it did not work.

Roy shouted again, 'This is typical of the bloody awful way HW does things.'

Certainly HW handled it wrongly in sending me as an embarrassed and junior intermediary, but with good intent.

Roy perhaps should have chuckled, commented that HW never changed and firmly suggested that it would be better face to face between the two top politicians.

Back to H. Wilson, and I made him go off to see Roy. He was there three-quarters of an hour. Meanwhile we hear that Heath has gone to the Palace and a phone call from No. 10 tells us to expect a call from the Palace.

Finally HW returns, looking down. Roy has made an objection. *Not to his own* appointment at the Home Office but to Peter Shore at the revised Board of Trade, being an EEC negotiator. Roy has refused to join the government till this is settled, since Peter is violently anti-European.

Interestingly, Marcia immediately says that Roy is right. Says one cannot both demote him ministerially and humiliate him on Europe. I strongly agree and we begin to press HW to adjust to meet Roy's view.

Back to 5 Lord North Street and stand around waiting for the call to the Palace. HW upstairs shaving.

We set off to the Palace. HW and Mary in front in Harold's own small

car driven by Bill Housden. We follow in a large Daimler limousine –
Marcia, Joe, Albert, Gerald Kaufman (who I like, he is quick and funny)
and me. Quite a Mafia. We drive to the Palace, through the cameras and
the cheering crowd at the gates.

We wait for an hour while HW is in audience with the Queen. Marcia
talks about previous times, how chilly it is in the Palace and how there are
no drinks. We discuss how to impose ourselves on the civil servants. For
a start, when HW came out from seeing the Queen, Joe goes to his car
and travels in it, sending Robert Armstrong, the principal private secretary,
in the back car.

Back to No. 10 Downing Street and everybody feels marvellous. Means
a great deal to Marcia and Joe because of the horrible circumstances in
which they were booted out last time. This is rubbing out the past, paying
off old scores.

Through the big black front door of No. 10. About 30 staff lined up in
the front hall and along the corridor leading to the Cabinet Room to greet
HW. But I sense a feeling of hostility and discomfort. Top civil servants look
very smooth, trying not to show their horror. I am relieved to spot Robin
Butler* among the private secretaries. Nice man, friend of William Plowden.*

We go through and stand around uncomfortably outside the Cabinet
Room. Then HW introduces Joe, Marcia and myself to the civil servants
and says, 'Why not go to Marcia's room?' So off we go to the small room
she had last time, adjoining the Cabinet Room and looking westwards
across the No. 10 garden towards St James's Park. A private secretary brings
tea and biscuits.

We set off on a tour of the house, guided by Robert Armstrong, who
looks very unhappy indeed.

Our plan is to establish our presence and authority.

Joe goes off discreetly to his two rooms at the front of the house and
sacks Heath's press officer and his deputy, who were believed to be very
Tory partisan.

I went to my suite of rooms along the corridor leading from the Cabinet
Room to the (locked) green door connecting to the Cabinet Office – 'the
Wiggery', very handsome. My room overlooks Downing Street, with lovely
high ceilings, a sofa and TV in my office and huge 18th-century portraits
on the walls.

Then we reassemble in Marcia's room and relax and drink.

I went off again and began to organise the private dining-room upstairs
which HW has suggested. I get a kitchen at the top of the house, insist
on a grill and a fridge permanently stocked. We will use the small state
dining-room on the first floor, between the pillared reception room and
the great state dining-room. It has room to seat up to ten people.

Also telephone John Pardoe, who says that Jeremy Thorpe had told them at the Liberal meeting that he did not think Heath was serious in the coalition offer. Just trying to put the blame on the Liberals for not forming a coalition. John Pardoe wants to keep in touch.

Go with Joe into the Cabinet Room and HW telephones Len Murray to bring the TUC to Downing Street tomorrow as the first move in government. Also tries to get the CBI, but they are all out at social engagements.

Am very worried HW cannot announce his Cabinet immediately – because of the problem with Roy Jenkins about Peter Shore. Don't want leaks of divisions. Harold telephones Roy again, but makes no progress. We are pressing Harold to compromise.

Then ministers start to arrive to see HW.

Elwyn Jones delighted to be Lord Chancellor.

George Thomas* effusive as Deputy Speaker.

Fred Peart* disappointed at Agriculture.

Michael Foot very nervous and withdrawn. Clearly no idea he has the terrible job at Labour (Employment). His first Cabinet job at 60. A gamble! I suggested it and think it will work.

Roy Mason* ebullient at Defence.

Eric Varley* content at Energy.

Benn also comes in to learn that he is going back to the Department of Industry.

We finish at midnight. Go back to Lord North Street to get our coats and then home in the limousine with Marcia, Kaufman and Eric Varley, dropping them off on the way.

HW has promised to get my release from the LSE through.

The election campaign is now finally over. Government begins tomorrow.

# CHAPTER 2

## The New Labour Government
## A Budget, Irish Problems – and 'Scandals'
## in Number Ten

*March–April 1974*

[ E ]ntering Downing Street inevitably changed the working style, rhythm and priorities of Harold Wilson's personal staff in March 1974. We were now part of government. Britain's problems became our problems, often leading to our failures, rather than being opportunities to score party successes in the electoral game.

Each of us in Mr Wilson's personal staff in Downing Street acquired governmental functions. We were given the status of temporary civil servants and we had to establish functional relations with the regular Civil Service machinery. Joe Haines returned to his 1970 job as head of the Prime Minister's press office. Marcia Williams again took over the political office, with Albert Murray and her sister Peggy working under her.

I, aged only thirty-nine and until now a Reader in Politics at the London School of Economics, had a particularly delicate task for a new boy in Whitehall. I was urgently required to create a new institution in central government, against the scepticism and occasional hostility of some of the regular civil servants. The Downing Street Policy Unit was to give the Prime Minister advice on all policy areas. I had initially to establish liaison and then to maintain continuing co-operation with all branches of central government (and especially with the Cabinet Office as the dynamo of the administration) in order to secure full information on what was happening in Whitehall. Yet I also had to preserve the independence of the Unit from the fatal embrace of the regular bureaucratic machine. I had to appreciate and pursue the political dimension of all policies. Yet the Policy Unit must not become a mere voice of partisan ideology or transgress on the territory of direct relations with the Labour Party which was so jealously guarded by Mrs Marcia Williams. These objectives and constraints required endless negotiations during my first weeks in Downing Street about access to confidential papers and to ministerial and official committees or to the Prime Minister himself. But they had to be done successfully, since in Whitehall information and access are the sinews of power. At the same time I had rapidly to find and recruit a team of policy advisers capable of operating successfully at this high and testing level. I was most fortunate in this latter endeavour and my young team worked incredibly hard and performed with great success. Without them I personally could have achieved very little.

In the event I secured my personal right to receive all confidential papers which went to the Prime Minister except those concerning secret defence and intelligence matters (although I could and did see these in the Prime Minister's box when I wished). I could attend all Cabinet committees chaired by the Prime Minister (which were most of the important ones) and go to other ministerial committees on prior request. It was in these Cabinet committees that the deepest discussion of policy options took place. I did not normally attend full Cabinet in Downing Street, but I did sit in on some Cabinets with the Prime Minister's permission, and went to all special Cabinets at Chequers.

I and my staff also attended official inter-departmental committees and mixed committees of ministers and civil servants where I felt the Prime Minister had an interest. The main constraint was time and not protocol. This complex web of policy discussions was for me a goldmine of information and the essential source for my direct briefing to the Prime Minister, which in turn depended above all on my location inside Downing Street and my ready, personal and informal access to him at all times. Consequently, most of the personal conflicts with the official machine described below were actually to secure, maintain or extend my rights of access to Whitehall information and to communicate to the Prime Minister. Even when seemingly petty, they were usually concerned with the crucial process of power in Whitehall. In the end, with the help of marvellous staff members, we created a Policy Unit which was both an integral part of Whitehall and yet independent of the machine and which, against the odds and under five different Prime Ministers, different political parties and various directors, survived for thirty years.

Actually for the Prime Minister's personal staff, their least difficulties concerned the regular civil servants in the Downing Street private office (though tensions inevitably arose with them and are chronicled with the excessive but transitory heat of the crisis hour in the following pages). Downing Street is a relatively small building, in fact two seventeenth-century town houses joined together back to back. Apart from the Cabinet Room and several main offices on the ground floor and the state reception rooms on the first floor, it contained a typing pool in the basement garden rooms, corridors of offices on the second floor and, at the top of the house, a long and thin, bleak apartment for the Prime Minister's living quarters (though after 1974 Mr Wilson declined to occupy them) and some bedrooms for staff or guests sleeping overnight. In all, there were little over a hundred employees, including messengers, security people and typists. No other head of government of a leading world nation is directly served by so few. This smallness is a great advantage to 'outsiders' arriving as the Prime Minister's personal entourage. Everybody in the house gets to know one another very quickly. There is little scope or time for hierarchy or ceremony even among the tiny band of regular civil servants themselves, so it is easy for the outsiders to fit in on the only basis which works in Downing Street – the different contributions of each to serving the Prime Minister.

Of course it also helped us that with such a small total staff, we outsiders could not be swamped by the regulars. Of the hundred or so people in Number Ten in 1974, only nine had frequent access to the Prime Minister to advise on serious questions of government and politics. Half of these were civil servants working in the two private offices which stood in line next to the Cabinet Room, looking over the Number Ten garden and into Horse Guards Parade. In March 1974 these key officials – themselves on three- or four-year loan from other departments – were the principal private secretary, Robert Armstrong; the private secretary responsible for foreign affairs, Lord Bridges; the private secretary covering domestic and especially Treasury policies, Robin Butler; the diary secretary, Mark Forrester, and the private secretary supervising parliamentary affairs, especially the Prime Minister's responses to Parliamentary Questions on Tuesdays and Thursdays at 3.15 p.m., Nick Stuart.* (Armstrong and Bridges were replaced in 1975 by, respectively, Kenneth Stowe* and Patrick Wright.*) The other half of the senior advisory team were from the 'Kitchen Cabinet': Joe Haines covering the press and broad political advice; Marcia Williams and Albert Murray covering the Prime Minister's relations with the Labour Party organisation and his Huyton constituency; and myself monitoring government policy.

It was a good balance between bureaucrats and pirates, and on the whole it worked well. The main tensions, as the following pages painfully demonstrate, arose not between 'us' and the regular civil servants but within the 'Kitchen Cabinet' itself. The most astonishing and alarming experience for me (but less surprising to others who had been in Downing Street with Mr Wilson in 1964–70) was to observe the amount of the Prime Minister's precious time which was spent in 1974–76 not on Britain's looming economic crisis but on petty problems within his personal team.

Equally disappointing, on reflection, was our excessive concern with media criticism, at least during these first months in office. In fact the capacity of Britain's newspapers to damage a Labour government ought to be limited by the transparency and extravagant viciousness of the Conservative bias of most of them. Their compulsive contempt for facts, truth or fairness should, in a fair world, neutralise the damage they try to wreak, whether on politicians, royals or any individual whose character or success arouses the native spite and envy of many journalists. But it does not work out so simply. Newspaper comment, however bilious, biased and untrue, is not accepted by politicians as the price of an abrasive democracy nor brushed aside, as it should be, with the contempt it often deserves. In fact newspapers were in 1974, and probably still are three decades later, the loudest public voice heard daily in Downing Street. Even seasoned politicians bruise – and it is clear from our experience how easily a Prime Minister can be diverted by press criticism from his main priorities of winning elections and governing the United Kingdom. However, given the enormous pressures upon him, it is remarkable how much Mr Wilson achieved. He was certainly helped by the vast political experience, the indomitable humour and the remarkable tolerance which he brought to this impossible job.]

### Tuesday 5 March 1974

My first morning in No. 10 Downing Street. Arrive 10 a.m. Cheering crowds and pushing photographers outside as I go in. Straight to my room, which is on the ground floor between the Cabinet Room and the Cabinet Office and conveniently close to the bottom of the stairs up to the Prime Minister's study. I phone Marcia, who I have not been able to pick up this morning since I couldn't get an official car.

See Joe in the press office. Then to my room, where the previous occupant, Robin Haden, Heath's press officer, previously from the Foreign Office, was sitting making phone calls. I went away to leave him in peace and give him time to move out.

HW was still seeing and appointing new ministers. I talk to Roy Jenkins (Home Secretary) and Tony Crosland (Secretary of State for the Environment) before they go in, and to Lord Shackleton,* who is not taking a job because he must earn some money. (HW therefore later calls him Lord Shekelton. In fact I like him. He helped me very much on my book on Herbert Morrison.)

Placated Marcia for not having collected her.

Finally took over my room. Visited by two of the private secretaries from private office in turn, trying to work out what I (and Marcia) are doing. I am firm and insist on seeing all Cabinet papers. Also warn one of them that I won't be frozen out. Also tell them they must not ignore Marcia.

Have coffee in Marcia's room with Marcia, Mary Wilson and two secretaries. Then we go to my room with Marcia and Albert to discuss HW's official diary. Eliminate most of the inherited Heath engagements, especially various boating and dinghy clubs.

This meeting goes on till lunchtime. A civil servant suggests a prime ministerial visit to China. I am attracted, but Marcia puts her foot down. She later tells me that the civil servants are only interested in trips abroad. She dislikes Chinese politics and also thinks HW must deal with UK problems.

Lunch in the new dining-room upstairs: HW, Marcia, Joe, Albert, me, Gerald Kaufman and the party secretary, Ron Hayward.

HW in good form. Nice lunch. Beef with plenty of good wine. Also English cheese – which pleases HW, who dislikes French food.

Discuss appointments – peerages, how to promote incompetents out of Transport House so that it can become efficient. Also some remaining junior ministerial appointments in the government. I press the case for Edmund Dell.*

Also discuss the case for a TV ministerial broadcast by HW as the new Prime Minister – pressed by Kaufman, opposed by the rest of us.

Afterwards had to go into a meeting of relevant ministers with the leaders of the CBI. They look a bit shamefaced. Curiously most of them are wearing red ties.

Harold Lever and I exchange funny notes across the Cabinet table. Still not sure where he is going to work.

Interesting to see Dick Marsh,* the former trade unionist and Labour minister who is now a successful boss, on the other side of the table with the CBI. Has obviously been living well. Michael Clapham*, their president, is a bit supercilious, but well informed. Their director-general, Campbell Adamson,* seems cowed. Benn and Shore speak as well. But Marsh's is the best intervention – about the chaos in nationalised industries financing.

Afterwards to my room.

Visited by Chris Foster* from LSE with some helpful suggestions for my staff. I want to get him in the Cabinet Office Think Tank (the Central Policy Review Staff, CPRS) if I can.

Then saw John Harris in my room. Discuss question of Roy Jenkins and HW. He says how angry Roy was yesterday. I say I understand. We agree to keep them in touch and to make sure relations are good. He says they have 'no intention to play it rough'. I said if they did it would be the end of Roy in this Cabinet. He agreed, but said never forget that Roy doesn't care; beyond a certain point he would rather resign than stay. I agreed. That is his strength.

He says the main problem yesterday was that Roy knew HW had seen other ministers face to face. Why not him? We agree they must lunch together – and we must keep in touch.

Meanwhile Robert Armstrong, the PM's principal private secretary, has sorted out my LSE position. The director, Walter Adams, was marvellous – positive, immediate, generous. I spoke to him afterwards and he was delightful and funny, pressing me to screw the Civil Service for a lot of money (some hope!).

Spent most of the rest of the evening with Marcia, Joe, HW and R. Armstrong.

Raised question of my status. Press for deputy secretary, as agreed. Not much hope since the Civil Service opposes. Marcia supports marvellously.

Out through the front door with HW and home to Kentish Town in an official car by 9.30. The earliest in four weeks!

## *Wednesday 6 March 1974*

Fluctuating day.

Morning phoned Marcia before leaving home – she was very depressed. Row with HW last night *over me*. Harold had refused to support me against the Civil Service for me to be a deputy secretary. She is now refusing to come in to No. 10. [The recent head of the Policy Unit is graded as a second permanent secretary.]

I go in. HW is at the National Executive Committee and then at the Parliamentary Labour Party. I dealt with some papers, the telephone, questions of security, etc. Still have trouble recruiting staff because we have no official status or title in Whitehall.

Marcia arrives but is difficult and refuses to talk. She sits with Mary and things are very tense.

Ministers come and go and I discuss the political scene with Jim Callaghan (Foreign Secretary), Michael Foot (Employment), Denis Howell* (Minister of Sport) and Brian Walden,* who is going to refuse a junior post because he told me that he wants to earn a lot of money. I have known Brian ever since Oxford and I bet him he won't refuse – to strengthen his resolve (but he did).

Long talk with Robert Armstrong. He thinks I should be an undersecretary (which he is). And after his lunch with Sir John Hunt,* the Cabinet Secretary, about which official papers I shall see. All fishing for what I will do in my new job, since there has never before been a policy unit in Downing Street.

Terrible lunch. We all go upstairs to the small dining-room. We discuss the CPRS and appointments. [The Central Policy Review Staff was established in the Cabinet Office by Edward Heath in 1971. Harold Wilson seemed inclined to abolish it in March 1974, but B. Donoughue argued strongly for its value and its retention. Mrs Thatcher abolished it in 1983.]

Suddenly Marcia blows up. Already upset because we were eating whitebait. She says she hates them looking at her from the plate. The PM solemnly announced that they were whitebait from the Home for Blind Whitebait, so she need not worry. I added they were also volunteers.

Broke the tension for a while, but then she blew up over Harold and me having a polite and friendly conversation together. She said that it was disgraceful in view of HW's lack of support for me over my status and in view of her having suffered rows on my behalf. She stalked out. HW followed, his meal unfinished. Gloom. Joe left. Albert quite rightly felt it was a terrible waste not to finish the lunch and went right through to the port and a cigar.

I went to the Prime Minister's study, which is on the same first floor as the dining-rooms but across the other side of the house, looking over the garden and St James's Park towards Buckingham Palace. HW was with Joe finishing dictating his speech for the debate on the Queen's Speech opening the new Parliament. Obviously did not want to be disturbed.

Down to Marcia who has her coat on in her room and is 'leaving for ever'. Very upset! I am very silent, miserable and decide it is not worth staying.

Albert arrives and Marcia attacks him, saying he is only interested in getting a seat in the House of Commons. Albert fights back brilliantly and talks to her for two hours and finally she takes her coat off. I have left and work in my room. The first Cabinet papers arrive.

Tea with an apparently pacified Marcia and discuss HW's draft for the Queen's Speech. She is quick and sees everything that is not there. We then go through lists of junior minister possibilities. I argue strongly for Bill Rodgers, David Owen and Bob Maclennan.* She dislikes the latter but is surprisingly favourable to Bill and David. Later we hear that David has declined a post, but will think about it. HW comes back and wonders why David declined. Discuss his child with leukaemia. HW is very sympathetic to him despite all of David's attacks on HW. No rancour at all.

But obviously rancour towards Bill Rodgers. HW may have vetoed him for Defence.

Go to see Harold Lever, Chancellor of the Duchy of Lancaster, in his palatial rooms through the locked doors into the Cabinet Office. Elegant but gloomy, with no people. He will have to fight to be heard. Talk to my old LSE friend Ray Richardson (Lever's new special adviser) about it. We must work together. They are off to dinner with Healey, who is treating Lever very well and trying to maintain good relations between the Treasury and him.

Then sudden excitement back in No. 10 about the possibility that the miners would settle their strike. Civil servants report that the two sides are agreed and on the phone wanting the PM to authorise a settlement. We press HW *not* to get involved and to leave it to ministers. HW rightly rebukes the civil servants for not consulting other ministers. Insists they send for the Chancellor. So Healey comes in and Michael Foot. But they cannot find the Energy minister Eric Varley (who was apparently at the opera with Gerald Kaufman) and nobody at all is at the Ministry of Energy – at the time of the coal settlement! HW furious. Wants to sack the permanent secretary. And when Varley arrives he gets a terrible rocket – in front of Albert and Marcia. (Joe and I slipped out discreetly.) Marcia ticks HW off. He mustn't do this to ministers in front of juniors.

### Thursday 7 March 1974

In the morning I telephone Marcia from home. She was ill. Had fainted in the night. Not coming into the office this morning. I offered to bring her in by car, but she declined.

Went in to Downing Street at 9.30. HW seeing ministers. I talked to Jim Callaghan. Saw Albert Murray, who is very depressed about his insecure position in the PM's entourage. He is a marvellous cockney and we must help him.

Spent the morning rushing around. Saw Lever in the Cabinet Office. Saw HW. Also Joe Haines, and spent time doing routine things with security and with Civil Service Establishment about my new position. HW told me he had instructed Harold Lever to get me a deputy secretaryship, but at the Cabinet Office. I later phone Lever and find he has forgotten. I am pleased because I decide I would rather have a lower position as under-secretary in No. 10 than a high position in the Cabinet Office. Access matters more than status.

Return to my room at noon. There waiting are Mary Wilson, Marcia and HW's long-time housekeeper, Mrs Pollard (also from a Northamptonshire village close to where Marcia and I were born). They want me to recruit a cook for No. 10 to provide meals at all times. We spend some time discussing this. I had not realised I was also to be head of catering, but it appears so. I have already secured a fridge, an infra-red stove and a lot of frozen food. Now we need personnel.

Gerald Kaufman joins us. A family gathering.

But Marcia is jumpy. We go off upstairs to lunch – HW, Marcia, Joe, Albert and myself. Discuss appointments. Marcia starts a row over the exclusion of Bill Rodgers from the government. She thinks it is wrong and a political mistake. Joe and HW say that he was not a complete success as a minister previously. She says nor were most of the people he has appointed. It would be a stupid error, possibly a disaster, to leave Bill out.

I sit silent at first because they all know I am a friend of Bill's. Then I said I thought he was very capable and disagreed with their criticism. But could not see how my intervention at this stage would help.

At the end of the meal Marcia walks out in a temper and HW is clearly upset. She had attacked him viciously in front of the waiter. He was very calm and patient with her. I get the feeling that everything he does in politics is to please her. He does not care about the people, the party or himself. She is the daughter who he delights in, however outrageous, and who he is working to please. It is amazing to watch. His patience with her is endless.

He leaves the table and Joe goes to help him with the next speech.

I go downstairs and have some appointments. I went into Marcia's room and she is there with Albert, with her coat on. She has a temperature. Is leaving. We see her out and I said I would telephone her later.

Back to my room to see various people. See Ray Richardson just before 5 p.m. Discuss the problem of Harold Lever not being interested in the nuts and bolts of political organisation. Must strengthen him and his staff or he will lose influence.

Telephone LSE to enquire who is giving my scheduled lectures. Find out they expect me to. So I dash by taxi with Ray and give a lecture off the cuff.

Back to No. 10 at 7 p.m. and send for Albert and discuss his job problem. Then a civil servant arrives and says the PM wants me. Go to him and Joe in Marcia's room. Discussing ministerial appointments. Discuss Bill Rodgers and David Owen. I support both and come out strongly for Rodgers. Say that everybody knows he is a friend and this is why I have been silent before. But really it was ridiculous to exclude him. He was good in government – and could be dangerous as an opponent because a superb organiser.

Joe is against, but HW is clearly receptive.

A victory celebration party had been arranged for this evening and food was coming. While I was at LSE it was cancelled because Marcia was ill. I did not know. So my wife Carol arrived at 8.30 – the only guest at the party.

Joe and Albert had gone home to get an early night.

Carol, HW and I had a drink together in the study. He was relaxed and very funny. Told Carol that it was all 'a pantomime': 'it is a riot, quite chaotic'. He said 'Nobody outside would believe it. A total pantomime.' In this mood nobody could help but like him.

Marcia phoned him and Carol and I left the room. I showed her round No. 10. HW was on the phone for 40 minutes. When he finished he came to join us in the Cabinet Room. We chatted, then left together. He said nothing about the telephone call.

Carol and I went to dinner with our old friend Denis Howell at the Sportsman Club. He is disappointed at again being Minister of Sport. We discuss appointments. He said we must sack the director of the Sports Council, Walter Winterbottom.* But I don't want to sack him. Walter has foolishly snubbed Denis while being in opposition, but is very good and has essential technical knowledge. Discuss appointments to Sports

Council and other bodies. Would like to get some of our LSE people on.

Home very tired, midnight. Message to phone Marcia. Did so. She is very depressed and neurotic. Talked for 75 minutes. Attacks Joe, Albert and me. Says we are all out for ourselves. Ganging up against her. And that I am out to replace her. She says she will retire to her country house and wait for HW to sack us all and come personally to ask her to return.

She was also disturbed by what she called my 'coolness'. Because I never got angry or upset. She also attacked HW bitterly and said he did not understand how to deal with civil servants.

She felt upset that she had carried the brunt of supporting Bill Rodgers at lunch.

Then it all came out. That HW was no longer consulting her. And I had not telephoned her this evening. She suspected because we all wanted to appoint the government without consulting her. Quite paranoic. Yet still shafts of bright perception and immense intelligence and judgement among the neuroses.


## Friday 8 March 1974

Spent restless night thinking about the conversation with Marcia. Decided to offer my resignation. Have not come into this, taking massive cut in income and mistrust of old political friends, to sit up half the night being accused of self-seeking. Even worse were the attacks on Albert.

Arrive at No. 10 at 9.30 a.m., before anybody else. Sort out my letters and papers. Then go to see HW. Tell him two points:

(1) If I stay, have decided to accept a lower position in No. 10 rather than be a deputy secretary on the staff of the Cabinet Office. I want my position to be totally at No. 10. And I don't want him bothered by my personal problems any more. It means a cut of £7,000 p.a. in my income.

(2) I report that Marcia has talked to me, is afraid I am replacing her, and that I do not wish myself or him to be in that position. Therefore he has my resignation in his pocket from that moment. And when he wishes to exercise it, I promise to say to *everybody*, private as well as public, that it is because of my heavy family commitments, with no mention of Marcia's jealousy and hostility.

He is very charming, says he appreciates the offer and that the fact that I have made it means it won't have to be exercised. He tells me that Marcia has at one time or another demanded the resignation of all his previous assistants, including G. Kaufman and J. Haines. And when HW has suggested he might sack them, each time she has reacted by saying that if he did she would resign and tell the press that he was betraying his loyal aides.

Then off to my room to work. HW sees a succession of people, including Roy Hattersley, Crowther-Hunt* (who he wants to put in charge of constitutional reform, especially the 1973 Kilbrandon Report on the constitution which recommended against independence for Scotland or Wales but is in favour of devolving more government power to them), Bill Rodgers and, finally, my longest-standing friend, Gerry Fowler.*

Gerry Fowler looks as if he has enjoyed some riotous nights. At first HW had resisted my pressure to put Gerry in the government – mainly because he felt people out of the Commons till now should wait a little. But now he has apparently appointed him to Education. As with Rodgers, HW resists the arguments, goes away, then concedes in his decisions.

Incidentally, next day I saw Harry Kissin,* who told me:

(a) HW had intended to make Harold Lever *only* Minister of Arts until he and, to a lesser extent, I and Harold Evans pressed the importance of giving Lever an explicit economic function.

(b) He said that HW was thinking of putting Michael Foot into Europe until I suggested the Department of Labour that Sunday evening at the end of the election campaign. My view is that, as he implied at the time, Wilson was already playing with the idea and I confirmed him.

Marcia did not come in to the office at all today and I did not telephone. We had a very pleasant lunch upstairs – HW, Joe, Albert and myself. Joe and I put Albert next to HW and made sure there was discussion of his problems of a parliamentary seat and money. HW agreed to act and that Albert should travel to Liverpool with him that afternoon. (We had finished off the speech before lunch.)

Also discussed the problems of the party organisation in Transport House. Ron Hayward, the party secretary, has asked for a Privy Counsellorship and a knighthood and is pushing himself forward into the limelight too much. Terry Pitt, the research officer – HW had asked Tony Benn, Pitt's close ally, to take Pitt as his junior minister in the Lords, but Benn's admiration apparently fell far short of employing Terry, and HW and Benn had quite a row. Now decided to put Pitt with Crowther-Hunt on Kilbrandon and devolution, where Pitt is quite an expert.

Roy Jenkins had been in to No. 10 to see HW this morning, to complain, as HW later told us, that although they are 'the two most important men in the government', their relationships were poor. They apparently went over the history of clashes over the past three years. Afterwards HW said they both felt better that it was off their chests. HW pointed out he had given Roy John Harris as a peer and junior minister, despite the latter's constant attacks on him. I hope Roy will settle down now. HW said he still thinks Roy is the natural successor to himself – though Healey looks an ominous challenger.

HW off to Liverpool. At last I can begin to deal with my office. Recruit two personal assistants. Talk to Ray Richardson and Chris Foster from the LSE about others. Also see George Weidenfeld* – nice to have my publisher at last show an interest, having left me completely dissatisfied with his firm's earlier handling of my biography of Herbert Morrison. He wants 'to build up the social contacts of Labour supporters'!

Finalise my position as under-secretary with the Establishment Officer. He reveals that the sticking-point is that I must not earn more than the PM's principal private secretary. I don't see why not, since I am not in the Civil Service hierarchy. But for other reasons prefer not to argue. Then go to see H. Lever and tell him not to bother to raise my case with Robert Armstrong, who is dining with him tonight. Lever is still fairly optimistic that the Budget will go his way. I hope he does not underestimate the capacity of the Civil Service machine to deceive him with flattery. I tell him he *must* get *staff* and must back his special adviser Ray Richardson for a higher position.

Interview a possible secretary, Brenda Phipps. Seems good and I say yes. Then Joe comes to complain. She was the best secretary working for him. The Civil Service had simply told me she was free and due for re-allocation without consulting him. Divide and rule, I suspect. Clearly I must keep in touch with the rest of the team on everything!

Home by 8 p.m. The earliest for a month. Actually saw my girls, Rachel and Kate, before they went to bed. And had dinner with Carol. HW must go off on more trips.

### Monday 11 March 1974

Incidentally last week HW made Harold Lever Minister for the Civil Service on Thursday morning – when he told him to get me appointed deputy secretary.

At Thursday lunchtime Marcia objected because she felt Lever would be too soft with the civil servants. By the evening, HW asked me if Lever had dealt with my problem and I had to say no. Next morning the job was taken away from Lever and given to Ted Short, the Lord President.

*Monday* – Arrived at No. 10 at 9.30. Worked all morning on papers and beginning to make appointments to the office. And clearing up the backlog of messages with my excellent new secretary Brenda. Try to see HW but he is busy.

Telephone broken down again – although the engineers were in all Friday morning and all Saturday morning. Nice to know that No. 10 suffers from the same technological incompetence that ordinary people suffer from. (Or were they bugging me?)

Saw HW with Marcia at lunchtime (she had sent me a gentle and affectionate apology). He complained that I had not contacted him since Friday – must not let that happen again. He likes the team to be in touch. It is his family. He says Marcia is much happier now.

The civil servants provide two bottles of champagne for his 58th birthday. The battle for possession is on.

At lunch I invite Geoff Bish,* the head of research from Transport House (who is chippy but capable), and two of the new policy advisers – Frances Morrell (with Tony Benn at the Department of Industry) and nice and clever David Lipsey* (with Tony Crosland in Environment). Explain the functions and establish liaison. Useful, though they are clearly in the dark and will have to fight hard to beat their ministry civil servants.

After lunch chat with Marcia about future politics. She is obviously afraid the Liberals will bring us down and wants the party organisation operating to plan for an election a year from now – opinion polls and constituencies. She is always looking ahead politically.

Then to my room. Interview lovely David Piachaud* from the LSE for a job as social policy adviser in the new Policy Unit and the potential research assistants. Letters and papers.

Policy issues beginning to come up – rates, pensions. I need staff soon.

Also the problem of Harold Lever's recent broadcast on French TV when he questioned the idea of a referendum on the EEC. HW and Joe Haines are angry and I am used as intermediary. Lever must be careful.

Evening party in the drawing-rooms for junior ministers, to whom HW read the Queen's Speech policy proposals. Talked to Gerry Fowler, Bill Rodgers, Denis Howell and various other old friends.

Some complaints from them about Roy Jenkins taking in John Harris as junior minister but not looking after others who had been equally loyal to him.

Drinks with HW, Albert Murray and Marcia afterwards. Home by 10.45.

## Tuesday 12 March 1974

[The Queen opened the new Parliament on Tuesday 12 March 1974. The new Labour government's programme included commitments to income redistribution, food subsidies, increased pensions, a rent freeze, repeal of the Conservative industrial relations legislation, public ownership of land development rights and of the aircraft and shipbuilding industries, and re-negotiation of the UK's entry terms to the European Community.]

Arrive 9.30. Try to get settled in the office and deal with some staff recruitment.

Much of rest of the morning I work on HW's speech in the Commons this afternoon on the Address.

Lunch with HW, Joe, Albert and Marcia. Discuss theme of 'conciliation'. Then off to the Commons. I sit in the PM's official box for the first time and hear the first day's debate on the Queen's Speech. House sober, but many interruptions of HW. Some silly. Strange to sit beside the Labour ranks – Bill Rodgers, Gerry Fowler, Phillip Whitehead,* all old personal friends sitting nearby. HW's speech was restrained and serious whereas House in a tetchy frame. So not good reception. But right approach nationally.

Back to No. 10 with Albert. Work in my room till 7 p.m.

Then see my old friend Will Plowden, from the Rothschild Think Tank in the Cabinet Office. He says they are worried about their future. Try to reassure him – and later tell PM he must see and reassure Victor Rothschild,* which he is doing tomorrow.

Will also warns of the Civil Service's hostility to me especially. I detect that. Not worried. But must get my staff. One has dropped out today.

PM returns from his first weekly visit to the Palace very happy. Queen apparently did not like Heath and has made this clear.

We talk. I put in a paper on economic strategy, against the deflationists. Then home early – leave the office by 9.15 p.m.

*Wednesday 13 March 1974*

9.30 arrive.

Now am into the daily office routine. Recruiting staff, dealing with papers.

Lunch with Joe and Albert in the Press Gallery in the House of Commons.

Then to the LSE to clear my desk and see various people before fully departing on my two years' leave.

Back in Downing Street clash with the civil servants in No. 10 over access to typing facilities. The pressures to squeeze me out begin. I fire a warning shot across Robert Armstrong's bows. I still think we can all work together. But if they are silly, their team must be broken up.

Evening drinks and talk with the PM. All kinds of comic problems. And

Barbara Castle pressing for massive additional expenditure in her Department of Health and Social Security.

HW is in splendid form. But he feels underworked. The ministers are doing it all. He is acting as just a 'sweeper-up'.

## Thursday 14 March 1974

Day dominated by the growing threat that the Opposition might defeat the government in Monday's vote on the final day of the debate on the Queen's Speech. I don't think so, but obviously the Cabinet discussed it today and HW takes it seriously.

Lunch devoted to discussing it in the small dining-room in No. 10.

Marcia and Albert, and soon Joe and myself, think we should seek another and decisive early election if we can. Because we will win. Tories would be blamed for causing another election if they defeated us on the Queen's Speech.

HW more cautious. Very concerned we should not look as if we want another election. Marcia keeps pressing him – he must decide if he does or does not want an election. Clearly he doesn't want the sweat of a fifth election. He suggests we might ask the other parties to co-operate in getting a shorter 12-day campaign.

Anyway under *no* circumstances must we adopt the Chief Whip Bob Mellish's* scheme of simply accepting the Opposition amendment. Cannot go on like that. Nor can the government allow itself to be humiliated, at the whim of the Opposition.

I suggest the Tories don't really want an election and will run when faced by the choice. Nobody else agrees. Marcia and Albert strongly feel that we should work to get an election now because the outlook will be worse later.

At one point HW puts the suggestion – I suspect agreed at this morning's Cabinet – that if we are beaten on the Address we should say we will take a vote of confidence after the Budget a week later. Joe points out this is not sensible. And the Queen's Speech is a better programme to fight the election on than the Budget.

During the afternoon I do the draft suggestions for Joe to write HW's speech tomorrow at High Wycombe. To be tough – warning the Opposition – we will accept no nonsense.

Much of the afternoon spent working on papers and dictating letters. Adrian Shaw has now joined us in the office (as our research assistant). Slowly becoming a real office.

HW and Marcia left early – at 9 p.m. Joe and Albert already gone. So I went home. Another early night! And perhaps only a few more days in office and then electioneering again. Hope not.

*Friday 15 March 1974*

An average day. Morning arrived early to attend the weekly 'Prayers' meeting – Mellish (as Chief Whip), Callaghan (Foreign Secretary), Healey (Exchequer), HW, Armstrong, Hunt (Cabinet Secretary) and myself – to discuss next week's government business.

Barbara Castle phones twice to interrupt the meeting. HW, irritated, tells us he has changed his private number to prevent Barbara phoning him all the time.

Next week the Monday Commons vote is the main item. But there is also Tony Benn's statement on Concorde – some awful figures to come. On Thursday the Cabinet will discuss – and Healey will press for cancellation.

Discuss weekend speeches by ministers attacking the Tories for electioneering. Complete next week's agenda.

Then the officials are asked to leave while ministers discuss political tactics. I am an official!

Morning in the office – appointments, letters, the press release on my job (delayed because of diplomatically waiting till Victor Rothschild was reassured by the PM that my Policy Unit was not intended to replace his CPRS).

Take Albert out for lunch. (HW and Joe are lunching with the *Daily Mirror* people, to say thanks for their support in the election.)

Afternoon flogging on. Feel very tired. Worked on the High Wycombe speech, threatening the Tories with an election. Joe and I did the draft. HW has strengthened it. He knows he has them on the run.

See Ray Richardson, then visit Harold Lever, who has big plans to deal with inflation by borrowing to keep down prices. We are threatened with nine price triggers and 40% inflation in two years. [The incomes policy inherited from Edward Heath involved a mechanism for triggering automatic wage and price increases.]

Lever keeps me and I miss Wilson before he goes off.

See Margaret Jackson*, who is intelligent, pretty and the recent Labour candidate for Lincoln. [Now Margaret Beckett, later Secretary of State for the Environment in Blair's government.]

Talk to Marcia, who is worried about Terry Pitt of Transport House making trouble because he is unhappy working on devolution in the Cabinet Office.

Home exhausted.

*Points from this week*:

H. Wilson says Lord Home (and especially Lady Home) wants Heath out from the Tory leadership. 'He is like me. He wants revenge.'

HW is very perky in the day and then usually slumps around 9 p.m. If he drinks, he becomes very strange and aggressive. His brow lowers and a very strange look comes into his eyes. Rather hunched and brooding.

Marcia has been in much better mood. But still touchy about being excluded.

## Sunday 17 March 1974

I went for lunch at Chequers, the Prime Minister's official country residence, with HW, Marcia, Mrs Wilson and eight businessmen from the so-called 'Office Trust' who had helped Labour financially in Opposition – mainly Jewish.

Chequers is a handsome Elizabethan house outside, with lovely grounds, garden and an indoor swimming-pool, though a bit fussy and panelled inside.

HW took us all on a tour and told all the stories and had the history of the house at his fingertips.

Mary Wilson told me she was very angry with me. She had read my biography of Herbert Morrison [Bernard Donoughue and G.W. Jones, *Herbert Morrison: Portrait of a Politician* (1973)]. Objects to my references to Morrison's sex life – and especially to sex problems with his wife. Said that should not be written. Also felt it was hurtful to Morrison's daughter, who is a close friend. She obviously did not like Herbert – and said I should not have tried to be so fair to him. I said that as an author one had to tell the truth. She said not for 50 years. I felt she was talking about my assumed future biography of HW.

It was a beautiful evening. We had tea in the only small and comfortable room. HW, Albert, Mrs Wilson and myself. The PM is very relaxed about tomorrow's Commons vote and pleased with the reception to Friday's speech.

Discuss the next election. He is inclined to make it a short campaign, make only a few speeches and spend most of the time running the government. That is my view too. He is delighted by the idea of being – with Gladstone – the only other PM to have four administrations. Says that would mean he would have the right to lie in state in Westminster Abbey. He seemed to like the idea. He obviously likes setting records, or being the first to do things.

## Monday 18 March 1974

Barely saw the PM in the day.

Worries are circulating in No. 10 about the *Daily Mail* publishing a scandal about Marcia's brother Tony and land deals. This is the story which nearly broke at the end of the election campaign.

Morning work on papers. At last getting on top of these.

Long lunch with Marcia, Joe and Albert upstairs. Much time wasted attacking me and my role in the Campaign for Democratic Socialism supporting Gaitskell, and defending HW for standing against Gaitskell for the leadership in 1960. 'To unite the party.' Marcia insisted he had never wanted the leadership. 'All he wanted was to be Chancellor for longer than Gladstone.'

They were bitter about how Sam Watson, the Durham mineworkers' leader and a strong supporter of Gaitskell, attacked HW in a hotel lobby in Scarborough in 1960.

Ganging up on me. All disliked the CDS. Albert said it made him turn left, because it forced people to choose, which middle-of-road people didn't want to do.

Also discussed our views on officials in No. 10. Albert thinks all must go. Marcia unsure. But she phoned later to say yes. Must go. And we will have a meeting late this evening to discuss how to do it.

The vote on the Queen's Speech looks OK. Tories running. I am sorry if we win – would like an election.

Feeling good today after the weekend. Adrenalin running. Could cope with anything now.

Went to the Commons for the winding-up speeches of the debate by Willie Whitelaw* for the Tories and Ted Short for us. [The Conservative motion on the last day of the debate on the Queen's Speech deplored the absence of a statutory incomes policy. Michael Foot as Employment Minister had attacked statutory incomes policy as a cancerous growth, but secured the Tory abstentions by promising not to repeal stage three of Heath's incomes policy. This commitment meant that the impending monthly increase in the retail price index would automatically trigger price increases, thus perpetuating the inflationary spiral.]

Anarchic atmosphere. Shouting and drunkenness. Whitelaw spoke reasonably, if too loud, but when he announced the Tories would withdraw their amendment our side erupted. Derision. Tories looking sheepish and Heath years older and thinner. Liberals furious and tried to get the Speaker to take their amendment. Pardoe shouting 'Disgraceful.'

Ted Short was pedestrian. Ploughed on through interruptions. Yet his flatness effectively quietened the House. I felt it was OK. Defused things.

Afterwards HW was in excellent form. Triumph and revenge written over his face. We all had drinks and laughed and joked.

But Marcia and I had mixed feelings. We didn't want to win. We wanted an election now.

[This period of political manoeuvring in March 1974 raised interesting questions relating to the role and prerogative of the modern British monarch.

After the inconclusive general election on 28 February 1974, the Queen did not automatically send for Harold Wilson to form a new administration because, although he commanded the largest party, he did not have an overall majority. As the sitting Prime Minister, Mr Heath was entitled to attempt to win majority support from the other parties. He could also have informed the monarch of his wish to remain in office in the new Parliament and seek support for his proposed programme in a vote on the Address. It was believed at the time that Her Majesty was not enthusiastic about her Prime Minister taking this course, but she would presumably have accepted it. Had Mr Heath chosen this path and then been defeated on the Address, he would certainly have been expected to resign. The Queen would then presumably have asked Mr Wilson to form a government. She might or might not have asked for the advice of her outgoing Prime Minister on this. In fact after the failure of Mr Heath's efforts to remain in office in early March 1974, she did, if only as a courteous formality, ask Mr Heath's advice — and he not surprisingly told her to send for Mr Wilson as the leader of the largest party in the new Parliament.

Now that Mr Wilson as the new Prime Minister was approaching the vote on the Address without an overall majority, the constitutional possibilities remained intriguing. Were he to be defeated, Mr Wilson would be expected to resign. He might then have requested from the monarch a dissolution of the infant Parliament and a fresh general election. But the Queen would not have been bound to agree, especially if it was widely believed that another election after so brief an interval would produce no greater certainty of a clear result. Her constitutional obligation would have been to take the course which offered the best prospect of continuing the legitimate government of the country with the least disruption. She might have invited Mr Heath to try again to form a government with majority support from within the existing Parliament; or asked a leading political figure to attempt to form a national coalition government (as in 1931). However, in the circumstances of the time she would most likely have granted another dissolution. In the event, as Mr Wilson had calculated, whether because they preferred his government or because they could not face or afford another quick election, the minority parties chose to support and provide a majority to Mr Wilson in the debate on the Address.

During these days Downing Street was vibrant with debate on these constitutional proprieties and possibilities. The uncertainties in prospect underlined the essential role of the monarchy as a non-partisan instrument providing a constitutional path out of such a political impasse and securing the continuity of legitimate government in Britain.]

*Tuesday 19 March 1974*

Routine office day.

But lunch upstairs very odd. We had with us some of the election team: Ron Hayward and Denis Lyons, Peter Davis and Bob Worcester* (who talked endlessly about opinion polls).

We never got down to the business of organising the next election.

Civil servants wandering into the dining-room with parliamentary questions. Mary Wilson came in and sat down and said nothing. HW irritated, walked around the dining-table and drank several brandies.

Then to the House for PQs. Had our regular Tuesday (and Thursday) briefing session beforehand in the PM's huge Commons room spotting possible supplementaries to questions from the Tories. None came up. The Opposition is totally demoralised. Like after 1945 but without a majority.

Drinks party at No. 10 in the evening. Very tired – and hungry. No food as usual.

Home 11 p.m.

*Wednesday 20 March 1974*

Row between Marcia and HW over lunch arrangements. So they are going to the House to eat with Ron Hayward. She objects to the three of us (Joe, Albert and me) eating 'in style' at No. 10. Marcia thinks we are conspiring to exclude her. Joe very angry and ready to quit!

Evening more drinks at No. 10. Exciting only because of news of an assassination attempt on Princess Anne. Messages coming and going between the police and No. 10, and HW very excited. A true journalist.

I was with Victor Rothschild when it happened. At his flat in St James's Place overlooking St James's Park. Had gone to discuss the relations of my Policy Unit with his Think Tank in the Cabinet Office. He opened by suggesting we merge them and I take over. 'I am getting old,' he said, 'and you are young.'

I resisted, pointing out that they are *totally* different operations (and therefore I would *not* put him out of business).

He seemed relieved and we chatted happily for two hours. He says he hates the civil servants and has been hurt by Heath's abusiveness.

*Thursday 21 March 1974*

Hard-working but satisfactory day. Beginning at last to prepare policy memoranda.

Lunch with HW and the others. He discussed today's Cabinet and how it had gone on too long. He had brought up Concorde in the hope the French would kill it. And argued to get free contraception by convincing the Tories it 'saves expenditure on maternity grants'.

Also firm for setting up a Royal Commission on the Press. He hates the press. Wants revenge for their attacks on Marcia, he says.

But dilemma! The *Daily Express* group look like folding. He hates it, but wants to save it because if it goes that will help the *Daily Mail* group, who he hates even more.

We agree that Harmsworth, the reactionary owner of the *Mail*, must lose his North Sea stake.

Evening drinks with Will Plowden of the CPRS. Said Rothschild is now *very* happy.

Cabinet meets in the evening on the proposed Industrial Relations Act. Getting worried about liberalising picketing.

Afterwards went to Marcia's room. Albert and HW already there. HW absolutely at his best. Relaxed, funny, self-deprecating. Telling us about the Cabinet – how he had to make M. Foot report on the Industrial Relations Bill. Foot had forgotten about Parliament and was intending to make his announcement outside of it.

Constant banter from Marcia and the rest of us, with HW trying to get a hearing and calling on us to be serious – though clearly enjoying it and not minding at all. This is how he relaxes – talking about politics, but frivolously and surrounded by a close political family. Everybody knowing he is PM but pretending not to respect that. Again the *Pantomime*. He was pleading for food, for sandwiches, but Marcia insisted that he sign her letters before he got his sandwiches. So he sat there signing and grumbling, but chuckling away as Marcia was strict with him and ordered him to do his job before he got his reward. A straight mother role. But very engaging. The rest of us had several drinks and lots of laughs before going home, leaving HW with his sandwiches to gobble down before seeing Max Aitken* and Lord Goodman (who is both HW's personal lawyer and the adviser to the newspaper industry) about the possible collapse of the *Daily Express*.

### Friday 22 March 1974

Lunch upstairs with the PM, staff and Terry Lancaster of the *Daily Mirror*. Discussed next election strategy. I pressed HW that he must have an ace up his sleeve to dissolve Parliament on. He agreed. Good lunch, with everyone constructive – except when Marcia tried to persuade Terry to sing some old campaign songs.

HW off to his Huyton constituency and I at last get an early night –

home by 6 p.m. and Carol and I walk up Swains Lane to the pub in Pond Square, Highgate, have sandwiches, and back home to music and early bed.

## Weekend 23/24 March 1974

### Saturday

Telephone flap from Harold Lever over the coming Budget. Threatens resignation because of the Budget attack on the rich and destroying confidence in the City. Calm him down. But arrange for him to see HW before the Budget Cabinet on Monday.

### Sunday

Marcia is apparently neurotic about a *News of the World* paragraph forecasting her getting a life peerage. Joe Haines told me she had decided to emigrate. HW spent hours talking to Joe about it, denying it, and threatening revenge on the press.

Joe also told me that Marcia was very upset – especially by the threat to bring her before the court in the Michael Halls case. And HW is threatening to break George Wigg, who he believes is behind the Halls case, with exposures on his private life. [Halls was H. Wilson's principal private secretary during his previous Labour administration. Halls died in office in 1969 and his widow claimed compensation on the ground that the stress of working at No. 10 under Wilson and Marcia Williams precipitated his death.]

And HW and Marcia had a row on Saturday.

Not the best way to spend a pre-Budget weekend.

## Monday 25 March 1974

HW told me that he was finding the workload light – less in a weekend than any night as President of the Board of Trade [1947–51]. He now works well at Chequers. Went through five boxes on Saturday morning and Sunday evening. He was trying to phone Marcia on Sunday afternoon but she had gone to bed – taken the phone off.

A good day. Feel fresh from sleep and playing football with our local team on Hampstead Heath at the weekend.

Marcia not in No. 10. Phone her three times at home to try to comfort her. She says she is not coming here. Is going to emigrate. Everybody is against her.

Work all morning on papers and with staff.

Also have half-hour with HW in the Cabinet Room on the Budget.

Convince him Lever is right. Healey presentation is wrong. Too insensitive to City confidence in his general threats of higher taxation. Not to *change* tax proposals. I agree with redistribution. But must be specific and not create uncertainty.

Lunch with Albert Murray at St Stephen's pub, across the road from the Commons.

HW lunches in No. 10 with Dick Crossman* – thin, weak, dying, barely able to talk or eat. I walked in St James's Park in the sunshine a little and came in after lunch to see Crossman hobble out of No. 10 – probably for the last time. I walked back to Marcia's room with HW. He is upset by Crossman. Says he won't live till midsummer. Perhaps a reminder of mortality?

He tells me about the Cabinet discussion of the Budget. How he opened the discussion to put Lever's point. Supported by Callaghan and Jenkins. So easily won. Also pushed Healey to have something helpful on mortgages.

Saw Tommy Balogh, now a junior minister at Energy, who is worried about our retreat on North Sea oil and concessions to the big oil companies – and Ray Richardson (Lever's very able special adviser) about the Budget. What a marvellous friend Ray has become. Tough, funny and totally loyal.

In the evening the PM saw Lord Goodman about the press attacks on Marcia. Convinced they spring from George Wigg. Is out to get him by the balls.

Then with Joe and the PM to Marcia's room – she was still not there – for drinks and talk for an hour. Very relaxed and amusing. HW at his best now. Also proud of his summing up in Cabinet. Says it is based on his training in the Cabinet secretariat 30 years ago – 'the most important time for me'.

Also again said his main ambition had been to bring in more Budgets than Gladstone.

## Tuesday 26 March 1974

[The first Labour Budget introduced by Denis Healey on 26 March 1974 increased income tax and corporation tax and also extended VAT. It increased pensions and some social benefits, leaving it broadly neutral in demand terms – but adding to underlying price increases by 1½%.]

Marcia again did not come in to Downing Street.

Saw the PM first thing in the morning to discuss the Budget again and the need to press Healey on helping to keep mortgages down and on not destroying confidence.

Worked till lunch. Went to the LSE to lunch for the first time since leaving.

To House of Commons for questions – went off well and frivolously.

Back to more work. PM busy all the time at the Commons with the Budget.

So I went off to a George Weidenfeld party in his luxurious Chelsea flat.

Lever, Kissin, the Tory MP Paul Channon* and his lovely and charming wife Ingrid. Sat next to Susan Crosland,* the journalist Kenneth Harris,* and John Freeman's* ex-wife Catherine.*

Also spoke to John and Miriam Gross,* Lord Drogheda from the *Financial Times* and Lord Goodman. Relaxing, enjoyed it. Finally tired and left for home at midnight.

## Wednesday 27 March 1974

In at 9.30 a.m. Saw PM and discussed problems of building societies and how to keep down mortgage interest rates. And Healey's failure to get across the question of rising prices for the nationalised industries. Didn't blame inheritance from Tories enough. Also discussed PM's next speech on Friday.

Worked on a policy paper. The Policy Unit team is now getting together well. Lunch at the Cabinet Office mess. Foul. But interesting chat with Robin Butler and Nick Stuart from our private office. Trying to establish good relations between us. Very important.

Worked all afternoon in the Unit till the TUC meeting.

Meeting of the government with the TUC General Council in the Cabinet Room.

[Under the 'social contract' the Labour government was committed to work closely with the trade union movement. Here as elsewhere such consultations are recorded. The unions certainly had ready access to Number Ten but in no way did they 'run the country' or Harold Wilson, as later alleged by Conservative propagandists.]

The PM opened with a general statement on what the government had done so far. Hoped a good start.

Sidney Greene* (National Union of Railwaymen) replied that the Economic Committee of the TUC was delighted with what done so far. Raised the four points which concerned them:

Delay in repealing the Industrial Relations Act
No family allowance increases
Delay in new wealth tax
VAT kept

HW spoke defending no increases in family allowances – said we did pensions, rents and food. Couldn't do everything.

Michael Foot spoke explaining that we could not repeal the Industrial Relations Act simply and quickly. Bill Wedderburn* of the LSE had advised. Any simple repeal would take away all the existing legal protections for trade unions – 1908, 1875, etc. So must be done carefully.

Healey explained the economic problems. Only had one week to prepare his Budget.

On VAT he is considering having two rates in the next Budget.

On *gifts* tax, more details tomorrow. Will include discretionary trusts. The legislation will be in the second Budget – but applied retrospectively as from this Budget day.

On *wealth* tax: terrible problem of evaluation. Must not rush it and get it wrong. The Green Paper will not be about *principle*, but about how to carry it out.

Wilson intervened to explain the problem with *nationalised industry prices*. (Something Healey did badly in the Budget and Wilson was annoyed about earlier this morning.)

Healey explained that the total nationalised industry deficit is due to be about £1,400 million. So had to make big price increases. Still a subsidy of £500 million. Creates problems for the retail price index.

Healey radiates enormous physical energy and confidence. Obviously great physical strength and stamina. He said he hopes to reflate the economy a bit later in the year. But the increase in GNP over year as a whole will only be up about 1% (though rising to 2½% by end year) due to losses in three-day week.

Len Murray, general secretary of the TUC, then asked some questions about VAT, payroll tax and economic growth. Murray said on Healey's output prediction we would have *higher unemployment* next winter than last. Real cancer. He said that:

*Nationalised industries investment* has not been looked at yet, but hopes that price rises will enable more investment. Tom Jackson (general secretary of the Post Office Union) later denied this was possible.

The atmosphere was extremely friendly and jovial. (Lawrence Daly of the miners' union was very shaky, his hands trembling.)

The PM intervened to discuss our plans for mortgages and building societies. Scanlon said this was not the time to put forward his pet theories. But their main fear is that the Labour government would delay a repeal of the Industrial Relations Act and then be beaten on it in Parliament, and so we would have done nothing and the engineering industry is about to go on to a four-day week because of disputes. And worried that these strikes will be presented as a battle against the government and against counter-inflation policies. Is not – but press will misrepresent it.

HW is looking very fit and happy. As Joe said, he is years younger than at the start of the campaign. Is really enjoying being PM this time round.

Michael Foot replied to Scanlon. Sounds much more confident than when he took office three weeks ago. Speaks powerfully and with enormous lucidity and passion. Still speech-making rather than analysing, but down from stratospheric to mere conference level. (The meeting was in the marvellous 18th-century Treasury boardroom in the Cabinet Office. Present were the TUC and HW, Denis Healey, Harold Lever, Michael Foot, Ted Short, Barbara Castle, Shirley Williams and Tony Benn.)

Foot's colouring is odd. Very pale when quiet. Quite pink when speaking.

HW summed up saying he is 'always available' to the TUC but best for them to continue with M. Foot and he has no desire for protracted meetings around the table at No. 10. Not suggesting continuing the dialogue with the TUC.

Afterwards from 8 to 9.15 I had drinks with HW and Albert. Discussing Albert getting the Newham seat at the next election.

Also relaxed chat. HW reread his own answers to PQs in the Commons on Tuesday. Still pleased with his jokes – which were good.

No reference to today's snide piece about me in the *Guardian*.

Home 9.30 p.m.


## Thursday 28 March 1974

Joe told me the story of how Marcia and Harold met. Mid-1950s. There were believed to be a lot of Gaitskellite plots against HW. He received an anonymous letter giving him full details. He was grateful. One day he saw a secretary from the Labour Party's general secretary's office at a bus stop. Marcia. Gave her a lift. She revealed she was the letter writer. Linked.

Joe said this was 'typical. She creates enemies for him, exposes them, then reassures him he has a friend in her.'

Normal office morning. Now feeling on top of the job in 'office' terms. Keeping up with the flow of paper. Allocating jobs to my assistants. Occasional memos to the PM. The difficult part is to know how to play him. The civil servants are now filling his diary from morning to night with semi-appointments, leaving little time for the political side to see him and discuss strategy or any points which come up. Joe is complaining we never see him now. The civil servants have grabbed him. At one point I raised this with HW. Always difficult to tell how he reacts. Impossible to see through his eyes. Looks at me without revealing anything. But he later says he is not happy with his diary.

Lunchtime with Will Plowden at a Leicester Square Indian restaurant.

Talk shop. Also William's future. He would find returning to university too unchallenging. And the Civil Service too boring.

Late afternoon Claus Moser* comes to see me. *Very* helpful. Says the Civil Service are keen to co-operate. Says the permanent secretaries at their weekly meeting have twice discussed how to relate to my Unit. Obviously a positive desire to integrate me.

He says the Civil Service had had enough of the Tories. Tells story of Lord Carrington* just before election saying he was hoping for an early election, because the time had come to deal with the unions. And after the election Carrington said, 'Poor Ted. Bad judgement on the election timing. And he has nothing but politics. The rest of us have other fish to fry.'

Also how the Tory minister Peter Rawlinson* in a Cabinet committee opposed the idea of a survey of the attitudes of the unemployed because they would not be literate enough to fill in a form.

We talked for three hours. He drove me home and drank here.

Told me another story about Heath. How he took Heath to the opera, in the royal box at Covent Garden. At the end Heath didn't say thanks. Just said, 'Not a very good performance, was it?'

### Friday 29 March 1974

In to 9.30 'prayers' meeting to discuss next week's government business. Callaghan worried about his Brussels EEC speech. Healey subdued after the Budget. HW looks tired – went to visit Marcia the previous evening and she kept him very late. (She later told me on the telephone that she 'gave him it with both barrels'. Because he was 'getting happy and complacent'. She also thinks 'he has outwitted the rest of us'. Says his politics is 'all about people. He is not interested in policies at all, just people.')

Still everyone says how relaxed he is compared to 1964–70.

Marcia still doesn't come in to her office in No. 10. HW goes off to Liverpool to his constituency at 10.30 a.m. – complaining that the speech Joe had done was too short. Doubt it is too short for that audience.

We all feel that the political honeymoon is over. For privacy I went into the lavatory with HW and said I felt that the Budget was going sour and we had to move fast to compensate. Need more politics. He feels that Healey has no political touch.

At lunch with Joe and Albert the conversation begins with Marcia. Joe says he is fed up. Is willing to quit. He is disgusted that so much time is absorbed by her obsessions and nervousness. 'She has always dragged HW down. Just think what he would have achieved without her.'

Then discuss election strategy. We must look ahead and plan the next election. This is the first week without a lunch in No. 10 with HW. We are losing contact. But Joe thinks this is the same as last time, and happens because HW loves his civil servants and doesn't want to think of the horrors of elections and politics.

One marvellous story. After the 1970 defeat HW stored his private papers in Marcia's garage. Then they fell out and she would not let him get at them. So he went out there one night with Marcia's brother Tony, broke into the garage and stole the papers back. As Joe said, what if the police had caught him? Joe wanted to write the headline 'Ex-PM apprehended for breaking and entering.'

HW has been trying to phone Marcia all this week, but she often left her phone off and refused to answer. She told me on the phone, 'I'm getting him worried. He knows I am up to all of his tricks. He will come out here soon and I will keep playing with him. He will suffer. He knows I've got his number.'

Worked at a high pace all afternoon producing three memos for HW's weekend box. Then entertained Grieveson Grant friends who reported on the City's reaction to Budget. Nervous about liquidity. [Grieveson Grant were a top City stockbrokers where B. Donoughue had been a consultant until the election. He became partner in 1983 until the firm merged with Kleinwort Benson in 1986.]

Incidentally today's *Sun* had a front-page article on me and 'Labour's Political Mafia'! This follows up the PQ in the House of Commons yesterday. Silly Bruce-Gardyne* named me as 'a Marxist' heading the Political Mafia. Strange to sit there in the official box, in a full Chamber, and hear myself named and attacked in this way. I did not feel a flicker of concern, except amusement. Still feel above it all. Untouched and unworried. Such a marvellous job – yet may end any day and then will go back to LSE. The Tories look a poor lot in Opposition. I have hardened and can take this with no trouble.

Afterwards walked back from the Commons to No. 10 with Robert Armstrong and discussed it. He rightly said that the key is to convince yourself that what you are doing is right. After that one is impervious. Still very difficult to get close to him.

Home early – 6.30 p.m. – to look after the children. Carol in the country.

*Weekend 30/31 March 1974*

Beautiful sunshine. I went to our Suffolk cottage at Wickhambrook and had a lovely time with Carol and the children.

The newspapers full of leaks about our schemes for the building societies and plans to scrap Concorde. Talk to Joe, who is concerned.

Also I was telephoned by HW, who is complaining about too much work. He is seeing Brian Faulkner from Northern Ireland tomorrow, and he has no brief. Also other important engagements. Says his diary is too crowded. He is obviously not happy with how his life is being organised. Not clear if this is just the absence of Marcia being taken out on others.

Joe told me that the German magazine *Stern* has a big article on Marcia – hostile to her; her alleged land deals and profits; and how HW's last private secretary, Michael Halls, was allegedly killed by the strain of handling the HW–Marcia situation and the widow is now suing and making terrible allegations against Marcia.

HW very agitated. Again these Marcia questions dominate Downing Street politics and shut out the more important governmental issues.

I also discussed subsidising mortgages with HW. Tell him that the Treasury is being sticky. He says the Cabinet will have to instruct them. Because it is an election pledge. He is totally committed to carrying out everything Labour promised. Again to erase the bad memories of U-turns in 1964–70.

## Monday 1 April 1974

All morning meeting at the Treasury on mortgages. The permanent secretary, Douglas Wass, in the chair – very good. Treasury wanted to raise interest rates. We each reported that our ministers – especially the PM – would not have it.

So proceeded to go through the alternative options. No great enthusiasm for the Harold Lever devices, but they have to come.

Returned to No. 10 for lunch. HW arrived from a Churchill ceremony, so on the spot we decided to have lunch together. Excellent discussion on tactics, especially on mortgages. Very good. HW clear and decisive and very friendly.

Afternoon I worked on papers, drafting memoranda, answering letters, saw Ray Richardson, etc.

5 p.m. I went to see Barbara Castle with my staff at her office at the Department of Health and Social Security, so we got liaison moving. Barbara very enthusiastic, especially that I have David Piachaud with me in the Policy Unit and that we are so keen on pushing the social services side. Dear Jack Ashley* also there. Says they are all very deferential towards me, being at No. 10.

Barbara is pretty again, if highly made up. HW says she looks 10 years younger. But why did she have all her regular civil servants with her? This inhibited me from presenting my plans for close and direct relations with her special advisers.

Back again at No. 10 get a message to phone Marcia. Also Albert has a letter for HW delivered by hand from her.

I telephone. She is violent. Accuses me of conspiring to organise a lunch with HW and without her. Denounces everybody. I listen for half an hour, then have to put down the phone and go to see Harry Kissin. He arrived to see HW in the study to discuss the Budget and get his peerage offer. Is also worried about HW and Marcia. He is very perceptive, has known them a long time, and realises the problem. I was still depressed from the telephone conversation with Marcia but reveal nothing of this to him. Also see Harold Lever to discuss mortgages and his excellent speech this afternoon.

Then drinks with Albert discussing the Marcia problem.

HW emerges with Kissin at 9 p.m. and calls me into the lavatory with him. Discuss the Budget and this week's Cabinet over a pee. Relaxed and totally without side. Presumably there are no listening devices in the lavatory!

I left at 9.30 and went very late to the Central Office of Information dinner in Soho for French political aides. Everybody tired. I discussed my role. Hungry, but they had finished a slap-up dinner, so I just had coffee.

Two other of our political aides there – Vicky Kidd from the Lord President's office and Adrian Hamm from the Treasury. Bright and perky – and very young and enthusiasts about their roles.

Afterwards waited half an hour for a taxi, carrying a cup of soup and sandwich I had bought from a take-away shop. Home midnight.

## Tuesday 2 April 1974

Spent the morning in the office and joined the PM in a meeting in the study with Barbara Castle and her junior ministers about providing better vehicles for the disabled. HW was good – had even more ideas than they did. Creative and positive. Barbara skittish and obviously enjoying her harem of men.

Phone Marcia at her request. She refused to come to lunch, claiming I did not want her to. Also accused all of us of being idle and doing nothing.

Worked till lunch, then to his club with Sir John Hunt. Walked through St James's Park in the sun to Pall Mall. He wants to sort out my job. Wants definitions of our work activities and to clarify my relations with civil servants and ministers from other departments. Feels must get it cleared up, PM to approve and then will get co-operation from Whitehall. Feels in the end my problem will be ministers not civil servants, especially if they think I am spying. He is very helpful and clear, and obviously wants to co-operate – and not be squeezed out. Think I can work with him.

Had another meeting with him and Robert Armstrong in the afternoon, where we took the definition of my job much further. He will draft a paper. I will inspect closely. Told him I would not consider matters not included as being forbidden.

He said that the main problem is that some of the other political advisers are of poor quality. How to give me full access, but not them. Think it can be done.

See Joe who says that the PM is very pleased with my work. Also that HW thinks Marcia is jealous of me. Also that Marcia's sister Peg and Michael English (the Labour MP for Nottingham) are friends. And that whenever Peg had a marriageable man, Marcia intervened against him.

Evening spent on masses of papers, especially economic. Really building up now. This is the test. To cover the material and attend meetings and also be on personal attendance to HW. Feel very tired tonight, though everybody says how fit I look. Must keep on top, and clear, and selective and decisive.

John Hunt came to show me privately his Cabinet brief. Important gesture. We must co-operate with the Cabinet Office – but not be swallowed. They have numbers and established access – but not location in No. 10. Each has something the other lacks. Deals can be done.

Robert Armstrong is also much friendlier after this afternoon's meeting. Perhaps he feels cleared to be more open with me now. He told me that he had been to the Queen to discuss Heath's peerage list – one of whom was accused in the Profumo or Lambton* scandal, but is actually innocent. Had to be cleared. This is what held up the list. [Lord Lambton resigned from the Heath government on 21 May 1973 following newspaper allegations concerning call-girls, etc.]

Balogh also came in to see me and gave me an advance paper for the Energy committee. To prime HW.

Denis Howell phoned to ask me to test HW on restructuring the Sports Council. He says HW is reluctant to sack Roger Bannister* before the election. (Quite right!)

Ray Richardson in again to report on mortgages and Lever's plan to hold down mortgage interest rates. Good progress. Wass being very helpful at the Treasury.

It is all flooding in now.

### Wednesday 3 April 1974

Morning in the office. George Jones* from the LSE dropped in to discuss the role of the PM's department.

Day dominated by newspaper scandal stories about Marcia and land deals – involving letters with apparently forged signatures by HW. The *Mail* and *Express* devote full pages to it. *Evening Standard* and *News* follow.

Questions in the House. Calls for suspension of Marcia by Labour MPs. [The signatures were proved to be forgeries and Ronald Milhench* was sentenced to three years' imprisonment for forgery in November 1974.]

HW didn't return for his planned lunch in No. 10. Marcia didn't come in. So Joe and I lunched together. Grim talk. Feeling that the press are awful and that Marcia and her family had been foolish. Exposed HW.

Afternoon in the office. Also visited by Ray Richardson and Lord Porchester.* But dominated by the impending Marcia crisis.

HW had a long meeting with Lord Goodman and another lawyer. They issued a writ for libel against the *Mail* and the *Express*.

In the evening I went to see Harold Lever, and Harry Kissin was with him. General feeling that Marcia should resign – or HW remove her – but I know it won't happen. They are psychologically essential to one another.

Came back from Lever's room through the Cabinet Office and down past the private secretaries' offices. Saw HW coming out of Marcia's room with Joe. He called me into the Cabinet Room with Joe. He was dictating a Commons statement on Clay Cross – another scandal involving Labour local councillors. I had tried to persuade him not to do it. To let Ted Short do it. But he wanted to take it on. Said Short did not properly understand relations between the National Executive Committee and the government. And also Short was collapsing under the strain of Clay Cross. So he would do it. 'That is what I'm here for,' he said. But intertwined with Marcia, meant a bad day tomorrow. He knew it was 'going to be rough'.

[Labour councillors at Clay Cross in Derbyshire had been surcharged for their refusal to implement the Conservative Housing Finance Act of 1972. The Labour Party conference in 1973 resolved to indemnify them for the surcharge, but the new Labour government refused to abide by this and the surcharge was upheld on legal appeal in August 1974.]

Then we discussed the newspaper scandal. He was violent against the press and said, 'If they want it dirty, they can have it dirty.' He said he would reveal the truth about:

1  Some other Tory ministers who he warned as being involved in the Lambton affair, and how the Tory government and police kept the prostitute Norma Levy abroad so she could not give evidence against them.
2  Jeremy Thorpe and alleged homosexuality, including alleged blackmail.
3  George Wigg's second family.
4  Max Aitken, the proprietor of the *Daily Express*, and his Australian mistress.

He proposed using Parliamentary Questions to ventilate it. I said he should forget this muck-raking and not stoop to the gutter levels of the press. He should elevate the issue on to a political level and say the press campaign was the rich hitting back at Budget redistribution.

Joe said the press could now go for Marcia and expose everything – her two illegitimate children, two houses, several personal domestic staff, all on four thousand pounds a year, etc. All the people who dislike her will hit back.

We sat around the Cabinet table – Joe, Albert and myself – discussing how to deal with it.

HW was angry and sad. Deeply hurt. He turned to me once and said, 'You should go and see Marcia. She has been with me for 18 years. You have been here for only a few weeks. She gets all this. Go and see her, for only 15 minutes. She really does like you.' He also asked me to write to her.

His hatred of the press shone out. Here he needed the affection and loyalty of those around him.

### Thursday 4 April 1974

An incredible day. From the beginning dominated by newspaper scandals about alleged land speculation involving Marcia.

HW wanted to make a personal Commons statement and drafted one. Joe and I thought it was terrible and sent him a memo *into Cabinet* saying it was 'inviting disaster'. He came out, and reluctantly agreed. Instead we suggested that we get Marcia's brother Tony Field to issue part of it. Joe went off to phone him to get him to do it.

I had to see prospective staff and Dick Leonard* for an interview, and in between was dashing down to Joe in the press office and to see HW to make plans.

Also phoned Marcia. Pathetic. In tears. So I arranged to go out and see her, immediately after Parliamentary Questions.

Lunch with Joe at the press restaurant in the House. He was savage against the press.

Afterwards to HW's Commons room as usual before questions at 2.30. Marcia was on the phone to the PM saying the press were blockading her house. He asked us to go and remove them.

Albert and I took a taxi to her house in Wyndham Mews, Marylebone, W1. Gangs of seedy press louts and photographers were there, blocking the road and entrance to her house. They have been ringing the bell, beating on the door, pushing letters through and climbing on the window-sills to try to look in and to take photographs. When we go in Marcia is in tears and totally destroyed. They have destroyed her. She is also angry with HW. She says he has abandoned her and just looked after himself.

We went out to buy champagne and ice-cream to cheer her up. The photographers take us. I lost my temper and go for them. One ran away and hid behind a car. I went for the other and was about to demolish him when Albert held my arm. I was lucky. I would have smashed him. Which would not have been good for me or the PM. They are male prostitutes and vultures.

We bring back the ice-cream, put the champagne in the fridge and play with her two little boys. Delightful and sad. They are blockaded and cannot go out to play. This sadly is the true British gutter press.

I tried to get the police to clear them out. A panda car came, and left without doing anything. Terry Lancaster of the *Mirror* arrived with another bottle of champagne and we all took some consolation.

Finally Albert and I left in the *Daily Mirror* car (carrying cameras to pretend we were photographers).

Back to No. 10. HW still furious with the press. Discuss a strategy to freeze out the press. PM to attend nothing. Joe to ignore the lobby. Good stories to go to a few decent journalists.

Also no aid to newspapers in trouble. This could kill the *Express*.

HW thinks we can turn it to our electoral favour in the long run. As underdogs to Tory press. But in the short run it is very difficult.

Heath and Thorpe are both very co-operative – partly because each wants the press held off.

Wilson is also convinced we must now have the Privacy Bill, which was cautiously recommended by an earlier Royal Commission.

We talked for one and a half hours about this – and about mortgages and interest rates, where he is very pleased with Lever. Healey's star is low. HW says, 'Healey can resign if he likes.'

What a curious day. I have my team here working on high-level government policy. I am away fighting the press and defending the PM's political secretary.

Marcia also told us an incredible story of how on her brother Tony's wedding day he called in the police to her house in Wyndham Mews and formally accused her of stealing his money and his passport. She threw them all out and claims she has never talked to him since.

There must be an odd streak in that family!

### Friday 5 April 1974

Incredible and distasteful day. After working in the morning with my staff, I went to have coffee with HW, Joe and Albert. Talk about the Williams and Field family land scandal which now dominated the press and all our thoughts. The PM's mind is full of writs and further attacks on the press. Does not seem able to get above the details of whether it was land 'speculation' or 'reclamation', and not to realise it is now serious politically, reflecting on his judgement, threatening him politically. We as advisers have also not been strong and clear enough. But we never sat down for long enough to discuss it. It is clear now that he ought to have:

a)  made sure that Marcia and her brother made statements and issued writs from the beginning, and then made sure
b)  he made a firm statement to the House reassuring it that he had nothing to do with it.

Marcia's voluntary resignation until after an inquiry would have helped. But she would not – and he would not ask because, as he insisted, that would be to admit guilt, and she is probably innocent of anything except imprudently being a sleeping partner to her brother's business activities. His position is less defensible, especially while working in HW's private office.

We were discussing the press and how to get revenge – and George Wigg, who HW says is behind it all, plying information to his old friend Chapman Pincher of the *Express*,

This discussion went on right until the moment when the Irish PM, Liam Cosgrave,* arrived to discuss that other irrational and insoluble problem – Ireland. Then the PM went off. But beforehand he asked that the three of us should go with Marcia to his solicitors to serve the writs this afternoon.

We went up to the reception rooms upstairs at lunchtime when the Irish talks had broken for drinks. We had to confirm whether it was wise for us to take an official car. Decided yes.

Seamus O'Sullivan from the Irish party came over to me. We had met at Harold Evans's for dinner. Very jovial and remembered me, and had noted that I had gone into No. 10. We discussed Ireland and I promised him to put in the right words.

The three of us – Joe, Albert and myself – left No. 10 at 1.25 p.m. and went in a black Wolseley to Wyndham Mews. The press were gathered and they jostled and photographed us as we arrived. Marcia seemed quite cheerful to be going out at last and very pleased to see all of us. Basically she needs reassurance that she is loved and wanted – not that she always works positively to produce either response. But when friendly she can be touchingly honest and direct in her relationships.

We had not eaten any lunch, so we swallowed dry biscuits and cheese.

I also ate Peggy's egg and bacon and drank a Guinness from the fridge.

We set off through hordes of photographers. The press had behaved appallingly, sitting and standing on the window-sill, trying to see through the windows, and bribing boys to bang on the door, ring the bell, and shout obscenities through the letter-box about HW and Marcia.

We drove to Gray's Inn. The lawyers said it would take an hour, so we left her and walked in the glorious sunshine through Lincoln's Inn Fields to my office in LSE, where I sorted out some of my mail.

We returned to the lawyers at 4 p.m., but had to wait for another one and a half hours. Finally four writs went out, and one is to go to the *Express* on Monday. Marcia was in good form – highly tranquillised – and very pleased with her lawyer.

We returned to Marcia's house in Wyndham Mews. Terry Lancaster of the *Mirror* was there. We had champagne again. Then heard the bad news from Walter Terry (who works for the *Express*) that the *Express* was going to run the story of Marcia's two children – of which he is the father. She collapsed in tears. We desperately tried to get in touch with HW, who was in a car going to Oxford. The police were sent to intercept. Also talked to Lord Goodman, who tried to get hold of Max Aitken, the owner of the *Express*, apparently in a plane flying from Bermuda to London.

Constant telephoning. But HW does not phone. Marcia says he is hiding from her. I phoned 10 Downing Street – they say he has not yet arrived at Oxford. Very hysterical atmosphere.

Joe left in the official car to go back to Downing Street. I left at 8 p.m. to go to Downing Street to clear my desk of papers. Marcia was obviously feeling deserted. Albert and Lancaster stayed.

I went home late for dinner with Ron Higgins of the *Observer*, and with our friends Betsy Reisz* and Tom and Celia Read.* In the middle of the hors d'oeuvres the Prime Minister phones me. He is in a telephone booth at Oxford Labour Club, with people milling around, and kept shouting to people to 'close the bloody door'. He said Marcia was in a desperate position. I must go round 'and pull the telephone wires out of the wall to stop her speaking to the press'. I was angry, feeling I had spent enough time in Wyndham Mews. But I agreed, finished my course, apologised to my guests, and left behind a rather puzzled table of guests.

At Wyndham Mews the atmosphere was in fact better. Lord Goodman had sent for the *Express* editor and stopped the story. (N.B. the father of Marcia's children is an *Express* political journalist!) So we sat around planning to get Marcia away to the country for the weekend.

Terry Lancaster also drafted a statement for her to sign and print in the *Mirror*, but Albert and I advised against. This was the first sign of suspicious behaviour by him. Journalists are journalists, I suppose. Otherwise

he is splendid. He left at 10.30 p.m. Albert and I stayed till midnight, by
when Albert was tiddly, and afraid of going home to his wife, and the
Williams and Field sisters were in a state of nervous collapse. We pushed
them upstairs to bed and left. By then there were no press left – although
earlier they had incessantly rung at the door, and tried to take photos through
the windows. At one point I poured a whisky and water over some from an
upstairs window and they complained bitterly.

As Joe said, they are 'vultures working for jackals'. I have never seen
the press in action before. No decent society should allow them to behave
like this.

I drove Albert to Charing Cross and then returned home – to find the
dinner party still in swing, and we continued till after 2 a.m. Ron Higgins,
whose judgement I respect, knows a lot about the Wilson entourage, and is
sensibly very concerned I should not become too close to them and 'paranoid' about the press, but also afraid that we shall have revenge and finish
the *Observer*, which is financially weak.

Very tired, and I privately decided not to get sucked too far into Marcia's
personal hell. But how can one abandon her before these vermin? I am
not a *friend* in any true sense, but she needs them now and I am a reasonable substitute. Certainly I could not abandon her now.

Actually the business about exposing her young children to such pain
shook me and I could easily have killed the journalist – like treading on a
louse.

## Weekend 6/7 April 1974

Disaster on Saturday evening. Harold Evans telephoned from the *Sunday
Times* to say that the *Observer* had a picture of me with Marcia next to
their story of land deals – implying I was part of it. Evans advised me to
phone up Donald Trelford,* deputy editor of the *Observer*, who Harold
said is almost the only decent human being left in Fleet Street. Get him
to change it. I did – and he did. The first edition had gone – terrible. But
second edition OK.

Felt depressed and decided to resign. It is all so *dirty* and I feel I want
to wash my hands every hour. And is it worth exposing oneself to these
vultures?

In the morning I still felt the same, but Carol strengthened me, saying
do nothing rash. And Joe was marvellous – 'Don't give in to the bastards,
fight 'em, don't give them the blood they want', etc. Then saw the *Observer*
second edition and felt better.

Off to the country, near Henley, to walk in the woods with the children
and picnic. Lovely, relaxing, and return revived, with plans for my Unit

next week. Phone Joe and HW and am relieved he is making a statement. (Last night when he phoned me three times HW was full of writs and not intending to make a statement, but I was firm and said he must speak to the Commons before going on TV. Nobody understands why he says nothing. In fact he is trying to duck it and hoping it will go away.)

Some recollections from these events:

– especially Marcia phoning HW and screaming at him and saying he was a machine, not a human being, and that he had always promised her this would not happen and that he would protect her. She accused him of abandoning her and hiding. She was savage and threatened 'to tell everything' about him. Joe says she is often fantasising and makes allegations which have no basis in reality. She is 'just sick'.

– HW went to Paris on Saturday for ex-President Pompidou's memorial service. He was embarrassed by President Nixon's effusive greetings and insistence on walking down rue St Honoré with him – 'that will lose me the election,' said HW. He was so worried about being seen on TV with Nixon that he immediately gave an interview to the BBC – something he did not normally do – in order to cut out the street shots taken earlier.

Nixon apparently saw HW with Janet Hewlett-Davies, the assistant press officer, and came up and said, 'Harold, is this the young lady you are in trouble with?'

'No,' said Harold, 'but I would like to be.'

'If you do,' said Nixon, 'I will send you my congratulations.'

[President Nixon was then under attack over the Watergate scandal and was eventually forced to resign office on 9 August 1974.]

## Monday 8 April 1974

All day on the Marcia land scandal. In the morning sat in the study upstairs with HW, Joe and Robert Armstrong correcting HW's draft statement for the Commons this afternoon. The PM was in very good form, taking criticism. Relaxed and cheerful.

At 11.30 he went off to see and lunch with Michael Manley, the PM of Jamaica.

Joe, Robert and I did fresh corrections to the statement before lunch. Then Joe and I went across to the Commons press restaurant for lunch.

Joe told me a story of how three years ago on Mary Wilson's birthday Marcia was angry because HW had taken Mary out for a birthday lunch instead of having lunch with her, and so in revenge she told Mary some hurtful sexual information about herself and HW long ago. It produced a terrible crisis, and HW – who told Joe the allegation was totally untrue –

broke with her for a while. Joe also said Marcia claimed that Mrs Wilson had a Polish friend in Rome – which Marcia was threatening to tell the press last Friday evening. Mary is remarkably stoical amid all this nonsense.

Back to No. 10, where we met with a fresh draft – including large legal interpolation by Lord Goodman. These infuriated HW and he got very angry, cutting out passages and writing in fresh passages. He was suddenly upset and in a very bad condition to deal with the statement. I was afraid that he would be drawn into angry exchanges. I tried to calm him and told him not to be angry but to show prime ministerial disdain.

In the end he did very well in the Commons. The occasion was an anti-climax. Subdued House. Silly questions after – partly because the Speaker (Selwyn Lloyd) chose an odd selection of questioners.

Afterwards HW was delighted, and puzzled by the lack of serious questioning. He went back to No. 10 where he did a TV recording for ITV. This went very well. The ITV people were friendly and HW came over very well.

Afterwards we had drinks with them, and then with a selection from the lobby – the serious newspapers – who had a long off-the-record interview. HW told them the stories of harassment of Marcia – with some exaggeration. Finally broke up around 7 p.m. after a whole day on scandal.

Home by 8.15 p.m. – the earliest non-Friday departure yet. Tired. And worried that my office is getting neglected and my team uncertain what to do.

## Tuesday 9 April 1974

Arrived 9.30. Straight to see John Hunt in the Cabinet Office about his paper on my position and the Policy Unit within the Whitehall machine. Also raised with him the question of the man imprisoned in Rhodesia. The *Sunday Times* had the story. The Rhodesians had sent an emissary to bargain: if no publication of the details of their massive sanctions-busting, they would release the man. Hunt arranged a top-level meeting at noon.

Back to my office while the Cabinet was meeting. Still trying to get our work programme moving and very depressed at these diversions. Want to submit a team paper on election strategy.

Lovely Kay Carmichael* came in from Scotland for her first day working on Scottish affairs with the Unit, cheering me up.

After Cabinet at noon I went with Robert Armstrong back to Hunt's room in the Cabinet Office. MI5 and 6 were there and the Foreign Office. Heard full details of the Rhodesian case. Decided no reason for not publishing details of sanction-busting. I thought the FO and others were encouragingly firm about wanting to hit the Rhodesians. Publication would help that. Afterwards discussed my Unit and cleared the details with Hunt, for submission to the PM.

To lunch at the Athenaeum with Jim Hamilton,* a delightful and capable Scot, deputy secretary in the Cabinet Office. I find, grudgingly, that some of these civil servants are refreshingly sane and helpful. Thinking of the situation in No. 10, if I had to choose between the Bureaucratic and the Neurotic, I know which way I would go.

Back through the park in continuing glorious sunshine. Robert Armstrong joined us. He had also been eating at the Athenaeum with Sir William Armstrong,* just about to leave his position as head of the Home Civil Service.

Went into No. 10 from Horse Guards Parade through the back gate and the garden. Robert and I picked up our files and went off together to the Commons to deal with PQs. The first question named me and asked about my 'Political Unit'. Part of the preparation to repel this attack was to issue the names of the members and have them circulated in the parliamentary papers. The questions were fairly nasty, emphasising the need for positive vetting and mentioning land deals.

HW left to spend the night at Windsor with the Queen. Mrs Wilson was annoyed because she did not like writing a letter of thanks signed 'Your humble servant', and last time they had worked out an alternative draft, which private office had now lost. So she had to work it out again.

I then had a meeting with Murray Fox, the next Lord Mayor of London, who is very keen to improve relations between the City and Whitehall. I told him:

a) Make this the theme of his mayoralty.
b) *Invite* a Royal Commission on the City.
c) Meet the Governor and decide to set up a proper representative body for the City.

He took copious notes and seemed to agree.

Home by 8.30 and out to the Flask pub in Highgate with Carol for beer and pie. Never so much appreciated the civilised company of sane women, and a decent English pub.

Called in on the *Sunday Times* editor, Harold Evans, on the way back, at his house on top of Highgate West Hill. Drank a bottle of wine and discussed the whole Marcia business. He is marvellously professional and funny. Being with him it is hard to believe that the scum of the *Sun*, the *Daily Mail* and the *Express* are of the same profession – or 'low trade' really.

*Wednesday 10 April 1974*

Depressing day. Arrived early at No. 10 and found nobody there. HW not yet in from Windsor. So I got the office moving – including complaining to *The Times* etc. about calling the Unit 'political' instead of 'Policy'. Also talked to John Crawley at the BBC.

I emerged again from my office at 10 a.m. and found HW in with Joe in Marcia's room. Joe revealed he had been told that:

a) The Tories were spreading the rumour that MI5 wanted Marcia removed on security grounds.

b) They were circulating photostats of the legal documents in the Michael Halls case. These cite evidence that acting as an intermediary between HW and Marcia was such a strain that it brought on Halls's heart attack.

c) The *Daily Express* has alleged evidence of tax evasion by H. Wilson (Watergate!). HW then revealed that he had been looking for his tax file and it was missing – possibly stolen. Joe said, 'The plumbers have been in.' [The Watergate scandal in Washington began when agents of President Nixon – known as the 'plumbers' – burgled the offices of his Democratic opponents.]

Joe later told me that HW was completely naive about money, uninterested in it, and if Joe asked for £1,000 HW would simply give it to him. He had no idea. Marcia often gave him *whole* chequebooks to sign and he signed the lot in advance. Joe is convinced that the only real worry is about the deal with the *Sunday Times* on his memoirs. In order to reduce tax on *income*, he sold the manuscript to them for a large amount of *capital*. This was arranged by his lawyer, Lord Goodman, and his accountants.

I listened, and felt more and more depressed. Joe was angry and said this was part of the campaign to destroy HW and Labour. True. But *these could succeed*. Land speculation, tax avoidance – never mind Marcia, this was all too much in contrast with HW's speeches and Labour's programme. He could become a liability.

HW was clearly rattled. He went off to Cabinet at 10.30, but came straight back and asked me to see Joe and arrange a meeting with Lord Goodman *today*. Also to think how to put the screws on George Wigg, 'who is master-minding all this'.

Marcia is issuing her statement about her and her family's speculation in land today. HW was happy with that. 'She doesn't know my motives – I want it out of the way for Easter – a bad time for the press. And it is not too bad. Could be worse. Better to get this out, then she cannot put out a really wild one herself.'

Then I went at his suggestion to phone Marcia, who I have not talked to since Friday. She was crazy, incoherent, violent and abused me. Said that we were enjoying life at No. 10 and leaving her to be persecuted. She didn't want sympathy from any of us. Albert was interested only in getting a parliamentary seat. Me in getting on. Implied threat that she would turn the press on us. She said, 'There must be plenty in all your private lives that can be exposed . . .'

I had frankly had enough and ended the conversation as soon as possible. It was absolutely ridiculous that a Labour government elected to help millions of people, and its PM, should be totally absorbed in comforting and being attacked by this woman. She is suffering terribly. The press is behaving like gutter rats. Even so, her insistence on attacking all who try to help her, on insisting that they put her before everything else, is intolerable. I have now been through every emotion – sympathy for her, anger at the press, irritation with her, and now, finally and totally, exhaustion and being fed up and wanting to wash my hands of it.

When I asked if she was going to the Scillies with HW for Easter she replied, 'Yes, if it will embarrass the King Rat. That is what he is. A King Rat.'

After that I simply got on with my work.

Late in the morning Albert returned, almost in tears, having gone out to her house to comfort her and simply been abused. Albert was totally fed up, and said enough was enough.

We saw HW in the study before lunch. He was very rattled. Going off at tangents to talk about Rhodesia, or revenge on the press, and how it would all rebound in our favour, and nobody was interested in the scandal – it was all blowing over. We pointed out Albert's problem of needing a seat. He dismissed it, saying, 'We must nurse this for a while.' Joe has pointed out how he always talks about Marcia as if about a loved but sick child.

I was pleased to get out and go to lunch with Joe. I felt very low. Almost soiled. I didn't come in for this. I hoped that we would really get down to making a *great* Labour government which would improve the life of ordinary British people. Now there is a grey pall about it. I no longer feel excited to enter No. 10, proud to see the Labour Cabinet meeting to discuss our programme. *Not* because I believe the smear campaign. On that, I don't know. But because British society could descend this low. It has convinced me that I don't want to go into public life. I don't want to devote myself, or make sacrifices for my family, on behalf of some 'public weal' ideal. It is not worth it. Our society is diseased and sick. I want to live privately with my family. That of course is the way that Weimar fell in Germany and Vichy came about in France.

I was revived by going after lunch to the DHSS to discuss providing better vehicles for the disabled. Here were sane, nice people sitting round a table concerned with the plight of the most underprivileged. For one and a half hours I felt it was worthwhile. We made progress and afterwards Alf Morris,* the very decent Minister for the Disabled, asked me to stay. He said how touched they were that No. 10 should show such interest and how these officials went away uplifted and encouraged by my presence as the symbol of the Prime Minister's commitment. We also discussed the next issues we could concern ourselves with – employment for the disabled, a research institute for the deaf, etc. I felt revived by doing something worthwhile at last.

Returned to No. 10 at 4 p.m. Worked on my papers and cleared my desk for the first time in a week!

Then went to see Joe and Albert. Albert had been back to see Marcia. Sigmund Sternberg* was trying to persuade her to go abroad at his expense. Terry Lancaster still trying to get his personal statement from Marcia (it came out later in the *Mirror*).

Apparently Marcia 'went berserk' in Albert's phrase, and after a hysterical explosion went upstairs. Albert left, with Lancaster upstairs knocking on her bedroom door and shouting, 'Now, now, Marcia, come out now.'

Incidentally, at 4.30 p.m., the moment I got back in from DHSS, I received a phone call from the Prime Minister. He had just been phoned and abused by Marcia, on an open line through No. 10, accusing him of keeping her statement. 'You know, Bernard,' he said, 'I gave it to Albert at 1.30. You know that, but she won't believe me. I have tried to get hold of Joe and Albert and Bill Housden. I can't find them. Will you try and find them?' I went downstairs and met Bill Housden, the PM's driver. I told him about the missing statement. He said, 'But I delivered the statement to Marcia half an hour ago, and was photographed doing it.' I went into the press office and there was Joe sitting working. I said I was losing touch with sanity. Joe was calm and firm as usual – though he did insist on Albert and me agreeing to a pact whereby none of us would resign without giving the other two 24 hours' notice – 'a 24 hours' veto', as he called it. Joe thought if we all resigned together, it could bring HW down. I said I thought the threat might force HW to break with Marcia to save himself. Joe referred, as often, to Asquith and Venetia Stanley. He is afraid Marcia will finally destroy HW. I agree – but fear that there will never be a clear moment when HW has the choice between Marcia and destruction. It will be a slow erosion, like waves under a cliff, and then he will be gone.

Albert was drinking but I refused. I don't feel like drinks, cigars or anything. I just want my family and sanity.

So I leave early and go home. It is Rachel's 9th birthday – she looks lovelier than ever.

## Thursday 11 April 1974

Last day before the Easter holiday. Government machine clearly winding down – flow of papers almost stopped. Some of my staff already on holiday.

I was working on a paper for HW's holiday reading: on election timing. Pointing out that by winter things will be getting more difficult – unemployment, inflation, fresh surge of union wage claims, most of the *easy* election pledges implemented, the remaining ones difficult and could mean trouble. Points to an election this year, i.e. June or October (I prefer latter). But there is a problem of precipitating the election. People don't want the bore of another election. Yet we can win now (16% ahead in NOP) and need the secure majority.

Marcia's statement is published today in the *Mirror* – Joe wrote most of it, taking out the whingeing and pathetic self-excuses and putting in a bit of dignity. All the papers took it up. Dignified, odd bit of pathos. Made a good impact. HW more pleased with it and felt this would help silence the wolves. Together with holidays and new sensations bound to come up elsewhere.

Joe and I had lunch together in the House of Commons Press Gallery. Albert not in today – he must be totally fed up with the battering he has taken from Marcia and because his hopes of getting the seat at Newham have had a setback.

Joe is worried about his own position with the press. He has damaged his relations with them out of anger and loyalty on HW's behalf. HW actually told Joe to discontinue lobby briefings. But Joe thinks that later it will be held against him that his relations with the press are not better. Joe is immensely detached and lucid. Totally loyal to HW but in no way sycophantic and ready to walk out at a moment's notice if no longer useful. He has no ambition and no material needs.

Absolutely honest, straight and simple. Puritanical – he slightly disapproves of my liking for the good life, but forgives it.

Back to No. 10 and finish the memo in desperate hurry. Do photostat copies myself. Put in large envelope 'For PM's Eyes Only'.

HW comes in and we chat. He goes upstairs to the study. As he goes, I tell him we must get away from 'diversions' and back to the mainstream of policies after the holiday.

He had no appointments in the afternoon or evening before going to the Scillies on the midnight train. Joe was staying with him for the rest of the day and the evening, because he gets lonely, bored and at a loose end with nothing to do.

I slipped off home and packed up the family of six in the old Ford Cortina, then off to the cottage in Suffolk for eight days.

## Easter Holiday, 12–21 April 1974

In Suffolk I found I was exhausted, frequently falling asleep in the day, and very irritable. Unable to relax and get interested in anything. Adrenalin has no outlet.

Weather dry, but grey, cloudy and cold. I stayed around the cottage most days, reading Proust and *Day of the Jackal*, and enjoying the log fire.

On Easter Monday I phoned the Prime Minister in the Scillies from the red public phone box at Thorn's Corner, Wickhambrook. Seemed very unreal to be phoning Britain's Prime Minister from a remote Suffolk phone box, putting coins in the box. He had been out walking and had slept in the sun.

Discussed Eric Heffer* who, as a minister, had broken collective responsibility by attacking the government over sending warships to Chile. HW said he had originally decided to sack him but then thought it better to warn him and let Callaghan, as the aggrieved Foreign Secretary, rebuke him in public.

HW complained there was not enough work for him to do. Obviously resents playing 'centre-half' and letting his ministers score the goals.

Talked to Joe on Friday. He had been to Ulster with HW the day before. Found it very depressing. Just a military occupation and the Army very angry with the restraints put on them. Wanted mandatory justice. A sign of what a cancer Ireland is. Britain's Algeria, brutalising the whole community.

Some reflections on HW after our first session in Downing Street:

– He sees it all through people. Not interested in policies. If he likes the people (Israel) he supports the policies.

– His lack of interest in policies is reflected in our difficulties in getting him to discuss what *ought* to be done in any area. Is interested in what is electorally desirable. And in what the manifesto promises – because he is so committed to keeping his promises and not doing U-turns. The rest he may be interested in at the time of ministerial meetings, but not outside Cabinet Room.

– Problem of my job is what actually to send to him. He doesn't want a mass of extra paper. And I don't know what he is saying to ministers in his own memoranda. Never see these.

– He hates confrontation. Hence when he saw Swann* of the BBC he assured him that we had no complaints against the BBC. So he won't complain to his civil servants about filling up his timetable with nonsense. And is pleased when I clearly get on well with the civil servants. In an odd way he uses Joe and Marcia to put their teeth into people, on his behalf.

– He lacks genuine deep passion. This is why he doesn't understand Ireland – or Bill Rodgers! And what he likes in Marcia, who compensates for his lack of it. And why he can forgive virtually all his political enemies (except Ernie Bevin and Hugh Dalton, his enemies in Attlee's 1945–51 government). It is as if he dissociates from his personal body, and any attacks on him do not hurt. But he resents attacks on the Labour Party, with which he has merged. So he forgives (and promotes) those who attack him personally and publicly; but claims he punishes those who 'attack the party', e.g. he claims Bill Rodgers was attacking the party when he said that it was doing badly, wouldn't win the next election, and by implication didn't deserve to. This distinction he draws is not always convincing.

– He does enjoy political pressure, and gives way to it. So the only way to get something, as Marcia says, is 'to kick him in the back'. And this *encourages* that kind of behaviour from others.

– Seeing the mediocrities, trimmers and self-seekers around him in politics, it is not surprising he is cynical, self-assuredly playing them off against one another, constantly plotting how to please one, sidetrack another, hold them together in the end. Like a circus master, running the show and making sure he doesn't get eaten, no longer noticing, even puzzled at, the applause for the show.

– Astonishing how he works through the day, 15 hours, without getting tired or wanting a nap. The work itself generates his energy. Also he paces himself. Lets others get excited and make the arguments. Often he does not listen, I suspect. It is difficult to tell whether he is listening or not, whether he has taken a point on board. His hooded eyes look blank often, as if behind transparent shutters. Impossible to tell what registers. He obviously has to sift the endless verbal battering of suggestions and ideas. He never takes a note to remind himself. He just sifts and remembers what he wants to and deals with it later.

Joe says that you know when he has really taken something hard between the eyes because he blinks a couple of times. Otherwise his face is generally impassive. I think he looks remarkably fit. His skin seems very *thick and pink*, giving an impression of stamina.

– But he has an irritating habit of talking through one. Interrupting in the middle of a sentence and talking through it on something else. This is partly the politician's megalomania, interested only in what they have to say, rarely listening to anybody else. I know of no exceptions to this among the many politicians I know who are over 50.

– He obviously enjoyed appointing the new Archbishop of Canterbury [Donald Coggan]. Ought not to interest him – but quite the reverse. He loves dabbling in this kind of Establishment game. Picking the man for any job.

– His attitude to the land deals scandal was often unrealistically detached. He was fascinated by every detail, like a connoisseur not a participant. He summoned me one day and described the plot. 'This is Agatha Christie. We are at the last but one chapter. It still could be any one of five who did the forgery. So, Bernard, who did it? Tell me your scenario. How will the last chapter finish?' I couldn't answer. I had not followed the details closely. It irritated me to have our attention diverted from serious things, like mortgages or vehicles for the disabled. But HW paced up and down the room fascinatedly going over the details. He remembered every detail and date and had obviously spent most of his time in the Cabinet trying to fit together the pieces in the jigsaw.

– He never takes exercise. Spends his days in No. 10 and in the Commons. In the car from one to the other. Never seems to feel a desire to walk in St James's Park – or go to Regent Street to look in shops. A totally insulated life. Spent in five rooms – Cabinet Room, Marcia's room, his study and, in the Commons, his room and the Chamber itself. Fifteen hours a day either in meetings, or with the Kitchen Cabinet, or in his room at the House. His knowledge of what the government is doing is taken from his boxes of papers. And his knowledge of the outside world is derived almost wholly from the newspapers. They are reality for him. This is why he reads them so avidly and gets so hurt by them. He is very interested in the world of newspapers. But does not realise that most journalists are totally different from him, being malicious and envious and unforgiving.

Every morning he reads all the newspapers. This is his dose of ordinary life – vicariously he absorbs other people's problems. So he is very concerned about 'rising prices' but in fact has virtually no experience of them. He rarely buys anything. He spends money almost as rarely as the monarch. He never carries money. Almost never goes out into town. Never to a restaurant, almost never to cinema or theatre. Certainly never to a concert (though he likes Gilbert and Sullivan), rarely mentions his family. In fact completely cut off from everyday, ordinary reality. Lives in a political cocoon. Many of his parliamentary colleagues probably do the same.

# CHAPTER 3

## Preparing for the Next Election – and More Troubles with Marcia and the Press
### April–May 1974

*Monday 22 April 1974*

I spent the morning on papers accumulated over the holiday.
12.15 dropped in to private office and found HW and Joe and the private secretaries discussing N. Ireland, etc.

Then HW went off upstairs with Joe, Albert and myself to the study for a long talk. (He was not going to lunch with us until Marcia returned. She had clearly forbidden it. So he ate alone in the flat off a tray, the same steak which we ate in the dining-room below him. Then he came and joined us for coffee. In order to be able to tell Marcia that he was not eating and conspiring with the Mafia!)

We discussed election timing – June, October, or 1975? Pros and cons. He was mainly afraid of:

1) being held responsible for precipitating the election;
2) what he called 'the big yawn' – people bored with elections and staying home.

But he was stronger for an early election than I had realised.

Joe didn't like October, which I preferred.

In the end HW decided we should plan contingently and *strategically* for an October election and *tactically* for a June election. Keep the option open. He also wanted to use the Common Market question to precipitate the election – and hold the referendum at the same time as the election! This all worries me. Could split the party – and therefore lose. [Joe later informed me that HW had told him in March that he preferred 10 October for the second election, but had sworn him to secrecy.]

Also discussed the proposed Royal Commission on the Press – which HW was setting up as revenge for the newspapers' headlines over Marcia and the land deals. Joe and I discussed members for it. And for an inquiry into broadcasting.

Altogether two hours of serious discussion.

Went to visit Harold Lever in the afternoon. Worried about Labour's attitude to the Common Market. Thinks must fire a shot across HW's bows. Is going to see Roy Jenkins. Lever has a brilliant mortgage scheme to bring interest rates down. He is very critical of Tony Crosland for not giving him public credit for the recent successful negotiations with the building societies. Tony never believed they would succeed! [The government made a loan of up to £500 million to the building societies to enable them not to raise mortgage rates above 11%.]

Evening with John Hunt, finalising our agreement defining the relations of the Policy Unit to the Cabinet Office.

Then endless letters and papers – and home at 9 p.m.

HW left early for Grange Farm, his country house in Buckinghamshire. There are few committees and papers this week.

I telephone Roy Jenkins to have a drink, but he was in France. Lucky him!

## Tuesday 23 April 1974

I worked all morning on papers and saw John Hunt, who told me that Victor Rothschild of the Central Policy Review Staff was worried we were getting an oil expert in competition with him. [I decided not to in order to maintain sweet relations with the CPRS.]

Also saw HW about the proposed Press Commission.

And yesterday's disastrous leak to the press by Michael Foot's department on the repayment of fines to unions prosecuted under the Industrial Relations Act. No consultation. Complete breach of rules. Wilson will tell Foot off tonight.

Don Ryder,* HW's favourite entrepreneur, came in to see PM and apparently told him that his International Publishing Corporation is very happy with government and the *Mirror* would give massive support in the next election.

Lunch with my staff and Robin Butler from private office and Chris Brearley from Cabinet Office and Susanne Reeve from the CPRS. To improve diplomatic relations between the central departments working directly to the Prime Minister.

Afternoon meeting with David Lea,* the economist from the TUC, about better relations with TUC. He also said No June election – TUC would not stand an election before the repeal of the Industrial Relations Act is on the statute book – and that will not be before July!

Then to Bob Sheldon,* the junior minister in charge of the Civil Service, to discuss the role and problems of special advisers.

Back to No. 10 drinks with the PM – who had clearly already drunk a lot – because he is bored. Discuss press, etc. He is confident of winning next election. Also amused by the engaging naivety of Michael Foot!

## Wednesday 24 April 1974

Saw very little of the PM today. He was at the Labour National Executive Committee where they raved about Chile.

I worked on papers and had a big meeting with John Hunt and all my staff, explaining the rules of the game for securing privileged Whitehall treatment for the Unit.

Off to lunch to my stockbrokers Grieveson Grant. Interesting man from M & G – David Hopkinson* – putting up proposals for selling more gilts by encouraging unit trusts to buy gilts. I asked him for a paper – and later discussed it with the PM and with Harold Lever on the phone. Will follow this one up. The City is also worried about its relations with Whitehall and we discuss how to improve that.

Back at 3 p.m. and saw HW. Discussed

1) Benn and British Leyland – nationalisation. Rumour that Benn is encouraging the militants to strike so the firm will go bankrupt and have to be nationalised.
2) Gilts and how to introduce Hopkinson's idea of making unit trusts' dealing in gilts tax-free.
3) Leaks – handling of news is bad at moment, especially on Defence matters.

HW had lunch with Joe and Robert Armstrong and Albert upstairs. He apparently asked complainingly where I was. Have to be careful about going out for lunch unless the PM is clearly engaged elsewhere.

Rest of the afternoon on papers, dictating documents, drafting letters, talking to Joe and Albert.

Also meeting with Balogh on the North Sea – he wants a negotiating committee to deal with the oil companies, led by Lever. Also worried about pay policy under Phase III of the inherited Heath incomes policy – all special cases are being treated ad hoc. There is no strategy or order of priorities. This will blow up in the end – and annoy the TUC.

My staff are now settling in. Today Richard Kirwan (Housing), Richard Graham (Industry) and Gavyn Davies (Economics) went to a beautiful big new room in the Cabinet Office. Whitehall imperialism. And it will be quieter in here with fewer people.

Basic problem is still to make sure that their excellent work is utilised – and does not just disappear into a void.

Evening to dinner with Ron Higgins of the *Observer*, who every time I see him keeps pressing me to keep a diary and regrets that he did not write one when he was secretary to Ted Heath. I tell him how busy I am.

## Thursday 25 April 1974

Day of the big Cabinet meeting renegotiating the terms of Britain's membership of the EEC, which I attended.

Most interesting was the general discussion at the end.

Especially Jim Callaghan, who first set out the renegotiation timetable: prepare negotiating position by June. Put to Cabinet. Then summer break. Then serious negotiations with EEC partners in the autumn.

Most important was his general statement that we must face the fact that the EEC exists and is acknowledged to exist by the rest of the world. (Astonishing that a Labour Cabinet needs to be reminded about this simple reality.) That Labour had not quite taken this on board but did now. And that on balance his position was to hope we could negotiate what we wanted while still *in* the EEC.

The Left looked stunned – Peter Shore, Judith Hart,* Tony Benn and Michael Foot, all sitting together at the far end of the table.

Even the PM looked agitated, and he asked Robert Armstrong to open the windows and let in some fresh air. The Labour Party has needed that for some time.

Then Michael Foot – obviously prearranged – intervened to talk about the implications of EEC membership for British parliamentary sovereignty. But this suited the pro-marketeers. Meant very muffled reply to Callaghan from the antis. Off the main point – and the right-wing pros could agree with a lot of what Foot said. And Shore unable to reply because had already spoken at length.

Denis Healey then spoke and said our bargaining position could be stronger in the autumn because

a)  Europe would need us in the Defence appraisal that was going on.
b)  Europe would need us in the big energy crisis which would arise in the autumn when he predicted the Arabs would again cut off oil.

This was helpful since it was pushing back the time for a final decision. The antis want a quick decision – out.

Roy Jenkins then summarised the position as he saw it. Timetable, with serious negotiations not till autumn. Said any quick decision to pull out would be 'very grave'. This was obviously a clear warning to the PM that he and his pro-EEC friends would then resign.

Then he went on to ask for an analysis of the alternatives to the EEC. Clearly prearranged as a way of exposing lack of alternatives.

But probably unnecessary since things were looking good for the pro-marketeers anyway. The PM shrewdly pushed it off, since it would open a whole argument on whether the alternatives had been fairly presented or not.

Shirley Williams then asked for a statement of the Commonwealth attitude. Clearly prearranged to expose the fact that the Commonwealth itself did not believe in the Commonwealth option.

(Afterwards HW said to me that he had 'spotted in the morning that the antis had met to arrange their interventions and in the afternoon it was clear that the pros had met. I was the only one who did not have a meeting about this meeting!')

It finished with Benn making a very demagogic speech about 'the British people' wanting a socialist industrial policy of the kind he was going to announce, since without it we would suffer terribly, and in the EEC it would not be possible to survive. Then he attacked HW for putting him on only one Cabinet committee. But by then people were preparing to leave, and tired. Healey fell asleep for 15 minutes in the middle of Shore's speech. So it ended very well for the pros, the antis looking grim, and with a timetable ahead till the autumn.

HW clearly is hoping to get the election out of the way before this EEC question all comes to a head. Most significant was the move of the middle – Jim Callaghan, Denis Healey, Fred Peart – towards a position of believing we could get what we wanted from *within* the Common Market. If this continues, the pro-marketeers can keep quiet and let things run. But interesting is how HW will react – with Jim Callaghan now taking a position more on the pro side than him on the EEC issue.

All the Cabinet attended lunch. I sat with Lever and Joe – and Lever was next to HW. HW had lost his voice but was in cheerful form. Very proud of the government. Said 'It is even better than 1906'!

Later I had a meeting with the 1971 Group of (Labour) Businessmen about their papers on National Enterprise Board and on management training. Very tired.

## Friday 26 April 1974

Spent all morning preparing the PM's speech to the Shopworkers' Union (USDAW) on Sunday. I contributed very little. Mainly Joe, who had obviously worked hard and late.

Lunch with Robert Armstrong. He is immensely able and self-assured. Going to the top. [He became Cabinet Secretary in 1979 and was head of the Civil Service from 1981 to 1987.] Is now co-operating much better with me and obviously preferring good relations to hostility.

We discussed need to improve the government's relations with the City and to get in City people to lunch. I would like us to work together on this. And a possible Royal Commission on the City.

In the afternoon Lever went to see HW about the problem of property companies collapse in the present financial crisis and his other ideas – e.g. helping building societies to keep down mortgage rates. I saw HW afterwards and clear that Lever had not made much progress. He must put it down on paper.

Tried to fix a meeting with Victor Rothschild of the Cabinet Office Think Tank, but he is very busy.

HW said he would probably go to see Marcia this evening. She has been attacking me. Told HW that I was the source of the *Private Eye* attack on her and of the *Sunday Times* material about her. Crazy. Also attacking Albert and his staff.

The last time I talked to her she put the phone down – and later told HW I was trying to get her to leave the country. (I had said that in her position 'I would want to get away from it all'.) Now I learn she is going away anyway. Rudi Sternberg* is helping her.

When I left at 6.15 p.m. HW was still there. Reluctant to leave for the weekend. How could he ever retire?

Not really a good day. Don't feel I did anything.

## Saturday 27 April 1974

Albert Murray went for the Newham selection conference for its parliamentary candidate at the next election. Eliminated early. Was quizzed about his 'other interests' as a member of HW's private office.

When I talked later to Joe he was furious. Blamed Marcia. Said he would destroy her one day. Total and loyal sympathy to Albert.

I talked to Albert and he was shattered. His wife Anne is fed up. I am afraid he will leave the office. Tragic. He is pure salty cockney and marvellous to have around.

Lunch with H. Kissin. His peerage has been delayed and he is worried why. I don't know. He is also perturbed that Healey has been spreading the story that the Treasury has completely frozen out Harold Lever, who has no influence. This will be fatal in the City. Kissin is clearly very nervous.

I came home and phoned Lever. He is furious and says he will personally announce that the government will change its intentions on overseas earnings tax. Then Healey will have to climb down. That Healey is the one man who could lose us the election.

## Monday 29 April 1974

Morning spent in the office. HW upstairs in the study drafting his statement on the Royal Commission on conflicts of interests arising out of the affair of T. Dan Smith. [The Labour local government politician from the north-east was convicted on 26 April and imprisoned on charges of corruption together with Andrew Cunningham.]

Lunch with Joe and Albert. Latter very depressed and threatening to resign and issue a statement denouncing Marcia. His whole career at stake. Joe, keen to protect the PM, tries to warn him off.

In the afternoon I went to the House for the statement on conflicts of interest in public life, quietly received. HW very witty and relaxed. All seems well.

He was still in good form when I had half an hour with him in the study. Discussed election timing – obviously June is disappearing. He is afraid of 'the big yawn', as he says. Thinks people happy and don't want an election.

He is very pleased with his style – low profile, intervening rarely and then with impact.

But when I saw him later he was annoyed. Ted Short (the Lord President and Labour's Deputy Leader) had not issued his personal statement on his relations with Dan Smith as promised. Had gone off electioneering for Vicky Kidd, his pretty political adviser. Goodman was vetting the statement. HW furious. Wanted it out before his own, because he had planned to 'blanket' Short. Now Short will get bigger treatment. HW had also clearly been drinking heavily.

Still getting on well with Robert Armstrong – who will now stay on till after the election, although his normal three-year period is already completed. PM is thinking of Derek Andrews as his successor as principal private secretary, because he and Marcia know him from the time when he worked in No. 10 in the earlier Wilson administration.

## Tuesday 30 April 1974

Several illicit Labour Party relationships reported to No. 10, including Ian Mikardo and Renée Short (not a beautiful pairing) and one leading left-wing Cabinet minister.

I wonder. I have learned to distrust all press rumours. The place is full of unsubstantiated gossip. This gossiping sickens me.

Exhausting day. Started 8 a.m. with Henry Kissinger's* Washington aide,

Hal Sonnenfeldt. Breakfast at Claridge's. Interested in my job and its prob-lems. Then world affairs. Had heard, quite rightly, that this administra-tion is insular. Till 9.15. Then he asked for my private address – and to see me 'outside the official network' in future.

Back to No. 10 for my *positive vetting* for security clearance. Kindly old Special Branch man. Waste of time. Mainly details of birth, marriage, death, etc. obtainable from public records. Then one casual question about my view on 'the role of the monarch'. I disguised my recent policy recom-mendation to blow up Buckingham Palace!!

After him had two *Time* magazine men, Smith and Gort, and discussed till lunch – which was with Geoff Bish from Transport House and Jack Straw,* the special adviser from DHSS. In No. 10. Good discussion on our proposed Policy Unit paper on *small policy issues* which mean a lot to people.

Beforehand long discussion on Ted Short's statement on his alleged association with Dan Smith and its treatment in press. Disgraceful head-lines smearing him. He is a straight man. But he did not handle the state-ment well.

HW keen to hit back at press. This still absorbs his attention. He is pleased to have a colleague united in this battle.

Afternoon to Parliamentary Questions. Another question on me leading to an attack on the Unit being paid for from party funds. [This was untrue. The Policy Unit was established as part of the Civil Service, paid for from public funds, with its members temporary civil servants and subject to all Civil Service rules and constraints, though without the normal job security.]

Then an attack indirectly on Marcia. HW lost his temper and the general atmosphere was not good.

Afterwards I had a meeting with Alf Morris, the junior minister at the DHSS, on vehicles for the disabled. There is a debate tomorrow and he wants to make a statement. I later see HW, who is not very enthusiastic, but I push him a bit.

The meeting with Ted Short on making the declaration of MPs' inter-ests compulsory. HW supports this. He has promised a free vote – on the assumption that Labour and Liberals will vote it through. He also wants a declaration of journalists' interests. Apparently some lobby journalists use the lobby to get privileged information – e.g. on the government's policy on trade towards South Africa or Eastern Europe – and then are paid by the relevant trade association to pass it on. Short is rather weak on all this. Inclines to give way to Tory demands for only voluntary regis-tration. HW stiffens him. On this issue HW has endless energy, endless desire for revenge. They really have hurt him.

George Wigg phoned the PM this morning. 'I was cool,' said HW.

*Wednesday 1 May 1974*

9.30 a.m. I was sent for by the PM. HW discussed his proposed counter-attack on the press – in May Day speech in Glasgow to denounce press for taking on the role of the Opposition.

Also plans to put down motions calling for details of the financing of Ted Heath's yacht.

He looked older and tired this morning. Said he thought the press had reached new depths over Ted Short allegedly receiving £250 expenses from Dan Smith over 10 years ago. Also regretted that the PLP did not rally to their defence. [Smith claimed on television that he had paid Short £250 expenses in 1960, though offering no evidence there was anything improper in this.]

While the PM was in the Defence committee and at the PLP, I dealt with Policy Unit papers.

Also saw Sir John Hunt. Learned that Henry Kissinger is very optimistic about a Middle East settlement.

I put to him my concern about how the Treasury are treating Harold Lever. Hunt said Lever never read his committee papers and this irritated people. We agreed that we must get staff to brief him. But I warned Hunt there would be serious trouble if Lever resigned. We agreed Healey lacked sensitivity – and to discuss this further.

Hunt – who is very helpful in many ways – said he felt this Labour government read too many newspapers, and the last Tory government listened to BBC radio too much – and claimed it was run by communists.

HW summoned me and Joe and we went over the press campaign for 45 minutes till 1.30 p.m. Then discussed election timing. HW favours the autumn. I suggest late September. He wants to announce it at conference. But wants to get Cabinet approval.

Marcia had attacked him for mentioning *Private Eye* in the Commons and so raising her problem again.

At first he said we could not have a September election because (grinning) 'Marcia is on holiday then'.

Very late for lunch with Tom Bridges, Robin Butler and Mark Forrester from the private office. They all felt the media were the main obstacle to government in the country, knocking everything, regardless of party.

After to the DHSS to discuss vehicles for the disabled (very complicated). Then brief meeting with Balogh about North Sea oil.

And off to the *Observer* to discuss their strike, etc. with David Astor and Ron Higgins. They offered me money now to write on Downing Street when I retire, but I declined courteously.

Back to Commons where HW wanted me to help get a university place for an Israeli friend. We relaxed with drinks and chatted. Bob Mellish and Ron Hayward came in. PM had little to do. No appointment. Complained nowhere to go to eat. He is lost without a work programme.

Coming back to No. 10 in the car, we read that Alf Ramsey has been sacked as England football manager. [Sir Alf Ramsey had been manager for 11 years, including 1966 when England won the World Cup, and was replaced by Don Revie of Leeds United.]

I said, 'He should have resigned at the top.'

HW replied, 'We all find that difficult to do.'


*Thursday 2 May 1974*

9.30–10.15 I saw PM before Cabinet. Still on the Ted Short problem. He is anxious to step in and make a statement on Short's behalf. I feel Short should speak up for himself. I hear he is in a bad way.

PM still furious with the press and keen to attack them in his Glasgow speech – I dissent. Scots want a speech about Scotland not about the London press.

During Cabinet I went to see Rothschild about liaison with the CPRS. He began with an attack on John Hunt and the Cabinet Office for trying to undermine him. I like him and feel we can work together. But he will have a problem interesting the PM in long-term policy.

Lunch with Desmond Hirshfield* in the Lords.

PQs – including more on the CPRS and indirectly attacks on me. PM in sparkling form. Tories seem subdued.

Also announced the Royal Commission on the Press under Maurice Finer* as chairman.

Back to No. 10 with Robert Armstrong.

Marcia has written letters to Albert and to one of the private office secretaries attacking them for the Trooping of the Colour arrangements. And attacking No. 10's new cook.

I have *not* received a letter from her. Ominous. Albert's letter was very rude, simply addressed to 'Albert' – no 'Dear' or 'Yours sincerely', etc.

PM went to the PLP and attacked the press. Short also attacked press at today's parliamentary lobby. It is taking too much of the government's time.

Incidentally it is crazy that the PM still has to eat on his own in the flat or at the House of Commons because Marcia has forbidden him to eat with 'the Mafia' in the No. 10 dining-room.

I am worried about HW's Glasgow May Day speech. The Scottish Office draft is terrible. Joe and I have no time to do it. No progress on our proposed Privacy Bill or other things, because absorbed in day-to-day press questions.

Home 8.30. PM at dinner with the Queen of Denmark.

NB: He told me the Cabinet discussed election timing and were 10–8 for *not* holding election in June.

## Friday 3 May 1974

9.30 went up to the study to see the PM. I am relieved that he has decided to take our advice and cut the attack on the press from his Glasgow speech. Instead will attack the Tories.

He came in to join us for lunch – the first time in weeks, and was in sparkling form. Very funny and obviously happy. As if last night's speech to the PLP had purged the venom from him. We were joined by two secretaries from the private office.

Afterwards he said how pleased he is that the relations between the political and private offices were working so well.

Fairly relaxed afternoon. Periodic visits to the PM's study to discuss parts of the speech. Joe did part of the Scottish section, and I did the rest. We had a hilarious meeting to finish off the speech around 6 p.m. Plenty of drinks. The PM severely warned Albert that after positive vetting the Special Branch had discovered something serious which Albert had hidden – he is a supporter of Millwall Football Club.

I met Mrs Wilson coming up the stairs and she complained that they were supposed to be going to a reception and were late. I told HW and he looked mock-frightened and sent Albert out to placate Mary. That failed and so HW went out and tried to persuade her to go off alone first. He came back in and we continued to gossip and joke.

Then a private secretary arrived with the message that 'Mrs Wilson is waiting in the car.'

HW left then and I went out with him.

That evening I went to a party at Bill Rodgers's house in Kentish Town. Roy Jenkins was there and we had a long talk. He seemed very interested – and sceptical – about my analysis of HW's character.

*Saturday*: Kissin telephoned very worried about Lever. He had been demoted to bottom of the printed Cabinet list and was in a highly nervous state. Pity – it will weaken his influence. I am trying to help.

The Short 'scandal' bubbles on. Some pressure for him to resign. We think should not. No reason to. He has done nothing proven wrong and is a decent man. It is just the biased malicious press. But the corruption concern grows. The spotlight will turn on others.

The PM's Glasgow speech seems to have gone well. Heckling, but a good reception.

I talked to him on the telephone at Chequers about Short, etc.

## Monday 6 May 1974

Morning spent mainly with Joe or on Unit papers. But also had a long talk with HW in the study.

He confirmed no June election. Also annoyed with Short at continued statements. Said he must shut up.

Lunch with Marcia's friends Peter Davis and Denis Lyons, HW's unofficial public relations advisers. PM summoned Joe and me from it at 2.30 to discuss election arrangements. Wants me to investigate the Election Business committee – arrangements whereby the Civil Service provides briefs for ministers in the campaign. Obviously secret and a possible misuse of the Civil Service.

4.15 saw Michael Cudlipp*, a long-standing journalist friend who is going to Glasgow to help found the co-operative newspaper from the ruins of the collapsed Scottish *Daily Express*.

5.15 Kissin came in to discuss the problem of Harold Lever. Apparently he was in a very bad way at weekend. Emotional and angry because of demotion in Cabinet order. Kissin seeing HW at 6.30 to tell him to cheer up Lever and back him up.

I returned to my papers and staff, and to think of names for the impending honours list. We are very short of ideas. Especially of women.

Could not get away in time for a concert with Carol at 7.30 p.m. Must clear my desk before tomorrow.

At 7 p.m. a private secretary comes in to say the PM has ordered a lunch tomorrow for himself, Lever, Joe and me.

Bill Housden, HW's driver, said he was fed up with Marcia – she is attacking everybody. PM has not seen her for two weeks!

Kissin, who has observed the Harold and Marcia relationship for many years, says she will never return. I wonder.

## Tuesday 7 May 1974

Went in at 9.30 to complete my positive vetting. The Special Branch officer was interested in whether I had avoided the exchange controls to buy my French house! A Labour colleague had told them of my recent acquisition and queried whether I had done it legally. Why don't they ask the Bank of England? I will produce the relevant documents giving permission.

PM interrupted us and I went upstairs to the study. Discussed the election – he inclines to late September. (Asserted he was only joking about Marcia's holiday.)

Also going on the attack against Tories by stirring up the Lord Lambton affair.

Discussed last night's TV programme seeming to imply corruption by Reginald Maudling.*

Later I had a good meeting with John Hunt and the PM about the government's next six months' work programme. I criticised the lack of economic content, especially no *monetary* policy. Also problems of Tony Benn rushing his programme for extensive controls over industry and more nationalisation without consulting Cabinet colleagues.

PM is also keen to raise some international loans and critical of Healey for not doing so. Later at lunch with Lever, Joe and Robert he pressed Lever to go ahead and raise loans to support sterling if he could.

Before lunch he had seen the Russian Ambassador. At the end they talked in Russian and the Ambassador asked him to visit Russia. He replied non-committally, but it later emerges that he would like to go. It would be nice to go with him.

Then PQs in the House. Went off very quietly. Tories obviously trying to be respectable and not to be muck-raking.

Afterwards we sat and chatted for an hour in the PM's room in the Commons. Maudling made a personal statement that he would sue the TV. HW would not go to the Chamber because 'it would seem ghoulish'.

He reported to me that Marcia had phoned to say she was going to issue a statement that she had resigned as his *'political'* secretary. Just remained his *'personal'* secretary. He said 'she is very disturbed at the moment'. Joe told me she is expressing great jealousy and animosity towards me.

Had another meeting with John Hunt. I said I was not too happy with the lack of supervision of monetary policy and the danger of hyper-inflation. He promised to slot it in to the Cabinet Economic Strategy committee. Later I put this to Robert Armstrong. At first he objected on the ground that the Treasury wanted to keep monetary policy to itself and Downing Street should not interfere. I said that was not good enough. Failures of monetary policy had brought down previous Labour governments. Must not let the Treasury do it to this one. That Roy Jenkins and Lever would not allow it. Healey lacked the authority to do it. The whole issue must go to ministers and to the PM. Think I made some progress here.

PM said he would *not* have a Royal Commission on the City – had used up his allowance of Royal Commissions. So Armstrong and I decided to proceed with inviting City people to dinner at No. 10 to improve relations.

The Engineers go on total strike. We are pleased as this means no newspapers. Scanlon, the engineering union leader, asks to come with his executive committee to No. 10 for the PM to settle. HW refuses. No more bread and sandwiches at No. 10!

HW left for dinner with his son Giles. I was home by 8.15. Carol ill in bed.

### Wednesday 8 May 1974

Coffee with Joe. I also saw John Harris in Whitehall. He thinks the press is discrediting the whole parliamentary system, and a lot of journalists are unhappy about it – he named Jeremy Isaacs of Thames TV.

Rest of the morning in the office.

Lunch at No. 10 with Harold Evans and James Evans, legal adviser to Thomson newspapers. Beforehand we had drinks with the PM – who was in good form. Said he used to think the three best newspapers in the world were British – *Financial Times*, the *Sunday Times* and the *Guardian*. But now he crossed out the *Guardian* because it is too 'soggy'.

Afternoon worked on papers. And saw Hunt who said the permanent secretaries had met today to discuss my Policy Unit and agreed to support it – because the PM did not have a department. So now have clearance at all levels.

Saw the PM briefly when he returned from seeing the Queen – in very happy form. He is in excellent shape this week.

Marcia asked me to phone her – and then when I did she accused me of trying to steal her job. Because I invited P. Davis and D. Lyons to lunch. She said that was her job.

Albert and Joe are fed up with her. Bill Housden is criticising her. The PM is distancing – not seen her for two weeks. To Joe he said he had 'quarantined' her for a fortnight.

Carol is unwell, so I went home early – 7.45 p.m.

Engineering strike called off because 'anonymous' donors (I know them) paid the Industrial Relations Court the £68,000 fine which the union refused to pay.

Very tired today. But feel content. The PM is in good form and is not suffering too much nonsense from elsewhere.

### Thursday 9 May 1974

Arrived 9.20. PM spent most of the morning in Defence committee (OPD) and Cabinet.

I went off shopping – first time out in daytime London since February!

Returned and found that the PM had asked for me half an hour earlier. Inevitable.

I went up to the study to see him and we discussed next Tuesday's speech on the press. Theme of open government – the government to offer to relax the Official Secrets Act, contempt of court, etc. In return for prevention of intrusions by the press on privacy of private individuals. A good theme – and the deal we agreed at lunch with Harry Evans. Better than simply attacking press.

Then lunch with private office, Joe and Albert.

PQs in House. Very quiet. PM relaxed. Says he is now worried it is too easy. Wants to widen his range of strokes. Said, 'Like Boycott, though you should never try to hook early in your innings.' [Geoffrey Boycott was a Yorkshire cricketer Wilson admired.]

Returned to the office to work on papers.

Went to the PM 5.30–6. Told him his speaking arrangements were not good enough. Not going to marginal seat areas. He said we must start planning his next election speaking programme.

6 p.m. saw Israel Gatt of Israel Labour Party – very nice.

Home 8 p.m.

*Friday 10 May 1974*

A day dominated by Marcia. In the morning we were working on the speech for the Post Office Workers Union Conference on Sunday. HW was in tremendous good form. Cheered by opinion polls showing Labour – and him personally – miles ahead.

Before lunch we discussed his future official and party trips:

- abroad to Moscow and Helsinki;
- home to more marginal constituencies. I produced my map of marginals. Albert suggested a meeting with Reg Underhill of Transport House and Marcia to plan a campaign of meetings. HW interrupted to say 'With or *without* Marcia!'

He was so happy to be discussing politics with us, planning the future, that he said he wanted to come in to lunch. We ate – HW, Joe, Albert and me – planning the late September campaign.

At the end, as he was finishing his cheese, the phone rang in the dining-room. It was Marcia demanding to speak to HW.

She shouted at him for about 10 minutes. He couldn't get a word in and finally slammed the phone down. I had meanwhile shut all the doors so that other Downing Street staff could not hear.

HW looked very black and said he would take coffee in the study.

Joe went with him and apparently told him that he and Terry Lancaster both agreed she was now worryingly unstable. HW said, 'You think she is going round the bend?'

Joe said she 'has a sharp mind'.

HW replied, 'Except that she uses it against her friends.'

We discussed it afterwards. Joe said it was typical. Whenever HW was feeling good, she moved in to drag him down. Albert said that 'The old vulture just sits on his shoulder and keeps pecking away at his neck.'

The PM saw some official visitors and then left for Chequers, hurriedly, at 3.45 p.m., without seeing any of us.

We all felt down. Especially when Terry Lancaster from the *Daily Mirror* phoned to say that Marcia had phoned him to denounce Harold and the rest of us. Lancaster said 'she was raving'.

Bill Housden, HW's driver, told me she had attacked him, accusing him of not telling her enough when she quizzed him daily.

Home early and out to see the film *Day of the Jackal* (about an attempt to assassinate de Gaulle) with Carol and our friend Nori Graham. Could give somebody ideas!

Sunday to Lord Porchester and his lovely wife Jeannie for a marvellous day at Highclere, his estate.

# CHAPTER 4

## Lady Marcia; the Irish Problem
## May–June 1974

### Monday 13 May 1974

R elaxed day. PM at Chequers in the morning dealing with N. Ireland.
I spent time with Joe preparing a speech for the next day, again on
the press. Lunch with Joe and Albert at the House of Commons.

Afternoon with the PM discussing speech – and fuss by Judith Hart
over the Crown Agents, who are scandalously involved in speculative
property.

Then to the TUC to see David Lea. TUC are trying to have a veto
right over whoever I appoint on the TU side of my Unit. I refuse.

Later I attend a No. 10 reception for Commonwealth Parliamentary Union.

Then in the evening I spent a delightful hour with HW. He sent the
private secretaries home and sat and reminisced with Albert and me.

One revealing point: discussing when he insisted on the great England
footballer Stanley Matthews getting a knighthood. The then Head of the
Civil Service [Laurence] Helsby* kept objecting, on silly Establishment
grounds, because he didn't like football. HW said he insisted, although 'I
was nervous of him, nervous of those mandarins, you know.'

Also said he had to attack the press in the debate tomorrow. I said, 'You
must ride above that.' He said, 'I can't ride above Marcia if I don't attack
them.'

### Tuesday 14 May 1974

Day mainly devoted to the speech on the press for the Commons wind-
up.

HW adopted our theme – *not* to attack press. But discuss the Harold
Evans themes of more information to the press on government and more
protection of ordinary individuals from press intrusions.

Went very well. Totally quiet House. Tories surprised he did not get
violent and obsessional. And pleased. Ended up applauding.

A great success.
Home 10.30.

## Wednesday 15 May 1974

[On 15 May 1974 the Ulster Protestant Workers Council organised wide-spread strikes by Protestant workers as part of their campaign against the new power-sharing Executive and the Council of All Ireland. The new political arrangements had been agreed in December 1973 at the Sunningdale talks between the UK, the Republic of Ireland and the Northern Ireland political parties, following on the suspension of the Northern Ireland Parliament in March 1972 and a referendum in 1973 which confirmed majority Ulster support for the continuance of the border. The new non-sectarian Executive took office in January 1974, but a growing number of Protestants protested against the concessions made by Brian Faulkner and his 'moderate' (in Northern Ireland terms) Ulster Unionist colleagues. Splits arose in the Unionist Party, ultimately leading to Faulkner's resignation and a loosening of the traditional ties between the Ulster Unionists and the mainland Conservative Party.

On 16 May there was a total transport strike in Belfast, and the following day a Protestant bombing campaign in Dublin and elsewhere in the Republic killed twenty-eight people and injured over 100. On the 17th there was a total strike in Ulster and a state of emergency was declared by the authorities.

Until the 28th most services in the Province were not functioning, and on that day Faulkner and the other Unionists on the new power-sharing Executive resigned. On the 29th the British government replaced the Executive with direct ministerial rule and the Ulster Workers Council, having achieved its aims, called off the fifteen-day strike.]

Exciting day in the office. Saw very little of the PM, but spent the day on two memoranda:

1  Opposing proposals to raise top salaries. This would be disastrous politically – but the Civil Service strongly recommending it and Ted Short's Cabinet committee foolishly and weakly not resisting. Comes to Cabinet tomorrow.

2  Opposing a Healey-Crosland proposal to put the whole of Lever's proposals for a mortgages and National Housing Finance Scheme into a sort of Royal Commission of Inquiry which would take years to report. Means no action on mortgages – which we must have for the election. They are pushing it through quickly because Lever is in America.

The PM must act on these – signs that the government is becoming bureaucratised and losing its political touch.

Good lunch with Tony Lester[*] and Healey's political adviser Adrian Hamm – both reporting difficulties with civil servants.

Alarming rumours that Anthony Benn is being rebellious. Refused to show PM a speech he was going to make on workers' participation. When his permanent secretary pointed out he must show it because it 'anticipated government policy', he replied that it was precisely because it did so that he didn't want to show it.

Benn is playing his own game, building a platform to make a bid for the leadership.

Home 8.30.


## Thursday 16 May 1974

Triumph! Both memoranda effective. PM stopped the top salaries and the building societies proposals.

Unit meeting. Thrashed out problems.

Interview with a security man about one of my staff. 'Is he vulnerable to subversion? He has a beard.'

Parliamentary Questions in the afternoon. Just a knockabout.

Later to see Judith Hart and Ralf Dahrendorf,[*] and then to the LSE Hon. Fellows' dinner.

Drinks with Ken Berrill[*] from the Treasury – very cynical – 'no point in doing anything before an election. Then we shall have to change the policies.' I would like some tough action on economic policy now.


## Friday 17 May 1974

Still pleased to have had some success at Cabinet yesterday. Unit morale needed this. Basic problem is that HW is only sporadically interested in policy – and then mainly for its political implications, electoral or inner-party. This is why the Unit is quite big enough with only half a dozen members.

9.30 attended the weekly business meeting in the study. At the end Healey and Callaghan raised question of the 'Lever plan' for dealing with the oil crisis by recycling debt. Both against and critical of Lever for flying this kite. Obviously the civil servants in both departments have been complaining to precipitate attacks on Lever. Trying to make HW think less of him, to defuse his impact and influence on the PM. Callaghan had a file of FO briefs criticising Lever. Healey piled in with relish. I deliberately stayed behind to hear this, although the business meeting had ended. Short, Mellish and the diary secretary had left. Robert Armstrong and

John Hunt also stayed for it, so I assumed they knew it was coming. Afterwards we left the study together, but they slipped off into the state room for a private conversation.

Pat Moynihan,* the American Ambassador to India, dropped in for an hour to chat with me. A nice man, very humane, an old LSE student and friendly to England.

At 11.15 the PM sent for me and I was there with Joe and him till 1.15. No speech this week so we just discussed various political and personal matters. Robert Armstrong dropped in often. He is fighting to dominate the PM's ear. He is very good. But HW sometimes draws the line between what he calls the 'family' and the civil servants. But Robert's job and self-respect involve total access. They often nearly take over HW – he is very deferential towards civil servants. But he usually draws the line in the end. Simply says, 'I want Joe, Bernard and Albert to come to the study.'

We had a long talk about the election. HW is still afraid that June would produce 'a long yawn' and low turnout by our people. But he definitely said he doesn't want to risk going on through the winter. So he is firmly for a September/October election. Probably last week of September.

He said he was going to see Marcia tonight – and then added 'or tomorrow'. Said he hadn't seen her for three weeks.

She wrote me a friendly letter. Also a friendly letter to Albert. Joe said she had been phoning HW with policy suggestions. Joe says she has now failed in her attempt to intimidate and bully HW to come crawling to her. So 'she will now try to wheedle her way back in. Don't underestimate her. She means to get her influence back. But she has discovered she can only push HW so far. He has taught her a lesson!'

George Wigg phoned HW that morning. HW said he 'was a bit frosty to him'. Wigg is suggesting that Harold Davies,* the Labour MP, is behind the leaks attacking Marcia (perhaps because he used to be MP for Leek – as good a reason as any other in their eyes).

I also reported that the documents that the *Sunday Times* had about *thalidomide* showed the limits Distillers had gone to and that a minister had allegedly lied through his teeth to Parliament on this subject – briefed by civil servants themselves briefed by Distillers.

Lunch with Joe, Albert and two private secretaries. Discussed Heath and the last election. They said the Tories were convinced they had to have an election soon or could never win. Knew they could not defeat the miners – wanted an election before that. But Tory back-bench discontent was the major factor pushing Heath not to compromise.

In the afternoon I drafted letter to Heath on 'anonymous donors' to the Labour Party and also did a green memo on the economic situation. [My memos to the Prime Minister were, at his request, typed on distinctive green paper, so that he could find them quickly in his red box.]

Evening spent hour and a half with Tony Crosland, who has been very helpful to my man specialising in the housing field. He says land nationalisation will be late, because John Silkin is just not up to it. He spoke with great admiration of the Civil Service machine.

He is for a June election, but concedes nobody knows.

He was savage about the 'Jenkinsites'. Said he was 'very glad I have broken with that gang'.

[Crosland and Jenkins had been closely identified in the 1960s but now appeared to differ on some policy issues – including Crosland's support for high public expenditure and Jenkins's total commitment to Europe. Crosland also felt that such supporters of Jenkins as William Rodgers and Shirley Williams were too 'right wing' and semi-detached from the mainstream of the Labour Party. The views expressed here may have been more savage than Crosland's normal position.]

HW had left for the country at 3.30 p.m. Beautiful day – and glorious weekend. I slept, read, drank a lot of beer and played a marvellous game of football on Sunday morning.

## Monday 20 May 1974

Spent the morning working at my desk on exceptional flow of papers. The PM summoned Joe and me before lunch and told us he was considering giving Marcia a life peerage. He had seen her over the weekend. Obviously she had pressed him because he said he 'could not see any reason for saying no'.

Joe raised a long list of strong objections. HW listened and then said, 'Yes, the press will give me a hard ride for a while, but I don't mind that.' He went on to say this was a good time to do it since it was just before the holiday and when a lot of other news was emerging which would swamp it. Then two weeks' parliamentary recess. 'Two weeks is a very long time in politics,' he said with a smile.

Joe continued to press, at least for delay till after the election. I said she would now be a public figure and could not be protected by any privacy Bill. But I did not press support for Joe as hard as he had wanted – mainly because I was astounded and could not work out what I thought. I never dreamed this would happen.

HW had a meeting so we left, but then we went up to the study again at 1–1.45 discussing it and other matters. Including his plan to reopen the Lambton affair.

After tea I went back up to see him and raised the matter again, suggesting delay. But he was very firm on it now – though adding, 'Maybe she won't accept it anyway.' Mainly he felt the timing immediately before the Bank Holiday would help it to slip through.

Later discussed Ireland, where a state of emergency was declared yesterday in reaction to the Ulster Protestants' strike against the proposed setting up of the Council of All Ireland. Tonight there is a 'mini-motorman' (security exercise). After that what? Agreed we needed a small contingencies committee on Northern Ireland – to consider 'the unmentionable' – British withdrawal from Northern Ireland. He said that what was not tolerable was British troops being shot by both sides. But we also discussed drawing new boundaries between the north and the Republic. We also saw it as 'the crunch'. He said law and order had gone. Ted Heath's political solution of the Sunningdale conference was about to collapse – if that went there was nothing but 'the unmentionable'. He suggested he was in favour of 'a sort of Dominion status'. The committee had to be 'cool, strong, with vision and without leaks to the press'. Meant must be small – HW, Jim Callaghan and the Lord Chancellor. Said he would put in Roy 'but for leaks from John Harris'.

Long talk. In the study in the evening sun, looking over St James's Park. Drinks – Robert Armstrong, Joe, Albert HW and me. A good talk – and a feeling we were on a precipice.

HW said the Irish were very worried and had been co-operating well on the border.

General feeling that Merlyn Rees is doing a good and honest job as Northern Ireland Secretary, but not quite big enough for it. HW is obviously hankering after a big move under himself. He said, 'We must not get into a Vietnam.'

I did not leave till 9.30. Still lots of papers to look at. But not tired. Feel very good and on top.


*Tuesday 21 May 1974*

Humdrum day. Morning spent on papers and one and a half hours with the PM – discussing Ireland mainly. Robert Armstrong sat in the study with us most of the time and inhibited the discussion of politics.

Lunch with private office.

PM went for PQs at the House. He was looking different, less well, perhaps from drink – but also how he used to look when Marcia had been at him. 'Got at', as Joe said. To me it was sour, guilty and shifty. The first time I had seen that look in weeks. And he was not so good at questions – one about me from the Scottish Labour back-bencher Willie Hamilton,* which he fumbled.

Later I had a succession of visitors. But Robert Armstrong told me that the Chief Whip, Mellish, had warned him there would be 'consternation' in the PLP over Marcia's elevation. She wrote me a very happy letter. She is sitting at home waiting for her peerage. The peerage has brought her happiness and HW has bought himself a little peace by giving it to her.

### Wednesday 22 May 1974

In the morning HW had the Public Enterprise committee. He has taken the chair from Ted Short in order to keep a rein on Tony Benn. On forming a workers' co-operative at the motorcycle manufacturer Norton Villiers he had to instruct Benn to draw up a proper paper and consult his colleagues – but '*not* to come back with a referendum of the shop stewards'.

On Harland & Wolff shipyard at Belfast HW insisted on no decision on further subsidy (£70 million in past four years) until the strikes of Protestant workers ended.

Then to HW's study where we discussed Ireland and also spent an hour choosing the members of the Royal Commission on the Press.

Lunch with Harry Kissin at Guinness Peat. Commodity men. Harold Lever was the main guest and he spoke very well.

Back to the Unit, preparing a paper by Richard Graham on Concorde. Tony Benn has put in an incredibly populist paper for building the 16 Concordes. Full of patriotic guff.

But I waited especially for the expected paper on top people's salaries (including senior civil servants). For tomorrow's Cabinet. At 7.30 p.m. it had still not arrived. Yesterday the Cabinet Office circulated a paper instructing that all papers for Cabinet items must always be circulated 36 hours beforehand – but civil servants' salaries are apparently an exception! They are trying to slip it through.

6 p.m. I held a party for my Unit. HW came and chatted.

Then we had dinner at No. 10 with the *Daily Mirror* people and Joe, myself and HW.

The PM was not in best form. Talked an enormous amount, very anecdotal. But they seemed to like it.

One vignette. Before dinner HW himself dictated the letter from Marcia accepting his offer of a peerage to her. Then he automatically took out his pen to sign it. The secretary stepped in and just stopped him in time.

Incidentally more scandals emerged today concerning Glamorgan local government and Labour connections to it.

### Thursday 23 May 1974

Arrived a little later than usual – 10 a.m. – just as the Defence committee was breaking up. There was a 15-minute break before the full Cabinet and

H. Lever came to my room with Joe to talk about the No. 10 press office, which is now going to take over handling Lever – from the Treasury press office – to emphasise that he is under No. 10 and not the Treasury.

Lever told us that Healey had accused him of being 'in cahoots with that man Donoughue'. I tried to get him to oppose the increase in top people's salaries. He had not read that Cabinet paper because it came so late.

During Cabinet I chatted with members of the Unit – no problems. We decided to focus on the Treasury and public expenditure next.

Saw Joe at midday and he was exploding with anger. The prospect of Marcia's peerage had now got him worked up. 'It's just greed,' he said.

Apparently she had crossed out the 'happily' from the acceptance letter HW had drafted for her – as if she were a reluctant acceptor instead of having pressed for it!

Joe said it was the same with her CBE. She asked for it, although Joe refused one, and then went around telling people how as a socialist she refused to go to the Palace to collect it. Then the next week she sent back dozens of her letters to the typists because they had forgotten to type 'CBE' after her name.

Joe was furious and bent on seeing HW again to try to delay it. He also said he would not handle the press side of the announcement. Marcia had sent in a message through Robert Armstrong explaining in detail how Joe was to handle the publicity. Joe simply replied, 'Balls.'

At 1.15 p.m. the Cabinet broke up, having spent most of the morning on Concorde – delaying a decision, with some people not as firmly against building them as previously. Benn apparently put his bad case rather well.

HW came out of the Cabinet Room and Joe asked if we could see him. We went up to the study. Robert came up as well but waited outside in case we needed him. Joe put his points firmly – for delay till after the election. If we were beaten, her peerage would be an appropriate farewell reward. If we won, we could do anything. But to do it now would revive the attacks. And as a member of the legislature in the Lords she could not claim privacy – Joe also said that we could not defend her now as before.

HW got very angry. He started attacking the press. Said this peerage was a reward for her loyalty when there was too much disloyalty around. It was his way of 'telling them to get stuffed'.

He also said that it was hard on Marcia, after 18 years together, that we had 'replaced' her. 'You three have taken me over, where it used to be only her.' That completely silenced me, since I felt guilty on that score. Not Joe, who kept pressing on. I added general support. Albert was silent and looked worried.

Finally HW said, 'Well, I've decided and that is that.'

Very uncomfortable. I went off to lunch with Lionel Robbins* at the Lords, arriving terribly late at 2 p.m. – and left him at 2.30 for Questions in the Commons.

At our briefing session in his Commons room in preparation for Questions HW was clearly edgy and wild, moving between moments of humour and frivolity and others of lowering ill temper. He had drunk three neat whiskies while we were with him before lunch. He had clearly drunk more at lunch, and now downed several large brandies. I was worried he would be dragged into some indiscretion at Questions, but fortunately the Tories went on and on about Chile, which he had covered on Tuesday, so although it was boring, he showed more of his recent sparkle and authority.

He went straight off to the Abbey for the installation of the new dean. (Generally he comes and sits in his room afterwards to discuss how Questions went.)

I went back to my room in Downing Street and worked on papers and then went down to see Joe and Albert in the press office. We were all feeling nervy. Unusually for me, I was drinking gin and tonic.

At 6.30 the PM returned from the Commons to find that an emergency meeting had been called to discuss Northern Ireland. The top military brass were there and the Defence minister. They were concerned with the total collapse of government in Northern Ireland and the need to re-establish authority – or get out. I saw HW when he came out of the Cabinet Room and he said to me, 'It is shit or bust. This will push Marcia off the headlines. We need 10,000 more troops.'

Albert and I were in Marcia's room when they all went back into the Cabinet Room. Appropriately we watched *Dad's Army* on her TV. I was still enjoying the gin and tonic and began to find the whole situation amusing. But my serious concern was whether conceivably HW had actually *provoked* the Irish thing to draw attention from Marcia – but later it was clear this was not so.

Incidentally Joe (who went home early, with no knowledge of the Irish crisis) told me that late in the afternoon HW had phoned him to ask if it was possible to delay the announcement of Marcia's peerage. He had apparently lost his nerve. Joe said no, too late. He had summoned a lobby to give them the news, and the *London Gazette* was already printed.

Joe was worried he had gone too far in opposing it. 'That has shortened my time here,' he said.

I doubt it. HW knew he was right, and will later respect him for it.

(Robert Armstrong suggested to us that perhaps Marcia should become a dame as a compromise.)

The meeting on the Northern Ireland crisis finally broke up after 9 p.m. HW took Albert and me into the lavatory and seemed very excited. 'This is big,' he said. But he thought that the generals were losing their nerve and he had tried to stiffen them.

He then went off to a private dinner with George Wigg – to threaten to expose him and his second family unless he laid off attacking Marcia. [Details of Lord Wigg's private life had come into Mr Wilson's possession, allegedly with the help of a private detective.]

What an incredible end to this day. Dinner between the British PM – after eight hours of whisky, Marcia and Ireland – and Wigg, who has been trying to destroy him by feeding the press with the material on the land deals.

As he left, HW said, 'I shall have to stick to water tonight.'

I went home to have supper with my old friend Denis Howell. We chatted till 11.30 p.m. He thought the Marcia peerage was silly but not too serious. He thought it would confirm the feeling in the PLP that 'she has something on him'. Denis is always sensible.

### Friday 24 May 1974

Did not go into No. 10. HW was at Chequers with the Irish political leaders.

Went to see Bill Rodgers at his home nearby, just back from New Zealand. He thought the Marcia thing was hilarious, but not too serious.

He was for a late September election still. Also thought his boss Roy Mason was simply not up to it as Secretary of State for Defence.

Most of the papers ran the Marcia story as their front-page lead – 'Lady Marcia' most of them said – with the usual reports of MPs being shocked. My feeling today was that it had not gone too badly. Most people seem not to take it very seriously.

But the interesting thing is how HW has been in worse form this week, looking tired, edgy, drinking more, and brandy not beer. He looks 10 years older. Is much less cheerful. Looks like he did at times in the February election, surly and lowering.

No PM since Churchill has had such a range between his best, which is superb, and his worst, which is tatty. It is worst when he feels under attack – and she secures that feeling by attacking him and planting the idea that others are attacking him. Then he shrinks intellectually and starts to hit out at imagined enemies, and especially the press.

### Friday to Tuesday 24–28 May 1974

Went for the bank holiday to the cottage in Suffolk. HW was deep in Ireland on Friday and Saturday – when he made a very poor broadcast, which I played no part in writing. Joe was away as well.

I telephoned Joe every day during the holiday. He was still furious over the Marcia peerage, especially since the press attacked him for having denied it beforehand. He did so because HW denied it to him – and now says he only meant to deny the rumours that Marcia would join the government. Joe feels professionally damaged. Also irritated with Marcia telling the press 'what a big surprise' it was – when she had demanded it!

Joe says if HW puts Marcia in the government he will resign immediately.

I am also worried that HW has lost his *feel* for Ireland. Not yet got it right. And he is still irritated with Joe for having opposed the peerage.

On Tuesday the Irish Executive resigned, HW returned from the Scillies and we came back from Suffolk, both earlier than planned because of Ireland. Sorry to leave the sun and glorious rich countryside. I read *The Odessa File*. Good, but not as good as the *Jackal*.

Also read Marcia's book *Inside Number 10*. Very good record. Curiously though it is least good on HW – no penetrating insights. And none of her characteristic poisonous attacks on people. Praises them all, including Wigg. Terry Lancaster must have ghosted the vitriol out of it.

### Wednesday 29 May 1974

Very satisfactory day. Dealing with Ireland. The handling of it over the weekend – by the civil servants in the Northern Ireland Office – was not good. HW's broadcast on Saturday, attacking 'spongers' in Ulster, was disastrous. It was the first statement by the PM in this government in which Joe and I have played no part.

I came in at 10.30, dealt with papers and then went down to the hall at 11 and met the PM as he came in. Went up to the study and Joe and Robert Armstrong came to join us later. I told him that he could not get Ireland right because nobody could, but he must get the English political end right. And I insisted that the 'unmentionable' must now happen. Harold agreed. He began to describe the scenario, with 'something like Dominion status' for the north of Ireland. Also take up Joe's idea to separate the constitutional, financial and military aspects of disengagement and have a separate timetable of withdrawal for each of them – in that order.

Merlyn Rees, the Northern Ireland Secretary, came in at noon and told us that the Protestant workers' strike was over. The Protestants have won. They have succeeded in destroying the experiment with Catholic participation in the power-sharing Executive. His position is that he is *pleased* the new power-sharing Executive established after Sunningdale has resigned, because it frees his hands to take direct action. And he thinks the Protestants have become very fascistic.

Drinks in the study and then lunch – HW, Joe, Robert Armstrong and me. Robert is fighting vigorously to keep his place in the entourage, joining in all our meetings.

At lunch we had a long discussion. Robert Armstrong is clearly worried by our consideration of withdrawal from Ulster. He suggests that we should abolish the Council of Ireland proposal and hope to get back to the general principle of power-sharing between Protestants and Catholics. I said that if we capitulate to the Prots they will use that blackmail weapon again and again to make sure there is no effective sharing of power. HW is basically on my side. Robert is clearly worried and later I see him in animated conversation with John Hunt. The machine is preparing a counter-offensive. It does not want any moves towards British withdrawal from Ulster.

[A month earlier during a meeting in the Cabinet Room Robert Armstrong wrote and passed to me a note reflecting on our earlier discussion of the Northern Ireland problem.

Note from Robert Armstrong to BD in the meeting with CBI 29/4:

> The stumbling block on Ireland is anything which smells of unification;
> The Council of Ireland smells of unification, *whatever* safeguards and stops we build in;
> The Council of Ireland is a concession put in basically for the sake of the Southern Irish government;
> The Irish government must now realise that they have pushed this too far and that the Protestant backlash exists *and is decisive*;
> . . . we should use this situation to save power-sharing in Northern Ireland, dropping the Council of Ireland part of Sunningdale but possibly agreeing to ad hoc cross-border co-operation on matters of common concern.

In my reply I wrote: 'PM referred to his meeting with Brian Faulkner on 1 April 74. Faulkner said he was going to try to water down Sunningdale anyway to a less meaningful Council of Ireland. So the retreat from Council of Ireland began before this strike.']

In the evening HW went off to give a TV broadcast – and then to dinner with Lady Marcia, who is apparently delighted with her title. I phoned Kay Carmichael in Glasgow. She had heard the whole story of the peerage, of the telephone conversations between Marcia and HW. Must be a very close leak to somebody.

Joe is furious still. He says again that if she gets a post in the government he will resign immediately.

Off to a Weidenfeld party in the evening.

*Friday 31 May 1974*

Went in at lunchtime. Lunch with the private office and Albert. Still status problems about who sits at the head of the table. I do – but Robert obviously feels uncomfortable in front of his juniors when I take over.

Maurice Finer came in to see me at 4 p.m. and we agreed a good list of names for his Royal Commission on the Press. Cut out all the MPs and one or two other lightweight names. Included Basil Yamey* – my suggestion – and Oliver McGregor,* who is a friend of Maurice.

I left Maurice in my room with Robert Armstrong and went upstairs for a long chat with HW, who had just come in. He seemed slightly subdued and less cheerful than usual. Don't know why. We discussed the Royal Commission – and also my idea for sending my old friend Michael Cudlipp to N. Ireland as Rees's press officer to improve his image. HW says he has approved this appointment, but must clear it personally with Rees first.

Then I took Finer and Robert up to chat to the PM – whom Finer had not met. They discussed names for the Press Commission – down to a dozen and it seemed to go well.

Then I dashed home to look after the children while Carol is still taking her exam.

Talked to Albert on the phone later that evening. He said that Robert Armstrong had come in to the PM's study later and got back on to Ireland, trying to push HW against British withdrawal.

Bill Rodgers came round to see us at home and we drank a bottle of wine together. He looks very well. But is obviously not stretched as a junior minister at Defence. Really he would like to go to N. Ireland. I put his name forward to Joe for this job earlier in the week, but the hostility to him in Downing Street is still too great. Bill would do it very well.

He made one point – that the government, and HW in particular, gives no impression of energetic radicalism. It is relaxed, competent – but not hungry to get things moving. This is absolutely right, especially where HW is concerned. Late in the election campaign he coined the slogan 'Life will be quieter under Labour', and that is really how it is.

But for how long? I smell a massive financial and economic crisis. Nobody in the government seems aware or concerned.

I put this to HW on Friday afternoon in the study. He doesn't believe it. I'm more pessimistic. A series of property, banking and financial crashes, accompanied by a world recession, could produce a dreadful situation here.

## Monday 3 June 1974

PM at the Parliamentary Labour Party discussing Ireland in the morning.
    I saw Robert Armstrong, who is very pessimistic about the economy.
    And Joe, who is still being attacked for denying Marcia would get a peerage (and join the government!). Very depressed and angry. Thinking of resigning. Wants gesture of support from HW.
    Before lunch I had an hour with PM discussing:
    – Joe and the press. PM said he intended to attack the lobby and cease providing them with any facilities.
    – Chapman Pincher's proposed attack on Marcia as a security risk. Martin Gilbert* is doing the counter-attack. PM has also seen Lord Goodman about it.
    – Ireland. We discussed my – Bill Rodgers's – suggestion of Jimmy Hoy* as a junior minister at the Northern Ireland Office, and HW liked it very much.
    Lunch with Joe and Albert.
    Afterwards I worked on HW's speech for Tuesday in the Ireland debate. [Both Houses of Parliament had been recalled from recess to discuss the situation in Northern Ireland.]
    And studied the PM's *very* secret memo on a scenario for withdrawal from Ireland and giving Ulster Dominion status, which I had originally suggested to him. It was personal to Robert Armstrong, with copies only to Hunt, Joe and myself.
    Evening to dinner at Buckingham Palace. I sat next to Prince Philip. Others there included Harold Lever and Lord Cromer.* All very pessimistic. Afterwards went for drinks with my old friend Lord Porchester – who told me there was a rumour I was living with Marcia. Perish the thought.

## Tuesday 4 June 1974

Spent the morning working on HW's Ireland speech. The civil servants made a massive attack to force him to leave out a sentence saying N. Ireland could 'go it alone'. Joe and I resisted – lost the words but kept the idea fairly clearly.
    There were nine people in the PM's study. The private office is trying to colonise the study, which was our last bastion.
    His speech went down quietly and quite well.
    Evening saw Kissin. He said HW had made him a firm promise to him to get rid of Marcia.
    In the evening I sat at the window of the white boudoir watching the

rehearsal of the Beating of the Retreat. Beautiful soldiers and horses on a glorious evening.

At least it is a day when Irish policy has been pushed a little nearer to sanity.

## Wednesday 5 June 1974

Morning mainly working on HW's speech for the NUGMW conference at Blackpool.

PM in excellent form. Still praising the Unit's 'Little Things Mean a Lot' paper. Said he wants to send out prime ministerial minutes supporting it.

He is angry with Transport House for the string of policy statements they are producing. Also with the Foreign Office for its continuous pro-Arab line.

Also discussed new junior ministers for N. Ireland.

Lunch at Grieveson Grant in the City – very worried about the financial position of the country.

Back to papers. And Victor Rothschild dropped in – very friendly and keen to get PM thinking about inflation. He feels strongly there may be a crisis soon.

Then Carol's Uncle Louis came in fresh from New York, with the same fears.

Joe is still very down. Robert Armstrong has appointed a man Joe sacked from the press office as secretary to the Press Commission. Joe sees this as a deliberate snub to him and part of the wider Civil Service campaign to cut us down to size. He asks me to fight it because he 'dare not lose' on this one. I shall do it, in my own way and time.

PM made a broadcast, attacking the Russians over their attitude to the Panovs, the ballet dancers. Tom Bridges and the FO very upset, because of relations with USSR. I told Bridges this was the PM's natural reaction to the FO's pro-Arab line. He always moves instinctively to protect friends under attack.

## Thursday 6 June 1974

Morning – went to the Department of the Environment for a special meeting of permanent secretaries to discuss land nationalisation. Very depressing. The DoE permanent secretary described it as 'municipalisation of land, a terrifying prospect'.

They produced some very practical objections which will have to be dealt with if the scheme is to work. But it was easy to see how ideas get squashed. Calling this meeting was a deliberate tactic to rally opposition.

I was very firm and told them the PM expected them to get on with the job.

Lunch with Joe – who is still very depressed – and Robert Armstrong, who is still pressing to be included in everything. Also discussed Marcia – she has been attacking Albert and me viciously. Yesterday morning she fainted and had the doctor. By lunchtime she was out lunching with Terry Lancaster, who says she is 'euphoric' about her peerage.

Afternoon with papers. Carol comes in at 5.30 p.m. for Beating the Retreat. HW has been to Blackpool for the NUGMW conference. Left at 12.45 – back 6 p.m.

### Friday 7 June 1974

Fairly relaxed morning. Dealing with papers – which are beginning to flow again after the holiday. Including two superbly pungent ones from Rothschild on 1) North Sea oil and 2) nuclear reactors. I think he is an excellent thing and must be kept on if possible. His memoranda always stand out a mile – authoritative, no nonsense, no fudge, no punches pulled.

Phone Basil Yamey, who is almost certainly going to serve on the Press Commission and pleased I put him on.

Joe still concerned about the battle with Robert Armstrong about the secretary for the commission. The PM has deliberately intervened to veto Robert's choice – because he came from the No. 10 press office (under Heath – Joe got rid of him). The PM told me he was angry with the civil servants for 'trying to pull a fast one'.

It was typical of the PM. Joe had a bad week with attacks on him in the press. So HW moved in to give him victory on this. He always does this with all of us, stepping in to give a boost when we are a bit down.

Had lunch with the secretaries and Joe and Albert. Planning how to implement the 'Little Things' programme.

Afterwards HW asked Joe and me to join him in the study to discuss the Swansea speech for Sunday. He was in bubbling form, handing out cigars and drinks. We quickly went through the speech. HW inserted a piece on the Common Market, suggesting this was what the next election was to be about.

He left at 4.30 p.m. and we were all preparing to go. Then things started happening. John Hunt dropped in for a drink and stayed over an hour. He was quite excited that the Irish Price sisters had ended their prison hunger strike. [Marion and Dolours Price, convicted for IRA bombings in London, had been on hunger strike to try to secure their transfer from Brixton to an Ulster prison. Roy Jenkins as Home Secretary handled this with great skill.]

And the Russians had relented and agreed to let the Panovs emigrate – HW had refused to attend the opening night of the Bolshoi unless they did this.

Also the draft of the Crossman Diaries had come in – volume I is to be published in November. Hunt says it is appalling. Terrible attacks on all the Labour leaders, especially Callaghan, Castle, Soskice* and HW and named civil servants. Hunt said it would bring the whole system into disrepute and would certainly be disastrous for this government to have its members denigrated in this way. (He says B. Castle is described as 'a boring old bag'.) It would be terrible if newspaper extracts appeared before or during an election campaign. Hunt says they will threaten the Official Secrets Act but with no hope or intention of using it. We agreed that I may have to talk to Graham Greene* of the publishers Jonathan Cape privately.

We also discussed economic strategy and incomes policy, which is just not being properly grappled with. It is not properly in the government machine at all. Just in separate committees of the Treasury and Employment. Nothing has come before ministers. Also the Treasury computer has broken down, so their forecasts are late. We agreed to put it all to the ministerial committee on Economic Strategy over the next two weeks – it has not met for the past two months! Economic policy is simply operating privately in the minds of Healey and Foot. It must be brought out and made coherent, and the PM must take grip of it. My excellent economic adviser Andrew Graham, the economics fellow from Balliol College, Oxford, is very pessimistic, believing that the whole thing will fall apart at the seams in the autumn. He says the Treasury is simply waiting, cynically and fatalistically, for that to happen, so they can move in and impose a massive freeze. They see the whole attempt to get a social contract as a political charade. This fits in with what Ken Berrill of the Treasury said to me.

Hunt says he thinks Len Murray is being very helpful, but is surprised that Foot is not pushing him harder.

Lever put in a devastating memo late in the evening, warning the PM of a total collapse in financial and industrial confidence unless we reassure people more. He suggested moderating the wealth tax and other tax proposals.

Meanwhile Anthony Wedgwood Benn's machine is roaring on, with proposals for government intervention in industry on an incredible scale. It will emerge soon as a Green Paper. Totally unrelated to the real world of industry. But a suitable populist platform for him.

Albert has been in touch with Marcia – she is still complaining about not being invited to Beating the Retreat, Trooping the Colour, etc. She is also attacking Albert and me in savage terms to Terry Lancaster.

Geoffrey Goodman of the *Daily Mirror* told the PM that Roy Jenkins had gone to a meeting of the Oxford University Labour Club and been very critical of him, accusing him of lack of leadership. Joe was furious and told me, partly blaming me for it. HW was much more tolerant, as he usually is of Roy, simply saying that Roy was 'going through a difficult time since the death of his mother'.

Also learned that Crosland at DoE was still trying to scupper Lever's mortgages scheme, to keep it all in DoE under an outside committee (which would take two years to report), and trying to put off any scheme for a Housing Finance Corporation. I phoned Lever later that evening and warned him to get a grip of it – he did not have a representative at the meeting because he and his tiny team were at a Treasury meeting.

I phoned Michael Cudlipp in Brighton to tell him we had finally arranged for him to go to see Merlyn Rees about becoming the press man working with Rees in Northern Ireland. The PR there has been very bad so far. Cudlipp was fairly cool at first, but he phoned me back on Saturday sounding much keener after thinking about it, and he will see Rees on Sunday. But it is clear that Frank Cooper,* the top civil servant at the Northern Ireland Office, is against it because Cudlipp is an 'outsider'. He would prefer an ordinary information officer from within the service. It is incredible. They are always looking after their own, regardless of the real needs. I spoke to the private secretary at the N. Ireland Office on Saturday and think I convinced him at least not to oppose it. Hope Cudlipp does not let me down, since I have gone out on a limb, and taken the PM with me, on this.

There was a final crisis at the weekend. The *News of the World* had a front-page story about a 'security scandal at No. 10'. It was about the Marjorie Halls law case and referred to Marcia having the children in 1968–70, implying this made her a security risk and that HW forced Michael Halls to cover it up.

The PM spent Sunday preparing a statement of denial. Joe was against this, saying it would simply draw attention to it. The PM ignored him, but finally agreed not to put out a statement when Marcia herself complained.

But clearly there is more trouble ahead on that front.

# CHAPTER 5

## Enter Left: Tony Benn and Industry Policy
## June–August 1974

*Monday 10 June 1974*

Quiet morning in the office. Lunch with the private secretaries and David Piachaud from the Unit discussing progressing our 'Little Things' paper.

Afterwards the PM sat for an hour with Joe and me in the study. He had just returned from a Trinity House lunch, in morning dress. Obviously lunched well.

He was back on the *News of the World* article and was arguing he should report them to the Press Council. Joe argued against (Joe is getting worried about always being against him on these matters). The PM said if the Press Council could allow unsubstantiated reports against a PM, without checking with No. 10, 'that should finish the Press Council'. Joe continued to argue against and in the end HW agreed to defer it till he had discussed it with Goodman tonight.

It was clear that Marcia – who the PM saw twice on Sunday – had been at him. She had attacked him on this. And on the Trooping the Colour ceremony – he sent for the secretary and asked to see the seating plan on his stand. That is what she had been complaining about. He also said to Albert that he should keep a check on the number of letters going through the political office – which again she has been saying to Albert. HW has obviously been under pressure.

He also sharply criticised Robert Armstrong for trying to spring his friend into the Press Commission as secretary. 'His first black mark,' he said. And then said, 'He will have to go in October even if we don't have an election.'

I saw the Foreign Office brief for the PM's meeting with the Saudi Arabian Ambassador. Violently anti-Israel. HW had scribbled furiously on it rejecting many of the points. The FO never seem to learn. Just because they hate Jews doesn't mean they can persuade the PM.

I was given the typescript of Crossman's diary to read, at HW's suggestion. Very thick.

I had a nice long letter from Prince Philip following our conversation at dinner at Buckingham Palace setting out his position on Ireland – with some good suggestions on getting the two sides together.

Wedgy Benn circulated another paper on saving another bankrupt and hopeless firm. Just a few more millions. He had seen the shop stewards who had convinced him.

Home 9 p.m.

### Tuesday 11 and Wednesday 12 June 1974

Dominated by Tony Benn. Questions on Tuesday were about him. All reports from departments and committees are that he is completely in orbit, issuing statements, announcing he is consulting the shop stewards on every conceivable subject. An increasing number of people say he is bonkers. Ministers at yesterday's Public Enterprise committee have been phoning in to say so. Monty Finniston,* chairman of the British Steel Corporation, said so today – when a small fire had occurred at a BSC works, causing £207 worth of damage, and Benn stepped in to close the works and announced he would not open it until there had been full consultation with all workers and all residents.

Yesterday evening at 5.30 HW sent for Joe and me and said he was taking over the handling of all Benn's industrial policies. Otherwise there will be a total collapse of confidence and no investment. He sent Joe to give the story to the *Financial Times* – whose man gives all stories to the *Guardian* as well.

HW said that Benn is 'completely mad'.

Today the papers carried the story. HW was pleased – especially after an excellent Energy committee on nuclear reactors.

The rest of the day I spent on papers – and on the Crossman Diary, which is full of criticism of his colleagues and especially of the Civil Service. The Cabinet Office is preparing to intervene and suppress.

Marcia has been creating all kinds of fuss over the Trooping the Colour, trying to get Albert and me off the stand. Insisting on her own nominees having seats. And for Beating the Retreat sending instructions to private office that their guests must *not* be given any drinks. It is pathetic.

### Thursday 13 June 1974

HW grabbed me at 9.30 before the Cabinet and discussed the Benn problem. He intended to lecture the Cabinet – praising them after these first 100 days but also saying that Bennery was the only thing going wrong. A question of presentation rather than policy. He asked me to go and check

Benn's statements against published party policy. I did, and took him a note into Cabinet. The basic point is that Benn is carrying out the long 'Labour's Programme 1973' and ignoring the milder manifesto.

HW also said to me for the first time that he thought it might be better to hold the election in the spring of 1975 'otherwise in the autumn they will think we are getting out from under our problems'.

I said no – I was afraid of a hard winter, with fuel prices, etc. He agreed he was afraid of a hard winter.

But he is clearly worried by the boost to Tory morale given by Benn.

Ironically Benn did not attend Cabinet so HW was deprived of the chance to reprimand him. I took him some material in at the start of Cabinet, but he was not able to use it.

Lunch in the kitchen with Joe and Albert and the private office boys. Afternoon questions – HW squashed George Gardiner and was very pleased with himself.

Later he dictated his speech for tomorrow – meant to put his position on Benn, but ended up much too Heath-bashing. So next day's press thought it was actually defending Benn.

Home 9.30 p.m.

– Incidentally I saw Rothschild 6.15–8 p.m.. To discuss the economy. He still wants ministers to discuss it over dinner. I like him, but he is obviously dangerously wicked in conversation.

### Friday 14 June 1974

9.30 prayers meeting to consider next week's government business. HW discusses Benn with Mellish and Callaghan. All agree he must be clipped. Apparently last night Edmund Dell was going to give a speech with a slashing attack on Benn. HW vetoed it. Doesn't want an image of ministers squabbling. But is a sign of the trouble Benn is causing and the danger of a right-wing backlash. HW said he was sending for Benn on Monday to dress him down. He also said, 'I must face his resigning. I can face that, though.'

Then PM went to the funeral of the Duke of Gloucester at Windsor and afterwards to Liverpool. I worked in the office. Stayed till very late with Andrew Graham's memo on economic strategy and one by Richard Kirwan on nationalisation of land.

### Saturday 15 June 1974

Trooping the Colour. A beautiful day and we took the children in fairly early. They loved seeing the office and house they have heard me talk about.

Just before the start I saw Albert, who said that Marcia had persuaded the PM to stop Albert and me (and our wives) having drinks after the ceremony – when there were hundreds of guests including junior private office staff. Albert was sad and humiliated in front of his wife – this of course was the intention. This woman is trying to destroy Albert by public humiliation and to exercise her paranoia on me. It is so sad and depressing that HW participates in these pathetic and petty manoeuvres over such trivial matters. She exercises her power over trivia. She doesn't care whether the Labour government succeeds economically or fails. She cares only about the petty social snobberies, who sits and eats and drinks with whom – and whether she has a peerage.

Sex came up at lunch with Harold Lever, who told me that the PM had told him that Marcia had told him that I was sleeping with *the cook* – and taking her to parties. I have of course never seen her outside of No. 10 and inside only at table. It shows how barmy 'the mad Duchess' – as the private office calls her – is. For my sake I prefer this rumour about the cook to the earlier rumour that I was living with the Duchess herself.

I also talked to Lever about his press relations. He continues lovably uncontrollable and gives Joe a lot of trouble. He promised to do better.

Joe was furious when I phoned him on Sunday morning. He was sorry for Albert. He says that Marcia has damaged the self-respect of many men – citing Tommy Balogh and Walter Terry, reducing them to servile ciphers. She does it by finding their weakness – often ambition or sometimes sex – using it to control them, and then sweetens them by occasional goodies, including office or peerages. She is trying now to exploit Albert's need for a job and a seat. We must stand by him.

For me, I don't care a damn about her attacks and rumour-mongering or the regular letters she sends by Bill Housden to HW demanding that I am sacked. But I am saddened and humiliated to see a Labour Prime Minister reduced to conniving at all this. She drags him down, diverts his mind on to the paranoid trivia which obsess her.

The final question is what is the basis of this hold she has over him. Surely not just some sex relationship long ago, if there ever was one. So what? He needn't go through the humiliations we have seen just to keep that quiet. Who would care? Certainly not Mary, who has learned to live with all this by now and handles it with dignity.

Some think it is more serious, something involving money, and she is squeezing him the whole time. But I have no idea if there is any truth in it or what it might be.

I just don't know. It is possible that she simply has over HW the same hold she has over other men, and some women. She attacks them and then gives them sweeties. This is what they need. Maybe she has over the years reduced HW to this tragic and pathetic dependence. Lever thinks so – and that HW keeps soldiering on, knowing he will retire from politics one day, and perhaps can then break away from this dominance which he resents and yet needs.

One last item. She hates the cook – without having met her. Hence the attempt to spread rumours about her and me. She is also playing the old game of humiliation. She has persuaded the PM to move the cook out of her room into a miserably tiny one. The superficial excuse for this is very impressive. We must have PR advisers in at No. 10 helping to win the next election. So Peter Davis and Denis Lyons are being brought in – to the cook's room, on the PM's instructions. It is pathetic to see a Prime Minister of Britain forced to spend his time on this trivia when he hasn't found time to deal with the economic problems which are ruining us.

## *Monday 17 June 1974*

I went in determined to raise with HW the question of Marcia's malicious rumour-mongering about me. He came in from Chequers at 11 a.m. I ran into him near the Press Association tapes outside the private office. He said, 'Come up to the study.' I went up – Joe was still at the dentist – and he handed me a letter from Benn with a copy of a resolution he was putting to the NEC demanding a two-day conference on the EEC – completely overthrowing the delicate compromise HW had established. HW was livid. He began to prepare the ground. He telephoned Callaghan – at Dorneywood and just off to Ottawa. He arranged for Michael Foot to come in and for Jack Jones to come in to lunch. If these were detached from Benn, he was in the clear. He cancelled lots of other appointments and we discussed tactics. We decided to make it a question not of policy but of procedure. Benn was simply using the party machinery and the press to launch attacks on his colleagues. He either played the game or must go.

Then Roy Jenkins and Ted Short came to discuss the IRA bomb explosion at the House of Commons.

Afterwards we continued discussing Bennery till Arnold Goodman came to lunch.

At one point HW thought of cancelling tomorrow's trip to Germany to be here to deal with Benn. I said no – play it, like Macmillan, as a 'little local difficulty'. He agreed.

But he also revealed that Marcia was coming in to the office again from Thursday, as were Peter Davis and Denis Lyons (for whom she has arranged the promise of peerages). I saw immediately what this was. It was her own Mafia. Having failed to force HW to get rid of us, she was bringing in her own Mafia. Also putting them in the cook's room – as a way of humiliating her. Two birds with one stone.

We were depressed and humiliated that HW goes along with this nonsense. Albert is afraid he will lose his job. She will try to push him out. Joe is cold furious. He is very tough and will expose her in the end.

We had lunch with the private office and opened lines up to them. We are all going to be under attack and need some common ground. Despite all their public-school conservatism, we, even Joe and Albert, have more in common with them than with Lady M.

Another curious incident. Rothschild asked to come and see me. He wanted to borrow my excellent economic adviser Andrew Graham for three days to write the CPRS economic brief to the Cabinet. He has *three* economists in the CPRS but apparently doesn't think they are much good – I suspect he is trying to make them resign. He was a little surprised when I said I would clear it first with the PM. I talked to Andrew and we decided to sleep on it.

I still like Rothschild. Fertile and funny. But he looks sick to me.

### Tuesday 18 June 1974

Morning in the office.

PM Questions.

Then off to Germany. To Northolt – where HW held up the flight while he phoned Marcia from an open phone in the reception hall – apologising for not phoning before and saying he had 'tried three times since lunch'.

An Andover plane. We discussed tomorrow's Bonn talks with Chancellor Helmut Schmidt* and read briefs.

Landed 6.30 p.m. Armed reception, tanks and red carpet. Then fantastic helicopter ride from the airport to the Frankfurt football stadium for Scotland's World Cup game against Brazil. Clipping over the tree-tops on a glorious summer evening.

Marvellous game – 0–0, but Scotland very unlucky.

Afterwards celebrations, TV interviews and the racing cavalcade of Mercedes and motorbike outriders 100 miles up the autobahn to Bonn. Arrived at the residence at 1 a.m. – and had strawberries and wine with Ambassador Nico Henderson* and his delightful wife.

Stayed the night in the hotel which Hitler used to meet Chamberlain in 1938. Overlooking the Rhine, tugs waking us up early in the morning.

### Wednesday 19 June 1974

Woke early and breakfasted in my room. Then back to the residence. HW took Joe and me apart on the balcony and said he had just learned that Heath was to speak in Thursday's debate on industrial policy. Should he?

I said no – seems inadequate time to prepare. Better to get Healey to talk about the need for industry to invest more. He rejected this and decided to wind up. Wired London to prepare a draft and meet us with it at Gatwick.

Joe and I shopped in Bonn with Joe Stone,* HW's doctor. Interesting talk. [Stone was at this time suggesting a controversial solution to eliminate Lady Falkender's influence over the Prime Minister, but I was not sure how serious he was.] Also noted how clean and optimistic everything was, how smart and efficient the shop assistants are. This is the spin-off of a successful nation.

Went to the Chancellery for the end of the Wilson-Schmidt talks – which had obviously gone very well. Then press conference at the embassy, cavalcade of Mercedes to Cologne airport and flew home.

HW in very good spirits. The whole trip had done him good. He was very impressed with Schmidt and with how 'deep' the talks had gone. HW is now beginning to lift his eyes above our own backyard and think of the world stage again.

At Gatwick he went off to a NATSOPA conference at Brighton and we went to London – and home.

Apparently he came in at 7.30 p.m. with Albert and dictated the draft of tomorrow's speech. Then off to see Marcia.

## Thursday 20 June 1974

In the morning we went through the draft speech, which seemed quite funny, and also discussed what to do about Benn, who is still completely in orbit.

The PM had seen him for one and a half hours on Monday and ticked him off, but he takes no notice and continues to put down motions at the NEC effectively attacking his Cabinet colleagues and giving his policy papers to the press before the Cabinet sees them.

At Cabinet this morning HW gave a lecture on the need to stop this kind of behaviour if we are to win the election, but it does no good.

Marcia came in to lunch with HW and Ron Hayward, and Joe and I were demoted to eat in the pantry. Joe is by now burning with hatred for her, for dragging HW down.

HW was looking grey and tired. He was flat at Question Time. He wound up the debate at 6.30 to 7 p.m. and it went wrong from the start. The Tories were in better morale and shouted him down throughout. His voice was weak and his jokes missed. Everyone noticed that he was not talking about industrial policy at all, just knockabout at Heath. His own benches were silent. At the end we were soundly beaten by 21, with all the Opposition parties voting against.

[The vote was 311–290 against extending state control of industry and creating the National Enterprise Board. The previous day the government suffered its first defeat on a major issue, by 308–300, rejecting a clause of the Finance Bill on trade union benefits.]

I went back to No. 10 and worked. The Beating the Retreat ceremony was on, but I had declined to go. Marcia was there with all her rich friends.

Went to a nice dinner party at Philip French's* with Bill and Silvia Rodgers and Joe Rogaly.* Home at 1 a.m.

## Friday 21 June 1974

9.30 weekly business meeting. Very interesting. HW says the lost Commons vote makes no difference. We cannot hold an election in July because of Scottish holidays. But it is useful to have some defeats as 'filling up the cup'.

Then Callaghan and Healey raised the question of Benn. HW was inclined to say don't take him seriously, he is not well, not sleeping well, etc.

Callaghan disagreed and said Benn knew exactly what he was doing – a calculated campaign to get the leadership. He rebuked HW very firmly and said something would have to be done about it. Healey agreed – and I talked to him afterwards and firmed him up.

Later in the morning I went to see Benn at the Department of Industry, to arrange for my policy adviser to have access to his department. He said OK, but don't know what is going on, and his civil servants are Treasury spies anyway. He said to keep in touch with his special assistant, Frances Morrell, who attends all his top meetings. She is a very large woman.

Benn outlined his strategy – to win over the workers, then management, then the small businessmen – 'I will get us the Poujade vote,' he said.

[Pierre Poujade was a French politician who campaigned on a nationalist basis, appealing especially to the lower middle-class 'shopkeeper' electorate.]

He looked very grey and tired. His driver later told me that he was working till 3 a.m. every morning and then getting up early. But the gleam in his eye is clear and unwavering. He is certainly odd, but I don't think he will crack. Destiny is guiding him and so he doesn't need sleep.

But he was boorishly rude to his officials.

In the afternoon I worked on papers and then went home early to see Carol, who had come home from four days in France.

Evening to dinner with our neighbour Wally Fawkes – Trog the cartoonist, as well as a great jazz clarinettist – who is marvellous. Home at 1.30 a.m.

Some reflections. Marcia now has HW in her claws again and he is losing blood fast. He looks more tired and his political judgement is off.

His speech went badly. And he is *drinking* more – brandy from midday till late evening, when he is very slow and slurred. Yet during the three weeks when he was away from her he drank only beer, and drew our attention to it and how much better he felt.

Obviously she was once exciting to him. Like heroin – but now the kicks are painful.

What is her hold over him? Bill Housden, HW's driver, told me he had evidence that money was behind it. She controlled all the outside donations to the Labour Party – and all HW's finances. He said nobody else saw anything of it. Perhaps there was something there. Perhaps he received money he shouldn't and she held it over him – though it would be for party expenses and not for himself, since he is not personally interested in money. But I have no evidence of this and don't know what Housden's alleged evidence is.

Housden also said there was some story about a hotel in Liverpool as well in May? – St George's Day? – 1956. This had come up once, somebody had said they knew about it and this created great panic.

Incidentally she had attacked the PM for taking me to Frankfurt and Bonn, and apparently had said the press should expose it and had telephoned Terry Lancaster at the *Daily Mirror* to tell him to do so.

On the aeroplane HW asked Robert Armstrong to move the cook into a smaller room.

The main policies we are pressing now are land nationalisation, building society rates, North Sea oil nationalisation and Benn's industrial policies. A lot of big things coming up to Cabinet now.

But what is most striking is how little discussion there is of economic strategy. I have often raised this with HW. He says D. Healey is not ready. I fear that disaster will overtake us before the strategy is ready.

One last point – John Silkin came to see me. The press were after him about some land deals his family had done in South Wales. I advised him to tell everything, set it all out and give the *Sunday Times* the lot. Not to let it out bit by bit like Short, or issue writs like HW. He promised to do so. I then rang Harry Evans who agreed to delay the story a week on the understanding that Silkin would be co-operative.

## Monday 24 June 1974

Depressing day. In the morning in the office, reading papers and talking to the staff in the Unit.

Lunchtime we went off to lunch at Guinness Peat with top brass from the City. I sat between the chairmen of Barclays Bank and Commercial Union.

HW talked a lot, very mixed, some poor stuff against press, some good in explaining how Wedgy Benn is not the government.

Coming back in the car with Robert Armstrong and myself, HW suddenly said, 'Harry Kissin is going too far. He is attacking Marcia. Trying to save me from myself. Two of his friends have turned Queen's evidence.'

I did not say anything in response.

Back to the House of Commons where he made a statement on our having made a nuclear test – and got a roasting from our back-benchers.

At No. 10 we had a meeting on the building societies with the PM in the chair. Healey was very strong, overriding other people. Tony Crosland was clear and clever, but somehow lost his case. Peter Shore was badly briefed, completely misunderstanding the question of composite rate tax. Lever was good and put up some ingenious scheme for giving the building societies a bond as a guarantee if they ran down their reserves instead of raising their lending rates. The PM backed Lever and Healey was very co-operative to Lever. So they will try this clever scheme to try to avoid more subsidies.

We went upstairs to the study for a chat. Joe and I said we were afraid of the Liberals going into coalition with the Tories. HW said he was not afraid of this. The Tories would lose from it. I could not follow his argument.

Went down to discover that he had vetoed my going to Brussels for the NATO meeting. This is at Marcia's insistence. She had complained bitterly that I went to Frankfurt. I was furious – and hurt that he told the private office and not me. This damages my status with them. I don't mind about not going to boring Brussels. Carol will be delighted. But it is a depressing example of the influence that woman has over him on all trivial matters.

He later explained to Joe privately. He also said how much he wanted Joe, Marcia and me to work together in the next campaign. Joe said to him it was difficult because of how unpleasant she was to us and how much disliked she now is. HW also revealed that the source of the story against Kissin was Harold Lever.

I get more and more depressed and cynical about politicians. Who can be trusted to stand up, simple and firm?

I went home early, walking to Charing Cross with Joe to see him off on the train. He is such a warm and straight friend. Open in his criticisms of me, but I know I can rely on him.

Incidentally, Robert Armstrong really grows on me. He is much more relaxed now. He does his job superbly. Firm and formal when he needs to be. But friendly and helpful to me, often guiding me over difficult patches.

*Incidentally*, Joe told HW that he had never known such intense dislike for Marcia. HW said he knew a lot of people were trying to persuade him to separate from her – 'but I cannot face the consequences'. *Not* he didn't want to.

## Tuesday 25 June 1974

Decide not to go in this morning. I was a bit peeved at being crossed off from the Brussels trip – even though I didn't want to go. I preferred that I – or he – should decide I shouldn't go, not Lady Falkender.

I went shopping and to the bank, and to the LSE to clear up several outstanding matters: I returned at 1 p.m., hoping the party would have left. It hadn't – and the man at the door had a message from the PM telling me to go straight up to the study. I went and found everybody there while HW was dictating the core of his Sunday speech to the Socialist International. Then the party for the NATO meeting in Brussels set off. He left myself and Robin Butler from the private office in charge of getting a final draft ready.

Had lunch at No. 10 and then spent the afternoon working on papers and taking the rare opportunity to discuss policy questions with the members of my Unit.

No. 10 was delightfully quiet and relaxed. With the king away, everything ticked over more slowly. Like a racing car idling between races. The private office was half empty. I missed Joe. It seemed odd not to see him in the corridors or dropping in for a cup of tea.

I went across to the House for PM's Questions – taken by Ted Short as deputy leader and Lord President. What a difference! The briefing session was desultory and humourless. I couldn't hear what Ted said. He got into a flap when he couldn't find one answer. It looked very ominous and Albert and I were very worried about what would happen.

In fact it went well in the House. Ted was very good. His dry style put the Tories down very effectively. And he made one fortunate error. Talking about Wedgwood Benn's policies he said there would be a *white* instead of a *green* paper. There was no authority for this. There was panic afterwards and HW was contacted in Brussels. HW immediately said marvellous, don't put it right, this is exactly what we want. It leaves the policy decision to the government and stops Benn's 'great debate' intention in its tracks.

I gather Benn was very upset.

In the evening Carol and I went to dinner at the French embassy. The other guests were MPs and journalists. I sat, just by chance, at a table with David Steel* and his wife. He started to discuss the new Liberal tactic of coalition and obviously planting a warning. He prefers to ally with Labour but was trying to say that there could be a coalition without Labour. I have put this to HW, but he discounts it, saying that if you look at the seats, the Liberals cannot benefit unless some Tory MPs stand down – and the Tories won't have that.

Steel is a wise and decent man. I wish he was in our party.

I also talked to Bob Maclennan and some Scottish Labour MPs. They are very worried about the Scottish position. They think the Scottish Labour Party – and Willie Ross – are behaving suicidally and giving the Scot Nats seats on a plate.

## Wednesday 26 June 1974

A very relaxed day. The PM didn't return till 7.15 p.m. so I took the chance to catch up on paperwork and did some revision of the PM's speech on oil and international money for Sunday.

John Silkin came in to see me. He has given all the material on his 'Welsh land scandal' to *Sunday Times* and that seems to be going OK.

## Thursday 27 June 1974

In the study with PM first thing discussing his coming speech and also hearing about Brussels. He had asked Chirac* what the French response would be if we proposed cancellation of Concorde and Chirac said 'négatif'.

Then had a meeting of the Policy Unit while the Cabinet was meeting. Unit discussed public expenditure – the outlook there very bleak.

I saw Reg Prentice, the Education minister, after Cabinet and talked to him about the school building programme. Terrible cuts – and grants going mainly to rich Tory areas. He agreed to send the PM a minute to try to get help. Politically it will be bad. The expenditure in inner London is only 49p per student – compared to a national average of £15, and of over £30 in places like Barnet. He told me of scandalous behaviour by his senior civil servants. The department had been allocated a little more money to spend and the senior officials had promised it to the chairman of the UGC for the universities without consulting him or any other ministers. In fact this money could have been invaluable for further education and for schools. Gerry Fowler, who is sound on these questions, had exploded and threatened to resign. Prentice realises that this was a deliberate move to commit him, but he is obviously afraid of upsetting his officials.

In the afternoon I attended the Cabinet Energy committee to discuss Varley's White Paper on North Sea oil. Amiable meeting. Much concern at the leaks from the department to the press.

In the evening I saw John Silkin, who was very happy with his meeting with the *Sunday Times*.

And to a literary party in Vincent Square with Carol and my close friend Graham Greene. GG is very worried about the Crossman Diaries – he is both an executor *and* the publisher with a financial interest in publishing.

But the government is putting heavy pressure on him. John Hunt had a meeting with Graham and threatened him with the Official Secrets Act. 'Harold may put me in the Tower,' he said with a typical chuckle. Graham says he is more worried about the damage the diaries will do to Labour's election chances. I lied to him by saying that HW was not taking much interest in the question and that it was 'all the Civil Service'. I don't want newspaper stories saying that HW is paranoid and imposing massive censorship.

## Friday 28 June 1974

A quite tremendous day. I feel physically and mentally on top of the world and my job, and so much is happening on all fronts.

I drove in and parked in Horse Guards Parade and was in No. 10 shortly after 9 a.m. I distributed the overnight papers, read my mail and then went upstairs to the 9.30 meeting in the PM's study to discuss next week's business. This went through quickly. Then PM, Callaghan and Healey began discussing Benn. Callaghan insisted that the PM must 'put him down'. Healey said that was precisely what he was going to do at this morning's Cabinet committee.

I talked to Callaghan outside the Cabinet Room and pressed him to intervene, because he did speak for a broad section of the party. He promised to do so – he also said it would be risky to sack Benn, but best to push him so that he resigned on a policy/procedural question. So we must get this nationalisation issue out of his hands and into a wider interdepartmental committee.

I sat in on this Cabinet committee – which is now called Industrial Development and replaces the old Public Enterprise committee which had Short in the chair. The membership has also been strengthened and now contains all the big guns except Roy.

Benn opened with a defence of his paper on industrial policy and a reply to some of the criticisms he had already received. He also made the extraordinary statement that what injured confidence in industry was not the uncertainty which he was creating but the certainty of Healey's Budget, Crosland's rent freeze and Shirley Williams's price code. Since all were present, this hardly lined up the committee behind him.

Healey spoke first and was very rough. He took Benn apart and described the paper as full of irresponsible rhetoric.

Callaghan followed and was even more savage. He said he would not have it and they had better understand it was either the paper or him.

Crosland made some brief and very sharp observations.

Shirley Williams's attack was the most closely argued and fully backed with evidence. It was a textual critique. She concluded with a very strong statement about the crisis she saw facing the country and that this paper could push us over the edge.

Lever supported this.

Benn sat there looking very pale, first rocking back and forwards in his chair and later scribbling furiously, no doubt for his diary.

There were some minor contributions before Benn replied. Quite skilfully he argued that what he was proposing was in the manifesto and was about issues which had been fought in the party for 20 years and he implied that his view had won. At times he seemed to threaten the others with the revenge of the party, the unions and 'the people'.

HW summed up, saying that another draft would have to be done and it would be considered in a mixed committee of ministers and officials.

Afterwards Robert Armstrong said that he had never in his whole career seen a minister so mauled by his colleagues. Yet Benn seemed unabashed. I mentioned this to Healey in the lavatory afterwards. He said, 'Yes, it's like cutting moonbeams.'

In the afternoon I talked often to John Silkin. A fresh crisis. The *Daily Express* had picked up the rumours of his property deals and wanted to print them before the *Sunday Times* printed the facts on Sunday – which would, as the *Express* knew, kill the story. Newspapers are not interested in facts. We decided to do nothing, but wait.

Crisis in the afternoon. Marcia had over the telephone been rudely bullying one of the juniors in the private office and he had put the phone down on her. She had immediately sent in a complaining letter by hand to the PM, and the official was frightened. I went to see him and Robert and said, 'Don't be afraid, stand firm and we will stand by you.' Joe later went and said the same. This alliance with the private office, which I have been trying to build up, is very useful.

In the evening we went to the study and spent three hours with the PM finishing the speech. It went slower and slower, and we drank more and more, and ended generally in very good condition.

It is a reasonably good speech now.

## Saturday 29 June 1974

Harold Evans dropped in home at breakfast to say they might not use the Silkin story at all, because there was little in it. He also revealed that they knew a lot about Marcia.

The day was spent on the phone to Silkin and the PM. The *Express* had run the story and the BBC had broadcast very biased versions of it. So we protested and issued a statement – including a trailer for the *Sunday Times* story.

## Sunday 30 June 1974

Pulled a ligament playing football. Tragic.
So spent the rest of the day watching the World Cup on TV.

## Monday 1 July 1974

Average day.
Main point the evening when Carol and I went to the American Ambassador's for dinner. Beautiful evening. Lovely house overlooking Regent's Park.

Present – the Levers, the PM, Senator Javits and very attractive Mrs Javits from New York, Senator Hugh Scott and wife, etc. I sat next to Mrs Heinz (soups), who was delightful. The food and drink were terrific.

The PM and Lever left in the middle to go and vote. PM returned and sat for an hour with Lauren Bacall, the actress widow of Humphrey Bogart, who clearly took his attention.

Home at 1 a.m. Very rare for the PM to go out to a function. He should do it more often – though curiously he kept making snide references about Harold Lever always going out to dinner, as if guilty at being there enjoying himself.

## Tuesday 2 July 1974

As I arrived in Downing Street, Bill Housden was driving away from the door in the PM's car. He pulled up and talked bitterly of Marcia's attacks on him. She had called him a liar, accused him of being friendly with Albert and me – clearly a criminal offence – and of conspiring with Albert to prevent her attending the Socialist International at Chequers last weekend. She had ordered him not to come into her house, but to leave her letters (which he took round to her house every day) on the doorstep.

Bill, who gives me the latest information nearly every day, had complained to the PM, who had said, 'It was best not to have anything to do with her.' The PM apparently has not communicated with her for a week. Bill said he had nearly had enough and dare not tell his wife, who would make him leave – 'and then it would be in the newspapers within 48 hours'.

Went in to work on papers. PM was at the party liaison committee – where Ron Hayward apparently complained about the proposal to bring Peter Davis and Denis Lyons into No. 10.

Attended Cabinet committee on building society finance at 10.30 a.m. Lever's scheme for an asset bond not going to work, but PM still backs him and Healey very patient.

Rest of the morning in the Unit. Nice lunch with Joe, Albert and Nick Stuart from private office.

Question Time went very smoothly.

PM returned around 6 p.m. and Joe, Albert and I went up to the study till 7.30 p.m. Discussed election plans for the autumn. Also John Silkin – PM still thinks he may put him to Industry if Benn can be persuaded to resign. (Another savage minute from the PM to Benn tonight about Benn's activities on the NEC.)

HW had clearly been drinking a lot. He was heavy and slow. He had nothing to do this evening and asked for all of his boxes to catch up on the reading he didn't do over the weekend.

I had put in a minute on the need to spend more on schools in the inner-city areas – which get nothing under the existing scheme.

I walked to the door with him. No. 10 was virtually empty. He went off to the House and I went to Caxton Hall, where Jim Callaghan was giving the Herbert Morrison Memorial Lecture. Appropriate, since he is the last of the great Morrisonian figures in the Labour Party.

A dingy hall, one-third full, mainly of those curious old ladies with glasses and small hats who make up the women's section of the Labour Party. What on earth can they make of 'multilateral disengagement'?

Afterwards I went with Callaghan and his special adviser Tom McNally, and Percy Clarke from Transport House, to a TV producer to discuss Jim's next party political TV programme.

Left at 9.45 and went home.

### Wednesday 3 July 1974

The PM was engaged most of the morning. He went out to lunch with the press and apparently was the worse for drink. This was embarrassingly obvious when the Cabinet committee on Energy met in the late afternoon. He rambled and ministers looked embarrassed. I was sorry. But he recovered remarkably before the meeting was complete.

We had a great success in the Unit. Grants for school buildings are only for *new* schools in expanding districts – which tend to be prosperous and Tory. Urban areas, especially city centres – Labour – get little or none. Prentice was passively accepting this at Education. I got the Unit and the private office to draft a minute from the PM to him telling him to alter the principles of allocation.

Apparently the top officials in Education are quite scandalous, trying to bounce the minister and give all the money to Tory areas or to universities.

In the evening we watched the World Cup here at No. 10 – I have a

TV in my room – and then on to a dinner party at George Weidenfeld's house. Sat next to Lady Pamela Berry, who was silly. There were too many people, except for dear Tommy Balogh and delightful Mrs Diana Phipps, so Carol and I left for home very early.

## Thursday 4 July 1974

Saw the PM between the Defence committee and Cabinet. He was in good form. But has decided not to take Albert to Bradford on Friday – probably a reflection of having seen Marcia the night before – their first meeting in over a week.

After Cabinet I talked to Tony Crosland and walked across the street with him. He is very worried that land nationalisation is going to be a half-baked scheme.

Questions went very easily in the House.

The PM is furious with Benn, who ostentatiously abstained on the EEC vote last night. He sent another severe prime ministerial minute – but says he wants Benn to resign only on a procedural not a policy question, to limit the party row.

Benn looked very grey and tired in the committee discussing nationalising shipbuilding and aircraft. It went fairly smoothly since most people accept these – and anyway Benn was most conciliatory in manner, only once referring to the shop stewards of Bristol and their expectations from government.

The PM left at 6.30 to go to Bradford as University Chancellor.

I worked till 9 p.m.

The PM was in much better shape today and not drinking much. We were relieved, having earlier discussed whether we might have to tell him it was in danger of destroying his authority.

## Friday 5 July 1974

PM away all day in Bradford. I went to the doctor's beforehand for the hamstring torn playing football on Sunday.

At the Unit we worked on briefs on economic reflation – urging that it be done through regional grants – and on financial assistance to Opposition parties.

Lunch at Grieveson Grant in the City. Very nice, sensible group of people.

Came home early and baby-sat while Carol went to a National Union of Teachers party.

*Weekend 6 and 7 July 1974*

Saturday evening to Brian Murphy's party in Muswell Hill. Peter Davis got into argument with Albert, attacking Joe.

At the same time a woman formerly with Transport House got me in a corner and began to attack Joe – and to praise Marcia, saying her judgement was better than his and how much closer to the grass roots she was. (I refrained from mentioning the three houses, several servants, children to private school, peerage, etc.) She also implied that she knew that Denis Lyons and Peter Davis were coming into No. 10 to squeeze Joe out.

On Friday the *Spectator* carried George Jones's article on my Policy Unit. Rather praising, and apparently Marcia got on the phone to the PM – at Bradford University where he was giving out degrees – to denounce me. Then on Sunday the *Observer* had a silly piece saying that HW was ignoring the Left – and blaming me and H. Lever! Apparently Marcia was furious again – because it even suggested that I have some influence. HW phoned Joe to complain and was angry with me.

It is bizarre when articles saying (a) that he has high-level advisers and (b) that he has poor advisers create such hatred in Lady Falkender simply because they mention anybody but her as having influence.

Incidentally I don't feel I have much influence at the moment. He has distanced himself again. He takes note of the memoranda but is definitely less accessible personally. This is because she is attacking me and he is trying to prove to her that he doesn't make much use of me. That is why he won't take me to Paris and may even strike me out of the *Guardian* lunch next week. Then once she is satisfied, he will characteristically make it up in other ways.

But the attacks on Joe are very ominous. He thinks this is the opening of the offensive against us all – leading up to Lyons and Davis moving in. To replace us *all*, so Joe must be attacked as well as Albert and me.

If so, this will be the big battle. Because Joe is as hard as steel. I'm not sure that Denis and Peter, whom I like, have the necessary marbles to tangle with him. It could be bloody. I don't mind at all – in fact I quite look forward to some serious axe-work instead of fencing around. Of course I – and Albert – will be marginal because we are comparatively recent in loyalty. And I will be attacked as a Gaitskellite. But Joe will need some beating and I will happily stand or go with him. Joe says if he goes he will first tell HW that he is going to spill the beans on Marcia.

I saw Harold Lever on Friday, who told me more of his weekend talk with the PM at Chequers – to which he said he was summoned solely to confirm or deny certain accusations. Marcia had reported to the PM that George Weidenfeld had overheard Lever, Kissin and Goodman plotting to save HW from Marcia. This was presumably when Weidenfeld must have added something about Kissin trying to control HW through me. The story is fitting into place. Weidenfeld passes on tittle-tattle to please Marcia. She elaborates on it to try to turn HW against Kissin, Lever, Goodman and Donoughue. All her enemies dealt with in one big lie. There is, as often, a kernel of truth in her allegations. We would like to see her removed. But where she is wrong is in accusing a conspiracy to do so. Sadly we all in fact accept that she is there to stay – she has HW by the short and curlies and will never let go till she has squeezed the last squeal out of the poor devil. Such a pity. He has such marvellous gifts and is basically such a kind man.

Joe points out that the excessive drinks in the past two weeks reflect the pressure she is putting on him.

Always at times like this I am depressed by the seediness of it all. The way that Britain's PM is dragged down into petty behaviour about trivial matters. The back-biting and stabbing, which obviously satisfies some people's personality frustrations and which many MPs seem to relish. It all brings it home to me that I don't want this life for very long. I hate seeing my name in the paper. I hate feeling I should explain to anyone – including the PM – that I did not do whatever the latest rumour says I did. It all leaves a nasty taste in my mouth. Yet I love the job, am fascinated watching it all and do not intend to be hustled or intimidated by the squalid questions of some of the mediocrities I see around. Reassuringly I don't feel scared or worried as I did in the first few weeks when things went wrong. I'm going to ride over it, or out, but I'm not going to be dirtied by it all.

It helps watching Robert Armstrong. Now I have a full view of him. Superbly efficient, tough, professional. The best of the British Civil Service. He has been very helpful to me – though quite properly would leave me to sink if I go wrong. He works enormously hard and has very safe hands. An impressive man.

## Monday 8 July 1974

HW did not come in till late morning – and then out to lunch at Shell – so I spent the morning in the office reading papers and getting some briefs ready for this evening's box – on concessionary bus fares, on nationalisation and on possible dates for the election. We have drafted a paper showing the pros and cons of each date.

Joe was out to lunch – and I had John Grant* in – but beforehand he told me of his meeting with the PM. The PM had insisted on seeing Joe alone and had asked Robert Armstrong and Albert to leave the room. Then had said Marcia was raving about the *Spectator* article describing the Policy Unit and a piece in the *Observer* referring to me as her successor. Joe defended me and also reported the attacks on himself. The PM said that people were spreading it around that Joe was saying, 'Marcia is mad.' 'I did not deny it of course,' said Joe. Marcia has summoned the PM to see her tonight, 'to explain if she is his political and personal secretary or just his personal secretary'. HW is apparently shaking in his boots.

In the afternoon Henry Kissinger came to see HW, and after that we attended the Cabinet Energy committee on the North Sea oil paper. Quite good, with Willie Ross performing well and making some positive suggestions.

Before the meeting I had followed the PM into the lavatory and asked to see him alone afterwards. He looked embarrassed and tried to duck it, saying he thought his programme was full. I pointed out that, apart from his tailor, who was coming to fix his trousers, he had nothing till his vote at 10 p.m., so he agreed.

We went up to the study at 6 p.m. and talked till 7 p.m. It was quite remarkable. I opened on the *Spectator* article by saying Joe had now confirmed that I had actually taken the author George Jones into the press office to tell them of his intentions and to get their clearance and they had actually sent him material for the article.

The PM accepted that, but said – as I knew – that it wasn't the point. The point was that the article suggested Marcia no longer had a major role and she was raving about this. 'She is very jealous of Albert too,' he added, as if to make it easier.

I explained that the article was written a month ago. And that I had suggested insertions stressing the important roles of Marcia and Joe.

HW was delighted at this and begged me to find the original and let him have it, preferably before his meeting this evening – which clearly terrified him. He looked haunted and hunted, yet glowed with relief when I gave him the facts and desperately tried to reassure me, pouring me out a large whisky, telling me it was perfectly OK for me to go on holiday before the Commons rose and then rambling on about Marcia and what a hard time she had had which made her behave in this 'strange' way.

He then rambled on about Crowther-Hunt and Scottish devolution. He apparently had not realised that Crowther-Hunt had been pressing for legislative devolution over the past four months. HW had encouraged him in pressing forward with a Scottish Assembly without realising it must have something to do – which meant a Scottish Executive. Now the PM is desperately trying to torpedo it by refusing to give them any money to do anything with.

Crowther-Hunt, who came to see me this morning, is bewildered and kept saying, 'But the Prime Minister was encouraging me, and I kept telling him about devolution, but he apparently didn't understand what I was talking about.'

I left the PM at 7 p.m. and found the tailor outside, and also Lord Goodman, who had come to discuss something to do with Marcia – I suspect to explain his role in the story of the 'Kissin plot' against her.

HW retailed the story of this plot to me – and confirmed that H. Lever had spilled the beans. Lever told him that Kissin was trying to control HW through me and was, in his words, 'trying to save me from myself'. That it came to Marcia from Weidenfeld, who also told him, and that he summoned Lever to Chequers.

I went back to the Unit and worked on more papers, briefs and letters – including one to the Treasury recommending an increase in regional grants as part of the reflating package.

John Hunt also sent for me to show me a minute he is preparing on my suggestion to keep a closer eye on impending bankruptcies so that we are not swept away in a chain reaction of financial crashes.

Came home at 9.30 p.m. – and then went after supper at 10.30 to see George Jones and collect the originals of the *Spectator* article. First I went in to the House of Commons and sent a letter to HW, who was eating in the restaurant with Crosland and Shore. The letter simply said that I had traced the original article and would bring it in tomorrow. He leapt to his feet and waved an excited thumbs-up sign to me, like a boy at a fair who has just found his lost purse.

Incidentally, Joe told me that HW said to him: 'They must not try to separate me from Marcia. That would be fatal.' Joe read into it an admission of the terrible hold she has over this poor man.

## Tuesday 9 July 1974

Morning in the office, working on the National Enterprise Board proposals and economic papers. PM at Cabinet and then to meet Malaysian monarch.

Douglas Wass phoned from the Treasury to say the Policy Unit could not be represented on the Budget committee nor see papers. Our first setback. Typical of the Treasury, thinks it has only to tell people what to do, not involve them in the argument.

Lunch at the stockbrokers Hoare Govett, where a bunch of Tories say that the *present* situation is what they want – Labour but a minority.

PM's Questions went easily.

Saw Roy Jenkins after, who asked me 'to have a friendly chat'. We stood in the corridor and he did not say anything and I rambled on between silences. At the end I asked did he want 'anything specific', he said no, just to have 'a friendly chat'.

Back to No. 10 for a Cabinet committee on the National Enterprise Board and nationalisation. Discussed the revised White Paper on industrial policy, drafted in the Cabinet Office under the PM's direction. Implies complete rejection of Benn, whose long original paper has been discarded.

Benn opened by saying this meant rejection of the party's intention and his own work. I thought this was an ominous opening, but then we were side-tracked by other ministers complaining about HW's scheme to put all assets of *existing* nationalised industries into the NEB. Benn said not even he had proposed that. HW said it was party policy, but was forced to climb down after some desperate searching through the party programme.

It was a bad start for the PM – and we had briefed him *against* suggesting this, which advice he rejected.

Then the meeting rambled all over the place. Long discussion about whether to specify companies, industries or to leave it vague. Each approach was judged likely to kill industry's confidence. The level was terribly low, and Healey left at one point glowering with disgust.

Tony Crosland and Shirley Williams were the best of a bad lot. It was quite the worst Cabinet committee meeting I have attended. HW did not chair it firmly enough, I think undermined by his bad beginning.

In the end, however, he picked it off the floor by suggesting a more pragmatic and limited approach which everyone accepted with relief.

I sit in on these meetings and conduct a hilarious exchange of messages with Robert Armstrong, who is perceptive and funny about these proceedings.

Earlier I had submitted to the PM the George Jones draft for the *Spectator* article. HW looked through and spotted I had made a mistake in the dates when I suggested they had been written. I simply had only a vague idea and thought it didn't matter. He was petrified of getting it wrong and half accused me of forging the manuscripts. Ridiculous really. He will have to send this evidence along to Marcia, who will then find me guilty. I don't give a fuck, but try to protect him if possible.

In the middle of sleazy episodes like this I feel a strong desire to lose the next election so I can get back to a cleaner life and so HW, with nothing more to lose, can perhaps get that woman off his back. Though perhaps he never will. Perhaps he needs her domination psychologically.

What a pity Roy Jenkins has apparently disappeared from the Labour political scene. He has completely dropped out of the government, never speaking, never appearing anywhere to defend the government. He is just a sleeping partner. Yet he could have *worked* at it, clearly distinct from HW and disagreeing with the Left, but working as a member of the team to earn his passage. Instead he stands aloof, disdainful, unhappy, trying to avoid contamination from his own party. Maybe he is proving himself a worthy coalition leader, as Joe suggests. What is certain is that his Labour support is dwindling.

Harold Evans dropped round this evening. He said more and more people in the Labour Party are talking of Jim Callaghan as the next leader.

[The memo from the author to the Prime Minister about the *Spectator* said:

## BD to PRIME MINISTER:

1. Attached is the original script for *New Society* written nearly four months ago, entitled 'Who has the PM's ear?' and containing paragraphs referring to Marcia Williams, Joe Haines, Albert Murray, etc.
2. The original paragraph is the last one on page 6 (photostat attached). In the margin, alongside sentence describing M's position and praise for her book, BD wrote:

'Must say: "(Marcia) has worked closely with him for 18 years and has exercised enormous influence."'
The author has inserted a sentence in ink along these lines.
NB. These scribbles in margin were meant to be 'thoughts' not the exact wording for the author to use.

3. The *New Society* rejected this article and it was sent months later without my knowledge to the *Spectator* with paragraphs on M and J, etc. omitted because subject had been narrowed to Policy Unit alone, and many other cuts. Apparently this latest script was entitled 'The PM's Policy Unit' but the *Spectator* changed that to the title published last week.

9th July 1974]

## *Wednesday 10 July 1974*

Morning on papers and preparing my tax forms for my tax accountant who came in for two hours in the afternoon.

Went to lunch at the Charing Cross Hotel with PM, editor of *Guardian*, Alastair Hetherington, and its political correspondent, John Cole.

PM talked at great length on the economy – he later said this was to reassure them he took it seriously. Quite a good discussion afterwards, ranging over the whole government's policies. PM was good – better than of late. He also drank only beer instead of spirits.

Went back to the House for Varley's statement on building more nuclear stations of British design. I returned to No. 10 and did not see the PM again. But Marcia came in to No. 10 this evening for the first time in months. She was – Joe told me – discussing whether to proceed with her writs against the newspapers at a possible cost of £12,000. She asked Joe what she should do – and he said, 'Sue – and declare yourself bankrupt if you lose.'

John Silkin is on to me every day about the press exposing the financial activities of his land companies. He seems to be through the storm now.

We have three speeches this weekend. private office and Joe are doing them, but I looked through the drafts this evening.

## Thursday 11 July 1974

In at 9.45 for Cabinet committee meeting on the plight of labour councillors from local authorities in default over the Tory Housing Finance Act. Nobody had any answer really. Willie Ross kept insisting we must pass an Act to rescue the Scots defaulters – some in Glasgow are responsible for £14,000 per head. But Mellish interrupted to point out that without a majority in the Commons we could do nothing.

Crosland was clear, responsible and resigned: nothing we could do to slow down the district auditors coming to a head in the autumn. And many of our people angry with the defaulters as self-publicists. He has a scheme for taking the money out of local authorities who have extracted too much in rents and giving it to the defaulters to pay with.

After this HW was at Cabinet, where there was another row concerning Jim Callaghan. The *Guardian* carried a report from the Transport House committee monitoring the EEC negotiations and said Peter Shore had attacked Jim.

Jim blew up. Shore denied he had said any such thing. And Benn had not attended because HW had written forbidding him. Roy, Healey and Lever were silent. But Lever told me afterwards that the Right is furious with the way the Left is getting away with everything. Yet they do nothing. Really they have surrendered. Roy is their head and he is sulking in his tent.

The officials were asked to leave the Cabinet Room while this was discussed.

I was supposed to go to lunch with Monty Finniston, chairman of the

Steel Corporation, but I cancelled when I heard of this row. Rightly so. The PM called us up to his study after Cabinet and we discussed this and other matters until 1.45 p.m. Then he went to the House and we ate at No. 10. He *never* eats here with us now. Terrified of Marcia.

In the evening we had a joint party with the CPRS. Rothschild was in a very gay and skittish mood. He said that he had dined with somebody who said to him, 'Bernard is so clever that he must be Jewish.' I replied that 'I should be so lucky.' And added that I had arranged things better for my children (my wife is Jewish).

Most of my Unit seemed well sloshed when they returned to No. 10.

I had a long chat with Will Plowden, who is still one of my favourite people.

Perhaps I was a little sloshed, since I forgot that I had brought my car in and parked on Horse Guards Parade, and when I left just after 9 p.m. I took a taxi home.

Incidentally I do not really feel at all tired these days. Often exhilarated, sometimes appalled, but I feel very much *on top* of the job. I feel I know when to intervene, when to brief and when to ignore something, and that is the key to this job.

## Friday 12 July 1974

Weekly business meeting. Delayed while HW and Mellish discuss the Commons crisis over 'nodding through' Harold Lever in the division lobbies when he was not in fact in the House – and the vote was a tie!

Reassembled at 11.15 for speeches. The PM has two in Wales – Bangor and Aberystwyth – and we have to do different ones. We go through them and get mixed up. There are countless drafts and the study is soon flowing in paper. Also there were too many people there. So in the end some of the agreed amendments were not put on the master copy, and we had the wrong version retyped.

Present were Joe, Albert, myself, Robin Butler, Robert Armstrong, and Adrian Shaw and HW. Too many for a speech.

We adjourned briefly for lunch – the PM went across to the House and then dashed back again.

We were interrupted in mid-afternoon by a letter from Heath about the Lever affair – clearly written in the hope of reaching No. 10 *after* HW had left for Wales and ignoring the fact that Lever and Mellish had explained it all to the Tory Whips that morning. A storm in a teacup, but HW took it very seriously and characteristically dictated a long reply, full of footnotes and excuses. Robert and Joe later shortened this, fortunately.

Then the copying machine broke down, so we were very late getting the press handouts. HW finally left for Northolt to fly to Anglesey at 5 p.m. – 45 minutes late.

I then went back to catch up on my papers and see a delegation from Grieveson Grant, worried, understandably, about confidence in the City.

Apparently the speeches went well. I went to Suffolk for the weekend, but first phoned Joe. HW was still fussing about Lever. He phoned at 8.30 a.m. on Saturday morning and wants to set up a select committee. Seems a nonsense to me. I talked to Lever, who claims to be untroubled but is clearly fussed. His problem is that he is undisciplined. And it worries him if the PM is annoyed with him.

I told him it would soon blow over and to forget it, but certainly not to keep issuing statements.

## Monday 15 July 1974

Morning – HW arrived late from Chequers. I worked in the office, dealing with mail and reading papers – today on the Concorde negotiating brief, cancelling Maplin airport, Scottish devolution, land nationalisation, etc. – a whole series of major policies flowing across my desk.

Callaghan came in at noon to see HW about the Cyprus coup.

After I went up to the study and saw HW alone for half an hour. Discussed present political situation – including latest unpublished NOP poll showing Labour 8% ahead.

Lunch with all from private office. Afterwards Robert Armstrong talked to me about the meals being too big and so we agreed to have only two courses – though it later transpired that some wanted sweet and I wanted the first course.

After an afternoon of papers and meetings and visitors and phone calls HW sent for Joe, Albert and me at 6.30 p.m. He was worried about a rumour that the *Express* was saving up for the election a story about him and some financial question – land or tax. He began to get violently anti-press and talked of 'roughing it up' with them and devoting a television programme to attacking the press. He said he had never done a land deal in his life. The tax issue worried him more. He claims that his tax papers are missing – stolen, he says. Definitely had gone by the end of the election campaign. He was not sure whether they went from Lord North Street or the room near Victoria station, provided by Marcia's friend Eric Miller,* chairman of Peachey Properties, where large amounts of Wilson papers are stored.

Then it emerged that two box files were missing from there – one of his papers and one of Marcia's. This obviously worried him. He told Albert to go and check it out thoroughly and then to report it to the police as a theft – to get it on the record if the Tories have got the papers to use in the election campaign.

At one point he muttered something about his 'Board of Trade papers from 1947'.

We got back on the election and Joe and I stressed that if the press ran a dirty campaign he should play it cool and not be caught off balance. He agreed and said, 'Yes, I really need a thug to handle this for me. I need a George Wigg so that I can stand above the battle.'

He said that, 'The weak link is Marcia. She gets so very upset in these situations.'

We then discussed the mini-Budget due next week. I argued that we needed an attack on price inflation rather than public expenditure to counter employment. He said he hoped for a mixture of both, with a regional employment premium (REP) and something to deal with company liquidity as well.

I'm not sure you can have everything in the package and keep sterling safe, but he was very clear where we stood. We discussed election strategy. He wants to run it as a team again. But resists Joe's pressure to hold the election on a Saturday. He still wants to announce it as a public holiday – it is difficult to do that in Scotland, for he thinks after an election people would just take a further holiday.

Then Mellish came in with more Tory proposals to redress the 'Lever vote' last week. Highly complicated and quite impractical.

HW wanted to announce he would go for a select committee of investigation – but first said he wanted to make sure Lever had nothing to hide. So he sent for him.

Lever came – it was now about 9.30 p.m. and Joe and I were getting hungry. HW went with Lever and Mellish into the white boudoir, while the rest of us – Armstrong, Joe, Robin Butler, Freddie Warren* from the Whips Office, and myself – stayed behind.

They returned and Lever had spilled the beans. On the evening of the vote he had been playing backgammon with a notorious gambler. He was very contrite, though I thought it was hilarious – especially where it appears he had written a false appointment into his diary at home to hide the gambling from his wife, and the Tories had chased up this false appointment and found him not there. The Tories came out badly. They had set spies on him, and their Whips had phoned his home under false names. They knew he was absent long before the division, but pretended to be shocked afterwards by the discovery. Just silly schoolboys playing tricks.

HW said it was high farce, but he meant to use it seriously by exposing the 'Tory Watergate'. Lever pleaded with him to let it drop, but he wouldn't. In a bizarre outburst the PM said that Lever had not suffered 1% of what he and his family had suffered and now he had a chance 'to grab them by the balls as revenge'.

So it all ended, part serious, part farce. HW was brilliant and funnily mock-serious in his interrogation of Lever. 'You mean you deceived your wife,' he said at one point in mock-astonishment. Poor Harold Lever was so shattered and contrite that he could not see the funny side. Nor could Mellish, who was fed up. But we felt at the end the PM was overreacting. Must try to stop a select committee or major statements tomorrow. It is all very unfair on dear old Lever.

## Tuesday 16 July 1974

PM at Liaison committee and at Cabinet – which he was very happy with. The Concorde brief went through easily, and dropping Maplin airport. London weighting caused more difficulty, but I gather Michael Foot was very good.

In the Unit we were working on the Health Service collapse. BMA demanding to see the PM. We are pushing that its delegation should include *all* the unions and representatives of the junior doctors.

Joe and I went up to see the PM after Cabinet and before lunch. Discussed Cabinet – and also the Lever issue, which continued to bubble. HW was now cooling off a select committee – Lord Goodman had phoned him to say Lever was not sleeping and it was imperilling his health.

Lunch with private office. Afterwards to the Commons for a very quiet Question Time. PM played it very tight. But later the Lever questions exploded, the Speaker ruled that the Bill should come back to be corrected, and when Short opposed this he could not get sufficient support from our side, so we lost. A dismal end to a silly affair, inflated beyond all belief. Brings Parliament into disrepute.

I did not see the PM again today. He had a meeting with Goodman, then to the Palace, then to the Commons. I worked on Kilbrandon Scottish devolution papers, which are very boring and show Whitehall retreating terrified from devolution. Then economics – I have been pushing the PM to see Healey and discuss the mini-Budget, and to try for anti-inflation price cuts rather than reflationary public works expenditure. He has now arranged to see Healey tomorrow. I sent him a brief and some background notes.

This evening the government was defeated by 25 votes on a clause of the Finance Bill. Clearly a bad day for morale. I talked to David Owen earlier in the House and he was fairly pessimistic, thinks things may collapse before October.

John Hunt, however, thinks Labour will have a majority of around 20.

I went to see him about the election business committee, set up to deal with questions put to ministers while campaigning, and the PM has made me his deputy to chair the committee and liaise with Transport House. We are getting it set up ready for the autumn.

I talked to Tony Crosland before Cabinet, and he is still worried about land. He says John Silkin has no political sense whatsoever, and is wildly over-optimistic about the prospects there. He is also complaining that Frank Allaun and others in Transport House are monitoring him on his land policies. Allaun has written to the PM advising *no* White Paper on land before the election because it will be a rushed compromise.

Home at 8.30 p.m.

## Wednesday 17 July 1974

Met Denis Healey in Downing Street at 9.20 this morning and we discussed last night's defeats on the Finance Bill – which had given away £120m of public expenditure. He was furious and said Robert Carr,* the Tory Shadow Chancellor, had told him they didn't really mean to do it. I told him to go on the radio and denounce them as irresponsible – and not to alter his mini-Budget next week.

Inside was another crisis. Photostats are circulating of alleged bank accounts in Zurich held by Ted Short. Short was in the study with the PM and Lever – brought in because of his expertise in bank accounts! Short denied everything. I talked to Lever for an hour. He was trying to use his Swiss contacts to get confirmation on the account, but had no luck. He said that Short was either a remarkably convincing liar, or the bank account was a remarkable forgery. It looked completely convincing, though apparently it is easy to forge with photostats. It was certainly genuine Swiss bank paper. The amount was 103,000 francs put in in 1971–72.

Harold Evans later told me that the press rumour was that this was some of the Poulson money – and that the photostats were circulated by Short's previous secretary. The PM seemed convinced it was genuine, but we counselled caution – not to go out on a limb.

I talked to Short just before lunch and he was remarkably calm – just a bit angry that people should go to such efforts to smear him. If it is a smear campaign, it is remarkably sophisticated, needing a Tory 'dirty tricks' department. [It was a forgery and Short was the innocent victim of yet another press smear. Later revelations suggest that the dirty tricks might have come from the security services.]

Cyprus also blew up today, with an Athens-sponsored campaign against President Makarios, who is alive, and the RAF rescued him and brought him back here. He arrived at No. 10 after lunch with masses of cheering

Cypriots. The Turks arrive this evening to ask us to declare war with them. The PM is very hawkish, but the chiefs of staff are worried. They apparently argue it would take a fortnight to mount an operation – although we are there already! – and are very worried about all the British wives and children scattered around the island. Our impression from the Turks who came to dinner this evening is that they won't take that long. They came hoping to issue a press statement afterwards to the effect that we were both jointly intervening. When they didn't get this, they said they would do it themselves anyway and then sat back to enjoy their meal. HW was very impressed by them.

At lunch I went to Boodles Club with two counsellors from the French embassy. They obviously hoped to pump me ahead of the PM's visit to Paris tomorrow. I responded with calculation. Said on Concorde that we had no fall-back position, so there was no point in their pressing for more than 16 planes. On Channel oil, we must solve it jointly. On reflation, we were doing it as an anti-inflation measure and so it would be foolish to weaken sterling because of it. And on the EEC, we recognised that nothing could happen until after our election, so there was no point in squabbling. What was needed was for French President Giscard* and HW to establish a working relationship. [Giscard had succeeded as President of France on 19 May 1974 after the death on 2 April of President Pompidou.]

Afternoon on papers and evening. The flow of policy material is enormous at the moment – masses of social policy from Barbara Castle, land nationalisation still flowing and in heaps of difficulties. The Cabinet Office is painfully redrafting the Benn industry policy. My adviser is not happy with it. Says it is very turgid, lacking the dynamic virtues of Benn's original paper and now very confused.

Everything is being rushed through to get it in the shop window before the recess.

Home 9.30.

## Thursday 18 July 1974

Morning the PM had the Defence Review (cuts) and Cabinet, where they deal with the Cyprus crisis. I worked in the office. Feeling very tired today. Have a virus – sore throat and very tired. Need a holiday.

Lunch at No. 10 and then PQs. Rather irritable House. As HW said, they want to be up and away. In the middle of briefing for questions he went off to phone Goodman to try to stop *The Times* doing a profile of Marcia and referring to her children. After questions he saw Goodman at No. 10. Then he and Joe went off to Paris.

At 7.30 I went off with Albert to the Wilson archives in the office near

Victoria provided by Eric Miller of Peachey Properties. I hoped to find some interesting material, but it was just boxes of recent speeches, clippings, etc. It was not clear whether anything important had been stolen, as HW suspected.

## Friday 19 July 1974

The PM in Paris. I spent much of the day with David Piachaud on social policy. Put in a few briefs for the weekend and then out to dinner with David Sainsbury.* Ill in the night and felt rotten all next day:

*Saturday*, when the Turks invaded Cyprus and I should have been at No. 10. The PM was there, having flown back early from Durham and not gone to the Miners' Gala.

[One consequence of the successful Turkish invasion of Cyprus was the abdication three days later of the right-wing Athens dictatorship which had initiated the crisis by its coup against President Makarios on 17 July.]

## Sunday 21 July 1974

Bill Rodgers came round for a drink and told me a lovely story about the Ministry of Defence. Despite the Cyprus emergency, *neither* the permanent secretary nor the relevant private secretary of Roy Mason bothered to come in to the office this weekend. Mason went in on Saturday morning, but couldn't get into his office, then couldn't work his intelligence telephone system because his civil servants were not there. A private secretary had the master key – and apparently 'does not like coming to work on Saturdays'. Finally on that Friday evening the Defence officials had said they were all prepared because they knew in advance that the Turks would invade at dawn. Bill asked when precisely did the sun rise in the Mediterranean and they admitted they had forgotten to check.

[I went on holiday for a few days, taking the family to my new holiday house at Céret in south-west France on 23 July and returning at the weekend of the 27th–28th. While I was away Denis Healey introduced a mini-Budget on 22 July. Its main objective was to reduce price increases by 2% a year through reducing VAT from 10% to 8%, relieving rates increases, and more food subsidies. It thereby eliminated the price increases induced by his March Budget and was on balance expansionary. At the end of the Budget debate on 24 July the Liberals indicated they would not vote against the government and so the Conservatives decided not to press a vote – though twenty-eight Tory back-benchers broke ranks to vote against the government. This was one of several indications of the tactical confusion existing among the Opposition and their reluctance to force an early election.

Despite its minority, the government passed thirty-eight Bills through Parliament between March and July. However, in total the Labour government suffered eighteen Commons defeats in that period and on 21 July the Government Chief Whip, Bob Mellish (who was that week promoted to the Cabinet), announced publicly that 'this Parliament is no longer feasible' – thus preparing the way for the Prime Minister's dissolution of Parliament in September.]

## Monday 29 July 1974

Back from France, having established the family safely in our house in the Pyrenees.

Began with the committee on recycling of waste materials. Then the Cabinet economic committee (MES), which discussed wealth tax and then capital transfer tax. The schemes seemed sensible enough. Lever was hostile – too hostile really – and he clearly irritated ministers, including the PM, who later said he thought Lever should be more modest when his personal wealth was at stake. In fact Lever is fairly immune from all of this, financially. His concern quite understandably is general financial confidence. But it is also true that, politically, he would be wiser to go softly on matters affecting the rich.

Went to lunch with Lord Kissin at the Lords, where he was taking his seat. Nice ceremony. Introduced by Jennie Lee* and Goodman – who looked like a huge pantomime dame in his robes and cocked hat. Interesting to me since I had described this ceremony in the Morrison book without actually ever having seen it.

Back in the afternoon and we began work on the PM's speech for the PLP – dealing with the party outburst over Roy Jenkins's speech calling for moderation. Decided to take even-handed approach, criticising Benn as well, but mainly praising the government. The PM dictated it and was very good from the beginning.

[Speaking at Haverfordwest on 26 July, Jenkins argued that Labour must not ignore 'the great body of moderate, rather uncommitted opinion' and would not win a proper majority unless these moderates were attracted. He added that 'it cannot be done upon the basis of ignoring middle opinion and telling everyone who does not agree with you to go to hell.' This sensible statement of current and forecast future political reality was ignored by a majority of Labour Party activists for another thirteen years.]

In the evening Lord Kissin came in to see the PM – who sent for me to sit in 'as witness'. In fact I had to leave early because John Hunt had arranged to see me about devolution. The Civil Service was and is furious with Norman Crowther-Hunt, whom they describe as 'totally dishonest'. The Civil Service is afraid that we are breaking up the UK. Norman Crowther-Hunt is producing a constitution a day to meet the various pressures. This evening there were *four* alternative drafts of the White Paper available.

The PM asked Joe to come up from holiday in the evening and we went over the draft PLP speech until after 10. He also contacted Denis Howell and instructed him to go as Minister of Sport to the airport on Tuesday to greet the British Lions back from South Africa. Heath had invited himself and the PM felt the government should be there – while making clear our disapproval of apartheid.

Went home very late and bought fish and chips, which I took into our friends and neighbours Tom and Celia Read to eat and chat.

PS: Missed out the afternoon meeting of the Cabinet drafting committee on Benn's industrial policy White Paper. The new draft done by the Cabinet Office was very vapid. I was told afterwards that Benn was on the counter-attack and the PM was resisting him quite well. Healey was spasmodic, but strong, and Shirley Williams was very good indeed. For a long time it looked as if there was no hope of agreement. Michael Foot was saying that the paper was not worth publishing – too defensive. In the end the PM began to see ways of bridging the gap and we all went off to redraft it in the Policy Unit and the Cabinet Office. But still a long way to go – and Benn clearly not willing to accept the restraints we are trying to put on him.

## Tuesday 30 July 1974

In the study first thing discussing revised drafts of the PM's PLP speech and adding bits to get the balance right. PM is obviously nervous about it, but senses that the timing is opportune – people want to get the squabbling over – and this will do it.

Cabinet committee on Kilbrandon devolution at 11 a.m. Very depressing. Everyone now getting frightened at what we are doing – Ross, the Scottish Secretary, rebuked them all

[My notes:

Ross        Savage attack on Crowther-Hunt. Accepts modified Scheme A – 'no halfway house'. Must be legislative devolution – with no Secretary of State. 'The pass has already been sold by the NEC. There has been too much panic about the Scottish National Party.'

| | |
|---|---|
| Healey | Very troubled – we are drifting into the break-up of the UK. Must say 'minimum to get us through the general election – and then with a majority we can deal with this seriously'. |
| Crosland | 'But for the electoral politics, it would be appallingly irresponsible to take such a major constitutional change with such little consideration.' |
| Jenkins | 'All ministers are at fault for paying too little attention to this. Therefore we should announce the minimum commitment and announce that we will deal with this properly after the election.' |
| Welsh Sec. | Wants elective Assembly and devolution of Secretary of State for Wales' powers, transfer of his powers to the Assembly. |

Rest agree on minimum – schemes 3 and 4. But accept that some legislative Assembly is minimum and promise to delineate power.

Notes end.]
[The government produced its White Paper on devolution on 17 September. It was vague in many respects, reflecting the hostility of the Scottish Secretary, William Ross, but clearly offering more devolved power to Edinburgh.]

Then Cabinet. Lunch at No. 10.

Afternoon PQs – final PQs of the session and went very quietly. Beforehand the PM telephoned Marcia. About the Industry paper – and about his meeting that afternoon with Harold Davies, who he now thinks is pushing the attacks on Marcia.

The PLP speech apparently went very well. Afterwards we went together to the farewell dinner for Sir Alf Ramsey, the ex-manager of the England football team. The PM was very good in his speech, ad-libbing away from the text, which was a little too stiff. I sat with Billy Bingham of Everton, and we had a fascinating talk about modern training methods. Very enthusiastic audience – and not back till after midnight, so I decided to sleep at No. 10.

Looking back, the saddest thing is the demise of the No. 10 lunches. Earlier the lunch talks with the PM, Joe, etc. were when we planned strategy. But Marcia has forbidden it, so he dare not even come in to eat. Very sad.

*Wednesday 31 July 1974*

Woke up early in No. 10 in one of the guest rooms at the top of the house, woken by Big Ben and the clock on Horse Guards Parade. My drip-dry shirt was nice and dry, but my socks still wet from overnight washing. Went downstairs, very quiet and cool, and cleared off some early papers, and then out to breakfast in the Strand.

Back in to No. 10 at 9 a.m. and settled down to my papers. A marvellous start. On top from the beginning. Went up to the study to see the PM. Discussed the Industry White Paper – and the need to put some spice into it. Also the Short affair, now it is clearly a dirty tricks forgery, as the police have confirmed. We discussed how to turn this back on the Tories. HW wanted simply to sue the *Express* journalist Chapman Pincher for libel. I wanted to make it a political attack – though I still fear that the forgery may be by some lunatic on the *Labour* side, especially from the north-east.

Afterwards I went back down to my room to deal with papers and talk with the Unit.

Lunch with Albert and Nick Stuart from private office.

2.30–5 p.m. a very tense meeting of the Cabinet Industrial Development committee to discuss the latest draft of the Industry White Paper. This was a Cabinet Office version completely rejecting Benn's ideas. Indeed so much so that it was purged of all life, and I had suggested to the PM beforehand that he could afford to give something back to Benn, especially in terms of a strong planning agreements system. In fact the PM gave away much more. He had had lunch with Marcia and came in determined to please the Left. Benn recovered a lot of ground. Lever resisted throughout, but the PM was very short with him. Shirley Williams was good while she was there, but had to leave early. Healey was strong when he intervened, but was usually silent. Crosland was intelligent but erratic and never secured anything. Barbara Castle slept through much of the meeting.

In fact it was mainly a dialogue between the PM and Benn, with the latter often winning, quoting extensively from the PM's own speeches, having brought photostats along. He also read long and unintelligible extracts from Labour's Programme 1973.

At the end Benn asked for and got the job of rewriting the introduction – when it came round later it had dropped all reassurances to the private sector, so I had a meeting with Robert Armstrong and we redrafted it again together and went to the PM for his approval, which he immediately gave, obviously very pleased. Though he looks at me oddly when he sees me getting on so well with Robert – who is proving a brilliant and affectionate ally. My Policy Unit is redrafting the main body of the Industry White Paper, with Andrew and Richard Graham working night and day.

The PM had a long meeting with the British Medical Association and the appalling Dr Stevenson in the evening. I took the chance to go home by 8 p.m. and take my Israeli brother-in-law out for a drink. He leaves England early tomorrow.

### Thursday 1 August 1974

In the office most of the morning while the Cabinet dealt with land nationalisation, etc. Lunch with Robert, Albert and Nick.

Afterwards the PM did a TV interview with Robin Day, who was very fair to him and who also said to me that my Morrison biography was the 'best he had read in years'.

I saw Lord Kissin – who told me about the financial provisions for Harold Wilson's political office since 1957.

I was supposed to attend the Cabinet committee on devolution but instead chose to work on redrafting the Industry White Paper, with Richard Graham from my Unit and Robert Armstrong.

An excellent day, beautiful and sunny, feel relaxed and totally on top of the job. The PM has been in excellent form – and boasting he is drinking little.

In the evening I took out to dinner at the Reform Club marvellous Jack Ashley and Alf Morris.

Also had a long talk to Shirley Williams on the phone, preparing for tomorrow's Cabinet on the Industry White Paper. Tell of our amendments and fears. She promises to help.

### Friday 2 August 1974

In at 9.15 and see the PM in the hall outside the Cabinet Room. Discuss Jack Ashley and I press for promotion and an honour for him [Jack was given a CH] – and get approval to push ahead with a survey of the deaf as preparation for setting up an Institute for the Deaf.

The PM went into Cabinet, which apparently was very good. On the Industry White Paper Lever and Callaghan and Shirley were very strong and Benn was completely defeated. The PM produced the revised introduction written by myself, Robert Armstrong and Richard Graham, and this was accepted with acclaim. Everyone went away very happy – except Benn.

[The main changes introduced in the Policy Unit redrafting were that company planning agreements were made voluntary, not compulsory; the nationalisation of the pharmaceutical and machine-tool industries was omitted; and there was a commitment to no further extensions of public control during the next Parliament. The White Paper – entitled *The Regeneration of British Industry* – set out proposals to set up a National Enterprise Board as a new source of investment capital for private industry and the creation of a system of planning agreements for industrial firms. It was published on 15 August 1974.]

I spent an hour with Ken Berrill, who is taking over the Think Tank from Rothschild. Very able, abrasive and abrupt, but I like and respect him and hope to get on well.

Had a reception for Adrian Shaw from my Unit at lunch, getting married. The morale and spirit of the Unit is good. Very able and nice bunch. Marvellous work on the Industry White Paper.

Lunch with Susanne Reeve, Rothschild's assistant, who is clearly worried about the future of the CPRS Think Tank.

Back for final clear-up and goodbyes. Nice talk with Robert Armstrong, who is such a pleasure to work with.

The PM had been due to go to the Israeli embassy for lunch with the Panovs, the ballet stars released from Russia. Marcia had arranged this. But the Russian Ambassador called in to protest so at the last moment HW called it off.

In the afternoon a fresh crisis blew up about the Health Service, and Barbara Castle was buzzing around. Clive Jenkins and Mikardo* had also been in No. 10 but fortunately I didn't meet them.

On Saturday the Cabinet Secretary telephoned me at home to say how much he and the Prime Minister liked the final Policy Unit draft of the Industry White Paper. This has been a great triumph for the Unit and will ensure that we are in future taken very seriously in Whitehall.

Then I flew to rejoin the family on holiday in France.

## CHAPTER 6

# The Second 1974 Election:
## Winning a Majority, and Kitchen Cabinet Manoeuvres
### September–October 1974

*Monday 2 September 1974*

I went into No. 10 for the first time since a month's holiday in my house in France. There I completely relaxed and had a marvellous time with the family and with my friend Jacques Pomonti.* Have never felt so close to Carol and content to spend time with her and the children.

From abroad I was able to see England a little clearer. It looked in a terrible mess. Falling apart socially as well as economically. Seems very frail compared to France, which is becoming a giant again.

Also felt that Labour would win the election – certainly in terms of votes vis-à-vis the Tories. We are the only serious government team around. But a multi-party result could produce a coalition or another minority situation. In any case, *neither* party has an approach or policies anywhere on the scale needed to solve the problems. Ours are the best, and they are sentimental and irrelevant.

Spent much of Monday with Joe. Discussing the problems of the election team, now Marcia has set up her counter-team with Peter Davis and Denis Lyons. We have problems being civil servants needing to stay in No. 10 and not to be seen doing too much party work. Will she move the centre of operations elsewhere to outflank us?

Evidence came in the first draft of HW's speech for the TUC on Thursday. Very good first 80%, then a curious gimmicky insertion about 'a Declaration of Interdependence' – including memorably original phrases such as 'no man is an island' and 'the bell tolls for us all'. Joe was livid. This was all from a paper by Davis and Lyons suggesting that this Declaration of Interdependence should be the theme on which we fight the election! Marcia was giving it her full backing.

In the evening Robert Armstrong came to see me with the hilarious news that they had discovered that one of the female civil servants working in No. 10 was a high-class call-girl involved in both the Norma Levy and the Janie Jones sex scandals. A strange girl, middle class, pleasant, very well dressed, perfect manners, but curiously lifeless. Certainly I wouldn't pay for it. She will have to be discreetly moved on. She was appointed under Heath and predictably the official vetting investigation had completely missed this lucrative sideline.

Went to dinner with Harold Lever, who was in fine form. We thought we would win the next election, but agreed to enjoy life together even if we lost.

Home midnight.


## Tuesday 3 September 1974

35th anniversary of the Second World War.

Spent the morning answering correspondence accumulated over the holiday. The PM returned at 2.30 looking very bronzed and cheerful after his holiday in the Scillies. [The Wilsons had bought land on St Mary's Isle in the Scillies in 1959 and built a bungalow there which became their normal holiday home.]

I went to see him at 5 p.m. just before the Cabinet committee on land nationalisation. Split between Crosland, who wants an 80% tax levy in the interim period before the full scheme, and Healey, who seems to want no White Paper at all because of Bank of England pressure over business confidence and fears property companies will collapse. I supported Crosland – who I had seen earlier in the afternoon. In the meeting the PM was poised between the two, inclining to Crosland until Lever intervened with a clever suggestion to help limit tax on property companies *not* making profits. Accepted gratefully by all. PM was delighted. Said to me afterwards, 'If he comes up with more winners like that, he can keep going back to Deauville every week.'

Afterwards Joe, Robin Butler and I met in the study with the PM to discuss his Brighton speech to the TUC. Joe piled in with his usual courage and bluntness. Totally demolished 'the Declaration of Interdependence' as a gimmick. The PM was very uncomfortable, reached quickly for a drink and said he was 'wedded to it'. Butler and I joined in. I said that this theme did not arise from the rest of the speech, which contained three quite different themes. HW said desperately, 'I like them all – let's say that we will make a Declaration of Interdependence based on those three themes.' Joe piled in again, so the PM said, 'Let's leave it for tonight and meet tomorrow.' This will be fascinating. It is a battle over words, but really between people. Marcia has forced this in, and the PM dare not drop it. But he knows Joe is right.

Dinner with Harold Evans and home late.

*Wednesday 4 September*

All day working on the speech for tomorrow's TUC at Brighton. Joe suggested many changes, I a few. HW surrendered a lot of the Declaration of Interdependence stuff, but kept some – which sounded OK now, since it is no longer false and inflated. We were in the study all morning and all afternoon. But HW went out to lunch.

Carol and the family returned from France today having had a horrendous Channel crossing.

In the afternoon we were cheered to learn that Hugh Scanlon of the Engineers Union had capitulated and agreed not to oppose the social contract at the TUC.

In the evening John Grant came in to No. 10 and we discussed tactics for the election – and still certain for 10 October, which had been HW's chosen date since late July. [John Grant, the Labour MP for the safe Labour seat of Islington East, was to act as Wilson's press assistant in the campaign. He attended the daily campaign committee instead of Joe Haines – who, as a civil servant, could not attend it.]

It has been arranged that Joe and I will do the election speeches here in No. 10, working in the flat. Albert would also be here with the political office. But the PM will be mainly at Transport House. This has all been worked out with Marcia in the Scillies. It is clearly her tactic to get HW away from us in the campaign. But really, as civil servants, we could not function as last time, in Transport House all the time. Joe and I accept this. She is bound to win on that. In fact HW told Joe later that he wanted to create the same sane and successful team atmosphere as last time and that he hoped to see us each morning and evening – apart from the speeches. He also then decided to arrange a dinner for next Tuesday at No. 10 with Joe, Albert, me plus Marcia, Peter Davis and Denis Lyons. This is meant to be a reconciliation meeting. It is typical of HW. After two weeks with her he returned committed to all kinds of schemes to freeze us out and put in her, Davis and Lyons. Then once he is back he starts looking for compromises. He balances the factions among us just as he balances the right and left wings of the party.

Home at 9 p.m.

*Thursday 5 September 1974*

[In his TUC speech at Brighton this day Wilson effectively launched the general election campaign. He listed the Labour government's achievements since March and contrasted the present peaceful situation in Britain with that seven months earlier when 'we inherited a deliberately divided and embittered nation with man set against man, brother against brother'. He made references to the earlier 'darkened streets' and the three-day week, which were to become the staple diet of his campaign speeches.

Significantly he gave great praise to the 'social contract', which Labour offered 'between all our people'. On the previous day, the Trades Union Congress had endorsed the social contract. This probably repaired the break created between Labour and the unions by Wilson's attack on trade union power in the White Paper *In Place of Strife* in 1969. The need for such a rapprochement was accentuated when two anti-EEC left-wingers, Jack Jones and Hugh Scanlon, took over the Transport Workers Union and the Engineers Union, holding between them 30% of the vote at conference.

Tony Benn was probably the first Labour politician to use the general term 'social contract' in its contemporary British meaning in his 1970 Fabian tract *The New Politics: a Socialist Renaissance*. Then James Callaghan adopted the concept and told the 1972 Labour Party conference that 'what Britain needs is a new social contract' and claimed that Labour's current policy document *Programme for Britain* was 'the charter for the new social contract'. Labour's *Programme for 1973* called for 'a far-reaching social contract between workers and the Government' and in that year an agreement between the party and the TUC, initiated by Jack Jones, the leader of the Transport and General Workers Union, was published covering prices, rents, taxes, pensions and transport. Thus Labour and the trade unions were moving towards a comprehensive agreement under the heading of the social contract. But it had not been finally worked out in detail when the February 1974 election was suddenly called, and the Labour manifesto was only able to refer in general terms to 'the new social contract' between the party and the TUC. The social contract was finally documented and recommended by the TUC General Council in June and was now made TUC policy in September in time for the election. Basically it meant that in return for such promised Labour policies as price controls, food subsidies, rent freezes, pension increases, greater industrial democracy and especially the repeal of all Tory industrial relations legislation, the unions would moderate wage claims in line with inflation, as calculated by the retail prices index. There was no mechanism for enforcing it on individual unions.

For Harold Wilson in the forthcoming election campaign and afterwards the social contract became an all-purpose political phrase conveying and implying an image of social justice, conciliation and co-operation in industry and society at large, a general style of peaceful government as an alternative to Mr Heath's abrasive and confrontational style, as well as a specific anti-inflation policy which hopefully would help to avoid the need for a statutory incomes policy.

As such it became a vital tool for Wilson in defining the difference between the Labour and Conservative approaches to government – made more clear, on this same day, 5 September, when the guru of New Toryism, Sir Keith Joseph,* made his seminal speech at Preston stating that the only cure for inflation was strict control of the money supply even if rigid monetarism involved increases in unemployment.]

Cabinet all morning. I worked in the Policy Unit. Then went down to meet the ministers coming out of Cabinet. Talked to Tony Crosland, who is pretty confident about the election. Also to Lever, who is full of tax amendments to the land nationalisation scheme. And to Roy Mason about our intentions to save small businesses – he is concerned with Barnsley Brewery. Hoped to have a word with Shirley Williams, but she nipped off for lunch with Roy Jenkins.

I went to lunch with stockbrokers Grieveson Grant, who are very gloomy about City confidence.

Home early to see Carol and family. Also to watch the PM's speech at Brighton TUC. A bit dull, but it seems to have worked as an election opener.

### Friday 6 September 1974

The PM returned from Brighton at 10.30 a.m. We gathered in the study to discuss the reception to the TUC speech. He was very pleased. Privately the TUC had been very favourable also.

All pleased with Tory splits – Keith Joseph attacking Heath on incomes policy and Geoffrey Rippon,* their Shadow Foreign Secretary, supporting private armies for citizens defence. Definitely more optimistic. PM decided not to refer to Joseph's attacks – which would unite the Tories. To let them argue among themselves and leave Healey to make our attacks. The PM is still talking of himself as needing to 'keep a low profile'. Also that he must not refer to Heath at all, let alone attack him.

We also worked on tonight's speech in Lancashire. Mainly a rehash of the TUC speech. At lunchtime we suggested the PM come in to lunch with us in No. 10. He looked scared and got the private office to book him a table elsewhere – anywhere.

Home 8.30.

[At the weekend the Prime Minister went to stay with the Queen at Balmoral to get approval for his intention to announce on 18 September a general election for 10 October. This date had the attractions that it was after the end of the Jewish High Holidays, after university students had returned to their (often marginal) university towns, and in a week without any scheduled announcements of economic statistics.]

## Monday 9 September 1974

At the weekend the *Sunday Times* printed a firm story that 10 October was the election day. Joe said that the PM would suspect me because I had seen Harold Evans on Tuesday. In fact I did not tell Harry and the *Observer* and everybody else seems to have got wind of the date on Saturday. Lots of people know, in Transport House and the Civil Service.

I was 40 on Sunday – and scored a marvellously satisfying 30-yard goal in Dartmouth Park United's first game of the season on Hampstead Heath.

This morning the PM arrived back from Balmoral earlier than expected. We had a long talk in the study about electoral strategy. At one point HW said it was going so well now that he almost wished the date was earlier, on the 3rd October. Now he is clearly geared up he doesn't like waiting. I raised with him the question of the Irish vote – and the campaign among Irish residents *not* to vote Labour because of internment in Ulster. Did some work on it and later put in a memo. Also tried to get hold of Merlyn Rees, but he is delayed in Belfast.

Also the question of small breweries, where Shirley Williams's department is being very sticky. Got the PM's support to go through to her and try to get some action – to defend Greene King beer in Suffolk as well as Barnsley Brewery. And to arrange that he visits Alf Morris on Friday in Liverpool when the White Paper on the disabled is launched. As always, he was very quick to spot the political significance and to support any action required. But, also as usual, he did not come to lunch. Joe, Albert and I ate away from the private office. Discussed our strategy for the campaign. It is clear that Marcia is trying to freeze us in No. 10 while she has her team at Transport House.

Joe recalled from HW's previous government that in 1968–69 she was one of the main forces behind the disastrous *In Place of Strife*, wanting an attack on the trade unions. She wanted the election in June 1970 – and then a quiet 'walkabout' campaign. She wanted it conducted from No. 10, with Transport House frozen out. She won and Labour lost.

In the afternoon the PM gave Joe a secret copy of the Tory (unpublished) manifesto and said only Joe and I were to see it. Not even Albert. We spent much of the afternoon discussing it – and especially its direct bid for a coalition.

[The Tory manifesto was published in three national newspapers on the next day, 10 September, well before the Conservative Party schedule, and its launch had to be brought forward to the 12th. The culprits were never identified, though trade union printers were suspected.]

I reported this to the PM just before he saw King Hussein of Jordan and said he must take the coalition threat seriously.

Also discovered that the White Paper on the disabled had nothing on three-wheelers, so I spoke to the PM and got him to sign a minute drafted by the Unit insisting on some sentences on government action to help disabled people to buy four-wheel cars.

Rest of time on Unit papers.

In fact the flow of papers has definitely slowed down. The calm before the storm.

Home at 8.30.


*Tuesday 10 September 1974*

Went in early to see Merlyn Rees before his meeting with the PM at 9.45. I am worried about the alienation of the Irish vote in the UK because they think we are doing nothing about internment, etc. Our Irish policy seems to have lost its momentum. I saw Merlyn and he had some figures with him showing that the number of internees had dropped – he later phoned and said the figures were not quite right.

I went to the office and dealt with mail and papers. Also a lot of tele-phoning to catch up on. Later in the morning we all met upstairs in the PM's study to begin preparing the strategy for the election campaign. Lunch as usual.

2 p.m. The PM had a meeting with the Northern Ireland SDLP – Fitt,* Hume, Curry, Devlin (who was terrible) and two others. Except for Fitt, they made a bad impression. Rambling and vague. Blaming us for all the troubles, to cover up their own impotence. They predicted Ulster would blow up again soon and that the Protestants would go for a UDI – and wanted us to make firm declarations that we would use force against them if they did. Also that we would explicitly accept the Irish dimension as at the heart of it all. They also attacked Merlyn personally, and the PM got fed up. Had to throw them out at 3 p.m. Yet Ireland depends on them. An unimpressive shower, but the only decent human beings left in Northern Irish politics.

Afterwards the Cabinet Industrial Development committee. A series of liquidity crises – Ferranti totally bust, Aston Martin bust, etc., etc. Saved Ferranti but not Aston Martin.

At one point, when Benn was making a moving appeal to give more money to a workers' co-operative under the receiver, Lever collapsed with laughter and was unable to control himself. Healey was totally scornful –

but they paid up because of the election. Benn took all this scorn and contempt in very good part, as if knowing that time is on his side.

Then to the great political meeting – PM, Marcia, Peter Davis [recently elevated as Lord Lovell-Davis for assisting Harold Wilson and Marcia with public relations] Denis Lyons, Joe, Albert, Terry Lancaster from the *Daily Mirror* and myself. This is HW's attempt to re-create the harmony of the last election by merging the two teams – his team at No. 10 and Marcia's alternative Mafia.

We three, Joe, Albert and I, went to join the PM in the study. But then the PM disappeared. After waiting there for half an hour Joe walked out, saying he had a job to do, and if the PM decided to hold one meeting instead of two, he would be prepared to attend if summoned.

Then messages came through to go to the flat, where we found the PM plus the other four having tea. On to business and Marcia set the pace. Where should we be based? Transport House. Recognised Joe and I could not go there, and Albert had already been told to stay in No. 10. Who would do the press relations? Peter Davis offered, and I felt this had been discussed before. But Terry Lancaster intervened to say Joe must really be in charge and so only needed an assistant to answer the phone. At this Peter Davis withdrew somewhat, and it was decided to get Jean Denham from Joe's press office to resign for the campaign and work for him at Transport House.

Then Marcia asked what about speeches, who and where to write them? The PM then said, 'Well, Marcia will of course be in charge, but Peter Davis will be helping to mastermind it.' I then intervened and said speeches could not be written by a committee. Lancaster said Joe must write them. I said yes, the committee should feed in ideas, but then leave Joe (and me) to work on them. This could not be done at Transport House so it had to be at No. 10 – in the flat. This was eventually agreed.

So we had won the mini-battles, resisting the moves to replace Joe and keeping some of the work in No. 10, where we have to be based anyway. Marcia kept going on about the need to be based in Transport House – which is true, since the officials there must have ready access to the PM. But to her it was a way to get things away from us. It also backfired. In the end we decided that Transport House was so important that Albert must be there – thus reversing her earlier decision that he should be in No. 10 in charge of a defunct political office.

We then decided to repeat, as in the February election, the morning tactical meetings at Lord North Street after the Campaign committee and before the press conference at Transport House. Joe and I would attend. So in the end it all went well. The attack on Joe had been blatant, but resisted.

We broke up at 6.30 to go downstairs to a party for Transport House officials. I in fact ducked it, went back to my office, did some reading and slept a little, since I felt a bit off, with a bad stomach. When I went up at 8 the atmosphere was generally drunken and in particular tense. Ron Hayward had discovered that the PM was giving the group of us dinner that night to discuss the election campaign without inviting him. In fact the PM had originally meant to invite him, but Marcia vetoed it!

Hayward went through the roof, attacked poor Albert and then walked out of the party. The PM sent Albert to run after him and fetch him back, but he would not come. Later it was decided to invite him and the Transport House people to lunch at No. 10 to discuss the campaign strategy, but Hayward refused, saying he 'did not want to be placated'. Meanwhile Percy Clarke, the Transport House press officer, who is always friendly and helpful to me but who others find difficult, told me that No. 10 treated the staff of Transport House like dirt. He warned Joe. Later Peter Davis and Lyons attacked Percy to me, claiming he had twice lost his nerve and walked out of campaign meetings in his stockinged feet, having forgotten he had taken his shoes off under the desk for comfort. It seems a bit of a jungle and was glad I came late. In the middle of the room a large Australian girl stood weeping with emotion because the PM said he had once lived for six months in her part of Australia.

This was all in the main reception room and the blue and white boudoirs, surrounded by lovely, if a bit pansy, furniture and paintings. They went on drinking for hours. The PM withdrew to hide in the study. Mary left. Marcia went off to talk to John Schofield Allen, who told her that Harold Evans – i.e. me – was the main source of press attacks on her. Allen is fortunately and finally leaving his undefined job at Transport House; his place in the bar of the nearby Marquis of Granby pub will be difficult to fill, at least for all the hours he was there.

Finally Alf Richman, with his customary delicacy, switched off all the lights, and people got the hint and left. We adjourned to the study and gossiped – joined by Terry Boston. We went off late to dinner in the small dining-room. The atmosphere was tense because Marcia had launched fresh attacks on Paddy, the pretty and excellent cook, claiming she is a security risk, bankrupt, and insisting she be sacked by election day. [Paddy later married Robert, now Lord Armstrong.] HW responded by ignoring Paddy throughout the meal and not thanking her afterwards.

Conversation was rambling. Most of the decisions had been taken. Except what to do with Alf Richman. It was agreed that if he went to party election meetings this time we might lose the election because of the resulting alienation of party workers, so he had to be stopped. But HW dared not tell him, so we spent an hour dreaming up a job for him. He is to stay at home to monitor the television.

Afterwards we were in the study till midnight. A lot of desultory talk. But HW did give a very good summary of this day's timetable of decisions as he saw it – with all our victories.

He made a long digression on how he would deal with press smears.

I said that after an initial denunciation he must not get dragged into a battle with the press, but must ignore them. He said that was right and he needed people to stop him following his 'first and not always my best instincts'.

Went home in a taxi, very tired, with Peter Davis.

### Wednesday 11 September 1974

Lively and exciting day. The PM in excellent spirits, repeatedly calling me to the study to discuss ideas and developments. The election has taken over. He is distancing himself from the civil servants and bringing the old team back in.

He dictated ideas for tomorrow's Stockport speech. Then we discussed strategy, including agreeing to a Sunday pre-election campaign strategy meeting. Also some policy points. Many of the Unit's 'Little Things' policies are now coming home – concessionary fares on railways, protecting small breweries, saving the pint measure, all came through today.

I was also in touch with Alf Morris to get some liaison with the PM on Friday for his launching of the disablement White Paper in Liverpool.

[The government produced a rush of White Papers before dissolving Parliament: on sex discrimination (6 September), consumer protection (10 September), pensions (11 September), land (12 September), the disabled (13 September) and devolution (17 September). Whitehall convention bars the issue of such policy documents once the campaign is under way.]

Also set the Unit to work on several chunks of the Stockport speech – on education, balance of payments, 'confidence'. But somehow the speech didn't get written and the PM was very worried by the late afternoon. We had been rushing in all directions, a hectic day. He was seeing Liam Cosgrave, the Irish Premier, for dinner. Therefore he could not attend a farewell dinner for Israel Gatt, the Israeli Labour Party man. I went instead and took a letter from the PM.

Just before going I got the latest Labour Party Bob Worcester poll – showing us 11% in the lead. I managed to tell the PM and he seemed very pleased. He introduced me to Cosgrave, a very quiet man.

Home at 9 p.m., but constantly on the phone to No. 10. The speech – and the minute we are putting in on the public expenditure review, which threatens to repudiate most of our next election manifesto. Andrew Graham and David Piachaud from the Unit doing a splendid job here.

*Thursday 12 September 1974*

PM in Cabinet all morning. Mainly on public expenditure – where they decided to delay most of the decisions which would have run completely contrary to our manifesto commitments. The excuse is the lack of decision on defence cuts. But electoral politics was clearly important.

We met in the study after the Cabinet till nearly 2 p.m., discussing the final details of this evening's speech at Stockport. Then the PM went up to the flat.

We all sat lunching in the small dining-room when he came in to tell us something, while protesting loudly that he was 'not lunching here'.

After lunch Robert Armstrong and I had a talk. Robert told me that HW has ordered that the cook must go. Sad, because it is a victory for Marcia, who hates her, probably because she is pretty.

We prepared several chunks of the speech in the Unit, especially that on the trade figures, which are remarkably good. Just good luck. The outlook is still grim and once the election is over we have to get down to the horrors of inflation. I have told the Unit this – that we cannot bear going on with electoral politics much longer. We simply must start briefing on what we think *ought* to be done.

At 5.30 I went to see Anthony Lester, special adviser to Roy Jenkins, at the Home Office. I told him my reservations about Roy's political inactivity in the past six months – that he seemed to opt out too often and left the Right leaderless. Tony pressed me to say this to Roy's face. I said I would prefer to and was very uncomfortable at never having had a serious talk with him. Tony said this is because Roy is shy and that it is necessary to pile in.

So we went in to Roy's enormous room – it was the one Herbert Morrison occupied 30 years ago – and had several large gin and tonics. After some desultory talk about the Civil Service, in which I praised Robert Armstrong, it emerged that Roy would like to replace his present permanent secretary with Robert. I said what I thought – that Roy should take a more active part leading the Right, and also in the campaign showing his loyalty to the party, including knocking any idea of joining a coalition; that I thought Harold Wilson thought more of Roy than vice versa; that HW was a much improved figure. (Here Roy agreed strongly, saying that in 1964–70 most of their time was spent discussing plots and press smears. Plus ça change!)

At the end – after two hours and two of the largest gin and tonics I have ever drunk in my life – we broke up. I felt much happier and now able to talk to him straight. I also felt we had buried the memory of that comic opera situation in March when HW was forming the government and used me as a messenger to Roy.

Roy summed up, laughing, by saying in future he would 'try to love HW more'. I interrupted and said that was not what I wanted. I wanted two things: (1) more active leadership of the Right and (2) more active participation in the campaign than last time.

Went home feeling drunk but cheered.

## Friday 13 September 1974

Went in late to No. 10 because the PM stayed at Chequers overnight after returning from Stockport. When he arrived we went upstairs to the study and began to discuss strategy for the campaign – the keynote speech in Glasgow on the 23rd, when to refer to strikes, national unity, etc.

He was more interested in discussing the press. Today's attacks on Lord Brayley,* a junior Defence minister, who had made financial contributions to the party, have renewed his paranoia and fears of smears on him in the campaign.

Saturday: The PM went to Paris to meet President Giscard d'Estaing. Joe phoned us and said he kept going on about how brilliant Marcia was and how she was somehow responsible for the flow of White Papers! He was also criticising me for having dinner with Harold Evans. And he was attacking Joe for being too dour! This is all her. The last kick was when he told Joe that we would not after all be lunching during the campaign with him and her in the flat. He said we were to eat separately in the dining-room and join him later. This is the reverse of what was decided earlier and can only be because of her pressure. Joe is feeling very bolshy. He says HW didn't like the fact that Joe kept opposing him. Joe apparently told him he must treat the EEC seriously when briefing the European journalists. HW was proposing to be flippant.

Sunday evening Harold Evans came round. Said the Civil Service is being very heavy over the Crossman Diaries and threatening him with court injunctions, etc. I also criticised him for a proposed series on the wealth and houses of Labour ministers. Unworthy of them. He also said that he was thinking of bringing the *Sunday Times* out in favour of Labour.

But obviously we have a tricky time ahead. Marcia is for the moment totally controlling HW and trying to turn him against us. I talked to her doctor, Joe Stone, on Thursday about her. He referred to her megalomania and indicated it would be better if Harold would get rid of her. He said she 'would love to sit on the white horse at the Trooping the Colour'.

## Monday 16 September 1974

The PM was in a joint meeting of the Cabinet and the National Executive Committee to approve the manifesto, held in the large state banqueting room from 9.30 through lunch to the afternoon.

I had a meeting with Bob Worcester and Peter Davis – with whom I still get on well – about opinion polls. Worcester brought his latest material, which is generally encouraging, and we discussed how to run things in the campaign. I also suggested one or two ideas for our questionnaire.

Finished with them at 11.45. Then had a meeting with Cabinet Office officials about the Election Business committee, a secret government committee which services ministers with briefs and replies to questions and letters on policy matters during the election. It is a way in which the Civil Service helps the government of the day in the campaign. The defence and explanation is that statements on policy must be in line with government decisions, as otherwise they might wobble and embarrass the machine. I am the effective link man, the PM's rep, on this committee. I am also the link to Transport House.

Harold Lever dropped in to the Unit for coffee, being bored by the NEC meeting. He was in splendid and very funny form.

Before lunch Joe and I went upstairs to the study. The PM was rather brusque with Joe. So we went off to the House of Commons for lunch. When we returned at 2.30 p.m. there was a message saying the PM wanted us immediately. He wanted a draft on the social contract to include in the manifesto. Joe drafted a piece which I thought excellent. Joe took it in to the NEC meeting and the PM was very surly. He said, 'Where have you been, what have you been up to?' And then said the draft was no good and it wasn't what he wanted, and he sent us off to find his earlier speeches. We did this. Joe was upset and angry.

We took the pieces back up to him. Shortly after he sent for us in the study. He was very jumpy and drinking brandies with frightening rapidity. He said the NEC meeting was in a crisis over the Common Market. Roy Jenkins had reopened the whole referendum question and also rejected a time limit. Peter Shore, Ian Mikardo and others were moving anti-Market amendments. He thought the whole thing was breaking up and they might have a disastrous split. He then ran back to the meeting.

Half an hour later the PM sent for us again. He was still drinking brandy, but was now beaming with happiness. He said he had solved the problem and they had approved the EEC section without amendments at his suggestion. He had played off Shore and Jenkins and appealed to the centre.

He was also now going out of his way to please Joe. We had sent in a note saying that we – Joe and I – thought that Michael Foot's introduction to the manifesto was too flat and gloomy. He said he totally agreed. We now sat down to rewrite it completely. He dictated, and we interrupted with suggestions. He now included Joe's earlier rejected piece on the social contract word for word, and said how good it was.

We worked under tremendous pressure. It was 4.45 when we started on this crucial part of the manifesto – and the Transport House press conference was at 6.45. By then it all had to be run off and handed out. And at 5.45 the PM was seeing the Zambian Foreign Minister. We finished with three minutes to spare.

I then went to my room and read papers and Joe went to do a first draft of the ministerial broadcast for Wednesday. It seemed to me, when he finished, very good. I made a few suggestions, and we gave it to the PM when he returned at 8.30. But he didn't want to discuss it. He was in a strange surly mood again. Albert later phoned to say he had been criticising Joe to Transport House people. Specifically because Joe wants to stay at St Ermin's Hotel during the election campaign, as last time, and Marcia is refusing to pay from office funds. Apparently Joe went through the roof when he heard this and is on the verge of a big row. We must hold him for four more weeks.

[The Labour manifesto, entitled *Britain Will Win with Labour*, was launched that day, 26 September, having been previously discussed between the Cabinet and the NEC at Number Ten on 25 July. It included a key pledge on the EEC giving 'the British people a final say through the ballot box'. On nationalisation it outlined the 1973 commitments to nationalise the pharmaceutical, road haulage, construction and machine-tool industries. It was broadly based on the February 1974 manifesto. The only new commitments were to repeat the Tory government's Christmas bonus of £10 for pensioners and to Scottish and Welsh assemblies with some legislative powers. One central phrase stated 'At the heart of this manifesto and our programme to save the nation lies the contract between the Labour Government and the trade unions.' Another described the battle against inflation as Labour's 'first priority'.]

## Tuesday 17 September 1974

The PM was occupied most of the morning with some African visitors and his lawyer over some newspaper problem. I dealt with Unit papers and also worked on Joe's version of the PM's election broadcast. But generally a relaxed morning with no great pressure.

The PM and Joe went to lunch with IPC (the *Mirror* newspapers). I went to lunch separately at Manzi's and had some beautiful fresh herrings and scallops.

Afterwards we had a brief meeting in the study and the PM was very friendly. Then he went off to Transport House with Marcia to try to restore relations with Ron Hayward and did not return till 8 p.m. Joe then had a final draft of the speech for him and he said he would read it – and he suggested we go home.

He was also drinking again, and had obviously had enough by 8 p.m.

Joe is in a very delicate position. The row over his staying at a hotel during the campaign has come to a head. Marcia is refusing to pay from office funds. Joe has booked his room at St Ermin's as usual during an election campaign. [Joe Haines lived in Tunbridge Wells, did not drive and could not take his train as usual because of the extraordinary hours worked during the election campaign.]

This puts the onus on her to explain why he should not have the usual facilities. In fact of course she is trying to humiliate him, as she has often humiliated Albert Murray. But Joe is made of flint. He won't submit. She is trying to mobilise the PM against Joe. HW is bewildered and miserable – giving in to her by criticising Joe, but then trying to show that he appreciates Joe's marvellous qualities. So HW is swinging between rudeness and over-affection. Joe is deeply hurt and furious, and saying that if he goes he will have revenge.

In the end of course the PM will always give in to her. Bill Housden told us that in the car he had heard her demanding that HW should not agree to what Joe wants. After the election Joe will probably, as he says, have to go. If so, my days will be numbered. But we will not be humiliated. The point is that neither of us needs her or him. It is nice to work here, but we don't need it. So she cannot, as with other previous members of HW's Kitchen Cabinets, either buy us or frighten us.

## Wednesday 18 September 1974

Dismal day. In the morning the PM was in the Cabinet and the Defence committee. We continued to work on the script of the ministerial television broadcast, which is now quite elegant.

The PM summoned us to the study at midday. He said Marcia – who had been sent a copy by official car in the morning – had attacked the television script and demanded a different one. So he was now re-dictating. His version was not very good – in fact terrible. Much more party-political, with snide attacks on the Tories. We tried to get some philosophy and uplift into it, but he resisted it.

We took lunch with the civil servants while the script was being typed.

When we resumed after lunch there were a load of problems, because it didn't flow at all. The TV people were all set up in the lounges waiting while we sweated to make something out of his rambling prose.

Marcia arrived at 4 p.m., ignored us all and made a few suggestions. When it was done she walked out, and was not around while the PM did his broadcast and two other interviews. He was not good, no style, just flat and all the old predictable phrases.

There was due to be a large meeting of the electoral team, with all the political office staff, at 6 p.m. Marcia had summoned it, but at 7.30 everybody was still sitting around waiting. She was upstairs in the PM's flat holding a separate planning meeting with Lord Lovell-Davis and Denis Lyons.

The PM had a drink in the study with Joe, myself and John Grant and then suddenly slipped out. He had ordered tea for us all, but ran out of the room after pouring his cup without drinking it.

I went off to the Unit to see David Piachaud who was drafting an excellent piece on unemployment for the PM's adoption meeting speech tomorrow in Huyton.

At 8 I went down to the press office. Albert arrived looking very unhappy. Marcia had picked a row with him because he had been talking to the civil servants in the private office. She accused him of plotting with them behind her back. Then she accused him of being no good at organisation or anything. The alternative meeting of the election team had apparently begun upstairs, and HW had said – at her prompting – that Joe and I were not to be invited. There had been some shuffling from room to room to hide from us. Absolutely ridiculous. It is a pantomime farce, but too petty to be funny. I did not give a damn, since I had anyway arranged to go to the cinema with Carol – a marvellous film called *The Sting* – and was grateful to get away. I simply walked out, without ever being able to give the PM the unemployment speech he had asked for. But Joe was seething and ready for a fight. The ridiculous thing was that Jean Denham, who had resigned from No. 10 especially to handle the press at Transport House, was not at the meeting either. She was sitting with Joe in Joe's office, waiting for the scheduled meeting to start, but was not summoned to the alternative meeting because that would have involved telling Joe, who would have answered the phone. This ridiculous business is typical of Marcia's way of operating. 'The Princess of Trivia and Pettiness', as private office call her.

Clearly we have been squeezed out of running the campaign. Joe had been asked to do the weekend Southampton speech and was working on it – but apparently Davis and Lyons and Marcia were doing the same speech at the same time upstairs. I don't mind at all and feel very detached, like a camera or a fly on the wall recording all this nonsense. In a way, the more bizarre and awful it is, the more fascinating. But I am still sad and angry to see the Labour Movement led and controlled in this way. All those people out there working and hoping and paying their subscriptions, sacrificing themselves for a Labour victory. In here, just petty manoeuvring.

Next morning I discovered that things had got worse for Joe last night. The PM had said to him, 'Why should we spend £200 so that you can have breakfast in bed?' (about Joe going to stay at St Ermin's during the campaign). This hurt Joe very much since he has never claimed any expenses, never had a rise in the past four years working for HW in opposition, and in 1970 he had slaved away on the Wilson memoirs for months without return – or at least he was paid £4,000 by the publishers, but was not paid a penny salary by Harold that year for all the press work he did.

Also once Joe went into the study. HW, Davis and Marcia were drinking coffee together. HW dismissed him from the room.

HW was also drinking brandy heavily before he did his final TV broadcast, on *Midweek* at 9.30.

Bill Housden told us next morning that HW and Marcia had a row later and he gave her a rocketing. He told her that nobody could work with her, that she always assumed that everybody was wrong except her and that all the team were upset at the changes in the ministerial broadcast which she had forced him to make.

It was clear to us that he knew the broadcast was bad and that Joe's version was better. He knew she was responsible and could not bring himself to admit this, but he was clearly upset.

[On 18 September the election was officially announced by Mr Wilson and the following day Parliament was formally dissolved. It had lasted only 199 days.]

*Thursday 19 September 1974*

The PM was clearly still upset in the morning. Very jumpy and distant. When he came back from the campaign committee he told Joe that he was going away to Chequers for the weekend to think about the campaign. He didn't want any help with speeches (except today's at Huyton which was mainly done by David Piachaud of the Unit and *very* good.) He knows that his hopes of merging the factions into one harmonious team have failed because she won't work with us and is trying to squeeze us out. He wants a happy team and has gone away to think about it.

After lunch Joe received a letter from Marcia capitulating completely on St Ermin's. Partly because of HW last night. But Joe says he will have to pay for that victory – and suspects that she would only have given way if promised something more by HW in the long run. He thinks Harold has asked her to be nice to us in the campaign and then he will get rid of us afterwards – probably with Davis replacing Joe.

In the afternoon the PM went to Huyton for his adoption meeting. We heard that *Private Eye* has printed a piece accusing Harold Evans of agreeing not to print the Crossman Diaries before the election in return for getting a scoop on the election date. We discuss it in private office. Suspicion is on me again – but James Margach of the *Sunday Times*, who wrote the story, has told Joe that he got the story from somebody else at Transport House.

I feel very relaxed about it. At least I did tell HW that I was going to see H. Evans, and I did not tell Harry the election date.

I talked to H. Evans this evening and he confirmed this.

### Friday 20 September 1974

When I arrived at No. 10 HW, who was at Chequers, was already on the phone asking me to talk to Michael Foot to get him to make a speech attacking the Tories on unemployment. I phoned Foot at home before he set off for Wales and he agreed to do so.

HW had also been on the phone to Joe and had been very sharp with him. Said Joe had upset Marcia – 'by comparing her to Frances Morrell' (Benn's large lady special adviser whom he takes everywhere).

Joe was upset. The Frances Morrell suggestion was incredible. It stemmed from a conversation between Peter Davis and myself, discussing Benn's appearance in a proposed party political. Joe took no part because he was not in the room at the time, though Marcia was. Over this petty matter the PM is involved in a row at the start of the election campaign when there is so much else to think about.

The PM stayed at Chequers all morning and for lunch, still trying to sort out his election strategy – and what to do about the tensions in his team.

Even worse, this morning's *Daily Express* carried a piece by its journalist Chapman Pincher (who has links with the security services), claiming that Marjorie Halls (the widow of HW's previous principal private secretary) had been bought off by Douglas Allen,* the head of the Civil Service, and that the issue of her claim for damages would be finally settled by the next minister for the Civil Service, who was to be Marcia.

Apparently Marcia 'went through the roof', according to Bill Housden, and intends to issue a writ. The PM was distracted and spent half the morning talking to Lord Goodman. He also told Joe he was going to devote tonight's big speeches at Portsmouth and Southampton to attacks on the press, and that this would be the handout.

I went out at lunch to see Shirley Williams at her office. We discussed the Common Market. She was afraid that Peter Shore was going to say something wild and asked me to convey to Harold that if Shore did so the pro-Marketeers would have to respond, and then the balloon would go up.

We also discussed the situation after the election. She is fairly pessimistic that there will be a split in the Labour Party. I share this view really, but stress to her that our moderate side must not detonate the time bomb ticking away – partly because there is still a remote chance that we will win. I told her that Callaghan and Wilson were both better on the EEC and might keep us in.

I did not say, what I had said to nobody, that I am now more pro-Market than previously because there is *absolutely no* alternative. If HW took us out, I would resign.

On the way back, after a couple of sandwiches and coffee for lunch with Shirley, I called in on Ron Hayward at Transport House to establish liaison for the Election Business committee. He was overtly friendly, as ever, and had clearly had a good lunch.

When I got back into No. 10 at 2.45 p.m. the PM was there and had left a message for me to go up to the study. He was there with Joe and Robin Butler working on tonight's speech. The atmosphere was tense, he was very jumpy, with his coat off, snapping, and surrounded by a confusion of papers and speech drafts. Joe was desperately trying to put some order into the speech.

From me he wanted statistics on prices and I went to get some from the Unit. He was also asking for material for Monday's Glasgow speech which he is going to dictate at Chequers over the weekend. I got the material. But there continued a most terrible rush.

He had drafted a piece attacking the press, which was to go out to the press. It was terrible. Joe and I felt unable to oppose him on it – he knew where we stood and his hostility to us stood out a mile. Then, as he left the room to interview Lord Chalfont (who is going to leave the Labour Party and feels this momentous news must be conveyed personally to the PM), he turned to Joe and said, 'Take out all that stuff attacking the press. It's not a good idea to do it.'

We were immensely relieved and Joe crossed it all out with great relish and had the press release typed.

While he was in the drawing-room talking to Chalfont the phone rang in the empty study. I went in and answered. The operator said that Lady Falkender wished to talk to the PM immediately. So I went through and interrupted them and told the PM. He said, 'Tell her I will phone back in a minute.' I returned and told the operator. As I finished, Marcia broke in and said, 'If that is Bernard Donoughue, I will tell him to stop this nonsense.' I coldly reported that the PM was coming to the phone shortly. She said, 'You'd better tell him to come straight away or there will be trouble.' I put the phone down and went back to Joe to work on the speech, which was still in a mess 20 minutes before the train to Southampton left Waterloo.

A secretary came running in from the political office saying that Lady Falkender had been on again demanding that the PM phone her – this was three minutes after she had talked to me. We sent in a message with one of the private secretaries.

HW came out and ran down the stairs to Marcia's room to telephone. He came back five minutes later, sweating and looking very upset. We went in the study and he said, 'She is in a terrible state, a terrible state.' He then started to attack the press and said he had to put back in the speech his attack on the press. She had insisted on it, he said, with the exception of one paragraph referring to the press digging up her parentage.

So we had to get another version of the press release retyped, putting the attack on the press back in. HW meanwhile started to pour himself stiff brandies.

Somebody phoned, who I took, from the conversation, to be a doctor, and at one point HW said, 'Yes, she is in an impossible state. You must give her plenty of them' – which I took to be tranquillisers.

At the last moment the PM checked through the speech and found it was in the wrong order, so we had a terrible flap. People were running in and out, up and down stairs, bringing drafts and messages. Total chaos.

Just before he left I managed to mention Shirley Williams's message on the EEC, but it was not clear whether in the rush he was able to take it on board.

He finally left in the car for Waterloo only minutes before the train was due to leave, and then skidded to a halt in Downing Street because they had forgotten both the speech and Albert!

Joe and I went off to enjoy the calm after the storm, but very depressed about the speech and everything. This is a terrible start to an election campaign.

Incidentally Robert Armstrong has gone off to see Douglas Allen about the Marjorie Halls story, where Douglas has clearly not got it right. He was understandably trying to get it out of the way before the election, but his timing made it look as if he was trying to buy her off before the election. Before he went, Robert took me in his office to praise and support Joe and me. He knows we are in bad odour for having opposed the PM on the party political broadcast and on his attacking the press. He said,

'The trouble with Harold Wilson is that he has, allegedly, surrounded himself with sycophants. Thank God at last somebody is standing up to him against bad influences.' OK, nice of him. But how do we preserve any influence when she opposes everything we say?

In the evening I had the Policy Unit home for a pleasant dinner. They know nothing of these squabbles and really are a remarkably able and pleasant group. To bed at 2 a.m.

### Saturday 21 September 1974

I woke at 6.30, worried that the PM had not been sent enough material to work on his Glasgow speech. Had a quick breakfast and then phoned Joe. He thought private office had sent it all. I phoned Robin Butler, the relevant private secretary, at home – but he had gone to play golf. I phoned the duty clerk at No. 10, who said that the only brief with the PM was something the Unit put in on Scotland. Disaster. HW is expecting a mass of stuff to read and dictate from.

I drove in to No. 10 and gathered together various papers, briefs and statistical digests. I put these together into a substantial packet and sent them off by messenger to Chequers. I phoned HW, who was remarkably friendly, said how pleased he was I had gone in to No. 10, criticised the private secretaries (unfairly in my view) and then talked about the EEC. He had been thinking about Shirley's message about the EEC and asked me to tell her that he would do what he could. Also asked for speech material next week.

Went home. Called in on Bill Rodgers on the way. Phoned Joe, who said the PM had phoned *very* friendly. In the afternoon Bill came round and we discussed the campaign. He is quite optimistic, but thinks the Liberals will do well.

Joe phoned to say our latest private daily poll shows a lead of 8%. We agree that is better than the earlier 15%, which was completely unreal.

### Sunday 22 September 1974

Played football in the morning. Slept and bathed and read papers in the afternoon. Then drove in to No. 10 via Lord Kissin's house in Hampstead. He told me that he was getting messages that things were not good. And that HW meant to drop Joe. He said that Lord Goodman was appalled by what he knew, saw and heard.

Arrived at No. 10 at 7.30, just before the PM arrived. We went upstairs for the planned strategy meeting. But Marcia was not there, nor Davis or Lyons. It was clear that the original plan for a unified team was not working. Marcia is trying to squeeze us out by simply refusing to come to meetings with us. And Davis and Lyons apparently follow suit and hold separate meetings with her.

The PM was in splendid form, though drinking too much. He had dictated a long and good speech, very much along the lines of the Policy Unit draft which Kay Carmichael and David Piachaud had worked on. He repeatedly praised the briefs I put in on Saturday. I felt this was part of his constant effort to try to keep everybody happy. But we had a very jolly evening. He said to me that he 'hated all elections' but was relieved now that this was under way.

He left around 10 and Joe and I went over the speech draft, suggesting amendments. Then Joe went off to retype corrections and redraft some weak passages.

We had not eaten, so Albert cooked us some soup and toast after midnight. I went to bed upstairs in a No. 10 bedroom at 1 a.m. Joe stayed up working after that. He and Albert are staying in the PM's flat.

## Monday 23 September 1974

Awoke in No. 10 at 7. Raining and blowy outside looking over Horse Guards Parade. Had breakfast in the flat with Albert. Then downstairs to my office at 8.45. Began to organise my staff to do the corrections and inserts to the Glasgow speech – of which there were 23. It was a major job and the whole Unit was frantically busy researching and drafting. We also had a major typing problem. We cannot use civil servants in an election campaign. We are supposed to use the political office secretaries. But some of these are over at Transport House with Albert. Of those that remain, two are totally uncooperative. One refuses to do any work at all. Albert dismissed her, but Marcia intervened to get her reinstated. So we had only one girl, working like mad, and the office was like a railway station in the rush hour, with people rushing in and out carrying sheaves of paper, and there were so many parts of drafts that it was nearly impossible to maintain control of one basic master draft. I was in sole charge because Joe was away at the press conference with Albert at Transport House.

Anyway I had to leave at 9.45 and go to 5 Lord North Street for our morning strategy conference, as originally arranged. Harold Wilson was there, looking nervous, and Joe, but nobody else turned up. Marcia was sitting in Transport House up the road, and had apparently refused to come. Albert was still there too, and Davis and Lyons somehow failed to come to our meeting but were up in Transport House with Marcia.

We had a discussion about the speech and agreed that it was right, as the Unit had advised, to concentrate it wholly on Scotland and make the press handout wholly on Scotland.

Joe asked where Marcia was and HW said, 'I don't know.' Then HW said he must go to Transport House and off he went. We returned to No. 10, Joe only briefly before going back to Transport House for the press conference.

We all worked on the speech in Downing Street till after 1 p.m. Then Peter Davis and Denis Lyons arrived at my office door saying they had come for lunch in No. 10. We went upstairs and found the PM in the study with John Grant, and he said we should take Grant in to lunch as well. We went in, and the cook, who has just been told she is getting the sack and must spend less on food, said, understandably, that she had not cooked for three extra people and simply had no food for them. Lyons then started to complain that he 'never asked to eat at Buckingham Palace anyway'. Joe then lost his temper and piled into Lyons so fiercely that the latter, who weighs well over 20 stone, began to sweat and had to sit down. It was an embarrassing and ridiculous situation, and an ominous start for the election 'team'. It was resolved when Robert Armstrong came in with the usual civil servants for their lunch and, swiftly sizing up the situation, withdrew with an appropriate mixture of understanding and contempt. Then we all sat down to an uncomfortable lunch, with the three outsiders eating the civil servants' meals.

Over lunch Davis and Lyons revealed that the PM had asked them to draft tomorrow's speech at Leicester on the social contract. Joe looked a bit steely, but I didn't mind at all. If they could do it well, that would ease the burden on us; if they could not, the sooner that incapacity was revealed the better.

After lunch Joe and I went down to my office to gather together and check the draft of the keynote Glasgow speech. It was nearly 40 pages, and much more solid and serious than HW's speeches usually are. I was pleased with it. We took it to Transport House. I deliberately stayed outside and Joe took it in. He came out two minutes later and said that HW wanted me up there. So we went up to his room – the first time I had been back to it since 1 March. It looked different – it now had only two desks, one for HW and one for Marcia. She ignored Joe and me and never said a word to either of us in the hour we were there, rechecking the speech with HW for the handout (including persuading him to take out a section attacking the press in Scotland). He left late and in a great rush. Joe and I went back to No. 10. I began to deal with the backlog of official papers and the ordinary work of the Unit.

At 4.30 Peter Davis phoned. He said that he and Lyons, who since lunch had been working in their little room on the third floor of No. 10, had finished tomorrow's draft speech for Leicester and asked me to come up to discuss it. I agreed, and suggested that they ask Joe as well, which Peter was clearly reluctant to do. I asked how long it was. Peter said, 'Three pages

– how long are his speeches usually?' I said, 'Well, we processed 37 pages this morning, so you have some way to go.' I then went up and collected it and returned to my room to read it. It was not good.

Joe came in to see me half an hour later and said he had had a long talk with them. They had admitted they could not write election speeches and said they never wanted to. They just wanted to suggest themes and approaches in speeches (at which I have always found them helpful and imaginative). They begged Joe to do the speeches, and not even to put their three pages to the PM.

Davis apparently said to Joe that he realised that he was being used as a pawn in Marcia's game and did not intend to let it go on, since he did not want to write the campaign speeches. So Joe went off to write the Leicester social contract speech. Lyons said he did not feel well and went home. Davis went to Transport House to talk to Marcia – he said to persuade her 'not to behave like a silly child'.

The rest of the afternoon and evening we worked on various drafts for future speeches. I had sandwiches for supper in the PM's flat. We watched TV and the PM looked very good in Glasgow, but we heard by telephone that it was total chaos there. Nobody was on duty at the hotel (Richman disobeyed orders). The garden girl arrived late. The duplicator was taken to the meeting hall instead of the hotel – and then broke down. Apparently they were still running off the press release of the speech *in the hall* while the PM was making his speech.

Kay Carmichael, who was in the hall, phoned later and said the PM fluffed a lot of lines and looked tired, but the audience was enthusiastic and the seriousness of the Scottish content seemed to have made an impact.

Marcia came in during the evening and we all gathered uncomfortably in her room. We decided to try to make it work as a team by letting bygones be bygones – for the moment. Apparently Peter Davis had given her a good lecture and she agreed to be more sensible.

I took some briefs to 5 Lord North Street at 11 p.m., came back to No. 10 to watch TV and went to bed here at 12.30. I slept very badly. It is a terribly noisy house, with doors banging, clocks chiming, and at 2 a.m. a large policeman walked into my bedroom, wearing his helmet and then left, slowly, as I stared at him, without saying what he wanted.

*Tuesday 24 September 1974*

I rose feeling tired and cold (no heating yet in No. 10). Had a delicious large breakfast in the kitchen in the flat. Then met Joe and we went over to Harold's house in Lord North Street. Marcia was already there and we telephoned Peter Davis and Denis Lyons to join us.

The atmosphere was much better. Marcia was co-operative and going out of her way to be friendly. The PM in very good form. We discussed Joe's basic draft on the social contract for Leicester and then the PM dictated an extra piece challenging the Tories on what would be their substitute.

Then at 11.15 I went to Transport House. I walked with Peter Davis, who told me of his talk with Marcia the previous evening, in which she had promised to join the team. I did not go into Transport House but went back to No. 10, working on papers and speech drafts.

Lunch upstairs in the small state dining-room with Joe, Davis and Lyons, and John Grant. Very useful. Planned future big speeches on housing, the style of government and the EEC. The PM joined us after lunch for coffee. We discussed with him the problem of the EEC and Peter Shore provoking a row. I told him to talk to Shore before any press conference and make sure he said nothing silly.

At this point the PM was still committed to speaking on the EEC tonight – and would dictate it himself. But later in the afternoon – after he had gone to Leicester – he left a message with Marcia saying he would do housing instead. So Joe had to sit down, with a big brief from my Unit, to draft a speech.

I went home – to see Carol and the kids for the first time since last Monday, to eat and change my socks. Had a lovely time, sitting on the settee, drinking vermouth, with one of my girls tickling my back and the other scratching my scalp, both of which I enjoy greatly.

Drove back in to No. 10 with Carol. My friend Jacques Pomonti phoned while we were here, from Paris, and promised to send me the memorandum he had written for Mitterrand on the women's vote.

Then I went up to the flat where Joe and Albert were finishing supper. Joe had finished a very good housing speech and we read and checked that. Then discussed the Lord Brayley problem. Suspicions about his business activities meant a likely investigation under the Companies Act – or an inquiry by the Director of Public Prosecutions. Joe felt that HW must get rid of him as junior Defence minister quickly, and I agreed. So Joe drafted a memo and put it to the PM in his overnight box.

We all walked round to Lord North Street to put our briefs and memos through his letter-box at 11.30 p.m. Then Joe went home. Albert and I returned to No. 10. In fact the PM arrived there shortly after, from some very good meetings in Leicester. We chatted a while. He had brought a draft for tomorrow's press conference, pushing the Tories on the social contract. He then went back to Lord North Street. I went upstairs to bed and read John Le Carré till 1 a.m., then fell asleep.

## Wednesday 25 September 1974

A day of disasters. Started nicely. I cooked myself breakfast in the No. 10 kitchen. The PM saw the Attorney-General, Sam Silkin,* about Brayley in the study and then we all went together in the car to Transport House. Gathered in HW's room and went over the press handout and other tactical points. He went into the press conference and I went back to No. 10. It all seemed sunny – the weather and the outlook. The latest poll shows us 14% ahead. And the Tories are clearly very low.

I was sitting in my office reading papers at 1.15 when somebody rushed in and said, 'Shirley Williams has announced she will leave politics if the referendum decides against the EEC.' Joe and the PM were furious. It had been a very good and impressive press conference until Shirley said this right at the end. Uproar. Headlines bound to be – and were – 'Shirley – I quit government.'

We discussed this over lunch and also tried to focus on tomorrow's speech on prices.

The PM came in with *his* draft version of Brayley's resignation statement. It made it clear that HW was sacking him but also was full of silly references to the press. HW said Marcia wanted *even more* attacks on the press in this resignation letter. We discussed it and opposed this. Robert Armstrong was very good, as always, and had drafted an excellent alternative statement without reference to the press, with a covering note saying all three of us strongly preferred this. HW was clearly worried and kept saying how Marcia wanted something in about 'hounding by the press', but in the end he gave way.

He spent an hour with Brayley, and with Mellish, who is a friend of Brayley. Brayley apparently very broken up, and claimed he had decided last night to blow his brains out.

The PM finally left in a great rush, minutes before the train to Ipswich. Brayley did not leave till afterwards, through the Cabinet Office side door. We were all relieved it had been finally done – though Joe and I had wanted him sacked a fortnight ago when it first came up.

Joe went off to brief the press and to write the next speech – all in two hours. I simply could not do it. I went upstairs to my bedroom, listened to Bach and Mozart on a cassette recorder I had brought for this purpose and wrote up this record of today so far.

I feel a bit down. The campaign is going wrong. They are small things and may not lose us the election, but they are silly and inefficient. They leave a bad taste. All the divisions of the Labour Party, and the murky people around HW, showing the tips of their icebergs.

In the evening Joe and I went out together to Janet Hewlett-Davies's flat for supper. She is Joe's excellent deputy press officer and lives in Ashley Gardens near Victoria. Returned afterwards and dealt with tomorrow's speech.

PM dropped in to No. 10 on way back at midnight and reported on the speech and the meeting in East Anglia, which apparently went very well.

## Thursday 26 September 1974

After breakfast at No. 10, I went across to Transport House for a strategy meeting. I prepared a statement on the social contract. The PM also saw Peter Shore in advance of our press conference to make sure he said nothing silly on the Market.

Reports from the press conference at Tory Central Office were that they have nothing to say. Very low-key.

I returned to No. 10. Discussing drafts of future speeches with the Unit when news came over the tapes that Roy Jenkins had spoken in support of Shirley, saying he too would leave politics if the referendum went against the EEC.

This is bizarre. Yesterday evening I had *two* conversations with Anthony Lester, Jenkins's aide, in which he assured me that Roy was not going to say anything, and I passed this on to HW, as was clearly intended. So both Shirley and Roy have said one thing and done the other. I felt depressed. I telephoned Lever, who was puzzled by Roy's timing and his phrasing. I told him that it was sad to discover that our side is as lunatic as the Left. Nicer, but just as bloody barmy. It is not clear who is trying to win this election. Both the Tories and our lot are clearly trying to lose it.

[Jenkins actually issued a statement saying that he would resign from a Labour government which was pledged to take Britain out of the Common Market – different from the version discussed in Number Ten.]

In the afternoon I dealt with a lot of routine business and then went home in the evening for two hours to see the children while Joe did a speech handout on City problems.

I returned at 8.30 to meet for supper in No. 10 with Marcia, Joe and Albert. I had arranged for the cook to leave four steaks in the kitchen for us.

I went down to the Garden Room to get the keys to the kitchen. I found the duty clerk and three pretty garden girls down there enjoying a good meal – off our steaks. They had eaten our dinner! When I pointed this out they were petrified and set off in an official car to buy replacements from a hotel or a restaurant. I did not tell Marcia, and we delayed, watching television, till a pale girl came to apologise and offer us our replacements – which cost them £10. I roared with laughter. Marcia laughed too, but I suspect she felt it was another Civil Service plot against her.

We had a midnight discussion and decided that tomorrow's speech must try to recover ground lost by the Common Market diversions. Had to get back to confrontation and to prices. So the PM will speak on housing, but the press handout will be on confrontation.

In bed by 12.30.

## Friday 27 September 1974

Woke late after my first good night's sleep here in No. 10.

We gathered early at Lord North Street – Joe, Marcia, Davis, Lyons and myself plus the PM. Dictated a bit of tonight's press handout. Also discussed Common Market strategy – I want him to make a major speech before Enoch Powell intervenes next Thursday.

The press conference apparently went off quietly. Before lunch we all gathered in the study at No. 10 for fresh thoughts on tonight's speech. We are aware that things have slipped – our poll now shows us only 2% ahead – and we want to *get control* again. Not just to react to diversions like Shirley, Roy, Brayley, etc. After lunch we went back to Transport House to check the final draft of the handout. Also preparing for tonight's TV appearance.

On the way back Joe told me that Ron Hayward had told Marcia and HW that somebody was leaking the campaign strategy from No. 10 to the press and implied it was me. I really cannot be bothered with the nonsense of this bunch of mediocrities. In fact Joe and I laughed – we would like to know what the strategy is, let alone leak it! One thing is certain: if we had a strategy, Hayward would be capable of leaking it, but not of understanding it.

In the evening Joe worked on the main section of the speech, while I and the Unit worked on the Welsh part for Saturday. This latter worked out very badly. The draft from the Welsh Office was terrible. The rehash from my Unit was terrible. I tried to make something of it, but the result was also terrible. Somehow I do not have a Welsh touch.

At 11.30 p.m. when Marcia arrived I had nothing worth showing. HW arrived towards midnight, in a bad state. He had been heckled by the Irish in Hornsey and his meeting was virtually broken up. Then afterwards he was lost by his police escort. Albert and Jean were in another car and they were lost before ever getting to the meeting. So it was chaotic. They were late for the meeting. Albert's car broke down three miles from the meeting and, suspiciously, outside a pub. He had to run and thumb a lift to get to the meeting before it ended. HW was tetchy and had drunk a lot.

Marcia immediately piled in, screaming at the exhausted HW,

complaining that the BBC had shown nothing of the speech on television and focused only on the Irish hecklers. She shouted at him to make him complain to the BBC. They had a row – while I sat in the next room still trying to draft the Welsh piece. Marcia suddenly stalked out shouting at him, 'You have become a garrulous old woman,' and left.

I went in to join him, Joe and Albert. HW was in a bad mood: he said Joe's speech had not been good, that they had forgotten to include parts he asked for, that I had totally failed to organise the Welsh speech, etc. He blamed everybody. We were in Joe's press office. The PM was sitting in Joe's chair, grumbling away to himself. We sat around looking glum. This went on till nearly 1 a.m. when he telephoned Swann, the chairman of the BBC, to complain. He rambled on for a while, with Swann clearly trying to butter him up at the other end.

After this, Marcia telephoned in and they had an argument, which ended with HW slamming the phone down on her. He moaned at us again and then wandered off down the passageway and home to Lord North Street.

I then went to my office to prepare some notes to help Joe do my Welsh script tomorrow morning. Thank God for Joe! His stamina for speech-writing is endless. I simply could not do it.

Albert came to my room at 2.30 a.m. and fell asleep in my chair. I went to bed at 3.15 a.m. – to get up at 7.30 ready for the next day.

### Saturday 28 September 1974

Woke up feeling low and tired and depressed. Too little sleep. The campaign going badly (yesterday's Labour Party private poll showed that our lead had come down every day since Tuesday – from 12% to 8% to 5% to 2%).

I listened to some Bach to regain sanity and then went to cook myself breakfast in the No. 10 kitchen. When I went downstairs I found Joe there, finishing a seven-page Welsh handout. Then we went out and nervously across to Lord North Street. We found the PM in excellent form, praising the speech by Joe and happy with his Welsh section. We discussed strategy for this morning at the press conference and then all went cheerfully to Transport House. HW's resilience is incredible.

The PM left for Wales at 12.15 and Joe, Marcia and I stayed behind and discussed tomorrow's speech. An excellent discussion and the first time we had restored the harmony and creativity of our February discussions.

Lunch with Joe at St Ermin's. In the afternoon Carol and the family came into No. 10. In the evening I slept a little at No. 10, then had supper with Albert and Joe and suddenly decided to go home. In a taxi at 10 p.m., feeling exhausted as if going on holiday to the seaside. It was lovely to lie in my own bath and in my own bed.

NB: This morning's private party poll had shown our lead up again to 11%. HW said he simply did not believe it. He thinks we are about 5% ahead.

## Sunday 29 September 1974

Drove in from home very early to HW's house in Lord North Street. Beautiful sunny day, cold and bright, and London deserted. Began by discussing Heath's speech last night, full of wild talk about 30% inflation and everything collapsing. We see this as part of the Tory strategy to create a sense of cataclysmic crisis, like 1940, as a build-up to the necessary co-alition. HW decided he must reply to it and he dictated a long, rambling piece which he inserted, to Joe's apparent dismay, into the middle of his very tight and very funny speech. Joe also felt it was a mistake to keep reacting to the Tory attacks and that we should be setting and keeping to our own strategy. Joe and the PM had a bit of a row.

In the middle of these discussions, before we could move on to the main agenda of planning the *whole* of next week's strategy, we were bizarrely interrupted. The film star Gina Lollobrigida arrived to photograph the PM, and this went on for three-quarters of an hour while we – Joe, Marcia, Davis, Lyons and myself – sat in the cramped room downstairs, together with two typewriters and typists banging out the PM's dictation. It was no way to run a campaign.

Finally we got rid of Lollobrigida and finished correcting the PM's amendments, but by then it was time for him to leave for Peterborough. So we never discussed strategy.

A final flap because of a train crash. So we had to switch him to a car.

Joe and I went to St Ermin's for a terrible lunch. Back to Transport House afterwards to discuss tomorrow's speech with Marcia. Then I went off to meet Carol and the kids for a walk in St James's Park, then home for the evening. Again a pleasure to get home, away from all of this.

The PM was expected back early from Northampton. He told us to go home early. He was going to go direct to Marcia's house.

## Monday 30 September 1974

Drove in from home, feeling better for sleep in my own bed. Arrived at No. 10 at 9.15. Picked up Joe and went to Transport House. Walked back from there with the PM and had the usual meeting in Lord North Street – Mary always brings us very good coffee and biscuits.

Our poll shows a lead of 7%.

Discuss strategy, but make very little progress. It is mid-campaign blues. Also that nobody can see how the campaign is going. The only new issue is Thatcher's* 9½% mortgage commitment, and everybody is frightened of that – and furious with Tony Crosland for failing to deal with it. Apart from that, we don't even know what the main issues are – though HW is increasingly focusing on the social contract (which simply means 'peace and quiet'), prices, unemployment and the EEC.

So we do a mainstream speech on those issues for Hatfield and Welwyn tonight. Plus some housing, and of course always the harking back to the darkened streets of last February. In the afternoon I had an unfortunate row with Harold Lever. He had given an interview with the Press Association (without permission) and his line was very similar to Heath's election line this week – gloom and impending catastrophe. This worried me, in case there was a headline 'Lever supports Heath'. So I suggested he modify it. Lever went crazy, swearing at me and saying I was acting as the Treasury's tool in trying to silence him. Incredible. I hadn't talked to the Treasury and was only trying to protect him. Still, I won't do it again. I think Lever was jumpy and nervous because he is to appear at the press conference tomorrow.

Our doctor friends Philip and Nori Graham came to visit in the evening with Carol and we went out to eat pizza. A lovely evening.

The PM returned from Hatfield and Welwyn at midnight. Looking very surly and unhappy. Complained about the speech. Obviously the meetings were less good. Also Joe and I suspect that he senses another move by Marcia against us. Things perhaps are not going quite so well. I walked Joe back to his hotel. A bit worried because HW is worried. We also discussed ways of hitting back at Thatcher. Exposing the fraud of her mortgage scheme – that it benefits only a few, and those the better off.

[As shadow Environment Secretary, Margaret Thatcher had published on 28 August a pledge to keep down mortgage interest rates to a maximum of 9½% and also to abolish the domestic rating system within five years of election. On 27 September she reiterated the 9½% mortgage pledge and added a guarantee that mortgages would be 'cut' by Christmas. It received enormous media coverage. The polls quickly showed an unprecedented rise in the number of respondents stating that the Conservatives were 'making promises they could not afford to keep'.]

## Tuesday 1 October 1974

Woke up early in No. 10. Beautiful morning, the sunshine lighting up Horse Guards and all the tall buildings beyond. Breakfast in the kitchen, reading the papers. Bacon, sausage, eggs, coffee, orange juice and toast.

Joe and I met with the Unit and set them to work on the mortgage problem. Then off to Transport House to collect HW and walked back to Lord North Street. He complained about his speeches, wanting them shorter and condensed. But then suggested all kinds of extras, and also dictated some inserts. So it ended up longer for tonight. He was speaking on the EEC. Joe had written a good piece, all about the referendum. But then HW added a piece about the Common Market being in a shambles which was bound to upset the marketeers and was quite different from the neutral tone Joe had established.

Back to Transport House for the press conference. I saw Michael Foot, who was very confident and said he had been to Scotland, which was much better than in February.

Lever was at the conference, speaking on mortgages and was very good. Also Shirley Williams, who was excellent – she is making more appearances at morning conferences than any other minister. After the conference and just before he left for Lancashire, HW was told that the ITV strike was on. Marcia immediately said, 'Get them to No. 10 and settle it.' HW agreed and off he went.

I then went back to lunch at No. 10, and Joe, Peter Lovell-Davis, Denis Lyons and John Grant came to join me by 2.30. We had another good talk on strategy, especially on the Oxford speech next Monday, which we want to be 'uplift' on philosophy and 'Little Things' that mean a lot to ordinary people. In the afternoon I worked in the Unit.

Marcia had said she would come in at 5.30 to help sort out the speeches, but she didn't arrive till 8 p.m. By then we were in some chaos because HW had leaked that he was going to solve the ITV strike at a meeting tomorrow and there would be an announcement tonight. This leak was on the TV news. All hell broke out. Michael Foot telephoned from Northampton to say he didn't want it. Len Murray phoned to say the TUC didn't want it. Nigel Ryan phoned from ITV to say they didn't want it, but if there was a meeting he wanted personally to be invited. The political correspondents phoned. Everybody said it was a mistake, but they all wanted to take part.

Joe was furious. He couldn't get on with his speech. He said it was a typical balls-up from 1964–70. A Marcia gimmick, which HW took up and leaked before he had thought it through or consulted anyone. Beer and sandwiches at No. 10. Just at the time when we were boasting that we had set up a great new conciliation and arbitration service to settle strikes.

Marcia phoned HW in Bolton and had a note sent up to him on the platform telling him to come down immediately and speak to her. He gabbled his speech and was finished in 40 minutes. But there was no rescuing it.

Joe was exhausted. I went to the kitchen and cooked him and me a steak. Then I drove him exhausted to the hotel and then drove home myself, getting there at 1 a.m.

Interestingly, today's Transport House canvass reports showed a big drop in the swing to us, especially in London marginals. Down to only 1–2%.

## Wednesday 2 October 1974

Came in to No. 10 by tube and in the office at 9.15. Went to Transport House to collect HW and back to Lord North Street. We corrected and expanded tonight's speech on unemployment. Also rehearsed HW for his television interview with David Frost.* One question is to be 'What is your biggest mistake?' HW said privately it was probably the 'timing of devaluation and not floating the pound in the 1960s'. But he would not say that on television because it would remind people that Labour devalued. So he will probably say something anodyne like his opposing military withdrawal from east of Suez too long. I said he must be natural and personal and not turn it into a party political.

We discussed the need to counter Thatcher's mortgage policy and will do a housing speech tomorrow. But still they are all paralysed by Thatcher. Nobody has answered it properly.

Our poll today remains steady – 8% lead. Also a dramatic rise in the number of people saying the parties are promising too much, coinciding with Thatcher's 9½% promise.

As usual the PM gave me several points for the Unit to check up and I came back to No. 10 before lunch to check them. A quick lunch with the usual five of us.

Afterwards HW was interviewed by David Frost. Very good. Very relaxed and personal. His best answers were rehearsed beforehand. But he survived questions on Marcia and the press very skilfully without blowing up. Mainly because he likes Frost.

Marcia incidentally is being very friendly and quite sane. The point about her is that she behaves appallingly when she is removed from the centre of things and believes everyone is plotting against her. But once she is back at the centre, with the help of masses of tranquillisers, she is amiable. At election times she is perceptive and makes good suggestions. Providing the men around her flatter her ceaselessly – and Peter Davis does this very well – she works very well in the team.

In the afternoon I was working on the Welsh handout for Friday. John Morris had sent a draft which was quite good – though perhaps written by somebody whose first language was not English!

Our friends the Reads dropped in to No. 10 during the day, which was nice. I might as well show my friends around, since we may be here for only another week.

Joe looks very tired. In the evening he was jumpy, unable to make much progress on the housing speech and irritated with the constant interruptions. He threw a secret FO telegram at one of his staff. He is terribly overworked, running an office and writing a speech every day. If he falls ill, we shall be in some difficulty. There is nobody among the hangers-on, or in Transport House, who like him could write a speech a day that HW could give and sound convincing.

Apparently there was a terrible row in Transport House tonight. The BBC was making a film about the team around Harold Wilson. They were trying to interview Marcia and Albert, but Ron Hayward intervened to try to stop it. He felt that he was the only important man around the PM and the programme should be about him. When I told the PM later he said that Hayward is 'one of the vainest and silliest men' he knows. In the Labour Party that is quite an achievement.

I was in the office till 1 a.m. when the PM came in. I was finishing the Welsh speech, checking out some facts that the PM phoned through to ask for. Our unemployment analysis – that Keith Joseph's monetarist policies mean 1½ million unemployed – has become headlines and the press is asking for the 'authoritative source' behind it. It is Andrew Graham from the Unit really who does the serious work, with Gavyn Davies, but we must hide as civil servants.

HW was looking tired but cheerful when he came in. Three polls tonight show us 7–9% ahead. I telephoned Anthony Lester in York. (He was asleep in his hotel.) He said Roy Jenkins was enjoying his canvassing tour and was very good at it. But none of the local MPs think we are going to win by very much. Too much apathy among our people. Our regional adviser said it felt 'like 1970'. I don't agree. We are definitely well ahead. But it is a fragile position, could be altered by anything serious, and we still have to get our vote out. Though one gets little feel here in No. 10 – quiet, stately, quite removed from the reality of life. And Transport House simply leaves the impression that nothing so incompetent could or deserves to win anything.

### Thursday 3 October 1974

Woke in No. 10 at 7 and listened to some Bach. Usual morning routine. Nothing exceptional today. The polls are still steady – 6–8% lead.

Spent most of the afternoon at Transport House. HW was there most of the time, since he did not leave till after 6, for meetings in west London. Occasional interruptions by the press and TV.

In the evening Joe and I returned to No. 10, where I worked on the Welsh part of tomorrow's Cardiff speech and he worked on the national handout. This evening the BBC were making a film of the HW team at work in the election. Joe and I could not take part because we are civil servants. So Davis and Lyons and Terry Boston sit in as substitutes.

At 11 p.m. Marcia and Albert come back to No. 10 in a great tizzy.

Ron Hayward had refused to allow them to be filmed. Because they were part of the No. 10 Mafia. He was the only important person in the life and success of Harold Wilson. It was apparently an incredible megalomaniac performance.

Joe and I, who had worked like maniacs all evening while these idiots squabbled over who did most to win the election, were so sick that we went off and didn't wait for HW to return. I went to the RAC Club to have a quick dinner with Harold Evans. He told me he was going to sue *Private Eye* for saying that he agreed not to publish the Crossman Diaries in return for getting the date of the election from me. He told me that his lawyers said I could sue too. He told me the sources of his evidence. First somebody at the TUC told his journalist James Margach it was not going to be 3 October but would be shortly after that (clearly HW was the leak to the TUC). Then somebody from the Home Office told Harry it would be the 10th. Then he sent Margach to cross-check with Joe and especially Ron Hayward at Transport House and it all added up. He also told me that they had decided not to publish Crossman on 27 August – while I was still on holiday in France.

I told Harry that Marcia had reported to me that John Allen was the source of some of the *Private Eye* stories against him – and that Allen got them from one of Harry's staff.

After dinner I phoned Joe, who was very low and going home – so I went home in the PM's car.

### Friday 4 October 1974

Drove in to Downing Street. Picked up the Welsh speech I had done from John Morris's draft; and went with Joe to Lord North Street. HW was already there – and furious. Ron Hayward had opened the campaign committee by attacking HW's 'entourage at No. 10' and accusing us of leaking the last poll figures to the press. This implies Marcia, who was the only one to get them from Bob Worcester. HW had walked out in anger. Apparently Bob Mellish had then tried to conciliate, but it was not a good start to the last stage of the campaign. Hayward's vanity and jealousy are growing intolerable.

We quickly dealt with the speeches and then went over to Transport

House. HW said he now wanted to go over to the attack, to sharpen up the speeches, attacking the Tories more. He also wanted more on unemployment. We agreed to do this, but are troubled that we go from day to day picking up issues and dropping them. There is no clear, simple, centrally controlled strategy as in February.

The polls showed us 7% ahead – 41%–34%–21%.

Joe and I lunched alone at No. 10. Joe is feeling depressed. His work is taken for granted. Also he is upset by rumours of a fresh *Daily Mail* smear campaign, against HW. Somebody had communicated to us from the *Mail* and the *Express*. Apparently the unions at the *Express* have warned the paper against printing any more smears. The *Mail* unions are less firm.

In the afternoon I worked for several hours on tomorrow's Scottish handout for the Edinburgh speech. Bruce Millan* had sent in a very good draft brief and I turned it into a speech. Joe was working on the main speech.

In the evening we watched the BBC programme on HW's campaign team, which was hilarious. Joe and I could not appear, as civil servants. So we put in Terry Boston, Peter Davis and Denis Lyons working on the speeches with Marcia and HW. In fact Terry Boston, who carries the PM's baggage to meetings, was featured most prominently of all. He is sweet, a very welcome member of the team and a calming influence within it – though (or perhaps because) I have never heard him say a word other than 'Well, I'll be blessed' or 'Bless my soul'. Joe calls him 'The blessed Boston'. I don't care about getting no media credit, since I loathe publicity.

I stayed up until well after one in the morning, checking the Scottish speech and waiting in case HW came back from Cardiff to No. 10. He was due to, but at the last moment went straight to Lord North Street, so he did not even collect his speeches to read overnight. This happens more and more now: he simply accepts what is written for him, which is mainly what Joe writes.

## Saturday 5 October 1974

I overslept in No. 10. Had to dress in two minutes and dash to Lord North Street without shaving and without breakfast.

Our main issue of discussion, after dealing with the two Scottish speech handouts, was the *Daily Mail* threat. Our information was that it was a story about HW's wealth. We discussed ways of pre-empting or countering this, but could do little until we actually knew what was in the story.

We also drafted – which meant Joe effectively – a statement for this morning's handout attacking the proposal of a coalition in the Tory manifesto, as a con trick. It was good, I thought, and went down well.

We went across, as usual, to Transport House at around 11.15 to prepare for the press conference. After that we had long rambling discussions on the *Daily Mail* while Joe and I desperately rushed the Scottish handouts on to stencil.

There were other rumours about other smears planned by the Tory press – especially against Anthony Benn, who is now alleged to live an active sex life, and they even smear his wife, so some Tory journalists claim. I don't believe a word of it. But it makes each of them infinitely more human and attractive than previously. I cannot see how these rumours, true or not, can other than do good to Anthony Benn's image – hitherto that of a computerised Boy Scout.

Joe and I went off to lunch at St Ermin's. Still discussing the enigma of HW – the hold that Marcia has, the sad air of seediness stifling such great talent. 'The vultures are coming home to roost,' said Joe.

I went back to No. 10 for a while, leaving Joe to sleep at the hotel before doing his next speech stint. Then I drove home to see Carol and the children. I bought some cakes for their tea and some smoked salmon for Carol and me. I put a bottle of 1971 Sancerre in the fridge and we drank it with the salmon in the evening, all lying on the bed, Rachel and Katie, Carol and me, with occasional interruptions by the twin boys, while we listened to *These You Have Loved*. Corny, but absolutely marvellous after the madness of Downing Street.

Incidentally Marcia has completely collapsed since hearing about the smear intentions of the *Daily Mail*. Trembling, afraid, taking sedatives and showing little interest in the campaign or the speeches.

In the evening Anthony Lester phoned to ask what I thought of Friday's party political broadcast. I had thought Roy was excellent and Shirley, but the programme itself was bitty and superficial. He said that Roy thought the party's television producers had no idea of what to do or what they wanted to do.

Out at the Flask pub in Highgate village later in the evening for a pint with our delightful friends Huw and Rachel Pierce. 'There *are* normal people out there,' as Albert always says.

Today's Worcester poll showed us 10% ahead – 43–33–19.

## Sunday 6 October 1974

I drove in from home at 9.30, after reading the newspapers, with three polls showing us 4/5/10% ahead. It all looks good from the outside – so good that there is danger of complacency.

Inside it seems more dodgy. Today's Bob Worcester poll shows our lead down from 10% to 5%, with the Liberals picking up the previously undecided.

And we have to face tonight's *Daily Mail*.

HW was very concerned at the morning's gathering in Lord North Street and taking the wrong line. On the press his reactions are always wrong. He wanted to *write an article* in the *Mail* on Tuesday refuting all its allegations about his so-called wealth and tax affairs and claiming that they had stolen the documents from his house. He was running upstairs to telephone Goodman every five minutes.

I said he must not get into an argument, get into detail or mention a robbery. He must dismiss it with contempt, like Baldwin. Joe agreed – but was pessimistic that this could lose us the election. Joe blames Marcia, again. She handles the money side. She is involved with land deals, Marjorie Halls, the Terry children, now a story about HW leaving her a lot of money in trust.

She was shattered again today, looking ill and shaky. Clearly afraid of what would come out. She ranted against Arnold Goodman, saying that he was 'the most evil man who had ever interfered in British politics'. She had a simple approach. She wanted HW to get the newspaper unions to strike and stop the *Mail* from coming out. She was pressing Albert to assist in this.

HW was very worried – but not frightened like her. He did not seem afraid of what would be revealed, but was clearly losing his nerve about being the cause of losing the election.

I don't think it will lose the election. People are inured to press smears and they now know that HW and Marcia are not angels. They take them, with all his faults. But it will dismay some of our party workers.

HW was late leaving for Birmingham. We had no time to discuss tomorrow's speech. But we did manage to extract a promise from him that he wouldn't say anything to the press tonight and we would all prepare a statement for tomorrow.

We also arranged for Roy Jenkins to fly to Guildford to see the damage from this latest IRA bomb incident. [IRA bomb explosions on 5 October 1974 at two public houses in Guildford caused four deaths and many injuries.] I spoke to Roy on the phone and he was clearly reluctant to go. I later realised that he must have suspected it was a manoeuvre to get him away from today's mass rally in Birmingham which HW and Roy are addressing.

This wasn't so. Originally Marcia suggested that HW go to Guildford in order to get some television coverage. Joe opposed that as a gimmick and said the Home Secretary would be more appropriate.

Joe and I went for quite a good lunch at a steak house – much better than St Ermin's. We are still low in spirit. Ahead of us is an afternoon of waiting for the *Daily Mail*, drafting a reply to it, writing a speech for tomorrow in Oxford without having given any thought to the subject and waiting till the PM returns after midnight. And outside it rains and blows and is cold, day after day. We agree even more that it will not hurt us if we lose.

Incidentally this morning at Lord North Street after HW had left Joe said to Marcia that we would do what we could to help, but we ought to know if there was anything terrible which we did not know of still to come out.

Marcia said no, the only money HW had was from his book (£240,000). This was in trusts 'set up to make sure the tax was paid' and £12,000 from the sale of his Hampstead Garden Suburb house in a building society. She did not mention, which Joe knows, that she received part of the book royalties in trust for herself and the children.

Joe asked about payment to the party from supporters. She said that all comes to her, then goes to Lord Goodman, who pays it into a Harold Wilson office account. One sum of £1,200 had been paid into the London branch of a Swiss bank.

[This bank account became the subject of press criticism of Wilson. At the time there were exchange controls on British residents and use of foreign banks was viewed with suspicion. Newspapers implied that Wilson was attempting to evade exchange controls, which was clearly untrue – but truth was not the newspapers' concern.]

I am writing this in my room at No. 10. It is dark outside and pouring with rain. Carol has gone to the airport to collect our friend Jacques Pomonti arriving from Paris. I hope to go home soon to see them – and to take the side of venison which Harold Lever, typically, sent me as a peace offering after our row earlier this week.

Glimmers of decency, sanity and humour, lighting up among the surrounding gloom.

I went down to Joe's room in the evening and we drafted another statement to the *Daily Mail*. Joe also did a draft television script for the PM's final broadcast on Tuesday.

Marcia and her sister Peg came in and we drank some tea together. Albert was also there. We had the television on, and generally it was again like Euston station. It is significant that Joe's room is now the centre of these social activities – it used to be Marcia's where everybody gathered.

Towards 9 p.m. Albert received a phone call to go to a pub near Blackfriars to meet some newspaper printing union friends. Marcia went home to dinner and I set off home to see Carol and Jacques – though they had still not arrived when I got there. We ate together and then I telephoned No. 10. Joe told me that apparently there had been a major bomb scare at the *Daily Mail* building. Also some kind of dispute in the 'reading room'. They had a difficult day on the *Daily Mail* apparently.

The *Mail* first edition appeared later carrying a large front-page letter addressed to Harold Wilson claiming there was no truth whatsoever in the incredible rumours going around that the *Mail* might publish a smear story about Wilson in that edition. This letter was very long and repetitive, clearly written hastily at the last moment to fill the gap left by the smear story which had been written ready for publication but suddenly dropped at the last minute.

Goodman had also been in contact with the *Mail* proprietor, Harmsworth, and somebody at the Newspaper Proprietors Association. They all knew what the smear story was going to be – Goodman told HW the details. This was when the *Mail* offered him a 'right of reply'.

Apparently one of the NPA people had recently been opposed by the *Daily Mail* for the presidency of something and was very willing to have revenge. He had been in touch with a key NATSOPA official and each agreed that if there was trouble at the *Mail* they would not be available to resolve it. This plus the dreadful bomb threats led the *Daily Mail* to take the view, so sincerely printed at the last moment, that they had never had any intention of publishing a smear story.

## Monday 7 October 1974

General relief that nothing today in the *Daily Mail* – and clearly won't be anything in the press now. In an odd way HW's tactics have paid off, making them afraid of smear campaigns.

Little fresh in the morning, except our poll showed us 14% ahead. Joe was feeling unwell today. In the evening he wrote tomorrow's TV script.

I went out to dinner with Carol and Jacques Pomonti. Returned. Marcia there in Joe's room. We read the TV script which was quite good – but Marcia thought not good enough – a bit flat. She was right, but we were all so sympathetic to Joe for the work he has done that we dare not say so. Anyway, it is better than I could do.

HW returned from Oxford in a strange mood. He rejected Joe's draft completely and said he would dictate his own. This he did. It was terrible. Marcia said so and left, saying HW had now completely converted her to the virtues of Joe's version. So we all went to bed – at about 1.30 a.m.

I did not get to sleep in No. 10 till 4, kept awake by worries about not having a satisfactory TV script for the PM tomorrow and by that bloody chiming clock in Horse Guards Parade. Our poll lead today was 14%.

*Tuesday 8 October 1974*

A rushed morning. Typically, HW abandoned his last night's dictation of the TV script without an argument. He said, 'You know, I just have to get these things off my chest, then we can forget about them.'

Joe locked himself in a small room and within an hour produced (1) the TV script, (2) today's radio script and (3) tonight's speech for Rochester and Chatham. They were excellent and accepted without a murmur.

At the press conference Roy Jenkins was superb, hammering the coalition idea out of sight.

In the afternoon I spent three-quarters of an hour alone with HW in his room at Transport House. I told him that if we won on Thursday he must spend the weekend quietly thinking about the economy. That would be the only question: all other policies must go overboard. He must get the economic strategy right and get hold of the Treasury. He said he would see Healey immediately we got back.

The electoral games are over now. Reality from now on.

[The current economic indices were bad. They showed national output rising by less than 1%, consumer expenditure falling, export growth diminishing, the balance of payments and the domestic sector heavily in deficit, unemployment rising towards one million and inflation heading for 20%. But price rises had been limited by Healey's July Budget to only 8% since Labour took office in March – while wages had rocketed 16%. On 3 October Ford offered its workers an immediate increase of 23.7%, with further stages totalling 14.9% by April 1976.]

I also raised with him questions about the membership of his next Cabinet. I stressed that Benn must move from Industry, perhaps to Social Services, with Barbara Castle going to Education. He thought that was not a bad idea. He said he had to move Mellish from Chief Whip, so I said why not put him to Housing and he agreed, saying that he would like Silkin back as Chief Whip, so that was simple. I also pointed out that Hugh Jenkins* was unpopular at Arts and suggested Lord Donaldson* instead. He again said that was a good idea.

Then I pushed it too far and suggested moving Shore away from Trade (where he is very damaging against the EEC). HW looked suspicious at that and said he could only do that if he moved Hattersley as well – to keep the balance. 'I mustn't upset the Left,' he said.

Then he suddenly got up and 'Perhaps I shouldn't change anything. Why change a winning team? It would be better to do it in six months.'

He went off to Chatham and I went back to No. 10.

HW returned early – at 10.30 p.m. – and asked Joe and Albert and me, with Terry Boston, up to the study. He was in superb form. We all had drinks and cigars. We told stories about the February election and discussed this one.

He was fairly confident of the result. Today's party poll shows us 9% ahead and tomorrow NOP will show 12½%. But he admitted that it had been more difficult than February. Then the issues were simple and he claimed that he never contemplated defeat. Now it was harder to get hold of. But he thought we would win and was glad that the 'Mafia' had put its money on a 30–60 lead.

He told stories from 'the early days' and also said that he was now prepared for defeat, though not expecting it – prepared psychologically because he could go out with his head up high, having won in February against the odds, washing away the memory of 1970 and having run a first-class government and a good campaign. He preferred to win, but now he was prepared to accept a defeat which would be honourable.

We all looked forward to Thursday in Liverpool. He was so excited that he had no more serious speeches. 'I hate elections,' he said, 'but this has been a marvellous campaign and it is all because of the marvellous team I have.'

Slightly tipsy from the brandy, I set off home at half past midnight.

## Wednesday 9 October 1974

The day started jumpily. We heard that the national polls were narrowing. Then Bob Worcester reported that our lead had dropped to 4% – from 14%, in two days. But I was confident. I said that I never believed it was as high as 14% and I don't believe that we have lost 10% in two days. I feel that we are about 5–6% ahead, that it may narrow a little and that all depends on getting out our vote.

We worked on a press statement for the press conference knocking the coalition and on Joe's draft for the eve-of-poll speech at Liverpool. Then HW went off to Liverpool at lunchtime.

It is too late to do anything now. I drove home at 3.30 p.m., went to bed at 5 – and slept 14 hours unbroken till 7 on Thursday morning.

Woke refreshed and thank God it is all over. I am happy to resign now. It would be nice to have two election victories under one's belt and retire. Do we get a Lonsdale belt for that?

## Thursday 10 October 1974

*Election Day.* Started fine but a forecast of rain. I went straight to Transport House. We all gathered in HW's room. He was back from Liverpool in great form. Obviously confident – but, like me, mainly because it is over.

He left for Huyton with Albert and others at 11, after voting in Westminster. Joe and I go up to Liverpool with Mary and Marcia this evening, on the plane.

Back to No. 10, where I had a long chat with private office about the economic crisis afterwards. Then the same with my Unit. General air of relaxation.

Had a splendid final lunch at No. 10 with Joe and the private office staff. Farewell to Paddy the cook – Marcia has succeeded there. I wonder if it's me next.

I wrote up this morning's section of the diary and now for the plane and Liverpool. How odd if it went wrong!

Drove out to Heathrow with Joe and Mrs Wilson. When we reached the small Hawker Siddeley jet the other four were already on board – Marcia, Jean Denham and two secretaries. Beautifully smooth flight – and marvellously beautiful hostess. Marcia was very jumpy on the flight, swallowing sedatives washed down by brandy. Also she and Mary were getting at Joe and me.

It was cloudy and rainy and we began to get worried about turning out our vote in the evening. Landed before 7 and drove in a three-car motorcade to the Adelphi. Still looking the same as in February. It has a nice, solid, provincial feel.

HW was out touring the polling booths so we gathered in his suite. The same as last time. But not the same atmosphere, Prickly and sour. Marcia sat there glowering. She criticised Albert several times. When I went out – to the bar for a quiet whisky before going to my room to phone Carol and listen to a concert on the radio – she apparently said that I had 'gone to leak to the press as usual'. When Joe and I went out together she implied we were going off to plot. I didn't like the feel of it.

My belief at this time was that we would certainly win, but not by much – I thought 20–25.

I went back into the suite at about 9.30 p.m. and HW was already there – he obviously wasn't staying in the constituency till the close of poll. Turnout was down in Huyton – as the TV reported it was everywhere. We were all subdued, eating sandwiches, drinking beer and waiting for the 10 o'clock news. We repeatedly phoned Transport House in London for news, but it was clear that they had very little idea of how things were going, especially in London and the south. It had been raining and the general party organisation is awful. Very few full-time agents and no systematic organisation.

The TV news came on and said turnout down. Then the BBC announced the results of its final opinion poll – taken *after* people had voted. It showed a landslide to Labour and all the TV pundits announced we would have a majority of over 100. ITV was more cautious, but still suggesting a majority of 40. For a few moments we were elated. Then a poll at Keighley showed a swing to us of only 1%, and people began to scale down their expectations.

When we heard that the turnout was down as much as 10–12% in some Labour strongholds HW got very agitated. 'We might as well go home,' he said. 'We've lost.' But then it was clear that Tory turnout was down as well.

We set off to the Huyton count much earlier this time – before 11 and the first result. Just before we left Marcia went into the bedroom and summoned HW after her. I stood near the door and listened. She was demanding that Albert should *not* be allowed into the count and also attacking Harold for giving Joe and me tickets to the count.

As we were leaving, HW told Albert that he should not go to the count but should give his ticket to Terry Boston. Albert, who cares very much about these things, looked pained and humiliated. HW knew he was being a rat and shortly afterwards went to his cigar-box and gave one of the entourage a cigar 'for Albert'.

As we left the hotel, Joe and I gave Terry Boston our tickets for the count, since we refused to go in if Albert, who was the only one who really and personally cared to be there for HW's triumph, was excluded.

We went in a motorcade to the Huyton count. We arrived an hour too early and sat in the large lounge watching the results on TV. HW was cheered by the Lancashire gains, though it was obviously going to be very tight. From now on we thought in terms of a majority of 5–15.

After the count HW came back to the lounge and told Joe and me not to come to the victory celebration at the Huyton Labour Club. Marcia had clearly demanded this. I was delighted, but Joe was angry. HW suggested that we stay there and take down the results for him. But we said fuck it, we would go back to the hotel. So, with Albert, Joe and I drove back separately to the hotel, while HW went off to his celebration of triumph, with Marcia, Terry Boston and Alf Richman – who of course had made the greatest contributions to the victory. Joe had only written 33 speeches and two television scripts in 19 days!

We sat in the hotel watching the results till 4 a.m. HW returned around 3. Everyone gathered and champagne was sent for. HW thanked the team and we drank to victory, though totally without enthusiasm. I had a headache and didn't finish my champagne. I slipped out and went to bed. Joe did the same. It was a dismal and sour end. No doubt our victory, but no pleasure in it.

The reasons are minor. Anyone looking back on the slights we experience would think they are too trivial to notice. We do notice for two reasons. Albert is hurt by the attacks on him because they are carefully selected on the small things he cares about – such as being there at the count symbolising HW's victory.

I care because of the accumulation of pettiness and trivia. I am appalled that the Prime Minister of Britain and the leader of the Labour Party, at such a crucial moment in history, should have his time taken up with such trivia, should be used as an agent in her pettiness, should himself be humiliated by being forced to humiliate people he likes at her bidding.

## Friday 11 October 1974

I woke in the Adelphi at 7 a.m. and phoned Carol, went down to breakfast and did not join the main party until just before our departure at 10.30 a.m. Marcia was already playing up. She was complaining that it was going to be terrible from now on, with more press smears, etc. 'Why,' she asked HW in her most plaintive voice, 'should I and my poor family have to carry the burden when you are enjoying yourself as Prime Minister?' This I have learned to recognise is the preparation for her to demand some major gesture from him. I wonder what it will be this time. The Exchequer?

She had obviously complained about Joe, Albert and me travelling on the plane back with HW. He asked for the list of seven passengers and stared at it for a long time. This was a moment of crisis. Joe and Albert had decided to have a row if there were any further humiliations. The three of us stood in a circle around him. He looked at her, at us, and then handed back the list without a word.

On the plane Marcia turned to me and launched an attack on me, in relation to lunch at No. 10. 'It is disgraceful,' she said, 'you are eating with those civil servants, joining them, instead of getting them sacked. And you appointed that cook to feed them. It's got to stop.'

I ignored this and she sat agitatedly through the rest of the journey, occasionally swallowing a pill of some kind.

We went straight from Northolt to Lord North Street. In there HW handed Marcia a letter and said, 'That's good news.' She threw it back at him and said, 'Now you are back I'm having nothing to do with that. You won't need me any more.' He looked frightened and tore up the letter.

They all went to Transport House. I couldn't face it and went back to No. 10. When Joe came to lunch he told me that when they got there Marcia shut the door of HW's office in his face and he and Albert were left standing in the corridor. When HW emerged he had decided – or been persuaded – to do a ministerial TV broadcast on Monday. We all thought this was wrong. The public have had enough of politicians on TV – but she has clearly told him to do it and will tell him what to say over the weekend at Chequers.

In the early afternoon we all gathered in the study at No. 10 and then went across to Transport House for the victory party. As HW started his speech the alarm bells rang and we were all evacuated because of a three-minute bomb warning – as if anything had *ever* happened in Transport House in three minutes!

It was too much for me. The comic opera had gone on long enough. So I evacuated back to No. 10 and packed my stuff for the weekend. Before I left Robert Armstrong came to see me. The PM had come back unexpectedly to No. 10 for 10 seconds to tell him that he had decided to discontinue the No. 10 lunches from now on.

I hope he gets a minute to think about the country's economy, in between acting as messenger for Marcia's hostilities. The nation is going bust. He is at a moment of political triumph. And he spends his time as a messenger on these pathetically trivial matters of who eats lunch in No. 10.

[The result of the October 1974 election was:

| SEATS | VOTES |
| --- | --- |
| Labour 319 (+18) | 39.2% (+2.1%) |
| Conservative 277 (-20) | 35.8% (-2%) |
| Liberal 13 (-1) | 18.3% (-1%) |
| Celtic nationalists 14 (+5) | 3.5% (+0.9%) |
| Northern Ireland 12 (no change) | 3.1% (-) |

The national swing in votes to Labour should mathematically have produced a net Labour gain of 25 seats instead of the 18 won, giving a more comfortable majority than the overall majority of three achieved. The deficiency occurred mainly because of a below-average swing (only 1.2%) in the Conservative-held marginal seats.

Labour's share of the national poll was the lowest of any majority government since 1922. But its lead of 42 seats over the Conservatives (who had their second lowest total since 1950) was one of the largest margins since 1950. The third parties, with 39 seats, were unusually strong though rarely united.

The published opinion polls on election eve had shown Labour leads stretching from 5½% to 14½%, with an average lead of 9.3%. Labour's private polls conducted by MORI detected a drop in Labour support and the Conservative recovery over the last few days, pointing to a final voting lead of 5% and an overall majority in seats of 5–10. The late Conservative appeal for a national coalition appears to have drawn away some Labour support.

The personal approval vote for Harold Wilson fell between May and September 1974 from 60% to 47% – though Wilson was still well above Heath (29%). Wilson suffered a 6% fall and a negative scoring of 1.7% in his Huyton constituency.]

## CHAPTER 7

# Attack on the Policy Unit
# October 1974

[The Downing Street Policy Unit, which is the centre of the action in this chapter, was a new institution in Whitehall, established by the author on the Prime Minister's instructions in March 1974. Harold Wilson then said that he wanted the Unit 'to be my eyes and ears'.

The official press release from Downing Street announcing its formulation stated that the Unit would 'assist in the development of the whole range of policies contained in the Government's programme'.

The three characteristics which distinguished the Policy Unit from what had existed before in No. 10 were:

1  it offered systematic policy analysis;
2  it was independent of the Civil Service machine; and
3  it worked solely for and directly to the Prime Minister.

It was a policy powerhouse and without the skilled and dedicated work of its members the author could have achieved little in his role as Senior Policy Adviser in 10 Downing Street.

The members of the Policy Unit, recruited frantically in the early weeks of Harold Wilson's third administration, were designated as temporary civil servants with no security of tenure – their appointments terminated automatically when their Prime Minister left office. Among the senior advisers of the Policy Unit between 1974 and 1979 were:

Andrew Graham, Fellow in Economics and later Master of Balliol College, Oxford;

Gavyn Davies, an Oxford economics graduate later a partner in Goldman Sachs and chairman of the BBC;

David Piachaud, then lecturer, later Professor of Social Policy at the London School of Economics;

Richard Smethurst, then an Oxford economist, later Provost of Worcester College, Oxford;

David Gowland, then lecturer, later Professor of Economics at York University;

David Lipsey, previously special adviser to Anthony Crosland, later journalist on *The Times* and *The Economist* and Labour peer;

Elizabeth Hartley-Booth, previously with the Labour Party research department;

Kay Carmichael, then lecturer in social policy at Glasgow University;

Richard Graham, previously with British Airways;

Richard Kirwan, housing economist at the Centre for Environmental Studies;

James Corr, later executive with the World Bank.

For a more detailed study of the Policy Unit's role see the author's *Prime Minister* (1987), esp. pp. 2–25.]

## Monday 14 October 1974

Came in to No. 10 at 9.30, dealt with papers and letters.

The PM arrived shortly after 11, but did not send for me before lunch. Joe went up and they discussed news from Lord Goodman that the *Daily Mail* has the stolen Wilson tax papers – Murdoch having turned them down. But, apart from that, Joe said he felt frozen out, a very cool reception.

There was lunch – I don't know for how long.

In the afternoon the PM sent for us and we went over the script for his TV broadcast, making many changes. Our main aim was to reassure industry and the City.

I talked to him afterwards, saying that all that mattered now was getting the economic thing right and that I was worried that the Civil Service did not seem to be good with priorities – they mix up the crucial with the peripheral. He agreed and said something about wanting the Policy Unit to be 'more involved in that from now on'. I hoped this meant approval for the Unit, but now know him well enough to have doubts. It may imply change – downwards, or out of No. 10.

Then he recorded his TV broadcast. Joe and I watched, very bored at many of the tired old phrases. But in the end it probably did some good, certainly no harm.

Afterwards we sat and had drinks with him and the TV men and then I went home. It feels uncomfortable. I said to Carol I have a sense of impending trouble, some attack coming. Now that Marcia's attempt to replace Joe has failed, the pressure will switch to me.

In bed I almost resolved not to renew my contract. My job is now in one sense done. The elections are won. Labour is firmly back in power. The Unit is established and functioning. I have lost the excitement. That is crucial. I no longer get a kick coming through the big black door of No. 10.

This of course is our weakness. Joe and I are so fed up with seeing a PM and Labour leader humiliated and diminished that we want to get out.

## Tuesday 15 October 1974

Cabinet this morning.

Beforehand I went through to the Cabinet Office to see John Hunt, the secretary to the Cabinet, to discuss the future. I told him that I had heard that the Civil Service wanted 'to regularise' me; that I was never irregular, but refused to be tamed; that my Unit were pirates and must remain so. He was very understanding, told me that the Civil Service meant me no ill, but he understood that Marcia Falkender did. We agreed to meet and plan better co-ordination in future.

I came back and saw Shirley Williams and Roy Jenkins before Cabinet. In good form and we joked about my constant pressure on ministers to save local breweries and reform the licensing laws. Shirley clearly thinks I am a soak.

Then an excellent two-hour meeting with the Policy Unit, planning the future. I told them I did not ever want to hear again about electoral considerations. They must all say what they think. I am concerned now about the Policy Unit's reputation and place in history, as one small reform in central government.

No word from the PM before or after Cabinet. Lunch as usual.

This afternoon I worked on papers. Also Joe told me that Bill Housden, HW's driver, had reported on the weekend. Marcia had spent most of the time at Chequers. She and the PM had been rowing and shouting most of the time. Above all she was demanding that I be sacked and the Policy Unit disbanded.

Joe's reaction was to say if I went, he would go. He had told Housden this, to feed back. I cooled him and said that might not be the best thing to do. We will see.

Back at 6 to see Ralf Dahrendorf, the Director of the LSE, and prepare the way for when I return there. He is helpful. Given the choice, I would like to see the EEC negotiations out of the way – and work for a sensible decision on it. If we recommend withdrawal, I would resign anyway. If not, I could leave happy.

Home at 8. Have not seen HW all day – the first time ever, I think, at least when he is in London.

Joe told me that he had heard from Robert Armstrong that the security services still had not completed Marcia's positive vetting – and that the PM was intervening to try to stop it. Robert is not certain that she would pass and is very jumpy about what to do.

## Wednesday 16 October 1974

No sign of HW in the morning. Nor did he send for Joe or Albert. At 11 he went to the Cabinet Energy committee on North Sea oil taxation. I didn't go, but stayed in the office reading papers and answering letters which had accumulated during the election.

At midday I asked Robert Armstrong to come to see me to discuss the future of the Policy Unit. He was very friendly and open. He knew that Marcia was moving against me. He said how much he now enjoyed working with me and that he now believed there was a role for a policy unit in No. 10. He also appreciated that while I was taking the flak, he was protected. We agreed to watch the situation and to act together (with Joe). We had lunch in No. 10.

The afternoon went like the morning, with no sign of HW.

At 7 p.m. he sent for Joe. Joe told me afterwards that it was a very awkward meeting. Joe did not sit down and there was a mutual coldness. But HW tried to win him over by telling him the details of his proposed reshuffle. Joe told him that some of them were complete thick-heads, and then left. Joe was angry because he knew that HW had waited until Marcia left – she has been in every day this week – before inviting him up. HW was afraid to be seen by her when he was talking to Joe or any of us. None of us is prepared to function on that basis.

In the evening there was a party at No. 10 to celebrate the victory. Mainly Transport House people. Carol came and she and I went with Joe. We had a quick drink and left before HW made his speech – in which he profusely thanked Alf Richman, Terry Boston, etc. for their major contributions to the campaign, but no mention of Joe.

We drove home at 9.15. I felt low and irritated. But still unable to believe that he will do anything, however craven and unfair, just to satisfy her. So I don't really believe when it comes to it that he will get rid of the Policy Unit just because she demands it.

## Thursday 17 October 1974

Cabinet this morning, mainly discussing a rather woolly CPRS paper on economic strategy. (Apparently Shirley Williams piled into it very heavily.)

In the late morning Joe sent for me and said that he had heard from our usual source that HW had completely capitulated to Marcia and had agreed to demote and transfer the Policy Unit from No. 10 into the Cabinet Office. [Bill Housden, the Prime Minister's driver for many years, also assisted Lady Falkender in many capacities, including chauffeuring her and ferrying her mail from Downing Street to her home. He was often unhappy and frequently held informative conversations with Joe Haines, Albert Murray and the author.]

Curiously I felt very cool. This was finally the crunch. And I could see quite clearly. I would wait for him to raise it and then simply say I was not going to the Cabinet Office – nor would most of the Unit. We had come to do one particular job in Downing Street and that was that. I would resign immediately.

Joe and I arranged to see Robert after lunch. We met at 3 in the Cabinet Room. By then I was feeling very tough indeed and rather looking forward to the fight. I was also looking forward to leaving, since I have had enough of this shabby lunacy. The thought of spending all of next week, half-term, with my wife and children – normal, decent people! – was marvellously attractive.

Joe spotted that I was thirsty for a fight and opposed my suggestion that I go up to the study and have it out immediately with HW. Robert was wonderfully cool and constructive. He suggested that he should go to see John Hunt and get him to tell the PM on Monday that there is no room for the Unit in the Cabinet Office. Then we have the crunch.

Robert also later said that he felt the PM's behaviour was 'utterly contemptible'. I repeated this to Joe later, who looked very sad and said that for the first time, after devoting six years of his life to HW, he began to view him 'with contempt'.

At 5 I went for the first time to the important meeting of deputy secretaries in John Hunt's room in the Cabinet Office. This is weekly, to prepare the coming Cabinet committee business. It was valuable recognition to be invited. And interesting. Our main concern was the Treasury's continuing refusal to bring economic policy to the Cabinet. This has long been the heart of our trouble. There is *no collective* discussion of economic policy. The Treasury keeps it to itself.

Later I chatted to Judith Hart. She had been sacked by the PM after lunch today because of security reports suggesting her communist associations. Later the security reports were shown to be unfounded, and HW saw her at 6 and reappointed her. A farcical situation. [The telephone tapped material was completely misinterpreted by the security services. This episode reflected Wilson's ambivalent attitude to the security services: rightly objecting to their attempts to smear himself and Marcia but perhaps too ready to accept their often ill-informed judgements on his colleagues.]

The strain is apparently showing on HW. Joe went to see him at 4 in the afternoon and found him the worse for drink

Incidentally, I saw Jim Callaghan in the morning, who said he had heard that things were 'bad again in No. 10'. He said, 'Harold seems haunted; but he'll never get rid of her.' He asked me for a drink and chat at the Foreign Office – which I later arranged for next Tuesday.

I felt calm but flat later, and left for home before 7.

### Friday 18 October 1974

A day of terrible pressure made worse because other people know what is going on and are watching with that mixture of fascination and schaden-freude which is normally exhibited when somebody else is being tortured in public. Two friends from the CPRS and one from the Cabinet Office communicated to me sympathetically and asked what was going to happen to me and the Unit. Robert Armstrong told me that Crowther-Hunt knew of the proposals to put us in the Cabinet Office – presumably from HW. My staff are beginning to look anxious and must be told one way or the other soon.

I spent the morning in No. 10 with little to do. Did not see HW. Nor did Joe. The PM sits up there in his study, or in with Falkender, while we are in our rooms.

Joe told me that some time ago when Marcia's brother announced his intention to get married she tried to break this off by recruiting back into the office a former girlfriend of his, to try to set the two of them off again. When that failed she insisted Tony have the sack. When he came back from a holiday he found his successor appointed and sitting at his desk. At the wedding she walked out in the middle of the service and flew home in HW's private plane, forcing HW to come back by train. At the airport she arrived at the wrong exit and was apparently delayed for some time because she did not have a passport.

Joe and I had a sombre lunch together. I said that I was absolutely clear and firm. I would not accept any more nonsense dictated by her which was meant to destroy the Policy Unit. This must be clarified by early next week. Any nonsense and I will go – and not silently.

In mid-afternoon I found the whole feel of the place so distasteful that I decided to go home early and see the family. Before leaving I saw Robert and made clear my position. He offered full support and was quite open that he felt as threatened as me and that, if I lost, they would all lose. 'The appetite of this tiger will grow with feeding,' he said.

It is reassuring for me to have Joe Haines and Robert Armstrong with me. So different. One is a bristly cockney, the other a warm and diplomatic civil servant of the highest order. But both totally decent, honest and honourable.

It will not of course prevent me from taking the brunt of the flak. Each of them has a first loyalty to the PM. Joe has long been set on curbing Marcia, Robert only recently, but he told Joe privately that this was now essential to protect the PM. But the point is, as Joe said, that fighting her might 'involve casualties'. I am the front-man casualty who may have to be sacrificed. I accept that, though I insist on doing it in my own way.

I can understand Joe's point of view. He almost wants me to go, providing I issue a statement blaming her. Robert would prefer me to stay, providing that meant that Marcia had clearly lost this particular battle. But if my departure results in a scandal which drives her out of No. 10 and back to Wyndham Mews for the next year, that is a price worth paying to protect HW.

I am the price. But I don't mind. I want to get out of this lunatic atmosphere. I am delighted to have two such comrades-at-arms behind me.

Incidentally, this morning we had the prayers meeting on next week's government business in the study. It was the first time I had seen HW since Monday. He glowered at me. He then launched off into an attack on the Labour right wing for plotting conspiracies and holding meetings to plan preventing the Benn parts of the programme going through. Callaghan and Healey looked at him with amazement, pointing out that the only plot was a meeting by the *Tribune* Group to try to prevent the plans for aid to industry. Wilson then said that on the Legislation and Queen's Speech committee the Right had caballed to exclude Benn's proposals. At this point Mellish interrupted to 'get the facts straight'. It was no plot. There was a timetabling problem fitting in all four nationalisation Acts, and they had all agreed that one might have to be delayed, but it was purely a question of time. HW then started muttering and said, 'It is all part of what they are up to. It goes back to Jenkins's speech in July' (at Haverfordwest).

Robert and I looked at one another in depression. I had heard about the plots syndrome, but did not expect it to start so early. Robert afterwards said that he felt it was all directed at me. I had felt so too. Callaghan and Healey looked as if they wondered what the hell was going on. What an atmosphere in which to approach the terrible problems ahead.

– Saturday morning I saw Harold Evans. I told him that I had been blamed for and accused of the leaks of our party polls to the *Sunday Times*. Harold roared with laughter. He said the *Sunday Times* reporter John Barrie got them from Harold Wilson himself! This gets ever more bizarre. Here we have HW believing another one of Falkender's smear stories against me, when he knew that I didn't do it because he did.

[Other events of greater long-term political significance were also taking place at this time. On this day, 18 October, the Prime Minister made a small reshuffle of his government. Among the changes were: John Silkin in the Cabinet as Minister of Planning and Local Government; Gerald Fowler to be Minister of State at the Privy Council Office responsible for devolution; and John Smith* to his first appointment as Parliamentary Secretary at the Department of Energy.]

## Monday 21–Thursday 24 October 1974

This is the story of the whole week – because for me the week had only one story, the build-up to the denouement with Harold Wilson over the role of myself and the Policy Unit, and each day was spent waiting and preparing my position for that.

Monday went very quietly. I spent several hours in session with the Policy Unit analysing the economic crisis and seeking a solution. It is my plan to do this every day now, so that we reach a genuinely *Unit* view, utilising the various valuable specialisms and points of view that the members have.

On Monday evening HW sent for Joe and spent an hour with him, not discussing much, but generally re-establishing relations. Joe felt that HW was in a better mood.

I talked to Harold Lever in the evening. He strongly advised me to swallow everything, to go along with HW and Marcia until an opportunity came for a better job and 'then go quietly to something better'. This is what I call the 'Weimar approach', and I leave him in no doubt that, though it is full of wisdom and would suit an older man, it is not my style. He is clearly worried when I make it clear that I mean to play it tough. He is worried that I will issue a statement saying why I am going – because of her intolerable interference. I deliberately left him with the impression that I would – though I might or might not. He got very agitated and said that I must not get angry and do anything which could damage my future. I am in fact completely calm and am calculating that in this first *major* conflict with Lady Falkender I have to be flinty and leave them in no doubt that I cannot be bought off or pushed around.

Tuesday was spent in a similar fashion. Bizarre really. The PM sits in his study. I in my room, Marcia in hers. We come and go, but never see one another.

I went to lunch at Grieveson Grant in the City. Such nice and civilised people. It makes me hanker even more for the real world – not least when Michael Beaumont said to me that they would like to renew the old arrangement. [I had worked as a consultant to Grieveson Grant before going to Number Ten. Michael Beaumont was the outstanding partner in one of the City's most successful private client departments.]

Over lunch, while discussing the economic crisis, my mind was racing over the options available to me. I decided that there must be a rapid crunch solution, and to bring this about by handing in my resignation.

I went back and saw Robert Armstrong. We went into the Cabinet Room and sat at the Cabinet table and talked for half an hour. I told him that I was not going to put up with this nonsense much longer and that I proposed to resign. My concern was what I then did – whether to go quietly or with a statement. That I wanted to do the thing which would seem right to me in 12 months' time. If it meant a statement, I wanted his help.

Joe incidentally had already said that if I resigned he would refuse to go to the lobby to announce it and would not allow his office 'to brief against me, which is the normal practice when anybody resigns'.

Robert was very good, clearly sympathetic and in full support. He said that if I went I should have an honour, a knighthood or a peerage, as a public sign that I was not going because I had failed in the job.

He and John Hunt saw the PM at 3.45. Hunt said what we had asked him to say – that he would not take me and the Unit into the Cabinet Office. So that manoeuvre was blocked. Then privately Robert, as he reported later, put the boot in and said that I was on the point of immediate resignation. HW then admitted that he had not discussed this with me and promised to see me tomorrow, Wednesday, having thought about it overnight. These two senior civil servants have been extremely helpful.

Meanwhile I briefed the two senior members of my staff to prepare them for a possible explosion. Andrew Graham understood the situation easily because he was here before in 1967–70. He is a brilliant protégé of Tommy Balogh at Balliol College, and knows all about Marcia's tricks. His instinct was to be nice to her and send her flowers in the Balogh way, but he is a very tough guy personally and he understood when I said I was not compromising at all.

Dear David Piachaud was totally shocked and bewildered.

In the evening Carol and I went to dinner with our old friends Will and Veronica Plowden. Again the necessary retreat to civilised and sane people in order to survive days spent in the zoo.

Wednesday – spent much of the day waiting for the call which HW had promised Robert. It did not come. But HW sent for Joe and talked to him for over an hour about his great plans for me and the Unit. He told Joe that Marcia was withdrawing, that I was to have her room and I would become 'head of the Kitchen Cabinet'. He even said I might be in charge of Albert and the political office. Joe said he was very happy and keen to be nice about me. He said how good I was and how he wanted to issue a press statement saying that I was more important than ever. He was very critical of the Civil Service and made several attacks on Sir John Hunt.

He was going to tell me personally about his great plans for me – but he never got round to it.

So I still had not seen him when I left at 7 p.m. for Barclays Bank headquarters in the City for a meeting of the Political Economy Club to hear Jeremy Morse[*] talk about the international monetary situation. I sat opposite Sir Keith Joseph and we talked at length about various social problems. He said he had heard very well of me and the Unit. He was pleasant and interesting but obviously very jumpy about his recent speeches and current bid for the leadership. Later in the meeting he just sat with his head in his hands.

Thursday – a day of waiting for the promised meeting, which never came. Bill Housden said that HW and Marcia had decided to capitulate and that when the meeting took place it would be 'a time for olive branches'. Joe also received the same message. Late in the day I saw Robert, who said I was to be invited to lunch at the Athenaeum on Friday, with her – and when Joe would not be there because he was due to take a day off.

So this would be it. I cannot say that I looked forward to it. I was sure that she would not capitulate totally. She would be preparing for her next attack. My problem is that I must make some concessions to help HW out of his problem, but not to the point where I give up any principle.

In the day I continued with the Unit. Also saw Alf Morris about ways of avoiding tax on the compensation to thalidomide victims. A very nice and sincere man. He is being very helpful to my brother, who suffers deafness. David Butler[*] from Nuffield College also dropped in. He is an old friend of Tony Benn and told me that when he saw Benn in Bristol in this campaign for the first time he was frightened by him – by 'the gap between reality and his fantasy'.

Also saw Ken Berrill about future co-operation with the CPRS. He referred to Benn and said he was one of the few real fanatics he had met.

## Friday 25 October 1974

This is presumably the day. I did not go to the morning 'prayers' meeting in the study, but stayed in my office and held another meeting with the Unit on the looming economic crisis.

Robert Armstrong came in to confirm that the lunch was at the Athenaeum.

Bill Housden had a long talk with me. He said it was going to be a peace-making day and everybody was supposed to be happy afterwards. He reconfirmed that a putsch had been intended, but now Marcia had retreated. He overhears all the conversations in the car, some to Chequers, and she tells him things.

I went into her room at 12.45. She was there with Albert. She said that we were *not* going to the Athenaeum because she had come in the wrong clothes! Probably she didn't want me to be seen out with her and the PM.

HW came in and asked me to go upstairs with him for 10 minutes. He sent for a bottle of champagne and talked for half an hour while we drank it.

He said he had given a lot of thought to the problem. There was no truth in any of the rumours I had heard. But he did want a different role for me.

He said he had, as PM, three roles: administrative, which he did with Robert Armstrong; Party, which was Marcia; and *Political Policy*, which was me. He wanted me to be 'a mixture of Schlesinger and Kissinger'. He wanted to change my title.

He suggested that I give up the day-to-day running of the Unit – maybe they should be moved. Here I objected, saying that their briefing was essential to me.

Finally he said he wanted me to have Marcia's room next to the Cabinet Room, as a symbol of my elevation to be 'head of the Kitchen Cabinet'. Marcia was going to be withdrawn somewhat from affairs.

I said little and simply tried to work out what was behind all this, some of which Joe had already told me.

We then collected Marcia and went upstairs to lunch. She immediately denied any basis for the rumours that she was trying to get rid of me. Revealingly she said that she had already denied it to Peter Davis, pointing out that she 'could not get rid of you and your Unit'.

She seemed to support HW's proposals and said I would have to organise HW's official social life too, arranging more parties and dinners for the GLC, etc. I didn't like that. Joe had warned me that one recurring ploy in destroying earlier people was to give them too much to do – and then attack when they inevitably failed to do it all.

She then went on to discuss rooms. She seemed to want for herself the lovely suite occupied by the Church of England appointments people. She also pointed out that various other rooms were free – but when I said that I would take them for my overcrowded Unit, she reacted strongly. She attacked the Unit and said that none of them should be in No. 10. They were not senior enough. She said that No. 10 should only be for very senior people – which is total balls, since No. 10 has always contained bright young people. Even the principal private secretary is only an under-secretary. I pointed this out and also asked which of the Unit was inadequate. It transpired that she had no idea who was in the Unit.

From this point on we niggled and after HW left had quite a row. She wants the Unit out. I resisted and she lost her temper. The more angry she got, the colder and calmer I felt.

The irony of this is that she strongly supported HW about having a Policy Unit in the first place, though perhaps she expected it to be under her thumb. She left at 3 p.m., arguing with me all the way down the main corridor and across the hall to the front door of No. 10 and shouting at me that I was 'ludicrous' in front of Bob, the policeman on the step.

Then I returned to my room. Not clear if I have won a total victory, as Albert thinks. Or if they have retreated from this battle in order to weaken me for the next by detaching me from the Unit and from the Civil Service (by calling me 'political'). Nor am I sure if he is double-crossing me on her behalf; or double-crossing her as well, by pretending to weaken me when not actually doing so.

HW left early for Chequers and went out of his way to be friendly to me in front of the others. I am relieved that this round is over, but wary. Handling the threatened changes in the Unit will be the tricky thing next.

Saw Ronald Higgins in the early evening and then went home with relief to an early bed.

Saturday. To *La Bohème* at Covent Garden. Marvellous, and absolutely what I wanted.

Incidentally Joe is now clear what room changes she wants: me to her small room; she to the palatial Church Commissioners' rooms; the Commissioners to be squeezed into my Unit's room; my Unit out in the street. This could be what it is all about.

# CHAPTER 8

## Back to Serious Government – and the Economic Crisis Looms
### October–November 1974

*Monday 28 October 1974*

The PM did not arrive until 11.30. I decided to act as if the past two weeks had not happened. I dropped in for a chat. He was very friendly and said he wanted Joe and me to work on the speech – a very long version of which had been sent from Chequers.

Joe and I spent an hour making corrections. Then we had lunch. After lunch we did not have a chance to talk to him because he saw Lord Wigg, and then the police arrived to discuss the theft of his tax papers. This is being taken seriously. It is thought to fit in with other robberies at Buckingham Palace Road and from Lord Goodman's office. I have been burgled as well. It looks like a mini-Watergate. HW doesn't seem very worried.

Joe saw him afterwards and put to him the fact that very few people had access to his house so as to know where to find his tax papers. Whoever did this *knew* what he was looking for.

In the evening we had the party for ministers to hear the Queen's Speech with the legislative programme for the new session. This is the second one I have attended. Much water under the bridge since the last one. I mixed with old friends, talking to Bill Rodgers, Roy Jenkins, David Owen, Shirley Williams, Denis Howell and Harold Lever.

Went home at 8.30 and on the TV heard the terrible news of an attempt by the IRA to bomb Denis Howell's wife.

In the Unit we are getting more worried about Tony Benn. He is handing out money to whoever is broke and to any group of shop stewards who threaten a work-in. No discipline, no criteria. Total scandal in some cases. But the Treasury seems to have no fibre, no control. Demoralised.

*Tuesday 29 October 1974*

HW very friendly. Spent most of the morning discussing his speech today on the Queen's Speech. Then he went across to Parliament for the opening.

At noon Joe and I went across to his room in the House to make some more alterations. He came in just before having lunch with Kaufman and Marcia. He seemed very jumpy.

We came back for lunch at No. 10. Then back to the Commons for the debate.

Heath opened, trying to be serious and to raise the crucial questions on the economy. His arguments were absolutely on the right lines, but he was very nervous and somehow went flat – sitting down to almost total silence from his own back-benchers. Another election defeat has damaged him.

HW rambled on for nearly an hour, reading out a list of past quotations to prove that he had always warned of the coming economic crisis, constantly harking back. Everybody felt he was still fighting the February election. By the time he finished many people had left. Each of these leaders had been bad in his own typical way. Each party privately thinks that it is time for a change of leadership.

Afterwards I went for tea with Harold Lever in Eaton Square. He told me that HW had sent for him a fortnight ago, on the Monday after the election, to tell him that he was going to move me to the Cabinet Office. Now that seems to be forgotten! But it will be raised again, I'm sure.

Back to No. 10, where I read through my papers before going home early at 8 p.m.


*Wednesday 30 October 1974*

Quiet day in the office. Did not see the PM. The Unit are working on a major economic paper.

In the evening I went to Wembley with Denis Howell to see England beat Czechoslovakia 3–0. Good game and pleasant evening.

Before leaving I put in a green paper memo to the PM warning him that Benn's proposals on the Industry Act, to come up tomorrow at the Industry Cabinet committee (IDV), were a dangerous step to the left and a significant reinterpretation of the White Paper. Because he wants (1) powers to direct a new NEB, (2) £1,500 million for acquisitions and (3) powers for compulsory acquisition without going through full parliamentary procedures. This must be stopped.

PM went to *Ralph Reader's Gang Show* in the evening. He was a keen Scout when young, rising to be a King's Scout, and likes this kind of entertainment.


*Thursday 31 October 1974*

The day dominated by Cabinet, and now with Benn, Judith Hart and Joan

Lestor in trouble over their activities at the party's National Executive Committee.

At Cabinet was Simonstown (South Africa): the visit of the British Navy, plans to withdraw from the base following the defence review, and the fact that at yesterday's NEC Benn, Hart and Lestor had voted for a resolution condemning the government for allowing the Navy to visit Simonstown on an official visit. This despite the fact that they privately knew we are proposing to give up Simonstown. It is part of their annual effort to prove to the Left that they are militant, in the weeks before the NEC elections.

The Cabinet was apparently very violent and HW gave Benn, etc. a public dressing-down. But it went on so long that they had to reconvene in the afternoon to discuss more Simonstown and then Benn's proposals at the Cabinet committee on industrial policy (IDV) to shell out £4 million to help some workers co-operative in Liverpool which makes radiators and orange juice. Healey had brought this to Cabinet as an issue of principle which the Treasury must win. Lever said Healey was bound to win – and offered Ray Richardson odds of 20–1.

*But*. The meeting dragged on into the evening. The PM left – as did Short, Jenkins and Crosland. The Left stayed on. Lever spoke strongly, but Shirley Williams was inexplicably silent. Jim Callaghan was in the chair and in the end the decision went to Benn. A terrible defeat on a crucial principle of whether we are rigorous or promiscuous in doling out money to every Tom, Dick or Harry who comes begging. A bad defeat for Healey as Chancellor – another symbol of the Treasury's current demoralisation. And cause of further demoralisation. The Treasury certainly no longer dominates government business. I always opposed that domination. But now, unless some of it is restored, in the cause of responsible finance, the country will be bankrupted.

In the afternoon the PM wrote to Benn and the other two about their NEC behaviour. Very stern letters drafted by Robert Armstrong. Demanding letters of apology and promises of good behaviour. And saying that failure to do so will be taken as resignations. HW said this was the kind of procedural issue – over collective responsibility – on which he wanted to catch Benn, rather than on a Left-Right *policy* issue.

Home at 9 p.m.

Had lunch with Anthony Lester at the Garrick. Discuss EEC strategy. I want the Right to be rigid and uncompromising. He told me that Jenkins has an arrangement with Reg Prentice – who is not pro-EEC – that either will resign if the other goes. In the afternoon Gerry Fowler came to see me and told me of rumours of this Jenkins/Prentice agreement. Also that back-benchers are beginning to ask when HW is going to retire.

## Friday 1 November 1974

At the weekly business meeting in the study at 9.30 they discussed Benn and Hart and Lestor. HW said he had sent letters and would not see them till they replied. Callaghan was furious and said he was considering breaking off relations with the NEC, and thought other ministers should cease attending.

I saw Healey on the way out. He was furious with Benn over the defeat in Cabinet and said threateningly that after the coming Budget there would be no money available for any further nonsense. I told him that people were ready for some traditional Treasury toughness.

Liam Cosgrave, the Irish Prime Minister, came in for a meeting – which apparently did not go too well. The Irish do not make a good impression here, even with their friends (who include HW and Joe and me).

I went to lunch at the House of Commons with Joe.

Spent the afternoon working on a long paper from the Unit on the impending economic crisis. Finally put it in at 8.30. Very gloomy. All depends on the social contract, which is very leaky. The wage settlements this month will decide it – and the prospects are not good.

What worries me most is the *lack of coherence* in the economic policy. Healey, Lever, Williams, Benn are all putting up separate schemes which are in fact interdependent. All stands or falls on what Foot does about wages at Employment. But there is no overview, no strong co-ordinating hand, i.e. no Prime Minister running it. That is why we are putting in our overview paper calling for clear decisions and drastic action. But not optimistic.

Went home to have drinks with Harold Evans. He is gloomy too. Thinks it will collapse on the union wages front.

I am very tired again. Probably a reaction to the pressures of the past weeks.

Sleep for most of the weekend.

Anthony Lester telephoned to tell me that Nico Henderson had told Roy Jenkins about Marcia's attempt to get me the sack. The grapevine is extensive!

## Monday 4 November 1974

After dealing with letters, I went up to see the PM in the study, sitting with Joe. They were discussing the theft of the PM's papers – how the police are supposedly leaking the stories to the press. Then we discussed top salaries: the PM hinted they might cut ministers' salaries as a gesture. He also said the test was coming for Michael Foot – of whom he spoke much less warmly than previously.

Then the CID came in to interview him, so we left and I worked in the Unit.

HW had read our weekend paper and pronounced it 'gloomy but difficult to fault' and added his commitment against a statutory incomes policy.

I had lunch with Tommy Balogh at the French Club in St James's Place. We talked policies. I wondered if he would say anything about Lady Falkender and his role there, but he didn't and so we left it. Really I was rebuilding fences. He is a creep to her, but I like him and accept him as he is. Certainly is not going to change at his age.

Joan Lestor has written a woolly reply to the PM's minute, arguing rather than surrendering, so she is getting another rocket. Benn and Hart had not replied by teatime, so they got a reminder from Robert Armstrong.

The PM has decided to cancel the Industrial Development Cabinet committee (IDV) until Benn has replied satisfactorily one way or the other.

This afternoon Transport House phoned the press office to say they had heard a rumour that I had resigned: party headquarters is behind events as always.

Home early tonight.

Before leaving I learned that Judith Hart has now replied, saying in four pages what Joan Lestor said in one page. She gets the same rocket. Benn has still not come through, and he gets a reminder.

Andrew Graham attended the Cabinet committee MES (Ministerial Economic Strategy) in my place. He returned in great despondency. He said that the PM had chaired it badly, ducking all the serious questions and saying that they could not deal with anything until after the Budget. He also said everybody was terribly complacent – especially Crosland. Andrew feels we must have a terrible crisis, probably a foreign exchange crisis, before anything will be taken seriously.

[This evening on the fifth day of the debate on the Queen's Speech the government had a majority of 14 on the first division of the new Parliament on an Opposition motion regretting Labour's proposals to nationalise the aircraft and shipbuilding industries. Next day on the final day of the debate it had a majority of 40 on a general motion moved by Margaret Thatcher attacking the government. In this debate Michael Foot stated unequivocally that the government had no intention of bringing in a pay freeze or a statutory incomes policy.]

## Tuesday 5 November 1974

I saw Tony Crosland before Cabinet and discussed local authority finance, rates and Clay Cross. I said I was worried some municipality might go broke. He seemed complacent, though not clear what to do if it happened.

Benn has written an argumentative reply to the PM's letter – not disagreeing but stringing it out. So Robert Armstrong drafted another very firm reply demanding total acquiescence.

We had lunch at No. 10. Afterwards PQs, when the PM was in lively form, but jumpy and drinking a lot of brandy. Joe told me later that Marcia had been attacking him both because of his proposed trips to Washington, Moscow, Iran and Australia (telling him he should not go abroad) and for his handling of the Benn affair. She is pressing the PM to pull back and let Benn off the hook.

In the evening the PM saw Healey about the Budget. I left for home early.

### Wednesday 6 November 1974

Came in early and saw the PM near the Press Association tapes beside the door to the private secretaries' office. Discussed his schedule meeting with Healey – on which Andrew Graham had put in a good paper. PM said Healey was going to raise prices, and 'the Left won't like it'.

Rest of the morning with the Unit, especially discussing the proposed Scottish Development Association with Richard Graham and Adrian Shaw. Then lunch with Carol and dropped in to Sotheby's for a sale of drawings by Laura Knight – the first time I had been there in ages. I still like the smell of paintings. I bought a lovely drawing of children bathing.

Came back and went with Kay Carmichael and Richard Graham to see Willie Ross about getting better access to the Scottish Office. Ross is in some ways an impressive figure – stern and craggy and full of integrity, and trying to be master of the whole field of Scottish affairs. But he rambled on from subject to subject, and only after a quarter of an hour did he ask us who we were and where we came from. This is the same characteristic that I see in so many politicians as they get older: vanity, talking endlessly, never listening to anybody else, in fact never really noticing who they are talking to.

Back to No. 10 at 5. Put in a memo suggesting an architectural competition for the new Scottish and Welsh Assemblies. Chatted with Joe. Apparently Benn and the others have now capitulated completely.

Also to Robert Armstrong about the next honours list – Denis Lyons, Briginshaw (General Secretary of the print workers' union), some old lags. HW even put in Rudi Sternberg, who is connected with the Swiss bank which went broke with an account of HW's, but Robert Armstrong made him take him out. [Sternberg was subsequently elevated as Lord Plurenden.]

Joe went up to see the PM in the evening. But I went home earlier to see the kids.

Tonight the PM is going to a George Weidenfeld party. Marcia is going, together with T. Balogh, E. Varley and G. Kaufman. Apparently she insisted they all be invited. Even the PM.

[*The Donoughue diary for Thursday 7 and Friday 8 November has not been located.*]

## THE PRIME MINISTER'S ENGAGEMENTS
## THURSDAY 7 NOVEMBER 1974

| | | |
|---|---|---|
| 10.30 a.m. | Cabinet | No. 10 |
| 2.30 p.m. | Briefing | H/C |
| 3.15 p.m. | Questions | H/C |
| | H/C | |
| 5.30–7 p.m. | Soviet Ambassador's reception (Mrs Wilson) | 13 Kensington Palace Gardens. |
| 6.00 ? | PLP | H/C |
| 8.15 p.m. | The Other Club, lounge suit or black tie | Savoy Hotel |
| 10.00 p.m. | Party by Sir Joseph Kagan* (Mrs Wilson) | Grosvenor House, Park Lane. |

## PRIME MINISTER'S ENGAGEMENTS
## FRIDAY 8 NOVEMBER 1974

| | | |
|---|---|---|
| 9.30 a.m. | Weekly diary meeting | No. 10 |
| 10.00 a.m. | Foreign Secretary | No. 10 |
| 10.30 a.m. | Sir Claus Moser | No. 10 |
| 11.30 a.m. | Minister for Sport | No. 10 |
| 12 noon | Lord Feather | No. 10 |

*Monday 11 November 1974*

Cabinet this morning at 10.30 to discuss the Budget. That went quite quickly, although it annoyed Benn and the Left. But Cabinet was then

stuck for one and a half hours on the trade union Bill – closed shop, etc.
Jenkins apparently got very angry and in the end Foot was forced to
compromise and sent off to negotiate with the TUC.

At lunch with private office we discussed the PM's speech tonight at
the Guildhall. We all agree it is terrible – tired repetition of paragraphs
from his election speeches.

I met him in the hall coming back from lunch and he seemed in very
good humour. We all went up to the study to work on the speech and he
was in better form than any time since the election. No glowering looks
or hunched shoulders. As if some burden had been lifted.

We took some of the repetition out of the speech and improved it a bit
– though it really needed rewriting from scratch.

After that Joe and I stayed behind for half an hour's general chat. About
Roy Jenkins – whom the PM still finds difficult to understand because of
his 'emotionalism'. And Ted Short, whom he sees as soon 'fading out'.

Also discussed the honours list, which he said he is still working on,
without revealing details.

In fact we know that Denis Lyons is in, but Rudi Sternberg (suspected
of being a double agent) has been taken out.

Incidentally, HW had not read the papers in his weekend box. private
office said they didn't know why not, but the PM spent Saturday 'with
Marcia and her brother Tony Field'.

The police were in again today discussing HW's missing tax papers. He
seems to enjoy all this, as a diversion from serious business.

## Tuesday 12 November 1974

Budget day.

Spent the morning in the Unit discussing industrial policy – which the
government does not really have: it has an anti-unemployment policy which
Benn dresses up as an industrial policy.

Saw HW before lunch. Still in good form. Discussed the EEC, where
we are reaching common ground now he realises I am not *theological* but
simply pragmatic (there is no alternative!).

Lunch at No. 10 and then to the House for questions. Very quiet.

The Budget raises prices enough to destroy the social contract; but does
not do anything enough to replace it.

Evening to *Pygmalion* with Carol.

[The Chancellor Denis Healey introduced a full-scale Budget (his third
in 1974) on 12 November to try to control the growing economic crisis.
He introduced a gifts and capital transfer tax to replace estate duty and a
new petroleum revenue tax on North Sea oil. He increased nationalised

industry charges. Pensions and social security benefits were improved. Most significant for industry were the measures – especially stock and investment relief and modifications of price controls – worth £800 million to relieve pressures on company liquidity. The government had majorities of 258, 27 and 38 on the key divisions on 14 November.]

*Wednesday 13 November 1974*

Fascinating morning in the IDV Cabinet committee discussing Benn's proposals for an Industry Bill: (1) planning agreements and (2) a National Enterprise Board.

On planning agreements he was pushed hard on why he wanted powers to *compel* firms to give information, even though they were not intending to have planning agreements or take government money. He ducked it. Unfortunately the PM, in the chair, never *forced* him to answer questions but in fact helped him out of corners. Callaghan, Lever, Jenkins and Healey all piled into Benn, but he just ignored them.

In the end the PM set up an official committee to report on this – a device he frequently uses to tame Benn. Or *hope* to.

On the National Enterprise Board the PM again stressed his desire for a revived IRC (Industrial Reorganisation Corporation), as he established during his previous administration.

The main clash came over the amount of money. Benn wanted £1,500 million. Healey only £300 million. This was never resolved and the meeting will have to continue next week. This committee now contains 14 Cabinet ministers and is virtually a Cabinet in itself. I went out at lunch to the Romney St Group, in the Reform Club, to talk to them on special advisers. Quite lively. I was careful to stress that I didn't have problems with the Civil Service, and this produced some scepticism from the audience. But I don't want press articles saying I am not getting on with them.

Afternoon in the Policy Unit.

In the evening the PM entertained the new Labour MPs and they had a long discussion in the Cabinet Room. A very mixed bunch – why should these be the chosen representatives to the nation's Assembly in 1974? Nothing in terms of ability, etc. picks them out. Just a random sample – with quite a lot of Tribune slogans.

Margaret Jackson seemed the best – and the best-looking.

Afterwards met Harold Evans at the RAC. The Crossman Diaries crisis is coming to a head again.

# CHAPTER 9

# Edging Towards the European Nettle
## November–December 1974

[H]arold Wilson's fourth administration now in the autumn of 1974 opened the second phase of Labour's handling of the question of Britain's entering and remaining in the European Community.

The first phase had been triggered by the Heath-Pompidou agreement, which secured British entry to the EEC on 1 January 1973. That presented a serious problem to the Labour Party, which was fundamentally divided on the issue, with a majority both in Parliament and among constituency party activists certainly against entry. As leader, Wilson's task had been twofold: to preserve party unity and to keep the membership option open for a future Labour government to stay in the EEC (which meant preventing the party while in opposition committing itself in principle against membership of the EEC). With typical skill and flexibility he achieved both objectives. His solution was a commitment to renegotiate Britain's terms of entry and then to hold a referendum or an election to legitimise the final decision. Those commitments constituted a clever compromise which held the party together during the two victorious election campaigns of 1974.

The renegotiation of Britain's terms of entry had been signalled with two major speeches by Foreign Secretary James Callaghan to his European ministerial partners on 1 April and 1 June 1974. Wilson became more directly involved during his visit to Paris on 14 September, six days before he called the election. This was the first of a series of quarterly Heads of Government meetings organised by the new President of France, Valéry Giscard d'Estaing. Although the question of Britain's EEC membership was not on the formal agenda, the British Prime Minister raised it over lunch, stressing that he objected to the present formulation of the Community Budget and that he would resist any move towards political union.

Labour's position was soon set out more fully and clearly in its election manifesto. There a number of issues were listed on which the government promised to secure concessions – changing the EEC Budget, reforming the

Common Agricultural Policy (including guaranteeing access to Commonwealth food products), opposing political, economic and monetary union,
and maintaining national discretion on VAT levels and regional policy.

Harold Wilson's prime concern in the renegotiations was to secure
enough concessions to satisfy his manifesto commitments and to keep his
party united. He had to extract enough bargaining victories to demonstrate
to his left-wing critics that he was fighting for Britain against Brussels, while
at the same time not alienating the Right by forcing a break with Europe.

Wilson set up two Cabinet committees to handle the renegotiations,
which are reflected in the following pages of this diary. He himself chaired
the senior European Strategy committee (ES), which ensured that the manifesto pledges were being met. James Callaghan chaired the second committee
(EQS) monitoring the detailed negotiations. The former was essentially a
party management role, the latter a policy monitoring role. Wilson and
Callaghan were a brilliant combination working together. But it was a huge
and stressful burden for two men aged around sixty, on top of their myriad
other duties and with barely a majority in Parliament behind them. Not
surprisingly, Wilson is seen in the coming months to suffer symptoms of
stress and ill health.]

## Thursday 14 November 1974

Spent the morning at the Department of Industry discussing 'industrial
policy' with Benn's two special aides, Frances Morrell and Francis Cripps.
In fact it was full employment policy rather than industrial policy. They
are putting round a paper saying that no firms should be allowed to go
broke and no workers should be made redundant. Nowhere did they
mention the implications for industrial efficiency or for public expenditure – I pushed Cripps and he finally estimated the cost at £1.5 billion a
year.

Went to lunch at the Connaught with my old friend Clifford Barclay*
and Robert Clark (of Stock Conversion).

Back for PQs in the House, which went very quietly.

Then to the Unit to go through a lot of papers.

At 5.30 went to see Jim Callaghan in his magnificent room at the Foreign
Office (which was also Herbert Morrison's room).

We discussed politics and the Market very gingerly. He stressed that he
didn't want to be PM. He was also very clear on the Common Market and
thought it was important that:

(1) The Cabinet should reach an agreed recommendation risking
resignations, rather than let everybody go their own way.

(2) He and HW should take a similar view. This he felt could keep the party together. Otherwise it would fall apart.

(3) HW should give him the normal support to a Cabinet minister when he had completed his negotiations and reached a balanced conclusion.

(4) 'To pull out would mean a siege economy, and I don't know how long the British people would stand for that.'

I concluded from this that he will end up for staying in. But he did add that if the referendum decided to stay out, we must obey. And then that he thought it would go the way that he and HW jointly recommended.

He was also critical of Healey for being too slack in his management of the economy and for failing to understand the gilt market.

I came back and completed work on papers for tomorrow before going out to dinner with Carol at the Sainsburys' (David and Sue).

PS: Robert Armstrong tells me that the PM wants Don Ryder of the International Publishing Group to head the National Enterprise Board. He has asked Benn for his suggestions – so far nothing.

## Friday 15 November 1974

In early to No. 10 – at PM's overnight request – to see the statement going out about the Crossman Diaries. Hunt has drafted it explaining why it is necessary to protect Cabinet secrecy. I said to Hunt that the statement implied they never would allow its publication. He denied this, saying that less than 20% of the content was at stake. In fact I know that the publishers have submitted a greatly amended text, but Hunt rejected it, saying that it was virtually all unacceptable. Hunt was very irritable with me when I raised it. He knows I am a friend of Graham Greene, the publisher/executor, and of Harold Evans, who is going to serialise it. It seems to me that Hunt was much too heavy earlier on, trying to frighten them into not publishing, and is now trying to get out from under and switch the responsibility on to the PM.

At the weekly business meeting in the PM's study, Mellish reported that the Tribune Group was in disarray and some of its now moderate members were unhappy with the way the hardliners were behaving.

The PM then raised the question of top people's salaries. He asked what was happening to the report: the Civil Service had deliberately hidden it, and Michael Foot told me that *he* as the minister responsible still hasn't seen it, three weeks after asking for it. It affects top civil servants' salaries and they mean to slip it through. The PM got cross and told Robert Armstrong and Hunt to get him something on paper quickly. He then mentioned the idea of cutting ministers' salaries at the same time. At this

Ted Short blew up, saying this was intolerable and that their pensions were determined by the salaries. Healey intervened equivocally, and I felt that the PM might be defeated on top salaries because ministers would want to keep their own salaries untouched.

At 10 a.m. we came down from the study and into the Cabinet Room for the Cabinet committee on European strategy. This proved a very heated meeting and went on until after midday without reaching a clear decision on the main issue – whether to implement on 1 January the tariff charges required by the Treaty or to refuse.

Callaghan recommended implementation and said a failure to do so would jeopardise his whole negotiating position in Brussels. This was clearly what the Left wanted to do – and Shore, Benn and Foot spoke against implementation, Shore very naughtily on cost-of-living grounds when the effect is virtually nil. Short also curiously supported the Left. Healey, Lever, Jenkins (who left early), Peart and Shirley Williams supported Callaghan.

When summing up, the PM appeared to be coming down – or at least summing up – in favour of the antis. Also during the meeting he had favoured them – after an hour and a quarter no pro-marketeer had been able to get in, whereas Shore and Benn had each spoken twice at length. Shirley became agitated, interrupted and said she must reserve her position. The PM looked very jumpy. But found a compromise whereby we would *ask* the EEC to delay implementation, but, if they refused, it would be brought back to Cabinet.

Afterwards HW went into Marcia's room and apparently – so she told me later – attacked the pro-marketeers and said that the committee was loaded in their favour. This is not true of course. It has three pros, three antis and three doubtfuls (Healey, Peart and Callaghan). On this occasion the doubtfuls turned pro on the merits of the case.

Went to lunch with Yoram Peri, the new Israeli Labour representative in Europe. Delicious lunch at Prunier's – but very depressing on the Israeli situation.

Came back and had a meeting with Janet Whitaker on problems of part-time workers. She is a civil servant and the wife of Ben, former Labour MP for Hampstead.

Then Tom McNally, Jim Callaghan's able special adviser, came in and we discussed the EEC and problems of relations with Transport House.

Finally had a tense meeting with Andrew Graham and David Piachaud of the Unit about putting in a paper to PM this weekend.

The Cabinet is holding a strategy meeting at Chequers on Sunday. The CPRS has put up a poor paper and will be there to present it. We will not be: all special advisers have been excluded. My people are furious and obviously thinking of resigning. I agree it looks ominous. It is ridiculous to have a Cabinet strategy meeting drawn up by civil servants, some of whom are known Tories. Looks like 1966–70 all over again. HW retreating into the machine. We put in a strong memo to that effect.

In the evening Graham Greene came home to fill me in on Crossman. Said that Foot might resign over it – and had privately said he would prefer to be Minister of Overseas Development!

## Monday 18 November 1974

Ill in bed with gastric flu. But I learned from No. 10 that the CPRS presentation at the strategy weekend at Chequers was badly given and badly received.

## Tuesday 19 November 1974

Spent the day in the office catching up on papers.

Saw Marcia briefly to discuss the PM's visit to Dublin on Thursday for Erskine Childers's* funeral.

Parliament Questions went very quietly.

Visited Gerry Fowler in the Lord President's office in the afternoon, with some of the Unit, to discuss devolution.

He later telephoned to say that Ted Short had complained that his special adviser, Vicky Kidd, had not been invited.

Still feeling shaky.

## Wednesday 20 November 1974

Cabinet this morning on Defence cuts.

Worked in the office.

Lunch with Eric Miller, a property millionaire friend of Marcia's who apparently finances some Labour activities.

Afternoon in the office reading. Very quiet.

Incidentally, I heard that Marcia was pleased that I had dropped in to see her – the first time since our famous champagne lunch – and put out the word that she would like me to do it again. I will, for serious discussion, but not for any nonsense.

## Thursday 21 November 1974

PM in Dublin today for Childers's funeral. Joe went with him. A grey and wet day. I am pleased I didn't have to go anywhere.

Before Cabinet I talked to Wedgie Benn, the first time face to face since

March. Discussed our visit to his special advisers and said that I felt we really need an industrial policy. A sort of national plan. Ten years ago Labour had a plan but no instruments to carry it out. Now it is getting the NEB, the Industry Act, FFI Bank, etc, but has no plan.

I am deciding, slowly I realise, that Benn and Bennery could be useful in getting this country's manufacturing industry out of its mess. Not his ad hoc subsidies to any bunch of shop stewards. Not his marginal co-operatives. But the NEB at the van of a proper policy of industrial regeneration. He would not be my chosen instrument – he is too fanatical. But he is all we have, and if controlled might just pull it off.

Spent rest of the morning in the Unit discussing the EEC. Went out in the afternoon.

Returned 6 p.m. as HW returned from Ireland. Went upstairs for a party he was giving for the journalists who followed his election campaign. Unfortunately he turned it into a formal press conference, answering questions just as he does at any press conference, sitting surrounded by a circle of journalists in the white boudoir.

His answers were all familiar, having been given a thousand times – except his curious suggestion of Richard Wood* for the Tory leadership.

Marcia and I got very impatient. We agreed to leave and walked out into the 'blue boudoir' next door. There we chatted in a friendly way, and slowly a stream of journalists came to join us. Finally HW surrendered and came in as well, looking pleased. He was very friendly to me, obviously feeling that the war was over.

At 10, just as we were leaving we heard of the terrible IRA bombings in Birmingham, so we didn't get away for another hour. [This IRA atrocity led to the government rushing through Parliament all stages of the Prevention of Terrorism (Temporary Provisions) Bill.]


*Friday 22 November 1974*

Morning in the Unit. Lunch with Marcia discussing next week's party conference speech. Agreed it must be new, with conclusive ideas, on the economic crisis, and she took away lots of notes to Chequers. Workmanlike rather than friendly.

Off to Suffolk at 7 p.m.


*Monday 25 November 1974*

Came in to No. 10 around 10 a.m. and worked on papers and then dealt with correspondence. Around noon went in to see Marcia – still very friendly. She said that HW had done a draft party conference speech based mainly on the points we agreed on Friday. One third on the problems of inflation and one third on industrial problems and the need for more investment. She said that on Saturday HW was resistant to doing a new speech and kept complaining that all he needed was the copies of his old speeches to do another regurgitation. But Marcia apparently impressed my point that he must do a fresh one and he relented. He took off the notes I had given him and dictated a remarkable *30* pages, very good, very strong on the dangers of inflation, etc.

Joe and I had lunch, then in the afternoon worked on the draft.

In the evening we met at 7.30 p.m. in the study with the Prime Minister, Marcia, Joe, Albert and myself. Soon moved to the little dining-room because of a bomb scare. Then worked till nearly 10, improving the speech immensely. A very happy and constructive meeting. HW was clearly delighted that we were all getting on so well and at one point said to Marcia, 'It's just like the good old days, the old team all working together.'

Afterwards Carol and I went to the French embassy for a very late supper. The clever economic counsellor made it very clear that the French do not give a damn whether we stay in the Market or not!

### Tuesday 26 November 1974

PM at the National Executive Committee this morning, preparing for the party conference.

Joe told me he was thinking of making ministerial changes on Irish policy. Putting Jenkins in overall charge and Prentice in Ireland. Rees then to Education, because PM thinks he is exhausted.

Joe and I went to Marcia's room at 12.30 and began to revise the conference speech. The PM came in from the NEC, having done some revisions of his own. We discussed changes in the text till 2 p.m. when we broke for lunch.

I have contributed more to this speech than to any previous one since February.

House of Commons PQs in the afternoon – fairly quiet.

Talked to Bryan Magee* for half an hour at the House about the pleasures (?) of being an MP.

Then back to No. 10. Worked on more revisions of the speech and also interviewed some prospective members of the Unit to cover the EEC.

### Wednesday 27 November 1974

Morning in the Unit. PM at the party conference, which is being held late and in London because the general election caused the usual October gathering at the seaside to be cancelled.

Lunch at No. 10. Afternoon very good and interesting. In the study with the PM, Joe, Marcia and Peter Davis discussing the final draft of the speech. I have had more influence on this than on any previous speech, trying to get realism on the menace of inflation. The PM accepted most of my alterations and left me to draft the peroration at the end – very 'uplifting' after a long serious piece on the NEB.

Marcia insisted that a piece attacking the City on tax evasion be put in. Perhaps right, in party terms, since the weight of the speech is against the unions. But curious that the PM actually doesn't understand the details of these tax dodges and gets it all wrong. He simply doesn't understand finance.

We stayed on working on the speech until 10.30 p.m. in the evening. I was supposed to be taking Carol and the Plowdens to the theatre, to celebrate our wedding anniversary, but I had to drop out. Not popular.

The PM and Marcia are treating me very solicitously. Several mentions of last Friday's *Economist*, which had referred to me suffering a 'pincer attack' from Marcia and John Hunt. Joe tells me that the PM now blames Hunt for 'that trouble over Bernard'. Very unfair. John was actually very sensible and helpful over it all.

## Thursday 28 November 1974

Went to the Labour Party conference in the Central Hall Westminster to hear the PM's speech (I sat on the platform). He gabbled a bit but was still impressive, very strong and clear. The audience was quiet and attentive, though cool. No standing ovation.

I talked to several people in the corridors afterwards. All agreed it was a first-class speech which would be appreciated by the serious commentators, but not one for the party activists.

The general mood of the conference is not good, with a lot of Bennery extremists around. The NEC elections were OK – no changes, though Benn moved to the top, displacing Foot.

Went for lunch at the Banker (*Financial Times*). Very interesting. Back to Commons for PQs – still quiet, with the Tories lacking the sting they had before the election.

Then back to No. 10 for a meeting with one of Denis Howell's civil servants, on the need for a Football Levy Board to raise and distribute money in support of football.

Meeting of Deputy Secretaries in the Cabinet Office. Very worried about Europe. Benn and Shore are trying to rupture the negotiations – Benn by opposing the Regional Fund, Shore by opposing the new tariffs.

Then a series of receptions in No. 10 – All Blacks Rugby XV, foreign delegates from the conference, and finally to dinner with Golda Meir of Israel at the Churchill Hotel. Quite a day. Feel in excellent form – as is the PM and everybody here.

The Golda Meir dinner was remarkable. I sat at a table with Ellis and Alma Birk,* Kilroy-Silk,* Frank Judd* and Albert. HW arrived late and made an average speech, apologising for Britain *not* voting *against* the PLO resolution at the UN last week. Golda replied for half an hour, exposing and demolishing Britain's hypocrisy. A fantastic speech. Slow, quiet, totally convincing and immensely moving. I was quietly weeping and so were many around, who sense that Israel might be abandoned and destroyed in the near future.

I stayed on afterwards to talk with Yoram Peri, who has replaced Gatt as the Israeli Labour Party representative in Europe. Not home till 1 a.m., but feeling in excellent form.

### Friday 29 November 1974

In early for the weekly morning prayers meeting. Only Healey and the PM there. Rest at the party conference. Afterwards to the Unit. Then saw Marcia to discuss the Middle East. Agree HW must do something to recover lost ground and show Israelis we have not gone completely Arab. Decide to persuade HW to use the coming Paris Summit to attack the UN pro-Arab resolution and say that the EEC must not be used to push us into votes like that.

Then Policy Unit meetings in the morning and afternoon discussing the Regional Fund in the EEC. Benn is trying to get the UK to revise its position on the Regional Fund (as Shore is on tariffs) and wants to rupture renegotiation.

We put in a paper saying this is intolerable. But the Regional Fund is in fact peanuts to us. What matters is regional *policy* – and renegotiating articles 92–4 of the Rome Treaty.

In the evening I went with HW to the *Daily Mirror* conference party at St Ermin's. Everybody in good spirits. Met Ian Mikardo and discussed Middle East. And talked to Michael Foot – who seemed happy and in party mood – about top salaries.

Then back to No. 10 for a reception for Labour Party regional organisers. Very pleasant and Marcia very friendly. But ended with a row with somebody from Transport House, who was as paranoid as they all are there. Attacking HW's speech because it *supported* Benn's position on the NEB. Said this was unforgivable inconsistency, since previously HW had been against Benn. All the conspiracy theories, suspicions, etc. came pouring out. Pathetic. Joe let them have several broadsides.

I was supposed to go to a farewell dinner for an LSE colleague, but I didn't get to the restaurant till 11.15 p.m. – and met them coming out, so no dinner. Home at midnight. Tired, but a good week.

Incidentally, at the *Daily Mirror* party Michael Foot was full of praise for Denis Healey – said he is the best Labour Chancellor ever from the Left's point of view. Interesting for the future leadership?

## Monday 2 December 1974

[Britain's renegotiations of its Common Market membership had continued apace throughout the autumn of 1974. All serious disagreements which could not be resolved at these detailed ministerial and official negotiations were carried forward to the two Heads of Government Summits in December and March. The first was in Paris on 9 December with Giscard d'Estaing again in the chair. The Labour Party annual conference, delayed by the October election until 28 November, was used as part of the political preparation for the December summit. Callaghan had arranged for Helmut Schmidt, the German Chancellor, to address conference on the EEC questions. Afterwards he stayed with Wilson at Chequers and the two leaders struck an important deal. Schmidt promised that Germany would support Britain over amending the Community Budget providing that Wilson would come off the fence and declare firmly and publicly his support for Britain's continued membership of the Community (assuming the terms were right). When Wilson agreed the deal Schmidt said that the British Prime Minister should now visit Giscard in Paris and make an equal declaration to the French in advance of the coming summit. Wilson did this on 3 December, as is referred to in the diary below. He then made his public declaration to a domestic audience in his speech to a gathering of London Labour mayors on the following Saturday.

By then Wilson was effectively committed to securing that Britain remained in the EEC. At no point in private did he ever discuss the possibility of pulling out of Europe. He went to the Paris Summit in a positive frame of mind. In Paris, with the overt support of Schmidt and the covert assistance of Giscard, significant progress was made towards finding a solution to the budgetary problem – through a complex mechanism which promised to correct the existing budgetary bias against Britain.

Back from Paris, Wilson quickly moved to establish the timetable for the referendum on Britain's membership of the EEC. It was agreed that the renegotiations must end by Easter, that the Referendum Bill would then be rushed through Parliament and that the referendum be held by June 1975 at the latest. At this point Roy Jenkins finally accepted the referendum device, which he had previously opposed. The Labour government would during the early months of 1975 be primarily occupied with the final stages of the renegotiations and preparations for the referendum.]

Interesting morning in Cabinet committee on European strategy – the EEC renegotiations.

Again went over the ground on increasing tariffs on 1 January. Shore still very angry. Majority strongly against him – not only pro-marketeers but also Healey, Peart and Callaghan.

Foot pressed his parliamentary sovereignty piece, but in the end it was clearly lost. Shore then asked to be able to raise the matter in the Council of Ministers this afternoon. This was agreed, providing he made only a statement agreeing with Callaghan. In fact he made the statement, then called a press conference and immediately denounced the EEC.

The Regional Fund item went more easily, with the PM speaking very much as we had briefed him – that it was regional *policy* which mattered, not the regional *fund*.

While we were sitting there, Robert Armstrong told me about the weekend. He passed me a note saying, 'We have had an extremely interesting and (for those who think like you and me) very heartening weekend. HW showed more of his hand than ever before – perhaps because he had the conference behind him.' This meant that HW was moving into an openly more pro-EEC position.

In the afternoon I worked in the Unit. Then HW summoned me to the study, with Joe. He was in very jovial form.

Said he opposed Ted Short's plan for a new scheme for special advisers, taking them out of the Civil Service. Unnecessary and will create a row in Parliament. Better to leave things as they are and make special arrangements for the few who want to be parliamentary candidates.

In the evening dinner with the Governor of the Bank of England, Gordon Richardson,* here at No. 10. Plus some City people. Very interesting. Till midnight!

PM on splendid form. Something has recharged his batteries – possibly getting conference behind him. He made very favourable references to my writing of parts of his speech.

## Tuesday 3 December 1974

Went to the PM's study with Joe to talk to the PM about the Common Market. It is now absolutely clear to me that he wants the UK to stay in. He went through the manifesto commitments, ticking them off one by one. He said that the only two sticking-points were that we must get a concession on *cheap food* – access from the Commonwealth – and we must get some compromise on *parliamentary sovereignty.*

He was fairly confident he could do this. His approach now is to get the negotiations out of the hands of the bureaucrats in Brussels and into the hands of the political leaders. He thinks that he, Schmidt and Giscard can sort it out.

He is also going to visit the other EEC capitals – plus Norway – in the New Year, while Callaghan is visiting Africa – 'This will get Jim off the Market for a while.'

He was in bubbling form. Obviously he has come to grips with the EEC and now wants to do it all himself. He also said I should go with him to the Paris Summit.

Today he is off for a quick one-day visit to President Giscard in Paris. Schmidt arranged this after leaving Paris on Sunday. He telephoned here yesterday and arranged it. It is not clear what it will achieve, but is part of Schmidt's desire to get things moving positively. It should get things moving ahead of the coming EEC Summit.

Also apparently HW told Schmidt that he would positively recommend staying in the EEC if the negotiations are successful, and Schmidt is keen for HW to tell that to Giscard in Paris.

Then I worked in the Unit. Saw the PM and Marcia again before lunch. Discussed need for a tougher Defence review next year.

Quick lunch with Joe. Then out with Carol doing Christmas shopping.

Back to find the PM trying to get hold of me from Paris. Wants us to gather evidence of 'press smears' to give to the Finer Commission on the Press.

Out in the evening to dinner with Yoram Peri and the Israelis.


## *Wednesday 4 December 1974*

Took my time going in. HW flying back from Paris. I arrived as he arrived, just before 10.30 – when we had a meeting of the Cabinet committee on Ireland (IRN).

Very good. Frank Cooper from the Northern Ireland Office very clear. Rees and the generals good. Quite optimistic because shootings and bombings are down. But really the political position is hopeless. All they have to offer is the Convention and they have little hope from that. Ahead stretches an endless period of direct political rule – which is why HW wants to get some movement towards pulling out.

Interestingly – and typically – they rarely discuss the ultimate *political* objectives. They get bogged down in the details of day-to-day administration, almost as an excuse for ducking the real issues and choices. I could see this was making Jenkins impatient. Finally, after a couple of hours' discussion of the details of imprisonment, etc., he intervened. He said that everything he heard made him more convinced that Northern Ireland had nothing to do with the rest of the UK. He said that although the whole discussion was about how to impose the civilised standards of Britain on Northern Ireland, the real prospect and danger was of the barbaric standards of Northern Ireland spreading to the rest of us. He wanted further discussions soon on the general issue of the future.

Ted Short followed and argued that all the Irish needed was 'good government, and therefore we should fully integrate them into Great Britain'. Several people laughed at this. But really he and Jenkins had put the serious alternatives. The officials' view, of an endless series of short-term direct-rule expedients, means in fact long-term direct rule without it ever having been discussed and agreed; and this is the worst of all policies – or non-policies.

HW was clearly sympathetic to Jenkins and ordered that more papers be prepared. He looked pale. Last night he was ill from eating oysters with Giscard in Paris, and only got about five hours' sleep. Apparently he is always ill after oysters.

Afterwards I went to Marcia's room and she was very angry at the oysters story. She disapproves of 'abroad' anyway and of France and French food above all. So when he came in she gave him a thorough ticking-off. She also attacked him about the bakers' strike and the shortage of bread and told him to get hold of Michael Foot to put pressure on for a settlement. Unfortunately Foot is never willing to get into conflict with the unions. He wants to be loved by them. HW said, 'Michael is getting very laissez-faire, I'm afraid.'

In the afternoon I worked in the Unit, until 4.30 when I went up to the study. Discussed British Leyland with the PM, giving evidence of their terrible management. He asked for this on paper at the 5 p.m. meeting of the Cabinet Industry committee (IDV). Also discussed the EEC. He is definitely looking for a way to stay in.

The IDV meeting was fascinating. First British Leyland. Benn said that the banks' accountants had discovered that the situation was much worse than the company realised; that they would not be able to pay the wages after Christmas and would have to close down Austin-Morris at Cowley. Benn was clearly very excited at this plum coming into his NEB lap and certainly gave the impression that the company had come to him for help and were resigned to public ownership – later I gathered that they had done no such thing and that their bankers were considering increasing the overdraft without actually involving the Department of Industry at all. Most people present supported the intervention and saw British Leyland as an obvious candidate for the NEB – although Jenkins and Crosland both argued for a 50–50 holding. The committee decided not to let Benn make any announcement, obviously afraid that he would commit them further than they wanted to go.

Then moved on to aircraft nationalisation. Here Benn had put in so many papers that the committee had great difficulty keeping track of the discussion. Crosland objected to taking the discussion to a conclusion so late in the evening. Benn got very angry at this and said he could not wait any longer. Then Jenkins piled in, stating that he could not accept the first objective of the nationalisation as set out by Benn, which was to maintain the present workforce in employment. He said this was to perpetuate all the mistakes in our aircraft policy over the previous five years. Benn got very angry, his eyes popping completely out of their sockets, as he protested that he had never been responsible for starting a single aircraft project (he had not cancelled any either, he admitted). Jenkins came back at him – and Benn suddenly went very calm and said that he saw a lot of sense in something Tony Crosland had said about not going on with this this evening, but dealing with it next time. Total somersault. And then he added that he would like 'to consult with the industry' in the meantime, which means, of course, to mobilise the shop stewards.

I did not hear the end of the discussion because HW sent a message down the table asking me to go and get Joe and Albert to help entertain the new February back-benchers who had come in to No. 10 for a drink. I did this, talking mainly to Betty Boothroyd*, who seems very sensible. Then I went to the German Embassy for a reception. Met some nice Germans, including Ralf Dahrendorf, now director of the LSE, who is in splendid form. And chatted to Margaret Jackson, who is clearly getting a little cooler on her boss Judith Hart.

Home at 10 p.m.


## Thursday 5 December 1974

When I arrived in No. 10 the PM was already in the Economic Strategy committee before Cabinet, discussing the mineworkers pay situation. Andrew Graham went along on my behalf and told me that the PM was showing much more interest than usual.

Cabinet had an enormous agenda. It did not properly deal with top salaries. This item had led to a row in the Unit since the civil servants refused to let members of the Unit see the papers. I was allowed to see them in the private office! I refused to go along with this, but could not get access for Andrew Graham and David Piachaud. They argued, quite rightly, that it was ridiculous for them to deal with and brief the PM on the social contract if top salaries – including top civil servants' salaries – were excluded. They asked what on earth the secrecy was about this particular group of salaries. And why should the circulation be limited only to those who had a vested interest in getting them through? This is when you see the Civil Service really at work. They have had this top salaries report for over three weeks. Almost nobody – not even Michael Foot – has been allowed to see it. The issue has been on the agenda for Cabinet committee several times, but no papers have ever been circulated and it has always been removed from the agenda late in the day. Now it has come direct to Cabinet – with the papers being circulated only a day before and only to Cabinet ministers. On a *really* important matter like its own salaries, the machine is *very* impressive.

I was telephoned this morning by the admirable Pat Nairne*, who is head of the Common Market Unit in the Cabinet Office. He asked me out to lunch at the Oxford and Cambridge Club. We went and discussed the EEC. He had already learned that I was going to the Paris Summit with HW and was very keen to pick my brains on HW's views – and to feed in a few things.

Went straight from there to the Commons for Question Time. Beforehand at briefing a message came through from Wedgie Benn that the press had got hold of the story that British Leyland was in trouble and he wanted to make his statement to head them off – he mentioned the *Sunday Times* and added there was 'an avalanche' of enquiries.

HW looked suspicious. Before giving permission he telephoned Healey at the Exchequer and asked a civil servant to phone British Leyland. Healey told him that Benn had been on to the Treasury saying he wanted to make a statement and that 'No. 10 was in favour'. British Leyland reported that they had had no press enquiries 'except from Mr Benn's own office'.

We then discovered from private office intelligence that the Department of Industry had not had any extra enquiries – and that Benn had just been to lunch with the *Sunday Times*.

It was quite clear to everybody that Benn was trying to bounce us into a statement – including the intention to nationalise.

Benn came to see the PM after Questions (which went slowly and quietly), but HW refused permission for a statement. That was at 4 p.m.

Afterwards I chatted to HW, who is in splendid form, and we drove back to No. 10 together.

I worked till early evening. Then went to a CCPR (Central Council for Physical Recreation) party – where I had a brief talk to Roy Jenkins and a long talk to John Gilbert* from the Treasury, trying to convert him to a Football Levy Board. Afterwards to a National Union of Teachers party.

## Friday 6 December 1974

Still feeling in high spirits. Everything is going fine at the moment. The atmosphere in No. 10 is excellent and I am enjoying the job immensely. Not really looking forward to leaving now – and must sort that out.

Went in early to the weekly 'business' meeting at No. 10. Everybody was steamed up because the press is full of the British Leyland story. The *Telegraph* got it in their first editions and everyone else followed. It looked as if Benn had bounced us after all.

I saw Joe after the meeting, at around 10 a.m., and he was furious. Wants to persuade HW to deal with Benn and stop this constant bouncing us into extensions of public ownership. Talked to Robert Armstrong, who agreed and feared a run on sterling. So he cancelled the PM's 10.30 meeting with the Church Commissioners and we went up and discussed the situation. The PM, who had been very cool compared to the other ministers in the earlier meeting, was now getting angrier at the way Benn treated him. He decided to set up a private inquiry into the leak – and instructed Douglas Allen, as head of the Civil Service, to do it.

[Benn announced the partial nationalisation of British Leyland to provide the necessary working capital for the continuance of the company, Britain's only native, mass motorcar manufacturer. Sir Don Ryder was appointed to chair an inquiry into the company's prospects.]

Then he saw Len Murray briefly, and after that we set again to discuss a speech the PM is giving tomorrow to the London mayors. He is going to devote it to a serious statement of our position on the EEC – basing his position firmly on the manifesto. If we get the negotiating points there, he will recommend to the British people that we stay in. If no, no. This is shrewd – since it is firmly based on the party manifesto. It is also good for the marketeers, since it now looks as if we will get the concessions. It is clear that he is now fascinated by the Market problem. He sees it as a challenge – to stay in, get the terms and hold the Labour Party together. He never talks of actually pulling out. When discussing what happens if we don't get the terms, he always avoids actually saying 'we come out'. He always says something like, 'It won't be acceptable to accept terms which are damaging to us . . .'

At lunch I dropped in to see Marcia. Tommy Balogh was there. They were discussing the Market and how Tommy, who as a Hungarian hates all foreigners, must make an anti-Market speech. I stopped him by saying that HW was going to do that and did not want anybody else upstaging him.

HW then came in for his usual pre-lunch drink in Marcia's room. She screamed at him because the press was saying that he had come off the fence in favour of the Market and had promised Giscard that if we got the right terms he would recommend staying in. She shouted at him several times, 'Harold, did you say that to Giscard?' He avoided it for a while, but she went on and on, and he finally denied it completely. [Though we all knew he did commit himself in Paris, as he had to Schmidt at Chequers.]

He then promised he would make an anti-Market speech this weekend to redress the balance. Earlier he had explained to me that he must keep the balance and that the pro-marketeers were not doing their cause any good by pushing the view in the press that he had changed, or by leaking what he had told Giscard.

After lunch HW sent for me and Joe, and with Robert Armstrong we sat in the study until 6 p.m., finishing off the speech. It is very good, finely balanced – and in no sense anti-Market. He was even talked into keeping in the bit about recommending staying in the Market if we get the right terms. So it will now be on the public record.

Incidentally at lunchtime I sent for my friend on the *Telegraph*. He told us that their industrial correspondent obtained the British Leyland story around 5 p.m. yesterday – 'It was a Department of Industry placing'! So Benn did leak it.

Then HW went to Chequers. I went back to the Unit, where we are preparing a brief on the EEC.

And Carol came in at 8 p.m. and we went to a very nice dinner party with Richard Graham.

Incidentally, when I saw John Hunt at yesterday's weekly meeting of Cabinet Office Deputy Secretaries to prepare next week's business (at 5 p.m.) I told him that future historians would be astonished, and if we have a crisis would be shocked, to learn that this autumn the two subjects which are *almost never* discussed at any Cabinet or Cabinet committee are (1) inflation and the social contract and (2) overseas finance, sterling, oil, etc.

These are the two issues which could make or break Britain in 1975.

He doesn't disagree, but won't, I suppose, be able to do anything about it.

*Monday 9 December 1974*

We flew to Paris from Northolt in the Andover at 10 in the morning. Joe missed the plane – he was delayed in the traffic – and drove straight to and along the runway as we climbed into the air above him. (He then took a commercial flight from Heathrow.)

Drove from Orly airport to the embassy in a great cavalcade of cars and police escorts. Lunch there with HW, Jim Callaghan and the civil servants. Then spent the rest of the afternoon sitting around, reading briefs, apart from taking Joe on a quick shopping tour along the boulevards. A grey day, threatening to rain, but Paris as always lively and invigorating.

HW returned at 6.30 with Callaghan and they reported to us on the Summit discussions. An afternoon mainly spent on institutional EEC questions which do not interest us very much. They then went off to dinner, and we ate in the embassy and afterwards sat in the elegant Duff Cooper library and chatted over coffee.

The PM and Jim Callaghan returned just after 11 and we began a briefing session for tomorrow on the Budget and the Regional Fund. I could tell the PM was unhappy. He was spoiling for a fight. Suddenly he launched a massive attack on civil servants – especially Michael Palliser* of the Foreign Office and Pat Nairne of the Cabinet Office – for being too pro-Market and not understanding the need to get cheap Commonwealth food – especially New Zealand lamb and butter. He asked them factual questions about the amount of imports in 1971, the EEC sugar arrangements, etc., which they understandably could not answer, and he denounced them for this. He was furious, and everyone was embarrassed. He was rougher than I have ever seen him. At the end Jim Callaghan intervened and said that it was all right making these criticisms, but what did the PM conclude? The PM shouted that 'From now on I will take my briefing from Bernard (me) and his Unit.'

I could feel myself blushing and I sank in my chair.

We broke up – it was now 1 a.m. – and the PM signalled to me to come to his room with him. He was delighted with himself. He said (unfairly) that the civil servants were mediocre as well as too pro-Market. And 'They must not think they have captured me and now it is all plain sailing.' He then revealed that on Saturday Marcia had attacked him for being too much in the pockets of the civil servants. He clearly felt he had demonstrated to her, in her absence, that he was not. He said, 'I'm so pleased that you came along.' He clearly meant me to report to her.

Robert Armstrong and John Hunt came into his bedroom to talk to him. He walked out with them, chatted, said good-night pointedly and then asked me to come back in and went over the whole occasion again with relish as he got undressed. He stood there in his voluminous shorts, beside the antique four-poster bed, chuckling away. I finally got to bed at 2 a.m. – but *he* had to get up at 7!

It was clearly partly a calculated attack. He wanted to warn the civil servants that he was not a prisoner of the pro-marketeers. He wanted them to fight harder for his seven negotiating points. But he was also genuinely angry. They had been pushing too much recently – for top salaries, against Israel, on honours, on lots of little things. Their briefs were too blatantly pro-Market. It finally all boiled over. He also wanted to redress the balance

after his Saturday speech, which had been widely interpreted as meaning
he was off the fence – into the Market. He was especially looking over his
shoulder to the Left, and to Marcia. Two steps forward, one back.

## Tuesday 10 December 1974

A glorious, sunny winter's day. Paris looking sparkling. I woke at 8 and
felt marvellous. Breakfast in bed, shower and then to the embassy. The
PM had already gone to the meeting of the Heads of Government at 9.
We sat around in the embassy for a while chatting about last night. The
general view was that Michael Palliser had pushed the PM too far and
forced a backlash. I knew it was more than that. Pat Nairne was very
concerned and came to have a talk with me about how to get their briefing
more right politically. The PM has been critical of him, but I find him
sound and very nice and straight.

I went out shortly after 11 a.m. and took the car across to the National
Assembly for coffee and then on to the conference centre in the Avenue
Kléber to find Joe for lunch. Joe was due to give the briefing on the morning
session, but he was very late. When he had not arrived by 1.15 p.m. I
sensed that something was wrong and went back to the embassy. Apparently
there was deadlock in the negotiations. Giscard had refused to give an inch
on the Budget. The seven others had supported Britain, but the French
were intransigent. At this the PM interrupted and said, 'There is no point
in going any further in the negotiations,' and there they broke up.

The PM went straight on to lunch. I went back to the hotel and had
an expensive (and not very good) lunch and then had a small rest.

There Joe Stone (the PM's doctor) told me that Marcia had telephoned
that morning saying that her brother Tony was unwell and demanding that
the PM and Joe Stone should leave the European Summit and return as
soon as possible from Paris to do something about it. As her doctor, Joe
thinks she is 'not properly balanced'.

HW returned at 4 p.m. looking unwell and took Joe Stone up to his
room. Apparently he was suffering from an attack of 'racing heart', which
often strikes him at times of pressure. After a while he came down and
said he wanted to dictate what had happened in the afternoon discussion
on the Middle East. But when the secretary arrived he said he didn't want
to – and after she had gone he said he refused to dictate to her ever again
because she had leaked to her police boyfriend stories and gossip about
life with Marcia in the Scillies in the summer. Joe and I exchanged glances.
Marcia has clearly been criticising her. Probably HW admired her in her
swimming costume on the beach!

Then HW reported that Schmidt had privately assured him that there was nothing to worry about on the Budget – he would 'fix it'. Schmidt said that Giscard had the problem of getting his Foreign Minister off the hook of opposing us. (But he also wants to please his Gaullist critics and may not move, we fear.)

The PM then dictated his note on the Middle East discussion. Apparently Schmidt had made an anti-Israeli speech saying that all the Europeans must put pressure on the Israelis to climb down. He also criticised the French for being so pro-Arab that they might push the Israelis into a war of desperation. HW then attacked the French and made a pro-Israeli speech. He says that the Dutch and Danes did the same, with the Belgians muttering support. By this time Schmidt had fallen asleep.

The PM went back late to the Summit – well after 5 p.m. – and after a phone call from Callaghan. I think this was a deliberate move to show his toughness and willingness to pull out of the Summit.

We learned that the foreign ministers had made no progress. The Italians had put forward a resolution supporting us on the Budget, and the rest of the seven supported, but the French still opposed.

I went out shopping – including buying four kilos of sugar as stock against the threat of rationing at home. Then to the hotel to write this. Then back to the embassy for dinner with the Ambassador while we waited for HW to return with – we hoped – the communiqué agreed.

At the embassy for dinner – with the Ambassador, John Hunt, Robert Armstrong, Tom Bridges and Antony Acland* from the Foreign Office. During the meal we periodically received messages from the Quai d'Orsay that things were going well and they were 'on the brink of a breakthrough'.

We adjourned upstairs to the library and took coffee. Then the bells rang and the PM came sweeping into the courtyard outside in the Ambassador's Rolls. The civil servants had a hurried discussion and decided that 'in order to avoid a repetition of last night' it was desirable that not too many people be present to receive him. They decided that it should only be the Ambassador, Robert, Joe, Tom Bridges and myself. The rest hung around outside.

HW came in, looking less tired than this morning, and reported on the evening's session. He had been irritated by long delays over translations and efforts by the French to slip through translations which modified the agreements. He clearly did not think he had made good progress – though all the civil servants felt he had achieved a great success, everything we wanted on the Budget, with a reference to the Brussels Commission to set up 'a correcting mechanism'.

Jim Callaghan came in, took off his shoes, looked tired and said HW had been 'very rough' on the others. We all 'debriefed' while waiting for the press conference which HW and Jim Callaghan were giving – it finally started after midnight and went on quietly for an hour. The PM especially was playing everything down, partly not to rub it in to the French, partly not to upset his left wing at home.

After the conference we wanted HW to go to bed, but he insisted on staying up and discussing the achievements. He asked for all the civil servants to come in and invited their views in turn. He was obviously being nice to them to make up for the previous evening, but it meant I did not leave the embassy till after 2 – and then I went for drinks with Tom McCaffrey*, the Foreign Office Press Officer, and Gore-Booth, who is at the embassy here. Not in bed till nearly 4.

### Wednesday 11 December 1974

Up at 9, had breakfast and then saw my Parisian friend Jacques Pomonti, who advises Mitterrand, for an hour. He told me that Mitterrand does not like Wilson.

I telephoned the embassy and was told that the PM would not leave the embassy before 11.30 at the earliest. So we set off from my hotel, walking slowly, at 10.45, buying some lovely fresh bread on the way to take home to Carol. As Jacques and I reached the embassy entrance we saw a line of motorcyclists revving up their engines and a cavalcade of cars waiting behind the Rolls. HW was standing on the embassy steps waving goodbye. He saw me, grinned and waved to me to hurry up, so I said a quick goodbye to Jacques, sprinted across the gravel forecourt and leapt into a Citroën, and within seconds we were roaring and wailing through Paris. We were in the air from Orly before 11.30 – and a good thing I did not delay any longer from the hotel!

The trip home in the Andover was awful. Very bumpy and several people looking green.

In the afternoon at No. 10 I worked desperately catching up on a huge pile of papers. Then on a memo to HW strongly urging that the Cabinet tomorrow *reject* the top salaries report (including £3,000 p.a. extra for me!). Ridiculous to be giving some people an *extra* £250 a week when the miners are just about to put in their claim.

Home early – 7.45 p.m. – and went to see my lovely Rachel in her school play.

### Thursday 12 December 1974

Cabinet at 10. HW reported on the Summit and apparently Shore, Foot and Benn attacked him for giving too much away. HW replied angrily that he was 'not an innocent abroad' and was negotiating with the Russians 'when some of his critics were still at school'. They also took top salaries and agreed a compromise along the lines HW had suggested in his own memorandum. It still means top chairmen getting *rises* of over £5,000 p.a. and seems to me likely to bring the social contract even further into disrepute.

HW had to leave in the middle of Cabinet and send for his doctor Joe Stone. He had a repeat of the 'racing heart'. Much worse than in Paris. He told Joe that he could not remember what he had read in his briefs this morning. Joe Stone ordered him to take three days' rest, and all his engagements for the rest of the week were cancelled. He had a light lunch in the flat and then went off to Chequers until next Monday.

A bad day for health. Today I was to be visited by my friend Senator Krichefski from Jersey. He had telephoned to tell me that he had some very personal matters to explain and that he would need a full hour. This morning I received a telephone call to say that he had a heart attack and died in his car on the way to Jersey airport. I may never know what his secret information was.

Spent the afternoon reading a mass of papers – mainly on devolution and Scottish problems.

Sterling is very jittery and the Bank is having to intervene heavily in the forward market. Price inflation is now 18%. It looks grim.

Left early to go out to dinner with our friend Huw Pierce – and John Crawley from the BBC. Very pleasant evening – home 1 a.m.

## Friday 13 December 1974

Heard this morning that Maurice Finer, who we have put in charge of the Royal Commission on the Press, is in hospital to have a lung removed – cancer. A week full of casualties. [He died very soon afterwards and was replaced as chairman of the Royal Commission by Professor O.R. McGregor.]

Worked on papers and then had a Unit meeting in the morning, planning our programme of work ahead.

Went to the LSE for lunch. General air of demoralisation there, because of shortage of money. At the moment am enjoying the No. 10 job so much that I feel no great urgency to return to LSE. This will change of course once we run into bad times again. At the moment it is exciting and invigorating beyond belief.

Back to the Unit to work on a paper on the Scottish and Welsh Development Agencies, but decide in the end not to put it in. Not substantial enough. Must make sure that our memoranda are selective and weighty.

Home by 8. No. 10 just does not seem as dynamic when the boss is away.

Harold Evans dropped in for an hour. Very contemptuous of John Hunt over the Crossman Diaries affair.

## Monday 16 December 1974

Came in early for the IDV Cabinet committee at 10 a.m. – on the nationalisation of aircraft; on section 7 powers to the Secretaries of State for Scotland and Wales; and the development agencies.

Aircraft went through with little dissent.

Section 7 powers was a battle to keep these powers with Benn's empire. He lost – and they went to the Scots and Welsh Secretaries. Not because their case was better. Benn had a good case in arguing that he should not be reduced to a Secretary of State for Industry in *England*. But there is so much suspicion of him now that he often loses when innocent or virtuous.

The final item was his attempt to prevent redundancies by compelling firms to stay in business even when losing money: by preventing them from selling assets; and forcing them to give three months' notice of more than 10 redundancies. He was opposed from all sides – even by Peter Shore. Benn is suffering from his own previous bad behaviour. Yet unemployment is a terrible threat – and he is the only person raising it and trying to put up solutions, however half-baked.

Both Bill Rodgers and Gerry Fowler were in the Cabinet committee meeting. Gave it a friendly feeling, seeing people I had known for so many years – Gerry now for almost 30 years! I sent him a note saying that this was a long way from the Horse and Groom public house in Northampton, where we used to drink when schoolboys after playing rugby on a Saturday.

The PM looked very seedy early on, but he drank a lot of water and his colour improved. He took a lot of interest and guided the meeting well.

I had lunch with Lady Birk at the House of Lords. Very bright and pleasant. Needs some political advice since she has to cover an enormous field in Environment.

Afterwards went to the House to hear the PM make his statement on the Paris Summit. Went very well really. Heath did not help by praising him. But HW dealt well with his critics behind.

But he did seem fragile, slow of speech and groping for phrases. Joe was worried and later telephoned for Joe Stone – who said don't worry, it is OK.

The PM went to *Swan Lake* at Covent Garden in the evening – and was savagely attacked by Marcia for doing so.

I worked on papers till 9 p.m. Then went home.

## Tuesday 17 December 1974

Ireland Cabinet committee at 10. Always fascinating. Proposals for a cease-fire, Convention elections, etc. The situation there seems much more promising now, with less violence than for years.

I sat next to Patrick Wright, the nice new private secretary covering foreign affairs and replacing Tom Bridges. He is an 'Arab' and I passed him a note comparing the IRA with the PLO. Just an opening shot.

Went to the PM's study afterwards. Discussed a statement on the disappearance of the Labour MP John Stonehouse* – where the PM knows nothing. He also said that nothing else on the Crossman Diaries had come up.

Had lunch at No. 10. Afternoon at Commons for Questions. Very quiet. All the sting and excitement has gone out of them now the election is over.

Afterwards the PM made his statement on Stonehouse saying that he was not a spy, and this went down well.

Came back to discuss a Policy Unit paper on the economy, put into the PM's box tonight. My staff are very worried by the proposals for massive rises in nationalised industry prices. I'm not sure this is right. It will help the borrowing requirement but could completely bust the social contract – if it remains to be busted. Wages are already rising at 25% and prices are up 25%. We are threatened by hyper-inflation even if the miners settle.

We worked on the economic paper until after 10 p.m. – Andrew Graham, David Piachaud and myself. Just one break in the middle to attend Tom Bridges' farewell party. I was supposed to go to a dinner of LEFTA, the Labour finance group, but by the time I got to St Ermin's Hotel at 10.30 it was over. I drove home, buying some Chinese food on the way, and finally had supper in a sleeping house at 11.30 p.m.

## Wednesday 18 December 1974

Went straight to the Treasury for a 10 a.m. meeting of some special advisers on a paper by our Richard Graham about industrial policy. Two of the advisers – including our Treasury host – did not arrive till nearly 11. The two advisers from Industry, F. Morrell and F. Cripps, performed very badly. Mrs Morrell is one of those large aggressive women who gravitate naturally into politics where they can exercise their frustrations. The Labour Party is full of them. So really a waste of time.

I dashed back to No. 10 at noon for a special committee on the Crown Agents, who have been investing in bad property, possibly fraudulently, and are now bankrupt to the tune of £85 million. A terrible story. There may be criminal proceedings. Decide to bail them out and set up an inquiry. None of the ministers present seemed to understand property finance – including Healey. Lever was not there – deliberately excluded by the civil servants, I was told, so I mentioned it to the PM as we went into the Cabinet Room. He ordered them to send for Lever, but unfortunately he was not available.

Curious episode of Mellish's resignation! I went to Marcia's room and she was holding a private meeting with the PM about Mellish's resignation as Chief Whip, just announced on the tapes.

Mellish had been furious about the rebellion by 58 left-wingers on Monday night – including eight parliamentary secretaries – voting against the Defence decisions. HW had done nothing about this. In fact yesterday was so busy we barely had time to discuss it – and then he felt it best to ignore it (as I did at the time).

Apparently Mellish grew angrier and angrier and wrote a letter of complaint to HW. It was not a letter of resignation – I saw it, and it was just complaining about the Tribune Group and that Mellish did not want the bloody job of Chief Whip in October anyway.

Robert Armstrong put the letter in the PM's secret box at 6.30 p.m. last night. The PM did not see that box – so he knew nothing about it till he heard about the resignation. He was furious with Robert – though he might also blame Mellish for resigning without making it clear in his letter.

There was great confusion. The press office had been denying the resignation. Search parties went out to find Mellish, who arrived (after several drinks) and the PM had to be dragged out of a lunch with the Prime Minister of Mauritius.

They had a long talk. The PM appealed to Mellish's loyalty to the party, told him how important he was, that if he went, the government would fall and be replaced by a national coalition. So Mellish yielded and agreed to soldier on.

Then the PM decided not to announce this till 9.30 in the evening – forcing the newspapers to get their first editions wrong and the BBC news to miss it (at 9 p.m.). Typical of him to play games with the media. But it began to leak later, because Mellish talked!

Spent the afternoon on Policy Unit papers and went to the political office party in the evening.

Joe told me that Michael Foot is threatening to resign over top salaries.

Apparently HW followed our brief closely in the Economic Strategy Cabinet committee discussing nationalised industries' prices. Shirley Williams and Barbara Castle also protesting.

*Thursday 19 December 1974*

The Cabinet this morning were discussing top salaries and then NHS consultants' salaries. On the former Michael Foot was taking a brave stand. The civil servants were asked to leave, as interested parties. But still most of it went through. Incredible really – an extra £6,000 to permanent secretaries! An extra £120 a week when we are about to confront the miners and try to stop them getting more than a *total* of £60 a week. Makes a farce of the social contract and Labour's claims to get greater equality. The Unit has briefed HW twice telling him he must reject the TSRB report by Boyle.* He has fought them, but the civil servants meant to slip it through. It did not go to any Cabinet committee. Straight to Cabinet, twice, with papers in ministers' overnight boxes. HW is just not prepared to fight the Whitehall machine. There were some compromises – deferments and phasing – to prevent Michael Foot resigning. But the civil servants were all grinning from ear to ear afterwards. As one official from the Cabinet Office said to me, 'Now we have got our increase, the Treasury can bring in its bloody wage freeze.'

The NHS consultants also got their massive *offer*, because Barbara Castle was desperate to buy them off. (At lunch Marcia supported the consultants and said she was afraid they would give up private practice in the NHS if they did not get their extra 40%.) The whole wage front is collapsing.

Went to Marcia's room at lunchtime. HW came in. Spent most of the time with HW repeating what went on in Cabinet and Marcia attacking the civil servants.

I slipped out for a sandwich at 1 p.m., taking Andrew Graham with me to discuss the economic crisis. We can see only the two alternatives of high unemployment, which we reject, and a statutory wages policy, which HW said again today he would not allow. Andrew and I are hoping to construct an alternative policy and put the paper to HW over Christmas.

Questions very quiet. Though the Tories are beginning to put on pressure about the EEC – referendum, etc.

Afternoon worked on papers. Evening with Carol to dinner with Gough Whitlam,* Australian PM, at No. 10. The Australians were very boring and some of their women were very large and seemed the worse for drink. But I had a lovely time sitting with the tennis player Virginia Wade, who was intelligent and amusing as well as beautiful.

Home by 1 a.m. Woke several times in the night suffering from the gastronomic excesses. (Some lovely 1955 burgundy.)

## Friday 20 December 1974

Felt a little bleary this morning. Took aspirin and drove in very slowly with the window open to blow away the cobwebs.

PM had an important early meeting with Jenkins, Callaghan and Short on the EEC referendum. Apparently they agreed a timetable of ending negotiations by Easter; then a Referendum Bill; then a referendum by end June.

I worked in the Unit on papers and we had a meeting in the morning.

Dropped into Marcia's room before lunch. HW came in from his talks with Whitlam, very tired and bored because Whitlam is heavy and not very inspiring. They decided they could not face dinner on Saturday alone with the Whitlams and so we began desperately to think of extra names to lighten the party. This was interesting and sad. HW said that dinner with the Australians should be an occasion for 'family and *close* friends'. So we tried to think of some. HW couldn't think of any. So we ended up with the same old group of people – Kagan, Eric Miller, Jarvis Astaire,* Peter Davis, Denis Lyons and Albert. The point is that *Harold doesn't have any old, close friends*.

HW went off to lunch with Harold Lever; and I gave him a list of questions which he should raise.

We had a final Christmas lunch at No. 10. Turkey and Christmas pudding and a farewell gift to the cook. Our house lunches are all coming to an end because Marcia insisted. In future we shall have to go out, and spend more time and money on it. Ridiculous.

There was a meeting of the Cabinet Economic Strategy committee from 2.30 to 4.30 p.m. Covering the miners and the general economic situation (based on a dramatic pessimistic paper by Shirley Williams).

Then a party for handicapped children – very moving and harrowing.

Later I did a memo on nationalised industries – where the civil servants are trying to get a 'no change' report slipped through without any ministerial discussion at all. They are circulating it on Christmas Eve and suggesting that it be taken as approved unless they hear to the contrary by the New Year – an old tactic. I strongly urged the PM to have it discussed by a full ministerial committee. We must modernise and restructure the nationalised industries to meet the need for greater efficiency and accountability.

Home at 9 p.m. Still feeling in excellent spirits.

## Monday 23 December 1974

A very relaxed day. Prepared a memo on wages for the PM. Otherwise festive chat.

In the evening we had the No. 10 staff Christmas party. Shortly after it started I was sent for and told that George Weidenfeld the publisher was in the tiny waiting-room. I had nothing to do with his being there, but went down to talk to him. He sat there in the near dark, rather pathetic, very lonely and forlorn.

Apparently Marcia had promised to go to dinner with him later in the evening. She cried off at the last moment – and in compensation invited him to the No. 10 staff party, along with the switchboard girls, typists, cleaners, etc. Then she didn't arrive till very late, so he was left waiting for an hour in the waiting-room. I happily chatted with him. He will presumably get his compensation in some future honours list. [He did, made Lord Weidenfeld in 1976.]

The party was quite good fun. With Robert Armstrong playing the piano and others singing. At one point Mary complained that a funny version of a popular hymn was blasphemous!

HW was in splendid form.

I went on later to George Weidenfeld's for an excellent dinner. Talked mainly to my old friends John and Miriam Gross, but also to Lady Melchett. As usual there were several beautiful blondes, looking as if they had recently exhausted the resources of a rich ex-husband. Some may have memoirs to publish. I steered clear, because I know George gossips to Marcia and it all comes back to No. 10 in a highly exaggerated form.

Home at 1 a.m. and off in the morning to Suffolk for Christmas.

# CHAPTER 10

# New Year 1975:
## Scotland, the EEC and Escape to Washington
### January–February 1975

*Wednesday 1 January 1975*

Has been a glorious Christmas. Sunny and mild. And Suffolk quiet and beautiful.

Came back to London yesterday afternoon. Today is New Year, a bank holiday, and the office is supposed to be closed, but I went in to No. 10 in the afternoon. First had lunch with Harold Evans at the RAC Club – where I also had a swim. Livened me up after a very late New Year's party. Only three hours' sleep. Harold told me that the Cabinet Office had rejected the proposed extracts from the Crossman Diaries and he was now thinking of pressing ahead and publishing without permission. He feels that John Hunt (the Cabinet Secretary) has been trying to push him around.

No. 10 was very quiet and dark, with most rooms empty. Just a few policemen, the duty clerk, and Patrick Wright, the nice Foreign Office private secretary in private office.

I worked for two hours on a large backlog of papers, Then Joe came in at 4.30 p.m. and the PM shortly after – to meet the Church leaders of Northern Ireland. The PM was not due back from the Scillies till tomorrow. Really he is bored there and always looks for an excuse to get back early. The 'Irish crisis' is usually a good enough excuse.

We went up to the study and discussed the collapse of Burmah Oil. Alleged to be gross mismanagement. The Bank of England has stepped in quickly – to keep it out of the hands of Benn. Suspicious. If the government got Burmah we would be able to break the bargaining power of the oil companies in the North Sea – not least because it would give us another 22% of BP, making over 70% in all!

I did not go in to the Irish meeting, since it was bound to be a lot of blather. Continued to read papers, and then went down to talk to the PM when he came out at about 7.30. Told him that *Private Eye* had libelled me again. He gave me permission to sue – but asked for 10% of the proceeds!

New Year's honours list due out tomorrow. Rudi Sternberg a peer. (He gave £15,000 to the party.)

Went home at 9 p.m.

## Thursday 2 January 1974

Went in at midday. HW came in then from Chequers and we went upstairs to discuss his proposed speech in Liverpool tomorrow, attacking the strikers at British Leyland.

He was very pleased with the press coverage of the honours list and was generally in good form.

We improved the speech a bit – though he would not accept my efforts to get him *not* to say that the threat of unemployment was greater than the threat of inflation.

Finished at 1.30 – when we went down to see Marcia, the PM saying, 'I haven't seen her for about 10 days.'

Joe and I went to the House of Commons for lunch. Bill Rodgers came over to join us. Discussing John Stonehouse, Joe said that Harold did not reappoint him to the government this time because he was 'such a liar'.

At teatime I went up to the study with Joe and we had a long chat with the PM on several matters – including Burmah Oil, where I am very suspicious that the Bank of England is pulling a fast one on us. He was still in good form. I told him about the Crossman Diaries. He said he was keeping out of it. He suddenly said of Crossman, 'Dick died as he lived, a bloody juvenile delinquent.'

Then I went down to the Unit, where with Andrew Graham, David Piachaud and Richard Kirwan we began thrashing out an economic package to put to the PM. Had a discussion for four hours. Going round and round on wages and unemployment. All that is certain is that each is going much higher! HW has not made things easier by repeatedly promising (1) he would not allow high unemployment; (2) he would not have a statutory wages policy; and (3) he was opposed to deflation, import controls, etc. That closes quite a few options!

Home at 8.30 p.m.

Joe tells me that the PM has decided to deal with Benn 'in his own way'.

The PM was due to have lunch with Lord Brayley today at the Caprice. Cancelled at the last moment because the Board of Trade say there may be criminal proceedings against him. Joe intervened. HW is naive on these things.

## Friday 3 January 1975

Saw little of HW today. When I arrived he was not there. I went through papers and then had a two-hour Unit meeting, attempting to thrash out an economic package.

Also tried to get hold of Eric Varley, to discuss Burmah Oil and see if the Bank of England *should* be left to handle it.

And Denis Howell to discuss the financial problems of sport.

Both fixed for next week.

Lunch at House of Commons with Joe, in the Strangers Cafeteria – very sordid. Strolled around St James's Park after.

In the afternoon I completed the office papers, did some dictation, and went off early to drink a whole bottle of good white burgundy before going home. I feel it is necessary to be *braced* for 1975!

## Monday 6 January 1975

When I arrived in No. 10 shortly before 10, HW was still not there. He did not come in till noon. He had been to the charity concert in Birmingham the previous night, back to Chequers at 1.30 a.m., and sat up till after 4 a.m. talking to Albert and Janet Hewlett-Davies from the press office. Apparently they had a marvellous time and HW received a tremendous reception. Still I'm glad I didn't go. Prefer to have supper with the children and go to bed to read a book.

Went at 11 to the Treasury, with Andrew Graham, to talk to Sir Douglas Wass, who is the permanent secretary. I wanted to ask for more access for us into Treasury thinking so that we could brief the PM better. He was not very helpful. Said it was all being done by a steering committee of Treasury secretaries, reporting to Wass. He could not see what the PM's special interest was. He said that they were sorting out the options and admitted that the Chancellor might *not* wish to mention *all* the options to ministers. Apart from the important committee on Short-Term Policy (STEP), there is another doing contingency planning for disaster – including ration books, etc. And import controls. But not apparently measures to block sterling. Wass conveyed no sense of urgency and said that he felt it was several months before he anticipated a major change of direction on the economic front. He was accompanied by Bryan Hopkin, chief economic adviser, who is a very grey figure, falling asleep throughout.

I told Wass I was not satisfied with what he had said and wanted closer liaison – or else we would have to mobilise the PM and other ministers. He took the point and promised further progress after more thought. I wonder! The sad thing is that the PM would be very reluctant to back us up. He doesn't like interfering with the mandarins.

Before lunch I dropped in to Marcia's room. She was clearly in a bad mood. After a manic period of happiness before Christmas she is now obviously on the depressive down curve and looking around for somebody to attack.

Bill Housden told me that she has been attacking HW savagely. Mainly because he did not telephone her on New Year's Eve – which is his wedding anniversary, the gesture he must make to show he cares for her as much as Mary – and did not visit her on New Year's Day. But he certainly came back on New Year's Day so that he would see her. The Irish meeting was just a cover.

Housden said that she had blamed him, the driver, for the PM not telephoning. She had threatened him with the sack, and had then said, 'Well anyway you won't be able to go on any overseas trips, I'll stop that.' Poor old Bill was all of a tremble and talking of leaving, as usual.

HW came in to join us in her room at about 1.15. They began to discuss the finances of the political office, which are apparently in a bad way. Ron Hayward has refused to pay some of the office expenses. They both attacked him. HW said they would have to save money – by not replying to any more Transport House letters. (He also said that Hayward was trying to organise an NEC attack on him over the EEC.) She said they might have to get rid of some staff – and that 'the trust will have to cough up some more money. Eric Miller will have to pay up.' HW then recalled that '£50,000 was paid in to the party at my direction and half of it was supposed to cover the expenses of this political office.'

I then slipped out quietly and went, very late, to lunch with Denis Howell at the Reform Club. We discussed sport finance, on which I am preparing a memo for the PM in reply to a slightly mad letter from George Wigg. Howell was savage about Tony Crosland, whom he thinks is ineffective, and resents still not being made a Privy Councillor – ten years after becoming a minister.

Returned to No. 10 to talk to Eric Varley about Burmah Oil – but he was delayed at a Cabinet committee and we put it off. But it meant I missed HW's meeting with Michael Foot on the EEC. They agreed:

(1)   no speeches till negotiations are complete;
(2)   then ministers to go their own way, but without personal attacks;
(3)   nothing on the EEC while Jenkins away in USA.

Foot was also apparently perfectly happy with the PM's speech on British Leyland attacking the strikers. Joe told me all this.

I then worked on a memo, with David Piachaud, on the NHS consultants' battle with Barbara Castle. When I later saw HW he said he thought she had mishandled it. Maybe, but the consultants have been terribly greedy.

Slipped over to the Banqueting Hall in Whitehall for a reception to launch an appeal fund for the Shakespeare Memorial Theatre. Littered with old actresses and pretty young boys. Saw Denis Howell again, and also the new Lord Pitt.

Back to the office for final clear-up of papers and then home by 8.45 p.m.

A very full and interesting day. Because the flow of papers was less, and I had time to think and to talk to people.

I saw HW wandering about at 8.30. He complained that there was no work to do. 'I cleared my boxes yesterday and I've nothing to do,' he said. Then he wandered off down the passage.

## Tuesday 7 January 1975

Went in by tube because Carol needed the car. Nice change to walk to the station and read the *Guardian* on the train. Arrived by 9.40. Went through Unit papers.

Claus Moser, the head of the Statistical Office, came at 11 to discuss the machinery for economic policy. I told him our dissatisfactions with Wass yesterday. He agreed it is wrong to keep all the serious talk in an internal Treasury committee and he will talk to Wass. He also offered me two tickets for *Traviata* at Covent Garden on Saturday with Joan Sutherland, but unfortunately we are booked to dinner. He is always kind.

To lunch – alone – with George Weidenfeld. Very pleasant chat, especially the gossip. He tested me out on Marcia but I played it very neutral.

Back to No. 10 at 3 and worked with Richard and Andrew Graham on a memo on nationalised industries. The civil servants have recommended that the Commons select committee report recommending an outside inquiry into the way Whitehall runs the nationalised industries should be rejected – because it means outsiders looking at them. They tried to slip it through without even consideration by ministers. We persuaded the PM before Christmas to have it brought before committee. Now we are drawing up arguments to have the outside inquiry.

I went up to the study to see the PM at about 5.30. He was with Robert Armstrong having a general talk about the hijack of a plane at London airport by some Arab terrorists. PM was very excited and full of plans to trick and capture the hijacker.

I finally managed to brief him on what Harold Lever wanted to see him about this evening:

(1)  He wanted a bigger say in the coming Washington talks.

(2)  He didn't want HW to allow the Treasury to bring in a massive deflationary policy under the excuse of a sterling crisis (which is very likely). The stock market has been firmer on rumours of an incomes policy plus squeeze package. Seems a bit premature, but certainly what the Treasury wants.

I went back to the Unit while Lever was with HW – but telephoned him later. Lever was not happy and has decided not to go to America. Says HW does not understand. Lever does not want to go to be paraded as a symbol of Labour's financial respectability. He wants to negotiate with Kissinger. But Callaghan and the Foreign Office won't have that. And of course none of the civil servants support Lever. I don't know why, but they are all, including Robert, against him. Not personally. But as a pirate.

I worked till 8.30 p.m. and then Carol arrived with our close friend Graham Greene to pick me up and Graham took us out to dinner at the French club. Just for social chat, and to discuss Carol's book on Everest which he is publishing. We did not discuss Crossman at all. The curious thing was that, although I had told nobody I was seeing Graham, and he told nobody, the *Daily Mirror* telephoned him at 6 o'clock to ask him to confirm that he was going to visit No. 10 today. Either it was pure guesswork or somebody had leaked – which could only be the switchboard or somebody who read my diary. It left us all feeling eerie.

Ate well and drank too much. Home at well after midnight and awake much of the night with a stomach upset.

## Wednesday 8 January 1975

Drove in and went to the Ireland committee at 10 a.m. Very subdued. Almost nobody said anything. Bill Rodgers was present and came to my room for a chat and coffee afterwards. He was unhappy with the way Merlyn Rees is handling it. Rees was very emotional and excitable. Bill also thinks his decision to announce the end of special category prisoners could jeopardise the truce.

HW seemed preoccupied in the committee and not very interested. I learned from one of the private secretaries that he sat in 'the control room' last night directing the hijack affair till midnight. It ended successfully and he apparently enjoyed himself enormously – just like a schoolboy.

I went up to the study at about 11.15 and he was there with Robert and Joe.

We discussed lotteries, appointments to nationalised boards, Benn, Ireland and then got on to economic policy. In the middle of this Bill

Housden interrupted us to report that Marcia was ill – her fainting fits again. (These usually occur when HW's foreign trips loom up.)

Discussing economics HW suddenly went quiet, looked at the ceiling and said seriously, 'I wonder if the Chancellor has got an economic strategy.'

Joe said, 'I wonder if Healey is sitting next door saying to himself, "I wonder if the PM knows that I haven't got a strategy."'

We had a long discussion. I stressed that we must not let the Treasury keep it to its chest until too late and then spring some horrible package on us.

HW said, 'I'm afraid that the rats have got at Denis.'

The PM put up several suggestions, which hardly amounted to a strategy. He wanted to ease hire purchase on cars to sell the stock of British Leyland. He wanted the Treasury to start buying shares and buying property to get the markets up. He then sent for Lever again to mollify him.

I went downstairs and was told by private office that HW had given instructions that I should go to Washington with him – and stay on a few days after with Harold Lever. A sudden switch of intention. It appears I am very much in favour now – he also asked me to go to NEDC with him this afternoon.

It all helps.

Went to lunch at the *Financial Times*. Lord Drogheda was there, with Freddie Fisher, the editor, and their columnists Sam Brittan, David Watt and Joe Rogaly. Robert Armstrong came too. It was lively and amusing, and they were a very attractive bunch, frequently squabbling among themselves. I enjoyed it, but talked too much, and a bit wildly about inflation. I was trying to play devil's advocate by pretending that inflation did not matter, but it didn't work and I ended up with them not impressed, thinking I was all for letting inflation rip.

Dashed back and went off straight away to NEDDY at Millbank Tower. Travelled with the PM and he was in splendid form. We went up to the meeting and HW introduced me to the members, some of whom I knew. The director is Ronnie McIntosh, who I used to know through Bill Rodgers in the old Department of Economic Affairs days. He has become a bit pompous, which is a pity, as he is nice.

The meeting was fascinating. Though one sees the weakness of NEDDY as a *forum*: very general, not time for every member to speak, and no time to pursue any one subject for long.

The papers – on investment – were good. The discussion less so. The CBI people – Campbell Adamson, Michael Clapham and Ralph Bateman* – were particularly weak and left private industry making a poor impression.

Finniston, the chairman of British Steel, spoke well on the need to maintain investment in the public sector.

Scanlon attacked the CBI and said that private industry never invested enough, whether profits were high or low. He demanded bilateral talks between the CBI and the TUC so that private industry could make a commitment to invest. Jack Jones of the Transport Workers supported.

Len Murray argued against unemployment as a cure for inflation. He said that the unions, brought up on Keynes, grab higher wages to increase consumer expenditure and create jobs. So it was better to deal with it through investment to create jobs.

Basnett of the General Municipal Workers and Jones also said that unemployment would not lead to lower wage claims.

We went for a drink after, at 5.30. I talked to Shirley Williams. She was very friendly. I urged her to press HW to collectivise the economic policy-making process.

Back at 5.45 for the Cabinet Energy committee on the proposal to deal with the collapse of Burmah Oil. Lever was critical of it – partly because he didn't want to include the 51% holding of Burmah's North Sea stake as part of the package. Mainly, as I knew, because he was angry at not being consulted. Benn said nothing, although the decision to use the Bank of England as the rescuing vehicle rather than the Industry Act was a clear rebuff for him.

Afterwards Eric Varley came to my room. I told him my concern about the Bank of England deal, and that in this case I favoured public ownership to give the new BNOC a power base, owning Burmah and controlling BP. He did not seem to have clear views either way, but said 'the main point was to keep it out of Benn's hands'. He went on to say that he had long believed that Benn was decent and well meaning, if over-enthusiastic, but he now believed he was 'positively malevolent'. He drank some whisky and promised to keep me closely in touch, and that above all they would not allow the Bank to sell the BP shares without consulting us at No. 10.

I also took the opportunity to canvass him on tomorrow's Industrial committee discussion of the nationalised industries. He clearly had not followed it and would speak to the brief of his permanent secretary, Joe Ramptor,* who is very right-wing and one of the main agents behind trying to get the outside inquiry rejected.

After he left we worked on our memo on the nationalised industries and finally put it in at about 8.30 p.m. Then Carol telephoned to say she was feeling ill, so I decided to go home.

In the hall Bill Housden offered me a lift home in the PM's Rover so I accepted. He told me how Marcia had been attacking him every day. This morning she was so awful that he finally plucked up courage and walked out of her bedroom where she was lying sick – and went downstairs saying that he could not put up with any more. After a few minutes the Asian maid came down with a long letter of apology. He said her style of life was fantastic and needed at least £20,000 a year. 'She throws her money around so much in the shops that I sometimes get frightened,' he said. He said she continues to attack me violently. 'It is all jealousy.'

I got home at 9.15 and found Carol very unwell.

## Thursday 9 January 1975

Went in early for the IDV Cabinet committee meeting to discuss the response to the Commons select committee report on nationalised industries – calling for an external inquiry, which officials rejected and we supported. Before the meeting I talked to Benn, who was very sympathetic and said that since I had last talked to him about it he had done some thinking and decided we were right. In the meeting Joel Barnett led off for the Treasury arguing – not very convincingly – against an inquiry. Benn knocked him down very effectively, and was supported, surprisingly, by Crosland. HW then produced his own pet compromise – a very clever one – to use NEDDY as the forum for the inquiry, taking outside views. This was accepted. The civil servants went out muttering that the machine would be furious at having lost this one.

Benn came up to me outside and said, 'That is a great victory for the Policy Unit.' I thanked him for his very effective support.

The Cabinet then met, mainly discussing social service questions and family allowances for one-parent families, which went through.

I saw Don Ryder who came to my room at 12 and stayed an hour. He outlined the terrible problems at British Leyland and we established a good rapport.

Went for lunch to Grieveson Grant in the City, always very useful, since they have several people who really can think about the political problems of the financial situation.

Went to the deputy secretaries meeting in the Cabinet Office. Not much business next week and then a terrible timetable after that. Had a clash about getting oil recycling on the agenda of the Cabinet committee on External Strategy. The Treasury doesn't want to put anything on paper because Healey wants to keep it all to himself, and the civil servants were supporting this. I kept pressing, on the basis that the PM should be thoroughly briefed before Washington, and in the end Hunt came in to support me.

In the evening I was just setting off to the theatre – *Equus* – when the PM sent for me. Joe and Robert were there. PM in excellent, jovial form and offered me a drink. Obviously wanted to chat, before Lord Goodman came in later. I was wearing my coat and said I was taking my wife to the theatre. He replied with a grin, 'What, is it her birthday?' To HW wives only enter life on formal occasions.

Before that, John Hunt had asked me to go to his room, with Robert, at 6. He then raised the Crossman question, knowing that I had mentioned it to the PM after meeting Harry Evans and talking to Graham Greene. He was very jumpy and said the PM couldn't have two lines of communication. I pointed out that it was just one occasion and not a continuing situation – and added that I had told Evans that the PM was not very involved and I would *not* be talking to him again about it. Hunt then got very jumpy and said that the PM was involved and he was reporting to him regularly. I said that anyway it was my job to report to the PM anything that concerned him and I certainly could not completely control what other people raised with me.

*Quite* enjoyed *Equus*. Home to bed at midnight.

## Friday 10 January 1975

Went in to the weekly business meeting at 9.30, but after that the PM had a series of personal meetings – including with the *Daily Mirror* about the strike threat to newspapers and with the CBI.

I worked on papers and went to lunch with a relative.

In the afternoon worked in the Unit on a paper on sugar – since the negotiations are collapsing. Went on till 9.30 at night when I finally put in the memo – basically putting the case for rationing.

Left a very silent and empty No. 10 and home very tired at 10 p.m.

Joe told me that Marcia is now drawing and spending £600 in cash per month. Her salary is £4,000.

Also worried about the honours system.

## Monday 13 January 1975

HW was late in from Chequers so I took my time, going in via the LSE. Spent the morning mainly working on papers. HW didn't arrive till 12.45. We had a brief discussion about the state of the press – with the *Express* apparently on the point of calling in the receiver.

The *Daily Mail* has a front-page story that HW is going to retire this summer to take over an Oxford College. Housden says that this has infuriated Marcia – not because it says he is going, but because it says he is doing it because of Mary's wishes.

Had lunch with Clifford German. An old school friend, he is now on the *Daily Telegraph* and we avoided all sensitive issues. He told me that the *Telegraph* sales are down 100,000.

HW spent the afternoon at the Commons and in audience with the Queen.

I worked on papers. Saw Robert Armstrong, who feels that the economic situation is about to collapse – and says the Governor of the Bank and Wass of the Treasury feel the same and have told Healey that 'the present government measures have failed'. Obviously the machine is seeking for a freeze. I told him that the PM will not have another wages policy.

Went to Maurice Finer's memorial service as the PM's rep – at Stationers Hall. Very moving. Lionel Robbins spoke, and McGregor, Charles Wintour from the *Evening Standard* (about to be closed) and Finer's partner and first pupil, Michael Sherward. The Lord Chancellor, Elwyn Jones, took the 'chair'. Lionel wept openly. I did privately. Such a waste, just as Maurice was approaching his peak. He is the first 'non-family' death which has affected me deeply.

Back to No. 10 to see Frank Price, chairman of British Waterways, who brought a gift from the organisers of the Birmingham Charity Show for HW, and also to convey the low morale of BW, which has long been a Cinderella.

Then a party upstairs for one of the political office secretaries who is leaving. HW made a nice little speech. We privately discussed the *Express*. I want him to let it go bust, and get somebody else to run the *Standard*. It is ironical that he, hating the newspapers, gets so frequently involved in trying to rescue them. Marcia was there, Gerald Kaufman came and it was small and informal and very nice. But I was suffering from a heavy cold and left at 8.15 to go home to whisky and bed.

## Tuesday 14 January 1975

Went in late because the PM had a party liaison meeting – in fact he cancelled it.

Saw Joe who was very angry because private office and the Foreign Office were plotting to get Donald Maitland, Heath's former press officer and friend, on the Washington trip. Maitland had committed himself totally to Heath, and HW replaced him as Ambassador to the UN when we came in. He is also a friend of the private secretaries and they have been trying to help rehabilitate his career by including him on the PM's trip. Joe vetoed this – so they persuaded Callaghan to bring him in *his* party. Callaghan came to see HW about it this morning. We were both worried that HW would give in. But in fact he stood fairly firm and said he would not have Maitland in on any function he was at though Callaghan could take him on his own to places. Later I heard the private secretaries discussing it. One said, 'It looks as if he's had it.' The other said, 'You will know if he is coming, because there will be some sharp feedback from Joe.'

Cabinet dealt with cancelling the Channel Tunnel, apparently without trouble; don't expect the French will be happy. [The cancellation was announced to Parliament on 20 January.] I saw the PM after Cabinet and discussed the newspaper strike.

Also saw Marcia, who was very concerned that she had been excluded from next week's dinner with David Frost (I put this right) and delighted because Ron Hayward has been attacked in the press for owning two properties.

Lunch with Joe at House of Commons discussing our submission of evidence to the Royal Commission on the Press. Recalling the events of the February election and the April land deals – now seeming so very far away.

At briefing before PQs HW was in excellent form. Said he is still nervous, especially at beginning of any new session. 'I hate it,' he said, 'I hate it more the more I do it.'

We also discussed Benn's letter about the complaint by his accounting officer (permanent secretary) that some of his expenditure was indefensible. Benn claims he wasn't properly warned and that the civil servants only oppose Labour expenditure. Not really convincing – but enough of a case to make it difficult for HW to hang him on this.

HW had an easy time in Questions. The Tories are in such a bad way that they cannot unite to attack us.

I came back afterwards with Robert, and worked on papers, including a draft which Sam Brittan had sent me.

Was feeling a bit off all day, with a heavy cold and sore throat. Went home early – at 7 p.m. – because we were having Jack Ashley and Alf Morris and wives to dinner. They were delightful. Jack is remarkable, full of life and humour and mixing in with everything despite his total deafness. The relationship between him and Alf Morris is wonderful to watch – the latter full of affection and concern, and constantly bantering and joking at one another's expense. Morris is absolutely genuine and devoted to his life passion of helping the disabled. Most MPs are partly cynical, partly phoney, often interested only in self-publicity without any deep principles at all, just loving being MPs and making the necessary noises. Alf is totally genuine.

Broke up well after midnight.

## Wednesday 15 January 1975

Went first to see Sigmund Sternberg at Star House. To discuss scrap metal policy for the public sector – and the need for a general inquiry into commodities. While there, my secretary Brenda phoned to say that the PM wanted to see me. So I drove in fast from Kentish Town. Met HW near the tapes in No. 10. He was just off to a meeting to launch Women's Year. He said he had explained to Joe what he wanted.

I went to see Joe who said it was about the press. The *Guardian* and *Telegraph* were in a bad way, and the *Express* nearly closed last Saturday. He wants the Unit to examine ways of subsidising the papers – or at least making sure that the *Guardian* and *Telegraph* don't go. So we started on that this morning.

For lunch I went to Save and Prosper Unit Trust, where we had a good and serious discussion on how to help industry with its financial problems. When I emerged I had some clear ideas in my head. The problem is how to follow them up and get something done. Moving that machine! There is no obvious point of input on these industrial/financial questions. This is why Harold Lever is the only hope – and he has great difficulty. The Treasury offers little hope.

Came back at 2.45 and went straight back on to the press question (HW was still at the Commons). The Unit is now functioning very well. Much more co-ordinated and all contributing well as a team. By 5 p.m. we had a draft paper sketched setting out the options.

At 6 I went out and was picked up by Lord Kissin and taken to the house of Philip Kaiser, where I met Ronald Spiers, the new counsellor at the American Embassy, who is close to Ambassador Elliot Richardson. We discussed the coming Washington visit. I praised Lever as somebody to be taken seriously and stressed the subjects in which the PM was interested. Kaiser said he would see me in Washington, and I arranged to see Spiers again after I returned.

Went back to No. 10 and we finished off our draft on the press. Talked to private office about where I would stay in Washington. I *ought* to insist on staying in Blair House, to demonstrate status. But it is small and will be crowded. I want some privacy and so will probably settle for a hotel.

Home at 9.30.

Two quotes from yesterday. The PM said:

'I hate reading speeches.'

'Benn cannot be on a winning ticket every time. There are too many tickets.'

HW went to the International Women's Year meeting today. He told Joe not to send Janet Hewlett-Davies as press officer because Marcia was jealous of her.


*Thursday 16 January 1975*

Went in early for the Cabinet committee (IDV) on the Industry Bill (information powers) – now finally through – and the nationalisation of shipbuilding. HW was not in there at first. He was upstairs with Michael Foot discussing the crisis in the newspaper industry.

After the meeting I discussed newspapers with Shirley Williams – and the possibilities of taking newspapers out of the price code. Like everyone else she wishes it was the appalling *Daily Mail* which was going bust.

During Cabinet I worked in the Unit, including a meeting on our paper on helping the newspapers.

Lunch at the Commons with Joe where we discussed and prepared the PM's evidence to the Royal Commission on the Press. Joe said that his source for the *Daily Mail* episode was Lord Goodman.

Before lunch we had both gone up to the study and had a long chat with the PM. About newspapers. And his next private secretary – we favour the internal promotion of Robin Butler, now the private secretary covering Treasury policies, but the Civil Service is against, he is 'too young', and they prefer a 47-year-old deputy secretary from the Cabinet Office.

The PM was in excellent form. We were in the middle of discussing a package of aid to newspapers at 1.30 when Marcia stormed in, shouted to him, 'You are supposed to be downstairs' and stormed out again. HW quickly left, beckoning us to follow, and we went up to the political office for a farewell party for one of the typists. She was obviously in a bad mood and attacked HW for being 'against Tony Benn. He is awful to him.'

As we left at 1.45 Joe said goodbye loudly and added that now we had to eat out we had to get to the restaurant before it closed. Actually I am not wholly sorry about closing the No. 10 dining-room. I get out more, more exercise, less claustrophobia. But it does mean that we get less work done at lunchtimes, and the internal information network – especially between us and private office – is less efficient.

During briefing for PQs at the Commons Marcia telephoned and HW left the room. When he returned he was virtually running, looking black, and he slammed the door after him. But he soon settled down and seemed still in good form. She is after him, but hasn't got him down yet.

I returned and went to the Deputy Secretaries meeting in the Cabinet Office. Then Norman Chester*, the warden of Nuffield College, Oxford, came in, and we talked about a football levy.

In the evening the Unit agreed a line on our paper on newspaper finance, and I sat down and wrote it, finishing at 9 p.m. We recommend (1) that newspapers are out of the price code; (2) a newsprint subsidy; (3) a big operation to end over-manning, similar to that done to end casual labour in the docks. Gavyn Davies did an excellent job on some tables for the appendix.

I was very tired going home. My friend Alfred Garfield came in to supper, but I could barely converse. Also have an ominous feeling things will start going wrong again. Either an explosion by Marcia, or an attack on me by the press. Why do I bother to help them?

## Friday 17 January 1975

All day at Chequers to discuss devolution on the DS Cabinet committee. The big black Rover came to collect me at 8.30 a.m. and then on to pick up Robert Armstrong. We reached Chequers by 10. Streams of other ministers arriving and we all gathered to have coffee in the main reception room, before a blazing log fire.

A group of ministers – Crosland, Elwyn Jones, Prentice – were discussing devolution and saying that Ted Short has been going too fast and too far without thinking much about it. They are out to slow it down. Tony Crosland took me on one side and said he wanted to speak early, on the English provincial backlash against Scotland, and I conveyed this to John Hunt.

Also had a long chat with Merlyn Rees, who seems much more relaxed, despite the IRA ending the ceasefire. He said the IRA is completely divided, and the Catholic community in the north is angry with them for ending it. He seems fairly confident that we shall remain on top – though I have noted how his moods swing from elation to depression and back again very fast.

We all filed into the large conference room shortly after 10.30. The ministers sat around the long table. I sat with Joe and a few other civil servants at the side. It was turning into a lovely day, cold, but very sunny. Chequers, although a dreary house inside, is in a marvellous location. It was very restful, having most of the government here, with no telephones, other meetings, etc.

HW opened by telling them he wanted a Second Reading debate on devolution in the morning. General views and no decisions.

He straight away brought Crosland in, who spoke ably and strongly for slowing down the process.

Prentice and Varley followed in similar terms. All felt we were on slippery slope towards the break-up of the UK.

John Morris, the Welsh Secretary, then intervened to say that we had promised devolution to Wales and would have to deliver it.

Edmund Dell argued that to have Scottish elections in 1976 or 77 would be disastrous for Labour, and would mean having a Scottish Assembly which was anti-Labour – because of the unpopularity of the economic prospects. Then Elwyn Jones spoke strongly for slowing down 'the most important decision of our lives'.

Barbara Castle said that we must devolve to stave off separatism, and if Willie Ross said there was no alternative we would have to do it.

Ross then came in as Scottish Secretary to say there was no alternative. We were committed. HW then spoke, saying he was not now summing up, but wished to agree with B. Castle that the only way to avoid separatism was devolution. He then went on to stress electoral factors – we must not force the Scot Nats in the Commons to vote against us, or to gain strength and win Labour seats in Scotland at the next election. He denied they were taking any firm decision and was worried about the English back-lash, but concluded, 'We must get devolution rolling forward.'

Rees followed, against speedy action now, because it would disturb his Northern Ireland situation.

Short intervened to say that he wanted the Bill ready in 1975, but no Scottish election for years – which seemed curious to some. His argument was that we must get a Bill through while we still had a Commons majority – which he thought would not be for very long.

Jenkins spoke long and impressively. He said frankly he was a 'go-slower' because he 'didn't like the look of the destination'. He was 'afraid of the slippery slope to separatism'. He saw no reason to rush things and exposed some inconsistencies in Short's arguments.

Benn came in, and was very weak at first, arguing that the workers were against devolution because it would break up the UK trade union move-ment. He then improved, pointing out that it was wrong to take this deci-sion before we had taken the decision on the EEC. He concluded by supporting Jenkins on slowing down.

Peart also took this view.

Gerry Fowler, Lord Shepherd* and Sam Silkin were not called at this stage.

This general discussion took an hour and a half and was of a very high standard. Also the speakers were 2:1 against rapid devolution and against Ted Short, who was looking very irritable.

They then turned to discuss the first detailed item – which was whether to give the Scots a Cabinet system, like Whitehall, or a committee system, like the GLC. Short strongly preferred the former. Many speakers opposed both. Jenkins, Crosland, the Lord Advocate (King Murray, who is impres-sive on first observation) and Elwyn Jones spoke for examining a compro-mise approach, a hybrid of local and national government, along lines suggested by Crowther-Hunt. This was a confused discussion with the ministers responsible for devolution, Short, Crowther-Hunt and Gerry Fowler, all disagreeing with one another.

HW summed up broadly along the lines advocated by Short. I thought this was a mistake, and so did Joe, because he ran the risk of annoying the majority of the committee.

We went downstairs and had a good buffet lunch, served by three not very attractive girls (Joe said they were clearly hand-picked by Marcia). I talked to Tony Benn, Dell and Gerry Fowler – who thinks we are now too far committed to extreme devolution to withdraw, and if we try to slow down it will provoke separatism.

Joe and I went for a stroll around the house after eating. He told me that he was going secretly to see an IRA contact that evening, because they wanted to reopen negotiations. He had told them before agreeing that if there was any violence he would not come (there had been none so far today). Albert is to be the regular contact man.

Apparently Marcia has been creating a terrible fuss over Ireland. She says that HW is responsible for the end of the truce because he had refused to use her brother Tony as the intermediary. (The IRA had mentioned him because they thought he was still close to HW.) She also thought that in any renewal of violence she would be their first target. According to Joe and Bill Housden, she telephoned HW at Chequers last night, while Joe was there, and began attacking HW, and demanding that we immediately concede all the IRA demands. HW lost his temper, told her to 'stop screaming at me down the telephone' and to 'keep out of things which you don't understand'. He said to Joe that he was about fed up with her. Joe said he thought she had been a bit better recently. 'Not with me she hasn't,' said HW.

We went back in, and after a quick coffee the meeting resumed on various points of detail and technicality. The afternoon's proceedings were much more desultory. HW was tired. Crosland went to sleep. They all rambled. Ted Short was not at his best. He is obviously badly briefed. He had with him a very thin brief from Vicky Kidd, who sat just behind him.

Towards the end a crisis arose. Short said that the committee had approved his papers in principle. Jenkins intervened to oppose this, and said he must reserve his position. He was supported by Crosland, Prentice and Benn. HW tried to support Short and railroad it through, but Jenkins continued to resist and it was clear that the committee was against Short, in general, on the speed of proceeding, and on the Cabinet system. HW then did a clever retreat and it was agreed that Short would bring more papers to the committee, that Crowther-Hunt would put in a separate paper, and then they would see.

I talked to Tony Benn afterwards, and he said that Short would never get it through Cabinet committee. 'We were just putting down markers today,' he said.

Also had a long chat with Jenkins. He is going to continue to oppose Short. He said he was much more optimistic about the EEC – though not about the economy. He seemed in much better shape now he has had a couple of weeks away in America.

I then went downstairs and sat down by the fire with Elwyn Jones, chatting over a drink.

HW went first in to a small meeting over Ireland. (The IRA are still divided. The Army apparently captured Seamus Twomey yesterday but decided not to imprison him.)

Then HW had a long talk with Roy Jenkins. Afterwards he told me that they had mainly discussed the EEC and the economy. On the Market they had agreed how to handle it, with Roy agreeing to ministers going their own way. (The PM is going to make a speech on this very soon.) On the economy, Roy had expressed his worries, especially about public expenditure and the borrowing requirement. They had a long and clearly very friendly talk.

HW came down at about 6 p.m. and had a drink. We chatted about various matters – including the press strike, the new chairman of the Royal Commission (Jim Gower or Alan Bullock?), and general gossip. He was in excellent form and obviously didn't want us to go back to London at about 7.15. I had to leave, because Carol was away and I had to get back to put the children to bed. Robert was pleased to have an excuse for getting back.

I also talked to Robert, there and on the way back in the car. He is leaving No. 10 for the Home Office after Easter. Replaced by Ken Stowe from the Cabinet Office. I told him that he must tell Stowe to play the game with Joe and me and that he would lose if he started any nonsense.

Robert told me that there is more Poulson scandal stuff to come.

Home at 8.30. Very tired but pleased with a very good week. Later Joe told me he had a 1½ hour talk with John O'Connell, who had spent the whole previous night talking to his namesake, David, of the IRA, and that they were willing to extend the ceasefire if some political progress could be made.

## Monday 20 January 1975

Went in early, in the office at 9 a.m., at HW's request to look at his speech on the EEC referendum. A good draft from him, setting out the alternatives open to the government in how to handle it.

Then saw Denis Lyons 10–10.30 about government advertising – where HW thinks there is a racket which should be stopped. No racket, but some changes needed.

Curiously HW was recommending setting up a Civil Service advertising agency. Despite all the evidence that the Civil Service does most commercial things very badly. Because he is instinctively a centraliser. And because he dislikes all private business and profit.

Later worked on papers. There was an incredible pile of documents, several feet high.

Saw HW about the guest list for the visit of the New Zealanders to No.10. Agreed a number of changes. Marcia wants David Frost, etc. I agree and also put in the cricketer Brian Close and the footballer Derek Dougan. I have persuaded private office that it is sensible to give way on these trivial social matters, about which Marcia cares so much, and then hopefully we won't be bothered on serious questions of policy.

Incidentally Marcia is now pushing HW to arrange a job for her brother Tony in the Department of Energy – where Eric Varley will be responsive to her wishes. Tony is presumably broke after the failure of his land deals.

Lunch with Harold Lever at Eaton Square. Discussed the arrangements for our visit to America.

Back to No. 10 and two solid hours of papers.

Joe said HW was expressing great irritation with private office. In revenge he might add Andrew Graham from my Unit to our Washington list.

In the evening I spent hours drafting a long memo on sports finance in answer to a letter from George Wigg.

Home at 9.30.

## Tuesday 21 January 1975

Because of telephone calls I did not see HW – or any other Cabinet people – before this morning's Cabinet, which was devoted entirely to EEC questions: the referendum, 'agreement to differ' between ministers, no personal attacks, etc. But afterwards HW was in great form, delighted by the good humour of Cabinet and the way they had all seemed happy with the compromises agreed. Because each side is confident that it will win. Each side mixes with people of its own opinions.

I worked on papers and on three briefs – on COI advertising, on HW's idea for releasing HP controls to help the car industry, which I oppose, and on raising new finance for sport.

Saw Marcia who is clearly still very jumpy.

Went to lunch at the House of Commons with Joe. He told me that HW had been 'pushing him too much'. The PM was very pleased with the Unit's paper on help for the newspaper industry – but resisted my proposal for a major scheme to end overmanning because Heath had once proposed something like it.

After lunch I went straight to HW's Commons room for PQ briefing. HW in superb form, joking and confident he could handle anything. He went over this morning's Cabinet again, saying how good it was. Then he suddenly said he didn't know how he could get out of attending Labour's Special Conference on the EEC – which he intends to treat as purely advisory. He said he had no idea what he could say to them, and perhaps they should arrange to call it at the same time as the Commonwealth Conference.

Going in to Questions I saw Gerry Fowler, who was very violent in attacking last Friday's Chequers meeting. He said they were all stupid and not interested in the arguments. Then he concluded that we had promised devolution so we must give it – or he would resign.

I went into the box in the Chamber, and Gerry came in and continued talking to me from the gangway throughout the PM's questions – which seemed to go OK, although wages are coming up more and more.

Went back to No. 10, and talked to Jacques Pomonti, who phoned from Paris about some advice he is giving to Mitterrand. Then back to papers and memoranda in the Unit.

At 7.30 Frank Judd phoned and asked to talk to me about Defence. HW had suggested this. So I went over to the Commons and drank with him for two hours in the Harcourt Room – Bill Rodgers was there eating with Roy Jenkins and Lever with Jim Callaghan. Judd is very nice, I like him a lot. He is worried about South Africa and Chile. But above all about Defence expenditure, where he thinks we are not radical enough. I agree and we decided to try to do something about this year's Defence review – asking what Defence needs Britain has in 1975, and starting from there.

Home at 10.15 p.m.

## Wednesday 22 January 1975

Didn't see the PM this morning because I thought he was going to the NEC, where they were discussing the referendum on the EEC. In fact he decided at the last minute *not* to go, but nobody told me.

At 11 there was the Cabinet Energy committee, but only discussing nuclear reactors so I decided not to go. Worked in the Unit. Massive flow of papers especially on the EEC referendum. We are preparing briefs on various subjects for next week's visit to the USA.

Went with HW and Joe for lunch at the Charing Cross Hotel with the *Guardian* – Alastair Hetherington, John Cole and a management man who was very pleasant. We had decided not to discuss Ireland, on which Cole is obsessive, or 'editorial freedom', on which Hetherington is obsessive. Talked about Europe, Heath and the Tory leadership, and especially newspaper finances – on which HW told them that I was doing the main work. He was very relaxed and I think he made a good impression – better than the last time we lunched here.

One thing he said was that had he been beaten in February or October last year 'I would have resigned the following afternoon.'

We returned to No. 10 at 3.30 p.m. He was very interested in the stock market situation and is keen to see it as high as possible. He goes to the tapes every hour and rubs his hands as the index goes up and up.

He also attacked private office again, saying Robert was pushing him too far, and that he had had enough of the efforts to push Donald Maitland back into the limelight.

The PM went to the House of Commons and I went over later to the Cabinet committee on industrial policy (IDV). This started at 5.30 and went on until 8.15. Not because of any major difficulties but because every item was tricky.

I was interested to note the different atmosphere in a Cabinet committee held in the PM's room at the Commons compared to the Cabinet Room in No. 10. Much less formal – a smaller table, people chatting and joking, less deference to the PM as chairman, with officials mixed up sitting close to the ministers. I sat next to Shirley Williams who arrived last as usual, looking very nice with her hair unusually well styled, and sat through the first half of the meeting reading *The Economist* and occasionally leaning over to make a funny observation on the whole proceedings.

The first item was on money for the Scottish Development Agency. Here Willie Ross was asking for better terms for Scotland than for England – to which Crosland strongly objected. But Ross simply wouldn't give way. He kept fighting for nearly an hour and finally they gave in. HW then asked him at least to smile in return, but Ross dourly refused. He is obstinate, craggy, and totally uninterested in anything except Scotland's interests. But I like him. Very much his own man. Nothing phoney about him, or packaged for the media. Straight out of the 19th-century manse.

Then they dealt with Tony Benn's request for more money for the National Enterprise Board. Ryder was present to support this – and to give warning that British Leyland would need much more than £500 million for itself. Dell argued against for the Treasury and others made criticisms. But mainly, I felt, because it was Benn. His case was strong. The NEB is meant to be a serious investment instrument. It cannot be that if it is only given twice as much money as the little Scottish Development Agency. In the end they agreed to raise the amount from £700 million to £1,000 million. (I saw Benn later and he was quite satisfied, pointing out that he still had £400 million under the Finance For Industry. 'Then I'll have £2.5 billion,' he said, chuckling and rubbing his hands like a gambler who was on a winning streak.)

Dell was also reasonably happy, believing he had forced British Leyland money to come out of the FFI's £1,000 million, and so had really limited it. But Benn told me that he could get round this.

The final item was the proposed new Scottish *Daily Express*. This is a terrible ramp. The government is putting up £1.3 million to buy this plant from Beaverbrook Newspapers – who are putting back £0.5 million, but pocketing the other £0.8 million (nobody else would buy the building at that price – or any other probably). Robert Maxwell has promised £100,000 – but we know he won't deliver. We have insisted that the Scottish public shows it *wants* the paper by buying £0.175 million worth of shares. They promised this. Now they say they probably won't buy them. So the only backers apart from the government are Beaverbrook (who is broke) and Maxwell (who is a mystery).

Because of this Peter Shore split off from Benn and opposed the project. Benn insisted we proceed because the workers were so enthusiastic. But HW pressed him three times on how much money his beloved trade unions were putting in, and in the end Benn sheepishly admitted they had not put up anything yet. HW then said, 'It sounds as if you'd better have a flag day.' However, they could not stop the issue of the prospectus for the shares because it was legal – and we would be blamed for stopping it. We had to let it go and then see if the issue failed. If it did, and Beaverbrook picked up the underwriting shares, we would have a problem!

We dashed back to No. 10 for dinner with David Frost and his girl-friend, Caroline. HW and I were late and the others were already upstairs when we returned – except Marcia, who as always arrived very late. Supper actually went very well. Frost is a nice and admirably approachable and ordinary person. No great genius. But none of the horrible excesses which usually go with stage people. His girl was attractive, positive, and wore a transparent blouse with *no* bra. This shocked Marcia. Joe sat next to her at dinner all evening, but HW turned his back on her – Joe said he was afraid Marcia would catch him talking to her. My wife Carol sat next to Mary and tried to make conversation. Not easy. She said afterwards she was amazed how totally *middle class* Mary is.

I mainly talked to Marcia, who was in lively form. It is always better to have her present at these dinners. Without her, HW expects everybody to listen to him, and he does go on at great length, with endless anecdotes. But Marcia refuses to be silenced and starts up alternative conversations around the table, which makes the evening much livelier.

HW talked to Frost for nearly three hours. Every so often Frost would shout 'fantastic' or 'super' or roar with laughter. But I don't think he ever managed to get in a whole sentence of his own.

We adjourned to the white lounge. People were very relaxed and it all went well. (HW said to me that it was the first 'non-business' dinner he had had in ages and he really enjoyed not having to think about an agenda or watch his words.)

Tommy Balogh dropped in for coffee – in case Marcia wanted a lift home – and Carol talked to him. He told her he missed not being in No.10 at the centre of things. But that I was better suited to the job because I was 'cooler' than him.

Drove home at 12.30 a.m. HW was very reluctant to bring it to an end and we all slipped off very much against his will. He had clearly drunk quite a lot, but without getting surly, which is a good sign.

He still had five boxes to read, and private office tell me that he worked till 2 a.m. and read all his papers for Cabinet.

## Thursday 23 January 1975

Dashed in early – feeling a little bleary – to get there in time for the Cabinet committee on Ireland at 9.30. The PM was around looking sprightly despite working till 2 a.m. and the meeting started seconds early, before everybody was there.

Merlyn Rees made a long and rather rambling statement, very vivid in language, conveying sharp and memorable pictures of the situation in Ulster, but somehow sounding like he is part of the problem, not above it. He is clearly a Celt – his mother was Irish, his father Welsh – and his lovely wife is Irish. There is not much shape to his argument, just vivid colours to the impression he wants to give. A very nice man, who cares deeply about the Irish problem, but perhaps not a political heavyweight.

Afterwards the Cabinet discussed HW's statement on the EEC referendum to Parliament this afternoon. No problems apparently.

I went off to work on papers in the Unit.

Dropped in on Marcia just before lunch. She was in good form, very chirpy about last night's dinner, clearly relieved that the Frost girl is not as beautiful as she feared, after all. Also discussed her plans to have a series of City dinners – she said she wants the PM to meet right-wingers in the City to demonstrate that he is really human.

I went off to see Robert Armstrong about it. He said the PM had told him and he has 'asked the Governor of the Bank for some names'. That is the problem here. We really want the kind of people that the Governor would *not* want to come.

The PM came in briefly, and then went to the House, Joe and I travelling in the car with him. I raised with him the question of Robin Butler – who we had wanted to succeed Robert Armstrong as principal private secretary, but the machine vetoed. Robert has now told me that Butler is going to be moved quickly even before his three-year term is due to end in July. The PM said that the Civil Service had tried to bounce this through him before Cabinet by sending him a paper in a hurry agreeing to Robin's successor. The PM said he spotted they were pulling a fast one, so he said no, and wanted to think about it. He told us he really wanted to know what Robin thought and wanted, and he asked me to find out.

Joe and I then had lunch together in the Press Gallery restaurant. Afterwards we went down to the PM's room for briefing for Questions and I told Robin Butler I wanted a private word with him.

The PM was in fine form before Questions and there was nothing down to worry about.

Before Questions I went with Butler into the lavatory and told him that Robert Armstrong had told the PM this morning that he was to be moved within a few weeks, and the PM wanted to know what he wanted. Robin was stunned. He said that Robert had sent for him *yesterday* and told him that the PM had asked for Butler to be moved because he wanted somebody with more of an economic training. Robin had believed this and had been deeply saddened that the PM wanted him to go. I assured him that the PM had not asked for this – and had known nothing about it till this morning. Butler was shattered and said he felt betrayed by the Whitehall machine, and simply could not understand why they should lie to him.

Questions raised few problems – except the repeated complaints that the PM did not answer enough questions. His statement on the EEC referendum also went reasonably well, despite some Tory sarcasm about the decision to allow the Cabinet ministers to go their own way. HW admitted this was a unique constitutional step, abandoning collective responsibility.

HW came back to No.10 for a Cabinet committee on external economic policy – mainly dealing with petro-dollars, oil for oil deals, and indexing oil prices, and in preparation for HW's Washington visit. The Treasury had tried to avoid having this because they don't want the PM to get a grip on these questions – they want to keep them to the Chancellor – but I and Lever had forced them.

Before the meeting I told HW what Butler had told me. He was astonished, said he had expressed no views on Robin going and certainly had not asked for an economist because he had Andrew Graham and the Policy Unit. We had gone into the corner of the Cabinet Room while all the ministers were kept waiting outside. HW swore about Robert. These are curious Whitehall games.

I then went back and worked in the Unit. The PM went out to dinner with Lord Aldington* and Michael Swann to discuss the BBC's finances in the evening – Swann apparently is always very concerned about his own salary.

Was able to get home by 8.15 p.m. – the earliest in a long time.

## Friday 24 January 1975

In at 9.30 for the weekly business meeting. Callaghan, Healey, Short and Mellish there. Not much business to discuss for the PM, as he goes abroad on Tuesday. So they had a general chat.

On the EEC Short expressed concern over some details. Said they must decide whether to have the Commons debate before or after the referendum. HW said definitely before. Also on whether to count the votes by constituencies or centrally. They have not yet decided. Short said he thought all kinds of things could go wrong. HW just grinned impishly and said it would be exciting and they could only deal with the problems as they came up. He wasn't going to get depressed in advance.

Mellish said it all proved how crazy it was to commit themselves to a referendum. HW and Callaghan both turned on him and said nonsense – without the referendum formula 'we could never have won two elections'.

They turned to devolution. Callaghan (who was not at last Friday's Chequers devolution meeting) said he wanted Short to know that he thought they were going much too far too fast. Healey agreed. Short pointed out that much earlier on Callaghan had supported devolution. 'Ah,' said Jim, 'that was before we won the election.'

Afterwards the PM set off for Canterbury for the enthronement of the new Archbishop.

Before he left Joe suggested to him that we should give a police escort to Margaret Thatcher – to help her subtly in the leadership contest with Heath. Because Joe said we wanted Heath beaten. 'He is still the most dangerous.' HW agreed at first, and then wavered – he said he feared Thatcher as well, especially as a woman.

I then went back to the Unit and worked solidly for the next 12 hours on preparing briefs for the PM – we have to get our Washington briefs in by the weekend.

On Saturday Joe told me that the Irish contact has been in touch again, O'Connell.

On Sunday the *Sunday Times* published the Crossman Diaries, with no prior publicity. Joe has strongly urged the PM not to bring in the Attorney. But we have to see what Hunt does.

## Monday 27 January 1975

In early, keen to see the PM's reactions to our memoranda – very good. Strongly in favour of my minutes on sports finance. I will go and see Wigg and then see if we can get a proper new Sports Levy Board. Also approved of our economic briefs for Washington.

Went with Joe to private office to talk to Robert Armstrong about the *Sunday Times* publishing the Crossman Diaries. Robert said that 'the lawyers are breathing fire and brimstone', and I got the strong impression that he shared this view, wanting to punish the *Sunday Times*. Joe and I set out the case for doing nothing – because we couldn't stop publication anyway, since there were so many copies around. Robert listened carefully. Then John Hunt came in – obviously on the same subject. We put our case and he was obviously very angry. I said that stopping publication could be very damaging to the PM. He said, 'That's all very well, but what about me?' He spoke again about how the PM was responsible as well – he clearly feels he has been left carrying the baby, which is true, but he has been the one who cared most throughout. He said that the Attorney might act anyway, because law officers are quite independent of politics. I said I needed convincing of that, in view of the past history of many law officers intervening – or not intervening – in line with their political interests. Hunt's strong face is curiously colourless, and his mouth flickers in a quick smile. His eye are fierce. He could run a machine very efficiently on behalf of any ideology. I prefer Robert, whom I always like even when conflicting.

I retreated to the Unit and went through papers, dictated some letters. Also talked to the Unit about their work while I'm away in the USA. The PM came in just after 12 having been to have his portrait painted by Cowan Dobson in Edwardes Square.

We all stood and chatted round the tapes, still astonished that the stock market went onwards and upwards.

Then the PM went into Marcia's room. Joe warned me not to follow. Apparently she is very touchy. Housden said that there was a lot of flak on Saturday evening. This morning Joe dropped in and she had just received notice that her writ for libel against the *Evening Standard* was about to come to court. (Her legal fees are already £15,000.) Joe warned her of the dangers of going to court since they might upset her in the dock. She denied this was possible. He said what if they asked about the children? She went through the roof – proving his point. She said she would bring us all down. She would destroy Harold Wilson, who she said was up to his neck in the land deals. She would drag down Joe and Albert and me with him. All the usual old stuff. She said she would earn her living writing books about us. Joe said he would earn his living reviewing them.

I dropped in to her room after HW had left at 1.15 to go to lunch with Barclays Bank. She was still very edgy but I just laughed. She said she would subpoena me as a witness. I said no need, since I would arrange to be on the jury. Poor Albert sat there trying to sweeten her. It is not the way. The only way is to stand up and say, 'Get stuffed.'

I went to the LSE for lunch, and dropped in on a few friends.

Back after lunch and then went with Andrew Graham to sit in on the pre-Washington briefing session with Healey, Callaghan and Lever. Healey was being very hawkish with the Americans, saying we must stick with a European anti-American line. But he was dovish on the Arabs – we must not unite in Europe to upset the Arabs. On the Middle East both he and Callaghan argued strongly that we must not join in any contingency planning for the Middle East in case we get involved on the American side. 'We don't want to know,' said Callaghan. This may have been shrewd, but seemed terribly cowardly and a real sign of a power in decline. Healey reported that the Americans are in terrible confusion, with all their top people fighting one another. He said Kissinger told him that it took him two hours to get through to President Ford what Nixon grasped in ten minutes. We broke up at about 5.30 and Robert and Hunt stayed behind, obviously to discuss Crossman.

I gave them 10 minutes and then went up to the PM's study. I told HW that Joe and I wanted a word with him. He chatted happily and gave me a drink while he waited for a phone call from Prime Minister Manley in Jamaica.

I went downstairs while HW saw the Romanian foreign minister. I saw a Finnish MP friend, Per Stenbach, for half an hour, and then went up to see HW again. Joe and Janet came up as well. Joe and I stressed that he must not get involved in a legal battle with the *Sunday Times*, which could only damage him, win or lose, and divert him from more important things. He said that Hunt had been much more dovish in their talk this afternoon – certainly because he is afraid of being isolated and has decided to compromise, not wishing to fight exposed battles with nobody else's head above the parapet.

Robert Armstrong came in, with some tiny excuse for interrupting. HW immediately told him that he had been thinking about it, and had decided 'we must do nothing'. So that is that. Providing they don't pull any fast one, it looks as if we have won this one. But I don't count any chickens.

We sat and chatted till 8.30. The PM is still in excellent form, drinking only beer, clearly on top of his work, enjoying life and for the moment not worried by Marcia.

Incidentally she also said to Joe that HW had only 'a few months to go before he retired'.

Home 9.15 and packed for the US. My first visit in 16 years – and I am using the same suitcases! Very battered, but nostalgic.

## Tuesday 28 January 1975

Took Carol and our daughter Katie to the hospital on the way in, for a check-up on Katie. Then drove on to No. 10, in pouring rain, with my cases for Canada. Got in at 10.10 a.m.

The PM should have been at the OPD (Defence) Cabinet committee. But he was alone in his study and had left a message for me to come up. I went and he started talking about Robin Butler. Said that the Civil Service had tried to have him moved and replaced by a Treasury man. HW had resisted. But he then said it was made more difficult because Marcia was attacking Butler and saying he lunched with *Private Eye*. I pointed out that Butler knew the appalling editor of *Private Eye*, Richard Ingrams, and had lunched with him once several years ago, but had deliberately not seen him since. HW seemed relieved. He asked me to tell Marcia this. He then said she was 'going through the roof about everything. It is always the same before I have a trip abroad.'

I suggested that she was obviously worried by the *Evening Standard* libel case coming to court. He said she was mainly worried about the fees – £15,000 so far. I suggested that it might be best not to go to court. 'She cannot pull back now,' he said.

Otherwise he was in excellent form. He said he would go in to see Marcia after Cabinet, and then asked me to go to see her after that and 'tell her about any Civil Service plots you have discovered. That would please her.' He then went down to Cabinet.

I had a brief chat with Roy Jenkins about television licences. He wants to raise them to £8.50 for monochrome, £17 for colour. The Unit wants to put the colour up to £18 and leave the black and white unchanged, as it is mainly the poorer sections of the country who have black and white.

During Cabinet I prepared for departure with the Unit, allotting work for the next few days.

Cabinet broke just after midday. HW went in to see Marcia. I went to see Joe. HW came out half an hour later and went upstairs. Albert, who was present, told me it had been very heavy in there. So I went in and discussed various business matters with her. She was obviously very jumpy and started attacking me. So I went out and back to my room. I went to the Commons for lunch with Joe and as we left HW was in there again and I could hear Marcia screaming at him. Later Albert told me that HW was there till 2 and they had a terrible row, with her attacking him violently throughout.

I then left for the airport with Joe and his able assistant Jean Denham. When we went on board the VC10 Joe was furious because we had been allocated seats right down the back of the plane among the garden room secretaries. HW, Callaghan and Lever were up at the front of the plane in spacious compartments, together with the civil servants. They are playing their games again.

The journey took eight hours, against strong winds. Very quiet and smooth plane, but cramped for working, reading our briefs and eating. Joe and I discussed the PM's Friday speech and Joe went off to type a draft.

Just before dinner we went up to HW's compartment and discussed it with him. He was in good form – though earlier Joe Stone told me that HW had sent for him privately and 'told me something very confidential. He had to get it off his chest.' He implied it concerned Marcia and added, 'Don't worry, he knows where his real loyalties lie.'

Mary was looking very pale and lying down in a bunk. The Levers told me that she had snubbed them very rudely.

The flight was beautiful because it was sunset for four hours. When we landed at 8 p.m. local time – 1 a.m. our time – it was pitch black, cold, and snow everywhere. There were Canadian officials, a mass of press men with flashing lights, and then we were whipped off in a great long cavalcade of enormous cars.

Ottawa seemed quite pretty, very spacious, with the houses snuggled under deep snow. Very nice were the thousands of skaters on the frozen canal that runs right through the city.

We went direct to the High Commission, a very stately house – just the PM and Mary, Robert and John Hunt, Patrick Wright, Joe and me. Had drinks and Prime Minister Trudeau dropped in to say hello. Curiously lined face. But slim young figure and moves very lithely.

I was now very tired and so we left and went 300 yards down the road to the Gatehouse, where we were staying. Went to bed exhausted – it was only 9.30 p.m. local time, but 2.30 in real time. Very comfortable suite and had a lovely long sleep till 7 a.m.

Lay in bed for an hour, writing this, listening to the local radio, and looking out of the window at the snow – it is 12° below freezing out there and heavy snow is forecast.

### Wednesday 29 January 1975

Felt beautifully refreshed from my long sleep. Took my time getting up, showering and washing my hair. Finally went down for breakfast and in the middle was summoned by HW up to Government House. It was beginning to snow heavily. Went up the long curving drive to Government House and found HW already in his room dictating an outline for Friday's National Press Club speech. Joe, Robert and John Hunt already there.

At 10 o'clock he set off for the official talks. I was picked up by Gordon Smith of the Canadian Cabinet Office and went in to his office to meet a bright Trudeau aide – Mike Kirby – and another Cabinet Office man, Pesche. We had a very good talk. Incidentally, Smith told me they had heard over the bureaucratic network that Hunt had 'snuffed me out'.

Returned 11.30 and we had a briefing for HW and Callaghan before their talks with Trudeau. Then off they all went in cavalcade. I was taken to an officials' lunch in a large official dining-room. Rather boring. Though I sat next to Trudeau's political secretary, Bob Murdoch, and we discussed our job problems. He said that their civil servants were not allowed near anything to do with appointments, travel arrangements, seating, etc. This was all controlled by the political aides. 'The key to politics is access; you must control access,' he said. I agreed. This is a change which must come in England.

After lunch I went to the Trudeau residence, which was a nice detached house near where I was staying at Rideau Gate. The prime ministerial lunch was still going on when I arrived so I sat in a side-room and waited. I could hear the buzz of conversation, and especially the light drone of Trudeau's voice from the dining-room.

After a while Bob Murdoch arrived. He took a telephone call and told me there was a two-hour delay on the plane out because of snow and freezing rain.

I told HW when they emerged from lunch. 'Don't tell the officials,' he said, 'or they will fit something else in.'

So we went back up to Government House and had tea while we waited till 6 for our plane departure. They produced tea, very formally, served by military attachés. HW and Mary and the Levers were in the main lounge with the governor-general and wife. The GG is French, has had a stroke and had difficulty in speaking. We were bored and irritated with waiting, but finally we all set off in cavalcade for the military airport.

They were spraying something on the wings to de-ice the plane, so we had a cup of tea while waiting. Then off to Washington – the first time in 16 years! So much in between. Jobs, marriage, children, growing middle-aged. I was very excited. The flight was only 1¼ hours. Joe was typing parts of the speech and I sat up front with Robert revising other parts of it.

As we descended to land at Andrews military air base, Washington, I went back to a seat, between two Foreign Office secretaries. The plane began to shudder a bit, and I thought it was the deceleration of the engines. The girls were a little worried and I reassured them. But then the plane began to pitch and toss, shuddering violently, its wings rising and falling so one minute we were looking straight down at the ground only a few hundred feet below, and the next we looked up at the stars.

I was now very worried and realised something was wrong. The girls were rigid with terror and gripped my hands, one of them digging her fingernails in till blood flowed. I thought this was death and wondered how Carol would explain to the children. We were now very close to the ground and the plane was rocking madly. Suddenly the pilot gave it full power, overshot the runway and zoomed up again. We had been down to about 50 feet.

We then half-circled and came in to land the other way. The plane was still being buffeted, but not as badly as before. I looked round and saw everybody totally still and silent, most of their eyes closed. Tremendous relief when we landed.

The crew told us that there had been freak turbulence over the airport and we had been caught up in a hot-air storm.

HW went to congratulate the pilot. We all left the plane silently. It was astonishingly hot – 72° after the sub-zero snow of Ottawa. It should have been exciting, but I was so exhausted by the experience that I did not really enjoy it.

We drove to Blair House opposite the White House, where the PM and the main officials are staying. Then straight to the embassy for dinner.

It was much later than scheduled and I could see that the PM was very tired. In the briefing discussion after we had eaten, sitting around the table in this grand salon, he began to show his irritation. He openly criticised the Ambassador, Peter Ramsbotham,* for not knowing who he was sitting next to at the White House dinner tomorrow. When we broke up he went on one side with me, said he was furious and launched a violent attack on the Ambassador, the Foreign Office, their extravagance and incompetence, etc.

I went back in the car with him Joe, Robert and Hunt. He was still complaining and continued in a bad mood while we sat downstairs in Blair House having a night-cap. Went to bed at 1 a.m., still wondering what had really upset him.

### Thursday 30 January 1975

Woke early in Blair House and unable to get to sleep again – it is midday British time. Went down and had breakfast, walked around the block to smell the air of Washington on a glorious, fresh, sunny morning, then joined HW in his suite to work on Friday's speech and on this morning's speech at the White House reception ceremony.

HW told me he was very tired. He too had woken at 4.30 and been unable to get to sleep again. He blamed the poor Ambassador. Basically he would have liked to have gone straight to bed last night without the embassy visit, which he saw as a waste of time. He was also nervous about today's meetings. 'This is the most important day,' he said 'and they should have made sure I got my sleep. That should have been the first priority.'

Shortly after 10 we drove round to the lawn of the White House.

We assembled in rows around the rostrum – I was in the front row. Beyond us were ranks of colourful soldiers and marines in full uniform, with bands playing. Beyond that in the distance across the garden and the meadow beyond was the Washington monument poking like a great finger into the blue sky. The sun was shining gloriously bright and fresh. Crowds of people were on the grass, some waving Union Jacks.

The band struck up 'Rule Britannia' as HW drove up in his car. President Ford came out of the White House to greet him and they went first to inspect the guard of honour, then out onto the rostrum.

Ford made a warm and impressive speech of welcome. We were a little worried because HW's speech, which we had put together hurriedly that morning, was short and tatty. Worse still, it was typed on a card which blew away in the wind as he started. I heard his tense north-country voice snap out, 'I'll have that back,' and a senior American army officer ran after it and retrieved it from the grass.

After the speeches we all filed up the steps into the White House, were received by Ford and drank coffee. I met there Arthur Hartman, who is a Kissinger aide in charge of European affairs, and his lovely wife Donna, whom I had known in London 10 years ago.

Also saw Hal Sonnenfeldt, Kissinger's aide.

I went down into the Cabinet Room for a meeting of economic advisers. It looked onto the gardens. There were flags on the walls and emblems of battles from the Second World War. A picture of Eisenhower looked down on the long oval table, and portraits of President Truman and Lincoln were on the other side, less prominent than Ike.

There were 13 Americans round the table including Bennett (who did most of the talking), Tom Enders (Energy), Sonnenfeldt and Elliot Richardson.

Derek Mitchell from the Treasury was in the chair for the British and he handled it well. The Americans were not impressive. They were hoping to get their economy moving by the third quarter of 1975, but it was clear they did not really understand the crisis. They told us that their computer forecasts had been wrong every time in the past three years.

The general level of analysis did not give me encouragement for the future of the Western world.

I left with Robert Armstrong at 12.30 to go back to see HW after his meeting with Ford and Kissinger.

HW reached Blair House at about the same time as we did. He was obviously pleased with the talks. He said that Ford could be another Truman, and that American morale was better than for a long time. Things had gone smoothly and he felt that he had 'known Ford all my life'.

John Hunt read out his summary of the talks, which was not very informative. It had clearly been friendly but not very profound.

They then went off to the Kissinger lunch. I went out to the house of an embassy official, in the hills around Washington. Very pretty, but boring, and I stayed only 35 minutes.

At 2.30 I went to join HW's party and we went off for tea with the Foreign Relations committee of the Senate. HW spoke at great length and answered questions at even greater length – one answer was 26 minutes. I timed it. He is getting worryingly long-winded these days, full of anecdotes about politics a quarter of a century ago.

I sat at a table with Senators Ed Muskie, George McGovern and Hubert Humphrey, each of whom seemed soft and finished. Very few American politicians have a sharp edge.

We returned to Blair House and worked a little on the Press Club speech and then on the PM's speech of thanks at tonight's White House dinner.

HW dictated a piece for tonight, which was terrible – pseudo-Churchill. So Joe, Robert and I altered it and effectively produced a different speech while HW went off to bath and change. We then all changed into dinner jackets – I had a flap because I had forgotten my black tie and Robert had to loan me one.

We drove in cavalcade to the White House, where the ceremony was fabulous. A band played as we went up the steps, and we gathered in the large recital room as the other guests arrived – film stars Danny Kaye, Cary Grant, Kirk Douglas, etc. A glittering array. I was with Joe and we wandered around from room to room, enjoying ourselves at the thought that such unlikely people as ourselves should be there in the White House.

Then the President and HW received us all in line. As I shook hands with the President, HW leaned across to me and said, 'I've gone back to my own bloody speech. They had taken away my Gettysburg bit.' God only knows what the Gettysburg bit was, but he was clearly out to stop us writing his speeches.

We went in to sit down in the dining-room at nine round tables. I sat next to an incredibly garrulous wife of a senator from Alabama. But also with Mike Mansfield, Elliot Richardson, Senator Griffin from Michigan, the broadcaster Alistair Cooke and the mistress of Warren Beatty the film star, so it wasn't too bad.

After dinner we went back to the recital room and listened to some songs by a coloratura soprano, Beverley Sills, who was fabulously vital and sensual. The men loved it, though it wasn't my kind of music.

A band was playing in the reception area and Ford led the dancing, but HW said he was tired, and he and Jim Callaghan left. Joe and I stayed till 12.30 but then we had to go.

I went to bed reluctantly. A wonderful day, full of colour and movement and interest and excitement. Not much serious politics really, but that doesn't matter.

## Friday 31 January 1975

A cold, wet morning. Appropriate for our visit to Arlington cemetery, to put a wreath on the grave of the unknown soldier and to see the Kennedy graves. Suitably sombre. We walked, bareheaded, in the rain. Acres of white crosses in all directions. The John Kennedy grave brought back all the emotions of that time when we heard he had been shot and I could not believe it. Again this sense of passing time I get here, because it is all so long ago when I was last here, before marriage, before jobs, four children ago. A whole youth gone.

But the Robert Kennedy grave was best, simple on the hillside.

On return to central Washington Joe and I went shopping, and then off to the National Press Club. It was absolutely packed. The food was filthy, quite uneatable. But I was introduced as one of the guests of honour, so that made up for the uncooked fish.

HW's speech was good. Tight and serious. And went down well. He also answered questions well.

Afterwards I went off separately to the Woodrow Wilson Center at the Smithsonian Institute and then back for a press conference at Blair House.

HW was tired, but relieved the serious work was over. We sat in his room in the early evening and read the English papers – he is much more interested in these than in the American. He read everything on the coming Tory leadership election. That is his real interest – the British parliamentary scene.

We went to the embassy for a very good dinner in the evening. I had a long chat with Nelson Rockefeller and Happy, his wife. Both were easy and completely without side.

Also talked to Elliot Richardson, Al Ulmann and some senators. They were all discussing Congress shop and using the occasion to do some lobbying.

As often on this trip I am conscious of how unimportant Britain is. The Americans are kind, but they are naturally not interested in our parochial problems. They are much less informed on British politics than people were when I lived here in 1959. Britain has slipped from their consciousness. It is sad and makes us aware how we have got so much wrong in these last 20 years.

Came home at 12.30. I sat up in Blair House and talked to the security men until after 1 o'clock. I knew that once I went to bed, the trip was over. Everybody else was already asleep. They have to leave for the plane before 8 in the morning, and I will stay on with Harold Lever.

## Saturday 1 February 1975

Poured with rain. I sat in an empty Blair House, which was like a railway station after the last train has gone.

Talked to my old friend, Judy Davison. Then went to the embassy.

Went out to lunch at Tony Rawlinson's, the Treasury man at the embassy. Slept in the late afternoon.

Dinner alone at a French restaurant. Cost $25 – and not very good. But nice sense of freedom – with a huge black Cadillac waiting outside.

Afterwards to coffee with John Midgley of *The Economist*. Stayed till 1.30 a.m. Much nostalgia for when I worked on *The Economist* back in 1959–60.

## Sunday 2 February 1975

Woke to 3 inches of snow.

Diana Josephson, an old friend from Oxford long ago, picked me up and took me to breakfast at the famous Watergate building.

Then we drove out to Mount Vernon. Beautiful in the snow, high above the Potomac, with a destroyer swaying at anchor way below. We walked and talked of Oxford nearly 20 years ago.

Lunch at the Hartmans, which was absolutely delightful, certainly the nicest meal I have had in America. Such a lovely family. Also there was Joe Sachs, who I last saw in 1958, now at the World Bank, and his very charming wife.

In the evening to dinner with Hella Pick of the *Guardian*. Very relaxed – the Hartmans there also.

Home 1.45 a.m.

## Monday 3 February 1975

Took the train to New York. Three hours. Very sunny, not very beautiful country. But gave me time to read the newspapers and relax.

Then, bang, New York, even higher and busier – but also dirtier than last time. Went direct to lunch with *Business Week* magazine. On the 39th floor of the McGraw Hill building. Harold Lever talked for hours about petrodollars. I dreamed, looked out of the windows up the East River to La Guardia, watching the planes float in and zoom out, and realised how much better it is to come to New York as I did in 1958–59, free as air, walking the streets and smelling everything. This VIP stuff is too air-conditioned.

Went to tea with David Rockefeller* at his First National Bank. Nice, but no genius.

Then back to a dinner for bankers at our Carlysle Hotel. Very interesting, considering. Lever was very good. I sat next to Paul Volcker*, who was charming, funny and very clever. It could have been much worse.

I was tired afterwards and went to bed at midnight.

## Tuesday 4 February 1975

Press conference with the oil trade press – Lever on North Sea oil.

Then I went for a walk down 5th Avenue beside the Central Park. Very cold – 22°F – so I went in the lovely Frick Museum.

Lunch at the Harvard Club with various journalists. Lever talked non-stop on petro-dollars and North Sea oil. Then back to the hotel – but I slipped off to the Metropolitan Museum and saw the Impressionist exhibition and all those Rembrandts. Fantastic.

Came out in the dark, bought a hot pretzel from a stand, and walked home eating it. Tried to find some presents for Carol and the children, but not much success.

Decided to go to no more conferences or dinners with petro-dollars on the menu, so I slipped into the bar and drank American beer for hours and hours (I don't think it is alcoholic at all).

Home tomorrow. A pity to leave America after 16 years. But I don't like being alone here. I miss the children.

Bed at midnight.

## Wednesday 5 February 1975

Up at 7.15 a.m., left the hotel at 8.15 a.m., driving through snow and slush to the airport. Disappointed to find a VC10 instead of a Jumbo. Took off half an hour late. Long and boring flight, losing five hours. Home just before midnight.

# CHAPTER 11

## To Dublin, and the EEC Renegotiation
### February–March 1975

*Thursday 6 February 1975*

[During the first two months of 1975 the Labour government continued with its complex and difficult renegotiation of Britain's terms of membership of the European Community. The main problems arose with Tony Benn over regional policy, with Peter Shore over trading issues, and with William Ross over various Scottish issues. The outstanding questions mainly concerned the Community budget, iron and steel, and New Zealand food imports. These were brought for resolution to the summit of European Heads of Government in Dublin on 10–11 March 1975.

Wilson went to Dublin convinced that the terms already agreed were satisfactory and that he and his Foreign Secretary would be able to recommend them to the British public as a proper basis for Britain's continued membership. The shrewd and generous assistance of Schmidt and the German delegation at the Summit made that outcome even more certain. After Dublin, the challenges to Wilson were to hold his Cabinet together during the referendum campaign – when ministerial colleagues were allowed to argue for opposing sides – and finally to secure a clearly positive vote on 5 June.]

Drove in to No. 10, feeling very tired. Enormous amount of paperwork to catch up on.

Saw HW briefly before and after Cabinet.

Lunch with Joe. Apparently Marcia has been behaving wildly and HW told Joe and Albert that he has had enough and wants to get rid of her.

She told Joe that HW is going to announce his retirement at this autumn's party conference – and go at Christmas. Joe said she is also attacking me again, blaming me for everything.

HW looked tired before Questions. But friendly. He gave a speech of praise for Ted Heath, who retired on Tuesday. [Edward Heath was deposed by Margaret Thatcher in the Conservative Party leadership election.] Some *Tories* objected – because it wasted part of Question Time. Afterwards HW was a bit shocked – 'After all he was Prime Minister of Britain.' We discussed it in the car going back from Parliament to No.10. He saw it as typical of the Tories' ruthlessness.

He doesn't think much of Whitelaw.

We worked for half an hour on two speeches – one for Friday in Liverpool and one on stabilising commodity prices at Leeds on Sunday.

HW had a succession of visitors and then went out to a private dinner with Marcia's friend Eric Miller, the chairman of Peachey Property, so I worked in the office till after 9 and then left. Feeling very tired, and again that brooding, ominous sense of an impending disaster. Cannot trace it. Probably just jet lag.

## Friday 7 February 1975

HW away in Liverpool all day.

I went in late. Dealt with backlog of correspondence.

Visited by John Hale, chairman of the National Gallery trustees – and my teacher when I specialised in the Italian Renaissance in Oxford 20 years ago. Still very charming, though the years have left their mark on him.

Lunch with my publisher friend Graham Greene. He thinks HW could do more to bring in the Labour Establishment 'socially'. I told him that HW is not really interested – only in the PLP, and then not socially. He is pleased with the Crossman outcome but speaks very critically of John Hunt, whom he described to me as 'nearly the most insecure man I have ever met'. [On the Crossman Diaries affair the court had found in favour of the publishers and against the government law officers' application for an injunction.]

Back to work on papers.

Also saw Ken Berrill from the CPRS, who dropped in to rebuild fences after the episode of the NEDDY inquiry into the nationalised industries. He said I had won a victory. I said I did not want victories – I simply did not like the way the machine operated on that occasion.

Stayed late in the evening working on a memo on (1) New Zealand and EEC negotiations (New Zealand PM is coming on Monday) and (2) on Wedgie Benn's proposals to minimise compensation terms for nationalisation by (a) giving the trade unions a statutory right to advise on the terms and (b) deducting any state aid given in the past 10 years.

Home at 9.

Still very tired, depressed and vaguely worried. I feel in my bones that something is going to go wrong.

Incidentally the Treasury vetoed HW's proposed speech on commodities. Healey thinks commodity prices will go down and so we must not give any guarantees or make any long-term agreements. That seems short-sighted: when world trade turns up commodities will rocket up again.

HW wants to make an initiative on commodity stabilisation at the Jamaica Commonwealth PM's conference – and the PM *did* give his commodities speech, despite Treasury.

### Monday 10 February 1975

Stayed home in the morning and worked on correspondence I should have dealt with at the weekend, but I was then too tired. The jet lag really hit me. I felt tired, depressed and worried about the future.

Drove straight to the American embassy for lunch with Ron Spiers, the excellent new minister there. He said their impression of the Washington visit was good. He was very impressed by the Labour Cabinet, especially Shirley Williams. Also thought Henry Kissinger wouldn't last very long as President Ford's adviser.

Back to the office in the afternoon. PM still not back from Chequers, where he was meeting the New Zealand PM Rowling. He returned at 6, looking harassed, and went straight into a Misc Cabinet committee to discuss compensation for nationalisation. [Cabinet committees which were not regular committees in permanent policy areas, but set up ad hoc to consider particular issues were designated miscellaneous – or 'Misc'.] Benn was pressing for minimum compensation. Lever for maximum, Healey was unclear, and the PM was not interested and left after half an hour. So it decided nothing. HW went to interview Professor Jim Gower for the new Press Commission and then to change for dinner with Rowling at No. 10.

This was a marvellous party. We had introduced some younger, livelier people than usual and it went with a zing. I mainly talked with the sportsmen I had put on the invitation list – Cliff Morgan, Derek Dougan and Brian Close, whom I drove home. Marcia enjoyed it, though at the beginning she complained bitterly that she had been placed next to a golfer. Home at 1 a.m.

– After the Misc meeting Tony Benn came to my room for a talk. Mainly about public appointments, where we both agree there is room for opening things up.

### Tuesday 11 February 1975

PM was with his lawyer David Freeman from 9.30. I went up at 10.30 to see him before Cabinet and we discussed the NEB board – Benn intends to put his left-wing adviser Stuart Holland on it, which would not help its image from early on.

The statement on increasing the Queen's Civil List was due to be made by the PM today. But it had leaked to the press. Also it was bad timing to have it on the same day as the miners' discussions, so HW decided to postpone it for a day. I had not been in on these discussions on the Civil List. Partly because I was away in the USA. Partly because I was not sent copies of the papers – which I consider a tribute. It is the result of the top salaries episode. Deliberate exclusion in case I made trouble. In fact the monarch has a good case – on the figures if not the timing. But the machine moved to slip it through without a thought of any political embarrassment to the government.

Cabinet was mainly concerned with EEC referendum questions and did not reach much agreement. Mainly divided on the question of information to be provided and whether to distribute 'arguments for and against'. In fact it doesn't make much difference. The form of the question is much more important.

I saw Lever after Cabinet and he invited Joe and me to lunch at Eaton Square.

Back to the Commons for PQs at 2.30. Apparently Marcia has been attacking HW again. He looked tired, but was in good form otherwise. Questions went quietly. The Tories were waiting for the results of their leadership ballot, so they were not too interested in the proceedings.

The PM has started drinking brandy again – often a sign he is under heavy attack.

We returned to No. 10 and he had a briefing session with the Foreign Office. I didn't bother to go. Joe and HW later told me it was terrible. About a dozen people from the FO turned up and talked in old-fashioned cold war terms. They were most concerned that HW should *not* use the term 'peaceful coexistence'. (He wanted to, and eventually did, quote Clem Attlee as saying 'The alternative to coexistence is co-death'.)

I went off to have dinner with my friends the Porchesters and Jocelyn Stevens, editor of the *Daily Express*, who has a lively wife, but he seemed under great stress, constantly attacking me for my politics.

Then to Buckingham Palace for a very successful party. Henry Porchester guided us round. I talked with the Duke and at great length to the Queen – about the Civil List, about horses and especially about her possible visit to the USA in 1976. She is keen but refuses to get mixed up with other monarchs, etc. And not sure whether to go on 4 July – which she considers 'their day'. She was very bright and interesting.

Talked to her secretary Martin Charteris and his deputy Moore, who are very different characters, the one very political, the latter a civil servant.

Talked to the Tory MP Ian Gilmour,* who was furious with the election of Margaret Thatcher to the Tory leadership and was talking of leaving politics.

Incidentally we were at the House of Commons when the Tory result was announced, just after 4 p.m. The PM waited in his room to hear it. He looked a bit down when he heard. Because he now had to face a new opponent. He said to me, 'After 10 years of studying the opponent like a hawk, learning every part of his character, now, at my age, I've got to begin all over again.' He then poured himself a stiff brandy.

We left Buckingham Palace at 1.30 a.m. and got to bed at 2.

### Wednesday 12 February 1975

Went up to see HW when I arrived in No. 10. He was complaining about the Foreign Office and how reactionary they are. He seriously means to try to move towards détente with the Russians.

I worked in the Unit in the morning, mainly with David Piachaud on part-time employment and on Defence spending – where we hope to promote some cuts.

Then lunch with Joe at the Commons. He told me that Marcia has gone completely wild again. Is in full cry against me. Was furious and jealous that I went to the Palace and not her. HW went in to see Joe in the press office this morning and asked why I was at the Palace. Joe told him it was because of my friend Henry Porchester and not instead of Marcia. He said HW beamed with pleasure and ran off to tell her. She is also blaming me for the way in which the Civil List increase was slipped through Cabinet and thinks it is linked to my going to the Palace. A plot whereby I act as the Queen's agent to persuade the PM to agree to her increase in grant: totally bonkers. Marcia knows I was in the USA when it was decided and has been told I did not see the papers, but is not interested. Her paranoia about me must be fed. I don't give a damn. But so sad that HW still keeps bending to her whip.

We met at 3 p.m. in the PM's room at the House of Commons to brief for the Civil List statement. HW got a rough passage in the House, reading it with many interruptions. Then at Questions after, he was quite brilliant. Destroyed the opposition on both sides. Witty thrusts. Standing at the despatch box in complete command. Have never seen him so good.

This was because it was Thatcher's first day as Tory leader. He was showing off to her, showing what a real professional can do. She looked very pale and tense throughout, realising what an uphill task she has. The rest of the House loved it – except that the Tories realised that they have not changed their *real* problems by changing their leader. They need to change *our* leader.

Denis Howell phoned me afterwards and said that the tea-room was packed with Labour MPs buzzing with excitement at HW's marvellous performance.

A very good boost for him. He was delighted with himself afterwards. He told me he had been very nervous and gloomy beforehand and had expected it to go badly. He felt so unwell this morning – no doubt assisted by Marcia's attacks – that he thought he would have to go to bed and let somebody else make the statement. He also had three brandies before going into the Chamber. He had another two to celebrate afterwards.

We went back to No.10 together afterwards in the car. I told him that the Unit was working on Defence cuts and that he must press for détente in Moscow or we would never get the right climate for cutting expenditure.

He went into the CBI meeting and then back to the Commons.

I went to the LSE to see the director, Ralf Dahrendorf, about extending my leave till Christmas.

Then back to finish off papers.

Joe was staying overnight at No.10 ready for the early start tomorrow for Moscow. I am pleased I am not going, even though I was excluded mainly to placate Marcia after Washington. Too exhausting and the subjects do not greatly interest me, except the broad subject of détente. I will have a few quiet days in London to think about government policy for the rest of the year.

Home by 9 p.m.

## Thursday 13 February 1975

HW left for Moscow first thing this morning. I'm pleased I have not gone since I need a rest and feel a cold coming on.

Went to see George Wigg at 11 in his flat near Victoria. Strange mixture of obsessions and real ability. Discussed finance for sport and he came round to my point of view and agreed to support a Sports Levy Board, covering all sport.

Then to lunch with an Israeli, Eran, nice Foreign Office man who is also studying at LSE.

Back to see Denis Howell and get more support for my sports levy scheme.

Then Professor Peter Self * dropped in for an hour and a half to discuss the LSE government department, which he chairs.

So it was 8 p.m. before I could begin to read papers. Fortunately the flow is less when the PM is away.

Home 9.45.

## Friday 14 February 1975

Meeting with lovely Marie Patterson from the T&G, now chairman of the TUC, about part-time employment which is mainly a female problem and on which we are minuting the PM, having inspired the Department of Employment to do a very mediocre report on it.

Felt worse and worse from my cold, so went home at lunchtime and to bed in the afternoon. Pleased I'm not in Moscow feeling like this.

– Albert says Marcia is still insisting that at party conference HW will announce his resignation for Christmas. She says he has started moves to buy a flat. Some hints that he might then marry her! I still cannot believe it. He is loving the job and is currently fed up with her.

## Monday 17 February 1975

Stayed home with a heavy cold. HW was in Moscow – achieving great successes with the Russians. Carol was at college, so I looked after the children, which I enjoy enormously.

## Tuesday 18 February 1975

Held Unit meeting discussing a paper on the state of play on the EEC renegotiations, which we will put in to the PM at the weekend.

HW didn't come in till 11.45. He had dinner last night with Kissinger and stayed at Lord North Street resting.

I met him in private office and we walked out along the passage chatting. He was obviously very pleased with his Moscow success and claimed it was the politicians who had done it. The Foreign Office had not wanted to push for anything, but he meant to make positive progress. 'It will please the party,' he said 'and not only the fellow travellers.'

Joe and I went to lunch at the Commons. They had obviously had a marvellous time in Russia and had been given the full treatment – opulence, massive meals, great cavalcades of cars, etc. For the first time it made me a little regretful I had not been, though I still have a rotten cold. Briefing and Questions went very quietly.

Afterwards I sat in the PM's room with him for three-quarters of an hour. Discussed economic questions and I briefed him on Andrew Graham's view that he will have to take *one* unpleasant option – and it would have to be import controls if it is not wages policy. We are worried that he has closed away options by firmly ruling out import controls, export subsidies, wages policy, deflation, unemployment, etc. He said, 'In an emergency you mean.' This will presumably be his let-out, for opening closed options.

We drove back from the Commons to No. 10 together. He went into the Cabinet committee on Economic Strategy – discussing exports, imports and the property market (including proposals for the government to buy up to £1,000 million of property to get it moving again). I sent in Andrew Graham and went to have a long talk with Frank Judd about Defence expenditure. He is a bit sceptical of our ability to make further cuts, but David Piachaud and I are pressing on with this. The draft Defence White Paper has just come round and it is *terrible*, full of cold war language, could have been written by John Foster Dulles [Eisenhower's Secretary of State and cold war warrior].

Afterwards went up to the study at 7 p.m. HW was there with Albert and Janet Hewlett-Davies from Joe's press office. They had obviously had several drinks. I had one and after a brief chat about Moscow and the delights of the ballet, HW went up to his flat and I went back to the office to read the enormous backlog of papers.

HW said it was marvellous to go to the Bolshoi Ballet in Moscow – *at* the Bolshoi, instead of, as usual, the Bolshoi coming to the Kremlin to perform.

HW said that Callaghan had sent a message to him asking how it felt to be sitting in the Czar's seat at the Bolshoi. HW replied by asking how it felt to sit in Rasputin's seat!

HW is obviously getting on very well with Janet.

Albert told me later that HW is helping to negotiate the purchase of 1 Wyndham Mews, next to Marcia's existing house, for her and her mother. Costs £12,000 for a 12-year lease. Three houses are better than two (including the one in the country).

## Wednesday 19 February 1975

Saw Bill Rodgers in the morning. He came in to discuss possible Defence cuts. Very prickly at first because of feeling of disloyalty to his Secretary of State. Bill has his usual total and almost irrational loyalty to his department's position. Privately he will admit that Defence expenditure is excessive by nearly £1,000 million. They are building totally unnecessary and useless cruisers and buying far more planes than we need. This is because the military chiefs made a high opening bid, assuming they would have to give up a lot – and they didn't! The Cabinet let it all through without a murmur. Bill said they were 'flabbergasted'. But openly he will concede nothing and defends them to the last.

Went to lunch at my stockbrokers Grieveson Grant. Very pleasant and encouraging – the City is clearly more balanced than last year. Not necessarily much more optimistic, but with much less hysteria than previously.

Yoram Peri, from the Israeli Labour Party, came to quiz me about HW's Moscow visit and the Middle East. I get a terrible sense of impending tragedy there. Everybody is abandoning the Israelis – to the great pleasure of our Foreign Office, who of course were never attached to them and have almost no Jews on the staff. Today HW was having lunch with some Egyptian (Reggie Maudling came – a shambling giant, looking totally punch-drunk as he shuffled up the stairs of No. 10). private office were delighted to have an Arab in. For much of the Foreign Office it is a kind of love affair, with lots of mutual conservative attitudes and politics thrown in. Some of them would stand by and watch Israelis massacred without a murmur of protest. I now understand appeasement between the wars much better. Czechoslovakia was their Israel. And the present apologia for the Arab terrorists is just their Nazi apologies updated.

At 4 I went to the Cabinet committee on the EEC (called EQS) and there was a fascinating discussion on Europe and Regional Aid. Benn had put in a wild paper attacking the whole EEC policy and he spoke to it with great rhetoric, as if addressing a mass meeting of shop stewards, ending with the claim that 'This is 1910 all over again, the Lords against the People, and the People must emerge triumphant.' The dozen people around the table looked a bit uncomfortable. Even Michael Foot, never slow with the rhetorical flourish himself, shifted uneasily in his seat.

Shore and Foot supported Benn. Interestingly, HW brought in Crosland, Callaghan and Peart against them. None of these is considered to be in the 'pro-Market' camp. Yet they were quickly being driven there. The antis very foolishly made personal attacks on these three. So a fierce argument developed – without a single outright pro-marketeer taking part. I was particularly interested to see Crosland taking a more positive stand. He has sat on the fence on so many issues in the past 12 months, looking amused, quizzical, contemptuous of the muddled arguments of others but unwilling really to fight to knock them down. He looked tougher today and came out firmly for the Market.

The PM showed interesting signs of how he will handle a 'pro' position. He repeatedly emphasised his intention to throw our weight about with the Brussels bureaucracy – *after* staying in. He also spoke very fiercely about the iniquities of the Paris Iron and Steel Treaty and how we must change that fundamentally – *not* of course part of the renegotiations and not the Rome Treaty. He also went out of his way to agree with Benn wherever possible – which meant he is going to take the opposite line in the end.

After the meeting – which showed a clear majority against Benn but decided to take the question to Cabinet – HW had a private meeting with Benn in the study. I don't know what they discussed.

I then worked in the Unit and went home at 9.30.

*Thursday 20 February 1975*

In early to attend the Cabinet committee on Northern Ireland. Little new
in it. Merlyn Rees always gives a long and picturesque report. He is flanked
by his top civil servant, Frank Cooper, and his top soldier, General Frank
King. They participate like ministers – the only other Cabinet committee
where outsiders take part is OPD, the Defence committee.

Worked through the morning in the Unit and then had lunch with Joe
at the Commons. Briefing and questions were fairly dull and routine.

We returned and went to a terrible Misc Cabinet committee meeting
on compensation for nationalisation. Benn and Lever arguing, Benn for
ridiculously low and Lever for generous compensation. Healey and HW
occasionally joined in. The four of them sat with lists of share prices in
Swan Hunter and Hawker Siddeley over recent years and tried to work
out a fair price. Wilson, Healey and Benn are clearly very ignorant of financial matters. It was one of the most fatuous discussions I have yet heard.
They could not agree and suddenly HW got up and walked out, having
asked for more information on 'how Clem Attlee did it'.

HW went to a NATSOPA party and then went to Chequers with Janet
– he told Albert he was not needed.

I had a delicious dinner at the Mirabelle with Denis Howell. Denis and
I plotted putting some pressure on the Treasury to get more money for
sport.

*Friday 21 February 1975*

HW in Newcastle. Making an Education speech. I have slipped up. It was
my job to put in a piece giving reassurance to the universities. It was left
out at the first draft stage, for inclusion at our final discussion – which we
never had. So it is out. And the universities will feel even more demoralised. Otherwise all day spent on memos – on the economic outlook and
on my Sports Levy proposal.

*Monday 24 February 1975*

Still feeling ill from an acute sinus infection so I went to the doctor on
the way to the office and was put on antibiotics.

HW was at the TUC/Labour Party liaison committee in the House of
Commons and I worked in the Unit.

Went up to see the PM shortly after midday. Briefed him on Chile –
where the Foreign Office and the Treasury had been in cahoots to misrepresent the alleged advantages of continuing loaning money to Chile and

the cost of breaking off. Tom McNally has done an excellent job of flushing out the truth – including the fact that when the Foreign Office was instructed by ministers to send a questionnaire to the Treasury to get the hard facts, the FO man went to the Treasury and allowed the Treasury to draft the questions so that they could *avoid* giving the facts.

Went to lunch with Anthony Lester. He is still enjoying working with Roy Jenkins, but like me feels he must give up within a year. He said Roy is very depressed about the way Healey is running the Exchequer and obviously would like that job. Though he says Roy is happier now being back at the Home Office, having been deeply depressed at first.

Lever dropped in to see me at tea, coming from a chat with HW. Said it was friendly, but did not really get down to brass tacks. Lever is not sure how we should handle the economy. Says 'soldiering on' may be as good as any other alternative.

My view is that there are different ways of soldiering on. We are going blindly, nakedly and in no particular direction. We could be better armed economically and march more purposefully.

At 5.30 the Misc Cabinet committee on fixing the petroleum revenue tax met. Lever was for only 40%. Balogh and Andrew Graham were for 50%. Varley and the Treasury were for 45% and this compromise won. In fact it didn't matter much since the money differences were not great (if you take less in PRT, you get more in corporation tax).

The PM had a dinner for the main charity organisations. Apparently he promised to institute a major survey of poverty – and to give the job to the Policy Unit. A feather in our cap, but God only knows what we can achieve. I wasn't there – sent David Piachaud from the Unit.

Went home to bed early with a terrible headache.

*Tuesday 25 February 1975*

Spent the morning working in the Unit. The PM was at the Cabinet committee on Economic Strategy (MES), which apparently went very smoothly. Andrew Graham was there representing the Unit and told me that nobody except Jenkins raised any concern about the progress of the economy. 'They are just going to sit and wait for it to hit them,' he concluded.

I went up to see the PM before lunch and we had a drink. Long discussion of a threatened rebellion of junior ministers on the Queen's Civil List issue. He said he wouldn't sack them now, but would drop them after the EEC referendum when he 'intended to have a reshuffle'. He thought one or two might choose the martyr's road before then – he mentioned Eric Heffer and John Grant as two he would happily lose.

Lunch at No. 10 again! Robert Armstrong has arranged for his wife to come in without remuneration to cook lunch on Tuesdays and Thursdays. For pre-Questions discussion. The PM apparently said it was a good idea, though Marcia will obviously go mad. But there is no way she can attack this. Robert's wife is discreet and no threat to her.

Briefing and PQs went very quietly. Definitely a quiet patch. Mrs Thatcher does not seriously intervene. Each of them is trying to avoid the other, sizing one another up. HW thinks she will wait for a big debate to make a splash. But Robert Armstrong doesn't think she has the stamina.

Margaret Jackson [Beckett] came back with me for tea.

She is upset about the EEC. Afraid the government will organise a Commons debate and vote *before* the referendum to get a parliamentary majority for staying in, so as to influence the referendum. Says the anti-marketeers see this as a 'pro- plot'. It is clear to me that the antis are getting worried about the result. She admits that a decision to pull out would do most damage to the party because the pro-marketeers would leave – though she is sceptical about Shirley Williams, whom she clearly dislikes.

She also claims that it is impossible for the government to negotiate satisfactory terms because she helped in the drafting of our requirements and they 'drafted it so that the terms were impossible to get'.

Went to the Cabinet committee on Industrial Development. Quite remarkable.

First item was the Meriden Co-operative. Everybody attacked Benn, claiming he had misled them in the past, insinuating that he was misleading them now. HW was very rough on him. All designed to limit Benn to the existing £4.9 million commitment and to stop his repeated tactic of bouncing back for more and more money.

Then they deferred Benn's request to aid Alfred Herbert, the machine-tools company, which is in a terrible way. This time they asked for more information. HW was again very peremptory with him.

But when it came to the third item – a paper from the Treasury setting out very well what should be the criteria for granting aid to industry – exactly the kind of thing necessary to deal better with situations such as arose with Meriden and Herbert – Benn escaped. He ignored Healey's arguments and asked for delay. He totally misrepresented the Treasury paper – and then tacitly admitted he had not read it. He attacked his own officials for betraying him, and the Treasury officials for putting forward Tory policies. He tried to intimidate his colleagues by saying 'watch out when some of your constituents come up to ask me for aid'. It was a wild and intemperate performance. Yet Healey did not really fight back. And the PM, who was late for another meeting, agreed to defer discussion till another meeting – which may be some weeks. Benn was pleased – and Healey furious. He complained to Lever and to me outside No. 10. But really he should have been tougher. It was a Treasury paper, and he didn't win. Benn successfully deferred it, without a leg to stand on, just by fierce opposition. Healey could learn something from that.

Afterwards I worked in the Unit till 8.30 and then went home.

– Incidentally, at Questions today the PM promised to meet the CBI's complaint on the Industry Bill – which commits him on the record – and has minuted Whitehall on the same lines. It is a constant battle between him and Benn. [Benn had introduced the Second Reading of the Industry Bill on 7 February 1975, setting up the National Enterprise Board and providing for a limited extension of public ownership. Its Third Reading was taken on 3 July 1975 – by then under Eric Varley as the new Secretary of State.]

## Wednesday 26 February 1975

Discussion with Richard Graham of my Unit – who warned me that the civil servants are still trying to overcome the Cabinet committee (IDV) decision to get NEDDY to study the general relationship between Whitehall and the nationalised industries. So I telephoned Ronnie McIntosh of NEDDY – arranged for him to come to see me next week. Apparently the Cabinet Office are backing the Treasury line. There is clearly still a battle ahead. This is just the kind of thing that the Crossman Diaries describe: the machine taking its own line regardless of ministerial decisions. I shall lose, but they won't win in the end.

Wigg has sent the PM a nice letter saying that I have totally converted him on the Sports Levy Board. But when I spoke to Roy Jenkins he was a bit cagey – he wants to hold it up while he does a complete review of gambling and betting. That could delay my Levy Board until it is too late.

We did a brief for tomorrow's Cabinet on the Defence Review, pointing out that the cuts are totally phoney. We are really spending *more* than the Tories would have done. It is probably too late, but we have alerted Barbara Castle, Callaghan, Lever and Healey, so at least I hope there is a discussion. I can never hope that HW will take the *lead* in these questions – especially when he has sat on the Cabinet committee which has been deceived, indeed has chaired it. But if enough ministers raise questions, he may see the opportunity to retreat a little. Building those three cruisers is madness.

Had nice lunch with my old friend Clifford Barclay at the Coq d'Or.

Saw the PM at teatime. He was in a very happy mood, though worried about the number of speeches ahead of him. He obviously wants Joe and me to do some more. I discreetly left the room and dashed to Euston to take the train to Glasgow. I have to go a day in advance of the PM's flight tomorrow because (1) I have been forbidden to fly because of my sinus infection and (2) there is a rail strike tomorrow!

The train journey was a nice chance to catch up on reading – and writing.

– Judith Hart telephoned me this morning to tell me about some Chile Solidarity committee propaganda she wants to send me. It is clearly communist in origin and language.

## Thursday 27 February 1975

Woke in Glasgow – the airport hotel – to find everywhere enveloped in freezing fog. Such a pity, with a whole morning off. I had met a man on the train yesterday who offered to collect me from the hotel at 9.30 and take me for a ride. He was on time and we set off driving north. For 30 miles we could not see the side of the road. Then the fog lifted as we drove alongside Loch Lomond and it looked astonishingly beautiful.

Did 100-mile journey. Back to lunch with Kay Carmichael at the university – freezing cold because of a strike which cut the heat off.

Back to the hotel to meet the PM – but he could not land because of another strike at the airport. Scotland seems to be falling apart. Everything on strike. Glasgow itself is bleak and depressing with piles of rubbish everywhere (there is also a dustmen's strike!). So the PM was diverted to Prestwick and arrived an hour late.

We had dinner with the Scottish TUC and then long talks afterwards, until 1 a.m. There were five communists among the STUC and some of the exchanges were quite sharp.

To bed at 1.30 a.m.

## Friday 28 February 1975

Had a briefing session in the PM's hotel room before meeting again with the Scottish TUC at 9.30 till 1 p.m. Some of the Scottish contributions were terrible – rambling and pointless, especially from the chair.

Lunch was interrupted by a demonstration of steel-workers outside the windows. Lots of shouting, police, TV cameras, etc. From then on the meeting was more desultory, with poor attendance and a lot of repetition.

In the evening we went to dinner with the Scottish Council of Industrialists. Stuffy and boring. The PM was getting tired.

Back to the hotel, after a visit to the Scottish *Daily Record*, at just after 1 a.m. The hotel was packed with Welsh rugger supporters, up for Saturday's international. When the PM entered they all cheered and sang some lovely Welsh songs to him. Although very drunk they were orderly and very friendly.

I sat up having a drink until nearly 3 a.m.

– Next morning went to open the Scottish Labour Party's new head-quarters and then flew home in the early afternoon. PM tired but enjoyed being away from London.

## Monday 3 March 1975

Day dominated by a row over a speech by Reg Prentice at the weekend suggesting the social contract is failing. In fact it is, and what he said is unanswerable, but HW was furious. Partly because the speech was attacking Michael Foot. Partly because HW doesn't like Prentice. Partly because – and this is where Prentice was foolish – the speech was not cleared with any other ministers despite firm instructions as recently as last Thursday's Cabinet that this should happen.

But there is also a hidden motive, typical of HW, which emerged at our discussions in the study this morning. HW is still planning to drop Benn after the referendum. But – believing always in balancing the Left and Right – he wants to attack the Right as well as a cover. So he is attacking Prentice and plans to drop him at the same time. 'He is my Richard Marsh,' he said in the study.

Apparently Jenkins telephoned HW yesterday and said that if HW punished Prentice he, Jenkins, 'would have to consider his position'. HW of course does not mean to punish Prentice now. Nor was he afraid of Jenkins's threat – 'Jenkins won't go before the referendum,' he said. 'He wants to be there to vote in Cabinet for staying in.'

Private office told me that HW phoned Prentice on Saturday evening and was very rough with him. But Prentice was apparently fairly tough in return and quite unrepentant.

Lunch with John Hale, at the Athenaeum, discussing the impact of the wealth tax on works of art and gifts to the National Gallery – of which Hale is chairman.

Afternoon at No. 10 doing a TV broadcast for Granada.

HW spent half an hour with Marcia and was praising the 'brilliance of her ideas'.

Incidentally I must see John Hunt. He sent for a copy of the Policy Unit's brief on Defence and has complained to Robert Armstrong that I do not co-operate with him – which means go along with the machine's tactics. I shall see him tomorrow. He must realise, as I said to Robert, that I am not in his department.

An interesting example of manipulation: last Thursday's Cabinet decided that Cabinet would have another discussion on future Defence spending. The minutes say that there will be 'further consideration' but no mention of the Cabinet doing it.

The minutes also quote a White Paper as saying that there may be revised expenditure after 1977. In fact the White Paper said 'After 1976'!

Felt very tired from late nights, so went home early, at 8 p.m. It is just a year since we formed the government. Feels like a hard lifetime ago.

## Tuesday 4 March 1975

Spent the morning in the Unit dealing with letters, papers, etc. The PM was upstairs with little to do. I saw him before lunch and raised the question of university teachers' salaries – in which I have an interest. The DES is refusing arbitration and has let university salaries slip below those in technical colleges. The PM has asked for details. Later I talked to Maurice Peston,* Prentice's excellent policy adviser. It will be put right in the long run but the universities are going to suffer a demoralising squeeze for a year or so.

Had lunch with Joe. He told me that the PM had described Marcia as 'totally unreliable'. Apparently he is now finding the job very exhausting. The Paris attack of heart palpitations worried him. And he says he hates Question Time more and more. But he is still undecided when to retire.

Today's PQs was rough but boring. Just a long slanging match about the social contract. Also constant Tory jibes about the split between Prentice and Foot. The PM sees Prentice's statements about trade unions not keeping to the social contract as a right-wing plot – he even said to me at one point it was 'all part of a leadership plot'. Roy Mason had confirmed that to him. I don't know. Prentice's speech seems unexceptionable to me, but he was quite wrong in not consulting his colleagues and officially clearing it. On the whole it is a mountain out of a molehill. But the PM doesn't like Prentice, thinks he doesn't matter and is looking for a way to punish him.

Then I worked on a minute to the PM suggesting that the Common Agricultural Policy should be on the agenda for Paris. Later I saw on the TV news that the agenda was already fixed. Then Robert Armstrong telephoned me to beg me not to put in the memo because it might destroy the Dublin negotiation. I would not agree to that. But will consider how to handle it tomorrow because the memo is now out of date. Cannot influence the agenda now, too late. But I still would like something to come out of Paris on reforming the CAP – this would strengthen the *pro*-Market case. Make the renegotiations seem a greater success.

*Wednesday 5 March 1975*

Went in early at 9.30 for the Cabinet committee on compensation for nationalisation, but when I got there I couldn't face it, after the last two experiences. So I went into the private office to talk to Robert. I found HW in there. He looked guilty, like a schoolboy caught stealing an apple, and said sheepishly, 'I'm playing truant.' I said so was I and that I couldn't face another meeting like the last two. HW looked very relieved and asked me upstairs to the study for a talk.

I raised with him the coming Dublin Summit on our EEC renegotiations. I said that the Unit had intended proposing to put the CAP on the agenda, but it was now probably too late. He said it was too late. That Jim would be furious. That he had promised Giscard not to raise anything as fundamental as the EEC pricing system. I said that in this case we must make it clear that we are not raising anything else with the Europeans. He agreed and said that he would make this clear from the beginning in Dublin.

I then raised his style of campaigning in the referendum. I said he should not campaign like a committed doctrinaire. He should show that he understood the doubts that people feel and then, at the end, despite everything, declare firmly that we should stay in. He agreed.

Joe then came up. HW told us that he hoped to finalise everything in Dublin and have the crucial Cabinet on 18 March. And a statement to Parliament and a White Paper before Easter.

I said that what worried me was the 3 months gap to the referendum. The uncertainty could damage sterling. The PM agreed, saying he did not like the prospect of Cabinet ministers disagreeing for 3 months. So we agreed he should press Ted Short to try to rush the referendum Bill through Parliament and get the referendum earlier – probably in the first week of June.

Then the officials arrived for the first Dublin briefing – Robert Armstrong, Patrick Wright, Pat Nairne and John Hunt from the Cabinet Office, and Michael Palliser (from Brussels). They took HW over the points for Dublin – the Budget, New Zealand food and steel. They were clearly optimistic of getting a reasonable deal on both the EEC Budget and New Zealand, but uncomfortable about steel. The PM seemed fairly bored with it all.

Robert Armstrong is off to Paris today to try to soften up the French in advance. They also discussed sending somebody to talk to the Germans, together with a letter from HW to Schmidt, to make sure they support us. Apparently the Germans are very divided. And the Berlin kidnapping has distracted them.

Callaghan came in at 11.30 with more Foreign Office officials. He looked very tired. His face has gone moon-shaped, like Churchill's did. But he was very firm on the issues. At one point he frightened the officials by suggesting that we might break off in Dublin and take renegotiations to another meeting. But HW opposed that, saying he would rather go on through the night.

HW then put his (my) arguments about (1) bringing the referendum forward, (2) his own style of low-profile campaign.

Nobody dissented. Callaghan seemed strongly in agreement.

The whole discussion was on the assumption that (1) we would accept the renegotiations as sufficient; (2) that HW and JC would recommend staying in to the Cabinet; and (3) the Cabinet would recommend staying in to the country. There were few ifs. Their minds were made up.

After the briefing session, I went back to my room with the Cabinet Secretary John Hunt. We had a very heavy session. He complained about the Unit's memorandum on Defence. He said it was inaccurate, but what emerged was that it was inconvenient. We argued quite fiercely. He foolishly tried to bully me and I got angry in return. In the end he retreated and said that next time I should attend OPD, the Cabinet committee on Defence, which I welcomed. He is obviously not accustomed to having younger people argue and resist him. His commitment is completely to the Whitehall machine. But I suppose that is his job

We had argued till a quarter to two. I was very hungry. In Whitehall I met Gerry Fowler and we went off to the Commons together for lunch – a terrible plate of sausages and chips. Interestingly, he was against Foot in the recent Prentice-Foot quarrel.

Back to No. 10 where I spent the rest of the afternoon working on papers. Did not see HW – who was at the House with a series of discussions on the Finance Bill – until the evening reception for Commonwealth delegations. I spent it talking to Margaret Jackson [Beckett], Judith Hart and Fred Peart – who was happily sloshed.

Interestingly, Janet Hewlett-Davies said that 'Marcia has shot her bolt'. I wonder what led her to think that. HW must have said something. I will believe it only when it is finally, unchangeably true. When I went in to Marcia's room at lunch to invite her to the reception for policy advisers, HW was in there. But he left immediately. He was talking about her 'brilliant idea' for Saturday's speech. It emerged that the brilliant idea was that HW should appeal for restraint on wage claims!

### Thursday 6 March 1975

Drove in, arrived just before 10 a.m. and went up to the PM in the study. Joe was sent for and we discussed the EEC and Saturday's speech by the

PM at Taunton. HW was also attacking the press, saying that the lobby must be abolished. He is still obsessed by the press, reading every article, reacting, fascinated by the papers yet talking as if he wants to abolish them.

He raised with me the question of steel and the EEC – the Treaty of Paris. Ways of getting round it so that he could argue in the referendum campaign that we had done a good deal to maintain our sovereignty.

He went downstairs to Cabinet at 11 a.m. They slipped through the Defence Review in three minutes. John Hunt had drafted a minute for the PM explaining that everything had already been agreed – so there was no need to delay it any longer. This was a direct rejection of the Policy Unit minute – and I believe not strictly true. The odd thing is that HW signs it and lets the machine get away with it, although it means trouble later when we will have to cut social expenditure and cannot cut Defence because of this commitment. He knows that but he won't fight them. In fact afterwards he was laughing at Barbara Castle for having protested and boasting that he had deliberately failed to hear her protests. I have been defeated. But the machine cannot win on Defence for ever. Economic realities will prevail. But it is *incredible* that a Labour government, with its long traditions of hostility to excessive Defence spending, just swallows all this so meekly. The Left doesn't say a word. Not even Michael Foot, whom I had lobbied strongly in Glasgow. Because of how the Cabinet system works. Each minister looks after his or her own territory. They leave Defence to Roy Mason and the Chancellor. If Healey, an ex-Minister of Defence, agrees, then the rest go along, including the spending ministers – Crosland, Castle, Benn and Prentice – who will later have to cut their own programmes by the amounts that they could have saved on Defence.

I went to lunch with Michael Palliser, our Ambassador to the EEC. Took him to the Little French Club. Very pleasant and interesting man. Totally pro-Market, but intelligent with it. He was in HW's private office 10 years ago. He said, 'It is good to see the old wizard again.'

Walked back across the park to the Commons where we briefed for Questions. Very quiet again. HW said, as often before, 'I hate Questions.' We discussed taking some day-trips abroad on Tuesdays and Thursdays so that he could avoid PQs.

I dashed back to the Cabinet Office between 4 and 5 for the regular weekly meeting of the Deputy Secretaries on the future agenda of Cabinet and its committees. We decided not to have the referendum on the Cabinet agenda next Thursday in case it opened up the question of the Common Market decision before it is properly discussed – which is now to be on Monday and Tuesday 17 and 18 March. This was arranged to allow a meeting of the Parliamentary Labour Party on the EEC on Monday evening. HW wanted to be able to *report* to them after the first Cabinet meeting on Monday morning, but *before* the actual decision was taken. So he would have a good excuse for not telling them anything!

Dashed back to the House of Commons for another briefing for the Dublin EEC Summit. Had a row on the way over because Donald Maitland from the Foreign Office had called in at No. 10 and had taken the Downing Street car I had ordered to the Commons, and it was pouring with rain! A little thing really, but Maitland was part of the Heath regime and it is always annoying when the staff show their preferences. It is inconceivable that I could have borrowed a reserved Foreign Office car.

The briefing meeting went quite easily. The Treasury man was badly briefed. He knew that the Treasury wanted to argue against the Kissinger plan for a floor price for oil, but admitted to the PM that he didn't know the arguments because he hadn't been properly briefed. I opposed them, arguing that the floor price was in our interests, as an oil-producing nation.

When the meeting broke up, HW indicated that Joe and I should stay. He shut the doors and said he was not happy with the briefing he had got on steel. He thought Callaghan had misled him. He asked me to get photostats of the relevant papers and minutes of meetings (so that private office would not know he was interested) and he asked me to put in a Unit brief setting out the steel issue. He thinks that the FO is trying to bounce him. If so they are foolish. Once he gets conspiratorial he is likely to cause trouble. I understand the FO position. As on the continental oil shelf, they want to avoid sensitive issues in Dublin by hiding them from him. I think it is better to bring them in the open and then persuade him not to take them up.

I went back to No. 10 and organised the Unit to do the steel briefs. Then I went with Robin Butler from private office to have dinner at Grosvenor House with Chris Collins from the Jockey Club and Andrew Waites, where we discussed the financial problems of the racing industry. They can see British racing declining fast, but the old fuddy-duddies who run the Jockey Club haven't a clue how to deal with it. I was interested to see how it fitted in with my scheme for a Sports Levy Board.

Left shortly after midnight and in bed just before 1.

## Friday 7 March 1975

In early. Kissinger arrived at 9.30 a.m. HW introduced me to him, but I did not go upstairs for the talks because I wanted to see how the Unit was progressing with the EEC and steel.

Chatted to Healey for 10 minutes while he was waiting to see the PM after Kissinger. He clearly has not made up his mind on a Budget strategy and is delaying the date as long as possible. He said that local authority expenditure was the biggest single problem for him. He also digressed about an article in a recent economic journal which proved that Nicky Kaldor* was wrong in believing that it would increase growth and productivity to get more labour into manufacturing. I suddenly got the feeling that he was making the mistake of getting involved in the intellectual arguments of economists, following every theoretical hare, in order to prove he is as intellectual as them. This would be fatal and exhausting. As Chancellor he needs to decide what the central issues are and take a broad economic and political judgement on them.

Kissinger came out, with Arthur Hartman from the State Department, who had time only for a few words, and Ambassador Elliot Richardson. They left in their great black cars and the pouring rain.

I had a brief meeting with William Plowden from the CPRS about poverty, which the Unit is now beginning to tackle. Williams handles it in CPRS. In ten minutes he gave me a complete run-down, clear and precise. He is very good.

David Piachaud from my Unit has also produced a long paper for me on Poverty, which I had to digest before passing it on to John Hunt.

At 11 a.m. went up to the study for a briefing on Dublin again. HW had Joe and me alone for a while and we discussed steel again. He asked for more information. Then everyone assembled – Palliser, Armstrong, Wright, Pat Nairne, Michael Butler* from the Foreign Office, and Hunt and Joe. Callaghan was delayed, but we started, first discussing steel. Then Callaghan arrived and we had reports from Pat Nairne, who had been overnight to Dublin, from Robert Armstrong about Paris and from Michael Butler who had been to Bonn.

Nairne had seen Garrett Fitzgerald,* found him sick in his dressing-gown and not well informed on next Monday's meeting, which *he* will chair. He did not even seem to know what would be on the agenda. However, he agreed to our proposals *not* to take the agenda in mechanical order, but to start with the main issues at dispute, the Budget and New Zealand, and leave everything else to fit in.

Butler reported that the Germans were divided, angry that we had raised steel, and everything depended on Schmidt – who was still suffering from the after-effects of pneumonia, with his doctors advising him to go to bed and *not* to go to Dublin.

Robert reported on the French. Someone called Brussellet had obviously been helpful, though a bit patronising. Oil in the English Channel seemed the worrying question. Brussellet said that the French would probably decide to move in and start drilling in the disputed area around the median line between the Scillies and Brittany. He said it was 'rather mean' of us to dispute with them on this – although there is thought to be a large oilfield there which could be worth £100,000 million.

The Foreign Office men then all began to murmur that we ought to give way. Callaghan said he agreed, rounded on me, said he knew I was arguing to the contrary and he wanted me to state my case. In fact I didn't because others intervened. The FO men all said that we had no hope of winning anything at international arbitration and we were risking upsetting the French. It was terrible. The FO always want to give away *real* benefits in return for the intangible assets of not upsetting somebody. They would give away a whole oilfield in order to be loved at their fucking cocktail parties. I was furious, but completely isolated in the argument that followed, I told Oliver Wright that our Foreign Office had given away everything except our oil and now they were trying to give that away and it had to stop. It was about time the FO started representing our interests to foreigners, and not the other way round. It is rare for Jim to support them in this attitude. We broke up in a strained atmosphere, and I was sweating, with anger and partly no doubt from nerves.

The PM had Elliot Richardson in for lunch to celebrate his arrival as US Ambassador.

Joe and I were not invited. But Marcia had invited herself and George Weidenfeld. Joe was angry and insisted he should attend. I would have done the same, except I had agreed to go to lunch with the Israeli Ambassador. This was not a great success. It was right out in Swiss Cottage and took hours to get there. Also the food was awful. But Carol came – so I had a chance to talk to her about domestic matters which we had not been able to deal with for days. And I sat next to the wife of Carl Foreman, the film director, and she was both bright and pretty.

Dashed back to No. 10 after lunch to get on with the steel brief. I gave a lift to Jennie Lee, the former Arts minister and widow of Nye Bevan, as another guest. I had not met her before. She seemed conceited and boring. Perhaps an off day.

When I arrived the Americans were just leaving so I had time to talk to Richardson and especially to Ron Spiers, the new minister, who I like a lot.

Joe had a row with the PM coming down the stairs. HW agreed yesterday that Joe should do his big speech next weekend. We had discussed some themes and ideas and Joe had already done notes. But Marcia had subsequently got at HW and got him to agree that she and Peter Davis should have a role in writing it. Davis then telephoned Joe, who explained what he had in mind for the speech. Davis then passed on these ideas to Marcia, who passed them on to HW as their brilliant creations. HW then agreed that Davis and Marcia should do the speech along those lines. When Joe heard this he questioned HW, who was evasive and guilty-looking. So Joe snapped, 'They can do the bloody speeches, I'm not having anything to do with it,' and stalked off.

Later Peter Davis came in and sat in Marcia's room attempting to concoct a speech. She always does this when she has been out of favour. She intervenes on a speech, claims she has brilliant ideas and brings in one of her allies to try to demonstrate that HW doesn't need Joe. It is predictable and usually successful in the short run – except of course that they simply cannot do a high-level speech and HW will end up having to do it himself.

HW left early for Chequers. I worked in the Unit on the steel brief and we finally finished it at 9.30 p.m. The whole Unit worked on it very intensively, and I was pleased with the result. I felt so wound up that I did not want to go straight to bed. So I telephoned Carol and we went out for a couple of pints at the local pub. Still the most relaxing activity I know.

But really I am exhausted. Feel I have used up very deep reserves of strength. Will have to rest and sleep a lot this weekend in order to restore my batteries for Dublin.

Incidentally in the EEC briefing this morning HW spoke throughout as if he was for staying in Europe and the government would conclude that way. At one point he said, 'The floating voters are with us now.' When Callaghan again spoke of an inconclusive Summit and the possibility of another meeting afterwards, HW chipped in that he did not want that and would rather work through Tuesday night to get an agreement.

## Monday 10 March 1975

Off to Dublin for the EEC Summit. Took off in a Comet from London airport at 10. It was grey and drizzling with rain, but cleared as we approached Ireland.

On the plane I read briefs and also worked with the others on a draft of the PM's proposed statement to the Summit on steel and our need to control private investment. He said he liked the Policy Unit's brief and had used it in his draft – especially our view that the only way to maintain some sovereignty in this area without amending the Treaty was in fact to extend public ownership.

The scene on the PM's plane on one of these flights is quite special. People are buzzing around, reading, discussing and drafting papers. Secretaries are typing. Groups of people stand around the PM's seat and put suggestions. Girls are dashing about serving refreshments. Time passes rapidly. We had descended very low over the Irish coast before we settled down in our seats. Ireland looked lovely, green and fresh in bright sunshine. Then we all shipped off in the familiar cavalcade of large black cars. I sat with Tom McNally and McCaffrey from the Foreign Office. We felt that in an IRA ambush we could all plead our Irish ancestors.

Went straight to the hotel – the Burlington, a new one, out on the Wicklow Road. Comfortable, but indistinguishable from any other hotel in the rest of the world. We had lunch there. Then Joe and I *walked* to the Castle. Gave me some fresh air and also refreshed my memory of Dublin, as we walked with the ghosts of Yeats, Joyce and St John Gogarty down Baggot Street and past St Stephen's Green.

The Castle is ideal for the meeting. Huge, secure and with every facility. From the beginning it is clear that the Irish are organising it well.

We had a quick briefing meeting and then Wilson and Callaghan went into the famous Patrick's Chamber where the meeting was being held – small and elegant. They sat in alphabetical order around the table, just the PM and the foreign minister from each country. Fortunately the French and Germans sat next to one another, which is essential if we are to get the compromise we need.

The afternoon session on the EEC Budget did not go well. They were pursuing very complicated formulae proposed by the Germans. Nobody could understand them and anyway they did not meet our needs. Basically we wanted the EEC commissioners' original proposals, but amended to take out limitations on our rebates based on a two-thirds formula and also to take out provisions where we would get nothing if we were in balance-of-payments surplus. The Germans, who would have to foot the bill, were agreeable to our position, but wanted a ceiling of £125 million – which would diminish in value with inflation and the rise in the EEC Budget. The French insisted on the balance-of-payments qualification.

By dinner they had made no progress whatsoever. The Heads ate separately at the Irish PM's residence, Iveagh House. We all ate there as well, but in a separate room. After dinner they were due to go back to the Castle to resume business. But in fact they stayed at the dinner table till very late negotiating – except for the Italian Premier, Moro,* who wandered off to the Castle, got lost and was not recovered till very late.

The advisers hung around in their dining-room and some became noticeably drunk. I mixed with the Germans in order to try to discover their sticking-points. As usual their men were impressive but humourless, and their women attachments were ravishing.

The Heads of Government came out at nearly midnight and went into a lounge for coffee and brandy. HW took us into a large lavatory – the PM, the Foreign Secretary and six senior advisers – and we discussed the latest position. We agreed that the latest German suggestions were still not good enough and we must aim to get back to the Commission's proposals and then amend them.

When HW returned from the lavatory conference to the lounge he was greeted with a chorus of 'Happy Birthday' – it was after midnight and already his 59th birthday.

They broke towards 1 a.m. and we set off. I went with Tom McCaffrey to the Shelbourne and we sat drinking with journalists till 3 a.m. I stuck to vodka and orange to avoid hangover. But it was after 3 when I got to bed – and had to be up early in the morning!

*Tuesday 11 March 1975*

Dull breakfast in bed. Listened to the Irish radio – where the first news item was that eight IRA prisoners who had appeared in court on a charge of attempting to escape from court had again escaped from the court!

Into the Castle by 9.30 and had a briefing before the session at 10.

HW was in good form and seemed confident. Callaghan was very good in briefings, forcing the officials to explain the latest complicated formulae in very simple terms.

After the session began, Joe and I slipped out and strolled down the quays by the Liffey. We went into a junk shop and bought some old stamps. The proprietor invited us into the back room, where he had a blazing fire and made us coffee. He chatted away with a string of stories. He frequently said he was 'a peaceful man' as a prelude to some heroic story of how he had knocked some desperate fellow clean out of the Hibernian Hotel.

Joe and I lost track of time and we scurried back to the Castle only to find that we were late for the mid-morning briefing. We decided not to try to explain to HW, who might not have been sympathetic.

The morning session dragged on until 1.30 p.m. They had made virtually no progress on the main issues of the budget and New Zealand cheese, but at least they cleared off the other agenda items.

We had a standing buffet. The Heads ate separately – and the Irish produced a birthday cake for HW. He was immensely touched and came dashing out to take us into the lavatory to tell us – he also told Joe to inform the press!

The afternoon session began at 3 and they then went on right through the evening. We were depressed at the lack of progress but it was a fascinating scene. We waited in groups outside the chamber. Prime Ministers and Foreign Secretaries would come wandering out to take their advisers into corners. It was like an oriental market, with a buzz of different languages; long slack periods; and then a rush of excitement as people came out with more news.

At 5.30 p.m. HW came out and took us to our delegation room. He said they were in deadlock, unable to find the formula to meet all our needs.

The German Chancellor Schmidt – who looked ill and tired from his recent pneumonia – was leaving at 6.30. But the German Ambassador had told us not to worry – they were working on a formula which would do the trick.

I saw Schmidt leave, wearing his Hamburg fisherman's cap and looking very morose.

Then HW came out, and Jim, with details of the German proposal and a formula devised by the French President Giscard to meet us on the balance of payments. It looked satisfactory and suddenly everything rushed to a settlement – with New Zealand cheese swept in with it. The tension lifted, everybody was rushing about laughing and drinking, and then dashing off to the airport.

The British stayed and ate more buffet at the Castle. Joe and I felt happy and sat on the famous throne drinking champagne, last used officially by George V.

I went with HW and Joe to a series of press conferences and then went off with Tom McNally and McCaffrey to various bars. I finally got in at 2.45 a.m. feeling very pleased with life. Dublin was looking beautiful. The Irish had managed things marvellously. The EEC had performed well. The British had got all they wanted. It was quite clear from how they spoke that HW and Jim Callaghan were wholly committed to staying in the Market – though they hid this in public.

### Wednesday 12 March 1975

Set off late for Dublin airport. Fortunately we picked up the PM's cavalcade, otherwise might have missed the plane.

On the way back I worked on the PM's statement to Parliament that afternoon.

HW was still in high spirits. He said how good it was to get away from London.

Back in Downing Street at 12.30 and I had to leave immediately for the LSE where I was having lunch with the director, Ralf Dahrendorf, and Reg Prentice. Dahrendorf was brilliant, but some of the professors present were old, pompous and unimpressive.

Back to the Cabinet Office for a 2.30 meeting of permanent secretaries to discuss co-ordination of policies on Poverty. Then across to the House at 3 to discuss the PM's draft statement. This was only finally typed at 3.29 – and he went into the Chamber to give it at 3.30.

A quiet reaction. The anti-marketeers on the Labour benches seem resigned to the fact that the PM and the Cabinet and Parliament will decide to stay in the EEC. Their objective is now the *PLP* and the *referendum*.

We all dashed back for talks with Pierre Trudeau at 4.30, which continued till after 6. Trudeau was very impressive – quick, sharp, perceptive and often very amusing. The people around him were good too. They give an impression that Canada is really going places. I took the chance to talk again to Bob Murdoch, whom I had met in Ottawa six weeks ago (it seems a lifetime).

Afterwards we gave a dinner for Prime Minister Trudeau. Very successful We had invited a much wider selection of people than usual – showbiz, sport, intellectuals – and the whole thing went with a bang. I left with Carol at 1.30 and it was still going on. HW was obviously enjoying it enormously, though he had had so little sleep that his eyelids were hooded down, almost completely hiding his eyes.

Marcia sat haughtily in a corner talking to Weidenfeld (who was her escort) and Hugh and Antonia Fraser. She always makes a fuss about not enjoying these occasions – though not such a big fuss as she makes if she is not invited!

Joe told me Marcia had instructed the PM that she and Albert must go with him to the Jamaica Summit and I must not. Apparently she was in a very bad mood when he returned from Dublin – as always when he has had a big success. But then, according to Bill Housden, she took several purple hearts and became euphoric for a while.

Joe also told me the full 'royalty' story, which explains her fury when I was invited to Buckingham Palace. She claims that her mother is the *il–legitimate* daughter of Edward VII. One of the king's officials, named Falkender, took the blame, and that is why she took the title Falkender. But really she is in direct line to the throne – and that is why the Queen is afraid to invite her to the Palace!

# CHAPTER 12

## The EEC Crunch in Cabinet
## March–Easter 1975

### Thursday 13 March 1975

Felt desperately tired in the morning. The children came into our bedroom at 6.30 and, despite Carol's efforts, we could not keep them out. I got ready slowly and did not get to No. 10 until after the Cabinet had begun. The ministers spent a long time discussing the details of the referendum. HW told me afterwards that Benn wanted to start campaigning immediately, even before the Cabinet takes its decision (next Monday and Tuesday).

I worked desperately to catch up on the backlog of papers.

Had lunch in Whitehall with Joe, and then to the House of Commons for Questions. Nothing particular came up there. The PM again said how much he disliked them.

Afterwards a second meeting with Trudeau to complete the unfinished business from yesterday.

Then a reception for the political advisers. HW was very good moving around and chatting to them. I was struck by the variety of standards among them, some very good, some poor. Marcia came and sat on the settee with Stuart Holland, Benn's friend, throughout.

I was shattered by the evening, but then had to go to a dinner in Admiralty House for Roger Bannister. Tony Crosland was there and gave a good impromptu speech. Drove home at midnight and staggered gratefully into bed.

### Friday 14 March 1975

Awoken at 6 again by the children. It was Katie's birthday and she came up with the others to open her presents.

Went in to the weekly diary meeting in the PM's study at 9.30. Mellish made a savage attack on Ted Short – he is always after Short's job as Lord President.

In the discussion at one point HW again said, in relation to the EEC, 'the floating voters are now with us' – meaning pro the Market.

Later we met to clear HW's speeches for this weekend. I stayed on alone with him afterwards and we discussed the appalling long period until the referendum. HW said he wished it was next week – and he blamed Jenkins, who had insisted that they should not introduce the referendum Bill until the renegotiations were over. Now we have to wait for the Bill to go through the House.

We discussed ways of stopping too much dissent among ministers. I suggested that he should put out the word that he is going to have a reshuffle after the referendum – and he would be influenced by how ministers had conducted themselves. This would warn the moderates not to do too much campaigning – and would prepare the way for sacking some of the extremists – not because they had taken a particular line over the Market, but because they had neglected their work in their ministries. He agreed enthusiastically. He said he would get rid of Benn, Prentice and Ross.

HW went to Wigan before lunch.

I went to lunch with Bill Woessner of the American embassy. Then back to the office to clear off my correspondence.

Robert Armstrong told me that the Chancellor intends to increase taxes by £1 billion and to cut public expenditure by the same amount. This is unavoidable, but will create a hell of a row. This is when they will regret not having cut more off Defence! Healey is going to see the 'spending ministers' next week. Grim times ahead!

Went home at 6 p.m. and collapsed into bed at 10.

## Monday 17 March 1975

Today the great day – the Cabinet meets on the EEC. I was dying to be there beforehand to see how HW was facing it, but I had broken a tooth and had to go to the dentist. When I arrived at noon it was still in full session, but reports were filtering out: Peart, previously a staunch anti, had made it clear he was now for the Market, and again the antis had foolishly attacked him, driving him further into the pro camp; Healey had shown a pro-hand; Ross still raspingly against.

Merlyn Rees came out of the Cabinet Room to look at the tapes for any news on Ireland. I asked him how it was going. He said it was OK – and revealed he is now safely pro! He said that John Morris was as well – 'He has given a commitment to Jim.' He said that HW should have a word with John Silkin, since even he was swingable. (I put this to HW at lunchtime and he said he would arrange to speak to Silkin later.)

Shirley Williams came out to telephone, and we talked briefly. She was bubbling with optimism.

Roy Jenkins came out to telephone but I did not get a chance to talk.

I was sitting outside the Cabinet with Ray Richardson, Lever's excellent adviser, who I have not seen much of lately. Marcia came out and sailed off to lunch with Lady Hartwell* of the *Daily Telegraph*. Albert said, 'She took her normal morning fistful of purple hearts before going.' She lunches frequently with Hartwell, Lord Pritchard and John Cordle, all Tories, and Weidenfeld.

I was supposed to have lunch with Will Camp* and the management of British Leyland, but I called it off at the last moment because the Cabinet went on and on – finally breaking at 1.40 p.m. It had covered all the specific manifesto negotiating points except sovereignty, which they will take tomorrow morning. Apparently it had been a very low-key meeting – as HW wanted – with statements from individuals and no fireworks.

I walked to the door with Jim Callaghan, who was looking pleased. He had put up a brilliantly ingenious suggestion: that HW should go round the Cabinet table *twice*. The first time would take views on the Market. The second would ask if people wished to register their dissent and ask for a licence to campaign against the Cabinet majority decision. This – as HW agreed later when we discussed it – will enable people like Eric Varley, possibly Silkin and Ross, to stick to their principles in opposing the EEC, but then to decide from loyalty not to oppose the Cabinet majority.

I stood outside the Cabinet Room with the PM and Janet Hewlett-Davies until well after 2 p.m. HW was clearly pleased with the Cabinet – mainly because it contained no recriminations, though the civil servants said it was rather dull by the standards of this government.

I went to lunch with Janet and then to French Railways to collect my holiday tickets. We walked back across the park, in brilliant sunshine after rain, feeling very rested after a weekend's good sleep, and delighted that this long Common Market trail has come so far without disaster. The Cabinet will clearly go well. Parliament will go well and I think the referendum will be OK. It is a triumph for HW so far. He has held the party together and put us in a position to stay in the Market. Nobody else could have done that. Some would have kept us in – and split the party. Some would have kept most of the party together (excluding the Jenkins group) but taken us out. HW has kept the balance. He has known what he intended since the Paris Summit. The problems now are the PLP and the party conference.

After lunch I worked on papers and then went to see the PM. Discussed Judith Hart (who was coming, at my suggestion, to see him this afternoon), and Commodities. Also went over the two-stage plan for tomorrow's

Cabinet. He said that Varley, with future leadership prospects, must decide not to dissent. Ross also perhaps. But anybody who was thinking of the NEC elections would have to go the other way.

He looked tired. Albert said that Marcia had seen him and attacked him against the EEC. He was pretending to her that he had not yet made up his mind. She also told him he ought to have a big press conference afterwards. Joe was against this. So were Robert and I. I went into the study with him and said it was dangerous and could go wrong. It was best to make Parliament his main platform. He obviously agreed – but was looking for somebody else to provide the excuse for turning down Marcia's suggestion. He said that if Jim opposed it he could drop it. So Robert had a word with Callaghan on the stairs (he was coming in to see Judith Hart). So Jim opposed, and HW immediately dropped it, recalling that the last time he gave a mass press conference with Jim in England was the day after devaluation in 1967 – 'and that was a disaster'. This was typical of HW. Afraid to oppose Marcia himself, he gets somebody else to do it for him.

At 5 p.m. we had the meeting of junior ministers in the state dining-room at No. 10 to report to them on the EEC. HW opened with a very flat statement, briefly summarising the negotiating achievements on the terms. He read his brief so quickly and so softly that many MPs clearly did not hear.

Seventeen ministers spoke – nine against and eight for, though some were cautious. All but one were publicly identified by their position and announced that (1) the renegotiations were a great success; (2) they had not altered their position one bit.

The exception was David Ennals,* who said he had swung to a pro position as a result of renegotiation.

The antis made the strongest speeches – Heffer, Stan Orme, Margaret Jackson, Frank Judd, Stanley Clinton-Davies* all making campaigning speeches. The leading pro-marketeers did not speak, leaving it to Bob Maclennan, Hugh Brown,* Ernie Armstrong,* etc. to make their case. Bill Rodgers was silent, as was John Harris, and David Owen spoke only about the nature of the coming campaign. This was a deliberate policy, as Bill Rodgers later told me.

But most significant was the silent majority. Gerry Fowler said these were people like him – who had changed into a 'pro' position, but preferred not to stand up and admit it.

The meeting broke up, without rancour, at 6.30 and HW went off to a long meeting of the PLP.

I had a drink with Michael Cudlipp, did some work on papers and then went home at 8.30. HW told me he was going to come back to No. 10 to dictate his statement for the Commons tomorrow, but there was no sign of him.

Not a bad day. By tomorrow lunchtime we will know the Cabinet score.

## *Tuesday 18 March 1975*

Drove in early to get there before the 9.30 Cabinet on EEC. Met Wedgie Benn in Horse Guards Parade and we walked together to No. 10. I said that it was a pity the referendum was so far ahead. He disagreed and said that it was too soon: such an issue required a really long campaign!

I stood with the ministers outside the Cabinet Room. They seemed friendly and relaxed. No sense of crisis. HW came downstairs from the study and moved among them chatting. Some of them asked for coffee to be served this morning – it never is for Cabinet, in the hope that proceedings will hurry up. Benn was the only one to order tea – and he asked for it to be served in his own personal tin mug.

Fred Peart, Shirley Williams and Barbara Castle were all late.

I then went to the office, cleared the backlog of papers and had a long briefing from David Piachaud on poverty, in advance of this afternoon's meeting.

Every so often I went into private office or to Joe, and we received reports from the secretaries who had been inside the Cabinet Room. The disappointing news was that Silkin, Varley, and then finally Ross had all spoken against. There was not a vote in the sense of paper or a show of hands. But they went around the table, each person stating his position clearly for or against. At the beginning HW and Callaghan both said they were pro; though HW claimed he had been in doubt until recently.

Varley was a particular disappointment. He has been created by HW. He is a typical Centre man, with no need to support the Left, but who should be seen to be supporting the leadership and the majority. Many of his natural constituency – Fowler, Strang,* Ennals – have decided to swallow their objections to the original entry and decide to stay in. He will offend a lot of people, to no purpose. Later I understood. Joe told me that Marcia got hold of Eric out of Cabinet during the coffee break and was ranting away at him to vote against – against HW, her boss. Gerald Kaufman, who intriguingly shares a flat with Varley, has also certainly influenced him.

Ross is a different case. He was anti, and does not change his mind easily. He also needs to outflank the Scottish Nationalists. But this may finish him as Scottish Secretary. He has few supporters, and now HW could drop him in favour of Bruce Millan. Ross's previous supporters were pro-marketeers who will now abandon him.

The final vote was 16–7 (Ross, Varley, Silkin, Foot, Castle, Shore, Benn against). Unfortunately the device of going round the table a second time and asking if they also wished to register dissent did not work to dislodge any in the minority. It was late – 1.45 – and it was done quickly. Too quickly for anybody to climb down. HW admitted after that he should have asked to see them each privately beforehand about dissenting.

I walked to the door with Jim Callaghan who said that he was very pleased and actually expected a vote of 15–8. He also pretended to HW and to me that he was surprised by John Morris's vote – but Merlyn Rees told me that Morris had pledged himself to Jim a few days ago – presumably on condition that Jim did not tell anybody.

We had lunch at No. 10 while HW revised his Commons statement in the study.

A crisis arose when we learned that (a) the dissenters were giving a press conference this afternoon and (b) various dissenting ministers were appearing on TV. We told HW and he was furious. He ordered that Ross and Varley be telephoned and told this was against the rules – and he would like to see Varley before Questions.

He also sent a message to the BBC that he would refuse to be interviewed if they put a dissenting Cabinet minister on with him. Robert phoned Charles Curran at the BBC, who replied OK but he would put on a dissenting junior minister. This was foolishly provocative. So HW blew up, just before going into the Chamber, and announced that he would not appear on BBC at all. Robert went off to phone Curran again, who gave in, and the BBC later interviewed Douglas Jay.* Then instructions were sent to all private offices saying that no ministers must appear at all on television that night, and that any junior minister who wished to dissent must register it with No. 10. This was all done in great haste and flap while HW was going into the Chamber. By the time I went in with Robert, HW was already halfway through Questions. These went quite well, with nobody really interested – though I was interested to see Ted Heath back for the first time, looking very sour and unhappy sitting all alone. HW welcomed him back but took the opportunity to use him to attack Mrs Thatcher.

His statement took half an hour to read, and then 45 minutes of questions followed. Curiously low-key and good-humoured. HW rode the questions comfortably. There was a clear sense that Parliament were decisively in favour and that the referendum would be OK.

Afterwards we went back to HW's room and he was so delighted to have it over that he offered drinks to everybody. Jim Callaghan and Tom McNally came in briefly before going off to a press conference at Lancaster House.

I returned to the Civil Service Department for a meeting on World Poverty with the three most senior permanent secretaries, Douglas Allen, John Hunt and Douglas Wass. David Piachaud had prepared an excellent paper for me.

Douglas Allen supported me and the paper throughout the meeting (I suspected because he wanted it off his hands). Wass expressed doubts about involvement in more spending – though we were not proposing much. And Hunt looked troubled and said he was troubled. In the end I got what I wanted, which was that the Policy Unit should continue to handle it, direct to the PM. These three top mandarins were not as impressive as usual on this occasion, though I felt they were trying to be helpful and did not want to be exposed as being too negative. Really it is an impossible issue.

I went back to No. 10 at 6.30 and briefly saw the PM. He had just completed his TV interviews including that with the BBC – and apparently all went well.

I then worked in the Unit till 8.30 p.m., preparing a brief with Andrew and David on two-tier petrol pricing – which we oppose – and on abolishing vehicle excise duty, which we support, and on the Budget, where we want something more positive than just cuts in public expenditure and rises in taxes: we especially want aids to investment and retraining.

Came home feeling very jaunty and bright. Have now had three early nights in succession and the effect on my system is remarkable. My brain is really working quite quickly.

– P.S. the PM was very pleased when I said, 'Ted Heath took the British Establishment into the Market. You will take in the British people.'

## *Wednesday 19 March 1975*

Cabinet committee on Economic Strategy – Andrew Graham attended.

Afterwards HW took Denis Healey to his room where Healey revealed his plans to cut public expenditure by £1,000 million and asked permission to bring this to tomorrow's Cabinet – with a late paper. He also, Robert told me, said he was worried about leaks from the Treasury, and he accused me and the Unit of leaking. I did not know this till they had gone off to the PLP meeting on economic policy. I was furious and wanted to go and see Healey and tell him not to make such allegations without evidence. But I cooled down, and promised Robert not to, since it would make it clear that he had told me what happened. Still it shows Healey in a poor light. Everybody knows the Treasury is leaky as a drain, including Denis himself. It was pretty poor behaviour to accuse somebody behind their back to the Prime Minister, and absolutely without evidence.

Went to lunch with Lord Stokes and Barber at British Leyland. They explained the historical background of their troubles, and claimed that given time they would get it right. They are very critical of the banks and the City, who they claim do not understand industry.

Worked in the Unit during the afternoon. The PM saw Forbes Burnham, and afterwards had Tommy Balogh to his study in order, through him, to convey to Varley his disappointment about the EEC. I saw Tommy afterwards and said I thought it was terrible that the PM's closest friends were against him and Varley must *publicly* make it clear that he is not campaigning with the Left.

Went up to the study with Joe and chatted with the PM. We came back to this theme of his being abandoned by his friends and those he had personally promoted. The PM agreed. He said 'even Charlie Morris'*. It goes back to his first PPS, Barbara Castle, and includes Morris, Fernyhough, Kaufman, Varley, Balogh, Shore – none of them would be where they are without HW.

He then began to get angry and said that none of the junior ministers who have joined in this will get promotion. He added that Willie Ross and Barbara were 'very vulnerable'. He said he might promote Brian O'Malley* in Castle's place and Bruce Millan instead of Ross at the Scottish Office. [In fact James Callaghan dropped both Castle and Ross when he succeeded Wilson as Premier in 1976.] He then added that he would get rid of Prentice at the same time as getting rid of Benn.

At 8 p.m. he went across the House for votes. I worked in the Unit with Andrew Graham and David Piachaud on a brief on Healey's public expenditure paper. This latter was a terrible botched job, just a list of random cuts cobbled together by the permanent secretaries. Showed no sign of thought, of 12 months dealing with the problem. Superficial – just £1,000 million across the board, including investment.

I went home shortly after 10. After 11 Joe telephoned. The PM had just learned that the anti-marketeers had put down a motion at the NEC attacking him. He attacked Joe, and blamed Joe and me for not having warned him of this in our earlier talk. (I did not know – Albert had forgotten to tell me.) He shouted at Joe, 'This is the end. It is the end. The end for all of you as well as me.' Joe said he was unfair, and put the phone down.

HW then, we learned after, summoned Foot, Castle and Callaghan from their beds to his room. He blasted off so savagely at Castle that she offered her resignation, which he did not accept.

He did not get to bed until 2.30. And in the morning (Bill Housden told me today) was in a worse mood than he had ever seen him. 'Not even reading the newspapers,' said Bill.

*Thursday 20 March 1975*

Dramatic day. I went up to the study at 9.45 am. The PM was there, looking grey and angry. Ron Hayward had already been and gone – having been told, I gathered later, that the PM would not tolerate an NEC motion against his Common Market line, with the party organisation then campaigning against him. The PM just barked, 'I am waiting for the Lord President.' So I withdrew.

He went into Cabinet at 10.30 and ordered that no officials attend. The Cabinet then discussed the situation. HW began, I was told, by criticising the way the dissenters were conducting matters. This discussion continued for a while and then HW walked out and went upstairs to his study, leaving the Cabinet in charge of Short. This was his hint to them that he was willing to resign. Short went up to see him at one point, and Callaghan at another. The Cabinet continued until after midday on this one item, with the PM out of the room most of the time.

I waited outside Cabinet for a while and chatted to ministers as they came out for a break – especially to Shirley Williams. They all seemed a bit depressed.

At one point HW went into Marcia's room and Joe went in to join them. Joe said that the close friends of HW who were now campaigning against him – Kaufman, Varley, Charlie Morris, Balogh, etc. – should be ashamed of themselves. Marcia blew up and said they were doing the right thing, and the people who should be ashamed were Joe and the people he talked to – meaning me. Joe got angry and asked her to name them. As always when confronted directly, she didn't answer. So Joe walked out and slammed the door. HW said nothing in this exchange, but later told Joe that he agreed, they ought to be ashamed. (But not in front of Marcia of course.)

We had lunch upstairs in a climate of crisis. Afterwards to the House for Questions. The PM was still angry, but beginning to relax more.

Questions went reasonably well, considering we all feared he would make some mistakes and mix it with Thatcher while he was so distracted. In fact she still looks scared stiff and does not take him on. The Labour ranks were very thin.

I went back to No. 10 to get on with work and then went to a reception at the National Gallery to see the new Caravaggio they have acquired.

Carol came and we were due to go from there out to dinner with Brian Macarthur, an old journalist friend of ours. I telephoned to No. 10 from the Gallery as I was leaving and was told the PM had returned to the study and was there with the staff. So I dashed hack, leaving Carol in my room, and went up. Joe was there with the whole of private office. The PM was drinking beer and had handed drinks around to the others. He was remarkably relaxed – though deeply tired. He had decided to go to Chequers to spend the day tomorrow, calling off his engagements at No. 10. He even talked of going walking with the dog, but we all knew he would end up dictating speeches.

I raised with him the fear – which Harold Lever had phoned me about, and which I already had – that if the motion in the Commons by the 'antis' reached 160 signatures – over half the party – this would be equal to a defeat for him on a motion of confidence. He became edgy, and said that he had dealt with that and he now expected the number of names to be *reduced*. He was under the impression that Michael Foot was now working to persuade people to take their names off. Foot was also going to try to get a more moderate motion passed at the NEC. So he was superficially more confident, his tactic was to threaten them with the disaster of his resignation, and to use Foot to reduce the opposition. But deep down he seemed tired and unsure. His methods are still oblique. He hints at what he will do. One thing he doesn't do is to sack somebody and tell the rest they will get the same treatment. This is because he is uncertain of his power – which in my view is enormous, since without him there is no Labour government. It will break up.

Went late to Brian Macarthur's and then home at 1 a.m.

### Friday 21 March 1975

PM at Chequers – where he dictated 18 more pages of his Aberdeen speech, all devoted to explaining the guidelines of how dissenters should behave, including the hint of a later reshuffle.

I spent an hour with Ronnie McIntosh discussing the proposed NEDC study of the Nationalised Industries. Tried to firm him up to resist Whitehall pressure to make the study narrow and meaningless.

Had lunch with my staff at the Little French Club. Worked afterwards on the PM's speech, in the Cabinet Room with Joe, Robert and Robin. Then I went to Oxford for a feast at Nuffield College. Sat next to Len Murray and lobbied him in favour of the NEDC study of the nationalised industries. Talked to Tony Crosland, who was very sceptical of whether HW would ever discipline anybody, or even hold a reshuffle.

And I talked to Ted Heath! He was very sticky at first. But I got him talking about the Civil Service, and he was very critical, saying that the servicing at No. 10 was inadequate and that a PM did need outside advisers to keep an eye on the mandarins.

### Monday 24 March 1975

PM did not arrive from Chequers till nearly midday. So I worked on my papers in the Unit.

There was a Cabinet committee at midday on Energy – security of atomic fuels and the proposal to have a two-tier petrol price. I decided not to attend and apparently they did not decide anything, since the Treasury put up a smoke-screen against any changes. Even the proposal to abolish vehicle excise duty, which makes sense from any point of view, was blocked by the Treasury – despite the fact that everybody supported recouping the lost tax from petrol duty.

I went to lunch at the Reform with Bob Worcester of MORI, who wants to do some polls in the referendum campaign. He also mentioned the bad reaction to the PM's lunch with the new American Ambassador Elliot Richardson when Weidenfeld and another were invited – both directors of Weidenfeld.

HW is going to Northern Ireland tomorrow. He arranged this last week when totally fed up over the activities of the anti-Market ministers. He said last Thursday, 'Bugger them, they can stew.' And also added that it would be a proper punishment for Barbara Castle, who would be arguing for a pensions uprating, and without his support would probably lose. Joe said that HW is tired and fed up with it all. This is why he likes to go away on foreign trips – to get away from his colleagues.

Just before lunch I saw Eric Varley and we walked out into Downing Street together. He was more optimistic on the conduct of the EEC campaign. But he said Barbara Castle was 'the most extreme of them all'.

After lunch I went up to the PM's study and with Joe and Patrick Wright from private office we discussed HW's speech in Belfast tomorrow. I was very unhappy with the draft. Completely pro-Protestant. No sense of the 'Irish dimension'. Appeared to promise to underwrite the Protestants whatever they did, with no sense of a policy beyond the Convention. So we changed the balance a bit. HW said that the Northern Ireland Office – who are all Protestants – are trying to push him back from his more positive Irish policy.

HW then had a string of meetings – with Harry Kissin, with Prime Minister Ecevit of Turkey, with Poniatowski from France, and then a long meeting with Healey, Callaghan, Crosland, Jenkins, etc. about the economic and the party situation.

I walked out into Downing Street with Tony Crosland. He is cheerful at the moment, conscious that H. Wilson approves of him – actually believes he will emerge as the next leader. I am not sure about that, but it is clear that he would be made Chancellor of the Exchequer if Healey went now. Crosland expressed doubts about the way Healey is conducting the Exchequer. Healey, although at times very impressive, operates in snatches, erratically, with no sense of continuing dominance.

The PM gave a reception for the people who worked on the Moorgate tube disaster. I did not go to it because there was a flood of papers and I wanted to clear my desk. But I went to the evening dinner at No. 10 for the Governor of the Bank of England and various City dignitaries to discuss the economy. Not very enlightening. The PM said afterwards that they were 'a boring lot'.

After they had gone, at around midnight Robert, John Hunt and I stood around upstairs and discussed the Crossman Diaries and the proposal to set up a committee of Privy Councillors to review the rules governing memoirs of ex-ministers and civil servants. It is quite clear that their intention is to get a tightening of the rules. They are having great difficulties finding Privy Councillors who have any knowledge of the problems and needs of the writing of contemporary history. The PM wants Charlie Pannell,* Michael Stewart and as many judges as can be obtained. I pressed for Edward Boyle, Julian Amery and having some respectable historians – Asa Briggs and Robert Blake – at least as assessors. The outlook is not good. When I suggested the 30-year rule might be eased a little, Hunt nearly went through the roof.

Home just before 1 a.m.


*Tuesday 25 March 1975*

PM went to Northern Ireland today. So I took the opportunity to go to the bank and arrange various matters – including depositing another eight notebooks of this diary and applying to the Bank of England for permission to do some repairs on my French house.

To the office and dealt with papers, letters, etc. and began preparing our brief on commodities in advance of the Commonwealth PMs' Conference.

Went to lunch with Harold Lever.

Joe tells me that Marcia is mounting another attack on me – mainly because she wants to stop me going to the Jamaica Summit and to get Albert there instead. What petty games they play.

Worked in the afternoon. HW returned from Ulster at 6 p.m. but I hid up the passageway to the press office so I would not be caught up in long meetings and then slipped out. Went home early to collect Carol and take her and Will and Veronica Plowden to a delightful Michael Frayn play at the Hampstead Theatre Club.

The Cabinet met for much of today. This is the meeting that the PM wanted to miss – this is why he went to Northern Ireland.

Apparently it went quite briskly under Ted Short. The main item was Denis Healey's Treasury paper suggesting cuts of £1,000 million in public expenditure. It was really a disgraceful paper. Not because of cuts in public expenditure, which I support. But because it is so crude. No figures. No strategy behind it. No argument. Just a broad cut across everything. No more sophisticated than in 1966.

Apparently Tony Crosland made a brilliant and devastating attack on it. Pity HW wasn't there – this was Crosland's bid for the Treasury if Healey falls.

But Jenkins, Callaghan – as ex-Chancellors – and Shore supported Healey. Even Lever, though on the ground that it was better than raising taxes.

The Cabinet met all morning and again in the evening at 5 p.m. I mixed and chatted as usual with the ministers. The atmosphere is remarkably relaxed and friendly – none of the hysteria and animosity which the press claims is present.

HW came in at 6 while the Cabinet was still sitting. But he didn't want them to know he was here, certainly not to go into Cabinet, so he slipped up to the flat in the lift, changed into a dinner jacket, and slipped out again to attend some Gilbert and Sullivan at the Savoy. He finds G&S preferable to the Cabinet – though not too dissimilar I imagine.

## Wednesday 26 March 1975

The PM went to Transport House this morning for the crucial National Executive meeting on the EEC. He was fairly confident beforehand that he would get an amendment to the critical motion which was going to commit the party organisation to campaign against the government. He has put the pressure on Ron Hayward who is, as always, desperately trying to be on everybody's side. Jim Callaghan has also done some splendid lobbying. HW has done little. Joe says he used to do more in these situations, but now he could not care too much, because he is getting fed up with it all.

I spent the morning with Tom McNally and John Lycon from the Commonwealth Secretariat, discussing the coming conference at Kingston. They want the PM to speak on special advisers, and Tom and I are proposing to brief him. Callaghan is strongly in favour.

We are also in the Unit working on Commodities and on World Poverty, which will be on the Commonwealth Prime Ministers' agenda, so the case for me going to Kingston is very strong. But apparently Marcia is still telling HW that he must not take me. I would like to go, and think it will be silly if she stops me; but don't care much either way.

Had lunch with Joe at the Commons. We are both very tired, looking forward to the Easter holiday and a bit depressed. The PM still seems below par. He has done several *party-political* things without consulting either of us – including allowing Robert to draft the guidelines for ministers in the EEC campaign and writing threatening letters to dissenting ministers. The NEC went fairly well. HW secured an amendment which meant that the party organisation, like ministers, could go various ways in the campaign. It would not be committed to campaigning one way or another. But Shirley Williams told me this afternoon that it was a terrible meeting, messy and nasty, and the PM had not supported her in her battle with Benn at the NEC. The odd thing is that HW still sees himself as fighting a *middle* course between the pro-marketeers and the antis. He does not seem to have adjusted to the fact that he and the government have now publicly joined the pros! There is no middle way now.

At 4 p.m. I went to the Cabinet committee on Industrial Development (IDV). Benn was proposing to spend £5 million to take a stake in Ferranti, which is allegedly bankrupt. It is six months since he last brought this one to committee and nothing has been done since, except to lose a lot more money. Nearly everybody attacked Benn – especially the PM, who was savagely contemptuous in some of his remarks. Healey also led an effective attack and maintained it consistently. Benn was clearly beaten. It was decided to put Don Ryder in, now he has finished with British Leyland, to negotiate to buy Ferranti and then to try to put it right. He was authorised to put it into receivership if that was the only way to bring the Ferranti brothers to heel.

Incidentally I am more and more worried about Ryder. HW treats him as the whiz-kid who can solve all problems. In fact he seems prepared to take on everything and to have more than a touch of megalomania.

The PM left in the middle of the meeting and went to do some TV recordings. Healey took over while they discussed the problem of providing more and better information on firms in trouble. The discussion became totally disorganised (not Healey's fault). They rambled all over the place, Benn talked a great deal. In the end they took the right decision to systematise the information coming to them, but it was a terrible discussion. The holidays are necessary.

I went back to the Unit to complete my brief for the Kingston Summit and also a draft on Commodities. The PM went to the Palace for his audience so I went home to write this and get an early night.

Am looking forward to going on holiday to France tomorrow. The government feels terribly messy.

# CHAPTER 13

## The Budget – and Preparing
## for the Referendum
## April 1975

*Monday 7 April 1975*

B ack from France late on Sunday night. Had a lovely holiday – but very cold. Also telephoned Kissin, near Nice, who told me that when he visited HW just before Easter he kept complaining about leaks to the press and made it clear he meant me. Kissin warned me that he got the impression from HW that my telephone was tapped.

Ridiculous about press leaks, considering the trouble I take *not* to talk to old friends who are journalists. If I ever did talk – what a story!

Went into the office and started working through the mass of papers accumulated over the holiday. Also had talks with the Unit about the Budget, where we fear a very negative approach next week. Decide to brief in advance. Try to get something positive especially on investment. The irony is that I support many of Benn's policies on investment. We need some Bennery without Benn.

The PM came in mid-morning. We gathered in the study – Joe, Robert and Nick Stuart from private office, Pat Nairne from the Cabinet Office and me. Discussed the PM's speech to open this afternoon's EEC debate. Very good speech, with few problems.

Joe and I then went to lunch to the Commons. He said HW was trying to trap Benn into resignation by not giving him the right to make appointments to the NEB.

Apparently Marcia went to the Scillies over Easter to stay with HW – she was flown there in Eric Miller's private plane. As a result, HW did not phone Joe once. If she had not been there, HW would have been on the phone constantly.

HW's speech went quite well, with very few interruptions. The dissenting ministers were absent from the front bench, except for Eric Varley, who is apparently now trying to show his loyalty.

Went back to the office with Robert and then worked on papers and letters. Had a long discussion in the Unit with Andrew Graham and

David Piachaud about the Budget. Preparing a brief.

Home at 8.30 to an empty house – Carol and the children are in Suffolk.

## Tuesday 8 April 1975

Graham Greene arrived at 8.45 a.m. with his American lawyer to collect me, to discuss the problem of the American attack on the British publishers' sales agreement, which the Americans see as anti-Trust. We drove to the Ritz and had breakfast. Graham said that things had improved since I sent the minute from No. 10 to the Board of Trade. When the Publishers Association went to see the Board of Trade recently the civil servants had this minute on the desk.

Amusingly, Graham said that George Weidenfeld had insisted that nothing would happen unless he were appointed emissary to Marcia to raise the issue and that I was quite the wrong person to use.

Walked back across the park in the cold sunshine to No. 10 and went in to a Cabinet committee on Energy. On BNOC, on the Burmah Oil situation – which is bad – and on North Sea oil participation. Very subdued. Just reports from ministers and little discussion. HW looked very grey in the chair, as if his mind was on something else. Not at all rejuvenated by his holiday. Probably the EEC question is weighing him down.

After that was Cabinet, which went badly. On the date of the referendum, Willie Ross is being very difficult, saying that the new Scottish local authorities won't be ready to carry out the referendum until the end of June. We are committed to having it as soon as possible – 5 June. The Cabinet decided to push the Scots, but Willie was obdurate and pessimistic.

They also discussed the question of ministers *voting* against the government in tomorrow's EEC vote. It was *never* HW's intention that they should do this. The 'agreement to differ' was to allow them to *campaign* in the *country* and excluded Parliament. But this was never made explicit and now the dissenters insisted on voting against. HW wanted to forbid this, and Jim Callaghan was strongly against. But they got little support. Crucial was the fact that Healey supported the dissenters.

I went to lunch with Joe at the Commons. We discussed industrial and economic policy. I am very worried about the Budget – Healey seems to have no strategy.

Afterwards Question Time. Very little interest. HW seemed relaxed enough and said he was 'feeling skittish'. In the Chamber most of the questions were on the splits in the government, with lots of attacks from our own back benches over the gag on dissenting ministers speaking in the debate.

Went back to No. 10 and later saw Joe Saxe from the World Bank, and then home to have dinner with our close friends the Grahams.

## Wednesday 9 April 1975

Came in late. The PM was at Windsor with the Queen. Then he saw John Silkin about his land nationalisation plans and after that spent an hour with Harold Lever, who was worried about Healey's Budget.

Lever came to see me beforehand. He seemed nervous and tired. He said he dare not tell me what was in the Budget and therefore could not discuss with me what he was going to say to the PM. (In fact I know what is in the Budget and will be told what he says to the PM.) I was saddened to see dear old Harold Lever so intimidated. I still love him best of all the politicians, but I wish he had a little more steel.

Went to lunch at the Etoile with my old friend Clifford Barclay and the new director of the LSE, Ralf Dahrendorf – who is as brilliant and attractive as ever.

Back to No.10 to have my smallpox inoculation for the trip to Jamaica. Joe Stone did it in the press office. Joe Haines, Janet and I had privileged treatment.

I went back to my room and Robert Armstrong came up to see me. He said the PM had taken him on one side in the study that morning and then, very furtively, had said he wanted me to be taken off the list for Jamaica. He said he wanted me to be in charge while he was away, to monitor the EEC developments for him.

I was naturally furious. This was a cowardly lie. It was because Marcia had insisted, as Joe had informed me in advance. But HW did not have the guts to tell me himself. Nor even to tell Joe, who he knew would have said what he thought of it. It is a typically petty thing. But it does humiliate me in front of officials who have seen the circulated list of the Prime Minister's advisers and then see my name removed on his instructions It damages my credibility in Whitehall – and is intended to.

At first I wanted to go straight over to the Commons to confront him. But Robert – and Joe who joined us – advised against. So I waited and worked in the office.

At 7.15 Joe and I went over to the Commons to hear the EEC debate. We particularly wanted to hear Eric Heffer, who was going to break the guidelines and, as a minister, attack the government. HW is then going to sack him.

I sat in and heard Heffer – who was not very good – and then went for a drink with Tom McNally. Ironically, he told me that Callaghan was very keen that I should go to Jamaica so that Tom and I could prepare the paper on special advisers, which will be a major item of discussion there. After all, I am the senior special adviser in Whitehall.

I went back with Tom at 9.30 to go into the official box to hear Callaghan wind up. But there was only room for one, so Tom went in and I went back towards the PM's room. In the corridor I met Eric Varley and we sat down to talk. He seemed very nervous, almost emotional and obviously not happy about voting against the EC membership.

As we were talking Marcia came up. She chatted away merrily, having just had dinner with HW, and then I said I wanted a word with her. We went into the PM's room. I shut the door. She looked worried and began to talk about Varley. I said I wanted to talk about Jamaica. Had she opposed my going? She began to shout and scream. She shouted that she did not want to talk to me now and she never wanted to talk to me again. I repeated my question and she screamed that she had never discussed Jamaica, who went was nothing to do with her, and she had never heard who was going until this evening.

I said that I was not sure I believed her. She then began screaming incoherently and opened the door to get out. I stuck out my leg and slammed it shut with my foot. She shouted repeatedly that she had nothing to do with it and didn't want to know anything about it and then she fled from the room.

I went out into the corridor. She sat in the adjacent secretaries' room, abusing me to her secretary Doreen Andrews, Albert and Bill. She kept shouting, 'He is a nasty piece of work.'

I walked towards the Chamber when I heard her shout. She came up the corridor and began ranting very loudly.

John Silkin came up with his wife to say hello and she denounced me to him. Then Lever came out of the lift and she told him that I had called her a liar, and tears were welling up in her eyes. I said very little. She ran back down the corridor.

I walked off with Lever, who was going to the Chamber. He pretended that nothing had happened. Probably it is a question of age and experience. When I am older I shall learn to swallow this shit and nonsense in order to get on with bigger things. Not yet though.

I walked back to No.10 and sat down, at 10 o'clock, to dictate a memorandum to the PM attacking the Chancellor's proposals to cut public investment and suggesting that what we need is *more* capital investment not less. This is also meant to be an attack on the rest of Healey's deflationary Budget, the details of which we pretend not to know. In conclusion I pressed the PM at least to *talk* to Healey about the Budget. Not with any great hope. Really the PM is not interested. He wants to wash his hands of economic policy – leave it to Healey to carry the can.

Incidentally, Joe tells me that HW now wants Crosland as his successor.

[On 9 April 1975 the House of Commons approved by a majority of 226 the government's recommendation that Britain should continue its membership of the European Community. A majority of Labour MPs (145) voted against the Labour government's recommendation, including seven Cabinet ministers and over 20 junior ministers.

On the following day Edward Short, the Lord President, introduced the second reading of the Bill providing for a referendum to be held on 5 June 1975. It was passed by a majority of 64 and went through its third reading on 24 April and through the House of Lords on 6 May 1975.]

## Thursday 10 April 1975

Took my time going in to No.10. Reflecting on last night I think it all a bit farcical, but am delighted I put the boot in. I don't want to fight about trips to Jamaica, or anywhere, which are trivial. But am delighted to confront her. It was striking how *petrified* she was when faced with a direct question about her behaviour.

The Cabinet met on public expenditure and agreed all the cuts on social expenditure – but cut Defence by only £110 million instead of the £200 million which Healey wanted. HW supported Healey, but Mason threatened to resign, and Callaghan, Lever, Jenkins and Peart supported him. It is crazy that a Labour government always ends up giving in to the military while being ruthless not only with social services but also with investment – half the cuts were in capital formation.

We had lunch upstairs, Serena Armstrong [Robert's wife, who had replaced the original cook, sacked at Marcia's insistence] producing some marvellous roast chicken.

Then to Questions. I had thought of not attending but Joe said I must behave as normal. In fact HW behaved in a quite extraordinary way, digressing to praise me and the Policy Unit every few minutes. It was so irrelevant that I was embarrassed. Joe said it was the most marked demonstration of support for me that he had ever seen. The bizarre fact is that he *approves* of people standing up to Marcia, which he would love to do but dare not.

He said that he wanted the Unit to join with the CPRS in monitoring public expenditure and briefing the Cabinet on the political implications. This had arisen at Cabinet because of criticism – especially by Crosland, who HW has now chosen as his heir – that the economic papers presented to Cabinet by the Treasury are inadequate.

Questions went well, with HW knocking the Tories for six on several occasions.

The Cabinet committee on Economic Strategy at 4.30. To discuss the railway wage claim – on which Michael Foot recommended giving way, saying, as always, that this was not the claim on which to make a stand, but also describing a 30% settlement as OK because it was 'the going rate'. This is totally to ignore the fact that the guideline he is supposed to have agreed with the TUC is around 20% (the current rate of price increases). If any rate that is the going rate is OK, then *any* going rate must be OK – so why not 50%!

At the end Roy Jenkins said that he felt this was the last moment of a dying voluntary policy, so he saw no point in fighting it. Better to get on with the new policy for the next round. Foot replied that he did not see any reason to change the voluntary system. HW then intervened with snide and sarcastic references to 'those who want to give up the voluntary system but have nothing to replace it'. This was clearly directed at Jenkins, who looked very uncomfortable but did not reply. Crosland to his credit intervened to say that he thought the present wage situation was intolerable, he had ideas how to change it and he hoped they would have a meeting soon to discuss it.

Afterwards HW went to the Commons to work and I went home.

*Friday 11 April 1975*

Travelled in early with an artist friend, Alan Aldridge, and attended the weekly 9.30 government business meeting. Jim Callaghan was remarkably optimistic about the EEC referendum vote at the coming special party conference. Thinks it is possible to win the AUE as well as the NUR – and to get down to a very narrow vote.

Question of the Argentine threat to invade the Falkland Islands came up. All agreed that the solution was to send out Joan Lestor,* the Foreign Office junior minister, 'who' HW said 'would deter anybody'. Callaghan was against the Foreign Office policy of capitulation and wants to settle it privately with HW.

Healey left early to work on his Budget speech, which he described as 'less contentious than previously'.

Afterwards I had a long talk with HW. He referred to my not going to Jamaica, without explaining it, and then said he was very worried about leaving No. 10 unattended for ten days after the party conference. 'There is nobody here on the political side I can trust,' he said. 'I want you to use your espionage network to keep an eye on all that is going on.' Curious, since he does have a political office run by Marcia.

He then said he also wanted me to go to the United States and prepare the ground for his visit there after Jamaica. He wanted me to discuss the current financial and economic situation, to investigate the boycott of Jewish banks and to look into some international trade questions. He said he had thought of sending Lever but thought I would be better. He specifically mentioned that he wanted me to talk to David Rockefeller and Hal Sonnenfeldt, Kissinger's assistant. He was very expansive – 'Go before the weekend. Stay on after we leave. Go to New York.'

It may be a sop. An olive branch. But it will be exciting.

Went home early to see Carol and the kids, back from the country. Not a bad conclusion to an intense week.

## Monday 14 April 1975

I went in early. HW was at Lord North Street seeing Allon of Israel. He returned at 11 for the Cabinet to discuss the Budget. This went on until nearly one. When it broke I went to lunch with Harold Lever.

Before Cabinet I talked to Michael Foot, who was claiming that the top salaries award led to lots of trouble, because it made it difficult to be tough with the less well off – I don't know if this is an explanation or an excuse.

Lever told me that there had been no really serious discussion of what Healey was proposing. Crosland was silent. Benn made his points about the need for investment. The trouble is that very few of them have the knowledge to pick up the numbers straight away. Lever says Healey claimed his measure would create only 20,000 extra unemployed. This cannot be true – a deflation of £1.75 billion in this fragile economic climate must do worse than that.

My view is that it is a negative Budget, solving a few, but not enough things in the short run and nothing in the long run. In fact it can be argued that there is nothing anybody can do about the short run until the wages question is dealt with. So we might as well ignore it and at least try to get the long run right.

Lever is very jittery about being excluded from receiving papers and from attending so many committees. This is the doing of the Treasury and the Cabinet Office. Though I have noticed Wilson cool about him recently. Lever said HW is 'more paranoid than ever about press leaks'. In fact he is the victim of a wider freeze-out – which is disgraceful in view of how often he has been right.

In the afternoon I worked on my papers.

Saw Ken Berrill in the evening to discuss the CPRS proposal to present better papers on public expenditure. He said that everybody was furious with the Treasury for putting out such crude proposals at the last moment. This was an opportunity to achieve more *collective* government in economic affairs – something I have been working for.

John Hunt phoned to ask if he could circulate our Unit paper on commodities – which the PM had praised fulsomely in a minute to him.

Home at 11 p.m.

Tomorrow the Budget, which could crack the party further. The PM has taken little part in it and shown little interest – Lever told me that when he went to talk to HW about the Budget, he did not ask a single question or make a single comment. Yet it could destroy him.

## Tuesday 15 April 1975

Budget day. Very few papers coming through; government business seems to have come almost to a halt. I went off to the Central Council for Physical Recreation for its general meeting and lunch at noon. Talked to Denis Howell, the cricketer Ted Dexter and the Duke of Edinburgh. Ended much earlier than I expected so I walked all the way back from Brompton Road to No. 10, in the first sun we have seen for months.

Before Questions, the PM seemed lethargic and not very interested, though still basically in good form. Questions went stickily. He was playing for time, but rather heavily.

Went back to the office to listen to the Budget reports on TV. It is received quite favourably, as a serious approach to the problem. My personal view is critical. It tries to deal with the short-term problems: the public sector deficit and the balance of payments deficit. As such it does not go far enough, still leaving a huge deficit. Over the longer run, it achieves nothing. I would have preferred a Budget with a much bigger switch into industrial investment. Risky in the short run, but at least meaning we entered the next upturn in better shape.

[The Budget claimed to deal with inflation. It raised income tax by 2p and increased National Insurance contributions. Excise duties were increased, lifting prices an estimated 2.75%. Public expenditure for 1976–77 was cut by over £1 billion.]

In the evening I took Andrew Graham to a meeting of the Political Economy Club discussing the Budget. Sat between Peter Jay – who was quite favourable – and the right-wing economist Ralph Harris, who is not pro-Healey. But the general discussion was poor.

Home at 11 p.m. with a terrible headache.

Incidentally Marcia was burgled at the weekend – two TV sets were taken from her weekend home in Buckinghamshire. She denied they were both colour. She said, 'The maid's set is only black and white.' Now that is true socialism!

*Wednesday 16 April 1975*

In the morning HW saw Callaghan about the Argentinian threat to the Falkland Islands and then went to the PLP on the Budget – which was apparently surprisingly mild.

I saw Tom McNally to discuss various South African and Rhodesian questions, also our paper on special advisers for Jamaica and the PM's speaking engagements for the referendum. So far he has arranged very little. I want him to make a big effort in the last week.

Lunch in the City at Grieveson Grant, who were properly sceptical about whether the Budget will get it right.

Saw the PM in the afternoon and we discussed his referendum campaign. He is still unclear and doesn't seem to want to get too involved – but he will have to. He must win or he is finished. He seems very cheerful and relaxed, as if he has privately taken an important decision. Perhaps because he thinks he will get rid of Benn. He told Callaghan, 'I have a rod in pickle for him.' On Tuesday night there were press rumours of Benn's resignation and HW said to Joe, 'I would sleep better if it were true.'

In the evening we had the farewell dinner at No. 10 for Robert Armstrong. HW made quite a nice speech and Robert a very kind one, referring with affection to everybody he had worked with. He is really a remarkable public servant, one of the best I have dealt with. Firm, honest, tough, but much warmer than most of the others. If he has a fault, it is that he sometimes equates the national interest with the interest of the Whitehall machine. But I have found him a good friend and guide. At first there was some natural mistrust between us and I resented his strong presence. But once we came to know and trust one another it all changed. He has helped me out of my difficulties. He has a sense of the complexity of human nature – that evil is often mixed with good, that everything is farcical as well as serious. He is of course quite conservative and very attached to the traditional institutions of the Establishment – monarchy, Church, public schools, etc. But not creeping deference, not because he wants favours from the Establishment, but because he thinks those values, that stability, is the best of Britain. I don't actually agree with all of that. But I do think he is the very best of the Establishment. Robin Butler and Pat Nairne are ones of his calibre.

*Thursday 17 April 1975*

Came in shortly after 9.30. Went upstairs and found HW on his own in the study, looking at his weekend speeches. He is under remarkably little pressure at the moment. The flow of papers has almost stopped, presumably because of the Budget. HW is trying to leave the referendum to Jim Callaghan as far as possible. He has opted out of the Budget. So he seems totally relaxed. Possibly irresponsibly too. Perhaps he can see his way through these problems and is simply waiting for things to fall into place.

We talked about the referendum campaign, and I stressed the need for him to build up into a strong peak in the last week. I also persuaded him to allow the pro-marketeers to use his photograph on their pamphlets (last night he said no, so I waited overnight and tried again, at Shirley Williams's personal request).

We went downstairs to a Cabinet committee on the Crown Agents scandal, which passed quietly. Things now seem under control.

Cabinet was at 11. Almost wholly concerned with whether to give a vote to holiday-makers and people living abroad. Jenkins was pressing for this. The PM – and Short – had wavered, but were now against in case it set precedents for elections. It was rejected 11–9 in the end.

In the middle HW sent out for a memorandum I had shown him – from Gerry Fowler to the Lord President, setting out the arguments against. I sent it in to the Cabinet Room, with a message not to let Ted Short see he had it.

Ron Spiers came to see me from the American embassy. We set up some meetings for me in the USA. He had just seen the US Ambassador to Jordan, back from Washington, who said that the State Department was in collapse, demoralised by South Vietnam and Cambodia, and with no policies whatsoever for the Middle East. He said Kissinger was in very low form. Might go at any time – though we have heard that before.

Went then to a meeting in Marcia's room to discuss the arrangements for the PM's referendum speaking campaign. She said, of course, that we had it all wrong. He wasn't doing enough. He must cancel his Whit holiday in the Scillies. He must not go to Plymouth, which was 'badly anti-Market'. She left everybody in no doubt that she was galvanising the action. In fact it didn't make much difference. Cancelling his Scillies holiday is just a way of punishing the poor bugger – and she will have him round the corner to nag. Anyway, it is ironical that she is complaining that nobody is doing enough to win the referendum when she has been bitterly *against* the EEC all along and has done nothing so far except encourage the anti-marketeers who were voting against the PM in the Commons! But Joe and I went along with it, since we do agree it is better for the PM to do more rather than less (he couldn't do much less!) in the campaign. She seemed uncomfortable and never looked straight at me, but made no reference to our clash last week.

Afterwards Robert told me that at last night's dinner, when she sat next to Martin Charteris from the Palace, she said as she sat down, 'I want you to know that I hate you and all that you stand for.' This is true. Perhaps because she had not been invited to the Palace or had her claim to royal blood, as a descendant of Edward VII, recognised.

We had lunch upstairs – the last to be cooked by Serena Armstrong. So that experiment ceases. In fact there have been fresh attacks on it. Last week Mary Wilson told Robert that her cook, Mrs Pollard, objected to Serena using the official kitchen (though Mrs Pollard never uses it, since she uses the flat kitchen). And HW told Joe that other people in No. 10 might object to us using the small dining-room. Presumably they have both been put up to it. Now we have to find another part-time cook.

Questions was again very flat and boring. All the spice has gone out of it since the election was won. The only interest is to see Margaret Thatcher sitting there looking petrified; like a rabbit in front of a stoat. And Ted Heath sitting, waiting, stonily in the corner seat below the gangway, with no sign of life until HW puts the boot into Mrs Thatcher, when a wintry smile crosses his face.

Last night at No. 10 for Robert's farewell dinner was Ted Heath's first visit to No. 10 since he was defeated 12 months ago. He looked tense and sad and barely spoke to anybody, though I had a brief exchange with him. He was looking round to see how things had changed.

After Questions Joe and I sat down with the PM to discuss his referendum campaign diary. I had also arranged, at his request, for Jim Callaghan and Tom McNally to attend. At the last moment, mysteriously, even sheepishly, HW revealed that he had cancelled Callaghan's attendance. He didn't properly explain why, but Joe and I knew from Albert that it was on Marcia's instructions – because we had arranged it and not her. Didn't matter. We had a long discussion and got the details well sorted out.

Afterwards Harold asked me to go in the car with him back to No. 10, where he chatted amiably enough. He said once again how he hated Questions these days. Also that he thought Mrs Thatcher's voice was terrible.

I went to the office and cleared my trays, though there is still not much to do. Then to Robert Armstrong's farewell party in the reception rooms. In fact I drank too much on an empty stomach and found myself at one point chatting up Mrs Thatcher's secretary, Caroline, who is very attractive, bright and sexy, and later went to a Bloomsbury pub with Nick Stuart from private office.

When I woke up this morning I felt very sluggish and sorry for myself.

*Friday 18 April 1975*

HW not there. He stayed overnight at Chequers and then went off to meetings in Birmingham.

I went first thing at HW's request to Hampstead to see Lord Kissin –
travelling in with him afterwards in his beautiful Rolls-Royce. He feels
shut out because HW has not consulted him on his Kingston commodities initiative.

In the Unit Richard Graham, our industry specialist, brings me
intriguing news. Monty Finniston, chairman of the Steel Corporation,
wants to make Marcia a full-time board member at £22,000 a year!

We went out for lunch with the private office to the Anglo-Belgian Club
to pay another farewell to Robert Armstrong.

Still sorry to see him go. He has helped me through some difficult times.

His successor, Ken Stowe, is a totally different animal: small, quiet,
obviously grammar school, probably has voted Labour, with no touch of
the Establishment about him. But he is shrewd and very able and very
nice, and Joe and I are very happy with him. He told me at lunch that
when he was introduced to Marcia she was totally cold and hostile. He
said he thought of Lady Macbeth. I told Colin Peterson, who runs the
Church of England side of No. 10, that he might have to arrange an
exorcism.

We all completed the afternoon in a dreamy fashion. I put in a brief
and then retired early to see the kids for a change, especially since Carol
is not well.

The week of overlap between Robert and Ken has been funny. For the
first three days Robert sat imperiously at his great desk, receiving visitors
and giving orders, while Ken sat at a little table and wooden chair beside
it, occasionally being thrown a paper by Robert. Yesterday I noticed that
Ken was at the big desk and Robert squeezed at the little table. This must
be what they mean by being 'phased out'.

I wrote today's diary this evening – the first time I have ever been able
to write Friday's story on Friday. Normally I am too exhausted and write
it on Saturday morning. Tonight not, which is a sign of how much less
work we have at the moment.


### Monday 21 April 1975

PM at a liaison meeting between the TUC and the NEC on the social
contract. He later said it was 'very friendly' – which means they did not
deal with it honestly. With wages going up at 30% there is no social contract.
It works only one way.

I worked on papers in the Unit.

David Rockefeller came in to see the PM just before 12.30 and I took
him to my room, where I arranged to see him when in New York.

Lunch with Joe at the House of Commons. He told me that the PM is relying more on Janet – she stayed at Chequers last Thursday and Friday night. But Marcia is getting wind of it so there will be trouble.

Had a meeting with Michael Myer and Hector Hawkins from the CPRS. They are very worried about swallowing the *whole* of the Ryder Report on British Leyland – which involves investment of £2.8 billion with little return. Foolishly they have agreed not to submit a memo to Cabinet – and now have no way of getting a word in. So I decide to put in a brief.

Pat Nairne came through from the Cabinet Office to raise sensible problems about referendum declaration day – *when* to announce the result, especially if it is no. The PM has not thought about this – it is nearly too much to get him to think about the campaign a month ahead, let alone about the result.

I went to the study where the PM was planning the Kingston visit with Joe, Patrick Wright, Ken Stowe and Janet. Made me a little sad not to be going. The PM is obviously excited about the trip.

Then he suddenly got very jumpy and left the room, came back and began walking up and down. Everybody got the message and left – then Joe told me that Marcia was coming in to see him (perhaps about the honours list which he was clearing at the weekend).

I stayed a few minutes and raised the question of opinion polls. He was reluctant to have official government polls in case he is accused of spending money for partisan purposes. He is obviously still keen on getting some private polls done but doesn't seem to have thought it out.

Sat for a while in private office with Ken Stowe, who is taking over private office very smoothly and co-operating very helpfully. Joe and I are very happy with him.

Home at 8.30.

## Tuesday 22 April 1975

Discovered on arrival that an IDV Cabinet committee had been slipped in to discuss industrial democracy. The PM apparently was not too pleased, but it has been hanging around a long time. I was not too pleased either, as we did not have the chance to put in our brief.

The meeting was very diffuse. Benn inevitably pushing for rapid progress (which we broadly support). And interestingly, Peter Shore opposing. The problem is that the Labour MP Giles Radice has got a Private Members Bill calling for more industrial democracy through its 2nd reading because the Whips forgot to shout 'no' in the Chamber! After a lot of waffle it was decided to set up an inquiry and bring out a White Paper for legislation next year. Healey and Benn clashed again – and Healey lost again.

The Cabinet discussed British Leyland and decided to accept the Ryder Report – which is fairly dismal and offers little return on £2 billion investment. After Cabinet I was supposed to go to the Reform for lunch with Ken Stowe, but he was delayed till nearly 2 p.m. with Ryder, who was very worried about leaks and what would happen to British Leyland shares. They did not know whether to suspend the shares or not.

So I went across to the Commons and had lunch on the terrace with John Smith, who is very impressive, and Donald Dewar,* who was down from Scotland for the day. Told me horrifying stories about corruption in Glasgow.

Went to Questions. Again drab. The PM kept saying how he hated Question Time and was looking forward to getting away to Jamaica for a fortnight.

Questions were wholly devoted to question number one – on the referendum.

I went back to meet Tom McNally and we drafted the paper on special advisers for the PM in Jamaica. Then back to Commons for a big briefing on Jamaica. It seemed that half the Foreign Office were there, but it was boring and nobody had anything to say. John Hunt seemed unable to explain why we were there. So much brains, experience – and cost – and little to offer.

I then returned to No.10 and worked on the special advisers brief for Kingston till 8.30. Then went home.

## Wednesday 23 April 1975

I went in a little late, thinking that the PM would go to the NEC. But he decided not to. He said he couldn't bear to face them squabbling and back-biting. So we spent the morning with him in the study. We mainly discussed Wedgie Benn, who had put a paper to a Transport House committee suggesting that the government should direct pension fund money into the NEB, etc. Seventy copies of the paper had been distributed, but none were sent to No.10. HW was furious and decided to punish Benn by not letting him make the British Leyland statement tomorrow. This would also make it clear that major government policy was not in Benn's hands.

HW was also trying to work out whether Mrs Thatcher, who is going to Turkey tomorrow, would still be in the House for the statement. So he sent for the airlines timetables and sat working out the times of flights to Istanbul, before concluding that she would be absent. Then he worked out some jokes at her expense.

Went to lunch with Joe at the Reform! My first attendance since being elected. Had to wait hours for the fish. I didn't know where to find anything, and Joe had to help me – with some disdain, since he disapproves of the whole club thing.

Attended a small Cabinet committee in the PM's room at the House of Commons on handling the announcement of the referendum result. Still assuming it takes three days and will be finished on Sunday, we don't actually know at what time the count will finish. Should there be an announcement at a fixed time or just as it happens? Especially important if the result is 'no'. Decided on a fixed time around 9 in the evening. Healey and Callaghan were there and they stayed on afterwards to discuss the handling of Benn on Leyland. Also Callaghan's intention to sack the PPS of his Junior Minister, David Ennals – who is Rod MacFarquhar,* one of the best young MPs. Because MacFarquhar had led the revolt in favour of votes for overseas Britons. Also, I suspect because Callaghan was preparing the way to discipline some left-wingers (MacFarquhar is on the right). For a start it enabled him to talk HW out of appointing a left-winger, Brian Sedgemore, as PPS to Albert Booth.*

I went back to No. 10 and spent an hour with Tom McNally finalising our paper on political advisers for Jamaica. After this I went to private office and with Joe and Ken Stowe worked on the draft British Leyland statement for tomorrow. It was rather too much backward-looking, reciting all the past failures and too little about the future. We changed that.

Carol came in at 7.30 p.m. and waited till we had finished. Then we went to the Deputy High Commissioner for Australia for a dinner for Alf Morris. Jack Ashley and Fred Jarvis* were there. The Australians were very dull. But nice to see Alf and Jack again.

Home at midnight.

## Thursday 24 April 1975

Saw Lever before Cabinet. He had a meeting with HW the night before, who said that I was looking after two matters – the referendum polls and something else I did not know about. I prefer to stay out as much as possible.

Also saw Shirley Williams about the opinion polls. Try to discover what the pro-EEC organisations will do before we spend anything. They are getting their material from the umbrella organisation which employs Humphrey Taylor of ORC – Bob Worcester's opposite number on the Tory side.

Marcia has ordered Albert to take my name off the list of people in No. 10 to get tickets for the Special Labour Party Conference on the EEC on Saturday. Albert, who has become a sad shadow of his former self, simply obeying her and running errands for her, obeyed. Petty and ridiculous. I simply telephoned a friend at Transport House and within ten minutes I had a special ticket.

Joe and I went to lunch at the House. I left early to meet Jacob Rothschild about the Arab boycott of Jewish banks. Then back to the House to go through the PM's statement on British Leyland. Ryder was there – and Lord Stokes telephoned in the middle to say he would appreciate it if the PM paid a tribute to him at the time of announcing the terrible situation into which he had guided Leyland.

[Today the government published the Ryder Report on British Leyland with proposals for the government to buy a large stake in the equity and to inject new capital of £1.4 billion to avoid imminent bankruptcy.]

Questions were boring as usual these days, One nice point. The PM was objecting to Michael Heseltine* replying for the Tories on British Leyland and said that this was 'a job for a man and not a lad'. Everybody took this to refer to Benn on our side as well. Afterwards the PM said he had not realised what he was saying, but on reflection was quite happy with it.

At 5 we had a briefing for Kingston. Better than the last one. In the Cabinet Room.

Afterwards my friend John Murphy dropped in for a drink and then I went with Carol and Philip and Nori Graham to a musical, *A Little Night Music*, which was slight but entertaining.

The PM went to the British Academy dinner where he spoke for 45 minutes.

He always asks Janet to travel in the car with him. Albert and Bill Housden have been commenting – which means that Lady F will be alerted.


## Friday 25 April 1975

Weekly business meeting in the PM's study at 9.30. Only Short there, as Healey was away in Turkey, Callaghan was working on his conference speech and Mellish was not well.

HW and Short began by discussing the government programme ahead. HW said, 'It is quite clear that we won't do the Queen's Speech.' He said they should let the nationalisation of shipbuilding and hovercraft slip. Also the abolition of private hospital beds. He said he did not support this in principle anyway. And he said Barbara Castle 'is behaving like a bitch. We gave her everything she asked for last year. She is just an old woman in a hurry; no sense at all.'

Short pointed out that Castle was 'quite the worst' at the last meeting of the NEC on the referendum – 'just vitriolic'.

There was little to do about next week's business as the PM will be away in Kingston.

I went down to the office for coffee, but the PM immediately sent for me to discuss the conference speech. With Patrick and Joe we worked on this till midday. I had been very unhappy that the speech was so pussy-footing. So careful to show respect to the views of the anti-marketeers. Nowhere in the first draft did HW actually say that he was in favour of staying in the EEC! But Joe strengthened it in various places, and I got him to put in a passage saying that the decision to pull out now was quite different from a decision not to support entry in 1971 – aimed to enable waverers/doubters to switch to pro. But my main concern was to get a firm ending. In fact HW had realised this and quickly decided to put in the conclusion from his Commons speech. But his first instinct is still to continue acting as if he is the middle-way broker between the pros and antis. In fact he has got to lead the pros and win, or else he is finished. Joe has realised this and is pushing him to take a stronger line. Marcia is opposing this, wanting HW to hedge his bets so that, if the referendum vote is no, he can then claim he was never strongly in favour anyway and so could hang on to the leadership. She also made two alterations to the speech, watering down Joe's firm-line sentences, one of her changes actually implying that we need to be in the EEC during the oil crisis but could then pull out again once things ease. HW said that was her intention and he amended her amendment to remove that implication.

The speech was now much improved, but still very low-key. We shall have to firm him up a lot more.

Joe and I went to lunch at the Commons and then back to a frustrating afternoon. I had cleared my desk – still far fewer papers than a few months ago – and wanted to get home to see Carol and the children. Had to wait 2 hours to get a meeting with Joe and private office to clear lines of communications for next week. The PM has asked me to send a telegram each day on the political situation. Any crises will delay my departure for Washington.

Joe came to stay with us overnight, so we can go together to the party conference tomorrow morning. It is held around the corner.

We went for a walk over Hampstead Heath. Discussed the reaction to a referendum 'no'. We are both convinced that HW will have to go to the Commons and ask for a vote of confidence, and if he doesn't get it will have to resign.

Joe also discussed the Marcia business. Her houses, expensive style of living, several servants, children at private school – all require a very high income. The circle of rich men who court her may help. Eric Miller must be next for some recognition.

Had a nice supper with Joe and Carol and then to bed at midnight! Tomorrow the EEC conference, a charade which will demonstrate only that the Labour Party activists represent nobody, not even the party – just themselves.

## Saturday 26 April 1975

Went with Joe to the Labour Party special EEC conference. It was held at the new Sobell sport centre in Islington, only five minutes from home and a marvellous change not to have to travel away for conference.

We arrived at 9.30, and HW was already there with Mary. Joe and I went up to join him in the political office. He was obviously edgy and not enjoying the experience of being in a conference minority. We walked down to the platform with him and then retired to find a seat in the main part of the hall. It was not full – 20% of CLPs did not bother to send delegates – so we didn't bother to sit in our reserved seats. Just as the proceedings began Marcia arrived with Eric Miller, with Albert tagging along behind. They had come from Eric Miller's Churchill Hotel according to what Albert told Joe. She went up on to the platform and sat behind HW in full television camera view. She left poor Eric Miller on his own. And Albert was in the doghouse with the PM. Having waited for her, he was not in time to see the PM, who wanted him. For one thing they had forgotten to bring a lectern so the PM had nowhere to rest his speech. He had to hold the 30 pages in his hand, which he hates, since he has a fear of dropping them, or of turning over more than one page at a time.

The PM's speech went very quietly, no cheers and no heckling. But clearly the majority of the hall were against him. For the first time at party conference he did not get a standing ovation.

It was quite an enjoyable and lively occasion, rather like a market, with people walking about, chattering, drinking tea or beer, all while the speeches were going on. Everybody knew the result was a foregone conclusion.

Roy Jenkins made a strong and good speech, quite uncompromising. Some of the antis spoke in identical King Street clichés, and the *Morning Star* was much in evidence. [The Communist Party headquarters were in King Street, Covent Garden.]

HW left the platform in the late morning and went upstairs with Marcia. Joe went to join them – and HW asked him to leave. They had the Israeli Ambassador there and apparently Marcia had fixed their meeting, in the middle of conference, hours before HW went to Jamaica. The Israelis were considering inviting her to Israel for a holiday, taking her children and her Filipino maid. Albert is also going with his wife and children. Presumably a perk to compensate for his not going to Jamaica. This was what the PM was involved with in the middle of this crucial party conference.

Joe was shocked. His puritanism still cannot stomach this kind of thing. He is also worried about alleged connections with an arms dealer who was trying to sell British submarines to the Libyans. This was referred to in a telegram to the Foreign Office from our Ambassador in Libya.

Joe walked out and refused to go back at lunchtime, so I stayed and had lunch with him. We went to a fish and chip shop and took our fish and chips and sat on the grass in the sun. Very tasty. Then I went home to look after the children.

Joe phoned later and said that Foot finished with a below-par speech. The majority against – less than 2 to 1 – was much better for us than we had expected.

## Monday 28 April 1975

Went in early to a near silent No. 10: almost deserted, with a strong sense, clearly detectable, that the boss is away – in Jamaica.

Telephoned around to get the feel of the post-conference situation. Everybody is concerned about the Left's move to call a special NEC meeting on Wednesday to make the party fight a full campaign against the EEC. Shirley Williams is at the centre of the counter-attack, so I keep in close touch with her.

Saw Evelyn de Rothschild at 11 for an hour to discuss the continuing boycott of Jewish banks. He is balanced and well informed and cleared this one up for me.

Telephoned Joe in Jamaica at 1 o'clock – 8 a.m. their time. He was in bed, with the sun blazing outside. I was a little bit envious, though it is a glorious day here in London.

To lunch with Robert Armstrong, who took me to the Athenaeum (much emptier than the Reform). Robert has only just moved today into the Home Office as deputy secretary, where he is running police and prisons. He is a remarkably wise and warm person. I shall miss him around No.10.

Went to the bank afterwards and then to RAC Club for tea with Harold Evans, who gave me some Washington contacts.

Back in No. 10 I did some more telephoning and then drafted a telegram to the PM describing how, according to Shirley Williams, Fred Mulley,* as chairman of the NEC, was not standing up sufficiently to the Left. He gave a specific pledge to conference on Saturday, in reply to a question from Ennals, that the party machine would not be used to campaign. Hayward set out similar guidelines in March at NEC. Fred should insist on this.

They are all intimidated. They know that this campaign is all orchestrated as part of Benn's leadership bid, but very few have the backbone to

stand up against it. The trouble is that the Labour Party is full of inver-
tebrates – not kosher.

Came home at 8 p.m. In fact am quite enjoying looking after the political shop. Will probably not go to Washington till Friday so I can assess
the political situation here after Wednesday's NEC.

## Tuesday 29 April 1975

Spent much of the day communicating to people involved in the EEC
battle, especially in relation to Wednesday's NEC meeting. Shirley Williams
and her adviser John Lyttle are at the centre of the 'pro' manoeuvres and
doing a fair job. Stimulating opposition to Benn's move to have an election campaign against the Market. Several unions have responded. And
Transport House revolted, with a staff vote against servicing such a
campaign.

Had decided to go to Washington on Friday, when I received a telegram
from our Ambassador there saying 'Please come on Thursday', so I will
do that. I talked to Joe in Jamaica several times. Sounds very cheerful and
enjoying the sunshine.

No. 10 is absolutely dead.

I sent my daily telegram to the PM on the political situation in the
evening, then Carol came in with her friend Ron Smedley for a drink.
Home at 9 p.m.

Telegram to Jamaica:

The position Tuesday evening is that the anti-marketeers still have a
majority at tomorrow's NEC and there will apparently just be a quorum.
All the pro-marketeers will attend and will probably be supported by
Jeger* and Hickling. Attendance of several anti-marketeers is in doubt.
But opposition to their manoeuvre has been demonstrated today
throughout many levels of the party.

Four trade unions have protested to Hayward about the use of their
money for the anti-campaign (APEX yesterday voted 6 to 1 against
withdrawal from the Common Market).

Five junior ministers – John Grant, John Smith, Arthur Davidson,*
Barry Jones* and the Lord Advocate – today wrote to Hayward
protesting that such a campaign would 'result in bitterness and intol-
erance within our ranks'.

The National Union of Labour Agents has written to Cartwright
expressing strong opposition to proposed campaign.

The NUJ chapel in Transport House passed motions of protest
and this discussed at Annual Transport House Staff meeting.

There are moves within the PLP to get a protest statement, by pros and antis, probably under the Manifesto Group umbrella, but outcome of this is still uncertain.

Mulley and Hayward have been active, seeing several protagonists. They appear more optimistic.

Central point is that to press this issue against such wide opposition suggests that some people are playing for very high stakes indeed.


*Wednesday 30 April 1975*

Great triumph. Shirley Williams telephoned to say that the Left capitulated at the NEC and did not even press their motion. All over in half an hour.

Lunch alone at the Reform.

Afternoon at No. 10 getting briefing for Washington and leaving arrangements for running the Unit.

Off to Washington at 9.30 in the morning. Very exciting.

# CHAPTER 14

## Washington Again,
## May 1975

### Friday 2 May 1975

Yesterday flew to Washington. The plane was three and a half hours late, which was infuriating. Wasted the whole day. But first time on a Jumbo, which is very comfortable. Like a great ocean liner ploughing through the sky. The loveliest point was flying over Greenland. We had gone very far north to avoid strong headwinds, north of 60°. Greenland was layers of snow-covered mountains stretching far towards the Arctic. It was brilliantly clear, and from 37,000 feet we could see each individual iceberg in the sea below. We arrived at 7 p.m. local time, but midnight real time. I was tired. Went for a short walk and had a milkshake in a hamburger bar to acclimatise and then to bed.

Woke at 4 this morning and unable to get to sleep again. So had a shower and shave and lay on the bed reading my briefs till morning tea arrived at 7. It is the Hay Adams Hotel – old, faded and genteel, but with some pretence at service and far better than those plastic airport places.

The embassy car arrived at 7.45 and drove me to the embassy where I had breakfast with Peter Ramsbotham, the Ambassador. I now appreciate him much better than last time. He is an individual personality, not smooth, reflective and far better than the average smooth Foreign Office type.

We discussed the PM's Kingston speech, which has gone very well but upset the Americans, especially their Treasury, who don't want any commodity agreements because they don't believe in interfering with the so-called 'free market mechanisms'. He said how difficult he found it to communicate with HW – and he asked me to tell him that Americans are stopping investment in the UK because of the rate of inflation.

Went to see Arthur Hartman at the State Department at 10 and we talked for an hour – Cyprus, EEC, Ireland, Middle East. He is very sympathetic and always calm – an ideal foil to Kissinger.

Afterwards back to the embassy to make some telephone arrangements

– and to phone No. 10 to discover Labour had lost 200 seats in the local elections.

Back to the State Department to have lunch with Frank Sieverts, who is now running their programme to deal with all the Vietnam refugees and whom I had not seen since Oxford in 1958. Just the same – charming, boyish, simple, just a little greyer in his Kennedy haircut.

We walked over to the Treasury building, near the White House. The sun had finally come out and it was beautifully warm as we walked. The grass was green, the White House gleaming, the air rich with the smell of Washington early summer. For the first time it felt like the America of my first visit in 1958. It needs the sun.

At the Treasury I saw Chuck Cooper, assistant to Bill Simon, who is very serious and very equable. A bit worried that their reflation programme will stir up inflation again. But their rate is less than half ours. Cooper is the most impressive American official I have yet met. All the facts at his fingertips. Clear analysis. Obviously not very interested in the British problem, but no reason why he should be.

From Cooper to Sparsky, a slick young man dealing with commodities. Very rushed and not in control. Too concerned with his whiz-kid image. Won't stay. But important because the Americans are worried by the PM's Kingston initiative and we have to ease some of their fears.

On to Tom Enders, back in the State Department, a very tall, ambitious and somewhat arrogant man. Only had a few minutes with him because he was summoned to see Kissinger and the President. Arranged to see him again on Monday.

Went back to the hotel around 5 p.m., feeling tired and jet lag begins to hit, but also feeling exhilarated. Exciting whirlwind day. Much better than just hanging round in the entourage of the PM.

Talked to my Oxford girlfriend Judy Davison and telephoned Barbara Hower, the writer, who is Harold Evans's friend.

Fell asleep, and woke at 7.50 p.m. – yet had to be at the embassy at 8 p.m. I showered and shaved in a flash and dashed off to get there at 8.15! Drinks on the lawn, talking mainly with Bill Colby, head of the CIA, General Scowcroft, Kissinger's assistant, and Hal Sonnenfeldt. Dinner was quite pleasant. Sat next to Marjorie Sonnenfeldt, who is really very bright and natural and quite untouched by her husband's important position.

Home at 1 a.m.

## Saturday 3 May 1975

Woke to glorious sunshine. Quickly breakfasted and then walked past the White House and across the grass to the Washington Monument. Beautiful feel of spring – warm, fresh smells, people lolling and looking. On the grass was a kind of fete, with music, stalls, etc., given by Inter-Action – all the community groups trying to live different 'more natural and non-commercial' life. Very pleasant, with bands and little children playing. I sat there until one o'clock. Then off to lunch with Barbara Hower. In Georgetown which was bustling and beautiful, like Chelsea on a smaller and more intimate scale. Lunched at a nice small Chinese restaurant. Then I walked a long way towards my hotel. Watched the Kentucky Derby on TV – some very ungentlemanly behaviour by the jockeys – and then fell asleep. Awakened by the chauffeur after sleeping for hour and a half. Dashed off to Arthur Hartman and had delightful dinner with him and his family.

Broke up at 11.30 and then went to a dance party given at Averell Harriman's house in Georgetown for the distinguished journalist Joseph Alsop on his retirement. The whole of present and past Washington politics was there – Kissinger, Cabot Lodge and a whole range of senators, congressmen, society hostesses (including my friend Mrs Liz Stevens, who accompanied me), journalists, writers – Truman Capote, Ward Just, etc. A beautiful house, with dancing to a 1950s band in the main lounge, a marquee stretching into the garden – and secret servicemen behind every tree. Very inbred feeling, everybody gossiping intensely about politics, and a strong sense that it was a society column occasion. They were all in dinner jackets. I wasn't and felt relieved to be in decent clothes.

It began to pour with rain later. I had sent my driver home so I had to thumb a lift with a very elegant society lady. Back to bed at 2.30 a.m. Again quite a day. In fact the morning was nicest – because closest to the atmosphere and feel I can still remember vividly from when Carol and I were here together in 1959.

## Sunday 4 May 1975

The car picked me up at 9.45 and we drove off to the Maryland eastern shore to visit Joe Saxe of the World Bank. It had poured with rain all night and was grey and damp in the morning. We drove first to Annapolis, a lovely old state capital, walked by the waterfront, and had coffee in a fish market. Then drove on the remaining 30 miles to the east shore of Chesapeake Bay.

Joe Saxe's home was beautiful, old and wooden, right beside the bay shore. We sat in rocking chairs, drinking and looking across the water, which was totally still and without any boats. After a huge lunch of fresh crab we walked along the shore to a beautiful but deserted mansion. It was a wonderful rest from Washington. A small community of fishermen in a remote part of Maryland. It is easy to forget that there are any Americans who are not politicians, journalists or truck-drivers.

Back in Washington in the evening I rested in the hotel and watched a terrible but irresistible old Western film. Had a sandwich and beer downstairs in the bar and then went to bed.

## Monday 5 May 1975

Had to move to another hotel this morning, which was a bore. The Hay Adams is fully booked, so I transferred to the Sheraton Park – huge factory of a hotel further out.

Went to a meeting with Joelson, lawyer to the Publishers Association, at the embassy at 10.30. Then back to Congress to see my old friend Paul Sarbanes for lunch. He is an outstanding Democrat congressman for the 3rd district of Maryland. I knew him at Oxford and he married Christine Dunbar, a nice English girl who was at college with Carol. He is now well established and thinking of running for the Senate. [He later became the first Senator of Greek extraction for Maryland.] Also very exercised about the Cyprus situation, since he is from a Greek family. Also with us was John Brademas, the other 'Greek' congressman. We ate in the Congress restaurant – bean soup, etc., surrounded by other American political figures, though I recognise very few of them these days. Afterwards Paul took me on a tour of the House of Representatives, and I sat in the gallery while he went down to vote and talk to colleagues. It feels very different from the Commons. People walk about and talk in the chamber. Also the membership seems much younger.

Off to the State Department, first to see Jack Davison, Judy's husband and also a friend of mine when I was at Harvard, who works on the NATO desk, and then to complete my meeting with Enders, adjourned from Friday. This was quite satisfactory, covering the whole field of commodities, oil, Concorde, trade, etc. He is a graceless person, obviously a bit arrogant and rude, but able. It was a serious hour and very useful to me.

Back to the hotel for a shower and a rest, and then Paul Sarbanes and Christine came round for drinks and we had a delightful hour of reminiscences. They went off to a dinner. I took the car to Georgetown, had a beer and ate a hamburger, walking along Wisconsin Avenue, and then home to watch the film on television, and then to sleep at around 12.30.

## Tuesday 6 May 1975

Very relaxed – and funny – day. The car collected me at 8.15 and we went to the airport to take the plane for the day to New York. The sun was blazing and it was a real southern summer day. I booked in, but realised that I didn't want to go to New York, and especially not take two aeroplane journeys there and back, on such a day. Shortly before boarding, I retrieved my ticket, telephoned to cancel my meetings and left. I took the local bus to the Greyhound bus station and then took a Greyhound bus to Baltimore and looked around the city for a little while. The sun helped, and I could see streets of fine old houses, but the squalor and total collapse of urban living in America was striking and sad. It is now an almost totally black city. My taxi driver was very vicious about the blacks. He said that they had destroyed this town and that now the crime was terrible.

Had lunch at an excellent restaurant called the Chesapeake. Clam chowder and lots of seafood. I felt completely free. Nobody knew where I was – the embassy thought I was in New York. I was doing private things, not lists of official meetings, and spending my own money. I sat in a corner, eating, drinking beer and then coffee, smoking a cigar and feeling very relaxed. I started to walk back to the Greyhound bus station, but passed the railway station, walked in, and found there was a train to Washington in a few minutes. There were only half a dozen people getting on, in a run-down Penn. Central railway station, at the back end of a town I had never visited before – but one of them was familiar. It was charming Mrs Paul Volcker, whom I had met in New York in February at the dinner given by Harold Lever for the bankers. She is crippled with arthritis and had been to Baltimore to get better braces for her feet. It was a remarkable coincidence – and means somebody in Washington may learn that I was in Baltimore and not New York. That will throw them! Mrs Volcker drove me back to the hotel. Her very able husband is just finishing the term teaching at Princeton, and then takes over as head of the New York Federal Reserve Bank.

Showered and then off to the Kennedy Center for a party given for the film actress, Raquel Welch. She was striking, but not beautiful, and clearly not too bright. Her bosom was much smaller than I had been led to believe. I travelled up in the lift with her and walked into the party with her, but I did not recognise her: had to be introduced. Various senators and congressmen came to the party – as well as Kissinger. He worries me more and more. Clearly very full of himself. Like a great bullfrog, and apparently basking in the limelight of film stars, etc. Hal Sonnenfeldt was also there, looking not too happy with the frivolity of it all.

I was with my friend Liz and her husband George Stevens – a film producer – and went on with them to an indoor tennis tournament in Arlington. Virginia. A dozen politicians playing with some media men – including the columnist Art Buchwald, who stands fixed in one spot and lobs back every ball, underhand, high, hilarious and causing the opposition to make mistakes from laughing. Spent most of the time with Liz and with the Heinzes. John is from the soup family and is congressman for somewhere in Pennsylvania. Teresa is beautiful and Portuguese [and later the wife of Senator John Kerry]. A very bright pair. Home to Georgetown at 11.30, where I had a cup of tea at the Heinz home, a lovely and unusually large and stately Georgetown residence, and then back to bed at 12.30.

## Wednesday 7 May 1975

Went shopping in the morning to buy gifts for the children. Right out of town to a shopping centre to get real Western belts.

On to visit Henry Brandon, the *Sunday Times* correspondent here, who was in the George Washington hospital after a heart attack. He seemed very perky and we gossiped about politics. I wondered if I would like his job, in a rather morbid way. Liz Stevens came along and we had a quiet hamburger lunch together afterwards. She is always nice to be with. Then I raced off to the embassy along the end of Massachusetts Avenue to meet the PM's party flying in from Kingston. They arrived at 2.30 p.m. looking very brown and happy. It had obviously been a very successful expedition to Jamaica.

After a brief gathering in the embassy, HW and Callaghan went off to the White House to see the President and Kissinger. I went back to the hotel and did some telephoning. Then Joe and Janet came in to see me and we went back to the embassy. There we gathered in the library and the PM came to tell us about the hour with President Ford. This was mainly on the Middle East, where the Americans are very worried and trying to get some fresh initiatives moving. Also a bit on commodities, where they gave cautious approval to HW's initiative. At one point we went to the Chancery building attached to the huge embassy building, and HW and Jim Callaghan gave a press conference. Not very long. Not many journalists there. The inevitable questions about the decline of Britain and the inflation. HW ducks these – he had another row with the Ambassador in the car coming from the airport when Ramsbotham started pressing on him the American concern about our rate of inflation – but at some point he will have to take it on board.

HW was very happy and clearly still pleased to be away. He was very keen to hear me report on the domestic situation. We had some drinks and then broke up at about 8, when he was having dinner at the embassy with Kissinger, Joe Fowler, Senator Fulbright, Rumsfeld (Ford's aide) and Joseph Sisco, with Jim Callaghan.

I had been approached to have dinner with the minister at the embassy (at his house) and Joe with the information officer. But we dropped out and went off into Georgetown for supper, just us and Janet. A nice fish restaurant on Wisconsin Avenue. I had clams, then jumbo prawns stuffed with baked crab meat, and lashings of beer. Excessively fishy, but delicious.

Afterwards back to the embassy, where we sat and waited for the dinner to end. We walked in the garden, beautifully tended and laid out, with the blossoms out, a very warm and starlit evening, brightly romantic, with the guests at dinner visible through the lighted windows – except for the unromantic armed police guards hiding behind every tree with their radios burbling away. Kissinger loves all of these trappings of power. One of the policemen told me that before leaving home Kissinger used to telephone and summon a police-car escort, with wailing sirens and flashing lights. It was finally stopped by the police, who pointed out that not only was it extravagant – since K has his own detectives anyway – but it was contrary to security. Everybody in the neighbourhood knew when Kissinger was leaving and which way he was going because of this damned police siren.

They broke up at midnight and Callaghan, Wilson and the Ambassador came to talk to us. Callaghan revealed that Kissinger had mentioned a secret new American 'general plan' for the Middle East. Not just step by step, but covering the frontier, Jerusalem, the Palestinians, the lot. This he will discuss with Gromyko at a secret meeting soon. They also have a plan to offer the Turks 30% of the land in Cyprus, though they are not optimistic of a settlement on this basis.

We broke towards 1 a.m. when Jim Callaghan, as always, said he wanted to go to bed. He is very careful to look after himself these days. He doesn't drink. He takes a siesta every afternoon, and always leaves functions early in the evening. As his press officer McCaffrey said, 'Jim is preserving himself for the nation.'

HW was still showing his dislike of the Ambassador, Ramsbotham, especially by talking loudly to somebody else while Ramsbotham was talking. He finds him a snob and inefficient on details – e.g. there are *never* any recent newspapers available. In fact, I think he is very intelligent and I like him a lot. His manner is rather aristocratic and toffee-nosed, but he has been warm and kind to me and I think behind the manner is a very individual and highly capable man.

Back to the hotel – and bed – at 1.30 a.m.

*Thursday 8 May 1975*

Up at 7.30 a.m. No breakfast because the hotel – the Sheraton Park – is terrible, with no service at all. Joe pointedly asked the counter clerk the way to the nearest Salvation Army hostel since he wanted some breakfast. We went out and wandered the streets in search of food and coffee, but without luck. Finally we drove to the embassy, where the Ambassador served me some delicious eggs and bacon left over from the PM's breakfast. The PM joined Joe, Janet and me at the breakfast table and talked about English politics and the press, and about abolishing the parliamentary press lobby. Getting ready for home – but still in excellent form.

We left in cavalcade at 9 a.m. driving to Andrews military airforce base on a glorious sunny morning. The trees and fields beside the motorway were rich and blazing with blossom. I didn't want to leave. This has been my best visit ever. Because Washington is beautiful and fascinating. Because Americans are just so nice and easy to get on with. And because I was there on my own, in my own right, and not just as one of an entourage.

Within minutes of reaching the airfield we were boarded and in the air, flying up the Eastern Seaboard. I settled in my seat to read papers but after a few minutes the PM sent for Joe and Janet and me and we went to join him in his compartment. We stayed there for three hours until lunchtime, drinking coffee, then beer later. We gossiped. He told us how he would deal with Benn. He had worked out a timetable for the Industry Bill with the report stage coming after the referendum when the government's amendments would be introduced – contrary to Benn's wishes. He also said that his moving Benn to another position was full of 'irony'. He seemed full of confidence that he would manoeuvre Benn into resigning over procedure rather than policy.

He was extremely cheerful. He said, 'The one thing I cannot face is going back to an economic crisis.' He was also counting the days to the Whitsun holiday, and complained that the NATO conference had been fixed in the parliamentary recess, so he would not be able to use it to miss Question Time, which is one of his major ambitions these days.

Above all he was delighting in Janet's company. The question is how Lady F will react to this. Apparently the moment her sister Peg returned from Jamaica to London at the weekend to report, Marcia started telephoning the PM in the middle of the night. She probably has wind of competition and will move in to stop it.

HW had lunch with the civil servants, and then sent for Joe and Janet and me and we gossiped again. We discussed Bob Worcester's suggested poll questions for the referendum campaign, with which he was pleased. He also quizzed me on the problem concerning British publishers. I was unclear on some of the technical aspects. He corrected me and remarked gently that political advisers seemed to him strong on principle but weak on detail. He was correct in this case, so I will put it right this weekend.

Also discussed British local government, where he thinks that the wasteful expenditure on staff and expenses is disgraceful.

We landed at Heathrow at 9.30 p.m., absolutely punctual, as always with the RAF. Just before landing, the PM revealed that Marcia was meeting him. When the luggage was cleared through Customs people began to go home. Jim Callaghan came up and said, 'Shall we go off then?' HW revealed that he was waiting for Marcia – who had not arrived. Jim laughed and cried, 'Hard luck, hard luck. If you will arrange for these women to meet you,' and sauntered off, laughing contemptuously. The rest of us left one by one. I was travelling with HW's doctor, Joe Stone, and we were nearly the last to go at about 9.50 p.m. As we left, the PM drove off in his official car to drive round the perimeter of the airport. Partly to get rid of the cameramen who would think he had gone home. Partly because he didn't want to stand there forlornly waiting for Marcia to turn up. She in fact arrived at 10.30 p.m. The PM spent the time waiting there forlornly in the lounge or off on his perimeter drives to pass the time. This humiliating tactic brought him down to earth on returning from an international trip and triumph.

I was home at 11 p.m. – which is only 6 p.m. Washington time – and I unpacked, read, and wrote this about today's events until 2 in the morning, when I finally felt tired. (I got my facts on the PM's pathetic wait at the airport from his private secretary the next day.)

# CHAPTER 15

# The EEC Victory
## May–June 1975

### Friday 9 May 1975

D id not see the PM at all today. Was in my office catching up on papers
and preparing several memoranda.

Heard more from Patrick Wright, the Foreign Office private secretary,
about the Libyan submarine affair. Apparently the arms dealer has written
to Marcia claiming that he has a letter from her demonstrating some
involvement on her part and that the PM intervened personally to stop it.
She has sent a minute to the PM denying this, and claiming that all she
did was 'to acknowledge his many letters'. This could be true. She then
accused Robert Armstrong of being responsible for it. There has obviously
been a substantial correspondence.

Also Patrick told me that the earlier diplomatic telegram from our
Ambassador to Libya mentioning her in a memo has disappeared from
confidential files in No. 10, and there is no record of it being taken out.
It looks as if it may be boiling up. There is a letter from somebody called
Brook saying that the rumour of No. 10's involvement is widespread in
the Ministry of Defence.

I worked on memoranda – on Benn and British Steel, on the machinery
for deciding public expenditure, on opinion polls about the EEC – until
9 p.m. and then came home.

Our private Worcester EEC poll shows the pros 70–30 ahead. But also
that the doubters are (1) women (2) in Scotland and the north, and (3)
among unskilled Labour voters. And it suggests that what is required is a
more positive lead from HW. I briefed accordingly.

### Monday 12 May 1975

The PM spent the morning with Len Murray and Michael Foot mainly
discussing proposals for a government inquiry into industrial democracy.

I worked on papers, did briefs on machinery for better controlling public expenditure, and on social policy, and then had lunch with Joe at the Commons. He told me that Marcia had Terry Lancaster of the *Daily Mirror* at Chequers at the weekend and that Terry had told him that she was violently attacking me to him.

A small crisis blew up in the afternoon when the chairmen of the nationalised industries held a meeting. They had been privately in touch with the Policy Unit and formed the impression – wrongly – that the PM would like to see them. Dick Marsh was about to announce this to the press when I heard about it and intervened to try to stop them. The PM doesn't want to see them for the moment – especially if they wish to criticise Benn. He told me that he doesn't want to get involved in attacking Benn any more – 'It is overkill already.' Actually all he has done is to brief the press that he will move Benn after the election. Typical of his oblique approach to leadership, always trying to avoid dealing with issues directly and head on.

Home at 9 p.m.

## Tuesday 13 May 1975

At 10.30 I attended a Cabinet committee on Social Policy, based on a good paper from the CPRS written by William Plowden. The PM liked it, everybody praised it, and it was decided to publish. In the middle of the meeting the PM left to talk to Joe about how to handle the lobby on the issue of the nationalised industries. He still thinks of the press all the time. Whenever we meet in the corridors he generally stops to chat about 'Isn't the press bloody awful today?' or 'Have you seen that terrible article in the *Guardian*?' I rarely have seen the pieces which offend him since they don't seem important to me. But he actually compares different editions of the same paper to compare ways in which their mistreatment of him alters from edition to edition.

He had a meeting at noon with John Hunt, Douglas Wass from the Exchequer and Healey to discuss the handling of public expenditure. John had put in a good paper in support of changes, to take decisions away from the Treasury – who on recent evidence have no feel for these questions at all. We briefed for more radical changes, bringing in ministers and political advisers so that there was a wider range of options and more political elements in the choices – whether of expenditure increases or cuts. When I talked to the PM a few minutes before the meeting he was well informed and fully supporting us. But Hunt later told me that at the start of the meeting he pretended to know nothing about it – in order not to be seen as initiating attacks on the Treasury. Fortunately Healey took a positive line and Hunt got most of what he wanted. Healey can be very good and independent on the handling of economic issues.

Lunch at the Reform Club with William Plowden.

Parliamentary Questions. Very dull. Nothing of interest.

I went to see the PM in the late afternoon about opinion polls on the referendum. I am managing the polls done by Bob Worcester. We already have the first two results – showing a big 'pro' lead but the need for HW to take a more positive role, especially in Scotland and the north. Now Callaghan wants to initiate more research and daily meetings in the early morning. HW told me to attend as his representative and to liaise with the research the Foreign Office is doing and to show Callaghan our poll results.

I was supposed to go to a No. 10 dinner in the evening on film finance. But I was not too keen on one or two of the guests, so I declined to go. Joe dropped out as well. Prefer to go home – at 9.30 p.m.

*Wednesday 14 May 1975*

Arrived at 9.45 for a 10 o'clock Cabinet committee on Defence. The first item was a proposal to spend over £100 million building a sea-based Harrier jump-jet aircraft – to operate from the new cruisers we are building at ruinous cost. Roy Mason put the case, cleverly confusing whether it was *essential* or *useful* to have this extra item. Then Field Marshal Carver, the able C-in-C of the Defence Staff – who, unexpectedly, has a stutter – supported him. On the ground that we needed to stop the Russians' Bear reconnaissance aircraft in 1982.

Healey then intervened and was really very good. He completely demolished the Defence case. He pointed out that two carriers in the West Atlantic, with *one* aircraft on deck and 19 below, was marginal to the problem of Russian attack – even assuming that the Russians were kind enough to choose that bit of the Atlantic where the two carriers were (and not to sink them, which would certainly happen in the first two minutes of any such war).

Mason then abandoned the Defence argument and put the case that the aircraft industry needs employment. Healey pointed out that was a totally different approach. But everybody else supported Mason. Callaghan described how frightening it was to be in a destroyer off Ireland in 1940 waiting for air support. Jenkins and Lever said our national credibility depended on no more cuts in Defence. Shore said he was 'totally convinced' by Mason's arguments. Beswick said that it was essential to employ 5,000 people. HW joined in and said that the exports of the Harrier were essential – although in fact there were no firm orders yet.

Mason said that we must build the sea-based Harrier because then the Shah of Iran might buy a cruiser from us. He had said the Shah would quite like a carrier with jump-jet Harriers on it. But there was no commitment or firm order at all.

On this evidence this government is bound to lead the nation into bankruptcy. The Chancellor was on the right side, but everybody was against him – despite having a deficit of £10,000,000,000. We must have big cuts in public expenditure. Yet if a Labour government won't cut Defence, what will it cut? Capital investment? This is crazy.

I was so furious that I walked out after this item of the agenda and did not stay for the others. We simply cannot go on spending 6% of our GNP on Defence, and borrowing 6% from abroad. Reality will hit us over the head before the end of 1975.

Went back to the office and processed a lot of papers. Then saw the secretary of the Cabinet from Fiji about our special advisers paper which the PM presented in Jamaica.

To lunch at Wheeler's with Michael Cudlipp, who is advising Merlyn Rees, the Northern Ireland Secretary, as PR. He said that Merlyn Rees now begins to acknowledge what I believe and have often argued to Michael – that we will have to withdraw from Northern Ireland at some point within 5–10 years. He has a great respect for Merlyn. Thinks he must be taken out of this job before he gets too tired – though Joe tells me that Merlyn has told HW he would like to stay there till the end of the year. Perhaps because he is afraid of being put into Education, which he and everybody sees as a dead end.

Back at Downing Street I met HW just back from a good lunch with the Archbishop of Canterbury. We went into No. 10 together and discussed matters very vaguely. Then he went off to the Commons to meet Gerry Fitt of the SDLP – which he had forgotten about. Patrick Wright went with him and told me later that he was in poor shape. Marcia telephoned as he arrived and he refused to take the call at first. Instead he went and had a stiff brandy. Then he said he would take the call in his room, and then personally locked the door to keep everybody, including the Irish who then arrived, outside. When he invited them in, Patrick was present and said he was 'not with it at all'.

Something is worrying him. Albert told Joe that yesterday HW said he was 'completely fed up' and was thinking of 'throwing it all in'. Certainly she is back on at him, and he is back on the brandy. He returned to No. 10 for a party in the garden of No. 10 given for the United Nations Association and was still, according to Joe, over the top. Joe ordered several photographers out of the party, but the PM countermanded the order. Joe became very depressed and told me that he was thinking of resigning. He is tired and fed up. I must make sure he does not go. Joe is essential to the sanity of No.10.

Joe told me that while he was having lunch with the Israeli Ambassador at his residence today Marcia telephoned. She was clearly haranguing the

Ambassador, who was unable to get a word in edgeways. She was apparently demanding to attend a reception for the Russian ballet dancers, the Panovs, tomorrow. She claimed that she was personally responsible for their release from Russia. In the end the Ambassador conceded and invited her to the reception. She certainly had been involved in the release of the Panovs.

However, Bill Housden tells me that she is not now going to her planned holiday in Israel.

In the evening Hugh Brown came in from the Scottish Office to discuss Scottish fishing rights. Very critical of Willie Ross.

Then a Unit meeting on local authority expenditure.

Finally home at 10 p.m.

## Thursday 15 May 1975

Came in at 9.15 to attend the first meeting of the special committee set up to plan the government's referendum campaign. In the Foreign Office, in the Ambassadors Waiting Room with Callaghan in the chair. Also there from the Commons were Shirley Williams, Roy Hattersley, Mellish, Bill Price, John Grant, and several Foreign Office officials.

Bob Worcester gave a clear visual presentation of the current state of public opinion, based on our private polls and the public opinion polls – all of which are showing the pro-vote at between 60% and 70% and the antis at 35% or below – and with the pros more committed to vote.

The doubtfuls concentrated among the working class, especially women, and especially in the north and Scotland. It is a very simple 'target vote' situation.

What is required is also simple – for the PM and the Labour leadership to campaign actively to persuade these basically Labour voters to support the EEC. Callaghan is very willing and is taking an active role. But the PM still does not have *any* speaking engagements during the referendum campaign. Joe and I set up a programme several weeks ago but Marcia intervened and abolished it on the ground that it was her job and not ours to organise his political speaking engagements. Since then she seems to have done absolutely nothing. It was very embarrassing at the meeting. We had before us on the table very impressive programme diaries, showing the speaking engagements of all the main participants between now and 5 June. There was one striking absentee from the list – the PM. He had none. People obliquely raised queries about it and I headed them off.

Two main problems emerged at the meeting.

First was the TV programmes – the BBC as usual is being difficult, selecting participants for their entertainment value rather than for their ability to put a case. We decided to send for Swann and Curran the bosses of the BBC tomorrow and have this raised.

Second is the relationship of our campaign to that by the Umbrella all-party organisation campaigning pro-Europe. They are fairly elitist and right-wing and their campaigning reflects this – hence they are not likely to have much effect on precisely those people that our research shows must be influenced – the D/E social groups in the north. Yet they are doing the TV broadcasts allocated to the pro-side by the broadcasting authorities. We decided to try to establish closer liaison with them in order to influence them and to press the BBC and ITV to give time for specific *government* broadcasts.

Jim chaired the meeting very well and forcefully, and is clearly enjoying taking the initiative and leadership on this. I walked back to No.10 with him for the 10.30 Cabinet, and we discussed future strategy, and especially the need to raise more money for more market research on waverers and switchers. We arranged that I would liaise with Roy Hattersley on this.

The Cabinet met on Arms to South Africa, and to redefine the guidelines for ministers appearing on television, to make it possible for them to appear together and present different views.

I worked in the Unit and also did some telephoning about getting more market research.

We had a long Unit meeting on public expenditure, trying to get at some alternative options, so that the next time the Treasury tries to bounce through some cuts – and this is inevitable – we are ready to try to introduce some political and intellectual sense into it. The level of argument in current Treasury papers is abysmally low and reflects their demoralisation. If they were published there would be a revolution.

Went to lunch with Ted Croker, the secretary of the Football Association, and Lord Brabourne from the film industry. Discussed pay TV – which attracts me as a way of raising money for my proposed Sports Levy Board.

Back to the Commons for Parliamentary Questions. Again the briefing was uneventful and the PQs quiet. The Opposition seems to have lost all its sting. HW is on top, but without being pressed too hard – which is a good thing since he is very tired and drinking too much brandy again. He even complained of being sleepy this afternoon, which is rare. He looks flabby and his eyes are red and watery.

He returned to No. 10 to record an ITV interview. I saw the end of it – not bad, but nothing new, except a slightly firmer commitment to staying in the Common Market.

Afterwards I talked to him about his referendum campaign speaking programme – or lack of one. He said it would all soon be under way, and this morning he had exploded at Albert – who is not at fault, of course, but it is HW's way of blaming Marcia without actually having the courage to do so. I told him that it was embarrassing at this morning's meeting and people were critical. He took the point and said it would now all happen.

We went downstairs together from his study to attend an Industrial Development Cabinet committee. I thought he was too tired to chair it, especially with an official dinner this evening, and suggested I should ask Ted Short to do it, but he declined, saying he must be there for all committees discussing Benn topics.

This committee was dealing with Benn's proposals (1) for a government receiver to take over firms going bust, (2) to prevent foreign firms closing down their subsidiaries, by freezing their assets, (3) to set up an Investment Bank to put money into firms rescued by Benn and (4) to discuss the criteria for government financial assistance to industry.

I attended part of the meeting, but then it broke up for ministers to go across to the Commons for an unexpected division. I went to my office for a cup of tea with Ken Berrill and then neither of us could be bothered to go back in. I was tired, and two hours of Bennery were more than I could take. God knows how the PM sits through it all.

The evening dinner was for the Fiji Prime Minister and his delegation on its way back from Jamaica. I had invited several friends – the Lewises from the LSE, and John Hale from the National Gallery.

We were all upstairs for drinks until 8.50, waiting for Marcia who arrived with Gerald Kaufman 20 minutes late. We immediately filed into the state banqueting room and sat down. After a few seconds Marcia got up, strode down to the back of the room, and shouted at Patrick Wright, the civil servant from private office, 'Don't you dare ever again allow people to sit down if their food is not ready to be served immediately. Go and do something about it immediately.' Patrick, who is a distinguished, intelligent and civilised man, just sat there and said nothing and did nothing. He told me afterwards that he had not come across this kind of low and boring behaviour before and so he did not know how to respond. We agreed that next time a two-fingered gesture would be appropriate. Fortunately the food arrived and Marcia went back to her seat next to Kaufman.

The meal went pleasantly. The PM made a charming speech of welcome. Just as the Fiji Prime Minister was rising to reply, Marcia stood up and stamped out of the room. She is heavy on her feet, so everybody heard and noticed. Poor pathetic Albert ran out after her.

Joe and I discussed it but had no idea what it was all about. But he had never seen such rudeness towards an official guest. People around were whispering.

After the meal the mystery was cleared up. Marcia returned to the reception room with her friend, the property developer Eric Miller, and brought in the singer Frank Sinatra. She was fawning all over Sinatra, who looked very American-Italian and had a large bodyguard with him. She took the PM off to talk to Sinatra.

Joe blew up. All his puritanism came out. We gathered that she wanted to attend the forthcoming Sinatra concert. Eric Miller, who is desperate to be in the honours list, was the go-between. To me it was all rather silly and did not matter very much, though I felt sorry for the Fiji guests, who did not get much time to talk to the PM.

We left at midnight, by when the PM was looking very tired.

### Friday 16 May 1975

Went at 9.30 to the daily Referendum Campaign committee in the Foreign Office – though Jim Callaghan was not there, as he is in Blackpool giving a speech. Bob Mellish was there, Roy Hattersley in the chair – and very good in guiding the meeting, very assured and well informed – together with John Grant, Bill Price, Tom McCaffrey (Jim's press officer), Tom McNally, Michael Butler and John Weston from the Foreign Office, and some people from the referendum unit sitting on the sofas at the back of the room.

Some procedure questions. Worcester's presentation; discussion of topics; discussion of TV and press problems – and some further discussion of the PM's role.

I went back to No. 10, where the PM had a meeting with Michael Swann and Hardiman Scott from the BBC, which apparently went well. The PM will now make a major appearance on TV in the final few days, as will Jim Callaghan.

After that he had a meeting at my suggestion with John Hunt and Douglas Allen on improving the procedures for making public appointments and selecting a wider range of people, especially in view of the new public boards we are setting up. This is something that Richard Graham from the Unit and I initiated last summer. Now it has come full circle with a committee report. We had briefed the PM for firm action. I should have attended the meeting really, but had another Unit meeting on public expenditure, for which I was already late after the referendum meeting.

After lunch I saw the PM and he reported on the meeting at length, saying that the Unit must play a major role in the process of trawling for better appointments. Apparently he gave that instruction to Allen and Hunt. He was in much better form than yesterday, looking brighter and less harassed.

Incidentally the Israelis telephoned No. 10 last night to ask for Marcia. They said that they had arranged her visit to Israel and that she was due to leave today (Friday). But they had now heard a rumour she was not going. Joe and I checked – apparently she is not going, but didn't bother to inform the Israelis, who had arranged and paid for the visit. Nor did she bother to tell Albert and his wife, who were invited and expecting to go away today. Poor Albert. He didn't know whether to pack his cases or not. But he dare not ask her.

Joe is getting very fed up. Most of the irritations are minor, on very trivial matters. But that is the appalling thing – the way the Prime Minister and the government of Great Britain are diverted by trivialities. That is what turns our stomachs – when there are so many critical problems, to see the Prime Minister and ourselves diverted in this way. Joe is very tired and is capable of blowing the lot. I ought to ignore such trivialities, but I get irritated at constantly hearing of her attacks on me and attempts to persuade the PM to get rid of me. I try to ignore it in public and get it off my chest at night into this diary.

Worked in the Unit in the afternoon completing a brief on world poverty with private office. Then home at 6.30 p.m. and out to a delightful dinner with Brian Knox, a brilliant partner at Grieveson Grant, the stockbrokers.

## Monday 19 May 1975

Some recollections from last week: HW told me on Friday that he thought 'Roy Jenkins is finished. Crosland is much better now.' He thought Crosland was much better placed for the leadership. He also thought that 'Healey won't get it when I go.'

Harry Kissin told me on Sunday that Michael Foot had a malignant cancer of the testicles. It has been operated on and he may recover. Kissin also said that Foot dislikes Marcia. That is allegedly why he would not serve in the 1964–70 government. Foot served in Wilson's Cabinet from 1974 because he had been assured that the old Kitchen Cabinet had been replaced. Kissin said that he was given the same assurance by HW. The fact that I was shown the proposed Cabinet on 4 March 1974 was supposed to be proof of this. But apparently HW has since told Kissin that he had to have Marcia around. He was vague about the reason, but left the impression he had no choice. Kissin thinks it is because HW is afraid somebody else will be hurt.

– Today. Went in to the Referendum Campaign meeting at 9.30. Nothing new. Callaghan again good in the chair. We decided to push prices and fight the antis on jobs.

All the polls are still steady at around 60/40–70/30 and it is hard to see how we can lose. But there is a long time to go.

Back to No. 10 to work on papers and read HW's draft speech for the

CBI. He had pondered this at the weekend and it is really first-class: firm on the EEC and on the economy. Encouraging. He is obviously picking himself up again.

He was at a liaison meeting at the TUC all morning, discussing a Jack Jones proposal for a new form of wage restraint, linking wages more closely to price rises.

I saw him just before lunch. Then I went out to have lunch with Monty Finniston at the British Steel Corporation. Very embarrassing. Since today the whole issue of steel closures comes to a head, with more marches, rallies and Benn attacking Finniston. It would be fatal for me to be seen going there, for it would be thought that HW was interfering.

Finniston and I tried to have a discreet lunch, discussing non-contentious matters, but in the end I advised him to cool things, treat it as a political situation and play it long. Later in the day we heard that he had made a compromise with the unions to defer the closures for a month – by when Benn should have been moved. After lunch there were crowds outside, and TV cameras, so Finniston took me down to the underground garage and out through an iron gate at the back.

He is an intelligent and sharp man, who clearly cares about the BSC. But perhaps a bit short-fused and not very politically adept. A manager's man rather than a politician's – which is as it should be.

I walked back to No.10, through St James's Park in glorious sunshine. Hard to believe that everything inside is falling apart, when everything outside looks so beautiful and fresh.

Worked in the Unit. Then saw Joe – who told me that the *Daily Mail* had discovered the story of Marcia not going to Israel and had telephoned to enquire. She and the PM were furious. They decided she had to go. Dare not be exposed on treating the Israelis so cavalierly. So she is going this weekend – under the pretence that HW wishes her to carry a personal message to the Israeli PM.

Albert is not going.

At 4 p.m. I went to the Cabinet committee on Northern Ireland. Long rambling discussion on the proposed convention and afterwards. And prospects for prolonging the present truce. Apparently our sources of information are diminishing during the truce. Because our informants have to be *arrested* and interrogated by the security forces to provide a cover for them to pass on information. Now they are not being arrested, as there is a truce, and they have no other safe way to pass on information.

It is clear that the Protestants are behaving much the worse of the two sides – more killings, more intimidation and gangsterism in their own areas, with big protection rackets.

At the end HW said that when the convention failed we might have to pull out our troops. Jenkins supported this strongly. Even Merlyn Rees said it was necessary progressively to distance Ulster from the rest of the UK.

Afterwards HW and Jenkins went upstairs to discuss the EEC campaign. Joe and I then went in to clear tonight's speech at the new Labour Museum in Tower Hamlets. The PM left at 5.45 and was back by 7.30. I was home by 8 p.m. Still very tired and looking forward to the holidays.

## Tuesday 20 May 1975

Referendum Campaign committee in the Foreign Office at 9.30. Callaghan in the chair – but Hattersley away abroad. No new polls – except analysis showing worrying volatility beneath the static surface majority to stay in.

By now the PM's programme has firmed up nicely and after the holiday he will be speaking virtually every day.

I walked back to No. 10 with Shirley Williams who was delightful, relaxed, confident, but quite disorganised as usual. She is an extremely attractive bundle of old-fashioned girlishness. In the meetings she frequently pulls Callaghan's leg, but he seems a bit slow in reacting.

Back in No. 10 I went up to the study for coffee and to work on the PM's speech to the CBI tonight. It is very good – strong on the Common Market, very tough on industrial policy. Not many changes needed.

We finished just before lunch. Ken Stowe stayed behind to clear various points. I went back upstairs and could hear the telephone ringing in the study. HW was not answering it. Ken Stowe later told me that HW said, 'It's only Marcia. She is not well. Joe Stone has been giving her drugs. I've heard all about it.' I waited in the lobby outside the study door and the phone rang for the messenger. Marcia was demanding that the messenger find out why the PM was not answering her. The poor little messenger went in to the PM, who said he would phone later, but also said to the messenger, 'Remember, you haven't found me.'

The outside telephone rang again. I was standing next to the messenger and heard him reply to a string of questions, including one whether it was me in there with HW. Then it rang again and a man's voice was phoning at Marcia's request, pressing the messenger to tell the PM to come straight away and talk to Marcia.

Finally the PM came out with Ken. I joined them and we went down-stairs to private office and he was there for half an hour chatting away to us all about every subject under the sun – including fixing his speaking engagements – before finally, at 1.35 p.m., going to telephone her from her room.

I met him coming out 10 minutes later looking very grim and grey. I then took him back in again and told him of Finniston's offer yesterday to give Marcia a job on the Steel Board. At first he welcomed it, saying, 'It might make her a bit happier.' But then he saw the problems. I said he must be very careful not to get too closely involved in BSC affairs and he agreed.

Press enquiries about Marcia's failure to go to Israel last week led her to explain that she had been prevented from going by illness.

At lunch in No. 10 I tasted the food of our latest cook, recruited by Robin Butler. Very good and nice to be eating in the house again – though we have to eat in the *pantry* as part of the compromise package. The PM has been under great pressure from Marcia to prevent the lunches. The compromise is that we eat lunch, but not in the dining-room. She had also tried to stop us using the kitchen, on the basis that Mrs Pollard, the PM's cook, might want it. This is ludicrous, since Mrs Pollard uses the kitchen in the flat, and the state kitchen is about 100 square yards in area. The PM abandoned this argument under pressure from Ken.

The private secretaries told us that there was a Home Office inquiry into an alleged scandal about Frank Sinatra being given privileged treatment through Customs last weekend. The airport authority refused this at first – partly from suspicion that Sinatra's friends might carry guns – but then a telephone call came from Chequers. Apparently Eric Miller was at Chequers on the phone saying, 'We would like him to get VIP treatment.' It was implied that the PM was behind this, though Ken Stowe is not sure he was.

Parliamentary Questions went quietly again.

Finished the day's work in the Unit. Then home quite early, at 8 p.m.

### Wednesday 21 May 1975

Took the tube in and went to the morning meeting of the Referendum Campaign committee. David Ennals in the chair. Not much new to report. Shirley was very agitated about this morning's NEC. The Left has put forward, without warning, a proposal that Transport House should not even circulate the engagements or speech dates of pro-marketeers. This is just silly spitefulness. There has already been a big row in Transport House. Ron Hayward has already acted as if the decision is taken and Percy Clarke was furious and threatened to resign. The idea behind this manoeuvre is to prevent pro-Market speakers getting any party publicity and so getting any audiences.

Shirley took me out of the room with her and went to telephone Jim Callaghan, who was at the BBC. She also asked me to go to talk to the PM and suggest that he go along to the NEC.

I went to see the PM who was about to dictate his speech for tomorrow's economic debate. He was against intervening, thinking it rather trivial, and would arouse more sympathy than it would do damage. I went back to the Foreign Office to see Shirley and we drove together round to Transport House for the NEC. The final irony was that as we arrived Shirley realised that she had got the time of the meeting wrong – it was much earlier in the morning, so she might have failed to get there anyway.

Back to the Policy Unit at No. 10, where I had a meeting with Andrew Graham and David Piachaud to discuss this evening's brief on public expenditure. The Chancellor has circulated papers suggesting cuts in public expenditure of £3 billion by 1978–79. We don't oppose this, as public expenditure must be controlled and reduced. But the Chancellor makes no serious argument for it, and his method – just lopping x% off everything – is typical of the way the Treasury does things. Unthinking and unselective, with no political philosophy behind the cuts.

Went for lunch with the PM and Joe at the Charing Cross Hotel with the *Guardian* – Alastair Hetherington, Peter Preston, who is replacing Hetherington as editor, and the nice management man, Peter Gibbings.

It was a delightful lunch. The PM was very relaxed, and talked very convincingly about his ideas for a 'national dividend' with TUC and CBI agreeing beforehand on the right division of the national product between wages, investment, exports, public and private consumption, etc. Then do the Budget accordingly and use a tax regulator to make mid-term adjustments.

The *Guardian* people were more optimistic than last time about newspaper finances. But Preston seemed subdued beside Hetherington. Perhaps he will gain in confidence once he really takes over.

Back to No. 10 where we all assembled in the study to work on the PM's draft of his speech for the economic debate in the Commons tomorrow. Went easily with few problems. The draft was adequate and mainly composed of passages which he had given before. Then just before we had finished the telephone rang. It was Marcia and she was obviously going on and on. HW could barely get a word in. Within two minutes of his putting the phone down it rang again and it was her again. HW tried to reassure here that something was OK and that he had personally spoken with somebody to put it right. After this HW was very unsettled and seemed unable to concentrate on the speech, which ended in a bit of a mess.

We broke up and went downstairs.

Joe told me some background. Yesterday Mrs Miller, Eric Miller's wife, had apparently telephoned Marcia to complain about her friendship with Miller. Marcia immediately collapsed and took to her bed ill. Joe Stone was sent for and applied sedatives. This is why she did not come to the office yesterday.

Now she is definitely *not* going to Israel with Eric Miller this Friday.

Went back to the office and worked on our brief on public expenditure. Completed it just in time to fly off to the Mermaid Theatre to take Carol to see Shaw's *Doctor's Dilemma* with our friends the Grahams. Drab production but still enjoyable because Shaw writes so well.

Incidentally HW now has worked out his programme to hang Benn after the referendum. Cabinet committee at Chequers on the Industry Bill on Friday 13 June. Cabinet on Monday. TUC and CBI on Tuesday and Wednesday. And Cabinet reshuffle at the weekend. He actually hopes that Benn will resign after the Friday meeting, when Benn's amendments will be dropped, and the government's amendments, meeting the CBI's fears, and also improving HW's power to make all appointments, will be agreed.

## Thursday 22 May 1975

Went into No. 10 before going to the Referendum Campaign committee. Saw the PM, who has made major alterations to his speech this afternoon. He went to the Cabinet committee on Economic Strategy at 9.45 and I walked across to the Foreign Office for the meeting. Quite an instructive discussion on how to press the issues of prices and jobs. Our polls still showing rock solid 70–30 after elimination of Don't Knows.

Cabinet at 10.30 a.m. Beforehand HW took Harold Lever into the Cabinet Room and – I learned later – asked him to become Minister of the Arts in the reshuffle. But HW was not clear and Lever was too bemused to ask whether this appointment was instead of, or in addition to, his economic job. I saw Lever after Cabinet and he was in a tizzy and asked to see me soon. Ray Richardson, his special adviser, phoned later and said HL would not accept if it was just the Arts.

Apparently the PM now definitely wants to bring the Arts under No. 10 and Lever is the only way he can do it. He may wish to appoint a Lord to do the day-to-day business but he needs a spokesman in the Commons – and clearly cannot be a spending minister himself. I wonder why he wants the Arts under No. 10. Show business, I suppose.

The Cabinet discussed public expenditure. They passed HW's proposals for new procedures of control without any trouble. Then on to the Treasury's papers. These were blocked by Crosland, by Benn – who said that 'time and events' would 'make it all irrelevant' – and by Castle. Nobody supported Healey, who was understandably looking quite forlorn by the end of the meeting. He is politically isolated and disagrees with his own officials. He needs support from somewhere. He won't say straight out that he is allowing unemployment to rise, partly to discourage excessive wage claims psychologically, partly to make room for manoeuvre on the next upturn in 1976–77. He tries to avoid giving any explanation, which leaves everybody dissatisfied – as does the crude Treasury technique of making cuts by simply taking x% off everything.

The PM came out of the meeting halfway through to go to the toilet, saw Joe and me, and said, 'It's very rough going in there.'

Afterwards one of the private secretaries said he thought he had seen the beginning of the end for Denis Healey. Not because he is trying to do unpopular things – though he is, has to, and that is always difficult. But because he doesn't know how to carry people with him. It is a very lonely job. And the old Treasury 'bounce' won't work any longer. There are too many members of the Cabinet who won't be treated as if they are economic idiots – especially Crosland.

After Cabinet Joe, myself and the private secretaries waited to clear the speech for this afternoon with the PM – we only had till 3.15 and we had still not been through the 38-page draft together.

But HW went in to see Marcia and he stayed on and on. We stood around outside. Nick Stuart went in to remind him. Finally at 10 minutes to 2 most of us went off to lunch. Joe stayed behind to work on the speech, but he was fuming and furious. He, Nick and HW finally finished the speech at 2.30 – then we all had to dash to the Commons to brief for Questions.

The Economic debate was poor but fascinating. Mrs Thatcher started quite well, serious and criticising the government's economic policies seriously. But she never made a *speech*, just a string of briefs. It got worse as it went on and by the end the Tories were looking glum.

HW beamed delightedly at her failure, and from the moment he got to his feet it was clear he was going to win the battle. Actually there was even less economic content in his speech than in Thatcher's, but it was a real speech, with themes, with light patches mixed in with the serious, and ending with a savage denunciation of the Tory arguments. He made no attempt to present a government policy. He simply performed, like a matador, and by the end Mrs Thatcher was effectively despatched. How far the solution of the country's economic problems was advanced was not clear, but the Labour back-benchers looked happy.

Back to No. 10 to clear up the Unit's business before the holiday.

Kissin came in to see the PM at 6.30 and apparently, Kissin told me later, he was in excellent form. He teased Kissin about his coming reshuffle and bet that he would not guess what would happen to Benn.

Kissin did not guess Energy.

HW also apparently praised me, but was critical of Harold Lever – who phoned me in the evening.

Michael Foot came in for a talk before the holiday. Still looking grey and ill. I talked to him for a while, but found him very unforthcoming. He is actually very guarded and discreet.

We all went upstairs at about 8 p.m. and HW dictated his statement tomorrow on the problems of the textile industry – and why we cannot impose import controls. Then general chat. He was very pleased with himself after today's debate. He had drunk a lot of brandy but it did not show. Parliamentary successes are the things which give him most lift.

Home at 9.30.

## Friday 23 May 1975

Today was supposed to be a holiday for me. But HW decided to come in – to do his textile statement. Not very good, with little specific to offer, and not well received by an almost empty house. Then back to No. 10 for a TV interview with Robin Day. Not bad, though he lapsed into the inevitable attacks on the press, which afterwards in the study he always regrets and at the same time defends. It is a compulsion beyond his control.

To lunch with Harold Lever at 1.30 where we discussed problems associated with his Arts appointment. Is he intended to be just a front-man? Then home at last at 3.45. To Suffolk.

## Wednesday 28 May 1975

Feel refreshed from lovely Suffolk holiday. Went straight in to the morning EEC campaign meeting in the Foreign Office. Hattersley in the chair. Our latest polls show a slip to the antis – mainly previous don't-knows moving anti.

In to No. 10 where I clear a backlog of papers. The Unit is still discussing public expenditure. See Joe, who is still badly bruised from a road accident he suffered last week.

Apparently HW is furious with Roy Jenkins for his personal attack on Benn. And is doing detective work on who has leaked to the papers the story of Marcia's behaviour at the Fiji dinner. He got hold of the dinner list and the list for Trudeau, which had a leak as well, and is comparing them for common names. It boils down to Joe, Albert and me, plus Peter Blaker, the Tory MP, who seems due to get a bad reputation for gossip, regardless. I certainly did not.

Took Patrick Wright to lunch at the Reform.

Afterwards to see Harry Evans for coffee at the Garrick. The *Sunday Times* is doing a hatchet job on Benn this weekend. But like all journalists Harry is fascinated by the way Benn has taken over this referendum. He will lose it, but it has been *his* referendum, from inception to the end. He has charisma.

Back to No. 10. HW returned from giving a speech at the General Municipal Workers Union which I arranged. Not many people there, but it was a platform. Not much coverage either, because ITV is on strike and the BBC did not bother to come.

He did two more TV recordings at No. 10 – including more attacks on 'some newspapers'. It is paranoia now.

We also discussed future speeches. He is unhappy with the briefs on food prices in the EEC – including the Unit brief. Says they are lies. But not clear what he wants. In fact he is still trying to present a *balanced* argument, when what is needed in the last week is an authoritative statement by the PM.

He asked me to prepare his Saturday speech at the Midland regional rally. I won't enjoy that.

He then saw Harold Lever, and Terry Lancaster from the *Mirror*. I had half an hour with Lever afterwards. He had come to clarify the position on the Arts, but in the end did not raise it. He is still very good fun, the most vulnerably human of the ministers.

HW left for Chequers at 7.30.

I walked up Charing Cross Road, bought a salt-beef sandwich, and then taxi home to watch Leeds sadly beaten in the European cup final.


*Thursday 29 May 1975*

Went in to work on draft of HW's speech for Saturday. Robin Butler and I put it together in time for the PM to have with him on the plane today going to the NATO meeting in Brussels.

Went to lunch by myself at the Reform, then back in the afternoon for a long meeting with Ted Croker, secretary of the FA, about sports finance and pay TV. He is the best of the sports people.

Joe phoned from Brussels to say that the speech was not what the PM wanted. Has changed his mind again – for the 4th time.

He is very jumpy about his speeches at the moment. Partly because he is not getting the newspaper coverage which he normally assumes to be his right. Partly because the situation in the last week of the campaign requires very firm and unequivocal speeches. His style so far has been to give carefully balanced and subdued arguments. He is clearly unhappy at having to come out so firmly in favour of the Market – because, as Joe says, he is emotionally anti-Market. He is required to be in favour, but he is really a Little Englander, and at heart he agrees with every word that Peter Shore says. So he fights to the end against actually telling people to vote yes. On the radio this morning he gave a long exposition of his approach to the EEC, but never actually brought himself to say he was for staying in. He is also being irritable towards Joe and myself because we are pushing him to be more assertive.

Came home early, at 7.30, and went to a nice supper with Helene Hayman,* the young Labour MP, who has just moved in to the house across the road.

## Friday 30 May 1975

Referendum campaign meeting at 9.30. Hattersley in the chair. Our polls still totally static, around 70–30 after eliminating the don't-knows.

Big fuss about John Gilbert, a Treasury minister, going on to the radio claiming that VAT and other taxes will go up if we stay in the EEC. Quite wrong for a Treasury minister to make statements on future taxation. Everybody is trying to get Healey to repudiate him. But Healey is shrewdly hiding in Paris, out of touch with his private office, having told his private secretary that he does not want to get involved. Denis has still not made *one single* speech in favour of staying in the Market. Just a press statement last weekend. The Left will not thank him. While the Right are furious with him. Late this evening Shirley Williams and John Lyttle phoned me from South Wales to ask if she should attack Gilbert on radio. I said no – wait to see if the press or TV pick up the VAT story. If not, why draw attention to it. So far they have ignored it.

Back in No. 10 I worked on drafting a section for the PM's speech in Glasgow on Monday. Talked to Kay Carmichael in Glasgow and then wrote a piece about how Scottish culture had always been more European than England's.

Lunch at White's Club with the minister and counsellor from the French embassy. They are worried, quite properly, about us being bored with Europe and not wanting any progress on EEC matters after the referendum. HW is bound to want to hear no more of it. Better if the Foreign Office takes over.

When the officials returned from Brussels they said that the PM had not been in a good mood. Had been openly rude to Giscard, by ignoring him and claiming he would refuse to have dinner with the Belgium Prime Minister Tindemans.

Marcia was on the phone to him for half an hour in Brussels. Wants the PM to write to Eric Miller. She also apparently phoned Mrs Miller at 4 in the morning.

Went to the theatre in the evening with Carol and our friends the Reads. To see *Travesties* at the Aldwych. Bit pretentious, but immensely entertaining.

To bed at 1 a.m. Surprisingly tired after a lighter week than usual.

*Saturday 31 May 1975*

Joe phoned to say that the PM had been on to him twice to say how pleased he was with the speech briefs we did.

The PM is an incredible worker. Having flown back from Brussels he immediately worked on today's speech and on a *Daily Mirror* article, phoning Joe with corrections at 11 at night.

*Monday 2 June 1975*

9.30 campaign referendum meeting. John Morris, the Secretary for Wales, in the chair. Also there – Mellish, Ennals, Grant, Bill Price and the usual Foreign Office crowd. Polls still absolutely static – 69–31. No reason to change our strategy. But continued concern was expressed at Healey's attitude – he still hasn't made a speech. And refuses either to deny Gilbert's statements about VAT going up in the EEC, or to let Dell and Lever deny them. I phoned Lever after the meeting and he said he would issue a statement, but later he contacted me and said that Healey had vetoed it.

Back to No. 10 and read over the PM's Glasgow speech – he was still out at Chequers. In the first draft he excluded my two pages on Scotland, but Joe and Robin Butler both pressed for their inclusion so they went into the second draft.

The first draft was 56 quarto pages long – about two hours – and would certainly have converted the Scots to independence from Brussels, Westminster, etc and especially from HW! We later got it down to 30 pages.

Went out to lunch with Joe. We went to Fleet Street to collect my new shoes from Baseley's, to the LSE to telephone, to the Aldwych to eat, to the Strand to buy stamps and then walked back to No. 10. A cold, bright day and a pleasure to get out in the fresh air.

Joe thinks HW has lost his quality and it would be a mistake if he used the referendum victory as an excuse to go on for ever. He thinks it will be a March 1976 departure – but sees the pull of the Queen's 1977 Jubilee. [Wilson announced his resignation in March 1976.]

We each believe he should make a clear victory statement on Friday – saying this ends the argument, now we must unite and solve our problems. Or if we lose, he should say he will go to Parliament for a vote of confidence, and shortly will retire.

Back at No. 10 I spent the afternoon reading Lord Kennet's 'Europe plus 30', an EEC proposal for setting up a forecasting institute. More Brussels bureaucracy at great expense.

The PM came in from Chequers to record a TV interview before going to Glasgow. On the way he dropped in on Marcia. Afterwards she telephoned

Albert to tell him to tell Joe that the PM was very depressed, thinking of retiring, and we must all rally round to cheer him up and make him go on. Joe put this to HW, who apparently just shrugged his shoulders and said he threatened to go to stop her getting at him.

The papers are on to the story of interventions from Chequers by first Eric Miller and then Albert speaking as if with the PM's authority, to get Sinatra privileged treatment at London airport. The PM has ordered Joe to deny that any such instructions were given from Chequers. It is true that the PM didn't. But others did.

Joe also senses that the PM suspects him of being the source of leaks. The PM has asked him to place a story 'with a gossip columnist'. Joe is too fly for that and will state that he doesn't know any. If he did do it, that would be seen as proof that he is the source of leaks, which obsess the PM more and more. He gossips freely in front of anybody.

The sad thing is that so much energy and ingenuity is spent on the newspapers, and so little on policy. That is why the EEC guidelines on dissenting ministers voting fell apart – because HW had never thought them through.

He is showing his usual 'pre-election' irritability – made worse because the press and TV are giving him very little coverage. This is understandable. His speeches are now commendably *firm* for going in, no equivocation at all. But they are long and rambling. He is not using Joe at all, so all his sentences are half a page long and totally unquotable.

Home at 7.30. More confident we will win, but keen to end it and get on with economic policy.


## Tuesday 3 June 1975

At the campaign referendum meeting in the Foreign Office. Callaghan not there, but Shirley Williams was there, Roy Hattersley, Grant and Price, and John Morris again in the chair. No new ideas. There had been a slip away from us – 66–34 – but still an apparently unassailable position, so no reason to change tactics.

Shirley Williams told us about a terrible row in the organisation 'Britain in Europe'. Mrs Thatcher is furious at the publicity given to Heath – who is now far ahead of her in the polls – and has violently attacked Whitelaw for allowing it. She has forced them to drop Heath from their propaganda.

Back to No. 10 where we worked on the PM's speeches for tonight – and for tomorrow in Cardiff, which was not much better. Very tired. Firmly pro – but flabby and tired.

Kay Carmichael telephoned to say that his Glasgow speech went very well, especially our Scottish bit.

Apparently, Janet told me, when he got back from Glasgow at midnight Marcia went to meet him at Northolt. She took along the Israeli Ambassador to have a discussion about Middle Eastern problems – at midnight, after a mass meeting in Glasgow! Finally he got away to Chequers and in the car said to Janet, 'Marcia must be going round the bend.'

I went out to lunch at Grieveson Grant, in the City. Very lively as usual. No ill-will to the government, just puzzled that we are doing nothing on the economic front.

Spent the afternoon reading. Rather bored. Waiting for the referendum on Thursday. Confident it will go OK, but just nagging doubts. Memories of 1970.

The PM came in to record a radio interview and then saw Healey – who had asked to see him about his 'position in the Cabinet after the referendum'.

A very slack day really, which leaves me feeling restless. The PM is also grouchy and looks unhappy. Perhaps a bit nervous. But also fed up. He hates the referendum. He dislikes having to make speeches in favour of the referendum especially when he gets so little TV and newspaper coverage. He needs a fresh boost. The poll on Thursday may give it. But it may depress him further by opening up the vista of economic mine-fields ahead.

I came home at 8 p.m. Then heard on the news that his meeting at St Pancras Town Hall had been disrupted and he had been unable to deliver his speech – which must have been a relief to all who know how bad it was. But useful politically. He immediately called a press conference to denounce the extremism of the antis – and got publicity his speech would never have got.


## Wednesday 4 June 1975

The PM did not come in today. Stayed at Chequers till teatime and then went by road to Cardiff – he prefers the car to aeroplane.

Ken Stowe told me that Healey came in last night to talk about the reshuffle after the referendum. The PM raised the question of John Gilbert's behaviour, and Healey defended him saying he didn't want to lose him. The PM then said he was not going to move Dell from the Treasury – he had thought of putting him to Industry, but now felt he needed somebody more left-wing. Healey raised the question of Prentice: half defending him, saying he had done nothing wrong, though was not a success as Minister at Education.

The PM did not show his hand very much. No hint of his plan to put Benn to Energy.

I went to the final meeting of the Referendum Campaign committee in the Ambassadors Waiting Room at the Foreign Office. Jim Callaghan in the chair. The poll figures were not bad – 67–33 – but the more detailed issue polls were all moving against us. Callaghan said he sensed the public mood turning against us and felt that 'in another week we would be in trouble'. I did not agree with this – nor did Bob Worcester. The change was too marginal. We then discussed Callaghan's speech at the final rally in Cardiff tonight. He proposed to put up a series of questions to the antis, which they had so far failed to answer. I strongly disagreed, saying that at a rally they simply wanted a strong affirmation of how to vote. People have had enough of arguments and questions. They want a lead. John Morris supported me, as did John Grant, and Callaghan quickly accepted and scribbled a few speech notes.

I also suggested that we should start to create modest expectation of a result – say 15% lead. Then if we got a 20% lead – less than the opinion polls predicted – it would look like a victory and not a disappointment. Callaghan did not agree. I had in mind the post-referendum situation, and the need to crush the Left and emphasise how little public support they had.

These morning meetings have been very good. Well chaired, especially by Callaghan and Hattersley. Well briefed by Bob Worcester, who covers every point we could conceivably be interested in. Good mixture of politicians – except for Mellish, who is crude and unconstructive – and civil servants. Nice to start the day with some tactical and strategic political thinking. And Jim is a much better listener than HW. Also has many less hidden prejudices which threaten to disqualify the advice or adviser regardless of the quality of the advice. I partly envy Tom McNally his job.

Back to No. 10 and read and talk in rather desultory way – there have been no papers of any importance this week – which is symptomatic of how the referendum has totally halted all government. But the Cabinet Office's 'Forward Look' for the next three months is horrendous. A massive backlog of delayed policy decisions, especially in the economic and industrial field.

This prospect must be daunting to the PM. He told Janet on the way back from Glasgow that he now felt exhausted, and the job gave him little satisfaction. He said he still enjoys *being* Prime Minister, but is bored by much of the work. He told her he was thinking of going in October. This is 6 months earlier than he told Joe, but is part of a recurring theme. He has nearly had enough. How long can Prime Ministers hold on, once they lose the taste for power, with packs of candidates for the job snapping at their heels?

I went to lunch with Pat Nairne at the Reform. Was tempted to tell him about his coming knighthood, but he probably knows anyway. Well deserved. He is worried about the anti-Market ministers after the referendum and thinks they should be moved off the relevant committees. The club was full of top civil servants, whom I did not know but Pat Nairne pointed them out to me. The bureaucracy eats well – and shrewdly avoids the Cabinet Office canteen.

Slack afternoon at No.10. Some irreverent discussion in private office of tomorrow's Beating the Retreat ceremony. Marcia has submitted a personal guest list of 80. Not a secretary from No.10. Not Joe or me. Just a long list of supporters – Eric Miller, Rudi Sternberg, Sigmund Sternberg, Prince Radiwicz, etc., and several Israelis. The PM's only guest is General Gowon of Nigeria, who has recently broken off all relations with Israel, so the party could be an interesting one. A bomb under the stand would leave large blanks in future honours lists.

Michael Palliser came in to see me between 6 and 7.15 p.m. He had asked for the meeting but had nothing specific to raise. He has carried the burden of renegotiations in Brussels more than anybody else, so this is quite a moment for him, the end of a long odyssey – as it is for me in a lesser way. He is very old school, obviously an ex-guardsman. Not an intellectual genius, but impressively powerful, well balanced and sensible. Not somebody I would oppose lightly. Is going to be head of the Foreign Office in July and should be very good. His capacity for work is staggering.

Went home feeling rather nervous. Went out to a pub for a drink after supper, and then across the road to Helene Hayman, who had Dipak Nandy and others for supper. General view that Benn has made political ground dangerously.

To bed at 1 a.m.


## Thursday 5 June 1975

Referendum day. Awoke feeling edgy. Not because of any doubts about the results – I sense that the mood has swung our way again in the final hours. Just because it is the end of a very long haul. And I know from previous experience that there is always a reaction from HW after an election – last time he tried to push me out. There is bound to be some nonsense from the political office, and the economy stretches ahead, a minefield with no moonlight.

Went in to No. 10 late, having travelled to the West End on a bus with the children. Saw HW when I got in. He had just voted, and said that the turnout in his Westminster area was higher than a general election. He said that he had been feeling tired, especially after the St Pancras meeting, but was now picking up again.

I went to the noon weekly meeting of Deputy Secretaries in the Cabinet Office. We were dealing with the government's 'Forward Look' for the next three months. An enormous programme. Everything delayed by the referendum and now piling up. Too much to complete. Also it does all pile up incrementally, without much thought for priorities and without much sense that this is in fact our government's programme for the months ahead, or any idea of a strategy which must be built into it with some priorities. Hunt took it all in 10 minutes. I made a few comments, but was unable to get in on lots of good points raised with me beforehand by Unit members.

Had half an hour's chat with Ken Stowe back in No. 10 about staffing. Robin Butler is finally (and greatly to my regret) going back to the Treasury this summer. The Treasury is trying to put somebody in his place. We are resisting it, and hope to get Nick Stuart (the secretary for parliamentary affairs) promoted there. The assumption that the Treasury can always command a place in the No. 10 private office is anyway to be resisted. Spies are inevitable, but departmental espionage should not become a hereditary right. They must work for it.

Lunch at No. 10 with Joe and private office. Then again a rather desultory afternoon.

The PM saw Callaghan and Healey about plans to deal with the situation after the referendum result – Commons announcement, etc. Then Healey stayed behind and they discussed the timing of various meetings over the next two weeks. HW is seeing the CBI, the TUC, meeting of NEDDY, plus all day at Chequers on the Industry Bill, and they have to be careful to get them in the right order.

Hal Sonnenfeldt, over from Washington, telephoned from the Foreign Office and dropped in for a chat. He may come to supper on Sunday. He has been on tour with President Ford and says it all went remarkably well.

Gowon of Nigeria came in to see the PM. Then it was the Beating the Retreat ceremony on Horse Guards Parade. Lady Falkender's guests arrived impressively. A long line of new Rolls-Royces debouched into Downing Street a string of men looking as if they had spent most of their lives selling second-hand cars. When one of the secretaries in private office enquired if he ought to go to help to usher them in, Joe said, 'No, the only sensible thing to do is to go and fingerprint them.' Lady Falkender had sent round a message at the last minute inviting Joe and me to take one of the remaining spare places on the stand but we firmly declined.

I walked to Charing Cross with Joe and then up to Soho where I had a drink in the French pub, which I had not visited in two years. A bit seedy now, but still nice to stand in the evening sun with a pint of bitter and watch London buzz by. Then walked up to Cambridge Circus – another half-pint – and up Tottenham Court Road to Goodge Street. Sunny, warm and a touch of holiday time about London. The newspaper headlines were all about a landslide victory in the referendum. No sense, however, among the people around of a great day of decision. They did not look as if they had voted!

Took a 24 bus to Hampstead South, had another half-pint and then walked across the heath home. Fabulous sunset. Families playing on the grass. Home to listen to my new Beethoven string quartets on tape. Still trying to hold some special sense of a day of destiny. Bed at midnight. If it goes wrong tomorrow, we are out of a job. And the country in a mess.

## Friday 6 June 1975

Took my transistor radio in to the office to listen to the referendum results – and a bottle of champagne to celebrate. A glorious sunny day – European weather. The results were late coming in, expected shortly after 11, but did not really begin till well after midday, but then absolutely in line with the polls, a resounding victory!

HW sent in from Chequers a draft of his victory statement. Perfectly OK, except completely impersonal. No welcoming of the victory. As if he were not involved. So I telegraphed, through private office, suggesting that he should (a) personally welcome the result and (b) say it was a victory of approval for the government's recommendation.

He accepted (b) but ignored (a).

[Telegraph:

Prime Minister from Ken Stowe
Draft statement by the Prime Minister
I have shown your draft statement to Joe and Bernard. We have minor drafting amendments to suggest. The revised text follows:

The British people, in clear and unmistakable terms, have made their historic decision that Britain shall remain a member of the European Community.
Their verdict has been given by a vote, and by a majority, bigger than that achieved by any government in any general election since the war. No one in Britain, in Europe or the wider world should have any doubt about its meaning.
It was a free vote, without constraint, following a free democratic campaign conducted constructively and without rancour.
It means that fourteen years of national argument are over. It

means that all those who have had reservations about Britain's commitment should now join wholeheartedly, without stint, in the task of overcoming the economic problems that assail us as a nation, and work wholeheartedly with our partners in Europe, and our friends everywhere, to meet the challenges confronting the whole world.

There are two points for comment. First, we doubt if it will be clear by the time you speak that the outcome will be better than the election of 1931. The coalition government then got nearly fifteen million votes totalling 67% of those cast. It would make your statement clumsy to differentiate between a one-party government and a coalition. We suggest therefore that for this statement we play safe and say since the war, although you could add 'and it might turn out in this century'.

Second, Bernard asks do you wish personally to welcome the result by adding at the end of the first paragraph the words 'they have overwhelmingly supported the government's recommendation'?]

I telephoned Robert Armstrong in the Home Office to come and share some champagne. Because we had originally been the only two senior pro-marketeers in No. 10 and had seen the whole cycle from early hostility by HW to conversion in his final declaration after Dublin.

In fact, in my view, HW is still mildly anti-European, in the sense that *personally* he doesn't like Europeans, their style of life or politics. But he decided – probably after October, possibly from long ago – that a 'yes' position was in fact best for Britain, most likely to hold the party together (because the pro-marketeers were more passionately pro than the antis were anti and more likely to split the party) and most likely to be a winning position. So he suppressed his prejudices and took a pro-position. But in fact his prejudices kept coming out.

Robert and I had a pleasant drink – although my champagne had gone a bit flat – and then we went to a celebration party in Joe's room. I went on to lunch at the American embassy for Hal Sonnenfeldt, with Harold Lever, John Hunt from the Cabinet Office, and Ron Spiers from the embassy. I felt quite euphoric and enjoyed myself immensely. So much that I teased Lever and he lost his temper with me. Actually the stroke he suffered in 1972 – and age – have left their mark. He quickly loses his temper. His originally marvellous sense of humour doesn't now survive pressure for long. And he is worried if anybody else is doing the talking for long. But he is still very good, and we made it up and went off together to the pro-Market celebration party. This was a risk, since HW would strongly disapprove – it was full of Tories and Jenkinsites. I talked to Shirley Williams, Silvia Rodgers, Jennifer Jenkins, Dora Gaitskell – and some men as well, but no Tories. By the time Lever and I left – around 4 p.m. – the result was clearly tied up our way.

HW arrived back at No. 10 shortly after six and read his little statement on the doorstep. Marcia had come in a bit before. The whole staff gathered in the hall, like after an election, and welcomed HW in. He was just about to go up to the study with Joe, myself and the private secretaries to celebrate when he paused at the foot of the stairs and said, 'I had better go to see Marcia.' Shortly after a messenger was sent for to take in champagne, and then Jim Callaghan arrived to see him.

The private secretaries stood around aimlessly with the Foreign Secretary. I was not prepared to stand around waiting for this nonsense to end so I went to Joe's room to watch television. Joe stormed in, shouting that he was not prepared to be kept waiting while Marcia 'who has contributed nothing to this victory, except to bugger it up by her incompetence, sits there drinking champagne'.

I left with Joe and went to a party with an old friend Nicholas Deakin, ending up at a late-night Irish dance in the Forum, Kentish Town.

## Saturday 7 June 1975

Joe phoned to say that HW had later commented on our absence yesterday evening. He did not phone Joe but sent an enquiry to him through a junior in the press office. But Joe did not phone back.

Incidentally HW's pre-referendum prediction was a winning ratio of *13–8* – and too pessimistic.

[In the referendum ballot on 5 June 1975, declared on a high turnout of 64.5% on 6 June, the result was as follows:

17,378,581 or 67.2% voted YES
8,470,073 or 32.8% voted NO

The *Daily Telegraph* concluded on 7 June: 'The result is quite frankly a triumph for Mr Wilson.']

# CHAPTER 16

# A Botched Reshuffle – and Burying Bennery
## June 1975

*Monday 9 June 1975*

Drove in early to No.10. Dealt with letters and papers and saw a man from the Civil Service Department about salaries of special advisers. Some dramatic increases are scheduled simply because they are linked to Civil Service rates – anybody aged 26 gets £6,000.

Cabinet met at 11.30. I went down and chatted with Shirley Williams and John Morris. HW was upstairs with Callaghan discussing the reshuffle, which is now intended for this evening. It was intended to put Rees at Education instead of Prentice, but when Callaghan talked to him Rees said no, he totally refused. So HW has to think again: he has now decided to put Mulley at Education. I suggested Hattersley, but he would not have him.

The Cabinet was soon over and the PM went off to lunch. I saw Jonathan Charkham, the man they have put in charge of the new unit controlling public appointments which has been set up following our initiative a year ago. Can see why they chose him, originally a businessman, he will at least have some idea what the outside world smells like. And very straight.

Went to lunch at the Commons with Joe and afterwards sat on the terrace in the sun. Discussed the changes. I am very unhappy with them. Could cause trouble. Putting Prentice out of the Cabinet to Overseas Aid is a big demotion which I am sure he won't accept. And Mulley into the Cabinet is unexciting. And Judith Hart to Transport is a promotion, which she does not deserve. In sum – two promotions to the Left and demotion to the Right, and an older man into the Cabinet. Nothing for the younger people at all. This surely is a sign that HW is losing his touch. And also reflects the problem of his policy of balance above all, when there are no good young left-wingers coming up. This means he both has to keep all the existing senior left-wingers and then can have no new right-wingers. Also means he cannot promote his best young people – Hattersley and Rodgers – because they are from the Right. So HW is paralysed by his own philosophy of balancing the left and right wings.

We had a briefing in the Commons before HW's Commons statement on the referendum. Little to say. Joe and I had discussed his statement with him in the study this morning and he had refused most of our suggestions. He was irritable, in a bad mood and very short with both of us. Joe said he is always like this when reshuffling. But I think there is more to it than that. He resents the battles within his personal staff.

The statement was at 3.30 and a lot of questions followed. It was the first day that Parliament had been broadcast. The Left was fairly subdued from its shattering defeat last week and the right-wingers were looking very cheerful.

[The Prime Minister, after announcing the result of the referendum, said that for the first time throughout many years of controversy over Europe British membership had the full-hearted consent of the whole British people. Mrs Thatcher, Leader of the Opposition, joined with Mr Wilson in rejoicing over 'this excellent result, which confirms the earlier parliamentary decision'.]

Afterwards Mrs Wilson came to his room and there was a row between them because she had discovered he will be in Brussels for an EEC Summit on the day of the Royal Garden Party, to which they had invited guests. He insisted he would be back in time and shut up Patrick Wright when he pointed out that was not possible.

I walked back to No.10 in the beautiful afternoon sunshine. Went to Joe's room and we were again discussing the reshuffle when Tony Benn walked along the street and came in to No. 10. It was 5.45 p.m. I went out to the main hallway to see his mood. He was glowering blackly and looked straight through me. He sat on the small settee outside the Cabinet Room and read a magazine. A few minutes later HW arrived and took Benn into the Cabinet Room. They were out again within a very few minutes, and Benn left in his car. HW told us that he had made the offer of Energy. Benn had said that he needed to think about it and wished to discuss it 'with my wife'. He promised to reply by division time at 10 that evening. HW was clearly nonplussed. In fact he now wanted Benn to take it. He is afraid of Benn resigning, not only because of the trouble he will cause but also because he has not got a left-winger to replace him. He will then have to put Dell to Energy, and this will upset the Cabinet balance between Left and Right.

HW went back to the House of Commons. I went to the National Gallery with Carol and then we went out to dinner at the Little French Club. From there I telephoned Joe twice. They were all at the Commons in an atmosphere of crisis about the reshuffle. Benn had held a meeting in his room to mobilise support. Michael Foot and Ron Hayward were present and Foot brought a letter to HW's room asking for 24 hours' delay. Foot tried to leave it with the secretary and depart without seeing HW, but HW sent somebody after him and fetched him back. Then a similar letter arrived from Benn. While HW was thinking about this he talked on the telephone to Prentice in Stockholm – and Prentice refused to leave the Cabinet, if so he would resign. Then Roy Jenkins telephoned to say that Prentice had spoken to him. Roy said if Prentice went he would go too. Joe told me that HW was very angry and fed up. He was talking of going to the Palace and resigning. But Joe persuaded him to give Benn his 24 hours – because time was not the principle. And to put Overseas Development in the Cabinet, so Prentice and Roy would stay. This was the only way to hold the thing together. But clearly the whole exercise had gone terribly wrong – including not knowing that Prentice was in Stockholm today. Nobody checked! This all demonstrated how HW's authority has been eroded. He cannot sack anybody, or even demote Benn, because the senior ministers are all autonomous barons, with their squadrons of supporters who black-ball any moves. By giving collective support to their friends each wing prevents HW from making any alterations. This is intolerable, humiliating and totally destructive of Cabinet government. It is also quite the oppo-site of 'prime ministerial' government. Whether or not Britain is ungovern-able – which the academics argue wrongly has become 'presidential' under Wilson – this Labour Cabinet is becoming ungovernable.

I talked to Joe at midnight. He said that the way things were going we could well be out of a job within 24 hours.

### Tuesday 10 June 1975

The PM had an early meeting with Callaghan and then went off to London airport with Marcia to meet Rabin of Israel. Apparently he arrived at exactly the same time as Fahtmey, the Egyptian foreign minister, who was being met by Callaghan, and there was a minor farce as the two parties avoided one another. The Egyptians had not been told that the PM and Rabin were at the airport.

I met with Joe and Ken Stowe in Ken's private office and we discussed how the PM should react if things continued to go wrong and especially if Benn continued to refuse. One of our contingencies was to call a Cabinet and announce that, as colleagues were refusing to accept the will of the PM, he was going to the Palace to resign.

Apparently last night Marcia had to be paged at the Dorchester to summon her to the Commons for the crisis. She had discussed the Benn move with HW at Chequers on Sunday and they had assumed it would go without a hitch. She was dining at the Dorchester with Eric Miller. I have heard no more about Mrs Miller's attitude to their relationship.

We lunched upstairs and then went to the Commons for Questions. The

PM was not very interested. He told Joe that now he cannot stand the House: when he is there he hankers after No. 10 and when he is in No. 10 he hankers after Chequers. This is just part of the growing evidence that he is fed up with it all. He spends more and more time at Chequers. Often goes days without reading his boxes. Shows little interest in policies.

Questions went easily enough. Afterwards Jim Callaghan dropped in to report that Eric Varley – who had written a letter to Harold that morning saying that he would not take Industry if Benn resigned – refused to change his mind. This is Eric, created by Marcia and Harold, going out of his way to be difficult, threatening the whole operation of the reshuffle, which was now falling apart disastrously. I pointed out to HW that this was the second time in three months that Varley had bent over backwards not to be helpful – cf. the EEC. I suggested that perhaps he was trying to prove his independent manhood. HW said that it was 'too late for that' and that Eric was just neurotic, now unable to sleep at nights and generally very unhappy.

I actually like Varley a lot, though he is not a first division minister or politician. Last night Ken Stowe heard Marcia screaming at him over the phone, but he has not budged, so far. He does not trust Benn, but he is trying to establish his position independent of Harold. Harold and Marcia think that the good thing about Eric is that he will do whatever they want. They are now wrong. Once that was true – that is how he climbed up the ladder. But now he is *less* compliant than the others because he has to do more than anybody else to prove his independence.

Michael Foot came in at 4 p.m. This was the end of the deadline given last night to Benn. But Benn did not come himself. Incredibly, he sent Michael Foot as messenger, to plead on his behalf, that HW change his mind. He didn't and Foot went away looking black.

Nobody has seen Benn. He is not in his ministry. Nor did he turn up at the House, so the committee stage of his Industry Bill was abandoned. A chaotic atmosphere. The House and the lobby are now full of rumours though still, incredibly, no newspaper has got the story of the reshuffle details.

HW called us in, Joe, Ken Stowe, Ken Marks (HW's new parliamentary private secretary) and myself, and we sat around the table. He asked us each in turn what he should do. Starting with me, I said he could not give way to this blackmail or his authority as PM was eroded, but he would have to find somebody at Industry who was acceptable to the TUC, even a figure from outside the mainstream – I suggested Merlyn Rees or even Stan Orme.

Joe suggested a major reshuffle as a means of restoring authority, and if that failed to go to the Palace.

Ken Marks said that the PLP would support HW against Benn.

Ken Stowe analysed the alternatives clearly and well.

The PM then asked us to go on talking while he was thinking. He said it helped him to sort out the options. Then he announced his solution – all on the assumption that Benn would refuse – which was that he would *merge* Industry and Energy, under Varley or Edmund Dell (he said he could take a right-winger because he had 'no need to maintain balance in the Cabinet if the Left refuses to serve'). The key to TUC approval was that *he* would take the NEB under his own direction at No.10.

He was delighted with this scheme and was still chirping about it when Len Murray came to see him at 5.30. He was now ready to face the departure of Benn and even Varley if need be, though his view was that Eric would happily stay at Energy with its extended function in Industry.

Joe and I walked back to No. 10 for an hour. I was a bit angry because in front of the others HW had ordered me 'not to leak this or write about it even in a hundred years'. He really is paranoid about leaks. I do not leak, and he knows it. Joe has heard that Marcia is still spreading the same old poison about me leaking to journalists. But of course I have every intention of writing this up within 100 years.

We went back to the Commons again at 6.30. I had time only to call in my office, lock away some secret papers and clear my desk. Also approved a draft minute we were putting to the PM supporting a tough line against the railway strikers.

Back at the Commons they had finally tracked down Benn. He came along at about 7 p.m. looking very tense. He was in with HW for no more than five minutes and we could hear his voice raised very loud (Joe and I were sitting on the settee outside). Benn stormed out and marched past us looking rigidly ahead. It was absolutely clear from his face that he had refused. HW came to the door, his round face looking battered and blank, and he summoned us in. He told us that Benn had launched off into a rhetorical tirade, attacking HW, saying he was damaging the Labour Movement, citing his own father and grandfather, but then he concluded by accepting the job at Energy.

HW poured himself and all of us a drink and then admitted that by the end he was not very surprised but was disappointed. He was so attracted by his own scheme for merging Energy and Industry and taking the NEB himself, and with getting rid of Benn, that he was sorry when the latter said he would stay. On reflection though we all agreed that this was the best solution – our original intention – and we ought to be pleased. HW then looked up and said, 'But there will be turbulence on the next one. Judith will turn it down.'

Ernest Armstrong was found in the bar and came along to accept a junior post in Environment. Then along came Judith Hart, in a flouncy green summer dress and looking very overweight. I chatted to her outside about Chile. Her attention was clearly nearer home. I definitely got the impression that she was preparing to be difficult. In fact she was no sooner in than out. As she came out HW was behind her shutting the door and saying, 'And I know a lot more about the Labour Movement than you do' – apparently she had accused him of trying to destroy the Labour Movement by offering her the Ministry of Transport, a post she felt unworthy of her.

We all went in to HW's room again, like a Greek chorus commenting on each scene of the play. We now discussed who to put to Transport instead of Judith Hart. I suggested Bob Mellish, who has been complaining for years about being Chief Whip and really wanting a proper ministerial job. He would also be quite tough in talking to the railwaymen. He had also sent his secretary, Freddie Warren, along to the office a little earlier to enquire if he might be wanted. So HW jumped at the idea and sent for Bob. We all trooped outside again and sat on the settee, till Mellish came out again.

He had turned it down. Said he wanted to stay on as Chief Whip. I nearly fell over with shock and pointed out to him that he had always repeatedly asked to be moved. 'Yes,' said Bob, 'and now my fucking Dame Nellie Melba act is over.' His bluff had been called. He had repeatedly announced at each recess that it was his last appearance as Chief Whip. It was some consolation that he would not be able to bore us with reading that in the papers again. Mellish then became emotional and said that he did it for Harold. 'I love that man,' he said, his small piggy red eyes filling with liquid, possibly not water. I said that I was sorry since I thought he would have handled the railwaymen well. He suddenly looked worried, sucked his finger and said he wondered if he had made a mistake. He started moving back towards HW's room for a second interview, but Joe came out and said how moved the Prime Minister was at his self-sacrifice, and that clinched it. He was staying on. Bob then revealed (his true motive) that he did not like the idea of his No. 2 (Walter Harrison) getting his job as Chief Whip, which may have been his main motivation, and wandered off towards the Strangers Bar. (Actually he really wanted to be made Leader of the House and when that was not on offer preferred to stay as Chief Whip.)

Prentice then appeared, having been flown back from a Stockholm conference in a special RAF jet. Inevitably the commercial flight was strike-bound at Copenhagen. Inevitably also our message telling him to come direct to the Commons did not get through and he went first dramatically and at great speed into an empty No.10.

He looked quite relaxed and I chatted to Maurice Peston, his special

adviser and an old friend of mine, while Reg was inside with the boss.
Peston was jet-lagged and glazed by what was happening. But when
Prentice came out he seemed quite cheery.

We – Joe, the two Kens and myself – trooped back in and HW was
looking much happier. He said, 'I don't care a bugger what happens now.'

We discussed the Railway vacancy. I was trying to steer him towards
Bill Rodgers, via Stan Orme, by suggesting Orme first and then Bill as
the option. He didn't react at first, but later said he thought 'Northern
Ireland might be the answer.'

The private secretaries were desperately combing London by telephone
trying to find various junior ministers. Although people knew a reshuffle
was on, few had left their telephone number. Lovely Joan Lestor was finally
found and arrived in a skimpy sunsuit, looking red as a lobster. Michael
Meacher could not be found and was said to be working late in a committee
– which curiously did not sit that night. Barbara Castle was at a meeting
in Islington, could not find her driver, and so we had to send a No. 10 car
for her. Fred Mulley was in Scarborough, had been phoning all day to see
if there was any news and was clearly ecstatic when finally told. Tony
Crosland said he had to have a big drink when told he was getting Bob
.Mellish as junior minister – and then had another even bigger one with
relief when told Bob had refused. (John Gilbert was moved from the
Treasury to take Transport.)

Harold Lever came looking pale and worried. Last night he had telephoned HW to offer his advice. HW had snapped back that he didn't want
it, and his advice was that Lever should go to bed and then slammed the
phone down. Lever looked as if he feared the sack. In fact HW teased him
wickedly. He told him that constitutionally there was room for only one
extra paid member of Cabinet and it was a choice between Lever and
Prentice. Since Lever had shown such solicitude for Prentice perhaps he
would be prepared to make the supreme sacrifice – and then told HL he
would have to give up his salary so that Prentice could be paid. Lever was
relieved but still looked down when he left. I walked along the passage
with him. HW now treats him badly, almost contemptuously – perhaps
because Harold has never stood up to him, always tries to please him. That
is not the way with HW. He is a masochist; though he encourages sycophants, he ends up against them. He likes to be opposed and punished.
Lever never does that. He is too gentle.

At 10 o'clock we were still short of a couple of junior ministers so HW
decided to announce only the senior posts. We all gathered round the TV
set for the news on ITN – and HW was delighted that they were surprised
at the Benn-Varley switch. To him the greatest virtue of this manoeuvre
was that he had outwitted and out-scooped the press.

The initial reaction by commentators, including Eric Heffer, was prom-ising. No hint of trouble; but then at 10.30 Michael Foot and Benn arrived, and a few moments later Barbara Castle puffed in. She revealed that Peter Shore was expected though he never came. It was a deputation to protest about the reshuffle in general – and Judith Hart in particular.

We advisers sat in the outside room, hot and airless, for an hour and a half while these shop stewards of the Left ranted at the British Prime Minister. Whenever they raised their voices – which was often – we could hear the waves of rhetoric. Foot referred to 'the bleeding body of Judith lying on the battlefield'. Benn accused HW of doing terrible damage to the Labour Movement. Barbara Castle denounced Prentice and said he should be out of the government. They repeatedly said that it was a terrible injustice to drop Judith – 'pitched out' said Foot. HW pointed out that he had not dropped her; she had declined to take an important position. Barbara Castle said it was intolerable to expect a minister to go to Transport after being at Overseas Development – and HW quickly pointed out that she had done precisely that in the last Labour government. What it boiled down to was that they demanded that Judith be put in the Cabinet. HW refused. But it was humiliating that he should let them go on like this. He was explaining and justifying himself. He foolishly told them Jenkins had demanded that Prentice be in the Cabinet, instead of simply saying it was his decision and they must lump it. They said OK, then they were demanding that Judith be in as well.

Curiously Benn did not attack Prentice. He said it was a good thing that ministers should say what they think. He was not attacking Prentice, but defending Judith, which was to his credit.

HW was not good. He should not have allowed it to happen or to go on. Attlee would never have tolerated it. It was part of the erosion of HW's power, Just like a 15th-century monarch, when the feudal barons had exces-sive and independent powers. He said to them that he had never discussed his Cabinet changes with any ministers before. He should not have done it now.

In fact this whole exercise has been a botch from start to finish. He never discussed it properly with us and obviously had not thought it through. He never thought through the possibilities that Benn would refuse or delay, that Prentice would refuse or be supported by Jenkins – even though Jenkins had warned him that he would go if Prentice went. He had not thought out that Judith might refuse – or who to replace her with. Or that Varley would make conditions.

He knew this reshuffle was coming weeks ago, was constantly referring to the cleverness of his plan, but never planned it beyond the Benn-Varley switch. This is a sign of his decline, that the greatest political manager of this century in Britain tried his first small reshuffle in his fourth administration, just after a smashing referendum victory, and he ballsed it up. *Every* single senior appointment, except for Mulley into the Cabinet, went wrong. Benn, Prentice, Varley, Hart, they all resisted. This was the first political issue since I came in which was planned and discussed only by HW and Marcia. Joe and I were mainly excluded until the final stage.

After the shop stewards had left we sat in his room and talked. He sent for champagne and one of the private secretaries brought sandwiches – none of us had eaten since lunch. It was after midnight. We all felt thank God it was over without disaster. HW was very tired but boasting of his success. He said, 'It had poetry. It had humour. It had political subtlety. And the press did not guess it.' We said nothing. Joe and I left to walk back to Downing Street to get our cars. It was a lovely warm June night. We had left HW to take Janet home in his car. We felt there was not much to be proud of. There was a sense of impending collapse. Not of cataclysm. Just of erosion and final decline.

## Wednesday 11 June 1975

11 a.m. went to the special Misc Cabinet committee on railway pay.

Fred Mulley and Foot spoke for making extra concessions soon in the hope of buying off the strike quickly. Foot especially, in the choice of his language, seemed to be preparing the way for ultimate capitulation.

Healey was erratic. At first he spoke well for a firm stand and pointed out the consequences of capitulation, including provoking a sterling crisis. But later he came in and said that he would be happy to settle for 2% extra if it made the NUR give way – yet even Foot and Mulley had talked of only 1%–1½% to buy off the strike. Jenkins immediately intervened to point out the contradiction of having a 'firm' line based on a bigger concession than the 'soft-liners' were proposing. Jenkins himself was for a firm stand, as were Shore and Crosland, provided, he pointed out, it did not so sour relations with the TUC that it messed up policy on the next pay round. This latter point was also Foot's main argument for an early concession.

The PM summed up for a tough line – which was how we briefed. He agreed to get personally involved by seeing the NUR and the TUC, preferably before next week.

I went to lunch with Kissin and Aubrey Jones (the former Tory minister and chief of the Pay Board in the 1960s) while the PM had lunch with Fahtmey, the Egyptian Foreign Minister.

Aubrey Jones was pushing his idea for a commission to deal with wages – quite well thought out.

HW is completely conservative on education policy. When I said to him in the Commons that Mulley might retreat from our comprehensive policy, he said it 'might not be a bad thing'.

Got home fairly early in lovely sunshine and in time to see the children before they went to bed – which is a rare pleasure these days.


## Thursday 12 June 1975

Saw Lever before Cabinet for a chat. Nothing serious. The Cabinet discussed the railways and Healey took a fairly firm line, saying that there must be tough economic measures *before* July. The recent weakness of sterling has worried everybody. Though the Bank has played it better than usual, letting the rate go and not spending too much money.

Worked on a draft reply to the Tribune Group who had written a letter to HW complaining about his reshuffle. I enjoyed putting in the sentence that their letter was 'regrettably hysterical in tone and inaccurate in content'.

Lunch at No. 10. I enjoy these lunches. The team is still very happy and constructive. Ken Stowe is quite different from Robert Armstrong. Less bustle, less sense of authority, less charisma. But very good in his way, calm, completely safe pair of hands, very open in telling and consulting Joe and me. He has the team on a looser and more relaxed rein than Robert. These Downing Street civil servants are individually so good, it is sad that the final output from the *whole machine* is so unsatisfactory.

Parliamentary Questions very quiet again. We still meet to brief the PM for three-quarters of an hour beforehand, but it is generally relaxed and frivolous, with no tension. The PM can now handle Questions with very little preparation. The Tories have nothing new to offer. Yet he is still nervous, hates it and has a brandy before and after.

He came back to No.10 to see the Chancellor and then to see Bernard Lovell and Henry Ford. I had a meeting with our economists, Andrew Graham, Gavyn Davies and David Gowland, as we prepared our public expenditure paper. Also worked on a brief for tomorrow on the Industry Bill and on 'Poverty in the World' – where HW had raised the charities' expectations in the spring and is now showing no interest in any follow-through.

Came home around 9 p.m. to meet Bruce Grant, very old friend from our days in Harvard, who is now Australian High Commissioner to India. Sat up till very late talking and listening to music.


## Friday 13 June 1975

The big black Rover car collected me at 8.30 to go to Chequers for the all-day meeting on the Industry Bill. Janet Hewlett-Davies was supposed to be coming with me, but HW had asked her to stay with him overnight at Chequers to prepare the press briefing.

It was a glorious and very hot day. The countryside was rich under the blazing sun. It seemed a pity to be sitting inside listening to hours of discussion of detailed amendments to the Industry Bill, while outside the window was all that parkland and trees. It made me hanker for university again, so that I can drop everything and just relax.

Before going up to the long committee room I had coffee with Tony Crosland in a side lounge. He said he thought John Gilbert was a very poor appointment to Transport. He was also very critical of Healey. He also said he thought Prentice was getting into dangerously right-wing company. It is impossible not to like Tony. He is amusing, perceptive, indiscreet and of course phenomenally intelligent. He is very much HW's chosen successor these days. But I am not sure he would be willing to get sufficiently involved or to do tough and detailed things which are distasteful but have to be done. There is always something of the detached amused Oxford Don about him. But my God it would be a relief to work for him. It would be a pleasure to have a proper discussion about politics *and* to be trusted not to leak it. HW actually came into the room while we were talking, but turned round and scuttled out.

The meeting began at about 10.30 with the full Industry committee there – which is two-thirds of the Cabinet – except for Benn, who sent Balogh, his junior minister at Energy, along instead. This was a relief to all, since it avoided embarrassment. It also gave Eric Varley a better chance to establish himself as the new Industry Minister. He really did very well. He very cleverly took a firm Benn position on most policy issues – so underlining that his appointment was not a retreat from the party's manifesto, but a change of ministers. He was also surprisingly on top of the details. He told me at lunch that he had been up working on the papers till 1 a.m. then went to bed, but could not sleep and got up at 5 a.m. to work again. 'But I am knackered now,' he said. He is a nice unpompous lad.

The meeting went remarkably smoothly. There were differences of opinion, especially over giving information from companies to trade unions, with Lever and Foot disagreeing. But it was a normal civilised disagreement and HW was always able to find the necessary compromise. This shows that the problem *was* Benn. He made it appear an irreconcilable gulf of dogma, and his rhetoric upset the moderates who refused to give way. Without him it was not difficult to resolve a long list of problems over amendments to clauses which had seemed previously insoluble.

HW had clearly read his papers and was master of the details. However, he did take too much time over items of details where he was keen to show off his knowledge.

We broke for lunch at 1.15. I sat outside in the sun with Tony Crosland and discussed public expenditure problems while he had a pre-lunch gin and tonic. HW, Foot and Healey had gone off for a special meeting about railway pay – they are meeting the TUC about it late this afternoon.

We had a cold meat and salad lunch in the main hall. Very pleasant and relaxed atmosphere. Roy Jenkins came up and started to talk to me – but HW came up and intervened, clearly suspicious of plots. I moved off to talk to Eric Varley and then to Fred Peart, who is actually a charmer, a real human being with no side.

The afternoon session only lasted 40 minutes. The NEB guidelines were quickly completed and everybody rushed out and flowed down the stairs and out into the sunshine where lines of black cars extended down the drive and across the park. I leapt in with Harold Lever and we sped back to town. Most ministers were going to the Commons to vote to abolish hare-coursing – it was a free vote but HW had let it be known he wanted everybody to vote. Lever decided not to and went home to tea.

Joe came to see me and told me that he had raised with HW the question of my alleged leaking. He had told HW from his knowledge of the press he did not believe it was true and thought it was unfortunate HW kept referring to it. But a private secretary then came in and they did not take it further. But Joe as usual has been a solid friend.

He also told me that HW was concerned about rumours of plots involving Prentice and two GLC councillors, Stephen Haseler and Carlton, who are 'plotting coalition'. I know nothing about it.

Worked on a devolution brief, saying that it would be disastrous for the Labour Party in Scotland if we retreated now. In fact there is a big move to retreat, with Jenkins, Crosland and Healey leading it. Gerry Fowler phoned me to say that he would resign if we climbed down now.

The TUC came in this evening. Joe went and told me they were very critical of the NUR and urged the government to take a strong line – because they consider arbitration to be sacred and don't like a union to break arbitration any more than an employer.

When the NUR came round at 8.30 they were firmly told this. Foot warned them that nobody in the government was for supporting the NUR claim. This represents a hardening up by Foot.

### Weekend 14/15 June 1975

Joe telephoned today, Sunday, to say that there had been a terrible row between HW and Marcia after the Trooping of the Colour on Saturday morning. I did not go, although I had seats on the stand, because I could not face all that nonsense. Apparently Eric Miller did not go either, and

Marcia went berserk. Eric is quite prepared to take her for a meal, but he is apparently not prepared to leave a nice wife and family for Marcia. He wants an honour and is prepared to make some sacrifice, maybe to sign a few cheques. Marcia went wild and started to attack HW. They were in her room from lunchtime until after 5 in the afternoon. She was shouting and raving and threatening him. Albert (who reported to us in full) was there and tried to leave to take his wife home, but HW ordered him 'to stay as a witness'. So poor Anne Murray had to go home alone in the train.

When they finally broke up she told HW as she was leaving not to communicate with her again because he had sacked her. Within the next hour she then telephoned a dozen times to try to speak to HW, but Albert answered the phone and pretended not to be able to find HW, who was in the room.

## Monday 16 June 1975

I decided not to go to Chequers for the Devolution committee. Friday was enough Chequers for me for a while. Also we are working in the Unit on a paper on public expenditure which must go to the Treasury by Wednesday. This is crucial and must come first. So I went in and spent the day in at No. 10. Took lunch with David Piachaud at the Commons.

They returned from Chequers at just before 5 p.m. Apparently it went well with the PM leading strongly that we could not retreat from devolution. Healey's attack petered out, and Jenkins barely said a word.

They returned for an economic strategy committee on the railway pay situation and on a paper from the TUC on the next round of pay settlements. The latter was really quite good, suggesting some quite firm and constructive alternatives, and the committee plumped for the toughest.

Joe and Albert reported to me on Saturday's row. Apparently Marcia was quite distraught that Eric Miller did not come. She left the stand in the middle of the trooping to come inside to telephone him. Later she retired to the lavatory for a long weep. She accused HW of trying to abandon everybody by threatening to retire in the autumn – it is quite clear she does *not* want him to retire. She threatened to destroy him by revealing the details of some alleged deal between himself, Frank Schon* and Joe Kagan long ago. HW apparently defended himself by saying, 'I only did it for you.' Albert was present as witness for all of this.

Actually this may be the clue to why he is so frightened of her.

Went home at 8.30 and sat up with our Australian friend, Bruce Grant, until midnight.

*Tuesday 17 June 1975*

Took Bruce Grant in to meet his wife, just arriving on a plane. Then off with the PM to a meeting of NEDC which lasted all morning.

Main topics were the investment programmes of the nationalised industries and the future role of NEDC. A fairly quiet meeting. Monty Finniston was the outstanding contributor, completely on top of his job. Benn did not come – still sulking in his tent. He sent Balogh along.

Had lunch at No. 10. Then briefing for Questions, and Question Time, which was still very tame. The Tories are completely without any fire. In our preliminary discussions we anticipate far more embarrassing questions than they ever manage to ask.

We met the CBI to discuss the Industry Bill at 5 p.m. Very boring. They are of such poor quality. Watkinson adds a little punch. But they did not ask any pointed questions at all. Just rambled on. Bateman, the president, is quite the worst.

Afterwards I worked in the office and then left early, at 7 p.m., to go to the Old Vic to see a splendid performance of Ibsen's *John Gabriel Borkman*, with Ralph Richardson, Wendy Hiller and Peggy Ashcroft. Home at midnight.

# CHAPTER 17

## Crisis over Pay Policy –
## the Treasury Bounce Fails and the Policy Unit Wins
## June–July 1975

*Wednesday 18 June 1975*

Worked in the Unit all morning. The PM had two committees – on External Economic Policy and on the Continental Shelf Oil Policy – but I did not go. Preferred to be in the Unit for our public expenditure discussions.

At midday the PM sent for me. He said we must do something about wages. Must have some sanctions. He put up some ideas: sacking people in the public sector, stopping investment in the railways and in new coalpits. He even suggested setting up an insurance fund to compensate private employers who stood up to strikers – he is very anti-strikes at the moment. He asked me to get the Unit to look at his ideas and any others we could think of.

What was interesting about this was not the particular ideas, but the fact that *he* was taking the initiative. After a year of ducking the wages problem he is now beginning to come to grips with it. Because the referendum is out of the way – he only fights one battle at a time. And because opinion is ready for it, demanding it. He never gets ahead of the game.

Went to lunch at the House of Commons with Joe. Sat on the terrace with Helene Hayman, Gerry Fowler, and then spoke briefly to Phillip Whitehead. Nice to see my generation in occupation there as Labour MPs.

Back for a meeting in No.10 with the TUC on the Industry Bill. Big delegation with all the main leaders there. Went well, with Jack Jones quite the outstanding man from their side. They are much more impressive than the CBI – they know the detail, have done their homework.

Afterwards I worked in the Unit on public expenditure.

Then saw HW alone in the study and talked for three-quarters of an hour over a drink. Discussed public expenditure. And wages problems. Also the question of Harold Lever taking over the Arts. Typically HW is not going to sack Hugh Jenkins, the present Arts Minister, yet. 'I've done enough for the moment,' he said. And added that Jenkins 'needed the money'.

He quizzed me about the new Social Democratic Alliance, about which I know nothing.

He was very friendly and happy to talk. Because he was killing time – until Janet Hewlett-Davies returned from a party. She is obviously immensely fond of him, almost in a maternal way. I say good luck to him. After some of the women he has had to work with in politics he deserves a bit of affection, and Janet is nice and kind and warm and completely undemanding. HW beams like a boy with a new bicycle when he is with her.

I left at 8 p.m.

## Thursday 19 June 1975

Talked to Harold Lever on the telephone before going to work. He is seeing the PM this morning about his proposed job as overlord of the Arts. I talked to HW last night, and he is not yet clear, in no hurry and reluctant to sack Hugh Jenkins, whom he sees as inadequate, because he has no source of income apart from his ministerial job. Lever did not want it at first, but is now resigned to having it because HW wants him to. In fact it will detract from his economics and financial influence because he will be unfairly seen as 'not serious'.

Worked in the office on the public expenditure paper and on a new brief we are doing on pay policy for tomorrow's Cabinet at Chequers.

I went down to the hall outside the Cabinet Room after today's Cabinet was over. Fred Mulley took me on one side as he came out and said he wanted help finding a special adviser in his new post at Education. I discussed the excellent Maurice Kogan, a former civil servant and now education expert, with him and promised to talk to Kogan about it.

HW spoke to me again about pay policy and the need for sanctions. He was also worried about today's unemployment figures which are very bad. He asked the Unit to look at them and to see how best to defend them.

We had lunch upstairs. Discussed the Attorney-General's writ against the publisher of the Crossman Diaries. In fact I had talked to Sam Silkin, the Attorney-General, about it earlier this morning. His position was not militant. He said he supported relaxing the rules, but also defining the rules more clearly. He expected the Radcliffe Committee of Privy Councillors would recommend this by the end of the year. He could not understand why the publisher Jonathan Cape had gone ahead with publication before that report. He thought this had left him with no alternative but to issue a writ. I pointed out that he would get a bad reception because (1) he had not issued a writ against the *Sunday Times* when it serialised the Diaries, whereas he now picked on a small publisher, and (2) because he would be seen as part of the Civil Service conspiracy of secrecy.

I warned him he was in for trouble. He gave the impression of not being very involved in it and not aware of the implications. It is clear that the civil servants are behind this – and especially, I gather, the Treasury Solicitor's Office, headed by somebody called Basil Hall.

At lunch Joe and I complained bitterly to Ken Stowe that we had not been told or consulted on the decision to issue a writ. Ken then said that *he* had not been told either.

The PM has put down a written answer to a question today claiming that he has never been in touch with the Attorney-General over any legal initiative because the Attorney-General is independent of government. Joe says this is not true. He remembers the PM seeing Elwyn Jones and encouraging him to take action against Jonathan Aitken and the *Sunday Telegraph*.

We told Ken to go and see John Hunt to complain. He did this later and Hunt admitted that he had known about it and apologised for not telling us.

Joe and I made it clear that we were firmly against taking legal action. It was ridiculous to think that they could *stop* publication of the Crossman Diaries. If they stop Cape's, then the manuscript will be published privately, circulated, published in bits in *Private Eye*, etc.

Joe said that the PM had not consulted us because he knew we were against this legal action.

Today Joe has announced the abolition of the parliamentary press lobby. This is partly because it is an out-of-date system which produces journalists who are totally idle because they don't have to find out anything, they simply are fed with news by ministers. It is also because they have been breaching the secrecy code, and carrying information to Tory headquarters. But above all it is part of HW's paranoia about and hatred of the press. It is now a year since I first heard him tell Joe to stop the lobby. HW has not himself seen the press, except after Summit conferences, since he came to power. Not a single press conference in the UK, which is a bizarre situation. Rather like Richard Nixon, his relations with the press get worse as he gets older, and he stores up resentment from all the previous election campaigns, etc., where they have lied, misrepresented and criticised him. Yet he still reads every page of every newspaper, however trivial.

Went to Parliamentary Questions. HW was still nervous about the unemployment figure – and rightly, since the Tories gave him a hard time.

Afterwards I retired and sat down with the Unit – Andrew Graham, David Piachaud, Gavyn Davies – to a crash exercise in pay policy. We had some disagreements about whether to recommend a single norm, or as Andrew Graham wanted, a 'winding-down', decelerating rate. I think the latter is not practical and prefer David Piachaud's simple norm at a simple flat rate; though Andrew was very creative on the rest of the paper.

We slogged away at this brief till after 10 p.m., making poor Piachaud miss the first act of a play and holding up the official car taking the PM's boxes to Chequers. I had had a dinner guest at home – but did not get back till he was leaving, at 11.30 p.m.!

In our brief we were recommending a policy that was non-statutory, but backed by a whole battery of sanctions against employers and unions who breach the norm. This is really what HW has been hankering after for months. He cannot introduce a statutory policy, because he has said that he won't. But he must have sanctions because otherwise the voluntary policy will fail. So we have come up with a whole battery of sanctions – cutting investment in jobs, tax penalties, ending arbitration and comparability, discrimination in government contracts, grants, etc.

Now we will see.


### Friday 20 June 1975

I was exhausted and had decided, perhaps foolishly, not to go to the big Cabinet meeting at Chequers today on inflation and pay policy. I sent Andrew Graham from my Unit instead. I am feeling tired and jaded and want a relaxed day. Also I dislike that long car drive. But it is important that Andrew hears the arguments since he will be at the heart of our briefing.

So I went in late, had a nice lunch at the Ivy restaurant, spent an hour with Rob Spiers of the American embassy and went home early.

Andrew and Joe telephoned this evening. To report. A very good meeting. Strongly for *our* kind of industry policy backed by tough sanctions. Rejection of Jenkins and Prentice pressure for a *statutory* policy. But equally everybody except Benn and Foot for a strong policy *soon* – and a 10% norm. Benn was talking about 1931, and saying that employment was what mattered, not inflation.

Elwyn Jones, the Lord Chancellor, was apparently devastatingly good against a statutory policy. Jim Callaghan had switched from his previous opposition to a norm, to now saying he would accept it if practical.

The PM was showing a lot of irritation with Jenkins.

Andrew said what a pity it could not be televised. The quality of discussion was so good it would have completely restored confidence.

This is encouraging. We are clearly moving fast into a new phase of pay policy which *may* at last end the drift and self-deception about the TUC being able to solve the problems which only a government can in fact deal with.

[For Friday's Chequers Cabinet:

## BD to PM

*Pay Policy*

*The Problem*

There are two aspects which tend to dominate almost everything else:

(a) Some groups have the *power* to demand and get very much what they want (at least in money terms). Perhaps for the first time we have a society in which the income distribution in no way corresponds to the class structure.

(b) There is a strong sense of British *fairness* together with a heavily institutionalised use of *comparability* in wage claims.

The inevitable result of combining these two principles is inflation. *Present policy* has also faced the following additional difficulties:

(a) *General* unemployment on the scale experienced in the post-war period acts as only a minor restraint on wage claims. High unemployment in Wales matters rather little to the shop steward at Dagenham.

(b) It has failed to allow for the *different characteristics of the public and private sectors.* As the result of the increasing shift to plant bargaining, power is now decentralised in the *private sector* and held by the shop stewards and convenors. It is the shop stewards who now bargain money. As a result, *even if* the trade union leaders are co-operating in a voluntary policy they are too weak to restrain pay claims.

(c) In contrast, in the *public sector* bargaining is centralised and the government is the employer. This means that in any policy the government *has* to take a position – and the present policy has allowed settlements at much too high a level.

(d) In the public sector there is a widespread use of *comparability* as the basis for wage claims occurring *within* the wage round. In addition, in the non-nationalised part of the public sector, there is comparability with the *previous* round formalised in the pay research system. Thus civil servants, for example, will be expecting settlements of 25–30% in the *next* round on the basis of settlements by comparable groups in *this* round.

(e) There have been few *sanctions* to reinforce resistance to wage claims.

*The requirement for a new policy* (not statutory)
It follows from the above that a new policy must

(a) use the government's position as an employer;
(b) recognise the variation between the public and private sectors;
(c) attack the major problem of comparability, arbitration and pay research;
(d) be supported by new sanctions.

*Policy recommendations*
We *recommend* a new policy with the following characteristics:

### The Norm

1. There must be a specified *norm*, preferably agreed by the TUC and the CBI. This norm must be to some extent *redistributive* to gain political backing. It should be applied to the *wage bill* of *groups* of workers so as to give trade unions the option of higher pay per head against more employment.

2. The *choice* for this norm lies between either for simplicity a flat rate (say £5 per week), or some combination of flat rate plus percentage. (However, in the latter case we must take care that trade unionists do not use *both* the percentage and the flat rate to the full – this would be inflationary.)

### Sanctions

1. The *general* sanction of allowing unemployment to go on rising.

2. In the *public* sector (a–c = instruments of policy; d–e = ground rules):
   (a) Abandon pay research.
   (b) Resist all claims on grounds of comparability.
   (c) Refuse to let claims go to arbitration.
   (d) Recognise that at the end of the day some groups cannot be defeated – but there must be no settlements above the norm in the Civil Service nor for 'special cases' such as university teachers.
   (e) Control public expenditure *in real terms* so as to make *the trade-off between wages and unemployment* specific to particular industries, and drive this home particularly in those cases which breach the policy – e.g. reduce investment in railways or in new coal mines; freeze the BBC licence fee.

[Hand-written against (a)–(c) above: 'Instruments of policy (not sanctions)'; against (d) and (e) above: 'ground rules'.]

3. In the *private* sector
   (a) Insert a clause into the *Price Code* allowing the Secretary of State discretion to refuse price increases where they are the result of wage settlements beyond the norm.
   (b) Let the next *major* firm which has breached the norm and which requests assistance go bankrupt. (We might announce that Sections 7 and 8 of the Industry Act are not available in such cases.)
   (c) Use all other forms of persuasion, wherever discretionary powers exist, to exert pressure on private employers to resist excessive wage settlements, e.g., government contracts, regional incentives, investment allowances, etc.

4. As far as *trades unionists* are concerned, consider whether it might be possible without legislation to delay the repayment of tax rebates to strikers until the end of the tax year.

### Presentation and propaganda

1. This programme must be backed up by propaganda, not just to reinforce the sanctions but to press home the advantages of the policy. We need both sticks and carrots.

2. The norm and the target reduction in inflation must be explained and promoted as never before. The government must unleash on the country its entire promotional and propaganda potential – posters, TV and radio commercials, newspaper adverts, celebrities, all exhorting to keep to the norm to beat inflation. Ministers, the TUC and the CBI must get out and talk to workers at shop floor level, on chat shows, on phone-ins, etc. There needs to be a campaign manager with real flare and a promotional budget of several millions. (It should have nothing to do with the COI.)

3. The *slogan must* be simple, and those who attack the policy (e.g. McGahey) must be denounced and isolated.

4. The government must be prepared to finance opinion polls of groups of workers *including* their wives.

5. Information should be distributed on the consequences of breaking the norm on schools, nurseries and other parts of the social wage and on the danger of redundancy.

## Summary

*There must be a simple norm* that applies to everyone (but we must recognise that some will break it – when they do we must try wherever possible to make sure that there are employment consequences).

*There must be a carrot:*
The prospect of a drastic and rapid fall in inflation, to give people hope.

*There must be sticks:*
Against employers: all the government's economic armoury must be mobilised to prevent excess offers.
Against unions: the consequence of excess settlements must be evidently and actually a loss of jobs.
Against strikers: moral support for employers (and delay of tax rebates?).
Against everyone: no hesitation in bringing home the harshness of the choices both in word and in deed.

There must be a massive propaganda exercise to present the issue and promote the policy – an exercise as never before.
                                  Signed: Bernard Donoughue, 19 June 1975]

## *Monday 23 June 1975*

Drove in early. Cleared papers and then was interviewed by Professor Dror from Israel, specialist in government. And visited by Maurice Pechet, an American friend from Harvard. Maurice was in great form.

Lunch at the Commons with Joe. From his notes he reported more on the Chequers pay policy meeting: Shirley Williams had been good and much praised by HW. Crosland only spoke for few moments. Prentice said he supported a *full* statutory policy, *now* and *permanent*.

Lever was thought to be weak because he had no precise ideas for the general sanctions he proposed.

Mellish very good. John Silkin asserted that the Commons would not pass a statutory policy.

Elwyn Jones spoke on the hypocrisy of the last statutory policy, when he was Lord Chancellor and ministers were constantly phoning him to ask him not to prosecute for breaches of the policy.

Barbara Castle was for sanctions, but not statutory.

Jenkins felt we were approaching a catastrophe.

Healey said that we only had a few weeks, and if we did not get it right, there would be a sterling crisis and 2½ million unemployed.

Joe and I also discussed wages policy and our new ideas for strengthening sanctions. We are trying to construct a policy which is not statutory but which will stick. This is the only way to get HW off the hook of his commitment not to have a statutory policy.

While Joe and I were sitting on the terrace discussing wages policy – the terrace was virtually empty because it was grey and threatening rain – Sam Silkin came up to us. He said to us, 'We are going to remedy that point you mentioned the other day. I'll say no more.'

It was clear that he was referring to our conversation about the Crossman Diaries outside the Cabinet Room last Thursday when I had said it looked odd to prosecute a small publisher but not a big newspaper. He was clearly conveying that he proposed to move against the *Sunday Times* because of an article on Sunday comparing Crossman's version of events in 1966–70 with that in Wilson's own memoirs.

Joe and I decided to warn HW when we got back. This is ridiculous and exactly what we feared – war between the government and the press at just the time when we don't want any diversions from the economic front.

Went back to No. 10 but HW was not back yet. When he returned he went straight upstairs with Douglas Allen to discuss promotions to permanent secretary in the Civil Service.

Joe saw HW on the stairs and the latter said that we should report to John Hunt and discover what was going on. I was waiting outside Hunt's office when my secretary telephoned to say that the PM now thought that I must not mention Crossman to Hunt. So I went in and discussed wages with him and especially how to follow up the conclusions of last Friday's Chequers meeting.

When I returned Joe came to see me. He had had a terrible row with the PM. HW had sent for him and said that I was responsible for the Attorney-General taking out an injunction. It was all because of my friendship with the editor of the *Sunday Times*. He then went off into one of his fantasies about me always leaking stories to the press. Joe said that he felt his blood pressure rising and lost his temper. He pointed out that it was ridiculous to suggest that my friendship towards Harry Evans would lead me to persuade the Attorney-General to take Evans to court – some friendship! The madness of this suggestion is a sad sign of HW's unbalanced mind on the question of leaks to the press. Joe then said he was fed up with hearing about leaks and as press secretary in daily contact with journalists he had never heard any evidence against me. At this point HW intervened to say that I was responsible for a leak from the IDV Cabinet committee. That Robert had discovered the evidence and that I had apologised.

This was an incredible allegation for a PM to make. A total fabrication. I had discussed that leak with Robert. He had implied that some people suspected me – clearly meaning HW – but said that he had some evidence that the story, which was about the CPRS, originated from the CPRS. I certainly knew nothing about it.

HW had simply lied to try to justify his paranoia.

Joe stuck to his guns and accused Marcia of being behind these allegations, and of being 'obsessed' with me. HW apparently admitted this and said he had 'often told her that she was too obsessed with Bernard'.

Joe said they lost their tempers with one another and voices were raised. Then Ken Stowe came in and reported that the Attorney was moving because there had been a clear breach of the law by the *Sunday Times* and because Harry Evans had made this clear on television last night – about which I knew nothing. Joe said HW then climbed down and conceded it could not have been my fault.

I felt depressed, flat and fed up with the shabbiness and lunacy of all this. In fact through my contacts with Sam Silkin I had done the 'eye and ears' job and been able to give HW an early alert of the proposed injunction which he wanted to stop. Without me it would have happened without him being told. And then accusing me of instigating an injunction against my friend is so lunatic that it is matter for medical rather than political analysis.

HW then desperately tried to get hold of Silkin to stop him issuing the injunction. But Silkin said he didn't want to discuss it – and he refused to allow John Hunt to attend the meeting discussing it.

The irony here is that the Attorney is behaving exactly as HW always said he should – without any political interference. But of course HW does try to interfere – and now Silkin won't have it. The 'independence' of the law officers is inevitably a fiction some of the time, because their actions have grave political implications. Soon there will be a question of charges for bribery and corruption against another Labour politician. The PM and Cabinet will then almost certainly discuss whether to allow criminal proceedings or to have a judicial inquiry into the whole Poulson situation.

I held a Unit meeting on wages and inflation. We are developing quite an interesting battery of 'sanctions' to back up our 'voluntary' policy.

Carol came in at 9 p.m. and we went to a reception for Arnot Sutherland, the retiring senior partner of Grieveson Grant stockbrokers, at Bucks Club in St James. Delicious food. Nice company of sane, balanced friendly people. All terrible capitalists from the City. I wish some of our socialists were only half as nice.

## Tuesday 24 June 1975

Decided not to attend the 10 o'clock Cabinet committee on Energy – nothing interesting on the agenda.

Sent for the file on the 'leak' from the April IDV Cabinet committee meeting which HW had told Joe I was responsible for. There was Robert Armstrong's report saying that his conclusion was that the CPRS *were* responsible. So HW was simply lying or had been misled. I showed this to Joe, who said it was all part of the decline of HW. 'You could not imagine, seeing him now, what a brilliant Rolls-Royce mind he once had,' he said. Joe admitted that his mind was now warped by his obsession with leaks, the press, etc. Just occasional glimpses of the old skills.

Went to the Cabinet committee on Ministerial Economic Strategy at 11. Discussed the future of NEDC – including Healey's statement that if its director Ronnie McIntosh continues to act the prima donna he would send him 'for a very long walk' – and the PM's claim that 'all power corrupts and NEDC corrupts absolutely: it ruined Catherwood and Figgures' (former directors).

Joe and I had lunch upstairs with private office. Discussed the PM's political office, whose inefficiency has astonished them. Letters not answered for 8 weeks. Long minutes to the PM, rambling and repetitive, which require answers but are unanswerable.

Today's episode concerned a proposed dinner for the PM with David Frost at Frost's house tonight. The PM had agreed on condition that it was a small family affair with no outside guests. Last night Frost reported that he was also inviting Jim Slater* and Jimmy Goldsmith,* two of the extreme right-wing financiers most often attacked by Labour, and especially the PM. When told, the PM reacted strongly and said he would not go. He added that 'Marcia tipped me off they might add some extras. She was right as usual.'

When private office telephoned David Frost to say that the PM was 'otherwise engaged' and to hint that in future he should not ask Slater and Goldsmith, Frost, sad and bewildered, said 'but Marcia suggested that I ask those two'. The pursuit of millionaires.

On HW's retirement: Bill Housden tells us that last weekend at Chequers, sitting around the swimming-pool, Marcia referred with pleasure to the fact that HW had changed his mind about retiring in October. Mary then blurted out, 'Oh, but he has promised me that he is going in October.'

Joe then retold the story of Tony Field's wedding at Joe Kagan's house, adding the extra piece that when Marcia took the PM's plane to fly back, after their terrible row, it landed at London airport at the public end instead of the private plane end. She carried no passport and was questioned. Harold Wilson had to come back by train. When she finally got back to her house Tony was there, having looked in vain for his money and camera. What a circus!

This afternoon at briefing for Questions, we were discussing Idi Amin, the Ugandan dictator, and saying that his symptoms were those of madness, with periods of calm followed by mad ravings. 'I know,' said HW, 'I am surrounded by those symptoms.' Joe said, 'You mean Barbara Castle of course,' and HW just laughed.

The Attorney took out a writ against the *Sunday Times* today over the Crossman Diaries. The PM saw him at midday to point out the difficulties – but in a very 'proper' way, in order not to exercise political influence over him – but the Attorney stood firm. He said there had been a clear breach of the law and that was that. All his legal advisers told him that if he ignored the *Sunday Times* he would lose the case against the publishers Jonathan Cape as a consequence.

Questions went easily. Afterwards the PM sat with his brandy counting the Question Times left to do before the summer recess. Each one ticked off gives him pleasure. He is delighted to be going abroad so much in the second half of July. Of course if he *is* retiring in October, this means he is counting up and ticking off the remaining Question Times in his political life.

I came back after Questions and worked in the office. Also discussed staffing next year with Andrew Graham, who is always very wise.

The PM did a radio recording and then saw the Chancellor, the Lord President and Chief Whip about MPs' salaries. The proposal for £8,000 a year will be badly received and the PM has told Joe he will oppose it. We will see.

I saw Senator John Button from Australia, and then went home early, at 8 p.m., to baby-sit while Carol went out. Feel tired and dissatisfied.

*Wednesday 25 June 1975*

Went straight up to the study on arriving. HW was there with Joe. Ken Stowe joined us. Some general conversation about the current stories in the press. Then discussed wages policy. Joe has been putting up a number of ideas – including *phased* increases and allocating a *total wage bill* to an industry, which the PM at first resisted, but now, characteristically, retells to Joe as if the idea is his own.

I pressed my view that we need a voluntary policy which has enough sanctions and incentives built into it to make it stick. Using the public sector as the spearhead, maintaining firmly the norm of 10% there. And in the private sector using the price code and discretion about giving government aid to discourage industrialists from conceding more than the norm. Plus an incentive of increased family allowances if the norm is maintained.

The PM was quite receptive. He is now interested in getting this one right. Though he worried us by suddenly saying that he was not opposed to a statutory policy in principle, only in practice. This is what Jim Callaghan said at Chequers. We pointed this out. HW said Jim said it as part of his leadership manoeuvres – 'ready to lead the coalition'. He said they would argue against HW that he was 'the only obstacle to a coalition'. Here he was being completely political, thinking of himself and others simply in relation to the leadership. Suddenly he did not seem to have any fixed position on wages policy. He was just watching the others and making sure he was not isolated on a limb. This is why he wants to make sure that Jim is on all the economic committees dealing with wages – so that he is locked into any government policy which emerges. In these discussions I realise how politicians are completely different from anybody else: fighting battles about policies, appearing to care and to be identified with particular policy positions, but in reality their policy attachments are often very tenuous, and they do not find it difficult to change position. Perhaps the purpose and sanctity of a party manifesto is that it provides a rooted position, and consistency of attachment to policies, which as individuals they do not feel.

Went back to the Unit and worked on wages policy and public expenditure.

Went to lunch at the Reform with Robert Armstrong. He is more relaxed now and adapting into his Home Office job. He said he notices how much less work he has to do. And how less *politically* aware the civil servants are at the Home Office. No. 10 is a very special experience.

He still thinks HW will stay on till 1977, for the Jubilee.

He told me that John Cordle, a Tory MP who is one of Marcia's close friends and dining friends, is a very odd character, with curious relations with foreign governments as well as with Poulson.

A bad day for her. Eric Miller's property company is said in the papers to be in serious trouble. [The company, Peachey Property, and Miller were soon to be subject to Whitehall and police inquiries into financial irregularities. Miller committed suicide in 1977.]

After lunch I went with the PM to a big press conference in the Treasury to announce the amendments to the Industry Bill – meeting some of the CBI's objections and dropping some of the Bennery.

It was a packed hall. The chairman of the lobby asked why we had to have a press conference – obviously still bitter about the dropping of lobby briefings. But clearly a lot of journalists were pleased to be in on the act.

Walked back to No. 10 through the Foreign Office courtyard and round to Downing Street. In very hot sunshine. Just the PM, Joe and Janet, a private secretary, detectives and myself. As we crossed the street groups of pedestrians stopped and gaped.

Joe said that Janet is very supportive of the PM. She is going to check with him about his retirement plans.

The Unit gathered at 6 p.m. to discuss public expenditure, where our papers are developing well, questioning every sacred cow in the book. Followed this with a brief on wages policy for the PM's private meeting with the Chancellor, Shirley Williams and Callaghan tomorrow at 11.30. These are meant to be the unofficial core of ministers dealing with wages policy. The PM has said that above all he does not want Roy Jenkins on it. This is silly, since Roy is very good and will make his voice heard anyway and might as well be in the middle. Partly it is the personal dislike which has developed between them. Partly that the PM, in abandoning the Left as he now has, tries to smoke-screen it by being rude to the Right.

After a long discussion with the whole Unit on the broad lines of the paper, Andrew Graham and I finally finished it ourselves and had it typed in the garden room at after 10 at night. I did not get home to eat until nearly 11. Very tired. Yet awoke this morning at 4.45 and am writing this in bed now as the sun gets up and the dawn birds sing. Another beautiful day coming. But I am bound to be a bit tired. And beginning to reconcile myself to the thought of leaving No. 10. Like Christmas, this job is exciting, but it cannot be prolonged for ever. And it is clear that this Prime Minister should not go on much longer. The appetite and the spark have gone. He does not get much kick out of it so he should give up. Often he is simply going through the motions, like a veteran boxer.

Incidentally, Peggy Field, Marcia's sister and Mary Wilson's secretary, is to be paid partly by the Civil Service. There is a minute from the PM asking that the PM be reimbursed for her previous pay and that the money be sent to Lady Falkender. Curiously according to Joe, Peg's salary was already partly paid for by two outside sources – the *Sunday Times* and a friendly peer. Now the taxpayer is chipping in.

I received a transcript of the Milhench trial today. [Ronald Milhench was accused and found guilty of forgery in relation to the land deals affair.] One interesting point emerges: he *did* pay Tony Field's company, in which Marcia and Peggy have a stake, £340,000. So they may have made a huge profit. The problem, apparently, is that they used the money to buy more land which they now cannot sell.

On Crossman – John Hunt put in a memo saying he had been to see Michael Foot (one of Crossman's executors) to suggest that they all reach a gentlemen's agreement not to fight the court battle until after Radcliffe reports. He found Foot amenable and critical of the *Sunday Times* as irresponsible, but said Anne Crossman depended on the *Sunday Times* for money. Hunt concluded that Foot would not cause any trouble.

### Thursday 26 June 1975

Went up to see the PM in the study at about 10.30. He was already with Joe. He straight away said how much he liked the Unit paper on pay policy which we had put in last night. This was the line he was going to take at the secret Misc meeting this morning with Healey, Williams, Foot and Callaghan, i.e. to resist a statutory policy, but build teeth into the voluntary policy. He said that our suggestion to use section 7–8 of the 1972 Industry Act to withhold financial aid to firms which break the norm 'took my breath away' but once he thought about it he agreed.

He seemed much more confident. Just as with the referendum last December – as if he 'could see the way through'.

But he was afraid the Treasury would try to bounce us into a statutory policy anyway. So he dictated a Prime Minister's personal minute, along the lines of our paper, to send to the Chancellor instructing him to follow this voluntary policy backed by sanctions, and saying that the other two options of a purely voluntary policy resting on TUC co-operation or a statutory policy resting ultimately upon combined sanctions were out. This is because we know from the Unit's Treasury sources that Healey is telling his Treasury officials that we are going to have a statutory policy – while telling his ministerial colleagues and the PM the opposite.

[The PM's minute took the following lines:

### CHANCELLOR OF THE EXCHEQUER

You mentioned yesterday morning that the Official Committee on Prices and Incomes (PIO) is urgently preparing papers for us to consider next week as a basis for developing the anti-inflation policy for the coming year. I am anxious that these papers and our discussion should concentrate realistically on the approach which commanded most support in the Cabinet discussion at Chequers and should not waste effort in analysis of the two options for immediate purposes we effectively discarded; namely, on the one hand, a purely voluntary policy resting solely upon what the TUC can offer and, on the other, deciding now upon a statutory policy which in the last resort would rest upon criminal sanctions. Our objective is for the government to develop a policy of its own, which will be voluntary, which will command the maximum acceptance by the TUC and in the country, and which will embody acceptable targets for price and wage increases in the coming year. Such a policy would be supported by a range of measures, some of which might require legislation, which would fall to be undertaken by the government to encourage compliance with those targets by employers both in the public sector (and especially nationalised industries and local authorities) and in the private sector.

2. The Official Committee can best help us by study of a variety of measures open to the government which could support this approach. Many have already been suggested, by colleagues at Chequers and in the subsequent discussions, and I have in mind particularly:

(a) the form of wage target – i.e. percentage, flat rate, or a combination; consideration should also be given to a split rate of e.g. 5% initially plus 10% after six months, or even a system of quarterly payments;

(b) support for the 10% target by buttressing awards made early in the cycle with provision for an RPI linked addition later on, but only if there was a very high rate of RPI;

(c) a total freeze on the highest incomes;

(d) some degree of selective price stabilisation once the pay policy was seen to be working;

(e) the concept of the 'wage fund', whereby the existing wages bill, with the addition of the percentage or flat rate award, would set the limit within which individual parts of the public sector would have to accommodate their settlements so as to ensure that any excessive settlement is paid for by contraction of employment and/or restriction of services of immediate effect; alternatively, cash limits covering both wages and other expenditures;

(f) definition of the arrangements whereby higher settlements could be accepted as within the policy, provided they flowed from identified higher productivity.]

When the Misc met before Cabinet at 11.30 this is the line which the PM took. But John Hunt later told me that the permanent secretaries refused to believe this. They were all acting on the assumption of a statutory policy: they knew the Treasury had a paper written on this basis and also had the legislation for a statutory policy ready drafted. Hunt took out to lunch Ken Couzens* from the Treasury, who is being put in charge of pay policy, as chairman of the Prices and Incomes Official Committee. Hunt had laid down the PM's line; but Couzens was doubtful. He said that the PIO was due to meet next week and would have papers on the three options – voluntary with no sanctions; voluntary with sanctions; and statutory, as if it was still open to decision, and then the Treasury would try to bounce through the statutory option. Hunt made it clear that the decision was already taken, by the PM, for the middle option. So they agreed to allow circulation of the three papers on the options – including a strong one from Foot at Employment pleading for a combination of the voluntary approach – but also to have a chairman's covering note which would direct them towards the middle option.

Cabinet then met at 12 with little of significance on the agenda. Afterwards I spoke to Fred Mulley, who is worried about cuts in expenditure on Education, and says that everybody is for stopping university teachers' pay rises and for making the universities the first martyrs in the pay policy. I was troubled by this, not surprisingly. But Mulley seemed very clear and firm. He masters his briefs very well.

Shirley Williams took me back to her office for a drink before lunch. Her views on pay are very close to ours and she is happy with how the Misc Cabinet committee went this morning. Shirley is very attractive, easy-going, amusing, no side. Her officials obviously like her – she takes them out to lunch and they have regular briefings and general discussions. She keeps John Lyttle, her special adviser, well involved, and her junior ministers. Her weaknesses are that she is a bit disorganised, never punctual, and these add to her image of being *muddled*. In fact she is not particularly muddled on politics or policies, but she gives that impression. The fact that she dresses, stands, walks and sits like an over-full sack of cabbages does not help. In fact she has pretty eyes, a pleasant open face and a lovely open smile. If she could get herself 'organised', with all the trappings of efficiency, she would have to be taken very seriously indeed.

I asked her if she was content in her present job as minister monitoring prices – implying that I did not think she ought to be – and I said that one day she would have to put her foot down and ask for something better. She said she was content for the moment, and she did not want to move while prices were rocketing upwards. She would like to get them under control first.

I left Shirley at about 1.45, went to the bank, and then to the Commons cafeteria for a quick lunch alone. Joe and I go there more often now – it is cheap and fast. Today he was having lunch with the *Sunday Times*. I went out on to the Commons terrace and chatted with Mike Thomas, the Labour MP from the north-east. He said lots of Labour MPs are fed up.

Many of them are in financial trouble because their salaries have not gone up for three years. He said many were running into debt and some had to take money from outside interests – 'with all the Poulson dangers'. They are having to work very hard, with constant late nights on committees. And now there is a lot of discontent over the selection of the delegation to Strasbourg. Nearly half of the Labour list are anti-marketeers – and those who took a lot of stick for supporting the leadership feel bitter that they get no rewards. He was critical of HW's style of leadership, which is always to reward his enemies and ignore his friends.

Went straight up to the PM's room in the Commons for the 2.30 briefing on Questions. He was again counting the number of Question Times left till the recess and encouraging the officials to arrange more foreign visits so that he can avoid Question Time.

Questions were in fact quite tough, with the recurring question of when he is going to do something about inflation.

Came back to No. 10 for a meeting of the Cabinet committee on Industrial Policy (IDV), which is much less interesting, and less worrying, now that Benn has been moved. Actually some of Benn's pigeons are coming home to roost. The motorcycle industry has collapsed, including not only his beloved Meriden co-operative, but also the Norton Villiers Triumph company which was previously OK. Benn's handouts and rhetoric to the shop stewards cannot make up for the years of management incompetence and too little investment. A few years ago we had 70% of the American motorcycle market. Now the Japanese have almost totally replaced us. NVT make 14 motorcycles per worker per year. The Japanese make 150.

The committee decided to help Alfred Herbert [the ailing machine tools manufacturer] with £25 million – or else our machine-tool industry would have gone beyond recall. It was not a good meeting, very rambling, and too much detail to make the optimum use of the high-powered ministerial team present.

Before the meeting Tony Crosland took me on one side. He said he was appalled by the lack of coherence among the Cabinet committees on economic questions. That afternoon one committee had been discussing schoolteachers' pay, while another elsewhere was discussing university teachers' pay, and neither of them having any guidance on overall pay policy. He said we must have a central committee discussing pay policy. I did not reveal to him that this morning's secret Misc had been discussing precisely that, but promised to get something done. I mentioned it afterwards to the PM and to Ken Stowe, and the PM said that Crosland must be on the Misc which meets on pay next week, and Ken Stowe said he would tell Crosland tomorrow. I also discussed with Ken Stowe trying to get some coherence in the economic committees. We are going to look at this in the Unit. It is total anarchy at the moment, with several economic committees, no clear lines of distinction between them and most of the important economic decisions put to none of them but kept for the internal Treasury committees. What we need is one master committee which deals with overall strategy (the ministerial committee on Economic Strategy ought to do that but usually gets involved in a ragbag of ad hoc micro-matters). Then there should be a minimum of committees below that, ministerial and official, to take the detailed individual decisions and to service the strategy committee.

I went home early. The PM was in the study, and kept Joe there for some time chatting, but I decided not to stay. I walked up to Leicester Square and bought a salt beef sandwich, then took a bus to Kentish Town and bought some fish and chips, had a pint in the local pub in Highgate Road and went home to bed. I was feeling quite tired.

### Friday 27 June 1975

Had a Unit meeting on transport policy – for our public expenditure paper – and then had long meeting with Christopher Foster, the adviser from Environment, also about transport policy. In the middle I was summoned to the PM's study to discuss a speech that the PM is giving on Monday, on food and agriculture.

Lunch with Joe at the Commons. Afterwards went out on to the Terrace. Merlyn Rees came up and told us harrowing stories about Irish murders. My old friend from school, Gerry Fowler, was there, surrounded as usual by lots of pretty ladies. Chris Price* was arguing that the crisis was not serious and just needs us all to 'give up a couple of gin and tonics each'. Gerry Fowler also was feeling fairly relaxed, saying, 'We have all been here before in 1966.' I felt this was being a bit complacent.

Before lunch the PM saw George Weidenfeld, his and Marcia's publisher, James Hanson,* the multi-millionaire, and Alistair McAlpine,* the millionaire, all lined up by Marcia. The latter two are very right-wing and not wholly suitable for a Labour Prime Minister to be spending time on in the middle of an economic crisis.

After lunch I worked in the Unit. Our economic team, Andrew Graham, Gavyn Davies, David Gowland and David Piachaud, produced two serious papers – one on the competitiveness of sterling at present, one on the percentage of thresholds and of new money in current pay settlements. These are the kind of papers the PM likes best – very statistical, lots of graphs and tables, and some hard political conclusions. One of our conclusions was that if wage settlements continue at the present rate of 30% and sterling depreciates to maintain competitiveness, the rate against the dollar at the end 1976 will be $1.65! [In 1976 the rate fell to $1.65 in October and bottomed around $1.57 on 28 October – not bad forecasting by the Unit!] When I told him about this paper he got very excited and said, 'That settles it,' and added, 'There is no answer to that – except a tougher policy.'

My brother Clem arrived from France and collected me from the office. We went to Soho for a pint and then to Hampstead for dinner. Home by midnight.

This afternoon the injunction against the *Sunday Times* was heard. [The Attorney won the first round, but the *Sunday Times* won the appeal.]

## Sunday 29 June 1975

Today's *Sunday Times* had a very strong editorial attacking John Hunt and HW for their support for secrecy and opposition to open government. Very savage. But they asked for it and cannot say they were not warned.

## Monday 30 June 1975

The PM was away this morning visiting an agricultural show in Warwickshire. I came in to the office and found a flood of papers on wages policy. Things are moving swiftly – but curiously on several levels. The Treasury continues to circulate papers on the assumption that all three options – (1) a TUC voluntary policy, (2) a government-backed voluntary policy with financial sanctions and (3) the Treasury's proposed statutory policy – are still open (and hoping to get the last). But we and the Cabinet Office are working on the assumption that, by elimination of the 1st and 3rd and following the PM's firm personal minute to the Chancellor last Friday, the choice has been made for the 2nd option. So the Cabinet Office covering notes, and the agenda of the PIO (Prices and Incomes Official) committee are based on that assumption, with a lot of detailed work on the kind of sanctions we mean to impose to back up the voluntary policy. At the same time some ministers such as Foot assume that the three options are open and that we will go for the first, more voluntary policy, and he is holding secret meetings with the TUC to secure that.

In the morning – and throughout the day – the sterling rate sagged. Joe and I went to lunch at the Commons, full of an ominous sense that things were going to be taken out of our hands. Last week Joe said to Ken Stowe that he feared the Treasury would come knocking on the PM's door to say that the sterling rate had gone and so we must have their statutory package immediately. I had told John Hunt that I feared that the Treasury would let the rate down in order to create the crisis atmosphere in which to bounce their policy. Apparently the PM on Sunday at Chequers said to one of the secretaries that he expected the Governor of the Bank, Gordon Richardson, to arrive on Monday at 3.30 p.m.

He was an hour out. At 2.30 the Governor came striding in. The Chancellor had already gone bounding ahead to the Prime Minister's study, up the stairs two at a time. Gordon Richardson came over to chat to me. He seemed very jumpy. He said, 'We must act now. We must act *now*.' I asked if he meant precisely now, this afternoon. He said, 'Well, by tomorrow at the latest.' I asked what he meant by 'act'. He said, 'Make a statement.' I said what kind of statement. He said, 'To reassure foreign holders.' I was fishing to see if he wanted specifically a statutory incomes policy. He seemed to think so, adding it 'must have something about public expenditure', but mainly he wanted a statement which demonstrated we were doing *something*. He said, 'This government's whole credibility has gone.' I asked if deposits were actually moving out. He said yes and it was gathering pace, but he was not specific. I assured him that the PM was very apprised of the problem, but it was crucial to get things right. He said we must 'end this nonsense of getting the co-operation and consent of others, the trade unions, the Labour Party. We must act. People are ready to support tough measures.' I agreed that most people were ready, but suggested there were grounds for getting widespread support for such tough measures. Ted Heath had tried the action policy and it didn't get him far. The Governor agreed but felt that the situation – the economy and public opinion – were different now.

Although he was worryingly jumpy, Gordon Richardson is a nicely smooth man and much better than the governors of yesteryear. The PM will respond to his style. But the policy and consequences may be just as disastrous for a Labour government.

Richardson went upstairs to join the Chancellor in the study. I stayed outside the Cabinet Room as ministers began to gather for the 3 o'clock meeting of the Misc 91 committee which deals with the new pay policy – Foot, Shore, Williams, Crosland, Callaghan, Healey and the PM in the chair.

We were kept waiting a while and I sat with Crosland. He was strongly for our voluntary option B pay policy backed by sanctions and was going to support it in the meeting. He thought that there was no hope of reaching an agreement with the TUC on a completely voluntary policy, and if the latest crisis gave us an excuse for not prolonging the agony it would be a relief. 'But it will need firmer chairmanship than Harold normally gives,' he said.

I also talked to Jim Callaghan standing near the news tapes. He is incredibly political. He very obviously steered us off discussion of the pay problem and talked about Wimbledon. He always does this. Very friendly, but never showing his hand. He certainly knows that the PM has brought him into this committee in order to lock him into any unpopular policies we bring in. The PM is very afraid of 'coalition' moves. His approach is always to isolate Jenkins and to lock in Callaghan. Jim knows this, but goes along with it. He needs to be there at the centre. And his political instincts are so good that he will spot the moment when to break.

The PM, Healey and the Governor came down at about 3.20 and we started the Misc meeting (the Governor left looking pleased).

Healey opened by stating that the crisis had come, sterling was, in the Governor's words, 'crumbling' and it was essential to make an announcement tomorrow. It must be tough enough to reassure our depositors. We had lost $500 million of our $600 million reserves in recent weeks. The Nigerians and Kuwaitis were running down their holdings. We had 'to act to halt the haemorrhage now'. On policy he began by talking as if what he was doing was simply advancing our voluntary option B, while adding to it a legal sanction against employers – which was the Heath policy. But as the meeting progressed he said more and more about the sanction against employers, less and less about option B.

Foot joined in, very worried. He pressed Healey hard to say what he meant specifically, what he would answer to precise questions in the House. Healey ducked this, and pleaded that he had not had time to work it out: 'This has blown up very suddenly and I was out of the office this morning.' He asked to be able to make a short statement of firm intent, that the legislation would be 10% wage increases and retrospective to today. In fact he was not being completely honest. He knew exactly what the Treasury wanted – the statement of statuary incomes policy policy which the Treasury has proposed and has been waiting to bounce in for months.

Callaghan was interesting. He said that, based on his previous experience, we should let the rate go down. If sterling was cheap it would bounce back. Meanwhile we should talk to the holders and deal with the external accounts separately. There was clearly a lot of wisdom and experience in his comments – after all, the point of floating sterling was to avoid having to defend it with panic packages. Healey did not respond at all.

Crosland spoke to support our option B (a voluntary policy backed by tough sanctions) as the best approach and did not seem fully to appreciate that Healey was surreptitiously moving us off it.

Shirley Williams was a bit woolly, wanting a three months' freeze while we sorted it out – probably the worst of all worlds.

And Peter Shore was worried that we were not being tough enough to make it stick and restore confidence.

The last stages were dominated by Healey firmly rephrasing his approach and the PM repeating that sterling was 'crumbling' so we must act – but not by imprisoning workers. He would draw the line rigidly at that. Healey then said that he was going to see Len Murray immediately and was bringing Jack Jones back from the Transport and General Workers Union conference in Blackpool that evening. He concluded that he would have the statement on the new pay policy ready to hand round at tomorrow morning's special Cabinet at 9.30 a.m., but he would not circulate it beforehand.

[Notes on the Misc 91 meeting on 30 June 1975. Present: Shore, Foot, Williams, Crosland, Callaghan, Healey, Wilson.

| | |
|---|---|
| D. Healey: | Governor said sterling is 'crumbling'. Can't wait a fortnight. Reserves $6 billion. Last few days lost $500 million. Mainly Kuwait & Nigeria. Perhaps Saudis – but don't know because don't work through Bank of England. But all foreign governments selling. |
| P. Shore: | This small package won't carry conviction. |
| S. Williams: | Agrees. So prefer freeze and detailed package to come in 10 days – as planned. |
| J. Callaghan: | 'Let rate go and block deposits.' A wasted package will make things worse. 'We've been here before.' |
| D. Healey: | No need to do public expenditure if we do this on income. Quotes Jack Jones remark 'suspending wage bargaining for a year'. |
| Prime Minister: | We won't be rushed into something we believe to be unworkable – criminal sanctions. |
| | 'Legal limit of 10%' announced tomorrow. Will be retrospective. |
| | This is the package. |
| | The employers will be prosecuted and perhaps a 3 months freeze. |
| | DH is trying to avoid falling into the hands of the IMF, which would involve: PE cuts, tax up and Incomes Policy. |
| M. Foot: | This is a cut in real incomes as the sole measure, backed up by clever statutory sanctions. |
| | Whole burden on wages. |
| Prime Minister: | Must include prices. |
| D. Healey: | Yes, but cannot include other trade union conditions on social services, employment, etc. |
| A. Crosland: | Statement must include three things: |
| | (1) 10% norm. |
| | (2) Sanctions. |

|  | (3) Prices and food subsidies. |
| *D. Healey:* | Package must finally include, in second White Paper after a week: |
|  | (1) Food subsidies not phased out – but not mentioned tomorrow. |
|  | (2) Retail prices controlled. |
|  | (3) Three or six months' delay on price rise. |
|  | But these need a week to sort out. |
|  | (4) Public Expenditure cash limit. |
|  | (5) Temporary Employment subsidy. |
|  | But not details. Just say part of the final package. |
|  | (6) Investment must be maintained – at expense of dividends. |
|  |  |
|  | Must have let-out for current arbitration settlements to avoid seamen's strike. |
|  | Will publish White Paper. |
|  | DH says this is option B + sanctions against employers. In fact he is selling the Treasury's statutory policy as if it is really option B. |
|  |  |
| *A. Crosland:* | 'Almost relieved.' |
| *Prime Minister:* | Agrees. |
| *M. Foot:* | I don't share your relief. |
| *P. Shore:* | Worried it won't stick. |
| *D. Healey:* | 'To try to solve this problem by creating unemployment is nonsense.' |
| *S. Williams:* | Worried – would like 'to buy time' by a wage freeze. |
| *D. Healey:* | That would leave an impression of not having thought it through or having clear ideas. |
|  |  |
|  | DH is to see Len Murray immediately and get Jack Jones back from T&G Conference at Blackpool this evening. We will pay for private plane. |
|  | Cabinet tomorrow 9.30. Statement ready to hand round – not circulated before. |

Notes end.]

I walked out with Crosland and expressed my misgivings – that the Treasury had successfully bounced through their policy by wrapping it up in the language of our voluntary policy, as if the statutory part were just a small appendix. In fact the legal sanctions were the heart of Healey's case.

I came back in, and Joe and I started talking to the PM outside the Cabinet Room. We each expressed our worries, and the PM told us to come up to the study with him so that 'the others won't know'. There Joe and I hammered away at him. Joe said he viewed the prospect of a full statutory policy with dread. The party would split. I said it was a terrible mistake to bring in a policy this Monday that was significantly different from what he would have introduced next Monday had he the time. I also told him that the Treasury had been waiting for this opportunity and that Healey had told his officials that he would get them a statutory policy in the end. Both Joe and I said we suspected that the Treasury and the Bank were deliberately letting the rate go in order to provide the crisis background for their statutory policy 'bounce'. But the PM resisted. He said we must protect sterling and a statutory policy was the only way. He preferred to have a sterling crisis now rather than in the summer holiday. We might as well face up to it and get it over and done with. He thought Foot had taken it well and would be content with a statutory policy if sterling was crashing.

He went off at 5 p.m. to have his meeting with Tindemans, the Belgian PM, who is here to discuss EEC matters. It was clear that HW's mind was not on the EEC – and it appeared to be reconciled to a statutory wages policy.

At round 6.30 p.m. I walked down past the Cabinet Room and found HW pacing up and down talking to Joe and Robin Butler. Joe was pressing him hard against a full statutory policy, especially on the implications for party unity. I joined in, stating that it was wrong to be pushed off the policy course we were following because of this sudden pressure on sterling – at which the Treasury and the Bank might be conniving anyway. That it is wrong to take a different decision today from what we would have taken next Monday, given the time. I also said that there was no 'fall-back' position from a statutory policy. If it collapsed, the whole edifice went with it. Robin Butler put up a good case for taking the pressure on the sterling rate for another week until we had our whole anti-inflation package ready, with its voluntary pay policy and its public expenditure cuts.

HW became rather irritable. He said that Joe and I were being 'too political'. That our option B policy, 'voluntary with strong teeth', would not work, that only a full statutory policy would save sterling. When Joe said that a statutory policy had never worked so far, HW insisted that it had been a success in 1966–69.

The four of us stood there in the hall debating this critical phase of policy as guests began to arrive, and butlers and waitresses, for this evening's dinner for Tindemans. Finally HW called it a day. He would not budge on the statutory policy and went up to the flat to change.

I changed in my office and went to the official dinner, sitting next to Haya Clayton from the film industry and the wife of the novelist John Fowles. It was a good dinner and reception after, with lots of nice people, including the wonderful Arthur Askey. Marcia sat next to George Weidenfeld and behaved perfectly.

At midnight the Treasury sent round a copy of the Chancellor's proposed statement for tomorrow. Later John Hunt told us that when he went into the Treasury earlier there were at least 20 mandarins sitting round the table drafting. Douglas Wass, the Treasury permanent secretary, had flown back from an oil-rig to preside over this great opportunity for the Treasury to sell again all the old statutory policy stuff it had sold to poor old Ted Heath. John Hunt said that these were *exactly* the same people who had drafted Heath's pay policy – and the words which emerged were almost exactly the same. And look where that got Ted Heath!

I went downstairs into private office and read the draft statement with Joe and Ken Stowe. We all agreed it was disastrous. It did not reflect this afternoon's ministerial meeting. It contained no references to our policy of voluntary with teeth if possible. No reference to sanctions against employers, except a woolly bit on the price code. It was a stark reintroduction of a statutory policy to control pay bargaining, including intervention in the bargaining process. It was even honest enough to admit that it was the same as was done under Heath, regretting that it was necessary to do it 'again'.

Ken Stowe – who has been a tremendous ally throughout all this business – went straight upstairs to the reception, which was still in full swing, with several notable public figures now staggering around full of good drink, and told the PM that we were unhappy with the Treasury draft and wanted to talk to him about it. Apparently HW reacted with hostility again. He said, 'Bernard and Joe are neurotic about statutory policy. Tell them to put in a brief, but I don't want to discuss it.'

Joe and I were annoyed at this. After all, our 'neuroticism' was over what the Treasury was threatening to do to the Labour Party, the Labour government and to Harold Wilson as Prime Minister – for none of whom the Treasury have any reason to give a damn. We were convinced that that statement would split the party, drive Foot, Castle and Benn out of the Cabinet and almost certainly lead to HW's resignation as leader. We said this in our memo, which Joe typed as we verbally agreed the draft, sitting in his room at 1 o'clock in the morning as the guests drifted noisily away down the Downing Street corridor to the front door. We also did a detailed critique of some of the Treasury draft's omissions and defects. We then went home.

The memo said:

## PRIME MINISTER

We believe that the Cabinet are being faced with an attempt by the Treasury to stampede it into a statutory pay policy against every pledge which we have given. We are reinforced in this belief by the knowledge that no money at all was spent in defence of the pound on Monday.

The proposed statement by the Chancellor is a straightforward announcement of such a policy. It has no reference whatsoever about acting against employers, it is solely concerned with legal restraints against pay.

Paragraph five, on dealing with prices, is so inadequate it will be laughed at in the House.

Paragraph four sets the alternative to a statutory policy as the TUC policy. This is not the case. We have been formulating another alternative, part voluntary, part statutory, which stood a much better chance of success.

The phrase using the law in the pay bargaining process will lead to a split in the party. It is not, as we understand it, what the Misc decided today. It will lead to resignations from the Cabinet and the government.

The commitment on public expenditure, which has serious implications, is being made in advance of any proper consultation or discussion with colleagues.

We believe the Treasury are trying to bounce the government along the same old path they have trodden before, with incalculable consequences for the government and the party.

Joe Haines<br>Bernard Donoughue

I was woken up by the telephone in the middle of the night. It was Joe. The PM had just spoken to him on the phone. He wanted us to know that he 'agreed with every word in our brief', he was going to forbid Healey to circulate his proposed draft statement and was himself dictating a long minute incorporating our criticisms. Joe was jubilant, and I was relieved sufficiently to compensate for being woken up.

Had only four hours' sleep. Woke again at 7 a.m. this morning to write this and went on my usual morning run on Hampstead Heath – absolutely beautiful in the early sunshine, rich with smells of orange blossom and cut grass, and London waking in the morning haze stretching below. Quite a day.

*Tuesday 1 July 1975*

I was delayed in heavy traffic and infuriated because I did not arrive until a few minutes before this morning's special 9.30 a.m. Cabinet. The ministers were already gathered and Crosland immediately took me on one side and complained that it was now clear that the Treasury was trying to bounce through a Heath Mark II pay policy instead of a TUC Mark II (or a Wilson Mark I). I agreed and expressed my suspicions about the run on sterling. It is now clear that in fact little foreign deposits moved and the Bank did not intervene to protect the rate at all. They knew that the Kuwaitis had said they would move their deposits at $2.20 and the Saudis at around $2.17. Yet the Bank had let the rate go down to that level, with little selling pressure. It smells like a Treasury ramp.

Before Crosland and I could say much, HW came downstairs. Michael Foot had already been in – to threaten to resign if we issued Healey's statement. Wilson was able to reassure Foot. Healey sat there flicking through the papers in his box and looking very glum.

After they went into Cabinet Ken Stowe came up to me and said, 'You and Joe have earned your keep. There has been a monumental shift in the PM's attitude.' Ken said the PM had retreated from his statutory position and was now talking about a Treasury bounce. He had this morning forbidden Healey to issue his statement. But they still had to have a statement by this afternoon.

The Cabinet went on all morning. The PM had to cancel his briefing to give evidence to the Radcliffe committee on ministers' memoirs and his proposed visit to Canada House. They finally broke at about 12.30 and Jim Hamilton and John Hunt of the Cabinet Office were despatched to draft a statement along the lines of ministerial wishes – which meant a voluntary policy if possible, a statutory policy if necessary.

After Cabinet the PM went straight into Marcia's room, so the rest of us went upstairs for lunch. We finished quickly and went straight over to the House of Commons, where the Misc 91 group of ministers gathered to discuss the draft statement. It was a great improvement, stating that ministers preferred our option with a battery of sanctions, but failing all else would introduce a statutory policy.

Questions went comfortably for the PM and then the Chancellor made his statement. It was quite well received, and sterling and the stock market went up rapidly.

[In the afternoon Chancellor Healey had told a surprised House of Commons that the government would announce its decisions on inflation and incomes policy next week. He said that the government would have to legislate to enforce a 10% wage limit if voluntary agreements were not reached between the TUC and the CBI to satisfy the target for reducing inflation. He added that measures to secure compliance were well advanced.]

When I saw the PM in the early evening, after he had given evidence to the Radcliffe committee (for a 10-year moratorium on memoirs!) and before he went to the Palace for the regular audience I pointed out to him that we had rescued sterling with a compromise statement and without needing the ultimate deterrent. He nodded, went outside and repeated this to Andrew Graham, who has done so much excellent work on our policy in the Policy Unit.

In the evening I went with Carol to have dinner with Ron Spiers from the American embassy. The Ambassador was there and Ralf Dahrendorf, plus two quality journalists – David Watt and Peter Jay. Very pleasant. Home at midnight.

### Wednesday 2 July 1975

Went up to the study to discuss the weekend's speeches with the PM. These are progressing well: Joe is doing the draft for the Mineworkers conference, trying to make it tough; Robin Butler and I are doing the Welsh speech.

We discussed the incomes policy position as well. Joe and I stressed again the political problems in always going all the way with the Treasury. We told him that the Treasury had bounced him on Monday. He just listens, agrees and then does nothing.

In fact Robin Butler told me that coming back in the helicopter from the agricultural show on Monday morning the PM predicted that the Governor and the Treasury would try to bounce him into an incomes policy but he claimed that he would simply refuse. Yet within 10 minutes of the Governor telling him that sterling was 'crumbling' he had completely capitulated!

In the Unit we continued to draft and discuss our papers on the option B voluntary incomes policy backed by sanctions.

We had lunch with Alastair Hetherington, Peter Gibbings and Peter Preston from the *Guardian*. HW dominated the discussion. He also went on at great length about the Crossman Diaries business. He repeated his claim – which Joe privately questions – that he has never interfered with Attorney-Generals. But he revealed the gist of his evidence to the Radcliffe commission yesterday – that for *memoirs* (as opposed to contemporary histories) authors would have to submit their scripts if they referred to events within 10 years.

We went straight from lunch down to the Misc 91 committee of ministers on counter-inflation policy. They had before them a series of papers on particular financial sanctions which might be used – cash limits, price code controls, sections 7 and 8 of the Industry Act, etc., all of which had originated in the Policy Unit.

At the beginning the PM said he thought that 'officials were getting the bit between their teeth and this ministerial committee must have full control'.

The rest of the discussion was a bit disappointing, very detailed, with people seeming tired – including HW. Callaghan left after half an hour without having said anything. And Crosland came in late. Shirley Williams still seemed uncertain. Michael Foot once pointed out that he was not happy with any statutory policy.

Healey spent some time explaining an incident from the morning, when Jack Jones had claimed publicly that Healey had promised him there would not be a statutory policy. Sterling dropped. Then Healey, who was at NEDDY, issued a statement saying that he had not quite said this. Sterling rose again. Healey used this as an argument to prove that we must have a statutory policy to defend sterling. To me it showed something different – that uncertainty is the real threat to sterling.

The PM left at 4.30 to see Nelson Rockefeller. I slipped out as well, and went into the Cabinet Office, to the big conference room across the corridor from my room, for a meeting of the official committee on prices and incomes. It was a large meeting, with about 20 officials from a dozen departments. Ken Couzens from the Treasury was in the chair – a lively, bristly, witty little man in his early forties, with a pronounced south of England commuter accent, Purley or Chorleywood. He talked a great deal and the meeting, which went on for three hours, was dominated by him, Dirkes from Employment, Alan Lord* from Industry, Hugo Cole from Environment, and a good man from Prices and Incomes. I intervened a great deal, far more than I intended, but the whole proceeding was very disturbing and at one point I lost my temper.

Couzens repeatedly referred to the ministers, especially to the Prime Minister, and their policy proposals in most sneering terms. His Treasury contempt for politicians came pouring through and many of the other civil servants joined in the laughter. At the very beginning he referred to the ministerial Misc 91 which he had just attended as 'after that interruption we can now get back to serious business'. This serious business they had in mind was promoting a full statutory incomes policy – and they did this by pouring scorn on every detailed weapon in our option B 'battery of sanctions' – cash limits, price code, the lot. They had produced papers showing how impractical they all were. An example was our Unit suggestion to use sections 7 and 8 of the Industry Act – withholding aid to firms which had breached the norm. The Treasury paper described the difficulties, how it would involve massive new legislation, etc. How difficult it would be to recover grant money from firms which had already spent it. In fact, as I showed in argument, there was *no* need for new legislation, and we were discussing refusing applications from firms which had already broken the norm, not recovering money from firms which later broke the code. The Treasury of course knew all this. But they were out to show and exaggerate the weaknesses and difficulties of our policy. All their papers contain references to the fact that a full statutory policy will have 'none of these difficulties'. One of today's papers was a series of appendices on problems such as investments, fringe benefits, top salaries, etc. The introduction said blatantly that these were written 'on the assumption that a full statutory policy would be introduced'.

When I lost my temper I interrupted Couzens and said that some of us knew that the Treasury was trying to bounce a full statutory policy through, but that the purpose of this meeting was to examine the instruments of the alternative policy, not to exclude them.

After that he changed his tone a good deal. In fact he is an attractive man, not at all a Treasury smoothie. But other people were very aware of the battle that was going on. Later Ken Stowe told me that he had heard from John Hunt that 'Bernard and Ken Couzens had been clashing'. It must have been clear to others that here was the real battle going on – between the Treasury and No.10.

I came back from the meeting at 8 p.m. – it started at 4.45 – very furious with what had gone on, but pleased I went. I think we made our point. I reported to Ken Stowe that I was now worried that the official Prices and Incomes Policy should be in the hands of people who were so totally opposed to one of the alternative policies. Ken – who has supported us marvellously throughout – went off to see John Hunt, who in turn arranged to see Wass and Couzens. Hunt will make sure that the Cabinet Office has overall co-ordination of the Treasury work. This would normally not necessarily be any great consolation, but in fact there is a great deal of tension between Hunt and Wass over the control of economic policy, and in this situation Hunt will want to impose the No. 10 view because that is his power base over Wass. Even so, Ken Stowe told me that Hunt had said to him, 'But we are going to have a full statutory policy, aren't we?'

In the evening I went off to LSE to a dinner Dahrendorf was giving for the LSE special advisers working in government. Quite an encouraging bunch – and Dahrendorf has some interesting ideas on setting up a kind of Brookings Institute for policy studies above the new LSE library. [Sadly, by the time I had helped to negotiate millions of pounds of EEC and Treasury money for an EEC institute in London, the LSE and other London research organisations rejected it. Roy Jenkins, as EC President, together with Douglas

Allen of the Civil Service Department, gave tremendous support. Mrs Thatcher finally killed it in 1979.]

## Thursday 3 July 1975

I went in early to see the PM before Cabinet at 10 a.m. He was angry with the PLP which had sent him a delegation about MPs' salaries and was pushing him to give in on the Boyle Report recommendations. He had promised Joe and me that he would not give way on MP's salaries – because the effect on our new incomes policy would be very damaging – but he has given way under the first pressure. This has been a recurring feature of his style of late. Firm verbal assurances before a crunch, and then total capitulation under pressure.

I also spoke to him about Robin Butler, who is due to leave the private office in August. This could be a disastrous break in continuity in the middle of the crisis. He agreed. But when I suggested Robin staying to the end of the year, he said, 'Well, the beginning of the parliamentary session will do.' Is this another sign of retirement in October? Joe told me that Marcia had suggested to HW (hopefully) that the economic crisis might 'delay' his departure plans. HW replied, 'It might bring them forward.'

Tony Crosland saw me as he was going in to Cabinet and suggested that we have a private meeting.

The Cabinet did not discuss incomes policy – only MPs' (their own) pay, on which they decided to capitulate. At midday Healey, Foot and Shirley Williams went off to see the TUC.

Lever came out in the middle and complained to me that he was being excluded from the economic discussions – he is not on the Misc 91. He said he was not prepared to be a respectable front-man, if he was not properly included in the discussions. Ray Richardson tells me that he is close to resignation.

After Cabinet I walked out with Crosland and arranged to see him this afternoon during Questions.

We went upstairs to lunch. Afterwards we went across to the Commons for briefing, which was very short because HW was receiving a delegation of MPs about their salaries. He has arranged to make a statement after Questions.

I did not go to Questions – the first time I have missed them in 16 months, Instead I slipped upstairs to Tony Crosland's room to discuss incomes policy. His position is very close to ours. I told him about the Treasury 'bounce' and our fears about the consequences. He said he would have to support Foot. I said no – the answer was to get Foot to support him on the '*sanctions*' policy. Because the TUC voluntary policy was not a starter, Foot's first hope of avoiding the statutory policy, on which he would have to resign, was to plump for the middle course. Crosland agreed to speak early and strongly for our middle course at this afternoon's Misc 91.

I went back downstairs and met David Owen in the corridor. He said that the capitulation on MPs' pay would be badly received. Just then HW came up smiling broadly and said, 'Well, I got away with that one all right.' I said, 'Yes, but David was just saying that you won't get away with it in the country.' HW's face slumped and he mumbled, 'Well, you have more than one constituency. We have got away with it in the House.'

Edgar Faure, the French politician, then came to see HW in his room. I went off to see Alf Morris, the minister responsible for the disabled, on the terrace of the House of Commons. He told me of a big programme for the disabled in Germany and wondered how we could make use of it. I told him about the PM's forthcoming visit to Chancellor Schmidt and promised to try to get something on the agenda about disablement. He is going to send me the papers and I will see what I can do. Alf, like Jack Ashley, is a marvellous tonic, a sincere and genuine person in politics to help other people. He compensates for the shabbiness of so many of the others.

I dashed back for the Misc 91 meeting on counter-inflation – Callaghan was not present at all this time.

HW was not in good form. Tired and not on top of the subject. He failed to sum up decisions and spent half the meeting writing his speech for his next engagement. But he was clearly worried by the shift of ministers away from a statutory policy. Healey reported on their meeting with the TUC, which seemed to have gone well, with nobody objecting to the sanctions with a voluntary policy, and accepting a norm of a £6 flat rate – which is about 11½%. More than our 10% but good progress.

Crosland then intervened very effectively. He said he had now had time to think about Monday and Tuesday's discussions and he was not happy. They were sliding down the same fatal road which Heath had taken. He did not want a statutory policy, which would have a minimum effect on inflation and a maximum effect damaging to the government and the party. Shore and Varley came in to support this view. Shirley appeared to give it support, though I still find it difficult to work out her position.

Healey immediately looked worried. He was being isolated. He intervened to say that he was very tired, they must learn what the TUC had later decided and he hoped they would not take any decision now.

The PM looked pale and worried, sent for Tuesday's Hansard and read from it Healey's statement, pointing out, 'You did not commit us to a statutory policy, did you, Denis?' Healey agreed he did not, but looked terrible. Everyone was deserting him. Being Chancellor in tough times is very difficult. He exchanged grim glances with Couzens, who was sitting at the end of the table. HW intervened to reassure him that 'we are not taking any decision on a statutory policy now'. But Crosland added, 'Maybe not, but I trust we won't have one.'

I was very pleased with this shift. Crosland had been very good. I was sorry for Healey who finds it all slippery beneath him. He rarely gets much support in Cabinet. I was less sorry for HW, whose performance over all this has been lamentable. At first he said it was inconceivable that he would preside over a statutory policy. Then last week he sent his minute to Healey ordering a voluntary policy with sanctions. On Monday morning he told Butler he would not be bounced. On Monday afternoon he was bounced. On Monday evening he refused to talk to us and called Joe and me neurotics for opposing the bounce. In the middle of Monday night he telephoned to say he agreed, and forbade the Treasury minute. On Tuesday he was for a 'reserve powers' statutory policy, but firmly for the statutory basis, and believed his own sanctions policy would not work. Today he is visibly slipping back away from the statutory policy under pressure from the movements of other ministers. He now bends before every wind. Joe said to me afterwards, 'This is very sad. He won't stand up to or for anything. This is just the fag-end of a very great politician.'

## Friday 4 July 1975

The PM in Bradford all day acting as University Chancellor. I spent the morning clearing papers. Went to lunch with Joe at the Commons. He is very upset because the PM has forbidden him to see the Cabinet minutes for Tuesday – all the civil servants can see them but not Joe and me. The reason for this paranoia about leaks from people who are loyal to him must be medical. Dozens of civil servants will see these minutes. The last leak inquiry (when I was accused) showed that an under-secretary in the statistical office had leaked it. My journalist friend tells me that civil servants – including very senior ones – talk constantly to the press. But the PM goes on believing that civil servants are perfect and his own personal assistants are leaking against him. This is the process which I call 'shitting on those most loyal to him', which is a recurring feature of HW. It is why there has been such a turnover in the Kitchen Cabinet over the years.

Joe is threatening to resign. He said he would telephone the PM after lunch and simply say he must see the minutes. If HW refuses, he will go home and that is the end of him. Joe is deeply depressed – about the PM's desertion, about Lady Falkender – and is ready to go anyway.

Today's *Daily Mirror* had a two-page middle spread on Lady Falkender – 'Her ladyship at No. 10' – showing her luxuriating among the state rooms.

Joe got hold of the original text which she had approved – an incredible list of claims about her preferring to be a nurse or a social worker and about the remarkable efficiency with which she answers hundreds of letters a day. In the end not even the *Daily Mirror* with its total loyalty to the Wilson regime (rewarded by four peerages already) could bring itself to publish all of this guff. (I am keeping the original for future amusement.)

We returned after lunch and Joe phoned the PM in Bradford. He was grumpy, and gave permission but added 'without prejudice' – in other words without conceding the principle.

In the Unit we were working desperately hard to produce an alternative White Paper on Incomes Policy. When the Treasury draft came round it was terrible. Thin, flat and with no conviction – indeed with little policy. It read as if written by people who did not believe in it – which is true. They are working on the assumption that if ministers get an unattractive draft they will conclude that it is an unattractive policy. So we worked like maniacs till after midnight. Andrew Graham and David Piachaud did an incredible job. Richard Graham stayed on with us. We sat in my room for 6 hours without a break, surrounded by papers all over the floor, as we drafted, redrafted, and then scissored paper, pinned them together and fed them to Brenda. It was after midnight when we finally had the text – a dozen pages, plus a critique of the Treasury draft.

We sent copies to the PM, John Hunt and Jim Hamilton in the Cabinet Office and to Joe Haines and Ken Stowe. They were to be circulated by car tomorrow morning. I then went off to a party at the Hampstead Heath house of Brian Knox of Grieveson Grant, arriving at about 12.40. I needed to eat, having had nothing since lunch. I felt elated at the work we had done and yet so exhausted I felt faint. Finally to bed at 1.30 a.m.

## Saturday 5 July 1975

Woke at 7 a.m. still feeling tense and exhausted. The problem is whether we can properly feed our draft into the machine. If we can, I'm sure we will win.

At midday Sir John Hunt telephoned me. He had read our draft. He said he thought we were too harsh in our criticism of the Treasury, etc., etc., but finally came round to say that he had 'much sympathy with our approach'. He asked if he could show it immediately to Ken Couzens who had done the Treasury draft.

John Hunt's move was very significant and helpful. He knew and said that our draft was better and did not want to get into a position where it was a single choice between us and the Treasury – we would win and that would be a blow for the machine. So he was moving in to try to give the

Treasury a chance to absorb our paper into theirs before ministers realised there was even a choice. He also, quite properly, did not want rows in Whitehall and too many alternatives floating round when we only had a few days in which to produce the final policy.

Joe phoned later to say that our draft was infinitely better and that the new publicity unit which is being set up in Whitehall could do something with it, whereas the Treasury draft was like a local government hand-out. He was dictating this view to the PM at Chequers – though also adding some criticisms in order to make it clear we were 'not ganging up'.

### Sunday 6 July 1975

Joe told me that the PM had told him he much preferred our draft. John Hunt had telephoned the PM at Chequers, very worried, and had asked to bring down the Treasury team to Chequers to discuss the drafts. But the PM had refused.

We have clearly put the cat among the pigeons this time. But it is the only way to give our policy a fair wind – to write it up ourselves.

Joe warned me to watch out now. 'They will be out to get revenge on you. Watch your shoulder-blades.'

He also said that Janet had reported the PM as being 'terribly depressed' on Friday. Not just tired. But fed up with it all.

Lovely sunny weekend, with plenty of exercise, walks and a tough game of football in a temperature of 75°. Finally feel wound-down and relaxed. Sitting in the garden, writing the last bit of this, with Puccini flowing through the door and mixing with the orange blossom and the honey-suckle. A high intensity which periodically turns to an ominous sense of unease, like thunder beyond the sunny horizon.

– N.B. Marcia lunched at the Press Club off Fleet Street on Friday. She did not leave till 4.20 – and the PM's personal car was waiting in the street outside from 2.15.

– On 'Crossman' and Attorney-Generals, Joe says he was there when the PM sent for Elwyn Jones to discuss the possibility of prosecuting Jonathan Aitken and the *Sunday Telegraph*. HW gave a clear hint to go ahead, saying, 'It will balance Will Owen' (a Labour MP who was prosecuted under the Official Secrets Act).

### Monday 7 July 1975

Was not hurrying to go in – because the PM is off to the miners' conference today – when I learned from No. 10 that John Hunt wanted to see me and that I was due to go to a drafting meeting in the Treasury at

10 a.m. Apparently the PM had sent a brief giving his strong support for the Policy Unit draft White Paper. Ken Couzens in the Treasury had been instructed to work on this and I was to go along and join in the drafting.

I talked to Ken Stowe on the phone before he left for Northolt to fly to Scarborough. He said, 'It is game, set and match to you.'

I drove in quickly to Camden Town with Carol, and there leapt out of my car and into a taxi at some traffic lights. I was in Downing Street in fifteen minutes and went straight through to the Cabinet Office to see John Hunt. He had his regular Monday morning meeting there and came out to speak briefly. He said that he and the PM supported our draft and everybody would be proceeding on that basis from now on. The Treasury draft would be withdrawn and would be removed from the agenda of tonight's Misc 91 meeting of ministers.

I went round to the Treasury with Robin Butler – up the curving stone staircase and round those endless bleak corridors, rather like the wards of a posh Edwardian hospital. The names of the Treasury mandarins reeled off as we hurried past the curving line of doors – Wass, Henley, Hopkin, Kaldor, Posner (the last two anti-mandarins), Mitchell, etc.

Ken Couzens was at a table in his office, with two young Treasury principals helping with the drafting, and Donald Dirkes, the clever man from Employment. We began going through our draft and discussing suggested amendments. I asked to send for Andrew Graham. Couzens resisted, but I insisted. We worked until midday when Couzens went off for a meeting with the Chancellor and Douglas Wass. This went on till lunch, when I slipped out and took Lord Porchester to lunch at the Reform. (He has two good horses running at York on Saturday.) We also discussed local government problems – he is chairman of Hampshire County Council and very wise on these matters – and public expenditure.

Back to the Treasury shortly after 2. The rest were eating a salad lunch off trays. I was then interrupted over the next hour by the problem of this evening's meeting of the Home Policy committee of the NEC, which still has on the agenda a 'Benn' paper opposing incomes policy and supporting import controls, freezing sterling deposits, etc. Shirley Williams phoned several times and we agreed a strategy of persuading ministers not to attend. I talked to the Chancellor's private secretary, who said that Healey's view was that ministers *should* attend, to attack the policy – but of course he would *not* be able to go himself. I persuaded him of the virtues of the other approach and agreed that it would be welcome if this afternoon's meeting with the CBI went on so late that ministers would not be able to get to the NEC. Michael Foot was due to attend a *Tribune* meeting anyway. The only remaining problem was Ted Short. So I telephoned Vicky Kidd, his special adviser. She said that Ted was attending the NEC, because there was a paper on Scotland. He had not noticed the major economic paper and agenda item. I suggested that it could be embarrassing for him to take part in an attack on the government. She agreed and said she would talk to him on those lines.

We finished drafting the incomes policy White Paper after 4 p.m., and Robin and I went back to No.10. The sun still blazing – a glorious summer which I have missed completely in my endless days of committees and long office hours.

Rapidly went through my papers and then into the Cabinet Room for the 6 p.m. Misc 91 meeting. The ministers took a long agenda of individual items where decisions were needed – on control of local authority rates, on how tough to make the price code, on how to control the nationalised industries, what to do about wage increments, about the remaining wage settlements in the present round (including the poor university teachers!), etc.

The PM was poor in the chair, not on top of the subject, and not pushing the discussion to a decision. Ministers just held long discussions, and then moved on to the next item. This is how the Cabinet Office exercises power – the civil servants take the minutes and *they* decide what was the precise decision by the committee. The weaker the chairman – and tonight HW was very weak – the greater the influence of the secretariat.

The Chancellor had to leave at 8 p.m. to meet the TUC, with Shirley Williams and Foot, and the PM was keen to finish, so the meeting ended in hurry, rushing through the final items on the agenda.

Afterwards I chatted briefly to the PM. He was very pleased with his success at the NUM, where his speech, nearly all of which was written by Joe Haines, had gone well, and there was now hope they would climb down from their extreme demands of £100 a week this year.

He has sent minutes to various people saying how good the Policy Unit draft White Paper is.

He went off with Janet and I was grateful to take the opportunity to go home.

After the meeting I had also walked outside with Tony Crosland, who is still standing firmly on our option B of sanctions. It is crucial to my way of working to have senior ministers other than the PM who can be relied on to take a lead role in committee.

Home by shortly after 9 p.m., went to bed and read a little, and asleep by 11.15, which was very welcome.

### Tuesday 8 July 1975

Drove in, taking lively Helene Hayman, the young Labour MP who lives opposite.

Feeling very fit and well as we go into the crucial last 72 hours on the White Paper. I got up at 7 a.m. this morning and went for my morning run over the heath with John Carrier,* my footballing friend from the LSE. For the first time in weeks it was grey and damp, but it soon cleared up and was later blazing hot again.

Had a briefing session in the Unit with Andrew Graham and David Piachaud and then went with Andrew to the 10.30 meeting of the official Prices and Incomes committee to consider the latest draft of the White Paper. It was upstairs on the 2nd floor of the Cabinet Office, in Conference Room B. A huge table surrounded by representatives of nearly every department. Through the window was an incredible view across the luxuriant treetops of St James's Park, Green Park, right to Park Lane and Hyde Park, a carpet of treetop leaves to the horizon. Central London looking like rural Sussex.

Ken Couzens was in the chair and we went through the draft, para-graph by paragraph, with each department making its comments. These were generally negative. The central point is that few of these departments or officials show the least concern for the anti-inflation policy – that is except for the Treasury and No. 10. Their concern is for their depart-mental convenience. So when we are suggesting that departments should take into account the wages policy of firms before granting contracts, or tightening the price code, they all put up objections. They are not inter-ested in suggesting the best way around technical problems in order to achieve our anti-inflation objectives. They simply argue that the technical problems are insuperable, because they are inconvenient. The Department of Industry seems to be the one exception, and often Employment – because they deal with the real world of industry and know that in real life prob-lems have to be solved and departmental tradition and convenience are not the only criteria.

The meeting dragged on until 2.25 p.m. – four hours without coffee or lunch. Fortunately Ken Couzens is a marvellously lively and funny chairman. He still doesn't believe in our policy, but like a good profes-sional he is doing his best to see it through.

The one worrying thing is that he reported that last night's meeting with the TUC went very badly indeed. They were 'all at sixes and sevens' and resisted the idea of any legislation at all. Because of this he warned that we might be forced to abandon our sanctions policy – which depends on some legislation.

Andrew Graham and I were worried at this. We smelt a Treasury rat. Were they going to use the TUC resistance as an excuse for slipping back to a totally voluntary policy, and then the moment it was clearly a failure – which would be at the very first wage claim – they would again spring the full statutory policy?

At the end of the meeting we put in some more draft sanctions – on fiscal and monetary policy, on the need for profits to maintain investment, and on exchange rate policy (which Ken said the Treasury would not accept).

I dashed through to No.10 at 2.25, sprinted upstairs, gobbled down my lunch, and dashed back to the Cabinet Office for the Misc 91 meeting of ministers in a small room off the main hallway outside John Hunt's office.

Healey was in the chair, and this was a vast improvement. A much better chairman than the PM recently. He had a list of remaining questions on which decisions were required and took us through these and got decisions. But as a *Chancellor*, leading the *policy*, he was less impressive, all over the place. At one point he seemed to say that he would settle for a totally voluntary policy with no legislative sanctions. At another he said we must have reserve statutory powers or else the currency would go.

He attacked the language of our introduction as 'hysteria and fourth-rate journalism' – which meant that it was not in traditional White Paper style.

Foot was very rigid and uncompromising. He totally opposed anything but the minimum legislation. At one point he reminded Healey of 'what you promised me this morning'. Healey looked tired, and said, 'Yes, but this committee is bigger than just the two of us.'

It was clear that Foot was more optimistic that he could successfully resist any legislative powers. He had got Healey on the run. Foot was not compromising at all.

One problem was that Crosland and Shirley Williams, although firmly for our 'battery of sanctions' policy, were reluctant to take on the powers and implement the sanctions which those policies involved in their own departmental areas. They were keen on being tough in general, but not in particular in their own areas of responsibility.

And Peter Shore, understandably, argued that he found it difficult to decide what, and how severe, financial sanctions we should adopt until he knew whether we were going to have reserve statutory powers or not. If we did, then our other sanctions could be softer, if not, then they had to be stronger.

So the real crunch – especially with Foot – still lies ahead.

Late in the meeting Sir John Hunt intervened to say that, in view of the important decisions ministers had taken, they might wish the draft White Paper to abandon its present structure, be divided into public and private sectors, and return to the division into Pay Policy and Prices Policy. The ministers nodded. Hunt had bounced them back to the original Treasury draft, totally contrary to what the PM had said to him in a minute this morning and without even referring to the Prime Minister's preference, as the absent chairman on this committee. Hunt still cannot swallow the fact that a White Paper has been effectively written outside the Civil Service machine. He would rather have a bad White Paper, from the Treasury, than a better one from outsiders.

I was furious and he noticed me talking angrily to Robin Butler. He wrote a note fairly suggesting that I intervene to put my point of view.

At the end I intervened and said I wished to oppose the suggestion of the Secretary of the Cabinet to go back to the original Treasury draft, which made it impossible to bring out the full battery of sanctions in our middle option.

Healey said he did not know there was any difference between the two drafts. He looked angrily at me and said whatever the difference between the drafts it was quite clear what we needed – and then described *our* draft. Hunt grinned at me, conceding defeat for the moment, but promising to come back again if he got the chance.

Apart from anything else, as Robin Butler said, it put poor Ken Couzens in an impossible position – to have to go off and write a new Treasury paper in time for this evening's Misc 91 ministerial meeting at 8 p.m.

The meeting broke up shortly after 5 p.m. so that the Chancellor could go off to another meeting with the TUC and to address the PLP. He is looking very tired – his face deeply florid and his eyes very bloodshot. Much of his normal ebullience is gone. He is working incredibly hard and under terrible strain. Above all, he gets very little support from colleagues and too little from the Prime Minister. (I don't suppose my Policy Unit makes his life any easier.) Basically he is a brilliant macho loner. But politics is a collective game. He is not instinctively a team player.

I went back to the office. The backlog of papers is terrifying and there was a long list of people who had telephoned – including George Wigg, who had been very bullying to my secretary because I had not phoned him back immediately. But I had no time. Further meetings with private office, reports to the Unit staff, and finally a long talk with Joe. He is feeling very excluded at the moment because he does not attend the meetings which are occupying us all day. Also the PM is not giving him any credit for the work he has done on speeches. Joe did the best parts of yesterday's speech to the miners. But afterwards the PM referred to it as all his own except for 'one thought' which he credited Joe with. We don't know if he actually believes this. Does he suppress and forget?

The ministerial Misc 91 reassembled in the Cabinet Room at 8 p.m. Beer and sandwiches were served as we sat around the Cabinet table – fairly dry and unappetising ham sandwiches and one egg and tomato roll. Today has not been a gastronomic delight!

The Chancellor reported on his meetings. The PLP had been strongly for action, including statutory reserve powers. He said that the TUC were now willing to have reserve powers. They did not want compulsory notification of settlements. And wanted a £5,000 pay ceiling instead of £10,000. But otherwise they had made a lot of progress since last night.

Then Shirley Williams said she was happy to introduce a tougher price code – disallowing *all* labour costs, not just the excess cost over the norm, in any application for price rises arising from excessive wage settlements.

This put the heat on Tony Crosland with the local authorities. His position had been that he was unwilling to single out the local authorities for tougher treatment than anybody else. Now he had to accept the possibility of legislative control of local authority increases, just as in the private sector.

In the discussion on whether to spend £150 million on food subsidies and reducing rent increases Crosland was much more convincing for the latter than Shirley Williams for the former. Healey came out for splitting it 50/50. The PM ducked it by suggesting that they *each* have £150 million.

This led the Chancellor to state that he also wanted to announce his £2 billion of public expenditure cuts. At this Crosland got very angry and launched a savage attack on the Treasury, its policies, and especially its exchange rate policies. He then said that he did not believe there had been a sterling crisis last Monday and on his information there had been no selling.

At this I turned cold. This afternoon, after the 2.30 Misc 91, I had taken Crosland to my room and discussed the whole situation. Particularly I had pointed out that if he wanted the middle option, as he kept saying he did, then he must not weaken credibility by refusing to implement the particular financial sanctions in his local authority areas. As a background I mentioned that the Treasury would welcome such weakening in a policy they did not believe in in order to bounce back the full statutory policy. In passing I mentioned my doubts about the nature of last Monday's 'crisis'.

I was now worried he would name me as a source. Healey got very upset and claimed that there had been 'massive' selling. Peter Shore intervened and said 'but not from any OPEC country'. Healey agreed, and bumbled on about there being 'selling from Germany'. Then they moved on.

HW went out to the lavatory and when he came back he said we must now come to the central issue of whether or not to include reserve powers of statutory compulsion on employers. He favoured them. He had always opposed criminal sanctions against workers. But these powers were against individual employers, and they were only in reserve. He thought the foreign depositors and the City were 'fetishists' but they had to be reassured. The policy had to stick or sterling would go. And tonight the PLP had shown that it supported this policy.

Foot then intervened. He looked white and strained. He said he was bitterly opposed to statutory reserve powers. They were wrong. They were close to being a 'breach of faith' with the TUC. And 'some of us are committed, deeply committed against them'. It was clear here that he meant the PM as well. He concluded by saying that 'I beg and plead with you not to go ahead with this.' He was saying that if we introduced reserve powers he would resign.

The PM came back in, looking a bit embarrassed and guilty. He said he was fully committed, but that was against a full statutory policy. He was not against reserve powers to be used against 'individual rogue employers'.

Foot intervened to say that was a quibble – he implied it was dishonest – and said there was no real difference.

Healey looked very worried. He said our policy would not be credible without reserve powers. Sterling could disappear in 36 hours. He would simply have to come back to Parliament and admit that we were wrong and had not done enough.

Crosland gave a very clear and balanced summary, rather academic. He said it was a closely balanced choice. Does having the reserve powers give advantages in the protection of sterling which outweigh the disadvantages of losing some support from the TUC? He would like some guidance from the Chancellor. His own view on balance was for reserve powers.

Shirley Williams supported Crosland, but adding that the financial sanctions mattered more than the reserve powers and these must carry conviction.

Peter Shore came out strongly against the reserve powers. He went into a eulogy about our 'battery of sanctions' policy, saying we had invented a brilliant alternative to a statutory policy. He said they were so convincing that the reserve powers would not be necessary and would anyway never be used.

Varley was also against reserve powers. He thought we would not get them through the Commons. And also that they would lose us support of the TUC in the strikes which we inevitably faced next year.

Healey came back in to say that he had 'never favoured a full statutory policy'. But the country wanted statutory powers. And sterling needed it. However, he did not want a decision tonight. They must wait till after tomorrow's TUC.

Then Foot lost his temper and began haranguing them on their breach of faith with the TUC. He was still shouting angrily as the meeting broke up at 10.35 p.m.

Outside I walked out with Crosland and told him not to mention me as a source on the sterling question. We stood in Downing Street as the other ministers drove off in their black Rovers. He said he still sees it as finely balanced but inclines towards reserve powers.

I went back in. All the civil servants were crowded round the PM and the Chancellor at the door to private office. The PM detached himself and came to talk to me outside the Cabinet Room. I said it very much depended on whether Michael Foot was truly representing the TUC position. The problem is that the TUC people say different things to different people. And also Michael has a romantic view of the TUC as actually believing in their own rhetoric. I was not so sure. We agreed that the best answer was to get Jack Jones's view. So the PM took the Chancellor on one side and asked him to see Jones – not to ask what he supported, but to say that he proposed to introduce reserve powers and would Jones *oppose* this.

We then retired into private office and discussed future plans. Including meeting the nationalised industry chairmen, which the PM will not do if Dick Marsh comes along.

I went up to my office, where Andrew Graham and David Piachaud were waiting and I reported on the meeting. I then went off to the American embassy residence in Regent's Park. The Ambassador, Elliot Richardson, had invited us to a dinner for Peter Ramsbotham, our Ambassador to Washington, who is back here on holiday. Carol went on her own. I got there, without dinner jacket, at 11.30. Mrs Richardson gave me some strawberries and a glass of champagne.

I had a brief talk with Gordon Richardson and Harold Lever, and also with Ramsbotham, who was very nice and revealed that he had heard that the PM was angry with him over what he said about inflation on our last Washington visit. I told him not to worry. The PM often got angry at unwelcome truths.

We left and drove home shortly before 1 a.m. (I got up before 7 o'clock this – Wednesday – morning to write up yesterday's events. So much is happening. I must get it all down before it merges into grey generalities.)

## *Wednesday 9 July 1975*

Late going in because I was writing up all of Tuesday's events.

HW spent much of the morning with Joe and Geoffrey Goodman discussing publicity for the White Paper on incomes policy. Geoffrey is running the new publicity unit. I was in the Policy Unit catching up on papers. Also telephoning – Fred Mulley came through twice about university teachers pay, which looks very bleak. Also Denis Howell, about his White Paper on Sport, where we are doing too little. Great pity, but quite impossible to get any movement from the PM or the Chancellor while so absorbed in the economic problem.

I saw the PM before lunch and raised the question of the university teachers, who are going to be the only group to get no increase based on the cost of living in this round. He was sympathetic. But little we can do.

He is less sympathetic to the special advisers and is sitting on their pay increases. Really he doesn't like them.

I also put to him the case for having reserve powers of compulsion written in the Incomes Policy Bill. Everybody outside expects this. Without them the policy will lack credibility and won't stick as far as sterling goes. He agrees. He said he had told Michael Foot that by splitting the government on this he was hastening the coalition. HW was quite hopeful that Foot would stay – 'He says he is bitterly opposed, but not that he will go.'

HW is pinning a lot of hope on Jack Jones of the Transport Workers, who is seeing the Chancellor later today.

The PM and Joe went to lunch with some political correspondents. I went to George Weidenfeld's lunch for the new President of the World Bank, who was a delightful and immensely intelligent man. Sat next to the novelist C.P. Snow and opposite Elwyn Jones. Very pleasant. Also there were Lord Goodman, the philosopher Freddie Ayer and the socially elegant historian Hugh Thomas.

Returned and the trade unions had voted – 19–13 for a £6 pay norm. Not quite enough really, and the PM said it confirmed our need for a government policy with reserve powers. Apparently some of our friends voted against – Alf Allen because he opposes tighter price control, NALGO because of increments, Fred Jarvis of NUT – we don't know why. These will probably come round later.

I went through to see Ken Berrill at the Central Policy Review Staff in the Cabinet Office. We had been discussing with them whether they should put in a paper. In fact it is almost incredible that the CPRS has played no role at all in this whole economic crisis. Kate Mortimer has attended PIO meetings and is bright. But their input, as far as *Cabinet* is concerned, which is their main role, has been nil.

Berrill did not seem to have any ideas. I suggested he might put in some background briefing on sterling – after all, this whole crisis is supposed to be about sterling, but nobody has given anybody any facts about sterling, or about our exchange policy. Just the Treasury mumbo-jumbo about 'it is crumbling' and wheeling in the Governor of the Bank. Berrill said he thought that would be 'irresponsible'. On this he is very much the Treasury's man, there representing the machine. Also completely cynical. 'What is best for the Treasury is best for the machine – and that is best for Britain.' A very depressing meeting. I don't see how you can run a Think Tank, as an initiator of original and uncomfortable ideas, on this basis. A long way from Victor Rothschild – and not in the right direction!

The CPRS has now not submitted a serious paper since William

Plowden's excellent survey of social policy at the beginning of May.

Went into another Cabinet committee Misc 91 at 4.30 to discuss the latest draft of the White Paper. It reads much better now. Many of the amendments have improved our original. Dear old Ken Couzens of the Treasury was drafting away to the end. Incredible energy and speed. For the Treasury, and especially his prices and incomes section, this is their great moment. They have been sitting with nothing to do since Heath went. Now they are in the spotlight again and they are loving it. Suddenly ministers need them. But he is an endearing bloke.

The committee took the paper paragraph by paragraph. Very friendly atmosphere, good suggestions, few problems. The PM beamed and looked pleased with how it was all going. They deliberately left the central question of reserve powers till the end. This was the crunch.

But when they got there they decided not to face it. Healey preferred to put it off to the main Cabinet, where he will get greater support. Crosland pointed out that they could not agree anyway, and would just go over the same ground again.

So we broke up at 6.45. I went outside with Crosland who is quite firm for a reserve powers policy now – as he really has been throughout.

I went back in and up to the PM's study. Joe was there and Ken Stowe and Robin Butler. We discussed arrangements for seeing various bodies about the White Paper and for HW's press conference on Friday. Also the title. John Hunt came rushing through to suggest 'Attack on Inflation', which HW and Joe had agreed on ten minutes earlier.

HW was very friendly, handed out drinks and was clearly pleased with life. He praised the Unit's work quite deliberately to Hunt. Then he hustled us all out and sent for Janet.

Afterwards Joe revealed to me an incredible fact. Last week the PM had told Ken Stowe to forbid me to attend the Misc 91 on pay policy – at the same time as he gave the order that Joe and I were not to get papers. He had ordered that Joe and I be completely frozen out from this pay policy White Paper. Because Marcia had insisted to him that we be excluded. (This all comes down the regular grapevine.) I did not know then – Joe deliberately did not tell me in case it depressed me in our work in the Unit. And Ken Stowe, who apparently got a flea in his ear for not giving me the instructions, stood by me with marvellous loyalty. So I went blithely ahead, attending all meetings. Ken made sure we got all the papers. And in the end the White Paper was still basically '*ours*' – and the PM has been praising our work on it to me ever since. He has never referred to this episode again and proceeds as if it never happened. He saw me in the committees, received and commented on my briefings, discussed the pay developments and papers with me every few hours, and instructed the

Cabinet Secretary that our draft White Paper was his preferred approach. He has clearly totally suppressed the fact that he gave orders for Joe, me and the Unit to be excluded. This is crazy. But full marks to Ken and Joe.

Went home at 7.15. Dinner with Will Plowden.

### Thursday 10 July 1975

Cabinet members arrived around 9.30 to collect drafts of the White Paper and read them in advance of the 10 o'clock Cabinet. Ministers sat around in the reception rooms upstairs reading. I came into No.10 with the Attorney-General, Sam Silkin. He said he is feeling very sore about the Crossman Diaries affair, where he suffered a lot of criticism. He said, 'I suppose if you set yourself up as a target you must expect to get shot at.' I pointed out that one feature of the concept of ministerial responsibility was that if 'others' – civil servants or Prime Ministers – put up the idea, and it goes wrong, then it is the minister who carries the can. He complained that there was no way of answering back journalists such as Anthony Howard, because they can always have the last word. He gave the strong impression that he regretted having got into this one – and was telling me because I had warned him that it meant trouble. He also criticised the PM for taking the credit for other people's work that went right, but ducking out if it went wrong. I said that there was nothing unique in the PM there!

Fred Mulley also talked to me about university teachers' pay. Not very encouraging. It looks as if they will be the only major group to get no increase this year. We cannot find a way round it.

I then went to the Unit to read papers. We are also preparing to get back to our work on public expenditure – the Treasury has come up with its paper calling for cuts of £2 billion, perhaps £3 billion in 1979. But no suggestion of what the choices might be. Just the principle of cutting the £2 billion – typical of Treasury decisions. No details. No real arguments on figures. Bounce, bounce. Actually we support the need for cutting back future public expenditure commitments. But ministers must be given proper explanations and a proper choice. The Treasury *never* does this. It is afraid of serious discussion. It lacks the confidence to get any decision taken properly by open discussion. Deception and secrecy are its second nature. Often it *loses* decisions it ought to win because other people are suspicious and resentful of its tactics. It is the institutional equivalent of Tony Benn – having been caught out in sharp practice and double-talk, it ends up being questioned and opposed on everything even when sensible and right.

Patrick Wright, the private secretary covering foreign affairs, told me that Marcia had telephoned to demand that Monday evening be kept free for the PM to have dinner with the Israel Foreign Minister which she had arranged. This was without consulting Callaghan, when the Foreign Office is in the middle of very delicate negotiations over the Middle East, and Callaghan is seeing Kissinger this weekend. It could upset everybody. When Patrick raised it with the PM he 'looked very shifty' and instructed him not to tell the Foreign Office.

Cabinet continued right through until 3 o'clock in the afternoon – a five-hour meeting with nothing to eat. HW came out in the middle to go to the lavatory and said, 'It is going very badly.' He complained bitterly about Bob Mellish who, without being called, opened the meeting by saying that they would not be able to get the legislation through the Commons. This is not true. It would be an uncomfortable process, with a minority of Labour lefties, Tories and some nationalists opposing. But the coalition majority would be big. Mellish simply did not want the trouble. But he did great harm, by encouraging the Left and worrying the middle.

Six ministers spoke out against any reserve powers at all – Foot, Castle, Benn, Varley, John Silkin and Shore. The rest divided evenly between those who wanted strong reserve powers in the Bill *now*. And those – including Lever – who wanted them referred to, but *deferred* until somebody actually broke the £6 limit. This latter view prevailed at the end, and Healey accepted it, though with misgivings.

Benn apparently spoke about betraying the manifesto and the working people and, as always, appeared to be preparing the way for some future resignation which he never actually gets round to.

We had taken lunch upstairs in the pantry during the Cabinet, so we were ready to dash across to the House for questions when they came out at 3 p.m. The PM took questions without having eaten anything – just two brandies on an empty stomach. It went fairly quietly.

Afterwards the Misc 91 met again at No.10 to draft the final White Paper sentences on deferring the reserve powers. I did not bother to go. I am very tired and want to move on to the next mountain, which is public expenditure.

The PM then saw the TUC and after that Cabinet resumed to approve the final draft. At this meeting Healey put the central point – which the Governor of the Bank had put to him earlier – that foreign reaction would depend on home reaction. Therefore the papers must *not* talk about Foot and the Left defeating Healey, though to some extent that is true. This is a 'weaker' policy than seemed likely yesterday and than outsiders have been led to expect.

So I am a bit worried whether it will stick and will hold sterling. When Lever phoned me it was clear that he was a bit worried too. He wanted to go on the radio tomorrow to reassure people that this is a strong policy and that it is good for sterling. This seemed difficult since the Cabinet had decided on no broadcasts except by Healey, but I promised to do what I could.

After the meeting with the chairmen of nationalised industries, Healey came up to me in the corridor and asked what I thought about deferring the reserve powers. I expressed mild concern. He invited me through into No.11. We went into the ground-floor study, a small room with its walls lined with volumes of Hansard. I made the point about outside expectations. He agreed, and said he was very worried that we had not done enough. He said, 'Perhaps I should have put my position on the line more this morning. Perhaps I should have said I would not stay on unless we had the reserve powers . . . but it was such a finely balanced decision.' As throughout this whole difficult business, he continued to have doubts right to the end.

He said – rightly – that if the agreed policy did stick it was the *best* one because it had the biggest consensus. But if sterling ran away we were in real trouble.

I put to him the idea that Lever might go on the radio and support it. He agreed.

After half an hour I returned to No.10. Healey said, at the end of our meeting, 'I do wish the PM had supported me more this morning.' In fact he often suffers from a lack of support, even when right.

I went to see Joe and made the Lever suggestion. Shortly after, Joe phoned me to say that the PM agreed to Lever going on the radio 'providing the Chancellor agrees'. So I phoned Lever to tell him it was set up.

Incidentally Healey also said to me, 'I am so pleased that we did not go ahead with our original full statutory policy last Monday. I am so pleased Cabinet stopped it. That would have been a big mistake.'

And a final talk with Andrew Graham and with John Hunt, and came home at 9.15. Still feel tired and flat. And slightly ominous about tomorrow.

### Friday 11 July 1975

Another glorious and sweltering morning. Today we unveil the pay policy package. It still seems to me to be in the balance whether it does the trick, but I feel more optimistic than last night.

Drive in and go to the 9.30 a.m. weekly diary meeting for next week's business. Little to discuss since the PM is away much of next week. He is clearly jumpy and gets the meeting over within 20 minutes – grumbling at John Hunt for having fixed it at all. He has to make his statement at 11 a.m., and we still must discuss the text.

The moment Callaghan and Healey have gone (and Healey was more optimistic this morning, pleased with the general press coverage) we all assembled to go through the PM's statement. It was really very good – a bit too deferential to the TUC, and we had to alter the emphasis to make it the *government's* policy, not the TUC's, but generally strong and clear. We then went through Joe's draft of the PM's statement to the press conference to be held at midday – very well written.

We had finished at 10.40, but then were held up by problems in getting copies – every photostat machine in No. 10, and I think there are four of them, broke down this morning. But we finally had everything and set off in two cars for the Commons. There was a large crowd in Downing Street, loudly cheering the PM.

[The Prime Minister announced to the House of Commons the White Paper providing for a maximum £6 per week limit to pay increases, a figure consistent with the government's aim to reduce the rate of inflation to 10% by the summer of 1976. Only one settlement per annum was to be allowed and price controls were to be extended. He said the government rejected statutory policies based on criminal sanctions against workers: 'We intend to ensure observance of the new pay policy by the full battery of weapons available.']

The statement went well. In Questions afterwards the PM skilfully drew attacks from the Tories – which united most of his back-benchers behind him – and then from Sid Bidwell and our far Left – which reassured the foreigners in the gallery that he could not have given in to the extremists, since they were obviously annoyed. In fact the moderate Left – Neil Kinnock* and even John Mendelson* – were generally helpful.

The Speaker allowed Questions to run on for an hour and so we were very late getting to the Ministry of Defence. The press conference was in the big concourse there, and was packed with television cameras and hundreds of journalists. In fact it was too big for a good question and answer session. It was also very hot and stuffy, so I left halfway through. David Watt of the *Financial Times* followed me out. He thought it was a tough policy, much tougher than people realised, provided ministers stuck to their guns, and that it was a skilful political balance. Joe had seen him and helped him yesterday. He is much the most intelligent of the political commentators.

I went back to No.10. Marcia was in her room entertaining the film star Richard Attenborough, who had arrived in a large Rolls-Royce. Just the right image for today's announcement of national austerity and sacrifice.

Joe and Janet and I went to the Commons cafeteria for lunch – we eat there for 50p, compared to £1.50 in the Press Gallery. Austerity has already begun. In fact I quite like the cafeteria – no waiters, no journalists watching us, and out on to the terrace afterwards to watch the boats on the river and gaze at the South Bank skyline, which is quite altered from 20 years ago. I like the new St Thomas's Hospital buildings. I often sit there and think of Herbert Morrison spanning that river from Parliament to County Hall.

Went back to work in the Unit on a paper on public expenditure. The Treasury have put up a proposal for Monday's Cabinet to cut public expenditure by £2.3 billion. A typical Treasury paper. No real arguments – and no suggestion of what the cuts might be in particular. Just a global paper figure. No recognition that the range of alternatives was so great it could mean anything or nothing. Cuts in subsidies are inflationary. Taking a single percentage across the board, which is always the Treasury's preferred method, often costs more and is the least efficient way of doing it. No alternatives. No analysis. No guidance towards real choices.

Worked on our paper till 9 p.m.

The PM had left for his constituency Huyton in mid-afternoon.

At 5.30 Marcia sent a message through her secretary to say that the PM wanted a draft statement to be prepared immediately to go to all constituency parties. I saw Joe, who said, 'They can sod off. I'm going home.' So we left it till Monday.

Today's *Daily Express* had an article on Marcia going to Annabel's with Eric Miller, the property millionaire. Bill Housden said that I inevitably got the blame at first. But later poor George Weidenfeld was blamed – because he had been at Annabel's that same evening.

Home very tired at 9.30. This has been an incredible fortnight. Fortunately I have written it down daily, because I simply cannot remember one day from another. All the committees have merged. Each one of us now believes that the decision which we have finally reached was our original idea and position.

I am now bored with 'Incomes Policy', but wish 'Public Expenditure' was not coming so rapidly on the agenda.

Am still flabbergasted and a bit amused about the business of HW trying to exclude Joe and me from the White Paper discussions. Quite ridiculous. There were a hundred copies of each of those drafts circulating through Whitehall, yet he was trying to stop Joe and me getting them. Mad. He most distrusts those who are closest to him. He totally trusts civil servants despite repeated examples of them leaking to papers. But the funny thing is that I was able to ignore him because I did not know he had banned me, and he dare not bring it up. In the end he was coming up to chat to me appreciatively in committees from which he had banned me. He had ordered me not to get the papers, yet we were *drafting* much of the bloody papers, and he praised them. Crazy. All because of, on one level, his need to meet Marcia's demands to exclude us, while pretending they do not exist on another. This explains why he came up to me at the tape machine and said, 'I heard you have had something to do with the good drafting work that has been going on.' Yet that same day he had sent John Hunt a minute stating that he had read the Policy Unit paper and much preferred it to the Treasury draft. To me – and to Her Ladyship – he dare not admit that he knew all about it and approved and authorised it. He put it as a kind of rumour after the event, over which he had no influence or control (or else he would have to stop it).

Am ready for my holiday and looking forward to the PM being away in Brussels next week.

# CHAPTER 18

## The Prime Minister to Retire?
## July 1975

*Monday 14 July 1975*

Went in early. Talked to the PM for 15 minutes outside the Cabinet Room before ministers began to arrive for the 10 o'clock Cabinet. He was pleased with the weekend press, which had praised him for his political skill in producing last week's package. He also praised the Unit's briefs at the weekend – our piece on public expenditure and a brilliant paper by Andrew Graham recommending sterling guarantees. We discussed the Cabinet on public expenditure and he said he thought that even the Chancellor was 'a bit shamefaced' about the bounce he was attempting – £2.3 billion in cuts without any attempt to specify what they might be.

He went back to private office and I went down the passage to talk to Crosland. He was puzzled by a suggestion from HW – of which I had not heard – that Cabinet ministers should write to Prentice wishing him good luck against the Left who are trying to oust him from his seat. I could not see what could be gained by this either.

Also discussed public expenditure – Crosland thought the cuts were 'absolutely crazy' and 'could be the end of the party'. I pressed him to fight hard. In fact I had already suggested to HW that he give Crosland a good run in the Cabinet discussion, because he understood these things and was 'Chancellor of the Exchequer material'. HW said, 'He would be a good choice for the job.'

After Cabinet had begun I cleared my desk of papers. Then went down to see Joe. He is furious because he suspects Marcia of waging another campaign to get rid of him. There was a sarcastic piece in the *Spectator* last week saying she wanted to be rid of Joe. Then there was a piece in the *Telegraph* criticising him – just after she had lunch with Ian Waller of the *Telegraph*. Now she has asked Geoffrey Goodman to do HW's message to the constituency parties instead of Joe. He is still fed up and ready to go.

Out to lunch with Clifford German, an old school friend on the *Daily Telegraph*. Delicious fish at Overton's.

This afternoon the PM had a briefing for Brussels which I stayed away from. Then a meeting with the nationalised industry chairmen. I went and chatted to Finniston beforehand, but didn't bother to go in to the meeting.

Between these two, Joe was in the study having a talk with the PM about his retirement. The PM said it would be 'sooner rather than later'. He felt it was time to give the others a chance – he said that Healey and Crosland were already in their mid-fifties and he 'must not stand in their way'. He also said he was totally fed up with the party and found its behaviour intolerable. He was very tired after 29 years in high politics. He said he wished he could have a sabbatical and return refreshed. Joe sensed he also feared that the party would break up soon, and he did not want to be in charge then – though he might return afterwards!

Albert told me that on Sunday night HW and Marcia had a dinner at Chequers for their business supporters – Eric Miller, Sammy Fisher, Donald Gosling of National Car Parks, Jarvis Astaire, etc. Afterwards HW had told Marcia that he will retire in October. Marcia is of course against it. Albert is also against it since he will lose his job, and also he was hoping to get a free trip to America in October.

I think retirement is the right thing for HW. He either goes now, at the beginning of this economic trouble, or he waits to see it through, till 1977. He is also bored with it all. As he said to Joe, 'It is all déjà vu.' We need a fresh spirit at the top – somebody who will fight every inch over the next year because he wants to enjoy the benefits in the years after that. The trouble with HW is that he doesn't want trouble; he would rather go. So he doesn't plan or fight the big issues. Something which has its benefits two years away doesn't interest him.

Mary is also pushing him to go.

I left early – at 7.30 p.m. HW is having dinner at No.10 with Allon of Israel tonight. Marcia is coming for drinks only.

I went home to listen to Beethoven. If the PM goes in October – and I think he should – I shall be out of a job. I wonder what will happen to the Policy Unit. It all depends on who succeeds. [The Policy Unit was continued by Prime Ministers Callaghan, Thatcher, Major and Blair.]

## Tuesday 15 July 1975

Cabinet to discuss MPs' salary increases and possible cuts in ministers' pay. Beforehand the Lord Chancellor took me on one side and said that he thought we would lose whatever we did. Certainly an announcement of pay increases of £30+ a week for MPs is not an auspicious start to the counter-inflation policy.

Reports from Albert, Bill and the civil servants on last night's dinner with Allon. Marcia arrived for drinks beforehand – which went on for 1½ hours. Then she came in to dinner twice and sat at the table without eating. She finally got up and left, and later sent in a handwritten note to the PM – telling him to telephone her. He didn't till after dinner.

There is an astonishing 'security' development on someone concerned with the new publicity campaign against inflation. It is alleged that East European embassy money is involved.

Two depressing developments on the bureaucracy front. The PM is supporting a proposal to limit the number of special advisers to two per minister. Specifically this is to prevent Benn appointing a third adviser, Tony Banks,* who is very left-wing – he refused to sign his PV form. But it is also part of the general erosion of the special advisers' position.

Second, and worse, was a minute from John Hunt to the PM suggesting that he add a 'footnote' to his submission of evidence to the Radcliffe Commission on ministers' memoirs. This would propose the application to ministers' memoirs of a bar on publication 'possibly up to 30 years, as for Official Secrets'. It is quite clear what is happening here. Hunt wants the rules tightened. But he does not say that openly in his evidence to Radcliffe. So he gets the PM to say it. The PM is both for secrecy and a sucker for every Civil Service bounce – so he will probably support it. I exploded at Ken Stowe, and put in a note protesting at this reactionary approach. But I know it won't do any good.

Had lunch with Lord Wigg in the Lords dining-room – where the food is *very* good. Talked only about finance for sport, and especially horse racing. He gave me three insider tips for that afternoon at Kempton – two lost and one was withdrawn!

Questions went very quietly.

Worked all afternoon in the Unit – North Sea oil (where Lever is pushing for more compromise with the companies, which we are resisting) – and Sport finance, where I am desperately trying to find ways of getting more money into sport.

Evening to a party for the CCPR at Lancaster House, Then to dinner with our friends John and Tessa Murphy – and Anthony Sampson of the *Observer*, who talked about corruption in the Department of Energy.

Home at 1.15.

## Wednesday 16 July 1975

Went in at 9.30, but did not see the PM before he left for Brussels.

Cleared my papers. Then took much of the day off. Visited the Augustus John exhibition at the National Portrait Gallery, where I met Carol and Nori Graham. To lunch at La Napoule. Then home to see the children for a change – the boys especially have been complaining that I am never there to play with them.

In the evening walked across the heath to a pub in Hampstead. Then to a Weidenfeld party for Mme Giroud, the French minister. Also chatted to John Gross, Lady Antonia Fraser, David Frost and Shirley Williams and Bill Rodgers and Asa Briggs.

Home at 1.30 a.m. Feeling very fit and quite excited at the prospect of it all ending in October. What will come up afterwards?

### Thursday 17 July 1975

PM is still in Brussels, so I took my time going in. Then quickly completed the Unit papers and had a preliminary discussion on public expenditure cuts.

Lunch at the City Livery Club with Jonathan Charkham, discussing his new unit for improving procedures on public appointments.

Worked in the office in the afternoon and went with Robin Butler and Gavyn Davies for an hour to play cricket in the nets of Westminster School. The PM brought forward his return from Brussels but went straight to Chequers so no need to wait late. I left the office at around 7 p.m., called in at a reception at Heinemann, the publishers, then home by 8.30. Listened to music and taped a Beethoven string quartet.

### Friday 18 July 1975

In early after a lovely 7.30 a.m. three-mile run right round Hampstead Heath – Millfield Lane to Kenwood, skirting right up to the top of the heath then sweeping down to the ponds. Feel very fit and generally on top of life.

Had fixed a Unit meeting at midday to discuss our public expenditure paper. The PM came in from Chequers just as we were beginning and sent for me and Joe and the private secretaries to discuss his speech to the Durham Miners' Gala tomorrow. He had done the draft – rejecting one by Joe – and it was terrible: stale, boastful, full of his old clichés, with whole paragraphs repeated from previous speeches. Joe pointed this out, saying that it had nothing new in it. HW looked tired and touchingly said, 'Well, I don't have anything new to say, do I?' Joe replied sharply, 'Well, you might put some of your old ideas in new words.'

We didn't finish redrafting till nearly half-past 1. Joe and I then went to the Commons cafeteria, had a light lunch and then sat on the terrace until it started to rain. Joe said there were other signs of an October departure. The PM had told private office not to fix him any foreign trips after then. We discussed what to do afterwards, Joe is very tired and wants to rest for a while. He is a bit irritated that HW thinks he will automatically go to work for Lord Barnetson's local papers – whatever the job. This is why HW gave Barnetson a peerage. He says he got a firm assurance of employing Joe. Joe thinks this is a pretty cheap way of buying off an obligation.

For myself, he said that the Lords would fit in well with the LSE. But we both recognise it is unlikely. 'Marcia will veto it,' said Joe. I don't care either way.

Saw the PM after lunch and had a long chat about the gilt market which has been very strong – as my friends at Grieveson Grant predicted.

We then got down to our Unit brief, on which Andrew Graham, David Piachaud and David Gowland had done a tremendous amount of work. Finally completed it – 8 pages – at 8.30 p.m. The PM had left at 5.30 for the north. So I drove home, listened to music and went to bed.

I saw in the 'dip tray' this afternoon a brief from John Hunt on the Franks Report on the Official Secrets Act, which is being taken at a Misc Cabinet committee meeting next Friday.

The Franks Report was a pretty pale and cautious affair, much too restrictive for most people's taste and widely attacked as such. But Hunt sent in an enormous long brief arguing that Franks was dangerously liberal, and that at least seven whole new categories of papers should be brought under the proposed Official Information Act. The end result of his proposals, as he intends, would be an even *more* restrictive position than *now*. Because the restricted areas would be virtually as wide, while the new Act would be much more enforceable than the old Official Secrets Act.

Hunt relates how an official committee under Heath had already concluded that they must tighten up on Franks. He starts from that and suggests that another official committee be set up, partly to tighten up further, partly to delay action in case Roy Jenkins wins with his more liberal line.

He also argued about the congestion of the legislative programme and therefore there is no hope of legislating any reforms. And that in case there is a danger of it getting into the next year's programme, the PM should propose waiting until the Radcliffe committee had reported. So Hunt's strategy is to get a ministerial decision to tighten up the Official Secrets Act if possible, and to fall back on delay if that fails.

Incidentally, on the Radcliffe committee, the idea which Hunt and the PM were putting up is, basically, of a 'ten year untouched' and a '30 year limit'. There would be 'strict conventions for ten years and then a much more liberal regime'.

But the 'liberalism' of this second phase was not too apparent. The Hunt wrote in his memo that 'powers of disapproval, by the Secretary of the Cabinet or some other designated person, would need to apply for a period substantially longer than a decade – perhaps even for the 30 years of the Public Records Act 1967.'

Also goes on to define that the 'less strict' conventions would not apply to 'discussions with the Sovereign or with officials', which would be covered by the Public Records Act for 30 years.

This is all quite appalling.

The sad thing is that HW happily goes along with all this. He opposes 'open government' because the press would benefit from it – and because the civil servants oppose it and he wants to please them.

– On Saturday I talked to Anthony Lester to warn Roy Jenkins about what Hunt was plotting. He said that our original idea for a balanced package based on the Franks, Faulks, Phillimore, Younger reports had been dropped. Jenkins has been given Franks, while the Lord Chancellor, who is safely reactionary, has been given the rest. It will be difficult to rescue anything from this.

## Monday 21 July 1975

Worked in the Unit in the morning. The PM came in late from Chequers.

I went to the Commons for lunch by myself. The Scottish Labour MP Norman Buchan came up to me on the terrace in great agitation over devolution, which everybody sees as getting out of hand. Slipping into independence by default. They all blame poor old Crowther-Hunt, the minister in charge.

Saw the PM after lunch while he was waiting for Lever to come and complain about being excluded from the main economic committee. Then HW went across to the Commons to hear Mrs Thatcher open the economic debate.

I worked in the Unit. Saw bright John Zysmann, who kindly asked me to take a job with him at Berkeley University.

At 6 p.m. the private secretaries gave their annual pleasant party for the private secretaries from other ministers' private offices.

Joe and I attended for a while, then retreated upstairs to the study where the PM was working on his speech. Finished off the last half, with him pacing up and down, using Joe and me as the audience. He had made a lot of notes himself and dictated from them.

He thought Thatcher had been poor this afternoon. 'She is a dead loss,' he said.

Afterwards I went to the apartment of Philippe Cuvillier, the economic minister at the French embassy, who was giving a farewell dinner for Tristan D'Albis, the departing counsellor. Food surprisingly poor, but very nice people there. Carol and I left at 12.30 a.m.

## Tuesday 22 July 1975

Didn't bother to go to the Overseas & Defence committee.

The PM did not go to the National Council of Labour, so we all assembled early for his speech in this afternoon's economic debate.

He had already put round a draft of half of it, done last night, and he now dictated the rest of it. The challenge of the speech livened him up and it was just like old times sitting in the study while he paced up and down dictating.

Around 12.30 he became restless and jumpy – clearly fearing a telephone call – and we broke up and went downstairs. He went into Marcia's room. Mary came in as well. They were all going off to a lunch at the Savoy for the Variety Club of Great Britain, with Vera Lynn and a lot of film stars.

HW only stayed there three-quarters of an hour for drinks. But it really was frivolous. On the day of his big economic speech. And on a day when the Opposition was threatening to put down a motion to reject our economic proposals – and three dozen Labour back-benchers had said they would revolt and vote against us – he is dragged off to some showbiz affair.

Today was Adrian Shaw's last day working in the Policy Unit, so I took him to lunch at the Reform. Then afterwards went to the Commons and took Adrian into the box with us to watch the PM.

Questions went quietly. Geoffrey Howe opened the second day's debate for the Tories. It was a bit boring and respectable so I left the box and went to sit on the terrace overlooking the Thames. Margaret Jackson [Beckett] came over and we had a long friendly talk. She seems to have moved from the far left into a more central position now.

I returned to the box for the end of HW's speech, which went down OK – better than Thatcher yesterday, but not marvellous. Then Heath got up and made a quite superb speech, basically supporting the White Paper. He stood well into the centre of the Chamber, as if detaching himself from any party. He was relaxed, conciliatory, speaking without notes. He gave an analysis of the economic situation as he saw it. Free of the party restraints, of the need to please his own supporters, it all made sense. There was a sense of a great occasion in the House. Mrs Thatcher sat there looking very second-rate by comparison. At the end the Labour benches cheered just as much as the Tories.

[The Conservative official Opposition decided to abstain, but the Labour left wing forced a division and 54 voted against the government.]

Back in his room the PM was pleased with himself and very generous about Heath. He said it was 'very good' and 'his coalition speech'. In a sense HW today was part of the past, the partisan leader of the old monolithic parties, while Heath was the start of the new era – the break-up of the two big parties. HW knew it. That is all part of why he wants to go, and knows he should go.

To Joe he said afterwards, 'Well, I won't need my stop-watch any more' (to time his speeches).

Getting in the car to go back to No. 10, he said to Bill Housden, 'That's my last speech in the House' . . . and then after a pause added, 'In this session of course.'

He went off to the Palace for the audience with the Queen. I worked in the Unit and then went back to the Commons. I drank in the bar for an hour with Gerry Fowler, who is very worried about devolution, and then for another hour with Margaret Jackson, whom I find very lively company – and amusingly scathing about her former boss, Ron Hayward of Transport House.

Had a quick supper in the cafeteria with Bill Housden, who is convinced from all the discussions he hears in the car that HW is going in October, and then home at 10.30.

Carol and the children are away in Somerset.

## Wednesday 23 July 1975

Took my time going in – by a slow bus because Carol was away in Somerset with the car – and then regretted it. When I got into No. 10 at about 10.30 a.m. found a message from the PM sent at least half an hour earlier asking me to go up to the study. Joe was there, with Patrick Wright, and they had been working on HW's speech for the Helsinki conference next week.

We all chatted about yesterday's economic debate and how Thatcher looked finished.

The PM went down to the Misc 91 Cabinet committee on incomes policy. I decided not to go. It was concerned with nuts-and-bolts details and I preferred to work in the Unit.

Went to an excellent lunch at Grieveson Grant.

Back to an interview with David Butler of Nuffield College on the referendum. He said that the Britain in Europe outfit had no idea about our activities in the meetings with ministers and opinion polls in the Foreign Office. Also that people in Brussels had told him that HW had reassured them in May 1974 that he would recommend staying in.

At 4.45 I went to the Industrial Policy (IDV) Cabinet committee.

Began with a paper by Peter Shore on his Civil Aviation policy – cutting back British Caledonian and cancelling Laker's Skytrain.

Then the Court Line fiasco, with a report from the Commission of Inquiry and two independent accountants blaming Benn for it going wrong. Shore Benn, Short, Varley and Joel Barnett from the Treasury were for rejecting the report – which was unfair to Benn. Lever, Ross and Williams were for accepting it.

Anyway this was only a pipe opener for what was to come – a terrifying report on the collapse of our motorcycle industry, and, worse, the fact that Benn when the minister at the Department of Industry had allegedly written letters to various shop stewards giving assurances of government support without ever getting any government authority for doing so. Furthermore, his civil servants had dissociated themselves and the accounting officer (the permanent secretary) put on record that he would refuse to sign the cheques. Now that Norton Villiers Triumph is bankrupt and has come to us for £50 million, and its shop stewards have Benn's letter in their pocket, the chickens really are coming home to roost.

Incredibly, Benn rose before the start of this item and walked out, saying to the private secretary at the door, 'No need for me to stay; there is nothing else which concerns me.'

Varley looked furious, and in his opening made a sarcastic reference to Benn having 'more pressing business elsewhere'. As Benn's successor at the Department of Industry, Varley is being left to carry the can. Do we fork out all this money to meet Benn's promises – and it will all go down the drain since there are already thousands of motorcycles which they cannot sell now? Or do we refuse, and expose Benn for having committed the government without authority? [The government announced its decision to withdraw financial support from Norton Villiers on 31 July 1975.]

Shrewdly, Shirley Williams asked for it to be brought to Cabinet, where they can question Benn – provided he arrives.

The Prime Minister left at the end of this item. As he walked out he came over to me sitting at the end of the Cabinet table and said, 'This is a terrible case. It may force Benn out. But if he goes it will look as if he is going on Court Line as well.'

The PM then went off to present some medals somewhere, and on to a dinner of the veteran MPs who were elected in 1945.

I went off very briefly to a party in the Foreign Office. Met Roy Hattersley on the steps, ebullient as ever. We briefly discussed Reg Prentice, under attack from his constituency tonight, and the PM's excellent letter in defence of Prentice. Hattersley said that he assumed from it that the PM had fixed the NEC in advance, because leaders did not go out on a limb otherwise. I said I hoped so too. Frankly I don't know. Joe and I had pushed him last weekend to intervene to help Prentice. Now he has done so. But he didn't consult us about how to do it, or about the contents of the letter.

I nipped back from the party to No. 10 and immediately met Roy Jenkins coming out of the Industrial Development Cabinet committee, which was continuing, discussing planning agreements. I walked with Roy to the Home Office discussing the Franks Report on Official Secrets. I warned him of Hunt's intention to torpedo it. We decided to fight against any negative decision, and to be prepared to put it off till after the summer when the hysteria about Crossman would have diminished. But definitely no reference to an official committee; and no acceptance that a delay till the autumn meant no legislation next session. I feel more at ease with Roy now, especially discussing particular policies.

Back to No. 10, and immediately ran into Shirley Williams coming out of IDV. Walked out with her and told her of Barbara Castle's excellent letter to Healey asking for more information for Friday's Chequers meeting on public expenditure – and especially that the Treasury should reveal the range of alternatives it is *actually* considering. Shirley promised to write in support.

Then finally got back to my room and cleared my desk before going off to dinner with Peter Parker.* Met Harold Lever on the way out and he took me back to Eaton Square in his car, eagerly discussing the motor-cycle questions, and of course delighted at the mess Benn is in. He loaned me his official car to go to Peter Parker's house in Notting Hill Gate.

Incidentally, during the IDV committee the PM rose and went out looking worried. I asked Robin Butler what it was. He didn't know, but said that the PM had gone to Marcia's room for a long telephone call just before the meeting. I saw Joe on the way to the Foreign Office party and asked him. He said that a Special Branch officer had been to see HW to report that a man who had been courting Peg, Marcia's sister, claiming to be a doctor and keen to marry Peg, was in fact an international criminal and believed to have worked for the CIA. It smells bad.

The dinner at the Parkers' was very pleasant. Good food and wine. A lovely summer evening. I talked to John Thompson, now with IBA radio, whom I last met 15 years ago when he edited *Time and Tide* and printed an article by me on the New Left.

Peter and delightful Jill Parker drove me home at 1.15 a.m.

The cats were waiting at the door to be fed.

*Thursday 24 July 1975*

Cabinet at 10 a.m. – though mainly on parliamentary business, and especially the terrible state of the legislative programme. Unless something is done, they will be sitting throughout August. Decide to sit all night and all tomorrow and even the weekend until the Incomes Policy Bill is through the Commons. [The committee stages were completed in a marathon session this Thursday night, the report stage in another all-night session on 29 July and the third reading on 30 July.]

Beforehand, I saw Eric Varley, who was still fuming at Benn. 'He is a louse.' Varley said that Benn had left the Industry Dept in a terrible state. Varley 'faced a dreadful six months clearing up the mess'. He also said that his spies in Energy told him that Benn was beginning to get up to all kinds of tricks there. Eric is off to see the shop stewards at Triumph next week and is not looking forward to it.

Also had a brief talk with Tony Crosland about tomorrow's meeting on public expenditure cuts at Chequers – but in fact today's Cabinet decided to call it off because of the parliamentary crisis and the need for ministers to be in the Commons voting.

Saw Joe, who was very annoyed with the PM for not discussing his future with him. I can see Joe's temper getting thin. He is tired and a bit fed up with it all. He is sure to beard the PM before long. He is completely brave, open and honest. He will be unemployed when HW does go.

They went to Hamburg today for a half-day visit to see Chancellor Schmidt. Nothing particular on the agenda. Just that the PM realised *six* weeks ago that the unemployment figures would be announced today – and would be bad. So he asked for a foreign visit. Because he wanted to avoid Question Time on the day unemployment goes past a million. He has admitted this to us, with a wicked grin.

As they were taking off from Northolt, poor Mark Forrester, the appointments secretary in No. 10, nearly had to bring them back in to land again. Marcia telephoned to him to demand that the PM should see the Israeli Ambassador tomorrow. She wanted immediate confirmation.

Forrester declined to put this appointment in the diary because a Cabinet was scheduled for the time when Marcia demanded. So she immediately sent him a letter making all kinds of accusations against him.

Went to lunch at Eaton Square with Harold Lever. He told a bizarre but typical story.

George Weidenfeld came to see him recently and said that Marcia was complaining that Lever never invited her to any of his smart dinners.

She would like to be invited. Lever resisted a little, on the grounds that he only had friends to dinner – and also, he admitted, because he did not wish to be involved. But then it was intimated to him that the PM would like him to have her to dinner. So Lever conceded, telephoned, and made a date. On the evening he sat there with his wife Diane waiting. Marcia never arrived for dinner. She never telephoned, did not apologise afterwards.

We also discussed his Arts appointment, which is to be announced in August. He must be careful on this or it will look like demotion.

Went back to No.10 and then to play cricket at Westminster School.

In the evening for drinks with Peter Gibbings of the *Guardian*, and on to Bill Rodgers's home in Kentish Town for a party there with Carol.

Home at midnight.

## Friday 25 July 1975

Curious day. The PM was at Chequers in the morning – he went straight there from Northolt airfield last night. He drove in at midday and went straight to the Commons and stayed there over lunch. He saw the Israeli Ambassador there, and then went back to Chequers without calling back in at No.10.

Joe thought he was deliberately staying away. Certainly I never recall an occasion before when he came to London without coming to No.10.

I spent a fairly relaxed day.

Nice lunch at the Commons and sat on the terrace afterwards in blazing sunshine, talking to exhausted Labour MPs who had been up all night – Helene Hayman, Ray Carter,* Norman Buchan, Chris Price. Rather hysterical atmosphere, but festive and good fun.

In the evening went with Carol and our friends the Grahams to the Old Vic to see Molière's *Misanthrope*. Very lively production. Dinner afterwards, and in bed by midnight.

## Monday 28 July 1975

Decided not to attend this morning's Energy Cabinet committee – mainly concerned with technical problems to do with nuclear energy. Also a difficult problem on the coal industry, but still in its early stages.

But before the committee I went along to the hall outside the Cabinet Room and talked to Ken Berrill (about investment outside the UK which puts pressure on our balance of payments) and to Tommy Balogh (who was defensive about his new Secretary of State, Benn, saying that 'at least he doesn't give away our oil to foreigners').

Read through the papers in my box. The PM summoned me at 11.15 a.m. to go to discuss his Helsinki speech. He had done a draft over the weekend which was really very good. He was bright and perky. Obviously his weekend had done him good.

We were in the study till 12 noon. We then all went down to the Cabinet Room to have a briefing session on the PM's visit to Helsinki. This seemed unreal to me. Killick* and Tickell* from the Foreign Office, Hunt from the Cabinet Office and Ken Stowe, Patrick Wright, Joe, Janet and me from No.10. Vague discussion of 'the German position' on this, and 'the Russians are after that'. The PM asked, 'What do the Americans think about it?' ('Little until very late in the day,' was the answer.) Joe prompted him to ask about China, which was nowhere referred to. 'Best not to,' said the Foreign Office, and that was that. The only abrasive note was when the FO tried to steer the PM off any reference to 'peaceful coexistence'. He resisted.

On the way out, the PM said that if China came up, he would quote Clem Attlee's only known reference to the subject – 'A big place, China.'

It was so relaxed on such a sunny day in that still, elegant room that it was impossible to believe they were discussing détente and the issues of Germany's eastern frontier for which millions and millions had died. I reverted to an earlier habit and made up some verse on the pad in front of me:

> Old men
> sitting in a gilded room
> talk of peace
> and prepare our doom.
> Grey heads
> too long out of the sun
> nodding round the table
> chatter on.
> Maps, frontiers, lands beyond
> excite their blood.
> Roses and families among the trees outside
> leave them dead

[The author when at Oxford University was the President of the Poetry Society and editor of Oxford Poetry, but subsequently and shrewdly neglected this minor talent.]

Joe and I went to lunch at the House of Commons, eating for the first time in the cafeteria of the Press Gallery. Gratifyingly cheap. Afterwards we went on the terrace. Gordon Greig of the *Mail* joined us. He was on to the story about the sterling crisis and the economic package. He said the Treasury had briefed him against HW.

Back to No. 10, to read a long paper on industrial democracy. Also interviewed a professor from Geneva, interested in Parliament.

Joe phoned to say that the retirement of HW has been delayed from October to Christmas. He gave way under strong pressure this weekend from Marcia, who argued that there would be an international and a financial crisis if he went – it was not clear whose financial crisis was being referred to, perhaps hers. He yielded, but insisted that under no circumstances would he go on beyond Christmas. HW told Janet, who told Joe, this morning. Marcia also told Albert, who was delighted that his October trip to USA was now safe, and he also told Joe and me. Such are the gossip networks in No. 10.

I was a bit disappointed. I think October would be right for HW. He is on top of a political wave at the moment. To the public he is supreme. But privately we know he is blown, no more interest, no more ideas, no appetite for power. It bores him. He should go, before public awareness catches up with private reality.

The PM summoned Joe and me and the private secretaries back to his room in the Commons for a final run through his speech to the Helsinki peace conference. Poor Patrick Wright had been briefed by the Foreign Office to have a last go at getting the PM not to mention 'peaceful co-existence'. The PM went through the roof, just wouldn't have it. Said they were 'old-fashioned anti-communists'. Poor Patrick had warned the FO this would happen, but he did his job manfully like a good civil servant, and got a black eye for it. Joe and I just sat grinning, which Patrick ruefully said afterwards did not help.

Back to No. 10 to finish industrial democracy and have a long talk with Andrew Graham about getting an economist to replace him when he goes back to Oxford in the autumn, which will not be easy. He is superb.

Home at 9.30 p.m.

## Tuesday 29 July 1975

Not a good day. Hot and sultry, and threat of storms. I feel tired and jaded and disappointed that the PM has decided not to go in October but to stay till Christmas. I think he should go while the going is good – and so should I.

The PM was in Cabinet committee from 9.30 – on incomes policy – and then Cabinet from 10.45, where they had big battles on the collapse of Triumph motorcycles and of Court Line, both involving Benn. I talked to him before Cabinet about Crossman, where he expressed views strongly anti–civil servants.

Tony Crosland came out of committee to telephone. He asked me why Shirley Williams and Roy Jenkins had taken on the rescue act for Prentice – and felt it should not be right-wingers who did so.

I nobbled Bob Mellish about getting a machine to aid deaf Jack Ashley in the House of Commons to help him to follow debates. It costs around £10,000 and would change Jack's working life. Unfortunately the Commons Services committee is proving unhelpful – mainly because of the opposition of a Labour member! So Bob Mellish is going to write to the DHSS and to the PM – where I will give help too in getting a positive response.

Saw Joe before they left for Helsinki. He is tired too.

Then a meeting with Richard Graham in the Unit about his paper on industrial democracy. Not too happy about it – a bit evangelistic. But I am too hard on it because am tired.

## Wednesday 30 July 1975

PM away at the Helsinki CSCE conference till Saturday.

I took Carol and the twins into No. 10 in the morning and to the Changing of the Guard. Still sweltering hot weather, and London full of tourists. I feel completely whacked and want to get away on holiday.

Lunch with Douglas Wass at the Reform. He is gentle and sensitive, not at all the usual hard cynical mandarin. He was quite open about Healey – tremendous energy, hard worker, whose parents are both still alive in their nineties. An intellectual by inclination, so gets involved in intellectual arguments, but not of the very highest calibre, so sometimes loses. But above all he agreed with me that Healey is a 'loner'. His instinct – as when at Defence – is to bury himself in his department and he does very little to win other ministers over to his policies. He believes in pure reason. Wass says Healey goes to a committee and thinks that when he has argued a convincing case he has won the battle. 'He was totally deflated after his three recent defeats in Cabinet.' Having put the case he sat back, and could not believe it when he lost. Wass admitted that 'he got a bloody nose over public expenditure.' And kept referring to Crosland as the one who defeated him. Wass had told Healey that morning that he 'must make a friend of Crosland, not an enemy'. He admitted that Crosland was a cleverer economist.

We discussed public expenditure and the need for greater selectivity. He agreed but could not see a basis for selecting. And said that in the end the spending ministers always prevented a more rational approach, because they dominate the Cabinet numerically, and none of them is prepared to carry a disproportionate amount of the burden.

He was very concerned that the 'public purse' had only one representative in the Cabinet, against all the spending ministers. I agreed and said that was all the more reason why the Chancellor must become more open and political, winning over support – especially from the PM – in advance. It was also a case for having a second Treasury minister (the Chief Secretary) in the Cabinet, and I would put this to the PM.

Also discussed the Treasury reorganisation. They are setting up a complete new section on industry policy – I guessed with Alan Lord in charge, though he rightly declined to reveal. But it is a threat to Varley's Department of Industry, and I got the impression that they were not consulting Varley adequately.

He drove me back in his car. In Downing Street I pressed him again to let Andrew Graham attend his Short-Term Economic Policy committee. This is situated in the Treasury (with a Bank of England representative) and was meant by Wass to be the key economic committee – unknown to most civil servants or any ministers. In fact Wass says that it has not worked out as well as he expected. But he resisted having Andrew on – saying that it was not him but the Chancellor who objected, since he did want short-term economic policy to be 'his own'. I pointed out that this linked to the earlier problem we had discussed – the Chancellor's need to involve other people, especially No.10, if he were to get the support necessary to win his battles. Wass agreed, but added that Hunt, Berrill and Moser were there from No.10. I flared at this and pointed out that *none* of these was physically in No.10, and none of them briefed the PM, personally and privately as distinct from the Cabinet, on actual economic *policy*. (Hunt sends him chairman's *steers* for when the PM is chairing an economic committee. They often have a *policy* steer at the end pointing the PM towards a policy conclusion the machine wants. But they do not contain the *arguments*, in the way Andrew Graham and I set them out.)

We parted on this note, unfortunately abrasive, because he is a nice man and I can tell he wants to be helpful. I will try to keep in closer touch with him.

In the afternoon saw a nice Australian named Rose, who was a special adviser to the Liberals when in power. Then slept in a bedroom upstairs for half an hour, feeling quite drained.

Philip Graham came in for a drink and then we went together to meet our wives and see the new Pinter play *No Man's Land* at Wyndham's Theatre. The play is brilliant but bleak. And it was intolerably hot and oppressive, the air like treacle, the sky mauve and threatening rain. I left in the interval, my shirt wringing wet, and I drove home alone to buy beer to put in the fridge and wait for the others to come home. I lay on the settee listening to Bach's violin concerto, and the cat came and snuggled against me. She is my least demanding friend. A moment's peace. But still feeling low and ominous. Must get away.

## Thursday 31 July 1975

Went in with Helene Hayman. Worked over papers and did some briefs for the PM's weekend box, including one on finance for sport, in response to a long rambling letter from Wigg, and one pressing him to give support to providing Jack Ashley with a mechanical aid which will enable him to follow proceedings in the Commons. To me that is as important as anything else.

Went to see Gerry Fowler before lunch about devolution. He is very worried about the timetable next year. It looks as if the Bill will have 200 clauses. The danger is that it will take all the parliamentary time, will prevent other legislation getting through, and then would fail to get through itself. Just like House of Lords reform in 1968–69. He is very clear and convincing, and completely on top of his job. We had a quick lunch together at the Commons, and then I put in a note to the PM warning him of the devolution problems.

Went off to the Oxford and Cambridge Club after lunch to see Robert Armstrong. He had telephoned and asked to see me. It was about Labour Party matters, and how to get hold of the membership of General Management committees of local constituency parties where left-wingers are threatening sitting members such as Neville Sandelson. I am a bit out of touch now, and don't trust anybody at Transport House, but promise to help. I presume that Roy Jenkins is behind this, but I didn't ask. I still like Robert enormously. He has such a passionate interest in everything. In fact I miss him a great deal in No.10. I feel I can ask his advice on matters and he will understand the human considerations.

Went home at 4.30 p.m. to look after the children while Carol went to the doctor's. To bed early and fell asleep before 10. Absolutely shagged out. Would happily resign tomorrow just to get away from it all. This is very much an end-of-term feeling. The treadmill since before the last election has drained my deepest reserves. I must get away from events and newspapers and politicians, and just sit somewhere and read. This is when somebody needs a family. I desperately look forward to being surrounded by them, being private, and completely out of the 'public sector'. This is what is rarely understood. How the public stage is both invigorating, an adrenalin pump, and totally sapping. Anyone with a 'private' personality, as I have, must come to hate it. The only ones who survive to the top are those with predominantly 'public' personalities. Loving the stage, relishing publicity, liking crowds, liking people to be interested in everything they do. A sense of privacy, and of discrimination about people, is a positive disqualification for public life.

That is why I am counting the hours to going to France tomorrow – and the months till HW retires and I can get back to university. Of course I will soon get bored with it and hanker for public life again. But that is how life is – cycles of commitment and exposure, then a retreat and withdrawal.

# CHAPTER 19

## Party Conference at Blackpool
### September–October 1975

*Monday 8 September 1975*

Back from a lovely holiday in our house at Céret in France – an interesting part of which was a happy day visit from Roy and Jennifer Jenkins. Went very well – more relaxed than ever before.

But not too happy to be back. It is my birthday – 41 today – and I entered No.10 with no feeling of zest or excitement. It has become routine. Not much we can do in the economic freeze ahead. The Labour Party is in a bad way. And the PM is less and less interested in policies, as opposed to politics.

Joe told me that the PM is now talking of leaving 'during this year' (1975 or 1975–76 is unclear). That he still talks of Christmas, but Marcia, Albert and Bill are fairly confident he can be kept on longer. And that he has discussed it with John Hunt, who has pressed him to stay, telling him how indispensable he is to the nation. So all the flatterers and those with a vested financial interest are pressing him to stay – not referring to John Hunt, who is in neither category. Joe and I, who want him to go out at the top, before the deterioration which is privately obvious becomes publicly exposed, are not consulted – Joe is only given hints.

Last Friday I missed a fascinating visit by Soares,* the Portuguese Socialist leader, with Mitterrand from France, Den Uyl, premier of Holland, Brandt* of Germany and Palme* of Sweden*. In the morning and then lunch. Soares reported on the Portuguese situation – how his socialists now have most of the country except Lisbon, and most of the Army – but not the Navy, which is very communist. Even the Maoists support the democratic socialists. He expected civil war within a fortnight – though they wanted the communists to strike first. Then the socialists would withdraw from Lisbon where the communists have strong units, and take over the rest of the country. But they needed supplies – the Czechs are supplying the communists. He was fairly confident. The others offered support. Mitterrand was very tough on the French communists, who he said are just lackeys of Moscow. He said the Russians had been pushing him hard not to intervene.

I worked in the office all morning while the PM was on the way back from staying with the Queen at Balmoral. Not too many papers. The flow is much less now because our policies are all through the committee and White Paper stage and back in the departments for detailed drafting.

The PM arrived after midday, delighted with his golfing at Balmoral, but complaining about the lack of work and papers. He kept us talking in the private office till nearly 2 p.m. Then I went off to lunch with two of the private secretaries to catch up on what I had missed in the holiday – which was not very much.

But one of them reported that the machine felt that John Hunt had overreached himself in empire-building and that the Treasury was out to cut him down to size.

The PM sent for us all at teatime to discuss his future speeches, and especially that at party conference. He decided to begin his conference speech with a long catalogue of the government's achievements. When it was suggested that this was boring he said he agreed, but that 'boredom is often a useful instrument in politics. Never underestimate it.'

Marcia has suggested that I go to conference. I don't know if this is a trap or a peace move. I shall think about it.

At 5.30 the PM went to a meeting of the anti-inflation group under Sydney Jacobson and Geoffrey Goodman of the *Daily Mirror*. So I went out to the Reform Club for a drink with Alf Morris. Spent two and a half hours – he is an excellent and genuine man. One of the few MPs and ministers who genuinely cares about people, and especially the disabled. The exact reverse of most politicians in fact – no vanity, and concerned with the real issues and not just the image and the packaging.

I am interested in the problems of the deaf and discussed with him ways of improving the provision for the deaf, as I have with Jack Ashley. Then we got on to his political problem – that his department gives him no support, and especially Barbara Castle. According to him, she doesn't care much about the disabled, nor indeed about much apart from her own political career. She spends hours a day before the mirror dolling herself up. She often refers to Israel's Golda Meir and says that she will become a Prime Minister in her late 60s just like Golda. This was the first time that Alf had ever said a disloyal word about Barbara. In the past he was always discreet and loyal. But it is clear that he is fed up. He cannot even get any servicing – his wife comes in to type without pay. Fairly depressing. I shall help as much as I can. Home at 9 p.m.

## Tuesday 9 September 1975

In at 9.30. The weather is still hot, though with rain around. London looks shabby. England is in fact depressing. I realised this morning that HW is completely isolated from the remorseless relative decline of this country. He never goes abroad other than under the artificial circumstances of a prime ministerial visit, so he is unaware of the growth and strength of countries like France. He takes his holidays in the Scillies, which is unchanged since 1950, so he thinks the world is unchanged. The same is true of Marcia, Mary and Joe, who all holiday in Britain. Joe has begun to realise what has happened, as emerged on our Bonn visit, when the prosperity and cleanness of their town struck him. But none of the others.

HW is agitated about his submission to the Royal Commission on the Press and has got Joe working over all those old dreary clippings. He is also upset by a story in the *Evening News* that he is authorising the Russians to increase the number of their diplomats /spies in London. He said to me quite categorically that 'The Russians have never raised it and so I have never authorised it.' Joe was sent off to issue denials on that and HW was also thinking and talking of setting up a commission of inquiry into it. This nonsense is all because he hasn't enough to do – few papers, few committees and no Parliament. So he hangs around, reading the ticker-tapes and fussing about what is in the newspapers.

At 11.15 we had the only Cabinet committee of this week – an OPD on North Sea oil and the problems of negotiating the continental shelf. Important but technical. Interestingly Benn was very tentative, apparently not yet on top of his subject. Quite different from when he was at Industry, where all those years in the same subject had given him a complete mastery of the field.

Also interesting was another clash between Energy in the form of dear old Tommy Balogh, always passionate to defend every drop of British interest and British oil, and the Foreign Office (Ennals) suggesting as usual that we should give away half of our case to begin with in order not to upset the foreigners. This time they wanted to concede to the Irish that Rockall is not an island right from the beginning. This is a recurring feature of all these discussions. The Foreign Office seems more concerned with the foreigners' interests than with Britain's. Somebody needs to ask the question, 'Whose side is the Foreign Office on?'

I chatted to Tommy and he seemed very frail and said that he felt unwell. I do hope it is nothing serious. I am sorry that he acts as a lackey to Marcia. But he is really unique and delightful. I would miss him.

Farewell lunch party for a private secretary, Mark Forrester. Afterwards to the Cabinet Office mess for lunch with Andrew Graham to plan staff replacements for the Unit this year. Now that HW is clearly staying for most of the year I feel I can approach people. That Cabinet Office restaurant is appalling. Filthy food. Terrible service. But it is very much the Civil Service – austere, gossipy, no pleasure or frills, a place for fixers to fix things. Smells of boiled cabbage. It is only the second time I have been there and it still utterly depresses me.

The PM went off to a meeting at Transport House of the Cabinet and the NEC (which apparently went well, with Michael Foot and Jack Jones coming out firmly in support of the government's counter-inflation policy).

I worked in the office. Ralf Dahrendorf from the LSE came in at 6 p.m. for drinks. He is still bubbling full of ideas. Offered me a marvellous job to set up a new Brookings-style institute. We went off to the Reform for dinner and he brought me up to date on all the latest LSE gossip, saying I will have no problem about ending or extending my leave from the LSE.

Home at 10 o'clock.

*Wednesday 10 September 1975*

Went to Chequers for an all-day Cabinet on devolution.

The car came at 8.45, but it broke down on the A40 and I had to flag down Tony Benn's Rover and hitch a lift with him. My car was a new British Leyland Marina – which illustrates what their problem is about.

Benn was as always engaging and open. He clearly opposes devolution but is not interested enough to take a big part. He thinks 'it will never happen' and will run into trouble later, in the House.

But mainly we discussed the 'future scenario of British politics'. He sees many parallels with the 1930s. He saw a polarisation of the extremist minorities and the centre rallying and uniting out of fear. But he doesn't expect the extremism to be very extreme. He was interesting, sensible and perceptive. He is also concerned with the longer view. It is impossible not to like him. Also I realised looking back over the past 18 months that in general I have been impressed by his analysis of the problems, which is always penetrating. It is his solutions which are usually barmy – because he is trying to please his supporters on the populist left. Apart from Tony Crosland, there is nobody else with whom one could have such a lively car journey. (Though he did produce his old tin mug and drink tea at one point, just to demonstrate his affinity with the Upper Clyde shipyard workers.)

We arrived around 10 on a lovely morning. Many of the ministers were there, others were arriving in a rapid procession of big black Rovers. The exception is the brown Rover of the Home Secretary. (Herbert Morrison always had a police car – when did that change?)

I chatted to various ministers while we had coffee beforehand. Chequers

always looks lovely in the morning, spacious, sunny, less intense and oppressive than No.10, a feeling of relaxation, with the PM always in a light
holiday jacket and often in sandals. Curiously I always get fed up with it
in the day and want to get away early in the afternoon – as do others, who
get away after lunch as quickly as possible. Somehow it doesn't wear well.
I wouldn't want to be there in the evening.

HW was fussing about the *Daily Mail*. He had dictated another denial
of their story on the Russian 'spies'. Joe thought it was disastrous since it
opened up the whole story. John Hunt had also done a draft, which was
terrible since it revealed that in fact the Russians had raised the question,
and there was a possibility of increasing the number of Russian 'inspec-
tors' who supervised import purchases. Joe was absolutely against and in
fact offered a scoop story which the *Mail* would publish on this 'denial'.

It was ridiculous. Hunt and Ken Stowe spent much of yesterday and
today drafting and redrafting this denial. The PM was constantly grabbing
Joe to discuss it. In Cabinet he was repeatedly sending messages about it.
He was much more concerned with this piddling little story in the *Mail*
than with devolution. Yet what the hell did it matter? Perhaps it was guilt.
The longer it went on, the more it emerged that the Russians had raised
it with us – with HW and with Peter Shore – and there was a possibility
of an increase. His categorical denial to me earlier was quite untrue. It was
true that he had never overruled the security services. But it was not the
black and white issue he had made out. How often have Joe and I seen that!

The devolution discussion began at about 10.20 a.m. in the usual big
room, with paintings of various fat and bewigged English gentry looking
down on the long table around which sat some 20 members of Cabinet
(Lever, Silkin and Mellish were away) together with Hunt and Berrill at
the table; the Cabinet Office note-takers at a side table; Joe, myself and
two private secretaries from No. 10 sitting along one wall; and a secretary
and Ted Short's political adviser from the Lord President's office.

HW opened as usual by saying that Cabinets at Chequers do not take
decisions – though in fact all points agreed are later treated as decisions
on my observation. Indeed later this afternoon HW stopped discussion of
several items on the grounds that they had 'been decided in the morning'.

Ted Short then introduced the first of a long list of papers on the agenda,
beginning with very general points. He made the broad observation that:

a.  We are not devolving sovereignty.
b.  We must preserve the unity of the UK.
c.  We are allowing the Scots and Welsh to decide in some policy
    areas – housing, health, etc. – and were discussing the constitu-
    tional implications of this.

Early on Roy Jenkins intervened to ask if there was any intention to hold discussions with the Opposition. Partly because it was a constitutional matter. Partly because there would be parliamentary problems in getting it through.

HW surprisingly agreed, suggesting informal consultations before the White Paper and formal consultations after. In fact this proposal – perfectly sensible but open to 'coalition misinterpretation' – was a bit of a trap and HW should have left it to others to support. This was emphasised when Foot and Castle strongly opposed, and HW then began to retreat a bit, though not completely.

Healey and Callaghan then intervened to open up the whole question of principle, opposing the move towards devolution. Healey was sensibly afraid that once there were Scottish and Welsh assemblies, the Tories would have an excuse to reduce the Scottish and Welsh representation at Westminster – and so have a permanent Tory majority.

Callaghan said he was 'afraid of opening the doors to separatism' and therefore wanted the 'most moderate' proposal possible. Shirley Williams agreed: 'We are on the road step by step to separatism.'

Callaghan and Peart, Healey, Jenkins and Elwyn Jones all warned that the Westminster power to 'override' actions by the assemblies would be meaningless – never used or ignored. Jenkins said that the threat of override would frighten Westminster more than the Scots.

Then they moved on to individual issues in a long string of papers. Introduced by Gerry Fowler as junior minister with responsibility for devolution with great clarity and authority. Gerry definitely made a good impact here, as Tony Crosland said later.

Every so often the meeting dissolved into grumblings of doubt about the whole exercise. But always Willie Ross stepped in to say it was too late. He had warned them years ago and they would not listen or support him. Now they must live with it. In fact Willie was being Calvinist, rubbing their faces in devolution, holding them wriggling on the hook because they had not listened to his Cassandra warnings earlier.

HW was chairing the meeting remarkably firmly and well considering that he was totally bored with the whole question. He privately admitted he had not read all the papers, and was thinking more of the *Daily Mail* than of the British constitution.

We moved on through national standards, the professions (where the lawyers, as always, insisted on no interference with their sovereign rights to control their own profession and fees and milk the public without accountability), social services, education, transport (including a barmy suggestion that the Scots and Welsh should have their own railway systems).

I went out to phone the office at noon and I ordered coffee to be served in the room. I had no authority to do this – normally HW gives the order if and when he wants coffee – but I felt that the imprisoned Cabinet needed some relief.

The discussion went on till 2 p.m. when we broke for lunch.

It was the usual buffet salad. I went out into the garden to eat mine with Gerry Fowler. We discussed the appalling amount of envy, malice and suspicion in public life. He said he does not talk frankly to anyone in the party – it was always leaked on to HW or to Ted Short. We also discussed his prospective court case for drunken driving. Sounds like bad luck. He was remarkably relaxed about it. I told him not to resign or do anything rash, but definitely not to get a second prosecution.

Joe was feeling unwell, with a terrible headache. I get worried about his health and wonder if he has high blood pressure.

We resumed just after 3. Callaghan, Benn and Rees had gone. The ministers zipped through the rest of the agenda but at the end the proceedings deteriorated into dreadful squabbling. Healey went on and on, saying that the Cabinet had never agreed to devolution. He interrupted HW in a most boorish way. Crosland objected to this. Jenkins obviously was embarrassed by Healey's crude style but agreed with his argument. Ross was booming away at the end of the table that it was too late to object, devolution was a fact of life. HW was trying without success to restore order. For 20 minutes it was like a monkeys' tea party.

This was ominous because:

- Healey could make political capital out of it;
- a lot of heavyweights – Jenkins, Callaghan, Williams and even Crosland support his position if not his style;
- possibly a majority of Cabinet opposes devolution;
- HW does not support it either really. His position is that we are committed to it: we proposed it, we put it in our manifesto, and we produced a White Paper – therefore we cannot go back on it. But he does not believe in it.

So the next meeting, looking at the whole package, could be dramatic.

Joe told me that Callaghan had suggested to HW another referendum! HW was not too pleased.

It broke up at around 4 p.m., with Willie Ross booming on about the need to devolve agriculture to Scotland while ministers rushed desperately to the door and down the stairs. The black Rovers streamed up to the back door and swept off down the drive, out of the grounds and back to London. A tremendous sense of power and movement, but a terrible waste of cars and petrol.

I travelled with Joe and Nick Stuart from private office. We passed Tony Crosland and Gerry Fowler, each fast asleep in the back of their cars.

Joe had a long talk about Northern Ireland with Merlyn Rees who told him that at the weekend the UDA and the SDLP were ready to reach an agreement and to join in a coalition government. This would be agreed through the Convention and would have been a marvellous triumph for moderation and the Convention. But then Enoch Powell intervened, made a passionate speech against all dealings with the Republicans which, like devolution, would break up the UK. This won over their decision against power-sharing. He said that Powell was the decisive and evil influence, for selfish reasons of protecting his own political position.

When we got back to No.10 Joe phoned the *Daily Mirror*. They put their people on to this but could get no information. Even worse, Rees told Joe that Craig had told him personally about Powell. When the *Mirror* talked to Rees he said that Gerry Fitt had told him.

We wondered if Merlyn was feeling the strain.

HW stayed at Chequers for 10 minutes to discuss the future economic programme with Healey. They agreed:

1. To delay public expenditure decisions until after party conference.
2. To discuss industrial strategy and unemployment in Cabinet before party conference.

Typical of HW. Interested in the party implications of economic policy, not the contents of the policy itself.

He then came back and went to a meeting with Thatcher and the Tories to discuss Ireland and try to maintain a bilateral approach.

I felt tired and came home at 8.30 p.m.

Incidentally, while bored by devolution I worked out the age structure of the Cabinet. Remarkably top-heavy and old. Nine are over 60 – it will be 10 with HW in March. If this Cabinet continued until 1978 14 would be over 60 and 6 would be old-age pensioners.

There will have to be a lot of changes in the next two years. Yet HW has not brought on a middle-rank succession. Nobody between Benn and Jenkins. He won't be able to avoid a reshuffle if he stays on much longer!

## *Thursday 11 September 1975*

HW is still lost, with too little work to do. He stands around in private office chatting, or spends ages studying the news headlines on the Press Association's tape machine. He goes to the study if he has an interview, but does not stay there to read – because he does not like being alone.

I cleared off back papers and letters.

I went to lunch with Tony Crosland at his house in Holland Park. We had a drink beforehand and did not eat till nearly 2. Susan was there, very beautiful and curious about affairs at No.10. Tony is often very domineering towards her.

He was as always very gossipy, frank, outrageous and funny. He admires HW a great deal – probably deep down because HW has the political abilities which Tony lacks. He was also savagely correct on HW's failings. Tony says he finds him so boring that he cannot bear to talk to him. He claims that at the dining-room tables in the Commons, hearts sink when HW arrives, bringing his familiar string of anecdotes about when he negotiated the first Russian trade agreement in 1947. More fairly, he complained that HW never consults him when reshuffling his junior ministers, and doesn't seem the least interested in their relative abilities. 'My biggest criticism of Harold is that he doesn't care a damn for the calibre and quality of his ministers and government.' This is sadly true. His governments are determined by party balance, meeting past promises, paying off scores, and giving way to Marcia. Somehow it is part of his belief that nothing makes much difference. A mixture of luck and last-minute manoeuvring will make more difference, certainly, than marginally raising the overall quality of the whole administration by insisting on picking the best men. Perhaps, deeply in love with the Civil Service, he thinks that the political ministers are marginal to decisions anyway.

I came back to a series of meetings: with my old friend Philip Williams* of Nuffield College, who had come to interview HW about Hugh Gaitskell; with a young graduate from Edinburgh researching into policy units; with a young man from the World Bank whom I might employ in the Unit; and for this week's meeting of Deputy Secretaries in the Cabinet Office. At the latter Ken Berrill revealed that fresh horrors had emerged on the public sector borrowing requirement. The Treasury had miscalculated some figures badly and then sat on their mistakes for months. Now it seemed they would have to revise the borrowing requirement upwards by £3 billion! At a stroke! This is what frightens one so in Whitehall. The technical sloppiness.

Healey's last Budget was presented as a courageous offensive by an iron Chancellor. In fact the savings were swamped by this one miscalculation. We still have not cleared the skeletons out of the cupboard, let alone made progress towards getting public finance properly under control.

HW also saw Eric Varley, who came to suggest Hugh Scanlon of the Engineers Union for some top job. HW thought it was ridiculous and squashed it.

Marcia was in all afternoon, which is a rare occurrence these days. She was visited by one of the financial friends of Tony Field, Lord Arwyn, who was elevated in 1964. She fixed for him to have half an hour with HW.

In the evening Carol came in and we went to the dinner of the Inter-Parliamentary Union at Lancaster Gate. Terrible food. But nice Greeks, Spaniard and Michael Healey, the clerk of the Irish Dail. I was host at the table. Home rather tired at midnight.

### Friday 12 September 1975

Very quiet day. The PM was involved in preparation for his visit to Romania next week. I cleared my papers.

Had lunch with Joe at the Commons. He told me that a scandal is brewing over the use of airfields on the island of Diego Garcia. The press is on to a secret agreement between Britain and USA, and HW was responsible for the decision to keep it secret. Will be very embarrassing. The PM left at 2.30 to go to open a Thorn electronics factory. It was pouring with rain. Little paper or business, so I went home early to have tea with the children.

### Monday 15 September 1975

Peter Gibbings, chairman of the *Guardian*, came in to discuss the newspaper situation. He is a very nice, modest, balanced man. The *Evening News* is losing £3 million this year; *The Times* around a million. The NPA is pressing for government aid. Gibbings supports the idea, but is very detached and aware of Fleet Street's deficiencies – and of journalists'. He described the boundless hypocrisy of journalists in denouncing others for the personal vices which they have more than anyone else.

I went up to see the PM at midday before Nelson Rockefeller came in. Discussed various subjects he wanted for his conference speech.

Lunch for Rockefeller. I sat between two Americans – Warren, who is organising the coming bicentenary, and Marr, a former doctor who is now a special adviser to Ford. Also had a long talk to Len Murray, who was in excellent form. He said how much better the 1974 Wilson was than the 1964 Wilson ('always interfering in everything'). And that he, Murray, had just taken a long summer holiday, which no previous general secretary of the TUC dare do. We all agreed that the 'Kennedy' days of endless mindless work were over, and it was better to relax and think more.

HW talked to Nelson Rockefeller throughout the lunch, turning his back on Mrs Callaghan – and preventing Roy Jenkins talking to Rockefeller at all.

After lunch HW sent for us all to discuss his conference speech. He was beginning to get ideas on what to say. He particularly wanted to 'bring some vision' into it and wants a piece about the future and the need for the government to look ahead. I suggested that he specifically deal with the 'inner city' problem as one that loomed ahead. He agreed and asked us to draft something. He also said he wanted to be tough on inflation.

We went off to begin collecting material and drafting pieces for him to consider on the plane to Romania tomorrow. The PM saw Roy Jenkins and Ted Short about electoral reform. Jenkins wants to have a Speaker's Conference by the end of the year. Apparently HW was sympathetic, but said that a special committee should be set up to brief government representatives on the electoral implications for the Labour Party – and suggested that I and the Unit act in that role. Roy Jenkins was very happy. Short suggested that Transport House do it – but HW said they would not be good enough. He wanted something academically respectable which would understand the political side. So we have another task. Curiously I discussed electoral reform with HW the other day and told him that I was in favour of PR. I wonder if he is – and is using me to support it without actually himself supporting Jenkins?

Afterwards I went to the study to discuss the PM's speech for tonight's opening of the exhibition on 'The Work of Franklin and Jefferson' at the British Museum. I took him a copy of my book on the American War of Independence and he liked a quotation in it from Jefferson and incorporated it in his speech.

We went to this ceremony in two cars – the PM, Mrs Wilson, Patrick Wright, Jean Denham and myself – at 7.15. (The PM saw the Chancellor of the Exchequer beforehand, but I don't know what about.) It was a very nice occasion – Rockefeller and Elliot Richardson, the American Ambassador, are both very amiable, and the others from the embassy are interesting to talk to. Tony Crosland and Susan were there – I took the opportunity to tell him we are beginning to think about transport policy, and he reacted very quickly, inviting Richard Graham and myself round to talk with him so that we don't get too many wires crossed.

The speeches by Richardson, Rockefeller and the PM were in fact very good, but half drowned by the noise of the audience talking throughout – appalling bad manners and perhaps one more sign of the decline in standards apparent everywhere. Then we toured the exhibition. I went round part of it with Pearl Bailey, the negress jazz singer. She had flown overnight with Rockefeller, was flying tonight to Washington and tomorrow to Los Angeles, where she was appearing in the evening in *Hello Dolly*. Incredible.

Home at 9.30. The PM went to dinner with the Ambassador. I had soup and cold fried fish at home and watched a moving TV programme on Richard

Dimbleby. So long ago he died. Yet he seemed part of our adult life for ages – ever since our TV lives began, and back into the war on radio.

Perhaps we really are getting old. Also seeing him as a wartime correspondent I realise that is really what I would have liked to have been – a war correspondent, in a genuine war I believed in, when Britain mattered, and when newspapers and radio had standards. A form of public service bureaucracy. Now privacy is the only worthwhile possession.

## Tuesday 16 September 1975

In at 9.30 to work on further drafts for the PM's conference speech.

Left at 12 noon to go to the bank to meet the new manager about my appalling overdraft situation.

Lunch with Yoram Peri, the Israel representative in Europe. He told me that Marcia had never given any explanation of her not going to Israel in the summer. It was all lined up and she simply did not arrive. He had heard that one reason was that Eric Miller, who was due to fly her in his private plane, had failed to deliver.

I spent the afternoon working on the conference speech.

HW has given me the task of working on electoral reform and servicing the Labour representatives when the new Speaker's Conference is set up. He knows I am in favour of reform. His own position is quite unclear.

Home at 9 p.m.

## Wednesday 17 September 1975

Morning in the office.

Lunch with Jack Ashley at the Reform. Very moving – I often forget that Jack is in a world of total silence. We conversed for an hour and a half: his lip-reading is now very good. I told him of my desire to do something for the deaf, even after leaving Downing Street. We are going to stay close over the next few months. He sadly supported Alf Morris's view that Barbara Castle believes in nothing except publicity for herself.

George Jones came in this afternoon. We gossiped about LSE and about the organisation of central government.

At 6 o'clock, just as I was leaving to see Harold Evans, Michael Cudlipp telephoned to say that *Private Eye* had a lead page story attacking him and me – saying that I was responsible for appointing this terrible man Cudlipp to the National Enterprise Board. Not important really, but it is depressing. This country is riddled with envy for anybody who has succeeded at anything. This is the psychology of national decline. It is like France between the wars.

*Private Eye* itself does not matter, a bunch of retarded public school failures, feeding off the *Daily Mail*. It is a boil, but the pus comes from the social body of Britain. Envy. Malice. Delight in the pain and failure of others. Resentment at any success or achievement. These are the main components of the British psychology at this moment. That is why no economic plans will make any difference. The state of mind is that of a loser. And it could prove to be the feeding ground of fascism – *Private Eye* is already fascistic, racist and strongly anti-semitic.

I met Harry Evans at the RAC and then went on to the Lansdowne Club for a swim. Never been there before. A pool full of debs and their delights. Went for a drink afterwards. Harold told me that George Weidenfeld had asked him to lunch. Pumped him about me, asking if I was a source of information. Then went on to explain how Marcia was the main influence on the Prime Minister and that she alone was responsible for Kissinger's Middle East peace settlement. Harold recalled that it was very similar to the message sent to him a year ago through Tommy Balogh. It appeared that Weidenfeld had been instructed to convey the message. Juvenile. Home at 8.30.

## Thursday 18 September 1975

The PM still in Romania. I went in as usual at 9.30 and did not bother to look up the article in *Private Eye* attacking me. Worked on the PM's conference speech – I have now done a 10-page piece on the 'Future', the problems facing the government in the years ahead, and am pleased with it. Will put it in to him this weekend.

Went alone to lunch at the Reform. Met our solicitor friend Jack Black there and we ate together. Highly intelligent and delightful man.

Succession of meetings in the afternoon:

2.30 with Tessa Blackstone* to discuss the proposed CPRS study of Britain's diplomatic representation abroad – with a view to cutting it. We will give full support.

3.30 the weekly Deputy Secretaries meeting on future government business. Learn that the error in calculating the National Debt interest by the Treasury is £3.5 billion. Ken Berrill says this is the largest error he has ever known. The Chancellor is pretty angry.

Also the CPRS has been given the task of planning pay strategy over the next five years – the 're-entry' problem. This is part of Hunt's scheme to promote the CPRS, while 'regularising' it and fully integrating it into the Cabinet Office, all part of his empire-building. Ken Berrill goes along with this, he plays the Whitehall game and does not rock the boat. This guarantees CPRS a role, but quite different from Rothschild's approach.

It is now an extra wheel on the Civil Service coach, and not the grit in the oyster which was originally intended.

5.30 saw Kissin. He looks sick. Is also angry because HW has not answered his letters and has refused to see him. Feels he has been paid off with a peerage and dropped, like all the others.

6.30 Lovely Betsy Reisz came in for a drink. [The wife of the film director Karel Reisz and previously, as Betsy Blair, an Oscar-winning Hollywood actress.]

8.30 the PM arrived back from Romania. Apparently they all hated it. Smelled of a police state – they went for a 120-mile motor tour and never saw another vehicle. People looked very miserable.

We discussed the conference speech, the unemployment figures (which are not too bad), and the Treasury errors.

I told Joe about Weidenfeld's talk with Harold Evans. He thought it might be the prelude to another attack from Marcia. 'If you go, I go,' he said.

Home at 10 p.m.


*Friday 19 September 1975*

Took hours to get in to No. 10 by public transport – buses are hopeless now. Arrived just in time to go to the Defence Cabinet committee (OPD). Discussed Chile debt – Jim Callaghan showing impatience with the Left, and with Judith Hart in particular – and new guided missiles order. The latest are mainly from America and France, so they cost hard currency and do not create employment. Typically, announcing the cancellation of the 'Hawkswing', Roy Mason said simply, 'It is not the weapon we want.' I wonder what the military said when persuading the Cabinet to spend hundreds of millions of pounds developing it – 'absolutely essential to our defence needs in the 1970s . . .', etc.

Afterwards HW saw Reg Underhill from party headquarters. I went off to the office and continued to work on HW's conference speech. I have now done 10 pages which I think are good, and Robin Butler says are very good. Also Andrew Graham is putting in four pages on the economic side. It all reads like a serious speech, with a good deal about the future – inner-city problems, industrial democracy, etc. Whether he will use it is another matter.

Went to the Commons for lunch with Joe. He has seen Bill Housden who told him that Marcia had said, 'There is one person I cannot stand in this building – that is Janet Hewlett-Davies.' HW is apparently having Janet to Chequers on Sunday – and taking her to Manchester on Tuesday. Janet has been away on holiday.

There was an enormous row in Marcia's room before lunch. Her tax bill has arrived – with capital gains assessment of around £20,000 on her share of the land deals profits. But her brother Tony Field reinvested the profits in Welsh farmland, which has dropped to one-third the price he paid, and he cannot get development permission. So he has lost the profits, and has no money to pay the gains tax, but cannot even sell at a loss, so he cannot establish a loss (which anyway could not be applied backwards to a previous gain). He is short of cash and cannot pay Marcia's tax bill.

The Welsh land was allegedly sold to Tony at a high price by Lord Arwyn and somebody else who was given a knighthood by HW around 1970. When this was mentioned HW said, 'We know they are a couple of crooks.'

Marcia was screaming at HW that she was being 'persecuted'. She claimed that the Inland Revenue had leaked this information to the press before giving it to her. Also that they were distraining her and she had to pay by Monday. She was insisting that HW do something about it. He had summoned Goodman in. She was proposing to sell her third house in order to pay the tax bill. But it had been on the market for two years without any buyers – she is asking £38,000 for an ordinary semi-detached which is probably now worth no more than £20,000. The agents also say that it is dilapidated. She wants Goodman's property section – headed by a man called Mackenzie – to buy the house off her. Apparently Goodman was very reluctant and HW was being very equivocal (both Joe and Albert were there and heard this and reported to me).

It is odd that Paul Callan, the *Mirror* gossip columnist, knew of this tax assessment before she did. It is all part of the terrible decline in standards whereby officials handling personal and confidential information – in banks, in the Civil Service, in the Inland Revenue – send such information to the press.

After lunch I continued to work on finalising the conference speech. We put this in at 4 o'clock, when HW was due to go to Chequers.

HW went to the Commons to see Gerry Fitt and Merlyn Rees about Northern Ireland – and to instruct Rees to go on holiday. His officials are now concerned that he is showing signs of over-strain. Frank Cooper, the permanent secretary, sent a message to No. 10 requesting this.

HW did not leave at 4 after all. He began to dabble in the strike of blast-furnacemen, which was on the point of agreement, to set up an official inquiry. He telephoned Len Murray, who was at the negotiations, because the union leader Smith was not thought up to it.

Also Joe took him off for an hour to discuss our evidence to the Royal Commission on the Press. The PM keeps rambling on with hearsay evidence of journalists tailing Tony Field, etc., but none of it is evidence. HW has no idea what is real evidence. He is a sucker for rumours and smears and hints. This is why Marcia can so easily mobilise him against somebody. Just a few dark hints of plots. He never presses for the hard facts. And has no idea how damaging it would be for him to submit a list of rumours and half-truths. Fortunately Joe is being firm with him – and has also persuaded him not to give oral evidence to the commission, which would be fatal. Like Captain Queeg (Humphrey Bogart), once his paranoia was exposed his case – which could be quite strong – would collapse. A sharp investigator would destroy him in public on the question of the press.

He left at 6.45 and then I came home. Feeling low. Britain is a miserable sight. A society of failures, full of apathy, and aroused only by envy at the success of others. This is why we will continue to decline. Not because of our economic or industrial problems. They are soluble. But because the psychology of our people is in such an appalling – I fear irretrievable – state. Meanness has replaced generosity. Envy has replaced endeavour. Malice is the most common motivation. The current newspapers are the worst example of that. This is the social personality of a loser. It is time to go and cultivate our gardens, share love with our families, and leave the rest to fester. And if it gets intolerable – because fascism could breed in this unhealthy climate – to emigrate if need be. For the first time in my life I have contemplated – and discussed with Carol – the possibility of going to live in France or America.

### Monday 22 September 1975

HW came in from Chequers direct to a joint meeting of the NEC and the TUC. They discussed unemployment – and the government's proposals to try to create jobs. These are fairly pathetic, but are a gesture before party conference designed to show that we are doing something. Healey especially is worried about his vote for the NEC. [Healey lost his NEC place to Eric Heffer at the following week's party conference.]

I went in early to the office, read my papers and then dealt with HW's draft of his conference speech. He had clearly made considerable use of our briefs, using my piece on the 'themes' underlying the government's legislation, Andrew's piece on the economy, and the peroration which I did jointly with Kay Carmichael.

Ron Spiers of the American embassy came in at 11 o'clock. An excellent man. Makes me feel even more strongly it would be nice to go to the USA.

The PM was back by 12.30. He looked down – hunch-backed and black rings round the eyes. I recognised the signs immediately and slipped out of private office and went out to lunch at the BBC. With Brian Wenham, a nice man, and the editor of *Panorama*. They were intelligent and amusing. Yet the underlying tone of their approach was the same – knocking, cynicism, seeing their job as exposing. No constructive sense of how we can get this country off its back. Perhaps they are right. Perhaps we cannot.

Back at 3 and went to talk to Joe – and then to Albert. The PM is down. Marcia attacked him yesterday at Chequers. Partly over her tax (the PM has intervened somehow to prevent her from being distrained) and partly over the piece in the *Telegraph*, smearing her by implication as an alcoholic, which is certainly untrue and probably libellous. But mainly over Janet – Marcia arrived at Chequers unexpectedly yesterday and found Janet working there. Things are warming up on that front. The PM knows it and looks worried – he retreated to the flat before lunch and sent for Joe to come and see him there. This was so Marcia could not find him in the study. He also left by the front lifts and out through the front door so as not to pass Marcia's room.

Albert tells me that Mary is beginning to complain about Janet.

Cabinet met at 3.30 to discuss the measure to relieve unemployment. I talked to Tony Crosland beforehand. He was contemptuous of the measures – which include proposals to employ youths to clean our ponds (and to paint them, according to Joe). He feels they reflect the total demoralisation and sterility of the Treasury.

Crosland is also very depressed about the press smear campaign against him last week. He said that the abysmal level of media comment and smears made him feel he did not care much if he left politics or if the government went out. 'I don't care either way,' he said. 'I would be just as happy to get out and live a private life.'

The Cabinet went on for two hours – much longer than scheduled. We had a Misc committee meeting at 5 o'clock on a new radical survey of the social services. When we finally met in the Cabinet Room, it was clear that the PM and other ministers were in a hurry to finish. There was little serious discussion. Barbara Castle babbled on, but HW and other ministers rose and left. It was funny but sad.

Had a general chat with HW afterwards. He was hanging around in the hall, ready to go off to Chequers, but waiting for Janet.

Home at 7.30 to listen to, and tape, *Cavalleria Rusticana* and *Pagliacci*. I find music more and more important, as a civilised escape from people. As Patrick Wright said today, 'Man is vile.'

*Tuesday 23 September 1975*

HW away all day today. He is visiting Manchester and Birmingham. Janet has gone with him having stayed at Chequers overnight. Marcia has attacked him viciously over Janet and complained to Mary about her. And over his retirement. He mentioned Christmas again as his proposed departure date and Marcia blew up. She does not want him to go. That would remove her own power. HW appears very worried and frightened. That is why he was hiding upstairs in the flat yesterday. Trying to avoid Marcia. So he has altered his plans and is coming to stay in London tonight and Janet goes home.

I fear that he will change his Christmas retirement plans too. But Joe and I each agree he should go.

I worked in the office in the morning.

Out to lunch with Pat Nairne, who has just been appointed permanent secretary at DHSS. A nice and very able man. He wants a run-down on the ministers and advisers at DHSS. I stress that he must look after Alf Morris and Jack Ashley, and that the PM would be annoyed if their policy areas were neglected. He promised to take Alf out to lunch once he takes over. We agree Barbara Castle is terrible.

Back in the office I worked on a brief on Northern Ireland – the official paper on 'future options' was terrible. Suggesting a handover to the Protestants and then 'distancing' ourselves to wash our hands of the consequences.

Also did a joint brief with Joe on the need for a new law on privacy. Must get that going.

My dear old friend Stella Alexander came in at 6 p.m. and we had a brief chat and drink.

Home at 8, taking HW's latest draft of his conference speech to read for tomorrow's discussion. It still contains large chunks of our draft.

## Wednesday 24 September 1975

My personal depression continues. No longer the excitement as I come through the door of No.10. For all kinds of reasons. Because it is now so clear how little we can achieve. Because the year ahead will be bloody and barren. Because the PM has little more to give. Because I am slowly forced to realise that this nation is in sad decline. Also because I know my job must come to an end soon and, like the last days of a holiday, once that point is reached, one wants it to end now.

I drove in. The PM was seeing Merlyn Rees and an Ulster Unionist politician at 10.15. I had intended to see him beforehand, but private office warned me that he was in a bad mood, depressed and snappy. He had come in and complained that they were not handling Marcia properly. She had been on to him again this morning. I stayed clear.

The Cabinet committee concerned with Northern Ireland (IRN) met to discuss the Irish problem at 10.45. Beforehand I spoke with Roy Jenkins about his proposed Royal Commission on Gambling and pointed out that we must have an urgent interim report on finance for sport. He agreed that this was part of the 'deal' in which we supported his Royal Commission. He seems in good form, very friendly and relaxed.

IRN was a good meeting. The officials presented their paper – recommending that 'withdrawal' and 'integration' be eliminated as options; and that we pursue 'majority rule' (i.e. Protestant rule: Stormont Stage II) and 'distancing' – i.e. washing our hands of the consequences. Frank Cooper, the permanent secretary at the Northern Ireland office, who is first-class, put this mediocre proposal as skilfully as possible.

HW immediately moved in and dominated the meeting throughout. He pushed the 'Dominion status' solution I had put to him in an overnight paper and also exposed a lot of weaknesses in the officials' thinking.

Other ministers joined in the attack. Mason put the case for integration and for total withdrawal. Healey was for repartition and ultimate withdrawal. Jenkins for withdrawal ultimately, though cautiously. So the paper was rejected. No options were excluded. The PM's 'Dominion status' option was included, together with his suggestion that a paper be prepared to cover a sudden total collapse.

Nice to go to a good lively meeting, where the ministers have independent views, where the grey official line is overturned, and where the PM is committed and impressive.

During the meeting John Hunt passed me a note asking to see me next week about his forthcoming visit to New York for the Economic Summit. This is the meeting for which HW originally suggested me. It has now fallen to John Hunt – though he did not press for it, and is understandably nervous about it.

After IRN Janet went upstairs with HW to the study. Two private secretaries leapt out of private office to go upstairs to see the PM, but I stopped them to give her a chance to talk alone. Earlier this morning she told me all that the PM had said to her yesterday and on Monday evening.

He was very depressed and fed up after terrible rows with Marcia on Sunday. She had ranted away at him, telling him he was no good at his job, the civil servants manipulated him, he got everything wrong, if he got anything right it was her idea.

HW said he knows that she is 'clinically' not right. He said that her present bout of instability was as bad as that at the beginning of the year which so got him down.

He said to Janet that Marcia is totally obsessed and unbalanced about me. He then gave an interesting explanation. He said that she helped to introduce me to him, but then found that she could not control me. She hated me for this. She has to control everything and everybody. 'She is a monopolist,' said HW. And she disapproves of anything she does not control or get involved in.

She had denounced him for inviting the Bradford University people to Chequers, saying that Bradford was 'second-rate'. He replied that academic snobbery was the worst kind.

She denounced him about his plans to retire at Christmas. She said that I had leaked this information to other Cabinet ministers – at which he claimed he pointed out that had that been the case it would be published by now.

She complained that he had told Joe. HW said that Joe needed to know because of his future. 'What of my future?' she shouted. HW said to Janet that he thought Marcia's future was OK – 'She has all those nice houses.'

She accused HW of being responsible for her father's death and for the present bad financial state of her brother Tony. HW had telephoned Tony yesterday to offer to help him get a job.

Janet has been very upset. She said Marcia is 'evil' and she finds it unforgivable that Marcia deliberately tries to destroy the morale of the Prime Minister of Britain. She (Janet) is also afraid that Marcia will expose and exaggerate his friendship with Janet out of spite, not caring for the consequences for HW and the Labour government.

Janet went upstairs after IRN to express concern at his depression and see how he was. He said he felt better now. And his talk with Tony had eased some of the pressure.

Incidentally HW told her that after Marcia's children were born, their father Walter Terry was supposed to divorce his wife, marry Marcia for two years, then divorce her and go back to his wife. This was to give Marcia respectability, which HW says she craves. (Hence the peerage?) Terry agreed, but the lawyers vetoed it.

Marcia has also upset Albert by ordering him not to come to the Blackpool party conference till Sunday, and by taking up Alf Richman beforehand instead.

I decided not to attend the Misc Cabinet committee on the grisly story of the Crown Agents. Went to my office. Then before going out to lunch went upstairs to see HW. He was not in the study but in the flat. He looked very jumpy when I arrived, but he chatted on for 20 minutes about the conference speech, the Budget deficit and Ireland.

I went to the City for lunch with Gordon Pepper of Greenwell's, who is an expert on money supply. He predicts a credit explosion and inflationary disaster when the economy next expands. A bit obsessive, but well informed, and when I got back to the office I strengthened a brief Andrew Graham was putting in on the relations between the Treasury and the Bank of England – which are of course inadequate.

Worked in the Unit. Did a final check on the speech. Talked to Kay Carmichael about Scotland. To the journalist John Cole, who had come in to see the PM. John is one of the few remaining decent journalists who actually recognises that there is some minimum standard of factuality and fairness. I interviewed a new member of the Unit, Dick Smethurst of Worcester College, Oxford, who seems very nice and bright and will join us in October.

In the evening there was a reception at No. 10 for American businessmen who invest in Britain. Marcia was in the corner with George Weidenfeld. I chatted to Mrs Elliot Richardson for a while, and Douglas Wass briefly and then went home.

Home is now a greater delight to me than ever. One of the spin-offs of the pressures and horrors of this job is that it has finally made me appreciate the joys of my family. I have never loved Carol more, or wanted more to spend time with the children. Public life has nothing to compare with this. The glamour and the power mean very little in the end. Nothing is lasting. Nothing is genuine. In the end a civilised man must turn to those close to him, who were there years before the glamour, and will be there years after the power has been taken from my fingers. These are the permanent things. Love, affection, companionship. The trust to tell everything, and be told everything. The unquestioning pleasure at just being together. No wheeling and dealing. Just living our lives together. A small flourishing oasis of affection and generosity, shelter from that appalling desert of human meanness and envy beyond. When I am asked, 'What will you do after No. 10?' – this is the answer: 'Try, however fallibly, to live like a decent human being with those I love.'

## Thursday 25 September 1975

Saw HW before Cabinet. He seemed cheerful and relaxed – because he is going away for a week.

He asked me to get unpublished Gallup opinion poll material on his and Thatcher's leadership.

Saw Bill Housden who said Marcia was 'completely round the bend again'. She had attacked Albert for not arranging separate accommodation for her in Blackpool. She wanted a separate house rented for her, and had asked Albert (he told me) to try to persuade Eric Miller to pay for it. Albert had failed to do this, partly because he didn't like approaching Miller, mainly because he knew – as we all knew – that Marcia did not intend to go to Blackpool anyway. She just wanted everybody to go to a lot of trouble for her, and then she would turn it down. Apparently she had shouted at Albert that she would do nothing to get him a job when HW retired – and Albert had left the room and gone upstairs.

I also learned from Albert that the point about her row with HW concerning her brother Tony was that she wanted HW to fix a job for Tony on BNOC, probably on the board. This would have produced the most terrible outcry. Fortunately HW has resisted – so far.

HW left Cabinet early to complete his boxes in the study before leaving for the north. I went up for a talk.

I also saw Joe about the current smear campaign hinting at a relationship between him and Kay Carmichael. Agree we shall thump and flatten the first journalist we discover in this squalid campaign. I look forward to that.

I went to lunch at the Reform, alone, but I arranged to meet Bob Worcester on the way and he gave me the Gallup information. Including the news that the *Sunday Telegraph* is doing a survey this week asking whether HW should retire!

After lunch I chatted with Dick Leonard, the former Labour MP who is now Home Affairs editor of *The Economist*. Have always liked him. Nice to talk about *The Economist* – it is 15 years since I was in the old Ryder Street building with Donald Tyerman,* Will Plowden, St John Stevas,* Alastair Burnet.*

I went to an important Deputy Secretaries' meeting in the afternoon. Discussing the three months' forward look at the government's programme ahead. I made a lot of criticisms. The usual rag-bag of miscellaneous items with no coherence or strategy or sense of a programme. Yet this isn't the civil servants' fault. It is not their job to create a government's strategic programme. This is what the PM and the inner Cabinet should look at.

As usual the economic stuff was thin – with no external financing items at all. The Cabinet committee MES(E) which is supposed to deal with that is a total flop, dealing only with oil consumer-producer items which are as suitable to the Energy committee. The Treasury is keeping all of the external finance items away from the committee and close to its own chest.

Went to a lecture on the American Revolution by Jack Plumb* at the American embassy. Met Robert Tyerman – Donald's son – who wrote the piece attacking me in last Sunday's *Telegraph*. He said he tried not to do it but Kenneth Rose* insisted on having it done. They knew it was a smear, though he had softened the words.

Home 8.45 in pouring rain. Went to our friends and neighbours the Reads for dinner – and inevitably discussed for hours the problem of this country's decline (and the role of the media in it, since Tom works at the BBC).

Returned home at 11.30 p.m. and telephone HW in Blackpool. Told him the opinion poll background figures (27% of Tories oppose Thatcher, while only 12% of Labour people oppose HW).

Then I reported the Gallup intention to publish a poll on whether he should retire. I sensed him stiffen and I could tell he was not too pleased. When I told him they were testing the popularity of Benn, Jenkins and Healey as successors he said, 'What about poor old Callaghan?' He asked me to get as much advance information as I could and to phone him at the weekend

He was in his hotel room with Joe working on the speech.

## Friday 26 September 1975

Worked on papers, clearing my desk before going to Blackpool on Sunday. Joe telephoned. He was still working on the speech. Particularly concerned about the party section. He said Marcia was trying to get the PM to say nothing at all about the left-wing militants scheming to get MPs thrown out of their seats. But he still wanted to. I put in a strong word of support and insisted he must do so. It would look like terrible cowardice if he did not.

Went out for a nice lunch with Michael Cudlipp at Wheeler's. He was very interesting – and admiring about Merlyn Rees. Says he has only taken two small holidays in the past 18 months and has done a first-class job. Never neglects his constituency or Parliament. But is exhausted now. When he moves (in the New Year) Michael thinks he would make a good leader of the House. I think social security.

Came home early to collect the children from school and prepare for Blackpool.

Incidentally Marcia is still putting on pressure to find her a £200 a week house to rent in Blackpool. Alf Richman is up there looking for one, but not too hard I trust. We can usually rely on him to fail.

## Sunday 28 September 1975

Went to Euston with Carol and the children to catch the 9.15 a.m. to Blackpool for the party conference. The children love the station and the trains. Makes me feel sorry to leave them. It feels less and less worthwhile to be away from the family.

I sat with Bob Worcester on the train and we talked and read the newspapers. A beautiful morning. The usual curious sensations as we passed through south Northamptonshire – Ashton and Roade, past the fields I knew as a child, Blisworth and the canal in which I swam and fished. I have no great sense of nostalgia – those were bitter and harsh days of poverty, discomfort and little human affection. Yet I had dreams for the future which were sustaining. And assumptions about other people, their decency and humanity, which made the future road look encouraging. I knew nothing, for many years, of the malice, the envy, the pettiness which riddles the metropolitan middle class. I thought they were human beings like the farm labourers and factory workers and schoolteachers of south Northants. The only vermin I had met had four legs and lived in hay stacks (and my bedroom!).

The train ran very late. Bob Worcester and I had a tasteless British Railways lunch which cost £4. We reached Preston an hour late and I left the train to take a car – the office had assumed we would be late and miss our connection at Preston and so had provided one. That is pessimistic genius. Albert came in the car with me.

We reached the Imperial Hotel at around 3 o'clock. The lobby was already filling with the dross of Labour Party conferences – the Transport House hacks, gossip journalists, pathetic hangers-on like John Allen. I went upstairs to our suite. The PM was in the NEC meeting. He had a large corner suite, with a bedroom leading off for Mary and himself. Since we worked in the lounge until the early hours of most mornings it left her with virtually no privacy.

My room was small and poky, down a side corridor, next door to Joe's. There were lots of Special Branch detectives around, more than I recall seeing on any previous occasion.

Marcia was still not here. Joe and Alf Richman were sent to inspect a flat for her. It cost £100 a week. Joe came back and said it was pretty dreadful but HW, who came out of the NEC to deal with it, told them to book it. He said, 'We will call her bluff.' Adding, 'But £100 is a lot of money if she doesn't use it. Still we have had all of this before.'

We all knew that she would not come. Albert telephoned her with details but she refused to say if she was coming or not. 'I would not pass a message through you,' she said to him. Albert is still under attack and she is demanding his removal. HW is going to give way and probably will give Albert a peerage as compensation. Joe and I support this move, but are still insistent that we won't take peerages for ourselves from HW.

In the evening HW went to a series of parties and meetings. This is the usual conference round of receptions and speeches. I went to the first one, given by the International Committee of Transport House. But one speech from Ian Mikardo and the sight of all the usual hangers-on was too much for me so I retired and did not go to any more.

As I left the *Private Eye* lice were crawling around in the hotel foyer, already looking bleary with drink. I went upstairs to work on the speech.

We had dinner in the Imperial Dining Room, poor food, but delightful north-country waitresses, full of smiles and chatter. We had three tables – one for the PM, Mary and his sister Marjorie (who is a delight, enormous, jolly former primary school teacher: one can see all the nice, kind, funny side of Harold in her).

I sat with Joe and Albert and Ken Stowe at another table and the girls were at a third.

After supper Joe and I worked further on the speech, combining our corrections into one basic copy.

Bill Housden phoned Marcia while I was in the room. She did not indicate if she was coming. She was mainly interested in whether Eric Miller had been present at last night's charity concert which HW had attended.

Apparently the office had been instructed to buy first-class return train tickets for Marcia and her sister, although they clearly had no intention of coming.

HW returned after 11 o'clock. He was very tired and seemed a bit the worse for wear. He slumped in the chair and peered out from under hooded eyelids in the way he sometimes did in the election campaigns. His voice was slurred. At one point he mistook Albert for Joe. The brandy bottle was very low.

We went through the speech corrections. He did not focus very well, but in the end accepted all the corrections.

We discussed Reg Prentice and his supporters, who are behaving in a very silly way. But we agree, and I argued strongly, that the PM must not soften his attacks on the militant Left. Marcia has been pressing him not to say anything on this, to duck it, but we all agree he must attack. Joe is afraid it will get a bad reception. I am not so sure. HW is very good – he says that it is 'like shooting moose . . . you must not wing them, you have to shoot straight between the eyes'.

Shirley Williams and Roy Jenkins had both told HW that they were irritated with Prentice's wild behaviour.

I left Joe with HW at 12.45 a.m. to go to bed. HW and Joe discussed Janet and Joe told him that if anybody attacked Janet for their friendship – and he said he meant Marcia – he would defend Janet to the full. This was his way of warning Marcia off.

HW, on another subject, told Joe that he had considered the political consequences of all his actions 'from the day he was born'.

## Monday 29 September 1975

Got up at 7.15 and went for a marvellous four-mile run, right out of Blackpool towards Fleetwood, along the path beside the sea, and back along the cliff-top path. A grey morning, but it felt lovely tasting the fresh sea air and feeling my legs wake up and stretch.

I was back in the hotel before 8 – seeing the journalist Anthony Howard as I slipped upstairs to have a bath and breakfast. We gathered in HW's room before 9. Nobody knows if Marcia will arrive, but I am confident she won't – the demonstration of interest is what she wants: phone calls, train tickets bought, the special flat booked.

The team went off to the conference in the Winter Gardens at 9.15, in two black Rovers, with a police escort. I preferred to walk with HW's sister Marjorie, who is well over seventy, but very alert and funny. We agreed together that if there were any demonstrators, she would hit them and I would catch them. 'We will need a sweeper-up,' she said.

After the opening procedures on the platform the morning session was fairly tedious. I went around the hall chatting to various old friends (Joe was back at the hotel supervising the corrected draft of tomorrow's speech). Getting bored, I went out on to the sea-front and then took a tram to Fleetwood. It took over half an hour but I enjoyed it. Totally anonymous on top of an old tram. No famous people. Just rocking along the sea-front, through some dreary suburbs, and then to the port, which is quite nice on a cold blowy day like this, with views right across the bay to the Lake District mountains. Wish the children were here.

Back on the tram. The party had returned by the time I got back to the Imperial at 12.40.

At lunch it was noticeable that the Left is split up. In the old days they all sat at one table. Now they are split up around the room. Michael Foot is very separate – the Tribune Group have dropped him from their recommended slate (in favour of Dennis Skinner!).

HW is clearly in a better mood. He has got Marcia off his back and the speech is well advanced.

The afternoon session went quite well. Everyone agrees that the atmosphere is congenial and constructive.

We went back to the hotel and Joe and I had a session with HW on the speech. We went through it and finished all but the last six pages (with the peroration still to come). After dinner he decided to finish it off before going to the agents' dance. So we did it, including the peroration.

HW kept saying how remarkable it was that we had finished the speech so quickly and with such little fuss. This was probably the nearest he dare get to an implied criticism of Marcia. In 'the old days' apparently he was often working on it till 5 a.m. Joe says in those days it was total chaos, with bits of paper all over the floor, tears and shouting and hysteria. Now all is relaxed. HW went out to several parties and returned at midnight, somewhat sloshed but in a very pleasant way, joking and praising and chatting, and a great pleasure to be with.

He went to bed at 1 a.m.

I went downstairs and talked with Jock Stallard, my local MP. I voted against him at the original selection conference in my constituency party, but now consider him a first-class constituency member, charming, gentle and completely genuine.

Went to bed at 3 a.m. The foyer still had people sitting around drinking. I drank nothing all evening because I felt a cold coming on.

## Tuesday 30 September 1975

Up at 7.30 but did not go for a run – my head was heavy and my eyes streaming with a cold.

We went off to the Winter Gardens shortly after 9 – HW in the car, but Joe and I walked to get some fresh air. We arrived just in time to hear the NEC election results – Healey off and replaced by Heffer. Jack Ashley did very well to come runner-up. With a little luck he might replace Barbara Castle, his Secretary of State, next time round. Tony Crosland did badly, and told me later that he probably won't stand next time – which will help both Healey and Ashley.

HW stood up to speak around 10 o'clock, a cold and early time for a long speech. I walked around the hall to view reactions.

Incidentally one journalist told me that the latest rumour among the journalists here in Blackpool is that I have become Marcia's lover! They were discussing this in the foyer of the Imperial last night. This is just one more example of how ignorant and uninformed the press are – but how willing to spread any malicious gossip. Why not the Archbishop of Canterbury? He speaks to her virtually as often as I do, and probably has warmer feelings.

Harold's speech was very long and not well delivered. He read it, page after page, and they took it, quietly and seriously. The economic part – which we had written in the Unit – was blunt and uncompromising: no reflation without defeating inflation.

Then he came to the final bit on the party extremists and the result was electric. The audience came alive – and was soon cheering him. At the end he got a long standing ovation.

We gathered in his room behind the platform afterwards and he was delighted. He said he never expected it to be so well received.

I saw Shirley Williams who praised its courage, and Tony Crosland who said it was marvellous. At lunch I talked to Roy Jenkins, who was at the next table. He was less ecstatic, but thought it a good speech. It has obviously put the moderates in very good heart.

But I came back from the Winter Gardens on the special bus to the Imperial, and two left-wing MPs, Frank Allaun and Renée Short,[*] sat opposite complaining and planning to issue a statement denouncing Harold. Obviously his arrows had gone home.

I ate lunch quickly. HW was lunching with Larry Lamb of the *Sun*, and with Joe, in the next dining-room. (John Stonehouse sat at a nearby table.)

[On 13 October 1975 Magistrates committal proceedings were begun against Stonehouse, Labour MP for Walsall North, on charges of forgery, fraud and theft.]

I was feeling rotten with my cold and went to lie down in my room. I finally decided to go home to London. The speech was over. I missed the family. All that remained was the round of parties and gossip which I hate.

As I was preparing to go Joe and Geoffrey Goodman came up to me. They had been discussing with HW the problems of the counter-inflation publicity unit (the Civil Service machine is obstructing them and the official information services are out to destroy them). HW had apparently said that I 'had the best intelligence network in Whitehall' and suggested that I helped them to get round the officials direct to ministers.

I took the train at 5.15 and spent an hour waiting on Preston station for a connection. Raining, getting dark. Dreary, but at least going home. Travelled with the editor of BBC *Panorama*. Desultory conversation about the media – but at least a serious man.

Home to bed at 10 o'clock. The girls came in for a cuddle. Carol brought a hot lemon drink. Marvellous to be among human beings again.

# CHAPTER 20

## Autumn Miscellany – Crossman Diaries, Ireland, Chrysler, Industrial Strategy and the Prime Minister Stays On
## October–November 1975

### Wednesday 1 October 1975

Stayed home in bed in the morning feeling lousy.

In the afternoon talked on the phone to Harry Evans. He said he had heard from his journalists in Blackpool that John Allen was spreading malicious lies about me – including that I am Marcia's lover and that I leak official secrets.

I am uncertain whether to take legal action or to go to Blackpool and give him a good hiding. Talk to Joe, who is going to mention it to the PM.

The other news is better. The Crossman Diaries judgement has gone in favour of the *Sunday Times*, Jonathan Cape the publishers and the executors, and against the Cabinet Office led by John Hunt. Marvellous. Joe says that HW doesn't agree with the judgement – but that is not the point. The government should never have got involved in this. Joe and I advised against and the PM ignored it, preferring to go along with Hunt. I never dreamed that one day I would be grateful to a judge.

Ironically, I had breakfast with the Attorney-General Sam Silkin at the Imperial yesterday. He was totally confident that the case would go his way.

### Friday 3 October 1975

I spent Thursday at home, still suffering from a heavy cold, and depressed by the Blackpool experience. Although HW had been excellent in every way, the rest of the circus seemed appalling to me. An atmosphere of envy, hate and pettiness which cannot produce good government or a decent society. Just a morbid entertainment for the media.

Friday morning went into the office. First to see John Hunt. He was offering to include me in a new committee on Northern Ireland. Interestingly they are taking the issue out of the direct control of the

Northern Ireland Office, who have failed, and have too many commitments which prevent them from seeing the long-term future. This is no criticism of Frank Cooper, the permanent secretary, who is absolutely first-class. But they are locked in to the present vicious circle. So it needs a new institutional base. Inevitably John Hunt's solution is his own Cabinet Office. Everything is drawn into the Cabinet Office – counter-inflation, the next phase of wage policy, devolution, now Northern Ireland. Soon the 500 civil servants already there will not be enough. But it is still right to take it out of the Northern Ireland Office. He is offering me a part because he knows that I am interested and the PM is interested, so it is best to involve us from the beginning. The Foreign Office is sadly staying as far out of it as it can – this is because Jim Callaghan does not want to get mixed up in the Irish bog. In fact of course the FO is essential because the Republic of Ireland is essential to any solution. Also the FO does have some interesting ideas about a future Dominion status for Ulster, and a joint Anglo-Irish guarantee.

We also discussed Hunt's coming visit to New York for the Economic Summit. He showed me his brief. The objectives seemed reasonably cautious. He will find it testing, but he has admitted that and he did not press to go. Today the Minimum Lending Rate was raised from 11% to 12%. Looks black.

We also discussed the Crossman decision. He told me that all their messages were that the decision would go to the government. When they got to the court, Tony Hetherington of the Attorney's office said that he had information that the Lord Chief Justice would find for the Attorney on every point. This fits in with the confidence exuded by Silkin when he had breakfast with me on Tuesday. It was clearly a great shock when it went the wrong way. Hunt actually went to the court to hear the decision, assuming victory, which led to much comment. His predecessor Burke Trend would never have done that. Joe told me on the phone that the Cabinet Office reported John as being 'in a right old paddy' afterwards. To me this morning Hunt put all the blame on the Attorney. He claimed that he personally was always against going to court anyway and was now definitely against an appeal. He was certainly excluded by the Attorney from some of the discussions. The Law Office took the initiative. The question is, would the Law Office officials have gone ahead contrary to the Cabinet Office wishes and without consulting? I wonder. Hunt made a sarcastic reference to 'your friends on the *Sunday Times*'. He also said that Lord Justice Denning was itching to handle any appeal, and had already indicated the dates when he is available. Hunt thought Denning might enjoy overthrowing Widgery. But in general Hunt had not enjoyed his experience with the law – the fact that Lord Chief Justices prove unpredictable and unfixable (so unlike a good permanent secretary) had clearly shaken him.

He expressed grave concern about the publication of the second volume of Crossman, not because of the references to civil servants, but because of the embarrassments to politicians in the 'In Place of Strife' section. He may have been looking round for a further weapon to take up the fight for secrecy. But I sensed less enthusiasm than before. The chromium polish finish of the mandarin was a little scratched. But only temporarily. He will recover. Like all the best mandarins – and he is very good – he does not get sufficiently involved in any issue, does not care enough to get really hurt when they go wrong. The Crossman Diaries involved him more than most things – was more important than, say, Ireland, homelessness, etc. – because it concerned the power of the bureaucracy, and the secrecy which is essential to the successful wielding of that power. It exposes the sham of ministerial responsibility and so threatens the machine. But he knows that the mandarins will survive, finding new cloaks for their daggers, so by next Friday all will be forgotten.

On Ireland he told me that the former Labour minister and now EEC Commissioner George Thomson is the machine's candidate to be the next Secretary of State/Vice-Consul. I wonder why. I like George (though HW doesn't). But he is a Scot, which will personify the Presbyterian dominance. I wonder if they want him out of Brussels to make way for a friend?

After an interesting hour with Hunt, whom I love to watch and actually, despite my occasional criticising, do admire in action, I went back to the Unit and we discussed economic policy. David Piachaud is especially troubled that the Cabinet is going to swallow the Treasury forecasts – 1½ million unemployed through until 1977 – without ever being told that figure. This is true. The Cabinet rarely discusses the government's 'economic policy' as such. It is told the Budget, hours in advance, with little chance to discuss and without being told the figures on which the Chancellor bases his decisions. It discusses 'counter-inflation' policy – i.e. the level of wage settlements – but never the whole package. It discusses particular public expenditure cuts – but never the total unemployment consequences. Or whether there are alternative ways of reaching an agreed objective. Or whether that objective – e.g. a better balance of trade or a lower public sector deficit – is as important as some of the remedies.

I will talk to HW about this. We must try to collectivise economic discussion. If it is all left to the Treasury the whole thing will fall apart.

Went for lunch with my publisher friend Graham Greene. He was very cheerful about the Crossman decision and hopes to publish volume 1 before Christmas if there is no appeal.

He told me that George Weidenfeld had telephoned the President of the Publishers Association to warn him not to try to work through me – 'a course of disaster' he told him. This is my present publisher, who has also just written to me saying how he would like to have lunch with me since it is too long since we met.

Met the journalist Tina Brown in Charlotte Street as Graham and I came out of Bertorelli's. A very impressive girl. She reported to me more of what she had personally heard John Allen telling the *Private Eye* gang at Blackpool, inciting them to print smears about me. She said it was so poisonous that she would be willing to testify in court.

Went home to meet the children from school. Carol is away at an educational conference in Cardiff. So I cooked them supper and put them to bed. Will do the same tomorrow. Very pleasant. Mixing with sane, rational, affectionate, unwarped human beings. How can I keep them that way? How can we keep them like the decent, ordinary people I grew up with in Northamptonshire? Prevent them from slipping into the kind of human sewers flowing around the conference hall and the Imperial Hotel at Blackpool? This is the biggest problem for middle-class parents today. How to save their middle-class children from growing up like some other middle-class metropolitan professionals. Malicious and envious. That is worth working for. At the moment they are lovely.

## Sunday 5 October 1975

Joe told me that David Frost had telephoned him, puzzled about why the PM was refusing to come to dinner with him, Jim Slater and Jimmy Goldsmith. He said that Marcia had come to dinner with them, loved it, and stated quite firmly that the PM would want to have dinner with them. Joe said the reason was that these right-wing financiers were not the kind of people a Labour PM should dine with.

Also a flap about an article in the *Sunday Telegraph* claiming that the PM kept stocks of Gannex raincoats at No. 10 which he gave away as presents to distinguished visitors. Joe Kagan, the manufacturer of Gannex, had telephoned Joe to complain. Kagan said he had been trying to get hold of Marcia for three days but she never answered the phone. The allegations were made by a man named Caunt, who worked for the PLP, and had been in HW's political office during the 1970 election. Marcia had upset him and he was out to get her (he was also a friend of George Wigg). HW was apparently afraid that Caunt kept a diary and might spill the beans on events in No. 10. For instance he claimed that Kagan had made expensive gifts to Marcia before his knighthood.

[Caunt did keep a diary, a copy of which was later given to the author.

It gave the clear impression that life in Harold Wilson's entourage was as bizarre in those earlier days as it was now.]

The *Sunday Telegraph* Gannex story is nonsense in so far as it refers to No. 10 now in 1975. But it illustrates (a) how HW is vulnerable to alleged scandal and (b) that the press is ready to start another campaign. This story is nonsense, and was officially denied. But they still ran it on half of the front page.

It is even clearer that I must accept nothing from HW – peerage, nothing. I must go out clean.

When will the storm break?

## Monday 6 October 1975

Still feeling a bit wobbly. Went in at 9.30 and cleared the papers from my desk. Talked with David Piachaud about his excellent paper on the pros and cons of selling council houses to their tenants – and later with Richard Graham about his paper on transport policy. Andrew Graham was not here – today he returns to work half-time at Balliol. We shall miss him. He has been a tremendous engine to the Unit and I have relied on him enormously.

Saw the PM when he came in at 10.45 but then he went straight off to talk to the Italian Ambassador and then he stayed upstairs for meetings with Frank Schon and with the national agent from Transport House.

I spent a lot of time in private office catching up on the latest news. There is a very happy atmosphere among us all. Relations between the Civil Service private secretaries, the press office and ourselves in the Unit are excellent. It is a very cheerful 'house' with the right balance of serious work and relaxed fun.

The day had, however, started badly with a piece in the *Daily Express* saying that I had replaced Marcia as chief adviser to Harold. Everybody pulled my leg, but we knew it meant fresh trouble and prepared to issue tin helmets. She will get revenge for that.

Weidenfeld is advertising her book about Downing Street on the buses, with a picture of her face on the front of every No. 11 bus.

Joe and I went to lunch at the Commons. Soya, sausages and onions. Grim but cheap.

Back to a meeting of MES (Economic Strategy) on industrial strategy. Healey and Varley had put in a paper, mainly drafted by Department of Industry officials, which I thought was terrible. It said a future strategy should be based on identifying those industries which were growing and those which were declining, putting money into the former and not into the latter. This seems incredibly crude. How can we pick industrial winners?

All the other ministers attacked it – Lever, Foot, Short, Jenkins. Jenkins had a sharp clash with Healey, who has an irritating habit of constantly interrupting people and giving them lectures on their ignorance. Jenkins finally lost his temper. He told Healey to stop lecturing him. He said he wished he was himself as sure of anything as Healey seemed to be of everything. That they were not all as ignorant as Healey implied – they were simply not convinced that the few facts which Denis and they knew about this were sufficient to form a dogmatic opinion. Healey looked very flattened. HW sat there grinning. Though this is something he cannot do – the elegant superior rebuke. He envies Jenkins that capacity.

By the end of the discussion the paper was in shreds and tatters and it was agreed not to publish it immediately as originally intended. Healey and Varley agreed to go and think about it again. Which means that we still don't have an industrial strategy. Healey and Varley were right at least in pointing to the need to have one.

Before the meeting I had a chat with Michael Foot about the need to get the Treasury to reveal its unemployment figures – which I know are planned to be 1.4 million through the end of 1976 into the middle of 1977, and then only a small drop to 1.3 million at the end of 1977. I did reveal this to Foot. As usual he just nodded, combed his fingers through his hair, and edged away looking a bit startled. He did not seem to take it on board. But at the start of the meeting he interrupted the PM and said he wanted unemployment firmly on the agenda. The PM looked worried and reassured Foot that he had just been looking at the Cabinet's 'forward look programme' and it included a Cabinet on unemployment in the near future. The PM then immediately passed a note to the private secretaries telling them to put unemployment on the Cabinet agenda. Within seconds a copy of the forward look arrived on the table in front of us and the private secretary was writing instructions on it to include unemployment. Foot had no idea how effective his intervention had been.

After the meeting I had a long chat with Roy Jenkins who seemed in good form. I mentioned privacy to him, that we must tighten the law there in return for relaxation on the Official Secrets Act. He was sympathetic. I agreed to talk to Anthony Lester at greater length when I see him tomorrow. Roy also told me that he has in mind to make Victor Rothschild chairman of the Royal Commission on Gambling. This seems a marvellous idea. Victor would love the intrigues and penumbra of shady aristocracy. He could also do the mathematics which it would require.

Incidentally the PM has supported the joint minute which Joe and I put in on privacy – despite a minute from Hunt opposing it. So we may get some action there, providing we can overcome any stonewalling in the Cabinet Office.

The PM and Joe went to the Russian embassy to see a film of his Soviet visit. I went to my office and had further discussions on housing and transport policy.

My throat was beginning to feel very sore so I came home shortly after 8 p.m.

Graham Greene came round to dinner and was delightful as ever. He is worried about the possibility of an appeal against the Widgery decision on Crossman. He dare not start printing until he knows. I am fairly certain they won't appeal but I dare not give him even a hint.

Today I saw papers from the head of the Civil Service, Douglas Allen, and from Pat Benner in the Cabinet Office saying that they think it is unwise to appeal against the Crossman judgement. Benner admits that when one comes to examine the book closely it is hard to see what exactly offends – which is precisely what Judge Widgery says. Allen put a different argument – that in the present climate of hostility to the Civil Service it would be foolish to launch an appeal to win special protection for civil servants. So the machine – as Hunt implied to me last Friday – is definitely against an appeal. It is up to the Attorney now.

What struck me was how sensible and well argued were the Benner and Allen papers. Relaxed and cool. I talked to Ken Stowe in private office and said what a pity that the machine was not as balanced earlier, when a similar approach would have led them to conclude not to go to court. Ken agreed – but added that John Hunt had always been under the impression that he was doing what Wilson really wanted: that the PM had left him in no doubt that he wanted to suppress the diaries. Ken had formed the same impression. And he was there when the PM saw the Attorney, and felt that, in a careful way, he was giving Silkin the same impression.

This is curious. I don't disbelieve it. Hunt gave me the impression that he was genuinely doing what the PM wanted. Stowe said that though Hunt was for taking them to court early on, in the end he wanted a civilised agreement, to allow publication but within agreed parameters. But he thought the PM wanted suppression – while keeping his own head below the parapet. In fact Wilson and Hunt were both playing the same game, of trying to leave the impression that the other one was the main driving force.

Wilson as usual won. Hunt got the worst of every world. Nobody ever believed that he was willing [as he apparently was] in the end to accept publication – because he was so strongly against in the beginning and because he played the heavy mandarin throughout the negotiation. His own evidence in court was full of first person singulars. Graham Greene told me that Patrick Gordon Walker had originally submitted a statement saying that it was intolerable that any civil servant should say 'I' so often, and especially 'I could not allow' so often, with no mention of 'advise'. They were unfair to Hunt in the end, not realising that he had been carrying out what he believed were the Prime Minister's instructions and that he had become more flexible – certainly more so than the Attorney. But they were not wholly wrong. Hunt, as Cabinet Secretary, does represent what frightens so many people – the faceless power of the bureaucracy, overpaid and unaccountable. The sad thing is that HW will do nothing to curb this power.

– There is great criticism of the appointment of Sir Ronald Edwards to be the new boss of British Leyland. He is 65, deaf, and a right-wing union-basher. This follows the appointments of Kearton aged 67 at BNOC, and McFadzean (who is good) aged 60 at British Airways. I am going to talk to HW about this. We cannot run our very newest industries with old-age pensioners. Ryder is behind this. He is generally felt to be not a success, but HW still swears by him. It is typical of HW to try to deal with a problem by appointing an ageing whiz-kid and then pushing the whole problem over to him.

In fact they had terrible problems getting somebody to take on British Leyland. Lots of people turned it down. Why should they have the problems? Why should they take all the shit from the press, from TV, from all the carping critics? So lots of people just preferred to tend their own private gardens. I completely sympathise.

### Tuesday and Wednesday 7 and 8 October 1975

Tuesday and Wednesday and I was ill in bed again, this time with laryngitis. Lost my voice totally. The doctor came and said I must stay in bed till the weekend. But I became terribly bored. Read two very good volumes of Anthony Powell.

### Thursday 9 October 1975

Still feeling weak and my voice very croaky but am so bored I decide to go in to work – especially as I have some interesting appointments.

Went direct to the Bank of England for lunch with the Governor. A very ceremonial place. I was passed from flunkey to flunkey as I walked around the corridors and up the lift to the Governor's waiting-room. Gordon Richardson collected me and took me into the dining-room. Sidney Greene,* Hector Laing* and Lord Weir* were there already. Others came to join us – Ford the home controller, Kit McMahon* the overseas manager and one or two others.

In conversation I plunged straight in and pressed them on how they liaised with the Treasury and influenced the government. I asked them if nationalisation of the Bank in 1946 had made any difference – it clearly hadn't. We had some sharp exchanges. I thought McMahon was the best of them. They clearly treated Sid Greene as a tame poodle.

After lunch the Governor came down with me to the internal car park and we talked for 20 minutes. He was clearly worried about Healey's failure to get his way in the Cabinet. We discussed possible remedies. And agreed to establish a closer relationship.

Back at No. 10 I went up to see the PM in the study. He was particularly interested in my reports of the allegations of John Allen's *Private Eye* smear campaign against me. He said that Allen is sad and they only kept him employed in No. 10 to prevent him leaking stories if they kicked him out. He was given no serious work to do.

I also warned him not to get too optimistic about unemployment. On Monday Healey had talked of a 'dramatic fall' in unemployment in late 1976–77. But the Treasury's own forecasts show no fall till 1978. HW is still hopeful that it may have about peaked.

He went for a discussion with Karamanlis, the Greek PM, who is here on a visit.

I had tea with Alf Morris and Roger Sydenham from the Royal National Institute for the Deaf. He was a nice man and we discussed ways of promoting greater social concern for the deaf. It is astonishing that there is so little provision for 2 million people disabled in this terrible way.

Went to the Cabinet Office weekly meeting of Deputy Secretaries to consider next week's business. There was some irritation that unemployment had been put on the agenda. As a result the discussion of public expenditure was delayed for a week – because they did not want the papers relating to the two subjects to be with ministers at the same time! Hunt said, 'We must get unemployment out of the way before they think about public expenditure.' The reason was clear. The Treasury's proposed cuts in public expenditure will increase unemployment (though their unemployment consequences are never mentioned in the Treasury papers). So they want to get all discussion of unemployment out of the way before people know about the expenditure cuts.

John Pike, the financial secretary at the LSE, came in at 6.30 for a drink. He is quite the best administrator and organiser at the school. Discussed my future. He warned me that he thinks Dahrendorf's idea for a 'Brookings Institute' will not get off the ground very fast because the academics object to anything that deals with the serious problems in the real world. So he as good as said no need to hurry back.

Carol came in at 8 p.m. and I changed for the Karamanlis dinner. Rather subdued and stuffy. The guests were old and there was no reception. HW introduced me to Karamanlis afterwards and said that the Greeks should send somebody to study our system of special advisers.

Karamanlis seems a withdrawn figure, preoccupied and not very interested in the occasion. He is reputed to be interested in nothing but politics. However, some of the Greek women – and especially the Ambassador's wife – were very haughtily beautiful.

Home at 11.30, still with a sniffly nose and a croaky voice.

### Friday 10 October 1975

I drove in for a change. Arrived too late for the weekly diary meeting. Was greeted by the press office with bad news – the *Guardian* had a big front-page feature saying that Marcia is going to be Minister of the Arts – and that I have replaced her as the chief adviser in No.10. We all reached for our tin helmets and waited for battle to commence.

One of the private secretaries told me that she had telephoned HW in the middle of his talk with the Foreign Secretary this morning and was audibly shouting at him.

The PM sent for Joe immediately Callaghan left – I steered clear of any meeting. Joe told me that the PM was reacting well. Denying the story but not very worried about Marcia. Not being distracted or attacking others of us as a way of buying her off. He thinks that the story is either a pre-emptive strike by Hugh Jenkins to prevent HW sacking him as Arts Minister, or a plant by somebody like John Allen to try to create trouble. Anyway I could do without it. I prefer the reality of influence, and am quite happy to let Marcia enjoy the public glory. Once people start saying in public that I have replaced her, then HW will be forced to redress the balance.

Bill Housden reported that after dinner last night HW said 'only two more black-tie dinners' – implying that he is going at Christmas. Perhaps. But Bill thinks this is said to him with the intention that he should pass it on to Marcia and frighten her.

Worked much of the day in the Unit with David Piachaud and Gavyn Davies on our brief on selling council houses. We are still having difficulty in coming up with a scheme which will produce large sales of council houses and not look like the Tory scheme. But it will be worth it if we can.

Joe and I went for lunch at the Commons. There was a long queue for the public cafeteria so Neville Sandelson took us into the members' café. He sat next to Marcia at the Karamanlis dinner last night and expressed astonishment at how right-wing her views are – strongly in favour of private medicine and private education.

HW went off to Merseyside after lunch. We continued to work on housing in the Unit – with Joe joining in with many suggestions. I had hoped to get home early but did not get away till 7.30 p.m. when we put in our brief.

## Saturday 11 October 1975

The *Guardian* published today a letter from Marcia complaining about their story. Very curious letter, explaining where she worked and how important she was – and pointing out that I was only a civil servant having nothing to do with politics. It reeked of insecurity and hostility. Is bound to lead to stories about a 'rift' in No.10.

Typically the journalist had made no attempt to check the story with us.

## Monday 13 October 1975

Went first to the bank and then to LSE to sort out my pension situation. Reached No.10 at about 11 a.m. The PM was seeing Lord Goodman – about the question of the ownership of the *Observer*. (They want to sell it to the International Publishing Corporation who own the *Mirror*.)

I went through my papers. Talked to Joe. The PM has hinted again that he may retire at Christmas. He told Janet that was his intention 'at the moment'. He also said to Joe that he did not want to publish his Press Commission evidence 'till the New Year – for personal reasons'. But we must wait to see what happens when Marcia has put pressure on him. She, incidentally, told HW that she believed that I had planted the piece in the *Guardian* about her and the Arts. The PM told Janet he did not believe it.

I went out to lunch with Robert Armstrong at the Athenaeum. Pleasant as always. I still like him enormously. We discussed the triumvirate at the top of the Civil Service. Douglas Allen, head of the Civil Service, very able but with little power or influence, clearly bored and under-occupied. Suffering because William Armstrong, his predecessor, had interfered too much in politics, and when HW came in March 1974 he had said that he refused to have much to do with W. Armstrong (then still head of the Civil Service) and would instead operate through the Secretary to the Cabinet. This had made Hunt and killed Armstrong and his successor Allen. Wass at the Treasury is the third in the triumvirate. An old colleague of Hunt's, he does not trust him, and tried to freeze him out of economic thinking from the beginning – keeping him off the steering committee on economic policy for instance. So those two have been in jealous conflict – and Hunt has had his occasional revenge. This is why Hunt wanted to take counter-inflation away from the Treasury and keep it under the Cabinet Office –

and why he wanted us under his umbrella. So it is not working too well at the moment. Apparently 10 years ago Rowan at the Treasury and Trend at the Cabinet Office made a concordat, not to compete but to share, and this benefited them both. Hunt and Wass are running it differently, cutting one another's throats, to their mutual disadvantage.

Robert said people are getting worried about Hunt's empire-building. – definitely the Treasury view.

The PM had been to lunch with ICI and went direct from them to the Commons for the first day of the 'spill-over session'.

I went over there for the 4 o'clock Cabinet committee on the Franks Report on Official Secrets. I saw HW for a few moments beforehand. He complained that his Cabinet Office brief was incomprehensible. I warned him that the Lord Chancellor's Office would be sticky. And pointed out that privacy was civil law, under the Lord Chancellor, and could not be easily attached to the Official Secrets Act. He said he was now thinking of a code of conduct rather than a Privacy Act.

Jenkins opened the discussion with arguments for liberalising official secrets even more than Franks recommended. He wanted legislation on this over the next session.

Callaghan interrupted him to disagree, saying that the conduct of foreign affairs required secrecy. The PM indicated some agreement on this. Then a division bell interrupted us.

While the other ministers were away voting I spoke to Elwyn Jones. I said I had heard that his department was proving sticky on privacy and hoped that was not true. He beamed as usual and asked what the PM thought. I said the PM wanted something doing on privacy. Elwyn then said that he was not at all opposed to doing something on privacy and showed me his departmental papers. But he added he was totally opposed to any liberalisation on the Official Secrets Act.

This emerged when he spoke to the committee on Official Secrets, listing all the people who had been jailed under it (no politicians though, as Jenkins pointed out!). Elwyn could see no reason to ease the Official Secrets Act in any area. The Attorney broadly supported this, though he was prepared to go along with some of the Franks reforms. Healey also took this view.

HW then left to go back to No. 10 to meet Governor Wallace of Alabama. I travelled in the car with him. He was chuckling away at the opposition to Jenkins and seemed delighted there would be no progress on Official Secrets.

I decided not to go in to Wallace. He seemed very tiny in his chair. He had a doctor with him in case he was ill – apparently he vomits sometimes. He is also very deaf. He could not hear what the PM said. He also appeared not to know the difference between Holland and Belgium, nor what was meant by the EEC. The PM was complaining that he should not have had to see Wallace, but in fact I can remember him agreeing to see him and showing interest.

We all stood and chatted outside the Cabinet Room for some time, the PM very chirpy, singing away to himself – as if he has got rid of some burden and can see his way through.

Then he went off to the Commons to talk to Solly Zuckerman* about scientific research.

I went to the office and finished my papers, and went home at 6.45 p.m. The work burden is much less at the moment. Also the thought that it might end soon makes me less willing to take on longer-term commitments and thinking. I wish I knew one way or the other.

## Tuesday 14 October 1975

Went in early for a Misc Cabinet committee on the Motor Industry. It was a CPRS presentation, including film slides, in the beautiful big conference room A in the Cabinet Office. It constituted a devastating attack on our motor industry – showing that despite 30% lower wage rates, our production costs were much greater than in France or Germany because of low productivity. The PM was all for publication, as were Lever, Varley and Healey. But Shore was opposed – on patriotic grounds (he is a big jingo) and also because it would give ammunition to our foreign competitors. Unresolved.

Interestingly, the PM was completely lost walking back from the Cabinet Office to No.10 – just 20 yards along the corridor and through the door. 'I ought to know the way but you had better lead me,' he said to Robin Butler. He has no sense of direction at all and just wanders vaguely off.

Afterwards I went back to the office to clear my papers and then out to lunch with Grieveson Grant in the City.

Back for Parliamentary Questions at 2.30. The PM had lunch with Marcia (who dined at the Dorchester last night with Vere Harmsworth of the *Daily Mail* – which she is suing for libel!). The PM looked a bit harassed and was phoning her brother Tony to arrange to see him this Saturday. I heard HW tell him that 'your problem has now been solved . . . it is all cut and dried' – whatever that might be. Presumably getting a job for Tony, or paying his tax.

The PM was very nervous about Question Time – he told me in the corridor when going in to the Chamber that he was 'shit-scared'. He counted the number of Question Times till Christmas (20) and then criticised Patrick Wright for not having arranged more overseas trips on Tuesdays and Thursdays.

In fact Question Time was going quite easily until HW mentioned that he had been burgled eight times – and this in the context of his answer on his evidence to the Royal Commission on the Press. Immediately the Chamber was buzzing and the press gallery evacuated to their telephones. This was an error of judgement – no doubt brought on by the fact that he drank four brandies beforehand (and two afterwards). This is the first time he has drunk brandy heavily since the summer.

He was pleased with himself afterwards, using the usual similes from cricket – 'padding up', 'couldn't resist hitting one or two to the boundary', etc. But he knew he had made a mistake in referring to the burglaries. The press was bombarding Joe – and Scotland Yard were apparently very agitated.

Afterwards we returned to No.10. I saw Jonathan Charkham, and made more progress with his Public Appointments Unit, which will professionalise and depoliticise some of the patronage which is wielded by politicians and civil servants.

The PM went off to see the Queen – still in good form according to Ken Stowe who phoned me at home at 11 p.m.

I worked in the Unit, including our new economist Dick Smethurst, planning the week's programme, until going home at 8 p.m.

## Wednesday 15 October 1975

The newspapers this morning all carried details of the settlement of Harold Evans's *Private Eye* libel – £2,500 and total apology. They had no evidence whatsoever for their malicious allegations. I felt a bit depressed – had I sued them with him I would be a lot richer this morning.

Saw Joe, who told me that the PM had telephoned last night to Janet to say he expected we were 'disgusted' with him over the eight burglaries. She said not disgusted, but disappointed.

This morning HW was full of ideas on housing and pressing for the Unit to come up with its schemes for selling council houses. We are working on this but it is immensely complicated for a small group to deal with in a few days. Typically, HW is most agitated because he has a speech to the local government officers in a few weeks' time. HW approaches politics through speeches. It is the part of his political activity he takes most care over. He thinks that when he has spoken on economic policy, or industrial relations, something has happened, that he has done something about it.

Anthony Lester came in from the Home Office late morning to discuss the Official Secrets Act. They are very depressed after the ministerial meeting on Monday. Roy Jenkins also told me this outside the Cabinet Room this morning, when he was on his way, late, to a meeting of the ministerial committee on Economic Strategy. He thought he had not put the case well, but that the reactionary attitude of all the ministers was shocking. Lester told me that Roy was going to take the position that either the government announced in the Queen's Speech that it would go ahead with the manifesto commitment to liberalise the Official Secrets Act, or there should be no reference at all. He was not prepared to promote the Cabinet Office and Lord Chancellor's Office scheme for a more restrictive Act.

Bill Housden told me that he is now convinced HW will go at Christmas. Apparently HW told this to Goodman when he came in the other day, and has begun, in Bill's words, 'to make preparations'. I wonder if this means to take over from Goodman at University College Oxford.

But both Joe and Bill are now convinced. I am too really, since HW always told me that it would be no more than two years. But I have learned that nothing is certain – especially if Marcia gets on to him.

Lunch with Joe at the House of Commons. Tony Bevins, a good journalist now sadly on the *Sun*, whom I remember as an LSE student, came to join us. He had some story about £2 million from the funds for Britain in Europe now being available to form a new centre coalition party.

Went back for a meeting at 2.30 with Bernard Thimont from the Civil Service Department on payments for my part-time staff.

Then at 4 p.m. to see Basil Hall, the Treasury Solicitor, about a further libel of me in *Private Eye*, accusing me of giving 'tax evasion' advice and leaking Cabinet matters to the City. Spent an hour there, in a nice Georgian house behind Central Hall, Westminster. Rather stuffy man, but he melted and became human. His impression was that the piece was defamatory. But he made it clear that the Treasury Solicitor's office would not be available to help for any legal action. He talked about earlier episodes over Marcia and Walter Terry, and over Marjorie Halls.

Then back to No. 10 and spent a hectic hour on Unit matters, preparing our Unit papers on housing and a possible brief on industrial strategy, which comes up to Cabinet tomorrow. The revised paper from Healey and Varley is terrible. Vague, with no specifics on industrial policy at all.

I dashed out at 7 p.m. to go to see Harry Evans to discuss *Private Eye* – which jointly libels us again today. On the way out I ran into HW just returned from the Commons to go to a dinner for the Papuans (I have dropped out to let Ken Stowe attend). We talked for 20 minutes in the hall outside the lift. He was delighted at getting away so lightly in this morning's press on his burglaries gaffe. Also discussed the libels question. I told him I had been to see Hall. He pressed me to sue. He said that the lawyers always advised against, but he had always won, and so had Harold Evans.

I saw Harold at the RAC, where he was swimming. He was furious.

*Private Eye* gave him a legally binding assurance that they would make no further malicious references to him – and there are four in today's issue. All total lies. He has already issued writs and advised me to do the same.

His car drove me home at 9 p.m. Later my solicitor, Jack Black, phoned and said that now we must sue.

## *Thursday 16 October 1975*

Cabinet met mainly on the new paper on industrial strategy and on a proposal to set up a Royal Commission on the Health Service. The Queen's Speech was also on the agenda but we did not reach it.

Beforehand I saw Shirley Williams in the main corridor and we agreed that the industrial strategy paper would have to be improved.

Sam Silkin sat outside the Cabinet for at least two hours waiting for his item to be called (it wasn't). He told me he was worried about Reggie Maudling and the Poulson scandal. The shadow Attorney – Michael Havers* – had been to visit him to say that Thatcher was thinking of appointing Maudling to the front bench, but wanted clearance on Poulson. Silkin had indicated that there was no reason not to at present but the case was still developing. Thatcher had then appointed him, and it subsequently appeared in the *Guardian* that Silkin had given assurances that no proceedings would take place. This was untrue and worried Silkin. I told him not to worry. Nobody had followed it up so far. But just in case he should write to Havers and set out clearly on paper – or at least file a departmental memorandum – so that he had a firm record of what he had and had not said. He did not think any other public figures were involved, but 'some MPs had come perilously close'.

He is a nice man, if a bit ponderous. He seemed nervous and obviously hurt by the recent criticisms of his performance.

Joe told me that HW had said to him that he was feeling 'terribly tired'.

I worked in the Unit and then went to lunch in the Cabinet Office canteen with Robin Butler and Nick Stuart from private office. This was my first visit to the canteen as opposed to the restaurant. The food was awful, but at least it is self-service, and not the terrible slow business in the Cabinet Office mess.

Nick Stuart told me that in the last government Stuart Holland had the same troubles with Marcia, and finally resigned because of her.

Joe had been to lunch with his journalist friend who keeps us informed on Fleet Street gossip and returned with a report on the current press rumours. The *Mail* and *Express* are again discussing merger (with the *Standard* to be dropped, because the *Evening News* has lost £3 million this year).

The pre-Questions briefing was very short because the PM held a ministerial meeting to clear the announcement of the Royal Commission on the Health Service.

He was not drinking so much brandy today, and promised to 'keep his head down and to pad up to any balls off the wicket'. This he did. Questions were boring and rambling – he never got beyond the first question. But at least he did not put his foot in it.

Afterwards I saw David Owen and we discussed his boss Barbara Castle. He says that she has got it wrong, but insists that she must not be dropped now. There is no danger of this. HW never drops a minister under attack.

I dashed back to the Cabinet Office for the Dep Secs meeting on next week's business, but it was nearly over. The only change was that the unemployment Cabinet was being allowed to slip a week – and public expenditure too, which now puts it into November. This is because the Chancellor has only just seen the forecasts, and wants more time to think about them.

Douglas Wass came in for a meeting on the Civil List and I talked to him for 15 minutes while he waited for the PM to come out of his briefing on Prince Fahd of Saudi Arabia. He is obviously worried about public expenditure. He also said it was 'crazy' to be taking decisions on the economy three years ahead when we don't know what will be happening. The Treasury certainly hates planning. I also began carefully to explore with him the possibilities on selling council houses.

He said that all the troubles in 1972–73 over the credit explosion were the fault of the Bank of England – more than the politicians. 'Barber was taken for a ride. He didn't understand. But the Bank had no control.' I asked what we would do if there was a repetition in 1977–78. He replied that it would not happen because the steam had gone out of the property sector. I said what if it arose in a new sector, like North Sea oil. He looked gloomy. Then HW emerged from the Cabinet Room and went up to the study for the Civil List discussion.

The Cabinet committee on industrial policy (IDV) then met in the Cabinet Room with Jenkins in the chair. It was a gloomy occasion. Varley's paper predicted the total collapse of the shipbuilding industry, with nearly 70,000 unemployed. Varley wanted £100 million subsidy to keep it going until nationalisation. I thought that was crazy – to leave the new nationalised corporation with the burden of closing it down – and passed a note accordingly to Bill Rodgers who made a brave statement saying that the biggest impact would be in his own Stockton constituency, but we should face up to it and not subsidise the building of ships which would never be sold. Healey, Lever and Rees took the same line. Ross, Foot and Varley were for subsidy, but Jenkins was very firm and clear in the chair. So it looks like more unemployment disaster in the north, but no alternative.

Then Ross raised the question of the Scottish *Daily News*, which had run out of money and wanted £100,000 within 24 hours. This was not on the agenda. Foot argued strongly for giving them the money to keep the paper going for another fortnight. But Lever was impressively against and Healey was totally adamant. The argument grew heated, but Jenkins was again very firm in supporting the Chancellor.

I walked out with Jenkins, who was grinning, though complaining that he thought it would be a routine Cabinet committee, but HW typically left him to handle a lot of dynamite – which he did superbly well.

I went back to the Unit and we worked for two hours till 9.30 p.m. – on the housing briefs. Home just before 10 o'clock.

## Friday *17 October 1975*

The PM was away in the north today. I went in early to get working on our housing brief. But after a conversation with my solicitor, Jack Black, about the latest *Private Eye* libel on me, had to put housing on one side. The solicitor – who is very nice and intelligent – arrived at 11.30 and we spent the next hour and a half going over the facts, then to snatch a quick cold lunch together at the Reform and then to see a barrister in King's Bench Walk to take counsel's advice. He was nice, middle-aged, named Joseph. He was very clear and helpful and said he was in no doubt that I would win.

I was completely torn. It seems I would win. Yet I am not interested in the money, and I dread going through the whole bloody legal process – not to mention the course in character assassination which *Private Eye* will produce in order to try to frighten me into withdrawing. We decided to sleep on it over the weekend – I am going to the cottage – and then to act on Monday if we decide.

The fact that HW will probably retire in about two months – he now says he wants it all over and done with before he goes to the Scillies – also makes me reluctant. I want to be out and private. This will be a shabby legacy. But if I don't, people – and especially HW – may think the allegations are true.

I came back at 4 p.m. and saw Israel Gatt and Yoram Peri from the Israel Labour Party. They invited me to Israel in the New Year.

Then plunged into housing and finally got the brief off to the PM at 7.15 – and was at the Old Vic at 7.29 for Trevor Griffiths's *The Comedians*, which is enjoyable, though the 'message' is banal. I was immensely helped in the briefs by some brilliant work by my young adviser Gavyn Davies. In fact all of the team in the Unit are an immense support to me. I shall miss each one of them very much.

Incidentally, in the paperback version of her book *Inside Number 10*

Marcia has cut out Joe from the acknowledgements. Previously she had thanked him and described him as HW's 'constant guide and friend'.

## Monday 20 October 1975

Incredibly hectic, and really quite a satisfying day.

Went in early to find a mass of papers waiting to be dealt with. Also had a lot of people to telephone – including arranging for my writ against *Private Eye*.

Then in mid-morning I saw the PM's proposed statement on the Royal Commission on the National Health Service. Not good. So I telephoned David Owen and got the background. Clearly Barbara Castle has got it wrong, locked in on the private medicine issue, unable to see the whole picture clearly.

Owen was very clear – and admitted to me he was in total disagreement with his Secretary of State. I liked his approach – stick to the manifesto on separating pay beds from NHS hospitals, and this not to go to the Royal Commission; but put the rest of private medicine, including the licensing question, to the Royal Commission.

I went to private office and discussed it with Ken Stowe and Joe. They were sympathetic. The problem was that HW was out at the airport with Prince Fahd of Saudi Arabia and was going straight on to lunch with Don Ryder. We had no way of getting at him.

Anyway I dictated a memo and gave a copy to Ken Stowe.

Meanwhile the TUC came on the telephone. Jack Straw, Barbara Castle's special adviser, had suggested that the TUC make a statement in support of the government's line. We got hold of the PM just before he left Chequers for the airport and he said that he did not want the TUC to do anything before his statement. So we put them off.

It was all very hectic. John Gross, one of my oldest Oxford friends, came in to collect me for lunch and we went to the Reform. John was very pessimistic about the media world, which he sees as full of sick, nasty people. I think it is worse than that.

Then I walked down Whitehall to the Commons where the PM was having a special briefing with DHSS advisers on the NHS statement. The PM did not seem very interested while they were there. But once they left, he came to life and we had a proper briefing. And he got on the ball and completely took on board the distinction I was trying to make between separating private beds and suppressing private medicine.

His statement went very well, a clever balance between Left and Right.

Afterwards John Stonehouse made his statement about his disappearance. From the Tory benches. Bizarre, but not mad, and crudely calculated to advance his own cause. The Speaker clashed often with him, and the House looked embarrassed.

Back to my papers. Incidentally, after the statement the PM said he was very pleased with our document on selling council houses, which could prove 'a historic document'. He is pressing for urgent action on it.

Janet Whitaker came in to discuss part-time work at 7, and we went back, she to Hampstead and me to Kentish Town, in a taxi at 8 p.m. I was supposed to be at the Fahd dinner, but I withdrew because my Israeli sister-in-law is here.

A rapid and excellent day. So much better when there is a lot of work.

## Tuesday 21 October 1975

The PM had an early meeting of the TUC/NEC Liaison committee and then Healey came in to see him about the financial situation.

I worked on Unit papers, and also was constantly on the telephone to my solicitor about my writ on *Private Eye*.

At 11.30 a.m. I went to a meeting with a delegation from the Scottish *Daily News* in the Cabinet Office big conference room A. (This is the old Treasury boardroom, very handsome, with a throne at the back of the room.) The Scots made a strong case for the future of their paper, but could not explain why no Scots – including the Scottish TUC – would put money into it.

The PM looked very tired and tetchy. Robin Butler said he was very irritable and was complaining about having too many engagements. Probably this is part of adjusting himself to departure: finding it all too much, so it is right to go.

I left the meeting before the end to deal with more details of the writ and the press statement.

Joe came in to discuss housing and we had a rare disagreement. The PM had asked me to circulate our paper on selling council houses – which he described as 'fascinating' and a 'historical document' – to the Chancellor and Crosland. Joe wants to exclude one scheme because the Tories had pushed it. I refuse.

Lunch with David Owen at the Reform. He has become much more weighty and mature. He has a big job at NHS – his part is bigger than running the Ministry of Defence. He was very pleased with our co-operation yesterday and thought that HW had saved the day, when Barbara Castle, as with *In Place of Strife* six years ago, became too rigidly committed. He says the department is much too big and that things had deteriorated into a real mess there. Pat Nairne, the excellent new permanent secretary, has a big job in clearing it up.

Back to the Commons for PQs. Dull and of little consequence.

I returned to No.10 (the PM had a meeting with the BMA at the House). We had a Unit meeting on economic strategy. We are beginning to rethink our approach – envisaging that some reflation is possible, to get unemployment down, and if so, it should be done soon, both for economic and political reasons. But we must have more discussion. I enjoy these Unit meetings immensely. The team is very good indeed. It meant missing the BMA meeting, but that was well worth it.

Incidentally David Owen, who knows Healey well, thought he is not as good now as when at Defence, and that his weakness for completely changing his position had become more pronounced and dangerous. David thinks he ought to be moved.

Came home after the Unit meeting at 8 p.m. to watch the end of *Shane*, my favourite cowboy film. Feeling very depressed again. The enormous pressures of the job have eaten away my resilience for the moment. Small things and worries get me down in a way they did not before – sign I need a change. Also the fact I know it will all come to an end soon is demoralising. No point in thinking long-term.

Before leaving I went along to Joe's room. The door was firmly shut. A messenger told me that the Prime Minister was in there. I went back to my room and telephoned. Janet answered. She said that Joe was not there, he was at the House of Commons. So I left, meeting Joe coming in grinning impishly as I went out.

## Wednesday 22 October 1975

The PM went to Transport House for the NEC this morning at 9.30. I saw him afterwards and he said it was pretty awful, with the Left behaving stupidly.

Joe said that last night the PM had said how terribly tired he feels. The fact that there is 'nothing new' in the job makes this worse.

Ken Stowe came to see me to say that the PM had asked that the Unit does some quick work assessing the Treasury's National Income Forecast (NIF). When Healey came to see him he was very gloomy, saying that the balance of payments and the PSBR were going very wrong again together. The PM is sceptical of the Treasury – especially when it is pessimistic – so he wants independent advice. Ken had mentioned his wish for the Unit's involvement to John Hunt who had immediately said, don't worry, 'it is all in hand, Andrew Graham is working on it with Ken Berrill'. I reserved my position on that, and telephoned Andrew in Oxford, who reported that he was having only most general discussions with Ken, and would want to put in a paper from us. John often moves to keep things to the Cabinet Office and to cut others out. That is Whitehall.

Did final amendments to the papers on selling council houses and then had these circulated to Healey, Crosland and Lever.

Had lunch with Joe in the House of Commons. Back after lunch to clear my papers and to discuss with Richard Graham the plans of Kearton at the new British National Oil Corporation to take over BP (UK), which I no longer support, on confidence grounds – it would upset sterling, the gilt market and the negotiations with North Sea oil companies on partici-pation. But Richard makes a good case that BNOC does need its own downstream refining, etc. operations in order to attract good management.

Went at 6 p.m. to the French embassy to a farewell party for Cuvillier. Talked to Tommy Balogh, Robert Armstrong, John Hunt and Michael Woolf* (who was in Downing Street with Heath). Then to the theatre to see *Otherwise Engaged* (Simon Gray) with Carol and her sister Jill. Quite entertaining. Home 11 p.m.

Joe is clearly a little worried about going out into the big world after 6 years with HW. I suppose I am anxious too, which is why I get these bouts of worry. But am really looking forward to getting free again.

Incidentally Richard Graham from my Unit has not been invited to Robin Butler's farewell party – because Marcia has intervened to restrict severely the number of guests at a hated civil servant's party. Typical of the high political policy level on which she naturally operates. Private office now call her the Princess of Pettiness. Harsh, but she has worked hard for the title.

## Thursday 23 October 1975

Went in late because first I attended Rachel's school harvest festival. Carol's Israeli sister came in with me. All very quiet in the morning in No.10.

The Lord Chancellor telephoned to ask for some help on a constituency speech.

Lunch with Joe, Robin Butler and his replacement from the Treasury, Nigel Wicks, at the Press Gallery in the Commons. Robin is very nice about his relations with the Policy Unit. And says that Marcia is 'the only totally destructive person I have ever met'.

The PM had been in Cabinet dealing with the Queen's Speech and with the industrial strategy paper.

After lunch to PQs, which went very easily again, with the PM reaching question 6. Much faster and tighter than usual.

Back to the Misc Cabinet committee on North Sea oil and a proposal by Kearton, the new chairman of BNOC, to take over the UK interests of British Petroleum. The rest of the committee were firmly against, except for Benn. The latter has found the expansionist ambitions of Kearton very well suited to his own ambitions for extending the public sector. There was quite a clash between Lever and Benn, who is trying to push Lever out of the North Sea negotiations. HW seemed to be bending over backwards to be kind to Benn, who saw Marcia on Monday evening and yesterday lunchtime.

Afterwards the PM went to the Palace. Before going he had a word with me about the Treasury forecasts. He said Healey was coming to see him tomorrow, a bit panicky, and he wanted a quick brief.

I telephoned Andrew Graham in Oxford, and began discussions with Dick Smethurst in the Unit.

Then John Hunt came in to see me. He told me that the Chancellor was in a flap over the forecasts and was discussing two alternatives with the Treasury – import controls for 5 years, or a big step devaluation. Hunt and Ken Berrill were putting in a paper against import controls, which he showed me. Very sensible and well balanced.

I then got more rapidly to work, telephoning Andrew again, discussing with Dick Smethurst, and writing out a first skeleton draft. I also briefed Ken Stowe before he went down to Chequers to have dinner with the PM and stay the night.

Home at 10 p.m.


### Friday 24 October 1975

I cancelled my car to Chequers and decided to work on the economic brief rather than go to the devolution Cabinet.

Went in to the office early (Carol had left for Worcester at 5 a.m.!). Worked with Andrew all morning and finally telexed our brief to the PM at lunchtime. Then off for a nice lunch with Harold Lever and his family at Eaton Square. Lever had no idea of the Chancellor's flirtation with import controls.

Back in the afternoon. At 3.15 was summoned to the Commons, where the PM had arrived direct from Chequers for a vote on hare-coursing. The PM was only now reading my telex, partly because the machine had broken down at Chequers. We discussed our approach. The PM was tired and nervous about what Healey might press for. Then Healey came, alone and on the surface boisterous – in fact we are told by his Treasury officials that he is exhausted and worried.

Joe and I went back to No.10 while the PM had the meeting with the Chancellor. But Ken Stowe soon came on the phone to summon us back.

The PM was looking very pleased. He felt well briefed and had been able to control Healey, who in the end contented himself with going for an IMF loan. The PM looked relieved and full of smiles and signalled to Joe and me to wait behind till after Hunt and Ken had gone. He was obviously enormously relieved to have resisted what he feared would be a 'bounce' – though to be fair to the Treasury they didn't really want import controls either. They are simply in despair and not on all fours with their ministers.

Went back again to No.10 to discuss with Andrew a longer brief for this weekend, giving the statistical background to our short telex.

Had a series of phone calls. From my solicitor saying that *Private Eye*'s solicitor had been on to offer grovelling apologies. Also problems with home – Carol was not back, the children on their own, our telephone out of order, and I had to organise neighbours to help.

Then off to Covent Garden for *The Barber of Seville*. A delightful performance and marvellously relaxing.

Then heard this evening of Jim Slater resigning, bust and possible criminal charges. It is only a few weeks since Marcia was trying to arrange for the PM to have dinner with him!

## Monday 27 October 1975

Came in from a weekend at the cottage in Suffolk by train. A lovely autumn morning, the trees aglow, and nice to be racing through the fields on a train.

In the office by 10.30 – already missed Victor Rothschild, who came in to talk to Ken Stowe about the Gambling Royal Commission and asked to see me about his letter suggesting Tommy Balogh's transfer to BNOC.

I worked on papers and had a long chat with Robin Butler, who is going back to the Treasury, about the ridiculous power battle between Hunt's Cabinet Office and Douglas Wass's Treasury. It is reaching a point where policy considerations come second. Wass is not thought to be primarily at fault.

To lunch with Bob Worcester at the Reform. He incidentally told me that John Allen had come up to him and said that he and Marcia had been discussing my relations with Worcester – who is indirectly referred to in the *Private Eye* piece which libels me.

Joe was also at the club with Sigmund Sternberg, so we came back together. Joe told me that the PM had again discussed his departure with him. He has now put it off till March. He said that Marcia came to see him three times at the weekend and pressed him to carry on. She actually said that since he had called for 'A Year for Britain' he must give a year more himself. The effrontery of this nearly choked us both. HW had given way again, agreeing to go on until March, although he is worried that Mary will be furious again. I was furious. Because it is a sign of his weakness. He should take a decision and stick to it.

Joe has given him another date, in February for a changeover in March, with the idea of an orderly transfer of power, rather like the American President.

Apparently Janet was at No.10 with HW till very late on Friday.

I worked in the office till Tessa Blackstone and Bernard Thimont came in to discuss Foreign Office numbers and cutting down overseas embassies. Apparently Hunt has been trying to stop the CPRS doing this study of Britain's overseas representation, but Tessa has insisted and Ken Berrill has given them the go-ahead.

Went to the PM's meeting with the CBI at 6 p.m. in the Cabinet Room. Very rambling, discussing policies before the economic Summit.

The PM hung around afterwards, in the Cabinet Room, in private office and outside in the corridors gossiping. He is still firm that devolution must go ahead, but has doubts about the parliamentary timetable next year.

I left No.10 with him, as he went to the Commons and I went to Harold Lever's house for dinner. We briefly discussed the Hunt-Wass battle. He was well aware of it and gave me another example of the expansion of the Cabinet Office power. I said that the Cabinet Office now wanted to run economic policy. HW said, 'I don't want to run economic policy. I just want to stop them (the Treasury) running it.'

### Tuesday 28 October 1975

Went in to No.10 at 9.30 and straight upstairs to talk to HW in his study. Had a long discussion on devolution. HW is particularly annoyed with the ministers who have leaked details of Friday's Cabinet at Chequers. He implies Jenkins, and says in revenge he will give firm commitments to devolution in the Commons today. He also thinks that the Scottish Assembly, once operational, will cause a break-up of the Scottish Nationalist Party, because it is a coalition and the pressures of the Assembly, and the need to co-operate with other parties, will break it up.

We discussed the weaknesses of the government's team in the Lords. Balogh and Beswick will go. There are no replacements. He also told me to tell Bill McCarthy of Nuffield College (whom I had suggested for the Lords) that his peerage is going ahead slowly.

Joe came in and we discussed press matters. I complained to the PM about his inviting the Hartwells of the *Telegraph* to No. 10 without inviting any executives or proprietors from sympathetic newspapers. HW looked embarrassed, since we all know who has pushed him into this, and he agreed to invite Peter Gibbings of the *Guardian* to the next dinner.

Albert told us that on Monday Marcia told him and Bill that it was OK, they had their jobs for a little longer, because she had persuaded HW to stay on another 3 months. That is how they all see it. Anything to keep the gravy train going. In fact if the PM stays on much longer he will have to make a reshuffle. He will also run into the Budget and so make it diffi-cult for a successor to appoint a new Chancellor in time to handle a spring Budget properly. Moreover, we are about to lose our parliamentary majority, and devolution could bring down the government, as HW said yesterday evening. Therefore a new leader needs to be in early to get a grip in time before a general election. All this points to an early changeover. Given his boredom with the job, these are serious reasons why he should retire soon.

Bill Housden told me that John Cordle, the Tory MP who regularly takes Marcia out to lunch, has sent her three watches worth £1,000 each to choose the one she wants. She accepted, but HW has intervened and told her to send them back – Bill Housden acted as messenger carrying the watches.

On the retirement, Joe and Ken Stowe had a private meeting today to plan a timetable. An announcement around 14 February (13th anniversary of his election as Leader of the Labour Party in 1963). Then two to three weeks for the changeover.

HW is making his private arrangements. He has asked Goodman to get his house at 5 Lord North Street valued for sale. He has also asked for a valuation of his insurance policies.

He said to Joe that he is still worried about Mary's reaction to the delay till March because he firmly promised her Christmas.

At 11 o'clock Lord Goodman came in to discuss the *Observer* (the proposal to merge with the Mirror Group is going very slowly) and presum-ably to discuss private things.

I worked in the Unit. Also went with Ken Stowe to see Douglas Allen across Horse Guards Parade in the Civil Service Department about the problem of Transport House calling meetings of political advisers. The PM had asked me to do this last night. Ken was furious with John Hunt because, having overheard our discussion with the PM, John had gone off and acted with Douglas Allen himself. Ken is worried that John is trying to run all of policy in the Cabinet Office and to run No.10 as well. Ken realises he will have to fight to keep Hunt out of No. 10. John is certainly an impressive predator rampaging in the Whitehall jungle. Ken may be too nice to cope with it. But some prime ministers clearly appreciate Cabinet secretaries like that.

Another example came up later in the day when it emerged that Hunt had told Ken Berrill to see *The Economist* and inform it about how the Cabinet Office ran central government. Joe Haines, as the senior press officer, had advised the Cabinet Office not to do so, and the PM had expressly forbidden me to see *The Economist*. Whitehall is becoming a less anonymous place under John.

Went to lunch with Joe at the Commons Press Gallery. Afterwards to PQs. Beforehand the PM said that though he hated Question Time, he loved the briefing sessions beforehand.

Curious Fleet Street rumours are circulating about Guardsmen, homosexual scandals, royalty, a politics professor from the LSE and a famous pop star. I don't believe them. Typical of scurrilous rumour-mongers in the press.

After Question Time the PM had a private meeting with Healey to discuss the proposed approach to the IMF. I briefed him on the need to examine any strings and conditions, especially in terms of limits to domestic credit expansion.

Then the Defence committee (OPD) met to discuss arms sales, followed by the secret Misc on economic policy. The same group as met over the counter-inflation White Paper – Healey, Lever, Crosland, Varley, Foot, Shore, Callaghan.

I went in at the start, but the PM went on so long about secrecy and leaks that I left. I immediately arranged with Ken Stowe to get a full briefing afterwards – and Nigel Wicks gave me this later.

Chatted with Joe and with Albert and also finished off my papers.

The PM left the committee meeting early to go to the Palace. Crosland also left early, having apparently said little. He is clearly reserving his guns for public expenditure. Before the meeting he told me he was going to press hard for disproportionately high cuts in 'low-priority areas' – 'personal social services and education'.

After the meeting Harold Lever came to my room for a drink and talk. We agreed not to discuss any details from the Cabinet committee – though details are bound to leak and we are bound to get the blame anyway.

As I was leaving at 8.15 p.m. the PM returned from the Palace with Ken Stowe. We talked briefly about the new *Observer* editor, Donald Trelford, whom I know to be a decent man.

Back to dinner with our close friends the Grahams and home to bed by 11.30.

[Meeting of the special Misc Cabinet committee on the economic situation – 28.10.75

Chancellor: presented the Treasury forecasts for unemployment and the balance of payments until 1977.

PSBR – latest £11–12 billion. 1976–77 down a bit but still high.

Bank of England Governor: thought unemployment would be less bad – peak at 1.25 million in 1976. Wants early reflation – but not now. Won't rule out early in New Year, because perhaps people will then believe counter-inflation is working.

Chancellor: the options – (i) Step devaluation – 7% would be more than necessary to keep competitive; (ii) Import controls; or mix of the two. Still too early to decide.

External financial gap – up to £1 billion. May not need to do anything. But must ask for an 'oil facility' by 6 November. Derek Mitchell of the Treasury has seen Witteveen of the IMF. Total is £1 billion. Witteveen said we must not put in an application which fails. To succeed requires two things:

1. Commitment against import controls. But would be able to put them on selectively. Much later generally – but not soon generally.

2. PSBR: Witteveen was still acting on £9 billion and found this worrying – didn't seem to know about £12 billion now forecast.

Conclusion: we should go for (a) oil facility and (b) first credit tranche for the IMF.

Healey will see Witteveen this weekend, then back to this group (next Tuesday) and then to Cabinet on 6th. Not at this moment doing anything to reduce the PSBR.

Discussion:

Foot – said little.

Shore – very pessimistic about world recovery – not powerful or quick. He thinks only 6% recovery instead of Chancellor's 14%. Careful on textiles – we have a marvellous multi-fibre agreement. Don't bust it.

Callaghan – pessimistic, in year's time just as bad and then getting close to election. Let's do the tough thing now.

Crosland – said very little. Analysed employment, balance of payments, PSBR problem. Cannot win them all. Couldn't see his way through.

Lever – a bit frivolous and general.

PM – opposed general import controls, but may have to do textiles.]


## Wednesday 29 October 1975

I decided not to attend the Energy Cabinet committee at 10 a.m., which was mainly on processing nuclear waste. Also stayed out of the IDV committee on strategy for the aircraft industry nationalisation. Not much of interest there, and I had a lot of paper and staff work in the office.

HW went with Joe to lunch at the *Sunday Times*. Beforehand John Hunt came flapping into private office, worried what the PM would say about the Crossman affair, insisting that he should remember that throughout Hunt was acting on the PM's behalf. I could not guarantee that the PM would remember that.

I went to lunch at the Reform with Alan Lord, the new second permanent secretary at the Treasury in charge of their industry section. He was previously a bright star at the Department of Industry and began at the Inland Revenue. When I discussed and praised Lord to HW later in the day, HW said that he had found the Inland Revenue was the best training for administrators because they have big responsibility early on and because they have to master detail.

Lord is a very tall man, intense in style, not at all cerebral and detached like most mandarins, with what seems like a Scottish accent even though he is from Yorkshire. We discussed the economic field warily. He mentioned the problems the Treasury has with its minister changing his mind. Over coffee we discussed housing, and our plans for the sales of council houses. He seemed very keen and promised to support. I said that Crosland was weak on this, being afraid of criticism from Labour supporters. It would therefore be important for Healey and Wilson to promise to take some of the political flak in return for Crosland's support. We agreed to keep in touch on this.

On the way back across the park he told me about life under Wedgie Benn at the Department of Industry. He said it was terrible working for a minister who is interested mainly in party ideology. He said that Mrs Frances Morrell was 'stupid and horrid'. Benn's other adviser, Francis Cripps, was 'just a detached mind'. (Nicky Kaldor used to say that Cripps was 'the cleverest young man in Britain'. Now he says, 'When he was under my direction he was the cleverest young man in Britain.') And that Michael Meacher was the worst junior minister he had met in 25 years in government. Some civil servants clearly do have strong views!

Lord told me that he had seen Benn on that evening in the summer when HW had told him he was moving him from the Department of Industry. Benn was with his wife discussing it. Benn seemed very down and said that the referendum result was seen by everybody as a victory for the Right and defeat for the Left. Meacher then came in and pressed that they should continue to stand firm for an 'extremist' Industry Bill. Benn said no, there was no point now in pressing extremist policies.

This honest reaction by Benn, suggesting that he takes populism seriously, may also explain why he went to ground for the next few months, rarely saying anything in public or in Cabinet committee. He was apparently convinced until the very end that there would be a 'No' vote on the EEC referendum.

HW went straight back to the House of Commons. I went over there with Nigel Wicks, the new private secretary replacing Robin Butler, who is a nice and modest though very able young man. Interestingly the state education sector is taking over No.10. Robert Armstrong (Eton), Tom Bridges (Harrow) and Robin Butler (Harrow) have gone and been replaced by Ken Stowe (grammar school), Patrick Wright (minor public school) and Nigel Wicks (grammar school). With me at secondary modern school and grammar school, and Joe (Bermondsey Academy for Hello Sailors, he claims) this is a good meritocratic domestic move.

There was a meeting of a Cabinet committee on the problems of the British motor industry at 4 p.m. in the PM's room at the House. Further discussion of the CPRS report on future strategy for the car industry. Agreed to publish. And on the looming Chrysler crisis – the PM is going to meet the Americans soon. Ryder was very concerned that no aid should be given to Chrysler which would make his job at British Leyland more difficult. Ryder is beginning to show the pressure, his face like a newly shaved death-mask. But he remains compulsively optimistic – which I suppose is essential for that job.

After the committee HW was on the telephone to Marcia for a long time. Partly about running the Arts (he had spoken to Lever about changing the minister after the committee). Joe and I still wonder whether in fact HW did promise Marcia anything in this area. She was on the phone straight away to the PM to learn what Lever had said. There was also some discussion of something where she had a choice – 'you have the buyer's choice', I heard HW say. I suspect it is houses – Lord Goodman has recently processed the purchase of the house at 1 Wyndham Mews for her as well as her present one next door. I don't know who is paying. She was also on about the education of her children – HW sent for John Silkin to help her get them into the French Lycée.

[The Prime Minister also invited the headmaster of Westminster School into Downing Street to interview him to assist in this project of finding suitable private education for the boys. Lord Goodman was also pressed to help.]

The PM spent at least half an hour on the phone dealing with these major policy questions.

Afterwards Joe arrived and we went into discuss various questions with the PM. I wanted to call a meeting of political advisers and invite somebody from Transport House to discuss current government policies. But HW refused. I thought it might improve relations with Transport House, but that does not seem to interest him.

I went back to No.10 at 5.30 to see Norman Chester about finance for Sport, and to chat about Nuffield College, where he is warden. Then my brother Clem arrived and we went back to the Commons for a drink with Alf Morris and Jack Ashley (I have minuted the PM saying that he should help Jack get his special Palantype machine for following proceedings in the Commons, and the PM is writing to Short as Leader of the House accordingly).

Clem and I then went to see the comedian Max Wall at the Shaw Theatre. Marvellous three-hour solo performance. Incredible rapport with the audience. Home for refreshments and in bed at 1 a.m. (Carol is away in Suffolk with the children.)

## Thursday 30 October 1975

Up at 7 a.m. to go for my usual three-mile daily run around Hampstead Heath with John Carrier. Cold and misty, quite different from those steamy summer mornings, but still lovely.

In at No. 10 I talked to Fred Mulley about education cuts before Cabinet, and to Bob Mellish asking his help as Chief Whip for Jack Ashley's Palantype machine, and to Harold Lever about the Policy Unit's proposals to sell council houses, which he strongly supports.

Cabinet discussed (and approved) increasing dental and optical charges and also including a promise to introduce devolution legislation in the coming Queen's Speech.

Apparently Roy Jenkins said that this went beyond our electoral commitments. This is true, but HW then said that he had committed us to this at Tuesday's Commons Questions because of the damaging leaks after the previous devolution Cabinet at Chequers which suggested slippage. Short said he would resign now. Healey changed view and came out strongly for going ahead with devolution and having no more arguments. Afterwards the PM was very pleased with how it had gone. But it did seem that his position was mainly reached as a revenge on the 'leakers' – whom he always sees as Jenkins. He has also been impressed by the Scottish Labour MP John Mackintosh's argument that the Scot Nats will be destroyed in the new Assembly. He walked up and down in private office for half an hour afterwards discussing devolution. He said he would personally love to be a member of the Scottish Assembly. I pointed out the importance of the election date for that Assembly and that it must not be in 1977 – forecast to be the nadir of the deep recession. Labour would then be massacred. He agreed, but I did not feel he was really looking that far ahead.

Marcia has been attacking HW again. Joe told me at lunch at the Commons that she had also been attacking me and Janet. Joe has decided not to send Janet as press officer with the PM to Liverpool on Saturday (and so to stay at Chequers tonight). We also discussed the Israeli connection. Yesterday evening the Israeli Ambassador came to see HW at the House. Joe said he has been present when Marcia was screaming at the Ambassador in a wild and offensive way. But of course it is very important for them to have access to the PM.

Later Bill Housden told us that there was a terrible row last night. Marcia was upset about her visit to the French Lycée school. She liked the headmaster but did not feel the matron was sufficiently deferential to her. Marcia then apparently launched a big attack on HW for being so friendly to Janet. Bill said it was very nasty. Obviously the pressure is being turned on Janet.

We went down from the Commons restaurant to the PM's room for briefing for Questions – which started late because HW had a meeting with Eric Roll from Warburgs about Chrysler.

The PM drank a lot of brandy – certainly five by the time he went into the Chamber at 3.15 p.m. But Questions went OK. A lot of churning but no really clean or interesting exchanges. Thatcher now intervenes every time but she does not make much progress. In fact she looks bewildered, and has told people that she finds HW perplexing and she has no idea how to handle him. HW always uses the same devices in response:

– What public expenditure cuts will the Tories make?
or
– There is no ministerial responsibility for x, y, etc.
or
– Thatcher has never repudiated the policies of her (Heath's) previous government, etc.

Boring but effective.

At 5 p.m. we had a meeting with the TUC in the Cabinet Room. This was in advance of the economic Summit to be held at Rambouillet, but in fact the TUC simply talked about unemployment and import controls. The pressure for the latter was very strong. They said we 'must have protection to give us a breathing space to restore our economic efficiency'. They also attacked GATT as 'unsatisfactory' and 'in need of fundamental review'. The GATT review was to be permanent, the import controls only 'temporary' until British industry was restructured (50 years?).

Jack Jones said he was afraid that some of our industries would be extinguished by unfair competition – motorcycles already, next textiles, TV tubes, and now motor cars.

David Basnett supported this. They all attacked the Japanese.

The PM said we are opposed to import controls because of the balance of payments implications of retaliation. But if we can prove unfair competition, or industries will be destroyed, then he will act.

Healey was very rough with them, pointing out that there was no point in having protection unless British industry – including the unions – improve their performance. And he warned them not to say anything about import controls to the press, or else all manufacturers will start forestalling purchases and increase our imports. Denis was very impressive.

Hugh Scanlon then interrupted indignantly to ask, 'Why should you assume that we will go off and talk to the press?'

Tom Jackson shouted, 'Because we have always done that in the past.'

Scanlon looked furious but everybody else laughed.

In conclusion Len Murray said that there must be action on unemployment soon or there would be trouble from their members – clearly meaning opposition to the £6 wage limit.

Afterwards I went upstairs to Robin Butler's farewell party. I talked to Douglas Wass, Victor Rothschild and Robert Armstrong – who told me that the favourable reference to him in the first edition of Marcia's book has been eliminated from the paperback.

Marcia refused to come into the blue room where the party was held. She sat in the big room next door having her photograph taken by a famous society photographer. Everybody could see this going on – it was very rude to Robin Butler.

Incidentally Albert told us that she puts her hairdressing bills on the Labour Party account at No.10.

Home at 9 p.m. Feeling tired and had a bad headache.

A lobby journalist told Joe and me that both Thatcher and Maudling had briefed the lobby that Sam Silkin had given a firm assurance that Maudling was in the clear on Poulson. Silkin insists this is not so and has now published an answer to a PQ pointing this out.


### Friday 31 October 1975

HW was in the north all day.

I went in early to a 9.30 meeting in John Hunt's room in the Cabinet Office discussing the briefs for the economic Summit. Also there were Derek Mitchell from the Treasury, Tom Brimelow,* the head of the Foreign Office, a very grey and rigid man from Trade, and Kit McMahon from the Bank of England. (Interesting how Bank of England people are sitting on government committees: Wass brought in the Governor for the steering committee on economic policy – so Hunt gets in McMahon for this.)

The meeting went on for two and a half hours. Curiously the main brief made no reference to inflation. It talked as if the sole problem was recession, and all we needed was a touch of Keynes. Most of it was devoted to making sure that we came out against protection. I argued that it must also contain a let-out clause, that not all countries are equal, some will have to reflate before others, and the strong will have to carry the main burden.

Afterwards I invited Kit McMahon, whom I like very much, back to my room for a cup of tea. We discussed interest rates – and also the absence of external financing from the briefs, i.e. that we might want a declaration of support from those nations in balance of payment surplus towards the financing needs of those in deficit. When I mentioned this to Hunt later in the day he looked very jumpy and said he didn't think it was the right forum. God knows why not. If the head of the Treasury's external department, the head of the Bank of England's external department, and the head of the Foreign Office are not the right forum, who the hell is?

Joe came to my room a little agitated. The *Sunday Express* have been on to Janet saying that they have heard that she is 'the new Marcia Williams'. Somebody has put them on to this.

Bill Housden then came in to tell us more information about Marcia's current campaign to get a peerage for somebody, though Bill won't reveal who.

Joe and I discussed how to protect Janet. Her support, feminine warmth and relaxed humanity is valuable to the PM (and to us).

I was then so behind on my paperwork that I barely managed to get to Robin Butler's party (his personal one to say goodbye).

Went to lunch with Tom McNally, Jim Callaghan's political adviser. He told me how good Jim Callaghan is at protecting him. In Lagos the High Commissioner excluded Tom from all the meetings and had openly boasted beforehand that he would show them how to cut special advisers down to size. After the first meeting Jim took Tom for a walk in the garden, said he didn't like the smell of this, and asked why Tom wasn't there. Tom told him. So Jim went back, said he was tired, that he wouldn't be attending any more meetings, and that he would eat in his room henceforward. Jim never dealt with the High Commissioner again. I wish HW was as firm as that. It would be nice to work for Jim one day.

Tom also said that Jim is keen to reform the diplomatic service – which is exactly the opposite of what John Hunt and Ken Berrill tried to tell Tessa Blackstone and the CPRS was the Foreign Secretary's view. Jim is waiting till Michael Palliser takes over. He knows that there is disgraceful overmanning in the big embassies. Apparently the present Foreign Office head Brimelow keeps sending pathetic memoranda claiming that they have 'cut their staff to the bone', but Jim doesn't believe it. Brimelow is a shy and gentle man who supports the Labour Party (which must be a lonely position in the Foreign Office) and almost never sees Jim. He says his job is to run the department not to advise the Foreign Secretary.

During the row over the consumer-producer oil dialogue, when Jim told the Europeans we wanted separate representation as the only oil producer in the EEC, apparently Michael Butler, an able under-secretary, said to Jim that he, Butler, 'could not go to Brussels to tell my European friends that'. So Jim told him he had better find another job 'opposing Britain's interests'. The officials are apparently afraid of Jim. He sacked one of his private secretaries for sending a minute to No.10 claiming that something was the Foreign Secretary's view when in fact it was the departmental view and Jim was abroad. It might be interesting to see Jim at No.10. He is obviously tougher than HW in dealing with officials.

I rushed back and went straight to John Hunt's room for a fascinating meeting of the official committee on Northern Ireland. I protested at the beginning that they had not produced the paper on the 'Dominion status' option which the PM had requested. John Hunt interrupted sharply to say, 'The PM did not request, he said he did not exclude it.' I said, 'Well you have excluded it.' Some officials chuckled and I felt I had won that one.

We then went over the papers on 'Majority Rule' and 'Distancing'. Frank Cooper from the Northern Ireland Office was brilliant. Although he supports these options, he has no illusions. Although the policies he supports are blatantly pro-Protestant, he admits it, and shows no illusions about what a bunch of thugs they are. It is just that he sees no alternative. And he saw that we still did not have a long-term policy. As I said, 'Where is distancing leading to? It is not taking Ireland any further away.' Cooper was then very open to our 'Dominion status' option. So we then discussed it. Hunt was rather scathing and I got a little hot with him and with Arthur Peterson from the Home Office and the able man from Defence. They referred to all the weaknesses of the 'Dominion status' option – that we would then have no right to apply other political and economic sanctions – as if we have that right under any other option! I said what other sanctions? They flannelled. I said why aren't we applying them now? The only sanction we have under any option, including now under direct rule, is the Army – and in a few years we won't be able to use that. It was a good and fast argument for 20 minutes, which I think with Frank Cooper's subtle help, I won. Hunt saw this and as always, being a good professional, quite happily changed position and agreed to contemplate the 'Dominion status' option, especially when he realised that our Defence requirements could still be protected. Also when he realised I did not mean necessarily and precisely a Dominion under the 1936 Act. Just a new constitutional relationship under the Crown.

Back to the Unit. Put in a brief to the PM on Chrysler and on the coming economic Summit and then home at 8.30.

*Monday 3 November 1975*

The PM was away all day in Scotland to celebrate the arrival of the first North Sea oil.

I went in to No.10 at 9.30 as usual. Dealt with papers and a lot of letters.

Bill Housden dropped in again and reported to me on the PM's 'Black Sunday' yesterday. HW telephoned Marcia from Chequers five times, and she refused to answer the phone. So Bill drove him over to her house – she had been there all the time but refused to speak to him. Soon she started to attack HW violently for his friendship towards Janet. She ordered him to telephone Joe and forbid Janet to come to Scotland with the PM on Monday. The PM refused, saying that Joe would refuse to have interference with his staff arrangements. He told Bill Housden all about it afterwards.

Apparently Marcia is now down to only three servants at home, including the poor Filipino girl, Linda, who works eight days a week.

I went to lunch with Yoram Peri, the Israeli. He has been trying to phone Marcia at No.10 for several days on an important question concerning the Socialist International. She is never in – he commented on her curious working hours. In fact she is trying to freeze him out.

I went back to work in the afternoon, but left quite early. The PM flew back from Scotland to Chequers to meet the Chrysler Americans. Joe went down there. I decided to get an early night since there are several late ones ahead.

In the event, however, Denis Howell dropped round at 9 p.m. for a drink and a chat. He was quite interesting on Tony Crosland. Denis has worked under Tony on three occasions as junior minister. He said that in the old days of 1964–70 they would drop in on one another for discussions and Tony would keep an eye on everything. Denis says that now Tony is completely withdrawn. Denis almost never sees him. They have a ministerial meeting every two weeks – 10 ministers – and Tony insists that it does not go on for longer than an hour.

Denis must be frustrated, doing a job little different from 11 years ago. He said that John Silkin is totally idle. Gordon Oakes does all his work.


*Tuesday 4 November 1975*

No. 10 was fairly empty when I arrived, several of the others – Joe, Janet, Ken – being at Chequers with the PM. It was a lovely morning. Hampstead Heath had been glorious on my early morning run, with a carpet of frost lying on the meadows in the shade of the trees and the rest of the grass glowing in the morning sunshine.

Les Huckfield, the Labour MP from Coventry, telephoned me to say he was worried about the Chrysler situation. He was trying to hold the MPs concerned to a moderate line, but some, such as 'the wild Audrey Wise', were threatening militancy. He was going to put questions to the PM and wanted guidance on what would be helpful. I spoke to the PM when he arrived from Chequers. He was very gloomy about Chrysler and said that he had little to offer. Talks were still going on but it was clear that the Americans would not put in any more money after the end of the month. They even offered us the plant for nothing. Joe said the Americans were very impressive. HW was tempted to attack them and expose them, but Joe said they were calm, courteous, very well informed and with an immensely convincing case.

They pointed out that since taking over French Chrysler they had not lost a single day's work through disputes; in the same period they had not had a single day without disputes in the UK.

The PM was taking the line we (and the Department of Industry and the CPRS) took in our brief. No alternative to closure – but should do it in a phased and humane run-down.

Joe said that the PM had reported to him on what HW called his 'terrible Black Sunday' at Chequers. HW said that, when discussing Janet, Marcia's face 'went red with that mad look'.

The PM went in late to the OPD Cabinet committee to discuss arms sales to Egypt. I went back to my room to read a stream of papers on industrial bankruptcies, import controls and the bleak economic outlook. Then to lunch with Francis Sandilands, the author of the report on inflation accounting. A nice shy man.

Back to the Commons for PQs. Went rather well. The PM more informative, less procrastinating than usual. The Commons in a serious mood because of apprehension about Chrysler.

Back to No. 10. The PM had a briefing for President Sadat's forthcoming visit. I decided not to go. The Unit is preparing several economic briefs and I had to organise and supervise these – on unemployment, on the economic Summit, on the PM's big Guildhall speech.

I left at 8 p.m. The PM was still at the Palace for his weekly audience. Afterwards he was seeing David Frost and Jimmy Goldsmith at No. 10, brought in by Marcia. In fact she had arranged for the PM to go out to dinner with them, without confirming with him. He refused but agreed to see them privately in No. 10. This is a repeat of when she arranged for HW to go to dinner with Jimmy Goldsmith, Frost and Jim Slater in the summer. The same sniff of millionaires which she finds irresistible.

This morning I saw Tony Benn sitting outside the Cabinet Room waiting to go in to the Overseas and Defence Cabinet committee. We discussed *The*

*Economist* article on the CPRS. He then launched into an attack on the changes made in central government since he was previously in government in 1964–70, and particularly the development of a Prime Minister's department. He was quite sarcastic about the Policy Unit, saying it was unaccountable, and complaining that ministers do not see my briefs. He was clearly alluding to the PM's recent minute forbidding the policy advisers to attend meetings in Transport House. He said, 'I get minutes from Harold but I don't know how far you are behind them.' He seemed rather bruised.

## Wednesday 5 November 1975

Went to Chequers for the special NEDC meeting on the government's industry strategy.

I went down in the car with Janet. We got stuck in the traffic and arrived late, at 10.10 a.m. The meeting had already begun – though Peter Shore and John Hunt were delayed even later than us. Before going upstairs to the meeting we had a cup of coffee in the main hall, which is more modern than the rest, and lighter now the dark wood panelling has been stripped away. There was a blazing log fire and we sat comfortably, not too keen to go up. The drive had been hair-raisingly fast, over 95 mph some of the way, and I needed to rest and settle.

Upstairs, the meeting was packed. It was held in the usual long L-shaped room, which is panelled all round in dark brown wood, but which is not actually a dark room because of the large high windows. The oval table is even longer than that in the Cabinet Room with seats round it for 30 at a pinch. The wooden varnished floor is covered by a huge oriental-style carpet, thicker and less delicately beautiful than that in the reception-room at No.10. The fireplace is stone with ornate wooden surrounds – very attractive. The walls of the main part of the room have five large portraits, including Walpole by Van Loo, and two Van der Helsts, one a lovely 17th-century lady and another of a courtier. The white embellished plaster ceiling is high and helps to lighten the room. The four huge windows look over the gardens to the south and the parkland to the east. The outside brickwork is lovely, old and Elizabethan. (The inside feels more recent, and in places is sombre and heavy.) The park is beautiful this morning, trees still full of bronze leaves ranging to the horizon, mixed in with a few ornamental evergreens. The sun was shining coldly through a light November mist. Really a day for walking rather than sitting cramped over papers and bathed in cigar smoke, focusing on the depressing and insoluble problems of British industry. As the morning passed I was aware of the increasing background music of squeaking chairs as people, sitting hour after hour, stretched their stiff legs and eased cramped bottoms.

HW sat in the middle, with Healey and Varley as the main ministerial authors of the paper on his left, then Shore, Williams, Benn and Lever at the end of the table. To Wilson's right were Ronald McIntosh of the NEDC, then Dick Marsh, Monty Finniston and round the table to the opposite side were the CBI, where Watkinson has certainly added some needed weight. Then the TUC down the other half of the table – Allen, Murray, Jones, Scanlon, Basnett, and McGarvey linking up with Lever at the end.

Healey, Varley and McIntosh introduced the papers in a fairly low-key way. Murray and Bateman responded for the TUC and the CBI respectively, not particularly directed to the papers but more a repetition of their contributions to the Summit briefings – worries about unemployment or profits, investment or the tax squeeze on small firms, plus a mutual concern about imports.

The TUC people then led concerted pressure for more training of skilled men. Scanlon said this would get worse in the next two years and he called for one year's retraining for everybody.

Finniston was very good, clear and firm. He said that everybody agreed on the diagnosis of the problems but there was no consensus on the objectives or the solutions. He suggested high productivity to make us competitive abroad, and high quality of production and servicing. He criticised the paper for stressing too much flexibility, and constituting too big a retreat from planning.

McGarvey said in a threatening tone that there was no prospect of union co-operation on overmanning while there was unemployment. 'No hope in retraining people for nothing.' He said the paper 'means nothing to me because this is the language of the market place'.

Several CBI people attacked the concept of picking and backing industrial winners. Because winners change – only the market can pick them, not governments.

Campbell Adamson of the CBI said it was OK if they were deciding to give industrial policy priority; industry could only invest in a climate not hostile.

This priority for industrial investment was definitely the theme of ministers. Only Jack Jones spotted that this meant downgrading other policy demands – including social policies.

Shirley Williams said they were all too relaxed in their timetable. On the brink of disaster. Must act now. She suggested that they mobilise all the vacant places in the colleges to provide retraining courses. She also suggested doing a deal with industry, giving some relaxation in price controls in return for guaranteed investment in new jobs.

Healey and Varley then summed up, proposing further working papers and committees on 30 key industries to report back by January.

The trade unionists said they were still puzzled at what the objectives of the policy were.

We broke for lunch shortly after 1 p.m. Eric Roll of Warburgs merchant bank talked to me about the Slater Walker rescue. He was doubtful about the honesty of one of the leading protagonists, but he said the outside directors were presented with it as a fait accompli.

Also talked to Michael Foot at lunch about unemployment. He is very worried about the political situation next spring, when he thinks things will be wrong for us, and the Tories will make a push. He wants some money spent now to get the government over that difficult patch.

The afternoon session was quite short because HW took people on his conducted tour of Chequers. I am sure this was because he knew that Foot's paper on manpower, which was the afternoon agenda, was unsatisfactory and would come under attack, so he protected Michael by limiting the discussion.

We broke at 3.30 and everybody streamed back to London. The PM had a press conference in the Treasury. I didn't go because we were preparing a paper in the Unit on unemployment. Anyway I left at 6 p.m. to go to the American embassy for a lecture on the American Revolution 1774–83 by my old Harvard supervisor, Bernard Bailyn. When I returned No.10 was empty. Andrew had put in our paper. The PM had left for Chequers again.

I travelled part of the way home in Ken Stowe's car and we discussed how to handle the council house sales questions, where Crosland is trying to delay us. Crosland had asked to see me about it. Private office replied no, if he wanted to talk he must talk to the PM direct. Crosland said OK, but now the PM says he wants Crosland to talk to me. So I will go to talk to Crosland about the politics of it, and will invite some officials from DOE and No.10 to discuss the technicalities. Perhaps we can then make some progress – but not in time for the PM's speech at the local authorities conference (which delay was I presume one of Crosland's objectives).

Home at 9.30.

## Thursday 6 November 1975

The PM slept at Chequers, then went direct to London airport to greet Sadat of Egypt arriving for his official visit and was back in No.10 by 9.50 a.m.

Cabinet at 10.15 discussed unemployment. Apparently it went 'well', with little difficulty for the Chancellor. John Hunt said that Foot was 'statesmanlike'.

I went for lunch at the Reform with Dahrendorf and Douglas Allen, mainly to discuss Dahrendorf's idea for a new Brookings Institute at LSE, housed on the top floor of the new library. Allen was very helpful. A highly intelligent man who seems to me wasted at CSD. He doesn't play silly bureaucratic games or empire-build.

Dahrendorf also said I would have no problems with my departure date from No.10 to return to LSE, whether to extend or terminate early. [This proved optimistic and Dahrendorf was unable to deliver. Within a few months the author was told by the authorities of the LSE that he must immediately choose between either leaving Number Ten or resigning his career tenure at the school. Not appreciating the choice, which infuriated Prime Minister Callaghan, he resigned.]

I did not go to PQs after lunch – one of the few I have ever missed. Because there was a meeting of the official Ireland committee in the Cabinet Office to take the revised papers following the previous meeting. It went smoothly. The papers were good, and Frank Cooper had produced an annex on Dominion status which seemed very sensible. We are beginning to hammer out a policy for the longer term which begins to make some sense: 'distancing', by means of a minister resident there and by trying to develop indigenous institutions of government from the local level upwards; accompanied by a return to 'Majority Rule' with real safeguards for the Irish minority; evolving towards either a satisfactory form of government within the UK, or towards a new constitutional association of a Dominion kind. It may not work – nothing ever has in Ireland – but at least it gives us something sensible to work towards strategically instead of just staggering from day to day.

Afterwards we had a quick meeting of the Cabinet Office Deputy Secretaries to discuss business for next week – when the PM has a horrendous programme.

The PM had a special committee on Chrysler at the House this afternoon, from which I am excluded on grounds of 'commercial confidence'. Ridiculous. Joe was there and said it was a 'depressing' meeting. Ministers were trying to duck taking the inescapable harsh decision of closing it down. HW is clear on this. He wants the closure phased, and if possible to preserve the Iranian order at Linwood. But there is on the present operations no long-term future for Chrysler. Every job saved for Chrysler is a job lost for British Leyland. Apparently Willie Ross sat there saying that we could not close it – but without having an alternative. Peter Shore left early. So they are going to continue the negotiations but with little to negotiate for. The Americans have left Britain.

The PM stayed on at the House till after 6, so I went on to the reception at the Russian embassy to celebrate the November Revolution. It is a great ugly fortress of a building. No cars were allowed through the gate so guests had to walk up the drive, eyed by numerous security guards and the various cameras and electronic devices which they use. Inside it was packed and a most terrible scrum. The refreshments were hard to find and guests were hunting in packs looking for them. There was a sea of broad Slavic faces. Never have I been in such a large crowd with not a single pretty face in sight. I found Robert Armstrong in a corner and we decided to leave early.

In fact I drank more than usual because wherever I found any of the rare drink supplies I felt compelled to have some in case no more appeared. So I had two vodkas, then a glass of Russian white wine (not bad) and some red wine, with caviar in between. This was not a good way to start a long evening. Because I went on to a dinner given at the LSE by Dahrendorf for its government department. All the old professors emeritus were there – Oakeshott, Smellie, Robson, Schapiro, Greaves, as well as the current stock, the best of whom is my old friend George Jones. It was curious to be back in the academic world again, with long meandering discussions about very little. Dahrendorf handled them well and is clearly brighter than anybody there except Michael Oakeshott, who was delightful and anarchic as ever.

Walked to Euston with George Jones and then took the tube. Home at midnight.

## Friday 7 November 1975

Went in early to be there before 9.30 for the weekly diary meeting in the PM's study – though we have not had many in recent weeks. I came in through the front door with Jim Callaghan, who is clearly continuing to enjoy life. Nothing much came up at the meeting.

Callaghan stayed on afterwards to discuss the Egyptians with HW. Sadat was here for talks all morning. HW looked tired – he did go briefly to the Russian embassy last night, and then went on to a reception at Grosvenor House where he stayed till half-past midnight.

I went to the Unit and worked on papers. Also was visited by Carol's Israeli cousin – it seemed appropriate while the Egyptian President Sadat was in the Cabinet Room.

Joe told me that the lobby has the rumour that he is having an affair with Janet. He reported this to HW and they both roared with laughter. Curious how the press just always gets it wrong.

Went to lunch with Ambassador Elliot Richardson at the American embassy. He is very bullish about Britain and clearly very pleased with his political prospects in the USA. He is going back to be Secretary for Commerce on 16 January – a pity because he only arrived here in the spring. Ron Spiers was rather worried about who his successor might be. Richardson is said to have a drink problem, but that is probably the typical malicious gossip of the envious. He drank two Bloody Marys and some wine, but was perfectly OK. He does have a very drawly voice, which sounds slurred even when completely sober. But he has certainly been a success here and I am sorry he is going. He is fascinated by politics and genuinely interested in what is going on in Britain. It is clear that they all assume that HW will stay on for a long time now.

Felt very tired when I returned. HW summoned Joe and me and Nick Stuart to his study shortly after 3 p.m. to discuss his Lord Mayor's speech at the Guildhall. This went on for hours. We finally broke up at about 5.30. Within 10 minutes the PM summoned us back again to discuss his Commons speech on the debate on the Queen's Speech. Then we gossiped over the whole political field. He served us with drinks and this went on till after 7 p.m.

Earlier in the day the PM had taken me on one side to 'warn me' about the Israeli diplomats in Britain. He said that they were all intriguing. That someone called Wenger was scheming with Gatt to get rid of the Ambassador, and he attacked several others. I could not work out what he meant. So I went up to the flat while he was changing for tonight's Sadat reception and raised it with him. I said I did not get involved with any Israeli intrigues. They contacted me firstly because we had mutual friends and relatives in Israel and secondly because Marcia never answered the phone to them. (He said, 'That's true. She's never there.') And that I would not snub them because of my strong attachment to Israel.

He then went into some curious explanation about how one of the Israeli representatives was suspiciously close to Gerald Kaufman, but they had now fallen out, and Marcia was upset, and the Israeli Ambassador was involved. It was not clear how I was concerned, but he implied that Marcia had suggested to him that I was involved in the intrigues against the Ambassador. I don't think he believed it. He was simply giving way to pressure. By the end he was standing there in his pants chatting away about Israel. He also said he was afraid of what Mary might say tonight sitting next to Sadat because she is very anti-Arab.

The Unit was working on an economic brief. It was not ready when I had to leave them and go upstairs to the Sadat dinner. I arrived as the guests were going in to the dining-room. It was unsatisfactory and I felt guilty having left Andrew Graham and the others in the Unit to get on with the work while I buzzed in and out. But that is a difficulty with this job: it is two jobs, dealing with HW and various problems relating to ministers and civil servants, and also running the Unit. At times it is necessary to sacrifice one for the other. Fortunately the Unit members are absolutely first-class, and of course are far more technically expert than I am in many policy areas.

The dinner was OK, not too long. I sat next to the film star Stanley Baker's wife, and to Ron Hayward's wife who is very nice indeed. Ron is lucky.

Marcia had brought as her guest John Cordle, the Tory MP she goes around with. He has been mentioned in relation to the Poulson scandal. [Cordle was later persuaded by his party Whips to resign his Commons seat over his association with Poulson.]

The reception afterwards was quite pleasant, though not as lively as usual. There were so many fat Egyptians and so many businessmen after their contracts that it left less room than usual for lively young guests. But I had a pleasant talk with Diana Rigg, who is remarkably intelligent for an actress.

Patrick Wright told me that last night the PM sidled up to him, gave him a piece of paper with Marcia's handwriting on it, and without looking at him said quickly, 'Invite them to the reception tomorrow.' On the paper were the inevitable names – Sir Joseph and Lady Kagan, Mr and Mrs Eric Miller, Sir George Weidenfeld. Patrick questioned Eric Miller's name on the grounds that he was an active officer and financier in various pro-Israel organisations. Rather like inviting Arafat of the PLO to the Israeli reception. The PM apparently looked embarrassed and said it is OK, because 'Miller doesn't get on well with the Israelis either.'

Pretty Mrs Miller was glaring at Marcia, who looked worried, and poor Eric stayed away from both of them.

We stayed until midnight.

Incidentally Janet told me today that HW had said to her that Marcia only wanted him to stay on as Prime Minister so she could 'stay on the gravy train'. He also seems still committed to retiring before the Budget. He has talked of selling Lord North Street but keeping a flat in town.

# CHAPTER 21

## Public Expenditure Crisis – and Playing Poker With Chrysler and Games With the Doctors
## November–December 1975

### Monday 10 November 1975

Into the office early. The PM was coming up from Chequers and did not arrive till after 11 a.m. I shut myself up in my room and read the two Treasury papers on public expenditure for Thursday's Cabinet (very long and involved arguments) and a very good but again very long CPRS paper on Ireland.

At 11.30 there was a briefing for the Rambouillet economic Summit. Beforehand John Hunt slipped upstairs to talk to the PM in his study. A little thing, but significant. Normally he would clear this with private office. No.10 is Ken Stowe's territory. But John Hunt is trying to colonise it. Later Ken said there was 'tension' between them. Hunt has put the squeeze on Joe and me at various times and now is squeezing Ken. Ken is quite upset about it. HW won't intervene. He is a timid mouse before the senior civil servants.

The briefing was very pedestrian, with little emerging. Both the Chancellor and Harold Lever were good. The main discussion was about whether we should insist on an independent note-taker, since we did not trust the French to record it fairly.

After the meeting I went to the Reform for a quick lunch and chatted there to an old friend Bob Gavron.

Afterwards HW summoned us to the study and we worked on his speech for tonight at the Guildhall. And discussed the shape of the speech on the Queen's Speech next week.

HW shuffled us out before 5 – when he was seeing the Israeli Ambassador. This was totally contrary to promises given by Wilson to Callaghan on Friday morning after 'prayers' and again this morning after the briefing. Each time Callaghan had insisted that as Foreign Secretary he must be there when the PM saw the Israeli Ambassador. HW gave a firm promise, but two hours later Marcia telephoned from home (she did not come in today) to insist that HW see Ambassador Raphael alone this afternoon. HW gave way, to the great embarrassment of Patrick Wright in private office.

Joe told me that Marcia has also arranged for the PM to see the Spanish Ambassador at Lord Mountbatten's place.

The PM went to the Guildhall at 6.45. I saw him as he left, trapped tight in tails and stiff shirt which he hates. Mrs Wilson, Ken Stowe and Janet went with him. He was playing around happily like a little boy before he left.

I then went across to see Frank Judd, the excellent young Navy minister. He told me that Roy Mason was breathing fire over the further £450 million Defence cuts which Healey is proposing. But he is mainly concerned with Iceland, and worried about the current jingoism here which is talking of going to war with the Icelanders on behalf of a few trawler owners. He talked good sense and I promised to talk to HW about it on Wednesday.

Left him at 8.30 and went home. Suffering from a bad headache and eye-strain. The flow of papers in the office has suddenly become enormous and it is difficult to keep up, as well as all the other engagements. But at least I now know what is important and what to skip.

– Next morning Albert and Bill told me that HW and Janet returned to No.10 at midnight from the Guildhall and stayed chatting in his study till after 2 a.m. Bill was furious, since he had to wait downstairs and did not get home until 3 a.m.

## Tuesday 11 November 1975

I arrived just before Cabinet. Looked for Tony Crosland to discuss council house sales and Thursday's Cabinet on public expenditure, but he was late.

There was some nervousness in the house over a snide *Daily Mail* piece reporting the friendship between Marcia and John Cordle, the Tory MP who has been mentioned in the Poulson corruption context.

I worked on papers all morning. Also had discussions with the Unit on our proposed public expenditure brief. We must find a way to get through to the PM on this. He read our weekend brief but did not react to our arguments that it is not necessary to go for such big public expenditure cuts as Healey is demanding – £3.75 billion. It is clear that the PM is trying to stay out of this argument, leaving Healey and Crosland to fight it out – and Mason who has sent a telegram saying that he will resign if Defence is cut a further £450 million. But it seems that it will need more than one Cabinet to resolve this one and then HW will have to get involved, to find a solution.

After Cabinet I walked outside with Crosland. He said he would not accept Healey's proposals and that Thursday's discussion will have to be wholly about the total cuts. We agreed to have a drink tomorrow evening to discuss it (and when I returned from lunch he had already fixed it).

Had lunch in the Commons Press Gallery with Joe. Discuss the pressure John Hunt is putting on Ken Stowe in No.10 and agree to talk to the PM about it.

At Questions briefing the PM was sparkling and happy and claiming that he now loves Question Time. He thinks he now knows how to do it – 'getting stuck in positively' rather than cautiously 'trying to play out time' as before. 'It is football, not cricket.'

No reference to the *Daily Mail* at all – 12 months ago he would have looked black and started a witch hunt for the 'leakers'.

Question Time itself went well. Mrs Thatcher did not intervene – she never does on Tuesdays. The Tories looked very down.

Afterwards HW poured out drinks for us all to celebrate the end of the session – Parliament breaks tomorrow at noon (the Tories are putting on an all-night 3-line whip) and reopens for the new session next Wednesday.

At 4 p.m. we had the Cabinet committee on Ireland in the PM's room at the House. The papers were good – pointing to 'majority rule', 'distancing' to develop Ulster's own local political institutions, and perhaps ultimately to 'Dominion status'. But the politicians were not interested. Rees, Healey and Callaghan all said 'do nothing'. Just sit and wait. No new initiatives.

HW and Jenkins were the only two looking for something different in the longer term – separation from Britain. They were also the only two aware that the present quiet may not continue, and then there will be panicking calls for change. Better to plan change now while there is time.

But it was impossible to make progress with reluctant ministers. Especially Jim Callaghan who has experience in Ulster. HW diverted them into speculations about building a Berlin Wall between North and South Ireland.

Afterwards HW said, 'Only Roy agreed with me.'

Back to No.10 for Unit discussions on public expenditure, planning our briefs for tomorrow.

Then Carol came in and we went to the Tate for the Paul Nash retrospective exhibition – including my own *Romney Marsh*. Never thought I would have a picture hanging in the Tate. It looked beautiful.

Home at 9 p.m.


*Wednesday 12 November 1975*

The PM sent for us very early on and we worked on speeches – Joe, myself and Nick Stuart. First on his speech on the Address next Wednesday and then on the local government speech for next Thursday. On the latter Crosland and the Environment Department are putting on a bit of pressure against saying anything blunt and honest about the excessive spending in local government. I press the PM to resist this. He may upset a few councillors and officers, but most people are ratepayers and taxpayers and will expect him to tell the truth.

We broke at noon and I had a Unit meeting to discuss public expenditure for tomorrow's Cabinet. This is developing into a big battle. The Treasury wants £3.75 billion cuts. Crosland is talking of resigning if it is more than £2.5 billion. Mason sent a telegram saying he would resign if Defence was cut by £450 million.

I had lunch with Douglas Wass at the Reform. I like him more and more personally. Obviously he is technically very good. But I am not sure he is a tough enough mandarin to deal with some of the reptiles in the dark waters of Whitehall. He does not have that instinct for the jugular which marks out for success in the Whitehall jungle. So he is usually outgunned by the Cabinet Office.

We went over the ground together. He conceded that Crosland might be correct in that there would not be a resource problem in 1978–79; maybe there would still be high unemployment and free resources to expand investment and exports. (This is the heart of Crosland's critique of the Treasury paper.) But Wass insists that without the cuts we won't be able to borrow to cover our domestic and trading deficits. Therefore we must get public expenditure radically down and balance our external payments by 1978.

He may be right, and the price of ignoring him could be total collapse before 1978. On the other hand if Crosland is right, and the investment and exports won't happen anyway, and there will still be recession then anyway, then all we are doing is digging a deeper hole, and Labour will pay the price at the next election. It is a calculation of risks either way. The Treasury may be over-cautious, and inflict the maximum self-denial, because otherwise the risk is national bankruptcy. Crosland says why pay a certain political price at the polls and a social price in unemployment when the economic disaster may not come anyway – or the economic recovery may not come in a dramatic way and so we won't need the extra resources to feed into exports and investment and prevent an explosion of overheating in the economy.

Wass said that one problem was that Healey cannot resist the temptation to get involved in theoretical economic arguments. He is always joining in debate with the academic journals. He did the same on Defence strategy. The Treasury want him to form a clear and firm judgement and stick to it. Too often he gets involved in a theoretical argument and abandons his departmental position.

Wass said that the Treasury had asked Michael Posner, the Cambridge economist now advising the Chancellor, to do an analysis and critique of Crosland's paper and to brief Healey on it beforehand.

Drove back in Wass's car. In No. 10 the Governor of the Bank was with the PM making sure he supports the Chancellor tomorrow. I intercepted Richardson on his way out and we went over the ground. He feels that even the Chancellor's maximum figure for cuts is too small – because really he wants a fundamental shift in balance between the public and the private sector. He also has a fair point – that the cuts always slip anyway. The £1 billion cut in the last budget has already been more than lost in slippages in greater expenditure.

I went back to the Unit where we worked the rest of the afternoon on an economic brief for the PM. We argued the case for lower cuts than £3.75 billion. Economically because we believe Crosland is correct about resources. Politically because Healey's policy involves an actual real cut in public expenditure over the next three years – the first time a Labour government has done this. We believe that a figure of around £2.5 billion will secure the borrowing confidence without destroying the party and creating unnecessary unemployment in 1978–79. We also suggested that some extra possible cuts be agreed and kept on the shelf, to be imposed if it seems that the Treasury is proving right and there will be resource constraints later.

The PM went off to see the Ambassador of fascist Spain at Lord Mountbatten's house. This has been arranged by Marcia at Mountbatten's request. It would create a terrible storm in the party. It was all very secret. Patrick Wright told me that the PM looked very guilty when mentioning it and said that he did not wish to receive any Foreign Office views on whether he should do it or not. He has simply been told to do it. Marcia incidentally is ill with a throat infection. 'Unfortunately not a garrotte,' said Albert, who is presently suffering hell from her and is not feeling in a comradely frame of mind.

At 6.30 I went to see Tony Crosland in his departmental office. He was looking very tired and told me that he sleeps on his settee every afternoon.

We discussed the public expenditure problem. I had taken along some graphs demonstrating that his position was sound – historically there was no precedent for a simultaneous growth in exports and investment of the kind that the Treasury was anticipating and fearing.

But I warned him that it would be a test of muscle. HW would probably stand by Healey – and neither of those really believed that Crosland would resign. They did believe Mason would resign. On that basis Crosland would lose. He said he thought others might resign: Castle, Benn, Foot. I queried this. Barbara is tough and not a resigner and anyway

HW often says he would be pleased to get rid of her. Benn seemed to have decided merely to read his objections and Cassandra predictions into the record and then wait for the collapse. Foot seemed to have decided to see it through. I sensed Crosland weakening at this, and I decided that he would not go through with the fight in the end. I asked him what was his resigning sticking-point. He said it was (a) if his housing investment were cut and (b) if the total cuts meant an overall reduction in public expenditure.

He then switched to the Rate Support Grant. He is worried that we shall upset the local authorities by cutting the Rate Support Grant percentage. A ministerial committee had decided not to do this, out of fear of reactions from Labour councillors basically, but the Treasury were taking it up to Cabinet. I said I would mention it to HW. It seems that Crosland is worried by the reaction of local authorities to his own speech saying that the 'party' of local government overspending is over now. He is trying to mollify them. I understand that. He cannot attack them on all fronts. But nor is it our job to give way to the local authorities on all fronts just to provide a quiet life for the Department of the Environment.

Went back to No.10 at 3 p.m. and drafted our brief to the PM, informing him of the Crosland position.

Home at 10.30 p.m. Joe telephoned at 11 p.m. to say that the PM had met Professor McGregor, the new chairman of the Press Commission. The latter was very impressed by the PM's evidence on press bias and was particularly impressed by the section on 'door-stepping' by an 'anonymous academic'. This was revealed to be me, and McGregor said he was so struck by it that he would like it expanded. The PM was apparently very nice about me, telling McGregor that I was 'serious' and that the Unit had significantly altered the working of central government.

Joe was very keen to tell me this. He said he was worried that I was sometimes disenchanted with HW. And that what really mattered was what HW said to outsiders about me, not how he reacted to Marcia's hostile pressure.

Apparently the PM came back to No.10 this evening and spent some time in the study with Janet. He seems to be much happier and with much greater appetite for his work. He told Joe that he was again enjoying being PM now – which may mean a further delay in the departure date.

## Thursday 13 November 1975

This morning the great Cabinet on public expenditure. All the ministers were gathered in the foyer outside the Cabinet Room several minutes beforehand, in a hubbub of expectation. The PM came over for a chat and said to me and Lever that 'the crucial thing is to avoid resignations'.

I then briefed him on the Crosland position. He said 'come into here' and took me into the lavatory next to the waiting-room. While he peed I explained that housing investment was Crosland's sticking-point, and that he must be prepared to deal with the question of an absolute fall in public expenditure. He said that he would support Crosland on housing investment. But it was clear that in general he would support Healey. I suspect this is partly because he quite rightly feels that he cannot allow Healey to go on being defeated in Cabinet. Partly and again quite rightly he really does feel that public expenditure has grown too far too fast, and that we cannot raise taxes any more. He also calculated that in the crunch Crosland will climb down.

As the ministers were going into the Cabinet Room John Hunt came dashing up to Ken Stowe and myself and said that he had 'almost documentary' evidence that this morning's leak in the *Guardian* about the Cabinet discussion was 'done by Crosland'. I was immediately suspicious. This was too like an attempt to smear Crosland in advance. Later I discussed it with my economists and with Joe. All thought that there was clearly more than one hand in the leak – but the main source seemed to be the Treasury. But the best thing was that the PM seemed so relaxed about it.

Apparently he started the Cabinet by saying that this was 'the worst day of the year' and he hoped that they would conduct their differences in a civilised way. They did. Everyone afterwards said how friendly and polite the disagreements had been.

I worked in the Unit all morning. At the end of Cabinet I went down to hear the reports. Crosland left looking very annoyed. Healey seemed pleased. The PM reported that Healey had won by two votes – including himself and Callaghan, though the private secretary told me that Callaghan had not come down on either side, and he was not convinced it was not really the other way by one vote.

Clearly it was a razor-edge decision, and the PM had decided it for the Chancellor by having the right to count the heads himself and to sum up.

HW said that Healey was 'too soft' on public expenditure. He obviously felt that he had been forced to do the Chancellor's dirty work for him. He also complained about Barbara Castle prattling on and said that at one point he had to tell her to shut up.

However, the battle is not really over. The decision was to leave the Treasury to hold bilateral discussions about particular departmental cuts. This is the stage at which blood is traditionally spilt and where individual ministers may decide to resign. This is where the Treasury may give way on lots of little things and end up with slippage from their £3.75 billion total. So Crosland could recover a lot by the end. Especially since the PM supported our idea of keeping some of the cuts 'on the shelf', only to be imposed if clearly necessary in the future.

Joe and I went to the Commons for lunch.

Marcia is still away ill. So the meeting of the 'Office Trust' (Eric Miller, Sternberg, Sammy Fisher and several others who help to provide for the political office) has been cancelled. Albert says that he has never seen any political office accounts and thinks HW never sees them.

Since she is in bed, Bill Housden has spent the day doing her shopping and errands in the PM's car. One of the drivers has complained to CSD that the No.10 drivers cannot log all their journeys, and so claim precise overtime, and implied that it was because too much time was spent on non-governmental duties. I know that the other drivers are angry that Bill is always occupied on Fridays taking Marcia to the hairdresser's, shopping, etc. So they have to go away for the PM's trips to Liverpool, etc. and Bill usually stays in London.

I went to the weekly Deputy Secretaries meeting in the Cabinet Office. John Hunt continues to behave as if he runs No.10, and Ken Stowe is getting more and more irritated. Ken says that Douglas Allen is also fed up with Hunt's interference in his CSD work, especially appointments.

In the evening we had a dinner for top industrialists: Weinstock of GEC, Wright from ICI, Jack Cohen of Tesco, Knight from Courtaulds, Alex Jarrett from Reed, Orr from Unilever, etc. Except for Arnold Weinstock, who showed his LSE education by talking impressively intellectually, the level was poor. They went on and on about planning agreements. But clearly last week's Chequers meeting has done some good.

The ministers were good – especially Shirley Williams and Edmund Dell. HW talked too much, and was clearly bored. He said afterwards he was fed up having to give elementary lessons in politics to industrialists.

It dragged on till midnight. I sat with Ken Stowe and Adrian Cadbury, who is very nice and able, at the end. We ate a whole plate of Turkish delight, and John Hunt sent a very funny note down the table complaining that it had been the only plate of Turkish delight on the table and demanding an official inquiry into who had eaten it.

At the end the PM looked inclined to discuss the meeting with us, but I slipped out and took a lift home with Edmund Dell. He is clearly not optimistic about the general outlook. Even this morning's Cabinet decision did not encourage him – he thinks it should have happened a year ago.

Home at 12.25 p.m. (I had been running on Hampstead Heath as usual this morning shortly after 7 a.m. with John Carrier. It was a long day. But I feel very fit and somewhat happier than of late – as always when we get involved in serious policy issues.)

## Friday 14 November 1975

Drove in early to the office, taking the car all the way to Horse Guards for the first time in many weeks. Arrived 9.15 and cleared some papers before going upstairs to the diary meeting in the PM's study. Not much of significance emerged there. Healey and Callaghan were there but did not discuss yesterday's Cabinet.

Jim Callaghan incidentally is clearly enjoying being Foreign Secretary immensely. One thing troubles me: I sense that he is looking for a 'victory over the foreigners'. Over Iceland fishing, over oil in the EEC, over the economic Summit. But Britain lacks the basic strength of France. Above all we need co-operation from our allies to finance us through the deficits ahead.

The PM went off in morning suit for two hours to Cardinal Heenan's funeral.

I worked in the Unit. Then had a long meeting about the next honours list with Ken Stowe, Joe and Janet. I crossed out some right-wing academics, most of the architects, and some mediocre establishment musicians. Try to put in Max Wall and some other vulgar entertainers who our people appreciate.

Lunch at the House with Joe and Janet. In the public cafeteria – only 38p for fishcake and chips.

In the afternoon HW saw Goodman about the press, and then had another briefing for the economic Summit, which I chose not to attend since there is nothing new to say.

Worked in the Unit on briefs for the PM's local authority speech. We are producing evidence of the terrifying growth in Civil Service and local government staffing – the departments have refused to provide any figures, saying that it is too difficult to get them. This is disgraceful. They are up to their tricks again. Anything to protect their own job prospects. It is to the credit of the private secretaries in private office that they don't go along with this attitude.

Nigel Wicks, Robin Butler's replacement, is very good and co-operating marvellously. Confirms my view that the good young civil servants are very helpful and responsible. It is the second-raters and the older cynics who are the problem.

Finished at 8 p.m. and put in our briefs – the PM had left for Chequers at 4 p.m. and is off to France for the economic Summit tomorrow.

Home to a nice dinner with Nori Graham and Carol. Feel much less tired than usual on a Friday. Relieved I am not going to France. All of those phoney trappings of power mean nothing now. It is reality or nothing.

*Monday 17 November 1975*

PM away at the Heads of Government economic Summit at Rambouillet. I went in to No. 10 as usual. Cleared my papers by 10.45 and then went off to see Tony Crosland about our proposals for the sale of council housing.

David Lipsey and Mrs Carlton, Crosland's two political advisers, were there. They put up their objections to our schemes – which were basically political and relate mainly to the local government elections next May. They – and especially Lipsey and Crosland – made a good case; though I feel he is still too pussy-footing with the local authorities and afraid of anything which makes them protest. He simply doesn't want trouble.

We also discussed last week's Cabinet. Crosland sensibly understood that HW could not allow his Chancellor to be defeated again. This I think was one of his main reasons for supporting Healey. It was essential for the morale of the government that its Chancellor should be seen to be winning on tough policies.

I pointed out to Crosland that he must not be seen to be capitulating to the local authorities on every issue. Or else HW will react and feel he personally has to take a tough line.

Went off to a good fish lunch with Carol's uncle Louis in Charlotte Street and then to Oxford. Stayed overnight at my lovely old college, Lincoln College in the Turl. I really went to talk to the new rector, Lord Trend, who as Burke Trend was John Hunt's predecessor as Cabinet Secretary. I found him very impressive: clever, discreet, austere, with a clear idea of what central government is about. He looked after me marvellously – despite the fact that he had another guest – Archbishop Ramsey, former Archbishop of Canterbury – and his wife was ill. In fact this morning he brought me tea in bed, personally, at 7.15 a.m. and then cooked me egg and toast for breakfast. Totally without side. Still fascinated by government and politics. Lincoln is very lucky to have him.

Archbishop Ramsey is quite a character. Charismatic, and just a touch of the old rogue about him. His wife was also very strange. She sat on the floor and appeared to be under the impression that Ted Heath was still Prime Minister.

*Tuesday 18 November 1975*

Travelled up from Oxford on the 9 a.m. train like a commuter. The trains feel bigger and faster and infinitely more expensive than when I was a student.

Arrived in the office at 10.30. Learned that the PM had a chill and was not going to meet President Nyerere at Victoria. He came straight to No.10

and we straight away worked with him on his speeches ahead. HW looked shivery and said that his bones ached. He seemed to be falling for the flu, and said he had sent for his doctor, Joe Stone.

The PM's Commons speech is very good and providing that HW is well enough he should demolish Thatcher tomorrow.

Apparently the Andover plane returning from Rambouillet had a terrible landing again. Dropped 300 feet just short of the runway. And the flight engineer, who had been with us on the VC10 to Washington in February, said that the terrible experience when we landed there was the nearest he had ever been to death, and that the VC10 was definitely about to stall.

Lunch at the Reform with Ken Stowe. He told me that the PM was getting jumpy again about our having office lunches at No.10. But we intend to go ahead.

Cabinet this afternoon was apparently fairly traumatic. A long hassle on elections to the European Parliament – finally split virtually the same as the EEC vote. Then on electoral reform they overthrew Jenkins's proposal – agreed beforehand with HW and Short – to put electoral reform on the agenda of the Speaker's Conference. HW said he was in favour of sending it to the Speaker's Conference because that would kill it. But he accepted the majority against – though of course if the Tories insisted they would have to change their minds. A bad defeat for Jenkins. A pity. Our electoral system is ridiculous and could bring the whole political system down into disrepute.

Then a long discussion of Rate Support Grant. Finally, by a narrow vote, they overthrew Crosland – who wanted 66½%. But HW did not let the Treasury have its 64½%. He split the difference at 65½%, which was the worst of all worlds. It breached the principle of not giving local authorities any increase in public expenditure. But it offended them by not giving them as much as they wanted – the same as last year.

That is two defeats for Crosland in a week. A pity. But he is suffering from the massive unpopularity of the local authorities.

Afterwards HW and the private secretaries gathered in private office where he joked and told long stories, in cheerful form despite a sore throat and running nose. (Joe Stone also found his heart was racing again.) Then we went upstairs for the eve-of-session party always given to junior ministers to hear the Queen's Speech read. A nice party. They formally bang the doors closed in the big reception-room. Then HW reads the Queen's Speech and Bob Mellish as Chief Whip talks about the problems of parliamentary management in the session ahead.

I noticed how lonely and isolated Reg Prentice looked.

Took a lift home in Alma Birk's car.

Nice to be home in the warm with the children.

[The Queen's Speech proposed a heavy legislative programme for the parliamentary session ahead. It stressed counter-inflation through price controls and the need to bring down unemployment as a precondition to winning the anti-inflation battle. It promised: the nationalisation of aircraft and shipbuilding; legislation for Scottish and Welsh Assemblies after a White Paper; more housing construction; to phase out private practice from National Health hospitals; that pensions and social security benefits would be increased; and to abolish selection in secondary education. On 25 November, the fifth day of the debate, the government had a majority of 14 on an Opposition amendment attacking the government's economic policies, and of 6 on a Liberal amendment opposing the proposals to extend the Dock Labour Scheme.]

## *Wednesday 19 November 1975*

HW sent for Joe and me shortly after I arrived and we discussed his speech for the Opening of Parliament this afternoon. He still had signs of a chill but seemed much recovered. The speech was now very good and very tough.

We were in the study for over two hours. Then I left. Joe stayed behind and discussed H's planned trips for January to the Middle East. The PM said he was having second thoughts. He still intends to retire in February/March, and he thought it would look odd to go on major visits and then to resign immediately afterwards. He spoke of himself being 'a lame-duck Prime Minister'. Then he added – 'But of course they don't know I'm going, do they?'

Patrick in private office showed me a very disturbing letter. Marcia had sent HW a draft letter for him to sign and send to Prince Fahd of Saudi Arabia recommending her brother Tony, who was going there with three associates to try to get contracts.

HW had discussed it with Patrick and thought it would be a good idea to follow up the Saudi visit here with 'this initiative'. In fact dozens of our big companies are trying to get business in Saudi Arabia and none of them have been given this kind of support. Patrick is very worried. Joe and I recommended him to get his objections on paper and to keep a copy.

I went across to Parliament for the State Opening, which I have never seen before. It was pouring with rain and there was massive security around Westminster, but I got into the House through the underground tunnel from the tube station and then went up to Freddie Warren in the Chief Whip's Office. He took me to the members' lobby and we watched Black Rod come in procession, have the door of the Commons slammed in his face, and then knock on it to be admitted. Shortly after he returned to the

Lords followed by a procession of MPs – including John Stonehouse – to hear the Queen read the speech from the throne. We then had too much champagne in Freddy's room and watched the Queen return to the Palace in her golden coach.

Warren also told me about a difficulty with the honours list. One suggestion from No. 10 had been Illtyd Harrington – who has been seen around with Marcia. But apparently Bob Mellish had vetoed it.

Joe and I went to lunch at the House, in the reporters' café and then to H's room for a final run over of the speech. HW seemed very cheerful and gave the impression of having dined well at lunch – which was confirmed when he left the Chamber to pee three times in half an hour. He had a couple of brandies but did not seem at all on edge as he often is before a big Commons speech. In fact he was late going into the Chamber and missed the opening procedures.

Mrs Thatcher was very poor, brief and thin. Last time she had produced a long economic essay and got bogged down. This time she did the opposite, with a few aphorisms and political attacks. Her people looked glum.

HW spoke for 56 minutes. At first very low-key and uncertain. Then they started shouting and interrupting, and he became angry and took them on. From that point it became a powerful debating speech and he won hands down. It was obviously a much more serious speech than the House expected, completely destroying the Tory position on public expenditure.

Afterwards we went back to his room and went through his local government speech for tomorrow morning in Eastbourne. The Department of the Environment have continued to shower us with requests to remove all controversial points including any reference to the actual numbers employed in local government. They want to bleach it of all character, to blunt every bit of edge which is peculiar to H. He finally rebelled and rejected all their objections. They had overdone it. Joe and I were very pleased. I provided some telling figures on the explosion in local government manpower.

HW went to the Palace before setting off to Eastbourne in the car with Joe and Albert. I went back to the office and at last began to work through the day's papers. Left some unfinished and dashed off to the Criterion Theatre where I saw Tom Stoppard's *Rosencrantz and Guildenstern are Dead* with Carol. Clever, witty, but not very satisfying.

## Thursday 20 November 1975

Didn't bother to go in early today because the PM was at Eastbourne – where he was booed by the delegates for some of his criticisms of local government. I went to the barber's and travelled in slowly – arriving just before midday to find that the Dep Secs meeting had been moved to this morning. Went along to it. Some interesting discussion on how public expenditure was proceeding. The bilateral on Environment has already taken place. That on Defence takes place this afternoon. But even before it takes place both Defence and the Treasury have decided they won't agree and have already written their papers for OPD/Cabinet. Defence has made no attempt to assess where its cuts would fall, working on the assumption that it won't have to make them.

Apparently the Shah is not very interested in the 'through-deck' cruiser, so that is £500 million that can be saved.

Returned to No. 10 and found Carol already here for the Nyerere lunch. Joe and the PM returned from Eastbourne just before lunch. Apparently Albert is not in the New Year honours list – but will be in the resignation list. (But that means he cannot be put in the government.)

The business about Marcia's brother going to the Middle East continues. She has been on to the PM again today and he is sending a message to Prince Fahd. The Board of Trade and the Foreign Office have been alerted to provide all assistance.

The lunch was very nice and Nyerere was fabulous, amusing, warm and charismatic. Obviously a remarkable man.

Afterwards I walked around St James's Park with Dick Smethurst from my Unit discussing the prospects for import controls and changes in HP. These are rapidly looking up despite total and rigid and absolutely doctrinal opposition from the Board of Trade, which must be the last bastion of the Manchester School of liberal economics.

The PM had hours of talks with Nyerere in the Cabinet Room and then went to Misc 59 Cabinet committee on Chrysler. I did not go to this, but it lasted for 1¾ hours and the PM emerged very dissatisfied. He felt everybody had been negative, refusing to accept the tough approach, but unable to produce an alternative. He slapped down Varley at one point saying that he was too much in the hands of his officials. Afterwards Varley was complaining bitterly to Joe that if Harold wanted him to go he would go, and if he wanted Tony Benn he could have him. It was all a bit tense. Especially since it was disrupted by phone calls in the middle from Ron Hayward, Bob Mellish and Cledwyn Hughes, saying that the PLP was in an uproar over the decision to send a minister – Lord Shepherd – to Franco's funeral in Spain. HW and Jim Callaghan were brought out of the Chrysler meeting and took a tough no-nonsense line.

HW was also a bit worried about the reports in the *Evening News* that the Opposition groups would unite to defeat the government on a confidence motion at the end of the Address. He gave instructions that ministers should not go abroad.

After the meeting finished we gathered in private office and talked. The PM said he was fed up with his colleagues. I sensed that he was again ready to retire, and would be more so after his Rome trip in 10 days. He said he wanted no more state visits here for two years and wanted to abolish evening dress (he is off again to Claridge's tonight to a reception for Nyerere with the Queen).

Albert says that he is beginning to have trouble with his eyes.

He went upstairs to change – and to phone Marcia about her brother – at 7.30. I went off to collect Carol from the NUT and then came home at 8.30 p.m.

### Friday 21 November 1975

In too late to get to the weekly diary meeting. Sent Andrew Graham to the ministerial Economic Strategy committee. He reported afterwards that they had decided in favour of import controls on TV tubes, cars, and textiles, despite Lever's passionate opposition, though with a prior attempt by Shore to get the Japanese to restrict tubes as they have restricted car exports.

Apparently it was a very confused meeting and Andrew felt not everybody was clear on what they were deciding. Varley was very strongly for import controls. They also decided to ease hire purchase charges.

I worked on papers and then had a long talk to Joe. He is reverting to the view that HW should go. Now the pressure is on again HW is feeling the strain.

Apparently at yesterday's Chrysler meeting it became clearer that there is no solution. HW is pursuing compromises – run-downs, etc., to save Linwood, move Coventry to Linwood, etc. – not because he is optimistic they will be possible but because it is essential to be able to say that we explored every avenue to save it. Import controls are of course tied to the closure – so that we can prevent Chrysler replacing their lost UK production by Simca imports from France.

Went to lunch at Grieveson Grant. The former Tory Chancellor Heathcoat Amory was the main guest: now over 70, but bright as a button, witty and charming. Very up to date on what we are up to in government.

Also there was Ian Fraser of Lazards and Rolls-Royce, who is rather full of himself.

Returned at 3 p.m. The PM upstairs in his study. When he emerged I warned him that our letter of application to the IMF loan was in the Treasury and it contained some tough commitments. He should see it.

Afterwards worked in the Unit. Discussed import controls with Andrew Graham – I am against them but see no way round them. And the PM's Blackett Memorial Lecture with David Piachaud.

Then went home early at 6 p.m.

– There is a correspondence between Goodman and the PM which seems to envisage some big book by the PM on the working of government. [Harold Wilson's *The Governance of Britain* was published in 1976.]

## *Monday 24 November 1975*

My car (a 1967 Ford Cortina) has broken down again – the differential is bust – so I took it to the garage and did not get in to the office till 10.15 p.m.

Worked through a lot of papers. HW came in at 11 a.m. and I went down and we all gathered in private office. HW walked up and down with the private secretaries, Joe, Janet, Albert and myself standing around in a circle. He had redone his Blackett Memorial Lecture and was very pleased with the briefs from David Piachaud. But angry with Ron Hayward, Transport House and the NEC for their manoeuvres over Franco's funeral and caucuses to censure the government over its economic and industrial policy at Wednesday's joint meeting of the NEC and the Cabinet. He refused to go to this morning's high-level liaison meeting at Transport House because he is fed up with Ron Hayward. Actually he is irritated with the party and the endless mean manoeuvring that goes on. There are also rumours that Benn is planning some kind of resignation drama over unemployment/public expenditure. He made an ominous speech this weekend, and rumours are floating that he is preparing something. Maybe. Certainly this is part of H's jumpiness.

But I wonder if Benn will ever actually cut himself off from power. Surely it is better for him just to wait for Harold to go – and he may know about that, since Balogh is his Minister of State and he still talks to Marcia.

HW then became a bit worried about press coverage of his absence from the liaison committee. So he decided to pursue the Iceland fishing crisis as an excuse. He summoned the ministers involved to a meeting at No.10 and announced it to the press. There was nothing to decide on Iceland, just a report. I did not go to the meeting. I went early to lunch with Harold Lever, who has written some excellent papers recently – on reflation, against import controls, and for the building societies to loan mortgage money to a wider range of clients, including for the purchase of council houses.

Was told by Joe today that HW had approached a finance house to loan money to Marcia's brother Tony Field to pay his tax debts. Tony wants £60,000. He says that his land is now worth £300,000 – because he bought it without planning permission and it now has planning permission. The paper, a copy of which was shown to me, also says that the Field family put up £130,000 of their own money for the original investment. The land

– and Tony's £40,000 house at Blisworth – is being put up as collateral. The PM is personally asking that the loan be given.

At 3.45 I went in to a meeting with the Textile Unions in the Cabinet Room. Sad tale of unemployment and inevitable pressure for import controls (some of which we shall shortly do).

Goodman came in at 5.15 p.m. He has offered to act as mediator in the big dispute between Barbara Castle and the doctors over private medicine.

I returned to work in my office.

Then to a party for International Women's Year. Lots of nice ladies and I enjoyed it – especially the very pretty lady jockey, Jane Macdonald.

But annoyed because HW has struck me off the list to go to Rome next week. Apparently this followed a row he had with Marcia after lunch today when she insisted on my exclusion. Another victory for her on such a great policy issue! But it does damage me in the eyes of civil servants who have seen my name on the circulated list and then learn that the Prime Minister has given instructions for my removal. That of course is the purpose.

Home 9.30.

## Tuesday 25 November 1975

Did not go to the 9.45 Misc committee on altering metropolitan local government boundaries, which has upset Labour people locally – they decided to go ahead with some minor modifications.

After it Harold Lever came in to my office for a cup of tea and a chat.

Went to the Energy Cabinet committee at 10.30. Brief discussion on protection of our nuclear establishments – which was previously incredibly amateurish. Determined terrorists could get to the heart of Harwell in five minutes – and then blackmail us all. Nobody had any guns. Corrected now.

Then a long discussion on restructuring Burmah Oil. A dreadful situation, with potential liabilities of £1 billion, and a market capitalisation of only £50 million. Lever was for winding the whole thing down. Benn wanted to take the opportunity to nationalise its North Sea oil interests – thus giving the company some cash and expanding BNOC. This will also meet Kearton's appetite to turn BNOC into another great oil company. For a change other people support Benn. It seems the easiest way to give Burmah some money and at least get something in return. And it will get the North Sea oil out of Burmah before it goes bust, as it inevitably will.

Cabinet was delayed a quarter of an hour. HW was frantically holding discussions on Chrysler in corners with Eric Varley and with Willie Ross – who says he will resign if we let Chrysler go. Ross calculates he will be dropped soon anyway, and might as well go out a hero of the Scottish

Linwood workers. Ross says Millan will resign as well, but Varley told me he doubted if that was true.

Talked to Bill Rodgers and David Ennals about Iceland. Bill is due to make a statement later about 'sending in the Navy', but neither of them believed in militancy. We shall have to negotiate a compromise in the end. The trouble is that both Harold Wilson and Jim Callaghan are very sensitive to prove that Labour is never 'softer' than the Tories in foreign affairs – and the PM is definitely a Little Englander.

Cabinet was solely on Chrysler and went on until after 1 o'clock. Varley is still taking the ruthless line; shut it down as soon as possible. Ross and one or two others cannot face the resulting unemployment and are willing to pay anything to keep it going even if nobody buys the cars. HW is playing a much more devious, but sensible, game. He privately believes there is no hope, but feels that we must be seen to have tried everything, to have explored every possible alternative, so that in the end everyone accepts the inevitability.

I worked on my papers and talked to Joe. We cannot work out where the Field family made the £130,000 which it allegedly put into land speculation.

HW told Janet that he had a bad weekend from Marcia shouting and ranting at him, and in the end he told her that nobody was taking much notice of her any more because of her behaviour and because she was 'stabbing people in the back all the time'. Apparently she spent much of today attacking me, according to Albert.

There is something curious happening about Israel. Marcia phoned private office and said that HW was to go to have breakfast with Allon at his hotel the morning after he returns from Rome. (The Foreign Office will be furious about this.)

Incidentally on money, according to Joe, Lord Brayley used to provide parcels of money – stacks of fivers wrapped in brown paper – in Opposition to pay for the office expenses. Joe was often paid out of this – and declared it for tax.

After Cabinet the PM took Joe and me upstairs and we stood outside the study for half an hour discussing Chrysler. He is worried that Varley is being too brusque, and so pushing Ross into resignation. HW wants closure without losing any ministers. So he asked me to attend as his personal representative at the top-level meetings between Varley and Riccardo, the boss of Chrysler, tomorrow. I was delighted. My remit is basically to save Ross.

I also said that the PM must pick off Bruce Millan, Ross's junior, to divide the Scottish team.

Went off to lunch very late at the Commons Strangers café with Nick Stuart of private office. He is bitter against John Hunt for some reason.

The PM came into Questions briefing in high spirits. He had lunch with Bruce Millan and had got on very well. Had also been impressed and came away with a lot of ideas – especially on the need to look closer at Chrysler's tax position and at the precise redundancy commitments – which have never been properly worked out!

I left Questions early to attend a committee in the Cabinet Office on the British National Oil Corporation (BNOC). Dell in the chair (very good), Tommy Balogh and David Ennals, plus Ken Berrill (very well informed), Jack Rampton from Energy (very conservative) and Alan Lord from the Treasury. Examining the alternatives available for developing BNOC into a major oil company. I don't know why this actually has to be done, other than to satisfy the chairman Frank Kearton's ego.

The PM saw Balogh, who left the BNOC meeting to discuss his resignation as a minister and transfer to the board of BNOC. When I got back to No.10 HW was seeing Shirley Williams about tactics for tomorrow's Labour National Executive Committee. I saw Shirley afterwards and she was quite reassured – in fact found HW almost too fiery. He has certainly had enough of Hayward and the NEC Left and is now prepared to fight for Prentice because it means fighting against them.

Lever spent half an hour with HW discussing inflation and the arts. Then HW went off to the Palace. Later this evening he is seeing Benn about something, and then has a caucus meeting of the moderate members of the NEC to plan how to handle tomorrow's all-day session with the NEC and Cabinet at No.10.

I went off to an 8 p.m. meeting of my constituency general management committee in North St Pancras – the first I have attended as a delegate of the General & Municipal Workers Union. As usual most of the time was spent passing resolutions denouncing the government. Did not end till 11 p.m. I had no supper, so I bought fish and chips and got home just before midnight.

### Wednesday 26 November 1975

The PM went to the NEC meeting in the morning and then straight on to a lunch with the Thomson Organisation. So I worked in the office. Then went along to lunch at the Reform.

The news from the NEC was not good. They decided not to do anything about Prentice – despite a good firm statement by the PM warning them that they were getting completely out of step with the PLP. Then they voted 16–12 to do nothing about Trotskyite infiltration into the party, with Benn and Lestor voting with the majority. I saw Shirley Williams after lunch, arriving for a joint meeting of the NEC and Cabinet in No.10, and she was furious. She asked me to tell Healey when he arrived, and he reacted equally strongly.

The PM was quite late from the Thomson lunch, looking sour and hunched. He told Joe to leak his statement to the NEC, on the grounds that others had leaked from the meeting. In fact nobody had. So Joe phoned Bob Carvel on the *Standard* to leak some details, and then on the basis of that leak having already occurred, he leaked the whole of the PM's statement to the NEC to the rest of the press.

I went into private office at around 3.30, and the PM wandered in. He said that he was 'totally bored with the whole business'. He didn't like some of the NEC people upstairs. So 'my Cabinet can deal with them'. He went through and sat down in the armchair. The private secretaries gathered. Janet came in. I telephoned Joe. Then the PM just gossiped for half an hour. He returned to the meeting which was in the state dining-room – but not for long. Apparently Healey had piled into the Left.

John Hunt asked me to go and see him at 5 p.m. We discussed Chrysler. He said, 'I have just managed to bash into the heads of the Department of Industry what their line must be.' His position was perfectly reasonable – to play Chrysler along until after the PM returned from Rome. But he did speak as if he runs the Department of Industry. While I was waiting for him I heard him talking on the phone to one of his deputy secretaries, Jim Hamilton, and saying that 'We have decided to take this one in the Cabinet Office and you and I will have to intervene if the Treasury get out of line.'

I did not go to the OPD Defence committee on Iceland – where apparently there was a big clash between Bill Rodgers from Defence, wanting a moderate line, and Hattersley from the Foreign Office, wanting dramatic gestures from the Navy (he recently wrote a biography of Nelson) – because I went to the Chrysler talks.

I arrived at the Department of Industry in Victoria Street at 6 o'clock. 'Our' side had a briefing in advance of meeting the Chrysler people at 7 p.m. Varley was in the chair, looking pale and tired, but very tough and decisive in style. He has made up his mind that Chrysler must go into liquidation and that no 'rescue' can be viable. He is correct in his viability judgement. But he seems to be taking it too much for granted. Because it is logically the right thing to do, he seems to assume it will happen. William Ross and Bruce Millan were there from the Scottish Office, encouraged by H's apparent support, and being very fiery against closure, claiming that the alternative scheme for maintaining Glasgow's Linwood and closing Ryton at Coventry will be viable.

They are clearly out to do another Upper Clyde Shipbuilders – a government rescue of hundreds of millions which staves off inevitable closure for a few years. Anthony Part, the permanent secretary, was there with some officials from Industry, not particularly impressive. Ken Berrill, sharp as ever, and myself and Edmund Dell.

We went over the ground and decided we had to press Chrysler on how much they were prepared to put in to the compromise 'Scheme B2' and what were their other commitments to its success.

We went into the conference room and sat in line facing one another at two long tables. Riccardo, 'the Chicago flame-thrower', sat there with another Sicilian-looking gentleman on his right. They both had swept-back dark greying hair, sharp suits and flashy ties, and reminded me of stereotype nightclub owners from Hollywood films of the 1940s. I expected them to put on sunglasses at any moment and assumed that they had violin cases under the table. Eric Roll of Warburgs merchant bank was on Riccardo's left, presumably offering wise advice on English politics.

Varley put the questions on the viability of the compromise very directly. (The compromise is to move the Coventry plant to Linwood, concentrate the Hunter and Avenger models there, do the Iran contract from there, and keep the Dunstable lorry works open: so sacking 10,000 English workers and keeping 15,000, mainly Scots.)

Riccardo answered equally directly that this compromise was not intended as a viable commercial proposal on their part. It was concocted in response to our needs to prevent Scottish unemployment and to keep the Iran contract. He said it was 'politically viable, not economically viable'. This was despite the fact that they have produced figures showing a return to profit in 1977 after a £40 million loss in 1976. However, he pointed out that this profit projection assumed great improvement on the labour front. He added, 'We've not had much worker efficiency and co-operation since we've been here. In other countries we would not have these problems.'

Then when Varley pressed him on how much Chrysler would contribute Riccardo said it would depend on whether or not we wanted a) the Chrysler name to continue and b) that the Chrysler parent should have an equity share in the new operation.

It suddenly emerged that this was crucial to them, determining how much they would put in, but our side had never thought about it. Our officials could not see the difference. Chrysler said it made a great difference to them because it affected their tax position. But they would not say which way, with or without the name and the equity, meant more money and which meant less money. So our side did not know which alternative would produce more money from Chrysler or which would produce more commercial advantage to the new operation. Therefore our response was bewilderment. Dell put it to them straight that if they told us the difference we would say which we would prefer.

So that was inconclusive, a bit farcical, and will have to be the subject of another meeting.

Millan then pressed well on their projections for reaching a profit in 1977. The Chrysler UK manager – Lander – said it all depended on:

- higher volume sales;
- fewer shifts, less overtime, and so less premium payments;
- labour improvements.

Even then it would only produce 90,000 units a year – which is tiny by any standards (Varley calls it a 'Toytown car company'). It was fairly clear that the Americans did not really believe in this profitability, and that Varley and Dell did not either. But the Scots were still trying to make it sound credible.

Riccardo made it clear that once they had put in some money, that would be that. He said the parent company in the USA was in such a precarious position that it could not survive any open-ended commitment to a subsidiary which might produce further losses. They could only survive because of the tax-loss recoupments in pulling out of the UK. They must pull out by 31 December for tax reasons. And every day we delayed setting up the new compromise threatened the viability of that (it could not start for six months because of the need to move Ryton plant to Linwood – which Ryton workers won't allow anyway!).

So we agreed to meet tomorrow morning when Chrysler would tell us the sums they were prepared to put in to the new operation.

We broke up shortly after 8 p.m. and retired to Varley's room to debrief, assisted by glasses of whisky. We went over the ground again, with Varley saying it was not a starter and the Scots insisting that it is. Curiously there was no discussion of the questions Riccardo has asked – about equity participation by them and the new company keeping the Chrysler name. I suggested that we take some expert advice on the future commercial implications of this. They clearly had nobody to consult, and were not very interested since Industry is committed to closure. Finally an official from the Scottish Office said that he had a friend who was a motor salesman and he would telephone him. (He did so and said it was his friend's view that Chrysler's name was a disadvantage. But there was no serious research into this problem which Chrysler thought would be very important to us.)

I left the Department of Industry with Edmund Dell and we went to the Commons and had a nice dinner in the dining-room there. We discussed the situation. He is all for brutal closure. I pointed out that we must not have a decision at the weekend, when the PM and Callaghan are going to Rome, and that we must try to carry the Scots with us if closure comes.

I also argued strongly that we need some independent figures. It is crazy that we are acting on Chrysler's projections – to which they are not committed since they have no intention of being there in 1976. And they have a vested interest in giving optimistic figures since they want to tempt us into this quagmire in order to take off them a) the costs of redundancy and b) the odium of closing the plant. Edmund agreed. We then saw close friends Eric Varley and Gerald Kaufman sitting at another table and we joined them. We discussed tomorrow's meeting and planned what we wanted. I also put my point about independent figures. Eric agreed, adding, 'We have not bothered with figures in the department since we were convinced that this compromise is not viable.'

He is right: it is not viable, but it has to be seen to be not viable. While we are using Chrysler's optimistic profit projection, the Scots can persuade Cabinet to continue.

We broke up at around 11 p.m. I said goodnight to Edmund and took a taxi halfway home before I realised I had my car on Horse Guards Parade. Turned round and came back again, costing me a pound. Senile dementia is starting early.

Finally home at 11.45 p.m. Feel very excited to be involved in this. Love negotiations.

## Thursday 27 November 1975

Up at 7 a.m. and drove in at 7.45 a.m. Called in at No. 10 and then went across to Industry at 8.30 a.m. Waited outside Varley's room with Millan and Dell. We gathered in Varley's office for a few minutes and then went in at 9.05 a.m. There were only 7 of us from the government this time: Varley, Dell, Millan, Part, Berrill, and an Industry official and me.

The meeting was quite short. Riccardo said that if we wanted their equity and name, they would contribute:

a)  £20 million of debts to the parent company written off;
b)  £13 million, as 20% of the estimated £65 million needed for 1976.

If we did not insist on their name and equity, which gave them maximum tax advantage, since they would then be able to argue that they had totally closed and finished their UK operations, they would contribute:

a)  £20 million debts waived;
b)  £35 million towards the future of the new company.

So the difference was £22 million based on their tax considerations – which we are unable to quantify.

We did not react, but said that we would go off and consider it, and Varley would have to report to Cabinet.

To me it seems a poor deal – for us. But good for Chrysler. The money they would put in, £35 million, is certainly less than they would have to pay on liquidation. And they get rid of all the odium of future closure on to us, and avoid the odium of closure now. They ought to pay £100 million for that.

In other words, the compromise scheme is also not in their interests. They should pay for that. It also means we should be very wary of their profit projections.

We broke up at 9.30 and had a brief discussion. I suggested to Varley that he had a word with the PM and I arranged that. I then drove back with Ken Berrill and went to the study to report to HW. I was just in the middle when Barbara Castle burst in to talk about private medicine. She was fixing the PM to support her Bill to control private medicine. She succeeded. In Cabinet he supported her – though he has taken control of it out of her hands and he will chair a small sub-committee. She won him over by claiming that local authorities are being delayed with planning applications to build large private hospitals. He has a compromise in view: a holding operation, delaying planning permissions till after the Royal Commission reports. Seems sensible enough. Also with him in charge, we shall be able to restrain Castle who is looking for constant fights with the medical profession.

Cabinet was brought forward to 10 o'clock, and went through the morning. It approved H's compromise on private medicine, despite the fact that he refused to tell ministers what he had in mind. (He said afterwards that there was 'one member of the Cabinet who leaks our decisions directly to the doctors'. He didn't say who.)

On Chrysler, they authorised Varley to continue negotiations. Interestingly, the Left is not pressing hard for keeping it open. Benn is not arguing for maintaining employment. Because:

a) They want to demonstrate how nasty the multinationals are.
b) They want to get import controls on as many items as possible, and they know that if we rescue Chrysler there will be no import controls, but if we close it there will be.

So the battle is really between Industry and Treasury who want to close, and the Scots who want to keep Linwood.

The PM is beginning to wobble. He said to me that he was worried about Varley being too tough. And he would like to try to keep it open 'for a year or so'. This is because he won't be here then. He wants to put off the pain for somebody else to carry. He doesn't seem too concerned with the actual viability of the motor industry.

I took a quick lunch in the Cabinet Office café and then slipped off to the bank for money and to the National Gallery to buy Carol a card for our 16th wedding anniversary tomorrow. On the way back down Whitehall I caught up with Douglas Wass, the Treasury permanent secretary, who had been to buy a book, and we strolled down Whitehall together in glorious winter sunshine. After a brief discussion of Chrysler, he expressed worry about Burmah Oil. Ever since Tuesday's meeting the situation has deteriorated. Its liabilities are certainly £1,000 million. He is afraid of something called a Section 332 liability if the government intervenes. He said that Down, the Burmah chairman, is asking for an immediate government commitment to shore it up. And that the Governor of the Bank feels curiously committed to save it because he personally intervened last year. Wass obviously thinks we should stay clear and let it go.

I walked on to the Commons and dropped in to the PM's room where he arrived late for Questions briefing, having just had lunch for Michael Manley. Joe said it was a terrible lunch with the PM reminiscing, and then forgetting what Manley had asked. Joe said he was all over the place, and drank too much.

I left before Questions and went off to the Department of Industry for our third meeting with Chrysler. This was the briefest of all. Varley reported to them on the Cabinet meeting and asked for time to consider their financial proposal on the compromise scheme. He asked if we could put in consultants – Cooper Bros – to produce independent figures. We would then meet them again next Wednesday and put our conclusion to next Thursday's Cabinet. Riccardo agreed and we broke up. I got the impression the Americans were quite optimistic. They obviously think that we are more attracted by the compromise than in fact we are. Or they are counting on the Scots and the PM to bail them out – they may be right.

I walked back to the Commons at 3.30 p.m. and met Patrick Wright coming out. The PM's car flashed out, and a second No. 10 car followed and picked Patrick and me up and took us round Parliament Square and back to No. 10. Patrick said Question Time was terrible. The brandy showed, with the PM slurring some of his words. The Tories shouted him down towards the end.

Back in No. 10 I reported on the Chrysler situation and the PM again said he would prefer if we kept it going for a year. Then he complained about Question Time and told Nick Stuart to contact the Speaker and suggest that the grouping of questions should stop. It was clear he knew it had gone badly. He said to Joe that 'I don't like the House. I don't feel I know it any more.'

Joe also told him that Jimmy Goldsmith is described as a financial backer of the Tory Party in the Nuffield study of the 1974 election. HW looked very worried – after all Marcia has just put Goldsmith on the list of the PM's 'personal friends' to take to the PM's Freedom of the City of London ceremony, although he has only met him once.

Lord Goodman came in to see the PM about the doctors situation – he is now acting as mediator, although Barbara Castle won't have him as chairman of the Royal Commission. He stayed for nearly an hour and kept the officials waiting who were going to brief HW on the Rome meeting. They waited for half an hour outside the Cabinet Room while the PM was upstairs with Goodman. I went over and talked to Michael Palliser, who has taken over this week as head of the Foreign Office and whom I like a lot.

Joe told me that the *Observer* newspaper has given its terms for a *Mirror* takeover – £1 million plus complete editorial freedom. They are losing a fortune. The *Mirror* will say no.

The Rome briefing also overran so we did not have the usual Dep Secs meeting nor our arranged discussion with the PM on his Carlisle speech. He then saw Balogh – about Burmah Oil – and Donald Chapman about his peerage. The PM was supposed to go to Chequers then, and to the north tomorrow by car, but he decided to stay in town and work tonight and go by train in the morning so he could work then as well. He is very behind on his paperwork and again looking tired. He told Patrick that he felt tired and 'not very well – a bit fluey again'.

So I went home early at 8 p.m.

– Joe says HW has put off his visit to Israel on 25 January. Because Marcia is going to be there at that time for the bar mitzvah of Eric Miller's son. They are flying out in Miller's private plane. We don't know if she has told HW not to come at that time, or if he has decided he doesn't want to be there then.

– Wedgie Benn has cancelled his scheduled visit to the USA for 'secret' reasons 'to do with his career'. Maybe he has been warned that HW is going to announce his retirement at the beginning of December. That is why Tommy Balogh has resigned from the government now and got HW to put him on the BNOC board – using the patronage while it is there to secure his employment for the future.

– On reflection the Chrysler negotiations are a most curious game of bluff and chess. The Americans don't know if we really want the compromise. We behave as if we do – and the Scots do – but most of us really don't. They behave as if they are doing us a good turn in offering it – but really they want us to take it.


*Friday 28 November 1975*

When I arrived HW was already up in the study with Joe discussing the press coverage of the doctors' strike. We talked about the general problem. I told him that Cabinet received the impression he had moved over to the Castle side. He admitted he had a bit, but implied he would not end up there. And he complained about her.

He is delighted with the election results of the PLP Liaison committee. All six winners are moderate members of the Manifesto Group. The Left was annihilated – Mikardo, Allaun, Heffer. HW was delighted at this. It confirms the line he took at the NEC on Wednesday, though he said he wished the results had come out before the NEC.

We discussed the speeches briefly. He did a bit of amending and dictating last night. He doesn't look well. He went off to catch the 9.50 train and then was in the north all the time – two speeches today and two tomorrow. A terrible grind. He also prepared two more speeches for the next week. He sees politics through speeches – reading facts into the record; committing himself and his government in public in advance so he can later refer back to what he said earlier; perhaps to prevent himself from weakening and retreating later; attacking people he does not like. It results partly from him being a man of words rather than action. Partly because addressing audiences is his preferred form of communication, he doesn't like man-to-man discussion. But above all it comes from the fact that he has only ever, in his whole career, been a minister in one department, and that was nearly a quarter of a century ago. Most of his political life has been spent rhetorically – in Opposition inevitably, and in government as leader, without a department.

After he had left I had discussions in the Unit on strengthening controls of the banking system. Percy Clarke phoned me from Transport House in a flap. Michael Foot is due to give a party political broadcast on unemployment next Friday. But with Chrysler due to come up he has got cold feet and is withdrawing. Percy wants the PM to make a suggestion – or even to appear himself. We could not get hold of the PM so I left a message for him.

The private secretaries held a cabal in the Cabinet Room about domestic office matters – and especially John Hunt's increasing interference with them. They are in rebellion. Ken Stowe may have to raise it with the PM to preserve the independence of No. 10 from the Cabinet Office.

We all went to lunch at Beotys restaurant with Robin Butler as a final farewell gesture. He is enjoying the Treasury but says that he has been stuck right away from immediate economic policy. The Treasury always gives people a 'sterilisation' period after they return from No.10. He also said that one reason why the Chancellor is so reluctant to discuss policy matters with the PM is that he does not want Hunt to get his hands on it and start interfering with the Treasury.

I left Beotys in a cloudburst and got absolutely soaked running to Horse Guards Parade to get the car and go home to take the family to the country. We set off just after 4 p.m., but the traffic was so terrible that we turned back and decided to go tomorrow morning. So I sat down and wrote up today's diary.

## Monday 1 December 1975

The PM is in Rome today. I would have liked to have been there – and but for Her Ladyship would have been since I was on the originally circulated list until struck off at her insistence. It was still an interesting day.

Drove in to meeting of the inter-departmental committee set up to discuss 'World Poverty', following the meeting of the PM with the charities long ago. The PM supported their approach in order to send everybody away happy. Now it ends up with 16 senior civil servants around a large table in the Cabinet Office conference room C. Everybody agreed that there is nothing we can do about 'the universality of poverty'. But we are having to treat it seriously because the PM is supporting it. We went on for over two hours and did not get very far. The Ministry of Overseas Development were quite helpful. The Home Office tried not to participate at all. The Treasury woman was savage, and had far worse bite than any Treasury knight.

In the middle I was called out to take a phone call from Joe in Rome. The PM had suddenly remembered what I said weeks ago warning him about impending cuts in the expenditure on the Open University. He wanted a telegram tonight giving him all the details. I put David Piachaud on to this and also telephoned Fred Mulley's new special adviser, Stella Greenhall, and invited her to No. 10 this evening.

Went to lunch at LSE and then back to Downing Street. A heavy flow of paper.

Mulley's adviser came in but did not yet have much information. Nick Stuart got much more through the private office network. I drafted a telegram which we sent to the PM.

So far public expenditure is not going well. Defence is getting a lot of support. Ken Berrill and Dick Ross in CPRS support exempting Defence from further cuts – no doubt following John Hunt's lead. Crosland and Castle are still fighting, but Mulley has already accepted maximum cuts for Education.

Home at 9 p.m.

Telephoned by an old friend Gordon Wasserman, the husband of Hugh Gaitskell's daughter Cressida. *Private Eye* has phoned him asking for dirt about me.

## Tuesday 2 December 1975

I arrived late at Millbank Tower for the Chrysler meeting because none of the No. 10 cars turned up. I was surprised when I walked into the room to find Riccardo and all the Chrysler Mafia already there. Peter Carey, a senior official from Industry, was in the chair flanked by officials – no ministers present. Riccardo had Gene Caffiero on his left as usual, accompanied by five others and Eric Roll.

The American position was now different – and tougher than last time. They had clearly been rebuked back home for being too generous. They would not budge on their offer of figures of £35 million without equity or £13 million with. Riccardo also now claimed that the compromise was economically as well as politically viable – slightly different from last time. They dressed it up as attractively as possible, offering us use of future Chrysler models and engines. Riccardo also said that they did not accept the CPRS report on the future of the British industry and he would like Caffiero to talk to them.

Richard Bullock, Carey's prim and austere deputy, intervened sharply to point out that Chrysler were trying to avoid all the disadvantages of liquidation – to get the advantage of tax rebates, and they ought to pay more for that than £35 million.

Riccardo responded fiercely, threatening to bankrupt Chrysler UK and so pay none of its debts. He said, 'This is like a Middle Eastern rug market. You've guessed our problems. We will guess yours. You will have real problems if we have to bankrupt in the UK. We came to play as gentlemen, but if you prefer, we won't.' (At this point I expected smiling Gene Caffiero to take out his violin case and pump us all on our side of the table full of lead.)

This was Riccardo's tough spiel, apparently spontaneous, but I could see it was from a prepared script. He claimed it would cost the UK government £60 million extra if they did not take the compromise scheme. He then warned that they might reduce the £35 million offer.

Throughout he talked of three alternatives – £35 million, £13 million with equity, and bankruptcy. He concluded, 'Don't make the mistake of thinking that by putting the squeeze on us you will get a better deal; you won't.' He also refused to discuss their tax considerations.

We then broke up. They left. We had a brief discussion. The Industry people all insisted there was no hope. The Scots argued that there was. I said that the compromise made no commercial sense. But politically the government might want to go for it. Therefore it was essential to cost it properly. They should have a realistic estimate of the price of buying a temporary respite in what is bound to be an 'Upper Clyde Mark II'. Carey agreed and said they would do that.

I took Hector Hawkins (from the CPRS) back in the car. Then worked in the office where there is a heavy flow of papers on public expenditure, on the Burmah Oil fiasco and various other major policy areas.

David Owen, who though a junior minister is effectively the Minister of Health, came in at 12.20 p.m. to collect me for lunch and we went out to Chez Victor, which is still one of the best little French restaurants in London. We discussed the doctors' dispute which is coming to a crisis. He said that Barbara Castle thinks of nothing but the pay beds issue – she neglects the whole rest of the Health Service and Social Security. She is following the dictates of the unions involved. Since *In Place of Strife* she has decided never again to get out of step with the unions. Now she is in danger of destroying the Health Service and does not seem aware or to care. David also spoke loyally in her defence but admits she is the biggest obstacle to a settlement. [In 1968–69 Barbara Castle had proposed a brave policy of restricting trade union power which despite Wilson's initial support was defeated by union opposition and a Cabinet revolt.]

He suggested to me a compromise whereby we delayed the timetable on phasing out until after the Royal Commission.

He says she thinks she can rely on the PM. That their old relationship means that in the end he will support her. He also told me her public expenditure position. That she would give way on uprating social security benefits, but will insist on extra for the Health Service itself.

On the consultants' dispute, David seemed unaware of the compromise negotiation being conducted by Goodman, who was on the phone twice today saying he had formed the basis of a settlement – involving a delayed timetable on our part, and acceptance of the legislation by them. Barbara Castle knew of this and had initially indicated that she did not object.

Then suddenly this evening she sent in a hysterical message of complaint to No. 10 saying that she knew nothing about it, objected totally, that HW must not negotiate with the doctors while they are taking industrial action, and he must simply tell them when they come to No. 10 tomorrow to go away and go back to normal working. Total nonsense, for union consumption.

Goodman phoned the message and was very contemptuous of her. Otherwise the compromise was going well.

On return from lunch with David Owen I drafted a minute to the PM suggesting the compromise we had discussed.

The *Guardian* phoned me to say that the *Investors' Review* had a piece saying that I was returning to LSE because of my bad relations with Marcia Falkender. I denied it – but must write to Dahrendorf to clarify my position formally.

Went to Roy Jenkins at 6 p.m. He had just returned from Israel and was tired. We discussed the composition of the Gambling Royal Commission, and his public expenditure position. He is for maximum cuts, except on Defence, where he feels we are becoming a third-rate power.

We had a pleasant and relaxed talk. He asked about my future career and advised me not to go back to the LSE. He also asked why HW was against Harold Lever – and said his irritation with Lever had become more marked of late. I don't really know. I said that HW still gave Lever policy support on paper. Privately I wonder if he is preparing for Lever's departure or demotion, trying to prove he is no good as a preparation for being unfair to him, which is a psychological process I have often seen. Marcia has been attacking Lever to him.

Returned to No. 10 to finish and amend my brief on consultants. News from Rome was of a big clash between HW and the rest of the EEC 9 over Callaghan's claim for separate representation for the UK, as the only EEC oil-producer, at the next oil consumer producer conference. HW banged the table and talked about leaving the EEC and joining OPEC. But this was all face-saving for Jim in preparation for a climb-down. Before going to Rome the PM had long discussions on 'how to get Jim off the hook'. He knew he had to climb down from the beginning.

News was of a delayed departure from Rome and they would not be back till 1 a.m. HW communicated that he wanted tomorrow morning's breakfast with Allon of Israel delayed an hour because he would be tired.

I went home at 9 p.m., picked up Carol, and went back into town to the annual Jonathan Cape party, which was very nice as usual. Home again at midnight.

## Wednesday 3 December 1975

When I arrived at No. 10 the PM was already upstairs with Allon of Israel. He had switched the meeting from Allon's hotel. Partly because HW is very tired – he did not get in bed till 2 a.m. this morning. Partly because, as Patrick Wright insisted, it really is too humiliating for our Prime Minister to go off visiting people in their hotels. This meeting was all fixed up by Marcia. She created a big fuss last night. At the end of H's exhausting Rome Summit, after 11 hours of hard negotiation over our claim for a separate seat at the producer/consumer conference and then a humiliating climb-down, and a big press conference, she telephoned and insisted that the PM telephone her immediately. So late at night from Rome airport he phoned her and she had a blazing row with him. It was overheard by officials and later reported in full by HW to Janet – who told me, and it was confirmed to me by the private secretaries who were present.

Marcia was ranting about trips to Israel. HW had provisionally arranged to go in the last week of January. She objected. This coincides with the time when she will be there for the bar mitzvah of Eric Miller's son. She was claiming that this was a deliberate attempt by him to sabotage her visit, and to make it impossible for her to go with HW on his official visit. She blamed me and claimed that I had deliberately fixed his visit for this time. Absolutely crazy. Madness. Paranoia. HW has never discussed the Israel visit with me. It was all arranged through Patrick Wright in private office.

Afterwards Janet told us that HW said to her that Marcia is mad and even used the word 'evil' – this is the first time he has ever gone that far. He also said that he had 'put up with it for 20 years' and could 'not put up with it much longer'. He said that he must find a way of 'getting rid of her'.

The representatives of the medical consultants came in for negotiations at 11.30 a.m. Beforehand Barbara Castle went up to the study to see HW and attacked him for allowing this meeting and for interfering. As we all went into the Cabinet Room the PM turned to Joe and me, looking very tired and miserable, and said, 'She says that the main problem is that I am involved in this.'

It strikes me that Barbara has some things in common with Marcia: stridency, persistence, ambition, hostility towards anybody she comes in competition with, but impressive commitment and devilish cunning. While she was upstairs berating HW, I had a 10-minute talk with Lord Goodman sitting outside the Cabinet Room. He has been acting as go-between with the doctors and had done a good job in finding some common ground. But he said he was convinced that Castle is out to sabotage any compromise. He said that after three discussions with her yesterday he 'seriously doubted her contact with reality'. He had also heard what I heard from David Owen and others – that she is totally neglecting the rest of the Health Service while she pursues obsessively this marginal issue of the private beds. She is totally subservient to the unions involved, desperately and pathetically trying to make them forget her role in *In Place of Strife*.

At the opening of the meeting the PM responded to her pressure by pointing out that he was not negotiating and that only the Secretary of State could negotiate.

Rodney Smith of the Royal College and a colleague both made opening statements to the effect that (a) private medicine was essential and (b) that this battle with Castle could destroy the Health Service.

Goodman then put his compromise proposal:

1. The consultants accept the legislation and cease industrial action;
2. but timing should be discussed with them, and anyway not be so hasty;
3. and phasing out of private beds in NHS hospitals should be regulated and related to the existence of alternative pay beds in the area. Suggested some commission be established to advise on the availability of alternative beds, so there was no net loss of availability by phasing out of beds in hospitals.

The PM said he could not answer now. Must consider.

Castle sat silent throughout except for one intervention – to point out this meant some private pay beds might remain for ever.

On the Royal Commission the PM said wait until after these negotiations. If they come to nothing, then maybe the Royal Commission might have a contribution.

The appropriately named Grabham, the doctors' union leader, very nasty and right-wing, then intervened to say that his association was 'determined to maintain private medicine in the UK'. But the Goodman proposal was the best compromise, even though 'it does harm the NHS'. He said that there was 'no point in further talks with the Secretary of State, unless on the basis of the Goodman proposal'.

So it was decided to proceed. The doctors would wait for a response from the government.

As the meeting broke up Castle got hold of HW and began to berate him. She also insisted that any commission set up should be responsible only to her. It was clear she wanted to get HW to retreat from his role as mediator with Goodman. So I went and fetched the private secretaries and told them to get him out. They took him away 'urgently' into private office and shut the door firmly, with Castle loitering outside still hoping to get at HW again.

Goodman was also around waiting for a joint meeting. He asked for the lavatory and I went in with him for a pee. He said that Castle was the biggest threat to a solution. But he was content with the progress so far made.

HW went upstairs with Goodman and Castle for a final talk. Then she came downstairs and HW kept Goodman behind for a further talk. Castle hung around outside the Cabinet Office for a while. She clearly wanted to take very opportunity to get at HW.

I had a quick lunch with Kay Carmichael in the Cabinet Office canteen and then dashed back for a meeting of the Cabinet committee on Defence and Overseas Policy. It was to discuss the proposed Defence cuts. Healey had suggested £450 million off – still one of the smallest departmental cuts. Mason had offered £100 million – which we knew could be provided from anticipated departmental underspending, so in reality they were refusing to cut anything at all. And every day the newspapers are full of leaks and briefing from Defence pointing out what terrible consequences there will be from any further Defence cuts. Nothing about the disgraceful 'fat' in Defence – over a quarter of a million civilian civil servants, the ratio of 'chiefs' to 'Indians' having doubled in the past 20 years, with two admirals to every ship in the Navy, and massive expenditure on free trips all over the place.

John Hunt's brief to the PM was very unbalanced. No attempt to present a balanced picture or a 'chairman's steer'. Just a list of every tatty argument for maintaining every penny of Defence expenditure. John was a military man.

Constitutionally it is a disgrace. On no other item of expenditure is there a Cabinet committee beforehand to discuss the departmental arguments against cuts.

And on no other policy committee of the Cabinet are the customers represented. The service chiefs sit in and put the case for getting more money. After the meeting I asked the Chancellor when we would expect to see the vice-chancellors of the universities sitting in on a Cabinet committee to discuss Education cuts and the doctors sitting in on Health cuts discussions.

Shortly after the start there was a sharp exchange between HW and Healey. When it emerged that Cabinet might need to meet on Friday, HW said he might not be able to be there and Healey rounded on him and said, 'It might be better for all of us if you were not there.'

HW pretended not to hear. But shortly after he got up and walked out. I followed him out and went into the lavatory with him. He said, 'What I hate is seeing Healey going for the *Tribune* vote', which is a bit unfair, even if Healey was intolerably rude. As a former Defence Secretary, Healey knows how much fat and waste there is in Defence.

Coming out of the lavatory the PM stopped and put his head in his hands. 'I am so exhausted,' he said. He then began to talk about how in 1964–70 he used to take his dog for a walk to the pub, but never manages that now. He also used to play a lot of golf, but doesn't now. 'I don't get any relaxation,' he said. 'I'm so tired.'

Then he suddenly launched into an attack on John Hunt, saying that Hunt 'creates all these Misc Cabinet committees for me to chair so that he can run them. Hunt is empire-building and I have to carry the can.' We then went back into the Cabinet Room where the meeting was still on. As he was sitting down he got up again and came over to me and said, 'Why should I be involved in all these piddling little things, like these bloody BNOC appointments? It is just so John Hunt can have his hands on them.'

The ministerial discussion continued with nobody supporting Healey, and the PM deliberately talking loudly whenever Healey was intervening.

Jenkins made the best case. He said that our GNP had slipped behind so rapidly that the nation had not realised it. Yet if we adjusted our Defence as rapidly, we would become a third-class power in the eyes of the world. And that would not help the economic problem. It would be harmful to a solution because of its depressing psychological effect on the British people.

The PM summed up absolutely firmly for no Defence cuts. He said that Defence is a special case, 'more important than school meals, or social security for Irishmen with 18 children'. He said that in Rome Schmidt had warned him that Germany 'did not wish to use her strength for economic purposes, but would do so if she had to'. NATO mattered to Schmidt and 'if he thought we were playing fast and loose with NATO, he would take economic reprisals against us. We must take account of the political realities, abroad as well as at home.'

Callaghan supported this. He said Schmidt had described Britain as 'useless and ungovernable'.

Both of them seem to have come home from Rome with their tails between their legs. This is the first time I have heard HW admit that we are politically as well as financially in hock to the Germans.

I felt very depressed after this meeting. Joel Barnett and Healey from the Treasury looked very down as well. The PM went off to give the Blackett Memorial Lecture, and then out to supper.

I went to the opera, to *Rigoletto*, with Carol, and enjoyed it very much. Home to bed at 11.45 p.m.

## Thursday 4 December 1975

Cabinet this morning. It was supposed to deal with Chrysler and public expenditure, but it never got beyond Chrysler. Before that there was a terrible row about the new EEC passport. Passionate protests against losing our own British passport and Peter Shore protesting that it stabbed him 'in the heart'.

Before Cabinet the PM had the Chancellor in the study for ¾ hour.

Fred Mulley also came in early to see me. He was a bit worried that we had been quizzing his people about the Open University prospects. He also was trying to get support so that nothing more came off Education. I tried to mobilise him to take a stand for Defence cuts. He is very intelligent but I am not sure if Fred takes stands!

After Cabinet the PM spent a long time explaining to Joe and me his plans for a Chrysler rescue operation. He is still desperately keen to rescue something and has asked Harold Lever to go off and come up with some kind of scheme which would encourage them to keep Linwood going. The PM thinks that British Leyland could produce Land Rovers there. He is also critical of Eric Varley and Industry for not trying hard enough to save anything.

Joe and I went to lunch at the Commons Press Gallery. We discussed HW's health. Apparently he felt so ill in Rome that he nearly did not attend the conference. His doctor, Joe Stone, has given him instructions to cut down his work. Ken Stowe has been told to clear the diary. John Hunt has been told to reduce the number of Cabinet committees. But the next 10 days are still terribly heavy.

Joe Stone told Joe and me that HW 'is not the man he was a few years ago'. His heart flutter is getting worse, and was very bad in Rome. Joe Stone said 'One day he will have a bad attack and he won't be able to walk out of that very easily.' HW also finds it harder to shake off any cold or infection. That is why he seems still resolute to retire in February/March.

Question Time was not good, and afterwards he had to make a statement on the Rome conference He took a lot of stick because of our 'humiliating climb-down' over oil and was also strongly attacked from his own side. He looked lonely and a bit frail, his voice not strong, and I felt that the House sensed that the old lion was at last weakening. Once they get their teeth into him he could lose his mastery quickly.

Afterwards he looked miserable and poured himself a very large brandy.

He clearly had not enjoyed it. He said that he had repeated the defence of Jim's position so often that in the end he believed it – that it was worth demanding a separate seat in order to get in the end 'separate representation'.

I went back to No. 10 to attend the Deputy Secretaries meeting in the Cabinet Office.

The PM stayed at the House and spoke twice in the debate on the Queen's civil list. Afterwards he attended a meeting of the 'Office Trust', which means of the financiers who help to run Marcia's office. Apparently there was a terrible row afterwards between her and him.

I went to the flat of the German chargé d'affaires with Jack Ashley and Alf Morris. Very pleasant dinner. I also strongly backed Jack and Alf to go to Germany and see the German rehabilitation centres for the disabled.

Home at midnight and beginning to feel very tired. But life is full and interesting.

The only irritating thing is to hear again from Gordon Wasserman that *Private Eye* is telephoning people asking for 'dirt' about me. Then Denis Lyons telephoned to say that there had been a *Private Eye* lunch where Will Camp and somebody called John Addy had been inciting them to attack me. Who are these people? What a pathetic way to spend their time.

## Friday 5 December 1975

Cabinet resumed this morning on Chrysler at 9.30. Afterwards the PM left for the north by plane around midday. The Cabinet meeting was very difficult. Lever produced his financial plan, which was apparently too complex for many to understand. Varley and some others were clearly for closure. Foot was for rescue. Benn was for a siege economy, putting his case that our entire industrial base was being eroded. The PM kept them to Lever's plan, and so did Jim Callaghan, who chaired the meeting very well after the PM left. This will keep the Scots a bit happier, though Bruce Millan informed the PM that he is resigning on the announcement of the Chrysler closure.

Varley told me that he would resign if Chrysler were rescued.

And Reg Prentice's permanent secretary telephoned me to give me an oblique hint that he would resign – over cuts in Overseas Aid.

So there is an air of resignation.

Tommy Balogh did resign yesterday, ostensibly because it is his 70th birthday, but really because he knows HW is going and wants to get out into a non-political job while HW still has the patronage. He is replaced on the House of Lords front bench by Marcia's friend Peter Lovell-Davis, whom I have always got on well with.

Gerald Kaufman is also promoted while Marcia and HW still have influence. And HW's PPS gets a job at Environment. So it was not really a political reshuffle. It was HW sensibly finding jobs for his cronies (except for Joe and me) which will keep them going after he has gone. Nobody else spotted this.

Joe and I went to lunch at the Commons Press Gallery again. A *Daily Mail* journalist told us at 1.20 p.m. that a ministerial meeting with Chrysler had been fixed for 4 p.m. I was to attend that meeting, but at 1.20 No.10 still did not know what time the meeting was. The Department of Industry was arranging it. Leaks in Whitehall are getting faster every day!

I went back to No.10 to work on a public expenditure brief, but was summoned to the Industry Department for a briefing meeting at 3 o'clock.

I went to the briefing. Lever was there with Ross, Dell, Varley in the chair, and the usual bunch of officials except that Alan Lord was also there from the Treasury.

Lever set out the basis of his proposal – with the government providing £40 million towards the expected losses in 1976–77, and sharing the losses after that. There was some further discussion and then the Governor of the Bank arrived and asked for Lever, so he left and had a long discussion in another room, in fact until 4 p.m. when we all went along to the conference room to meet the Americans again. Lever then put his scheme following an introduction by Varley. He made the scheme – which is basically just a subvention to cover their losses – as attractive as possible, at one point offering them all the theoretical profits.

The American were clearly surprised by the generosity of the offer and asked for a break of 15 minutes to consider. They pointed out their time problem – they had to leave on Monday afternoon for a Wednesday board meeting in the USA. And added that they had a problem of bank finance and asked if we would get UK banks to loan to them (without parent guarantees, which they did not want to give).

We withdrew to Varley's room and then a terrible row broke out between Lever and Dell about the details of the offer. Dell said the Cabinet had authorised only a maximum of £40 million in the first two years. Lever said it was £40 million plus half of anything over £40 million in those two years, as well as sharing in years after then. Lever said he would not return to the negotiating table on any other basis. He launched into a savage attack on the Industry officials, whom he accused of not wanting to do a deal. Anthony Part, their permanent secretary, then looked very unctuous and said, 'Don't look at me. We are only civil servants. We do not take decisions. We merely provide the staff work.' This was the old story. The civil servants do influence the decisions till things start to go wrong; then they quote the constitutional mythology that only ministers take decisions.

Lever paced up and down the room. He said he wouldn't go back in. If he did and they retreated from his package he would walk out.

It was very emotional and embarrassing. It would have been terrible to break down on this point. I said, 'Our offer may not have overwhelmed them but it has certainly disrupted us.'

However, Lever's performance had the advantage of pleasing the Scots. One of the Scots officials said to me, 'Our ministers will be able to live with this now.' Willie Ross also told me he was pleased with Lever for fighting so hard for a compromise.

Finally we patched up the difference over the figures, agreeing to fudge it until tomorrow. It proved impossible to get any clarification about what Cabinet actually had decided. Dell tried to get Healey but he was on a train to Leeds. They tried to get Callaghan, who had been in the chair after HW left, but he was on a train to Cardiff. There was no point in getting HW since he had not been there for the summing-up.

My feeling was that Lever was probably right, since it was after all his scheme which Cabinet was discussing.

In his attack on the officials Lever accused them of 'deliberately raising unnecessary provocations' to sabotage the scheme.

We went back to the conference room. I walked with Varley, who said, 'I knew that once Lever was included he would fuck it up.'

Entering the conference room Eric Roll took Varley to one side, and they, plus Riccardo and Lever, went off for a conference down the corridor. Ross and Dell went to join them. When they came back into the room they announced that we would adjourn till tomorrow. The Americans had asked for the details on paper so that they could think about them.

We went back to Varley's room for fresh discussions. Another meeting was fixed for tomorrow at 11 a.m. Then we broke up. I travelled back in Lever's car. I reported to Nigel Wicks in private office and he sent a message to the PM after first talking to Industry and Lever – Lever said he was optimistic of a settlement, and Varley said he was pessimistic.

It was now 5.30 p.m. and I sat down to prepare briefs in No.10. We put in a paper on public expenditure, pointing out to the PM the probability of falling short of the £3.75 billion cuts and where he was likely to get concessions and what were the sticking-points of ministers.

Also a piece on import controls – which look barely worth doing on a small rag-bag of items for one year only. And on alleviating unemployment in Linwood.

Then I left for home, tired, but after a fascinating day.

*Saturday 6 December 1975*

I did not go to today's Chrysler talks. Carol was away so I stayed at home and looked after the children.

But Lever told me on the phone afterwards that he had upped the offer, after embarrassments about the £40 million maximum where the Americans had spotted our switch of position. They were now pushing for help with the investment programme and with bank guarantees, so the total package was up to about £85 million, but on that basis the Americans were looking interested. Lever was still angry with the Industry officials who he said maintained a very 'frosty' style.

*Sunday 7 December 1975*

Joe phoned from Chequers to say that the PM had asked him to ask me to draft a note to ministers from the Policy Unit about council house sales – and especially leasing, which he called 'life enfranchisement'. He has been worried by our public expenditure paper and is looking at ways to bridge the gap to the total.

*Monday 8 December 1975*

Went in early and immediately started work on the Housing paper which HW had asked for yesterday. He arrived at 11 a.m. and went straight into the Misc 59 on Chrysler. I was about to go in and was standing talking to Joe when John Hunt held up his hand to stop us coming in and slammed the door. He reappeared two minutes later to tell us to stop talking – at which Joe exploded.

I did not mind not going in since the PM had asked for another paper – on privacy – and I went off to discover the state of play on that, and on the Franks and the Phillimore reports. I telephoned the Home Office and the Lord Chancellor's Office and caught up on developments.

Alan Lord, a permanent secretary at the Treasury, also came in for a cup of coffee, having been shut out by John Hunt also. At the committee they decided to back Lever in increasing the loss subsidy and in giving joint bank guarantees.

Art Hartman, from the US State Department, telephoned to say he is here in London and I took him to lunch at the Reform. Very nice man. He is off to Vienna and then Brussels. Is concerned about our Defence cuts. On the UN he said that Kissinger was worried that Pat Moynihan might have started a panic of US opinion to leave the UN. There is also clearly some resentment about Moynihan's style and polished rhetoric.

Art said that Kissinger also has long periods of believing everything is going badly.

When I got back to No. 10, after walking through St James's Park in beautiful winter sunshine, there was a message saying to go straight to the Department of Industry for another Chrysler meeting. Got there at 2.50 p.m. Due to meet Riccardo et al. at 3 p.m. But Lever was missing. They telephoned him everywhere and finally chased him to earth in the House answering questions.

So we went into the conference room to discuss Lever's plan but without Lever. The Americans seemed very buoyant. They knew we were on the run. They now had losses of £73 million underwritten. Plus a joint guarantee on a £35 million loan. And they asked for us to put up the £55 million capital development – which we conceded. And then Caffiero produced another capital development scheme of another £35 million for making the new Alpine here – and they asked us for £25 million of that £35 million. This would keep Ryton going as well. So we ended up with us paying £140 million to keep nearly the whole thing going.

Our side was demoralised, with only Edmund Dell making an occasional objection. Then Lever came in late and spoke so warmly of Chrysler that he seemed to be on their side of the table. The Americans then went off to put the scheme to their Board.

I left with Lever and warned him that he might have gone too far. He must not react too much to the Industry officials, and give away everything to Chrysler. I was worried by the hostility to him which I had heard from Industry as well as from the Treasury.

We went back together to Whitehall, where another Misc committee was called at 6 p.m. to discuss the situation in Chrysler. I again did not go, because I had to draft the Housing brief. The Misc ended at 7 p.m. as I was leaving to go to see Tony Crosland at the Commons. Lever told me that he had thought about my warning, agreed he had gone too far, and so he had now agreed that Chrysler ought to give some kind of guarantee for £20m of the capital development. This would at least be a test of their good will.

Tony Crosland was sitting in his room drinking a large whisky when I got there. He told me that he had his medical check-up today and was cleared 100%. [Tony Crosland died fourteen months later.]

He repeated his insistence on not giving anything to the Treasury on Housing investment. He said that he would insist on more from Barbara on personal social services, from Education and from Defence.

He said that Jim Callaghan has become 'a real right-wing Tory' and that Jim and Roy were both 'very bombastic' on economic matters, repeatedly reminding people that they were ex-chancellors.

He thought that Healey would not get his £3.75 billion and that HW should prepare for that.

His good reason for excluding Housing was that it was crucial that we had a good housing record at the next election – since we won't have a good anything else.

Returned to No.10 at 8 p.m. and finished my brief and read the rest of my papers. Then home at 9.30 p.m.

The PM has told Joe that his departure is still 11 March – with an announcement on 25 February, after the NEC that day. He will enjoy keeping that lot in the dark. He will tell the Queen tomorrow.

Janet was at Chequers this weekend.

Marcia has been attacking Joe because of his so-called friendship with David Frost's girlfriend Caroline. Marcia considers David to be her contact and property and useful for a television series which HW is arranging with Frost through Goodman.

Bill Housden also told me today that Marcia is afraid that Joe will continue to work for HW after he retires and she is working to prevent that.

HW told Joe that he would have liked me to attend his dinner tomorrow with the newspaper proprietors. But Marcia would complain and 'She is still as obsessed as ever with Bernard.' Joe said, 'Well don't tell her Bernard is going.' HW said, 'Oh but she would find out – through the Hartwells.'

The row last Thursday was about peerages. Marcia was insisting on certain names, but HW resisted them.

HW is very removed from her at the moment. Bill says that HW is beginning to look after Mary more.

## *Tuesday 9 December 1975*

Cabinet started at 9.30 this morning to discuss public expenditure. I worked on a brief about the Franks, Younger, Phillimore and Faulks Royal Commission reports for tonight's PM's dinner with the newspaper proprietors. [These were : Report of the Departmental Committee on Section 2 of the Official Secrets Act, 1911, chaired by Lord Franks of Headington, 1972. Report of the Committee on Privacy, chaired by Kenneth Younger, 1972. Report of the Committee on Contempt of Court, chaired by Lord Phillimore, 1974. Interim Report of the Committee on Defamation, chaired by Sir Neville Faulks, 1974. Following these reports and with the backing of the Prime Minister, Joe Haines and the author attempted to negotiate an agreement with the press whereby, if they accepted some constraints on breaches of privacy, the government would make major concessions on official secrets, contempt of court and defamation. Sadly the press contacts rejected this, demonstrating that, whatever they might claim in self-righteous editorials, in fact they cared more about retaining the licence to breach individuals' privacy than they did about securing greater freedom of access to official secrets and liberalisation of contempt and defamation.]

Joe told me that the PM said to him that he really wanted me at this dinner but was afraid what Marcia would say, since she is 'obsessed' with me. This is all farcial, bearing in mind that I have been doing all the work briefing the PM for the dinner discussion, yet he dare not invite me to it. Fortunately I have better things to do than sit listening to the proprietors of our appalling press.

HW sent messages out from Cabinet asking for our brief on the Open University. Then on council house sales. Then on local authority maintenance expenditure. This included the information that it costs 25p to repair a water-tap washer in Camden. So he sent out a note asking someone to go out and buy a washer to find out how much it costs. The duty clerk said he had bought one yesterday for 2p. I sent in this information, adding that it ought to be possible to get a discount for bulk purchase.

At around midday ministers started coming out in a stream to go to the lavatory, etc. Roy Jenkins was in the waiting-room completing his Commons statement apologising for an official mistake in pricing TV licences. Eric Varley came out to telephone.

Harold Lever took me for a walk to a remote lavatory to tell me how clever HW had been over Defence. He and Crosland, Castle and Mulley had all said that they would not take any more cuts unless Defence did. So HW told Mason to go away and work out £275 million (out of £450 million) of cuts which did not diminish the front-line capability of NATO. This meant that the other ministers now had to start giving way – even though Defence's cuts were not yet precisely in the bag. HW has clearly moved on Defence. Our brief was devoted to convincing him that without cuts on Defence he would not get the £3.75 billion total.

HW then came out and took me into the lavatory. He said he was enjoying it and the Cabinet was very good-tempered, even though Barbara Castle and Fred Mulley had threatened to resign. He said that in October 1974 when he woke up after the election, he thought, 'Good, we have won' – then immediately his heart sank because he 'realised now we would have to deal with all those things we had put off between the elections'. This Public Expenditure Survey (PESC) was the main thing he had been dreading, but now it had come he was 'quite enjoying it'.

He was pleased with his move on Defence. He had allowed everyone a second reading statement and now wanted to move fast on the total.

He was also pleased with Crosland on council house sales – Crosland said, 'You are pushing at an open door.'

He said he was going to insist on protecting the Open University. He said, 'We all have our sacred cows, which other people think are bulls. Well mine is the Open University. I won't argue about the cuts. I just won't have 'em.'

He then took his top set of false teeth out and cleaned them under the sink tap in the lavatory. I couldn't understand what he said without them, just muttering through his gums.

Cabinet went on till 1.30 without reaching a conclusion and they decided to continue and conclude on Thursday morning. HW was confident there would not be too many problems.

Joe and I went to lunch at the Commons. He told a nice HW vignette which had been reported to him by Janet. HW had told her that last Thursday in the row with Marcia over her demands for peerages for friends, she had reminded him of his obligations to her from long ago. He said, 'Because of that does not mean that I have to spend 20 years' penal servitude afterwards.'

Question Time briefing went very gently and Question Time easily. HW seems more relaxed about it, takes it all at greater speed without getting too embroiled.

Afterwards back to No.10. Joe Stone came in to examine HW, who is clearly in much better health now. Then we went up to the PM's study to discuss his Guildhall speech over a cup of tea. I suggested that he insert some reference to John Wilkes, a radical politician in the City in the 1770s. Once when an academic historian I did research into him.

At 6 p.m. HW went off to tell the Queen about his future plans for retirement. I went to watch Rachel and Katie in their school play.

Before going Joe told me that Marcia has discussed a contract for another book with Weidenfeld and has asked the journalist, John Connell, to ghost-write it. He has apparently asked for 50% of the proceeds.

Late in the evening I got worried about Chrysler, on which we are putting in a brief, and had long telephone calls to Andrew Graham. The government's rescue operation is terribly profligate.

## Wednesday 10 December 1975

Went in to attend the Misc committee on BNOC and Kearton's plans to build it up. The first ten minutes were spent complaining about the Chrysler leaks in today's press, especially the *Financial Times*.

The meeting was very tense, dominated by the battle between Benn and Lever. Benn wants to take over BP's North Sea oil as well as Burmah's for BNOC. He also wants to take the participation negotiations with the oil companies away from Lever. Lever wants to go gently with the oil companies, and claims that the activities of Benn and Kearton are wrecking his efforts to reach an agreement.

The PM tried to keep them apart, and used Edmund Dell and Ken Berrill effectively as foils. In fact the Department of Energy does have a case – BNOC will be very weak if all it can do is acquire its participation oil from the majors and then sell it back to them at whatever price they fix for them to contribute. So it would help if the BNOC had its own downstream refining capacity. But I am wary of the empire-building ambitions of Kearton and the nationalisation addiction of Benn.

John Smith, the new Minister of State at Energy, was present and very good. He strikes me as serious, does his homework, speaks forcefully and with a lot of political sense. He will go quickly to the top if the Scot Nats give him the chance to hold his seat. [He became Labour leader in 1994.]

Afterwards HW said, 'What an extraordinary meeting.' He then went off to the National Council of Social Services to deliver David Piachaud's excellent speech.

I worked on papers. Then had lunch at the Reform – chatted to Alan Neale, the permanent secretary at Agriculture. And afterwards to John Smith, who asked to keep in close touch. He said that he told Benn after the meeting that he had 'thrown it away'. He said that Benn now delegates the departmental work and claims to be 'brooding' (presumably waiting for HW to resign).

HW told the Queen about his retirement last night. She was sympathetic. But apparently her secretary Martin Charteris is flapping and saying it will be a disaster.

Coming back from the Reform I saw Anthony Lester and we walked back together to No.10. Agreed to work together to get the UK to write the European Convention of Human Rights into British law.

He also told me of the terrible flap in the Home Office over the scandal of overcharging on television licences and the Law Lords deciding against the Home Office. Apparently the departmental lawyers completely ballsed it up, and were totally confident they would win. Jenkins had contemplated resigning if they could not get the money to repay those who had overpaid. He also gave his permanent secretary, Peterson, a rocket.

Joe came back after lunch, fuming against Marcia. She has been trying to knife him in the back through David Frost.

Last night at the newspaper proprietors' dinner, Goodman sat next to Joe and fiercely attacked Marcia's role in HW's life, saying that 'if it were not for that woman he would have been a great Prime Minister'.

We did a joint brief to stop a crazy DOE proposal to change the law retrospectively to overthrow the Law Lords' decision that people not connected to the sewerage should not be charged sewage rates. The DOE paper stated explicitly that the purpose was so that nobody should get any money refunded as a result of the court decision.

The PM had an Economic Strategy Cabinet committee, on the next round of the pay policy, in which they decided to go slowly and not tie it up till after the Budget. Andrew Graham, who attended on my behalf, thought the PM was pushing delay to wait for prices to fall next summer. I know it is because he won't be here to go through the agonies of the next negotiation.

We also prepared a small brief on tomorrow's public expenditure Cabinet. About £500 million still to get and not much more to squeeze. So we suggest a bit of Crosland's local government, a bit of Barbara's personal social services, and the rest off the contingency reserve (the latter to prevent any resignations).

There was a reception for the Everest climbers at 6.30. Harry Evans came and told me he had heard that *Private Eye* are 'staking out your house' to get a story. Also that Auberon Waugh claims to 'hate' me, even though I have never met him. Waugh is rumoured to be sleeping with his au pair and, as a Catholic, feels guilty and disguises it by publishing how sinful others are. Waugh is also poisonously jealous of Harry because of Harry's beautiful girlfriend Tina and has made this clear to her. That may be why he attacks him as 'Dame Harold Evans' each issue. And of course Harry is able and successful, which is unforgivable in the eyes of most modern journalists, especially at *Private Eye*.

Drove to Carol's school with her. She went to the children's Christmas play and I walked home. Sense of the end coming and not sorry. 'Demob happy,' as Joe says.

My friend Clifford Barclay told me that the PM's accountant David Freeman told him that I would be leaving No.10 soon. Obviously he knows something of HW's plans.

## Thursday 11 December 1975

Was collected by official car at 7.30 a.m. and set off in the dark of a cold winter morning for another meeting with Chrysler.

Beforehand we had a brief meeting in Varley's room where it was again made clear that the Department of Industry was unhappy with the situation.

The Chrysler people, straight off the plane from Chicago, looked as fresh as ever. Riccardo reported that the Chrysler board had discussed our suggestions, and they had also put them to the American banks (who have loaned the Chrysler parent $2 billion last year). They accepted all our proposals, and the only quibble was about how to spread the £28 million guarantees on capital development which we had asked them for.

Then we broke up to go back to Cabinet at No. 10. Varley and Kaufman were muttering all the time against Lever, and two of the Industry officials, Sir Anthony Part, the permanent secretary, and Bullock, were very open in their hostility to the deal – which certainly favours Chrysler excessively.

I dashed back to No. 10 in Ken Berrill's car. When I got there some ministers were already arriving for the 9.30 Cabinet on public expenditure. HW was late and I only got two minutes with him to brief him on Chrysler. John Hunt came rushing up and started shouting at me for some reason I could not discover. He is showing signs of nervous strain and behaving in a most odd way, ordering people about and flapping in all directions.

With Cabinet meeting I went to the Unit and cleared a huge pile of papers.

The Cabinet went on for four hours till 1.30 p.m. They broke briefly for coffee, and also at one stage HW took Healey and Barbara Castle, Mason and Crosland upstairs to the study to get some progress on concessions. In the end they reached £3.6 billion – partly with the help of cutting predicted interest on the national debt and partly by chopping some off the Civil Service expenditure. Afterwards HW seemed quite pleased. He expressed relief that – with Chrysler – this was almost the last big hurdle over (for him as PM).

I went to lunch with William Plowden at the Reform. He told me that Anthony Howard of the *New Statesman* had told him I was leaving No. 10, as had a visiting Australian academic. This is 10 days after I wrote to Dahrendorf asking for an extension.

William reported that the CPRS is in a very unhappy state. They feel that Ken Berrill is running them too much like a regular Civil Service department, and is afraid of upsetting the Establishment. They have demanded a weekend seminar to air their grievances.

Back to Question Time briefing. The PM was very relaxed. One of the questions was about the Policy Unit. A silly Tory described us as 'discredited Marxists'. The Labour side erupted with laughter and several shouted to me 'You never told us' or 'You could have kidded me'. I even saw one or two old Tory acquaintances – John Biffen and Leon Brittan and Margaret Thatcher – smiling. HW grinned widely and expressed astonishment.

When I went back to HW's room he was still laughing. I told him that I did not mind the 'discredited' bit, but nobody had ever called me a 'Marxist' before.

Gerald Kaufman talked to me in the corridor and said that Varley was going to resign. I questioned this, but Kaufman insisted. I asked what Eric wanted in order to keep him happy, but Kaufman seemed incapable of giving a clear reply. However, I discussed it with HW and suggested he must take it seriously. Not that I thought Eric would resign. But it was necessary to show that Eric was loved. HW was quite scathing about Kaufman and Varley, saying they 'often behaved like a couple of little girls, petulant and skittish'.

We all came back to No.10 for another Cabinet committee on Chrysler. Apart from Varley, Lever, Ross and Dell, there was also Healey, Millan, Booth (the junior minister at Employment), Ennals and Shore.

Before the start I talked privately with Eric and told him it would be foolish to resign – Labour Party supporters would say he had resigned to put men on the dole. Varley said, with some justice, that the whole industrial strategy was now lacking in credibility. He said 'even Bennery makes more sense than this'.

HW then took Varley off to chat in the corner at the bottom of the stairs. He told him that he, HW, had made two great political mistakes in his career – in resigning in 1951 and in standing against Gaitskell in 1960. That these nearly ruined his chances. He 'only won the leadership because he stood against a drunk' [George Brown]. Therefore he didn't want Eric to do the same – he 'could be leader in a few years'. Eric replied, 'I wouldn't have your job at any price.'

We all went into the Cabinet Room. Varley said he would simply report the details of the proposals, which he opposed, and he would put his own position more fully at Cabinet tomorrow.

Dell agreed – though adding that now we had made the offer, which he 'deeply regretted', we must go through with it. [Dell later informed me that he had intended to resign but that Callaghan dissuaded him.]

Healey was interesting and important. He was much more 'pro' the deal than Dell – in fact these two Treasury ministers were miles apart. He was attracted by the Iran situation (the Iran Minister of Finance had sent a telegram saying it would be 'disastrous' to confidence in British exports if we collapsed Chrysler). Also to avoid redundancy costs which he estimated at £160m. So 'on balance it is worth it for these contingency advantages'.

Others spoke in favour and HW summed up in favour with just a few loose ends to tie. He then concluded by saying, 'Let's be politicians.' The Tories would attack the scheme for spending too much. But we could 'take on the Tories – and Eric will have a great parliamentary triumph with our people'.

One embarrassment is that the CPRS is committed soon to publish its own report – which argues for reducing the size of the British motor industry. Ken Berrill said that was OK since 'we have now cut out the section which stated that Chrysler should be the first to close'.

NB: HW told me that when Varley said he was worried about the Chrysler decision being inconsistent with our Chequers industry strategy, HW said (or thought!), 'That was all a load of rubbish anyway.'

Afterwards I worked in the Unit, then went home by tube, walking to Trafalgar Square with Joe and Albert.

HW was supposed to see David Frost this evening, but cancelled it on Marcia's instructions, and rearranged a weekend meeting involving Goodman somehow. This is all mixed up with the idea of a big and very remunerative television series. Albert says that Marcia will get a nice share of this as HW's literary manager and executor. I don't know how much, or indeed how true that is.

Home at 8.45 p.m.


*Friday 12 December 1975*

Cabinet met at 9.30 to decide finally on Chrysler. The newspapers are full of Varley's threats of resignation – based on Gerald Kaufman's briefing of the press last night.

The vast majority of ministers were in favour of the rescue scheme – except for Roy Jenkins, Shirley Williams, Eric Varley – and Benn, who opposed it because he preferred import controls.

HW left the meeting at 11.30 a.m., after the Chrysler decision but while they were discussing import controls (on which they reached no agreement simply because there were too few people left). We all went off to the Guildhall for the PM to get the Freedom of the City. He was delighted with this, and even enjoyed riding in the open golden coach. The morning was sunny and cold, but very good for December.

The Guildhall ceremony was marvellous. I had not been there before. A nice little orchestra in the gallery, and full of the guests of the PM and the Lord Mayor. Actually the PM's 'personal guest list' was quite intriguing. It included Lord Brayley, Rudi Sternberg, Jimmy Goldsmith (who didn't show up), Eric Miller, Joe Kagan, Sammy Fisher, together with Tony Field, Marcia and Peggy Field. Joe said he had looked around to see if Inspector Knacker of the Yard was keeping the ceremony under observation. We noted that the Office Trust was well represented. In fact a number of HW's 'personal list' were much closer to Marcia.

[Brayley was made a peer by Wilson in 1974 and resigned from the government in 1974 after official accusations of financial malpractice. He was believed to help finance the political office.

Rudi Sternberg was made a peer as Lord Plurenden by Wilson in 1975, was reported by the Downing Street private office as being a Soviet spy, and was believed to assist in financing the political office.

Miller was knighted by Wilson in 1976 and was believed to assist in financing the political office. He later committed suicide after official allegations of financial malpractice at his public property company.

Kagan was made a peer by Wilson in 1976, was believed to have assisted in financing the political office, and was later imprisoned for tax irregularities.

Fisher was made a peer as by Wilson in 1974 and was a member of the 'Office Trust'.

Tony Field had served as Wilson's office manager, Marcia was Wilson's political and personal secretary and Peggy Field was Mrs Wilson's secretary.]

The 'special guests' were formally announced and marched up the central aisle to the stage. Marcia dramatically delayed her regal entrance until right at the last moment. On the stroke of midday the whole great gathering fell quiet to await the Prime Minister. At that moment she flounced in with creepy Gerald Kaufman and in a swish of stiff underskirts the two of them minced up the aisle. On stage she turned and smiled girlishly at the television cameras. The Lady Secretary certainly has style.

HW's speech of acceptance went down well, serious and statesmanlike, about Britain's problems and decline over the past 30 years (mainly described in terms of under-investment). But he looked old and tired to me, with dark rings and sunken eyes.

Afterwards we all walked to the Mansion House and had lunch. I talked to Shirley Williams about her opposition to the Chrysler deal – she is clearly worried about the long-term implications.

I sat next to a grumpy City Corporation official and opposite George Weidenfeld – who made some cutting remarks about my lack of friendliness. I replied by referring to his firm's apparent lack of effort to sell my book on Herbert Morrison.

The lobster soup was nice and I was just settling to eat my beef when Harold Lever came along and said there was another Chrysler meeting at 2 p.m. So off we dashed in his car to the Department of Industry, with not even a sight of the promised passion-fruit sweet!

In the briefing meeting we discussed a paper containing 14 points of detail which had to be settled with Chrysler before the final meeting.

With the Americans, Varley said smilingly that they would have read of our political problems – implying his resignation – but reassured them that there were no more problems. He would announce the deal next Tuesday, when there would be an order for Parliament to approve.

Riccardo asked for a break to consider our detailed points and they left the room. I talked to Ken Berrill and we discussed who should wind up in Tuesday's debate (Eric is opening). I thought of Dell or Ross. Sir Anthony Part stood by me and interrupted to say that Dell would refuse to speak in the debate since he had too much sense to support 'this kind of nonsense'. I told him that Dell would presumably speak if told to by the Prime Minister. He muttered on and clearly still totally refused to accept that the Department of Industry had lost on this.

The Americans came back and said they accepted our points, with a few details to be discussed. Riccardo said his advisers would stay to negotiate. They looked a bit glum at spending more nights in London hotels and pressed to start discussing this evening. Bullock, the Industry official in charge, showed reluctance, saying that he had a dinner party this evening. Throughout they have been hostile and unrelentingly discourteous to the Americans.

This Chrysler business has had some curious twists and turns.

At first we all agreed it had to close because of lack of financial viability. Even the PM. The concern originally was to make sure:

1.  that it appeared we had tried to save it,
2.  therefore the Scots would not resign, and
3.  the Americans would get the blame for the closure.

All the discussion on the American offer to put £13 or £30+ million into a scheme which we had responsibility for was on that basis. It was a question of each side wanting the ball in the other court when the final whistle went.

Then with the Scots – angry at the hard hostility of the Industry officials – threatening to resign, the PM told Lever last Thursday, 4 December, to come up with a compromise proposal, which promised at most to rescue some of Chrysler for a year or so (till after the PM has gone), and at least to have shown sufficient willingness, so that the Scots could in all conscience stay on.

The effect of Lever's initiative last Friday and Saturday was to come up with a scheme reversing the original situation – now we were putting in the money, much more, for them to continue with the bulk of the business on a permanent basis.

To the Department of Industry – and Dell from the Treasury – this was even worse. But they were not worried at first because they thought it was even less likely. Then when Chrysler accepted our package it became very difficult for us to withdraw. Varley saw this too late, and reacted emotionally by threatening to resign. But with Healey supporting the package Varley was lost – and not in a cause on which he could really resign. He could not resign in protest against a policy which prevents large-scale unemployment. Hence his animosity towards Lever – though he was only doing what the PM had told him.

My first reflection is that this compromise is the only course. The alternative is worse:

- 30,000 unemployed at a cost of £160 million;
- lost exports to Iran and the whole of the Middle East;
- increased imports of foreign cars – or import controls;
- Scotland closer to separatism.

It is a balance of evils. The disadvantages of our decision are clear – more public debt to bail out an American multinational to provide more car capacity than we need. Contrary to our industrial policy and Leyland policy. But on balance our decision is the least wrong.

As I left the negotiating room Lever commented to me that we must be careful that Ryder of British Leyland does not go on TV to criticise the settlement. Anthony Part came rushing up to me in the corridor and spat out, 'You are to have no contacts with Don Ryder.' I was astonished and asked him to repeat it – and he did. I told him that it was for the Prime Minister to decide whom I did or did not speak to on this issue where I was representing him personally. He then said I must not advise the PM to speak to Ryder. He said, 'Ryder is under the Department of Industry. I will go to speak to the Secretary of State.'

I returned to No.10, meeting Bob Maclennan on the way. He expressed concern about the way we are handling devolution, and was particularly critical of Gerry Fowler. I sensed that he wanted Gerry's job.

In fact the PM is thinking of moving Gerry. And Roy Jenkins wants to get rid of his junior minister Alex Lyon, who is a very difficult character. And the Attorney-General, Sam Silkin, is going to resign and go into hospital: he looks very ill and some suspect cancer. So there is another reshuffle building up. HW will duck and delay it if he can.

Back in No. 10 at 4.30 p.m. I went up to the third-floor flat where the PM was entertaining some of his guests – family, friends plus Joe and private office to tea or champagne to celebrate the Freedom of the City.

I went over and sat beside his armchair and reported on Chrysler. He instructed Joe that Ryder should not go on TV; and told private office to try to get Dell or Ross to wind up on Tuesday in place of Kaufman, whom Varley wants. He said at one point, 'Kaufman ought to be sacked for his behaviour over the past few days.'

After a couple of champagnes I went downstairs to the Unit and went through another batch of papers. Arranged for some LSE social psychologists to come and talk to the counter-inflation unit. And tried to prevent David Piachaud from resigning over the public expenditure cuts – which have been quite overshadowed by the Chrysler business.

Also intervened with the Department of Environment to try to stop them making retrospective charges for sewage disposal on people not connected to the mains. And began intervening with the Department of Education to make the authors public lending right wider. Must declare a vested interest here.

Finally home at 8.45 p.m. Very cold evening. Sleeting as I waited for the bus in Camden Town. Also have sore throat and a cold coming on. But still an exciting week.

## Monday 15 December 1975

Awoke feeling fluey – sore throat, heavy eyes.

The newspapers are full of attacks on our Chrysler compromise. In fact they are quite unrealistic. Won't face up to the real choices. We have committed a lot of money – but there was no option which didn't. Closing down would lose, according to Healey, £150 million in the first year in unemployment benefits, social security and lost tax revenue. The loss of Iranian exports, and the flood of imported cars to replace Chrysler, all made that option very expensive. Nor did we want to nationalise it. We don't have the management to run it. And we would then face paying all the costs if it closed in a couple of years – which it probably would. We want Chrysler's commitment – money and management. The brutal toughness of Riccardo is exactly what we need to bring our trade unions to face reality. Our own people, managers or ministers, have no guts – there are not two vertebrae to rub together in much of the whole Cabinet – so we have to import backbones.

Eric Varley has behaved foolishly and Kaufman treacherously. He was right to take a firm line on Chrysler. To prove his political manhood and to maintain the credibility of his industrial policy. But when the Cabinet went against him he for a time went into sulks.

[On 16 December 1975 Varley announced to the Commons the Chrysler deal, which he estimated as involving £162.5 million: £72.5 million committed over the next four years, plus a government loan of $55 million for capital expenditure and a further £35 million of medium-term loan.]

It was foggy and HW was late coming in.

At 11 we went to an economic strategy committee to discuss import controls. The final package we are putting up is very tiny. No cars now because of Chrysler. Varley has stopped pressing for TV tubes. Footwear is only restricted from East Europe. Even textiles are controlled in a very limited way. I don't think it is worth doing. Typical of the kind of Anglo-Saxon compromises which have fudged our policies in the past 30 years. We should either introduce sufficient protection to really protect our employment – and to hell with foreign reaction. Or not at all. This way we get foreign resentment and possibly retaliation, for nothing worthwhile. The problem is partly institutional. The Department of Trade is totally and ideologically opposed to any restraints. So major concessions are made to win Trade's agreement to a few piddling gestures. If it is right, we should overrule Trade and go fully ahead. If Trade is right, we should not waste time on protection. But in practice we get all this institutional horse-trading.

At the end of discussing import controls, the PM raised the question of Chrysler, and Varley's statement tomorrow. Many of the wounds showed and some of the arguments were dragged out again.

Joe and I went to the Commons for lunch. I was feeling lousy. Joe told me how Marcia had been at HW again this weekend, complaining that she was going to be thrown out into the world with no money, and HW thought only of himself – all leading up to pressures for him to stay on. There was also some argument about the New Year's honours list. The PM came in today and asked for Sigmund Sternberg to be given a knighthood. But the honours section resisted, saying that there was evidence of his having given money to the Labour Party, and so this would have to go to the Scrutiny Section. It was then withdrawn. Poor Sigmund. He has been open about his financial assistance to the party. His money has mainly (perhaps wholly) gone to the party for specific research assistance in policy areas which interest him. He is a very decent man.

Worked in my office in the afternoon.

In the evening Kissin came in to see the PM. Afterwards I hitched a lift home with him, to save going out in the fog. He told me that HW had discussed me for 20 minutes. Had been full of praise. Had said that I had chosen a brilliant team. That the Unit was essential to his style of government and to his success as PM. All very nice. But then HW said

a. I was too sensitive and hostile to Lady F.
b. I was too concerned about security and my future.

Very strange that. True. But I have never shown it and never mentioned it to him.

He did not reveal any intention to retire to Kissin – who is genuinely an old friend of his and usually gives him sound advice.

I went to bed with hot whisky and again feeling very feverish.

*Tuesday 16 December 1975*

I stayed in bed through until Tuesday 23 December, with bronchitis and severe sinus infection. Very unpleasant. So I did not go into the office again before Christmas.

But I kept in touch by telephone and Joe told me what he heard from Janet, Albert and from Bill Housden.

As the days went by it was clear from what Joe said that Marcia was getting her claws into HW again. He is planning some big television series for after he has retired – either with David Frost on 'past Prime Ministers' or with George Weidenfeld on 'Democracy'. The model is Alistair Cooke's 'America' – linking a big TV series with mass book sales.

At present they are still playing both TV ideas. HW is having dinner with Frost in the New Year. And he and Marcia had dinner with Weidenfeld in the week before Christmas. Frost is favourite – though Marcia has turned against him for not inviting her to dinner. Also she has been seeing a lot of Jimmy Goldsmith, who has apparently cast doubts on Frost's ability to finance the series. Joe and I don't yet understand it all – there are all kinds of manoeuvres going on. But she is definitely fixed on freezing out Joe from the moment HW retires (which she is also bent upon delaying as long as possible).

HW issued a writ against the *Daily Mail* for a Nigel Dempster piece saying that HW has become a 'brandy addict' and will retire on his birthday. He is suing against the first allegation. But Marcia is claiming that now he cannot retire on his birthday because of his writ. She is using this as a lever to try to make him stay on. But HW said to Joe that, though it meant he 'might have to change the timing', that could mean 'earlier'. He now thought it was a mistake to get too committed to a specific date, such as after the NEC meeting on 25 February, and for his birthday in March. He needed to be more flexible and perhaps make it a bit earlier.

Still I will wait and see. Lady F may be able to change his mind again over the Christmas holiday.

However, his plans are proceeding. He is going ahead to arrange his flat in Ashley Gardens as a pied-à-terre (Janet also lives in Ashley Gardens). HW has no idea of the number of people who know his secret – mainly because he refuses to admit how many people he tells himself!

Marcia has probably told Weidenfeld (for the TV series and a book), her sister, Bill, Albert – and they have all surely told their nearest and dearest.

Joe and I and Janet know.

So do Ken Stowe and John Hunt.

And Martin Charteris rang up in a tizzy to say that Harold Lever had told him – and that Peter Ramsbotham our Ambassador in Washington knew.

Goodman knows, and so presumably does David Freeman the PM's accountant. And the Queen. No wonder it gets printed in the *Daily Mail*.

Marcia is seeing Finniston about a part-time job on the Steel Board. No doubt there will be some honours in the film world which may open that door.

A mini-crisis arose in the Unit when the *Guardian* and the *Telegraph* printed stories saying that Richard Graham had written a paper for the PM proposing to cut the railways. Richard denied ever mentioning it, but curiously did have a paper that very day arguing – though in different details – that the railways should be cut.

The PM was very agitated. I was at home in bed. And after a long flap the papers published apologies. We believed that it was part of a shrewd PR campaign for the railway unions. Their PR man Will Camp obviously wants an official denial which becomes a policy commitment.

This story broke while the PM was in Ulster visiting the troops. Messages came from the depths of Armagh asking about Richard Graham.

I missed the No. 10 Christmas party. A pity because it would be my last in No. 10.

I went off to Suffolk for a lovely Christmas. No telephone or television. Just the old radio, a log fire and the children. Lovely. Though my cough did not completely clear up.

Back on Monday 29 December in the evening.

In the office for part of Tuesday. Lunch with Joe and private office. Not much happening.

Joe was very depressed. He has been in conflict with *The Times* over their description of him as 'a professional liar'. The PM has encouraged him and the press office has refused to give information to *The Times* until they apologise. Yesterday *The Times* asked for the honours list, and when Joe refused, they said they would get it from the PM – and did. HW told the duty clerk to give it to them. He said to Joe, 'You have got yourself on a hook and will have to get yourself off it': completely dissociating himself, although before Christmas he instructed Douglas Allen and the Treasury Solicitor to pay for Joe to sue *The Times*. Joe felt bitterly betrayed. He said, 'It is disgraceful, he is treating me the way he always treats his colleagues.'

Joe and I discussed our plans for what we call 'after ski-ing'.

I picked up a mass of papers and brought them home to read.

Stayed at home the rest of the week, looking after the children while Carol went to a NUT conference.

New Year's Eve went to a party at Jack Black's – my solicitor.

He said that *Private Eye* has asked for, and been given, a final extension till 12 January to submit evidence. What a grubby world. I cannot say that 1976 holds any fine prospects. Return to LSE – which will be a boring anticlimax. Further political, social and economic deterioration in Britain. Fortunately I have Carol and the children, compared to which nothing else matters.

# CHAPTER 22

# Irish Initiatives, Icelandic Retreats and Trying to Reform the Law January–February 1976

## Monday 5 January 1976

I went in to the office – the first time for a whole day in Downing Street for three weeks. All very quiet in No.10. The PM did not arrive till nearly midday. There were no crises. No committees till Wednesday. Only a trickle of papers. Some of my staff were still not back – one delayed by the bad weather in Germany. One of the private secretaries was away. The New Year in No.10 was certainly not coming in with a bang.

I worked most of the morning clearing my papers and writing letters. Also arranged a series of lunches with people I should see before I depart – if only, as in the case of Jim Hamilton from the Cabinet Office and Jonathan Charkham from the Public Appointments Unit, because I owed them a lunch.

HW came in at midday and I saw him in private office. He praised the Unit paper on monetary policy (urging the need for greater controls over banking credit if we are not to repeat the Barber disaster of 1971–73). I went back to finish my work and Joe went upstairs. There HW told him long and complicated stories of how the press tried to bribe people to get dirt on Tony Field and also some story from Brayley, about press 'dirty tricks'.

Brayley, incidentally, was a George Wigg product, having been in the Army with Wigg.

HW invited us for a lift over to the Commons in his car. He continued to praise the Unit paper in the car. He was friendly and cheery, but looked pale and tired, with black rings around his eyes.

The reason transpired when Bill Housden came to have a cup of tea with me after lunch. He said that HW had visited Marcia for three hours last night. She is still on at him to stay on longer.

Bill still thinks HW will go before Easter – and even perhaps in three weeks. He said that Mary is off to the Scillies soon to prepare the cottage there for his retreat after retirement.

(But Joe has heard from Ken Stowe that HW is talking of leaving later now, after his birthday, and after having a big farewell dinner for the Cabinet and Len Murray and Ron Hayward – and Stanley Baker and Sir Richard Attenborough and Frank Sinatra, etc.?)

Bill Housden says that HW has no lasting personal loyalty. Once he has gone, none of us will hear another word from him. 'Once you have served your purpose, you will be dropped, that applies to all of us.' Bill says he knows HW better than anybody, having worked closely with him for twenty years. In 1970 Bill never heard a word from him after his election defeat until HW was given the use of an official car – then he telephoned Bill to come and be his driver again.

He wondered what will happen about peerages. He said that at least 8 people have been personally promised them by Marcia – and there is only one more list. Bill thinks that Weidenfeld and Kagan are the most likely.

He said that HW had told him that he was afraid when Marcia telephoned and often 'went to hide'.

The PM returned early from the Scillies because he gets bored with the family.

The week before Christmas he went home early to Lord North Street. Next morning he told Bill that he wished he had stayed at No.10. He complained that when he got home Giles was watching the TV. There was nowhere for him to sit and read. He had nothing to talk to Mary about. So he was forced to sit there watching TV as well.

I said to Bill that I suspected there might have been a little slippage on retirement – and he went straight off to tell Albert. They discuss together everything they see and hear – and tell us all. They of course both want to delay as much as possible.

The PM sat in his study reading his boxes. Joe and I left him there uninterrupted. I finished my papers – including two very depressing ones: on Ireland, where there is now no long-term policy at all; and the Radcliffe Report on ministerial memoirs, showing a 15-year limit and a series of Boy Scout 'honour' rules, clearly written by William Armstrong to protect civil servants.

Went home early, shortly after 7 p.m., to take Carol her delayed birthday and Christmas presents – tapes of Janet Baker and Glen Campbell.

On the way out Ken told me that Ted Short wants to get rid of Gerry Fowler. He used to think he was the cleverest man in the government but 'now cannot stand him'. I still think that Gerry is very good.

### Tuesday 6 January 1976

When I arrived HW was already in the private office. I joined them – Joe, Patrick Wright and Ken Stowe. We discussed Ireland. The terrible sectarian killings have brought the crisis to a head. HW sent for Merlyn Rees, who was in Belfast seeing the politicians, and told him to come back here to a meeting this afternoon. I said there would be renewed pressure to move Merlyn (whom HW offered to move last summer but he refused). And perhaps he should go. He looks very tired. The basic question to Merlyn is where does he want the Irish situation to be in five years. I am not sure that he has time to look beyond today's latest killing in Crossmaglen.

Joe said he thought it was another Algeria. I said that the PM's original attachment to a move towards Dominion status should be pursued. HW began to pace up and down and to think on his feet. He began to play with the idea of an all-party meeting at Lancaster House to discuss security (not politics). He also wanted to tie the Tories closer into a bipartisan approach. So he would tell Merlyn to arrange a meeting with the Tories soon. But with Whitelaw, not Thatcher. So tomorrow, when Thatcher is flying abroad. He knew her plane took off at 9 a.m., so Merlyn was to contact her just after nine, and then contact Whitelaw as substitute. He is still very sharp on small tactics when he applies himself.

On security the PM wanted tougher measures. He wanted a policy of letting the troops shoot on sight anybody they suspected of being armed. Above all he felt a gesture of firmness was necessary. Though he said that no military solution was possible.

He then had several appointments – starting off with John Hunt, who came in carrying volume II of the Crossman Diaries in a large cardboard box.

I went to my room and read papers.

At 11 a.m. Leo Pliatzky came in. He has just been appointed Second permanent secretary at the Treasury in charge of public expenditure. He came to establish contact with me. He is a very lively rough diamond. Physically stocky and unpresuming. A strong north-country accent. Blind in one eye and just recovering from a gall bladder operation. He talks very freely, full of swear words and strong views on various individuals in Whitehall, e.g. William Armstrong the most impressive Whitehall mandarin he ever met, but a total failure; Douglas Allen, bright and nice, but too weak in controlling his departmental barons, and when he disagreed with Heath he was ignored and put out to grass – Armstrong was wheeled in to operate economic policy under Heath's direction. Douglas Wass – much tougher than is realised and more autocratic, constructing a Treasury hierarchy which he will control.

He was a close friend of Tony Crosland for many years but thinks him a failed boy wonder, with 'no political courage' and 'too lazy'.

He said he would have preferred to have Alan Lord's job on industrial policy, and had been advising Healey on that during the battles with Benn.

Now he was going to get public expenditure under control. 'I'm going to alter our fucking image,' he said. He admitted Healey was ambivalent on public expenditure. And said that they had just about educated him in the summer of 1974. But he went off to the election and came back 'with his head full of nonsense'.

Leo's first idea was to set up a Cabinet committee on public expenditure – containing the non-spending ministers. I promised to think about it and we will have lunch to discuss it in a month's time.

When he left we had a brief meeting in my office on selling council houses, where we are slowly edging DOE towards a more positive attitude – actually the officials are being quite helpful. The opposition to our schemes for selling council houses is on the political side of Environment.

As Joe left for lunch with Ian Coulter of the Steel Corporation he told me that HW had said to Janet that I had actually been brought in by Marcia to get Joe out. She also claimed that this was a pact between her and Kissin, who knew me beforehand. In fact I was told that Kissin wanted me there to get Marcia out. And I came with no intention of getting anybody out. But as it has turned out my firm alliance with Joe has made it possible for me to survive Marcia's ceaseless attacks on me. HW prefers not to take us both on. Anyway Joe is too valuable to him – and knows too much.

HW also admitted that Marcia was pressing him to stay on in office. He said to Janet, 'She would like me to stay on till I die in office.'

I went to lunch with Pat Nairne, who is clearly enjoying running the DHSS. He praises Castle for her resilience and courage in the face of constant criticism. But he clearly feels she is about clapped out. He says that the department is not in good shape either. It is mainly run by David Owen on the Health side ('Good but young and impetuous') and by Brian O'Malley on Social Security (a 'real true-blue conservative').

Pat also thought that Crosland was becoming a disappointment – 'too lazy'.

Incidentally he said that Barbara Castle never looks ahead – has no strategy whatsoever. He is trying to get her to think about where they should be by the end of the session. She doesn't think like that. He said Healey did at Defence. She just leaves everything to Owen and O'Malley and pursues the political issue of the moment. That of course may be one reason why she is such an effective politician.

We also discussed the Royal Commission on the Health Services. They hope Merrison from Bristol will take it – though he is about to be Chairman of the Vice-Chancellors. If not, he thought it might be Asa Briggs, the social historian, though he opposed him as 'too busy and muddled'. Barbara Castle wants Peter Parker, as a compensation for having been sacked by the Tories from her Ports Authority in 1970. I would fully support him. I also suggested Burke Trend. Pat said, 'Yes, but he isn't a member of the human race, you know.'

Dashed back to see my friend Maurice Kogan at No. 10 – he is in for a chair at the LSE and off to the USA next Tuesday. Agree to liaise but perhaps best for him if I don't interfere on his behalf.

At 3.30 we had the meeting on Ireland. Merlyn Rees reported in his usual breathless way, full of colourful detail and marvellous anecdotes.

The PM then said that he wanted a military initiative, even an over-response, to stress that we are doing something.

Merlyn was not too happy with this. He said it was only a question of 30 Provisionals and 30 Protestant UVF in Armagh doing all the killing. A big army was irrelevant to that.

(At this morning's meeting with Merlyn and the politicians in Belfast the police frisked the politicians and found one – Glenn Barr – carrying a gun into the meeting.)

Roy Mason as Defence minister was in favour of a stronger military presence. He asked to despatch the 'Spearhead' battalion straight away – the instruction was sent from the Cabinet Room. He also suggested sending in the SAS; using computerised intelligence information, closing the border; and designating Armagh a Special Security Area under martial law.

He said he was fatally weakened by not being allowed to use Gurkhas, or Northern Irish troops or the SAS – this was a quarter of the British Army!

The PM supported this and told them to send the SAS – just to Armagh – and to try to close the border to a few checkpoints.

Then the PM asked all but the ministers to leave. We officials did so – but Joe and I went back in immediately as previously arranged with him through the door from the private office. The PM had thought of this as a way to get the two soldiers – Carver and the CIGS – out of the room while they got down to politics. They then discussed his plans to involve the Tories tomorrow, but Whitelaw and not Thatcher. The PM sent for a railway timetable to discover the time of the earliest train Whitelaw could catch from Carlisle – he had to be telephoned there, after Thatcher has left England, but in time to catch an early train to London.

One of HW's objectives was also to freeze out Airey Neave,* the official Tory spokesman on Ireland, since HW suspects him of wanting to break the bipartisan approach and bring the Ulster Unionists back into the Tory fold.

We broke up at 5 p.m. The PM went upstairs to see the merchant banker Kenneth Keith. I went back to the Unit: discussed the PM's speeches with Andrew Graham and Dick Smethurst; and did a Green Paper brief to the PM supporting the abolition of the vehicle excise duty (and raising petrol tax) in opposition to Healey.

Called in private office and the PM was back there. Very pleased with
the Ireland meeting. And especially with the press headline about his
recalling Merlyn from Belfast. He said, 'It's always good when people are
coming and going to No.10. Gives the impression of things happening.'
The impression! That is unusual honesty.

We had a long jokey discussion on Ireland. He wants to send the
Gurkhas.

Joe told me that John Cole of the *Observer* had dropped in to tell him
that he had heard that both Joe and I were leaving. This has convinced
him that HW was retiring. Joe denied it.

Home at 8.15. Feeling cheerful and revived. Demob-happy.

## *Wednesday 7 January 1976*

PM already in private office discussing Ireland when I arrived. He said he
had been thinking about my suggestion yesterday for a cordon sanitaire
along the Armagh frontier. I raised it yesterday evening as part of a joke,
because I have been reading all about the British Raj in India and that is
what they did on the north-west frontier.

Went to my office and prepared for our meeting with officials to prepare
for next week's meeting with the charities. Pat Benner in the chair understandably still trying to offload it back on to us. David Piachaud and I
doing our best to remain constructive before a task we do not believe in.
Nor do I believe that the final Chequers meeting will take place – I have
fixed it for mid-May, by when we should all be departed.

Returned and discussed my new adviser Jim Corr's work programme
covering industry and devolution policy. He has still not been security-
vetted so he cannot see official documents.

Then Professor Richard Rose* telephoned from Strathclyde University.
He had a solution for Northern Ireland – put several Northern Irish politicians in the British government to demonstrate power-sharing. I asked
which existing ministers should we sack and what would the Labour Party
say.

Went to lunch with Joe and Janet. (There had been talks on Northern
Ireland this morning.) The PM is planning his Lancaster House all-party
conference. Joe had asked him what it would achieve. He said 'a headline'.
Such cynical honesty is engaging, except when it is every day.

When we returned Eric Miller was leaving Downing Street in his
personal taxi. He has bought a London cab and its driver and uses it for
visits when his Rolls-Royce would be embarrassing. He was seeing Lady
Falkender about her Israeli visit later this month, which he is paying for.

This afternoon HW had talks about Ireland with Willie Whitelaw and

Airey Neave. Whitelaw was very co-operative. Neave was more wary – perhaps he spots the intention to lock them in.

I worked on briefs on council house sales and on some economic sections of the PM's speech to the overseas bankers.

My solicitor telephoned to say that *Private Eye* has admitted it has no evidence or defence against my libel action.

Lord Fisher* phoned from hospital to say he would like to be a member of the Royal Commission on Gambling.

I phoned LSE to say that I could not be an examiner in the Government Department this summer because I expected still to be at No.10 – a deliberate red herring on the PM's departure date.

This evening three partners from Grieveson Grant came in to report to me on the state of the gilt market. It is very important we keep in touch with the City to assess the impact of the government's economic policy.

Left for home at 8.30 p.m. private office was furious because HW has agreed to see the Israeli Ambassador tomorrow morning at 8.30 – on Marcia's insistence and despite HW's promise to Jim Callaghan that he would never do this again.

## Thursday 8 January 1976

Drove in. Went up to the study to see the PM. Talked about his Ireland initiatives – the SAS men and extra troops have gone, Armagh to be a Special Emergency Area and, above all, his plan for a series of all-party conferences to discuss security, etc. He is very pleased with how it is all going and seems much revived. He has cut down on the number of Cabinet committees he chairs – no more IDV or EN (Ted Short is taking the former on Industry and Roy Jenkins the latter on Energy). In fact he enjoys dealing with big broad issues like Ireland and he then becomes politically creative. Most people attack him for never functioning on the big strategic issues. And it is true he does it too rarely – too often he is tactical, marginal or petty. But he can lift himself up, and do it well. Pity it doesn't happen more often.

I also raised with him the scare stories in this morning's papers about us nationalising the banks and car insurance. This must be scotched. I pointed out that he has a speech to the overseas bankers in a month's time and he could reassure them then.

Went back to my office and cleared off my papers. Also set the Unit to work on Ireland – especially investigating how the social security system there works and is controlled.

Went out to lunch with Joe and Gordon Greig of the *Daily Mail*. He told us the *Express* circulation is down to 2.3 million – the *Mail-Express* merger begins to look inevitable.

When I got back had to dash to a Cabinet Office meeting to prepare the first of the standing conferences on Ireland, for next Thursday. Discussed who would attend and how to organise the military briefing.

Afterwards Frank Cooper, permanent secretary at the Northern Ireland Office, came to my office for a cup of tea. Very nice, able, quite intellectual. He has remained remarkably sane and cheerful through the horrors of this Ireland business. Never appears to suffer the euphorias and depressions of Merlyn Rees. Merlyn is too involved in the day-to-day detail. But Ulstermen like his integrity and the fact that he cares about what happens to them.

Then I returned to the Cabinet Office for the Deputy Secretaries meeting to discuss business for next week. The PM has quite a light committee load – though a heavy parliamentary one, because of Ireland and devolution.

Defence cuts will come up. John Hunt, who is chairman of the Joint Intelligence committee, will help the Ministry of Defence get its way.

One example. The Cabinet took a decision last year that the whole Civil Service should cut staff by 10%. When the Lord Privy Seal this week circulated the letter instructing departments to implement this, Hunt added a sentence saying 'it may be assumed' that Defence could be excluded because of its other cuts. This is amending a Cabinet decision – without consulting ministers. I was furious and anticipate that Shirley Williams and Barbara Castle will raise this point.

Returned to work on suggestions for the PM's speeches.

Bill Housden told me that PM had said to him 'only 5 more speeches now'.

The PM gave a farewell party for the American Ambassador Elliot Richardson and his wife at 6.15. Just a dozen people: Michael Palliser, and Brimelow who has just retired as PUS at the FO, Michael Carey from Defence, John Hunt, the Richardsons and the Spiers from the embassy, private office, Joe, Carol and me. Very nice, Quite short – they left at 7.15 to go to the opera.

In the middle Mary Wilson came in in tears because the *Sunday Express* telephoned to ask her if she is going to collect her old-age pension when she is 60 next week.

Marcia also phoned to complain she had not been invited to the Richardson party. So HW told Patrick Wright off for not inviting her.

Interestingly, Albert told us that Eric Miller, whom he is getting to know well, now claims to be not so keen on Marcia.

Home at 8.30 and early to bed.

Still enjoying it enormously. Last autumn's depression has disappeared.

*Friday 9 January 1976*

When I arrived the PM was still at his breakfast meeting with the Israeli Ambassador. So I went to my office and cleared papers. Then went up to the study at 10.15 and joined Joe in a discussion of Northern Ireland. The PM is still thinking of ways to punish the Irish for their financial subsidies – now running at £600 million a year. He asked the Unit to work on this.

Also discussed devolution. He has to move Gerry Fowler. Ted Short doesn't want him. And anyway his job is complete – nobody will replace Fowler. But HW doesn't seem to have any ideas on where to put him. He had hoped to move Alex Lyon from the Home Office (Jenkins wants to get rid of him) and to put Fowler there. But the Lord Chancellor won't have Lyon (Sam Silkin is thought to be very ill and Peter Archer* would replace him). Odd that Labour is short of lawyers for the Law Officer positions.

The PM remains very cheerful and bucked by his Irish initiatives.

I left at 11 a.m. and went to interview Helen Liddell, the able research secretary of the Scottish TUC. She is leaving them soon – and says that the communists are systematically taking over at every level. Even secretarial vacancies are filled by communists. She also thinks that the Scot Nat tide is virtually unstoppable now.

Had an hour on transport policy with Richard Graham and then took Helen Liddell to lunch at Sheekey's restaurant – lovely scallops.

Back to talk to Arnold Lovell from the Treasury about vehicle excise duty. He is against dropping it simply and purely because it is a convenient tax. He says the Treasury should never give up 'a good tax'. The staffing situation on VED is disgraceful. They have spent a fortune computerising it – and still end up employing more staff to run it than before the computer.

But it was a useful talk with Lovell. I am very keen to keep relations with the Treasury sweet in the pre-Budget period. So I have deliberately shown them my paper on abolishing VED before circulating it to other ministers.

Joe came to tell me that HW has authorised Ken Stowe to tell Patrick Wright about his departure.

Last night HW had his dinner with Frost, Weidenfeld, Jimmy Goldsmith and Anthony Jay.* They withdrew from the ladies to discuss the big TV series. As they returned to the table Frost said, 'As for money, the sky is the limit.' But apparently afterwards Marcia was scornful and said, 'Frost hasn't got any money.'

The PM told Janet about it today and commented on Caroline Cushing's see-through dress.

In the early evening I worked on drafts of the PM's next week's speeches.

And Gavyn Davies had produced an excellent survey of the mechanism for financing Northern Ireland. We edited this and then put it in to the PM.

I went home at around 9 p.m.

## Monday 12 January 1976

Went in late because the car broke down again (it is nearly 10 years old) and I had to take it to the garage.

The PM had a briefing on his Commons statement on Northern Ireland, but I decided not to attend. He was very pleased with our weekend briefing on finance for Northern Ireland.

Took Robert Armstrong out to lunch at the Reform. It is clear that he has heard nothing of an early departure by HW. He says the Home Office is very slow-moving. Needs some new men. And that Roy Jenkins is very relaxed. If he does not win the next leadership election then he will leave politics. Interestingly the Home Office is often used for senior politicians whose careers have hit problems – Butler, Maudling, Callaghan in 1968, and now Roy – all ex-Chancellors.

Back to No. 10 and then to the House for HW's Irish statement, which went very quietly. Before that he had a meeting with Mason and Callaghan on Defence cuts. Afterwards Mason told me that his staff had become very bolshy about the cuts in Civil Service numbers and were refusing to co-operate and leaking information to the press.

Interestingly he showed sympathy for further rationalisation in Defence – merging the three services, etc. – but he needed time to do it. (Incidentally Joe has worked out that there are 56 information officers in Defence.)

Allon of Israel saw the PM afterwards and reported a very bad situation in the Middle East.

The PM came back to do interviews for the BBC and the Central Office of Information.

I was working with Gavyn and David on a paper on using financial sanctions in Northern Ireland. The PM was late finishing his interviews so we were delayed going to the reception at the American Ambassador's residence to say goodbye to Elliot Richardson. Talked to Roger Bannister and Donald Trelford of the *Observer*. As Carol and I left the Ambassador came across and was very charming. He said he admired my qualities of 'intellect and humour'. Always nice to be flattered.

Went on to dinner with Anthony Sampson of the *Observer*, whom I like a lot. Peter Parker was there lively and funny as ever. And Will Camp, whom I told off for his connections with *Private Eye*. Home at 1 a.m. feeling tired.

## Tuesday 13 January 1976

Went on an early morning run over the heath. Was evident that my bronchitis is not clear. Pains in the chest and a sore throat. Have arranged to visit the doctor. Trust it is nothing more serious.

Arrived at No. 10 just in time for the Misc 89 on the Radcliffe Report on ministerial memoirs. Very good two-hour discussion.

The PM and the Lord Chancellor in favour of accepting Radcliffe – 15 years delay on memoirs, but no sanctions to enforce them except the existing Common Law and Secrets Act.

Sam Silkin wanted stronger measures, including a law to allow the Crown to issue an injunction and claim damages for breach of copyright from anybody who offended – though he did think a shorter time period, 10 years, was appropriate. He was correct in pointing out that there is a balance between time and enforcement. The longer the time restraint, the less acceptable is enforcement.

Later on Mason and Callaghan were strong for a tough enforcement line.

Healey and Shore were for acceptance of Radcliffe.

The Cabinet Office 'bounce' was to try to get ministers to sign a declaration saying that they would not breach Radcliffe – this would provide exactly the legal instrument of enforcement which Radcliffe explicitly said was undesirable. So the Hunt position is: accept Radcliffe, which is quite liberal and avoids taking ministers to court – and then sign this document which we can invoke when taking you to court!

The PM was of course in an ambivalent position. The Radcliffe restraints stop people writing about other ministers' 'stewardships'. Only about their own. His stewardship is the whole government, so he can write about anything he likes.

Roy Jenkins spoke for half an hour and very well for a liberal interpretation.

Hunt talked to the PM for a long time afterwards in the Cabinet Room – and then took Ken Stowe in there – and it was subsequently revealed that Radcliffe was going on to the agenda of Cabinet on Thursday (to try to restrain volume II of Crossman) and that copies of the report would not be circulated to Cabinet ministers – they could inspect them for half an hour beforehand.

Joe and I talked to the PM afterwards. He had enjoyed the meeting. He said that 'the purpose was to restrain Jenkins'. I cannot imagine why, since Jenkins's position was not much different from his own, and was useful in restraining the reactionary lawyers and civil servants.

The PM was also very agitated about a story in the *Express* about only

20 SAS men being sent to Ireland despite all the publicity about big special measures. In fact it is fairly true at present though more will go.

He then went to tell off Lever for gossiping about his retirement. Lever had allegedly told Ramsbotham and Martin Charteris, who had reported it. So the PM was going to tick him off. I was pleased, since he should discover that I had not leaked to Lever, as is suspected. But sorry for Lever.

On this subject, the PM told Ken this morning that his plans for early March still stood, though Ireland might cause a slip of two or three weeks.

Lunch with Joe at the House. I felt tired and unwell, with the return of a throat and chest infection.

Questions went fairly easily, but not the PM's speech on devolution. We had not had time to discuss it collectively with him – the first time in two years. It was too hard on federalism for my liking. He was constantly interrupted and received little support from his own back-benchers, who are clearly unhappy about devolution, while having no alternative.

[The four-day debate on devolution took place between 13 and 19 January. Opening it, Wilson said that Labour's devolution proposals would lead to Scottish and Welsh elections at end 1977 or early 1978 and would embody 'the most fundamental constitutional development of this century'. At the end of the debate on 19 January, in three divisions the government had majorities of 71, 277 and 258.]

I went back to the office and worked on the Iceland cod war – David Piachaud has an idea for a compromise, based on us making concessions in the 'off' fishing season because this would not cost us much in lost fishing.

HW had a dinner in the evening with the counter-inflation unit – plus Gerald Kaufman, Peter Lovell-Davis and Lady Falkender. Joe went. To decide whether the Unit should go on or not. (It ought not. It has done its work.) I was glad not to have to go. Took a taxi home and straight to bed with lemon tea and aspirins.

*Wednesday 14 January 1976*

Delayed going in because my ancient Ford Cortina would not start and had to go to the garage again (it was in there on Monday and yesterday). Finally reached No.10 at 10.30 and prepared for the 11 o'clock meeting on poverty with the voluntary organisations. Also talked to my old friends Michael Zander from the LSE and Anthony Lester about setting up a Royal Commission on the legal profession. Anthony has persuaded Roy Jenkins – whom I saw in Whitehall in the street and chatted to. He was doubtful about trying to get Tony Benn's support on the ground that whatever Benn supports Healey opposes. I telephoned John Lyttle to get Shirley

Williams's support. Barbara Castle is away, but we shall approach her when she returns.

The meeting with the voluntary organisations about poverty was unsatisfactory. They understandably complained that nothing had happened for a year. They also wanted to know our thinking, which we were unwilling to reveal (since the whole point of the operation is for ministers to tell them about our policies, such as they are). They were not a very impressive lot, rather muddled and uncoordinated. But their aspirations are good and they have been let down by the PM on this – raising their expectations after a good dinner and then abandoning them to me to cover up. Pat Benner sat quietly as chairman and left David Piachaud and me to handle them. The main tactical problem was that we had decided to let them talk, while they wanted to hear our views. This led to a lot of sparring and some frustration on their part.

It went on for two hours and when it finished at one o'clock I had to sprint to the Reform to get there in time for lunch with Jim Hamilton. Astonishingly it is almost two years since he took me out to lunch, right at the beginning when I was just setting up the Unit. He is a nice, bright and extremely hard-working man – in fact the engine-room of the Cabinet Office. Obviously curious about when I am going to leave and where to, he kindly observed that he thought that I had made the Unit now a permanent feature of Whitehall.

Back at No. 10 the PM spent most of the afternoon in the study, reading his boxes and seeing visitors. I went up to see him, to try to persuade him to support a Royal Commission on the Law. His first reaction was just to refer the question of their incomes to the top salaries committee. But I think I persuaded him to support a broader committee of inquiry.

Also talked to him about Iceland fish. We had worked out the seasonal patterns of landings. It is clear that the first quarter is the season to make concessions in order to get the Icelanders to compromise – because we don't get much fish then anyway.

Incidentally Tom McNally tells me that an official in the Foreign Office failed to brief Hattersley properly for the Iceland negotiations, suppressing the fact that the industry would be content with 80,000 tons (we were insisting on 110,000). The official has now been 'moved'.

HW asked for our graph and tables to be put in his folder and in the Iceland OPD committee meeting at 5 p.m. He then read out our suggestion and said he would circulate the graph.

Of the other ministers Jim Callaghan was all for negotiation but pessimistic about the Dutchman Luns as a mediator. Roy Mason wanted to get the Navy out of it, since our frigates are very fragile and he was afraid that one of them could be sunk in a ramming. Very reassuring about our mighty modern Navy! Fred Peart was for using the EEC. Obviously we originally went too far out on a jingoistic limb. McNally says Jim is still for a tough line and hoping for a victory and does not welcome advice recommending compromise.

I left the Cabinet Room after the Iceland meeting and talked to Sam Silkin outside about the Radcliffe Report. He accepts that getting ministers to sign a paper which had legal force would be difficult but wants to do it anyway as part of the 'procedure for ministers'. He had met Harold Evans for the first time the other evening at the American Ambassador's residence and thought he was 'a fanatic' for open government. I pointed out that Harry's experience over thalidomide had made him a fanatic. Sam said, 'He is very tough. He said to me "It is granite against granite." He may be granite, but I certainly am not.'

Joe was very pleased about last night's dinner for the counter-inflation unit. He had proposed that it be wound up – it had done a good job, but it was set up for 'six months to a year', and the time was now up. The PM described this as a brutal approach but welcomed it and used it – used Joe – to do the job of bringing it to an end which he believes is right but always lacks the guts to do. They are agreed that Geoffrey Goodman is more valuable to the *Daily Mirror* than to the unit. Marcia was there flanked by what Joe calls 'Marcia's poodles' – Gerald Kaufman and Peter Lovell-Davis.

Apparently Sydney Jacobson at the *Mirror* was the most impressive person there.

Golda Meir came in to have drinks with HW at 6.45 p.m. I did not go since I had David Hopkinson in from M&G Unit Trust to tell us about confidence in the City. A very bright and sensible man, who was in Westminster as a parliamentary clerk so he knows how it all works.

I left when the Meir party broke up and walked up Whitehall with Joe. He said Golda was marvellous. She told them how she had been with Kissinger and Ford when news came of Congress voting to cut off military supplies to Angola. She told them that was why Israel could not put all of her trust in the US government.

HW went off for a while with Marcia. He later told Janet – whom he telephoned and summoned back from home to No.10 – that Marcia had been 'round the bend again' in her attacks on Mary (because Mary wants HW to retire) and in attacking Janet. Janet reported that she also denounced me and Joe – Joe especially for ending the inflation unit. She said this was a plot and insisted that it be retained and some other function be found for it – waste reclamation is one idea being discussed.

I reached home at 9 p.m. and watched the football on the TV. Bad stuff.

*Thursday 15 January 1976*

The PM seemed very haggard and jumpy after last night. Also worried about complaints that he won't allow Harold Lever to talk to the Commons select committee about Chrysler.

Inspector Ronson of Scotland Yard came to see HW at 10 a.m. about the thefts of his papers. Apparently they have sorted it out, but need to eliminate the last dozen prints on the papers. But according to Ken Stowe, Marcia refuses to be fingerprinted. The police are now considering how· to force her to be fingerprinted. Apparently a warrant was mentioned – though there is no suggestion that she did the dirty deed.

Before Cabinet I talked to Fred Mulley about the proposed reorganisation of our local schools – Camden, William Ellis and Parliament Hill – into comprehensives. He is being very helpful. But he says that his junior minister Joan Lestor is no help. She does none of the detailed work and it all comes to him in the end. Fred is underestimated by the outside world. Intelligent and sensible.

Cabinet had a rag-bag of items. It agreed to pursue Ted Short's idea of a committee including outsiders to look at parliamentary reform – Shirley Williams was very emotionally in favour of this. The Radcliffe recommendations went through on the nod, accepting the report as it stands with no real amendments – and no mention of ministers signing anything. The biggest discussion was on Defence cuts. As of this morning there was no agreement. Mason offered £175 million. Healey wanted £275 million. The PM got them together before Cabinet to try to hammer out a compromise but without any success. In Cabinet Callaghan gave massive support for Mason and there was a majority for his final offer – £193 million, which did give Healey his £3.5 billion of cuts, but meant very little in terms of Defence reductions. It is estimated that £100 million could not be spent anyway, and £50 million is German offset – which we may not get, and is not strictly a public expenditure item anyway – it is foreign purchases which may have happened regardless.

I saw Healey afterwards and walked into No.11 with him. He was disgruntled, but he had done a very hard and good job and was relieved to have his £3.5 billion.

Lunch with Joe at the House – he was furious with HW over the Geoffrey Goodman affair. Having at first praised Joe for preparing the way to wind up the counter-inflation unit, HW is now saying it was all too brutal and a mistake by Joe. This is because Marcia later decided it was her destiny to rescue Geoffrey Goodman from this cruel treatment and she has forced HW to retreat and ask Geoffrey to come and see him so that he can say how much he loves him, and how essential it is that he continues the unit, devoting it to waste recycling. HW has completely reneged on Joe and was too ashamed to talk to him this morning, scuttling off whenever Joe appeared. In fact Goodman achieved little, always marginalised and kept by the hostile Civil Service from seeing some papers because they were suspicious of his contacts with a communist East European embassy.

After lunch we went down to the PM's room in the Commons for the regular 2.30 Questions briefing – but he did not arrive. At five minutes past three we summoned Ted Short to stand ready to hold the fort, unbriefed.

The PM had gone to the Savoy to dine with the trustees of D'Oyly Carte Opera. His black Rover came skidding through the gates and he arrived in the room at 3.12 p.m. He was cheerful and relaxed and went in to bat very successfully.

I left immediately after Questions to go to London airport with Tom McNally to meet Hal Sonnenfeldt who was flying from Paris to New York via London. He brought some messages from Kissinger about the Copenhagen conference which Kissinger said he could not trust to put through the normal State Department and Foreign Office diplomatic channels. Kissinger was particularly concerned to convey that he did not, as alleged in some German newspapers, believe that a communist takeover in Europe was inevitable, or that communist participation in the government of Italy was inevitable. He simply wanted us to resist all moves towards co-operation between the democratic socialist parties and the communists.

Hal added that Kissinger had been extremely depressed, and worried about his wife's health, but was now OK again.

Tom McNally and I were held up for 20 minutes at the airport by security guards. They claimed – jokingly – that two people named Donoughue and McNally did not inspire confidence in the IRA security context.

We returned to Whitehall shortly after six, but sadly it was too late for me to join in the first all-party conference on Ireland. Apparently the military briefings and all the usual visual aids worked successfully.

I joined them for drinks when they broke up. Thatcher, Whitelaw, Neave and Gilmour were there from the Tories. Everybody seemed pleased.

Towards the end of drinks the PM was summoned into Marcia's room and took a long phone call from her. She had threatened to come in but this was averted. So he went off to Chequers – accompanied by Janet, who is needed for the TV interviews which he is to do tomorrow morning at Chequers.

I drove home just before 9.

Patrick Wright told me that the PM had come in to private office today, like a sheepish messenger, bringing a note from Marcia demanding that the Foreign Office be instructed to give special help to John Cordle,

Marcia's Tory MP friend, who is doing some business deal in Nigeria. The High Commission is to be instructed to gain access for him to some top Nigerians and to indicate governmental approval. Patrick is very wary in the letters he writes on behalf of the Prime Minister in such commercial matters.

## Friday 16 January 1976

HW was at Chequers today. I went in late to No.10. Sent to the PM an amended draft of McNally's report on our Sonnenfeldt meeting. Then dictated a draft piece on proposed reforms in Civil Service procedures for pay, etc. Set Gavyn to work on another Ireland memorandum. Cleared my papers.

Had lunch with Jonathan Charkham at the Reform and discussed the excellent work of his new public appointments unit.

Came back and completed the Civil Service memo and arranged with private office to have a collective discussion on it next week.

The Lord Chancellor came through on the telephone demanding an urgent private meeting with the PM to discuss how to prevent a Royal Commission on the Law. Fortunately I was in private office when he rang and I mobilised opposition to him. So he was delayed till the end of next week so that we could alert Roy Jenkins and Shirley Williams. I have promised private office that I will donate two bottles of 1967 claret to them if we succeed in getting this Royal Commission. Corruption, but in the cause of anti-corruption.

The Lord Chancellor then telephoned me to ask if I had any ideas for a speech he had to give tonight. I rambled on a bit, and then sent him round some points in a letter by special messenger. I did not mention the Royal Commission and nor did he.

While he was on, Israel Gatt came through from Jerusalem with a message for the PM from Rabin, asking us to oppose all alliances with the communists at the Copenhagen Socialist International.

The afternoon was an absolute rush and the hours slipped by. In the evening we worked desperately hard to get our brief on financial sanctions in Northern Ireland ready for the 8 p.m. box to Chequers. It was a terrible rush in the end, with my marvellous secretary Brenda typing furiously and pages of copy all over the floor. We finished at 8.20 and caught the box (which was held up for us by the duty clerk). Quite a good paper – Gavyn Davies did splendid work again.

I then sat with Patrick Wright for an hour while we chewed over various aspects of our respective lives. His lovely and very funny wife and their children see even less of him than I do mine.

Home at 10 p.m. Enjoyed today enormously. But still dogged by this chest and throat infection. Will see the doctor tomorrow.

## Monday 19 January 1976

HW is in Copenhagen today for the international socialist conference.

I went in fairly early to clear papers and correspondence. There was no response from the PM on our Ireland paper yet – though he had scribbled on Merlyn Rees's paper that he wanted any comments.

Ron Spiers from the American embassy came in. Obviously sorry Elliot Richardson has gone. Worried whether Mrs Armstrong, the new Ambassador, will be a serious person or 'just a Southern Belle'. He says that the embassy is already deluged with requests from the smart social set to invite her to parties, etc. He apparently had a big battle to enable Richardson to meet a wider audience. The list is controlled by an old dragon at the residence who tries to present the same lists as operated for David Bruce years ago.

An intelligence man came in to discuss the positive vetting of one of my staff. These people are incredible. Generally dim and with little political sense. He was worried that my housing man had a beard.

William Plowden dropped in to talk about a suggestion to examine the policy analysis function in central government. The job which the policy analysis reviews set up by Heath were supposed to do but no longer do. We agree that something is necessary. For instance on transport policy, the DOE paper will inevitably be quite inadequate, yet some thorough analysis of overall policy areas is necessary. I suggested that the Unit works with the CPRS on this and produce a joint paper. This is very important. The central policy capability is critical, yet is not functioning properly.

Went to lunch with Harold Lever. He is still convinced that HW is going to resign. And he is concerned what will happen to him and to me. His power depends on his relations with the PM. With a new man there he might be shut out – especially if I were not in No. 10 to represent him. So he wants me to stay on with any successor, and offered to speak to any successor about this. He isn't just concerned about himself, but is genuinely concerned with what happens to me afterwards.

He insists that he did not tell Charteris at the Palace about HW leaving – it was Charteris who raised it with him, saying that the Palace was 'concerned about the succession'.

Harold also told me the full story about Marcia coming to lunch with him. She had asked to be invited and he arranged a date to come with him and Diane. The lunch was prepared and they both waited but she did not arrive. He raised this with HW – who said it was because Marcia

did not want to eat just with him and Diane. She wanted to be invited
to his parties and to meet his (rich) friends. It was made quite clear.

So Harold Lever invited her to a small party – with all his friends there.
He has not invited her again.

He said that the serious press is growing more convinced that HW is
retiring.

And that Jimmy Goldsmith is prepared to put up £250,000 to destroy
*Private Eye*.

I left the office early and was home by 5.15 p.m. My morale is good,
though fed up with this throat infection.

Spent some of the day mobilising support for a Royal Commission on
the legal profession. Close contact with Michael Zander and Anthony Lester.
I have got private office supporting very well and blocking off the Lord
Chancellor's attempts to get at the PM and prevent proper discussion. We
have fixed a meeting with the Lord Chancellor on Thursday but in the
meantime are alerting other ministers who might want to participate.

## Tuesday 20 January 1976

When I arrived the PM was in private office discussing Saturday's speech
in Wales – he had slept at No.10 overnight.

I raised the question of the future of the *New Statesman* with him. Its
circulation is now down to 33,000 and he wants Kissin and Lever to buy
it. He had told Kissin he would do the negotiation, but now wants to stay
out of it and let them do it.

He was quite confident on Iceland. Luns has assured them that if we
withdraw our warships there will be no harassment and a compromise
should be found.

I also mentioned to him the bad situation in the Scottish Labour Party
which Kay Carmichael had reported to me. I said that the Sillars breakaway
people were not mad extremists but young moderates. He said, 'That is what
I expected.' He then digressed to say that people were wrong to think he
was worried by the prospect of losing his majority in Parliament. He said
he would quite like it. 'We need time to govern with less legislation. There
is too much legislation so we never get round to governing properly.'

He went to the study. One of his visitors was Mr Kudlick, his former
accountant, whom he was seeing about his stolen papers I presume.

The Geoffrey Goodman inflation unit affair gets worse. Geoffrey has
mobilised his friend Marcia to defend him and HW is weakening. Ken
Stowe told us that Geoffrey has not yet passed his security vetting because
of his close association with one or more communist embassies. It sounds
suspiciously bad.

We had our first lunch in No.10 under another new lunch regime. Private office and Joe and me. We discussed attacks on the Civil Service. The Lord Privy Seal had put in a paper asking the PM to give a speech saying what a perfect body of men, underpaid and overworked, civil servants are. I had prepared a paper suggesting various reforms in Civil Service procedures for settling pay, pensions, etc. and the reduction of the numbers of peerages, which he should do positively while attacking ignorant criticisms. The civil servants from No.10 were very sympathetic and we prepared a joint paper which Ken Stowe will put to the PM.

The PM was in Marcia's room for much of lunchtime, and afterwards at briefing he was in an ugly mood, snapping at everybody. He was particularly jumpy about the employment figures – 5.1% adjusted.

Question Time itself was very rough, with a lot of hostility from behind HW over unemployment. But he survived as usual. In the end there is nothing the questioners can do. The executive has the last word. The Speaker allowed Questions to go on an extra nine minutes, and then announced his own impending retirement. Must have been an emotional moment for him, but he made it nicely matter-of-fact.

After that Joe and I returned to No. 10 – Joe to write Saturday's speech, despite his conjunctivitis. I cleared my papers and left early to go to an X-ray unit in the slums of Holloway Road to get my chest X-rayed. Then home early, to play with the kids and to bed to read some more of Paul Scott's novels on India, which I enjoy enormously.

## Wednesday 21 January 1976

Strange incident in the night. I woke up at 5 a.m. with the feeling that all was not right downstairs. I went down and found an odd parcel in the letter-box. I took it to the study, away from the children, and went back to bed. Then in the morning called the police, but it wasn't an Irish bomb – just a book from Michael Zander.

Arrived at No. 10 to find a Cabinet had suddenly been called. To discuss Radcliffe and also Lever's appearance before the Commons select committee over Chrysler. On the former they decided to accept the report whole and publish. On Lever they decided still to forbid Lever to go before the select committee. I met Lever in the corridor on the way through to the Cabinet Office and he said, 'Funny thing is, they are right.'

But the PM was angry with him for allegedly leaking news of their discussion to the *Guardian*. The PM deliberately told only Lever and raised it verbally at the end. So when it appeared in the *Guardian* he said it could only be Lever.

Before Cabinet Tony Benn came to see HW about Kearton and his plans for BNOC. Afterwards I chatted to him about Herbert Morrison – he is giving the Morrison Memorial Lecture in July. We agreed to meet soon and discuss Morrison and the nationalised industries.

Interestingly, Nigel Wicks told me that Benn's private office are very fond of him, because he is so courteous and considerate. Now he seems very tamed. No longer thrashing round to thrust the manifesto down everybody's throat. He is doing a quiet job, and I presume waiting till HW retires or the government collapses because of unemployment, etc.

Joe is getting more angry and fed up with HW over the Geoffrey Goodman affair, where Marcia is making trouble defending her friend. Joe is threatening to put on paper the decisive versions for getting rid of the ineffective Goodman, who still has no security clearance.

Marcia is apparently quite happy at the moment. She is intensively building up contacts in the show-business and film world for after the PM has retired. Everybody still expects a birthday farewell on 11 March. Joe thinks it could be a little later in March. I would not be at all surprised if he kidded us and did it earlier – before the by-elections, before the next employment figures, etc. At the moment he looks grey and tired. He is doing nothing all day. He has passed on the Energy Cabinet committee to Roy Jenkins and the Industrial Policy committee to the Lord President.

The number of Misc Cabinet committees has been dramatically cut since Christmas. So he has much less committee work. Cabinet has less to do because public expenditure is over. He has ordered his daily engagements to be drastically thinned. He has cancelled all his proposed trips abroad. And he has only one speech arranged in February (two more this month). So he has almost ceased to function except in the House on Questions, at Cabinet once a week, and on isolated big issues and on Ireland and Iceland. He is now a part-time Prime Minister firing on only two cylinders. He has far fewer papers in his box – and does not always read them. He is ready to go now. Equally, at this pace, he could survive physically for much longer – but to what purpose? He is just a shadow of the man of two years ago. His objective remains survival – now physical as well as political.

Before Cabinet I also spoke to Fred Mulley who told me that he was fed up with Crowther-Hunt – gets everything wrong as junior minister at Education and creates more work. Fred said that he would rather have nobody, a vacancy, than Crowther-Hunt. He put this to HW after Cabinet and the PM agreed to move CH – back to the Cabinet Office in a swap with Gerry Fowler. In fact this meant putting CH in a non-job, since there is nothing to do with the second reading of the Devolution Bill – and then only the third reading – in the summer. It would get Fowler out of devolution, which Ted Short wants, though without promoting him since

it puts him back where he was in March 1974. And it would demote Hunt
by putting him back to devolution.

Fowler was held standing by to be called to No. 10 for much of the
afternoon, but then it was called off – because Crowther-Hunt had asked
for twenty-four hours to rethink it. He was considering possibly leaving
the government altogether and going back to Oxford. Poor Fowler telephoned me completely puzzled, asking what was going on. I could not tell
him, but assured him he was not going to be sacked.

A curious situation has arisen for Roy Jenkins. President Giscard of
France has suggested to HW that Roy be the next President of the EEC.
Schmidt, who would prefer a pro-German, has suggested Healey. (HW
was committed to Christopher Soames. Callaghan wants George Thomson
and doesn't want Soames. HW won't have Thomson.) But if Roy takes it
he will be out of the leadership race. It would be terrible if he announced
his acceptance in the next few weeks and then the party leadership came
up. I hope he decides to wait until after Easter. I would like to be able to
warn him but it would be a very dangerous move since it would be bound
to get back to Joe.

Curiously, John Harris had dinner with Marcia last night. It is possible
that she will have warned him, so Roy Jenkins may be alerted.

I saw John Harris at the Reform at lunchtime (I ate with Leonard Schapiro
of the LSE) with Roy Hattersley. But, although I sat with them at the big
table, I did not speak since they were surprisingly with John Allen.

Marcia is not after all going with Eric Miller in his charter jet of 180
people to his son's bar mitzvah in Jerusalem tomorrow. According to Albert
Murray she has fallen out with Eric, who has not been very flattering to
her recently. She tried all the old tactics. She blocked him from seeing the
PM. She refused to answer the telephone when he rang. She excluded him
from the No.10 Christmas party for crippled children, although last year
he provided all the toys and he and his wife Myra wrapped them personally. He wanted to provide more toys this year, and the kids would have
liked that, but she gave him the shut-out. So now they are enemies.

Instead for the Christmas party she used an American PR named Andrew
Neatorou, who is in showbiz with a lot of film star contacts.

This is also why she originally made HW change the date of his Israeli
visit – before he finally cancelled it. Because he was due to be there at the
same time as Eric Miller. She was not going. She did not want the PM to
honour Eric by seeing him in Jerusalem. It is bizarre. Albert and Bill hear
all of this.

After lunch I had a long talk with Kay Carmichael about Scotland –
she is so fed up that she is thinking of joining the new Sillars Scots Labour
Party. She says she started in the ILP and wants to end there.

I worked on a lot of papers and made some phone calls to mobilise further action on the Royal Commission on the Law. We have now ensured that the Lord Chancellor cannot have a private meeting with the PM to argue against it – because so many ministers have spontaneously shown an interest in the issue! So there will now be a ministerial meeting.

Finally came home at 8 p.m. – and played my first game of chess with Rachel – I declared it a draw when she had only her king and a pawn left.

Incidentally the PM saw Douglas Allen and Lord Shepherd, the minister responsible, this evening about the Civil Service. The private secretary said he showed no interest in it – neither in their request for a speech defending the Civil Service nor in our suggestions for positive reform. Just a blank boredom.

He spent most of the time at the Commons. And saw Thatcher later about the Radcliffe Report.

## Thursday 22 January 1976

Saw my bank manager early on, turning my huge overdraft into a ten-year loan.

Then had the DOE people – Peter Lazarus, David Lipsey, etc. – in to discuss our proposal for the sales of council houses. Beginning now to make progress. The officials are being very helpful. Joe has fed in some ingenious devices.

Lunch at No. 10 with private office. Discussed the Royal Commission on the Law and also the alleged scandal about Ryder's land deals in Sussex. Ryder has been on holiday in Egypt but has now returned to go to Ronald Edwards's funeral and to help find his successor at British Leyland. (They are thinking of Graham Dowson, the man from Rank, who doesn't look like a starter to me.) Joe and Ken Stowe each suspect that Ryder is in trouble. It all depends on whether he had foreknowledge of the planning permission and the net profits to be made.

Marcia has requested further help for John Cordle in Nigeria. He is linked with some scheme to sell the Nigerians dirigible airships to help their transportation problems. Patrick Wright is very embarrassed by the attempts to involve the Prime Minister – and eventually the Foreign Office – in these financial matters.

After lunch Joe and I walked over for Questions.

The suggestion of help from the Czech embassy to our friendly journalist has come up again (so HW is weakening in his defence of him) together with information and confirmation from the security services on John Stonehouse and the Czechs.

The PM seemed much more relaxed than of late at Questions briefing.

He had heard that Jeremy Thorpe may have to resign over the London & County Bank affair. The report is said to name and blame him.

HW also started talking about the CIA – and claimed that the former Labour MP Maurice Foley was paid by the CIA. No evidence. We have learned that sometimes he is right but sometimes it is total falsification, a residue of some old smear campaign.

Questions went very easily – including questions on the CIA. I then returned promptly to No.10. I worked on papers, wrote a minute on the Royal Commission on the law, and then went to the Dep Secs meeting in John Hunt's room in the Cabinet Office.

Gerry Fowler came to see me, puzzled about his swap with Crowther-Hunt. HW had told him that we needed a spokesman on devolution in the Lords and I supported that. Could not tell him that Crowther-Hunt had been effectively sacked from Education and moved to devolution for the few months until he returned to Oxford in the autumn (he is likely to be dropped altogether by HW's successor). Gerry will be better at Education. Crowther-Hunt's impact on Devolution is less predictable. It could lead to civil war.

A typical HW reshuffle – the single swap, to minimise changes, no new faces, no actual sackings.

But in No. 10 the PM had seen Roy Jenkins. According to Joe, Roy asked to see him to tell him that he was fed up with being Home Secretary, that he knew he couldn't be Chancellor or Foreign Secretary, but he would like to be Leader of the House. The PM might be willing to do this if he were staying. Instead he told Roy about the presidency of the EEC. Roy said firmly he was not interested, but would think about it. He looked unhappy and distracted as he left. I joined him outside, walked with him to the Home Office and fixed to see him next week. [Roy Jenkins became President of the EEC in 1977.]

Then home at 8.30 p.m.

*Friday 23 January 1976*

Went in for the weekly 9.30 diary meeting. Beforehand I spoke to Denis Healey, who was feeling quite optimistic about the economy. On the basis of a conversation with some French economists he now hoped that unemployment would peak earlier and start turning down in the autumn. He realised that there was little political pressure on unemployment from the grass roots, but he said that the Westminster and TUC pressure, however artificial, was from the people with whom we had to negotiate the next round of incomes policy. Sadly this is true.

We walked up the stairs together to the diary meeting – which was over in five minutes because the PM now has very few committee meetings. (He is also doing very little paperwork. There are papers in his boxes which have been unread for a week. He does not respond with interest to any policy suggestions, from within No.10 or from other ministers. His speech to the French Chamber of Commerce last night was tired and over-long – Patrick Wright told me it was a disaster and people were talking throughout.)

The Chancellor stayed on afterwards to discuss his dinner last night with the six TUC members of NEDDY. He said they were very close together on the next round of incomes policy, favouring a % increase which allowed some widening of differentials. He said Jack Jones was isolated in wanting a repetition of the flat rate. Pity. I think Jack Jones is right. The present policy is working marvellously and it would be crazy to risk it by opening up the whole basis of it.

I worked in the study for much of the morning, and did not see HW again. He went out to visit Lord Goodman, who has phlebitis, then saw Marcia, and then went off early to Chequers.

I went to lunch with Yoram Peri at Chez Victor – wine list very expensive. The Israelis are obviously very worried about the drift in British policy towards the Arabs. He said that the Israelis were aware that Marcia objected to them seeing me and wanted a monopoly of the Israeli contacts for herself. I said it was wholly up to them, but pointed out that my Israeli connection pre-dated my time in No. 10. I have family there. HW now, under pressure from Marcia, refuses to see Peri or Gatt. Her contact point is the Ambassador – the one Israeli I do not normally see.

Returned and worked on a paper on unemployment. Gavyn Davies has done an excellent projection of unemployment in 1976 – reaching a crude peak of 1.7 million in August, and 1.5 million in April. I put this in because HW is getting optimistic again, convincing himself that unemployment will turn down at any moment. I want him to realise that if he doesn't retire in March he will have to explain one and a half million in April. And it will be worse if he stays till the summer. Of course some of the April and August figures are students. But the adjusted figures also go on rising throughout the year.

Intellectually he has retired already.

Home at 7 p.m. Meant to go to Suffolk, but back too tired, so delayed our departure till the morning.

## Monday 26 January 1976

HW had a meeting with the Icelanders at 11 a.m. Callaghan, Hattersley, Peart and the officials were already outside the Cabinet Room at 10.45. I went to join them and talked to Hattersley, who remarked what a difficult lot the Icelanders were to negotiate with, and how the Marine section of the Foreign Office were terribly incompetent. While waiting, the Foreign Office and the Ministry of Agriculture officials and ministers were holding a heated disagreement over what should be our negotiating position. A lot of shouting, with Callaghan generally winning. It was not an example of good government. Perhaps these disagreements should have been ironed out before! But Hattersley told me that the Agriculture Department changed its policy position every two hours so they had to have fresh meetings.

HW arrived from Chequers only seconds before the Icelanders. He looked tired and pale and suddenly very old. This may be because he is getting old and is not well. Joe was not at Chequers. Janet stood in for him.

Yesterday evening HW had a dinner with Tony Benn and Kearton to discuss BNOC. Kearton was not impressive, HW told me later. Not on top of the subject. It was interesting that Janet was there. She had no official role.

Not that Marcia's influence has ended and I believe it will increase again when he leaves. There was a letter in today from Raymond Fletcher thanking HW for the help he had given to John Cordle and himself towards getting a big business contract in Nigeria. Fletcher's letter said openly that he was going to make 'a lot of money' out of it. So presumably would Cordle.

It seems that the birthday retirement on 11 March is now fixed. Marcia has told Albert, and has told Bill that he will be employed afterwards. Bill came up to me in the corridor and said, 'I have some information, but I cannot talk to you about it. I have been expressly forbidden to tell you. But Joe knows.' I went to Joe, who confirmed it was the retirement. It was Bill's way of telling me – by saying it was something he had been instructed not to tell.

Albert is very worried about what he will do afterwards. He is still hoping for a peerage.

HW talked to Albert on Friday before going to Wales. Without specifically naming the date he made it clear it was coming. He said that 'a new Prime Minister will have to get rid of Barbara'. It is clear that he cannot face the next reshuffle. He dare not tell Barbara – one of his oldest political associates – that she must go. He also said that Ted Short must go, but he cannot do it while Ted is deputy leader. He also talked a lot about the Frost TV programme he is going to make after retirement. (Marcia had lunch with Frost today.)

I wonder if Eric Varley knows. He put in a paper today about Kirkby manufacturing – the bankrupt co-operative situated just outside HW's constituency. Eric is suggesting a further loan of £400,000 to tide it over 'the next two months'. He admits it will be bust after that. Is this like Chrysler – 'buy it off till after I have gone'.

I worked the rest of the morning and then went to Grieveson Grant for lunch.

When I returned the lunch for the Icelanders was still going on, and then the talks resumed.

Apparently at one point HW and Callaghan were in the study with the Icelandic PM. HW wrote a figure of cod-catch on a piece of paper and showed it to Jim. He must have misread it because he immediately quoted a lower figure. This may have been deliberate. (HW told Janet this and she told us.) But as Joe said, this was bound to be the risk when Jim and the PM had not really had time to prepare their position in advance. It was all off-the-cuff.

I was in private office when HW came in at about 6 p.m. looking very battered. He was complaining bitterly. 'It is disgusting,' he said, 'there is nothing in the evening papers about the Iceland discussions.' In a way this sadly sums it up. There has been no serious discussion in here of the fish issues. No views or questions on the possibility of a compromise, or at what figure. Just irritation with the newspapers because Healey's possible reflation had won the headlines. That sums up too much of our experience here. 'Anything for a headline.'

I felt depressed and went home

Curiously I don't feel sad or elated about the final confirmation about his retirement. I have lived with it so long as a possibility. I want it to happen, because continued uncertainty is debilitating, and HW's oscillating is depressing. Yet life will be drab and flat when I no longer go through that door at No. 10 – when life returns to normal and not enough of interest will happen in a week to fill a single page of this book. But I won't be sorry to leave, especially to leave the periodic shabbiness and paranoia. But there have been many good and exciting times too.

### Tuesday 27 January 1976

Went in late, having first visited Camden School to see if it is suitable for Rachel to go there.

Had an excellent Unit meeting on taxation – we are examining the ways in which tax can help on incomes policy: e.g. if it is flat rate, then giving some tax concessions to the middle-income groups. Andrew Graham as usual led the way.

Had lunch in No.10 with private office. Discussion of whether to buy smaller cars for ministers as part of an economy image.

Questions went well. The PM was short and sharp. The House was full and in a reasonable mood. HW had been to lunch at the Old Bailey, but was back promptly.

I did not stay behind for a chat after Questions, but went back with Joe to No.10 and cleared some more of my papers, Also had a Unit discussion on unemployment: the basic puzzle is why, with so high unemployment figures, there is little political reaction. Our MPs are not receiving letters or protests. At Linwood more people applied for redundancy than were required. And employment agencies report they have vacancies they cannot fill. There is much here that the government does not understand. And that I don't understand.

At 6 p.m. I went back to the PM's room in the House of Commons for the Misc 80 Cabinet committee on the Franks Report on reforming the Official Secrets Act.

Roy Jenkins was very good for a more liberal position. But HW, Callaghan, Shore, Mason and Elwyn Jones were all hardliners: demanding that the criminal law be applied to a whole range of information – much wider than previously. The one consolation was when Healey – who was very good and very amusing – revealed that the Treasury itself did not believe that it was essential to send people to jail for revealing every economic item. It was the officials in the Cabinet Office who had decided that the whole economic area should be covered by criminal sanctions. They had not asked the Treasury, who are actually taking a commendably liberal line. But the hard line looks like winning – though it will be better when HW has gone, since on secrecy he is the worst of all.

The proposals to publish more official information are being resisted on the spurious grounds that it will need more staff, and the policy is to cut the number of civil servants.

After the meeting I stayed and talked with HW for an hour. He poured out drinks and talked in a very relaxed way. We discussed how to improve the unemployment figures. What it was like as a young man in the Cabinet Office – how he disliked doing the Cabinet minutes. Then he said it was necessary to do something about the Department of Education, including changing the permanent secretary. He said that it has poor-calibre officials, is 'just a post box' for the local authorities. He wants to take Science away from it, and the Arts. He clearly blames the department for Crowther-Hunt's failure there, though he admitted that Crowther-Hunt has a knack of upsetting people. He is going to talk to Douglas Allen about it.

He also recalled two years ago when we went to the Palace and he decided to keep Robert Armstrong as principal private secretary, but to sack William Armstrong as head of the Civil Service – 'he had become Deputy Prime Minister, he had to go'. He also said that William Armstrong had suffered a mental breakdown in the middle of the February 1974 election campaign.

He admitted that he had made a mistake over allowing the huge increases in Civil Service pay in December 1974. He said, 'I told Robert, I know what you are up to; but still I let them get away with it. The trouble is these Boyle Reports [on top people's pay]. How can you reject them?'

He is still a civil servant at heart.

– Incidentally in the Cabinet committee there was a very bitter exchange between Ted Short and Jim Callaghan. Jim accused Ted Short of 'letting me down' over setting up a select committee on Cyprus. Ted Short glared at him and snapped, 'I beg your pardon. I beg your pardon.' They then started a private row over select committees which slowly spread to the rest of the committee. Callaghan and Mason were totally against all select committees as a threat to executive government. They said straight out that it was more difficult to avoid questions there than at Question Time. Short and Healey disagreed. Even HW said he thought select committees were not a wholly bad idea and that they gave a job to MPs and that procedures could develop whereby ministers could avoid embarrassing questions. In my view it depends on the calibre of the members of the select committees. Some exploit and abuse the committees just for self-publicity, under the protection of parliamentary privilege, with no concern for the truth of what they say or allege.

Came home at 9.15 p.m.


## Wednesday 28 January 1976

I drove in. A lovely morning, crisp and sunny with frost in the air.

The PM did not go to the NEC (which decided to put MPs up for constant reselection in their constituencies). He was in the study for two hours with Joe discussing his 'skiing holiday'. Joe asked if he was absolutely firm about going. He said absolutely.

There are two dominant reasons:

1) He is worried about his health – in fact frightened.
2) But above all he said it is because he doesn't like the present PLP. He finds the behaviour of many of the back-benchers – especially the Skinners and Criers on the left – appalling. 'Just delinquents,' he said. He also specifically mentioned Joan Maynard.

He will tell the PLP on 11 March. And Joe will make a simultaneous statement. The only threat is the pending by-election – the Tories are threatening to hold theirs on the 11th.

I interrupted them in the study and discussed the Royal Commission on the Law. I showed him the excellent leader in the *Mirror* and told him about John Hunt's interest – Hunt has sent a memo saying that the PM has no need to read all the papers (mainly pro a Royal Commission) and that he will provide a brief. HW said he was now fully for a Royal Commission. He said he had changed the membership of the Misc committee discussing it to put on it Michael Foot and Jim Callaghan. He had also put on John Silkin, who had written to say he was in favour of a RC, although a solicitor. I felt very cheered.

Patrick Wright told me he was very worried because the PM had instructed him to send some confidential official documents to Marcia – mainly on the Arab boycott of Israel.

HW had a lunch with the Governor-General of Australia – Joe and I were not invited – so I went to the Reform for lunch with Bill Rodgers. He is looking very fit and in excellent form. We mainly discussed Iceland – which is not going at all well. The Icelanders break every promise and are totally unreliable. We are now discussing catch figures far below what they first offered a few weeks ago when we took such a jingoistic attitude in rejecting them. Bill is quite amused that Roy Hattersley, one of his rivals, has come a bit of a cropper in this. But so has Jim. He is very grumpy and going round complaining about HW. In fact on the international energy question and now on this he has taken a Palmerstonian approach at the beginning and then found that we don't have the gunboats to sustain it. Jim is also understandably annoyed with HW over the Middle East, where he finds HW always interfering. (HW claims that 'half the bloody Foreign Office came in on Saturday' to fix the UN resolution so that we abstained rather than voted against the PLO resolution at the UN.)

In the street outside the Reform we saw Ivor Richards, just flown in from the UN, and we gave him a lift in the car. I jibbed him about the UN and our role there. He made it clear that he is keen to get back into Parliament. He is already looking for a seat. I have always liked him since he was MP for Barons Court in the early 60s.

Bill dropped us both off at the St James's Park end of Downing Street and we walked through. As we got to No. 10, HW was seeing off the Australian. Ivor Richards told me he would like to see HW for five minutes, and I mentioned this to HW later, but he was too busy at this moment.

Went over to the Commons at 3 p.m. to discuss the PM's statement on Iceland. Actually he had nothing to say since the Icelanders had broken their promise to reply to our yesterday's offer. So HW's statement was just a holding operation. The situation is not good. The Icelanders say that any offer to us above 40,000 will bring down their coalition government. That level will ruin our distant fishing fleet. We have withdrawn our frigates on the Iceland promise not to harass, but they have now sent in their coast-guard boats to box in our trawlers so none of them can fish.

Afterwards HW went to visit Lord Goodman in hospital with phlebitis. I went back to No. 10. Michael Cudlipp came to see me for a two-hour talk about the National Enterprise Board. Ryder is obviously under pressure, hoping the land deal scandal will go away and obviously not discussing it with anybody. Michael has stayed right out of it.

Put in a brief supporting Shirley Williams on a revised price code.

Home at 10 p.m.

### *Thursday 29 January 1976*

Fascinating day, full of interest and variety. Also bright and very cold weather which seems to be killing off the viruses in my chest and I feel much better.

Went in early and attended the Economic Strategy Cabinet committee.

On the next round of price control everybody agreed that it was necessary to provide the degree of relaxation which would help industry to invest, while not letting prices rip to the extent which would alienate the TUC from the next round of incomes policy. The PM summed up in support of Shirley Williams, which was our approach and that of the CPRS.

The other item was on London weighting for civil servants being applied to MPs. It is all scandalous really. London weighting has increased by about 150% in the past three years. It is supposed to apply automatically to MPs. Michael Foot resisted this sensibly, saying it would upset many in the private sector to see MPs and ministers voting themselves a pay rise now. But Ted Short was afraid with our small majority of upsetting MPs and HW supported him.

There was a 20-minute break till Cabinet, and the ministers stood around in the hall chatting and telephoning their departments.

I talked to Shirley Williams, who has a terrible cold and a lovely husky voice. She was very pleased with how the price decision went.

Michael Foot was a bit unhappy with the London weighting situation. I suggested to him that it was desirable to abolish London weighting on grounds of regional policy. He was sympathetic but feared that the public service unions would be up in arms. We also talked of the notorious Civil Service pay claim a year ago. 'A terrible mistake,' he said. 'Its repercussions go on and on.'

I buttonholed John Silkin about the Royal Commission on the law. He said he was for it and I pressed him not to wobble under pressure from the profession. Elwyn Jones suddenly came dashing up, dressed in his black gaiters and white frills, and shouted at Silkin, 'John, you are letting us down, you are letting us down.' I intervened and asked, 'Who are the "us", Lord Chancellor?' He paused, and his face broke into a broad beaming smile. I suggested, 'The legal profession?' He said, 'And the government of course.'

I also confirmed with Roy Jenkins that we were meeting at 7 p.m. this evening.

The ministers then all streamed in to Cabinet to discuss Iceland and direct elections to Europe – where HW and Jim Callaghan are having a sour row because HW thinks Jim is trying to bounce it through too quickly and risks rousing opposition by over-haste.

Sam Silkin, the Attorney-General, was waiting outside Cabinet until his item was called on the agenda. We discussed the Royal Commission on the law – he is not opposed and feels it is politically inevitable anyway. He says that the main obstacle is Dobson, the permanent secretary at the Lord Chancellor's office, whom he described as 'an intolerable reactionary' (and Sam is not a raving radical himself). Dobson upset Sam over his answers to Jack Ashley's PQs on the legal profession earlier this week. Apparently Dobson wanted to give brutally hostile or negative replies. Silkin says they were arguing till just before he went into the Chamber, with Sam wanting to be more helpful. Really he should have told Dobson to go to hell. But apparently Dobson is pushing Elwyn into a reactionary position (not that he would find that difficult) and made Elwyn retreat after he had a private meeting with Jenkins and agreed to a commission in principle.

I pointed out to Silkin that Elwyn was in danger of getting into a very isolated and extreme position which would make it difficult for him to influence the terms of reference and membership of the commission. Sam said he was seeing Elwyn after Cabinet and would stress this point.

I went to see Joe and while there Marcia telephoned him. She opened sweetly with 'Happy birthday' but then accused him of being rude to her because he had complained about her fixing up for a friend of hers – Tom Blau – to have the right to photograph the PM on his 60th birthday without consulting the press office as the rules require. This would be a very valuable photograph for which Blau would get upwards of £1,000 from the press. Apparently he got £500 for some photographs last year of Marcia in No. 10, which she arranged without getting anybody's permission.

They had a sharp exchange on the telephone. As I walked back to my room from Joe's, past her room where the door was slightly ajar, she was screaming and shouting. I heard her say, 'What does that Joe Haines want, Albert? Does he want me to go crawling on my knees to him, Albert?'

Cabinet finished well after one o'clock. We had our usual lunch in No. 10 – lovely cooking by Sarah.

Marcia went to lunch with John Allen at the Etoile. This was presumably on his *Private Eye* expenses account.

Questions briefing went on sedately as usual. All a routine now. After Questions the PM came back looking very flat. 'This House is boring,' he said. 'It is too predictable. There used to be a time when its charm was its unpredictability. Now it is boringly predictable.'

He then stayed on for the Great Unemployment Debate – which did not worry us at all because we knew the Tories would not vote with the Left against us.

He also saw Harold Lever about his interim report on reorganising finance for the Arts. According to Lever afterwards they spent only two minutes discussing it. HW is not interested now. He does not really care very much about the Arts and anyway he won't be here when Lever makes his final report at Easter.

I went back to No. 10 to read papers and then went off to see Tony Benn. He was on the Embankment in a large office beside Millbank Tower (next to the Department of Industry). His beautiful big union banner – from the Witney branch of some trade union – hung on the wall. He offered me a pint mug of tea – which he drank himself while I had a round cup. To me only beer comes in pints. He was absolutely charming throughout as always. We began by discussing the Royal Commission on the Law, where he promised full support, and then went on to the Plowden Report on reorganising the electricity industry which is published today. He says his officials are all set to implement it straight away but he wants to find a reason to delay so that he can use it as an excuse to open up discussion of nationalised industries. We then discussed Herbert Morrison, and agreed it was time to rethink the public corporation concept. I suggested to him that a good reason for delay was the expected report on nationalised industries from NEDDY. He picked this up and agreed. I promised to alert him on progress on that inquiry and we planned to work together on electricity. I agree with him on this, and do think that he is the only person around who is interested enough to rethink the whole nationalised industry jungle. Interestingly he is now against size and large-scale operations and expressed sympathy for Schumacher and 'Small is Beautiful'. He seems much more relaxed, less fanatical and less tired than in 1974. Energy is suiting him. He is certain to be a force in British politics for the next fifteen years – but will he be content to be just a Cabinet minister?

The official car collected me from Benn's office and took me back to the Home Office where I spent a very pleasant hour and a half with Roy Jenkins – in front of a lovely coal fire, which was welcome since it was a bitterly cold evening.

We discussed the Cabinet committee on secrecy and official information. Also the Radcliffe Report on ministerial memoirs, where Roy told me that he would not sign any official document swearing to obey Radcliffe.

He added that Michael Foot would not either, and said that I should tell
HW. When I returned I told private office. Ken Stowe said it might be
too late, since John Hunt was already well advanced in bouncing this one
through – he had personally drafted some answer to PQs for the PM stating
that ministers would shortly be circulated with a document to sign. This
was put in the PM's folder – in the hope that he would say it in the
Commons and then that would be that. In fact it was never agreed, though
discussed, in Cabinet committee, and was never discussed at all in Cabinet.
I told Ken Stowe to tell Hunt that this bounce was simply not on. (Of
course, the PM would support Hunt if pressed; though he would be foolish
to press it against Jenkins and Foot, supported by Benn and Castle, who
are writing diaries and have an interest in this.)

But the main gist of our conversation was about HW's retirement. Roy
said that he had always felt that if HW was to do it this year it would be
on his birthday – which he had noted was a Thursday, when the PLP
meets. Also Lord Goodman had warned him before Christmas that he
thought HW might go soon, and after Christmas had said that he thought
it was now even more likely.

I reacted sharply to this and said that Goodman should 'not gossip'.
Roy said firmly that Goodman was not gossiping. He simply felt that Roy
should know. He said that he had told only three other people, who he
was sure would tell nobody.

He then asked me to confirm it. I declined. He asked me to confirm at
least that if it had not happened on his birthday it would not happen this
year. I again declined and said I thought it would be improper for me to
comment. He then said that was absolutely right.

Later, however, when discussing his future I commented – intending to
give him a helpful hint – that there was no need to take any decision till
Easter. I was in a real dilemma. I wanted to help him. But I must be
discreet. In the end I was relieved that Goodman had done the job of
telling him.

We drank two large whiskies and then I left at shortly after 8.30 p.m.

It was very nice seeing him and I feel completely relaxed with him now.
He said again how much he had enjoyed his visit to us in France last year.

After returning to private office to see Ken Stowe I went home at 9.30
p.m. Feeling much better, fitter, high morale and enjoying the last few
weeks of the regime. Partly because it is ending. It would be disastrous
for HW to go on for long. He has nothing else to give.

He went to Chequers tonight prior to going north tomorrow – and took
Janet with him as the press officer accompanying tomorrow's visit.

[This evening two dozen Labour MPs voted against the government on
its motion on unemployment.]

*Friday 30 January 1976*

PM away in the north all day (Marcia phoned him when he arrived there to complain that he had taken Janet with him).

I worked in the Unit. Saw my legal advisers Jack Black and Leslie Joseph about *Private Eye*. Had lunch with Eric Roll at Warburgs.

Back to do a brief on Ireland and another on the role of special advisers. Home at 9.15 p.m.


*Monday 2 February 1976*

The PM came in from Chequers at around 11.15 a.m. and went up to the study. Tony Crosland came in to see him about British Railways – he wants to sack Dick Marsh as chairman (or at least not reappoint him). He says Marsh won't do anything against the unions. We shall never get the numbers of railwaymen down while Marsh is there. I discussed all this with Crosland while he – and John Gilbert – were waiting to go upstairs.

Also talked to Don Ryder from the NEB who was hanging around waiting for the midday meeting on nationalised industries. He described how difficult it is to get good people for the nationalised industries – their pensions are the problem because these are linked to salaries. So we can only get people who have already qualified for a high pension – hence the only people we get, like Kearton or Ronnie Edwards, are over 65.

He also described how his deputy chairman on NEB tells things to Kenneth Keith of Hill Samuel – and it immediately gets leaked to Patrick Hutber of the *Sunday Telegraph*. Keith is fighting to keep Rolls-Royce out of the NEB.

At midday we had a meeting in the Cabinet Room about appointments in the nationalised industries – Healey, Crosland, Gilbert, Varley and Ryder.

Beforehand I had talked to Varley about Finniston at British Steel. Varley is very against – says he has messed up relations with the trade unions and is behaving very sillily. Healey agreed with this in the meeting. So Varley is looking for a new man at British Steel. And Ryder is looking for a new man to replace Edwards at British Leyland. They both want Ian McGregor,* from the USA, and began to squabble about who should have him.

Crosland is going to pick Peter Parker for British Rail, who is a lovely man.

They had few other names. The PM's contributions were very unoriginal – Aubrey Jones and Campbell Adamson. Healey went through the roof and said we must get some new blood – the PM has no new ideas. And knows no new people. Everything is frozen around 1966. All his proposals for appointments are Tories.

After the meeting Eric Varley told me that Michael Foot was suggesting Ian Mikardo for the Steel Corporation! Eric declined to give a view, but 'presumed HW did not want a by-election'.

HW nipped off to see Marcia – and stayed there till 2 o'clock, apparently under great attack. She has claimed that Janet is 'Joe's spy'.

Joe and I went off early to lunch in the House of Commons Press Gallery. He told me that the departure arrangements are for a 6 p.m. PLP announcement and then a press reception on the 11 March.

When we returned to No.10, HW sent for Joe and kept the rest of us away. Joe told me that they discussed two things:

(1) HW's idea that foreign espionage agents are trying to destroy British politicians. That the South Africans have planted the homosexual scandal on Jeremy Thorpe. And that the CIA have tried to get him.

(2) HW said that Marcia is 'more obsessive than ever before'. Obsessive in her hatred of Joe and me. And obsessively trying to stop HW from resigning. Then with unaccustomed perception, HW said, 'She doesn't want to give up the social life – dinner at the Ritz, evenings at Annabel's. She has all these friends hanging around her. They probably just want a peerage. When I go they will all disappear.' Joe was very pleased with this. It is so refreshing – and rare – to have such expressions of self-awareness from HW, without the delusions and the self-deceptions. But of course HW is perfectly capable of perceiving all this truth on one level; and then functioning on another level as if she is a saint.

Joe described to me how the political office operated. He said that in opposition HW had three bank accounts. Marcia controlled two of them. She paid money in and drew it out. Cheques came to her. HW gave her his chequebooks ready signed, leaving her to fill them in. HW never saw his bank statements. He did not – and does not – even see his own mail. Bill Housden collects it from Lord North Street in the morning and takes it to Marcia in Wyndham Mews, normally using the PM's official car.

I interrupted Joe and HW in mid-afternoon to raise this question of the college students registering as unemployed, which inflates the April, Christmas and August unemployment figures terribly. HW had sent a memo asking for them to be taken off the register last June. The machine is mainly a committee under Crowther-Hunt – he ballsed it up and produced a recommendation so complicated that nobody can understand it. And now it is too late to affect the Easter figures. HW is furious. Fred

Mulley and Gerry Fowler have phoned me to put the blame firmly on Crowther-Hunt.

I also told the PM about John Hunt's bounce on the Radcliffe Report, putting in an answer to a Commons supplementary question stating that ministers will shortly sign a statement that they will never write or reveal anything until they are 94. I pointed out that Jenkins and Foot won't sign. So he agreed that the supplementary should be removed. It looks as if we have resisted this one; but I think Hunt will return to it – certainly with a new administration.

In the late afternoon I worked on a revised version of our brief on financial sanctions in Ulster. And on a brief for tomorrow's Cabinet committee MES on the economic situation.

Interestingly, the PM had asked for a report on the activities of the intelligence agents of CIA, Russia and South Africa. Hunt produced for him a report on just the Russians. Presumably the South Africans and the CIA are spying on us in what the Cabinet Office considers a friendly way and so no need to report.

Home at 8.45. Still feel cheerful. Pleased it is coming to an end. That is right for Britain and right for HW. It is time for a new and fresher mind at the top. Apart from the sense of 'wind-down' it does not feel different now. No sense of the end of an era. Just the quiet ticking of an old clock.

## Tuesday 3 February 1976

The PM had a meeting in his study with Mason, Callaghan, Healey and Varley about special advisers taking part in the Transport House preparation for the next Labour election programme. The PM told Ken Stowe I should attend but the message did not reach me. Apparently he relented in his antagonism to special advisers attending Transport House committees, but they established firm ground-rules: the relevant minister should submit a paper on the current policy of his department; and the special adviser should attend with his minister to defend that policy. Not propose new ones. And not vote.

Afterwards there was the MES committee on medium-term economic policy. We put in a strong paper alerting the PM to the danger of high unemployment and a balance of payments crisis in 1977–79. The committee decided 'no reflation' but some minor jobs-creation initiative. Not really grappling with the problem – although the CPRS had put in a very good paper on incomes policy over the next five years.

I worked on my lecture to be given at the Civil Service College tonight. On the role of special advisers.

There was a curious memo from the PM on file, dictated on Saturday at Chequers, referring to Jimmy Goldsmith. He had been in touch with Marcia and she had persuaded the PM to see him on Saturday afternoon. Goldsmith wanted the PM to intervene with Lee Kuan Yew to deter the Singapore and Hong Kong authorities from pursuing Jim Slater and those of his associates alleged to have been cutting corners in the Haw Par business. The PM had covered himself by saying that anybody who was guilty should be accused – but he had still intervened, as PM, on sensitive commercial and legal matters, on behalf of business friends of friends of Marcia.

Had lunch in No. 10. Then to the House to watch the election of a new Speaker. A long succession of speeches – some funny, especially Derek Walker-Smith* – about the virtues of the retiring Speaker Selwyn Lloyd and of the new Speaker George Thomas. Then Thomas was dragged from his seat in the third row by Walker-Smith and George Strauss, the two senior members, and took over the chair.

Thomas is a charming, typically effusive Welshman, who has longed for this job and loves Harold for getting it for him. The only sad aspect is that his mother is not alive. He is a bachelor and was a complete mother's boy, worshipping 'Mam' as everybody in South Wales called her. When she died the light went out of his life. Apparently Jim Callaghan is not too keen on him. The Welsh Mafia is very complex.

I returned at 4 p.m. to No. 10 and then set off by car, in the sleet and snow, to the Civil Service College at Sunningdale.

It is a beautiful location, a fine old house, with new residential buildings among the trees, and lovely views across fields and low hills. It was very cold and snowing but I wondered if I would perhaps like the job as director.

My talk went quite well, with Pat Nairne a very friendly chairman. We all retired to the bar for beer afterwards and I went to bed at 11.30. Could not get to sleep so I read the Book of Ruth in the bible by the bed – the only book within reach.

## Wednesday 4 February 1976

Up at 7 a.m. Still dark and snowing heavily. Went to have breakfast alone and then to the station to travel up as a commuter. Arrived too early for my official car so I walked across Westminster Bridge to Downing Street. Felt very lively even though it was bitterly cold and nobody was in No. 10 when I arrived.

9.30 was a Misc committee on the law of privacy. The Lord Chancellor put the case for not having a new look. Others seemed to accept this – Jenkins, Shore, Mason, Healey. The Lord Advocate cautiously differed –

and the Attorney Sam Silkin. Then Ted Short piled in very effectively and said it was essential to have a law of privacy – and not difficult because other countries did so. The PM looked up at this and suggested a Green Paper. So I sent round the table to him a copy of the Labour manifesto commitment, which everybody had forgotten. The PM read it out and they agreed on a Green Paper – which was progress considering the bad start.

Afterwards the PM looked very pleased with himself.

Then Joe, Nigel Wicks and I went up to the PM's study and spent over an hour on the Birmingham speech for Friday. It seemed a long time since we had spent a morning up there. The PM was quite sparkling and very cheerful.

Afterwards I telephoned Helen Liddell at the Scottish TUC, who was very depressed by the situation up there, where the Scot Nats are destroying the Labour Party – in a by-election result today they have increased their majority by 500%. She says that the Labour Party there is quite demoralised.

Lunch with Robin Butler at the Reform. Very nice to see him again. The very best kind of civil servant. He is enjoying the Treasury, which he finds much more 'open' than when he left it, reflecting Douglas Wass's very civilised attitude.

Went by car from the Reform to the Commons where I saw Fred Mulley about getting students off the unemployment register at Easter. In the Policy Unit we have another scheme – to bring forward their summer grants payment so that they won't qualify for supplementary benefits.

But Mulley is not interested. He doesn't want any trouble. He doesn't want to bother the local authorities. His civil servants don't want to do anything. His private secretary was there making silly interventions. I contemplated thumping him on the nose. But ended up arguing with Fred and walking out rather intemperately.

I got back to No.10 too late for the 2nd Downing Street Conference on Northern Ireland – which was a film show on security which seems to have gone well.

At 6 p.m. we had a drinks/reception for Northern Ireland trade unionists, as part of the diplomacy of defusing the situation there. But the PM did not turn up. He was with Marcia, Weidenfeld, and Geoffrey Lloyd, the Birmingham Tory, discussing what to do with the latter's castle.

Joe and I were furious at the PM's ill manners and sense of priorities. At 6.40 I walked out – and a few of the Ulstermen had left already. I went to my room and then to the Reform Club for a meeting of the Political Economy Club – Brian Griffiths on the Bank of England and competition and credit control. I got bored and tired and ill-tempered by 9 p.m. and so I came home. I suspect that deep down I am jumpy about my next job, which may explain my bad behaviour with Fred Mulley in the afternoon.

## Thursday 5 February 1976

Arrived at 9.45 a.m. and there was a message from the PM for me to go up to the study. He was with Ken Stowe and we discussed the insoluble problem of getting students off the unemployed register. The PM was fed up with the Education Department. I explained the Policy Unit's option of advancing the payments of the summer term grants – also the problems with the Treasury interim proposals. I warned him that the department would suggest simply taking the students figures separately, which is certainly the easiest administratively, but may not do the trick since people will just add them back together again.

He was also concerned with the situation at Beaverbrook newspapers, where the unions have accused the management of wanting to close down and merge with the *Mail* and the *Evening News*. He is involved in this, having warned the unions through Albert.

We discussed the Royal Commission on the Law. He is now completely in favour. So are most ministers. This has been quite a professional operation lining up a majority in favour.

We all walked down to Cabinet. I talked to Joel Barnett about the students scheme, where the Treasury is taking a positive line.

During the rest of the morning I worked on papers.

Joe was very upset because John Hunt had arranged for the PM to give an interview to *The Times* without referring it to the press office. He blasted off at Ken Stowe and I had to cool him down. The appointment was cancelled. The point is that Joe is issuing a writ for libel against *The Times*. His office were going to strike for the day that the PM gave the interview.

Lunch in the No. 10 kitchen. Delicious steak and kidney pie.

Then off to the House for PQs. The PM was very cheerful, drinking Madeira. He had lunch with Roy Jenkins and Jim Callaghan and they had agreed to have a Royal Commission on the Law. He said, 'It's all fixed now that Jim and Roy agree. We might as well not have the committee meeting.'

Questions went easily on the first day under Speaker Thomas. He was firm with the long-winded and kept it moving swiftly.

Joe told me a curious story. He was in the study criticising John Hunt and HW silenced him by putting his finger on his lips. He walked over to the portrait of Gladstone, raised it and pointed to the wall behind. He was clearly indicating that the room was bugged. He whispered to Joe, 'We will have to go for a walk in the open.' Perhaps paranoid. But I believe that my room is bugged. Certainly my phone is tapped. On several occasions

HW has revealed a knowledge of some affairs which could only come from some form of bugging, since I had discussed it with only one discreet person, either in my room or on the phone. Kissin had earlier warned me that my room – which was once George Wigg's – was bugged. I had dismissed that, and tried to resist the kind of paranoia which surrounds HW and Marcia. But the evidence is growing. The Cabinet Office is of course the centre of intelligence activities.

HW went off to Birmingham by car. I went back to No. 10. Worked in the office. Went to the Dep Secs meeting. Then off to see Harry Evans at the RAC. He told me they had evidence that the cost figures for building Concorde were deliberately fiddled downwards to mislead the government. Also that he hopes to get Bernard Levin as theatre critic. So there is some good news.

Home at 8.30. The workload is now much less so I am less tired. The whole office has an air of running on only one cylinder. Fewer committees. Fewer papers. Less pressure. Few crises. The days go more slowly. Slowly drifting towards the end, rather like an old man slowly sinking to death, without pain or regret. I want 11 March to come quickly because it will be exciting. Now is flat. The end is all that we have to look forward to.

But when it comes it will be very flat afterwards.


## Friday 6 February 1976

The PM was away in Liverpool today. I went in at the normal time, cleared my papers, and then spent an hour with a Canadian civil servant sent to me by Gordon Smith in Canada. I am impressed by these Canadians. Again he was tough, direct and very radical in his attitude to the administrative machine.

For the rest of the morning the Unit met to discuss the role of special advisers. The PM and Ken Stowe have produced a draft minute which is terribly restrictive – not allowing advisers or ministers to take any part in the preparation of the next Labour election programme. He is suggesting that ministers submit to the NEC a draft of current policy and that nobody should go beyond that. I cannot see people standing for it. In fact of course he is not very interested in future policy, or in the role of special advisers in general. He just wants to have revenge on Transport House and the NEC for all the insults and public humiliations he has suffered from them.

Went to lunch at the Reform with Andrew Graham and discussed monetary policy – the Chancellor has replied with some nice bromides about our paper suggesting strengthening the Bank's control of credit in the banking system. We discussed how to report – trying to get the Treasury more directly involved. But I doubt if the PM in his present mood will want to have any bother about it.

Dashed back to draft a brief to the PM on the Royal Commission on the Law. Helped by an excellent minute from Anthony Lester. I had finished it when Alf Morris arrived at No.10 to take me to Sunningdale for his 'summit' on the disabled. Jack Ashley and Lewis Carter-Jones,* the other junior ministers, were with him and we had a good laugh in the car going down (my second trip in three days). Arrived at 4.30 p.m. We all went for a walk and then played table tennis. Alf and Lewis were beating Jack and me 20–5 when I noticed that it was time for the bar to open and we all adjourned.

Dinner was quite pleasant. I sat with Jack and Barry Jones opposite two other Labour MPs, Denzil Davies* and Ernie Armstrong. Plenty of wine and I felt sleepy by the time we adjourned for the first meetings. But listening to the disabled and their problems rapidly cleared my head. They make my problems and concerns seem very frivolous indeed.

Barbara Castle took me in a corner and told me to persuade Harold to give up his nonsense about special advisers. 'He always gets in the hand of his civil servants,' she said.

We adjourned to the bar at 10.30 p.m. and stayed there till midnight, when I left in my official car – finally to bed at a quarter to two. Tired. Too much beer. But enjoyed the visit immensely, and see the great potential of Sunningdale. It really could be made a 'think tank' for the Civil Service.

Joe's writs against *The Times* were announced today.

And HW is seeing Chancellor Schmidt tomorrow at Chequers.

## Monday 9 February 1976

I went in early for a Monday – after a lovely 3-mile run on the heath at 7.30 a.m., with the sun rising brightly over a London crystal clear, with all the roofs shining with frost and the grass sparkling.

The PM was late. He had been taken ill in Liverpool on Friday and had to come racing back at 90 mph with the heater blazing hot. He was very fluey and feeling shivering cold. What is curious about this is that it coincides with another European encounter – this time with Helmut Schmidt. Previously it was on every overseas trip – Paris, Rome, Copenhagen. Now he seems to get ill even when the 'Summit' is here. He got back by midnight, took four aspirins and a lot of whisky and went to bed to sweat it out. On Saturday he felt very rough while talking with Schmidt – and had four whiskies at Northolt while waiting to see Schmidt off – but he survived and was feeling a bit better by this morning, although his voice is very husky.

The PM came in late and we all talked with him in private office. He was completely taken up with the question of Angolan mercenaries. He wants to stop the recruitment of mercenaries. He is genuinely petrified of a right-wing coup in Britain using ex-servicemen as the shock troops. He said that they could recruit about 2,000 in a few years, using the addresses of ex-servicemen provided by the ex-servicemen's association and the Ministry of Defence. Since there are few troops based in the UK they could, he believes, carry out a coup d'état. For this reason he wants to have recruitment of private armies banned. So there was a big meeting in the Cabinet Room to discuss possible changes in the law, and setting up a committee of inquiry. I did not bother to go. It all seems to me like *Boy's Own* comic stuff and I don't see the point in wasting time on it.

Went to lunch at Rothschilds, with Victor and Evelyn de Rothschild. Very pleasant. Victor described his battles with Burke Trend and John Hunt. We then discussed the Arab boycott of Israel and how it was spreading everywhere, with Arabs insisting even on vetting the staff appointments of companies.

Back to the House of Commons at 3 p.m. for the PM's statement on Angola – and really nothing to say, except to promise another statement tomorrow.

Afterwards went back to No. 10 for the Misc 120 Cabinet committee on the Royal Commission on the Law. The lawyers' shop stewards were already gathering – the Attorney-General, Sam Silkin, the Lord Advocate, John Morris (who is a QC), sitting there discussing what a dreadful idea it was to have a Royal Commission. The Lord Chancellor came to join them. I felt very isolated until Edmund Dell arrived. I did not know where he stood and took him into a corner. He was absolutely sound.

The PM arrived and we went into the Cabinet Room. I suggested to him that he should ask all lawyers to declare their interest and asked him what would be the collective name for a group of lawyers – perhaps 'an interest of lawyers'? He chuckled and said, 'No, it is a cheat of lawyers.'

Elwyn Jones opened with a long quote from a letter from Professor McGregor arguing against a Royal Commission. (As Roy Jenkins asked later, 'Why on earth should he write to you spontaneously about this?') Elwyn was not very good, and the PM kept on interrupting him.

Then Jenkins piled in and argued unequivocally for a Royal Commission.

So we went on along the table. All the barristers – Sam Silkin, Lord Advocate, John Morris – against; but all the lay members – Foot, Shirley Williams's Minister of State, Dell, Millan in favour – plus John Silkin, which as a solicitor was very important.

The PM left the room in the middle of John Morris's long plea for lawyers. As he went out he signalled for me to come and we went into the lavatory. He was clearly enjoying it and asked me if I thought he had been

fair and unbiased from the chair. I said no – which was an understate-
ment. He replied, 'That does not matter. I did not pick the committee so
it is OK for me to be biased.' This struck me as a marvellous chairman's
principle. 'Only be unbiased when you have picked the membership of the
committee.'

He also asked if the Lord Advocate was 'OK'. I said no. He had been
earlier but from my discussion with him before the committee it was clear
that he had rallied to the barristers' shop stewards committee.

So when he went back in he intervened to say that it would be necessary to exclude Scotland from the inquiry since it has a separate legal
system. On this basis he did not call the Lord Advocate to speak until after
he had summed up the conclusions of the committee. In this summing up
he simply said that 'clearly the Committee was 2:1 for a Royal Commission'
and that was the decision.

I felt delighted going out. The Lord Chancellor came up to me and said
in his Welsh accent, 'You wicked man. I know all about you and it is all
your fault.' I replied that he had done a splendid job for his lawyers' trade
union. That seems to be the main function of the Lord Chancellor,
protecting the rich pickings for lawyers. I said he should be awarded the
Victoria Cross – posthumously – for bravery in the face of the Labour Party.

Roy Jenkins came up beaming and said he had 'never seen Harold
enjoying himself so much'. We also discussed an extra woman for the Royal
Commission on Gambling, and I suggested Margaret Allen of *The Times*
– whom he had already thought of and liked.

HW went up to the study with Janet. I worked on clearing the papers
which had been accumulating all afternoon. Then Graham Greene came
in for a drink and we went off to the Old Vic – meeting Carol there – to
see Ben Travers's *Plunder*. Afterwards Graham took us to supper at Manzi's.
Delicious. He is such a nice man. But we were not home till nearly 1 a.m.

I was greeted at home by a message from Frank Judd, the junior minister
at Defence. I phoned him. He was worried about some Sea Cat missiles
being loaded tomorrow for Chile. He was thinking of resigning. I telephoned HW at Lord North Street. He was still up and agreed that the
missiles should not go. So I phoned Frank Judd, who was very relieved
not to have to resign.

A very long but satisfying day, full of action and variety.

## Tuesday 10 February 1976

Another early morning run around the heath to try to restore my fitness,
eroded by all those weeks of semi-pneumonia. Again a lovely morning, all
crisp sunshine.

Arrived 9.40 and saw the PM before the Economic Strategy Cabinet committee. He was in private office and still full of the Angolan mercenaries. He wants the inquiry and also the law changed on recruiting mercenaries. (Thatcher is opposed to him on this; and wants the right of her Finchley constituents to volunteer and fight for Israel protected.)

He then went into MES to discuss the next batch of job creation measures and the abolition of vehicle excise and duty, which a majority wanted abolishing, though it was treated as advisory and not compulsory on the Chancellor.

I went off at 10.30 to the Cabinet Office to discuss our plan to remove students on vacation from the register of unemployment. The Education officials were still very negative, but the Treasury were very aggressive and the chairman was positive. My personal view was that it was now too late to do anything – but I mean to keep the pressure on the officials as a punishment for their desultory behaviour in the past few months.

I left before the end of the meeting, leaving David Piachaud to fight the battle. I went off to see Douglas Allen to discuss the Civil Service College. He has the right ideas, but it is clear that things are not going well. They have run it as a second-rate university, instead of a unique part of public administration.

We had lunch in No. 10.

Then across to the Commons for Questions. Marcia was there with HW, pressing him to intervene on the mercenaries question, and also fixing an appointment with George Weidenfeld. She also persuaded him again to refuse to see or talk to Israel Gatt or Yoram Peri from the Israel Labour Party. He capitulated on this and told Ken Stowe to tell the switchboard not to let any calls in. It is clear she wants to confine Israeli access to the one channel which she controls – the Ambassador, with whom I have no contact.

The PM looked very distracted, and he began drinking whisky – the first time he has drunk hard liquor at Questions for some time.

Joe told me that Marcia had spent three hours with HW on Sunday – mainly pushing him to stay on in office. She was encouraged by his reaction and today told Albert he could 'relax'. The new argument she used was that if Jeremy Thorpe resigned as Liberal leader it would be wrong for HW to resign as well. Joe was very concerned. We both agreed that it would be a disaster to stay on. The PM is only a shell of his former self. He is doing very little and taking little interest. He could not survive long like this – and might bring the government down with him.

He made another statement on Angola, then I went off to see Gerry Fowler in his room and discuss students on the unemployment register. Gerry told me hair-raising stories about how mediocre the civil servants are in DES, and how Norman Crowther-Hunt left total chaos behind.

I returned at 5 p.m. to write a paper and then held a Unit meeting on monetary policy.

Then home early to look after the children in case Carol had to go to see her mother, who is ill.

## Wednesday 11 February 1976

Arrived in No.10 at 9.30 p.m. Went down for the Economic Strategy committee at 10 p.m. Talked to Michael Foot about the Royal Commission on the Law. He said Elwyn Jones had charmingly but without blushes admitted he himself had drafted the letter he read out 'written by' Professor McGregor.

Also talked to Jim Callaghan about special advisers. I told him that I was concerned about the very restrictive rules which he and HW were making. He said that Tom McNally and I should get together to make some revisions. He said that he was worried about the 'bad eggs' among the special advisers.

The meeting of MES – on the next round of wages policy – was of a very high standard indeed, a great credit to this Labour government. Every minister contributed constructively. Healey did very well. He has genuinely opened this out to ministers and was himself very impressive. His morale became much better. Clearly the battle against inflation has been very good for him.

He put up the exciting idea of a 'Nil Norm' on wages, together with massive cuts in taxes. This would mean no increase in industrial costs but an increase in real spending power.

Other ministers were very attracted, although Varley and Foot doubted if the trade unions would go along with it. Still they agreed to explore it. Failing that, they will go for a fixed % rise in wages and tax concessions giving a reduction of price inflation down to 6%.

The PM was very pleased with the committee and with the idea of a big tax concession which would come as a lump sum in the autumn.

Afterwards my doctor Michael Model came in to visit me.

(I saw Shirley Williams after MES. She warned me that unfortunately she could not promise a 'Nil Norm' on prices, which would be ideal.)

Went to lunch at the Reform with Ken Griffin who has been a trade union adviser in the Department of Industry and who is thought to have been very successful. He was out to establish better relations between No.10 and the TUC. He wants me to appoint a trade union specialist. He also will arrange a lunch with Len Murray and David Basnett.

Walked back to No.10 and then a quiet afternoon in the office. The Lord Chancellor's Office are still being recalcitrant, refusing to produce terms of reference for the Royal Commission, but private office was excellent in ordering them into line.

The PM went off for an audience at the Palace. Carol came in and we had a nice dinner with Alf Morris and Jack Ashley.

Albert says that Marcia claims she has persuaded HW to delay his resignation – and he has actually indicated this to Ken Stowe, though for how long is not clear, and it still looks like the end of March.

Home at 9.30 p.m.

## Thursday 12 February 1976

Went in early for the OPD committee on sending ammunition and missiles to Chile – Frank Judd had written to me saying he would resign as Navy minister and I had briefed the PM suggesting that we should delay sending the missiles until after OPD has considered the whole question of our relations with Chile, which comes up in a fortnight.

HW came up to me outside the Cabinet Room and we walked down the passageway towards the front door. He said he completely agreed with my note on the missiles, had already talked to Roy Mason, and was waiting to catch Callaghan as he came in to put the same point. I was quite pleased. Jim came in and I slipped away while they talked.

The OPD meeting went as planned. HW opened by putting the case for delaying on the missiles. Mason did not disagree nor Jim so it went quite smoothly, despite problems with the legal adviser arising from the Law Department having lost the papers for two days at some point between here and Croydon.

Cabinet followed immediately. I talked to Tony Benn who gave me a copy of a speech he had made with references to Herbert Morrison based on our last meeting. We also discussed the nationalised industries problems and agreed to meet again soon.

Tom McNally came in to talk about special advisers. We drafted a long memo with arguments why they should be allowed to participate in NEC discussions of future party policy. Tom took away a copy to discuss with Callaghan and I gave Ken Stowe a copy to put in HW's weekend box.

Cabinet ran on after 1 p.m. and I did not see HW when he came out. I went to the Reform for lunch with John Smith, the junior minister at Energy. But I heard that HW had slipped the Royal Commission on the Law through without any comment.

I like John Smith. Very serious and competent, with a nice sense of humour. We discussed BNOC. He thinks Kearton is good, admits Briginshaw is bad but said that came from No.10 – and that Will Camp was put on by Tommy Balogh.

He is fairly depressed about Scotland.

Back to Questions. The PM seemed in a bad mood, snapping at everybody. And drinking whisky again. But when he is irritable he is sharper and intellectually more impressive than usual.

Questions went zippily, with the new Speaker taking it much more tightly than Selwyn Lloyd did at the end of his time.

And the Royal Commission was welcomed on our side.

I walked back with Joe. The signs of HW wanting to stay on are multiplying. Apparently Mary is now worried about what he will find to do if he retires. And Marcia keeps hammering away. It now seems that he doesn't really want to go. But as Joe and I agree, he is only surviving by doing very little. All kinds of problems are being swept under the carpet. No longer-term decisions are being taken. He needs a big reshuffle, but is ducking it. It is terrible really. We keep avoiding decisions on the basis that he will be going soon – and then he doesn't go. So HW's tendency to short-term thinking is compounded by all of us.

Joe said he would talk to him, and tell him that he had to decide, either to go or stay. If to stay then we had to work out a regime and he had to take some serious decisions.

Joe Stone came in this evening. He drove me home and said that HW is in better health now he is doing much less work.

In the Unit we are working on the 'Zero Norm' for wages and it doesn't look a starter. Too many problems.

Home at 8.30 and watched Paul Robeson in *Showboat*. Terrific.

## Friday 13 February 1976

An ominous date. I felt depressed today. Mainly because of suggestions coming from Albert, and hints from HW to Joe, that HW was thinking of staying on longer. He has referred to Marcia's argument that it would be wrong for him to go if Thorpe is going to resign as well (though that seems unlikely).

The tube was very slow going in – and our car is still out of action – so I missed morning 'prayers'. Apparently Callaghan raised with the PM the question of special advisers and the paper which Tom McNally and I had written. He intimated it was too liberal. Unfortunately the PM was a bit irritated that he had not seen a copy – but he had not read any papers last night anyway. He sat up in the study till very late with Janet. (On Wednesday night he phoned to summon her from home to come to have a drink and have a 'wake' to celebrate the sacking of Alastair Burnet from the *Daily Express*. Janet reported that at one point last night he said, 'Only a month to go now.')

I worked in the office all morning and was generally grumpy with everybody.

I took Ken Berrill to lunch but it was not a success. I like and admire him, but he is quite condescending to me. He also defended the level of Civil Service salaries with some ridiculous arguments. So I got grumpy again. Ken left at 2.15 p.m. and I walked up to French Railways in Piccadilly and sorted out my summer holiday. Everything on the assumption that I will be free and HW gone.

This assumption was reinforced, and some earlier doubts suppressed, when Joe told me that the PM had sent for him in the study and stated that his intention to resign was firm and unmoving.

I talked to Helen Liddell in the late afternoon – the Scottish position sounds beyond rescue. Then I went home, arriving at 9 p.m.

– Pat Nairne and his delightful wife Penny came to dinner on Saturday. Very charming man and straight. He referred to John Hunt as 'the iron fist in the iron glove' and said that Hunt firmly had Ken Berrill and the CPRS in it. He added that at the beginning John Hunt had assumed he would have a similar controlling relationship with me, but 'you handled that one very cleverly'. With both John Hunt and Marcia assuming they were going to control me, clearly my life and independence have been in grave danger. Fortunately I was blithely and naively unaware.

# CHAPTER 23

# Drifting Towards Retirement
## February–March 1976

### Monday 16 February 1976

The PM came in late from Chequers and went straight into the talks with Den Uyl, the Dutch Prime Minister. I didn't bother to go in to the Cabinet Room for their talks – and Patrick Wright later reported them as being 'extremely boring'.

The reception before lunch was quite nice – I chatted to the Labour MP Tom Bradley* and John Pardoe and Denis Hamilton* from the *Sunday Times*. But the lunch itself was a bit boring.

HW was looking flabby and sunken, as if his teeth were not fitting him. Joe reported that HW had said earlier that he was feeling fitter – but would not do so if he stayed in the job and worked hard at it. He is now clearly on course for 11 March again.

In the evening I went for dinner with Israel Gatt and Yoram Peri. They have been completely shut out by Marcia and are now unable to get access to the PM, although for years Gatt was accustomed to talk to him direct, and has now come with important news about Israel opening relations with Spain.

Before going I talked about the Israelis to Joe and Albert. Albert said that Marcia now hated them – Gatt and Peri. Partly because they persisted in talking to me. She had always been jealous of Gatt's access to the PM and wanted to force him into acknowledging her as the only channel, as she has successfully forced the Ambassador.

Joe advised me not to go to meet them, since Marcia had got the PM very agitated on the Israeli question, with all kinds of manoeuvring and back-stabbing. She would accuse me of interfering and the PM would say it was none of my business. This is right. But these are friends. I have family in Israel and I cannot have Gatt go back to Israel and say that I avoided him.

So I went to the Churchill Hotel and met them for dinner. I stated that Marcia was a problem, but that they must work through her since it was a party matter, concerning the International Socialists. She is the political secretary, not me. They planned how to get round it, and decided to go through Ian Mikardo.

Peri drove me home at midnight.

## *Tuesday 17 February 1976*

Up at 7 a.m. Telephoned Israel Gatt and told him to go gently. No need to press. By next time the obstacle may have been removed. He promised to do so.

Then off for my morning run around the heath at 7.30 a.m. on a very raw cold and dank morning.

In early to the office. The PM had a meeting with Ron Hayward – the regular 'High-Level Liaison' – and then I went in to talk to him about several things:

– John Hunt's letter suggesting a draft declaration be circulated to all ministers for them to sign promising to obey the Radcliffe Report. This went far beyond the Radcliffe Report – which anyway only suggested it for new ministers. And I pointed out that Jenkins had told me that he and Foot would not sign. Nor would Benn and Castle. They all have their memoirs to think of.

– Also told him of the latest NOP – with Labour 1% ahead, and that the Tory pollster Humphrey Taylor was leaving ORC, the Tory polling organisation.

I then went down to greet a delegation of sportsmen from the CPRS complaining of the lack of money – including Douglas Insole, the former Essex cricketer, who told me that he still plays football, and he is much older and fatter than me.

Joe then came in to warn me that the Israeli issue was boiling up and that I would catch some flak. Marcia has been complaining about me seeing the Israelis. The PM has raised it with Joe.

Well, I will wait for it. This is sad nonsense. To try to prevent me from seeing Israeli friends. Whether she is trying to black them out to give a monopoly to her other contacts, or to punish them for being friends of mine is as yet unclear; but I will discover.

We had lunch at No.10, and as previously promised I took two bottles of 1967 claret to celebrate the Royal Commission on the Law, on which private office had been very helpful.

Nigel Wicks pointed out to me that the BNOC appointments of Briginshaw and Camp had not come from No.10, as John Smith told me, but were put up by Benn in his paper (though was he inspired to include them, I wonder?).

Joe and I walked over to the House for PQs. He has had a long talk with the PM this morning. Joe suggested that Albert Murray should have a peerage, and the PM seemed opposed. So Joe asked what would Albert be able to do? The PM said 'go back in printing' – although Albert was not a printer, just a machine-cleaner. He obviously had not given much thought to it.

Joe then warned him that it would seem questionable to give a peerage to Weidenfeld, since it would be giving a pension, in expenses of £54 a week, to his own and Marcia's publisher. HW was apparently shocked at the amount of expenses and implied he was unaware of it. He concluded by saying that Weidenfeld would have to promise not to claim his expenses. But it looks as if George is at last to be crowned, a reward for long and devoted and often painful service to Her Ladyship.

Finally Joe said that the first person to get something should be Bill Housden – over many years HW's driver, valet, shopper, messenger and all-purpose personal assistant at all times of day and night, as well as chauffeur, shopper, messenger and spy for and against Marcia. The PM snapped back that he had given Bill something before. Joe corrected him and pointed out that it was Macmillan not himself who gave Bill the MBE. So HW said reluctantly that perhaps he had better give him an OBE.

Apparently the PM is planning not to do his resignation honours list till after he has gone. This is foolish. It leaves a new PM to supervise it – and may give the impression that he left in a hurry. But presumably he wants to do it with Marcia, away from our prying and disapproving eyes.

He was drinking whisky, heavily diluted, before Questions – which went very easily because of the speed at which the new Speaker took them.

Afterwards Eric Varley came to see him about tonight's vote to restore Eric's salary – which was cut by a vote mix-up last Wednesday. The PM impressed on him that he must not do anything rash if we were defeated again. I talked to Eric afterwards and he said that there was no danger – he would talk to HW about how to handle any such crisis.

[On 11 February 1975 the government had been defeated by 5 votes on a motion censuring Varley on the Chrysler issue. Today on the 18th the Commons voted by a majority of 18 to reverse that.]

Ian Mikardo came ambling along and dropped in to see HW – about Israel Gatt. I did not stay to see the outcome, though Joe later said that the PM was understandably very fed up with the whole Israeli thing.

I went off to see Barry Jones, the Welsh junior minister from the Shotton Steel constituency. He has 7,000 steel redundancies planned at Shotton, most of them affecting workers in his constituency. He wanted me to try to get the BSC to modify its redundancy plans. He is also wondering whether to resign from the government. I tried to persuade him not to.

Back to No. 10 where I worked on the Radcliffe minute, and on smaller minutes on Sport and on the opinion polls.

Also saw John Hunt's brief on Crossman Volume II where, on balance, he recommends against legal action to stop them publishing, but is going to write to them citing Radcliffe to try to delay publication for fifteen years. He recognises he won't succeed and as a final fall-back position has a number of cuts which he is demanding. These will probably be conceded. It was sensibly argued and well balanced.

Home in a taxi with salt-beef sandwiches, to discover my house had been burgled. My lovely grandfather clock; my father's brass horses and the old music box; and the stereo set. All beautiful things giving pleasure and memories, and irreplaceable. Very disturbing. So I lit the fire and sit here beside it writing this at one in the morning. No desire to go to bed. No music. Carol and the children in the country. Feeling bleak and damaged.

But curiously the sense of pleasure that HW is retiring is greater than the misery at this intrusion and loss.

– Incidentally tonight Joe obtained a copy of a letter Marcia had written to HW asking him to appoint a certain man called Evans to be Dean of Canterbury (he is now dean of a university college). Evans is a friend of John Vaizey and Vaizey is helping her to get her children into a private school – though she is still unsure whether to send them to King Alfred's, the Lycée, University College School or Westminster.

Vaizey has of course been a vicious public critic of HW.

– David Watt of the *Financial Times* told me that two Cabinet ministers (unnamed) had told him that they thought HW would retire soon.

– When Frank Church, the American senator, came yesterday HW quizzed him on the CIA and, according to Patrick Wright, made some wild insinuations about their activities.

### Wednesday 18 February 1976

Wasted the morning on the burglary. Waited for the fingerprint man – no marks, he wore gloves. Then went to Liberty's and other shops to get valuations on the losses – between £1,500 and £2,000.

So I did not reach the Reform Club till 1 o'clock, and went straight in to have lunch with Michael Cudlipp. He thinks that the furore about Ryder's land deals has damaged the NEB for the time.

Joe told me that Marcia is pressing HW to put Jimmy Goldsmith on the National Enterprise Board.

Went back to No. 10 at 2.30 p.m.

HW came up to me in the hall and asked me up to the study for a chat.

He gave me a brandy – he had a Madeira. We chatted for three-quarters of an hour about burglaries, etc. He seemed very concerned in case I had any papers stolen – I said I did not have any to steal. Certainly no burglar could read my writing in these diaries.

I expected him to raise the Israeli question, since Marcia has been complaining again about my friendship with the Israelis. I have been a bit slack getting involved here; but I no longer care. I don't want to expose HW to a lot of flak, but for myself I don't care very much.

HW was very friendly and amusing. He is obviously a bit bored with having so little to do. He had been to lunch at the *Daily Mirror* and was impressed and depressed by the fact that the new editor was aged 33 and was astonished to learn that HW had actually talked to Churchill. HW repeated this story to everybody in No. 10. He was relating it to his retirement decision – and taking it as further confirmation that he ought to go.

Shirley Williams came in to see him at 4 p.m. and came in to the study while I was there. She just came for a general chat.

Afterwards I went down to my office and caught up on papers. Also drafted him a brief for tomorrow's Cabinet discussion of private practice, suggesting that Barbara Castle sticks to the Goodman compromise.

And a list of possible chairmen for the Royal Commission on the Law.

HW also saw a security expert about the possible bugging of his study. He is convinced it is bugged and has arranged for a private security expert to come in and investigate. In No. 10! A bit late in the day!

I came home early at 7 p.m. – and sat waiting in the dark with a carving knife in order to greet the burglars in case they made a return visit through the still broken window, but to my disappointment nobody came.

## Thursday 19 February 1976

Psychological reaction to the burglary – very depressed to have lost the only personal things which my father left me. With Carol and the children away it all feels very bleak and sad.

I spent much of the morning dealing with the builder mending the window, etc.

Arrived at No.10 too late for the Cabinet – which dealt with unemployed students, getting them off the unemployed register, and with private medicine, deciding that Mrs Castle produce a White Paper which will prevent her from bouncing her way out of the 'Goodman compromise'.

Had lunch at No.10. Learned that my pressure on HW about the Department of Education had paid off. The permanent secretary is to be moved and Jim Hamilton from the Cabinet Office (a superb man) is to be put there. Very good for Education, but will leave a big hole in the Cabinet

Office. John Hunt has relied enormously on Jim as the engine room of the Cabinet Office expansion into all kinds of policy fields.

Parliamentary Questions went quite briskly and with no problems. (The Speaker has written to the PM to explain his tactics and to apologise for criticising the inordinate length of HW's answers.)

Afterwards I went to see Fred Mulley at his request. He was concerned about the change in his permanent secretary – and blamed me for it. He also wanted to discuss Camden School. He knows I am interested in the local schools and wanted to clear it with me before issuing a confirmation of a Section 13 to make Camden comprehensive. [My two daughters subsequently attended Camden School and I was not convinced that the changes we made were wholly for the better.]

Carol had returned from the country and came in to No.10 in the evening, as did my old friend Alfred Garfield.

We went to a delightful dinner with Ron Spiers at the American embassy. Pat Nairne and his wife were there, very nice, and still the easiest and straightest of all the mandarins.

Peter Jenkins the journalist was also there and we had a bit of a row about the seediness of the present British press.

Home at midnight.

## Friday 20 February 1976

In early for the 9.30 prayers meeting.

This morning's press is full of attacks on the Public Expenditure White Paper – which is down for debate on 8 and 9 March. The PM smiled broadly at this – because it puts Healey firmly in the firing line just before the leadership comes up. He does not want Healey to get it.

The PM was also pushing to get the Film Industry Report dealt with quickly. Marcia is pressing him on that. She wants to get a public authority set up, with public funds. Apparently yesterday in Cabinet, according to John Hunt, the PM told the Chancellor that he wanted some of the contingency reserve for the film industry. [Lady Falkender subsequently became a member of the Interim Committee on the Film Industry 1977–82 and of the British Screen Advisory Council 1985–.]

Bill Housden told me that after last night's 'charity dinner' in No. 10 (which raised £100,000 for charity, and for which a charge of £1,000 per plate was made) Marcia and HW had a 20-minute row in the car outside Lord North Street, with her still attacking him because he was retiring. As he got out of the car he said, 'After what you have said, I am even more determined than ever to go.'

The rest of the morning I worked on briefs – we are putting several in this weekend: on the 'Zero Norm' wage policy for the next round; on council house sales; on the latest opinion polls; on possible chairmen for the Law Royal Commission.

I went for lunch with Donald Trelford, the new editor of the *Observer*, at the RAF club in Piccadilly. A nice and bright man – remarkably similar in build and style to Harry Evans. I will try to get him an interview with the PM. He remarked on how eager the Chancellor is to talk to the press. When Trelford asked him to come at some time in the next three months, Healey insisted on making it this week.

Back to No. 10 and I finished the briefs. The PM went early to Chequers – having been to see Lord Goodman this morning, and also having another solicitor, Freeman, in. He is clearly tying up the loose ends.

I went home early at 6.30 to look after the children since Carol is attending an NUT conference this weekend.

Still tired and depressed by the robbery. And basically sad to think No. 10 is coming to an end now that I feel really on top of it. Yet also relieved to be out. Joe feels the same – though mainly relieved. He told me today he feels as if a great burden has been lifted from his shoulders. That is how I felt a few weeks ago.

## Monday 23 February 1976

The last week in February. Should mean only less than three weeks to go. But it is impossible to tell. HW keeps wobbling. On Friday he indicated to Joe that he might be slipping to a retirement date in late April and discussed this with Goodman. This morning he also talked of 7 April – the day after the Budget. He is worried about 11 March being a by-election date. Joe is trying to get him to think about 16 or 18 March, arguing quite rightly that it is either March or June, nothing in between – late April would be disastrous for the local election results.

The terrible thing is that at this late stage HW is still fiddling and wobbling as if a difference of a few days matters. Just like his obsession with marginalia in policies. When all that matters is that he should decide whether he is going or staying, and then to choose a day – any day – and stick to it.

This all shows how indecisive he has become – though this of course is the biggest decision of his life.

Bill Housden is still convinced from all the discussions he hears it is 11 March.

This morning the PM went to the liaison committee with the TUC where it was very quiet despite the public expenditure cuts.

I saw HW when he came in. He immediately asked for my list of chairmen for the Royal Commission on the Law – which he had telephoned about last night. I gave him my list. He said he inclined towards Norman Chester, the Warden of Nuffield College, Oxford, who chaired the Commission of Inquiry into Association Football on which I sat a decade ago. I had also suggested Alec Cairncross,* John Freeman or Eric Ashby.*

I also raised the question of a replacement for Joan Lestor, who finally resigned from Education this weekend. According to Fred Mulley she never did any work and her civil servants would not realise she had resigned since she rarely came to the office anyway. Fred will be pleased – he wanted to get rid of both his junior ministers, Crowther-Hunt and Lestor, and now they are both gone. They want Ernie Armstrong back – especially since the Education Bill is going through the Commons, about schools, and Fowler, Minister for Higher Education, is having to take it.

Interestingly they are nominating Lord Donaldson as spokesman on Education in the Lords. This is to make sure that Crowther-Hunt is not spokesman faute de mieux. Donaldson is not an educationalist, but it is felt by the department that he is better than Crowther-Hunt.

HW was reluctant to make an appointment replacing Joan Lestor quickly. He said he wanted to demonstrate that since she did nothing it was not necessary to replace her quickly, which was a bit harsh.

HW had also responded well to our Policy Unit briefs and despatched them to the various departments.

I worked in the Unit the rest of the morning on a vast flow of paper.

Then lunch at the Commons with Joe. We discussed the usual topic, and Joe said he would try to get HW to make a firm decision, preferably for March. Not that Joe wants him to resign. But as a totally loyal supporter, he wants HW to do the right thing, and realises that all this dithering is further evidence of decline. 'A Rolls-Royce has become an old Morris Minor,' he said.

Joe also reminded me of when we discussed with Marcia her libel suit and Joe had said she must not go to court in case they asked questions about her children. 'Then I will destroy Harold Wilson,' she screamed. How?

What happened on 23 April 1956 – 23/4/56, the date Joe and Bill and Albert always refer to as having great significance in Marcia's relationship with HW? [It was the date of the dinner which Labour Party leaders gave for the Russian leaders Bulganin and Khrushchev. It was attended by both Wilson, as Shadow Chancellor, and Marcia, as an employee at party headquarters taking notes. According to Wilson's biographers, this is when the personal contact between Wilson and Marcia began.]

After lunch HW came back to be interviewed about Attlee by Kenneth

Harris. I chatted to Harris in the waiting-room beforehand. His Attlee biography is clearly going to be even longer than my Herbert Morrison!

At 4.30 we had an odd Cabinet committee on the relations between BNOC and BP. All four ministers who dabble in that field were present – Benn, Lever, Dell and HW – as was Kearton from BNOC. They pretended to be united and promised to continue to explore all options. Really a waste of time put on to please Kearton.

I worked till 6.45. Then Professor Hilde Himmelweit from the LSE came in, and drove me to Islington, where I went with Carol to see Rattigan's *The Browning Version* at the King's Head. Very touching.

Home at 10.45.

### Tuesday 24 February 1976

Joe came to see me at around 10.45 a.m., having already had a long talk with the PM about his retirement. Joe had put his argument that it has to be March or June, and that April, just before the local elections, is crazy. HW picked March, but now inclines to the 18th, admitting that to do it on his birthday is a gimmick.

It is astonishing how indecisive HW is even at this late stage. Joe is making up his mind for him.

Janet and Bill Housden have reported to Joe and me on a terrible row between HW and Marcia last night. After a reception for police charity, she attacked him and pressed him not to retire. She is totally against him going.

She claimed that she and her family had worked their fingers to the bone for him and now he was abandoning them. They had never got anything in return, etc.

She threatened to publish to the world all about his friendship with Janet. He replied that he had kept the nine-page letter she sent him pressing him to intervene to try to persuade Eric Miller to divorce his wife, even rewarded by a peerage, so that Eric would be persuaded to marry her.

He said she had driven him to do the one thing he never wanted to do – go back to academic life. He would return to Oxford – which meant no job for her. She left the building in tears at 10.30 p.m. He then telephoned Janet at home and asked her to come round and he told her all of this till a quarter to one in the morning. (Bill Housden had also heard it independently and reported it to us.)

He has decided to make Norman Chester of Nuffield College, Oxford, the chairman of the Royal Commission on the Law – partly so that he can make a flying visit to Oxford this Friday and frighten Marcia into thinking that Oxford is part of his plan to retire to academe. When he and

I discussed it all later HW told me he thought Norman Chester was 'the best man for the job'.

Marcia has also been complaining about problems with the £65,000 trust which HW set up for her children from the royalties on his book of memoirs. She needs a lot of money for the fees for the private education of her children. She accuses HW of restricting her use of the money – which is anyway in trust for the children. (The trustees apparently are Goodman, his assistant Leighton Davies and Gerald Kaufman.)

Apparently at one point she said she would marry George Weidenfeld if HW retired – though it was not clear if this was a threat to HW or to George Weidenfeld. HW said OK. Poor George. What a supreme sacrifice. But I suppose he will still get his peerage.

Bill Housden had been alerted to get the car ready at 8.30 p.m. in the evening and did not get away home till 1 a.m.

The Lord Chancellor came in for a discussion on the Law Royal Commission at 11.15. We sat in the alcove outside the Cabinet Room and discussed his ideas for chairmen – Tom Brimelow from the FO; Burke Trend; Marcus Sieff from Marks and Spencer and also my friend Lord Porchester. He is quite adamant that my radical friend Michael Zander, who has exposed some of the disreputable activities of the legal profession, should not be a member.

Afterwards I went up to see the PM. He was not very impressed by Elwyn's list. Brimelow is 'over the top'. He is against Burke Trend. Sieff is too Tory. He still seems keen on Norman Chester, who was one of my original suggestions.

We then had a meeting over the proposed Green Paper on privacy. John Hunt brought in his Cabinet Office deputy secretary, Bill McIndoe, a very nice man, who has not had much time to get on top of this. We discussed it for nearly an hour. I pressed my ideas and the PM backed me firmly – and afterwards told John Hunt he wanted me to be associated with the drafting.

I nipped off at lunch to see the new paddle steamer on the Westminster Embankment, opened today as a floating art gallery.

At briefing before PQs the PM was in a jovial and skittish mood.

He is still obsessed with his belief that the South African Special Branch is involved in lots of dirty tricks in this country – and especially against Jeremy Thorpe. There seems to be increasing evidence that he is right.

Afterwards I saw Fred Mulley, who is pressing for a replacement for Joan Lestor. He needs assistance in getting his Education Bill through the Commons. He wants Ernie Armstrong back.

He also said he would like me as Minister of the Arts in the Lords! I would enjoy that – but it would have to come from a different stable. [The author was appointed Opposition Spokesman on the Arts in the House of Lords in 1992.]

I came back to No.10 and worked on my papers.

Then at 6 o'clock Sam Silkin rang and said he wanted to see me in the Commons. I dashed across, thinking it might be something serious. In fact he wanted me to help get a job for his son.

Afterwards Joan Robertson, an old friend, came in for a drink.

When I left the office at 8.30 the PM was still not back from his audience at the Palace.

## Wednesday 25 February 1976

The PM had a crucial NEC meeting this morning – probably his last. He went along to defeat the Left on the issue of calling a special conference to discuss unemployment, and also on the issue of MPs having to be re-selected every five years.

He came in at 11.30 looking very pleased with himself – although he was half an hour late for Thorn, the Luxembourg PM. Jim Callaghan is also ill with flu, so the talks were conducted perfectly well by Roy Hattersley.

I grabbed the PM as he walked up the corridor and told him that the Arab boycott was operating on a Euro-dollar loan raised today by the Electricity Council. Rothschilds and Warburgs were excluded. He looked worried because this was a public sector loan, approved by the Bank of England. But he said he could do nothing – it was too late.

However, I got private office to telephone the Treasury, who knew nothing. But that started the alarm bells ringing – and by this afternoon the Chancellor was meeting the Governor.

I worked all morning on papers and then went to lunch with Thorn – sitting next to Margaret Drabble, the novelist, who was very subdued.

Afterwards there was an OPD Defence committee at the House of Commons – on Anglo-Irish oil, and multi-combat aircraft. I decided not to go, and went to the National Gallery instead to see the new Rubens Rokeby Venus.

Back at No. 10, I raised the Arab boycott again with the PM and he authorised another intervention – which Nigel Wicks did to the Treasury. Shortly after he reported that it was OK. The Treasury and the Governor believed the loan should not proceed on boycott conditions. The Chancellor was going to tell the PM at the Parliamentary Labour Party meeting.

Apparently the PLP went well, with the Left smashed in all directions.

The PM then went off to see *The Gondoliers*. Not quite my cup of tea, but I can see the similarities with everyday life in No. 10.

I went to the British Museum, for the private viewing of the Thracian exhibition, with Nigel Wicks from private office, and we retired to the pub for some of the new Watneys Fine Ale afterwards.

HW said to Janet, 'It is March or June.' But he is still wobbling.

Incidentally:

– Yesterday as Harold Lever hobbled past us, HW turned his back on him and said, 'Ships that pass in the night.' Exactly what he said about Sigmund Sternberg when he was under attack 18 months ago – a cold abandonment, with no concern for past services rendered.

– One of the PM's obsessions is coming true. He has long believed that the South African espionage system – BOSS – is doing dirty tricks. Now there is some evidence that they are behind both the Jeremy Thorpe case and the Peter Hain case. They are out to discredit the Liberal Party because of the liberal influence against apartheid. A man called Wyatt has spilled the beans – involving an agent called Kamil who has apparently been attempting to blackmail the Anglo-American Diamond Company. It involves a journalist called Winter who works for the South African *Daily Express* and the South Africa police. It is a bizarre story, but there may be some truth in it. A Witwatersrand Watergate. HW is collecting information on this. It is incredible. I thought the PM was really paranoid, but he seems to have been right again.

### Thursday 26 February 1976

Arrived at 9.30. Ministers were gathering for the accommodation committee to discuss the dispersal of civil servants. (The Foreign Office is squealing loudly because it is required to send 500 to Merseyside. The PM said he quite understood their concern – 'There is a terrible shortage of golf-courses in Liverpool.')

I was going to attend but he came up to me beforehand and asked me to get the details of a motion passed at the NEC yesterday after he left – allowing Tony Benn to brief journalists. I found out and took it in to him in the Cabinet Room, but by then the committee was half over.

When it broke up I walked down the passageway towards the front door with the Lord Chancellor discussing the Law Royal Commission. We agreed it needed a strong 'professional' element – and I suggested an accountant friend, David Bacon. Also discussed the chairman. He now has doubts about Norman Chester as being quirky – which may mean not susceptible to pressure from the lawyers.

The Cabinet committee on Ireland met at 10.30 and they discussed the ending of the convention. They all agreed it had been a successful ploy in 'playing for time'. Now they had to find another one. Late in the meeting Merlyn Rees made a passionate and convincing plea for not taking a tough financial line against Ulster. This clearly reflected our paper on financial sanctions. He and the Chancellor have replied to our earlier paper conceding the enormous flow of money to Ulster – but he is pleading that it should continue.

[On 3 March 1976 Rees announced the dissolution of the Northern Ireland Assembly and the commencement of Direct Rule of the Province from London.]

Cabinet started at 11.30, after some film shots of Ted Short on completing 25 years in Parliament. Cabinet had nothing special on the agenda, but it went on till 1 p.m.

I saw a man who came to help me draw up my will! Then had lunch in No. 10 with the others from the office.

The PM kept us waiting for briefing while he saw Enoch Powell about Ireland. He said afterwards that Powell was 'very sensible'.

Questions was not good. The PM was uneasy, and began boasting about how many Jews he had rescued from Russia. It was embarrassing.

Donald Bruce came to see HW to say it was 'too delicate' to put on paper. PM refused to see him saying he was 'bloody lucky to get his peerage'. Albert said Marcia had been pushing on Bruce's behalf.

After Questions I dashed back to see my lovely Washington friend, Mrs Liz Stevens, who told me that Jimmy Carter would win the American presidential.

At 5.45 we had a Misc committee on the closed shop in the Civil Service. Foot was for it. Jenkins against. And the relevant minister Lord Shepherd for some scheme whereby civil servants would pay their dues to the Civil Service Union but not have to join the union. The PM was bored – and a bit harassed, looking somehow haunted.

This evening he had dinner with D'Oyly Carte. Beforehand he came up to me and told me about his three-hour talk with Jeremy Thorpe earlier this week – from 10.30 p.m. till 1.30 a.m. He is absolutely convinced that the South Africans are behind it all. And now there is some evidence that a South African impersonated Peter Hain to get him arrested and charged with theft. [He was acquitted on 9 April 1976]. The story gets more and more bizarre. The PM is loving it all, since it appeals to all his obsessions with plots, spies, leaks, conspiracies, etc. But, as usual, his instincts about this are not completely off the mark.

I went to Odin's restaurant to see Peter Hennessy[*] and went home at midnight.

*Friday 27 February 1976*

In for the weekly 'prayers' meeting. The PM looked very tired and pale after last night's dinner for the D'Oyly Carte. But he was chuckling as he went in – we arrived at the front door together – and he told me he was feeling 'very mischievous'.

At prayers he pressed for progress on the Film Industry Report – so that he can get the new Film Authority set up before he goes.

Healey, Mellish and Short were there – nothing of importance came up.

During the morning I worked on our brief on Crosland's new Transport paper.

Had a quick lunch with Claus Moser.

Spent the afternoon again on Transport and then on Ireland.

Home early – at 8 p.m.

It is now exactly two years since the eve of the election.

*Monday 1 March 1976*

So – March at last, due to be the final month, just two years since we came in.

A beautiful morning, cold and sunny. I felt rather tired, having been to the dinner of the Professional Footballers Association last night until 3.45 a.m. (and out to dinner with John Hale till 2 a.m. the previous night).

I worked in the office. The PM came in mid-morning and we all gathered in private office and discussed the usual matters – the press, Parliamentary Questions, Joe's draft for the PM's speech this weekend.

HW called Joe outside and told him that Marcia had been shouting and rowing with him this weekend. Constantly attacking him to try to make him stay on – even just for three months. But he claims to be sticking firm – though the date looks more like the 16th or 18th.

I telephoned Tom McNally who had just come back from Rhodesia. He is very pessimistic: does not think the white Rhodesians have changed at all – and that in a year there will be a war, and demands for us to be involved.

Went to lunch at the Reform where I met Thomas Balogh and his son. He confirmed that John Smith was right and it was No.10 which insisted that the dubious printing union leader Briginshaw goes on the BNOC board.

HW had lunch in No. 10 with Marcia and Weidenfeld. The latter arrived with a file of papers and we all assumed it was to do with the next book – HW on the government of Britain.

I met Marcia and Weidenfeld leaving No. 10 at 3.30. Neither of them acknowledged me. She has complained to Albert that nobody supports her in her campaign to make HW stay on. She also claims that she does not know the date of the resignation – but Mary does. She told Bill Housden in the car going home that HW had told Weidenfeld the date.

The Misc committee on the counter-inflation unit met at 9.30 – though it was very late in starting. HW treated it frivolously. The other ministers – Healey, Shirley Williams and Michael Foot – wanted the unit to continue and to have contacts with ministers. So HW suggested that I co-ordinate this. He said, 'Bernard Donoughue has contacts in every department.' Quite nice – but there won't be time to get it off the ground.

Afterwards I cleared my papers and then went to Ted Short's party to celebrate two years in office. HW came as well and Healey, and various MPs and officials, mainly from Ted's office. Very nice. Ted Short was in sparkling form, benign and smiling and entertaining his harem of young female staff. Very different from his stern public image. I have always liked him.

The Lord Chancellor came in at 5 p.m. to discuss the Royal Commission on the Law. We have still made little progress. He wanted Plowden as chairman, but the PM vetoed him as too Establishment. Elwyn vetoed Norman Chester as 'too old and quirky'.

The PM told him to look at my list.

Home at 9.30.


*Tuesday 2 March 1976*

Another lovely morning.

Before the Cabinet committee (MES) on Transport Policy I talked to Jim Hamilton of the Cabinet Office, whose appointment as permanent secretary at Education will be announced today. An excellent choice.

Crosland presented his Transport paper very sensibly. It recommends a switch from rail to road, the opposite of the manifesto, and it is packed with concessions to the railway unions.

Most people were worried by parts of the paper – especially the massive increases in fares involved.

The pro-railway sentiment of the older members also emerged – Ross, Lever, Short, Jenkins and the PM all spoke up for maintaining the existing railway system.

It went through in the end, though with strong doubts about the timing. We have to publish it either before the local elections or in the middle of the negotiations on Stage II of the incomes policy. Either way is politically painful – but we cannot wait till the autumn.

Crosland was very keen it should not go to Cabinet and the PM agreed, though I think that was wrong. It is too important to slip through Cabinet committee.

Afterwards I went to see Joe who told me about HW's talk with Ken Stowe last night, and Ken later confirmed it to me. This was before the PM went with Marcia to see the new boring film spectacular *Moses*. He said that he was now enjoying the job enormously. He said he was 'like a waiter under notice' – he could enjoy it because it wouldn't last.

He also asked Ken to approach the Queen about the farewell dinner with her. He wanted Ken to ask if she were willing to 'receive' Marcia. The latter believes that the Queen won't because Marcia is related to the Queen – being so she claims a direct descendant of an illegitimate child of Edward VII. Her chosen peerage title is her statement of claim to be of royal blood. (I don't know if she believes in the Divine Right and divine origin of royalty as well.) If the Queen continues to banish this competitor for her throne, then the PM says he won't invite anybody to the dinner except his family. But if Marcia is accepted as of true blue blood, then he will invite others – his Cabinet, Joe, me, everybody, etc.

Ken was absolutely bewildered by this bizarre request. God knows what the Queen will make of it. I imagine she would be quite intrigued and perhaps a little jealous to meet someone as powerful as Marcia – especially being such a close relative.

I also cleared various papers and draft speeches, and then had lunch upstairs in No.10 (including some delicious pancakes by Sarah because it is Pancake Tuesday).

It all looks set for two weeks' time. I think Tuesday 16th. Last night when I raised with him the question that Chile is on the OPD agenda for 10 March – which will lead to Frank Judd's resignation – he said, 'Delay it till the 17th, the 17th.'

The irony is that I raised this matter because I knew he would not want Judd to resign while he was PM. He reacted exactly as if he knew that I knew what I was concerned with. Yet officially I don't know anything! Why the hell does he think I suggested he might want the committee delaying for a week or so!

Briefing for Questions went very slowly. His whisky was 'off' and he sent for another bottle which took ages to come. He said, 'If they don't hurry up, I shall answer Questions cold sober, which will create a record.'

In Questions he was brilliant, demolishing the Tories, and Eric Heffer, Dennis Skinner and various other enemies of the Labour government with a series of sharp thrusts. I felt he was settling old scores, enjoying himself irresponsibly, in the last few days. He was chirpy and very pleased with the world. Retirement is good for him so far – though he told Ken last night he expects to receive the 'doctor's mandate to get the country out of the mess' after he has retired.

I came back after questions for a meeting with a man from the CPRS to discuss their study on the central machinery for policy analysis. It seems a very good idea to me. The whole PAR system has collapsed.

Then we had the special Misc Cabinet committee on the Film Industry. This was an incredible farce. Everybody knows it is a ramp to get public money for various showbiz friends through the new Film Authority. Healey openly calls it 'Wilson's benefit'. Healey and Jenkins declined to attend the committee and join in the charade. Lever looked embarrassed. Peter Shore supported it, although his officials had produced a paper completely demolishing it. Eric Varley loyally supported it. As did Hugh Jenkins, who has a film industry background. Ted Short pointed out that we could build twenty-five primary schools for the £25 million devoted to this.

Joel Barnett made a slashing attack on the whole idea. The PM summed up by saying that he agreed with most of Barnett's criticisms but 'the majority of the committee supported Peter Shore's proposal', thus totally excluding himself from responsibility for the final decision.

Ministers looked amused and a bit embarrassed.

The PM looked a bit ashamed afterwards. He treated the whole thing as a joke. Indeed halfway through the meeting he told a private secretary to go and fetch Janet Hewlett-Davies and bring her into the meeting. He sat there smiling.

It is as if after thirteen years of suppressing his personal feelings, he is now enjoying being a naughty schoolboy again. Quite endearing really. Very human. I like him for it.

But it is further proof that it is time to go.

For myself I am now enjoying it greatly and will be deeply sorry – traumatised – when it ends.

After the committee Tom McNally came in and we drank. He is looking for a Commons seat. He has been excellent to work with, but our partnership is due to end sooner than he thinks. [In fact within a month we would be working together in No.10 under a new Prime Minister.]

Marcia is trying to persuade HW to leak his intentions to retire to the Cabinet in advance. When HW told Joe this, Joe pointed out her motive – so that a 'Harold must stay' movement could be mobilised. HW had not thought of it.

Yesterday HW told the journalist Peter Hennessy that John Hunt was the best Cabinet Secretary ever. He said that Hunt was 'a borzoi' compared with Burke Trend's being 'too feline'. I agree that John is a very impressive Whitehall operator. He and I are bound to clash and disagree over policies from time to time, as well as the inevitable competition for the

Prime Minister's ear between the No. 10 and the Cabinet Office advisers. He and they are jealous of my privileged access. I also sense that he would like to bring No. 10 completely within his empire. But I admire and respect him as a highly efficient manager of the Whitehall machine.

## Wednesday 3 March 1976

The PM was with the Chancellor when I arrived this morning. Healey was reporting on the dinner last night with the NEDC and trade unionists. This is the first of the series to explore the next stage of incomes policy. Nothing precise to report but Healey was definitely optimistic.

We went to the NEDC meeting at 10.20 – the PM in the front car with Healey; Nigel Wicks and me behind.

The meeting was long and tedious. The PM attended and took the chair because it was his 'last' NEDDY.

They discussed the Treasury's 'Medium Term Assessment' without any figures. Then briefly the price code. Just a series of set statements round the table, with the trade unionists looking bleary and irritable. Dan McGarvey is a very unhealthy mauve.

The PM was bored and kept sorting out his pockets – he found and passed to me my Green Paper on Ireland.

He also gave Nigel a note on which he scribbled that he had heard that the EEC was going to abolish suet pudding and he wanted this stopped.

We all had a quick drink afterwards and then went by car – the PM, Joe and me – to the Charing Cross Hotel for lunch with the *Guardian* – Peter Preston, Peter Gibbings, Peter Jenkins and David McKie. It was better than usual. They asked some sharp questions and the PM relied less on anecdotes than usual. He put to them his theories about BOSS, the South African police out to get Jeremy Thorpe and Peter Hain.

Peter Jenkins asked him some pertinent questions about the future of Britain, and how to arrest the decline in British power. HW just looked blank. David McKie is quiet but young and impressive and seems entirely without malice – rare among journalists and probably a disqualification for high office in modern journalism.

We returned at 3 p.m. so that HW could see George Weidenfeld, who had been summoned at Marcia's insistence – they had a terrible row last night.

Then Misc 89 met to discuss the liberalisation of the Official Secrets Act – and went on for two and a half hours. It was quite clear that the majority of the committee – led by HW, Callaghan, Elwyn Jones, Mason and Shore – were for tightening everything up. Roy Jenkins would not have that and lost his temper several times. He said if we were not going to keep our promise of liberalisation then he would rather do nothing. He got some good support from Healey and from Ted Short, who is always craggily radical on this kind of issue.

Healey left for a pee in the middle, and as I opened the door for him said, 'This is balls-achingly boring.'

Jenkins and Callaghan clashed repeatedly, which is a pity since they are a natural alliance which could dominate the Cabinet. Each has a band of reliable supporters. Roy also has the liberal intelligentsia and the press. Jim has the party machine and some trade unions. They would be unbeatable together. But they do seem to irritate one another.

The meeting was chaotic at times, with half a dozen people talking at the same time and the PM unable to impose order. He tried to find a compromise in reclassifying papers, but it won't work.

Afterwards I walked to the door with Roy. We discussed what to do next. My view is to let it go into the sand. Better the bad old ridiculous Official Secrets Act than a new one which would actually work. 'Better the blunderbuss than the Armalite rifle,' I said. What the machine wants is a more repressive measure under a liberalising gloss. HW would be happy with that. Fortunately Roy Jenkins is not going to be fooled.

I was exhausted when we emerged at nearly 6.30 p.m. I went upstairs to change and then went to the Aldwych to see a very lively *Henry V.* Afterwards we went to the 'crush bar' at Covent Garden for food and drinks with our hosts from Grieveson Grant – very pleasant, though not home till after 1 a.m. (and on the heath running this morning at 7.30!).

HW is totally ignoring Harold Lever, who has declined to help out with the Field family 'slag heap' debts.

## Thursday 4 March 1976

Was caught in terrible traffic and arrived too late for the CPRS presentation on social policy in the Cabinet Room. I saw William Plowden and Tessa Blackstone afterwards and they seemed quite pleased. The PM also spoke well of it, as did Tony Crosland, though Fred Mulley seemed less impressed.

Cabinet went on for hours over Rhodesia and the conspiracy laws, where there was a lot of disagreement between Jenkins and the Left. The PM was looking very tired.

Albert told us today that after the party for Labour peers yesterday evening, Marcia came storming into HW's room and started to scream at him. She opened by shouting to Albert, 'Do you know that he is going to leave on the 16th?' She then accused HW of receiving parcels of money from supporters. He said that was true, but she had received all the money. On top of that he accused her of taking £90 a week from the office funds.

When she denied it, he pointed out that he had personally examined the stubs of the chequebooks. She ranted on and on, and he said that he was retiring in order to escape this kind of pressure. He said she had harassed him for 20 years and he could not put up with it any longer. He then sat down and read his papers while she went on shouting and then she finally sat on the settee and wept.

Albert tried to leave the room at the beginning of this; but HW ordered him to stay, saying, 'I need a witness.'

At the end she said she refused to go home in HW's car. So HW sent Albert to order a taxi. When he returned with that, she said she wouldn't take it, she would walk. But when she got outside and was faced with the unfamiliar experience of travelling home unchauffeured, she changed her mind and climbed into the 3.5 official Rover.

Lunch at No. 10. Questions went very easily and boring.

We went back to a briefing on tomorrow's Irish talks – HW was rambling and uninterested.

Upstairs to clear his two weekend speeches. Again HW was uninterested and accepted any amendments.

He then saw Barbara Castle on 'a private matter' – he told us afterwards that she came in to ask for a peerage, and said she had fixed it so that Jack Straw would get her seat in Blackburn.

I raised with him the situation in Education, where they are very short of a junior minister, with two Bills going through the House. He said he would do it tomorrow – it will be our suggestion of Joe's friend Margaret Jackson [Beckett].

Home – first seeing Professor Kedourie about my future at the LSE.

*Friday 5 March 1976*

The PM stayed overnight at Chequers, which is rare for a Thursday. He apparently feels safer from Marcia's attacks out there.

I saw him in private office when he came in the morning. He then went upstairs to discuss the results of the Lonrho inquiry with Peter Shore.

After that he began the talks with Cosgrave and the Irish delegation.

I worked on papers and especially on an excellent paper by Gavyn Davies on employment – showing that the number of people working, in jobs, is scarcely down on the boom of 1973 – and more than in the 1970–72 depression. Yet unemployment is sky-high – because more people are registering as unemployed.

Lunch with the Irish, which was very friendly. I sat next to Dermot Nally, from the Taoiseach's office. It is clear that their operation is very simple and primitive. But Nally is very good.

At the end of lunch Nigel Wicks from private office brought up news that there was a sterling crisis and the pound had dropped below $2. The PM got agitated and sent for the Chancellor, who arrived while the Irish were still in the reception-rooms. The PM looked very angry and snapped, 'What the bloody hell are you up to?' They then went into the study to discuss it.

Clearly there has been some mismanagement. The Treasury policy is to get sterling down to maintain our competitiveness. They also want to destroy the $2 barrier as a virility symbol. Therefore the Bank of England has been selling sterling recently. Then the foreigners joined in and it got out of hand, falling three cents in two hours. They did not want to intervene to maintain an artificially high rate, but they did not want to provoke a currency crisis. They had panicked, and the Governor came flapping across to see the Chancellor.

When Denis left he looked a bit defeated.

We then all went with the Irish into the Cabinet Room to settle the communiqué.

I went back to my room and was telephoned by Shirley Williams about some bad resolutions at Monday's Home Policy committee of the NEC. About Northern Ireland. I telephoned Merlyn Rees who was in a press conference, but he suggested I talk to HW to get him to intervene.

I grabbed HW as he left for Liverpool to speak to him on privacy and on Ireland. He refused to intervene, but suggested arguments they might put. He added, 'Northern Ireland should not be at the Home Affairs committee anyway: it should be at the International committee.' An interesting distinction – against direct rule from London.

I talked to Shirley and Merlyn Rees again and then settled down to the Unit paper on employment. We did several drafts and did not get away till 9 p.m. in the end. But it was a good paper and worth the effort. Gavyn Davies produces winners every time.

Joe is feeling sad that the end is coming – like me he will miss the excitement and the style. But he believes it will kill HW to stay on. He is just not fit enough any more.

The one obstacle to retirement now is Jeremy Thorpe. He is under great pressure to resign. The PM is worried that this will take the glamour off him. He also doesn't like the idea of turmoil in two parties at the same time. Marcia is pressing this point. But Joe is trying to keep him to his decision, and at present it seems firm – he has fixed a Cabinet for Tuesday 16th.

HW has now told Albert – 'before Easter'. He added, 'Bernard does not know.' Joe said that was for Marcia's ears. Of course he knows that I know. We have often discussed together its implications on the clear assumption that I knew. But he dare not admit it out loud to others in case Marcia learns and accuses him of telling me.

## Monday 8 March 1976

I barely saw HW at all today. I worked in the Unit this morning. He came in at 11.15 to see the Israeli Ambassador and I saw him slipping upstairs. He left early for lunch with the Lord Privy Seal and various officials from the Civil Service Department.

I nipped over to the Reform for lunch – sat next to Freddie Fisher, editor of the *Financial Times*. He keeps going on about how depressed he is with everything. I told him to stop moaning and to start rowing. But I know how he feels.

Dashed back for a 2.30 meeting of permanent secretaries in the Old Treasury boardroom in the Cabinet Office – a beautiful room.

The Treasury paper – on the next PESC review of public expenditure – was terrible. No figures. No strategy. Nothing. Nobody attacked it, until I did at the end. They all talked about the madness of public expenditure. Douglas Wass was very bland in the chair and Leo Pliatzky long-winded in his introduction.

The meeting lasted two hours then I dashed off to a meeting in the Treasury on top people's pay – which includes us senior civil servants. In Ken Couzens's room – where we thrashed out the White Paper last summer. This went on for two and a half hours. Just a man from the Inland Revenue, who said there would be 'a social revolution if we squeezed top pay any more'. A man from CSD who said that it would be impossible to recruit anybody unless we increased all top salaries – emigration, etc. And a man from Employment who declined to say what he thought, but felt that his minister [Foot] would oppose any increases.

I was so late that I was unable to go home as planned to settle my insurance claim. Also I missed the reception for Teddy Kollek, the Mayor of Jerusalem.

Meanwhile HW had seen a string of people – including Goodman and Weidenfeld. Yet he had not bothered to deal with the ministerial appointment to Education, although Ken Stowe raised it with him again.

Apparently HW said this evening that perhaps he should not retire after all. Because of Rhodesia, sterling, etc. He is still dithering. Incredible with only eight days to go. Such indecisiveness is itself a disqualification for continuing.

According to Albert and Bill, Marcia was at him after lunch, pressing him to stay on.

There is also according to Albert and Bill a letter from Lord Arwyn to her with proposals for fresh property speculation in Wales.

## Tuesday 9 March 1976

Perhaps a week to go.

I did not see the PM till just before lunch.

He had sent for Frank Byers,* the Liberal chairman, to tell him about the South African involvement in the Thorpe and Hain affairs – or at least their alleged involvement – mainly to strengthen the support for Thorpe. He does not want Thorpe to go now and steal the thunder from his own departure.

Then he saw Frank Schon: not about NRDC, which Schon heads, but because Schon and Arwyn are (according to Albert who sees most of her correspondence) apparently backing Tony Field in his business ventures, and especially in property speculation in Wales, where, according to Arwyn's letter, there is somebody called 'the Cardiffian' who is their Welsh contact. I hope he is not a Labour councillor on the planning committee!

I was phoned by the secretary of the Royal Commission on the Press to complain that the PM was interfering in their ground with his speech and Green Paper on privacy. Also that we had forgotten to send them a copy of the speech, so I warned the PM and told him to apologise when he saw the chairman this afternoon.

I had lunch upstairs, but did not go to Parliamentary Questions, where HW made his revelation on the South African connection. Nobody knows if he has any evidence, and he did not consult anyone before planting a question with Jim Wellbeloved. It is partly a diversion, to take their minds off sterling and to make it difficult for the Liberals to get rid of Thorpe in the near future. But he does also believe it.

I went to an official committee preparing for the Green Paper on privacy. They have an impossible task: trying to cover the Franks, Younger, Phillimore and Faulks reports as well as the PM's idea of a deal with the press. They are also excluding the Official Secrets Act and official information so there is not much in it for the press. I fought hard on official information and made sure that it was at least considered for the final package.

This evening HW finally announced Margaret Jackson as junior minister for Education, after pressure from all directions. Not a bad appointment though it will offend some who have been longer in the House. Joe and I pushed HW for it.

This morning the PM went through the arrangements for next Tuesday with Joe and Ken Stowe. He seemed to assume it was still all on – but he said that the point of no return would not be till Monday.

If he changes it is sure to leak.

The Israeli Ambassador knew all about his plans yesterday, and pressed HW to stay on (somebody had mobilised him).

John Hunt has now been told.

Went to David Owen's riverside house for a smashing dinner in the evening.

Home at midnight.

## Wednesday 10 March 1976

I decided not to go to the OPD Cabinet committee on the Falkland Islands. This is the effect of knowing it is coming to an end soon – there is no incentive to take part in the beginning of things where I know I won't be here for the end of them.

It ended about 10.45 and the PM invited Joe, Nigel and me up to the study for coffee and to discuss the Royal Commission's scheme for financial aid to the newspaper industry in general – and to rescue the *Observer* in particular. The *Observer* is the only paper with no viable long-term future, even if it gets aid.

We agreed that the *Observer* must be saved. Partly because it is a unique and excellent paper. And partly because if it collapsed then the unions would not co-operate with the rest of the redundancy schemes.

While HW saw L. Hooper – a senior intelligence man who has been looking into the South African connection – we went downstairs to Joe's room and discussed plans for rescuing the *Observer* – now mainly through a merger with the *Financial Times*.

After Hooper, we went back up to the study and the PM approved a basic rescue scheme which I had dictated onto a quick draft paper. He told private office to circulate it to ministers who are on the Cabinet committee discussing the Royal Commission's scheme.

The PM gave us all a drink before lunch – it is some time since we sat up there in the study and all drank together.

Merlyn Rees reported that his junior minister Stan Orme has had enough of Northern Ireland and wants a change.

The PM also means to drop Roy Jenkins's Minister of State Alex Lyon – whom Jenkins no longer wants – but he says he must wait till a general reshuffle – which will be done by his successor.

I had lunch with John Mackintosh to discuss the Policy Unit, which he wants to mention in the next edition of his book on the British Cabinet. We also discussed other matters, including devolution. He intends to stand for the new Scottish Assembly. He is a clever man, but there is something cold and lonely about him.

In the afternoon I worked in the Unit on papers.

During the afternoon sterling came under heavy pressure and fell to new lows. The PM saw Healey in the Commons while they were listening to the public expenditure debate. Healey reassured him. But HW was still worried when he returned and he took everybody up to the study for a drink to discuss the currency.

I decided not to go, and instead went out to the RAC Club for a drink with Harry Evans. We mainly discussed his private matters, though he did tell me all about the material on Jim Slater and Peter Walker, which was due to be published in last week's *Sunday Times*, but was suppressed by a High Court injunction.

I telephoned back to No. 10 to check that all was OK there before I went home. Private office told me that all was relaxed and that the Whips were fairly confident about tonight's vote on public expenditure.

The PM had gone to George Weidenfeld this evening for Marcia's birthday party.

I was home when I heard on TV that we had lost the Commons vote because 39 Tribune left-wingers had abstained.

[The government was defeated by 28 – the heaviest government defeat in recent memory.]

Even worse – the PM was not in the House for the uproar that followed our defeat. He had dashed straight back from the vote at the House to Marcia's party at Weidenfeld's Chelsea flat. This created great comment.

## Thursday 11 March 1976

The PM's 60th birthday. Curious that both HW and Marcia are Pisces. The fish that swims and is torn in opposite directions. Quixotic and ambivalent. Supposed to be the direct opposite of Virgos (me). This was the day when originally it was all supposed to happen – well, it might, but not what was planned!

I went straight in and up to the PM. He was thinking of having the vote of confidence next Monday to reverse last night's Commons defeat. (He had told Joe that last night's Commons defeat would make him delay his departure 'a week' but had convinced him more than ever that it was the right thing to do.) I was in favour of having the confidence debate today (for sterling reasons), as were private office. Technically it is not possible to have a confidence debate put down today – it had to be put down yesterday – but it could be done on the adjournment. HW came round to our way of thinking and agreed today was best. He would open the debate with a short tough speech. And he would sack the PPSs who abstained last night. I wanted him to sack them straight away without even telling their ministers, like Morrison and Attlee did in 1949, but HW wanted to wait until after the vote (to make sure we got their vote).

HW them did a radio interview before Cabinet.

I went down and talked to various ministers:

– to the Lord Chancellor about the Law Commission – he is happy with my suggestion of John Freeman as chairman.

– to Roy Jenkins about the confidence debate and to fix for us to have drinks together next Wednesday. I have deliberately chosen to do it after the resignation, then nobody can accuse me of leaking it to Roy.

Bill Housden and Albert were hopeful that last night's vote will make the PM put off his departure. I sat in the car with Bill for 10 minutes. He told me that the PM was furious with the Left and muttered something about them suffering 'after I have gone'.

The PM had arranged to see Martin Charteris this afternoon about Palace arrangements for his resignation – including dinner for the Queen. But he called this off because of this afternoon's debate. This led to fresh optimism for Bill – but then the Charteris meeting was rearranged for the evening. It really does look as if he is firm now. The Left have made him even firmer. Because, as he has often said, he no longer knows or likes the PLP; last night re-emphasised that.

HW was due to go for a birthday lunch with Mary today at the Epicure, where they have been for the last 20 years. But he called it off. Instead we all went to the study and prepared his Commons confidence speech. He dictated paragraphs. We produced some facts and figures. By 1.30 it was done. Very short and very tough.

We all then went to lunch in the kitchen. The private secretaries reported on two remarkable notes they had received from Marcia:

(1) asked them to arrange an official dinner party for 'the Prime Minister's friends – Lord Plurenden, etc.';
(2) asked them to arrange for HW to make an official visit to Washington in June (after his departure), at public expense, so that he could attend the D'Oyly Carte performances there (she is pushing him into all the D'Oyly Carte things – Hanson and McAlpine are rich fellow trustees!).

After a quick lunch we returned to the study to complete the speech. We then went to the House for briefing for Questions.

Various people came in – including Cledwyn Hughes, Jim Callaghan and Ted Short – to make sure that his speech stressed that this was not just a general vote of confidence in the government – it was specifically in support of the government's 'financial and economic policies' – i.e. a repeat of yesterday's vote. So the Tribune Group would either have to climb down, or bring the government down. We agreed with this and had written that in three times – at the beginning, in the middle and at the end. So there was no question of HW fudging it this time. He was taking them head-on – and if he lost, the government would fall. We could all be out of a job by tomorrow.

But HW said that if we lost, the final thing he would do before going to the Palace was to withdraw the whip from the Tribune Group, so they could not be endorsed as candidates in the ensuing election (though the NEC might reverse that).

He was a bit nervy and jumpy and drank quite a lot of Madeira. But he was very sharp. All his recent slackness and frivolity had gone. The challenge had tautened him and he was thinking fast.

Questions went quite quietly till towards the end, when Canavan,* a woolly Tribunite, intervened. HW slapped him down. Then Heffer came in and claimed that the Tribunites had not gone into alliance with the Tories. HW rounded on him, accused him of political 'promiscuity' and said it was just as bad to be 'a lapdog outside the bedroom door' as to leap into bed. Heffer looked winded and the House gasped. Our side cheered and it was clear that the bulk of the PLP were behind HW – in fact John Tomlinson his PPS had warned HW that the Manifesto Group would not support him with speeches unless he slapped down the Left.

After Questions we returned to his room for 20 minutes, while Ted Short dealt with next week's business.

HW was clearly feeling in fighting form and looking forward to the battle ahead.

His speech went quite well. A lot of shouting from the Tories – which helped to rally the Labour ranks behind him. The Left was totally silent while he rebuked them again and again for giving aid and comfort to the Tories.

Mrs Thatcher replied with a tough and crisp speech, her best yet.

Jeremy Thorpe made a strange rambling speech, all about the need for consensus – almost coalition. This was because the Liberals had decided to vote against us, even though Thorpe and Steel wanted to abstain. David Steel told me later that the Liberals were afraid that if they abstained it would be said that they were afraid of bringing about an election. It is also part of the internal Liberal battle – with some of them wanting to defeat Thorpe.

We then went back to HW's room and he gave us all a birthday drink. Or at least he said it was a birthday drink, but I suspected it was to celebrate this last speech as PM.

We then came back to No. 10 for the Cabinet committee on the newspaper industry.

HW had circulated my note on rescuing the *Observer*, though it was not so urgent now since the latest reports on its finances are a little more optimistic. The committee simply discussed the general approach to the report. A majority were for supporting aid to Fleet Street – but Varley was strongly against, on the very good grounds that they were incompetent management and pampered unions. On this basis we should support everybody. Certainly it was hard to make a case for giving state money to men, some over 70, who were earning over £100 a week and doing nothing.

The PM reserved his position a little – he was in favour of aid but said he thought it might not go through the House.

On sterling, since last Thursday we have spent some $700 million gross, $300 million net – and are spending more today. There have been no sales by big sterling holders, but a lot of general pressure. Today the net sales will probably double.

I went off at 6.15 to a party with Ron Spiers for the new American Ambassador, Anne Armstrong. She seemed an above-average tough, brittle masculine American Southern woman.

But I had the chance to talk to several politicians about tonight's vote. David Steel told me that the Liberals were voting against us, despite the contrary advice from himself and Jeremy Thorpe. He has behaved honourably in the recent Thorpe affair; but seems very depressed about their future.

Ted Short was pessimistic about tonight's vote – thought we might only squeeze by with a couple of votes to spare. Harold Lever was taking bets the majority would be less than 13.

Shirley Williams was very pleased with HW's performance this afternoon.

Eric Roll came up to me to ask what was happening to sterling – he is an outside director of the Bank, but they are told nothing.

I talked to Gordon Richardson, the Governor of the Bank, who seemed very unrelaxed, but was taking some pleasure from the fact that the French are under pressure as well.

Lord Goodman chatted and then left, feeling the strain on his leg, where he has recently had a thrombosis. Curiously Harry Kissin has had the same, and is being treated by the same doctor.

I travelled from Knightsbridge to the Chelsea embankment to George Weidenfeld's flat for the birthday party for the PM.

I enjoyed it. Partly from the general frantic feeling of having to enjoy the last moment. Partly because I spent dinner talking happily to an old friend, Miriam Gross; drinks beforehand talking to Jim Callaghan; and drinks after talking to Lord Goodman and the delightful Mrs Phipps.

The dinner party was at three tables. There was a top table for HW. Mary was not on it – she sat at my table. Marcia – who probably instructed George on the seating – was at the top table with the Prime Minister, along with John Vaizey of all people. He has often viciously attacked HW. But of course he is helping Marcia to get her children into private school, so he immediately qualifies for the top table. As did Noel Annan, who is also allegedly helping with the children, and certainly has little in common with HW at all. Basically the party contained a group of George's friends, Marcia's hangers-on, a few top politicians such as Jim, and Albert and me. Still the wine was unusually good. Weidenfeld buzzed, fluttered and flopped around like a blue-arsed fly.

Lew Grade was also there on the top table. At about 1 o'clock in the morning he started to do a solo tap dance for the PM's entertainment. It was a bit embarrassing to see this remarkably energetic but fat old millionaire of 69 performing like a dancing monkey, with Marcia's active and verbal encouragement. It did not elevate Great Britain's Prime Minister, who looked quite bemused – though it may of course lead to the elevation of Mr Grade. [Lew Grade received a peerage in Harold Wilson's honours list, as did his brother Bernard Delfont.]

Also on the top table was Nigel Ryan, a Tory from ITN who is an impressive flatterer of Marcia.

It was a good thing Joe was not there – he presciently called off on the false grounds of sudden sickness. It would have made him genuinely ill.

Jim Callaghan sat at my table and was very funny. In the middle of HW's birthday speech he started grunting, 'Speak up, speak up Harold, we cannot hear you.' This completely threw HW and he lost the track of his speech and gave up.

But Jim was very worried about the d§ivision vote. Not that we would lose, but that HW would suddenly slip off in the car to the Commons and leave him behind, missing the vote. With good cause. HW suddenly left like a bullet, and Jim had to leap up and dash after him. They returned half an hour later.

Jim has become very much the conservative elder statesman. He spent a lot of time talking about his Sussex farm and his family. He has moved on to a new plane of contentment – which next week's announcement may disrupt.

Jim left shortly after midnight. HW stayed till around 1 a.m. I stayed till 2 a.m. and then got a lift home.

Very tiring, but quite an occasion. We won the division by 17. Had we lost that would have been the end of the government. But I did not worry. It makes little difference whether HW goes to the Palace tonight or in five days' time. In some ways it would be more appropriate tonight. To go to resign and so miss the end of one of these Weidenfeld-Marcia social gatherings, which have nothing in common with the real HW at all. He is simply taken along and shown off to impress the rich natives.

*Friday 12 March 1976*

I missed the morning's prayers meeting because the traffic was so bad. A pity because I would have liked to observe HW this morning. Later on he looked pale and tired.

At 11 a.m. I went to the Treasury for a meeting to devise a 'Top Pay' policy. This is really very important. I am not convinced that we should have such a policy, but if so it must be done well. Yet here are five of us thinking up a policy virtually off the tops of our heads. In fact the tax system is the only efficient and comprehensive instrument. But the Inland Revenue man seems afraid of anything which to him seems 'confiscation' and says that would be 'over the dead bodies' of the Inland Revenue. I pointed out there were a lot of dead bodies around.

Went to lunch with Jonathan Charkham at the City Livery Club. Discussed theoretical future jobs for me – though he did not know this is an imminent question.

Came back and saw Lord Goodman again – he had come in to see the PM. We discussed taking over the *New Statesman*.

I was working on the latest Treasury paper – devaluation plus £1 billion reflation – when I learned we had been burgled again. So I set off home very depressed by it all. Just a TV set, but a terrible feeling of being violated by these intrusions. Before leaving I told the PM. He seemed almost pleased. He commented wryly that 'somewhere in South Africa House there must be a room full of grandfather clocks and TV sets'.

Home by 4.30 to find the house full of police. A terrible bore. So I did not go out in the evening with the Donaldsons. Carol went while I baby-sat – feeling another bad cold coming on.

# CHAPTER 24

## Resignation – With Such Honours
## March–April 1976

*Monday 15 March 1976*

This is the decisive week. Joe and Ken Stowe spent last night at Chequers going over the final resignation arrangements.

The only doubts were from the continuing currency crisis.

HW drove up from Chequers with his sister, Marjorie – she was here for her birthday party but was staying over for the last rites. On the way up they had the car radio on. At 11 a.m. the news announced that the currency markets were fairly quiet. Then Bill Housden heard HW say to his sister, 'It is all systems go.'

I was in private office when HW arrived. He chatted casually, but made no reference to the big event. For much of the morning he disappeared quietly upstairs with Ken Stowe.

Ken told me that the Queen is very concerned at HW's going. She doesn't want him to do it and there has been discussion of trying to get him to change his mind. Martin Charteris discussed this with John Hunt, and was quite properly dissuaded from taking such an approach. Not only because of the constitutional proprieties. But also because of the belief that HW is determined – and rightly so – to go. He has lost the appetite for power and the will to govern. That is why he has no alternative.

I went to lunch in the City with Grieveson Grant – having a terrible sinus cold, with my eyes streaming throughout the lunch. I gave no hint, but enjoyed playing with them as old friends by asking what would be the City impact if HW was run over by a bus tomorrow.

There is no sniff of rumour in the papers. Apparently John Junor of the *Sunday Express* heard from a legal source that the resignation was pending (I have learned he had dinner with Arnold Goodman on Friday!). He is said to have called together his four political correspondents and they all rejected the possibility of HW going, so the *Express* did not carry its great scoop.

I decided not to go to the Treasury committee to formulate policy on top people's pay. We are all too tense and jumpy about tomorrow. Some hypothetical incomes policy for a hypothetical government next year just did not seem other than too remote.

I hung around No.10, wandering from the press office to the private office and then to my own Policy Unit, chatting vaguely but really with nothing to say. The only thing worth discussing could not be openly discussed.

This evening there was a dinner for the Royal Statistical Society. Although it was HW's final dinner before the great announcement, I decided not to go. I could not face being trapped round a table for two and a half hours, continuing the charade of pretending this PM was still going to be in office after tomorrow – or that I would be. I arranged with the PM for Gavyn Davies to go instead and he was delighted. He is a good statistician and has earned a reward, doing marvellous work for me.

During the evening I drank a large amount of my own whisky, and then quite a lot of Joe's. Joe, Janet, Ken and Patrick sent out for fish and chips since they were all sleeping in London (Joe at Janet's, some of the others here in No.10) tonight completing the preparations for tomorrow. I joined them and we drank quite a lot of wine. Curiously I was mentally completely sober although I could feel the physical effects of the drink on my legs.

I arranged with Ken Stowe that I should sleep the night in the flat at No. 10. I then went off in the big black official Rover to collect some salt-beef sandwiches from Leicester Square. The others dispersed and I sat up, eating, drinking and watching television in my office – with still no hint on the media of tomorrow's sensation.

I wandered upstairs to the statisticians in the dining-room who were finishing dinner while HW was off at the Commons voting. I talked to Claus Moser, and from the LSE Roy Allen and Jim Durbin – with whom I had a bit of a row over the LSE dons' characteristic stupidity and parochialism in rejecting Dahrendorf's scheme for a Brookings policy studies institute there. Some day that would have brought the school external reputation and independent revenues which they will need when the state finds it cannot afford to support their relaxed life any more. I was tense and irritable, so when the dinner broke up I grabbed Gavyn Davies and he drove me home. He sensed something was afoot but had no idea.

Went to bed at midnight. I woke three times in the night dreaming that the telephone was ringing and HW was on the line to say he had changed his mind.

## Tuesday 16 March 1976

D-Day.

I woke before 6 a.m., made Carol a cup of tea, bathed and set off before 7 a.m. I walked to Camden Town and took a tube in to Charing Cross, walking through the Embankment gardens and into No. 10 by 8 a.m.

The policemen were puzzled. Already everybody was about. The police thought Crosland was resigning!

I had a long chat with Bill Housden before he went to collect the PM from Lord North Street at 9. He stressed how he wants the PM to give him some honour, just so he can face his family and friends. He is still hurt that HW thought he had given him something (it was Macmillan who did so). He wants an OBE or CBE so that he can take his wife to the Palace. I promised to push this through Ken Stowe.

Bill told me that the PM had told Eric Varley at Marcia's birthday party on Wednesday.

The PM told Jim Callaghan on Thursday when they were leaving Weidenfeld's party to go to vote. Going down the stairs HW said that he would be going soon and he wanted Jim to know in advance. But he did not give the exact date. He added that he would not be going into business or anything. Callaghan clearly did not believe it and came up to Bill Housden to say, 'You can't believe everything Harold tells you.' Bill replied, 'You can believe this one.'

The PM came in at about 9.15. I was in private office. He looked preoccupied. He was obviously interested to find me in so early and said, 'Have you had burglars again?' Then he went upstairs with Ken Stowe. They set off for the Palace at 10.10. I went to the front door and watched them as they drove off – there was not a single photographer or journalist, nor when they returned. Nor a breath of rumour in this morning's newspapers.

It is the best-kept secret ever.

HW sent for me when he returned. I sat in the study, on the settee as always. He paced up and down nervously. He told me why he was resigning and claimed that only four people knew. I saw no reason in beating about the bush, so I told him that I had known for some time. He did not comment or look surprised. He knew I knew, but was just going through the motions.

He told me that he thought the Policy Unit was a great success and that he would recommend his successor to keep it on. He added, 'It depends who it is of course – Denis Healey thinks he knows it all anyway.'

I went downstairs and ministers were gathering for Cabinet. It was clear that most of them did not know. I talked to Roy Jenkins about the meeting we have arranged for tomorrow night. I talked to Tony Crosland about having dinner with us at home on Saturday. Neither had any idea. Nor had Shirley, nor Elwyn Jones. But Harold Lever came up to me, nodded and whispered, 'D-Day?'

The PM sent for Jim Callaghan at five minutes to eleven and formally told him. Jim came down looking totally winded and his face completely changed colour. Joe said, 'Good morning' to him; he replied, 'Is it?'

The PM then told Ted Short, who looked almost in tears, and he took Healey into Marcia's room for two minutes to tell him.

Marcia came out and went over to the corner and told Peter Shore, who gasped loudly, 'No!'

Then they all filed into the Cabinet Room, a few minutes late.

No regular secretariat were allowed in to the Cabinet – just John Hunt, Ken Stowe and Joe.

The PM read his statement – which was long and dignified – very quietly in order not to be emotional. Joe said there were gasps. Michael Foot muttered, 'Is it irrevocable?'

When he finished they all looked poleaxed.

Jim Callaghan then made a brief statement, claiming that HW would be judged more kindly by history than by his contemporaries, which Joe said was perfectly judged.

HW then left the Cabinet and started to see a relay of visitors he had to inform personally – Ron Hayward from Transport House; Len Murray and Jack Jones from the TUC; Cledwyn Hughes and Frank Barlow (the chairman and secretary of the parliamentary Labour Party) to discuss the election arrangements – I talked to them in the waiting-room and they were completely bewildered. They wondered if they had to get it over with all in one day. I told them it should be done leisurely and with dignity. I said that HW's long and remarkable premiership should not end in a mad scramble.

For a while I sat outside the Cabinet talking to Douglas Wass, who was aware that the Chancellor's chances had not been improved by his performance in last week's economic debate. He was also worried about the preparation of the Budget.

I saw my Policy Unit members and told them. They were shocked – I thought Gavyn Davies would faint. Then I saw Thimont from the Civil Service Department – arranged by me weeks ago – to discuss the contractual position of my staff. We shall all get dismissal notes within the next few days. When HW goes to the Palace we cease to be employed – and qualify for three months' redundancy pay.

The PM had lunch in the flat.

We ate in No. 10 as usual. The atmosphere was subdued. I felt very flat. Having waited for this moment and built up to it, the climax is over. The next couple of weeks will drag.

We went over to Questions as usual. Briefing was not very serious.

The PM got a subdued cheer as he went into the Chamber. His Questions were devoted almost entirely to speeches of congratulations.

Heath was superb. But Thatcher got it wrong again, graceless, with some snide petty points and a call for a general election, which clearly embarrassed many on her own side.

[Edward Heath said: 'Any man who has been able to lead his party successfully as you have for thirteen years, to be Prime Minister for eight years, having won four general elections, deserves the fullest tributes for his achievement.']

After Questions I came back to No. 10 and discussed the situation with the staff.

Carol came in at 6.45 with Brian and Susanna Knox, who were taking us to the opera. In fact I stayed on at No. 10 and missed the first two acts of Szymanowski's *King Roger*. There was too much buzzing for me to leave.

At 4 p.m. we went to the farewell press conference in the Ministry of Defence. HW was jaunty and relaxed, announcing that he forgave the press for their sins against him. But it was not special, just another press conference, with no new insights.

I finally went to the opera at 9 p.m. and afterwards we went to an Italian restaurant and came home well after midnight.

So it has happened. Everybody was stunned. Nobody in the press expected it – when Joe told the lobby they were totally silenced.

In that sense it was a successful operation. It is good because HW had exhausted himself. He has nothing else to give: just like an old boxer shadow-boxing. He knows the moves and goes through the motions, but he has lost his punch and the appetite to fight.

Marcia lost this final and very important battle to keep him on the treadmill.

It is a sad time for Joe, who has no job to go to and whose life has been devoted to Harold Wilson for the past seven years. I fear that HW will drop him like a used glove – cheerio at the door and not another word or kind action. [Sadly this did happen.]

For me it is satisfactory. Two tumultuous years. Much pain, distress and exhaustion. My back under constant knife attack from off-stage. But in the end a fascinating job done – and the Unit with a good reputation. Nick Stuart and Ken Stowe both came separately to me today and said that they sincerely hoped that HW's successor would keep the Unit going because it provided something a PM needed.

When I left the PM had finished a long list of interviews, and had the press office up to the study for a drink. Later, Bill Housden told me, HW went round to George Weidenfeld's, and there had another row with Marcia. She kept interrupting and shouting at him. He told her again that she was the reason he was going. She said she was going home and was taking his car. He said she could go home but could not have his car. So she went into the next room to weep, and ordered a car.

HW told both Albert and Bill today that he would be happy to pay her salary of £4,000 a year if she would stay away and never come in to do any work. But of course he does not mean it. Otherwise he would not have gone over to see her on Saturday for two and a half hours of constant rowing.

## *Wednesday 17 March 1976*

I feel very dead this morning. All momentum gone. Have worked so long to make sure that HW stuck to his guns – now he has done so I realise that I am out of a job.

The PM was seeing Frank Schon and Joe Kagan this morning. According to Albert, about Tony Field's business interests. He then went to the PLP on the Budget.

I came in late and did very little.

Went to lunch with the French Ambassador. Others there were Bryan Hopkin and Lawrence Airey from the Treasury and various Frenchmen. A small meal with superb food. I declined to speak my bad French. The other English people spoke it – but appallingly.

Returned for the Cabinet committee on Economic Strategy (MES) – which was on the most important economic strategy paper of the year (further 10% devaluation and £1.5 billion reflation). I talked to Crosland beforehand about the leadership election. He was surprisingly optimistic, basing his hopes on the 1974 intake. He said that his main target was 'to beat Roy on the first ballot'. I cannot imagine it will happen.

Outside the Cabinet Room sat a most embarrassed group of ministers – almost all candidates. Callaghan, Foot, Benn and Jenkins. Healey came bouncing up, and he will certainly stand in the end. Jenkins asked him if he were keeping them guessing or keeping himself guessing. Healey said a bit of both. He is said to be paralysed. His friends in the Commons have told him that he will get annihilated. But if he does not stand that is humiliating capitulation. He is 59, and it is now or never.

But it looks all sewn up for Callaghan. This evening he had a long talk with HW at the Commons. HW reported that Jim was so confident of victory that he was 'almost preparing to come and measure up for new curtains at No.10'. HW shared that confidence. He also told Callaghan about the Policy Unit and strongly advised him to continue it. HW later told Ken Stowe, who supported this view. HW asked for various papers on the Policy Unit so he could give Jim the details.

Ken Stowe raised with HW the question of Tom McNally, Jim's special adviser, and suggested he might take Marcia's place as political secretary. Ken says HW smiled and said, 'No. There isn't really a job there. Nothing to do.'

Jim has told HW that he would continue to run the Foreign Office himself with Merlyn Rees as a stop-gap Foreign Secretary, until Healey has completed his Budget and incomes policy, when Healey would go to the FO.

This is interesting, that he would not put Jenkins there. But who to the Treasury to succeed Healey? Crosland?

The question now troubling Ken Stowe is the resignation honours list. This is supposed to be a small list of those who have worked personally for the PM. But Marcia has a book – which Albert has seen – which contains an enormous long list of names – with a lot of show-biz characters such as Lew Grade and David Frost as well as Weidenfeld. It includes people already committed to pay HW and MF for books and TV series.

It is her last chance to influence honours and she is going for the lot. But Ken told me that he won't have it. He is worried what a successor would think. So there is a big battle ahead. HW is trying to slip it through before he leaves but there is bound to be trouble.

In the evening HW was at the House, giving an interview to Jimmy Margach of the *Sunday Times* and then John Cole of the *Observer*. I went over to see Roy Jenkins. It was not satisfactory. His supporters were coming in and out to discuss tactics – Phillip Whitehead saw me and it is bound to get out that I was with him. Roy's mind was on other things. He is confident that his bandwagon is beginning to move. He kept asking if Healey would stand. After half an hour I left. He has much more important things to do.

I wouldn't mind him winning – but he won't. He might even be third after Callaghan and Foot. Actually Callaghan would probably be best for both the country and the party.

I called back in No. 10 at 8.30 but everybody had gone home. Even the private secretaries were gone. It was a dead house. The engine was stopped. Many lights were out.

The PM told me earlier that he felt 'very relieved'. He looks relaxed and well. But what on earth will he do with himself in the years ahead?

## Thursday 18 March 1976

I arrived before Cabinet. Talked to Crosland, who said his main ambition is to beat Jenkins on the first ballot and that he hopes to get support from the 1974 intake. We had discussed this briefly yesterday. But his problem is he has too little committed support. He hopes for the 1974 intake because they are uncommitted – or unknown – to the main candidates, or to him, not because they are committed to him. He is coming home to supper on Saturday. I hope this won't be interpreted as my particular support for him as leader, though I admire him greatly as a man; it has been arranged a long time.

I also talked to Elwyn Jones, who said that Harold's resignation was 'tragic'. HW took Cabinet as usual.

Ken Stowe came up to talk to me about the future of the Policy Unit. He said that he and the other private secretaries had held discussions. They had enjoyed working with the Unit, felt it had been a success, hoped it – and I – would continue; and that Ken would advise a new Prime Minister accordingly. I was very moved. I told him that I had made arrangements to go back to the LSE if necessary, so the new PM would have a free hand. Also that I had deliberately not replaced staff who left or went part-time. So it would be quite easy for a new PM to abolish the Unit, or keep it, and change it as he went along. Ken asked for a paper on the Unit, including details of the staff, and I sat down and drafted this.

We had lunch in No.10. I felt very subdued. Joe was obviously unwell, with a heavy cold, as well as nervous about his future. The strain is really beginning to show and he is suffering from nose-bleeding.

After lunch Carol came in to collect me and we went with Rachel to an interview at her new comprehensive school. Afterwards I came home and looked after the children.

The life and action has gone out of No.10 and the days begin to drag. The flow of papers has been cut off. We are a lame-duck presidency. Issues are being held over till the new man comes in. The private secretaries sit round gossiping. My staff are edgy and uncertain of their future. I now want it all to end quickly. It looked as if it might at first, with Jim Callaghan miles ahead. But now Healey is entering the race that makes a difference – he will pick up some of Jim's soft-middle support.

This morning Ken told me that last night HW had a long talk with Callaghan recommending he keeps the Policy Unit. Jim is very confident. The Whips also have had a canvass which shows Jim comfortably ahead. I hope the Healey intervention does not alter that. Despite his disadvantages in the leadership campign – aged 62, and a sense of déjà vu – Callaghan will keep us on the Wilson course, holding the party and unions behind the economic policies until we get inflation down. After that it would be nice to have a little more vision. Until that, it would be crazy to rock the boat.

## Friday 19 March 1976

The PM spent overnight at Chequers and went north today.

I saw Ron Spiers from the American embassy at 11. He thinks that Healey could win it.

At midday I went to see my solicitors about settling the *Private Eye* affair – £2,000 and apology and costs.

Then to lunch with Harry Evans. He said the *Sunday Times* staff were very anti-Callaghan. I attacked him for this and persuaded him to modify his editorial.

Back to Whitehall for a committee on Top Pay policy – but it had been called off, without telling me. I am a lame duck too now. I will carry no weight until the future is resolved one way or the other.

I asked Tom McNally to come over this morning because I had some poll figures for him. He came looking very agitated. He said that he had just seen Jim Callaghan and Jim wanted me to know that there was no truth whatsoever in the rumour in today's *Guardian* that I would be replaced by Tom. In fact I had not seen the *Guardian*. Tom went on to say that Jim wanted him to give me a message: that he would wish me to continue; that I 'must not do anything precipitate – in other words you must be at your desk when Jim comes in'.

He told me that Jim is making no agreements or alliances. That Crosland had 'put out feelers to him' (he would withdraw in exchange for the Treasury, I got the impression) but Jim had rejected them. Jim's strategy was to stay above it all and win without having sold himself in advance. He can leave the others feeling the pressure and making deals which backfire.

I also discussed with Tom what he would do in here. I stressed to him that I was completely relaxed about whether I went or stayed; and that I would help him in every way. He could join the Unit, be in charge of the Unit, or have Marcia's job. He replied that Jim had made an unequivocal offer to me to stay on. 'He is not making the same offer to Marcia,' he added with a wide grin.

I stayed on in the evening talking to Andrew Graham about preparing a general brief for the new PM. Then I went through the passageway to the Chief Whip's Office in No.12. I don't know why. I just felt a desire to wander along there.

Freddie Warren, who runs the Chief Whip's Office, and has done so for many years, sat at his desk in the corner of his room. His desk was covered with papers and bottles and glasses. There was an empty champagne magnum. Two half-empty whisky bottles. Freddie, who looks like an old bird, was fast asleep, upright in his desk chair, his glasses slipped to the end of his nose.

The policeman who was escorting me woke him up. Freddie saw me, immediately perked up, and said, 'Have a drink.' He poured me and himself enormous whiskies and started chattering. He said, 'Let's send for the gals,' pressed a button, and in came Dot, his delightful secretary, who has worked for him for nearly twenty years – Ted Heath was Chief Whip when they came.

Warren was sloshed, but completely intelligent in all he said. His body seemed inert, but his eyes were bright and his mind clear.

He talked about the job of previous Chief Whips. He likes Mellish, but finds the extent to which his Catholicism comes before everything else worrying. He said that if Shirley Williams wants something, that will come before the PM's wishes because she is a Catholic. He also said that everything has come to a halt because of the leadership change, and that Mellish is worried about the future.

He said that Mellish declined the job at Transport last June because he wanted to be Leader of the House and when not offered that he wouldn't take anything else.

Warren talked about patronage and honours. He said that Joe and I should have 'something big'. I said that we would not take anything from HW.

He then told me something very intriguing. He said that in the old days the Whip's Office handled quite a lot of patronage – after all the Chief Whip is the Patronage Secretary. But in 1966 this was taken from the Chief Whip by the Prime Minister, Harold Wilson. Patronage was taken into No. 10. He said, 'That gal Marcia insisted on it.'

He said that 'no other Whip' than John Silkin, the young new Chief Whip then, would have agreed to it – and implied that Silkin was only given the job on that condition. So it does seem that the Lady started on her career of controlling and disposing of patronage ten years ago!

I came home, carrying too much whisky, at 11.15 p.m.

## Saturday 20 March 1976

Tony Crosland came home to dinner, with Susan. Immensely, but endearingly, indiscreet. Savagely against Jim Callaghan. Obvious that his wife Susan is pressing him to stand. He has doubts. Asked me what I think – I say stand, but be prepared to be annihilated. Must stand to demonstrate his seriousness. He got angry when I would not reveal whom I or HW supported.

Joe phoned. Very depressed because HW is now up for sale for television interviews, etc. He is giving one to Chalfont – who resigned from the party last election to try to damage us. Marcia had lunch with him last week.

And when HW agreed to go on *Weekend World* TV programme this Sunday, David Frost phoned to protest, saying that he had already bought the exclusive TV rights to Harold Wilson – even while he is still in office.

Joe is deeply offended by the sight of the PM being offered for sale like any other commercial product.

## Monday 22 March 1976

Long dragging week ahead – with only the first ballot on Thursday. We wanted the elections to be dignified and not too hurried; but this is perhaps too leisurely.

The PM went to the Liaison committee and apparently they said very nice things about him. Then he went off directly from Transport House to the *Financial Times* for lunch.

I had a very rushed day.

A meeting of the Top Pay policy committee. Anthony Rawlinson from the Treasury has now joined it and we are beginning to make some progress – dropping quite a lot of the guff from the last paper.

I dashed back to No. 10 because we had to circulate to ministers our paper on selling council houses by 4.30 p.m. The PM had decided to go ahead with this – in Cabinet committee on Wednesday – and we have to circulate our paper 48 hours ahead. Gavyn Davies did an excellent first draft. We worked on it before lunch – in the Cabinet Office canteen – and then had a terrible rush to get it away in time. But it was quite good.

David Frost came in to see the PM about his TV commitments.

Then at 5 o'clock the Cabinet committee on the future of the film industry met. Everybody knew this was a farce. The PM actually described it as his 'leaving present' – he said that '£7.75 million' (the amount of grant) is 'not much for my leaving present'.

Joel Barnett from the Treasury completely knocked down the PM's arguments, but conceded the money – he said afterwards he could not 'resist the PM's candour about his motives'.

The PM was very jumpy when the committee talked of taking it to Cabinet and begged them not to do so. In the end they agreed.

Afterwards I went with Joe to the Gromyko reception at Lancaster House, where we had a row with decent John Cole about a nasty piece in yesterday's *Observer* attacking both of us. I also had a long talk with Tom McNally about his plans in No. 10, since we are all confident that Jim will win.

Bill Housden told Joe he draws £125 a week from HW's personal account for Marcia.

We returned from Lancaster House by car and I cleaned up before going to the farewell Cabinet dinner. I went upstairs to one of the bathrooms on the private secretaries floor and stripped off to wash and shave – mainly to freshen myself up.

We all gathered upstairs in the pillared white reception-room – the 23 Cabinet ministers plus John Hunt and Burke Trend (the present and previous Cabinet Secretaries), Douglas Allen as head of the Civil Service, Ken Stowe, Marcia, Joe and myself.

After some champagne we filed in to the state dining-room – which always depresses me a little with its dark wooden panelling lined with huge portrait paintings – and sat around the table in the same order as at Cabinet – this solved various status problems and especially the question of who would sit on the PM's right (John Hunt). I had a marvellous seat at the head of the table looking down it, so I could see everybody. It was a fascinating occasion. I felt like a fly on the wall. All the ministers were in high spirits, with great joviality. There were few signs of the tensions which the candidates must have been feeling. The table was buzzing with talk and laughter. It really is a remarkable Cabinet.

I sat with Joe, Bob Mellish and John Morris on my right; and Trend, Peter Shore, Tony Benn and Michael Foot on my left.

Trend seemed to have aged. He was very agitated about missing his train to Oxford and in fact left at 9.45 before HW spoke.

HW's speech was not very good. A few jokes and observations written on his menu. Off-the-cuff without having the virtues of sparkling spontaneity. In fact it was a very ragged performance and he lost the attention of his audience. But nobody minded since they were all supporting him on this occasion whatever he said.

Tony Benn then jumped up and read out an exchange of correspondence he had with the BBC in 1965 when they asked him to write HW's obituary. It was quite funny and typical of Benn – totally without nerves or self-concern. I could see that one or two ministers – especially Callaghan – thought it was impertinent of Benn, but on the whole he got away with it because of his brashness and good humour.

Ted Short had made the 'official' reply. Well judged. Brief, simple, no frills, but straight from the heart.

Roy Jenkins rose to say a few words and to tell a story, but he had great difficulty finishing it because Barbara Castle was talking loudly and interrupting him.

Elwyn Jones also told a nice story and then we filed off into the drawing-room (everybody had been paired). There several ministers were openly discussing the election campaign. Lever went off in a corner with Jenkins. Lever has been wavering in his support for Jenkins, but in the end supported him on the first round because, he said, with all his faults, he is the best candidate – the best Prime Minister we did not have. After that he will support Callaghan.

Roy came over to me late in the evening and was very kind, saying how high was the reputation of myself and my Unit. He looked very sad, as if he recognised that he will not do well enough to stay on long after the first ballot. But he was still charming and impressive to talk to. I felt very depressed. It would be marvellous to run the Unit under him.

We broke up towards midnight. I went home with Harold Lever and we had tea for an hour. Diane came in from the opera and joined us while we chewed over this fascinating situation. We both believe it will be Callaghan, are very content with that, and accept without too much concern that he may not wish to keep either of us on since we are both personal to Harold Wilson. Lever has often felt personally snubbed by Roy and resents it, but in the end he is a Jenkins man.

I returned home shortly before 1 a.m., feeling very exhilarated. How lucky to have the privilege to attend such an occasion. To have dinner with this, the greatest ever Labour administration, saying goodbye to Harold Wilson, its most outstandingly successful Prime Minister. It could not happen with Attlee or MacDonald since they did not retire in office with a Labour government. It may not happen again.

## Tuesday 23 March 1976

Already a week since the resignation day – it seems an eternity.

As I arrived at No. 10 people were going upstairs for the big joint meeting of the NEC and the Cabinet to discuss industrial policy. I could have attended, but as I saw the horrible Joan Maynard and various fellow trav-elling trade unionists come along the corridor I decided to give it a miss. It was anyway a charade – promised at the NEC to delay a row threat-ening there until after HW had resigned. Nobody believed it would achieve anything. There will be no serious decisions until a new administration takes over.

In fact Joe went into the meeting in mid-morning and found that HW had left the room. Others drifted away early and not many stayed for the beer and sandwiches lunch. Joe and I went across to the Commons for lunch in the Press Gallery. Joe was very depressed. He feels the hostility of all the journalists and knows it will not be easy for him to get a job in that field.

(Before lunch Cliff Lloyd and Derek Dougan came in to see me about the evidence of the Professional Footballers Association to the Royal Commission on Gambling.)

Questions were flat and the briefing boring – I went out for a walk in the middle. I saw Ian Wrigglesworth* and we had a chat about the campaign. He is a very good young Labour MP, organising for Jenkins. He seemed fairly happy with how things were going. His camp is showing signs of strong hostility to Callaghan, whom they see as much too conservative.

After Questions the PM saw Jeremy Thorpe. I went back to No. 10 and worked on my papers.

Carol came in at 7.30 with my dinner-jacket and I got ready for tonight's big dinner with the Queen. We all went upstairs and drank lots of champagne while waiting for her to come. She was introduced by the PM to everybody – Marcia gave a deep and well-practised curtsey, as only one member of royalty can do to another! The Queen was perfectly dressed, but I thought she looked a little tired and drawn from the pressures of the Snowdon/Margaret divorce problem. Prince Philip stopped and talked with me for five minutes, taking up the conversation we had about Ireland a year ago. Quite impressive that.

Dinner was good, with some 1945 claret and 1931 port. I drank much more than usual and enjoyed the occasion immensely – Patrick Wright's wife was marvellous company, witty and very Irish.

HW made a good short speech, and the Queen was appropriate in reply.

Then we had a very long session in the reception rooms. Nobody could leave till the Queen left and she stayed quite late. She stood near the corner and the distinguished guests were ferried over to her for a few words (Michael Foot for at least fifteen minutes). But Marcia was not conveyed, despite her royal lineage, nor George Weidenfeld, although they hovered nearby expectantly. We heard over the private office network from the Palace that although the Queen did not mind shaking hands with her at the beginning, she did not see any reason to devote time to talking to her.

Some of the guests were not wholly sober. Late in the party Patrick Wright came over to chat and confessed to having celebrated too much. He is also worried that Jim may not keep him on – which would be a great mistake since Patrick is absolutely first-class. While talking to Patrick and observing his symptoms of modest inebriation, I became conscious that I was unable to walk straight. It was quite harmless, but Patrick and I have never celebrated to such an extent at the office. For the first time I asked Carol to drive me home.

It was a delightful and colourful occasion, glittering but not too formal. Everybody was relaxed and there was a great sense of enjoying it. What a two days! I have loved it. I am pleased that it is all over. It is right that Harold Wilson is going now – he has lost all appetite for the job. And it is nice that the end is coming gently – perhaps too gently. These farewells are very pleasant – the problems will come later, when we are still dragging on, but with no more farewell parties to fill in the time.

*Wednesday 24 March 1976*

I woke feeling very tired – and facing another big function: lunch with Gromyko and the Russians. Went in late (the PM was at Transport House with the NEC, helping to defeat the Mikardo motion suggesting that MPs come up for reselection by the local parties every five years).

The Gromyko lunch was fairly boring. I was terribly tired. The speeches were much longer than usual and made worse by having them translated.

The room was littered with curious characters active in East-West trade. Including Lord Plurenden (Rudi Sternberg), who was not on the original guest list but was included at midday at Marcia's insistence (she had summoned him to her room). This was partly because she did not want to sit as arranged next to John Hunt – who was moved right down the table. Partly no doubt because Sternberg asked to be there, wishing to impress the Russians that he still has access to British government. (The Foreign Office have told me privately that he is a double agent!)

Afterwards we had the Misc Cabinet committee on Council House Sales, discussing the Policy Unit paper. Crosland opened very depressingly, talking about how we must not upset Labour councillors who don't like the scheme (no mention of the council tenants and Labour supporters who want to buy their council houses). Willie Ross was also totally opposed; Edmund Dell and Harold Lever not very helpful. Then Ted Short spoke very briefly and strongly in favour, followed by Ken Berrill in similar vein.

The PM intervened curiously. He completely abandoned Joe's Scheme A. He also attacked Scheme C. But in the end he summed up strongly in favour and ordered the officials to pursue it positively.

After that, chatting near the PA tape machine, he said he intended to pursue this issue as a back-bencher. He said that the meeting had been a good illustration of why old men should retire – and he specifically referred to Crosland and Ross. He said, 'They made up their minds in 1965 and they have been closed to new ideas ever since.'

Afterwards I saw Graham Greene, who discussed any books Joe and I might write – and also asked me if I would like to be chairman of Guinness Mahon Merchant Bank. He could not promise it, but his family owned it before Lewis & Peat and he thinks it is possible. I declined. It would be exciting and well paid. But I would like to do something more intellectually challenging if possible.

Meanwhile Ron Hayward and several Transport House officials arrived for a non-existent No. 10 reception for party officials. HW had agreed to hold this party as a farewell thank-you to the party organisation and many invitations went out. But then Marcia cancelled it because she received a last-minute invitation to a film premiere tonight and preferred to go to that.

But she forgot to arrange to cancel the invitations. I talked to Ron Hayward who was, understandably, furious.

I went home at 9 p.m. and watched the football on TV.

## Thursday 25 March 1976

In late again. This is the result of demoralisation. The PM has no more committees. The flow of paper has dried up. We are lame ducks with little to do. So immediately one feels tired, gets up late, goes to the office late, and generally falls apart. That is why I want this long election procedure to end: and either to get on with some work or to get out.

The PM had lunch with Lord Ryder (whose future at the National Enterprise Board seems even more in doubt, as the Department of Industry secretly prepares to get rid of him) and Jimmy Goldsmith. The latter was there at Marcia's insistence. He promised HW (who subsequently told Joe – adding 'Paris is worth a Mass') that he would make Marcia a director of some company connected with Cavenham Foods. It is not yet clear what honour he requires in return. [He expected a peerage and was disappointed with a knighthood.]

Questions were boring again – and briefing almost non-existent, since the PM did not come across till five minutes past three.

The only feature was HW making a savage attack on the Liberal MP Cyril Smith (who was not present). HW is using these final Question Times to pay off old scores – Heffer, Skinner, Tebbit, Smith . . .

HW has told Marcia that when he goes he wants to lead his own life and her to lead hers – I will believe it when I see it.

I went back to No. 10 and learned the result of the first leadership ballot at before 5 p.m. (it was to be declared at 6 p.m.). Jim had less than we expected, and Roy, and Benn more. Benn announced his withdrawal in favour of Foot (giving him 127 votes) and it suddenly looked as if Foot had a chance of a bandwagon victory.

I went upstairs to the reception for the Commonwealth Parliamentary Association. I talked to HW about developments on the ballot and the pressure it put on the right wing. He was very uncharitable about Jenkins.

Dear Arthur Bottomley took me on one side and asked if I was interested in his seat when he retires. His union NUPE are not very keen on their candidates so far. Arthur is a very kind and decent man – the best of the old Labour tradition. He is somebody else who was immensely loyal to HW and then was dropped totally.

I left the reception with Jack Ashley and went to the House of Commons to join Alf Morris for drinks and supper. It was a very exciting time with rumours and reports from the battlefield – especially when Jenkins announced his withdrawal. There was great relief on the right wing then. We saw Roy Hattersley and Tom McNally and they admitted to having been depressed by the low initial poll of Jim and the threat of a Foot band-wagon now he had Benn's votes. But the Jenkins votes (not all of them: some would go to Healey) could help Jim to win in the end.

I also saw Gerry Fowler, Frank Judd, Norman Buchan, and had dinner at the table next to Tony Benn – he was in his shirt-sleeves, with his wife Caroline, and two bearded young men, but I did not see any tea mug.

Jack and Alf were delightful as ever, and keen to give support to keeping the Unit on. Alf voted for Jim. Jack voted for Jenkins, and will vote for Jim next time.

(Helene Hayman voted for Michael Foot – but will probably switch next round.)

I talked to Ian Wrigglesworth, who had just come from the Jenkins meeting. Roy had argued for withdrawal. Two or three opposed but the others saw that it was the only thing to do. He might have lost votes on the next round – this way at least he can say that he was third on the first ballot and that he withdrew with dignity and honour so that the party can get it all over with and end the suspense.

Home at 10.30.


*Friday 26 March 1976*

The PM went home to Chequers with Joe last night. He did not say very much and said nothing about what Joe would do afterwards – other than to offer to telephone Barnetson of United Newspapers.

Late last night Jim Callaghan phoned HW at Chequers. He is being pressed by his advisers to go on TV and do something positive to tip the final votes. They have lost their nerve. Jim wanted HW's advice. HW told him quite rightly to keep his nerve and not to do anything silly.

Cabinet met this morning to discuss Europe and the European elec-tions. I came in late again and did not see the PM at all. (He saw Goodman later and then went off to see his proposed new office just off the Embankment near Transport House.)

I went to lunch with the *Guardian* – Peter Gibbings, the chairman and Peter Preston, the editor. Very pleasant and lively. Both very nice and Preston more impressive now he is on his own.

Then to the NUT to pick up Carol and home early – 3.30 – to collect the children. Seems years since I last came home in the light.

Feel very detached and not particularly keen to continue even if Jim asks. The prospect of fresh challenges in the outside world is quite attractive. But no doubt I will stay on, if only till the end of the summer.

## Monday 29 March 1976

I went to Manchester for the weekend to play in a marvellous charity football game at Stalybridge involving a lot of Manchester United and Manchester City professional players. I played in the back line with two former internationals, Dave Mackay and Nobby Stiles, and had another international Mike Summerbee in front of me. On the other side were Tommy Docherty, Tony Book and Mick Doyle. A crowd of 5,000 on a lovely day. And I had a good game. Euphoria afterwards!

Came up on the train with the Labour MP Tom Pendry this morning, feeling rather stiff (Docherty's stud marks are deep in my thigh!).

Straight to lunch with Bob Worcester.

Drifted through the afternoon. Saw Victor Rothschild at 6 o'clock about the Royal Commission on Gambling. He also offered me a job with Rothschilds! I will wait and see.

In the evening was the PM's party for the Labour Party helpers – delayed from last week. Except that Marcia had drawn up the list and it was full of her Tory friends from showbiz, some of whom are clearly on the record for having denounced HW politically.

Some of the Labour people were snubbed by not being invited – including Jean Denham from the press office, who was formerly with Transport House and has helped in eight general elections.

I chatted to Tony Benn, who was charming and said to me disingenuously, 'I thought this was a Labour party, so I brought my camera; but when I saw who was here I decided not to take any pictures.' He is perceptive and can be very funny.

It was mainly rich people and stage entertainers, many of whom have frequently denounced Harold.

I am so glad that Harold is going. This awful triviality is too much.

Home at 10 p.m.

## Tuesday 30 March 1976

The devolution Cabinet committee was cancelled. I did some clearing up in case tonight's ballot produces a firm result. I went up to the study and had a talk with HW – including inviting him to our Unit party tonight. He said again how relieved he feels it is all over. He does not seem particularly interested in what is going on now. Just as if he has cast off all interest with the burden.

Lunch at No.10. Ken Stowe and Joe are very depressed about the resignation honours list situation. HW is keeping it close to himself and we all
have fears about the kind of people who will be rewarded.

We set off to walk over to the Commons for what will be HW's last
Question Time. HW saw us leaving through the front door and called after
us to travel with him in the car. So HW, Joe and I set off for the last time
together along Downing Street, down the bottom of Whitehall, across the
south side of Parliament Square and swung into the main yard of the Palace
of Westminster – very appropriate in view of the storms which we have
come through together in the last two years.

Joe reported that John Silkin had told him that he believed Michael
Foot would win on this second ballot. HW grinned and said, 'That will
look like a bad miscalculation on my part.' He also said that he did not
trust Silkin's judgement.

The briefing was fairly frivolous, with much drinking and jokes about
my football game on Sunday at Stalybridge.

I wandered out in the middle and chatted to Frank White, the Labour
MP who refereed in Sunday's game, and Roger Stott,* who played on the
wing. There were some ribald comments about my robust tackling.

Also saw Ray Carter, who is a Callaghan man and deserves to benefit if
Jim wins.

Questions went as always. But not at all serious. The Tories are not
interested in him any more. But Thatcher put in a very heavy and humourless question and HW put the boot in return. He said afterwards that he
felt she had slipped a lot lately and would 'never get the feel of the House'.

After further farewell drinks – Madeira for us and back to the brandy
for HW – we filed back to No.10.

I was working in my office later when Joe came up, very depressed. He
has seen the resignation honours list. Some fifty names for peers and
knighthoods all in Marcia's handwriting on a sheet of lavender-coloured
notepaper and simply ticked by HW. It is a most odd list, led by David
Frost and John Vaizey. Joe and I know the reason for the proposed peerages in most cases.

The only action HW took was to strike out Will Camp. Ironically he is
the only one of them who ever did any political work for HW – though
not much, very briefly in an election campaign. HW thought he was too
close to *Private Eye*.

Among the proposed knighthoods are John Terry from the film industry,
Jarvis Astaire, the boxing promoter, and Jimmy Goldsmith. And two people,
Gosling and Hobson from National Car Parks, whom I have met at a gathering of people helping with the political office. [Hobson refused the offer
of a knighthood.]

There are other peerages – Kagan, Weidenfeld, Sternberg, Illtyd Harrington, and the showbiz tap-dancing brothers Lew Grade and Bernard Delfont – who will all create interest if not astonishment. The political office trust is well represented.

[Harold Wilson's resignation honours list, published on 27 May 1976, contained 42 names. There were nine Life Peers, including Sir Joseph Kagan, Sir George Weidenfeld, John Vaizey, Sir Bernard Delfont, Sir Lew Grade, Sir Joseph Stone and Albert Murray. The nine knighthoods included John Terry, Stanley Baker and John Mills from the film industry, and the businessmen James Goldsmith, James Hanson, Eric Miller, Donald Gosling and Sigmund Sternberg. MBEs went to Peggy Field and William Housden. Joe Haines and the author were not on the list, nor was anyone from the Downing Street Policy Unit.]

My Unit's party started at 5.15 in order to get the leadership election result at 5.30 – when HW was supposed to arrive. But Albert came to announce that Marcia had decided to hold an office party at the same time as mine and HW had to go to that. She presented four of her staff with jewelled bracelets as rewards for their long and loyal service. In fact, according to Albert, Eric Miller gave her five bracelets for this purpose. Eric is going to get a knighthood.

The Unit party went very well. John Hunt, Ken Berrill, private office, former private secretaries such as Robert Armstrong and Robin Butler all came and we had a great time. The ballot result was good – Jim ahead, Healey with only 38, and Foot decided to fight on to the next ballot next Monday. But it did mean another six days in limbo.

HW sent a stream of messages saying he was coming to the Unit party in five minutes, but Marcia held on. When her party broke up, she followed him to the study and kept him there for half an hour.

Eventually Harold came to our party at 7.30 p.m.! Two hours late. By now most of the guests were happily drunk – but nowhere near as under the weather as HW. He was walking slowly and heavily, his face vacuous and his eyes glazed. Still he came, and he talked to the members of the Unit for three-quarters of an hour and that was very nice. When he left he walked through the door and looked totally lost. He has no sense of direction at all. He turned back and asked Janet to show him the way back to private office – some ten yards down the passage.

HW then went to private office and discussed giving an honour (a CH) to himself with Ken and Janet. They also – as I overheard – tried to get him to take a more responsible attitude to his resignation list, but he was not prepared to listen. He is suicidal. He doesn't seem to care about the reaction to this final and scandalous use of patronage. He just wants to be rid of the whole thing and to buy off some peace with Marcia.

I went home feeling fed up with the whole business and unable to wait until it all ends.

## Wednesday 31 March 1976

The PM was having briefing for the Heads of Government meeting tomorrow in Luxembourg, so I did not bother to go in early.

Lunch at the Athenaeum with Robert Armstrong, who is keen to catch up on all the gossip. He is still very biting about John Hunt.

I went home early in the afternoon. But first talked to Ken Stowe about the honours. Marcia had suggested that one of my Unit have an honour – but not me, obviously as a way of snubbing me. Ken and Joe were outraged, and Ken went to speak to the PM. HW then said he meant to offer me something too – much higher. I told Ken I would turn it down – nothing would induce me to join this particular circus – but I wouldn't mind being offered just as a show of appreciation. Apparently HW says he is firmly going to offer me something. I stated that if anybody from the Unit were to have anything it should be Brenda, my marvellous secretary. Andrew, Gavyn and David also deserve acknowledgement for their marvellous work, and I told Ken that.

In the evening I went to the opera to see *Carmen*, which was lovely.

## Thursday 1 April 1976

The PM is off to Luxembourg – a real farce since he is not in the least interested.

I called in at my solicitors to settle the final details of my libel action against *Private Eye*.

Then to lunch with Harold Lever, who is rather worried in case he loses his job under the next PM. (Lever voted for Jenkins on the first ballot and Healey on the second.) He was very savage about HW, and especially his lack of standards or principles.

He told me the final story about Marcia's brother, Tony Field's £60,000 tax bill.

HW took him on one side and asked him to arrange for Lever's own private bank to have an anonymous account, into which certain people would pay money, and from which the tax bill would be paid.

Lever agreed. Then it was changed. The bank would loan the £60,000 to Tony, and receive as collateral his slag-heaps land. The interest would be paid and guaranteed by these same people – who were led by Frank Schon, and Lever thinks included Rudi Sternberg and Kagan. Lever told his bank only to do it on strictly commercial terms and without any element of political favour.

Schon then came to see him and said that he could not guarantee the interest payments for ever, but only for a few years. Lever said OK – but sign a covenant to buy the debt. Schon said that he did not want to have his name openly involved.

The bank then told Lever that the land is worthless.

Lever then said he would not do it because he could not be involved in other than a straight commercial transaction.

HW then sent for Lever and was very angry with him, saying, 'This is only a book-keeping transaction for you.' But Lever would not yield.

That was the last Lever heard of it. It seems to have been settled. Shortly after, Schon got his peerage.

I went back to the office and worked on our briefs for the new PM. Then Ray Richardson came in and we had a long chat about the future – LSE sounds depressingly parochial these days.

Harry Evans came in for a chat. Drove me some of the way home – rest by bus. Home at 9.30 p.m.

### Friday 2 April 1976

No.10 is like a morgue. No papers. The PM and Jim Callaghan and Joe and private office are away in Luxembourg. In the Policy Unit we are in suspense, uncertain of our future. Everything has come to a halt and there is a strong sense that the main excitements are past.

Anthony Lester came to see me. It is clear that Roy Jenkins did not expect to do as well as his supporters hoped. He expected to get just over 60. Bill Rodgers thought he might get 70–75.

Roy is obviously a bit depressed by it all. He is worried that his authority in the Cabinet has been weakened and he won't be able to get anything through. He is getting very interested in devolution and would like to take that on – but not if his authority is gone. He is thinking about the European presidency in this context. I suggest that he should not take it. It would be a mistake to bow out of English politics now, at his lowest point. He will recover in time.

Anthony Lester says he would not go with Roy to the Foreign Office, because he won't be able to contribute there. I am not sure that Jim will offer him the FO. Jim does not seem to like him – Roy approached Jim after the vote, but was brushed off very firmly.

Had an excellent lunch with Joe Rogaly of the *Financial Times* at Wheeler's. Afterwards I went up to a No.10 bedroom to sleep off the wine. Then David Watt came in for a talk – very pessimistic as usual.

Joe and the private secretaries returned from Luxembourg at around 6.30 p.m. Joe looked terribly tired and ill. I would not be surprised if he had a stroke. The end of his relationship with HW – and the dreadful way in which HW has treated him – has shattered him.

They said that HW had been at his worst on the trip – pompous and patronising and boasting.

Jim had been consulting HW on what to do about this, that and the other when he is in No.10. The FO says that he does little paperwork and does not talk to many people, but is quite decisive. It will be quite a challenge for me. If he trusts me I can have quite a lot of influence, given my experience here. If he shuts me out then I will go quite soon.

The future is very perplexing. It is hard to break my links – and security – with the LSE – but it may be necessary.

This is the end of Harold Wilson's last full week. The end of an era, as everybody says. He has left in great popularity, his undoubted virtues at last appreciated. But his faults are still there. Much was swept under the carpet. And the financial side of things may go wrong at some time, though that is not really his fault since he is personally not the least interested in money, rewards or honours. He has very simple tastes and there is absolutely no grand or pretentious side to him. He deserves to go out with some dignity.

## Monday 5 April 1976

Harold Wilson's last day. No.10 was very subdued. No serious business was going through. private office was quiet, the secretaries sitting at their desks reading newspapers. Nothing was happening in the Policy Unit.

I saw Anthony Lester for an hour in the morning over coffee. If Roy goes to the Foreign Office – as he anticipates but I don't – then Anthony will not go with him. But if he stays happily at the Home Office then he will stay with him, hoping to do more on devolution, which Roy has now strongly taken up. There is also the option of the European President, which neither Anthony nor I are keen on for Roy.

Mid-morning we got a sudden invitation to lunch with HW. He is going to give a farewell lunch. HW made sure that it was for his team in No.10, despite pressures from the political office to bring in outsiders.

I saw HW at the ticker tape and we chatted. He looked relaxed, with his face fatter and fleshier, as if lifting the pressure has taken away some of the edge. He could easily go vegetable, like Churchill. But he stressed how much he was enjoying it and what a relief it was 'not to have to think about my colleagues'. Yesterday there was great publicity for his walk to the pub for a drink with his dog and Mary. This was arranged and the press informed several days in advance, so it can hardly have been a casual spontaneous occasion. Later today I heard Mary say to him that perhaps it would have been better for them to go to church rather than the pub, but he was not impressed, especially since the cameras might not have been able to get in the church.

Incidentally, while we talked at the ticker tape he said to me, 'I don't understand why I am being attacked over the honours list. I have barely ever met half of them.' [Some fairly accurate details of his proposed honours list had appeared in the press.]

We gathered upstairs in the large reception-room – the pillared room – before lunch.

Beforehand he invited me into the Cabinet Room with him and he talked about the books in the bookcases which had been left by previous Cabinet ministers. He chatted on about various former ministers, guessing their birth and death dates. He was also looking for the book of the last Prime Minister to resign voluntarily from the office.

I wondered if this would be the chance for him to offer – and me to refuse – something in the honours list. He had again told Janet that he was definitely going to offer me something 'big', and he gave a similar impression to Ken Stowe. (On Friday he offered Joe a peerage, which was promptly declined.) He rambled on and seemed to be bracing himself for something – or perhaps waiting for me to ask, since Ken had warned him that I would refuse a peerage and he probably did not want to be snubbed. Then a private secretary came in and the moment passed.

Back to the lunch. We all assembled in the pillared room – Harold, Mary, Joe, Janet, Ken Stowe, Patrick Wright, Peggy Field and myself. The sun streamed over Horse Guards Parade and over St James's Park, where the first leaves of spring are showing. It is always very quiet up there, with distant sounds of traffic in the Mall or Whitehall. We stood around and drank and talked quietly. We were waiting for Marcia, who had a guest. The invitation time was 1 o'clock. At a quarter to two she still had not arrived – nor had Albert, who was pouring out the drinks for her and her personal guest. The Prime Minister and his wife, on their last day in 10 Downing Street, at their last meal there as Prime Minister, and his team of close personal staff, were kept waiting three-quarters of an hour by her. Harold Wilson went out as he came in, a remarkable man but too often humiliated and made shabby by this sad association.

We finally went into lunch in the small dining-room. I sat at the end, with Joe and Peg Field (who said, 'You have some steel in you,' when I mentioned my views on her sister). We talked among ourselves. Harold talked genially across the table, but never managed to get everybody else to shut up and listen. He was telling Ken Stowe about his plans to write a quick short book to come out in paperback quickly. He will sit at Grange Farm and write it in long-hand. Marcia was down the other end sitting next to Patrick Wright and exchanging acid remarks with Janet Hewlett-Davies.

It was after 3 o'clock when we broke up. HW went across to the House of Commons to get the ballot result. Before going he asked Joe to get Terry Lancaster of the *Mirror* round there quickly so that he could deny that he had leaked to the *Standard* the story that Roy Jenkins was going to leave politics to become President of Europe. Joe demurred on the grounds that the story was correct – and indeed he knew HW had leaked it to Charles Wintour, the *Standard* editor. So Lancaster was not summoned. But to the end HW was trying to manage the press and plant stories. To the end he was leaking himself and blaming others. Was his purpose in this story to weaken Jenkins in the new Cabinet?

Joe and Ken told me the ballot result early – slightly better for Callaghan than had been expected, though HW predicted the majority – 39 – exactly this morning. Foot had picked up very few of Healey's votes. Most people decided to vote for Jim and tell him they had done so. Even Crosland – who in my house three weeks ago was savagely denouncing Jim as a total disaster.

[The results of the three rounds of the Labour leadership contest were:

| 1st ballot 25/3/1976 | | 2nd ballot 30/3/76 | | 3rd ballot 5/4/76 | |
|---|---|---|---|---|---|
| FOOT | 90 | CALLAGHAN | 141 | CALLAGHAN | 176 |
| CALLAGHAN | 84 | FOOT | 133 | FOOT | 137 |
| JENKINS | 56 | HEALEY | 38 | | |
| BENN | 37 | | | | |
| HEALEY | 30 | | | | |
| CROSLAND | 17] | | | | |

Ken Stowe showed me the document giving the official Whitehall response to HW's proposed resignation honours list. It reported strong objections from the Bank of England, the Home Office and the Inland Revenue to six of those named. [Not all of those subsequently excluded from the proposed honours list were those subject to official objections.]

The resignation list is clearly running into trouble. It will not be ready this week. HW wants to put it out on Thursday week, because there are no papers the next day. Appropriately that is Maundy Thursday.

Joe gave a big farewell party in the press office at 4 o'clock. When I arrived his room was crowded and hot and the drinks were twice finished and had to be replaced. It was very sad for me, seeing Joe's last hour. He seemed strained and drained.

We heard that HW might not come back to No. 10, but was considering going straight to the Palace from the Commons to resign. I went to see Ken Stowe and told him to tell HW this was intolerable. He must come back and say goodbye to his devoted staff in No. 10. He must also come to Joe's party.

HW finally arrived at Joe's room at 5.30, with Marcia. As he entered the room everybody sang 'For He's a Jolly Good Fellow'. I stood quietly out in the corridor with John Hunt. I am not a good singer, and presume the same is true of John.

Harold Wilson then walked back to the front hall, waited till the car and everything was ready to go to the Palace and walked out through the front door waving to the crowd. He did not turn to wave goodbye to the scattered staff inside. (Including Marcia, who stood stiffly with tears welling up in her eyes. Her party is over.)

He had not even looked in to private office to say thanks and goodbye to the secretaries and duty clerks who had slaved all hours and weekends, rarely seeing their wives and children, to serve him.

He just walked out, slightly stooped, brushing back his grey hair, a plump little man in a crumpled suit apparently casting aside without a second thought or backward look the office, the house, which is the supreme object of many politicians' dreams and ambitions. It, we, had served our purpose. As Bill Housden says, sadly nothing sticks with him. No relations seem to matter beyond their current utility. Only today's and tomorrow's headlines matter. No regrets. No proud memories. No lasting traces. Ultimately, he sees himself, as he sees others, in his own words, as 'a ship that passes in the night'.

Yet despite all these reservations, which are sharpened and perhaps made more jagged by the tensions of our final hours together as a team in Downing Street, I was deeply moved as I watched Harold Wilson leave for the last time through the big black door of No.10. Despite all the irritations and frustrations of working for him, he is basically a nice kind man. And a remarkable politician – though in my time with him his great political virtues and skills were too often blunted and tangled up in the brambles of his own personal inhibitions, and especially the cross-pressures from others, to allow him to perform to his own full potential. He carried too much heavy luggage from the past. This prevented him from fulfilling the expectations of the great office he held, or for that matter even enjoying it. This also often prevented me from respecting him as much as a man with his great political ability and record deserved.

In fact I felt sorry for him as I watched him go, in an affectionate and

I hope in a completely unpatronising way. I don't know how he will cope in the real world of non-politics outside, after a lifetime of political power and fantasy. He won't know what to do with his time without the automatic flow of papers and business, and the support scaffolding of secretaries, drivers, etc. which is provided at the top of politics and government. He has too few genuine interests of his own, inside him, to keep him interested when he is on his own. He cannot go back to being an active backbencher. And I am not sure about his health, after all those heart murmurs. He will be lost. I don't know that he has many real friends – who will stick by him now that he no longer has real power, influence and glamour. Certainly Marcia won't allow him to see Joe or me now he has no need of our work. He will need Mary. She has the kind of solid north-country virtues which can be relied on to be there with him and support him when the hangers-on have deserted the ship.

Jim Callaghan had meanwhile gone from the Commons to Transport House and there waited the call from the Palace once Harold had kissed hands and left. I received a phone call from Tom McNally saying that he and John Cunningham,* Jim's very able PPS, would be arriving at the back door and asking me to let them in. So I stood down there waiting in Horse Guards Parade in the spring sunshine, everything quiet and normal, in contrast to the pandemonium of political commerce and journalists and tourists in Downing Street.

Tom McNally and John Cunningham did not arrive on time. A large black Rover came speeding up and braked in a cloud of gravel and dust. Out leapt Ken Stowe back from the Palace saying, 'Come on in, Jim is on his way and he is ahead of me.'

I paused and decided not to go in yet. Somehow it seemed presumptuous of me to be there clapping in the new man. I waited a few minutes and then walked down the garden path – first locking the back gate – in through the back door and up the familiar stairs. Mr Callaghan was already in and had gone up to the study.

I went to Joe's room. It was empty except for the litter of empty bottles and ashtrays. Joe had gone home for the last time, without our saying goodbye, also without seeing Jim come in. That left a gap which I felt almost like a sharp pain. His friendship, loyalty, shrewd political judgement and above all sense of fun had alone made it a pleasure to work here. Without his support I would probably have succumbed to the hostile crossfire long ago.

I went out into the corridor just as Tom McNally and John Cunningham – smart, straight and politically shrewd – arrived. I showed them to Marcia's room and recommended Tom to take it. Then I took them on a tour of the rest of the house so that they got a feel for it.

It was fascinating to see the new men coming in, as Joe and I did two years ago, full of excitement and a sense of power, not quite believing in it, being a bit obstreperous and humorously throwing their weight about, but understandably, really only testing their wings.

Tom McCaffrey quickly moved into Joe's office, but will have difficulty filling his place in No. 10. He told me that he wanted to sack Janet, Gerry and Matthew from Joe's staff. But he was worried about sacking Janet in case it was taken as a bash at Joe. So he will offer her demotion and wait for her to go of her own accord. Tom is beaming at everybody. He is quite open. He has waited for this power for 20 years and is going to enjoy it. But I didn't feel completely comfortable with him.

The new Prime Minister was already in the study and sent for the two Toms and John Cunningham to discuss his television speech. I went up, knocked, and walked in and after a while began to offer my views. He was very responsive. Finally he decided to sit down and redo it – shorter, and with more emphasis on restoring the traditional values. He told us all to get out and then redid it on his own.

Then he went into the pillared room and did his broadcast at the first attempt. I sat on the settee watching with Mrs Callaghan in the blue room. We discussed living in the flat at No.10 and I advised her against. She is intelligent and nice. She was very proud and supportive watching her husband in his first performance. That was good to see.

We all wandered around afterwards and then Jim announced he was going home – back to the flat in Kennington – to bed. This was about 9.45. I went to have a drink with the two Toms and then I went home too. We had changed trains without too many hitches.

But this was an unreal day. Only from tomorrow will we get back to government and find out what the new man is really like – and how he will run No.10.

# List of Persons Mentioned in the Diary

(Names with biographies are marked with a star in the Diary.)

**Acland, Sir Antony**
(1930–) PPS to the Foreign Secretary, 1972–75; head of Diplomatic Service, 1982–86; Ambassador to Washington, 1986–91.

**Adamson, Sir Campbell**
(1922–2000) Director-general of the CBI, 1969–76.

**Aitken, Sir Max**
(1910–85) Conservative MP for Holborn, 1945–50; director and chairman of Beaverbrook Newspapers, 1968–77.

**Aldington, Lord (Toby Low)**
(1914–2000) Conservative MP for Blackpool North, 1945–62.

**Alexander, Andrew**
Then City editor of the *Daily Mail*.

**Allen, Sir Douglas (later Lord Croham)**
(1917–) Permanent secretary at the Treasury, 1966–74; head of the Civil Service, 1974–77.

**Allen, John Schofield**
Worked for Wilson in 1964–70 government and courtier of Marcia Williams.

**Andrews, Sir Derek**
(1933–) Private secretary to the Prime Minister, 1966–70; under-secretary at the Ministry of Agriculture, Food and Fisheries, 1973; permanent secretary, 1987–93.

**Archer, Peter (later Lord Archer)**
(1926–) Labour MP for Rowley Regis, 1966–74, and for Warley West, 1974–92; Solicitor General, 1974–79.

**Armstrong, Ernie**
(1915–96) Labour MP for NW Durham, 1964–87; under-secretary at the DES, 1974–75 and at the Department of the Environment, 1975–79.

**Armstrong, Robert (later Lord Armstrong of Ilminster)**
(1927–) Principal private secretary to Edward Heath (as Prime Minister), 1970–74 and to Harold Wilson, 1974–75; deputy under-secretary at the Home Office, 1975–77; secretary of the Cabinet, 1979–87.

**Armstrong, William (later Lord Armstrong of Sanderstead)**
(1915–80) Official head of Home Civil Service, 1968–74; chairman of Midland Bank, 1975–80.

**Ashby, Eric (later Lord Ashby)**
(1904–92) Master of Clare College, Cambridge, 1959–75.

**Ashley, Jack (Lord Ashley)**
(1922–) Labour MP for Stoke-on-Trent South, 1966–92; PPS to the Secretary of State at the DHSS, 1974–76.

**Astaire, Jarvis**
(1923–) Boxing promoter, businessman and Muhammad Ali's tour manager in the 1960s and 70s; former deputy chairman of Wembley plc and Labour Party donor.

**Astor, David**
(1912–2001) Editor of the *Observer*, 1948–75.

**Balogh, Thomas (later Lord Balogh)**
(1905–85) Fellow of Balliol College, Oxford, 1945–73; Minister of State at the Department of Energy, 1974–75; deputy chairman, BNOC, 1976–78.

**Banks, Tony**
(1943–) Labour MP for Newham NW, 1983–97, and for West Ham, 1997–; member of the GLC, 1970–86; Minister for Sport, 1997–99.

**Bannister, Sir Roger**
(1929–) First person to run a mile in under four minutes, 1954; chairman of the Sports Council, 1971–74.

**Barclay, Clifford**
Accountant, educationalist and close friend of the author.

**Barnett, Joel (later Lord Barnett)**
(1923–) Labour MP for Heywood and Royton, 1964–83; Opposition Treasury spokesman, 1970–74; chief secretary to the Treasury, 1974–79; vice-chairman of the BBC, 1986–93.

**Basnett, David (later Lord Basnett)**
(1924–89) Member of the TUC General Council, 1966–86; general secretary of the General and Municipal Workers' Union, 1973–86.

**Bateman, Sir Ralph**
(1910–96) Deputy president of the CBI, 1973–74; president, 1974–76.

**Benn, Tony**
(1925–) Labour MP for Bristol SE, 1950–60, and for Chesterfield, 1984–2001; Secretary of State for Industry, 1974–75; Secretary of State for Energy, 1975–79.

**Berrill, Sir Kenneth**
(1920–) Chief economic adviser to the government, 1973–74; head of Central Policy Review Staff, 1974–80.

**Birk, Alma (later Baroness Birk)**
(1917–96) Journalist and parliamentarian; under-secretary for the Environment, 1974–79.

**Bish, Geoff**
Head of research at Transport House.

**Blackstone, Tessa (later Baroness Blackstone)**
(1944–) Lecturer, LSE, 1966–75; advised Cabinet Office, 1975–78; Minister of State for Education and Arts, 1997–2003.

**Booth, Albert**
(1928–) MP for Barrow in Furness, 1966–83; Minister of State at the Department of Employment, 1974–76; Secretary of State for Employment, 1976–79.

**Boothroyd, Betty (later Baroness Boothroyd)**
(1929–) MP for West Bromwich, 1973–92; Speaker in the House of Commons, 1992–2000.

**Boston, Terence (later Lord Boston)**
(1930–) Labour MP for Faversham, 1964–70. Assisted Harold Wilson in 1974 election tours, handling baggage and press.

**Bottomley, Arthur (later Lord Bottomley)**
(1907–95) Labour MP, 1945–83, for Teesside, 1974–83; Secretary of State for Commonwealth Affairs, 1964–66; Minister of Overseas Development, 1966–67.

**Boyle, Edward**
(1923–81) Conservative MP for Handsworth, Birmingham, 1950–70; Minister of Education, 1962–4; vice-chancellor of the University of Leeds, 1970–79.

**Bradley, Tom**
(1926–2002) Labour MP for Leicester NE, 1962–74, and for Leicester East, 1974–83; vice-chairman of the Labour Party, 1974–75; president of Transport and Salaried Staffs Association, 1964–77.

**Brandt, Willi**
(1913–92) Mayor of West Berlin, 1957–66; Vice-Chancellor and Foreign Minister of Germany, 1966–69; Chancellor of Germany, 1969–74.

**Brayley, Desmond (later Lord Brayley)**
(1917–77) Under-secretary for Defence, 1974; chairman of Canning Glass, resigned 1974 after Department of Trade inquiries into financial irregularities.

**Brimelow, Tom (later Lord Brimelow)**
(1915–95) Head of the Diplomatic Service, 1973–75.

**Brown, Hugh**
(1919–) Labour MP for Glasgow Provan, 1964–87; parliamentary under-secretary at the Scottish Office, 1974–79.

**Bruce-Gardyne, John (later Lord Bruce-Gardyne)**
(1930–90) Conservative MP for South Angus, 1964–74; PPS to the Scottish Secretary, 1970–72.

**Burnet, Alastair**
(1928– ) Editor of *The Economist*, 1965–74; editor of the *Daily Express*, 1974–76; broadcaster at ITN thereafter.

**Butler, David**
(1924–) Fellow, dean and senior tutor at Nuffield College, Oxford, 1956–64; author of many works on British general elections and the British political climate.

**Butler, Sir Michael**
(1927–) Head of European Community Affairs FCO, 1974–76; deputy under-secretary, FCO, 1976–79.

**Butler, Robin (later Lord Butler)**
(1938–) Private secretary to Edward Heath, 1972–74, and to Harold Wilson, 1974–75; Treasury, 1975–88; secretary of the Cabinet, 1988–98; master, University College, Oxford, since 1998.

**Byers, Frank (later Lord Byers)**
(1915–84) Liberal MP for North Dorset, 1945–50; Liberal leader in the House of Lords, 1967–1984.

**Cairncross, Sir Alec**
(1911–98) Head of the Government Economic Service, 1964–69.

**Callaghan, James (later Lord Callaghan)**
(1912–) Labour MP for South Cardiff, 1945–50, and SE Cardiff, 1950–83; Chancellor of the Exchequer, 1964–67; Home Secretary, 1967–70; Foreign Secretary, 1974–76; Prime Minister, 1976–79.

**Camp, Will**
(1926–2003) Lobbyist and communications consultant to Harold Wilson in the 1970 general election.

**Canavan, Dennis**
(1942–) Labour MP for West Stirlingshire, 1974–1983.

**Carmichael, Kay**
(1925–) Senior lecturer in social work and social administration at Glasgow University, 1974–1980; member of Policy Unit, 1974–76.

**Carr, Robert (later Lord Carr)**
(1916–) Conservative MP for Mitcham, then Sutton, 1950–75; Secretary of State for Employment, 1970–72; Home Secretary, 1972–74.

**Carrier, John**
(1938–) Lecturer in social policy, LSE, and friend of the author.

**Carrington, Peter, Lord**
(1919–) Defence Secretary, 1970–74; Opposition leader in the House of Lords, 1964–70 and 1974–79; Foreign Secretary, 1979–82.

**Carter, Ray**
(1935–) Labour MP for Birmingham, Northfield, 1970–79; parliamentary under-secretary at the Northern Ireland Office, 1976–79.

**Carter-Jones, Lewis**
(1920–2004) Labour MP for Eccles, 1964–87.

**Castle, Barbara (later Baroness Castle)**
(1911–2001) Labour MP for Blackburn, 1944–79; Employment Secretary, 1968–70; Secretary of State for Social Services, 1974–76.

**Channon, Paul (Lord Kelvedon)**
(1935–) Conservative MP for Southend West, 1959–97; Minister for Housing, 1972–74; Opposition spokesman on prices and environmental affairs, 1974–75.

**Chester, Sir Norman**
(1907–86) Academic, author and local councillor; warden of Nuffield College, Oxford, 1954–78.

**Childers, Erskine**
(1905–74) President of Ireland, 1973–74.

**Chirac, Jacques**
(1932–) Prime Minister of France, 1974–76; President of France from 1995.

**Clapham, Sir Michael**
(1912–2002) President of the CBI, 1972–74.

**Clinton-Davis, Stanley (later Lord Clinton-Davis)**
(1928–) Labour MP for Hackney Central, 1970–83; party under-secretary

for Department of Trade, 1974–79; Minister of State at the DTI, 1997–98; European commissioner, 1985–89.

**Cooper, Sir Frank**
(1922–2002) Permanent under-secretary at the Northern Ireland Office, 1973–76; Defence, 1976–82.

**Cosgrave, Liam**
(1920–) Irish Prime Minister, 1973–77.

**Couzens, Sir Kenneth**
(1932–2004) Deputy Secretary, Incomes Policy and Public Finance, Treasury, 1973–77; second permanent secretary, Treasury, 1977–82.

**Cromer, Lord**
(1918–91) Governor of the Bank of England, 1961–66; Ambassador to Washington, 1971–74.

**Crosland, Anthony**
(1918–77) Labour MP for South Gloucestershire, 1950–55, and for Grimsby, 1959–77; Secretary of State for Education and Science, 1965–67; president of the Board of Trade, 1967–69; Secretary of State for Local Government, 1969–70, and for the Environment, 1974–76; Foreign Secretary, 1976–77.

**Crosland, Susan**
Journalist, author and wife of Anthony Crosland (*qv*).

**Crossman, Richard**
(1907–74) Labour MP for Coventry East, 1945–74; leader of the House, 1966–68; Secretary of State for Social Services, 1968–70.

**Crowther-Hunt, Norman (later Lord Crowther-Hunt)**
(1920–87) Fellow and lecturer in politics, Exeter College, Oxford, 1952–82; member of the Commission on the Constitution, 1969–73; Minister of State for Education, 1974–76; Privy Council Office, 1976.

**Cudlipp, Michael**
(1934–2004) Journalist for *The Times* and the *Sunday Times*; consultant on PR to the Northern Ireland Office, 1974–75; National Enterprise Board, 1975–78.

**Cunningham, John**
Labour MP for Whitehaven, 1970–83, and for Copeland, 1983–; PPS to James Callaghan, 1972–76; party under-secretary for Energy, 1976–79; Minister for Agriculture, 1997–98.

**Dahrendorf, Professor Ralf (later Lord Dahrendorf)**
(1929–) Director of the LSE, 1974–84; warden of St Anthony's College, Oxford, 1987–97.

**Davidson, Arthur**
(1928–) Labour MP for Accrington, 1966–83; parliamentary secretary at the Law Offices Department, 1974–79.

**Davies, Denzil**
(1938–) Labour MP for Llanelli, 1970–; PPS to the Welsh Secretary, 1974–76; Minister at the Treasury, 1976–79.

**Davies, Harold (later Lord Davies)**
(1904–85) Labour MP for Leek, 1945–70.

**Davis, Peter (later Lord Lovell-Davis)**
(1924–2001) Public relations adviser to Harold Wilson, 1962–74; Minister of State for Energy, 1975–76.

**Deakins, Eric**
(1932–) Labour MP for Walthamstow, 1970–87; parliamentary under-secretary at the Department of Trade, 1974–76; DHSS, 1976–79.

**Dell, Edmund**
(1921–99) Labour MP for Birkenhead, 1964–79; Paymaster General, 1974–76; Secretary of State for Trade, 1976–79.

**Dewar, Donald**
(1937–2000) Labour MP for South Aberdeen, 1966–70, and for Glasgow, 1978–2000; Scottish Secretary, 1997–99; Scottish First Minister from 1999 until his death.

**Donaldson, John (later Lord Donaldson)**
(1907–98) Under-secretary at the Northern Ireland Office, 1974–76; Arts minister, 1976–79.

**Driberg, Tom (later Lord Bradwell)**
(1905–76) Labour MP for Maldon, 1945–55, and for Barking, 1959–74.

**Ennals, David (later Lord Ennals)**
(1922–95) Labour MP for Dover, 1964–70, and for Norwich North, 1974–83; minister at the FCO, 1974–76; Secretary of State for Social Services, 1976–79.

**Evans, Harold**
(1928–) Editor of the *Northern Echo*, 1961–66; editor of the *Sunday Times*, 1967–81; editor of *The Times*, 1981–82; close friend of the author.

**Field, Tony**
Brother of Lady Falkender.

**Finer, Maurice**
(1917–74) High Court judge; governor of the LSE, 1964–74; chairman of Royal Commission on the Press, 1974.

**Finniston, Sir Monty**
(1912–91) Chairman of British Steel, 1973–76.

**Fisher, Samuel (later Lord Fisher)**
(1905–79) Chairman of the London Labour Mayors' Association from 1953; Mayor of Camden, 1965–66; financier of the political office.

**Fitt, Gerry (later Lord Fitt)**
(1926–) SDLP MP for West Belfast, 1970–83; SDLP leader, 1970–79.

**Fitzgerald, Garrett**
(1926–) Fine Gael MP for Dublin SE, 1969–92; Irish Minister for Foreign Affairs, 1973–77; Taoiseach, 1981–82 and 1982–87.

**Foot, Michael**
(1913–) Labour MP for Devonport, 1945–55, for Ebbw Vale, 1960–83, and for Blaenau Gwent, 1983–92; political columnist, author, biographer and critic; Secretary of State for Employment, 1974–76; leader of the House of Commons, 1976–79; leader of the Labour Party, 1980–83.

**Foster, Sir Christopher**
(1930–) Economist at Oxford and LSE; special economic adviser, DoE, 1974–77.

**Fowler, Professor Gerald**
(1935–93) Lecturer at Oxford, 1958–1965; Labour MP for the Wrekin, 1966–70 and 1974–79; Minister for Education, 1969–70 and 1974–76; close friend of the author.

**Freeman, Catherine**
Ex-wife of John Freeman (*qv*).

**Freeman, John**
(1915–) British Ambassador in Washington, 1969–71; chairman of LWT, 1971–76; chairman of ITN, 1976–81.

**French, Philip**
(1933–) Journalist, film critic on the *Observer* since 1978, and neighbour of the author.

**Frost, Sir David**
(1939–) Television producer and presenter.

**Gilbert, John (later Lord Gilbert)**
(1927–) Labour MP for Dudley, 1970–97; Financial Secretary to the Treasury, 1974–75; Transport minister, 1975–76; Minister of State at the MoD, 1976–79 and 1997–99.

**Gilbert, Sir Martin**
(1936–) Historian and author, Churchill's official biographer and fellow of Merton College, Oxford, 1962–94.

**Gilmour, Ian (later Lord Gilmour)**
(1926–) Conservative MP for Norfolk Central, 1962–74, and for Chesham and Amersham, 1974–92; Defence Secretary, 1974.

**Giscard d'Estaing, Valéry**
(1926–) French Minister of Economics and Finance, 1969–74; President of France, 1974–81.

**Goldsmith, Sir James**
(1933–97) International financier, right-wing politician and friend of Lady Falkender.

**Goodman, Arnold (later Lord Goodman)**
(1913–95) Senior partner, Goodman, Derrick solicitors; legal and general

adviser to Harold Wilson; chairman of the Arts Council, 1965–72, and of the *Observer* Trust, 1967–76.

**Gordon Walker, Patrick (later Lord Gordon Walker)**
(1907–80) Labour MP for Leyton, 1966–74; Foreign Secretary, 1964–65.

**Gormley, Joe (later Lord Gormley)**
(1917–93) President of the National Union of Mineworkers, 1971–82.

**Grant, John**
(1932–2000) Labour MP for Islington East, 1970–74; Parliamentary Secretary for Overseas Development, 1974–76; under-secretary, Department of Employment, 1976–79.

**Greene, Graham Carleton**
(1936–) Publisher, nephew of the author Graham Greene; chairman of Chatto, The Bodley Head and Jonathan Cape, 1970–88; trustee of the British Museum, 1978–2004; close friend of the author.

**Greene, Sidney (later Lord Greene)**
(1910–2004) General secretary of the National Union of Railwaymen, 1957–74; chairman of the TUC, 1969–70.

**Gross, John**
Author, literary and theatre critic and friend of the author.

**Gross, Miriam**
(1939–) Literary editor of various newspapers.

**Hailsham, Lord**
(1907–2001) Conservative Lord Chancellor, 1970–82.

**Haines, Joseph**
(1928–) Political correspondent for the *Sun*, 1964–68; Harold Wilson's chief press secretary, 1969–70 and 1974–76; leader writer, *Daily Mirror*, 1978–90; close friend of the author.

**Hamilton, Sir Denis**
(1918–88) Chief executive of Times Newspapers, 1967–70, and Reuters 1979–85; chairman of Times Newspapers, 1971–80.

**Hamilton, Sir James**
(1923–) Deputy secretary at the Cabinet Office, 1973–76; permanent secretary at the Department of Education, 1976–83.

**Hamilton, Willie**
(1917–2000) Labour MP for Fife West, 1950–74, and Fife Central, 1974–87.

**Hanson, James (later Lord Hanson)**
(1922–2004) Chairman of Hanson plc, 1965–97.

**Harris, John (later Lord Harris of Greenwich)**
(1930–2001) Special adviser to Roy Jenkins, 1965–74; Minister of State at the Home Office, 1974–79.

**Harris, Kenneth**
(1919–) Journalist, on the *Observer*, 1950–84, and associate editor, 1976–84.

**Hart, Judith (later Baroness Hart)**
(1924–91) Labour MP for Lanark, 1959–83, and for Clydesdale, 1983–87; Minister of Overseas Development, 1969–70 and 1974–79.

**Hartwell, Lady (Pamela Berry)**
(1914–82) Socialite and wife of Michael Berry (Lord Hartwell), chairman and editor-in-chief of the *Daily* and *Sunday Telegraph*, 1954–87.

**Hattersley, Roy (later Lord Hattersley)**
(1932–) Labour MP for Birmingham Sparkbrook, 1964–97; Minister of State at the FCO, 1974–76; Secretary of State for Prices and Consumer Protection, 1976–79; deputy leader of the Labour Party, 1983–92.

**Havers, Sir Michael (later Lord Havers)**
(1923–92) Conservative MP for Wimbledon, 1970–87; Solicitor General, 1972–74; Lord Chancellor, 1987–92.

**Hayman, Helene (later Baroness Hayman)**
(1949–) Labour MP for Welwyn and Hatfield, 1974–79; Minister of Agriculture, 1999–2001.

**Hayward, Ron**
(1917–96) General secretary of the Labour Party, 1972–82.

**Healey, Denis (later Lord Healey)**
(1917–) Labour MP for Leeds, 1952–92; Defence Secretary, 1964–70; Chancellor of the Exchequer, 1974–79.

**Heath, Sir Edward**
(1916–) Conservative MP for Bexley, 1950–2001; leader of the Opposition, 1965–70 and 1974–75; Prime Minister, 1970–74.

**Heffer, Eric**
(1922–91) Labour MP for the Walton Division of Liverpool, 1964–91; Minister of State at the Department of Industry, 1974–75.

**Helsby, Laurence (later Lord Helsby)**
(1908–78) Permanent secretary at the Treasury and head of the Civil Service, 1963–68.

**Henderson, Sir Nicholas (Nico)**
(1919–) British Ambassador to Germany, 1972–75; to France, 1975–79; to Washington, 1979–82.

**Hennessy, Peter**
(1947–) Journalist on *The Times*, 1974–76, 1982–83; author; professor of contemporary British history, University of London, 1992–.

**Heseltine, Michael**
(1933–) Conservative MP for Tavistock, 1966–74, and for Henley, 1974–2001; minister at the DTI, 1972–74; Opposition spokesman on Industry, 1974–76; Secretary of State for the Environment, 1979–83 and 1990–92; Secretary of State for Defence, 1983–86; president of the Board of Trade, 1992–95; Deputy Prime Minister, 1995–97.

**Hirshfield, Desmond (later Lord Hirshfield)**
(1913–93) Founder and chairman of Trades Union Trust Managers, 1961–83.

**Hopkinson, David**
(1926–) Investment manager at M&G, 1963–87; chairman, 1975–87.

**Howell, Denis (later Lord Howell)**
(1923–98) Labour MP for Birmingham All Saints, 1955–59, and for Birmingham Small Heath, 1961–92; Minister of State for Sport, 1969–70 and 1974–79.

**Hoy, James (later Lord Hoy)**
(1909–76) Labour MP for Leith, 1945–70.

**Hunt, Sir John (later Lord Hunt)**
(1919–) Second permanent secretary at the Cabinet Office, 1972–73; Cabinet Secretary, 1973–79.

**Isaacs, Sir Jeremy**
(1932–) Television producer; chief executive, Channel Four, 1981–87.

**Jackson, Margaret (later Beckett)**
(1943–) Labour MP for Lincoln, 1974–79; PPS to the Minister for Overseas Development, 1974–75; assistant government Whip, 1975–76; under-secretary at the DES, 1976–79; leader of the House of Commons, 1998–2001; Secretary of State for Environment, Food and Rural Affairs, 2001–.

**Jacobson, Sydney (later Lord Jacobson)**
(1908–88) Journalist at the *Daily Mirror, Daily Herald* and the *Sun*; editorial director at IPC, 1968–74.

**Jarvis, Fred**
(1924–) General secretary of the NUT, 1975–89.

**Jay, Anthony**
(1930–) Television writer and producer; author of *Yes, Minister* and *Yes, Prime Minister*, 1980–88.

**Jay, Douglas (later Lord Jay)**
(1907–96) Labour MP for Battersea North, 1946–83; president of the Board of Trade, 1964–67.

**Jeger, Lena (later Baroness Jeger)**
(1915–) Labour MP for Holborn, 1953–59 and 1967–79.

**Jenkins, Clive**
(1926–99) General secretary of the Association of Scientific, Technical and Managerial Staffs, 1970–88; on the general council of the TUC, 1974–89.

**Jenkins, Hugh (later Lord Jenkins of Putney)**
(1908–) Labour MP for Wandsworth, 1964–79; Arts minister, 1974–76.

**Jenkins, Roy (later Lord Jenkins)**
(1920–2003) Labour MP for Southwark and Birmingham Stechford, 1948–76; SDP MP for Glasgow, Hillhead, 1982–87; Minister of Aviation, 1964–65; Home Secretary, 1965–67 and 1974–76; Chancellor of the Exchequer, 1967–70; deputy leader of the Labour Party, 1970–72; President of the EC, 1977–81; leader of the SDP, 1982–83.

**Jones, Barry**
(1938–) Labour MP for Flint East, 1970–83, and for Alyn and Deeside, 1983–2001; Under-Secretary of State for Wales, 1974–79.

**Jones, Elwyn (later Lord Elwyn-Jones)**
(1909–1989) Labour MP for West Ham and Newham, 1945–74; Lord Chancellor, 1974–79.

**Jones, Professor George**
(1938–) Lecturer and professor at LSE, 1966–99; close friend of the author and with him co-author of a biography of Herbert Morrison.

**Jones, Jack**
(1913–) General secretary of the TGWU, 1969–78.

**Joseph, Sir Keith (later Lord)**
(1918–94) Conservative MP for Leeds NE, 1956–87; Secretary of State for Health, 1970–74, and for Education, 1981–86.

**Judd, Frank (later Lord Judd)**
(1935–) Labour MP for Portsmouth West, 1966–79; PPS to Harold Wilson, 1970–72; under-secretary for Defence, 1974–76; Minister of State, ODM, 1976–77, FCO, 1977–79.

**Kagan, Joseph (later Lord Kagan)**
(1915–95) Chairman and managing director of Gannex Textiles; financed the political office; later imprisoned for tax offences.

**Kaldor, Professor Nicholas (later Lord Kaldor)**
(1908–86) Professor of economics at Cambridge, 1966–75; adviser to Denis Healey, 1964–68 and 1974–76.

**Kaufman, Gerald**
(1930–) Labour MP for Manchester Ardwick, 1970–83, and Manchester

Gorton, 1983–; parliamentary under-secretary at DoE, 1974–75; Minister of State at DTI, 1975–79.

**Killick, Sir John**
(1919–) Ambassador and a permanent representative to NATO, 1975–79.

**Kilroy-Silk, Robert**
(1942–) Labour MP for Ormskirk, 1974–83; PPS to the Arts minister, 1974–75; television presenter and, most recently, member of UKIP.

**Kinnock, Neil (later Lord Kinnock)**
(1942–) Labour MP for Bedwellty, 1970–83, and Islwyn, 1983–95; leader of the Labour Party, 1983–92; MEP, 1995–; European commissioner, 1999–2004.

**Kissin, Harry (later Lord Kissin)**
(1912–97) Chairman and director of various public and private companies in the City; adviser to Harold Wilson and financier of the political office; introduced the author to Harold Wilson.

**Kissinger, Henry**
(1923–) US Secretary of State, 1973–77.

**Laing, Hector (later Lord Laing)**
(1923–) Conservative businessman; director of the Bank of England, 1973–91; treasurer of Conservative Party, 1988–.

**Lambton, Lord Antony**
(1922–) Conservative MP for Berwick on Tweed, 1951–73; under-secretary at the MoD, 1970–73; resigned from Parliament in 1973 over call-girl scandal.

**Lea, David (later Lord Lea)**
(1937–) Secretary of the TUC economic department, 1970–77; assistant general secretary, TUC, 1977–99.

**Lee, Jennie (later Baroness Lee)**
(1904–88) Labour MP for North Lanark, 1929–31, and for Cannock, 1945–70; Minister of State for the Arts, 1967–70.

**Leonard, Dick**
(1930–) Journalist and broadcaster; Labour MP for Romford, 1970–74;

PPS to Anthony Crosland, 1970–74; assistant editor, *The Economist*, 1974–85.

**Lester, Anthony (later Lord Lester)**
(1936–) Distinguished lawyer and special adviser to the Home Secretary, 1974–76.

**Lestor, Joan (later Baroness Lestor)**
(1931–98) Labour MP for Eton and Slough, 1966–83, and for Eccles, 1987–93; under-secretary at the Foreign Office, 1974–75, and Department of Education, 1975–76; Labour NEC, 1967–82.

**Lever, Harold (later Lord Lever)**
(1914–95) Labour MP for Manchester Central, 1945–79; Paymaster General, 1969–70; Labour spokesman on Europe, 1970–72; Chancellor of the Duchy of Lancaster, 1974–79. The author was special adviser to Mr Lever, 1970–74.

**Lipsey, David (later Lord Lipsey)**
(1948–) Journalist and author; special adviser to Department of Environment, 1974–76, and to FCO, 1976–77; member of No. 10 Policy Unit, 1977–79; worked on *The Economist*, 1992–99.

**Lord, Alan**
(1929–) Principal finance officer to DTI, 1973–75; second permanent secretary, HM Treasury, 1975–77.

**Lubbock, Eric (later Lord Avebury)**
(1928–) Liberal MP for Orpington, 1962–70.

**Lyons, Dennis (later Lord Lyons)**
(1916–78) Public relations adviser to Harold Wilson, 1970–78.

**McAlpine, Alistair (later Lord McAlpine)**
(1942–) Director of Robert McAlpine & Sons, 1963–95; treasurer of the Conservative Party, 1975–90.

**McCaffrey, Sir Thomas**
(1922–) Head of news at the FCO, 1974–76; chief press secretary to the Prime Minister, 1976–79.

**MacFarquhar, Professor Roderick**
(1930–) Labour MP for Belper, 1974–79.

**McGregor, Sir Ian**
(1912–98) Chairman and chief executive BSC, 1980–83; chairman, NCB, 1983–86.

**McGregor, Oliver (later Lord McGregor)**
(1921–97) Lecturer in economics and professor of social institutions at London University, 1964–85; chairman of Royal Commission on Press, 1975–77.

**Maclennan, Robert (later Lord Maclennan)**
(1936–) MP for Caithness and Sutherland (Labour 1966–81, SDP 1981–88, Liberal Democrats 1988–97); under-secretary at department of prices and consumer protection, 1974–79.

**McMahon, Sir Christopher (Kit)**
(1927–) Adviser to the Bank of England, 1966–70; executive director, 1970–80.

**McNally, Tom (later Lord McNally)**
(1943–) Political adviser to the Foreign Secretary, 1974–76 and to the Prime Minister, 1976–79; MP for Stockport South (Labour 1979–81, SDP 1981–83); leader of Liberal Democrats in the Lords, 2004–.

**Magee, Bryan**
(1930–) Philosopher and author; MP for Leyton (Labour 1974–82, SDP 1982–83).

**Marsh, Sir Richard (later Lord Marsh)**
(1928–) Labour MP for Greenwich, 1959–71; Minister of Transport, 1968–69; chairman of British Railways, 1971–76; chairman of Newspaper Publishers Association, 1976–90.

**Mason, Roy (later Lord Mason)**
(1924–) Labour MP for Barnsley, 1953–83; Defence Secretary, 1974–76; Secretary of State for Northern Ireland, 1976–79.

**Maudling, Reginald**
(1917–79) Conservative MP for Barnet, 1950–74; Chancellor of the Exchequer, 1962–64; Home Secretary, 1970–72.

**Mellish, Robert (later Lord Mellish)**
(1913–98) Labour MP for Bermondsey, 1946–74, and for Southwark, 1974–82; Opposition Chief Whip, 1970–74; Chief Whip, 1974–76.

**Mendelson, John**
(1917–78) Labour MP for Penistone, West Riding, 1959–78.

**Mikardo, Ian**
(1908–93) Labour MP for Reading, 1945–59, for Poplar, 1964–74, for Tower Hamlets, 1974–83, and for Bow and Poplar, 1983–87; chairman of the International Committee of the Labour Party, 1973–78; chairman, PLP, 1974.

**Milhench, Ronald**
(1937–) Forger, convicted in November 1974.

**Millan, Bruce**
(1927–) Labour MP for Glasgow Craigton, 1955–83; and for Govan, 1983–88. Minister of State for the Scottish Office, 1974–76; Secretary of State for Scotland, 1976–79.

**Miller, Sir Eric**
(1924–77) Chairman of Peachey Properties, close friend of Lady Falkender and financier of the political office; committed suicide in 1977 while under official investigation for financial irregularities.

**Moro, Aldo**
(1916–78) Italian Foreign Minister, 1965–66 and 1970–72; Italian Prime Minister, 1963–68 and 1974–76.

**Morris, Alf (later Lord Morris)**
(1928–) Labour MP for Manchester, Wythenshawe, 1964–97; under-secretary at the DHSS with special responsibility for the disabled, 1974–79.

**Morris, Charles**
(1926–) Labour MP for Manchester Openshaw, 1963–83; PPS to Harold Wilson, 1970–74; Minister of State for Education, 1974; CSD, 1974–79.

**Morse, Sir Christopher Jeremy**
(1928–) Executive director of the Bank of England, 1965–72; deputy chairman of Lloyds Bank, 1975–77; chairman, 1977–93.

**Mortimer, Sir John**
(1923–) QC, playwright and author.

**Moser, Professor Claus (later Lord Moser)**
(1922–) Professor of statistics at the LSE in the 1950s and 60s; head of the Governmental Statistical Service, 1967–78; warden of Wadham College, Oxford, 1984–93.

**Moynihan, Patrick (Daniel)**
(1927–2003) Counsellor and consultant to the US President, 1969–73; US Ambassador to India, 1973–75; US representative to the UN, 1975–76.

**Mulley, Fred (later Lord Mulley)**
(1918–95) Labour MP for Sheffield, 1950–83; chairman of the Labour Party, 1974–75; Minister for Transport, 1974–75; Secretary of State for Education, 1975–76; Defence Secretary, 1976–79.

**Murray, Albert (later Lord Murray)**
(1930–80) Labour MP for Gravesend, 1964–70; Minister of State at the Board of Trade, 1966–68, and at the Board of Technology, 1968–70; private secretary to Harold Wilson, 1974–76.

**Murray, Len (Lionel) (later Lord Murray)**
(1922–2004) Assistant general secretary of the TUC, 1969–73; general secretary, 1973–84.

**Nairne, Sir Patrick**
(1921–) Second permanent secretary, Cabinet Office, 1973–75; permanent secretary DHSS, 1975–81.

**Neave, Airey**
(1923–79) Conservative MP for Abingdon, 1953–79; head of the leader of the Opposition's private office, 1975–79; murdered by the IRA in 1979.

**O'Malley, Brian**
(1930–76) Labour MP for Rotherham, 1963–76; Minister of Health and Social Security, 1974–76.

**Orme, Stan (later Lord Orme)**
(1923–) Labour MP for Salford West, 1964–83; Minister of State at the Northern Ireland Office, 1974–76; Minister of State at the DHSS, 1976–79.

**Owen, Dr David (later Lord Owen)**
(1938–) MP for Plymouth Sutton (Labour 1966–81, SDP 1981–92); under-secretary for Defence, 1968–70; Minister of State at the DHSS,

1974–76; Foreign Secretary, 1976–79; one of the 'Gang of Four' founders of the SDP in 1981 of which he was leader, 1983–87 and 1988–92.

**Palliser, Sir (Arthur) Michael**
(1922–) Ambassador and permanent representative to the EC, 1973–75; head of the Diplomatic Service, 1975–82.

**Palme, Olaf**
(1926–86) Swedish Prime Minister, 1968–76 and 1982–86.

**Pannell, Charles (later Lord Pannell)**
(1902–80) Labour MP for West Leeds, 1949–74.

**Pardoe, John**
(1934–) Liberal MP for Cornwall North, 1966–79.

**Parker, Sir Peter**
(1924–2002) Chairman of the British Tourist Authority, 1969–75; chairman of British Rail, 1976–83.

**Peart, Fred (later Lord Peart)**
(1914–88) Labour MP for Workington, 1945–76; Minister of Agriculture, Fisheries and Food, 1964–68 and 1974–76; leader of the House of Lords, 1976–79.

**Peston, Maurice (later Lord Peston)**
Professor of economics at London University, 1965–88; adviser to Secretary of State for Education, 1974–75, Prices 1976–79.

**Piachaud, Professor David**
(1945–) Professor of social policy at the LSE since 1987. Member of the Policy Unit, 1974–79.

**Plowden, William**
(1935–) Lecturer in government at the LSE, 1965–71; member of the Central Policy Review Staff, 1971–77; director-general, RIPA, 1977–88.

**Plumb, Professor Jack**
(1911–2001) Historian, fellow of Christ's College, Cambridge, from 1946 and professor of modern English history at Cambridge, 1966–74.

**Pomonti, Jacques**
(1936–) Personal friend of the author and adviser to French Socialist Party leader François Mitterrand.

**Porchester, Lord (later 7th Earl of Carnavon)**
(1924–2001) Held various senior positions in local government and on bodies governing horse racing; racing manager to HM the Queen, 1969–2001; close friend of the author.

**Powell, Enoch**
(1912–98) Conservative MP for Wolverhampton, 1950–74; Minister of Health, 1960–63.

**Prentice, Reginald (later Baron Prentice)**
(1923–2001) MP (Labour) for East Ham North, 1957–74, for Newham NE, 1974–77, (Conservative) for Newham NE, 1977–79, for Daventry, 1979–87; Minister of Overseas Development, 1967–69 and 1975–76; Education Secretary, 1974–75.

**Price, Chris**
(1932–2004) Labour MP for Perry Barr, Birmingham, 1966–70, and for Lewisham West, 1974–83; PPS to the Education Secretary, 1966–67 and 1975–76.

**Ramsbotham, Sir Peter**
(1919–) British Ambassador to Iran, 1971–74 and to Washington, 1974–77; Governor of Bermuda, 1977–80.

**Rawlinson, Peter (later Lord Rawlinson)**
(1919–) Conservative MP for Epsom and Ewell, 1955–78; Attorney-General, 1970–74.

**Read, Tom and Celia**
Friends and neighbours of the author.

**Rees, Merlyn (later Lord Merlyn-Rees)**
(1920–) Labour MP for South Leeds, 1963–83; Secretary of State for Northern Ireland, 1974–76; Home Secretary, 1976–79.

**Reisz, Betsy**
Hollywood Oscar-winning wife of the film director Karel Reisz.

**Richardson, Gordon (later Lord Richardson)**
(1915–) Governor of the Bank of England, 1973–83.

**Richman, Alfred**
Former journalist involved in Wilson's election campaign travels and travails.

**Rippon, Geoffrey (later Lord Rippon)**
(1924–97) Conservative MP for Norwich South, 1955–64, and for Hexham, 1966–87; Environment Secretary, 1972–74; chief opposition spokesman on foreign affairs, 1974–76.

**Robbins, Lionel (later Lord)**
(1898–1984) Distinguished economist; professor of economics at LSE, 1929–61; chairman of LSE, 1968–74.

**Rockefeller, David**
(1915–) Chairman of Chase Manhattan Bank, 1969–81.

**Rodgers, William (later Lord Rodgers)**
(1928–) MP for Stockton-on-Tees (Labour 1962–81, SDP 1981–83); Minister of Defence, 1974–76 and for Transport 1976–79; one of the 'Gang of Four' founding members of the SDP in 1981.

**Rogaly, Joe**
Journalist on the *Financial Times*.

**Rose, Kenneth**
(1924–) Journalist on the *Sunday Telegraph*, 1961–97.

**Rose, Professor Richard**
(1933–) Professor of politics at Strathclyde University, 1966–82.

**Ross, Willie (later Lord Ross)**
(1911–88) Labour MP for Kilmarnock, 1946–79; Scottish Secretary 1964–70 and 1974–76.

**Rothschild, Lord Victor**
(1910–90) Director-general of the Central Policy Review Staff 1971–74; chairman of N. M. Rothschild & Sons, 1975–76.

**Ryder, Don (later Lord Ryder)**
(1916–2003) Director of IPC, 1963–70; chairman and chief executive of

Reed International, 1968–75; chairman of the National Enterprise Board, 1975–77.

**Sainsbury, David (later Lord Sainsbury)**
(1940–) Director of J. Sainsbury plc, 1973–90; chairman, 1992–98; parliamentary under-secretary at DTI, 1998–.

**St John Stevas, Norman (later Lord St John of Fawsley)**
(1929–) Conservative MP for Chelmsford, 1964–87; Arts minister, 1973–74 and 1979–81.

**Scanlon, Hugh (later Lord Scanlon)**
(1913–2004) Member of the TUC General Council and president of the Amalgamated Union of Engineering Workers, 1968–78.

**Schmidt, Helmut**
(1918–) German Minister of Defence, 1969–72; German Finance Minister, 1972–74; Chancellor of Germany, 1974–82.

**Schon, Frank (later Lord)**
(1912–95) Chairman of National Research Development Corporation, 1969–79.

**Self, Professor Peter**
(1919–99) Professor of public administration at LSE, 1963–82.

**Shackleton, Edward (later Lord Shackleton)**
(1911–94) Labour MP for Preston, 1946–55; leader of the House of Lords, 1968–70; Opposition leader of the House of Lords, 1970–74.

**Sheldon, Bob (later Lord Sheldon)**
(1923–) Labour MP for Ashton-under-Lyne, 1964–2001; Opposition front bench spokesman on the Civil Service, 1970–74; Treasury minister, 1974–75; financial secretary to the Treasury, 1975–79.

**Shepherd, Malcolm (later Lord Shepherd)**
(1918–2001) Leader of the House of Lords, 1974–76.

**Shore, Peter (later Lord Shore)**
(1924–2001) Labour MP for Stepney, 1964–74, for Stepney and Poplar, 1974–83, and for Bethnal Green, 1983–92; Secretary of State for Trade 1974–76, for Environment 1976–79.

**Short, Edward (Ted) (later Lord Glenamara)**
(1912–) Labour MP for Newcastle on Tyne, 1951–76; Education Secretary, 1968–70; leader of the House of Commons, 1974–76; deputy leader of the Labour Party, 1972–76.

**Short, Renée**
(1919–2003) Labour MP for Wolverhampton NE, 1964–87; member of the National Executive Committee of the Labour Party, 1970–81, 1983–88.

**Silkin, John**
(1923–87) Labour MP for Deptford and Lewisham and Deptford, 1963–87; Minister of Local Government, 1974–76; Agriculture, 1976–79.

**Silkin, Sam (later Lord Silkin)**
(1918–88) Labour MP for Camberwell, 1964–74, and for Southwark, 1974–83; Attorney-General, 1974–79.

**Slater, James**
(1929–) Controversial financier; chairman of Slater Walker Secs, 1964–75.

**Smith, John**
(1938–94) Labour MP for Lanarkshire North, 1970–83, and for Monklands East, 1983–94; Minister at the Department of Energy, 1975–76 and at the Privy Council office, 1976–79; leader of the Labour Party, 1992–94.

**Soares, Mario**
(1924–) Portuguese Socialist leader and Prime Minister, 1976–85; President of Portugal, 1986–96.

**Soskice, Frank (later Lord Stow Hill)**
(1902–79) Labour MP for Birkenhead East, 1945–50, for Neepsend, Sheffield, 1950–55, and for Newport, 1956–66; Home Secretary, 1964–65; Lord Privy Seal, 1965–66.

**Steel, David (later Lord Steel)**
(1938–) Liberal MP for Roxburgh, Selkirk and Peebles, 1965–83, and for Tweeddale, Ettrick and Lauderdale, 1983–97; leader of the Liberal Party, 1976–88; first presiding officer of the Scottish Parliament, 1999–2003.

**Sternberg, Rudi (later Lord Plurenden)**
(1917–78) Financier of political office; allegedly a 'double agent'.

**Sternberg, Sir Sigmund**
(1921–) Chairman of the Commodities Research Unit Ltd and campaigner for inter-faith tolerance.

**Stone, Joe (later Lord Stone)**
(1903–86) Doctor to Harold Wilson and Marcia Falkender.

**Stonehouse, John**
(1925–88) Labour MP for Wednesbury, 1957–74, and for Walsall North, 1974–76; Postmaster General, 1968–69.

**Stott, Roger**
(1943–99) Labour MP for Westhoughton, 1973–83, and for Wigan, 1983–99; PPS to the Secretary of State for Industry 1975–76 and to the Prime Minister 1976–79.

**Stowe, Sir Kenneth**
(1927–) Assistant under-secretary at the Cabinet Office, 1973–75; principal private secretary to the Prime Minister, 1975–79; permanent secretary, DHSS, 1981–87.

**Strang, Gavin**
(1943–) Labour MP for Edinburgh East, 1970–; parliamentary secretary at the Ministry of Agriculture, Fisheries and Food, 1974–79.

**Straw, Jack**
(1946–) Labour MP for Blackburn, 1979–; political adviser to the Secretary of State for Social Services, 1974–76; special adviser to the Environment minister, 1976–79; Home Secretary, 1997–2001; Foreign Secretary, 2001–.

**Stuart, Nicholas**
(1942–) Private secretary to the Prime Minister, 1973–76; deputy secretary for Education, 1976–92.

**Swann, Professor Sir Michael (later Lord Swann)**
(1920–90) Chairman of the BBC, 1973–80.

**Thomas, George (Lord Tonypandy)**
(1909–97) Labour MP for Cardiff Central, 1945–50, and Cardiff West, 1950–83; Speaker of the House of Commons, 1976–83.

**Thorpe, Jeremy**
(1929–) Liberal MP for Devon North, 1959–79; leader of the Liberal Party, 1967–76.

**Tickell, Sir Crispin (later Lord Tickell)**
(1930–) Private secretary at the FCO, 1972–75; Chef de Cabinet to Roy Jenkins, 1977–81.

**Trelford, Donald**
(1937–) Deputy editor of the *Observer*, 1969–76; editor, 1975–93.

**Tyerman, Donald**
(1908–81) Editor of *The Economist*, 1956–65; governor of the LSE, 1951–75.

**Underhill, Reginald (later Lord Underhill)**
(1914–93) National agent for the Labour Party, 1972–79.

**Varley, Eric (later Lord Varley)**
(1932–) Labour MP for Chesterfield, 1964–84; PPS to the Prime Minister, 1968–69; Minister of Technology, 1969–70; Secretary of State for Energy, 1974–75; Secretary of State for Industry, 1975–79.

**Volcker, Paul**
(1927–) President of the New York Federal Reserve Bank, 1975–79; Chairman of the board of governors of the US Federal Reserve System, 1979–87.

**Walden, Brian**
(1932–) Labour MP for Birmingham, All Saints, 1964–74; Opposition front Bench spokesman for Treasury Affairs, 1971–73, and television broadcaster.

**Walker, Peter**
(1932–) Conservative MP for Worcester, 1961; Secretary of State for the Environment, 1970–72, and for Trade, 1972–74; Opposition spokesman, 1974–75.

**Walker-Smith, Sir Derek (later Lord Broxbourne)**
(1910–92) Conservative MP for Hertford, 1945–55, and for Herts East, 1955–83.

**Warren, Sir Alfred**
(1915–90) Secretary to the Chief Whip, 1958–79.

**Watkinson, Harold (later Lord Watkinson)**
(1910–95) Conservative MP for Woking, 1950–64; president of the Confederation of British Industry, 1976–77.

**Wedderburn, Professor William (later Lord Wedderburn)**
(1927–) Professor of commercial law at the LSE, 1964–92.

**Weidenfeld, George (later Lord Weidenfeld)**
(1919–) Founded the publishing firm of Weidenfeld & Nicolson, in 1948.

**Weir, William, 3rd Viscount**
(1933–) Member of the court of the Bank of England, 1972–84.

**Whitaker, Ben**
(1934–) Labour MP for Hampstead, 1966–70.

**Whitehead, Phillip**
(1937–) Television producer and Labour MP for Derby North, 1970–83.

**Whitelaw, Viscount William**
(1918–99) Conservative MP for Penrith, 1955–83; Secretary of State for Northern Ireland, 1972–73; deputy leader of the opposition, 1975–79; Home Secretary, 1979–83; leader of the House of Lords, 1983–88.

**Whitlam, Gough**
(1916–) Prime Minister of Australia, 1972–75.

**Wigg, George (later Lord Wigg)**
(1900–83) Labour MP for Dudley, 1945–67; Paymaster General, 1964–67; chairman of the Horserace Betting Levy Board, 1967–72.

**Williams, Marcia (later Baroness Falkender)**
(1932–) Personal and political secretary to Harold Wilson, 1956–83.

**Williams, Philip**
(1920–84) Fellow of Nuffield College, Oxford, 1958–84.

**Williams, Shirley (later Baroness Williams)**
(1930–) Labour MP for Hitchin, 1964–74, and for Hertford and Stevenage,

1974–79; SDP MP for Crosby, 1981–83; Opposition spokesman on home affairs, 1971–73; Minister of Education, 1976–79; founder and president of the SDP, 1981–88; leader of Liberal Democrats in the House of Lords, 2001–04.

**Wilson, Harold (later Lord Wilson of Rievaulx)**
(1916–95) Labour MP for Ormskirk, 1945–50, and for Huyton, 1950–83; leader of the Labour Party, 1963–76; Prime Minister, 1964–70, and 1974–76.

**Wilson, Mary**
(1916–) Wife of Harold Wilson.

**Winterbottom, Sir Walter**
(1913–2002) Director of coaching and manager of the England football team, 1946–62; director of the Sports Council, 1965–78.

**Wood, Richard (later Lord Holderness)**
(1920–2002) Conservative MP for Bridlington, 1950–79; Minister of Power, 1959–63; Minister of Pensions, 1963–64; Minister of Overseas Development, 1970–74.

**Worcester, Bob**
(1933–) Chairman of MORI since 1973, which carried out Wilson's and Labour Party opinion polls.

**Wrigglesworth, Sir Ian**
(1939–) MP for Teesside (Labour 1974–81, SDP 1981–87); PPS to Roy Jenkins, 1974–76.

**Wright, Patrick (later Lord Wright)**
(1931–) Head of the Middle East Department at the FO, 1972–74; private secretary for overseas affairs to the Prime Minister, 1974–77; deputy undersecretary, FCO, 1982–84; head of FCO, 1986–91.

**Yamey, Professor Basil**
(1919–) Professor of economics, London University, 1960–84.

**Zuckerman, Solly (later Lord Zuckerman)**
(1904–93) Chief scientific adviser to the government, 1964–71.

# Index

BD – Bernard Donoughue; MF – Marcia Falkender; JH – Joe Haines;
HW – Harold Wilson

Acland, Sir Antony 261
Adams, Walter 60
Adamson, Sir Campbell 60, 276, 554, 651
Addy, John 596
aircraft industry 69, 153, 237, 255, 264, 313, 379, 543, 571
Airey, Lawrence 701
Aitken, Jonathan 420, 453
Aitken, Sir Max 76, 87, 91
Aldington, Lord (Toby Low) 293
Aldridge, Alan 352
Alexander, Andrew 29, 31
Alexander, Stella 505
Allaun, Frank 165, 514–15, 586
Allen, Alf 462
Allen, Sir Douglas 191, 193, 257, 338, 339, 384, 426, 448–9, 522, 526, 541, 554, 567, 615, 619, 639, 661, 707
Allen, John Schofield 39, 182, 208, 511, 516, 519, 524, 525, 539, 648
Allen, Margaret 660
Allen, Roy 697
Allon, Yigal 353, 472, 577, 590, 591, 626
Alsop, Joseph 370
Amery, Julian 344
Amin, Idi 429
Andrews, Sir Derek 27, 109
Andrews, Doreen 350
Anglo-American Diamond Company 677
Angola 630; mercenaries 659, 661
Annan, Noel 694
Anne, Princess 75
APEX 366
Archer, Peter 625
arms deals 365, 377, 382, 542, 552, 660, 663
Armstrong, Anne 634, 693
Armstrong, Ernest (Ernie) 336, 408–9, 658, 673, 675
Armstrong, Paddy 182, 184, 196, 200, 221
Armstrong, Robert 48, 54, 545; becomes PPS to HW 58, 644; sorts out BD's LSE position 60; relations with BD 69, 83, 86, 93, 94, 95, 108, 109; and Heath's peerage list 86; 'going to the top' 108; and monetary policy 115; and attack on Lever 121–2; fights for HW's ear 122; inhibits political discussions 124; and MF's peerage 126, 127; and Northern Ireland 129–30, 132; pessimistic about economy 132; criticised for Press Commission appointment 133, 137; praised by BD 146, 155, 158, 171–2, 173, 226–7; on Benn 150; shortens HW's reply to Heath 161; discovers civil servant is call-girl 174; supports BD and JH 193–4; views on HW 194, 225; drafts Brayley's resignation statement 199; and MF's positive vetting 224; supports BD over future of Policy Unit 224, 225, 226–7; and MF 227; and BD's threatened resignation 229; letters to Benn on NEC behaviour 235, 237, 238; and alterations to HW's honours list 238; and EEC renegotiations 252, 258, 259, 261; and run on sterling 257; and Mellish's resignation 266; piano playing at No. 10 269; at *Financial Times* lunch 276; economic worries 280; at Chequers for devolution discussions 284; to be replaced by Stowe 287; accused by HW of pushing him too far 290; and City dinners 292; and Robin Butler 292, 293; and publication of Crossman Diaries 295, 296, 344; on Washington trip 299, 300, 301, 302; arranges for wife to cook at No. 10 317; begs BD not to put in memo on CAP 321; to Paris to soften up the French 322, 326; informs BD of Healey plans 334; against HW having press conference on EEC 336; tells BD he has been removed from Jamaica list 349; farewell dinners and parties 355, 356, 357, 358; further praise from BD 355; becomes

deputy under-secretary at Home Office 365; accused by MF of involvement in Libyan arms affair 377; celebrates referendum result with BD 402; and HW's allegations of leaks against BD 424, 428; adapts to Home Office job 430; sees BD about Labour Party matters 486; discusses civil service with BD 526–7; favourable reference to him eliminated from MF's book 548; on Home Office and Jenkins 626; at Policy Unit party 715; 'biting' about Hunt 716

Armstrong, Serena 317, 351, 357
Armstrong, Sir William 95, 526, 618, 619, 644–5
Arwyn, Lord 497, 502, 687, 688
Ashby, Eric 673
Ashley, Jack 84, 172, 281, 361, 450, 486, 489, 499, 505, 514, 545–6, 596, 648, 658, 663, 711, 712
Askey, Arthur 443
Asquith, Herbert H. 35, 98
Astaire, Jarvis 268, 471, 714
Astor, David 49, 111
Athenaeum, the 230, 231, 365
Attenborough, Sir Richard 467, 618
Attlee, Clement 101, 309, 411, 482, 673–4, 690, 708
Ayer, Alfred Jules 462

Bacall, Lauren 151
Bacon, David 677
Bailey, Pearl 498
Bailyn, Bernard 555
Baker, (Sir) Stanley 559, 618, 615, 715
Baldwin, Stanley 211
Balogh, Thomas (later Lord): and MF 140, 237; during election campaign 20, 22, 23, 26, 27, 28, 29, 30–1, 34, 36, 39; and North Sea oil 78, 105, 111; brings BD advance paper for Energy committee 86; at Weidenfeld parties 153, 239; Andrew Graham protégé of 229; lunches with BD 237; and EEC negotiations 257, 340, 341; misses not being at No. 10 292; and petroleum revenue tax 316; sent to meetings by Benn 414, 417; defensive about Benn 481, and British oil 490; joins BNOC 539, 578, 585, 596–7, 663, 679
Bank of England 175, 263, 270, 271, 272, 277, 280, 292, 343–4, 413, 442, 445, 485, 523–4, 532, 548–9, 655, 657, 676, 720; see also Richardson, Gordon
banks, nationalisation of 623
Banks, Tony 472
Bannister, Sir Roger 86, 333, 626
Barber, Anthony 4, 26, 339, 532
Barclay, Clifford 243, 318, 349, 605
Barlow, Frank 699
Barnetson, Lord 474
Barnett, Joel 32, 278, 478, 594, 656, 682, 706
Barnsley Brewery 178, 179

Barr, Glenn 621
Barrie, John 227
Basnett, David 35, 277, 547, 554, 662
Bateman, Sir Ralph 276, 417, 554
BBC (British Broadcasting Corporation): and Tories 111; biased coverage of election campaign 26, 28, 31, 36, 37, 38, 43, 47; interview with HW 93; biased version of Silkin story 150; films HW's team at work 207, 208, 209; opinion poll on election 216–17; interviews with HW 338, 339; and EEC referendum 381–2, 393; BD lunches at 503–4; see also Swann, Michael
Beaumont, Michael 228
Beaverbrook Newspapers 291
Beckett, Margaret (née Jackson) 71, 241, 255, 317, 323, 336, 476, 477, 685, 688
Benn, Anthony (Tony) Wedgwood 10; use of term 'social contract' 177; and election campaign 21, 36, 42, 47; appointed Secretary of State for Industry 55; rows with HW over Pitt 66; statement on Concorde 71, 126; rumoured to be encouraging strike at British Leyland 105; and EEC discussions 106, 107; industrial policies 115, 135; clashes with HW 121, 125, 138–9; puts resolution to NEC for conference on EEC 141; attacks colleagues 141, 143; outlines strategy 144; upset by Ted Short's 'fortunate error' in the House 147; attacked by colleagues over industrial policies 149–50; angers HW 152, 153; and Industry White Paper 158, 166, 169, 171, 172–3; forbidden to attend Cabinet meeting 160; scorned by colleagues 180–1; and Frances Morrell 191; and Tory smears 210; and right-wing plots 227; 'gap between reality and his fantasy' 230; actions worry Policy Unit 233; dangerous left-wing proposals on Industry Act 234; militancy at NEC 234–5; defeats Healey at IDV committee 235, 236; receives stern letters from HW 235, 236, 237, 238; further clashes over policies 241; against implementing European tariffs 245; may help manufacturing industry 246–7; displaces Foot in NEC 249; and EEC Regional Fund negotiations 250; and nationalisation of British Leyland and aircraft 254–5, 256, 257, 258; attacks HW on EEC negotiations 262; and unemployment policies 264; 'positively malevolent' 277; supports inquiry on nationalised industries 278; expenditure opposed by civil servants 281; and Scottish devolution 285, 286; requests more money for NEB 290–1; and EEC regional policy 306; proposals for compensation for nationalised industries 307, 308, 315; attacks whole EEC policy 314; success in IDV committee 317–18; and EEC referendum campaign 333, 337; attacked on proposals for Ferranti 346;

HW tries to trap into resignation 347, 355; defeats Healey over question of industrial democracy 359; and British Leyland 360, 361, 362; and campaign against EEC 365, 366; HW's plans for 375, 378, 390, 391, 397; his proposals dealt with in IDV committee 383; and steel closures 386; and public expenditure 390; and *Sunday Times* 'hatchet job' 392; takes over EEC referendum campaign 392; general view on 399; and Cabinet reshuffle 405, 406, 407; accepts Energy 408; protests about reshuffle 411, 412; sends Balogh to meetings 414, 417; on unemployment 421; his 'pigeons coming home to roost' 435; and pay policy 465; and Court Line fiasco 478; and collapse of motorcycle industry 478; 'getting up to tricks' in Energy 480; tentative on North Sea oil 490; discusses 'future scenario of British politics' with BD 491; clashes with Lever over North Sea oil negotiations 538; at Department of Industry 544; and EEC referendum 544; attacks Policy Unit 552–3; and rumours of resignation 575; and NEC vote 578; cancels visit to USA 585; and Chrysler 596, 608; and BNOC 603–4, 636–7, 642, 667, 674; popularity 637; discusses with BD Royal Commission on Law, Morrison, Plowden Report, and nationalised industries 649, 663; at Cabinet farewell dinner 707; at party for Labour Party helpers 713; and leadership election 711, 712, 720

Benn, Caroline 712
Benner, Pat 522, 622, 629
Berrill, Sir Kenneth (Ken): cynical 121, 135; and CPRS 173, 230, 353, 462; and NEDC inquiry into nationalised industries 307; reveals Treasury miscalculations 496, 500; well informed on BNOC 578, 604; and Chrysler 580, 582, 606, 608; and Defence cuts 588; criticised for running of CPRS 606; unsatisfactory lunch with BD 665; defends Civil Service salaries 665; in favour of council house sales 710; at Policy Unit party 715
Berry, Lady Pamela 153
Beswick, Lord 379, 540
Bevan, Aneurin 327
Bevin, Ernest 101
Bevins, Tony 530
Bidwell, Sid 467
Biffen, John 606
Bingham, Billy 170
Birk, Alma 250, 264, 570
Birk, Ellis 250
Bish, Geoffrey (Geoff) 68, 110
Black, Jack 500, 531, 533, 539, 615, 651
Blackett Memorial Lecture (1975) 574, 575, 594
Blackpool Party Conference (1975) 508, 510–15

Blackstone, Tessa 500, 540, 549, 684
Blake, Robert 344
Blaker, Peter, MP 392
Blau, Tom 648
BMA *see* British Medical Association
BNOC *see* British National Oil Corporation
Book, Tony 713
Booth, Albert 361, 607
Boothroyd, Betty 255
Boston, Terry 41, 42, 45, 46, 182, 208, 209, 214, 217, 224
Bottomley, Arthur 51, 711
Boycott, Geoffrey 117
Boyle, Edward 267, 344; Report on top salaries 449, 645
BP *see* British Petroleum
Brabourne, Lord 382
Brademas, John 371
Bradford University 153, 154, 507
Bradley, Tom 666
Brandon, Henry 373
Brandt, Willi 488
Brayley, Lord Desmond 185, 198, 199, 271, 577, 609, 617
Brearley, Christopher (Chris) 104
breweries, small 178, 179
Bridges, Edward 30
Bridges, Lord Thomas 58, 111, 133, 261, 265, 545
Briggs, Asa 344, 473, 620
Briginshaw, Reginald 238, 663, 667, 679
Brimelow, Tom 548, 549, 624, 675
*Britain Will Win with Labour* (Labour manifesto) 187
British Leyland 105, 254–5, 256, 257, 258, 271, 273, 276, 278, 290–1, 335, 339, 346, 359, 360, 361, 362, 491, 523, 545, 556, 595, 639, 651
British Medical Association (BMA) 164, 172, 536
British Museum exhibitions 498, 677
British National Oil Corporation (BNOC) 277, 348, 523, 537, 539, 576, 578, 603–4, 636–7, 642, 663, 667, 674, 679
British Petroleum (BP) 537, 538, 603, 674
British Steel Corporation (BSC) 138, 161, 276, 358, 386, 388, 615, 620, 651, 668
British Waterways 280
Brittan, Leon 606
Brittan, Sam 276, 281
Brown, George 607
Brown, Hugh 336, 381
Brown, Tina 519, 605
Bruce, David 634
Bruce, Donald 678
Bruce-Gardyne, John 83
BSC *see* British Steel Corporation
Buchan, Norman 475, 481, 712
Bucks Club, St James 428
Budgets: March 1974 77, 78, 79, 80, 82, 83, 85; July 1974 (mini) 163, 164, 167; November 1974

238, 239, 240–1; April 1975 325, 334, 339, 347–56 *passim*, 496

bugging 85, 656–7, 670

building societies *see* mortgage rates

Bulganin, Nikolai A. 673

Bullock, Alan 287

Bullock, Richard 588, 606

Burmah Oil 270, 271, 272, 273, 277, 348, 576, 584, 585, 589, 602

Burnet, Alastair 509, 664

Burnham, Linden Forbes Sampson 339

*Business Week* magazine 304

Butler, David 230, 477

Butler, Michael 326, 384, 550

Butler, Robin 54, 58, 545; relations with Policy Unit 79, 104; dislike of media 111; works on HW's speeches 147, 161, 175, 192; playing golf 194; too young for promotion 283; vetoed as Armstrong's successor and moved by Civil Service 292–3; attacked by MF for lunching with *Private Eye* 297; praised by BD 355; recruits cook for No. 10 388; works on HW's speeches 393, 395, 446, and Incomes White Paper 455; plays cricket with BD 473; farewell party 537, 548; goes back to Treasury 400, 449, 587, 655; at Policy Unit party 715

Button, Senator John 429

Byers, Frank 688

Cabot Lodge, Henry 370

Cadbury, Adrian 567

Caffiero, Gene 588, 600

Cairncross, Sir Alec 673

Callaghan, Audrey 497, 723

Callaghan, James xi, 10, 13, 19; adopts concept of 'social contract' (1972) 177; and election campaign 20, 21, 24, 25, 32, 42, 48; becomes Foreign Secretary 50, 61, 71; supports Lever 78; worried about Brussels EEC speech 82; rebukes Heffer over Chile 100; and EEC renegotiations 13, 106, 107, 242; criticises 'Lever plan' for oil crisis 121; attacked in Crossman Diaries 135; and Benn 139, 141, 144, 149, 172, 235; gives Herbert Morrison Memorial Lecture 152; talked about as new leader 159; and EEC 160, 192, 243–4, 245, 251, 252, 253; on HW and MF 226; considers breaking off relations with NEC 236; clashes with Benn 241; critical of Healey 243; at Paris Summit 258, 259, 261–2; and EEC referendum 268, 294; against Lever 275; and Maitland 280; back-pedals on Scottish devolution 294; in Canada and Washington 297, 298, 302; message to HW 313; and further EEC discussions 314, 322–3; supports Foreign Office over oil 327; at Dublin Summit 328, 329, 330, 331; and EEC 335, 336, 337, 338, 340, 341, 345, 348,

352, 357; supports Healey 345; keen that BD should go to Jamaica 349–50; and public expenditure 351; intends to sack MacFarquhar 361; in Washington 373, 374; laughs at HW for waiting for MF 375–6; wants more research on polls 379; at Defence meeting 379; chairs EEC referendum campaign committee 381, 382, 385, 387, 398; teased by Shirley Williams 387; and industrial policy 421; and wages policy 430; and sterling crisis 438–9, 440; not consulted by MF over HW's dinner with Israeli minister 465; and Scottish devolution 493, 494; pessimistic about economic recovery 543; protects his special adviser 549; keen to reform diplomatic service 549; on oil 550; tough with officials 550; and Northern Ireland 562; enjoys being Foreign Secretary 568; and Iceland cod war 629, 630, 641, 642, 643; and Defence cuts 631; wants George Thomson as President of EEC 638; and Official Secrets 644, 683; clashes with Short 645; against select committees 645; annoyed with HW over Middle East 646; clashes with HW over European elections 648; and George Thomas 654; and Royal Commission on the Law 656; and special advisers 662, 664; clashes with Jenkins 684; at HW's 60th birthday party 693, 694; told of HW's retirement 698, 699; and leadership election 701, 703, 704, 707, 708, 711, 712, 715, 718, 720; becomes Prime Minister 722, 723

Callan, Paul 502

Camden School 671

Camp, Will 335, 596, 615, 626, 663, 667, 714

Campaign for Democratic Socialism 50, 73

Canavan, Dennis 692

CAP *see* Common Agricultural Policy

Cape, Jonathan (publishers) 135, 419, 420, 429, 516, 590

capital transfer tax 168, 240

Capote, Truman 370

Carey, Michael 624

Carey, Peter 588

Carlton, Anne 569

Carmichael, Kay 94, 130, 195, 197, 222, 238, 319, 394, 396, 503, 508, 593, 635, 638

Carr, Robert 165

Carrier, John 456, 546, 567

Carrington, Lord Peter 82

Carter, Ray 481, 714

Carter-Jones, Lewis 658

Carvel, Bob 579

Carver, Field Marshal Michael 379

Castle, Barbara 10; threatens to stand against Jenkins as deputy leader (1970) 34; presses for more expenditure for DHSS 70; continually phones HW 71; discussions with BD 84, 85; 'skittish' 85; 'a boring old bag' 135;

produces masses of policy material 166;
sleeps through IDV committee 171; and
Health Service crisis 173; battles with NHS
consultants over pay 267, 274; and Scottish
devolution 284, 285; and Defence cuts 324;
and EEC 337, 340, 343; offers resignation
340; 'an old woman in a hurry' 362; and
Cabinet reshuffle 410, 411; and pay policy
425, 465; uncaring about the disabled 489,
499; ambitious 489; criticised by Owen 532,
534, 535; and public expenditure cuts 564–5;
prattles on 566; and private medicine 576,
583, 585, 589–90, 591–3; threatens to resign
602; criticised by Nairne 620; HW feels she
must go 642; and special advisers 658; and
the Goodman compromise 670; asks for
peerage 685; interrupts Jenkins's speech 707
Catherwood, Sir Frederick 428
Caunt, George 519–20
CBI 55, 60, 276, 277, 279, 318, 386, 387, 390,
400, 417, 431, 446, 554
Central Council for Physical Recreation (CCPR)
256, 354
Central Policy Review Staff (CPRS) 60, 61; relation with Policy Unit 71, 75, 76, 104, 112,
161; taken over by Berrill 173, 230; produces
poor papers 224, 245, 246; Plowden's work for
326, 378; HW wants Policy Unit to join with
351; and Ryder Report on British Leyland
359; and leaks 427, 428; plays no role in pay
policy crisis 462; given task of planning pay
strategy 500–1; 'in a very unhappy state' 606;
reports on motor industry 607–8; 682; presen-
tation on social policy 684; *see also* Rothschild,
Lord Victor
Chalfont, Lord 192, 705
Channel Tunnel 281
Channon, Ingrid 79
Channon, Paul 79
Chapman, Donald 585
Charkham, Jonathan 404, 473, 529, 617, 633,
695
Charlton, Michael 43
Charteris, Martin 309, 356, 604, 614, 628, 634,
691, 696
Chequers 72, 284, 553
Chester, Sir Norman 283, 545, 673, 674–5, 680
Childers, Erskine 246
Chile 100, 105, 127, 289, 315–16, 319, 501, 660,
663, 681
Chirac, Jacques 148
Chrysler Motors 545, 547, 550–2, 556, 573, 574,
576–86, 595–9; 600, 603, 605–13, 631, 668
Church, Senator Frank 669
Churchill, Sir Winston 30, 84, 128, 323, 670, 718
CIA 369, 640, 652, 653, 669
Civil List, Queen's 309, 310, 316, 532, 596
Civil Service: growth 568; cuts 606, 624, 626;
reforms 636, 639; salaries 267, 404, 645; 647;

665; dispersal to different regions 677; union
678
Civil Service College, Sunningdale 653, 654, 661
Clapham, Sir Michael 60, 276
Clark, Robert 243
Clarke, Percy 2, 22, 152, 182, 388, 586
Clay Cross, Derbyshire 87, 237
Clayton, Haya 443
Clinton-Davies, Stanley 336
Close, Brian 288, 308
Coggan, Donald, Archbishop of Canterbury 102,
294, 380
Cohen, Jack 567
Colby, Bill 369
Cole, Hugo 447
Cole, John 159, 289, 508, 622, 702, 706
Collins, Christopher (Chris) 325
Common Agricultural Policy (CAP) 243, 321,
322
Concorde 71, 76, 83, 125, 126, 148, 162, 164, 166,
657
Connell, John 603
Conservative Party: and election campaign 23, 28,
29, 35, 47, 48; in Opposition 70, 73, 83, 96,
110, 115, 119, 127, 165; win vote on industry
143–4; and Lever crisis 163; lack of unity
167–8, 178, 281; manifesto published early
179–80, 209; October election results 219,
220; leadership ballot 309; *see also* Heath,
Edward; Thatcher, Margaret
Cooke, Alistair 302, 614
Cooper, Chuck 369
Cooper, Frank 136, 253, 315, 502, 506, 517, 550,
556, 624
Cordle, Sir John 335, 430, 541, 559, 561, 632–3,
639, 642
Corr, James (Jim) 222, 622
Cosgrave, Liam 90, 183, 236, 685
Coulter, Ian 620
council houses, sale of 520, 525, 526, 529, 532,
533, 535, 537, 544, 546, 555, 569, 599, 602,
603, 620, 623, 639, 710
Court Line 478, 483
Couzens, Ken 434, 447, 448, 452, 454, 456, 457,
458, 463, 687
CPRS *see* Central Policy Review Staff
Craig, William 495
Crawley, John 96, 263
Cripps, Francis 243, 265, 544
Croker, Edward (Ted) 382, 393
Cromer, Lord 132
Crosland, Anthony (Tony) 1, 10; supports
Campaign for Democratic Socialism (1960s)
50; gives good statement on housing 21;
congratulates BD on campaign 53; appointed
Secretary of State for the Environment 59;
and Lever's mortgage proposals 104, 120,
136, 146; savage about 'Jenkinsites' 123; on
Industrial Development committee 149; and

land nationalisation 153, 165, 175; plans to help Scottish local authority defaulters 160; and devolution 170, 284, 285, 286, 415, 494; and Industry White Paper discussions 171; confident about election 178; fails to deal with Mrs Thatcher's mortgage commitment 204; and local authority finance 237; and British Leyland 255; and aircraft nationalisation 255; criticised by Howell 273; supports Benn 278; objects to Ross's request for better terms for Scottish Development Agency 290; and EEC negotiations 314; and Defence cuts 324; gives impromptu speech at Bannister dinner 333; sceptical about HW 342; as next Labour leader 343, 351, 385; attacks Healey's paper on public expenditure cuts 345; criticises Treasury papers 351; and railway wage claims 352, 412; and public expenditure 390, 391, 470; driven to drink by Mellish 410; critical of John Gilbert and Healey 414; praised by BD 414; appalled at lack of coherence among Cabinet economic committees 435–6; and sterling crisis 438, 439, 440, 441, 445; and incomes policy 449–50, 451, 455, 457, 459, 460, 463; praised by Wass 484; on HW 496; keen to discuss transport policy 498; scathing about unemployment policy 504; depressed by smear campaign 504; does badly in NEC elections 514; on economic situation 543; and council house sales 544, 555, 569, 603, 710; Howell on 551; and cuts in public expenditure 542, 561–2, 563, 564–5, 566, 567; and Rate Support Grant 565, 570; has medical check-up 600; criticises Callaghan 600; on Labour housing record 601; 'too lazy' 619, 620; choice of chairman for British Railways 651; and Transport paper 679, 680–1; does badly in leadership election 701, 702–3, 704, 705, 720

Crosland, Susan 79, 496, 498, 705
Crossman, Anne 432
Crossman, Richard (Dick) 78, 271; see Crossman Diaries
Crossman Diaries 135, 137, 138, 318; Graham Greene worried about 148–9; and non-publication by Harold Evans 185, 191, 208, 241, 244, 264, 270, 279; Foot may resign over 246; finally published in Sunday Times 294, 295, 296; court finds in favour of publishers 307; and proposal to set up committee to review rules governing memoirs 344; and writ against Cape 419–20; and Attorney-General's writ against Sunday Times 426–7, 429, 432, 446, 453, 464; judgement in favour of Sunday Times and Cape 516, 517–18, 522; and Hunt 522–3; and publication of Volume II 518, 619, 627, 669
Crown Agents 119, 265–6, 356, 507

Crowther-Hunt, Norman 66, 156–7, 169, 226, 285, 286, 475, 637, 638, 640, 644, 652–3, 661, 673
Cudlipp, Michael 114, 131, 136, 336, 380, 499, 510, 647, 669
Cunningham, Andrew 109
Cunningham, John 722, 723
Curran, Charles 338, 382
Curry, Austin 180
Cushing, Caroline 291, 292, 601, 625
Cuvillier, Philippe 475–6, 537
Cyprus 162, 165–6, 167, 645

Dahrendorf, Professor Ralf 121, 223, 255, 311, 331, 349, 446, 448, 491, 524, 555–6, 557, 606, 697
Daily Express 37, 76, 86, 87, 89, 90, 91, 95, 96, 150, 162, 171, 191, 209, 279, 280, 282, 309, 468, 520, 531, 623, 627–8, 664
Daily Mail 37, 38–9, 40, 72, 76, 86, 87, 95, 209, 210, 211, 212, 213, 222, 279, 283, 386, 482, 492, 528, 531, 561, 597, 614, 623, 656
Daily Mirror 3, 23, 24, 32, 46, 47, 71, 76, 89, 91, 98, 99, 104, 118, 125, 136, 187, 250, 251, 275, 279, 451–2, 489, 495, 502, 585, 630, 645, 670
Daily Telegraph 46, 257, 258, 279, 282, 335, 470, 540, 615
D'Albis, Tristan 476
Dalton, Hugh 101
Daly, Lawrence 80
Dartmouth Park United (football team) 179
Davidson, Arthur 366
Davies, Denzil 658
Davies, Gavyn 105, 207, 221, 283, 413, 420, 436, 473, 533, 626, 633, 641, 685, 697, 699, 706
Davies, Harold 122, 170
Davies, Leighton 675
Davis, Peter (later Lord Lovell-Davis) 2; and election campaign 20, 33; as HW's unofficial PR adviser 114, 116; as MF's Mafia 141, 151, 154, 174; promised peerage by MF 141; and 'Declaration of Interdependence' paper 174; gets peerage 181; and HW's reconciliation dinner 176; offers to do press relations 181; recommended by HW to write his speeches 181; attacks Percy Clarke 182; BD gets on with 186; at MF's alternative meetings 189, 190; and lunch at No. 10 195; gives up on writing election speeches 196–7; realises he's a pawn 197; tells MF off 197, 198; co-operates with BD and JH 197–8, 201, 203, 205; in BBC film 208, 209; at HW's dinner for Whitlam 268; passed JH's ideas off as his own 327–8; replaces Balogh in the Lords 597; works with counter-inflation unit 628, 630
Davison, Jack 371
Davison, Judy 304, 369
Day, Robin 28, 172, 392

deaf, the 230, 489, 499, 524, 546; *see also* Ashley, Jack
Deakin, Nicholas 403
Deakins, Eric 21
Defence committee (OPD) 115, 297, 315, 323, 542
Defence expenditure: Unit's memorandum on 289, 311, 323; draft White Paper 313; and cuts 310, 313, 318, 324, 351, 379–80, 501, 561, 563, 573, 587–8, 593, 599, 602, 624, 626
Delfont, Lord Bernard 694, 715
Dell, Edmund 60, 139, 284, 286, 290–1, 397, 405, 408, 567; and Chrysler Motors 578, 580, 581–2, 597, 598, 600, 607, 610; and BNOC 604, 674; and Royal Commission on the Law 659; and council house sales 710
Dempster, Nigel 614
Den Uyl, Joop 488, 666
Denham, Jean 181, 189, 201, 216, 297, 498, 713
Denning, Lord Justice 517
Devlin, Bernadette 180
devolution *see* Scottish devolution
Dewar, Donald 360
Dexter, Ted 354
Diego Garcia, island of 497
Dimbleby, Richard 498–9
Diplomatic Service 500, 549
Dirkes, Donald 447, 454
disabled, the 98, 110, 111, 179, 180, 183, 281, 489, 596, 658; *see also* Morris, Alf
Distillers: thalidomide affair 122
Dobson, Cowan 295
Dobson, Frank 648
Docherty, Tommy 713
Donaldson, John, Lord 214, 673
Dougan, Derek 288, 308, 708
Douglas, Kirk 302
Down, Sir Alastair 584
Downing Street, No. 10 9, 10, 17, 57–9, 197; cooks come and go 63, 112, 140, 141, 145, 182, 184, 196, 200, 317, 351, 357, 388; typing facilities 69; lunches 82–3, 170, 219, 317, 636, 681
Dowson, Graham 639
Doyle, Mick 713
Drabble, Margaret 676
Driberg, Tom 47
Drogheda, Lord 79, 276
Dulles, John Foster 313
Durbin, Jim 697
Durham Miners' Gala 473

Ecevit, Bulent 343
economic policies 135, 160, 214, 236, 268, 271, 276, 307–8, 312–13, 316, 435–6, 542–3, 548–9; *see specific issues*, e.g. Budgets; import controls; incomes policies; inflation; mortgage rates; public expenditure; sterling crises, *etc.*
*Economist, The* 222, 249, 290, 304, 509, 542, 553

Edinburgh, Duke of *see* Philip, Prince
education/schools 148, 152, 380, 412–13, 434, 546, 571, 587, 588, 595, 631, 671, 673; *see also* universities
Edwards, Sir Ronald 523, 639, 651
EEC *see* European Economic Community
Election Business committee 114
electoral reform 498, 499, 570
Elizabeth II, Queen 73–4; and HW 51, 54, 95, 116, 178, 280, 349, 477, 489, 574; and State Opening of Parliament 68, 571–2; and Heath 69, 86; talks with BD 309; and MF's ancestry 332, 681; and HW's retirement 604, 696, 709; *see also* Civil List
Enders, Tom 301, 369, 371
engineering industry disputes 80–1, 115, 116
English, Michael 86
Ennals, David 336, 337, 361, 365, 388, 395, 490, 577, 578, 607
European Economic Community (EEC) 5–7, 34, 49, 50, 242; as issue during election campaign 21, 22; renegotiation discussions and disputes 13, 53, 106–7, 166, 185, 192, 194, 198, 205, 223, 235, 240, 242–3; Benn and 141, 153, 314; NEC and 141, 186, 273, 340–1, 345–6, 362, 365, 366–7; and tariff charges 245, 252; Regional Fund 249, 250, 252; and Labour manifesto commitments 187, 252–3, 257, 259; referendum discussions 68, 103, 186, 199, 200, 251–2, 268, 287, 288, 289, 294, 309; HW's views 257–8, 259–60, 287, 314, 328; Paris talks 260–1; HW's statement on referendum 292, 293; further discussions 306, 314, 333–41 *passim*; and PLP 324–5; Dublin Summit 306, 321, 322–3, 325, 328–31; referendum campaign 343, 348, 349, 351, 352, 356, 357, 361; conference 363–4; campaign committee meetings 381–2, 384, 387, 388, 390, 392, 394, 395, 396, 398; referendum results 399–402, 403, 477
European Parliament elections 570
Evans, Harold (Harry): promises *Sunday Times* will say Heath should go 49; and Lever 66; and BD 90, 92, 95, 116, and discussions of deal with press 117, 119; and Silkin story 145, 150; on Callaghan as next leader 159; and press smear on Short 165; dinners with BD, 175; BD blamed for leaks to 179, 182, 191, 227; and Crossman Diaries 185, 241, 244, 264, 270, 279; and *Private Eye* allegations 191, 208, 529, 530–1; gloomy about economic situation 236; gives BD some Washington contacts 365; fascinated by Benn and EEC referendum 392; Attorney-General's writ against 426, 427; pumped by Weidenfeld about BD 500; passes on to BD John Allen's lies 516; warns BD about *Private Eye* 605; 'a fanatic' for open government 630;

gives BD information on Concorde 657;
modifies editorial on Callaghan 704
Evans, James 116
*Evening News* 34, 86, 490, 497, 531, 573, 656
*Evening Standard* 21, 86, 280, 295, 297, 531, 531,
579, 720

Fahd, Prince, of Saudi Arabia 532, 534, 535, 571
Falkender, Marcia, Lady (*formerly* Williams, née
Field) 2, 3, 8, 9, 14–18, 20; ancestry 332,
356–7; appearance 3, 22; early relationship
with HW (1950s) 81, 673; has affair with
John Allen (1960s) 39; and Walter Terry 507;
takes revenge on HW and Mary Wilson
(1971) 93–4; tries to ruin brother's wedding
89, 226, 429; and election campaign
(February 1974) 20–40 *passim*; takes tranquillisers 22, 35, 37; relationship with HW
14–15, 16–18, 22–3, 24, 27, 35, 38, 46, 63–4,
76, 140–1, 144–5, 351; praised by BD 3, 24,
32, 34; smear story printed about 37, 38–9;
backs Jenkins 39, 53; thinks Hayward no good
39; on election day 41, 42, 44–8; awaits
Heath's resignation 49, 50–1; first days at
No. 10 54, 56, 58, 59–60; rows with HW over
BD's status 61; further rows with HW 61–2,
and Albert Murray 62; favours Rodgers as
minister 62, 63; attacks HW 63–4; depressed,
neurotic and paranoiac 65; objects to Lever
becoming Minister for Civil Service 67;
apologises to BD 68; favours early election
70, 73; rows with HW over No. 10 lunch
arrangements 75; and press attacks 77, 78, 84;
threatens to emigrate 77; gives HW 'it with
both barrels' 82; relationship with HW
disgusts JH 82, 83; accuses BD of conspiring
against her 84–5; and further press reports
over land deals 86–7, 88–92, 93, 94, 96–7, 98,
99, 103; abuses BD and Murray 97; forbids
HW to eat with BD *et al.* 103, 112; attacks
BD as source of press attacks on her 108;
blamed for Murray's failure to be selected for
Newham 108, 109; complains about Trooping
the Colour arrangements 112, 135, 137, 138;
further unbalanced behaviour 114, 115, 116,
117–18; tries to 'wheedle her way back in'
122; awarded peerage 123–4, 125, 126, 127,
128, 129, 130, 132; further attacks on Murray
and BD 135, 139–40, 141; further press
stories 136; brings in Davis and Lyons 141–2;
in control of HW again 143, 144–5; attacks
HW for taking BD to Germany 145, 146;
insists he veto BD's Brussels trip 146, 147;
bullies private office junior 150; attacks her
driver 151; attempts to turn HW against
Kissin, Lever, Goodman, BD and JH 154–5,
156, 157, 158, 159; advised to sue press by
JH 160; and HW's missing box files 162, 163;
and demise of No. 10 lunches 170, 268

September 1974 – May 1975
sets up counter-team for election
campaign 174, 176, 179, 181; vetoes
Hayward 182; gets rid of cook 182,
184; megalomania 185; orders changes
to HW's TV script 188–9; accuses
Murray of plotting with civil servants
189; attacks on JH and BD 190–1,
194–7, 204; and further press accusations 191, 192–3, 199; and election
campaign 197–218 *passim*; persuades
HW to do TV broadcast 218–19;
positive vetting incomplete 224; attacks
Policy Unit 224, 225, 227, 228, 229,
230–2; attacks HW 238; insists HW be
invited to Weidenfeld party 238–9; on
better terms with BD 246, 247–8, 249;
further attacks on HW 254, and civil
servants 267; invites Weidenfeld to No.
10 party 269; angry at HW for not
phoning her on New Year's Eve 273;
has fainting fits 276; attacks her driver
who walks out 277–8; 'fantastic'
lifestyle 278; holds HW responsible for
end of truce in Ireland 286; pushes
HW to arrange post for her brother
288, 507, 509, 528; plans series of City
dinners 292; jumpy over *Evening
Standard* court case 295; attacks Robin
Butler for lunching with *Private Eye*
297; violent row with HW 297; further
wild behaviour 306; furious at BD's
Palace visit 310, 332; insists HW will
resign at Christmas 312; her 'brilliant
ideas' praised by HW 320, 323; and
speech-writing for HW 327–8; at
Trudeau dinner 332; takes 'fistful of
purple hearts' 335; and EEC negotiations 336, 337, 341; prevents BD from
going to Jamaica 344, 345, 349, 350,
351; flies to Scillies in Eric Miller's
plane 347 (*see* Miller, Eric); burgled
354; and EEC referendum 356, 357,
363; and Ken Stowe 358; and HW's
reliance on Janet Hewlett-Davies 359,
362, 375; tries to prevent BD having
party conference ticket 361–2; arranges
meeting with Israeli Ambassador 364;
invited to Israel but cancels trip 364,
384–5, 386, 388, 390, 499; keeps HW
waiting at airport 375–6; and Libyan
arms dealer 377; attacks BD 378;
harangues Israeli Ambassador 380–1;
abolishes programme for HW's EEC
campaign speeches 381; appalling
behaviour 383; brings in Sinatra 383–4,
388
May 1975 – April 1976
further demands on HW 387–8, 389,

395–6; relations with Israeli diplomats 397, 464–5, 480, 481, 546–7, 551, 558, 560–1, 577, 591, 623, 641, 646, 661, 666, 667, 670; her guest list for Beating the Retreat 399, 400; accuses BD of leaks 408; attacks HW over Miller 415–16; suggests guests for Frost's dinner 428; pleased that HW is not retiring 428–9; behaves perfectly 443; approves two-page spread in *Daily Mirror* 451–2; insists BD and JH are frozen out of White Paper on pay policy 463–4; entertains Richard Attenborough 467; campaigns against JH 470; gives dinner for business supporters 471; non-arrival at Lever lunch 480–1, 634–5; pressures HW to defer retirement 483; and Janet Hewlett-Davies 501, 504–5, 507, 546, 547, 551, 552; 552; rows with HW over tax bill 502, 504; inability to control BD 506–7; and Blackpool conference 508, 510, 511, 512; and *Guardian* stories 525, 526; right-wing views 525; dines with Harmsworth 528; cuts JH out of book acknowledgements 533–4; restricts guests at Butler's farewell party 537; presses HW to stay on 539–40; and Cordle 541, 559, 561; helped by Lord Goodman 545; cuts reference to Armstrong from book 548; refuses to go to Butler's farewell party 548; puts hairdressing bills on Labour Party account 548; arranges for HW to dine with Frost 552; illness 564, 567; wants HW to recommend her brother to Prince Fahd 571; insists on BD's exclusion from Rome trip 576; further rows with HW 577; mad and 'evil' 591; obsessed with BD 601; demands peerages for friends 601, 603, 618; asks Connell to ghost-write her book 603; makes HW cancel meeting with Frost 608; and HW's 'personal guest list' at Guildhall ceremony 608, 609; further rows with HW 613; and HW's TV ideas 614; presses HW to stay on 614, 620; not invited to Richardson party 624; at counter-inflation unit dinner 628, 630 635; attacks Mrs Wilson and Janet 630; refuses to be fingerprinted 631; and Geoffrey Goodman 631, 637; demands help for Cordle 632–3, 639, 642; builds up show-business contacts 637; lunches with Frost 642; arranges HW's 60th birthday photograph 648; 'more obsessive than ever before' 652; controls HW's bank accounts 652; rows with HW about retirement 661, 663,

671, 674, 679; and her children's education 669, 675; and Film Industry Report 671; and Weidenfeld 679–80; requests to be 'received' by the Queen 681; wants HW to leak intention to retire 682; rows with HW over financial irregularities 684–5; makes 'remarkable' requests 691; at HW's 60th party 693; further rows with HW 700–1; controls honours list 702, 705; receives money from HW 706; and the Queen 709; cancels No. 10 reception 710–11; writes guest list for HW's party for Labour Party helpers 713; and Policy Unit party 715; at HW's farewell lunch 719–20; at JH's farewell party 719–20

Falkland Islands 352, 355, 689
family allowance 79, 80
Faulkner, Brian 84, 120, 130
Faulks Royal Commission Report 601, 688
Faure, Edgar 450
Fawkes, Wally (Trog) 144
Fernyhough, Ernest 340
Ferranti 180, 346
Field, Anthony (Tony) 33; breaks into garage with HW 83; his wedding and MF 89, 226, 429; land deals 39, 72, 88, 89–90, 288, 502, 575–6; HW spends weekend with 240; as intermediary with IRA 286; HW pressured to arrange job for 288, 507, 509, 528; and Milhench 431–2; and Lord Arwyn 497, 502, 688; loan to pay tax debts requested by HW 575–6, 716–17; on HW's 'personal guest list' 608, 609; and property speculation in Wales 688, 701
Field, Peggy: and her sister 15, 33, 86; and election campaign 22, 27, 34, 35, 37, 38, 39, 40; works for MF 56; reports to her on HW and Janet Hewlett-Davies 375; salary 431; has stake in brother's company 432; courts an international criminal 479; on HW's 'personal guest list' 608, 609; awarded MBE 715; at farewell lunch 719
Figgures, Sir Frank 428
Film Industry Report and committee 671, 679, 682, 706
Finance Bill 164, 165
*Financial Times* 79, 116, 138, 249, 276, 467, 603, 669, 687, 689
Finer, Maurice 112, 131, 253, 263, 280
Finniston, Sir Monty 138, 160–1, 276, 358, 386, 388, 417, 471, 554, 615, 651
Fisher, Frederick (Freddie) 276, 687
Fisher, Sammy 471, 567, 608, 609, 623
Fitt, Gerry 180, 380, 495, 502
Fitzgerald, Garrett 326
Flask, The (pub) 95, 210
Fletcher, Raymond 642

Foley, Maurice 640
Foot, Michael 10; becomes Secretary of State for
    Employment 50, 55, 61, 66; and miners'
    settlement 62; and statutory incomes policy
    73; and Industrial Relations Bill 76, 80, 81;
    and press leaks on union fines 104; 'engaging
    naivety' 105; and EEC renegotiations 106,
    141; and economic policy 135; on London
    weighting 164; and Benn's Industrial White
    Paper 169; introduction to manifesto
    rewritten 187; agrees to attack Tories on
    unemployment 191; confident about election
    205; and economic crisis 236, 237; com-
    promises 240; and top people's salaries
    244, 250, 256, 266, 267, 353; against imple-
    mentation of EEC tariffs 245; and Crossman
    Diaries 246, 432; displaced in NEC elections
    249; praises Healey 251; and bakers' strike
    254; and EEC 273, 314, 337, 342, 365;
    attacked by Prentice 320, 323; and Defence
    spending 324; and railways wage claim 352,
    412, 415; has testicular cancer 385, 391–2;
    dislikes MF 385; and Cabinet reshuffle
    405–6, 407, 411; holds secret meetings with
    TUC 437; and sterling crisis 438, 439, 440,
    441; threatens to resign 445; and incomes
    policy 447, 450, 457, 459–60, 462, 465;
    romantic view of TUC 461; supports
    counter-inflation policy 491; dropped by
    Tribune Group 513; and unemployment 521,
    555; and industrial policies 532, 533; with-
    draws from party political broadcast 586; and
    Chrysler 596; resists London weighting for
    MPs 647; and Radcliffe Report 650; suggests
    Mikardo for Steel Corporation 652; and
    Royal Commission on Law 662; and wages
    policy 662; has fifteen minutes with the
    Queen 709; and leadership contest 711, 712,
    714, 715, 720
Football Association 28, 382
Football Levy Board 249, 256
Ford, Gerald, US President 296, 301, 302, 308,
    373, 400, 497, 373
Ford, Henry 413
Ford Motors 214
Foreign Office 94, 111, 121, 133, 137, 275, 309–16
    passim, 322, 325, 327, 329, 360, 482, 483,
    517, 549; Referendum Campaign committee
    381–2, 384, 387, 388, 390, 392, 394, 395, 396,
    398
Forrester, Mark 58, 111, 480, 490
Foster, Sir Christopher (Chris) 60, 67, 436
Fowler, Professor Gerald (Gerry): appointed
    Minister for Education 66; threatens resigna-
    tion over cuts 148; as minister responsible
    for devolution 228, 246, 285, 286, 289, 415,
    477, 486, 493, 495, 611, 625, 637; tells BD
    of Jenkins/Prentice agreement 235; friend-
    ship with BD 264; against Foot 323; and

EEC negotiations 336, 337; against giving
    people living abroad the vote 356; relaxed
    about economic crisis 436; had up for
    drunken driving 494; disliked by Ted Short
    618; back at Education 637–8, 640, 653, 661,
    673
Fowler, Joe 373
Fowles, Elizabeth 443
Fox, Murray 95
France/the French 148, 166, 174, 185, 258–62,
    281, 322, 326–7, 329; see also Giscard Estaing,
    Valéry; Mitterrand, François; Pomonti,
    Jacques
Franco, General Francisco: funeral 573, 575
Franks Report on Official Secrets 474, 475, 479,
    527, 601, 644, 688
Fraser, Lady Antonia 332, 473
Fraser, Hugh 332
Fraser, Ian 574
Freeman, Catherine 79
Freeman, David 308, 605, 615
Freeman, John 79, 673, 691
French, Philip 144
Frost, David 206, 281, 288, 291, 428, 473, 519,
    552, 601, 614, 625, 642, 702, 705, 706, 714
Fulbright, Senator James William 373

Gaitskell, Dora 403
Gaitskell, Hugh 1, 7, 50, 73, 496, 588, 607
Gardiner, George 139
Garfield, Alfred 283, 671
GATT 547
Gatt, Israel 117, 183, 250, 533, 558, 633, 641,
    661, 666–7, 668
Gavron, Bob 560
General & Municipal Workers' Union 393, 578
German, Clifford 279, 470
Germans/Germany 322, 326, 329, 490, 596; see
    also Schmidt, Helmut
Gibbings, Peter 389, 446, 481, 497, 541, 683,
    712
gifts and capital transfer tax 168, 240
Gilbert, John 256, 394, 395, 397, 410, 414, 651
Gilbert, Sir Martin 132
Gilmour, Ian 309–10, 632
Giscard d'Estaing, Valéry 166, 185, 242, 251, 253,
    254, 258, 260, 261, 322, 331, 394, 638
Goldsmith, Sir James (Jimmy) 428, 519, 552,
    585, 608, 614, 625, 635, 654, 669, 711, 714,
    715
Goodman, Lord Arnold: relationship with MF
    15; and press attacks on MF 40, 78, 87, 91,
    94, 132, 166, 191; as adviser to newspaper
    industry 76; and HW's tax affairs 96, 212;
    and Short 109; plots to save HW from MF
    154–5, 157; reports on Lever's health 164;
    looks like pantomime dame 168; appalled by
    everything 194; attacked by MF 211; and
    theft of HW's tax papers and Daily Mail

smear story 211, 213, 222, 233, 283; and
MF's house sales 502, 545; and merger of
*Observer* 526, 541; told of HW's retirement
530; and sale of HW's house 541; asked to
help find school for MF's boys 545; and
consultants' dispute 585, 589, 590, 591–3;
attacks MF 604; and HW's retirement date
615, 650, 696; illness 641, 647, 693; as
trustee for MF's children 675
Goodman, Geoffrey 23, 24, 32, 35, 38, 136, 470;
and counter-inflation unit 489, 515, 630,
631–2, 635, 637
Gordon Walker, Patrick 43, 522
Gore-Booth, Sir Paul 262
Gormley, Joe 32
Gosling, Sir Donald 471, 714, 715
Gower, Professor James (Jim) 287, 308
Gowland, David 222, 413, 436, 474
Grabham, Sir Arthur 592
Grade, Lord Lew 694, 702, 715
Graham, Andrew 221; pessimistic about
economic policy 135; writes memo on
economic strategy 139; Rothschild wants to
borrow 142; doing splendid job 183, 207;
knows all MF's tricks 229; attends Economic
Strategy committees 237, 255; works on Unit
economic paper 265, 267, 271, and memo on
nationalised industries 274; advises HW on
economic options 312, 313; on petrol tax 316,
339; prepares briefs for Healey 340, 347–8,
389; with BD at Political Economy Club 354;
writes industrial policy paper 420–1; at
Chequers Cabinet meeting 421; 'always very
wise' 429; produces serious papers on sterling
and pay settlements 436–7; works on Incomes
Policy White Paper 452, 456, 474; 'superb'
483; not allowed to attend Wass's Short-Term
Economic Policy committee 485; returns to
work half-time at Balliol 520; reports on
discussions with Stowe 536; works on briefs
for HW 538, 539;
Graham, Nori 118, 204, 362, 472, 485, 568
Graham, Philip 204, 362, 485
Graham, Richard 105, 125, 172, 222, 238, 258,
265, 274, 318, 358, 384, 452, 484, 520, 537,
615
Granada TV 320
Grange Farm, Buckinghamshire 42, 104
Grant, Bruce 413, 416–7
Grant, Cary 302
Grant, John 155, 176, 189, 196, 198, 205, 316,
366, 381, 384, 395, 396, 398
Gray, Simon: *Otherwise Engaged* 537
Greene, Graham 135, 148–9, 244, 246, 275, 279,
307, 348, 518–19, 522, 660, 710
Greene, Sidney (*later* Lord) 79, 523, 524
Greenhall, Stella 587
Greig, Gordon 482–3, 623
Grieveson Grant (stockbrokers) 83, 105, 133, 153,
162, 178, 228, 278, 313, 355, 385, 397, 427,
474, 574, 623, 684, 696
Griffin, Ken 662
Griffin, Senator Robert P. 302
Griffiths, Brian 655
Griffiths, James 43
Griffiths, Trevor: *The Comedians* 533
Gromyko, Andrei 374, 706, 710
Gross, John 79, 269, 473, 534
Gross, Miriam 79, 269, 693
*Guardian* 37, 81, 116, 138, 154, 159, 160, 274,
282, 289, 304, 389, 446, 525, 526, 566, 590,
615, 636, 683, 704, 712
Guinness Peat 125, 145–6

Haden, Robin 59
Hailsham, Lord 28
Hain, Peter 677, 678, 688
Haines, Joseph (Joe) 2, 545; appearance 3, 22, 41;
character and personality 3, 24, 32, 37, 41,
99, 226; relationship with MF 14, 15, 16, 23,
35; on HW 31, 32, 34, 36–7, 96, 101; and
election campaign 8, 9, 20–47 *passim*; back in
Downing Street 50–1, 54, 55, 56, 58; opposes
Rodgers's appointment 63, 64; attacked by
MF 65; loses best secretary to BD 67; angry
with Lever over EEC broadcast 68; writes
HW's speech threatening Tories 70, 71; angry
with MF 75, 82; complains of losing touch
with HW 81, 83; and MF and the press 87,
88, 89–91, 92; on MF 77, 81, 93–4, 97, 98;
angry at press smears against HW 96; vetoes
resignations 98; writes MF's press statement
99; worried about relations with press 99;
speech-writing 107, 112, 113; and Murray's
failure to be selected 108, 109; on MF's
behaviour 115, 116, 117–18, 122; objects to
peerage for MF 123, 126, 127, 129; on
Northern Ireland 129, 132; threatens resignation if MF gets government post 129, 130,
132; wins battle with Armstrong over Press
Commission secretary 133, 134; angry with
MF 140, 142, 143, 146; in Germany with
HW and BD 142, 143; attacked by MF 154,
155–6; advises MF to sue press 160; opposes
gimmicky insertion in HW's TUC speech
174, 175, 176; election speeches 176, 181,
186–7; clashes with HW in Paris 185; criticised for staying in hotel during election 187,
188, 190–1; and HW's attacks on the press
192, 193; loses temper with Lyons 196; takes
over speech-writing from Lyons and Davis
196–7; and Brayley resignation 198, 199; supper
with Janet Hewlett-Davies 199–200; campaign
speechwriting 199, 200, 201, 202, 203, 209, 210;
and complaints from HW 204, 205; exhausted
and depressed 206, 207, 208, 209; and press
allegations about HW's tax affairs 211–12;
writes HW's TV script 212, 213, 214; election

day in Liverpool 216, 217; clashes with MF 218; difficult relations with HW 222, 224, 225; agrees to resign if BD does 223; and HW's plans for Policy Unit 224–5, 226–7, 229–30, 231, 232; re-establishes relations with HW 228; and theft of HW's tax papers 233, 236; with HW at Childers's funeral 246; works on HW's party conference speech 248, 249; angry with Benn 257; in Paris for Summit 258, 259, 260, 261; worried about HW's health 264; lunch at House of Commons with Rodgers 271; at economic discussions 275–6; angry at attempt to get Maitland on Washington trip 280; at Chequers 284, 285, 286; and IRA 286; lunch with *Guardian* people 289; dinner with Frost and girlfriend 291; plans to help Mrs Thatcher in leadership contest 294

    **January 1975 – April 1976**
    advises HW on Crossman Diaries 294, 295, 296; warns MF against suing *Evening Standard* 295; in Canada 297, 298, Washington 299, 300, 302, 303, and Moscow 311, 312; and pre-Dublin Summit discussions 323, 324, 326; not invited to lunch for US Ambassador 327; rows with HW over MF and Davis writing speech 327–8; in Dublin 329, 330, 331; and HW and anti-marketeers 340, 341; tired and depressed 345; advises BD not to confront HW over Jamaica trip 349, 351; happy with Stowe's appointment 358, 359; reports on HW and Janet Hewlett-Davies 358–9; disapproves of Reform Club 360–1; strengthens HW's EEC conference speech 363; shocked at MF arranging Israel trip 365; enjoys Jamaica trip 365, 366; in Washington 373, 374–5; thinks of resigning 380; furious at MF's behaviour at dinner 383, 384; tired and irritated 385; bruised from car accident 392; foretells HW's resignation 395; suspected of leaks 396; angry at MF 403; advises on Cabinet reshuffle 406; defends BD 415, 426–7; and Crossman Diaries 420; announces abolition of parliamentary press lobby 420; puts up ideas on wages policy 429–30; and sterling crisis 437–8, 442, 443–4; forbidden to see Cabinet minutes 451, 452; approves Unit's draft of Income Policy White Paper 452, 453; feels excluded 458, 468–9; redrafts HW's Durham Miners' Gala speech 473; on HW's retirement and his future 473–4, 480; tired and irritable 474; realises how shabby Britain is 490; feels ill 494; advises HW on Press Commission 502–3; smear linking him with Kay

Carmichael 509; at Blackpool conference 511, 512, 513, 514, 515; cut from acknowledgements in MF's book 533–4; disagrees with BD over council house sales 535; worried about the future 537; rumoured to be having affair with Janet Hewlett-Davies 557; keen to tell BD of HW's praise 565; attacked by MF for friendship with Frost's girlfriend 601; negotiates with press on privacy 601–2; called 'a professional liar' by *The Times* 615; and winding-up of counter-inflation unit 630, 631–2, 637; has conjunctivitis 636; 'ingenious devices' regarding council house sales 639; suspects Ryder is in trouble 639; clashes with MF 648; furious at HW's bad manners 655; upset with Hunt for arranging HW's interview with *The Times* 656; warned by HW of bugging 656–7; issues writs against *The Times* 656, 658; and HW's retirement 664, 665, 672, 673, 674; advises BD about Israelis 666, 667; advises HW on peerages 668; obtains copy of MF's letter to HW requesting friend's appointment 669; mixed feelings that the end is in sight 672, 686; feigns illness rather than go to HW's 60th 694; goes over final resignation arrangements 696, 697; 'dropped like a used glove' 700; offended by HW's TV interviews 705, 706; depressed about future 708, and HW's honours list 714; does not receive honour 715; tired and ill 717–18; declines peerage 719; gives farewell party 720–1; does not say goodbye 722

Hale, John 307, 320, 383, 679
Hall, Basil 420, 530
Halls, Marjorie 136, 191, 193, 211
Halls, Michael 77, 84, 96, 136
Hamilton, Sir Denis 666
Hamilton, Sir James (Jim) 95, 445, 452, 579, 617, 629, 670–1, 680
Hamilton, William (Willie) 124
Hamm, Adrian 85, 121
Handler, Ariah (Arie) 416
Hanson, Sir James 436, 691, 715
hare-coursing 415, 538
Harland & Wolff shipyard 125
Harmsworth, Sir Geoffrey 76, 213
Harmsworth, Vere 528
Harrier jump-jets 379
Harriman, Averell 370
Harrington, Illtyd 572, 715
Harris, John 24, 25, 29, 30, 33, 45, 49, 52, 60, 67, 68, 116, 124, 336, 638
Harris, Kenneth 79, 673–4
Harris, Ralph 354

Harrison, Walter 409

Hart, Judith 106, 119, 121, 225, 234, 235, 236, 237, 255, 319, 323, 335, 336, 404, 408, 409, 411, 501

Hartley-Booth, Elizabeth 222

Hartman, Arthur 301, 304, 326, 368, 370, 599–600

Hartman, Donna 301, 304

Hartwell, Michael Berry, Lord 540

Hartwell, Pamela Berry, Lady 335, 540

Haseler, Stephen 415

Hattersley, Roy: and HW 51, 66, 214, 404; and EEC referendum campaign 381, 382, 384, 387, 394, 396, 398; discusses Prentice with BD 478–9; and Iceland 'cod war' 579, 629, 641–2; conducts talks with Luxembourg PM 676; supports Callaghan 712

Havers, Sir Michael 531

Hawkins, Hector 359, 589

Hayman, Helene 394, 399, 418, 455, 481, 486, 712

Hayward, Ron 20; row with Percy Clarke 22; complains about right-wingers 25; and discussions on Transport House 39, 60, 66; asks for Privy Counsellorship and knighthood 66; lunches at No. 10 143; complains about Davis and Lyons coming to No. 10 151; angry at not being invited to election campaign discussion 182; HW tries to restore relations with 188; overtly friendly towards BD 192; implies BD is source of press leaks 201; refuses to allow MF and Albert Murray to appear in BBC film 207, 208; attacks HW's 'entourage at No. 10' 208; refuses to pay political office expenses 273; and EEC 273, 340–1, 345, 365, 366, 367, 388; attacked in press for owning two properties 281; Margaret Jackson scathing about 477; interrupts Chrysler meeting over Franco's funeral 573; angers HW 575; has 'high-level liaison' meeting with HW 667; told of HW's resignation 699; arrives for non-existent No. 10 reception 710–11

Healey, Denis 10; and election campaign 21, 30, 37, 38; and miners' settlement 62; as possible successor to HW 67; at weekly 'Prayers' meeting 71; criticised by HW 82, 89, 115, 145; and EEC renegotiations 106, 107, 348; and Lever 108–9, 111, 120, 121, 126, 151; criticised by BD 135; and industrial policy 143, 158; attacks Benn 144, 149, 150; and mortgages 146, 151; defeated on Finance Bill 165; and Benn's Industry White Paper 169, 171; and devolution 170, 294, 415, 416, 493, 494, 546; and land nationalisation 175; scornful of Benn's policies 180; amazed at HW's attack on right-wing plot 227; defeated by Benn 235; and lack of coherent policy 236; clashes with Benn 241, 256, 317–18, 346, 359; criticised by Callaghan 244; supports EEC tariff charges 245, 252; praised by Foot 251; economic incompetence 266, 376, 280, 315; and oil recycling 278; and imminent economic collapse 280; hawkish on Americans, dovish on Arabs 296; on commodities 307–8; depresses Jenkins 316; and Defence spending 318, 324; and public expenditure cuts 334, 339, 340, 344–5; accuses Unit of leaks 339; criticised by Crosland 343, 345; in Turkey 362; and public expenditure 378, 389, 390–1, 459, 470, 563, 564, 566, 619, 620; and EEC 394, 395; and post-referendum reshuffle 397; and railway wages claim 412, 413; HW's minute to 432–3; and sterling crises 426, 438, 439, 440, 441, 442, 443, 444, 445–6, 447, 686, 689–90; and TUC 449, 450; isolated 450–1; and pay policy 457, 458, 460, 465, 466–7; under strain 458; Wass's analysis of 484; and NEC 503, 514; and Northern Ireland 506; and industrial strategy 520, 521, 530, 532, 533; his lecturing manner irritates Jenkins 521; criticised by Owen 536; gloomy over economy 536, 538; and import controls 538, 539; at secret committee meeting on economic policy 542–3; rough with TUC 548; at NEDC meeting 554; clashes with HW 593–4; and Defence cuts 593, 594, 631; and Chrysler 607, 611, 612; more optimistic about economy 640; and Official Secrets 644, 684; wants new blood in nationalised industries 651; impressive in meeting about wages policy 662; eager to talk to press 672; declines to attend film industry committee 682; optimistic 683; and leadership election 701, 703, 715, 720; *see also* Budgets

Healey, Michael 497

health service *see* National Health Service

Heath, Sir Edward 69, 75, 82; establishes CPRS (1971) 61; and EEC (1973) 242; incomes policy (1973) 4, 71; relations with unions 4; calls election 2, 4–5, 82, 122; attacked by Short 20; violent speech 23, 25; attacked by Powell 29, 31; election campaign 33, 35, 38, 40, 43; and Tory defeat 46, 47, 48, 49; coalition discussions 51–2, 55; resignation 52, 53, 74; older and thinner 73; co-operative over press 89; speaks in debate on industrial policy 142, 144; writes to HW about Lever affair 161; greets British Lions back from South Africa 169; abrasive and confrontational style 177; attacked by Keith Joseph on incomes policy 178; gives speech 'full of wild talk' 203, and 'flat' speech 234; loses to Margaret Thatcher 294, 306; 'sour and unhappy' 338; critical of Civil Service 342; smiles at HW's attack on Mrs Thatcher 357; visits No. 10 357; angers Mrs Thatcher 396; and Poulson case 427; pay policy repeated 443; makes superb speech 476, 477; pays tribute to HW 700

Heathcoat Amory, Derek 574
Heffer, Eric 100, 316, 336, 349, 411, 503, 514, 586, 681, 692, 711
Heinz, John 372
Heinz, Teresa 151, 372
Helsby, Laurence 119
Henderson, Lady Mary 142
Henderson, Sir Nicholas (Nico) 142, 236
Hennessy, Peter 678, 682
Herbert, Alfred (company) 317, 435
Heseltine, Michael 362
Hetherington, Alastair 159, 289, 389, 446
Hetherington, Anthony (Tony) 517
Hewlett-Davies, Janet 199–200; and HW 93, 272, 313, 362, 374–5, 413–14, 419, 431, 540, 549, 682; MF jealous of 282, 375, 501; on MF 323, 397, 506–7; lunches with BD 335; and trip to Jamaica 349, 359; on Washington trip 373, 374–5; Mary Wilson complains about 504; on HW's retirement 664; at HW's farewell lunch 719, 720; offered demotion 723
Higgins, Ronald (Ron) 91, 92, 106, 111, 232
Himmelweit, Professor Hilde 674
Hirshfield, Desmond 112
Hoare Govett 157
Hobson, Ronald 714
Holland, Stuart 308, 333, 531
Home, Lord and Lady 71
honours/peerages 60, 86, 279, 359, 568, 572, 601, 603, 608–9, 613, 615, 618, 668, 702, 705, 714–15, 716, 719, 720
Hooper, L. 689
Hopkin, Bryan 272, 701
Hopkinson, David 105, 630
Housden, William (Bill) 21; and MF 15, 98, 114, 118, 151, 225, 277–8, 567; on MF and Labour Party finances 145; repeats MF's conversations and rows with HW 188, 190, 191, 223, 230, 273, 279, 617, 671; and HW and Janet Hewlett-Davies 362; on HW's retirement 428–9, 477, 525, 530, 617, 642, 691; on MF's acceptance of gifts 541; on HW 618, 721; receives honour 668, 698, 715
Howard, Anthony 464, 513, 606
Howe, Geoffrey 476
Howell, Denis 1, 61, 64, 68, 86, 128, 169, 233, 234, 249, 272, 273, 274, 311, 315, 354, 462, 551
Hower, Barbara 369, 370
Hoy, James (Jimmy) 132
Huckfield, Les 552
Hughes, Cledwyn 573, 691, 699
Hume, John 180
Humphrey, Hubert 302
Hunt, Sir John 71; discussions with BD over job definition and relationship of Policy Unit to Cabinet Office 61, 85–6, 94, 95, 104, 105, 116; on Lever 111; compares Labour and last

Tory government 111; meetings with BD over monetary policy 115; at meeting on 'Lever plan' 122; and Northern Ireland 130, 132, 134; and Crossman Diaries 135, 149, 244, 264, 270, 279, 294, 295, 296, 307, 344, 420, 426, 427, 432, 516, 517–18, 522, 523, 543–4, 619, 669; prepares minute on impending bankruptcies 157; discusses Unit with BD 223; and meetings of deputy secretaries 225; backs BD 229; criticised by HW 229–30, 249; economic discussion with BD 258; in Paris for Summit 259, 261; supports BD on oil recycling 278; in Canada and USA 298, 300, 301; complains of BD's non-cooperation 320; at Dublin briefings 322, 326; and Unit's memo on Defence 323, 324; at meeting on World Poverty 338, 339; and Unit's paper on commodities 354; at briefing for Jamaica Summit 360; produces good paper on public expenditure 378; at referendum celebration party 384, 402; and pay policy discussions 433–4, 443, 445, 448; attacked by Sunday Times 437; and Unit's Incomes Policy White Paper 452–34, 457–8; wants rules on memoirs tightened 472; considers Franks Report dangerously liberal 474–5; presses HW to stay 488; empire-building 489, 541–2, 560, 594; and CPRS 500; in New York for Summit 506, 517; offers to include BD in Northern Ireland committee 516–17; Armstrong on 526, 527; and Unit involvement 536–7; opposes import controls 538; battle with Wass 539, 540, 548; and 'Dominion status' for Northern Ireland 550; and Stowe 560, 562, 567; accuses Crosland of leak 566; amuses BD 567; and Chrysler 579, 599; increasing interference 586; and Defence cuts 593, 624; shows signs of strain 606; knows of HW's retirement 614; and Radcliffe Report 627, 650, 653, 667; and devolution 638; interest in Royal Commission on the Law 646; 'the iron fist in the iron glove' 665; and James Hamilton 671; and privacy law 675; praised by HW 682; at Cabinet farewell dinner 707; MF does not want to sit next to 710; at farewell parties 715, 721
Hussein, King, of Jordan 180
Hutber, Patrick 651
Huyton Labour Club 44

Ibsen, Henrik: John Gabriel Borkman 417
Iceland 'cod war' 561, 575, 577, 579, 628, 629–30, 635, 641–2, 643, 646, 648
import controls 312, 392, 538–9, 547–8, 574, 575, 576, 598, 612–13
In Place of Strife (White Paper) 177, 179, 518
incomes policies: inherited from Heath 71, 105; Labour 22, 23, 26, 73, 115, 120, 135, 435–6, 447–51, 605, 653, 662; HW and 418, 419, 421,

422–6, 429–30, 432–4, 437–46; White Paper
and Bill 452–69 *passim*, 480; *see also* 'top
people's salaries'
industrial democracy 359, 377
Industrial Development Committees (IDV) 149,
180–1, 234, 235, 254–5, 282–3, 290, 317–18,
346, 359–60, 383, 435, 478, 479
industrial policies: and Benn *see under* Benn,
Anthony Wedgwood; Healey/Varley paper on
520–1, 530, 531, 532; NEC discussions 708;
*see also* industries, nationalised; Industry
White Paper
Industrial Relations Act (1972) 69, 76, 79, 80,
104, 432
industries, nationalised 60, 79, 80, 115, 144, 158,
240–1, 265, 266, 268, 274, 277, 278, 307, 315,
318, 322, 342, 378, 461, 651; *see also* aircraft,
motor and shipbuilding industry
Industry White Paper and Bill 158, 166, 169,
170–3, 234, 241, 277, 282–3, 318, 413–14,
418, 431
inflation 5, 6, 71, 73, 115, 163, 164, 248, 263, 265,
277, 354, 442, 472, 571; and counter-inflation
unit 438, 446–7, 450, 489, 515, 628, 630,
631–2, 635, 637, 680
Ingrams, Richard 297
Insole, Douglas 667
International Publishing Corporation (IPC) 104,
187, 244, 526
Inter-Parliamentary Union, London 497
*Investors' Review* 590
IRA 284, 286, 287, 330; bombings 134, 141, 211,
213, 233, 247
Isaacs, Jeremy 29, 116
Israel/Israeli issues 20, 137, 261, 353, 362, 365,
558, 630, 659; and MF 173, 364, 380–1,
384–5, 386, 388, 390, 397, 480, 499, 546–7,
577, 641, 646, 661, 666; *see also* Gatt, Israel;
Meir, Golda; Peri, Yoram; Raphael, Gideon
ITV 94, 205, 217; strike 393

Jackson, Margaret *see* Beckett, Margaret
Jackson, Tom 80, 548
Jacobson, Sydney 24, 489, 630
Jamaica Commonwealth Conference (1975) 308,
332, 344, 349, 352, 359, 360, 361, 365
Jarrett, Alex 567
Jarvis, Frederick (Fred) 361, 462
Javits, Senator Jacob 151
Jay, Anthony 625
Jay, Douglas 338
Jay, Peter 354, 446
Jeger, Lena 366
Jenkins, Clive 35, 173
Jenkins, Hugh 214, 418, 419, 525, 682
Jenkins, Jennifer 403, 488
Jenkins, Peter 37, 683, 671
Jenkins, Roy (*later* Lord Jenkins) 10; as
Chancellor of the Exchequer 4, 39; and EEC

6, 34, 49–50; and election campaign 21, 24–5,
26, 38, 41, 47; and HW 25, 42, 49–50, 52–3,
55, 60, 66–7; appointed Home Secretary 59;
and John Harris as his junior minister 67, 68;
and EEC renegotiations 106–7; interested in
BD's analysis of HW's character 113; differences with Crosland 123; and Northern
Ireland 124, 254, 387, 506, 562; and Price
sisters' hunger strike 134; criticises HW at
Oxford University Labour Club 136; has 'a
friendly chat' with BD 157–8; political inactivity 158–9; and EEC discussions 160;
gives speech calling for moderation 168, 227;
and Scottish devolution 170; has long and
productive discussion with BD 184–5; and
EEC referendum 186, 200; and election
campaign 207, 210, 214; visits Guildford after
IRA bombing 211; agreement with Prentice
rumoured 235; his 'emotionalism' not understood by HW 240; accepts referendum device
251–2; and British Leyland 255; and EEC
discussions 268; in USA 273; against Scottish
devolution 285, 286; has friendly talk with
HW 287; wants to raise TV licences fees 297;
depressed at Healey's running of the
Exchequer 316; wants to review gambling and
betting 318; threatens resignation over
Prentice 320; blamed for delay in EEC referendum 334; and economic issues 345, 351,
352; presses for people abroad to have the
vote 356; makes uncompromising speech on
EEC 364; and Defence cuts 379; angers HW
by attack on Benn 392; threatens to go if
Prentice goes 406, 411; and NUR strike 412;
suspected of plotting 415; and Scottish devolution 415, 416, 493, 494; and industrial
policy 421, 426, 431; supports EEC institute
448; given Franks Report 475, 479; supports
Prentice 484; visits BD in France 488; embarrassed by Healey 494; prevented from talking
to Rockefeller 497; wants Speaker's
Conference 498; and Royal Commission on
Gambling 506, 521, 590; irritated by Prentice
512; praises HW's Blackpool speech 514;
loses temper with Healey 521; and Official
Secrets 527, 529–30, 644; chairs IDV meeting
532, 533; and devolution 546; defeated on
electoral reform 570; advises BD not to go
back to LSE 590; and Defence cuts 590, 594;
and overcharging on TV licences 602, 604;
and Chrysler 608; wants to get rid of Alex
Lyon 611, 625, 689; Armstrong on 626; and
Radcliffe Report 627, 649–50; and Royal
Commission on Law 628, 656, 659; suggested
as President of EEC 638, 640, 720; wants to
be Leader of the House 640; and HW's
retirement 650; and railways 680; declines to
attend film industry committee 682; and
Official Secrets Act 683–4; speech interrupted

by Barbara Castle 707; and leadership election 702, 707, 708, 711, 712, 717, 720; and devolution 718
Jockey Club 325
Jones, Aubrey 412, 651
Jones, Barry 366, 658, 668
Jones, Elwyn: made Lord Chancellor 51, 55; suggested for Northern Ireland committee 124; 'chairs' Finer's memorial service 280; on devolution 284, 285, 493; and Crossman Diaries 420, 453; on statutory pay policy 421, 425; and Official Secrets Act 527, 644, 683; and Royal Commission on the Law 633, 635, 639, 647–8, 659, 660, 662–3, 675, 677, 680; and privacy law 654; and HW's resignation 699, 703
Jones, George 86, 154, 156, 157, 158, 499, 557
Jones, Jack 141, 177, 277, 386, 418, 440, 447, 461, 462, 491, 547, 554, 641, 658, 699
Jones, Janie 174
Joseph, Sir Keith 178, 207, 230
Joseph, Leslie 533, 651
Josephson, Diana 304
Judd, Frank 250, 289, 313, 336, 561, 660, 663, 681, 712
Junor, John 696
Just, Ward 370

Kagan, Sir Joseph 239, 268, 416, 429, 519, 559, 608, 609, 618, 701, 715, 716
Kaiser, Philip 282
Kaldor, Professor Nicholas 326, 454, 544
Karamanlis, Konstantinos 524, 525
Kaufman, Gerald: presses for Jenkins at Treasury 52–3; to the Palace with HW 54; praised by BD 54; presses HW to do TV broadcast 60; at Weidenfeld party 239; at informal party at No. 10 280; and EEC campaign 337, 340, 341; escorts MF to dinner for Fiji Prime Minister 383; and Israeli intrigues 558; promoted 597; and Varley's threatened resignation 607, 608; HW's views on 607, 611; at discussion on counter-inflation unit 628, 630; as trustee for MF's children 675
Kaye, Danny 302
Kearton, Frank 523, 537, 538, 576, 578, 603, 604, 636–7, 642, 651, 663, 674
Kedourie, Professor Elie 685
Keith, Kenneth 621, 651
Kennedy, John F., US President ix, 43; grave 303
Kennedy, Robert: grave 303
Kennet, Lord: 'Europe plus 30' 395
Khrushchev, Nikita 673
Kidd, Vicky 85, 109, 246, 286, 454–5
Kilbrandon Report (1973) 66
Killick, Sir John 482
Kilroy-Silk, Robert 250

King, General Frank 315
King Murray, Ronald (later Lord) 285
Kinnock, Neil 467
Kirby, Michael (Mike) 298
Kirkby, Merseyside: Golden Eagle 41, 44–5
Kirwan, Richard 105, 139, 222, 271
Kissin, Harry (later Lord): reports to BD on HW's appointments 66; at Weidenfeld party 79; worried about HW and MF 85; worried about his delayed peerage 108; and Lever 108, 113, 114, 146, 157; and HW's relationship with MF 132, 154–5; takes seat in the Lords 168; meeting with HW 168; tells BD about financial provisions of HW's political office 172; warns BD that HW means to drop JH 194; takes BD to meet Spiers 282; warns BD that HW suspects him of press leaks 347; feels shut out by HW 358; tells BD of Foot's cancer 385; reports on HW 391; ill and angry with HW 501; tells BD that HW praised him 613; his pact with MF 620; and New Statesman 635; warns of bugging 657; has phlebitis 693
Kissinger, Henry 109; optimistic about Middle East settlement 111; sees HW 156; and Lever 275; compares Ford to Nixon 296; meetings with HW 301, 302, 312, 325–6; Spiers's views on 308; floor price plan for oil 325; 'in low form' 356; and Hartman 368; at Harriman's party 370; 'like a great bullfrog' 372; loves trappings of power 374; and Middle East negotiations 373, 465, 500; worried about Moynihan and UN 599–600; views on communists 632; worried about wife's health 632
Knight, Sir Arthur 567
Knox, Brian 385, 452, 700
Knox, Susanna 700
Kogan, Maurice 419, 621
Kollek, Teddy 687
Krichefski, Senator Bernard 263

Laing, Hector 523
Lamb, Larry 515
Lambton, Lord Antony 86, 87, 114, 123
Lancaster, Terry 22, 47, 76, 89, 91–2, 98, 117, 118, 129, 134, 135, 145, 181, 378, 393, 720
land nationalisation 69, 123, 133–4, 139, 145, 153, 162, 165, 166, 172, 175, 178, 349
Lander, Donald 581
Lansdowne Club, London 500
Lazarus, Peter 639
Lea, David 104, 119
Lee, Jennie 168, 327
Lee Kuan Yew 654
Leonard, Dick 88, 509
Lester, Anthony (Tony) 121, 184, 200, 207, 210, 235, 236, 316, 475, 521, 529, 604, 628, 635, 658, 717, 718

Lestor, Joan 25, 234–5, 236, 237, 352, 410, 578, 631, 673
Lever, Diane, Lady 151, 163, 164, 298, 299, 481, 634, 635, 708
Lever, Harold 1; and election campaign 25, 27, 28, 31, 32, 45; appointed Chancellor of the Duchy of Lancaster 60, 62, 66; forgets to get BD Deputy Secretaryship 63; MF objects to his becoming Minister for the Civil Service 67; not interested in political organisation 64; optimistic about Budget 67; gives French TV broadcast questioning EEC referendum 68; plans to deal with inflation 71; threatens resignation over Budget 77, 78; mortgage schemes 85, 86, 89, 104, 108, 120, 146, 151; rumoured by Healey to have been 'frozen out' by Treasury 108–9, 111; worried by position on Cabinet list 113, 114; pressed by HW to raise loans to support sterling 115; oil crisis plan opposed by Healey and Callaghan 121; speaks well at Guinness Peat 125; accused of being 'in cahoots' with BD 126; at Buckingham Palace dinner 132; warns HW of collapse in financial confidence 135; mortgage scheme under threat 136; bad press relations 140; and snide references from HW 151; summoned to Chequers to discuss 'Kissin plot' 154–5, 157; and Commons crisis 161, 162, 163, 164; and alleged Short forgery 165; hostile to wealth tax 168; in fine form 175; and land nationalisation 178; laughs at Benn 180; puzzled by Roy Jenkins 200; quarrels with BD 204; speaks well at press conference 205; sends BD peace offering 212; advises BD to remain calm about threat to Unit 228; tells BD of HW's plans 234; bets on Healey defeating Benn 235; opposes Benn 241; supports implementation of EEC tariffs 245; excluded from committee on Crown Agents 266; economic plans opposed by HW 274–5; critical of proposals for Burmah Oil 277; Canadian trip 297, 298, 299; in Washington 303, 304, 305; argues for generous compensation for nationalisation 315; unsure how to handle economy 316; supports Healey's public expenditure cuts 345; worried about Budget and 'intimidated' 349; ignores MF's histrionics 350; and Defence cuts 351, 379; disagrees with Healey's expenditure cuts 353; excluded from committees 353; appointed Minister of the Arts 390, 392, 393, 418, 419, 481; loses temper with BD 402; treated badly by HW 410; disagrees with Foot 414; misses hare-coursing vote 415; and pay policy 425, 465–6; excluded from discussions 449, 475; and North Sea oil 472; delighted at Benn's troubles 479; and MF's non-arrival at dinner 480–1, 634–5;

and industrial policies 532, 533; clashes with Benn over oil 538, 603–4; writes excellent papers 575; and Chrysler 596, 597–8, 599, 600, 607, 609, 610, 611, 631, 636; and HW's retirement 614–15, 628, 634; angers HW over leaks 636; reports on the Arts 649; and BNOC 674; cold-shouldered by HW 677, 684; embarrassed by film industry committee 682; bets on vote of confidence 693; on 'D-Day' 698; supports Jenkins for leader 707, 708; and council house sales 710; savage about HW 716; tells BD story of Tony Field's tax bill 716–17
Levin, Bernard 657
Levy, Norma 87, 174
Liberal Party 48, 51–2, 55, 68, 146, 147, 167, 210, 219, 485
Libya/Libyans 365, 377
Liddell, Helen 625, 655, 665
Lipsey, David 68, 222, 569, 639
Lloyd, Cliff 708
Lloyd, John Selwyn 94, 654, 664
Lollobrigida, Gina 203
London School of Economics (LSE) 1, 6, 8–9, 26, 40, 52, 53, 55, 60, 64, 69, 263, 311, 349, 556, 557, 623; 'Brookings-type' institute 448–9, 491, 524, 555–6, 697
Lord, Alan 447, 485, 544, 578, 597, 599
Lovell, Arnold 625
Lovell, Bernard 413
Lovell-Davis, Lord *see* Davis, Peter
LSE *see* London School of Economics
Lubbock, Eric 51
Luns, Dr Joseph 629, 635
Lycon, John 345
Lynn, Vera 476
Lyon, Alex 611, 625, 689
Lyons, Denis 26, 31, 75, 114, 116; as Marcia's Mafia 141, 151, 154, 174; promised peerage by MF 141; and 'Declaration of Interdependence' paper 174; and HW's reconciliation efforts 176, 181; attacks Percy Clarke 182; at MF's alternative meetings 189, 195; clashes with JH over lunch at No. 10 196; admits inability to write election speeches 196–7; co-operates with BD and JH 197–8, 201, 203; in BBC film 208, 209; on honours list 238, 240; at HW's dinner for Whitlam 268; discusses government advertising with BD 287; reports to BD on *Private Eye* lunch 596
Lyttle, John 366, 394, 434, 628

McAlpine, Alistair 436, 691
Macarthur, Brian 341, 342
McCaffrey, Sir Thomas (Tom) 262, 329, 330, 331, 374, 384, 723
McCarthy, William (Bill) 540
Macdonald, Jane 576

McFadzean, Francis Scott, Lord 523
MacFarquhar, Profesor Roderick 361
McGahey, Michael (Mick) 424
McGarvey, Dan 554, 683
McGovern, George 302
McGregor, Sir Ian 651
McGregor, Professor Oliver R. 131, 263, 280, 565, 659, 662
McIndoe, William (Bill) 675
McIntosh, Ronald (Ronnie) 276, 318, 342, 428, 554
Mackay, Dave 713
McKie, David 683
Mackintosh, John 546, 689
Maclennan, Robert (Bob) 62, 148, 336, 611
McMahon, Sir Christopher (Kit) 523, 524, 548, 549
McNally, Tom 34, 152, 245; flushes out truth about loans to Chile 316; in Dublin 329, 331; prepares HW's brief for Jamaica conference 345, 349–50, 355, 360, 361; at Referendum Campaign committee meetings 384, 398; praises Callaghan for protecting him 549; reports to BD on Iceland 'cod war' 629, 630; and airport security 632; prepares a further brief on special advisers 662, 663, 664; depressed about situation in Rhodesia 679; his future position discussed 682, 701–2, 704, 706; as political adviser to Callaghan 712, 722, 723
Magee, Bryan 248
Maitland, Donald 280, 290, 325
Makarios, Archbishop 165–6, 167
Manifesto Group 586, 692
Manley, Michael 93, 296, 584
Mansfield, Mike 302
Maplin airport 162, 164
Margach, James (Jimmy) 191, 208, 702
Marks, Ken 407, 408
Marsh, Sir Richard (Dick) 60, 378, 461, 554, 651
Mason, Roy: becomes Defence minister 55; and Cyprus emergency 167; and Barnsley Brewery 178; and Prentice's 'leadership plot' 321; and Defence cuts 324, 351, 501, 561, 563, 593, 602, 626, 631; argues for jump-jet Harrier 379; and Northern Ireland 506, 621; and Iceland 629–30; and Official Secrets 644, 683; against select committees 645
Matthews, Stanley 119
Maudling, Reginald (Reggie) 115, 314, 531, 548
Maxton, James 11
Maxwell, Robert 291
Maynard, Joan 645, 708
Meacher, Michael 410, 544
Meir, Golda 250, 489, 630
Melchett, Lady Sonia 269
Mellish, Robert (Bob): 70, 71; and MF's peerage 124–5; and discussions over Benn 139; and defaulting local authorities 160; and Commons

crisis over Lever 161, 163, 164; announces Parliament is 'no longer feasible' 168; and Brayley 199; and Hayward's attack on HW's 'entourage' 208; HW's plans for 214; 'gets the facts straight' on 'plot' 227; reports on Tribune Group 244; resigns, then stays on 266; attacks Short 333; at EEC referendum meetings 294, 381, 384, 395, 398; turns down offer of Transport 409, 410, 705; and pay policy discussions 425, 465; helps Ashley 484; his Catholicism 705
Members of Parliament: declaration of interests 110; salaries 244–5, 429, 435, 449, 450, 471, 647
Mendelson, John 467
Meriden Co-operative 317, 435
Midgley, John 304
Mikardo, Ian 109, 173, 186, 250, 511, 586, 652, 667, 668, 710
Milhench, Ronald 87, 431
Millan, Bruce 209, 337, 340, 577, 578, 579, 581, 582, 596, 607, 659
Miller, Sir Eric: provides storage for HW's papers 162, 167; finances Labour Party 246, 273; and HW 268, 307; relationship with MF 347, 363, 364, 389–90, 394, 399, 406, 415–16, 468, 471, 622, 674; and Sinatra's visit 383–4, 388, 396; property company in trouble 430; and MF's cancelled trip to Israel 499; at Sadat dinner 559; at HW's Freedom of the City ceremony 608; relationship with MF cooling 624; and son's bar mitzvah 585, 638; gives bracelets to MF 715; knighted 609, 715; commits suicide 430, 609
Miller, Lady Myra 389, 394, 406, 559, 638
Mills, Sir John 715
mineworkers see National Union of Mineworkers
Mirror see Daily Mirror
'Misc' committees 308
Mitchell, Derek 15, 301, 543, 548
Mitterrand, François 198, 262, 289, 488–9
Model, Dr Michael 662
Morgan, Cliff 308
MORI polls 2, 220; see Worcester, Robert
Morning Star 364
Moro, Aldo 329
Morrell, Frances 68, 144, 191, 243, 265, 544
Morris, Alf: at discussions on vehicles for the disabled 98, 110; dines with BD 172, 281; and launching of disablement White Paper 179, 183; helps BD's brother 230; relationship with Ashley 281; given dinner by Australian Deputy High Commissioner 361; 'a sincere and genuine person' 450, 489; interest in German rehabilitation centres 450, 596; and lack of support from Barbara Castle 489, 499, 505; and discussions on the deaf 524; takes BD to Sunningdale 'summit' on the disabled 658; votes for Callaghan 712

Morris, Charles (Charlie) 340, 341
Morris, John, QC, Lord Advocate 206, 208, 284, 334, 338, 366, 395, 396, 398, 659, 660
Morrison, Herbert 184, 243, 468, 491, 690; *Herbert Morrison: Portrait of a Politician* (B. Donoughue and G. W. Jones) 1, 59, 67, 72, 168, 172, 609; Memorial Lecture 152, 637
Morse, Sir Christopher Jeremy 230
mortgage rates 78, 79, 83, 84; Lever's proposals 85, 86, 89, 104, 108, 120, 136, 146, 151, 575; Mrs Thatcher's pledge 204, 205, 206
Mortimer, John 36
Mortimer, Kate 462
Moser, Sir Claus 82, 239, 274, 485, 679, 697
motor industry 180, 214, 346, 528, 545, 547, 607–8; *see also* British Leyland; Chrysler
motorcycle industry 125, 435, 478, 483, 547
Mountbatten, Louis 561, 564
Moynihan, Patrick (Pat) 122, 599
MPs *see* Members of Parliament
Mulley, Frederick (Fred): as chairman of NEC 365, 367; appointed into the Cabinet 404, 410, 412; on railway pay 412; at Education 413, 419; and education cuts 434, 546, 588, 595, 602; and university teachers' pay 461, 464; and reorganisation of schools into comprehensives 631, 671; fed up with Crowther-Hunt 637; and removal of students from unemployment register 652–3, 655; on Joan Lestor's replacement 673, 675
Murdoch, Robert (Bob) 299, 332
Murdoch, Rupert 222
Murphy, Brian 154
Murphy, John 362, 472
Murphy, Tessa 472
Murray, Albert (*later* Lord): appearance and personality 41; and electoral campaign 2, 8, 20, 25, 27, 41; and election victory 42, 44, 45, 46, 47, 48, 50, 51; and MF 15, 56, 58, 59, 62, 65; depressed by job insecurity 63, 64, 66; wants early election 70; dislikes Campaign for Democratic Socialism 73; thinks all officials at No. 10 must go 73; eats 'in style' at No. 10 75; possibility of Newham seat 81, 97, 99; and MF 'problem' 84, 85, 88, 89, 90, 91, 92, 97, 98, 99; fails Newham selection 108; depression 109; attacked by MF for Trooping the Colour arrangements 112, 135; teased by HW 113; on MF and HW 118; as part of HW's 'family' 119, 122, 124; and MF's peerage 126; humiliated by her 139–40, 142; argues with Peter Davis 154; checks out HW's missing box files 162, 166–7; is moved from No. 10 to Transport House 176, 179, 181; attacked by Hayward 182; accused by MF of plotting with civil servants 189; cooks soup and toast for BD and JH 195; dismisses uncooperative secretary 195; late for Hornsey meeting 201; falls

asleep in BD's chair 202; on 'normal people' 210; at drinks with HW 214–15; excluded from Huyton count 217, 218; further attacks from MF 218; thinks BD has won over Policy Unit 232; at Golda Meir dinner 250; involvement with HW and MF 197, 306, 312, 313; on MF's drugs intake 335; forgets to tell BD about anti-marketeers 340; a shadow of his former self 361; comments on HW and Janet Hewlett-Davies 362; in the doghouse with HW 364; invited to Israel with MF 364, 385, 386; witnesses row between HW and MF 416; against HW's retirement 471; banned from Blackpool conference by MF 507; removal demanded by MF 511; suffering hell from her 564; witnesses another row 685; hopes HW will defer retirement 691; his peerage 511, 573, 642, 668, 715
Murray, Anne 92, 108, 140, 364, 416
Murray, Len 28, 32, 55, 80, 135, 205, 257, 277, 342, 377, 408, 440, 497, 502, 548, 554, 662, 699
Muskie, Ed 302
Myer, Michael 359

Nairne, Patrick (Pat) 256, 259, 260, 322, 326, 347, 355, 359, 398–9, 505, 535, 620–1, 654, 665, 671
Nairne, Penny 665, 671
NALGO 462
Nally, Dermot 685
Nandy, Dipak 399
National Economic Development Council (NEDC; NEDDY) 276–7, 278, 307, 318, 400, 417, 428, 447, 553–5, 641, 649, 683
National Enterprise Board (NEB) 107, 144, 157, 158, 241, 244, 247, 249, 250, 254, 255, 290, 308, 318, 347, 415, 499, 651, 669
National Gallery 307, 320, 341, 676
National Health Service (NHS) 164; and private practice 362, 571, 576, 583; and consultants' pay disputes 267, 274, 586, 589–90, 591–3; increased charges 546; *see also* Royal Commission on the Health Service
National Union of Journalists (NUJ) 366
National Union of Labour Agents 366
National Union of Mineworkers (NUM) 4, 23, 31, 32, 33, 62–3, 73, 80, 255, 262, 267, 268, 446, 455, 458
National Union of Railwaymen (NUR) 79, 352, 412, 413, 415, 416, 615, 651, 680
nationalisation *see* industries, nationalised; land nationalisation
NATO (North Atlantic Treaty Organisation) 146, 147, 375, 393, 594, 602
NATSOPA (National Society of Operative Printers and Assistants) 143, 213, 315
Neale, Alan 604

Neatorou, Andrew 638
Neave, Airey 621, 623, 632
NEB see National Enterprise Board
NEDC/NEDDY see National Economic
    Development Council
New Society 159
New Statesman 606, 635, 695
New York 304–5
New Zealand: food imports 259, 306, 307, 308,
    326, 330, 331
News of the World 77, 136, 137
newspaper industry 58–9, 209, 210, 281, 283, 288,
    497, 531, 533, 535, 541, 623, 656, 689, 693;
    see also Royal Commission on the Press and
    specific newspapers
Newspaper Proprietors' Association (NPA) 213
NHS see National Health Service
Nixon, Richard, US President 93, 96, 296, 420
North Sea oil 23, 26, 105, 111, 134, 148, 156,
    224, 240, 270, 277, 348, 472, 498, 537–8, 551,
    576
Northern Ireland: HW's attitude and policies 13,
    84, 101, 124, 127–8, 132, 253, 343; situation
    depresses JH 100; Protestant strike against
    Council of All Ireland 120, 124, 129, 130; and
    HW's attack on 'spongers' 129; Prince
    Philip's suggestions 138; and electoral
    strategy 179; HW meets SDLP members 180;
    Cabinet meetings on 253–4, 265; HW meets
    Church leaders 270; HW gives pro-Protestant
    speech 343; further Cabinet discussions
    386–7, 505–6; issue taken over by Hunt and
    his civil servants 516–17, 550; George
    Thomson as Secretary of State 518; BD more
    optimistic over policy discussions 556, 562;
    HW visits troops 615; sectarian killings
    618–19; HW wants to send in Gurkhas 622;
    HW has talks with Whitelaw 622–3; SAS sent
    in 623, 627–8; and financial sanctions 625,
    626, 633, 634, 653, 678; first all-party confer-
    ence on 632; HW fails to turn up at trade
    unionists' reception 655; new ploy for
    'playing for time' needed 677–8; HW against
    direct rule 686; see also IRA; Rees, Merlyn
Norton Villiers motorcycles 125, 435, 478
nuclear industry 146, 160, 342, 543, 576
NUJ see National Union of Journalists
NUM see National Union of Mineworkers
NUR see National Union of Railwaymen
Nyerere, President Julius 569, 573, 574

Oakes, Gordon 551
Oakeshott, Professor Michael 557
Observer 33, 49, 91, 92, 106, 111, 154, 156, 179,
    472, 526, 541, 542, 585, 622, 626, 689, 692–3,
    702, 706
O'Connell, John 287, 294
Official Secrets Act 116–17, 135, 529–30, 627,
    683–4, 688; see also Franks Report

oil industry 4, 5, 121, 166, 293, 325, 326–7, 418,
    550, 590; see also British National Oil
    Corporation; North Sea oil
O'Malley, Brian 340, 620
Open University 587, 595, 602, 603
Orme, Stanley (Stan) 44, 336, 410, 689
Orr, David 567
O'Sullivan, Seamus 90
Owen, Dr David 25, 62, 64, 164, 233, 336, 450,
    532, 534, 535, 536, 589, 620, 689
Owen, Will 453

Palliser, Sir (Arthur) Michael 259, 260, 322, 324,
    326, 399, 549, 585, 624
Palme, Olaf 488
Pannell, Charles (Charlie) 344
Panovs, the 133, 135, 173, 381
Pardoe, John 48, 49, 55, 73, 666
Paris, Iron and Steel Treaty of 314, 324
Parker, Jill 479
Parker, Peter 479, 620, 626, 651
Parliamentary Labour Party (PLP) 51, 61, 111,
    112, 113, 125, 128, 132, 168, 169, 170, 335,
    336, 355, 367, 408, 449, 458–9, 586, 676, 706
Part, Sir Anthony 580, 582, 597, 606, 610, 611
passports, EEC 595
Patterson, Marie 312
pay policies see incomes policies
Peachey Properties 162, 167, 430
Peart, Fred 55, 107, 245, 252, 285, 314, 323, 334,
    337, 351, 415, 493, 630, 641
Pechet, Maurice 425
peerages see honours
Pendry, Tom 713
Pepper, Gordon 507
Peri, Yoram 245, 250, 253, 314, 499, 533, 551,
    641, 661, 666–7
Peston, Maurice 321, 409–10, 745
Peterson, Arthur 550, 604
Peterson, Colin 358
Petroleum Revenue Tax 240, 316
Philip, Prince 132, 138, 309, 354, 709
Phillimore Report 601, 688
Phipps, Brenda 67, 68, 281, 452, 633, 716
Phipps, Diana 153, 693
Piachaud, Professor David: as social policy adviser
    in Policy Unit 68, 84, 183, 221; drafts excel-
    lent speech for HW on unemployment 189,
    190; shocked by HW's treatment of BD and
    the Unit 229; excluded by civil servants from
    seeing papers 245, 255; prepares papers on
    economy 271, consultants' dispute 274, and
    Defence 310; produces papers on poverty 316,
    326, 337, 338–9, and economic policies 420–1,
    436, 452, 474; worried about Cabinet
    accepting Treasury forecasts on unemploy-
    ment 518; writes excellent paper on council
    house sales 520; briefs HW for Blackett
    Memorial Lecture 574, 575; writes speech for

him 604; threatens resignation over public expenditure cuts 612; and meeting with charities over poverty 622, 629; puts forward compromise in Iceland 'cod war' 628; fights for removing students from unemployment register 661

Pick, Hella 304

Pierce, Huw 210, 263

Pierce, Rachel 210

Pike, John 524

Pincher, Chapman 90, 132, 171, 191

Pinter, Harold: *No Man's Land* 485

Pitt, Terence (Terry) 28, 32, 39, 52, 66, 71, 274

Pliatzky, Leo 619–20, 687

Plowden, Veronica 229, 249, 344

Plowden, William (Will) 54; speaks to BD about Rothschild's Think Tank 69, 76; discusses his future with BD 81–2; one of BD's favourite people 161, 229; gives BD run-down on poverty 326; writes survey of social policy 378, 462–3, 684; reports to BD on unhappy state of CPRS 606; suggests policy analysis review 634; reports on reorganising electricity industry 649; vetoed by HW as too 'Establishment' 680

PLP *see* Parliamentary Labour Party

Plumb, Professor Jack 509

Plurenden, Lord *see* Sternberg, Rudi

Policy Unit: creation of 9, 13, 14, 27, 50, 52, 56–7, 59, 61, 221–2; relationship with CPRS 71, 75, 76, 104, 112, 161; working well 79; liaises with DHSS 84; and Hunt 94, 95, 105, 116; and questions in the Commons 95, 110; misnamed by the press 96; settling in 105; success over top salaries and mortgages 121; memos to HW 122–3; 'Little Things Mean a Lot' paper 110, 133, 134, 137, 205; *Spectator* article on 154, 156, 157, 158, 159; clashes with Treasury 157; works on NHS collapse 164; redrafts Industry White Paper 172–3; attacked by MF 179, 222–32 *passim*; thrashes out an economic package 271; given job of instituting poverty survey 316, 326; praised by HW 351; produces papers on pay policy and public expenditure 418, 420–5, 430, 431, 432, 436–7, 446–7, 464, 468; prepares alternative White Paper 452–5, 456–8, 463–4; and further hostility from MF 463, 468–9; difficulties in running 558–9; 'discredited Marxists' 606; liaises with CPRS on policy analysis 634; party 715; future of 703, 471; *see also* Graham, Andrew; Piachaud, David

Political Economy club 230

Pollard, Mrs (cook) 63, 357, 388

Pomonti, Jacques 174, 198, 212, 213, 262, 289

Pompidou, Georges 166

Poniatowski, Prince Michel Casimir 343

Porchester, Lord Henry 87, 118, 132, 309, 310, 454, 675

Porchester, Lady Jeannie 118, 309

Posner, Michael 454, 564

Poujade, Pierre 144

Poulson (John) affair 165, 287, 427, 430, 531, 548, 559, 561

poverty, discussions on 316, 326, 331, 337, 338–9, 345, 385, 413, 587, 622, 629

Powell, Enoch 29, 30, 31, 33, 34, 37, 201, 495, 678

Prentice, Reginald (Reg) 47; and education expenditure 148, 152; and EEC 235; and Scottish devolution 284, 286; gives speech on failure of social contract 320, 321; HW's plans for 334, 340, 397; moved to Overseas Aid 404, 406, 409–10, 411; getting into 'dangerously right-wing company' 414; rumoured to be plotting with GLC councillors 415; supports statutory pay policy 421, 425; under attack from constituency 470, 478–9; 'wild behaviour' 512; lonely and isolated 570; and NEC 578; threatens resignation over Overseas Aid cuts 596

Press Commission *see* Royal Commission on the Press

Preston: Imperial Hotel 511–12

Preston, Peter 389, 446, 683, 712

Prevention of Terrorism (Temporary Provisions) Bill 247

Price, Bill 381, 384, 395, 396

Price, Chris 436, 481

Price, Dolours 134

Price, Frank 280

Price, Marion 134

Pritchard, Lord 335

privacy law 89, 505, 521, 527, 601–2, 654–5, 675, 688

*Private Eye*: attacks MF 108, 111; allegations against Harold Evans 191, 208, 529, 530–1, 605; libels BD 270; and Robin Butler 297; attacks BD for Cudlipp's appointment to NEB 499–500; 'lice' 511; campaigns against BD 519, 605, 524, 588, 648; and Will Camp 596, 626; BD's libel action against 533, 534, 539, 615–16, 623, 651, 704, 716; Goldsmith prepared to destroy 635

public expenditure 184; discussions 390, 431, 484–5; and Finance Bill 164, 165; cuts 148, 334, 339, 340, 344–5, 351, 354, 382, 389, 459, 464, 468, 470, 479, 480; crisis 561–7, 605; White Paper on 671, 687, 690; *see also* Defence expenditure

Public Records Act 1967 475

Rabin, Yitzhak 406, 633

Radcliffe Committee 344, 419, 445, 446, 472, 474–5; report x–xi, 618, 627, 630, 631, 636, 639, 649–50, 653, 667

Radice, Giles 359

Radiwicz, Prince 399
railways *see* National Union of Railwaymen
Rambouillet economic summit 560, 569
Rampton, Jack 578
Ramptor, Joe 277
Ramsbotham, Peter 300, 368, 373, 374, 461, 615, 628
Ramsey, Sir Alf 112, 170
Ramsey, Archbishop Michael 569
Raphael, Gideon, Israeli Ambassador 364, 380–1, 397, 480, 481, 546–7, 560–1, 641, 661, 666, 687, 688
Rate Support Grant 565, 570
Rattigan, Terence: *The Browning Version* 674
Rawlinson, Anthony (Tony) 304, 706
Rawlinson, Peter 82
Read, Celia and Tom 91, 169, 206–7, 394, 509
Rees, Merlyn 51; as Northern Ireland Secretary 124; pleased power-sharing Executive has resigned 129; and appointment of Cudlipp 131, 136, 380; and alienation of Irish vote in UK 179, 180; attacked by SDLP members 180; HW plans to move to Education 248, 404; mood swings over Northern Ireland situation 253, 275, 284; against Scottish devolution 285; gives picturesque reports on Ulster 292, 315; and EEC negotiations 334, 338; acknowledges Britain will have to withdraw 380, 387; tells harrowing stories of Irish murders 436; on Powell wrecking UDA/SDLP agreement 495; showing signs of overstrain 502; praised by Cudlipp 510; meeting with Whitelaw 619, 622; not happy with HW's plans for military initiative 621; too involved in day-to-day detail 624; against financial sanctions for Ulster 678; announces dissolution of Northern Ireland Assembly 678
Reeve, Susanne 104, 173
Reform Club 30, 172, 241, 273, 343, 360–1, 379, 398, 655
*Regeneration of British Industry, The* (White Paper) 173
Regional Fund, EEC 249, 250, 252, 259
Reisz, Betsy (née Blair) 91, 501
Reisz, Karel 501
Revie, Don 112
Rhodesia 94–5, 97, 355, 679
Riccardo, John 577, 580, 581, 582, 584, 588–9, 598, 600, 605, 610
Richards, Ivor 646
Richardson, Elliot 282, 301, 302, 303, 326, 327, 343, 461, 498, 557–8, 624, 626, 634
Richardson, Mrs Elliot 461, 508, 624
Richardson, Gordon 252, 438, 439, 446, 461, 523, 524, 564, 584, 597, 686, 693
Richardson, Raymond (Ray) 62, 64, 67, 71, 78, 84, 86, 87, 235, 335, 390, 449, 717
Richman, Alfred (Alf) 42, 182, 197, 217, 224, 507, 510

Rigg, Diana 559
Rippon, Geoffrey 178
Robbins, Lionel 127, 280
Robertson, Joan 676
Rockefeller, David 304, 353, 358
Rockefeller, Nelson 447, 497, 498
Rodgers, Silvia 26, 144, 403
Rodgers, William (Bill) 1, 50; exclusion from government by HW 62, 63, 64, 65, 101; finally seen by HW 66, 68; and Jenkins 113, 123; finds MF peerage situation hilarious 128; not stretched at Defence 131; describes Cyprus emergency 167; optimistic about campaign 194; at Cabinet meeting 264; unhappy with Rees's handling of Northern Ireland 275; and Defence cuts 313; and EEC negotiations 336; too right-wing for promotion 404; supported by BD for Railway vacancy 410; against subsidising shipbuilding 532; and Iceland 'cod war' 577, 579, 646
Rogaly, Joe 144, 276, 717
Roll, Eric 547, 555, 580, 588, 598, 651, 693
Rome, Treaty of 250, 314
Rome conference (1975) 587, 590, 591, 595, 595
Romney St Group 241
Ronson, Inspector 631
Rose, Kenneth 509
Rose, Professor Richard 622
Ross, Richard (Dick) 588
Ross, William (Willie): against Scottish Nationalists 25, 148; makes positive suggestions in Energy committee 156; and defaulting local authorities in Scotland 160; and devolution 169, 170, 284–5; analysed by BD 238; fights for better terms for Scottish Development Agency 290; and EEC 306, 334, 335, 336, 337, 338, 340, 348; criticised by Hugh Brown 381; and further discussions on devolution 493, 494; favours subsidising shipbuilding 532; and closure of Chrysler 556, 576–7, 579, 598, 607; and railways 680; opposes council house sales 710
Rothschild, Evelyn de 365, 659
Rothschild, Jacob 362
Rothschild, Lord Victor 69, 71, 75, 76, 104, 108, 112, 133, 134, 139, 142, 161, 173, 521, 539, 659, 713
Rowling, Wallace Edward 307, 308
Royal Commission on the City 108, 115
Royal Commission on Gambling 506, 521, 539, 590, 623, 708, 713
Royal Commission on the Health Service 531, 532, 534, 585, 589, 592
Royal Commission on the Law 628, 629, 633, 635, 639, 640, 645–6, 647–8, 649, 656, 658, 659–60, 662, 663, 667, 672, 673, 674, 675, 677, 680, 691
Royal Commission on the Press 76, 103, 104, 112, 125, 131, 133, 134, 137, 253, 263, 281,

283, 287, 490, 502–3, 526, 529, 565, 688, 689

Royal Statistical Society 697

Rumsfeld, Donald 373

Russia/Russians: dinner for Bulganin and Khrushchev (1956) 673; HW's meeting with Ambassador 115; and the Panovs 133, 135, 173, 381; and HW's policy of détente 310; HW visits Moscow 311, 312, 313; and British defence plans 379; and Mitterrand 489; diplomats seen as spies 490, 492; BD at embassy reception 556–7; intelligence agents 653; and Rudi Sternberg as double agent 710

Ryan, Nigel 205, 694

Ryder, Sir Don: HW's favourite entrepreneur 104, 244; chairs inquiry into British Leyland 257, 278, 290, 359, 360, 362; authorised to buy Ferranti 346; still trusted by HW 523, 534; and Chrysler negotiations 545, 611; and land deal scandal 639, 647, 669; on nationalised industries 651; future at NEB in doubt 711

Sachs, Joseph (Joe) 304

Sadat, President Anwar 552, 555, 557, 558

Sainsbury, David 167, 244

Sainsbury, Sue 244

St Ermin's Hotel 24, 31, 35, 38, 52, 187, 188, 190, 203, 210

St John Stevas, Norman 509

Sampson, Anthony 472, 626

Sandelson, Neville 486, 525

Sandilands, Francis 552

Sarbanes, Christine (*née* Dunbar) 371

Sarbanes, Paul 371

Save and Prosper Unit Trust 282

Saxe, Joseph (Joe) 349, 370

Scanlon, Hugh 27, 28, 80, 81, 115, 176, 177, 277, 496, 548, 554

Schapiro, Professor Leonard 557, 638

Schlesinger, Arthur ix, 43

Schmidt, Helmut 142, 143, 251, 253, 258, 260–1, 306, 322, 326, 331, 450, 480, 594, 638, 658

Schon, Frank 416, 520, 688, 701, 716, 717

schools *see* education

Scotland/Scottish issues 94; HW's Glasgow speeches 112, 113, 394, 396; demand for Scottish Parliament 23, 25; World Cup 142; and Tory Housing Finance Act 160; second election campaign 195, 196, 197, 205, 209, 210; development agencies 238, 263, 264, 290; devolution 25, 66, 156–7, 162, 164, 169–70, 187, 264, 284–5, 294, 415, 416, 475, 486, 491, 492–4, 540, 546, 611, 625, 628, 637–8; and EEC renegotiation 306, 337, 348; strikes 319; corruption 360; fishing rights 381; newspapers 114, 291, 319, 533, 535; *see also* Chrysler Motors

Scott, Hardiman 384

Scott, Senator Hugh 151

Scottish Council of Industrialists 319

Scottish Labour Party 148, 320, 635, 655

Scottish National Party 25, 285, 625

Scowcroft, General Brent 369

Sedgemore, Brian 361

select committees 645

Self, Professor Peter 311

sewage charges 604–5, 612

Shackleton, Lord Edward 59

Shaw, Adrian 70, 161, 173, 238, 476

Shaw, George Bernard: *The Doctor's Dilemma* 390

Sheldon, Robert (Bob) 104

Shepherd, Lord Malcolm 285, 573, 639, 678

Sherward, Michael 280

shipbuilding industry 69, 125, 153, 237, 282–3, 313, 362, 532, 571, 573, 579

Shore, Peter: kept out by HW because of anti-Market speeches 22; good at press conference 36; pushed Left by wife 40; appointment objected to by Jenkins 53, 55; and EEC 106, 107, 160, 186, 192, 198, 200, 245, 249, 250, 306, 314, 337, 340; badly briefed on building societies 146; attacks HW for giving too much away at Paris Summit 262; opposes Benn 264, 291, 359; supports Healey's public expenditure cuts 345; and Defence cuts 379; and NUR strike 412; and sterling crisis 438, 439, 440, 441; and pay policy 450, 457, 459, 460, 465; and civil aviation policy 478; opposes publication of motor industry figures 528; pessimistic about world recovery 543; and import controls 574; and EEC passports 595; and Official Secrets 644, 683; and film industry committee 682; told of HW's retirement 699

Short, Edward (Ted): insulted by Robin Day 28; appointed Minister for the Civil Service 67; gives pedestrian speech 73; and Clay Cross councillors 87; and conflict of interests issue 109, 110, 111, 112, 113, 114, 145; takes PM's Questions 147; opposes Speaker's ruling on Lever crisis 164; and press forgery smear 165, 171; seen by HW as 'fading out' 240; angry at idea of cutting ministers' salaries 245; special advisers scheme opposed by HW 252; and Northern Ireland 254; and EEC referendum 268, 322; and Scottish devolution 284, 285, 286, 294, 492; attacked by Mellish 333; in charge of Cabinet meetings 341, 344; introduces EEC Referendum Bill 351; against people living abroad having the vote 356; finds Barbara Castle 'vitriolic' 362; and NEC meeting 454–5; and electoral reform discussions 498; wants to get rid of Fowler 618; and parliamentary reform 631; 'must go' 642; clashes with Callaghan 645; and MPs' salaries 647; and privacy law 655;

gives party 680; and railways 680; and film industry committee 682; and Official Secrets 684; and confidence vote 691, 693; told of HW's retirement 699; speaks at farewell Cabinet dinner 707; and council house sales 710

Short, Renée 109, 514–15

Sieff, Marcus 675

Sieverts, Frank 369

Silkin, John: and patronage 705; and election campaign 36, 51; and land nationalisation 123, 165, 349; chased by press over land deals 145, 148, 150, 160; becomes Minister of Planning and Local Government 228; and EEC negotiations 334, 335, 337; and pay policy 425, 465; and MF's children 545; 'totally idle' 551; supports Royal Law Commission 646, 647–8, 659; and Foot's leadership bid 714

Silkin, Sam 199, 285; and publication of Crossman Diaries 419–20, 426, 427, 429, 437, 464, 516, 517; and Maudling and Poulson affair 531, 548; illness 611, 625; and Radcliffe Report 627, 630; and Royal Law Commission 648, 659; and privacy law 655; asks BD to get job for his son 676

Sills, Beverley 302

Simon, Bill 369

Simonstown, South Africa 235

Sinatra, Frank 384, 388, 396, 618

Sisco, Joseph 373

Skinner, Dennis 513, 645, 681, 711

Slater, James (Jim) 428, 519, 539, 555, 654, 690

Smedley, Ron 366

Smethurst, Richard (Dick) 222, 508, 529, 538, 573, 621

Smith, Cyril 711

Smith, Gordon 298, 657

Smith, John 228, 360, 366, 604, 663–4, 667, 679

Smith, Rodney 592

Smith, T. Dan 109, 110, 111

Snow, C. P. 462

Soames, Christopher 638

Soares, Mario 488

'social contract' 5, 23, 27–8, 35, 79, 177–8, 186, 187, 196, 197, 198, 200, 204, 236, 240, 320, 321, 358

Social Democratic Alliance 419

Social Democratic Party 7

Sonnenfeldt, Hal 109–10, 301, 353, 369, 372, 400, 402, 632, 633

Sonnenfeldt, Marjorie 369

Soskice, Frank 135

South Africa 169; arms deals 30, 382; trade with 110; Simonstown visit by Royal Navy 235; intelligence agents 653; and Thorpe and Hain 652, 675, 677, 678, 683, 688

special advisers 104, 245, 404, 419, 462, 472, 549, 653, 657, 658; BD and McNally prepare

brief on 345, 349–50, 355, 360, 361, 662, 663, 664

Spectator 154, 156, 157, 158, 159, 470

Spiers, Ronald (Ron) 282, 308, 327, 356, 402, 421, 446, 503, 558, 624, 634, 671, 693, 703

Sports Levy Board 294, 311, 315, 318, 325, 382

Stallard, Jock 514

Stanley, Venetia 35, 98

Steel, David 147–8, 692, 693

steel industry 324, 326, 328; see British Steel Corporation

Stenbach, Per 296

sterling crises 263, 275, 426, 436–41, 446, 462, 693

Stern, Der 84

Sternberg, Rudi (later Lord Plurenden) 108, 238, 240, 271, 399, 567, 608, 609, 691, 710, 715, 716

Sternberg, Sir Sigmund 98, 281, 399, 539, 613, 677, 715

Stevens, George 372

Stevens, Jocelyn 309

Stevens, Liz 370, 372, 373, 678

Stevenson, Dr 172

Stewart, Michael 344

Stiles, Nobby 713

Stokes, Lord 339, 362

Stone, Dr Joseph (Joe) 143, 185, 260, 263, 264, 298, 349, 376, 387, 570, 595, 603, 664, 715

Stonehouse, John 265, 271, 515, 534–5, 572, 639

Stoppard, Tom: Rosencrantz and Guildenstern are Dead 572

Stott, Roger 714

Stowe, Sir Kenneth (Ken) 545; replaces Armstrong 58, 287, 358, 413; discussions with BD 387, 388, 397, 400; and HW's reshuffle 406, 407, 408; and Crossman Diaries 420, 427, 522; and economic issues 435, 436, 437; supports Policy Unit 443, 445, 448, 452, 454, 463–4; clashes with Hunt 541, 650; and HW's resignation 614, 628, 696; suspects Ryder is in trouble 639; and HW's request for MF to be received by the Queen 681; supports continuance of Unit 700, 701, 703; and honours list 702, 714, 716, 720; at HW's farewell lunch 719

Strang, Gavin 337

Strauss, George 654

Straw, Jack 110, 534, 685

Stuart, Nicholas (Nick) 58, 79, 152, 171, 172, 347, 357, 391, 400, 495, 531, 577, 584, 587, 700

Summerbee, Mike 713

Sun 83, 95, 515, 530

Sunday Express 549, 624, 696

Sunday Mirror 35

Sunday Telegraph 47, 420, 453, 509, 519–20, 651

Sunday Times 94, 116; and HW's memoirs 96; and MF 108; and thalidomide case 122; and

Silkin's land deals 145, 148, 150; announces election date 179; and publication of Crossman Diaries 185, 191, 294, 295, 419, 426–7, 429, 432, 516; leaks to 227, 256; does 'hatchet job' on Benn 392; pays Peggy Field's salary 431; attacks Hunt and HW 437; has injunction on Slater and Walker material 690; HW gives interview to 702; anti-Callaghan 704; *see also* Evans, Harry

Sunningdale talks (1973) 120, 124, 129, 130

Sutherland, Arnot 427

Swann, Professor Sir Michael 100–1, 202, 293, 382, 384

Sydenham, Roger 524

Tate Gallery: Paul Nash exhibition 562

Taylor, Humphrey 361, 667

television licences 297, 602, 604

Terry, John 714, 715

Terry, Walter 91, 140, 211, 507

textile industry 392, 576, 613

thalidomide affair 122, 230, 630

Thames TV 29, 116

Thatcher, Margaret: pledges to keep down mortgage rates 204, 206; moves motion attacking government 237; becomes Conservative leader 206, 309–10; pale and tense 310; and HW 294, 317, 338, 341, 357, 360; looks scared 341, 357; defeated by HW in debate 391; furious at publicity given to Heath 396; rejoices at referendum result 405; and economic debate 475, 476, 477; discusses Ireland with HW 495; opposed by 27% of Tories 509; and Maudling appointment 531, 548; finds HW perplexing 547; and Question Times 562; gives poor speech 572; and Northern Ireland 619, 632; sees HW about Radcliffe Report 639; opposes HW on recruiting mercenaries 661; gives good speech 692; graceless 700; will 'never get the feel of the House' 714; kills EEC institute 449; abolishes CPRS 61

Thimont, Bernard 530, 540, 699

Thomas, George (*later* Lord Tonypandy) 55, 654, 656, 671

Thomas, Hugh 462

Thomas, Mike 434

Thompson, John 479

Thomson, George 518, 638

Thorn, Gaston 676

Thorpe, Jeremy 48, 51, 55, 87, 89, 640, 652, 661, 664, 675, 677, 678, 686, 688, 692, 693, 709

Tickell, Sir Crispin 482

*Time and Tide* 479

*Time* magazine 110

*Times, The* 96, 166, 222, 497, 615, 656, 658, 660

Tindemans, Leo 394, 442

Tomlinson, John 692

'top people's salaries' 22, 120, 121, 125, 126,

244–5, 250, 255–6, 262, 263, 266, 267, 353, 629, 645, 687, 695, 696–7, 706

trade unions 5, 79–80, 104, 115, 116, 179, 209, 240, 254, 277, 366–7, 462; *see also* NUJ; NUM; NUR; 'social contract'; Trades Union Congress

Trades Union Congress (TUC): meeting with government (March 1974) 79–81; on setting date of election 104; and Policy Unit 119; HW's speech to (September 1974) 174, 175, 176–7, 178; and ITV strike 205; and election day leak 208; Scanlon demands talks between CBI and 277; Marie Patterson chairman of 312; and NUR 352, 415, 416; and 'social contract' 358; and discussions on Industry Bill 400, 418; and pay policy 421, 437, 445–6, 449, 450, 455, 456, 459, 460, 461, 467; and NHS 534; presses for import controls 547–8; at meetings with NEDC 554, 555, 641; Griffin's plans for 662; *see also* Jones, Jack; Murray, Len

Transport and General Workers' Union 7, 47, 177, 277

Transport House: during election campaign 20, 22, 25, 27, 32, 34, 40, 46, 47–8; inefficient 60, 66; angers HW with policy statements 133; monitors Silkin's land policies 165; and second election campaign 176, 181, 186, 187, 189, 195; *see also* Bish, Geoff; Hayward, Ron

transport policy 436, 498, 634; *see also* National Union of Railwaymen

Travers, Ben: *Plunder* 660

Treasury 9, 81; and Lever 108–9, 111, 126, 204, 275, 353; lack of economic policies 115, 121, 135, 225, 233, 235; and industrial policies 265, 278, 282; vetoes HW's speech on commodities 307–8; 'in cahoots' with Foreign Office over loans to Chile 315–16; paper on industry deferred by Benn 317–18; and Kissinger oil plan 325; and leaks 339; and petrol duty 342–3; and public expenditure cuts 344–5, 353, 389, 390, 464, 468; and pay policy 'bounce' 432, 434, 436, 437–8, 441–4, 445, 446, 447–8; and Income Policy White Paper 452–4, 456, 463–4, 465, 467, 468–9; and Berrill 462; miscalculates National Debt interest 500; and unemployment figures 518, 521, 524; HW sceptical about 536; 'sterilisation period' in 587; policy on sterling 686; *see also* Couzens, Ken; Gilbert, John; Wass, Sir Douglas

Trelford, Donald 92, 542, 626, 672

Trend, Burke (*later* Lord Trend) 517, 527, 569, 621, 659, 675, 682, 707

Tribune Group 227, 244, 266, 413, 513, 690, 691, 692

Triumph motorcycles 480, 483

Trudeau, Pierre 298–9, 332, 333, 392

TUC *see* Trades Union Congress

Twomey, Seamus 287
Tyerman, Donald 509
Tyerman, Robert 509

Ulmann, Al 303
Ulster Protestant Workers Council 120, 124, 125
Underhill, Reginald (Reg) 22, 117, 501
unemployment 80, 191, 207, 264, 267, 277, 419, 420, 426, 480, 503, 504, 518, 521, 524, 532, 555, 563, 576, 641, 644, 649, 650, 653, 676, 685; and students 652–3, 655, 656, 661, 670; Tory attitude to 82, 207
unions *see* trade unions
United Nations Association 380
universities 148, 315, 321, 434, 435, 455, 462–3, 464; *see also* Open University
USDAW 107

Vaizey, John 669, 694, 714
Varley, Eric: content at Energy 55; and miners' settlement 62–3; his White Paper on North Sea oil discussed 148; gives statement on nuclear stations 160; at Weidenfeld party 239; and Burmah Oil 272, 273, 277; and devolution 284; and Petroleum Revenue Tax 316; and EEC 335, 336, 337, 338, 340, 341, 343, 347, 350; becomes Industry Minister in Cabinet reshuffle 318, 407, 411, 414; and pay policy 450, 460, 465; and collapse of motorcycle industry 478; angry with Benn 480; and Treasury's lack of consultation 485; suggests Scanlon for top job 496; his papers on industrial strategy 520, 521, 530, 532; at NEDC meeting 554; slapped down by HW 573; and import controls 574, 613; and Chrysler 576, 577, 579, 580, 581, 582, 583, 584, 595, 596, 597, 598, 606, 607, 608, 609, 610–11, 612, 613, 668; and Kirkby manufacturing 642–3; against Finniston 651; and wages policy 662; and film industry committee 682; against help for newspaper industry 693; told of HW's resignation 698
vehicle excise duty 339, 343, 621, 625, 661
Volcker, Paul 305
Volcker, Mrs Paul 372

Wade, Virginia 267
Waites, Andrew 325
Walden, Brian 61
Wales/Welsh affairs 145, 187, 201, 202, 206, 207, 208, 238, 263, 264, 284, 628
Walker, Peter 690
Walker-Smith, Derek 654
Wall, Max 546, 568
Wallace, Governor George 527–8
Waller, Ian 470
Warburgs merchant bank 547, 555, 580, 651, 676
Warren, Frederick (Freddie) 163, 409, 571, 572, 704–5

Washington, trips to 299–304, 368–76
Wass, Sir Douglas: helpful on mortgages 84, 86; liaises with Policy Unit 157, 272, 274; and economic situation 280; and spending on World Poverty 338, 339; and statutory pay policy 443, 448, 454; on Healey 484, 563; on Crosland 484, 563; on public expenditure 484–5, 532, 563; clashes with Hunt 526, 539, 540, 548; discussions with BD 563–4; worried over Burmah Oil 584; Pliatzky's opinion of 619; civilised attitude 655; bland 687; worried about Budget 699
Wasserman, Cressida (*née* Gaitskell) 588
Wasserman, Gordon 588, 596
Watergate scandal 93, 96
Watkinson, Lord 38, 417, 554
Watson, Sam 73
Watt, David 276, 446, 467, 669, 717
Waugh, Auberon 605
wealth tax 79, 80, 168
Wedderburn, William (Bill) 80
Weidenfeld, George (*later* Lord): finally shows interest in BD 67; parties 79, 130, 153; passes on gossip to MF 154–5, 157, 269; party guests chosen by MF 238–9; at No. 10 Christmas party 269; lunches with BD 274; invited by MF to lunch for new American Ambassador 327, 343; as MF's escort 332; and US attack on British publishers' sales agreement 348; unsuitable company for HW 436; at official dinner with MF 443; gives lunch for World Bank president 462; blamed for press leak 468; gives party for French minister 473; asks Lever to invite MF to dinner 480; lunch with Evans at MF's behest 500; warns president of Publisher's Association about BD 519; advertises MF's book 520; at Sadat reception 559; and BD's *Morrison* biography 609; and HW's book and TV series 614, 625, 668, 679; MF threatens to marry 675; told of HW's resignation 680; sees HW at MF's insistence 683; gives birthday party for HW 693–4; ignored by the Queen 709; gets peerage 269, 618, 668, 715
Weinstock, Arnold 567
Weir, Lord 523
Welch, Raquel 372
Wellbeloved, Jim 688
Welsh Development Agency 263, 264
Wenham, Brian 503–4
Weston, John 384
Whitaker, Ben 23, 26, 29, 30, 245
Whitaker, Janet 245, 535
White, Frank 714
Whitehead, Phillip 69, 418, 702
Whitelaw, William (Willie) 73, 307, 396, 619, 621, 622–3, 632
Whitlam, Gough 267, 268
Wicks, Nigel 537, 542, 545, 568, 598, 637, 655, 667, 676, 677, 683, 686, 689

Widgery, Judge 517, 522
Wigg, Lord George 51, 77, 78, 87, 90, 96, 110,
    122, 128, 129, 163, 233, 273, 288, 294, 311,
    318, 458, 472, 486, 617, 657
Williams, Marcia *see* Falkender, Lady
Williams, Philip 496
Williams, Shirley 24, 26, 123; and EEC renegotia-
    tions 107, 192, 193, 194; and Benn's industrial
    policy 149–50, 169, 171, 172; threatens to
    leave politics over EEC referendum 199,
    200; and election campaign 205, 210; pres-
    sured by BD to save breweries 223; and
    economic policy discussions 224, 235, 236,
    266, 268; supports Callaghan on EEC tariffs
    245; wishes *Daily Mail* would go bust 283;
    at IDV committee 290; impresses Ron Spiers
    308; disliked by Margaret Beckett 317; and
    EEC 335, 337, 341, 346, 361, 365, 366, 367,
    381; a 'bundle of old-fashioned girlishness'
    387; worried about NEC and EEC 388–9;
    and John Gilbert 394; at Campaign
    Referendum meeting 396; at pay policy
    meeting 425; liked by officials 434; weak-
    nesses analysed 434; content in present job
    434; and sterling crisis 438, 439, 440, 441;
    and pay policy 449, 450, 457, 459, 460;
    supports Barbara Castle 479; and Prentice
    484, 512; praises HW's Blackpool speech
    514; at NEDC meeting on industry 554; at
    meeting of industrialists 567; and NEC
    meeting 578–9; and Chrysler 608, 609; and
    parliamentary reform 631; and price control
    647, 662; and HW's retirement 698
Wilson, Giles 116, 618
Wilson, Harold: character and personality x, 1,
    11–14, 100–2, 128; and BD's diary ix-x, 43;
    and BD's employment ix, 1–2, 9; relationship
    with MF *see* Falkender, Lady Marcia; hatred
    of the press 13, 16, 58–9, 76, 87–8, 102, 110,
    111; election campaign (February 1974) 2,
    3–4, 6, 7–8, 20–40; speeches 8, 20, 22, 26, 31,
    35, 37, 44; election day 40–8; waits for Heath
    to resign 45–6, 47, 48, 49, 50–1, 52; appoints
    Jenkins to Home Office 52–3, 60; to the
    Palace 53–4; back at No. 10 54–5, 57;
    appoints ministers 59, 60, 61, 62, 63, 66, 67;
    and BD's threatened resignation 65–6; rela-
    tionship with Jenkins 66–7; 58th birthday 68;
    feels underworked 69–70, 77; and Queen's
    Speech 70; at Chequers 72; meeting with
    TUC 79–81; committed to carrying out
    Labour promises 84; and Clay Cross council-
    lors 87; and MF's family land scandal 89–90,
    93, 94, 96–7, 102, 103; meets Nixon in Paris
    93; spends night at Windsor 95; and allega-
    tions of tax evasion 96; at loose end before
    holidays 99–100; and timing of next election
    103, 107, 109, 111, 113, 114, 122; and Ryder
    104; and EEC discussions 106, 107, 134; and
    Short scandal 109, 112, 171; loses voice but
    cheerful 107, 109; Glasgow May Day speech
    112, 113; wants investigation of Election
    Business Committee 114; in good form 116;
    gives speech on press 116–17, 119; and
    Question Times 117, 124, 127; draws line
    between 'family' and civil servants 122; and
    MF's peerage 123–4, 125, 126, 127, 129; and
    Northern Ireland 124, 127–8, 129, 130, 132;
    and Lord Wigg 128; unworried about
    economic situation 131; and Panovs 133, 135,
    173; gives JH a boost 134; and *News of the
    World* article on MF 136, 137; and 'Benn
    problem' 138–9, 141, 143, 144, 147, 152, 153,
    158; in Germany 142–3, 145; defeated on
    industry vote 143–4; and City lunch 145–6;
    attacked by back-benches on nuclear state-
    ment 146; vetoes BD's going to Brussels 146;
    in Brussels 147, 148; and dinner at American
    Ambassador's 151; still backs Lever plan for
    building societies 151; at Bradford University
    153, 154; excessive drinking 145, 152, 155;
    and Scottish devolution 156–7; and *Spectator*
    article on Unit 154, 156, 157, 158; 159;
    discussions with *Guardian* people 159–60; and
    Commons crisis over Lever 161, 162, 163–4;
    and missing tax files 162–3; and Cyprus crisis
    166; to Paris for talks with Giscard d'Estaing
    166; resists Benn over Industry White Paper
    169, 171, 172; PLP speech 168, 169, 170
    **September 1974 – December 1974**
    cheerful after Scillies holiday 175;
    delighted with Lever on land nationali-
    sation 175; Brighton TUC speech 175,
    176–7, 178; and social contract 177–8;
    electoral strategy 175, 179, 181, 182,
    183, 185, 191, 194–5; unsuccessful
    meeting with SDLP 180; relations with
    Jenkins 184–5; and EEC referendum
    186, 187; drinking again 188, 190; rela-
    tionship with JH 186, 187–8, 190; elec-
    tion speeches 188, 189, 190, 192, 193,
    195–205 *passim*; and Brayley's resigna-
    tion 199; TV interview with Frost 206;
    wants to attack Tories more 209; and
    *Daily Mail* allegations about his finan-
    cial affairs 211, 212, 213; rejects JH's
    TV script 213, 214; and future appoint-
    ments 214; confidence growing 215; on
    election day 215–18; victory in
    Transport House interrupted by bomb
    warning 219; and stolen tax papers 222,
    233, 236, 240; TV broadcast 222;
    mutual coldness with JH 224, 225;
    plans for Policy Unit 225, 226, 228,
    229–30, 231–2; sacks Judith Hart 225;
    drinking too much 226; attacks right-
    wing conspiracies 227; makes govern-
    ment reshuffle 228; gives rambling

Queen's Speech 233–4; sends stern
letters to Benn, Hart and Lestor for
NEC behaviour 235, 236, 237, 238; and
honours list 238; to Weidenfeld party
238, 239; chairs IDV Cabinet
committee 241; and EEC renegotiations
242, 243, 245, 251, 252–3, 254, 257–8;
and top people's salaries 244–5, 262,
267; in Dublin for Childers's funeral
246; gives party for journalists 247;
Conference Party speech 247–8, 249; at
Golda Meir dinner 250; speech attacked
for supporting Benn 250; visits Giscard
d'Estaing 253, 254, 258; wants to pull
out of Northern Ireland 253–4; shows
more interest in economic strategy than
usual 255; and Benn and British
Leyland 256, 257; at Paris Summit
258–63, 264; has 'racing heart' 260,
263, 264; makes statement on Paris
Summit 264; goes to *Swan Lake* 264;
makes statement on Stonehouse 265;
and Mellish's resignation 266; will not
allow statutory wages policy 267; and
EEC referendum 268; bored with
Whitlam 268; no close friends 268
**January 1975 – April 1975**
bored in Scillies 270; gives BD permission to sue *Private Eye* 270; pleased
with press coverage of honours list 271;
gives speech attacking British Leyland
strikers 271, 273; and political office
finances 273; and Arab hijackers 274,
275; and Lever 274–5; dissatisfied with
Healey's economic strategy 276; at
NEDC meeting 276; and inquiry into
nationalised industries 278; attitude to
wives 278–9; refuses to have Maitland
on Washington trip 280; hates Question
Time 281, 324; and newspaper industry
280, 281, 282, 283, 291; and discussions
on devolution 284, 285; discussions
with Jenkins 287; and EEC discussions
287, 288, 289, 293, 306, 314; recommends Civil Service advertising agency
287; on resigning if he had been
defeated 290; interested in stock market
290; asks for a smile from Ross 290;
and dinner with Frost 291–2; and
Robin Butler 292–3, 297; portrait
painted 295; in excellent form 296; to
Canada 297–9, and Washington 300–3;
criticised for speech in praise of Heath
306–7; dines with Eric Miller 307;
commodity speech vetoed by Treasury
307–8; meets New Zealand Prime
Minister 307, 308; and Queen's Civil
List 309, 310–11, 316; in Moscow 311,
312, 313; dinner with Kissinger 312;

and economic situation 312–13; helps
MF buy house 313; gives education
speech in Newcastle 315; and Benn
317–18; in Scotland 319–20; attacks
Prentice 320, 321; finds job exhausting
321; Taunton speech 323–4; continues
to attack press 324; has US Ambassador
for lunch 327; rows with JH over
speech 327–8; and Dublin Summit on
EEC 306, 322, 323, 325, 326, 328,
329–31; 59th birthday 530; and EEC
referendum campaign 331–42 *passim*,
343; refuses to be interviewed by BBC
338; welcomes Heath back to the House
338; finds City dignitaries 'a boring lot'
343–4; visits Northern Ireland 343, 344;
at NEC meeting on EEC 345–6; attacks
Benn at IDV committee 346; still enam-
oured of Ryder 346; thinks phones are
tapped 347; tries to trap Benn into
resignation 347; and Commons debate
on EEC 347, 348, 349; asks for BD to
be removed from Jamaica list 349; uninterested in economic policy 350; praises
BD and Policy Unit 351; attacks
Jenkins on voluntary pay policy 352;
wants BD to go to US 352–3
**April 1975 – July 1975**
and EEC referendum campaign 355,
356, 361, 363, 364; hopes for Benn's
resignation 355, 390; and Lord Kissin
358; reliance on Janet Hewlett-Davies
358–9; prepares honours list 359;
furious with Benn 360; avoidance of
Mrs Thatcher 360; objects to Heseltine
replying on British Leyland 362; speaks
at British Academy dinner 362; and
BD's telegram to Jamaica 366–7;
Kingston speech upsets Americans 368,
369; in Washington 373–5; waits for
MF at airport 375–6; still obsessed by
the press 378; meeting with Hunt et al.
over public expenditure 378; and EEC
referendum campaign 379, 381, 382–3,
384, 393–7; 'in poor shape' at meeting
with Fitt 380; 'fed up' 380; tired and
drinking too much 382; writes first-
class speech for CBI 385–6, 387; and
Northern Ireland 386–7; lunches with
*Guardian* people 389; offers Lever Arts
in reshuffle 390; and speech for
Commons economic debate 389, 390,
391; 'despatches' Mrs Thatcher 391;
statement on textile industry not well
received 392; interview with Robin Day
392; at Brussels NATO meeting 393,
394; suspects JH of leaks 396; Glasgow
speech a success 395, 396; on referendum day 399, 400; victory statement

401–2, 403, 405; and Cabinet reshuffle
404–6, 407–12, 413; spends more and
more time at Chequers 407; and
railway strike 412; and comprehensive
schools 412–13; handles Questions with
ease 413; and Industry Bill discussions
413, 414; and meetings with TUC
about NUR 415, 416; and pay policy
418, 419, 421, 422–5, 429–30, 432–4;
relationship with Janet Hewlett-Davies
419; and legal action regarding
Crossman Diaries 420, 426, 427,
522–3, 543–4; and abolition of parliamentary press lobby 420; accuses BD
of leaks 426–7, 428, 451; and dinner
with Frost 428; and talk of retirement
428; counts Question Times left until
recess 429, 435; sees unsuitable
millionaires 436; and sterling crisis
436–7, 438, 439, 440, 441, 446; and
statutory wages policy 442–4, 445,
450–1, 453, 454, 455, 459; gives
evidence to Radcliffe Committee 446,
472; at Bradford University 451; JH
deeply depressed by 451–2; does not
credit JH for speech 458
**July 1975 – November 1975**
rumours and comments on his forthcoming retirement 471, 473–4, 483, 488,
505, 510, 525, 526, 530, 533, 539–40,
541, 559, 571; drafts bad speech for
Durham Miners' Gala 473; scathing
about Mrs Thatcher 475; gives
Commons economic speech 475, 476,
477; Helsinki speech and visit 477, 482,
483, 484; golfs at Balmoral 489; unaware
of Britain's decline 490; worried about
submission to Press Commission 490;
and press stories on Russian 'spies' 490,
492; at devolution discussions 492, 493,
494; and future economic programme
495; too little work to do 495–6; failings
savaged by Crosland 496; praised by
Len Murray 497; Romanian visit 497,
498, 500, 501; speaks at opening of
British Museum exhibition 498;
'dabbles' in blast-furnacemen strike 502;
and discussions of his evidence to Press
Commission 502–3, 565; pushes
'Dominion status' for Northern Ireland
506, 550; resists fixing job for MF's
brother 509; wants poll results on his
leadership 508, 509–10; at NEC meeting
in Preston 511; Blackpool conference
498, 499, 501, 512, 513, 514; refuses
dinner with Frost 519; accused of giving
away Gannex raincoats to distinguished
visitors 519–20; still swears by Ryder
523; interested in *Private Eye* smear

campaign against BD 524; has no sense
of direction 528; 'shit-scared' about
Question Time 528–9; mentions his
eight burglaries 529, 530; and council
house sales 529, 535; presses BD to sue
*Private Eye* 530; never drops ministers
under attack 532; 'terribly tired' 531,
535, 536; and import controls 538–9,
547; invites *Daily Telegraph* people
540–1; obsessive about secrecy and leaks
542; helps in finding school for MF's
boys 545; and devolution 546; and Mrs
Thatcher 547; in Scotland to celebrate
arrival of North Sea oil 551; and
Chrysler closure 556, 573; warns BD of
Israeli intrigues 558; and guests for
Sadat reception 559; sees Israeli
Ambassador alone 560–1; and public
expenditure debates 561, 564, 566, 567,
569, 570; secret meeting with Spanish
Ambassador 564; at Rambouillet
Summit 569, 570; gives Queen's Speech
570, 571; wins against Tories on public
expenditure 572; booed at Eastbourne
572; and Blackett Memorial Lecture
574, 575, 594; irritated by Hayward and
endless party manoeuvring 575, 578;
and Iceland 'cod war' 575, 577
**November 1975 – February 1976**
approaches finance house for loan for
MF's brother 575–6, 716–17; excludes
BD from Rome trip 576; worried about
Chrysler 577, 583–4; and NEC 578–9;
'all over the place' 584; complains
about Question Time 584–5; and
National Health Service 586; 'sees politics through speeches' 586; at Rome
talks 587, 590, 591, 594, 595–6;
attacked by Barbara Castle 591–3;
clashes with Healey 593–4; exhausted
594; attacks John Hunt 594; against
Defence cuts 594; and Chrysler rescue
595, 596, 606, 607–8, 610; heart flutter
getting worse 595; finds jobs for his
entourage 597; further interest in
council house sales 599, 602, 603;
announces retirement date to JH 601;
clever over Defence cuts 602; won't
have Open University cuts 602, 603;
tells Queen of retirement 603, 604; at
BNOC meeting 604; scathing about
Kaufman and Varley 607; awarded
Freedom of the City 585, 608, 609,
611; honours lists 608–9, 613, 618;
praises BD to Kissin 613; plans TV
series 614; sues *Daily Mail* 614; may
change retirement date 614, 617–18,
628; and press stories on cutting railways 615; visits troops in Ulster 615;

praises Unit paper on monetary policy 617; and Northern Ireland 618–19, 621–2, 623, 625, 626, 634; gives farewell party for American Ambassador 624; meetings with Israeli diplomats 625, 626; discusses TV series with Frost 625; in favour of accepting Radcliffe Report on memoirs 627; and devolution debate 628; and Royal Commission on the Law 629, 645–6, 656, 659–60; and Iceland 'cod war' 629, 635, 641–2, 643, 646; reneges on JH over Geoffrey Goodman 631–2, 637; requests help from Foreign Office for MF's friend 632–3, 639; at hostile Question Time 636; grey and tired and doing nothing 637, 641; relaxed at Questions briefing 639–40; has mini-reshuffle 640; makes bad speech to French Chamber of Commerce 641; retirement date fixed 642; on need to do something about Department of Education 644; admits mistake over increases in Civil Service pay 645; on select committees 645; dislikes PLP 645; rows with Callaghan over European elections 648; finds the House 'boringly predictable' 649; uninterested in the Arts 649; no ideas for appointments in nationalised industries 651
February 1976 – April 1976
suspects South African Special Branch in Thorpe scandal 652, 653, 675, 678; never sees own mail 652; at discussions on privacy law 655; fails to turn up for reception for Northern Ireland trade unionists 655; and bugging 656–7; and special advisers 657; taken ill 658; and Angolan mercenaries 659, 661; will delay resignation 663, 664, 665; looks 'flabby and sunken' 666; discusses peerages with JH 668; impressed at young age of Daily Mirror editor 670; against Healey becoming leader 671; and film industry discussions 671, 679, 682, 706; 'wobbling' on date of departure 672, 674, 677; chooses chairman for Royal Law Commission 672–3, 674–5; and Joan Lestor 673; at crucial NEC meeting 676; and Arab boycott on Electricity Council loan 676; sees Powell about Ireland 678; frivolous at counter-inflation meeting 680; asks Stowe to approach Queen about 'receiving' MF 681; 'brilliant' at Questions 681–2; bored at last NEDC meeting 683; lunches with Guardian people 683; and Official Secrets 683,

684; accuses MF of taking money from office funds 684–5; and sterling crisis 686; still dithering over retirement 686, 687; reveals South African involvement in Thorpe and Hain affairs 688; appoints Margaret Jackson to Education 688; approves financial aid for newspaper industry 689; and government defeat on public expenditure 690, 691; 60th birthday 690–4; retirement day 698–701; and honours list 702, 705, 711, 714–15, 719, 720; on Callaghan 701; TV interviews 705–6; shabby treatment of JH 700, 717–18, 721; at farewell Cabinet dinner 707; at dinner for the Queen 709; intervenes in council house sales discussion 710; uses final Question Times to pay off old scores 711; advises Callaghan to keep his nerve 712; at party for Labour Party helpers 713; criticises Mrs Thatcher 714; two hours late at Unit party 715; last day 718–22; The Governance of Britain published 575
Wilson, Marjorie 511–12, 513, 696
Wilson, Mary: and MF 93–4, 140; during election campaign 33, 40, 41, 44, 46, 47; to the Palace with HW 53; at No. 10 59, 63, 75; objects to BD's biography of Morrison 72; dislikes signing herself 'Your humble servant' to the Queen 95; annoyed with HW for being late 113; at Lord North Street 203; to Liverpool for election 216; and blasphemy at No. 10 party 269; 'totally middle-class' 291; in Canada 298, 299; rows with HW over engagement mix-up 405; wants HW to resign 429, 471, 540; and Janet Hewlett-Davies 504; anti-Arab 558; off to the Scillies to prepare cottage 617; and HW 618, 664, 722; upset by press 624; upstaged by MF 693; walks to pub with HW 718–19
Winterbottom, Walter 64
Wintour, Charles 280, 720
Wise, Audrey 552
Witteveen, Johannes 543
Woessner, William (Bill) 334
Wood, Richard 247
Woolf, Michael 537
Worcester, Robert (Bob) 2, 75, 186, 208, 343, 375, 509, 510, 511, 539, 713; polls 7, 183, 210, 215, 377, 379, 381, 398
Wrigglesworth, Ian 708–9, 712
Wright, Oliver 327
Wright, Patrick 58, 545; liked by BD 270; on Canadian trip 298; and Irish affairs 265, 322, 326, 343; reports to BD on MF and arms dealer 377; at HW's meeting with Fitt 380; shouted at by MF 383; and MF's arranged meeting for HW and Israeli Foreign Minister 464–5; works on HW's Helsinki speech 477,

483; tells BD that 'Man is vile' 504; criticised by HW 528; told by HW to invite MF's friends to Sadat reception 559; and MF's attempts to involve HW in financial affairs 632–3, 639; worried about MF and Israelis 646; at dinner for Queen 709; at HW's farewell lunch 719, 720

Yamey, Professor Basil 134
Younger Report 475, 601, 688

Zander, Michael 628, 635, 636, 675
Zuckerman, Solly 528
Zysmann, John 475